THE

UBS GUIDE

TO THE

EMERGING
MARKETS

THE

UBS GUIDE

TO THE

EMERGING
MARKETS

UBS
Union Bank of Switzerland

BLOOMSBURY

Disclaimer

This guide provides an outline of the background of and recent developments in the markets of fifty countries and does not purport to be a complete description of the markets referred to. The information on which this guide is based has been obtained from sources which Union Bank of Switzerland ("UBS") believes to be reliable, but UBS has not independently verified such information and does not guarantee that it is accurate or complete. Information and expressions of opinion contained in this guide may be subject to change without notice and may at any time be superseded. The UBS group of companies and/or any person connected with it accept no liability whatsoever for any direct, indirect or consequential loss of any kind arising out of the use of this guide or any part of its contents.

The editorial deadline for inclusion in the book was January 1997.

First published in 1997 by
Bloomsbury Publishing Plc
38 Soho Square
London W1V 5DF

Copyright © 1997 Union Bank of Switzerland

A copy of the CIP entry for this book is available from the British Library

ISBN 0 7475 2983 3 (hardback)
ISBN 0 7475 3290 7 (paperback)

10 9 8 7 6 5 4 3 2 1

Edited, designed and typeset by Book Creation Services, London

Printed in Great Britain by Clays Ltd, St Ives plc

Acknowledgements

We are grateful to the following individuals and to the many central banks, finance ministries, statistical services, stock exchanges and other organisations that have provided us with information, for their contribution to the publication of this Guide.

Our special thanks go to our three UBS editors: Constantin Vayenas, who did a fantastic job co-ordinating the editorial effort, Heinrich Siegmann and John Tatom; to Bill Jamieson our Consultant Editor; to Kathy Rooney of Bloomsbury; to Gill Paul, Melanie Porte and Tony Spalding of Book Creation Services. And many thanks to Lisa Spiro, David Robins and Peter Buomberger of UBS, Nigel Newton of Bloomsbury and, particularly, Jeffery Tolman of Tolman Cunard, without all of whom this unusual partnership would not have been effected.

Contributors

Consultant editor Bill Jamieson
Editors Constantin Vayenas, Heinrich Siegmann and John Tatom

Hong Kong: Richard Ligon, Angeli Mulchand, Qu Hong Bin, Aditya Samant; *Jakarta:* Urban Carmel; *Johannesburg:* Wayne Blignaut, Francois Gouws, Franco Lorenzani; *Karachi:* Shuja Alvi; *Kuala Lampur:* Yeo Kar-Peng; *London:* Deborah Bennellick, Catherine Blake, Sarah Docx, Pedro Fonseca, Terry Friedrichs, Robert Fugard, Peter Galbraith, Rupert Gordon-Walker, Natalie Kakish, Nicola Livett, Stephen Luker, David McWilliams, Alexander Mitcheson-Smith, Beate Moore, Angelique Moorhouse, Vikas Nath, James Oates, Charles Olivier, Zsolt Papp, Michael Perry, Tom Priday, Richard Reid, Guy Rigden, Ian Rowley, William Seward, Ina Sharikani, Matthew Shaw, Bashir Siman, Peter von Maydell, Sally Wilkinson, Duncan Woods, Emre Yigit; *New York:* David Dwight, Nicholas Harris, Ingrid Iversen, Lawrence Krohn, Rafaelina Lee, Tony Molestina, William Romary, Veronique Stolz; *Prague:* Spencer Nash; *Singapore:* P.K. Basu, Bibiana Chong, Lawrence Hatheway, Low Siew Kheng, Jaime Juan, Dominque Maire; *Tel Aviv:* Daniel Carasso; *Warsaw:* Maciej Radziwill; *Zurich:* Erdal Atukeren, Igor Azarov, Alain Geier, Martin Hood, Gioele Jaeger, Christa Marti, Andreas Michel, Carine Oesterle, Walter Stolber, Zsuzsa Szabo, Franzisca Taeschler, Friedrich von Schwarzenberg, Grant Weissenberger.

Contents

Introduction by Bill Jamieson   9

Emerging markets: The big picture   12

Emerging equity markets   25

Emerging fixed-income markets   32

Emerging currencies   45

Country sections   49

Glossary   784

Index   796

Contents

Argentina	49	Mexico	417
Brazil	67	Morocco	435
Bulgaria	84	Nigeria	455
Chile	99	Pakistan	464
China	115	Panama	476
Colombia	127	Peru	488
Côte d'Ivoire	142	Philippines	503
Croatia	151	Poland	522
Czech Republic	167	Portugal	544
Ecuador	183	Romania	558
Egypt	197	Russia	569
Estonia	212	Saudi Arabia	587
Ghana	222	Singapore	598
Greece	232	Slovakia	613
Hong Kong	246	Slovenia	627
Hungary	261	South Africa	640
India	281	South Korea	658
Indonesia	297	Taiwan	673
Israel	318	Thailand	687
Jordan	333	Turkey	706
Kazakstan	346	Ukraine	721
Kenya	360	Uzbekistan	732
Latvia	370	Venezuela	742
Lithuania	384	Vietnam	757
Malaysia	398	Zimbabwe	772

Introduction

O ver the past ten years the most engaging story in global economics has been the rise of emerging markets. The continuing success of the Pacific Rim economies, the turnaround in Latin America, the collapse of the former Soviet Union and the spread of market-driven economic reform, re-structuring and privatization programmes have triggered an unprecedented shift in global capital flows.

Since the early 1980s the total portfolio flows, foreign direct investment (FDI), official development finance and private debt finance from the mature industrial economies to the developing world, has totalled US$1,600 billion and is now running at more than US$225 billion a year.

It is difficult to picture what these huge figures mean. For reference, the aggregate amounts to twice the Gross Domestic Product of China. And the annual flow alone is equivalent to the combined GDP of the seven largest economies of sub-Saharan Africa, on the move, from north to south (or west to east) each year. Just taking the figures for FDI and official development finance, the flow since 1990 equates to the movement of six companies the size of Ford Motor Corporation from the mature economies to the developing world each year.

For portfolio investment, the figures are equally breathtaking. At the end of the 1980s the 24 main investible emerging markets had a combined market capitalization of only US$145 billion, or 7% of the United States, United Kingdom and Japan markets combined. By 1995 their market capitalization had increased to two trillion dollars, or more than 16% of the market capitalization of these three developed markets.

Fund managers and private investors, hungry for portfolio diversification and an opportunity to acquire stakes in the fastest growing sectors of the global economy, have poured some US$230 billion into emerging equity markets since the mid-1980s. These flows are volatile and sensitive to changes in interest rates in the US and to perceived emerging market risk. But the underlying trend in flows to emerging markets appears to be rising at around US$10 billion a year.

No previous decade has seen such a shift in capital resources. It is both appropriate and timely that the Union Bank of Switzerland should prepare us for the next decade with the most extensive guide yet published on emerging markets.

It is appropriate because UBS is one of the largest and most influential banks in the world. Its global emerging markets coverage – be it fixed income, equities, currencies or commodity products, and the relevant research and analysis – is formidable, as befits a bank that is a member of the world's leading exchanges with seventy overseas offices and a worldwide staff of 28,000.

This unique book, providing extensive historic, economic and political data on fifty countries, and with detailed information on the respective fixed income and equity markets, draws on the best of the bank's analysts worldwide. The quality of these skills is becoming increasingly recognised. The book also benefits from the bank's highly regarded global perspective.

It is timely because the emerging market story has now grown markedly more diverse and complex, placing a premium not only on individual country analysis but also on stock selection. Broad brush, indiscriminate exposure to emerging markets has given way to more sophisticated country by country analysis, with greater importance placed on the timing of asset and portfolio switches.

For bond market investors, emerging markets offer attractive spreads and generally improving credit worthiness. Growth has been spectacular: trading in emerging market debt has risen from US$734 billion in 1992 to US$2,740 billion in 1995. Returns on emerging market bonds in recent years have also been outstanding: the average annual return since 1991 has been 19% against 8% on US Treasuries and 7% on Standard & Poor's bond index.

A critical part of the research undertaken in emerging market fixed income is risk assessment across markets that have been prone to bank crises and failures. At least two-thirds of the International Monetary Fund's 181 members have suffered bank crises since 1980 and the cost of resolving these has approached US$250 billion. But much wider damage is done to confidence. More than ever, qualitative analytical skill is required to assess and interpret emerging country financial data.

But a host of questions now confront the emerging market investor. Has IMF surveillance data improved sufficiently to provide an early warning of, or avoid another Mexican-style crisis? How convincing are the turnaround stories in some of these economies? Are all the economies of eastern Europe benefiting from a rising tide of foreign investment, or are some headed for budget and currency problems? Will Russia succeed in improving its tax revenues? How are we to interpret the rise in current account deficits and signs of slowing grow thin some south-east Asian economies? What are the prospects for South Africa?

In one sense the term "emerging markets" has done the investor no favours. It suggests a group of countries whose economies behave as one homogeneous bloc, or where there are strong pan-regional convergence forces, such as western Europe. In truth, there is less a common "colour" than a rainbow. There are now large variations in economic and market performance, not only between regional blocs but also within them. These divergences are becoming so marked as to raise serious questions about the appropriateness and efficacy of the regional asset allocation approach. Individual countries are scattered like a broken string of pearls across the developmental cycle: Hong Kong, Portugal and Poland at one end, India, Morocco and Zimbabwe at the other.

Not only are there evident developmental disparities between emerging market economies, but there are also considerable policy divergences. Some countries such as Chile have achieved a radical re-structuring and liberalization of their economies and have taken privatization to heart. But, on the same continent, Venezuela has still to show a commitment to restructuring and reform. Others, such as Romania and Bulgaria, mouth the rhetoric of reform and privatization, but in the real economy property rights laws remain little changed to date.

Political instability brings a further dimension of risk. Thailand, South Korea and Bulgaria are three examples of worrying political turbulence to have emerged in 1996. These underscore the requirement of emerging markets to convert impressive sounding rhetoric and abstract statistical success into an improvement in living standards and growth in real incomes across a broad swathe of the population. The macro-economic picture only holds up if living standards generally are improved.

Meanwhile doubts have arisen over the sustainability of the Asian economic miracle. Critics point to a slowing rate of growth and/or deteriorating current account balances in countries such as Taiwan, Singapore and South Korea as evidence of serious structural slow-down: that some Asian countries are coming to the end of a technology-driven growth catch-up and that fresh stimulus is required.

Some sense of proportion should be kept in this debate: Asia's share of global exports in 1996 was up, not down, and Asia's market share in the US (its main market for most exports, particularly electronics) has not fallen. The Asia ex-Japan share of US electronics imports continues to grow.

But the debate poses searching questions on the ability of some of the more mature emerging market economies to make a further quantum leap in labour skills and technological innovation.

Thus, detailed individual country analysis and assessment has become paramount. This UBS guide is not only a detailed review of recent developments across fifty markets. For professional fund managers and private investors alike, its extensive data and quality of analysis on each of these countries make it an indispensable foundation-stone for the future.

Bill Jamieson
Economics Editor: Sunday Telegraph

Emerging markets

THE BIG PICTURE

Emerging markets command half of world output today...

"Emerging markets" have become a catch-phrase encompassing a wide-range of developing, reforming and newly industrializing countries in Asia, Latin America, Eastern and Southern Europe, the Middle East and Africa. These countries have grown considerably faster than the traditional "industrial" economies, many have received sizeable net capital inflows in recent years, and many are witnessing rapid financial market development. Any attempt to attach a precise definition to the "emerging markets" label is bound to be controversial, because, as Bill Jamieson put it in his introduction, there is less "a common colour than a rainbow".

The fifty countries covered in this volume have attracted the most interest from a very diverse investor base. The selected countries include highly developed service economies such as Hong Kong and Singapore with annual per capita incomes of over US$25,000 as well as poor, still largely agricultural countries such as Vietnam or Nigeria with per capita income levels at below US$300.

Similarly, some countries have sophisticated financial markets with a stock market capitalization two-to-three times their GDP (Hong Kong, Singapore, Malaysia, South Africa) while others have not yet developed stock markets at all. Some basic indicators for the countries covered are summarized in Table A.

...and two-thirds tomorrow

These countries have grown on average (GDP-weighted) around 6% annually in the last ten years – about double the annual growth rate of the "industrial" world (Chart 1). Asia's emerging economies have grown fastest at around 8% annually, with Latin America, the Middle East and Africa lagging behind, averaging around 4% but still outperforming the industrial countries (Chart 2).

The transition economies of (Central) Eastern Europe and the former Soviet Union (FSU) contracted markedly in the early 1990s. The Central European countries have since recovered and entered a solid growth path of 4-5% annually, whereas economic recovery in the FSU has progressed more slowly.

The growth differential with the "industrial world", which we expect will continue well into the future, has entailed dramatic shifts of world output. About one generation ago, today's emerging and developing economies accounted for about one-third of world GDP (measured in purchasing power parity). Their share has grown to one-half of global GDP today, and is projected to grow to two-thirds in another generation (Chart 3). Thus, within about half a century the locus of world output will have dramatically shifted, most likely also accompanied by similarly large movements of financial markets.

A: Basic country indicators (1996)

Asia	Population in millions	GDP in US$bn	Per Capita GDP US$	GDP Growth %	Foreign Debt US$bn	Foreign Debt % of GDP (end 10/96)	Stock Market Capitalization	Rating (S&P/Moody's)*	
Hong Kong	6.3	158	25101	4.3	—	—	440.1	A	A3
Singapore	3.0	93	30281	6.1	—	—	186.5	AAA	Aa1
South Korea	45.2	487	10727	6.6	125	25.6	138.8	AA-	A1
Taiwan	21.3	268	12520	5.4	48.9	18.2	273.6	AA+	Aa3
China	1234	773	670	9.6	110	13.5	113.8	BBB	A3
India	953.2	359	384	6.0	95	26.5	122.6	BB+	Baa3
Indonesia	196.8	221	1123	8.0	114.5	51.8	91	BBB	Baa3
Malaysia	20.2	96	4638	8.3	47.7	51.5	307.2	A+	A1
Pakistan	134.1	65	480	6.1	30	46.3	10.6	B+	B2
Philippines	70.1	83	1179	5.3	45	54.5	80.6	B	Ba2
Thailand	61.2	184	3028	6.7	94.5	51.2	99.8	A	A2
Vietnam	75.5	21	277	9.3	6.4	30.6	—	—	—

Latin America

Argentina	35	339	9679	3.2	110	32.5	44.7	BB-	B1
Brazil	168.5	761	4513	3.0	186	24.5	217.0	B+	B1
Chile	14.4	74	5140	6.5	21.8	29.4	65.9	A-	Baa1
Colombia	35.7	87	2432	3.0	27	31.1	17.1	BBB-	Baa3
Ecuador	11.7	19	1595	1.8	14.6	78.2	1.9	—	—
Mexico	96.6	300	3106	4.9	175	58.3	106.5	BB	Ba2
Panama	2.7	8	2898	1.5	5.4	69.2	1.3	BB+	Ba1
Peru	24	62	2587	2.4	30	48.3	13.8	—	B2
Venezuela	22.1	64	2881	-1.3	36	56.5	10.1	B	Ba2

Eastern Europe

Bulgaria	9.1	11	1244	-5.0	9.5	83.7	—	—	—
Croatia	4.8	19	3944	5.0	4.5	23.9	—	BBB-	Baa3
Czech Republic	10.3	54	5189	4.3	18	33.6	18.1	A	Baa1
Estonia	1.5	4	2945	3.5	0.4	9.3	—	—	—
Hungary	10.2	44	4331	1.0	29.5	66.7	5.3	BBB-	Baa3
Latvia	2.5	5	2152	2.5	0.6	11.1	0.2	BBB	Ba2
Lithuania	3.7	8	2051	3.5	1.3	17.1	0.9	—	Ba2
Poland	38.7	130	3353	5.0	45	34.6	8.4	BBB-	Baa3
Romania	22.6	33	1435	4.8	7.7	23.8	0.06	BB-	Ba3
Slovakia	5.4	19	3505	7.0	6.5	34.0	2.2	BBB-	Baa3
Slovenia	2	17	8572	2.5	4.4	25.6	0.7	A	A3

CIS

Kazakstan	16.3	22	1397	1.0	4.6	20.2	—	BB-	Ba3
Russia	146.3	476	3305	-6.0	115.4	23.9	37.2	BB-	Ba2
Ukraine	51.6	48	934	-5.0	11.3	23.5	—	—	—
Uzbekistan	22.9	21	914	-0.6	2.1	10.0	—	—	—

Southern EU countries

Greece	10.6	121	11624	2.2	26.7	22.1	24.2	BBB-	Baa3
Portugal	9.9	103	11025	2.5	13.0	12.6	24.7	AA-	A1

Mediterranean and the Middle East

Egypt	60.1	68	1123	4.0	28.6	42.3	14.2	BBB-	Ba2
Israel	5.8	93	15820	4.0	47.5	51.1	40.0	A-	A3
Jordan	5.8	7.2	1676	4.1	7.1	98.9	4.5	BB-	Ba3
Morocco	27.6	39	1407	12.0	23.4	60.3	8.7	—	—
Saudi Arabia	19	135	7106	1.8	25.2	18.7	45.9	—	Baa3
Turkey	63.9	175	2734	6.9	73.0	41.8	30.0	B	Ba3

Sub-Saharan Africa

Côte d'Ivoire	14.8	10	668	6.2	20.2	203.9	0.9	—	—
Ghana	18.3	7	402	4.7	6.1	82.0	1.5	—	—
Kenya	31.5	9	290	4.8	7.9	86.6	1.8	—	—
Nigeria	108.9	28	246	3.0	38.5	135.7	3.6	—	—
South Africa	42	126	3052	3.0	31.7	25.2	241.6	BB+	Baa3
Zimbabwe	11.3	7	617	6.5	4.4	60.5	3.6	—	—

*January 1997

Source: World Bank, IMF, Datastream, Standard & Poor's, Moody's, UBS

1: Emerging economies double growth of industrial world
Annual growth rates as % change

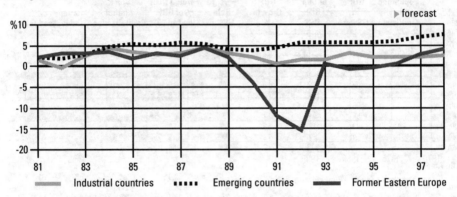

Industrial countries   Emerging countries   Former Eastern Europe

2: Asia leads growth
Annual growth rates as % change

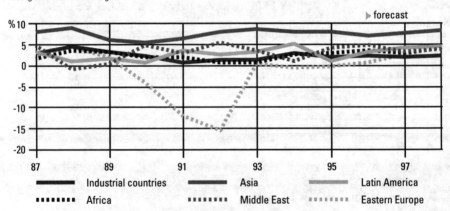

Industrial countries   Asia   Latin America
Africa   Middle East   Eastern Europe

Economic fundamentals have improved

An improving economic performance stems from better economic policies. Foremost, inflation has declined globally, including in historically inflation-prone emerging economies (Chart 4). Even Latin American and Eastern European countries suffering from hyper-inflation just a few years ago have made astounding progress – some of them reaching levels prevailing in industrial countries (e.g., Argentina 0.3%, Croatia 3.6% in 1996). In our fifty-country sample, inflation declined from 39% in 1995 to 17% in 1996, and is projected to fall to 11% in 1998. Nevertheless, inflation is not dead. About a dozen countries in Latin America, South-Eastern Europe, Central Asia and Africa continue to face considerable inflationary threats.

3: Dramatic shift in world output

% Share of world output

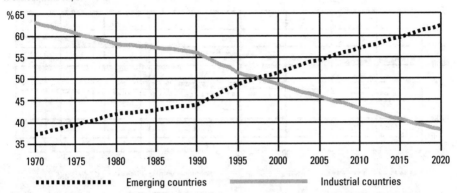

●●●●●●●●●●●●●●● Emerging countries   ▨▨▨▨▨▨▨▨▨ Industrial countries

4: Global inflation

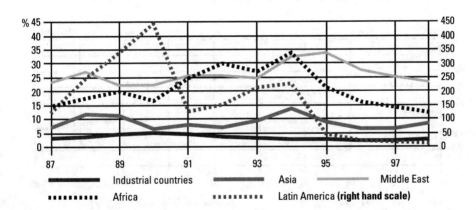

━━━━━ Industrial countries   ▨▨▨▨▨ Asia   ━━━━━ Middle East

●●●●●●●●●● Africa   ■■■■■■■■■■ Latin America **(right hand scale)**

Along with lower inflation, most countries have managed to improve their public finances. Deficits have reached about 2.5% of GDP and are declining further – on average, already below the Maastricht limit of 3%. Lower deficits, moreover, are accompanied by improving foreign debt ratios.

While foreign debt has nominally increased, especially for Asian and Latin American emerging economies (Chart 5), growing prosperity has led to improved debt-to-export and debt-to-GDP ratios (Chart 6). In the fifty countries covered, external debt amounted to 32% of GDP in 1995 but is projected to decline to 27% in 1998. Two out of every three countries have comfortable foreign reserve levels worth more than three months of imports. Still, about one out of three countries in our sample has foreign debt exceeding 50% of GDP and thus warrants some concern.

5: External debt rising...

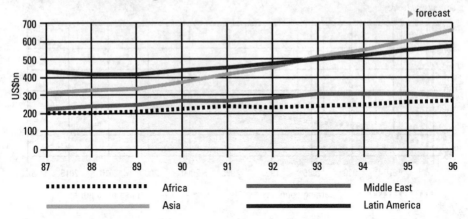

▶ forecast

US$bn

Legend:
- ▪▪▪▪▪▪ Africa
- ▬▬▬▬ Asia
- ▬▬▬▬ Middle East
- ▬▬▬▬ Latin America

6: ...but easier external debt servicing

As % of exports

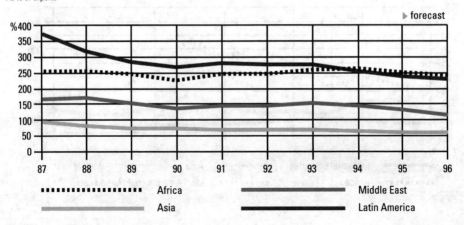

▶ forecast

%

Legend:
- ▪▪▪▪▪▪ Africa
- ▬▬▬▬ Asia
- ▬▬▬▬ Middle East
- ▬▬▬▬ Latin America

Capital needs remain high but keep shifting

The only major economic indicator that appears to be deteriorating somewhat is the current account. Current account deficits reflect imports of goods and services that exceed the country's exports, and investment exceeding national savings. As long as these deficits can be attributed to imports of investment goods or unusually high investment, which increase a country's competitiveness and export potential, sizeable imbalances may persist over an extended period without causing undue concern. However, current account deficits exceeding 5% of GDP or so for several years can be critical for countries with managed exchange

7: Aggregate net resource inflows rising

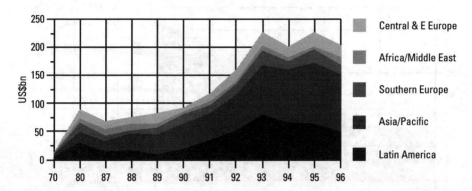

8: Rising share of private foreign investment
Aggregate net long-term capital flows to non-industrial countries

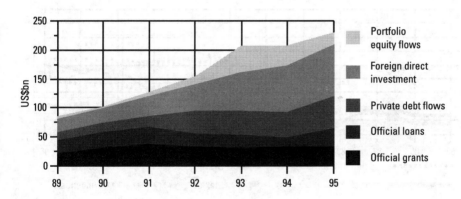

rates, where deficits are not backed by adequate foreign currency reserves and have been triggered by imports used for consumption or excessive government spending. The current account deficits of our fifty countries are projected to widen from 1.3% of GDP in 1995 to 2% in 1998. In nominal terms, this is an increase from US$65 billion in 1995 to around US$150 billion in 1998, but more than a third of the increase results from the dwindling current account surpluses of China and the four Asian "tigers". Yet, with the foreign exchange reserve build-up slowing, net capital inflows are projected to increase at a somewhat smaller pace that the current account deficit, rising about US$30 billion to US$219 billion in 1998.

9: Foreign direct investment flows by region

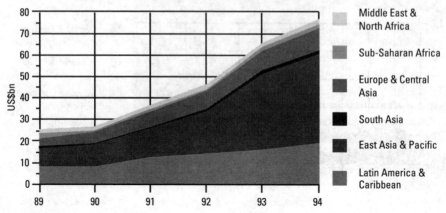

10: Improving sovereign risk (selected countries)

Institutional investor ratings: 0 - 100 / worst - best score

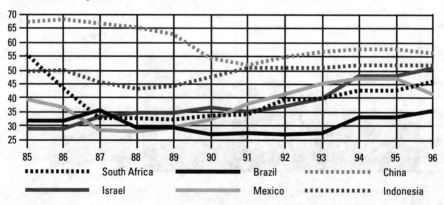

Widening current account deficits mean increased demand for foreign capital. Aggregate net resource inflows into developing countries have skyrocketed from about US$10 billion in 1970 to around US$200 billion at present (Chart 7). The increase has been particularly steep in the 1990s when net inflows more or less doubled. About half of the inflows are now going to Asia whereas Latin America's share has declined somewhat in recent years.

Not only the direction but also the composition of the flows has shifted markedly since the late 1980s. The lion's share of the capital nowadays comes from private sources: only about one-quarter are official grants and loans (Chart 8). Private debt flows have increased about fourfold, testifying to greatly increased emerging bond markets. Portfolio equity flows have also increased many times over. The largest source of funds is foreign direct investment

(FDI) which amounts to about 40% of total net flows (Chart 9). This may, indeed, be the most relevant signal for the emerging economies. Contrary to portfolio investments which may leave a country at short notice, the rise of FDI indicates the long-term commitment of international capital towards these countries. Still, banking and other financial activities in many emerging markets remain unduly restricted, as the stalling of financial services liberalization within GATS (General Agreement on Trade in Services) attests.

Political stability is improving

Various studies maintain that prosperity stimulates democracy which, in turn, enhances economic development. There is much evidence indicating that beyond a certain threshold rising income levels and economic reforms can only be sustained in a sufficiently stable and predictable political environment. Past evidence from countries such as Spain, Portugal, Greece, Taiwan or South Korea suggests that countries are unlikely to sustain per capita income levels above around US$8000 per year unless the necessary democratic institutions and processes are in place and functioning.

While certainly not all elements of western-type democratic systems are being emulated, and perhaps shouldn't be, a country must at least be able to ensure the rule of law, the protection of physical and intellectual property, an efficacious educational system, the orderly succession of leadership, and curtail discretionary infringement of government in the private sector. Most of these ingredients appear to be necessary for keeping today's economies, with their high degree of division of labour, functioning and internationally competitive in the long run. Internal stability tends to translate into external stability, the sine-qua-non for economic prosperity and the availability of capital.

Democracy has clearly been on the rise not only in central and eastern Europe but also in Latin America, South East Asia and more recently Africa. Many authoritarian regimes in power in the eighties have succumbed to democratic rule. Since country ratings implicitly or explicitly reflect a country's economic and political fundamentals as well as the strategic setting, they make for a rough indicator of a country's internal stability and external strategic risks. The rating agencies Moody's and Standard & Poor's currently rate the sovereign risks of thirty-eight out of the fifty countries in our sample (see Table A).

Twenty-two countries were rated investment grade (i.e., Baa3 and higher by Moody's; BBB- and higher by Standard and Poor's) and fourteen countries speculative grade. Two countries were rated investment grade by one agency and speculative grade by the other. (As recently as three years ago, Moody's rated only 21 countries from our sample, 11 of which were investment grade). Overall, emerging market ratings have improved significantly since the mid-1980s (Chart 10). Given that financial markets are evolving, additional countries are bound to be covered by the rating agencies.

Increased market scrutiny, in turn, should reinforce the resolve to strengthen economic and democratic reforms. The absence of this would obviously increasingly result in adverse market reactions.

Competitiveness rising

Emerging economies at present are still less competitive than today's "industrial" countries but they will be among the most competitive countries "tomorrow". This is the conclusion of two UBS studies on international competitiveness published in 1993 and 1996 (*UBS*

B: Asia most competitive 'tomorrow'

Competitivenes indexes and subindexes. All series connected to index numbers based on 100 for best performing country.

	Overall Index	SAVINGS %GDP index	INNOVATION INDEXES R&D spending %GNP	capital goods imports %GNP	export growth rate %	POLICY INDEXES inflation rate '89-94 avg. %	government consumption % GNP	real exch. rate % change
Singapore	96	100	21	100	87	96	100	100
Malaysia	91	73	na	85	100	91	79	82
Thailand	83	74	3	61	88	90	95	93
China	83	87	16	30	97	57	100	60
Japan	81	73	76	0	45	100	95	70
Korea	78	77	46	36	54	86	90	99
Ireland	76	61	25	70	45	97	63	97
Switzerland	75	61	73	26	5	95	74	97
Indonesia	75	76	4	36	62	82	95	87
Netherlands	72	54	48	42	22	95	68	91
Germany	71	57	64	17	5	92	42	97
Belgium	68	50	40	38	18	96	68	98
Austria	67	57	38	35	12	93	47	97
France	67	45	59	16	11	97	47	98
Sweden	66	40	76	26	8	94	0	91
Canada	63	41	37	24	35	100	32	94
US	62	32	66	6	37	95	58	96
Italy	62	44	34	11	14	90	53	92
UK	60	32	53	22	14	96	32	98
N. Zealand	60	46	21	25	34	100	68	96
Chile	59	52	16	30	44	63	95	78
Australia	59	42	33	19	24	99	53	97
Israel	57	30	82	38	52	68	5	100
Spain	57	45	20	11	38	88	53	91
Russia	55	78	21	47	69	10	68	na
India	52	46	21	2	46	74	90	91
Argentina	52	34	62	6	32	63	79	76
S. Africa	52	45	22	34	7	70	37	97
Mexico	50	39	3	19	33	70	100	93
Colombia	49	47	27	14	29	28	84	83
Hungary	49	40	27	40	11	37	5	97
Pakistan	47	27	23	14	38	71	74	90
Portugal	47	43	14	21	9	82	58	75
Egypt	46	16	3	27	27	69	74	99
Brazil	44	51	100	3	45	0	61	93
Poland	41	52	15	20	31	28	32	60
Nigeria	39	51	18	24	32	23	53	na
Iran	39	48	1	15	0	23	68	58
Greece	36	19	10	11	15	61	47	93
Turkey	33	41	12	12	46	18	79	95

Source: UBS

International, Issue 26, Winter 1996). The studies come to the conclusion that tomorrow's, that is in the next 10-20 years or so, competitiveness leaders will be Singapore, Malaysia and Thailand (Table B). Six out of the top ten countries are emerging economies from our sample, all located in Asia. (Japan is the most competitive "industrial" country at rank 5; Ireland the most competitive country in Europe ranked seventh; Hong Kong was omitted for methodological reasons).

11: Asian savings highest
As a % of GDP

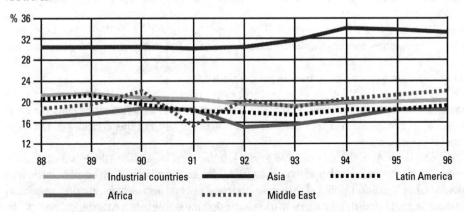

Legend:
Industrial countries | Asia | Latin America
Africa | Middle East

In addition to China, Korea and Indonesia, which are also in the top ten, Chile, Israel, Russia, India, Argentina, South Africa and Mexico show the best potential, but will depend critically on reinforcing the market-oriented policies and reforms they are pursuing.

Ultimately, countries distinguish themselves by the standard of living achieved by their residents. Not surprisingly, nations growing fastest tend to be those that are most rapidly becoming competitive in world markets. They are becoming attractive places to locate production and distribution centres. They are quick to develop new products and adopt processes that lower cost, or rapidly adapt products and processes developed elsewhere. In the end, they create the most competitiveness "problems" for other nations.

What are the keys to competitiveness? Our ranking is based on three main components reflecting a country's national savings rate, its propensity for innovation, and its policy environment. High savings are crucial since they can provide the bulk of the financing needs of new investments which ultimately drive growth.

Tapping foreign savings, as reflected in current account deficits, has become increasingly easy in our integrated world, but this source of financing remains relatively small compared to the amount of investment needed to sustain above-average growth. Chart 11 shows Asian saving rates in the last decade reaching 30% of GDP and more, and thus handsomely exceeding the rates of 20% and less that are typical for the industrial countries and many emerging market countries. The Asian states can be expected to maintain high national saving rates, and thus a competitive edge, thereby promoting policies that keep government spending under control, support funded pension schemes with defined contributions, introduce fiscal systems taxing consumption rather than capital or labour income, and encouraging corporate sector saving.

Investment quality is as important as high investment rates. In the 1970s, former communist countries "invested" up to 30% of GDP per year without, after all, increasing competitiveness or prosperity. Rather, investments must be accompanied by the development and utilization of new technology and process innovation which are allowed to operate in an open economy. As indicators of a country's propensity for innovation, we have used spending on research and development, capital good imports and export growth. Finally, on the policy level, stable prices, low government consumption, and a competitive foreign exchange rate have been found particularly important. Table B lists rankings based on these indicators for most of the countries covered in this volume.

Outlook positive, but beware of risks

On the whole, our outlook for emerging economies remains positive. Both the prospects for the next two years summarized in some of the charts above, as well as the competitiveness outlook spanning the next two decades or so, strongly support this conclusion, but there can be exceptions.

Southeast Asia should continue to ride on the crest of growth which has carried the region in the last decade. Huge infrastructure needs, high saving and investment rates, relatively stable legal and political systems, moderate government sectors, modest regulatory impediments, liberalizing financial markets and openness towards technological change are all factors likely to stay and to be conducive to growth.

Moreover, the region has benefited from persistent intra-regional migration of economic activity which is set to continue. Labour-intensive production keeps shifting toward low-wage countries while the more advanced countries have been successfully diversifying into higher value-added products. This pattern can be expected to hold in general, even though some particulars will change. Growth in the advanced countries in the region should slow somewhat but still remain clearly above the rate of industrial countries. Increasing integration into the global economy also means larger exposure to fluctuating demand for Asian exports, as last year's export slump testifies.

China seems set to be the growth engine for the region for some time to come, stimulating growth elsewhere but also increasing dependence on Chinese economic development and stability. Risks, above all, stem from political and strategic uncertainties still abundant in the region. Purportedly, few borders in the region are uncontested, bilateral rivalries abound, a regional security framework (such as Europe developed during the cold war) is at best rudimentary, and increasing prosperity and technological prowess have supported the build-up of military capabilities in many countries which may destabilize the region in the long run.

After the "lost decade" of the 1980s, Latin America has made remarkable strides in the 1990s in reforming its economies and improving fundamentals, especially in bringing down inflation. For the foreseeable future, the region seems to have entered a growth path of 4-5% annually. Deregulation and trade liberalization, especially in Mercosur, is progressing, yet much still needs to be done. Conditions and prospects can vary quite markedly from one country to another, and doubts persist whether sustainable growth can be achieved. Average savings of 15-20% of GDP (only half of Asian rates – see Chart 11 – Chile being the notable exception) are too low to fund investments without major foreign capital inflows. Moreover, privatization has moved at a modest pace only, while the state sector is still too large in most countries.

Probably more so than elsewhere, economic volatility can be traced to political inaction, which has often hindered improvements of tax systems, pension and civil service reforms, the restructuring of the banking system, privatization, and land reform. Foreign investors clearly would have erred had they abandoned Latin America in the wake of the debt crisis of the early 1980s or the 1994/95 Mexican peso shock. Nonetheless, careful country-by-country scrutiny seems to be particularly warranted in this region.

Most countries in Central-Eastern Europe appear to be mastering the transition to market economies. Russia and other former Soviet republics, however, are still in the midst of transition, whereas countries such as Romania and Serbia have not yet started transition in earnest, while Bulgaria has shown the fragility of transition efforts. While these countries are very diverse, on average they seem to be headed for a growth path of 4%. Fundamentals can be expected to improve further, especially when the sizeable informal economies find their way into official statistics, and democratic reforms and gradual integration with the European Union and Nato progresses.

Trade liberalization will open the large markets of western Europe, but will also increasingly force productivity gains in the east. Private foreign direct and portfolio investment inflows can be expected to foment investment, complemented by official finance.

Uncertainties emanating from developments in Russia pose a risk to all countries in the region, but should not be of undue concern especially in the central European countries. There is also the risk of some social backlash if inequalities widen significantly, unemployment rates rise markedly or severe austerity policies are imposed. Yet, this is unlikely to pose serious threats to the democratic systems already in place. Despite the astounding progress many of the countries have made, they still lag far behind Western Europe. Back-of-the-envelope calculations make it plain that it will take more than one or two generations for eastern Europe (assuming 5% annual per capita growth) to catch up to EU income levels (assuming a 2% annual growth rate).

Economic reforms, deregulation and privatization have recently also improved the prospects in some Near and Middle East countries such as Egypt, Israel, Jordan, or Morocco while other countries in the region have implemented change more slowly. This region is obviously particularly sensitive to international tensions. If tensions can be further reduced, or at least kept in check, continuing along the economic reform path will help prosperity which, in turn, should keep radical forces subdued and encourage political reforms as well. The countries on the Arab peninsula are no exception to this. While higher oil prices may be able to temporarily mitigate liquidity problems, economic reforms are required to stem otherwise inevitable internal economic imbalances.

Sub-Saharan Africa has been the only continent which has not yet shared in the growth of the 1990s. Unfortunately – notable exceptions such as Côte d'Ivoire, Ghana, Kenya, Namibia, and Zimbabwe notwithstanding – this is unlikely to change in the foreseeable future. The combination of external tensions, civil wars, pervasive poverty, inefficient economies, corruption and political instability has created a vicious mix in many countries which will be difficult to overcome. Nevertheless, Africa's largest economy by far, South Africa, faces better prospects and may provide a boost for neighbouring southern African countries as well. Overall, it has managed the transition to democracy far better than many expected and has embarked on reasonable economic policies. While political risks clearly exist, we remain guardedly optimistic that the country will be able to achieve higher growth rates in the years ahead.

The emerging economies covered in this volume should continue to outperform the developed countries as a group, their economic fundamentals are expected to improve further, they can expect further net capital inflows, and they should benefit from the ongoing liberalization of international trade and finance. All emerging economies face increased scrutiny by the markets with positive effects for some countries but negative for others. On the positive side, one should expect the relentless pressure for economic reforms, rule of law and political stability. On the negative side, there is the greater visibility of, and exposure to, economic and political weaknesses and associated risks. Globalization is not a zero sum game: if economic fundamentals improve and markets liberalize further, the winners will clearly outnumber the losers.

Emerging equity markets

EXTRACTING THE TRUTH
FROM THE MYTHS

The emerging markets investor-base is widening. More and more funds are either taking their first plunge or building on existing foundations. But misconceptions still surround these equity markets, mostly regarding the historic risk and return profiles of this asset class and its relationship with the developed world. This overview is aimed at both investors new to these markets, and those who are looking to increase their exposure.

MYTH 1
Emerging equity markets offer very high-risk and high-return assets: *Historically not true*
It is true that emerging equity markets have been relatively high risk. Chart 1 compares the performance of the US, Japanese and a composite European index with the longest available emerging markets' series – the IFC global composite index. As the accompanying Table A shows, emerging markets are very volatile. But they do not show extraordinarily high returns. Emerging equity markets, as an asset class, have outperformed no other major equity asset classes in dollar terms. Indeed, the IFC global composite index shows similar returns to Europe and the US with a higher volatility. But more surprising is that in dollar terms, the Japanese market has been more volatile than the emerging markets composite – and with a lower average return.

1: Total return of various equity asset classes (US$)

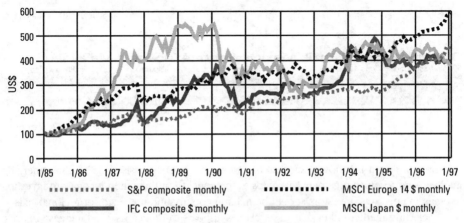

Source: UBS & Datastream.

A: Risk and return in various asset classes, Jan 86 - Dec 96 (US$)
*Risk is the annualized monthly standard deviation. **From 1991 onwards*

	Annual average monthly return %	Annual average monthly risk* %	Annual period return %
S&P 500 Composite	16.9	14.2	15.7
IFC Composite	16.7	22.5	13.8
M.S.C.I. Europe 14	16.6	16.5	14.9
M.S.C.I. Japan	14.6	26.8	10.6
J.P.Morgan Brady Bond Index**	21.5	13.7	20.4

Source: UBS & Datastream

A comparison of these indices hides as much as it reveals. One needs to look at the underlying data and global trends to discern what actually happened in the past 12 years:

All of the data compared here is in dollar terms. In the ten years to 1995, both the European and the Japanese currencies have risen strongly against the dollar. We consider returns in the larger emerging equity markets to be dollar denominated, given that their currencies are either pegged to the dollar or the dollar forms a large part of the basket to which their currencies are linked. Strong currencies have helped both Europe and Japan to outperform.

Emerging markets composite indices conceal trends in individual markets. This is shown by a comparative examination of the MSCI European Index. When it rises or falls, it is likely that underlying markets are moving in the same direction (albeit by different magnitudes). Most European markets enjoy very high correlation. This is not true for the emerging markets. It is a struggle to find two emerging markets as highly correlated as the weakest of the European markets' correlation. Even within economically integrated regions such as the ASEAN or the Mercosur, correlations are weak. Thus, any emerging markets composite index is a very poor indicator of the overall health of individual markets.

B: Correlations – France, Germany, Switzerland and the UK

60-month correlation	France	Germany	Switzerland	UK
France	1.00	—	—	—
Germany	0.75	1.00	—	—
Switzerland	0.72	0.72	1.00	—
UK	0.80	0.62	0.71	1.00

Source: UBS & Datastream

C: Correlations - Brazil, Mexico, South Africa and Malaysia

60-month correlation	Brazil	Malaysia	Mexico	South Africa
Brazil	1.00	—	—	—
Malaysia	-0.01	1.00	—	—
Mexico	0.17	0.26	1.00	—
South Africa	0.02	0.30	0.22	1.00

Source: UBS & Datastream

It is only during a meltdown, such as the Mexican currency crisis of 1994, that emerging markets tend to move together. This leads to the conclusion that when it comes to investing in emerging markets, investors should be making country and not sector or regional calls.

Selecting market rather than asset classes appears to reduce risk and increase returns. This is illustrated in Table D. In Scenario 1, investments were only in the developed world.

In Scenario 2, the investor allocated 10% of the portfolio to emerging markets. The risk declined – but so did the return. In Scenario 2, 2.5% of the portfolio was invested in each of the four largest and most investable emerging markets: Brazil, Malaysia, Mexico and South Africa. Although associated risk was not lowered as much as a 10% investment in the IFC composite, individual emerging markets offered better returns at lower risks than investing only in the developed world.

D: Diversification into emerging markets – risk and return
*Risk is the annualized monthly standard deviation
** The four emerging markets are: Brazil, Malaysia, Mexico and South Africa.
Portfolio exposure: 2.5% in each market.

	Annual return %	Annual risk* %
Scenario 1: MSCI World	11.3	10.3
Scenario 2: World + IFCG Index	11.1	8.9
Scenario 3: World + 4 Markets**	13.0	9.9

MYTH 2
Emerging markets' correlation with the developed world is rising and withering away diversification opportunities - especially as impact of foreign money is becoming more significant: *Completely untrue*

Chart 2 tracks the correlation of our four selected emerging markets with the S&P 500. Over the past five and one-half years, emerging markets' correlation has actually deteriorated to meaningless numbers. In early 1991, Mexico, Malaysia and South Africa were highly correlated with the US; the relationship subsequently declined. Brazil, seemingly, has improved its relationship – but it was trivial five years ago, and remains so even at today's levels. The relationships underwent big changes in October 1992 (after the effect of the 1987 crash was factored out), and in late-1993 as the emerging markets fever reached its peak.

2: Emerging market correlation with US is declining

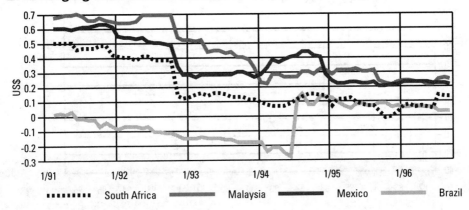

Source: UBS, IFC and Datastream

Readers should note that a decline in correlation from 0.65-0.70 levels to 0.3 (as in the case of Malaysia and South Africa) implies that the relationship is only one-fifth as strong. This is because the r-square - which measures the strength of the relationship - has declined from 0.5 to about 0.1 levels.

MYTH 3
The secret to performance in emerging markets is to adopt a bottom-up, rather than a top-down, investment process, because recent surveys have shown funds that employ a bottom-up process outperform in the long run: *Unlikely*

This may work out to be true for funds in the long run, but we believe it is a result of a relatively higher ability to pick stocks than markets. If dispersion of returns remains wide in markets, then picking the right market will drive performance.

An easy way to understand this is to compare the trends in European markets with the emerging markets again. In Chart 3, each drop line shows the dispersion of returns of European markets since 1982. Since the late 1980s, the trend is clear – dispersion of returns of European markets narrowed, as countries became integrated within the European Union and their monetary and fiscal policies started converging. As the economies began moving in lock-step, the equity markets returns started converging. So whereas in 1985 it paid to be a country picker in Europe because chances were that in the best market the investor out-performed even if his stock selection was poor, this was not true in the 1990s. By now, the advantage of selecting the right market has disappeared; it is more important to pick the right sectors and stocks.

The situation is quite different in emerging markets. In Chart 4, the dispersion of returns of the IFC emerging markets is shown in dollar terms. In most years, the dispersion of returns was wider than 150% and indeed moved off the vertical scale in seven years. It was only in the aftermath of the Mexican currency crisis that in 1995 returns were shocked into convergence – but still the dispersion was over 50%. Last year the dispersion widened to close to 175% again. This suggests that it still pays to pick countries in emerging markets

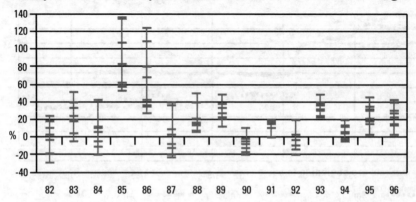

3: Dispersion of European markets' returns is narrowing...

Source: UBS & Datastream

4: ... but dispersion of emerging market returns is spread wider

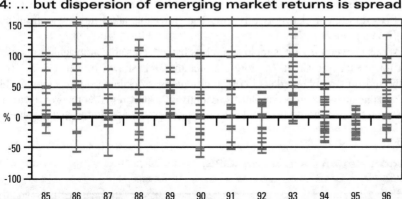

Source: UBS & IFC

because the economies are on different cycles and, therefore, equity markets provide widely dispersed returns.

In fact as Table E shows, the worst stocks in the best emerging market have almost always outperformed the best stocks in the worst emerging market. If you were the world's best country picker but the worst stock picker, over a year's horizon in emerging markets, you would always outperform the investor who is the world's best stock picker but the worst country picker. Obviously, the trick is to pick the best stocks in the best country, but failing that one must get the country right.

E: Worst stocks in the best emerging market outperform the best stocks of the worst emerging market
Equally weighted portfolio of stocks

	Best market	Performance %	10 worst stocks %	Worst market	Performance %	10 best stocks %
1985	Zimbabwe	154	77	Venezuela	-27	36
1986	Philippines	383	157	Nigeria	-57	-59
1987	Turkey	262	164	Brazil	-63	0
1988	Brazil	126	-32	Turkey	-61	-61
1989	Turkey	502	196	Venezuela	-33	-25
1990	Venezuela	602	400	Brazil	-66	-46
1991	Argentina	397	190	Zimbabwe	-52	-44
1992	Thailand	40	-28	Zimbabwe	-60	-50
1993	Turkey	234	44	Nigeria	-12	19
1994	Nigeria	191	48	Poland	-42	-42
1995	S Africa	18	-14	Sri Lanka	-38	33
1996	Venezuela	132	33	Korea	-39	30

Source: IFC

MYTH 4
Emerging markets are beginning to correlate with one another and country selection is less important: *Not true*

There is an indication that intra-regional markets are beginning to show rising correlation. In Charts 5 and 6 it is possible to see to what degree markets in Asia and Latin America respectively are moving in the same direction as regional economies integrate – but with the exception of two cases, correlation is very low. Therefore, this takes little away from our country selection argument.

Correlations between the IFC's regional indices have been stable at insignificant levels for the past four years (see Chart 7). More importantly, as is shown by Chart 8, the correlation of the most investable markets in different regions is declining. And as long as this correlation remains at the current low levels, country selection remains the key factor in relative performance, and should be of primary concern to the emerging market investor.

5: Asian correlations are rising (US$)
60-month rolling correlation

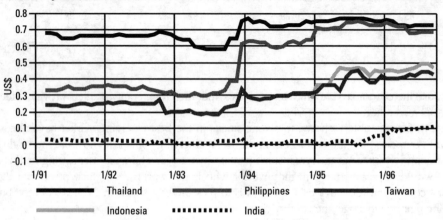

Source: UBS, Datastream and IFC

6: Latin American correlations are also rising (US$)
60-month rolling correlation

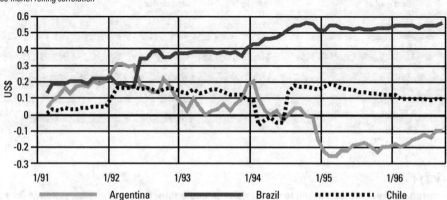

Source: UBS, Datastream and IFC

7: Inter-regional correlations are stable and insignificant (US$)
60-month rolling correlation of IFCI regional indices

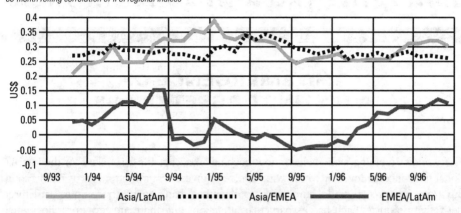

Source: UBS & IFC

8: Correlation amongst most investable markets in decline (US$)
60-month rolling correlation

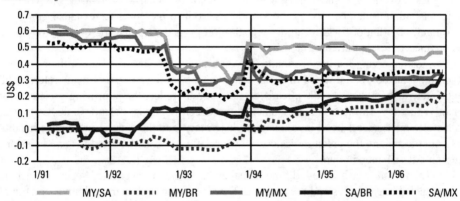

Source: UBS, Datastream and IFC

Emerging fixed-income markets

THE EMERGENCE OF
A DISTINCT ASSET CLASS

The world's emerging markets have now become an acceptable asset class for the international fixed-income investor with a wide choice of investment opportunities available, ranging from investment grade eurobonds to defaulted bank loans to complex structured derivative products. Each has its particular attractions and there are few portfolios which would not benefit from investment in one or more of the products which the emerging countries have to offer. The 1990s have seen the continuation of far-reaching economic and political reforms in emerging market countries.

The advent of democratic governments enjoying political legitimacy has enabled reformist administrations around the world to introduce measures to revitalize moribund economies by dint of fiscal rectitude, privatization programmes and the opening of closed economies to foreign investment.

Most emerging market economies have only recently embarked upon their entry or their rehabilitation in the world financial community. With the success of many reforms still ultimately to be judged, credit spreads do not yet fully reflect the improving prospects for many countries. Top tier countries, such as the Czech Republic, Poland, Chile, Colombia, Malaysia and Thailand are in investment grade territory, and there are clearly only a handful of countries where the credit indicators, which are fundamental for fixed-income investors, are on a deteriorating trend.

The factors which have led fund managers to invest in lower-rated securities include lower global interest rates and the increased flows of savings into managed funds and out of deposit accounts. A crucial recent development is the search for yield amongst insurance and pensions fund managers who have only just started to direct their resources of hundreds of billions of dollars towards lower-rated fixed-income instruments.

Mexico – 1982

The debt crisis, which erupted when Mexico defaulted on its international obligations in August 1982, precipitated an emergency which threatened major international financial institutions and brought lending to many countries to an abrupt halt. However, sovereign default was not a new phenomenon of the 1980s and it had been a peculiar 1970s notion that a sovereign nation would not default on its obligations – sovereign default on both internal and external debt has happened many times before and will undoubtedly happen again. Similarly, it was a particular 1980s notion that a borrower who had defaulted would never be able to access the international capital markets again.

Following the crisis of 1982, Latin American borrowers found the markets closed to

1: Total international bond issuance (US$bn)

Issuers domiciled in countries rated BBB or lower

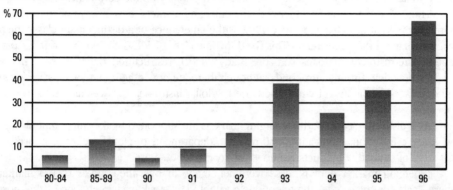

them for no more than three years and began borrowing again (albeit on a small scale) in 1986.

In the past, investment in emerging market fixed-income securities has almost always meant international foreign currency securities. Domestic currency markets were, with few exceptions, small, illiquid and often closed to foreign investment. This is changing rapidly.

The local markets of most countries in this survey are open to foreign investment in one form or another, although a totally open market where local and foreign investors have fully equal treatment is the exception rather than the rule. Most countries maintain some controls on their capital account which act as a barrier to the free flow of funds. In most cases, however, these restrictions exist to protect domestic monetary stability rather than to protect domestic investors and discriminate against foreign fund managers. For many countries, the example of how the rapid disinvestment of foreign funds brought Mexico to the brink of default in 1994 encourages extreme caution.

A wide range of fixed-income investments in international debt has always been available, although this has only developed into a large and liquid market in the past five years. The distinction must be made between bond obligations and loans, i.e. between investors and banks. In general, debt in bond form has always been fully serviced, even when a country has defaulted on commercial bank loans.

Only Costa Rica, Panama, and the former Yugoslavia (a special case in itself) have defaulted on bonds in recent years. Most bonds are in anonymous bearer form whilst loans are registered. If a country has severe balance of payment difficulties and would like to seek a rescheduling of its external obligations, it can get its bank (i.e. loan) creditors around the negotiating table; it cannot easily do this with bond holders.

What the market offers

Throughout the 1980s, many countries now considered "emerging markets" frequently accessed the bond markets. Hungary, Turkey, Greece and South Africa, for example, are already well known to many investors. Other countries, such as Bulgaria, the former Soviet Union, India, Colombia and Algeria, also borrowed publicly on the euromarkets.

Thus, what have now been termed "the emerging markets" have always been available to investors. What has changed, since 1989, is the emergence of a distinct asset class which has now entered the mainstream. This fixed-income class divides into roughly four sectors, namely, pre-restructured loans (or "pre-Brady" debt), restructured debt (mostly "Brady bonds"), new debt (mostly eurobonds, although there are now other types such as Yankees) and domestic obligations (of which there are US dollar instruments as well as local currency bonds).

As a distinct asset class, the emerging markets are supported by the full gamut of trading, sales, origination, syndication, and research departments of global securities houses. A vast array of derivative products are now also available.

Emerging market debt is also overwhelmingly an over-the-counter (OTC) market where deals take place over the telephone and not via a stock exchange. One of the most important developments since 1990 has been the rapid expansion of the investor base. The emerging markets have moved out of the realm of flight capital and the specialist fund and into the mainstream. It is now perfectly normal for a sophisticated investor to have some exposure to emerging markets.

However, amongst the universe of fixed-income investors, overall exposure remains tiny. In the past three years, many new investors have been buying emerging market bonds for the first time.

The completion of fifteen Brady restructuring deals (with three more agreed in principle) and the surge in eurobond issuance, means that the total outstanding volume of emerging market securities in bond form has surpassed US$360 billion (rated BBB or lower). All the major Brady deals have been completed and Peru, Vietnam and Côte d'Ivoire have also reached agreements in principal.

The well-publicised agreement between the Russian Federation and its commercial bank creditors was not a "Brady" deal as Russia did not seek debt forgiveness which is the defining aspect of a "Brady" plan. Similarly, the restructuring of the foreign debt of Morocco, Croatia and Macedonia.

In the case of Slovenia, the restructuring of that country's portion of former Yugoslav commercial debt was structured in such a way with compensatory payments that creditors were as well off as if payments had been made throughout the five-year period when the debt was in default following the dissolution of the former Yugoslavia.

Eurobond issuance has surged since 1990 reaching US$66 billion in 1996, nearly double the level of 1995, In the past two years, several countries accessed the eurobond market for the first time, including Kazakstan, the Russian Federation, Slovenia, Morocco, Jordan, Mauritius and the Baltic States. Many other countries are now actively seeking financing in the eurobond markets.

The preserve of higher-rated countries for many years, sovereign foreign currency credit ratings are now very widely used by emerging market issuers active in the international markets. The change in fashion means that it is now probably essential for a country to seek a credit-rating before issuing public bonds in the international markets.

Domestic markets are now also attracting a great deal of attention. With the move towards convertible currencies and the adoption of economic reform policies reducing

2: Emerging market bonds (US$)

JP Morgan Emerging Market Composite Bond Index (Dec 1993 = 100)

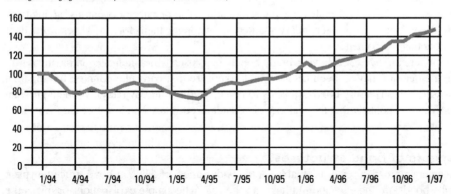

inflation, debt instruments denominated in local currencies will give further possibilities for portfolio diversification. As the majority of international debt (which is practically all liquid) is denominated in US dollars, the performance of these instruments naturally has a high correlation to the US Treasury market. Local currency markets offer investors the chance to diversify and this opportunity, for many investors, outweighs the drawbacks of local markets such as illiquidity and difficult settlement procedures.

Evaluating emerging market debt

Not only are the instruments available in the emerging markets frequently unfamiliar to investors, but the criteria by which they should be evaluated are often different from those in other fixed-income markets. Below, we have highlighted the major factors of which the investor should be aware.

Obligation seniority

Emerging markets offer a sometimes bewildering array of instruments, especially within the restructured debt sector. The most important aspect to appreciate (and the aspect which goes a long way to explain some seemingly strange anomalies in yields) is that different instruments are not regarded as equal obligations of the issuer; market valuations impose a specific hierarchy on sovereign debt.

Eurobonds have a higher seniority than Brady bonds which, in turn, are seen as safer investments than domestic foreign currency debts (Mexican Tesebonos, which very nearly defaulted three years ago, were domestic instruments denominated in US dollars). However, the opinion of the market with regard to obligation seniority has been undergoing some fundamental changes in recent years. The greatest cause for this has been the fact that the original bank holders of Brady bonds have sold a large proportion of their portfolios. Investors, rather than banks, are now the largest holders of these bonds.

The rating agencies have generally recognised this fact. Previously, where they were rated, Brady bonds would carry a rating one notch below that of other sovereign debt of the same issuer – they now usually carry the same rating. The practice of countries buying back their Brady bonds in the secondary market or swapping them for uncollateralized debt enforces this phenomenon.

Where an investor is buying Brady bonds, he is usually not interested in having collateral, the decision having been taken to seek exposure to a particular country, not a partial exposure to US Treasury bonds. In years to come, Brady bond buy-backs will be a growing trend and it is unlikely that the majority of collateralized Brady bonds will reach their maturity date.

Aspects of bond structures

The emerging market sector is notable for the wide variety of different bond structures; plain vanilla bonds are the exception rather than the rule. The simple explanation for this is the lower (or perceived lower) credit quality of borrowers. Issuers frequently have to add credit enhancements or sweeteners to their bonds to attract investors. This, of course, greatly increases the complexity of evaluating the true value of many bonds, and those investors willing to devote time to studying such structural considerations may be able to gain significantly higher returns.

Collateral

Under Brady Plan restructuring agreements, many of the bonds issued to refinance defaulted loans are collateralized by zero-coupon US Treasury bonds (or similar instruments for the small non-US dollar tranches). In addition, some rescheduling agreements incorporate rolling interest payments guarantees for 12 or 18 months.

These rolling guarantees form an important part of the correct evaluation of Brady bonds; whereas collateral against the principal guarantees one final payment, rolling interest payment guarantees will change in value over time as the remaining number of payments guarantees diminishes. Other bond issues have been collateralized by other types of assets and receivables. A further function of collateralization is that this collateral can be stripped from the bonds to create a purer form of sovereign risk which or course, would have a higher yield.

Ownership clause

Eurobonds whose equity is held partially or wholly by foreign shareholders, are frequently enhanced by ownership clauses which enable the bondholder to put the bond at par if the ownership structure changes. This enhancement means that these bonds would normally trade at a premium to wholly owned local companies.

Equity conversion

Certain Brady bonds are eligible to be tendered in debt-for-equity swaps or other type of exchange. Such an embedded option will increase the price of the bond in comparison with a similar non-convertible issue, but because of the wide variety of exchange options available, calculating precisely how such bonds should be valued has proved to be extremely difficult.

Dollar constraint clauses

These clauses have been contained in the prospectuses of several Brazilian issues and have caused concern to some investors. There are two basic types of dollar constraint clause and both concern a situation whereby the government prevents domestic companies from paying foreign currency debt.

The first (and more common type of clause) states that in that event, a bondholder can elect to receive payment in local currency instead, but does not diminish the rights of the bondholder to demand payment in the original currency of the bond. The second clause (which makes such bonds less attractive to international investors) states that the borrowers can fulfil their obligation by offering local currency at the official exchange rate. No benchmark liquid bond would contain such a clause.

Warrants and options

Some Brady bonds from oil-exporting countries include attached "value recovery rights" which increase interest payments if oil revenues rise above a certain level. Uruguayan Brady bonds have a similar option based on a trade-weighted basket of exports. These warrants can be detached and traded separately. In normal circumstances, Brady bonds trade ex-warrant.

Country credit factors

Although most emerging market countries have credit ratings, not only are there sometimes differences of opinion between the major rating agencies, but these ratings are frequently lagging indicators. In considering the credit rating of a sovereign borrower, two factors must be taken into consideration: the willingness to pay and the ability to pay.

Willingness to pay

The willingness of a sovereign nation to pay its debts is one of the most important factors when considering emerging markets, and is foremost a political question. If there is any crisis over foreign payments and certain economic hardships would need to be enforced to maintain payments, an amount of political stability is necessary.

Stability combined with legitimacy is the ideal combination but it is primarily stability which is important; for example the Soviet Union was considered a much better credit than the Russian Federation is now. Additionally, the regime's commitment to integration in the world financial and trading system needs to be high if such matters are not to be sacrificed for short-term domestic considerations. This ties in with obligation seniority and Nigeria is a good illustration: Nigeria has foreign debts of over US$30 billion and has defaulted widely. However, the country's negotiable debt is only around 10% of the total (the rest is bilateral and concessional) and is fully serviced - this is the debt which is important for maintaining relations with foreign banks and the Nigerian authorities place an extremely high importance on maintaining good relations.

Legitimacy of debt

When a country has made the transition from an authoritarian regime to a more democratic one (or vice versa), the new administration (as well as the population) may view obligations contracted under the old regime as less legitimate than any new debts. Thus old and new debt of the same borrower can have different values. This factor has hampered restructuring agreements with debtors arguing that banks should shoulder some of the blame for a country's predicament for lending excessive sums of money to irresponsible regimes. The recent argument in France over Tsarist debts shows how such disputes can persevere for decades.

Economic factors

These are important in assessing a borrower's ability to pay. What needs to be examined is a country's capabilities of earning sufficient foreign exchange to cover its obligations, which therefore makes ratios such as export earnings to debt service and foreign reserves more significant than many domestic considerations. Although a country might not be able to repay all outstanding principal at once if called upon to do so (indeed very few countries could - including most of the OECD), it may well be able to service its debts with ease. Some highly indebted countries, such as Sudan and Liberia, have few opportunities to raise foreign currency and to service debt so that the prices of their debt trade at substantial discounts to face value.

Local currency debt

The process of evaluating the relative attractiveness of investments in local market instruments is completely different to investing in foreign bonds. Factors which are important include domestic monetary policy, banking system liquidity and the outlook for exchange rates. Whereas a country cannot print foreign exchange to service debt but has to earn it, a government could, if it so wished, print its own currency (although many countries have laws in place to guard against this, these laws in many cases have not been tested over time).

With few opportunities to hedge currency risk efficiently, the outlook for the exchange rate can be the most important consideration in choosing or avoiding a local market instrument. Rules and regulations on trading local markets and repatriating profits can also change, sometimes frequently. Although the global trend is towards greater liberalization and the elimination of remaining barriers, and the wrath of international investors is feared by many governments, there can be no guarantee that an investor may suddenly find himself unable to get his funds out of a particular country.

Trading emerging market debt

In the emerging markets, different obligations trade in different fashions. Restructured debt trading is more dominated by professionals and can be highly volatile, whereas eurobonds tend to be bought by retail investors and can be relatively illiquid. Local currency debt markets are always dominated by domestic banks. Thus, classic trading techniques can yield poor results if applied without taking the special characteristics of emerging markets into account.

Brady Bond market

The market in restructured debt is notable for its high volatility. Benchmark Brady bonds are so liquid with such large volumes that a single investor cannot move the market. In addition, the instruments have durations of up to thirty years and thus are highly sensitive to political and economic events. Until recently, the typical Brady bond investor has been an arbitrageur who holds the bonds for short periods; institutional investors were more likely to put money

3: Brady bonds (US$)

JP Morgan All Brady Index (Dec 1990 = 100)

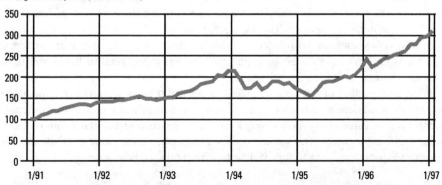

into emerging market equities or eurobonds. Although this is changing rapidly with a surge of institutional investment, volumes (particularly in benchmark issues) are not sufficient to affect the trading patterns of the market.

The relative inefficiencies of the Brady bond market means that traditional strategies, such as yield curve plays, are unlikely to produce satisfactory results in the short-term, although the rapidly increasing depth of the market implies that there could be significant gains awaiting the investor with a longer-term horizon.

In addition, the different forms and complexity of the instruments mean that they can react differently to events – remember that the collateral element changes in value independently of any local developments.

Despite reflecting an identical credit, fixed and floating rate Brady bonds will, of course, vary in price according to LIBOR. With falling rates, Par bonds have naturally given a much higher return than Discount bonds over the last couple of years. However, the liquidity and large outstanding volumes of Brady bonds does mean that very large tickets can easily be executed without moving the market. Trades of US$5 million can be made on a bid/offer spread as low as 1/8% in benchmark issues.

Sovereign loans

Traditionally a specialist market, trading sovereign loans is rapidly becoming more mainstream with reasonable liquidity in benchmarks such as Morocco and Russia. However, the vast majority of loans are extremely illiquid assets. Bid/offer spreads can be 5 points or more and it can take weeks to find a counterparty for an obscure asset.

This, of course, is the very attraction to some investors - potential returns are therefore enormous. The major obstacle to trading these loans is settlement procedures. Loans normally have to be assigned, a physical process which can take a number of weeks. The lengthy and expensive process of loan assignment has lead to the development of a number of ways to circumvent this: Euroclearable debentures can be issued against Nigerian Promissory Notes, for example.

Or an investor could buy one of the warrants issued by many investment houses which reflect the performance of loans without the problems of physically trading them. Loans can be the most volatile emerging market asset. Being frequently illiquid, a single investor can easily move a market. However, an active investor can easily see the advantages of this: very volatile assets subject to significant price swings can yield large returns. This sector is the only area of the emerging markets where commercial banks still have noticeable influence.

A large proportion of the loans are still held by the original lending bank and some banks actively trade their loan portfolios. The treatment of unpaid interest can have a significant effect on the value of non-performing loans. These assets normally trade with past due interest ("PDI") at zero cost. The amount of PDI can mount rapidly during default and the treatment of PDI during restructurings will be fundamental to valuing loans.

Eurobonds

Emerging market eurobonds still suffer from poor liquidity in general. US$250 million remains a large issue size and bid/offer spreads can be as wide as 1%. The more sophisticated frequent borrowers in the market now offer large and more liquid eurobonds and global bonds; Mexico, Argentina and Russia now offer bonds with issue sizes of US$1,000 million or more. Specialist funds and retail accounts remain the backbone of the eurobond market and bonds are often bought and held to maturity. Away from benchmark sovereign issues, the investor base remains relatively small which can lead to market saturation, particularly in a specific borrower class. Institutional investment is growing rapidly, however, though of course concentrated on the top tier of borrowers.

The retail element of the eurobond market places a strong emphasis on name recognition. Eastern European or Turkish borrowers have little problem raising funds in Europe or Japan, whereas the same investor can be unwilling to buy Latin American bonds of the same of better quality. German retail investors can be particularly name conscious, a fact which can sometimes lead to bizarre pricing. As well as being dependent on the fate of the sovereign credit of their domicile country, the yields of emerging market eurobonds will also be dependent upon the normal credit factors affecting any corporate bond. Some borrowers would be AAA rated if based in the US ("the right company, wrong address"), others have clearly more worrying factors, however well they are portrayed in the summary of the bond prospectus.

Local markets

With few exceptions, local currency markets are illiquid and investors should be prepared to hold their investment to maturity. Most markets comprise mostly short-term discount treasury bills which can be bought at an official auction or in the secondary market. The majority of investors in these markets are local banks which frequently have few other options for investment. The lack of liquidity, which characterizes the foreign exchange markets of many emerging market countries, can be a problem, though, and without due care, large losses can be made on foreign exchange transactions, thus cancelling out any return on the investment.

BRADY BONDS

Brady bonds are bonds that have been issued in the restructuring of commercial bank loans and other debt, whereby creditors tender their loans in exchange for new bonds. A "Brady plan" is officially known as a "debt and debt-service reduction agreement" (DDSR).

Countries that have completed Brady plans

Argentina	Dominican Republic	Nigeria	Poland	Brazil
Jordan	Panama	Uruguay	Bulgaria	Mexico
Philippines	Venezuela	Costa Rica		

Countries that have agreed a Brady plan in principle

Côte d'Ivoire	Peru	Vietnam

How a Brady Plan works

The basis of a Brady Plan is that the creditor banks realise that the debtor country will never be able to repay their outstanding obligations in full. Thus a compromise is struck. A committee representing the creditor banks will negotiate with the debtor country to decide how much a country can realistically afford to pay over time. Economic forecasts to establish how much a country can afford are usually drawn up in conjunction with the IMF.

Having agreed on how much the country can pay, this is compared to the outstanding debt. The difference is then reconciled in one of three ways: Discount Bonds (where the principal is cut), Par Bonds (where the debtor pays sub-market interest rates) and a debt-buy back at a mutually agreed discount.

In some cases, there is also an option for creditors who do not want to see the principal amount of their loans cut or receive sub-market interest rates; in this case, the creditor must agree to lend new money to the debtor in return for retaining the value the existing obligations. Interest arrears (past-due interest "PDI") has never been explicitly forgiven in a Brady plan (except the agreement in principle with Côte d'Ivoire which has yet to be ratified by creditors). In most cases, this PDI is rescheduled into a separate tradable bond. Occasionally, for example in the case of Peru, contractual unpaid interest is recalculated at lower rates which is for the debtor an effective cut in PDI.

The principal amount of par and discount bonds is usually fully collateralized by zero coupon US treasury bonds (or similar instruments for non-US dollar tranches) which are held by a third party. Thus creditors have the confidence that these obligations will ultimately be repaid. Frequently, several interest payments are also collateralized on a rolling basis; i.e. when the collateral backing a coupon payment is not used, this collateral rolls forward to back the next interest payment. An investor buying a collateralized Brady bond would thus not expect to lose all his money.

A menu of options is drawn up and creditors decide which option suits them best. Derivatives of the basic Brady bonds can become very complex because of the need to satisfy many different creditors whilst resulting in an overall debt-cut acceptable to the debtor country. For example, certain creditors may be attracted to long-term equity options, others might prefer discount securities for tax purposes; in addition, where there is a foreign policy interest, banks may have their arm twisted by their government to accept a particular option.

After a protracted process of rebalancing these options, a balance will be found which satisfies both sides. The final part of the agreement will usually be IMF blessing. Creditors need the comfort that the IMF agrees that the debtor country's economic plans and forecasts will enable the country to fulfil these new obligations. In many cases, new money will be lent by the IMF at concessional rates to buy the collateral.

Principal types of Brady Bond
Collateralized Fixed-Rate Par Bonds ("Par Bonds")
Par bonds are received in exchange for eligible debt tendered at face value. They offer the debtor permanent interest rate relief and protection from fluctuations in interest rates. The bonds are long-dated, usually 25 or 30 years, have a single repayment at maturity, and their principal is collateralized by specially-issued zero-coupon US Treasury bonds which are held at the US Federal Reserve Bank. There is usually also a rolling interest payment guarantee collateralized by "AA" or higher rated financial instruments which covers 12 to 18 months of interest payments. In certain cases, "value recovery rights" are attached to the bonds: under such rights, payments to bondholders can be increased according to formulae based upon the price of oil or a trade-weighted index.

Collateralized Floating-Rate Discount Bonds ("Discount Bonds ")
Discount bonds are received in exchange for eligible debt tendered at a discount to face value, thus offering the debtor permanent, partial relief on the principal owed. In return, the creditor receives higher interest payments, usually LIBOR plus 13/16%. In the case of Mexico and Argentina the discount was 35% , for Venezuela 30% and for Poland and Bulgaria it was 50%.

The bonds are long-dated, usually 25 or 30 years, have a single repayment at maturity, and their principal is collateralized by specially-issued zero-coupon US Treasury bonds which are held at the US Federal Reserve Bank. There is also a rolling interest payment guarantee collateralized by "AA" or higher rated financial instruments which cover 12 to 18 months of interest payments. As with Par Bonds, value recovery rights may be attached.

Front-Loaded Interest Reduction Bonds ("Flirbs")
Flirbs are received in exchange for eligible debt tendered at face value. They pay sub-market interest rates for the first few years and thus offer the debtor temporary interest rate relief and protection against future interest rate fluctuations. There is no collateral for the principal, although there is often a rolling interest payment guarantee collateralized by "AA" or higher rated financial instruments which covers 12 months of interest payments for the first five or six years. The trade-off for less collateral is a shorter average life. The bonds amortise after an initial grace period of up to nine years.

Debt Conversion Bonds ("DCBs") / New Money Bonds ("NMBs")
Debt conversion bonds are received in exchange for eligible debt tendered at face value, conditional upon the creditor providing additional new money ("New Money Bonds") equivalent to a certain percentage of the amount of its eligible debt. There is no collateral for either principal or interest payments, but the average lives of these bonds are shorter than

those of par or discount bonds. There are also some New Money Bonds issued by some countries in connection with previous refinancings prior to a Brady restructuring.

Interest Arrears Bonds

IDU bonds are received in exchange for a creditor's claim on certain past due accrued interest which has not been paid. No collateral is provided for these bonds, except in the case of Costa Rica. They have a variety of names such as Interest Due and Unpaid bonds "IDU", past due interest bonds "PDI", interest arrears bonds "IAB", or, in the case of Russia, interest arrears notes "IAN". These are all essentially the same thing.

Convertibles in emerging markets

The growth of the market for convertibles issued by companies from emerging markets has been one of the major features of recent years. Despite the volatility seen in emerging markets in general over this period, convertible bonds continue to grow in popularity.

What is a convertible?

The general definition of a convertible bond is that it is a fixed-interest security, that gives holders the right to convert into ordinary shares. It can be considered as offering both investors and issuers certain properties of both equities and bonds.

Features of a convertible:

◆ Coupon, a fixed amount, paid gross on known dates, either semi-annually, annually or quarterly.
◆ Convertible: the convertible is usually convertible into a known number of shares (there may be regulatory restrictions) for a known period of time.
◆ Redemption: this is not so straight forward. A convertible may be redeemed at a known amount on a set date. Alternatively a holder may be forced to convert on a set date. It may be that the company or the holders also have the right to redeem the bonds on earlier dates at known amounts.

New Issue volume in emerging markets (US$m)

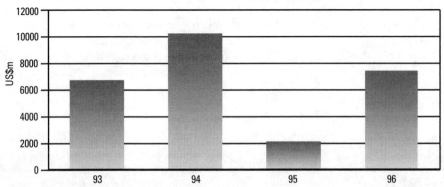

What are the benefits to investors?

Convertibles offer investors the chance to gain exposure to an underlying equity whilst at the same time holding a fixed-interest security. Convertible holders benefit from a know coupon flow and in most cases a known redemption. This gives the bonds fixed interest characteristics which should allow them to outperform the shares in a falling market. This defensive property should appeal to investors in emerging markets.

What are the benefits to an issuer?

The cost of financing a convertible bond will be below that of a straight fixed-interest bond from the same company, since the inclusion of conversion rights allows a lower coupon. Looked at another way, the company is able to issue shares at a premium to its current share price, which may not be possible with a straight equity placing. Finally, by issuing a convertible on the international markets the company is broadening its investor base.

Emerging currencies

THEORY VERSUS HISTORY

According to economic theory, there should be no excess return in the long run from holding a foreign currency (including the safest short-term asset, such as a treasury bill) in one country versus another. On average, the movement of the exchange rate will be offset by interest rate differentials, which makes the expected return on holding the foreign currency equal to zero. However, this theory assumes that the safest asset in each country is equally safe, or that there are no country risk premiums, so the theory is only a guide to interpreting historical evidence. Some currencies have earned persistent excess return over long periods of time. In this article we examine the causes of these excess returns in the developed countries, and then apply the lessons to the emerging markets.

Total return
The appropriate way to measure total return on a currency is to choose a base currency and then calculate the cumulative return from holding a foreign currency against it over time. This calculation includes the cumulative effect of interest rate differentials, which should (on average) offset the movement of the exchange rate.

The theory
According to economic theory, ignoring many factors, such as country risk, taxes, problems of inflation measurement and others, inflation differentials determine long-run exchange rate movements, as well as the intra-period interest rate differentials between two currencies. Where this is true, the total return from holding a foreign currency is zero. Interest rate differentials will exactly offset exchange rate movements. The corollary to this theory is that forward exchange rates are unbiased estimators of future spot exchange rates, which makes the expected return from currency hedging also equal to zero.

The historical evidence
Unfortunately, the historical evidence does not support this theory – risk and taxes for example, cannot be ignored. Since 1973, there has been a 33% excess return from holding deutschemarks against dollars, and a 50% excess return from holding Japanese yen against dollars. Within Europe, there has been a 60% excess return from holding deutschemarks against UK sterling, and a 33% excess return from holding deutschemarks against Swiss francs. Surprisingly, there has been no significant return from holding deutschemarks against either the Italian lira or the French franc. Overall, the yen has been the strongest of the 'big eight' currencies since 1973 on a total return basis, while sterling and the Swiss franc have been the two weakest, reflecting in the latter case a lower country risk premium than elsewhere.

1: Return for US$ investor

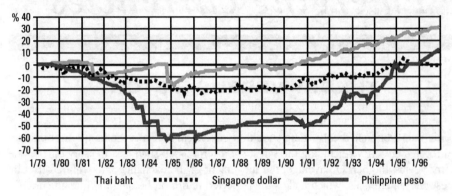

Thai baht   ■■■■■■■■ Singapore dollar   ━━━━━ Philippine peso

2: Return for US$ investor

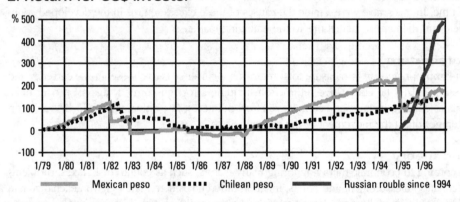

Mexican peso   ■■■■■■■■ Chilean peso   ━━━━━ Russian rouble since 1994

Understanding the yen

This evidence shows that the textbook theories of purchasing power parity (PPP) and interest rate parity are inadequate descriptions of the real world. The yen is a good example, because it has tended to appreciate faster than inflation differentials with the United States would suggest. This is due, in part at least, to that fact that productivity in Japan's tradable goods sector has converged rapidly with US productivity levels since 1973, while domestic productivity has lagged behind. Because of the widening productivity differential between tradable and non-tradable goods, Japanese export prices have fallen rapidly relative to consumer prices. Since 1973, the ratio of Japan/US export prices has fallen by 60%, while the ratio of consumer prices (CPIs) has fallen by only 27%. The exchange rate has fallen by 60% during this time, which is consistent with the fact that exchange rates move according to the relative prices of internationally traded goods, and not according to the prices of non-traded goods like housing and health care. Thus, using CPIs to measure real appreciations, not to mention inflation itself, can be problematic. The theory is really just an excellent point of departure.

A productivity gap

Because of the productivity gap between Japan's internationally exposed sector and its domestic sector, purchasing power parity, calculated using CPIs, has persistently underestimated the equilibrium value of the yen against the dollar over time. This accounts for the fact that PPP, based on CPIs, for US$/JPY is currently near 150, compared to an average spot rate of 109 in 1996. On a relative export price basis, equilibrium for US$/JPY was around 105 in 1996.

Biased forwards

Because the yen has appreciated faster than CPI differentials have suggested in the past, and because interest rates are set with respect to overall price inflation, closer to CPIs, interest rate differentials between the yen and the dollar have been biased predictors of the US$/JPY exchange rate. This means that forward exchange rates have persistently underestimated the degree to which the yen appreciates over time. This observation can be generalised to other countries with relatively rapid productivity growth in the tradable goods sector, and relatively slow productivity growth in the non-tradable sector. This pattern has been a hallmark of emerging markets: Germany and Japan after 1945, and the Asian tigers more recently. Developing economies tend to have the appearance of such rising real exchange rates in the long run, while mature economies often have steady or falling real exchange rates.

Real interest rates

While the excess return on the yen is explained by productivity differentials, the poor performance of the Swiss franc is explained by low real interest rates. Due to Switzerland's safe haven status and its high domestic savings rate, it has been able to operate with persistently lower real interest rates than neighbouring countries. These relatively low real interest rates mean that nominal interest rate differentials have persistently overestimated the degree to which the Swiss franc appreciates over time. There is thus a built-in penalty for holding Swiss francs in the long run, or, in other words, a risk premium on holding dollar or other short-term foreign currency assets.

Emerging markets

Based on these findings for the 'Big 8' currencies, the emerging market currencies ought to be good long-term investments. Emerging market currencies are (by their definition) characterized by high productivity growth rates in the export sector. This is similar to the Japanese yen after 1949. Some (but not all) emerging countries have high real interest rates as well, either due to political risk or due to a reliance on foreign capital. This is the opposite situation to the Swiss franc, and suggests that politically risky emerging markets should be good long-term currency bets, because there are returns to compensate for their higher risk.

High real rates

Chart 1 shows how three politically risky currencies have performed against the dollar. The Russian rouble has had extraordinarily high real interest rates since 1994, which has resulted in excess currency returns of 490% in the past two years. The Mexican and Chilean pesos have also suffered from high degrees of political risk, which accounts for the excess returns since 1979 of 180% and 130%, respectively.

High productivity

Emerging markets with high productivity growth have not always been good currency bets, like Japan, since 1979, however. For example, the Thai baht returned only 31% to US-based investors since 1979, while the Singapore dollar returned -1% in that period (see Chart 2). Less developed countries have actually performed worse than middle income countries, with the Philippines returning 12% to US investors since 1979 and India returning -64% in the same period. The lesson seems to be that real yields are the most important consideration for long-run currency investment, even more important than productivity performance. This is highlighted by the fact that the Latin American currencies have been better performers than most Asian currencies. Better still are high real returns that come from return on investment instead of risk premia.

Argentina

Area (thousands of km²):	2767
Population (1995, millions):	34.6
Population projection (2025, millions):	43
Population younger than 15 yrs (1991, % of total):	29.4
Urbanization rate (1993, % of population):	87
Life expectancy (1993, years at birth):	72
Gross domestic product (1996, US$bn):	339.2
GDP per capita (1996, US$):	9688
Average annual GDP growth rate (1990-96, %):	4.9
Average annual inflation rate (1990-96, %):	361.2
Currency (peso per US$, average 1996):	1
Real exchange rate: (1990=100, average 1996)	114.72
Structure of production (1994):	54% services, 37% industry, 9% agriculture
Main exports:	agribusiness products (cereal, beef, meat, fats and oils), chemicals, base metals, electrical goods
Main imports:	capital goods & passenger vehicles, fuels, spare parts
Main trading partners:	Brazil, US, Netherlands, Germany, Chile, Italy
Market capitalization of Stock Exchange (December 1996; US$bn):	44.7
Total foreign debt (% of GDP):	32.5
Next elections due under normal circumstances:	half of Chamber of Deputies, October 1997; Senate, May 1998; presidency and remaining half of Chamber of Deputies, May 1999
Credit rating: (Jan 1997, Standard & Poor's, Moody's)	BB-; B1

FORECAST: 1997-2000 (average)

	Worst case	Most likely	Best case
Real GDP growth (%)	2.0	3.9	4.5
Inflation (%)	3.5	2.3	2.0

■ POLITICS

Historical overview

Argentina was discovered by the Spanish in 1516, but strong Indian resistance prevented the Europeans from establishing a colony for over sixty years. In the power vacuum that followed independence in 1816, Argentina experienced decades of instability and political unrest. These were characterized by an armed struggle between the unitarios, who wanted a strong, liberal central government, and the federales, conservatives who supported decentralized provincial authority. For decades this bloody, vindictive conflict thwarted Argentina's development. Despite the adoption of a constitution in 1853, the de facto civil war continued until the end of the 1870s, when Buenos Aires was declared a federal district and the traditional rivalry between that city and the rest of the country was resolved. After 1880, commercial activity expanded together with foreign investment and immigration.

Argentina continued to prosper under different civilian governments until the Great Depression of 1929. With the economic crisis came the military, taking power in 1930. When Juan Domingo Perón won the presidential elections in 1946, he inherited a country exhausted by political instability and economic failure.

Perón remained in power until 1955, when a new military coup marked the beginning of three decades of almost uninterrupted and repressive military rule. Particularly dramatic was the reign of terror known as the "Dirty War" starting in 1976. It lasted six years and resulted in the death or disappearance of thousands of Argentines. The defeat of the Junta in the Falklands/Malvinas war against the United Kingdom in 1982 led to the demise of military rule.

In December 1983, Raúl Alfonsín of the middle-class Radical Civic Union Party (the Partido Unión Cívica Radical, or UCR) was inaugurated as Argentina's first civilian president after eight years of military rule. Alfonsín left office in July 1989 amid economic chaos, rebellion in the army and widespread discontent. His successor, Carlos Menem of the working-class Peronist Party (the Partido Justicialista, or PJ) was elected for a six-year term in May 1989, receiving 49% of the vote.

Recent events

Since Menem took office, his party has regularly won about 40% of the vote and holds a majority in both chambers of Congress. In May 1995, Menem was elected for a second term by almost 50% of Argentina's voting population, and the Peronists extended their majority in both the Chamber of Deputies and the Senate. Since then, however, Menem's popularity has decreased substantially as a consequence of the rigid Convertibility Plan, implemented in 1991 (see below) and the so-called "Tequila Hangover", the capital flight sparked by Mexican devaluation, which have led to record levels of unemployment.

Economy minister Domingo Cavallo, chief architect and executor of the Convertibility Plan, left the government in July 1996. He was replaced by Roque Fernández, who had been central bank governor and was another major architect of the Convertibility Plan.

Chronology

1516	Discovery of Río de la Plata by the Spanish
1580	Foundation of Buenos Aires. The region is under the administration of the Viceroyalty of Peru.
1778	Creation of the Viceroyalty of Río de la Plata
1810	First rebellion against Spain
1816	Independence
1810-80	Instability and civil strife
1853	First constitution
1880	Buenos Aires is declared a federal district

1880-1916	Conservative leadership, period of prosperity and progress
1891	Foundation of the Radical Civic Union (UCR)
1916-1930	Presidency held by Radical Civic Union
1930	Military coup
1930-46	Period of strong military influence or direct military government
1946	Juan Domingo Perón wins the first free presidential elections since 1930
1947	Creation of the Partido Justicialista, or Peronist Party
1955	New military coup and three decades of military intervention and repression begin
1970s	Violent confrontation between guerrillas, right-wing paramilitary groups and the military
1976-83	"Dirty War" under a new repressive military government
1982	Defeat in the Falklands/Malvinas war against the United Kingdom
1983	Raúl Alfonsín of the UCR wins the presidency
1989	The Peronist Carlos Menem is elected president
1990	Foreign minister Domingo Cavallo chosen to head the economy ministry
1991	Convertibility Plan implemented; formation of MERCOSUR
1994	Constitutional reform
1995	Re-election of President Carlos Menem
1996	Cavallo replaced by Fernández as economy minister

State organization

Argentina consists of twenty-three provinces and the federal district of Buenos Aires. Each province has its own constitution and government, with a governor as chief executive, a legislature and a court system.

Within each province, power is further delegated to the municipalities. Despite this federalist organization, the president, to whom the national constitution grants considerable power, often intervenes in provincial matters.

Constitution and government

The 1853 constitution defines Argentina as a federal republic with separated executive, legislative and judicial powers. Supreme executive authority is vested in the president, who is in charge of the armed forces and appoints the president of the central bank as well as the heads of civil and judicial offices.

The president is elected by universal suffrage and, since the August 1994 constitutional revision, is allowed to run for a second consecutive four-year term. The bicameral legislature consists of the House of Deputies and the Senate. The 257 deputies are directly elected by popular vote and serve four-year terms, while the 72 senators are elected by provincial legislatures for six years. After 2001, senators will be elected by popular vote.

Political parties
Partido Justicialista (PJ) or Peronist Party
Base of support in the labour movement
Founded 1947
Led by Carlos Saúl Menem

Unión Cívica Radical (UCR) or Radical Civic Union Party
    Centre
    Founded 1891
    Led by Rodolfo Terragno
Frepaso Demócrata
    Centre-left; alliance between Frente Grande, the Unidád Socialista,
    the Partido Cristiano and Politica Abierta para la Integración
    Social
    Founded 1994
    Led by Carlos 'Chacho' Alvarez

Legislature:
Senate: PJ (38 seats), **UCR** (17), **others** (13), four senators still to be elected (as of September 1996)
Chamber of Deputies: PJ (132 seats), **UCR** (67), **Frepaso** (21), **others** (37)

Next elections
Half of the Chamber of Deputies: October 1997; third of Senate: September 1998; presidency
and remaining half of Chamber of Deputies: September 1999

Other political forces
Labour
The labour movement, which is the base of President Menem's party, still has considerable political and economic power in Argentina. Following Menem's Convertibility Plan, privatization policy, deregulation and administrative reforms have led to record un-employment. As a consequence, union leaders are becoming more aggressive, provoking national strikes and mass demonstrations.

Military
The influence of the military, discredited by the country's defeat in the Falklands/Malvinas war and accused of serious human rights violations during its years of power, has declined considerably since 1983. Moreover, during the last five years, Menem's government has drastically cut military spending and reduced the armed forces to a fifth of their former size, sharply reducing the possibility of another coup. As a consequence, the military role today is confined to guarding Argentina's borders and taking part in international peacekeeping missions.

Central bank
The Banco Central de la República de Argentina was founded in 1935. It is governed by a board of ten directors, including the president and vice-president, who are appointed for six years by the executive branch of the government.

    The bank is responsible for the regulation and control of the banking and credit systems, the money supply and foreign exchange rate policy. However, this latter task is now considerably limited by the 1991 Convertibility Law, which established a fixed peso/dollar rate and prohibits creation of pesos except for the purchase of foreign exchange.

■ ECONOMICS

Historical overview

Argentina was among the most prosperous countries in the world as recently as 1930. Its wealth was based on a strong export-led agricultural sector. However, the economy could not adapt to the international environment that emerged after the Great Depression and the Second World War. As a consequence, Argentina entered a forty-year period characterized by state intervention and, in particular, protectionism.

Economic mismanagement resulted in massive capital flight and the exodus of business and educated workforce, while corruption and tax evasion increased dramatically. Prices rose sharply and output grew much more slowly than in neighbouring countries.

The period of terror at the end of the 1970s saw a worsening of the economy. Production foundered and the country's foreign debt exploded, while unemployment and inflation soared. The international debt crisis and consequent need to curb imports depressed economic output in the early 1980s. At the same time, monetary financing of public sector deficits further accelerated inflation.

In 1985, the Austral Plan, which included wage and price freezes as well as a pegged currency, initially succeeded in reducing inflation. However, since the government was not able to balance the budget, the central bank expanded money creation; consequently, inflation exploded again in the late 1980s, while economic output continued to stagnate.

Argentina's economic performance, 1961–95

	Average annual real GDP growth, %	Average annual consumer price inflation, %
1961-1965	1.7	23.0
1966-1970	4.3	19.3
1971-1975	2.8	64.4
1976-1980	2.2	192.9
1981-1985	-2.1	327.7
1985-1990	0.3	584.1
1991-1995	6.0	32.3

Source: IMF

Recent developments

Despite coming to power on a populist platform, President Menem and his former economy minister, Domingo Cavallo, have implemented radical structural reforms to eliminate the roots of Argentina's fiscal imbalances and hyperinflation. Measures have included deregulation of the economy, privatization of state-owned enterprises, liberalization of foreign trade and elimination of restrictions on foreign investment.

The key component of the reform programme is the Convertibility Law (see below). It re-established domestic and foreign investor confidence and initiated a period of strong economic expansion. Annual output grew an average 8.9% between 1991 and 1994, led by an increase in domestic demand, and inflation dropped from an annual average of 2,314% in 1990 to zero in 1996.

In 1995, GDP fell 4.6% in the wake of the Mexican currency crisis, as capital left the country and the subsequent credit crunch brought sharply higher interest rates. Moreover, the budget deficit worsened and reached 1.8% of GDP in 1996. Hence, the Convertibility Law continued to be crucially important to the pace of economic development. Despite a temporary increase in the value-added tax to 21% from 18% in April, average consumer prices increased only 3.4% in 1995, declining further to 0.2% in 1996.

The Convertibility Law

The Convertibility Law of April 1991 fixes the peso-dollar exchange rate and guarantees full convertibility of the local currency. Moreover, the law stipulates that foreign exchange reserves must be sufficient to back every peso in circulation and in bank vaults. Printing money to finance budget deficits is therefore no longer possible, because such money would not be backed by reserves. Thus, money growth that is not backed by reserves cannot be used to lower interest rates and stimulate economic activity. The central bank is not allowed to act as a lender of last resort. The law also prohibits the indexation of prices and wages. Increases in remuneration are permitted only if justified by rising productivity.

Economy

Although agriculture's share of GDP fell to 9% in 1995, about 30% of the economy is still considered dependent on this sector, as industry and services have developed around food processing, transport and other agriculture-related activities.

Construction accounts for 6% of total output, while manufacturing generates 27% and comprises mainly food, textile machinery and transport equipment. Argentina is virtually self-sufficient in energy, and the privatized oil company Yacimientos Petrolíferos Fiscales (YPF) controls about half of the oil sector. Services contribute 54% of GDP. The main components of the service sector are tourism, commerce, financial services and transportation.

Share of GDP by sector

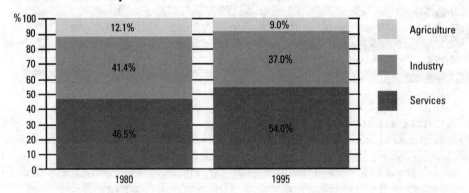

Source: Official data

Savings and investment

Argentina's saving and investment rates began to decrease dramatically in mid-1985. Saving as a percentage of GDP reached a low of 13.9% in 1993. Although it has improved slightly since then, it still amounted to only 17.4% of GDP in 1995. Investment decreased from over

25% of GDP in 1980 to 14.4% by the turn of the decade, then regained some ground, reaching a level of 18.3% in 1995.

Since 1991, substantial foreign direct investment (FDI) has helped to fill the gap between saving and investment. Net inflows, including direct and portfolio investment, increased from US$0.2 billion in 1990 to US$12.9 billion in 1993. The rise in US interest rates in early 1994 and the "Tequila hangover" in the wake of the Mexican currency crisis resulted in capital outflows, but those had ceased by the middle of 1995.

The US has become the dominant foreign investor in Argentina, followed by investors from Europe and, increasingly, from Chile, Canada and Brazil.

Trade

Argentina's economy was basically closed until the early 1990s. Although the Menem government has been trying to integrate the country into the world economy, merchandise exports were still equivalent to a modest 7.6% of GDP in 1996. Commodities have traditionally been Argentina's major exports. Agricultural goods, above all cereals and beef, still account for 23% of total exports, although down from 45% at the beginning of the 1980s. Manufactures of agricultural origin, mainly meat and fats and oils, represent 36%, whereas industrial goods, principally comprising chemical products, base metals and electrical and transport-related goods, account for 31% of GDP, up from 16% in the early 1980s.

Capital goods and parts were the most important components of imports in 1995, amounting to 40% of the total. Intermediate goods contributed about 36%, while consumer goods amounted to only 16% of foreign purchases.

In 1995, 29% of exports went to Brazil, Argentina's major trading partner. The US was second, with 9%. The Netherlands, Germany and Chile were also major destinations for Argentine exports. Imports were largely from the US (21%), Brazil (21%), Italy and Germany.

Regional links have been strengthened by the establishment of a customs union in the Southern Cone (MERCOSUR), which includes Argentina, Brazil, Paraguay, Uruguay and, since October 1996 with associate status, Chile.

Balance of trade in US$m

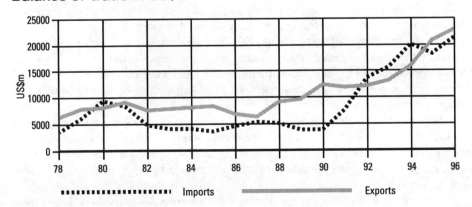

Source: IMF

Trade restrictions

Most commodities may be imported freely. Cars, can be imported only under a quota system. Import tariffs are divided into three categories. A maximum rate of 20% is applied on all consumer goods, while only 5% to 15% is applied on industrial imports and raw materials and 5% to 10% on agricultural products. There is 40% duty on capital goods. Generally, exports require no approval, except for a few sensitive materials. The only export duties charged are on oilseeds and some types of raw leather. Tariffs on goods originating in and traded among the members of MERCOSUR have been removed on 85% of all goods, and are expected to be eliminated entirely by the end of the century. A common external tariff was implemented by MERCOSUR in 1994.

Breakdown of exports (1995)

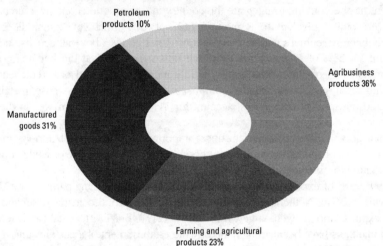

Petroleum
products 10%

Agribusiness
products 36%

Manufactured
goods 31%

Farming and agricultural
products 23%

Source: Republic of Argentina

Balance of payments

Traditionally, Argentina has enjoyed a trade surplus. But lower import barriers, increased domestic demand and the strong peso have boosted imports significantly since the structural reforms at the beginning of the 1990s. This resulted in a trade deficit in 1992, the first time since 1980. Depressed import demand as a consequence of the 1995 recession and the real appreciation of the Brazilian currency, and higher commodity prices, which fuelled export earnings, resulted in a trade surplus of US$2.2 billion in 1995 and US$1.4 billion in 1996, respectively.

Because of heavy debt service payments, however, Argentina's invisibles account has consistently recorded a deficit. As a result, the current account balance has been negative for many years, with the deficit reaching 2.8% of GDP in 1994. It improved in 1995 and 1996, owing to the increasing trade surplus, registering in an overall deficit of 0.7% and 1.2% of GDP, respectively.

Between 1991 and 1993, current account deficits were easily financed by large capital inflows. However, with the rise in US interest rates in early 1994, capital inflows began to slow, and capital outflows accelerated in the wake of the Mexican currency crisis. Inflows resumed by the middle of 1995.

Current account as a % of GDP

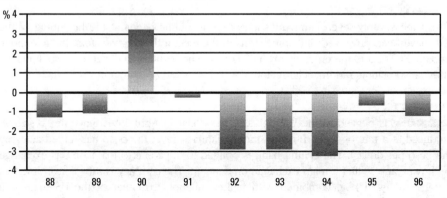

Source: IMF

Debt

Argentina remains one of the most highly indebted countries in Latin America. Its nominal foreign debt is about US$110 billion, up from US$62.1 billion in 1989. This is due not only to the renewed access of Argentine companies to international capital markets, but also to the economic disruption which followed the Mexican currency crisis. External debt as a percentage of GDP fell from almost 80% in the mid-1980s to 26% in 1993, but increased again to over 32% in 1996. Debt service payments, which dropped sharply from over 120% of foreign exchange revenues in 1983 to 26.6% in 1994, worsened again during 1995 and 1996, reaching 42.3% by the end of 1996.

Economic policy

Monetary policy

The central bank's function is limited by the 1991 Convertibility Law, which makes the institution effectively a currency board rather than a dicretionary monetary policy-maker in the usual sense. The Convertibility Law stipulates that central bank reserves must be sufficient to back every peso in circulation and in the vaults of private banks. This constrains the central bank significantly in the use of traditional monetary tools, such as buying or selling government securities to manage liquidity in the system. Printing money to finance budget deficits is no longer possible.

Fiscal policy

In the early 1990s, successful tax reforms increased revenues and reduced tax evasion somewhat. As a consequence, the fiscal targets set by the International Monetary Fund under the Extended Fund Facility were easily met. In fact, the government balance (excluding privatization proceeds) improved from a deficit of 1.9% of GDP in 1990 to a 1% surplus in 1993. Rising government spending and reduced tax revenues, however, caused the central government balance to slip into deficit in the second half of 1994. The 1995 economic crisis further aggravated the imbalance, since the cost of capital to finance the fiscal shortfall and to replace expiring debt increased considerably. As a result, Argentina experienced a deficit of 0.5% and 1.8% of GDP in 1995 and 1996, respectively.

Privatization

Most of the seventy-seven companies that were in public hands at the beginning of the 1990s have been privatized, including firms in the electrical energy sectors, the telephone company ENTEL and the oil company YPF. A few other entities have yet to be sold, mainly in the transportation and financial sectors.

Currency

The austral was pegged to the US$ at 1,000 per dollar in April 1991. Since the peso was introduced at a rate of 1 per 1,000 australs in January 1992, the peso has traded at parity (one peso per dollar). The central bank is obliged to intervene to maintain this exchange rate, buying and selling foreign exchange on demand. The currency is fully convertible.

The nominal peg, combined with higher inflation than that of the US, had until recently resulted in a strong real appreciation of the Argentine currency. But following the low inflation rates of the last two years, the peso's CPI-adjusted value has retreated some-what since late 1994, enhancing Argentina's competitiveness.

Argentine peso/US dollar exchange rate

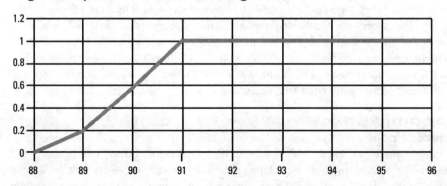

Exchange controls

There are no exchange controls; foreign currency can be sold or bought freely. No tax is imposed on foreign-exchange transactions. Banks are authorized to receive deposits and make loans in foreign currencies.

Banking system

The central bank is in charge of the regulation and control of the banking and credit system. The commercial banking industry is made up of 130 banks, including national official banks, state-owned provincial and municipal banks, domestic private banks, foreign-owned private banks and co-operative institutions. The market is highly concentrated, with the nine biggest institutions controlling about half of all domestic deposits and accounting for a substantial part of the US$100 billion total assets of the Argentine banking sector. Major banks generally supply the same services provided by international banks throughout the world.

Although consolidation in the banking sector is under way (reserve requirements are currently quite high, and a stand-by facility with international banks has been created as a safeguard against systemic risks), the system is still rather vulnerable to internal as well as external shocks, which affect credit availability and interest rates.

■ EQUITIES

Index performance (in local currency)

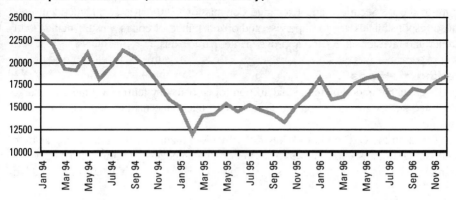

Key indicators

	Index performance %, in US$ terms	Market Cap. US$bn	P/E	Div. Yield	Weight in IFCI	IFCG
1994	-41.6	36.9	17.7	2.9	4.4	2.0
1995	8.6	37.8	15.0	3.5	3.6	2.0
1996	18.8	44.7	38.2	3.0	3.9	2.5

Sources: Local Stock Exchange, IFC, Bloomberg, Datastream, UBS

Structure

Argentina's main stock market, the Mercado de Valores de Buenos Aires (MVBA), accounts for almost 90% of the total securities trading volume. The remaining 10% takes place in eleven small independent exchanges, located in Córdoba, Mendoza, Río Negro, Rosario, Santa Fe, and La Plata. There is also a highly developed over-the-counter (OTC) market, the Mercado Abierto Electrónico (MAE), where trading volume currently exceeds that of the Bolsa. Most equity trading takes place on the MVBA Stock Exchange, whereas the corporate and government bonds are mainly traded through the MAE. As of the end of November 1996, there were 149 listed domestic companies on the MVBA, with a total market capitalization of US$47.7 billion.

The Buenos Aires Stock Exchange is divided into three departments, the Official Market, the Second Listing Section and the New Investment Project Section. Larger companies trade on the first market; however, liquidity remains limited for most of the shares. The ten largest stocks account for more than 80% of total market capitalization. Small and medium-sized companies have the benefit of simpler and less expensive requirements on the Second Listing market, while goods and services activities can register with the New Investment Project Section, created to promote access to the capital market. Such companies have more simplified financial statement requirements and do not need historical records. They do, however, have to provide a description of their projects as well as technical, financial and feasibility reports.

Regulatory authority
The Comisión Nacional de Valores (CNV) is Argentina's regulatory agency and is similar in nature to the US Securities and Exchange Commission (SEC). It is an independent entity whose responsibilities are to supervise authorized public offerings, ensure market transparency and investor safety, and approve market participants.

Trading methods
Equities are either traded by traditional auction (open outcry system) or via the OTC market. Most listed shares are traded on the OTC, a pure telephone market with no firm posted bids/offers.

Prices on the OTC do not usually differ by more than 1.5% from those prevailing on the floor. OTC transactions have to be reported immediately to the exchange via an electronic reporting system. Brokers using this system have access to real-time offers and bids.

Hours
The continuous OTC market starts at 09.30 and closes at 18.00, Monday to Friday. The auction market takes place from 12.00 to 17.00.

Settlement time and clearing
Cash: T; T+1; T+3; T+5; Forward: as per the contract between buyer and seller, settlement is up to 120 days. All shares in the official market are deposited in the Caja de Valores S.A. (Stock Clearing Corporation). This facilitates the clearing process. A computerized book-entry system is used for 80% of publicly traded securities, the remaining 20% being in bearer form.

Limits on price movement
The price of a share may not change by more than 15% in a single session.

Types of shares
Shares can be in bearer or nominative form. Some are registered, and are either negotiable or non-negotiable. Although a company is allowed to have different classes of shares, all stocks are required to have the same par value, stated in Argentine currency.

Most shares have ordinary voting rights. Some publicly held companies have several classes of shares in which each stock can have as many as five votes. Few preferred stocks (with no voting rights) are traded; however, these entitle shareholders to first rights on dividends and/or distributions of assets upon liquidation.

Stock indices

The three best-known stock indices are the Bolsa General Index (Bolsa Indice General), the Merval Index and the Burcap Index. The General Index includes all listed shares on the Buenos Aires Bolsa; these companies are weighted by their market capitalization.

On the other hand, the Merval Index, the official index of the Mercado de Valores de Buenos Aires is trade-weighted, and its composition is adjusted at the end of each quarter. Finally, the Burcap Index, which is managed by the Argentine Institute of Capital Markets, has the same constituency as the Merval but is weighted by stock market capitalization.

Commissions and taxes

Broker commissions are negotiated freely between brokers and their customers, but typically amount to 0.5%. There are no capital gains or income taxes on securities transactions for either foreign or domestic investors.

Disclosure of financial statements

Financial statements are required to reflect the true and accurate position of the company. Such statements are required to be audited and approved by an external accounting company. Every listed company must disclose quarterly and annual reports to the National Security Commission, the Stock Exchange and its shareholders. Listed firms are also required to disclose their earnings results as well as any relevant information that could have a positive or negative impact on the company's developments.

Shareholders' rights

Shareholders have the right to be informed of upcoming extraordinary and annual general meetings by an official notice, which must be published at least ten days before any such meeting and repeated for at least five days.

The notice must include an agenda and description of matters to be considered at the meeting. Shareholders who own more than 5% of a company's capital can request an extraordinary shareholders' meeting. Shareholders can vote by proxy, with the exception of directors and the corporation's employees.

Ownership limits for non-residents

There are no restrictions on the foreign ownership of exchange-traded or OTC stocks, warrants, options, or bonds. Non-resident participation in the stock market is quite significant. In fact, foreign investors own more than 50% of all free-floating shares available for public trading (representing 40% of all listed shares).

Capital and foreign exchange controls

There are currently no restrictions on inflows and outflows of foreign and domestic currencies. Foreign exchange deposits may be held in banks in Argentina.

Brokers

Individuals who meet all the securities market's network requirements and hold shares can become individual brokers and are allowed to act as market makers. This is also the case with brokerage firms. Trading must be conducted on the Exchange through these official brokers, who can deal for their own account and on behalf of third parties.

Sectors
The largest sectors (by market capitalization) represented in the Merval Index include petroleum (with about 40% market capitalization weight) and telecommunications (29%). Also important are banking (8.2% market weight), steel (4.5%) and food (3%) as well as electric power (2.8%).

ADRs
As of April 1996, there were twenty publicly traded Argentine ADRs, eight of which are listed on the NYSE.

Derivatives
Equity derivatives (mainly call options) are currently traded in Argentina on the Futures and Options Market (MERFOX). However, trading volume in these instruments remains modest. Trading of forwards, futures and options contracts is regulated by the CNV.

■ DEBT

The domestic bond market has largely developed since the 1991 Convertibility Plan, which fixed peso-US dollar parity. The following year, Argentina returned to the international capital markets. After a Brady-style restructuring of its outstanding external debt in 1993, it has been able to tap the eurobond market regularly in several currencies for various tenures. The increasing acceptance by both international and domestic investors signals continued success in Argentina's recovery from the debt crisis of the 1980s.

The Comision Nacional de Valores (the Argentine Securities Exchange Commission) regulates bond issuance and secondary market trading. The Buenos Aires Stock Exchange (BASE) supervises the activities of brokers, ensures transparency and drafts listing rules for new public offerings. The National Commission of Brokers Associations provides limited indemnity against failed trades.

Most Argentinian domestic debt securities are denominated in US dollars. Many have an amortizing payment structure and some pay after a grace period. The size of the market is about US$30 billion.

Letes
Letes are 90-day peso denominated government bills, issued for the first time in 1996 as a central bank monetary instrument. Twelve dealers are licensed to participate in auctions.

Cedulas
There are three Cedulas issues, secured by residential mortgages held by the government mortgage bank. They pay floating rate coupons linked to libor after an initial period paying fixed rates. Principal is repaid according to an amortization schedule.

Bote (Bonos del Tesoro)

Bote are US dollar denominated registered bonds issued by the government. They have 5- or 10-year tenures; principal is repaid quarterly after a 1-year grace period for 5-year bonds and 2½ years for 10-year bonds. Bote pay coupons of 3-month libor flat every quarter. Bote are listed on the BASE.

Bonex (Bonos Externos)

Bonex are US dollar denominated bearer bonds guaranteed by the Republic and are issued by the central bank. They are issued with 10-year maturities and repay principal in 8 equal instalments after a 2-year grace period. Coupons are 6-month libor flat payable semi-annually. Bonex can be leant to banks on an unsecured basis for 30 to 180 days.

Bocon (Bonos de Consolidacion)

Bocon are denominated in US dollars and pesos in registered form. Two instruments – Bocon Pre and Bocon Pro – were created in 1991, to repay government debts owed to pensioners and suppliers respectively.

Bocon are variable rate bonds which pay interest each month. The peso-denominated bonds pay the average domestic savings account rate and the dollar bonds pay 1-month libor flat.

For the first 6 years interest is capitalized through payments of Pay-in-Kind (PIK) bonds; thereafter investors receive cash. They have 10-year tenures; principal is amortized after a 6-year grace period during which a sinking fund operates.

Bocon are listed on BASE, trade electronically either on the exchange or through MAE and settle through the Caja de Valores in book entry form.

Bocon Pre (Bonos de Consolidacion Provisional)

Two are denominated in pesos and two in US dollars. They were issued in 1991 to repay debts owed to pensioners. The peso bonds were worth US$2.04 billion and the dollar bonds US$4.5 billion.

Bocon Pro (Bonos de Consolidacion)

Two Bocon Pro bonds with a nominal value of US$3.7 billion were issued in 1991 to repay debts to government suppliers. One is denominated in pesos and the other in US dollars. The peso bond pays interest at the local average savings account rate, and the dollar bond pays libor flat.

BIC (Bonos de Inversion y Crecimiento)

There are two peso-denominated BICs, issued by the central bank with a guarantee from the Republic of Argentina. BICs pay 0.9% over the central bank weighted average monthly cost of funds each month, and principal is amortized over the life of the bond. Only one, BIC 5, is liquid. They are listed on the BASE.

In 1997 the government intends to auction longer-term bonds for the first time. The first issue will be for US$500 million of two-year US dollar denominated bonds, called Bontes, which will be auctioned through the twelve dealers who participate in bill auctions.

Secondary market trading

Secondary market trading is mainly OTC via the Mercado Abierto Electronico (MAE) electronic system, although bonds can be traded on the BASE. Prices are quoted on nominal value in the OTC market but on the Exchange are they quoted at residual value (Caja de Valores statements show residual value). OTC trading hours are 10.00 to 18.00; BASE trading hours are 12.00 to 17.00. Coupons on bearer bonds can be clipped a month before paydate, and the coupons can be traded separately for a week.

Repurchase agreements can be transacted using the most liquid US dollar denominated bonds.

The security side of a transaction is normally settled for book entry at the Caja de Valores (central depository), which is owned by the Stock Exchange and member brokerage firms. Bearer bonds usually settle physically. Settlement is for T+3 through the Caja de Valores, or T+5 through euroclear.

Non-residents pay no taxes on either sovereign or corporate bonds. There are no restrictions on repatriating income or profits, and nor do foreigners need permission in advance to invest in Argentinian securities.

Eurobonds

The Republic returned to the eurobond market in September 1992: US$250 million, 8.25%, were issued at 300 basis points over US treasuries, with maturity on October 15, 1997. Subsequently several state enterprises and private corporations have issued in major currencies.

Argentina also plans to issue bonds denominated in pesos in 1997, starting with a 5- or 10-year maturity, according to the Finance and Economy Ministry in a report in December 1996. Peso-denominated Argentinean bonds, unlike the country's foreign currency bonds, are rated investment grade by the US rating agencies, so they could be bought by US investors who are not allowed to buy speculative grade paper.

Eurobond issues (US$m)

	1990	1991	1992	1993	1994	1995	1996
Sovereign	—	500.0	488.0	2,379.3	2,824.2	5,652.9	6,882.1
Private	21	375.0	1,339.2	3,860.0	2,760.0	1,964.4	2,517.1

Brady bonds

Argentina issued Brady bonds in April 1993. The bank loans were replaced by discount bonds and par bonds with a 30-year maturity. In addition, Argentina issued floating rate bonds (FRBs) with a 12-year original maturity against interest arrears. The par and discount bonds are collateralized with 30-year zero coupons and have a 12-month rolling interest guarantee.

Bond	Coupon	Collateral	Maturity	Currencies
Discount	6mth L+13/16	Principal+Interest	2023	US$, DEM
Par bonds	Step up	Principal+Interest	2023	
FRB	6mth L+13/16		2005	

Denominations of US$250,000:

1 30-year par bonds with a below market fixed coupon
2 30-year discount bonds paying 6-month libor plus 13/16%

Both instruments were issued in US$s and DEMs, collateralized by US treasury zero-coupon bonds and with 12-month revolving interest guarantees. They can also be tendered in privatizations.

3 12-year Floating Rate Bonds (FRB) paying 6-month libor plus 13/16%
FRBs are not collateralized but have sinking funds that operate after six years. They are not eligible for tendering in privatizations.

■ ARGENTINA: Economic indicators

Population and development	1990	1991	1992	1993	1994	1995	1996e
Population, million	32.6	33.0	33.4	33.8	34.2	34.6	35.0
Population growth, %	1.4	1.3	1.2	1.2	1.2	1.2	1.2
Nominal GDP per capita, US$	4343	5754	7539	8683	9720	9464	9688

National accounts							
Nominal GDP, US$bn	141.4	189.7	251.6	293.3	332.2	327.4	339.2
Change in real GDP, %	0.1	10.5	10.3	6.3	8.5	-4.6	3.5
Gross fixed capital formation, % of GDP	14.0	14.6	15.2	16.0	16.9	17.6	18.2

Money supply and inflation							
Narrow money, change %, Dec/Dec	1023.8	148.6	49.0	33.0	8.2	1.7	2.1
Broad money, change %, Dec/Dec	1113.7	142.6	61.6	46.5	17.6	-2.7	11.5
Consumer price inflation (avg.), %	2314.0	171.7	24.9	10.6	4.4	3.4	0.1

Interest rates *=latest figures							
Money market rate, annual average	3025.30	93.60	37.80	7.20	6.80	9.20	7.00*
Deposit rate, annual average	1518.00	62.00	17.00	11.00	8.00	12.00	8.00*

Government finance							
Government balance, % of GDP	-3.5	-0.1	0.6	1.1	-0.1	-0.5	-1.8

Exchange rates lc=local currency							
Exchange rate, annual average, lc/US$	0.49	0.95	0.99	1.00	1.00	1.00	1.00
Exchange rate, end of year, lc/US$	0.56	1.00	0.99	1.00	1.00	1.00	1.00
Real exchange rate 1990=100	100.0	94.6	109.7	122.2	122.2	115.7	114.7

Balance of payments							
Exports of goods & services, US$m	14800	14386	14729	15623	18509	23853	25700
Change %	25.8	-2.8	2.4	6.1	18.5	28.9	7.7
Imports of goods & services, US$m, fob	6846	11566	18388	20709	25601	23774	27350
Change %	2.8	68.9	59.0	12.6	23.6	-7.1	15.0
Trade balance, goods only, US$m, fob-fob	8628	4419	-1450	-2426	-4236	2237	1350
Current account balance, US$m	4552	-647	-5401	-7452	-9363	-2390	-4200
as a % of GDP	3.2	-0.3	-2.1	-2.5	-2.8	-0.7	-1.2

Foreign exchange reserves							
Foreign exchange reserves, US$m	4295	6005	9990	13791	14327	14288	18000
Gold at ⅔ of market price, US$m	1088	995	1000	1048	1119	1119	1123
Import cover (reserves/imports), months	7.5	6.2	6.5	8.0	6.7	7.2	7.9

Foreign debt and debt service							
Short-term debt, US$m	5652	8546	10172	9965	12153	14469	15900
Total foreign debt, US$m	60674	64416	71897	76648	90709	99506	110000
as a % of GDP	42.9	34.0	28.6	26.1	27.3	30.4	32.4
as a % of foreign exchange receipts	343.4	380.0	414.7	417.0	412.6	348.0	363.6
Interest payments, US$m	5617	5199	3383	3223	4240	5426	7100
Principal repayments, US$m	3195	2807	2181	2763	1598	5092	5700
Total debt service, US$m	8812	8006	5564	5986	5838	10518	12800
as a % of goods exports	71.3	66.8	45.5	45.6	36.9	50.2	56.4
as a % of foreign exchange receipts	49.9	47.2	32.1	32.6	26.6	36.8	42.3

Brazil

Area (thousands of km²):	8512
Population (1995, millions):	165.4
Population projection (2025, millions):	224
Population younger than 15 yrs (1991, % of total):	34.2
Urbanization rate (1993, % of population):	71
Life expectancy (1993, years at birth):	67
Gross domestic product (1996, US$bn):	760
GDP per capita (1996, US$):	4509
Average annual GDP growth rate (1990-96, %):	1.8
Average annual inflation rate (1990-96, %):	1205.6 (1996 = 16.8%)
Currency (real per US$, average 1996):	1
Structure of production (1994):	46% services, 43.5% industry, 10.5% agriculture
Main exports:	metallurgical products, transport equipment, chemicals, iron ore
Main imports:	capital goods, oil & derivatives, chemical products
Main trading partners:	US, Argentina, Japan, Germany,
Market capitalization of Stock Exchange (December 1996; US$bn):	217
Total foreign debt (% of GDP):	24.5
Next elections due under normal circumstances:	Senate, Chamber of Deputies and President: October 1998
Credit rating: (Jan 1997, Standard & Poor's, Moody's)	B+; B1

FORECAST: 1997-2000 (average)

	Worst case	Most likely	Best case
Real GDP growth (%)	3.0	4.5	5.5
Inflation (%)	15	7.5	6.5

■ POLITICS

Historical overview

When the Portuguese discovered Brazil in 1500, the country was inhabited by Indian tribes who had only a few possessions and lived off the land. The Portuguese invasion dramatically changed the native style of life. Colonists started to plant and exploit wood and sugar cane, enslaving the natives and sending them out into the fields. Soon trading in Indian and African slaves became Brazil's second-largest commercial activity. The gold rush of the 1690s also did little to develop Brazil, as natives were used as a source of cheap labour and died in the mines.

The Prince Regent of Portugal, fleeing the French invasion of Lisbon, arrived in Brazil in 1807 and established the United Kingdom of Portugal. His return to Europe fifteen years later opened the way to Brazil's independence, which it achieved without conflict. Slavery was abolished, a domestic market created, industry and infrastructure developed and a parliamentary system established, so that by the end of the 1890s, Brazil had become a modern state.

Brazil then experienced a succession of military and civilian presidents supervised by the armed forces. In 1937, president Getúlio Vargas shut down Congress and implemented an authoritarian system which lasted until the beginning of the 1950s. It was followed by a succession of fragile democratically elected presidents and military regimes.

In the early 1980s, the so-called Brazilian "economic miracle" started to fade. Opposition to the armed forces increased so much that the military government was forced to implement a policy of abertura (opening) and to hold presidential elections. In 1985, the victory of the opposition candidate marked the end of military supremacy in Brazil.

Recent events

In late 1989, Fernando Collor de Mello narrowly won the first direct presidential election since the early 1960s. But after allegations of corruption, he was impeached by Congress in September 1992 and replaced by his vice-president, Itamar Franco. In October 1994, Fernando Henrique Cardoso, of the centre-left Social Democratic Party (PSDB), won 54% of the votes in the first round of the presidential election and took office on January 1, 1995.

Although Cardoso's formal coalition enjoys a majority, party discipline is notoriously lax. Despite the fact that many of Brazil's governors and Cardoso's congressional opponents expressed support for his economic programme, it has become increasingly difficult for the president to pass the constitutional changes necessary to alleviate Brazil's fiscal burden.

Chronology

1500	Brazil is discovered by the Portuguese
1531	King João III of Portugal establishes São Vicente as capital of the new colony
1690s	Gold rush in south-central Minas Gerais
1807	French invade the Spanish town of Lisbon and the Portuguese prince regent flees to Brazil
1807	Rio de Janeiro becomes the capital of the United Kingdom of Portugal
1821	Return of the Portuguese monarch to Europe
1822	Independence in the form of a monarchy
1888	Slavery is abolished
1889	Constitution of the Federal Republic
1889-1985	Succession of military and civilian presidents
1930	Military install Getúlio Vargas in power
1937	Vargas takes complete control of the country
1945	Military force Vargas out of office
1950	Vargas is elected President in direct elections

1954	Vargas commits suicide
1980s	"Abertura" (opening)
1982	First direct elections for governor since 1966
1985	Democracy is re-established
1988	New constitution
1989	Fernando Collor de Mello wins the first direct presidential election since the early 1960s
1992	Congress impeaches president Collor de Mello
1994	Plano Real implemented
1994	Fernando Henrique Cardoso wins the presidential election

State organization

Brazil is a federal republic consisting of twenty-six states and a Federal District that includes the capital, Brasilia. Each state is divided into municipalities, which are further divided into districts. State and municipal governments are organized like the federal government. They are led, respectively, by a governor or a mayor and have legislative and judicial branches.

Constitution and government

According to the 1988 constitution, executive, legislative and judicial powers are separate. The president is the supreme executive authority. He can be elected for a single four-year term (President Cardoso is seeking a constitutional change permitting a second term) and appoints the members of the Council of Ministers, the senior military and the judges of the Federal Supreme Court.

The Congress consists of a 81-member Senate elected for eight-year terms, one third at a time, and a 513-member Chamber of Deputies elected every four years. Both senators and deputies are representatives of the twenty-six states. The judicial branch is made up of federal and state courts. Brazilian civil law is generally based on Napoleonic Law.

Political parties

Brazil's political scene is very fragmented, with eighteen different parties represented in Congress. As a result, coalitions are difficult to achieve. As democracy has only recently emerged, the ideologies of the parties are still not well developed.

Democratic Movement Party (PMDB)
> Centre-right
> Led by Paes De Andrade

Liberal Front Party (PFL)
> Centre-right
> Led by Antonio Carlos Magalhaes

Social Democratic Party (PSDB)
> Centre-left
> Led by Fernando Henrique Cardoso

Workers Party (PT)
> Left
> Led by Luis Inácio Lula Da Silva

Democratic Labour Party (PDT)
   Left-wing
   Led by Lionel Brizola

Result of 1994 elections to the Senate and Chamber of Deputies
Senate: PMDB (21 seats), **PFL** (20), **PSDB** (10), **PPR** (6), **PP** (6), **PTB** (5), **PDT** (5), **PT** (5), **others** (3)
Chamber of Deputies: PMDB (107 seats), **PFL** (89), **PSDB** (62), **PPR** (52), **PT** (49), **PP** (36), **PDT** (34), **PTB** (31), **PSB** (15), **others** (38)

Next elections
Senate, Chamber of Deputies and president: October 1998

Other political forces

Despite the success of democracy and successive cuts in the military budget since 1985, the armed forces still enjoy considerable power in Brazil. So do certain business groups, such as the Federation of Industries of São Paulo State, which are powerful in policy-making. Finally, the popularity of Luis Inácio Lula da Silva, leader of the potent Workers' Party, reflects the still powerful appeal of populism in Brazil, despite the momentum accumulated in recent years by progressive (reform-orientated) politics.

Government

PSDB and PFL, supported by PMDB and smaller parties.

Opposition parties

PDT, PT, PSB and others.

Central bank

Brazil's central bank executes the decisions of the Conselho Monetario Nacional (CMN), which is the supreme banking authority. The CMN is made up of representatives from both government and the private sector and determines monetary, credit and exchange rate policies. The central bank controls the money supply by setting the discount rate on loans to banks, currency bands, a daily Referential Interest Rate (TRD) and reserve requirements for the commercial banking system. It also can purchase and sell government bonds on the open market.

■ ECONOMICS

Historical overview

In the early 1900s, Brazil experienced high growth rates, based mainly on coffee and natural rubber exports. The Great Depression, the Second World War and the ensuing collapse of international trade put an end to this prosperous period and encouraged Brazil to embark on a policy of industrial import substitution. The government actively promoted industrial growth by protecting the national economy with tariff barriers and, most importantly, by establishing state-run companies. This strategy showed reasonable success until the early 1960s when the strain on public finances led to an acceleration of inflation and a sharp fall in economic growth. Military rule as well as reforms to the fiscal and monetary system brought a recovery. The subsequent "Brazilian Miracle" achieved annual GDP growth rates of more than 10% between 1968 and 1973, and of at least 5% between 1974 and 1980. The continuous growth of the budget deficit resulted in increasing inflation in the mid-1970s, but Brazil was nevertheless able to avoid hyperinflation in this period.

The second oil crisis in 1979 and the beginning of the international debt crisis in 1982 put pressure on the country's external balance and shrank output in the early 1980s. Moreover, loose fiscal and monetary policies as well as limited access to external financing after the outbreak of the debt crisis fuelled a rise in inflation. Various stabilization plans, namely the Cruzado Plan in 1986, the Bresser Plan in 1987, the Summer Plan in 1989 and the two Collor Plans in the early 1990s, failed to control inflation. On the contrary, the collapse of each of these plans further accelerated the price increases and eventually produced hyperinflation. Meanwhile, economic growth slowed.

Brazil's economic performance, 1961-95

	Average annual real GDP growth, %	Average annual consumer price inflation, %
1961-1965	N/A	62.6
1966-1970	6.4	27.8
1971-1975	10.6	25.7
1976-1980	6.7	52.0
1981-1985	1.2	149.9
1985-1990	1.9	665.7
1991-1995	2.7	827.5

Source: IMF

Recent developments

At the beginning of 1994, Brazil's government implemented the so-called Social Emergency Fund to reduce the fiscal deficit. This plan gave the central administration control over spending programmes and tax increases for a period of two years. The fund reduced the amount of revenues that would otherwise be transferred from the federal government to state and local authorities. In addition, the government implemented measures to increase tax revenues, such as an increase in personal income tax and a rise in the tax on financial institutions.

In response to rising inflation, the so-called "real unit of value" (Unidade Real de Valor, URV) was introduced in March 1994. The URV, which was not an actual currency but rather an accounting unit, was applied to wages, long-term contracts, credit transactions, household rentals, leasing and futures contracts. The central bank set the daily value of the URV in terms of the cruzeiro, the country's currency, in line with the evolution of the price indices. At the same time, the URV continued to be worth about one US dollar. The introduction of the URV paved the way for the initiation of the Plano Real.

The Plano Real was launched in July 1994. It entailed the introduction of a new currency, the real, which supplanted both the URV and the cruzeiro. By converting wages and public prices into URVs and then into reals, the plan allowed Brazil to wean itself away from the indexation mechanisms on which it had been dependent.

The plan has proved successful so far. Inflation has dropped from a monthly rate of 50% in June 1994 to less than 1% in 1996. Low inflation has brought stability and credibility to the new currency, helping to underpin economic growth. However, cheaper imports led to the restructuring or collapse of a large number of companies and higher unemployment. It also resulted in the first trade deficit since the beginning of the 1980s. Moreover, the budget deficit dramatically increased.

The Brazilian economy

Brazil is the tenth largest economy in the world and possesses vast natural resources and mineral reserves. The country produces large quantities of raw materials and processed foods, such as orange juice, sugar, cacao, soy products and meat, and is one of the world's largest coffee producers.

Shares of GDP by sector

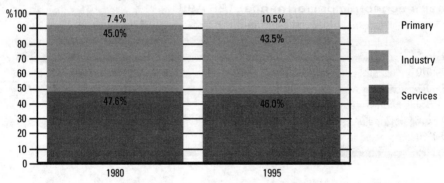

Source: Official data

Iron and bauxite are among Brazil's most important raw materials. In total, agriculture and mining account for 10.5% of the country's GDP. The industrial sector, which covers a large range of products, including vehicles, chemical goods, paper and textiles, provides for 43.5% of total GDP.

For decades, services accounted for about 50% of the country's GDP. The importance of the financial system, which had become the biggest part of this sector as a result of inflation-related gains from financial transactions, has decreased since the implementation of the Plano Real. Commerce, restaurants, hotels and tourism are becoming more important.

The informal sector is very important, employing an estimated 30 million people – equivalent to about half of the workforce in the formal economy.

Savings and investment

The economic instability and insecurity caused by inflation has resulted in extremely volatile saving behaviour in the last twenty years (between 10% and 31% of GDP). As a result, gross domestic investment, which remained above 20% of GDP during most of this period, could not always be financed domestically. In the beginning of the 1980s, the international debt crisis and the economic growth slowdown in industrial countries resulted in a sharp fall of capital inflows to Brazil. This obliged the government to borrow money from the central bank (printing money) to finance the gap between domestic savings and domestic investment. Foreign investment increased again in 1992, attracted by a dramatic rise in demand for consumer goods and the formation of MERCOSUR. Since 1994, newly won price stability has further boosted foreign investment.

Trade

Brazil's dependence on foreign trade is modest, since exports comprise only 7% of GDP. Manufactured goods – mainly metallurgical products, transport equipment, machines and mechanical instruments, and chemical products – account for 64% of total exports, while primary products such as iron ore, coffee and soybeans comprise 36%. The largest category of imports is capital goods, accounting for 39%, oil and derivatives account for 17% and chemical products 18%.

Brazil's relations with industrialized countries have traditionally been strained. In the 1980s, its role as an international weapons supplier, its rejection of calls to safeguard its natural resources (especially the Amazon region) and the protection of its domestic economy caused tensions not only with industrialized countries, but also with its neighbours. President Collor's commitment to open the economy significantly improved Brazil's foreign relations, culminating in the 1991 signature of the MERCOSUR agreement to establish a customs union with Argentina, Paraguay and Uruguay.

Brazil's main trading partner is the United States, which accounts for 19% of exports and 24% of imports. Argentina has moved up to second place due mainly to the recent increase in Brazil's oil imports and the elimination of trade barriers in conjunction with the MERCOSUR agreement. Other important trading partners are Japan, Germany and Italy.

Balance of trade in US$m

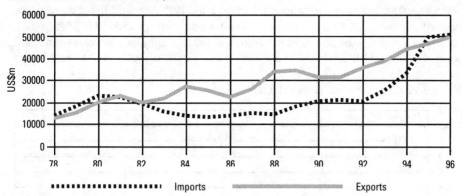

Source: IMF

Trade restrictions

Goods can be imported only by firms registered with the Secretariat of Foreign Trade (SECEX). With some exceptions, most imports must be approved by the Technical Department of Commercial Interchange (DITC). Selective measures of protection (tariffs on cars, toys, etc.) are implemented regularly. Some exports are prohibited or require the approval of the SECEX, but in general products may be exported freely.

Breakdown of exports (1995)

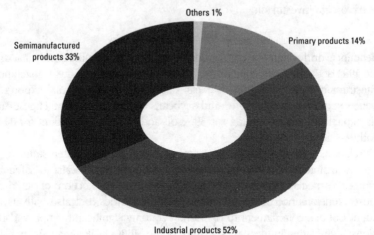

Others 1%

Semimanufactured products 33%

Primary products 14%

Industrial products 52%

Source: Official data

Balance of payments

Until recently, Brazil's trade balance had been in surplus since the early 1980s. Initially, the government supported the export sector, because the rise in international interest rates and the subsequent outbreak of the international debt crisis forced the country to increase its foreign exchange earnings. Hence, the trade surplus has generally financed the service deficits resulting from interest payments. However, the 1995 economic boom and the loss of competitiveness due to the appreciation of the Brazilian currency resulted in 1995 in the first trade deficit since the beginning of the 1980s and led to a significant increase of the current account deficit, which amounted to 2.6% and 3.2% of GDP in 1995 and 1996, respectively.

Current account as a % of GDP

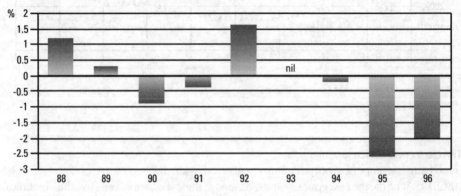

Source: Official data

In the early 1980s, the outbreak of the international debt crisis, the slowdown in economic growth in industrial countries and falling commodity prices put an end to external borrowing, significantly reducing capital inflows. In later years, financial outflows exceeded inflows. It was not until 1992 that renewed access to international capital markets and a rise of foreign portfolio investment resulted in a positive net inward capital transfer.

Debt

According to the World Bank, Brazil is a severely indebted middle-income country. Following the 1982 debt crisis, the country signed several debt rescheduling agreements, but was unable to comply with them, causing an accumulation of debt arrears to private and public creditors. In the first half of the 1990s, Brazil reached an agreement on interest arrears, restructured Paris Club obligations and concluded a rescheduling of its public-sector foreign debt under the aegis of the Brady Plan. This re-opened access to international capital markets.

The foreign debt of Brazil's public and private entities totals US$194 billion, or 25% of GDP, compared to 50% in 1983. Unlike 1982, the largest share of debt is currently in the private sector. Total debt service, which reached a peak of 89% of foreign exchange receipts in the early 1980s, fell to 43% in 1996. Short-term debt accounts for a third of total foreign debt.

Economic policy
Monetary policy

At the beginning of 1994, the government was forced to initiate a new stabilization programme to fight hyperinflation. The first stage of the plan involved measures to balance the government accounts, raise real interest rates and unify the commercial and parallel exchange rates. Subsequently, Congress passed a constitutional amendment setting up the so-called Social Emergency Fund, designed to give the government control over spending programmes and tax increases for a period of two years. The tight policy has brought inflation from an annual average of 2149% in 1994 down to 16.8% in 1996.

Fiscal policy

Until recently, Brazil's fiscal stance was loose. As a result, the central bank was obliged to finance the budget deficit and the consequent monetary growth fuelled inflation. The Social Emergency Fund in 1994 achieved an initial reduction in the deficit. But the improvement was achieved mainly by temporary expenditure cuts. The total public sector borrowing requirement, a deficit measure which includes inflation-distorted interest payments, remained high, amounting to about 4.5% of GDP at the end of 1996.

Privatization

Since 1991, the government has sold a large number of state-owned companies worth an estimated US$12 billion, mainly to Brazilian buyers. However, it has not found the political support to privatize large utilities, such as the telecoms, oil companies and the largest state-owned banks. Hence, the privatization programme is incomplete so far. Preparations for the privatization of the mining giant Companhia Vale de Rio Doce and the state banks of Rio de Janeiro and Minas Gerais are now under way.

Currency

In July 1994, the real was introduced as the new currency, supplanting both the cruzeiro and the "real unit of value" (the Unidade Real de Valor, or URV, an accounting unit applied to wages, long-term contracts, credit transactions and other contracts). Initially, the real was set equal to the US dollar and was allowed to float against the US currency within a band. This band has since been adjusted several times. However, the real has appreciated sharply in real terms, weakening the competitiveness of Brazil's products.

Brazilian real/US dollar exchange rate

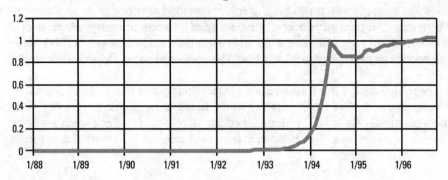

Banking system

The country's banking system is made up of state-owned commercial banks and universal banks, as well as development and investment banks. Restructuring started in the early 1990s. Within three years, some two thousand branches of important financial institutions were closed and the sector's labour force fell by 20%. Recently, banks were hurt by the new economic climate resulting from the introduction of the Plano Real, because they lacked the infrastructure and the credit culture necessary to evaluate loan portfolios in a non-inflationary market. Two of the country's ten largest banks, Económico and Nacional, collapsed, obliging the Banco Central do Brazil to intervene. The restructuring of the banking system in Brazil is not yet complete.

■ EQUITIES

Index performance (in local currency)

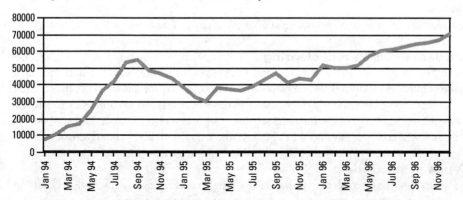

Key indicators

	Index performance %, in US$ terms	Market Cap. US$bn	P/E	Div. Yield	Weight in IFCI	IFCG
1994	67.6	189.3	13.1	0.7	16.7	11.9
1995	-22.1	147.6	36.3	3.4	10.5	8.7
1996	30.4	217.0	14.5	2.3	11.4	9.0

Sources: Local stock exchange, IFC, Bloomberg, Datastream, UBS

Structure

The Bolsa de Valores de São Paulo (BOVESPA) is the principal stock market in Brazil, followed by the Bolsa de Valores de Rio de Janeiro (BVRJ). Other stock exchanges are located in Salvador, Porto Alegre, Belo Horizonte, Curitiba, Recife, Fortaleza and Santos. However, about 85% of all equity trades occur on the BOVESPA.

The São Paulo Stock Exchange is totally automated. Its liquidation and custody systems are fully integrated and make use of real-time systems to register transactions and transmit information. As of November 1996, the market capitalization of the Bolsa de Valores de São Paulo stood at US$203.7 billion, with 550 publicly listed domestic companies.

Regulatory authority

The Securities Commission (CVM) is Brazil's regulatory agency. Its task is to maintain the integrity of all transactions of the Brazilian capital market. The CVM looks after the regulation and inspection activities of investors, financial intermediaries, stock exchanges and public corporations. There are also self-regulating entities within each stock exchange, to regulate dealing in stocks, commodities and systems for the negotiation, registration and custody of stock.

Trading methods

The primary trading method is through an open outcry system. There is also limited electronic trading through the Computer Assisted Trading System (CATS) in São Paulo and the SENN in Rio de Janeiro. The OTC market has had limited success in Brazil, owing to the success of formal market electronic negotiation systems like CATS and SENN.

Hours
The markets open at 10.00 and close at 16.00, Monday to Friday.

Settlement time and clearing
Cash: T+1, Financial: T+3. By law, clearing and custody of securities on the Brazilian capital markets must be conducted by companies created exclusively for this purpose. In São Paulo, the exchange itself is responsible for custody whereas CALISPA (Liquidation Cashiers for São Paulo S.A.) is in charge of the financial settlement of operations. In Rio de Janeiro, both custody and settlement are entrusted to CLC S.A. (the Liquidation and Custody Chamber).

Types of securities
Common and preferred shares, warrants, stock rights and receipts, subscription bonds and privatization certificates are traded on the Brazilian exchanges.

Stock indices
The most popular market index is the São Paulo Stock Exchange's BOVESPA Index, comprised of equities representing 80% of the stock exchange's cash transactions volume over the previous twelve months. The IBV Index (a market capitalization-weighted index, consisting of the most actively traded shares) is calculated by the Rio de Janeiro Stock Exchange. Finally, the I-Senn Index is a trade-weighted index of the fifty most traded stocks in the previous twelve months.

Commissions and taxes
Broker commissions range from 0.5% to 2.0% of the value traded on the Rio de Janeiro Stock Exchange. Commissions range from 0.5% to 2.7% of the value traded on the São Paulo Stock Exchange. There is a 15% tax on income (interest, premiums, fees, discounts, and profit participation) earned by foreign investment companies. However, as of January 1, 1996, dividends and cash bonuses earned by Annex IV portfolios (see below) became exempt from income tax withholding. Capital gains are subject to the IOF tax (Tax on Credit, Exchange, Insurance of Securities transactions), which ranges from 0% to 25%.

Disclosure of financial statements
Listed companies must disclose copies of their by-laws, financial statements, minutes from shareholder meetings, and a full description of the company's business and history to the Securities Commission and the exchanges. These disclosures must be updated.

Ownership limits for non-residents, capital and foreign exchange controls
Only approved institutional investors/broker-dealers can invest directly in Brazil. Approximately 90% of the foreign funds flowing into the Brazilian capital markets are under Annex IV, which permits foreign institutional investors to invest in Brazilian securities through an Institutional Investment Portfolio.

As a general rule, priority is given to long-term direct investments, particularly in those sectors likely to increase employment and income. Foreign capital is subject to regulations and prerequisites for the entry and repatriation of capital. All foreign investments must also be registered with the central bank in accordance with the Foreign Capital Law.

Brokers
By December 1995, there were 227 brokerage firms operating in the Brazilian capital market. The BOVESPA had eighty-six member-brokers, with another forty-seven brokers located outside of São Paulo, but who are authorized to operate on the exchange. The latter type of broker is called a permissionário (permitted member).

Sectors
The composition of the BOVESPA index is dominated by the utilities sector, with telecommunications accounting for 27% of the index's market capitalization, followed by electric power companies (22% market weight). In addition, the chemical/petrochemical sector (15% weight) and financial groups (11%) together account for almost one quarter of the BOVESPA index's capitalization. Also of note are the mining (7%) and steel (4.6%) industries.

ADRs
As of April 1996, there were forty-nine publicly listed Brazilian ADRs, with two (Telebrás and Aracrúz Cellulose) listed on the NYSE.

Derivatives
Equity derivatives, interest exchange derivatives and swap operations are traded frequently in Brazil. Commodity derivatives trading volume is not significant. Futures are traded on the Bolsa de Mercadorias e Futuros (BM&F).

■ DEBT

The Comissao de Valores Mobiliarios (CVM – Securities Commission) regulates Brazil's domestic bond markets. Financial institutions are supervised by the Banco Central do Brasil (central bank), which also conducts open-market operations, and manages foreign exchange transactions.

Public debt
Bônus do Banco Central (BBCs)
BBCs are discount bearer bills with maturities ranging from 35 to 56 days. They are auctioned by the central bank every Tuesday, using a competitive tender system.

Letra do Tesouro Nacional (LTN – national treasury bills)
LTNs are discount bills with 182-day maturities. They are sold in US treasury-style auctions every fifteen days. LFTs are 360-day discount treasury bills, and are auctioned according to no regular schedule.

Nota do Tesouro Nacional (NTN – national treasury notes)

NTNs are issued with floating or fixed-rate coupons in several series with maturities that range from 90 days to 12 months. They are the main debt financing instrument of the treasury and also represent the government's intention to extend the maturity of its short-dated obligations. They are sold in US treasury-style auctions, which are held on an irregular basis.

Notas do Banco Central (NBCs – central bank notes)

NBCs are issued by the central bank as a monetary policy tool, and like NTNs are pegged to the Referential Rate (TR). NBCs have terms of 6 or 12 months and pay interest semi-annually.

Bonus do Tesouro Nacional (BTN – national treasury bonds)

BTNs are fixed-rate bonds with tenures up to 25 years. No longer issued, they represent external debt converted into internal debt.

Privatization currency bonds

Privatization currency bonds represent the restructured debt of state-owned enterprises and are denominated in foreign currencies. They are sold at a discount and investors receive a stake in the enterprise at redemption. Issues include Agrarian Debt Bills (TDAs), National Development Fund Bonds (OFNDs) and Siderbrás debentures. No new primary offerings are planned, and the secondary market is illiquid. At redemption, holders can take stakes in privatized industries. Government issues are sold either by the central bank (BBCs) or the Treasury (LTNs, LFTs, NTNs, BTNs) off-exchange in US treasury-style auctions and then traded over the counter (OTC). They settle T+1 in the primary market and on the same day netted with reserves held at the central bank when traded OTC. Clearing is through the SELIC system (Special System for Clearing and Custody/Book Entry Liquidation and Custody System), owned by the central bank. All bonds are in book-entry form.

Repo transactions are not yet permitted.

Private debt

Bank Deposit Certificates (CDBs) and Bank Deposit Receipts (RDBs) make up the largest section of the debt markets. Liquidity was increased by changes in regulation that allowed ownership to be transferred at the holder's request. They pay fixed-rate coupons and floating- or variable-rate coupons indexed to the Referential Rate (TR) or inflation indexes (IGPM/IPCR), with minimum maturities of 30 and 120 days respectively.

Interbank Certificates of Deposit (CDIs) are traded on the interbank market and are used as collateral for financial institutions' trading operations. Trading is done over the counter, usually for one day, and reflects the expectations of interest rates for the next day's funds rate, called CDI-Over. Ownership is electronically transferred and settlement completed through CETIP (the custody system for private instruments). They are also actively traded at the São Paulo Commodities and Futures Exchange (BM&F). Corporates issue debentures with maturities of at least one year with floating rate coupons payable semi-annually. Leasing company debentures pay interest and amortize principal monthly.

Private debt securities usually settle T+1 in CETIP (Bond Custody and Financial Liquidation Centre), and are owned by ANDIMA, a self-regulatory capital markets association which is made up of 370 financial institutions.

Foreign investors
The real is not freely convertible, and some foreign exchange transactions must be registered with the central bank, and executed through an authorized financial institution.

Non-residents can buy debt securities through investment funds stipulated by the Monetary Council's Annex IV. Alternatively, they can circumvent certain diversification rules, by purchasing bonds through the CC5 mechanism.

Derivatives market
Bolsa de Mercadorias and Futuros (BM&F – Future and Commodities Exchange) is one of the largest and most active futures exchanges in the world.

Pre-Brady rescheduled debt
Several attempts were made in the 1980s to solve Brazil's arrears to official and commercial bank creditors within the wider context of the Latin American debt crisis. Deposit Facility Agreements (DFAs) were made in 1983, which were then converted into Multi-Year DFAs (MYDFA) in 1988. In the same year, Exit bonds (plus New Money bonds) were issued, which are eligible for tendering in debt-for-equity swaps, and Interest Due and Unpaid bonds (IDU), which can be tendered in Brazil's privatization programme.

In 1994, after the introduction of the Plano Real, a final debt reduction scheme was agreed with Brazil's London Club bank creditors. US$32.5 billion of outstanding external debt was converted into US$28.6 billion of Brady bonds.

Brady-style restructured debt
The following instruments were selected from the Brady Plan menu:

Eligible Interest bonds, Front-Loaded Interest Reduction bonds (FLIRBs), FLIRBs with Capitalization bonds (C-Bonds), the largest and most liquid Brazilian Brady, Debt Conversion bonds (DCBs), 1994 New Money bonds, Discount bonds and Par bonds.

Brazil can repurchase bonds in the market two-and-a-half years after issue; there has been speculation about a more formal exchange of Bradys for conventional eurobonds, following the success of the Mexico and Philippines transactions.

Eurobonds
Brazil and Brazilian banks, agencies and enterprises have issued 217 eurobonds in eight currencies since 1991, when Petrobrás launched a US$250 million two-year issue.

Eurobonds issues (US$m)

	1990	1991	1992	1993	1994	1995	1996
Sovereign	—	—	—	—	—	1651.8	1173.2
Private	—	290.0	2210.5	4788.1	4217.6	5427.7	4245.2

Brady bonds

Brazil issued Brady bonds in April 1994. The bank loans were replaced by discount bonds and par bonds with a 30-year maturity, front-loaded interest reduction bonds (FLIRB), and in addition, Brazil allowed creditors an option of putting in new money and receiving a more attractive debt conversion bond (DCB) for their original principal. Brazil also issued eligible interest bonds (EIs) against interest arrears. The par and discount bonds are collateralized with 30-year zero coupons and have a 12-month rolling interest guarantee.

Bond	Coupon	Collateral	Maturity	Currencies
Discount	6mth L+13/16	Principal+Interest	2024	Multiple
Par	Step up	Principal+Interest	2024	
FLIRB	6mth L+13/16		2009	
DCB	6mth L+7/8		2024	
"New" New Money	6mth L+1		2009	

Prior to the Brady restructuring, Brazil had issued some new bonds, which now trade alongside the Bradys. In 1988, Brazil issued "new money bonds" against new lending by banks (the so-called "old" new money bonds) and in 1992 the republic issued interest due and unpaid bonds (IDU) against interest arrears. In August 1989, exit bonds were given to those banks willing to exchange existing debt for a below market alternative in return for being excluded from the call for new money.

■ BRAZIL: Economic indicators

Population and development	1990	1991	1992	1993	1994	1995	1996e
Population, million	150.4	153.3	156.3	159.2	162.2	165.4	168.5
Population growth, %	2.0	2.0	1.9	1.9	1.9	1.9	1.9
Nominal GDP per capita, US$	2919	2516	2418	2742	3430	4162	4509

National accounts							
Nominal GDP, US$bn	438.9	385.8	377.9	436.5	556.4	688.1	760.0
Change in real GDP, %	-4.1	0.2	-0.8	4.1	5.8	4.4	3.0
Gross fixed capital formation, % of GDP	22.9	19.3	19.5	20.0	20.8	20.8	21.3

Money supply and inflation							
Narrow money, change %, Dec/Dec	2495.4	300.0	850.0	2131.6	2580.8	25.3	11.0
Broad money, change %, Dec/Dec	576.9	600.0	1592.9	2773.0	965.3	47.7	
Consumer price inflation (avg.) %	2901.0	411.0	965.0	1920.0	2149.0	76.0	16.8

Interest rates *=latest figures							
Deposit rate, annual average	9394.30	913.50	1560.20	3293.50	5175.20	52.20	24.30*

Government finance							
Government expenditure, % of GDP	13.1	10.3	17.5	17.5	16.5	16.0	16.6
Government balance, % of GDP	—	—	-2.2	0.3	1.3	-5.0	-3.9

Exchange rates lc=local currency							
Exchange rate, annual average, lc/US$	0.00	0.00	0.00	0.03	0.64	0.92	1.00
Exchange rate, end of year, lc/US$	0.00	0.00	0.00	0.05	0.85	0.97	1.04
Real exchange rate 1990=100	100.0	185.1	168.8	191.3	249.4	313.2	339.7

Balance of payments							
Exports of goods & services, US$m	35170	34938	39881	43595	49010	52641	53747
Change %	-6.2	-0.7	14.1	9.3	12.4	7.4	2.1
Imports of goods & services, US$m, fob	28184	28251	27984	34856	43495	63495	66486
Change %	16.6	0.2	-0.9	24.6	24.8	46.0	4.7
Trade balance, of goods only, US$m, fob-fob	10747	10578	15239	14329	10861	-3854	-5539
Current account balance, US$m	-3823	-1450	6089	20	-1153	-18533	-22740
as a % of GDP	-0.9	-0.4	1.6	0.0	-0.2	-2.7	-2.8

Foreign exchange reserves							
Foreign exchange reserves, US$m	7430	8020	22520	30602	37069	49707	57000
Gold at ⅔ of market price, US$m	1175	488	510	702	949	1172	1183
Import cover (reserves/imports), months	3.2	3.4	9.7	10.5	10.2	9.4	10.3

Foreign debt and debt service							
Short-term debt, US$m	17351	16827	21194	28931	36449	43734	46500
Total foreign debt, US$m	122752	124825	133614	147351	157061	173140	186000
as a % of GDP	28.0	32.4	35.4	33.8	28.2	25.2	24.5
as a % of foreign exchange receipts	330	334	309	316	292	289	319
Interest payments, US$m	10868	9493	8278	9269	8140	10643	11200
Principal repayments, US$m	8549	7000	4980	8066	9212	12180	13000
Total debt service, US$m	19417	16493	13258	17335	17352	22823	24200
as a % of goods exports	61.8	52.2	37.0	43.7	39.3	49.1	50.7
as a % of foreign exchange receipts	52.2	44.1	30.6	37.2	32.3	38.1	41.5

Bulgaria

Area (thousands of km^2):	111
Population (1995, millions):	9.1
Population projection (2025, millions):	9.7
Urbanization rate (1993, % of population):	70
Life expectancy (1993, years at birth):	71
Gross domestic product (1996, US$bn):	10.4
GDP per capita (1996, US$):	1143
Average annual GDP growth rate (1990-96, %):	-4.1
Average annual inflation rate (1990-96, %):	113.3
Currency (lev per US$, average 1996):	185
Structure of production (1994):	51% services, 35% industry, 14% agriculture
Main exports:	cigarettes, iron, wine
Main imports:	oil
Main trading partners:	Germany, Italy, Greece, Turkey, France, US
Total foreign debt (% of GDP):	83.7
Next elections due under normal circumstances:	legislative required by December 1998

FORECAST: 1997-2000 (average)

	Worst case	Most likely	Best case
Real GDP growth (%)	0	1.25	2.0
Inflation (%)	90	60	46

■ POLITICS

Historical overview

The first Bulgarian state was founded in 681. In the 9th century, Tsar Simeon established an empire in the Balkans which was incorporated in the 11th century in the eastern Roman (Byzantine) Empire, from which it received Eastern Orthodox Christianity. Following the decline of the Byzantine Empire at the end of the twelfth century, Bulgaria became independent. In 1396 it was conquered by the Turks and was ruled for five centuries by the Turkish Ottoman Empire.

Modern Bulgaria emerged from the disintegrating Ottoman realm during the 19th century. With Russian assistance, an autonomous Bulgarian principality was established, and in 1878 it was recognized by the Congress of Berlin. Bulgaria declared itself an independent kingdom in 1908. Following independence, its major problem was territorial rights over Macedonia which mounted in the Second Balkan War in 1913.

Bulgaria fought in both world wars as a German ally in a vain effort to re-acquire Macedonian and Thracian territory held by Greece and Yugoslavia. The alliances with

Germany not only failed to win new territories for Bulgaria, but also resulted in the country being put under Soviet control in the postwar peace settlement.

Shortly before the Soviet armies entered Bulgaria in September 1944, a coup installed a broad anti-fascist coalition. Soviet support ensured the emergence of the Bulgarian Communist Party (BCP) as the dominant force. Bulgaria was declared a people's republic in December 1947 and BCP dominance was consolidated with considerable violence against opponents and earlier allies, and also against factions within the BCP itself. A Soviet-style one-party system was established.

In 1954 Todor Zhivkov became First Secretary of the BCP and stayed in power for thirty-three years. Zhivkov forced Bulgaria to go through the familiar Communist experiences of collectivization, urbanization, and industrialization. Extreme loyalty to the Soviet Union in foreign affairs was combined with a few reform measures in the domestic economy. The regime in Communist Bulgaria until the mid-1980s was one of the least repressive in the region and one of the most internally stable.

Communist Bulgaria left many ethnic and economic questions unresolved, however. The first arose from Zhivkov's campaign of forced assimilation of Bulgaria's ethnic Turkish minority. In economics, Bulgaria inherited a heavy dependence on the COMECON market, uncompetitive industry and huge foreign debt.

Recent events

After the fall of Communist regimes in central Eastern Europe in 1989, Zhivkov was ousted from power, but Communist rule in Bulgaria was not abolished, it was reformed. In June 1990 the Bulgarian Socialist Party (BSP), the renamed Bulgarian Communist Party, won the first multiparty elections. Although it gained a parliamentary majority, the BSP agreed to the election of Zhelyu Zhelev, then leader of the opposition Union of Democratic Forces (UDF), as Bulgaria's first non-Communist president.

Growing political chaos and strikes led to the fall of the first BSP government in November 1990 and a new so-called "government of experts" was established. In July 1991 a new constitution was adopted, under which Bulgaria was declared a parliamentary republic. The UDF won parliamentary elections in October 1991, but a year later the government lost power following a no-confidence vote. A new "government of experts" ruled until 1995.

In the December 1994 general elections, the BSP again won a parliamentary majority, allowing the BSP leader Zhan Videnov to assume the post of Prime Minister of a BSP cabinet. The ruling coalition strengthened its power by winning local elections in October 1995. Despite strong pressure from the opposition and President Zhelev, as well as the internal conflicts within the BSP, the normal activities of the government were not impaired. Videnov's government not only survived two no-confidence votes, it also started a voucher privatization process. As a result of the ongoing economic crisis the Videnov government resigned at the end of December 1996. Following huge mass demonstrations, which brought the country to a halt, the governing Socialists and the opposition agreed to call early general elections in mid-April 1997. Until then, a caretaker government, led by Marian Sofiansky (UDF) will prepare the elections and begin negotiations with the IMF and the EU over economic aid for Bulgaria.

Half-way through the four-year term of the current socialist government, Bulgarian opposition candidate Petar Stoyanov, a reformist lawyer from the Union of Democratic

Forces (UDF), won the November 1996 presidential election run-off with almost 60% of the vote. Culture Minister Ivan Marazov, candidate of the governing socialists, received 40% of the votes.

Chronology

681	The Bulgarian state is founded
1396	Bulgaria becomes a province of the Turkish Ottoman Empire
1877	Russia declares war on the Turks in support of the Orthodox Slav subjects of the Ottoman Empire
1878	The Ottomans recognize an autonomous principality of Bulgaria at the Congress of Berlin; Eastern Rumelia and Macedonia remain under Turkish rule
1915	Bulgaria declares war on Serbia, entering the First World War on the side of the Central Powers of Germany, Austria-Hungary and the Ottoman Empire
1918	Bulgaria surrenders to the Entente Powers
1919	Bulgaria is forced to cede its Thracian territories and Mediterranean coast to Greece, its western frontier to Yugoslavia and to return Dobrogea to Romania.
1941	Bulgaria signs a pact with the Axis powers of Germany and Italy and, following the outbreak of war in the Balkans, gains western Macedonia from Yugoslavia
1944	A left-wing alliance takes power, dominated by the Bulgarian Communist Party. The Soviet army occupies Bulgaria.
1947	A new constitution abolishes all opposition parties and establishes a system based on the Soviet model. Bulgaria becomes a people's republic.
1954	Todor Zhivkov becomes leader of the BCP
1989	November: Zhivkov is forced to resign as General Secretary of the BCP and as President of the Council of State. The government announces the dissolution of the secret police.
1989	December: the National Assembly abolishes the "leading role of the BCP in society" and legalizes demonstrations and political parties
1990	June: in elections for the 400-seat new constituent Grand National Assembly, the Bulgarian Socialist Party (BSP; the former BCP) wins 211 seats, the United Democratic Front (UDF) 144 seats
1990	August: Zhelyu Zhelev, leader of the UDF is elected president in a parliamentary vote
1990	October: Bulgaria becomes a member of the IMF and the World Bank
1990	November: the Lukanov government resigns after agreement on the formation of a multiparty government under a non-party premier
1991	April: the Paris Club of state lenders agrees to the rescheduling of Bulgaria's foreign debt
1991	July: the new constitution is adopted by the Grand National Assembly
1992	Zhelyu Zhelev is re-elected in direct presidential elections
1994	In general elections, the BSP (in alliance, as the Democratic Left, with two small parties, BUPA and Ekoglastnost) wins a majority, taking 125 of 240 seats in the National Assembly
1996	The first round of Bulgaria's mass privatization begins. Videnov resigns as prime minister amid deepening economic crisis.

State organization

Bulgaria is divided into nine regions (oblast) formed from twenty-eight former provinces in 1987. The city of Sofia, the national capital, has its own regional status. Local authorities for all regions and districts are elected for thirty months.

Constitution and government

Bulgaria has been a republic since the abolition of the monarchy in 1946. In 1947 a new constitution declared Bulgaria a people's republic. The Bulgarian Communist Party became "the leading force in society and in the state". This principle was reiterated in the constitution of 1971. The present democratic constitution was approved on July 13, 1991.

The first chapter of the constitution declares that the Republic of Bulgaria is a republic with a parliamentary form of government. The constitution upholds principles such as political and religious freedom, free economic initiative and respect for international law.

National Assembly

The National Assembly of 240 members is the unicameral legislature of Bulgaria. It exercises parliamentary control over the country. Members are elected by proportional representation from thirty-five constituencies.

To qualify for parliament, a party must achieve at least 4% of the vote. Parliament sits for a maximum of four years, but early general elections are possible if a government loses a vote of confidence.

The key functions of the legislature are the enactment of the laws, the approval of the state budget, the scheduling of presidential elections, and the approval or dismissal of the members of the Council of Ministers (government).

President

The head of state is the president, elected by popular vote every five years. Although there is no executive role, the office has powers in emergencies, as well as a role in the security and foreign policy spheres and the right to return legislation to the parliament for reconsideration. The president is also the supreme commander-in-chief of the armed forces.

Council of Ministers

The Council supervises the implementation of state policy and the state budget, the administration and the armed forces, and the maintenance of law and order. Currently, there are twenty ministers.

Current government

President (sworn in January 19, 1997)	Petar Stoyanov
Prime Minister	Marian Sofiansky

A caretaker government, led by Marian Sofiansky (UDF) are now preparing general elections, which are scheduled for mid-April, 1997.

Governor, National Bank	Lyubomir Filipov
Parliamentary speaker	Blagovest Sendov

Main political parties
Bulgarian Socialist Party (BSP)
> Evolved from the BCP
> Left-centre
> The main factions within the BSP are orthodox Marxist and social democratic
> Led by Zhan Videnov. As a leader he favours humane Communism rather than social democracy.

Union of Democratic Forces (UDF)
> Formed as an anti-Communist organization in 1989
> Pro-market and right-of-centre
> Strongest in Sofia and other urban areas
> Led by Ivan Kostov

The People's Union (PU)
> Formed in 1994 as a coalition between the Bulgarian Agrarian National Union (BANU), led by
> Anastasia Moser, and the Democratic Party (DP), led by Stefan Savov

Movement for Rights and Freedoms (MRF)
> The party of ethnic Turks
> Led by Ahmed Dogan

Bulgarian Business Bloc (BBB)
> Smallest of the five groupings in the current parliament and the least stable
> Led by Georges Ganchev

Results of the recent parliamentary elections
The elections resulted in an absolute majority for the Democratic Left, an electoral coalition between the BSP and two minor parties. The remaining seats were divided between four other groups. After attempts to enlist other groups in a broad coalition, the BSP leader, Zhan Videnov, formed the government of the Democratic Left alone.

	% of votes	seats
Democratic Left	43.50	125
Union of Democratic Forces (UDF)	24.23	69
People's Union (PU)	6.51	18
Movement for Rights and Freedoms(MRF)	5.44	15
Bulgarian Business Bloc (BBB)	4.72	13
TOTAL		240

International relations
The post-Communist governments of Bulgaria have stressed that their most important foreign policy goal is to integrate Bulgaria into the industrialized world. Bulgaria joined the IMF in 1990 and became an associate member of the EU. Diplomatic relations with several Western countries were re-established in 1990 and 1991, and in 1992 Bulgaria became a member of the Council of Europe and the Consultative Committee of the Western European Union. In December 1995 Bulgaria's National Assembly approved an official application for full EU membership. Nevertheless, the BSP government is trying to balance its foreign policy priorities between integration with the West, and especially with the EU, and rapprochement with Russia.

Central bank

The existing legal framework in Bulgaria provides for a two-tier banking system with the Bulgarian National Bank (BNB) on the first tier and the commercial banks on the second. The law of the Bulgarian National Bank, enacted in 1992, provides for the bank to operate as bank of the state, reporting directly to the National Assembly. The BNB is independent from the Council of Ministers (the cabinet) and other governmental bodies.

The nine-member board of the Bulgarian National Bank is appointed for five years. The governor of the BNB and three deputy governors are appointed by parliament. The remaining five members are appointed by the president. The new members of the BNB board were appointed in July 1996, as the terms of previous members, appointed five years ago, expired at the end of June. The parliament extended central bank governor Lubomir Filipov's term another five years.

■ ECONOMICS

Historical overview

Communist rule transformed Bulgaria from a primarily agricultural country into an industrial one. Bulgaria's system of national accounts has changed only recently to the standard Western measurement of GDP from accounts based on the Communist-era concept of net material product (NMP). In 1939, 15% of NMP was provided by industry and 65% by agriculture. The figures in 1989 were 59% and 11% respectively. According to official statistics, between 40% and 50% of gross capital investment was devoted to industry during that period, and less than 10% to agriculture.

Industrialization created a standard range of heavy industries in the early decades of Communist rule. But over time, there was an increasing tendency to specialize, to fill niches within the Soviet economic bloc. A sizeable defence industry was also created during the Communist period, mainly for Warsaw Pact needs. In the late 1970s and 1980s, high-tech activities such as electronics and microbiology appeared in Bulgaria. The country became the leading producer of personal computers within COMECON. However, this equipment was grossly obsolete by contemporary Western standards. Tourism, agriculture and food processing were also promoted by the Communist regime. Bulgaria has traditionally been a major producer of fruit and vegetables, but also of tobacco, 90% of which was directed to the Soviet market in the late 1980s. Viticulture has also been developed extensively. In 1989, Bulgaria was the world's fourth largest exporter of wine.

Like most other Soviet-bloc countries, Bulgaria experienced a creeping systemic crisis from the mid-1970s. After the fall of Communism, stagnation gave way to an economic downturn. Output in most sectors fell, and there were sharp rises in unemployment and inflation. Between 1989 and 1994 employment fell by almost 30%, with unemployment peaking at almost 20% in late 1993. Bulgaria's foreign trade was badly hit by the collapse of the command economies of COMECON (dissolved in 1991), which had accounted for some 80% of Bulgaria's total foreign trade. In addition, Bulgaria's economy was seriously affected by UN sanctions against Iraq from 1990, and Yugoslavia from 1993 to 1995.

Recent developments

In 1994, after five years of decline, the Bulgarian economy started to recover, with modest GDP growth of 1.4%. Industrial production rose 4%, partially induced by a revival in exports. This was helped by an increase in trade with the EU and a revival in trade with former COMECON members. But inflation remained high, running at 120% at the end of 1994.

Economic activity strengthened further in 1995, again led by exports, with real GDP rising about 2.5%. Unemployment fell to 11.8 %, as the private sector absorbed workers laid off from the state-owned sector. Slower depreciation of the lev helped to cut inflation to 33% at the end of the year.

During 1994 and 1995, the improved trade performance was accompanied by a lower deficit on invisibles – services and net transfers. The current account deficit fell to about US$0.2 billion in 1994, and turned into surplus of US$0.3 billion in 1995.

Despite many positive developments in 1994 and 1995, the Bulgarian economy faced a serious crisis in 1996. The long delay in structural reforms, together with the absence of an effective monetary policy during 1995-96, were the main reasons for the financial crisis and the general loss of confidence. Liquidity problems in a growing number of banks caused a run on the banking system, with massive withdrawals of deposits in both lev and foreign currency in favour of cash holdings of foreign exchange. High debt service obligations have further weakened domestic liquidity.

The exchange value of the lev has plunged from just over 70 lev per US dollar at the end of 1995 to 122 lev, and in some exchange offices to 150 lev by May 1996. After intervention by the National Bank, the rate temporarily recovered to 106 lev, but dropped again dramatically. Meanwhile, debt service payments, higher than expected energy imports, high resident outflows and currency interventions by the National Bank to support the lev brought a collapse in Bulgaria's foreign exchange reserves from US$1.2 billion at the end of 1995 to US$518 million by the end of December 1996.

Government proposals to the IMF and the World Bank included significant tax breaks and accelerated privatization to attract foreign investment, the closure of about one hundred state-owned, loss-making firms, restructuring other companies, and rehabilitation of the banking system through merger and stronger supervision. The IMF responded by making a stand-by loan agreement with Bulgaria and disbursed the first tranche of US$115 million. Several of the measures, especially privatization, will be politically difficult for the government to implement. The second US$115 million stand-by tranche was delayed as of December 1996, pending action to close or sell a number of loss-making state enterprises and revision of the badly off-track macroeconomic framework. The state-owned Mineralbank and the First Private Bank, the biggest private bank in Bulgaria, were taken under special supervision.

Privatization began in January 1996, but progress remained limited. Moreover, the state intends to hold a controlling share of 33% or more in most enterprises. The highly subsidized state-owned industrial enterprises ran into trouble when energy subsidies and credits fell in 1996. Thus, following two years of output growth, the Bulgarian economy fell into recession. GDP is expected to fall by about 5% in 1996. The sharp depreciation of the lev, down to 1,000 per US dollar by late January 1997, has drastically raised prices. After single-digit monthly inflation rates for the previous nineteen months, the CPI increased at a double-digit pace in May and reached a peak rise of 26.9% in December 1996. The budget deficit, larger than the annual limit set under the IMF stand-by agreement, has become increasingly difficult to finance.

The Bulgarian economy
Industry
In 1995 industry accounted for almost 35% of GDP. Output fell by about 30% between 1989 and 1993. In 1996, increases in energy prices and a sharp cut in bank credits caused industrial production among state enterprises to fall 4%. Output declines were largest in key industrial sectors, such as metallurgy and chemicals.

Services
In 1995 services provided 51.2% of GDP. This has been the worst affected sector of Bulgaria's economy during the transformation, showing no growth since economic reforms began, a very atypical development in Eastern Europe. In 1995 the decline in the services sector was about 6%.

Share of GDP by sector

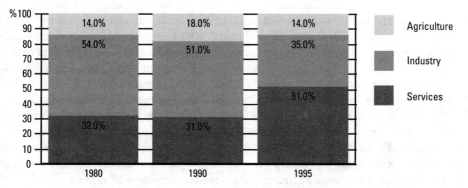

Source: Official data

Agriculture
Agriculture is the smallest of the three sectors of the economy. It produced 14% in 1995. Private farming was legalized in 1990 and by 1994 privately owned farms supplied more than 70% of total agricultural production. As a result, agricultural production increased in real terms by 10% in 1994 and by 12% in 1995.

Trade
Under Communist rule, Bulgaria was distinguished among other Eastern bloc countries by the unusually large proportion of its foreign trade (about 80%) that was conducted with COMECON countries. Almost 60% of Bulgaria's foreign trade was with the USSR. Despite subsequent diversification, the former USSR remained the main partner for several years after dissolution of COMECON. But in 1995 Bulgaria's principal trading partner became the European Union, accounting for about 38% of both exports and imports. Its largest individual trading partners are Russia, Germany, Italy and Greece.

Breakdown of exports (1995)

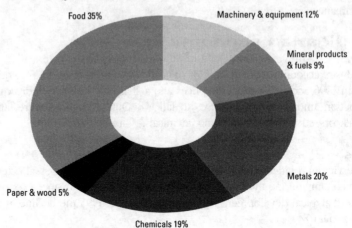

Source: Official data

The commodity structure of Bulgaria's foreign trade has changed radically since Communist rule collapsed. After the dissolution of COMECON, the share of machinery and equipment both in exports and imports, which traditionally had been strong, declined sharply. Meanwhile, agricultural goods and livestock became the largest items in Bulgaria's exports, and mineral products and oil rose to about 40% of imports. In 1994-95, the structure of foreign trade changed again, as Bulgaria became a low-cost producer of bulk commodities. In 1995 the share of industrial goods trade increased to 12% of exports and to 22% of imports.

Bulgaria's principal exports in 1995 were industrial goods, accounting for 65% of the total. Base metals accounted for 20%; chemicals, 19%; machinery and equipment, 12%; mineral products and fuels, 8.5%; wood, paper and glass products, 5%; processed food, beverages and tobacco, 35%. Industrial goods, fuels and mineral products were the main imports in this period.

Imports and exports as a % of GDP

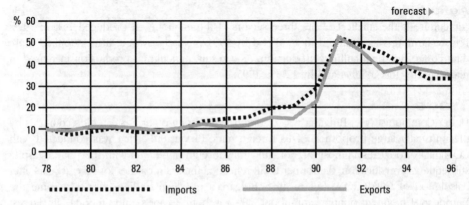

Source: UBS

Balance of payments

Bulgaria had current account surpluses until 1985, largely due to the surplus in trade with developing countries, which more than covered a negative balance of trade with OECD countries. The situation has changed dramatically, however, since 1986, when Bulgaria's foreign currency earnings (especially from exports to developing countries) fell as a result of the oil price collapse. Moreover, this reduction in hard currency income coincided with major new Bulgarian investment programmes in the 1986-90 plan period. Thus, during the late 1980s, large trade deficits with the OECD (about US$1.4 billion in 1986, and almost US$1.7 billion in 1989), combined with far smaller surpluses with developing countries, brought rising current account deficits. These were mainly financed by borrowing and swollen by increasing interest payments. The outcome was the loss of creditor confidence and a moratorium on debt payments in 1990.

Current account as a % of GDP

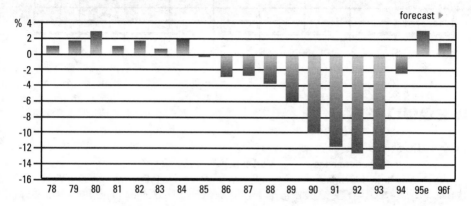

Source: Official data

Export volume growth accelerated to about 13% in 1995. Export gains were concentrated in energy-intensive sectors, which were implicitly subsidized by artificially low domestic energy prices. Exports also rose because of stronger demand in key markets, particularly among OECD countries, which now account for more than 50% of Bulgarian exports. Imports recovered in 1995 with a rise of about 4%, after a drop of 13% in 1994. The sharp increase partly reflected higher fuel imports for export processing. Moreover, the stronger lev encouraged imports of raw materials, which in turn sustained growth in domestic production.

Currency

The Bulgarian national currency, the lev, is internally convertible, although full current account convertibility has not been achieved. Exchange rates are determined on the internal foreign exchange market. After the serious 1996 financial crisis and the dramatic devaluation of the lev, the introduction of a currency board was intensively discussed at the end of 1996, and it seems likely that such a system will be adopted. Under the rules of a currency board, levs in circulation would have to be fully matched by central bank foreign exchange reserves and monetary gold. The exchange rate will be pegged to the dollar or to the deutschmark. Given the very low level of reserves at the end of 1996, substantial support from the IMF will be needed to implement such a proposal. Moreover, the need for a new government to be built which has to decide on the introduction of the currency board may delay its implementation and deepen the country's economic crisis.

Bulgarian lev/US dollar exchange rate

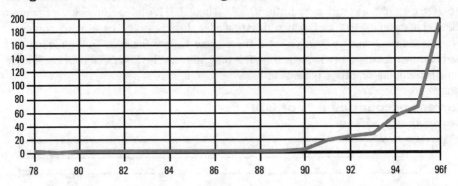

■ EQUITIES

Key indicators

	Index performance %, in US$ terms	Market Cap. US$bn	P/E	Div. Yield
1994	—	0.5	25.4	0.3
1995	-15.6	0.6	—	—
1996	-85	0.7	16.9	0.2

Sources: Local stock exchange, IFC, Bloomberg, Datastream, UBS

Structure

Since 1991, fourteen stock exchanges have been set up in Bulgaria. Most trading takes place on the Bulgarian Stock Exchange (BSE) and the Sofia Stock Exchange (SSE). Since it began trading in May 1992, the BSE has established itself as the main market for Bulgarian stocks.

At the end of 1995 there were eighteen companies listed on the BSE. Market capitalization rose by 27.2% to BGL4,389 (US$62.7) during the year. In addition to the official market, there is also a regulated market on the BSE for shares of the twelve large banks and insurance companies which are predominantly state-owned. Turnover during 1995 was BGL298 million (US$4.21 million). Market value as a percentage of GDP at the end of 1995 was 0.6%. The average price/earnings ratio was 17.86.

Regulatory authority

A Bulgarian Securities and Exchange Commission (BSEC) was set up in January 1996 to regulate and supervise the BSE. It is responsible for granting and controlling investment intermediaries, setting disclosure requirements and registering issuer prospectuses.

Trading methods

BSE trading is mainly by the traditional open outcry method, although it is supported by a computerized trading system. Buy and sell orders are entered into the computer and shown on large screens. Orders are then matched, and the trades registered after confirmation of purchase. Details of orders and trades are broadcast by Reuters. The BSE is setting up a real-time electronic trading system.

Hours

The BSE floor is open for trading from 11.15 to 11.45, Monday to Friday.

Settlement time and clearing

Settlement and clearance is organized on a T+3 physical basis through the BSE's clearing bank. A computerized clearing system is under discussion.

Commission rates

Commission rates on BSE share transactions are 2.2% of the transaction value.

Stock indices

There are four share price indices recording share dealing. Three of these follow specific markets (BSE, the SSE and the Balkan Exchange) while a fourth composite index, the Standard Business Data Index, is published daily by *The Standard* newspaper. The BSE index comprises all domestic securities and is weighted according to market capitalization.

Taxes

A withholding tax of 15% is payable by non-residents on dividends and interest. This rate can be reduced where double taxation treaties apply. Dividends issued by companies with a foreign partner are liable to a 10% withholding tax. There is also a stamp duty of 1% levied on the transfer of limited liability company shares.

Disclosure of financial statements

Every company must submit a prospectus, an audited balance sheet and a financial statement outlining past year's performance to the BSEC. Any significant changes in the activities, capital or management structure of a listed company must also be registered.

Shareholders' rights

BSE members must deposit a sum equal to 5% of average daily trading value to a fund as a guarantee against member default.

Capital and foreign exchange controls

Trades in foreign currency can only be done through banks and brokers licensed by the Bulgarian National Bank. Banks and other financial institutions may trade freely in foreign currency.

Brokers

The BSE has fifty-six members comprising twenty-six banks, three insurance companies and twenty-seven financial brokers.

Sectors
The principal sectors are energy, tourism, banking and trading companies.

ADRs
There are no Bulgarian ADRs.

Market comment
The Bulgarian equity market is relatively underdeveloped and liquidity remains low. It has attracted fewer foreign investors than other central and Eastern European countries. Future growth will depend on the pace of privatization and the liberalization of tax and customs regulations.

■ DEBT

The Bulgarian National Bank (BNB) acts as agent for the Ministry of Finance (MOF) for the sale of government bills and bonds. The BNB conducts auctions for discount and interest-bearing treasury bills, and treasury bonds denominated in Bulgarian lev and US dollars.

Sales of short- and long-term securities to finance the budget deficit are not governed by legislation, but are currently authorized by regulations issued by the MOF and BNB. Other medium-dated government bonds are issued in accordance with Council of Ministers decrees and with the 1996 Law on State Protection of Deposits and Accounts.

Treasury bills
Discount and interest-bearing treasury bills (paying a spread over basic interest rate) are issued with 3-, 6-, 9- and 12-month maturities. Bills are auctioned every Monday, and details are announced by the BNB three days earlier. Individual bids are restricted to half of the 70% of an issue offered for competitive bids – satisfied at the highest price first. Bids are submitted to the Government Securities Division of the BCB in multiples of 100,000 lev. Non-financial entities can only make non-competitive bids, which are filed at the average price of competitive bids. Settlement is 2 days later.

Treasury bonds
Bonds are auctioned on the second and fourth Friday of each month, for maturities of 15 months to 7 years. Settlement is 4 days later.

Direct sales
Some treasury bills are sold direct to individuals and non-financial institutions, through contractual arrangements with banks who act as agents. They include the BNB, the United Bulgarian Bank, the Bulbank and the Bulgarian Post Bank.

Long-term government bonds are issued to settle the non-performing credits of state-owned companies which are owed to banks. They are sold direct to institutions and individuals. In addition, long dated participating bonds are issued for Bulgaria's privatization programme.

The size of the government debt market in September 1996 was about 640.6 billion lev (US$2.9bn).

Secondary market trades are settled through the BNB, where transfers are notified and registered.

Overseas investment in government securities is regulated by the Law on the Economic Activity of Foreign Persons.

Eurobonds

In 1988/9 the Bulgarian Foreign Trade Bank (Bulbank) issued three international bonds in the Japanese Shibosai market. However, Bulgaria has yet to issue a eurobond.

Brady bonds

Bulgaria completed a Brady-style restructuring of its London Club debt in 1994. Commercial bank creditors were offered a menu of options consisting of Discount Bonds, Interest Arrears Bonds and Front-Loaded Interest Reduction Bonds.

■ BULGARIA: Economic indicators

Population and development	1990	1991	1992	1993	1994	1995	1996e
Population, million	9.0	9.0	9.1	9.1	9.1	9.1	9.1
Population growth, %	0.2	0.2	0.2	0.2	0.2	0.2	0.2
Nominal GDP per capita, US$	1293	799	956	1139	1125	1508	1143

National accounts							
Nominal GDP, US$bn	11.7	7.2	8.7	10.3	10.2	13.7	10.4
Change in real GDP, %	-6.5	-11.7	-7.3	-2.4	1.4	2.6	-5.0
Gross fixed capital formation, % of GDP	21.9	18.5	16.2	13.9	12.2	11.2	8.8

Money supply and inflation							
Narrow money, change %, Dec/Dec	9.9	27.5	40.5	27.5	55.6	42.7	—
Broad money, change %, Dec/Dec	16.4	125.0	42.1	47.5	78.6	39.6	—
Consumer price inflation (avg.) %	26.3	334	82.0	73.0	96.3	62.1	123

Government finance							
Government expenditure, % of GDP	65.9	45.8	45.3	50.7	43.3	39.4	—
Government balance, % of GDP	-12.6	-3.7	-7.1	-14.1	-5.4	-5.4	-10.0

Exchange rates lc=local currency							
Exchange rate, annual average, lc/US$	3.89	18.15	23.44	27.69	54.30	67.24	192
Exchange rate, end of year, lc/US$	7.10	21.70	24.49	32.71	65.70	70.70	439

Balance of payments							
Exports of goods & services, US$m	3349	4193	5151	4991	5276	6680	5840
Change %	6.7	25.2	22.8	-3.1	5.7	26.6	-12.6
Imports of goods & services, US$m, fob	4637	5104	6284	6543	5698	6479	5925
Change %	6.9	10.1	23.1	4.1	-12.9	13.7	-8.6
Trade balance, of goods only, US$m, fob-fob	-757	-32	-213	-885	-17	427	200
Current account balance, US$m	-1180	-842	-1090	-1515	-248	334	150
as a % of GDP	-10.1	-11.7	-12.6	-14.7	-2.4	2.4	1.4

Foreign exchange reserves							
Foreign exchange reserves, US$m	—	358	902	664	1002	1236	300
Import cover (reserves/imports), months	0.0	0.8	1.7	1.2	2.1	2.3	0.6

Foreign debt and debt service							
Short-term debt, US$m	2438	2484	2419	2363	138	—	—
Total foreign debt, US$m	9933	11226	12151	12585	10361	9050	9500
as a % of GDP	85.1	155.5	140.3	121.8	101.4	65.9	91.1
as a % of foreign exchange receipts	287	263	234	250	190	133	160
Interest payments, US$m	821	849	950	702	499	605	700
Principal repayments, US$m	1349	161	227	126	180	383	590
Total debt service, US$m	2170	1010	1177	828	679	988	1290
as a % of goods exports	83.0	27.0	29.8	22.2	17.3	19.3	28.7
as a % of foreign exchange receipts	62.8	23.7	22.7	16.5	12.5	14.5	21.7

Chile

Area (thousands of km²):	757
Population (1995, millions):	14.2
Population projection (2025, millions):	19
Population younger than 15 yrs (1991, % of total):	30.6
Urbanization rate (1993, % of population):	84
Life expectancy (1993, years at birth):	74
Gross domestic product (1996, US$bn):	74.1
GDP per capita (1996, US$):	5133
Average annual GDP growth rate (1990-96, %):	6.7
Average annual inflation rate (1990-96, %):	14.7
Currency (peso per US$, average 1996):	412.19
Real exchange rate: (1990=100, average 1996)	125.42
Structure of production (1994):	17.5% services, 27.3% industry, 55.2% agriculture
Main exports:	copper, paper, pulp, newsprint
Main imports:	fuels and lubricants, other intermediate goods, capital goods
Main trading partners:	US, Japan, Germany, Brazil
Market capitalization of Stock Exchange (Decmber 1996; US$bn):	65.9
Total foreign debt (% of GDP):	29.4
Next elections due under normal circumstances:	legislative: December 1997; presidential: December 1999
Credit rating: (Jan 1997, Standard & Poor's, Moody's)	A-; Baa1

FORECAST: 1997-2000 (average)

	Worst case	Most likely	Best case
Real GDP growth (%)	4.5	5.5	6.0
Inflation (%)	5.5	5	4

■ POLITICS

Historical overview

The Spanish conquered Chile in 1536, but the indigenous population always resisted Spanish domination. This continual unrest motivated Spain to impose drastic trade restrictions. As a result, Chile remained undeveloped until the second half of the 18th century.

Chile became independent in 1810, but it was not until the 1830s that the country drafted a constitution and held its first presidential elections. During the next 150 years, democracy was interrupted by only two brief periods of military dictatorship. Meanwhile, victories over Peru and Bolivia in the War of the Pacific (1879–83) allowed considerable territorial gains.

In 1970, an alliance of socialists, communists and radicals won the presidential election. New policies of government intervention and nationalization included a system of price controls, which resulted in increasing economic difficulties and political turmoil. Amid conditions of deepening economic and political crisis, General Augusto Pinochet Ugarte led a military coup in September 1973.

Over the next seventeen years, the populace suffered under a regime that ignored freedom of speech and human rights. However, the military implemented important economic reforms, including privatization and a radical overhaul of the country's pension system, paving the way for the success currently enjoyed by the Chilean economy. However, an economic crisis at the end of the 1970s forced the regime to submit a new constitution to the electorate. The 1981 charter, which stipulated a gradual return to democracy and ratified General Pinochet's presidency until 1989, was approved by two thirds of the population. Meanwhile, the debt crisis of 1982 prompted further economic and political liberalization.

Recent events

Democracy was re-introduced in December 1989, when Patricio Aylwin was elected president. Although Pinochet will head the army until 1998 and the armed forces still exert considerable influence, democratic structures are now firmly in place.

In December 1993, the centre-left Christian Democrat Eduardo Frei Ruiz-Tagle won the presidential election by an overwhelming 58% of the electorate vote. He has continued the economic policies of his predecessor, aiming to reduce inflation and maintain economic growth. In addition, Frei has emphasized social and educational projects and supported small and medium-sized enterprises, while overseeing the improvement of Chile's international trade links.

Chronology

1536	Beginning of the Spanish conquest
1541	Foundation of Santiago de Chile
1810	Chilean independence
1823	De facto dictatorship under the Interior Minister, Diego Portales
1837	Execution of Portales and return to democracy
1879-83	War of the Pacific. Chile triumphs over Peru and Bolivia.
1886	Election of José Manuel Belmaceda, reformist
1890	Civil war
1924	Military government under General Carlos Ibáñez del Campo
1925	Former civilian president Arturo Alessandri retakes power
1927-31	New military dictatorship
1932	Presidential elections and return of the radical Arturo Alessandri
1964	Eduardo Frei of the Christian Democratic Party wins the presidency
1970	Salvador Allende of the Unidad Popular (alliance of socialists, communists and radicals) becomes president
1973	Military coup engineered by General Augusto Pinochet Ugarte

1981	New constitution approved by plebiscite. Provides for eventual return to democracy.
1988	General Pinochet is rejected as president by plebiscite
1989	De facto re-introduction of democracy. Christian Democrat Patricio Aylwin elected president.
1989	Revision of the 1981 constitution
1993	Christian Democrat Eduardo Frei Ruiz-Tagle (son of former President Eduardo Frei) wins the presidency

Constitution and government

Chile is a presidential republic. According to the 1981 constitution, revised in 1989, the president represents the supreme executive authority. He is elected for a six-year term and cannot be re-elected. He appoints the members of the Council of Ministers as well as the judges of the Supreme Court, who are designated for life. The Congress consists of a 46-member Senate and a 120-member Chamber of Deputies. Senators serve eight-year terms and Chamber members four-year terms. The members of Congress, with the exception of eight senators, are currently elected by general suffrage.

The eight remaining senators as well as the head of the armed forces and the members of the National Security Council, which monitors the military, are still appointed by the former military government.

State organization

Chile is divided into thirteen regions and fifty provinces. As per the 1991 constitutional changes, local officials are now directly elected.

Political parties

Christian Democratic Party (PDC)
Centre-left; largest and most influential party
Founded 1957; major re-organization 1969, 1971
Led by Alejandro Foxley

Independent Democratic Union (UDI)
Right-wing; represents the military regime's economic and political elite
Founded 1983
Led by Jovino Novoa

National Renewal (RN)
Conservative
Founded 1987
Led by Andrés Allamand

Party for Democracy (PPD)
Centre-left; more liberal than PDC
Founded 1987
Led by Sergio Bitar

Socialist Party (PS)
Left-wing
Founded 1933
Led by Camilo Escalona

Result of December 1993 elections
Senate: **PDC** (13 seats), **RN** (11), **PS** (5), **UDI** (3), **PPD** (2), **other** (4), **appointed** (8)
Chamber of Deputies: **PDC** (37 seats), **RN** (29), **PPD** (15), **UDI** (15), **PS** (15), **others** (9)

Next elections
Legislative: December 1997; presidential: December 1999

Other political forces
Military
Although democracy was re-introduced in 1989, the military still exerts considerable influence in Chile. The armed forces are not subject to government authority, have a guaranteed portion of the national budget and still appoint eight senators. However, their power should be phased out in the next couple of years, as all the Senate members will be elected by general suffrage in December 1997. Furthermore, General Pinochet is due to retire by March 1998 and the new 1998 Congress is expected to implement further constitutional reform.

Labour
The country's main union confederation, the CUT, represents most of the labour unions and is backed by the powerful Confederation of Copper Mine Workers.

The labour movement and government maintain close ties, negotiating together with business on legislative reforms and other important labour issues. However, union concerns about new free-market reforms and disagreements on labour security reforms are intensifying. They have already resulted in large-scale strikes, mainly in the mining sector.

Central bank
The president of the central bank is appointed by the head of state. As per the constitution, the Chilean central bank independently formulates monetary and exchange rate policy. However, its link to the government has been very strong. The mid-1996 government decision to write off part of the debt that Chilean commercial banks owe to the central bank led to the resignation of its former president, Roberto Zahler, and has raised concern about the autonomy of the bank.

The central bank is mandated by law to promote monetary stability and facilitate foreign and internal settlements. The bank manages real interest rates on its short-term liabilities to achieve its inflation targets. (In 1996, December/December inflation registered 6.6%, compared with the central bank target of 6.5%.)

■ ECONOMICS

Historical overview
Chile has been hit by two severe economic disturbances during the past thirty years. The first was initiated in the early 1970s by populist policies and the first oil crisis, which resulted in severe recession, hyperinflation and a balance of payments crisis.

After the military coup in 1973, General Pinochet introduced free-market policies. Subsidies and price controls were eliminated, import tariffs significantly reduced, and state enterprises privatized. These policies succeeded in stabilizing the economy. But the outbreak of the international debt crisis and the drastic fall in the world price of copper led to a second economic disturbance in 1982, triggering a collapse of domestic output, a severe banking crisis and the suspension by the government of the country's foreign debt service. The peso was devalued several times, causing inflation and unemployment to rise and real wages to collapse. Chile's economic deterioration led to massive protests against the authoritarian regime.

Consequently, Pinochet was forced to pursue a policy of economic liberalization. State-owned companies were privatized, import tariffs were cut, a new pension fund system was launched and tax reform was implemented. As a result of these developments, the public and private sectors became more efficient, production more competitive internationally and the export base more diversified. Thus, after a two-year recession and a series of devaluations, the Chilean economy picked up throughout the 1980s. When Aylwin became president in 1989, he inherited the most dynamic and best run economy in Latin America.

Chile's economic performance, 1961–95

	Average annual real GDP growth, %	Average annual consumer price inflation, %
1961-1965	3.8	24.7
1966-1970	4.7	26.2
1971-1975	-2.2	208.2
1976-1980	7.5	72.1
1981-1985	-0.4	21.3
1985-1990	6.5	19.4
1991-1995	7.4	13.8

Source: IMF

Recent developments

Government policy in recent years has focused on tight monetary control, export growth and deregulation of trade and investment. The mandate has included social reform and increased expenditure on health, education and infrastructure. The continuation of stabilization policies has been rewarded by high investment, export-driven output growth and decreasing inflation. Chile's economy grew by an impressive annual average of 7.4% from 1991 to 1995, while annual average inflation declined from 27.5% in 1990 to 8.2% in 1995.

Economic growth of 8.5% in 1995 was caused mainly by a sharp increase in private consumption driven to a large extent by a dramatic improvement in the terms of trade. This growth also reflected soaring investment due to a resurgence in residential construction and to buoyant government spending. Strong domestic demand and the accelerating pace of economic activity pulled inflation higher and led to a tightening of monetary policy first in late 1995 and more dramatically in April 1996. By the end of July, the real rate on the 90-day central bank paper (the monetary policy benchmark) stood at 7.5%. The tight policy resulted in a soft landing for the economy, GDP growth slowing to 6.5% in 1996 while average inflation dropped to 7.4%.

The economy

The Chilean economy produces a wide variety of raw materials and manufactured goods. Over the last fifteen years, agriculture has experienced a modest expansion, while fishing and mining, especially copper, have grown rapidly and become the most dynamic tradeable goods sectors. Together, the three activities which make up the primary sector contributed 17.5% of total 1995 GDP.

The main manufacturing products are fish meal, wood pulp, steel, chemicals and cement. Due to the improvement in Chile's terms of trade, this sector faced increasing competition from imported goods, resulting in a quasi-stagnation of manufacturing output during the last two years. Services accounted for about 55% of GDP in 1995. Financial services, which have experienced ten consecutive years of strong growth, are becoming an increasingly important part of the economy.

Share of GDP by sector

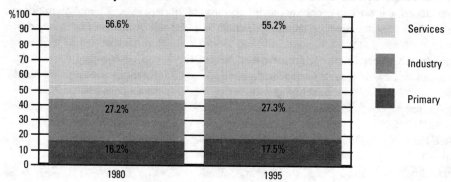

Source: Banco Central de Chile

Saving and investment

Since the mid-1980s, Chile has enjoyed the highest saving and investment rates in Latin America. Gross national saving rose sharply in the 1980s, thanks partly to the pension reform implemented at the beginning of the decade.

The private-sector pension fund system expanded the supply of capital for investment needed to fuel growth. It also stimulated the privatization process by providing new funds. Since the beginning of the 1990s, however, the household saving rate has remained stable and gross national saving has risen further, largely owing to government surpluses and retained earnings by businesses.

As a consequence, gross national saving reached 27% of GDP in 1995, while gross domestic investment amounted to about 28% of GDP. Those rates remain, however, below those of most emerging Asian economies.

Foreign investment continues to flow to Chile despite tight restrictions on capital inflows. Since 1974, over US$35 billion of foreign direct investment (FDI) has been authorized under the Foreign Investment Law (know as Decree Law 600, see below). Of this amount, US$15.5 billion effectively entered the country, most of it in the mining sector. The US provided 38% of these funds, whereas Europe and Canada supplied 25% and 13%, respectively.

Decree Law 600 intends to equalize treatment of foreign and national investors. Foreign investment projects of over US$5 million, investment in sectors normally developed by the Chilean government, and investment by foreign public entities, must be presented to the Foreign Investment Committee, which is certified to authorize them and to fix the terms and conditions of the contracts. Special regulations apply for the mining sector, as well as for investments of US$50 million or more. Foreigners can hold an unlimited amount of shares in Chilean companies. However, the capital invested must remain in the country at least one year.

Trade

Chile's economy depends heavily on exports, which represented 25% of GDP in 1995. Until the early 1970s, copper accounted for over 80% of Chile's export income. However, given that diversification of the country's product base has been an important goal of the Chilean government, this proportion fell to about 40% by 1995. Nevertheless, with mining products accounting for about 50% of total merchandise exports, the country's trade balance remains highly dependent on world commodity prices. Meanwhile, massive investment in value-added forestry products, such as paper, newsprint and pulp enabled manufacturing and semi-manufacturing sectors to soar from about 10% in 1970 to 42% in 1995. This helped reduce Chile's vulnerability to fluctuations in world metal prices.

In 1995, 56% of imports were made up of intermediate goods; 27% and 18% of capital and consumer goods, respectively.

Chile's major trading partners are the US, Japan, Germany and Brazil. However, trade with the MERCOSUR countries is expected to rise significantly since Chile joined the free trade organization, as an associate, in October 1996.

Trade restrictions

Most products may be freely imported or exported. Imports require a document, the "Informe de Importación", issued by the central bank. A uniform tariff rate of 11% is applied on all imported goods, with the exception of a few items such as wheat, spirits, edible oils and sugar. Tariff duties or surcharges are applied to imports of products that are subsidized in the country of origin or dumped in Chile.

Balance of trade in US$m

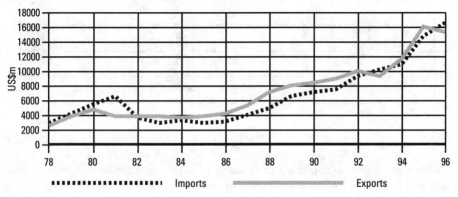

Source: IMF

Breakdown of exports (1995)

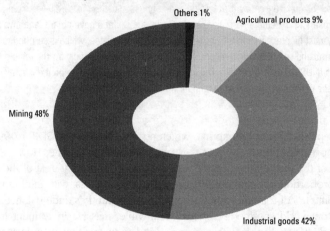

Others 1%

Agricultural products 9%

Mining 48%

Industrial goods 42%

Source: Central Bank of Chile

Balance of payments

Chile has enjoyed a positive trade balance for the last fifteen years (with the exception of 1993 and 1996). Because invisibles trade was regularly in deficit, due mostly to debt service payments, the country has had large current account deficits since the 1970s. However, the trend improved significantly at the end of the 1980s, and the current account deficit averaged 2% of GDP between 1990 and 1994. Although the current account registered a slight surplus in 1995, it fell back into deficit again in 1996 because of the higher price of oil, an essential import, and lower copper and wood pulp prices.

Chile's erratic current account balance, as a % of GDP

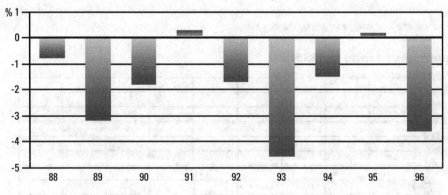

Source: IMF

The current account gap has been financed by strong capital inflows, which continue despite restrictions on foreign investment imposed by the central bank. Furthermore, the capital account balance, including portfolio investment, debt amortization and refinancing, has been in surplus since the mid-1980s. As a result, foreign exchange reserves have soared dramatically and in 1996 were equivalent to over ten months of merchandise imports.

Indebtedness

Chile is only moderately indebted. It never felt the need to negotiate a Brady-style debt reduction. As a result of debt reschedulings in the late 1980s and early 1990s, total foreign debt fell from US$21.9 billion in 1986 to US$17.3 billion in 1991. However, external debt increased again to US$21.8 billion in 1996 because of renewed access to international capital markets. Debt as a percentage of GDP dropped from over 100% in 1984 to 29.4% in 1996, whereas total debt service, including interest payments and amortization, fell from almost 70% of foreign exchange receipts in 1982 to 25.8% in 1996.

Economic policy
Monetary policy

The Bank of Chile has generally followed a restrictive monetary policy since gaining autonomy in 1989. However, the strong inflows of foreign capital, resulting from relatively high interest rates and a strong capital market, have tended to boost the money supply, making the task of controlling inflation difficult. As a result, the bank's grip on interest rates remained tight throughout 1996.

Fiscal policy

The dramatic worsening of the Chilean budget balance in the first half of the 1980s forced the regime to implement a new tax system, with a shift from income tax to consumption tax. Thanks to its highly efficient VAT system, and to strong fiscal discipline, Chile has achieved budget surpluses since 1987, and although the government has no formal surplus target, the 1997 budget balance is expected to remain positive.

Privatization

Large portions of the former state-owned companies returned to the private sector after the 1973 military coup, when a major privatization programme was launched. Since then, the state's policy has been to maintain a strong private sector. The only important exception is the nationalized copper industry, which is run by Codelco (the Chilean Copper Corporation). However, as new private mining projects were initiated, Codelco's share of total copper output dropped from about 75% in the beginning of the 1990s to less than 50% in 1995.

Currency

Historically, the official exchange rate of the Chilean peso has been adjusted in line with inflation. At the beginning of the 1990s, the central bank could not prevent a real appreciation of the peso and had to initiate several revaluations of the central peso rate against the dollar and extend its intervention band. In 1992, the Chilean peso was pegged to a basket of currencies consisting of the US dollar, German mark and Japanese yen, the weight of each currency in the basket being based on its relative importance in Chile's international transactions. Moreover, the peso was permitted to fluctuate within a wide band of plus/minus 10% around central rates whose evolution is governed by the gap between

Chilean inflation and that of the countries whose currencies compose the basket. The band was extended to ± 12.5% of the central rate in January 1997.

Despite exchange controls and the easing of the regulation on foreign investment by Chilean companies, net foreign investment continues to flow into the country. Net merchandise trade flows have also been strong, notwithstanding lower import barriers. The peso has therefore appreciated in real terms between 1994 and 1996, leading to further adjustments of the band.

Chilean peso/US dollar exchange rate

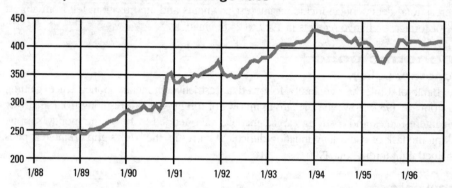

Exchange controls

In general, foreign currency can be exchanged freely either on the official or the informal exchange markets. Importers must purchase the foreign currency needed on the official foreign exchange market, which is controlled by banks and other financial institutions licensed by the central bank. Capital in foreign currency transferred into Chile must be registered at the central bank. The repatriation of profits and capital by foreign investors is subject to authorization from the central bank.

Access to the local market is restricted for offshore investors. All foreign borrowing is subject to a reserve requirement of 30%, which must be held in the central bank for one year and which bears no interest. Foreign borrowings must be sold through authorized banks, and repatriation is strictly regulated. However, the central bank is authorized to make exceptions to the general rules on the inflow and outflow of capital.

Banking system

The banking system is controlled by the Superintendency of Banks and Financial Institutions and by the central bank. Legal regulations on the banking system provide for the equitable distribution of credit and for protection against undue influence by political groups.

The system includes the central bank, one state bank, thirty-seven national and commercial banks as well as savings and loans associations. Consolidation of the banking system has increased concentration in the industry. Banks usually achieve high rates of return, thanks to economic stability. As a result of the banking crisis of the early 1980s, regulators and managements have developed rigorous credit standards. Bad loans are thus estimated at a mere 1% of total assets of the financial system.

■ EQUITIES

Index performance (in local currency)

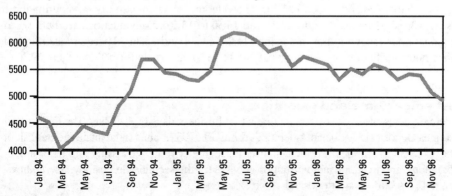

Key indicators

	Index performance %, in US$ terms	Market Cap. US$bn	P/E	Div. Yield	Weight in IFCI	IFCG
1994	41.2	68.2	21.4	2.4	2.3	4.8
1995	-2.9	73.9	17.1	3.5	1.9	4.4
1996	-17.2	65.9	14.6	4.0	5.2	3.4

Sources: Local stock exchange, IFC, Bloomberg, Datastream, UBS

Structure

There are three stock exchanges operating in Chile, the Bolsa de Comercio de Santiago, the Bolsa Electrónica de Santiago and the Bolsa de Corredores de Valparaíso. As at November 1996, there were 283 publicly listed companies on the Bolsa de Comercio de Santiago, with a total market capitalization of US$68.2 billion.

Regulatory authority

The Superintendencia de Valores is Chile's regulatory agency and is similar in nature to the US Securities and Exchange Commission (SEC). It is an autonomous institution, but is linked to the government through the Ministry of Finance. The Superintendencia approves and authorizes the registration of public securities, initial public offerings and the establishment of Stock Exchanges.

The Superintendencia also has the right to suspend trading of publicly offered securities.

Trading methods

Major stocks, options, dollars, futures, investment fund units (CFIs), and CFI rights issues can be traded through an electronic terminal called Telepregon. However, trading is also performed under an open outcry (traditional floor trading) and an electronic auction (trading of fixed-rate and financial intermediation markets).

Hours

General trading begins at 09.30 and ends at 17.30, Monday to Friday. However, hours vary depending on trading method. There are three traditional floor trading sessions (10.30 to 11.20, 12.30 to 13.20 and 16.00 to 16.30). The Telepregon system also operates during three sessions (09.30 to 10.20, 11.30 to 12.20 and 13.30 to 15.50). Daily auctions are held when traditional floor trading is not in session (11.20, 13.20, and 16.30). There are also limited trading hours for futures (in Telepregon, 09.30 to 13.20) and options (in Telepregon, 09.30 to 16.30).

Settlement time and clearing

Settlement takes place on a trade day plus two business days (T+2) basis. The Centralized Securities Deposit (DCV) began operating in August 1995. It aims to facilitate the deposit of publicly offered securities and their transfer through electronic processing and recording of transactions, and to supply administration services for the securities in custody. As yet, however, not all securities are deposited at the DCV.

Types of shares

Common and preferred shares, subscription rights, and corporate and government bonds are traded on the Santiago Stock Exchange.

Stock indices

There are three main stock indices in Chile. The most popular is the Selective Stock Price Index (IPSA), which is based on the forty most actively traded companies during the previous year and is a trade-weighted index. The General Stock Index or IGPA is calculated on a market capitalization basis using all shares on the Exchange. The Inter-10 Index comprises the top ten shares with ADRs, with significant trading volume on the Santiago Stock Exchange. There is also the ADRIAN Index which tracks the price changes of all Chilean ADRs.

Commissions and taxes

Commissions paid by investors for trading in securities are freely fixed by the brokers themselves.

Taxes (payable on a cumulative basis)

less than CLP 317,000	0.5% tax
between CLP 317,000 and 634,00	0.3%
between CLP 634,000 and 1,270,000	0.1%
between CLP 1,270,000 and 1,900,000	0.05%
amounts exceeding CLP 1,900,000	no additional tax.

Non-Chilean investors are subject to a 35% capital gains tax rate, while dividends are subject to a 35% tax.

Disclosure of financial statements

Every listed company is required to disclose quarterly financial statements to the Superintendencia de Valores. The December 31 financial statements must be audited.

Ownership limits for non-residents

Non-resident portfolio investment is subject to control by Chilean authorities in order to achieve limited and stable levels. Approval by Chilean authorities is subject to certain minimum holding periods, which depend on the size of the investment to be held in Chile. Non-Chilean investors who wish to invest over US$5 million must get prior approval from the Foreign Investment Committee.

Capital and foreign exchange controls

All foreign borrowing is subject to a reserve requirement of 30%, which must be held in the central bank for one year and which is non-remunerated. Foreign borrowings must be sold through authorized banks and repatriation is strictly regulated. However, the central bank is authorized to make exceptions to the general rules governing the inflow and outflow of capital or credit.

Brokers

There are forty-five brokers registered with the Santiago Bolsa de Comercio. It is possible to trade on the exchange only through these official brokers.

Sectors

The largest sectors (by market capitalization) comprising the IPSA Index include electric power (34% market weight), paper and pulp (22%), telecommunications (15%), beverages (8%), and financial companies (6.5%).

ADRs

There are twenty-one publicly listed Chilean ADRs, with seventeen listed on the NYSE. Due to restrictions on non-portfolio investment and a one-year capital repatriation requirement on equity investments, most foreigners invest via the ADR market, which is active and offers a good representation of the underlying market (the market capitalization of Chilean ADRs accounts for about 40% of the Santiago Bolsa's total market capitalization and almost 67% of the total market capitalization of the IPSA).

Derivatives

Options, futures (IPSA Futures, Inter-bank Dollar Futures), and Investment Fund Units (CFIs) are traded on the electronic trading system, Telepregon.

■ DEBT

The Securities, Corporate and Banking Laws govern the securities markets. The Ministry of Finance through the Superintendency of Securities and Insurance, and the Superintendency of Banks and Financial Institutions supervise trading on the stock exchanges. However, the over the counter (OTC) markets are not directly regulated.

Government debt securities are issued by the Banco Central de Chile in bearer form. The key central bank interest rate is the acuerdo. A small repo market exists out to one year, but most transactions are overnight.

PDBCs (Pagare Descontable Del Banco Central – T-Bills)

T-bills are discount securities with 30-day maturities and are auctioned weekly, on Wednesdays, by the central bank at a fixed rate. It is the benchmark interest rate for the rest of the debt market.

PRBCs (Pagare Reajustable Del Banco Central – T-Notes)

T-notes are issued with maturities up to 90 days. They are indexed, discount instruments used by the central bank in its conduct of monetary policy. Auctions occur twice a week, on Tuesdays and Thursdays at posted rates.

PRCs (Pagare Reajustable Pago Cupons – T-Bonds)

T-bonds are issued for terms of 8, 10, 12, 14 and 20 years, and are interest-bearing. They make up half the debt market.

Principal is amortized in equal instalments over the life of the bond. PRCs are auctioned twice a week, on Tuesdays and Thursdays. The amount on offer is announced in advance, and bids are allotted at one rate.

PCDs (Pagare Capitulo)

PCDs are issued with maturities of 5 to 15 years. They represent the external debt of the central bank converted into local bonds. Principal repayments are indexed either to the inflation rate (CPI), where interest is paid equal to the average domestic deposit rate; or to the dollar exchange rate, where the rate is spread over libor.

PDPs (Pagare Diferencial Cambiario)

PDPs were issued to subsidize private borrowers who have outstanding foreign currency debt. They have maturities of 6, 8 and 10 years.

Secondary market trading

Secondary market trading is mostly OTC through electronic screens, but can also take place on the Santiago or Valparaiso exchanges. Settlement is through the Banco Central de Chile in book-entry form. OTC trades settle on the trade date, and exchange trades settle T+1.

The Deposito Centralizado de Valores (DCV – central depository) was created in 1996. It is owned by the stock exchanges and financial institutions.

Foreign investment

Non-residents can repatriate profits after taxes at any time but can only remit capital after five years. In addition, they must have a diversified portfolio of investments, which places greatest emphasis on investment in listed shares. The foreign exchange transaction must be made through an authorized bank and at a rate within a 10% band of the central bank's rate. Investors must register with the Foreign Investment Committee, and appoint a local legal representative.

Eurobonds

Chilean utilities and private enterprises issued several yankee bonds in the US domestic market between 1993 and 1996. Chile has not yet issued a sovereign eurobond.

Eurobond issues (US$m)

	1990	1991	1992	1993	1994	1995	1996
Sovereign	—	—	—	—	—	—	—
Private	—	—	—	—	—	300.0	860.0

Restructured debt

In December 1990, Chile restructured its 1983–91 private and public sector debt by consolidating it into a US$3.2 billion loan denominated in US$, deutschmarks, yen, French francs, Swiss francs, Italian lire and Belgian francs. The loan has a 15-year maturity, pays libor plus 13/16% (or the CD rate) and amortizes in eighteen equal instalments from 1997. Chile also raised an additional US$1.4 billion in new money.

CHILE: Economic indicators

Population and development	1990	1991	1992	1993	1994	1995	1996e
Population, million	13.2	13.3	13.5	13.8	14.0	14.2	14.4
Population growth, %	1.6	1.1	1.7	1.7	1.6	1.5	1.6
Nominal GDP per capita, US$	2307	2582	3156	3313	3728	4737	5133

National accounts							
Nominal GDP, US$bn	30.4	34.4	42.7	45.6	52.2	67.3	74.1
Change in real GDP, %	3.3	7.3	11.0	6.3	4.2	8.5	6.5
Gross fixed capital formation, % of GDP	23.3	20.9	22.7	25.6	24.3	23.2	23.8

Money supply and inflation							
Narrow money, change %, Dec/Dec	17.8	42.7	29.9	22.2	22.5	19.4	12.3
Broad money, change %, Dec/Dec	23.5	28.1	23.3	23.4	11.3	25.8	—
Consumer price inflation (avg.) %	26.0	21.9	15.4	12.7	11.5	8.2	7.4

Interest rates *=latest figures							
Deposit rate, annual average	40.27	22.32	18.26	18.24	15.08	13.76	14.44*
Prime lending rate, annual average	48.83	28.55	23.92	24.30	20.34	18.16	18.16*

Government finance							
Government expenditure, % of GDP	20.3	21.2	20.3	20.8	20.4	20.7	21.0
Government balance, % of GDP	0.8	1.5	2.2	1.9	1.7	2.6	1.5

Exchange rates lc=local currency							
Exchange rate, annual average, lc/US$	305.06	349.37	362.59	404.35	420.08	396.80	412.19
Exchange rate, end of year, lc/US$	337	375	382	428.47	403	409	423
Real exchange rate 1990=100	100.0	106.9	112.5	113.0	116.8	121.7	125.4

Balance of payments							
Exports of goods & services, US$m	10285	11110	12439	11800	14450	19191	18496
Change %	7.4	8.0	12.0	-5.1	22.5	32.8	-3.6
Imports of goods & services, US$m, fob	9204	9531	11712	12778	13706	17960	19923
Change %	7.6	3.6	22.9	9.1	7.3	31.0	10.9
Trade balance, of goods only, US$m, fob-fob	1335	1588	772	-982	725	1384	-1227
Current account balance, US$m	-536	109	-703	-2096	-640	162	-2700
as a % of GDP	-1.8	0.3	-1.6	-4.6	-1.2	0.2	-3.6

Foreign exchange reserves							
Foreign exchange reserves, US$m	6069	7041	9168	9640	13088	14140	14800
Gold at ⅔ of market price, US$m	477.6	449.4	427.0	446.8	477.0	476.1	478.0
Import cover (reserves/imports), months	7.9	8.9	9.4	9.1	11.5	9.4	8.9

Foreign debt and debt service							
Short-term debt, US$m	3382	2199	3475	3487	3865	3510	3300
Total foreign debt, US$m	18576	17319	18964	19665	21768	21825	21800
as a % of GDP	61.1	50.4	44.4	43.1	41.7	32.4	29.4
as a % of foreign exchange receipts	171	145	142	155	142	107	110
Interest payments, US$m	1832	1636	1405	1129	1444	1540	1400
Principal repayments, US$m	1042	1036	1307	1668	1437	3726	3000
Total debt service, US$m	2874	2672	2712	2797	2881	5266	4400
as a % of goods exports	34.3	29.9	27.1	30.4	24.8	32.8	28.2
as a % of foreign exchange receipts	26.4	22.4	20.3	22.0	18.8	25.8	21.9

China

Area (thousands of km²):	9561
Population (1995, millions):	1221.3
Population projection (2025, millions):	1471
Population younger than 15 yrs (1991, % of total):	27
Urbanization rate (1993, % of population):	29
Life expectancy (1993, years at birth):	69
Gross domestic product (1996, US$bn):	772.7
GDP per capita (1996, US$):	626
Average annual GDP growth rate (1990-96, %):	10.5
Average annual inflation rate (1990-96, %):	10.5
Currency (renminbi per US$, average 1996):	8.37
Real exchange rate: (1990=100, average 1996)	72.87
Structure of production (1994):	47% industry, 32% services, 21% agriculture
Main exports:	clothing & garments, yarn & textiles, food
Main imports:	chemicals, textiles, iron & steel
Main trading partners:	Hong Kong, Japan, USA, Germany
Market capitalization of Stock Exchange (October 1996; US$bn):	115.3
Total foreign debt (% of GDP):	13.5
Next elections due under normal circumstances:	Congress is elected for 5 years: next election 1998
Credit rating: (Nov 1996, Standard & Poor's, Moody's)	BBB; A3

FORECAST: 1997-2000

	Worst case	Most likely	Best case
Real GDP growth (%)	10.0	10.5	12.0
Inflation (%)	12 to 15	10.0	9.0

■ POLITICS

Historical overview

China was first unified under the Qin dynasty in 221 BC. The dynasty's eleven-year reign was cut short by the emergence of the Han dynasty, which went on to rule China for more than four hundred years. The fall of the Han dynasty in AD 220 was followed by seventeen centuries of dynastic rule, including that of the Tang dynasty, which reunified China in 907. The last of these was the imperial Qing dynasty (1644–1911). Like many dynasties before it, the Qing collapsed under decades of pressure from internal revolts and external disputes with Western powers.

In 1911, China became a republic under the leadership of Sun Yat-sen. In the early years, power was spread among regional warlords. Then, after years of struggle, in 1927, the Kuomingtang (KMT) under Chiang Kai-shek established a new government at Nanjing, headed by Sun. During this period, Chiang campaigned actively to annihilate the growing Chinese Communist Party (CCP). He was eventually successful in driving the CCP from their rural base in southern China, and they fled to Northern Shannxi province in 1934–36 in the legendary "Long March". Ironically, hostilities between the KMT government and the CCP were replaced by a temporary alliance when the Japanese invaded north-east China in 1931 before launching a massive invasion in 1937. This union broke down completely in 1946 when the Japanese surrendered. Four more years of conflict ended when the KMT retreated to Taiwan and Mao Zedong stood before a sea of CCP supporters in Beijing's Tiananmen Square declaring the birth of the People's Republic of China (PRC).

The CCP immediately launched an economic reconstruction package, which showed early signs of promise. It was interrupted when the unrealistic policies of the "Great Leap Forward" (1957–60) coincided with several years of bad weather. This caused massive famines, which swept the countryside in the early 1960s. Mao's credibility was damaged by the disaster, and his power began slipping to factions headed by other senior party officials such as Deng Xiaoping. Faced with an intensifying power struggle, Mao called for a Cultural Revolution. This lasted ten years, ravaging much of China's society, and finally ended with Mao's death in 1976. After a series of wrangles, Deng Xiaoping emerged as the PRC's leader.

Recent events

In 1979, China ended centuries of isolation when Deng launched the "Four Modernizations" programme. It set a new course for the country's economic development by embracing market-led reforms and opening the country to foreign investment and influence.

China's gradual opening was put in jeopardy in 1989, when the death of the pro-reform general secretary of the CCP Hu Yaobang led to the most serious student demonstrations ever seen in China. Mass gatherings in Tiananmen Square criticized corruption within the government and called for political liberalization. When negotiations with government officials fell short of student demands, factory workers and professionals joined the students. The demonstration came to an abrupt end when factions within the government authorized the use of force against demonstrators on June 4, 1989.

While the political situation remained tense, economic reforms were given a boost in 1992 when Deng toured the special economic zones (SEZs) of the south. He gave his blessing to the sharp economic growth of the region, which was driven by the SEZs, and launched a new round of double-digit growth.

The following year, an ageing Deng gave up all formal government titles and chose Jiang Zemin, once party secretary of Shanghai, to be his successor. Deng's death, in February 1997, refocused attention on his legacy and the issue of the pace of economic reform. Jiang now holds all major official titles of government leadership.

Chronology

221BC	Qin dynasty unites China
907	After a long period of disunity, Tang dynasty reunifies China
1841	Britain defeats China in the Opium War

1911	China becomes a republic under Sun Yat-sen
1949	The Chinese Communist Party establishes the People's Republic of China
1960	The Great Leap Forward leads to massive famine
1966-76	Cultural Revolution
1978	Deng Xiaoping returns to the party leadership
1979-80	Deng launches economic reforms and the Open Door policy
1989	The PLA attacks student protesters at Tiananmen Square
1992	Deng visits the SEZs to promote economic development
1993	Jiang Zemin becomes head of state and party leader
1993	14th Communist Party National Congress adopts a socialist market economy platform
1994	China scraps its official exchange rate and floats the renminbi
1995	Beijing's missile tests in the Taiwan Straits strains China-Taiwan relations
1996	National People's Congress endorses the Ninth Five-year Plan
1997	Deng dies after a lengthy period of illness

Constitution and government

The Fifth National People's Congress adopted the most recent version of the constitution on December 4, 1982. It was amended in 1993. The constitution describes China as a socialist state under the democratic dictatorship of the people led by the working class and based on an alliance of workers and peasants. Despite this, China is commonly seen as an authoritarian one-party state.

The National People's Congress (NPC) is the apex of state power. Its three thousand members, who are indirectly elected by the provincial people's congresses, meet once a year to pass laws and treaties and nominate executives. The State Council is the highest state administration body. It is comprised of the prime minister, duty premiers and state councillors. Other ministries and commissions, as well as twenty-two provinces, five autonomous regions and three municipalities, report directly to the State Council.

Current government

President of State	Jiang Zemin
Chairman of NPC	Qiao Shi
Prime Minister	Li Peng

Political forces

Political power in China is in the hands of the Chinese Communist Party (CCP). Its highest authority, the Central Committee of about two hundred members, is elected at a party congress every five years. The Central Committee elects a fifteen- to twenty-member Politburo to direct policy.

Central bank

The People's Bank of China (PBOC), once a major state bank, became the central bank in 1984. China's first central banking law, launched in 1994, states that the central bank's main function is to make monetary policy and supervise financial institutions in China. Despite the significant improvement in credit management, the PBOC is still in the process of shifting from credit quotas and other administrative measures to market-oriented policy instruments.

■ ECONOMICS

Historical overview

In 1949, China's economy was suffering from the effects of decades of war. The government of the newly formed PRC spent its first three years concentrating on reducing widespread unemployment, curbing starvation and slowing racing inflation. Its policies were largely effective in reducing China's immediate problems, and gave the leadership time to work on reconstructing the economy. It chose a Soviet centralized planning model, directing domestic resources into developing heavy industry.

Attempts to orchestrate economic expansion were crippled by periods of poor planning and intense political struggle. The Great Leap Forward (1957-60) was an effort to accelerate economic growth, which ended when a massive famine swept the country. The central government attempted to increase industrial expansion through rural collectivization, abolishing wage incentives and launching an ill-planned steel production scheme. The failure of the Great Leap Forward and the resulting famine forced the central government to direct its efforts towards agriculture. This ensuing period of growth was cut short by renewed political struggles and disruption caused by the Cultural Revolution (1966-76).

The second generation of CCP leaders came to power two years after Mao's death in 1976. Led by Deng Xiaoping, they emphasized market reforms as a path to development. In 1979, they introduced a plan to reduce central planning in favour of a market-driven economy. This new package stressed privatizing agriculture, liberalizing prices, increasing industrial competition and opening the country to Western investment and trade. As a direct result of these reforms, the economy grew at a compound rate of 10% during the 1980s. Real per-capita income doubled and consumers gained access to an abundance of goods. By 1995, China had become the world's eleventh largest exporter.

Population

China's population was estimated at 1.22 billion in 1995. The growth rate has been reduced to 1.0% by the harsh one-child policy introduced in 1980. This is 40% less than the 2.3% growth rate in the early 1970s. If this trend continues, China could have a flat growth rate by 2000. This would lead to an older population in the long term, but concerns over this are overshadowed by concerns over rapid growth in the labour force in the short to medium term. About 6 million new entrants will enter the job market in each of the next five years.

The Chinese economy

Industrial production has largely driven China's economic expansion. Industrial output grew at a real compound rate of 11% during the 1980s, more than double the 5% growth rate for agricultural output. During this period, China's industrial production underwent a structural shift. Before Deng's reforms, more than 80% of industrial output flowed from state-owned enterprises (SOEs). Since reforms were instituted, much of the growth in industrial output has come from collective enterprises owned by townships and villages, private enterprises and foreign joint ventures. By 1995, SOEs were responsible for only 34% of output. At the same time, the services sector boomed, climbing from 20% of GDP in 1980 to 31% of GDP by 1995.

Share of GDP by sector

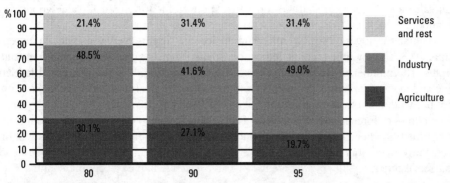

Source: Official data

Share of industrial output by sector

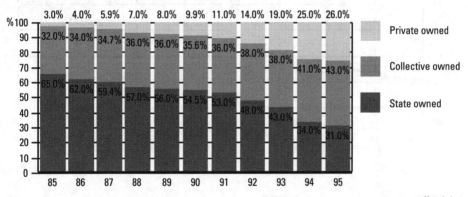

Source: Official data

Savings and investment

Like other Asian countries, China has high rates of savings and investment. Its 35% gross national savings rate since 1980 has been supported by cultural tradition and rising personal incomes. These savings have funnelled into investment and been responsible for gross domestic investment climbing to 40% of GDP in 1995. Foreign investment has kept pace with domestic investment. By 1995, China had attracted more than US$135 billion in foreign direct investment (FDI), making it the developing world's largest recipient. While overseas Chinese from Hong Kong and Taiwan dominate FDI, Western investors are pouring more capital into the country. This reached 27% of total investment in 1995 and is rising rapidly.

Balance of payments

China's exports have been growing by 16% annually since 1978. During this period, China's exports doubled their share of the world total. The mix of exports has also shifted. Agricultural exports fell from a high of 50% in 1980 to 15% in 1995. Exports of textiles, toys and manufactured goods have surged to represent 85% of total exported goods. In its Ninth

Five-year Plan, the government increased tax incentives for exports of electronics and other high value-added goods to shift the country's export profile towards high-value goods. On the imports side, manufactured goods represented 82% of the total in 1995.

During the 1990s, China has run a current account surplus every year, with the exception of 1993. The invisible account, led by tourism and shipping, has also maintained a large surplus. The number of foreign travellers has grown rapidly, driven by increased foreign trade and investment, creating a surplus in the travel account. The shipping account, however, has tended to run a small deficit of about US$1 billion per year.

Inflows of foreign capital, especially FDI, have maintained China's capital account surplus since 1989. Beijing's decision to reduce tax concessions for foreign investors will hit foreign investment, but China's market potential, cheap labour and land cost will continue to attract investment.

Exports and imports as a % of GDP

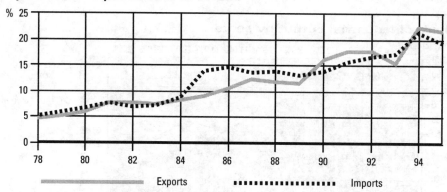

Source: Official data

Breakdown of exports (1995)

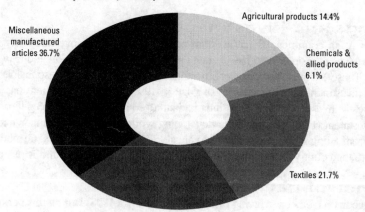

Miscellaneous manufactured articles 36.7%

Agricultural products 14.4%

Chemicals & allied products 6.1%

Textiles 21.7%

Machinery & transport equipment 21.1%

Source: Official data

Economic policy
Monetary policy
China's conflicting aims of subsidizing state-owned enterprises and controlling inflation through credit policy have led to several boom-bust cycles. As money supply has accelerated, fuelling inflation, China has then tightened monetary policy. This then chokes the SOEs, many of which have 70% debt-equity ratios, triggering working capital crises and feeding massive inter-company debts. In turn, this leads to higher unemployment as SOEs falter. Faced with this pressure, Beijing must pump credit into the state sector, starting the cycle over again.

Improvements in the condition of the state sector and banking reforms are helping China improve its monetary management. However, the central bank is only now mastering the use of sophisticated monetary mechanisms. In April 1996, the central bank started open market operations and is expected to continue broadening its range of available market mechanisms.

Fiscal policy
An inadequate tax base and inefficient tax collection have fed the central government's growing budget deficit over the past decade. The central government collected only 12% of GDP in tax revenues in the early 1990s compared to 24% in 1980. Beijing launched major tax reform in 1994 to increase the central government's tax revenues and reduce the deficit. The plan was designed to simplify the tax code and balance revenue division between the central and local governments.

Real GDP and inflation

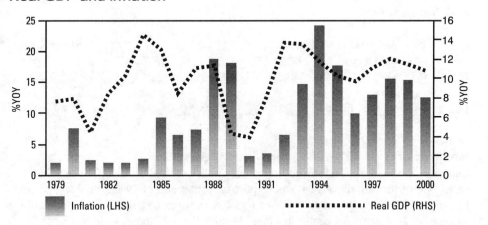

Source: Official data, UBS estimate

Currency
Chinese currency is still not convertible. During the 1980s China utilized a dual track exchange rate. Trade transactions by state sectors used an official rate, while transactions by foreign companies in China and some domestic companies were conducted at the "swap" market rate, which was closer to the market rate. In 1994, the authority unified the swap and

official rates and set up China's first interbank foreign exchange market. This effectively devalued the currency by 33% against the US dollar. Since then the currency has gained 5% against the US dollar on the back of surging exports and foreign investment inflows. As a further step towards the government's long-term goal of full currency convertibility, Beijing eased foreign exchange controls on trade transactions and debt service in April 1996, making the currency convertible for current accounts.

■ EQUITIES

Index performance (in local currency)

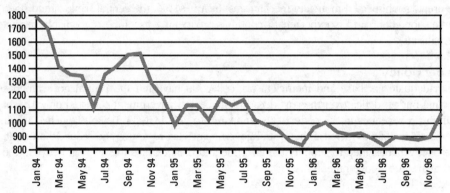

Key indicators

	Index performance %, in US$ terms	Market Cap. US$bn	P/E	Div. Yield	Weight in IFCI	IFCG
1994	-34.5	43.5	—	2.3	—	—
1995	-14.5	42.1	31.0	3.2	0.3	2.3
1996	89.4	113.8	27.8	0.8	0.7	3.7

Sources: Local stock exchange, IFC, Bloomberg, Datastream, UBS

Background

China's economic system reform and open-door policy created by Deng Xiaoping has provided one of the world's largest markets. Set up at the end of 1990, the Shanghai Stock Exchange (SSE) developed rapidly from a regional exchange to a national one, establishing its position as a securities centre in China. Besides the SSE, there is the Shenzhen Stock Exchange (SZSE), which is the financial centre in the South of China.

Structure

Both exchanges have A shares, limited to Chinese investors and B shares, solely for international investors. In September, the SSE's capitalization was US$52.2 billion in A shares and US$1.38 billion in B shares. The capitalization of the Shenzhen Stock Exchange was US$30.7 billion in A shares and US$1.97 billion in B shares. A total of two hundred companies listed on the SSE are A-share companies and thirty-eight are B-share companies. The SZSE listed 138 A-share companies and thirty-four B-share companies. International investors can also buy Chinese securities on the Hong Kong Stock Exchange. These shares are known as H shares.

The SSE has linked up with various international and regional exchanges. After its first linkage with the Fujian exchange in August 1993, twenty-three other exchanges were connected to the Shanghai exchange, strengthening the growth of the different regional markets. The exchange also has a memorandum of understanding with NASDAQ in the US.

Regulatory authority

The regulatory body supervising both exchanges is the China Securities Regulation Commission (CSRC). This body supervises both stock exchanges. Its powers were increased in August 1996, when the Chinese government removed the authority of local city governments to manage the SSE and the SZSE, as part of a strategy to improve the regulatory climate and make the regulatory authorities independent from government bodies. In a separate move, the SSE set up a special department with a computerized monitoring system for day-to-day surveillance of trades. B-share companies are required to disclose information in line with international regulations.

Market participants

The SSE has 577 members, of which 504 are international. The SZSE has 523 member brokers. The SSE's foreign account holders numbered 20,000 at the end of 1995. International participants are mainly institutional investors from the US and Europe. More than 50 countries are represented.

Trading methods

Both the SSE and the SZSE trade via computerized automatching systems. The SSE's computer mainframe executes five thousand trades per second. The SZSE also operates in scripless form. New issues are distributed by price auctions.

Hours

The Shanghai exchange is open from 09.30 to 15.00, Monday to Friday. The SZSE is open from 09.30 to 11.00 and from 14.00 to 14.30, Monday to Friday.

Settlement time and clearing

The Shanghai Securities Central Clearing and Registration Corporation, fully funded by the SSE, settles A shares on T + 1 basis or even T + 0. B shares are settled on a T + 3 basis.

Limits on price movements

At the beginning of its operations in 1990, the SSE imposed price limits in order to balance supply and demand. This did not create a real secondary market, but led to a market without trading, so in 1992 the Exchange scrapped the limits. The market has since been driven by the market mechanism and operation.

Taxes

There is a cash dividend tax of 20%.

Limits for foreigners

There are limits to foreign ownership in companies in the communications sector as well as media, power and armaments companies.

Stock indices

The main index is the SSE Composite Index.

■ DEBT

The China Securities Regulatory Commission (CSRC) was created in 1992 by the State Council to administer and supervise the formation of China's capital markets. The CSRC is an agency of the State Council Securities Policy Committee (SCSPC), and now assumes the authority previously vested with the Peoples' Bank of China (PBC) to formulate regulation of the country's embryonic bond market.

Public debt

The 1994 Budget Law stipulated that government must finance its deficit through bond issuance rather than borrowing. This caused a large increase in issuance of tradeable securities by the Ministry of Finance. The ban on corporate issuance in 1993 restricts the market to government and state enterprise bonds. Further expansion is likely, to fund China's infrastructure needs.

The State Planning Commission is responsible for bonds offered by state investment companies, provincial governments for regional enterprise bonds and the Ministry of Finance for state treasury bonds.

Primary market

The procedure for bond issuance takes several months, and new issue techniques are in an experimental phase. Interest rates have not been liberalized, which hinders the evolution of realistic benchmarks. Until 1996, bonds were placed according to mandatory administrative allocation. For savings bonds, an underwriting syndicate of specialized banks distributed bonds through their extensive branch networks. For tradeable bonds, the MOF selected an underwriting syndicate of securities companies. The system was established in 1994. Now the interest rate payable on bonds issued at par is auctioned, as the price for bonds coupons is set by the Ministry of Finance.

"Primary dealers" underwrite a minimum 1% of each new issue, and they then sell bonds to around one hundred "secondary dealers". The issue is listed twenty days later, usually on the Shanghai Stock Exchange, which charges 0.01% commission on each secondary market transaction.

A small secondary market in tradeable bonds operates on the Shanghai and Shenzhen Stock Exchanges, as well as OTC through the unregulated electronic Securities Trading Automated Quotation System (STAQS) and the National Electronic Trading System.

Treasury bills
Treasury bills are issued by the PBC for general budgetary purposes.

Savings bonds
Savings bonds are non-tradeable securities with coupons fixed each year (with inflation protection) and are designed for individual investors.

Tradeable bonds
Issued by the MOF, tradeable bonds have maturities ranging from 6 months to 3 years; bonds with terms less than 1 year now settle in book-entry form. Bonds pay accumulated coupons at redemption at the same time as principal repayment.

Subsidies
In July 1993, inflation-linked subsidies were provided for government bonds with maturities of three years or more. The subsidy was based on the difference between the consumer price index and three-year bank deposit rates, and is calculated on a monthly basis. Subsidies no longer apply to new tradeable bonds.

Foreign investors
Ministry of Finance officials have said that the market will open to foreign investors when the renminbi becomes fully convertible, but only if there is a fully functioning futures market, foreign firms have become primary dealers and the bond market has been connected to euroclear and cedel. Overseas interest in the credit, in the meantime, is satisfied by nine eurobond issues.

Eurobonds (in US$m)

	1990	1991	1992	1993	1994	1995	1996
Sovereign	0.0	0.0	0.0	588.1	1607.9	394.7	—
Private	0.0	0.0	0.0	88.0	0.0	45.0	—

■ CHINA: Economic indicators

Population and development	1990	1991	1992	1993	1994	1995	1996e
Population, million	1155.3	1170.1	1183.6	1196.4	1208.8	1221.3	1234.0
Population growth, %	1.4	1.3	1.2	1.1	1.0	1.0	1.0
Nominal GDP per capita, US$	320	324	368	455	420	547	626

National accounts							
Nominal GDP, US$bn	369.6	379.3	435.6	544.6	508.1	667.6	772.7
Change in real GDP, %	3.9	8.0	13.2	13.8	11.9	10.2	9.6
Gross fixed capital formation, % of GDP	35.2	35.4	37.2	43.5	40.0	33.0	32.0

Money supply and inflation							
Narrow money, change %, Dec/Dec	20.1	28.2	30.3	43.1	28.5	18.8	—
Broad money, change %, Dec/Dec	28.9	26.7	30.8	42.8	35.1	29.5	26.0
Consumer price inflation (avg.) %	1.4	5.1	8.6	17.0	21.8	14.8	6.5

Interest rates							
Deposit rate, period average	8.60	7.56	7.56	10.98	10.98	10.98	—
Lending rate, period average	9.36	8.64	8.64	10.98	10.98	12.06	—
Working capital interest rate	10.2	8.6	8.8	9.8	11.0	12.0	—

Government finance							
Government expenditure, % of GDP	19.5	18.9	18.3	16.8	13.2	12.3	12.5
Government balance, % of GDP	-0.8	-1.0	-1.0	-0.6	-1.3	-1.0	-1.2

Exchange rates lc=local currency							
Exchange rate, annual average, lc/US$	4.78	5.32	5.51	5.76	8.62	8.30	8.37
Exchange rate, end of year, lc/US$	5.22	5.43	5.75	5.81	8.45	8.29	8.45
Real exchange rate 1990=100	100.0	85.2	80.0	80.0	58.8	66.9	72.9

Balance of payments							
Exports of goods & services, US$m	57322	65824	78757	86805	119064	167483	174870
Change %	20.0	14.8	19.6	10.2	37.2	40.7	4.4
Imports of goods & services, US$m, fob	46706	54297	73799	98327	111472	149302	163480
Change %	-11.5	16.3	35.9	33.2	13.4	33.9	9.5
Trade balance, of goods only, US$m, fob-fob	9165	8743	5183	-10654	7290	16900	11500
Current account balance, US$m	11878	13083	6188	-11702	6532	17040	5000
as a % of GDP	3.2	3.4	1.4	-2.1	1.3	2.6	0.6

Foreign exchange reserves							
Foreign exchange reserves, US$m	29586	43674	20620	22387	52914	75377	90000
Gold at ⅔ of market price, US$m	3265	3063	2905	3043	3250	3249	3279
Import cover (reserves/imports), months	7.6	9.7	3.4	2.7	5.7	6.1	6.6

Foreign debt and debt service							
Short-term debt, US$m	16140	19146	23500	26255	29117	31847	31042
Total foreign debt, US$m	52751	59779	69509	84178	100536	106600	110000
as a % of GDP	14.3	15.8	16.0	15.5	19.8	16.0	14.2
as a % of foreign exchange receipts	87.0	85.0	81.4	91.1	79.9	60.9	60.2
Interest payments, US$m	2534	2954	2708	2630	3844	7092	7285
Principal repayments, US$m	3319	4123	5213	6729	6343	9500	9900
Total debt service, US$m	5853	7077	7921	9359	10187	16592	17185
as a % of goods exports	11.4	12.0	11.4	12.4	9.9	11.1	11.1
as a % of foreign exchange receipts	9.7	10.1	9.3	10.1	8.1	9.5	9.4

Colombia

Area (thousands of km²):	1139
Population (1995, millions):	35.1
Population projection (2025, millions):	49
Population younger than 15 yrs (1991, % of total):	34.8
Urbanization rate (1993, % of population):	72
Life expectancy (1993, years at birth):	70
Gross domestic product (1996, US$bn):	87
GDP per capita (1996, US$):	2437
Average annual GDP growth rate (1990-96, %):	4.2
Average annual inflation rate (1990-96, %):	24.8
Currency (peso per US$, average 1996):	1036.5
Real exchange rate: (1990=100, average 1996)	136.86
Structure of production (1994):	21% services, 29.3% industry, 49.7% agriculture
Main exports:	coffee, coal, oil and derivatives, chemicals, textiles
Main imports:	transport equipment, paper, iron, steel, wheat, chemicals
Main trading partners:	US, European Union, Japan
Market capitalization of Stock Exchange (December 1996; US$bn):	17.1
Total foreign debt (% of GDP):	31
Next elections due under normal circumstances:	Congress: March 1998; presidential May 1998
Credit rating: (Nov 1996, Standard & Poor's, Moody's)	BBB-; Baa3

FORECAST: 1997-2000 (average)

	Worst case	Most likely	Best case
Real GDP growth (%)	3.5	4.8	5.5
Inflation (%)	21	17	15

■ POLITICS

Historical overview

Colombia's capital city, Bogotá was originally founded as the capital of a new Spanish colony in the middle of the 16th century. The Viceroyalty of Peru, however, had sovereignty over the region until 1717, when a new territorial division of the Spanish possession created the Viceroyalty of New Granada. Subsequently, Bogotá became one of the principal administrative centres of the South American Spanish territories.

Towards the end of the 18th century, discontent and disillusionment with Spanish domination led to rebellions. After a prolonged and bloody civil war, the Viceroyalty of New Granada finally gained independence in 1819 and the Republic of Greater Colombia was created, encompassing what is today Colombia, Venezuela, Ecuador and Panama. From the beginning, the new state was torn between federalists and centralists, represented by two political parties, the Partido Liberal (federalist) and the Partido Social Conservador (centralist). More than a century of political division and turmoil followed, with civil wars and government insurrections alternating at a dramatic pace. Panama proclaimed independence in 1903, helped by the United States. This marked the beginning of an important dispute between Colombia and the US that lasted until the early 1920s.

After a period of relative stability, conflict between the Partido Liberal and the Partido Social Conservador started again in 1946 and led to "La Violencia", the most destructive civil war that Colombia has ever experienced. It lasted until 1957, when Liberals and Conservatives agreed to govern jointly for sixteen years.

Recent events

Although the struggle between Liberals and Conservatives has cooled, the new political stability has been threatened by a low-intensity guerrilla war, as well as significant drug-related activities. President César Gaviria Trujillo, who ruled the country from 1990 to 1994, proposed a national peace plan to overcome drug-related violence and political terrorism in conjunction with a constitutional reform to make the political system more democratic. He offered the guerrillas a voice in government if they agreed to lay down their arms. In response, two insurgent groups turned themselves into political parties: the Alianza Democrática, formerly the M-19, and the Ejército Popular de Liberación (EPL).

On August 7, 1994, Ernesto Samper Pizano, the candidate of the Partido Liberal, assumed the presidency after defeating his conservative rival by a narrow margin. Initially, he enjoyed strong support from the Congress since both the Senate and the lower house are dominated by the Liberals. However, allegations that the President's election campaign was partly financed by funds from the Cali cartel, together with the intensification of violent attacks by guerrilla groups during 1996, led to a dramatic revival of political tensions and to the US decertification of Colombia as a partner in the fight against drugs. In June 1996, Congress absolved President Samper of any wrongdoing in connection with the campaign finance scandal. Despite the political unrest, Samper has remained in power; however, he has lost some congressional support.

Chronology

1550	King Charles V of Spain establishes a new colony
1717	Bogotá becomes the capital of the Viceroyalty of New Granada
1810	First representative council created by the citizens of Bogotá; beginning of the civil war
1813	Proclamation of independence
1819	Creation of the Republic of Greater Colombia
1821	Annexation of Panama
1830	Ecuador and Venezuela gain independence from the Republic of Greater Colombia
1830	Brief military government
1832	First constitution of New Granada

1854	Brief military government
1863	Constitution approved, creating the Republic of Colombia
1886	New constitution
1903	Panama becomes independent from Colombia
1953	Brief military government
1946–57	"La Violencia", civil war
1957	Creation of the National Front; Liberal and Conservative parties agree to govern jointly with an alternating presidency
1974	Presidency ceases to rotate, but political stability continues
1984	Government and guerrilla groups fail to reach an agreement
1990	New negotiations between government and guerrilla groups
1991	New constitution
1995	President Samper faces accusations of corruption
1996	The US decertifies Colombia as a partner in the fight against drugs

State organization

The country consists of thirty-two departments and the capital district of Santafé de Bogotá, which are further subdivided into municipalities. Each department and municipality elects its governor, mayors, and legislature by universal suffrage.

Constitution and government

Colombia is a republic and a constitutional democracy. The 1886 constitution was totally revised in 1991 to strengthen the judiciary system, decentralize the executive power structure and provide for more congressional checks on the central government. It separated the executive, legislative and judicial powers. The president is directly elected for a four-year term and is not eligible for re-election. Legislative power is vested in a Congress of two houses, a Senate of 102 members and a House of Representatives of 161 members, which are both elected for four years.

Political parties

Partido Liberal (PL)
> Centre-left
> Founded in the mid-1840s
> Directorat: Emilio Lebolo, Luis Guillermo Giraldo, Luis Fernándo Jaramillo

Partido Social Conservador (PSC)
> Centre-right
> Founded in the mid-1840s
> Led by Fabio Valencia Cossio

Alianza Democrática (M-19)
> Left
> Founded in 1974 as a guerrilla movement; became a political party in 1990
> Led by Antonio Navarro Wolf

The Partido Social Conservador is divided into three factions: the official Conservative Party; the Nueva Fuerza Democrática (leader, Andrés Pastrana); and the Movimiento de Salvación

Nacional (leader, Alvaro Gómez). Each faction is represented in the current legislature. The Alianza Democrática, which was a significant player in the Constitutional Assembly, lost most of its strength in the 1994 elections and today is of little importance on the national level.

Results of 1994 elections to the Senate and House of Representatives
Senate: PL (59 seats), **PSC** (24), **others** (19)
House of Representatives: PL (94 seats), **PSC** (52), **others** (15)

Next elections
Congress: March 1998; presidential: May 1998

Other political forces
Guerrilla groups
Guerrilla groups began to form in the mid-1960s. Although negotiations in the early 1990s caused many groups to demobilize, rebel organizations still exist, the largest being the Fuerzas Armadas Revolucionarias de Colombia (FARC) and the Ejército de Liberación Nacional (ELN). Despite President Samper's initial success in inducing the guerrilla forces to (unofficially) negotiate, political agreements will not provide a complete solution, as many guerrillas are now motivated more by material gain (through drugs, kidnapping or extortion) than ideology. Moreover, many guerrillas have taken advantage of current political uncertainty (stemming from the corruption allegations against the president) to intensify their attacks against the military and the country's infrastructure.

Drug dealers
Drug earnings are known to have been diverted into legitimate businesses, politics, the military and the police force. Therefore, drug cartels have considerable power, having infiltrated many sectors of Colombian society. Despite the death of Medellín drug lord Pablo Escobar at the end of 1993 and the jailing of the Cali cartel leaders in 1995, Colombia's drug cartels are among the wealthiest and most sophisticated criminal organizations in the world; their reign is far from over.

Central bank
El Banco de la República was founded in 1923 to act as the country's central bank. Although it became independent in 1992, the minister of finance remains chairman of its board. Its main task is to defend the purchasing power of the peso through foreign exchange, credit and monetary policies, which are determined in co-ordination with the government. The bank is in charge of note issuance and the setting of reserve requirements.

■ ECONOMICS

Historical overview
Despite guerrilla activity and drug-related violence, Colombia's economy has been remarkably stable. GDP has grown steadily since the 1950s and, despite persistently high inflation,

the country has never experienced a period of hyperinflation similar to those of Argentina, Brazil and Peru. Moreover, its debt burden is relatively modest. Colombia, in fact, is among the few Latin American countries that have not defaulted on their debt since the Second World War. Colombia's economy is strongly dependent on real income growth in the tradeable goods sector. During the 1970s, real GDP grew steadily, largely through income gains from high coffee prices. However, soaring prices pushed up peso receipts and expanded the money supply, fuelling persistent inflation. Later, financing of government budget deficits by the central bank also stimulated money growth, and inflation became worrisome.

In the second half of the 1980s, thanks to the oil boom, the curbing of monetary growth, the elimination of inefficient subsidies, and restricted government spending, Colombia enjoyed the highest rate of GDP growth and one of the lowest inflation rates in South America. But inflation remained high by international standards, and the tight monetary policy implemented in 1991 to curb the increase in prices depressed domestic demand, resulting in an economic slowdown. Fiscal and monetary policies were subsequently eased, allowing investment to remain strong and further boosting output.

Colombia's economic performance, 1961–95

	Average annual real GDP growth, %	Average annual consumer price inflation, %
1961-1965	n/a	18.3
1966-1970	5.6	10.1
1971-1975	5.8	17.3
1976-1980	5.4	24.3
1981-1985	2.3	22.3
1985-1990	4.5	23.6
1991-1995	4.4	25.6

Source: IMF

Recent developments

In 1995, the government, businesses and workers agreed to a social pact on prices, wages and productivity, in an attempt to de-index the Colombian economy. In addition, the central bank maintained a tight monetary policy. However, these efforts were stymied by increases in government expenditure. As a result, inflation remained high in 1995 and 1996.

Heightened political turmoil, falling coffee prices and high interest rates slowed output growth in 1995 and 1996. The latter remained at a reasonable 3% pace, however, thanks to an increase in public spending and the buoyant energy (mainly oil) and financial sectors. In January 1997, President Samper declared a state of economic emergency aimed at addressing some of the concerns about Colombia's macroeconomy, most notably the magnitude of the government's fiscal deficit and the strong inflow of foreign currency. These inflows have accelerated money growth and put upward pressure on the peso, eroding the competitiveness of Colombia's tradeable goods.

The economy

For many years, Colombia was primarily a coffee-producing country, but the importance of coffee and agriculture in general has fallen significantly during the past few years, with the latter accounting for 21% of GDP in 1995. Manufacturing, including mining (especially oil and gas), comprised about 29% of 1995 GDP. Food, beverages, clothing and chemicals account for the majority of the country's manufactured goods, but mining activities have increased the most in recent years, primarily because of the rapid expansion of oil extraction and processing. Colombia is the third largest producer of crude oil in Latin America, and is also an important source of gold, emeralds, nickel and coal.

Finally, services made up almost one half of 1995 GDP. Tourism, transport and financial services are the most important components of this sector. In addition, Colombia's economy includes a significant informal sector. The production and trade of cocaine generate revenues estimated at about 5% of GDP.

Share of GDP by sector

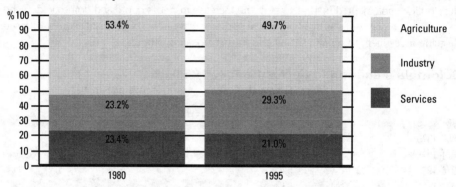

Source: Banco de la República

Saving and investment

Colombia's saving rate has been volatile during the past twenty years, fluctuating between 15% and 24% of GDP and falling to 17% of GDP in 1995, while gross domestic investment has remained stable at a somewhat low level of 20% of GDP.

However, the country has experienced strong inflows of foreign investment since the beginning of the 1990s. In 1995, foreign direct investment (FDI) grew approximately 50%, amounting to US$2.2 billion, and new sovereign debt issues totalled US$615 million. Despite the political crisis, this trend continued in 1996. The oil, manufacturing and financial sectors are the largest recipients of FDI, which comes primarily from the US, followed by the UK and Spain.

Trade

Until the beginning of the 1990s, Colombia's exports, which represent about 25% of GDP, were largely agricultural products, such as coffee and bananas. In 1991, the country began to diversify its export base, expanding oil and mining production. Colombia remains highly dependent on commodity prices, however, since its principal exports are petroleum and its derivatives, coffee and coal, which accounted for 18.7%, 18.8% and 6.1% of total 1995 exports, respectively. Principal imports in 1995 consisted of intermediate goods (43.8%), although the share of capital goods has increased to about 40% of total foreign purchases in recent years. The US is Colombia's principal trading partner; one third of Colombia's merchandise exports are sent to that country and about 50% of imports come from the US. The European Union is another important trading partner, although Japan's share of Colombia's total imports increased significantly in 1995 and now accounts for 17%.

Colombia is a member of the Andean Community, which includes Bolivia, Colombia, Ecuador, Peru and Venezuela. In this customs union, trade between Colombia and Venezuela is particularly important. The two countries have a system of common external tariffs, and merchandise trade between them is almost totally free, with the exception of a few agricultural products.

Balance of trade in US$m

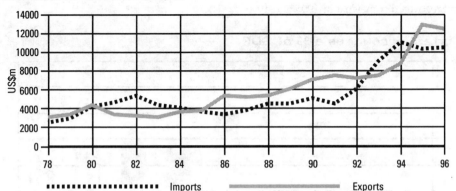

Source: IMF

Breakdown of exports (1995)

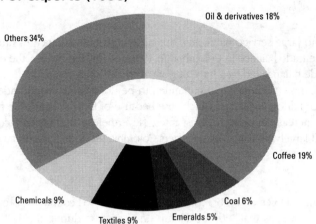

Source: Banco de la República

Trade restrictions

Import controls as well as administrative and quantitative barriers were eliminated in 1991. Although all imports require a licence and must be registered at the Colombian Institute of

Foreign Trade (INCOMEX), import requests are rarely refused, except for a few agriculture and communications products.

Exports of some products, such as gold and endangered animal and vegetable species, require the advanced approval of INCOMEX and the registration of the exporter. Export quotas can also be imposed in the event of domestic consumption supply shortages.

Balance of payments

Imports have risen much faster than exports since the beginning of the decade – more than doubling from 1990 to 1995 – owing to trade liberalization and economic growth. However, the slowing pace of economic activity and peso depreciation in the first half of the year moderated import demand in 1996. Hence, the trade balance deteriorated steadily until 1994, and recovered somewhat in 1995 and 1996.

Current account as a % of GDP

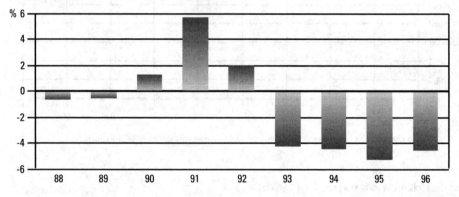

Source: IMF

Owing to large service payments, the current account balance has traditionally been lower than the trade balance in Colombia. In 1993 and 1994, however, the dramatic worsening of the trade balance led to a large current account deficit.

In 1995, the current account continued to be dominated by the trade deficit and the traditional shortfall on invisibles, which rose because of large debt service payments associated with an increase in dollar interest rates. Nevertheless, the current account deficit has been financed largely by FDI, which renders Colombia less vulnerable to sudden capital outflows.

Debt

The World Bank defines Colombia as a moderately indebted country. It is one of only a few Latin American nations that did not default on their debt during the 1980s. Recently, the Colombian government has pursued a policy of pre-paying its external debt by tapping international bond markets and shifting the maturity profile of its debt away from short-term liabilities. There has also been a shift in the composition of the debt away from the public to the private sector. Demand for Colombian bonds rose sharply in September 1995 after Moody's, the US rating agency, increased the country's debt rating to Baa3 from Ba1.

Standard & Poor's rated the country's bonds BBB- (January 1997). Colombia was thus the second-highest rated country in Latin America, after Chile.

Total external debt rose in nominal terms during the past three years, following the renewed access of Colombian firms to the international capital market. Total foreign debt has decreased in relative terms from 44% of GDP in 1990 to 31% in 1996. Debt servicing as a percentage of foreign exchange receipts has fallen from 44% in 1989 to 32% in 1996.

Economic policy
Monetary policy
According to the constitution, the central bank is responsible for stabilizing prices. In 1991, the Banco de la República implemented a tight monetary policy and introduced targets for monetary aggregates to curb the rise in consumer prices. However, large capital inflows, especially in 1992–93, as well as rapid growth in government spending since 1993, have largely frustrated attempts at monetary tightening and left inflation well above the pace desired by the central bank.

Fiscal policy
Public sector deficits in the second half of the 1980s were in large part due to public investment in the oil industry and increasing expenditures to combat drug-related and guerrilla violence. However, slight budget surpluses were recorded at the beginning of the 1990s, reflecting increased oil revenues, higher VAT receipts, and improved collection of income taxes. Since 1995, however, the fall in import tax revenue, and a worrisome increase in government spending generated a new public sector deficit. Fiscal policy remained expansionary in 1996, as spending on health, education and defence increased, and the public sector deficit reached 1% of GDP. This occurred despite an increase in VAT and a rise in oil revenues.

Privatization
The public sector in the Colombian economy has traditionally been less important than in many other Latin American countries. As a result, Colombia's privatization programme is relatively small. Some companies have been sold in recent years, mainly financial sector stocks (Banco de Colombia and Banco de Comercio). Electricity plants and some other industrial enterprises have also been privatized. Other banks, as well as companies in the electricity and natural gas sector, are still expected to be transferred to private hands.

Currency
Colombia's currency is the peso. It fluctuates freely within a 14% band fixed by the Banco de la República. Following the unification of the exchange rate system in January 1994, capital repatriation and extensive FDI caused the peso to appreciate in real terms. However, the 1995 political crisis reversed this trend and the peso twice touched the ceiling of the band during the spring of 1995. Consequently, the central bank introduced new regulations on the portion of commercial banks' total assets that may be denominated in US dollars or other foreign currencies, and the minimum reserve requirement on bank's foreign currency-denominated assets was gradually eliminated. Despite these measures, the peso depreciated by more than 16% in nominal terms and 2.2% in real terms in 1995. In the latter half of 1996,

however, the currency appreciated again in real terms, due to the diminishing political crisis, increasing amounts of investment entering into the country, rising private foreign borrowing, increasing oil revenues and the deceleration of the import demand. The continuing strength of the currency contributed to President Samper's decision to declare an "economic emergency" in January 1997.

Colombian peso/US dollar exchange rate

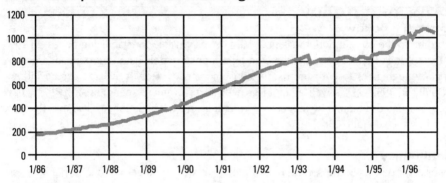

Exchange controls

All foreign exchange operations occur through authorized intermediaries at rates determined by the market. Transactions exceeding US$7,000 must be reported to the central bank. Exchange proceeds from exports must be submitted to authorized financial intermediaries within three months, or kept in foreign accounts at the central bank. Foreign currency accounts held at banks abroad must be reported to the central bank. Import and export payments can be made via such accounts.

Banking system

The Colombian banking sector is subject to tight regulations and close supervision by the "Superintendencia Bancaria." The sector includes 32 commercial banks, 25 financial corporations, 10 savings and loans associations, 31 commercial financing companies and two special credit agencies. In addition, there are 43 leasing companies, which are also controlled by the Superintendencia Bancaria. Of all these financial institutions, three are fully owned by the state, although the government owns stakes in several other financial companies. In recent years, steady economic expansion has resulted in rapid growth of credit and rising bank profits. The assets of credit institutions have grown from US$16.85 billion at the end of 1991 to about US$42 billion by the end of 1995. Although bad loans in the banking system increased with the recent economic slowdown, they have been confined to 6% of total loan portfolios (June 1996). Despite its good asset quality, however, the Colombian banking sector remains relatively inefficient by international standards. Substantial investment is needed to modernize the country's banking operations.

■ EQUITIES

Index performance (in local currency)

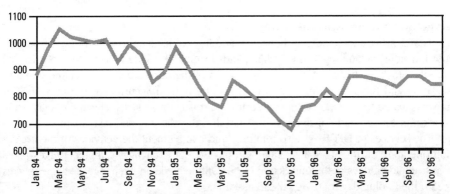

Key indicators

	Index performance %, in US$ terms	Market Cap. US$bn	P/E	Div. Yield	Weight in IFCI	IFCG
1994	26.8	14.0	19.5	1.7	2.1	1.2
1995	-25.5	17.9	11.3	2.6	1.9	0.8
1996	4.5	17.1	10.4	3.2	1.0	0.9

Sources: Local stock exchange, IFC, Bloomberg, Datastream, UBS

Structure

As of November 1996 there were 189 publicly listed companies on the Bogotá Stock Exchange (Bolsa de Bogotá), with a total market capitalization of US$16.7 billion. Stocks are also traded on the Medellín and Cali Stock Exchanges.

Regulatory authority

Companies listed on the National Securities Register (Registro Nacional de Valores), brokerage firms, and the stock exchanges (Bogotá, Occidente and Medellín) are supervised by the Superintendency of Securities.

Banking institutions and insurance companies are regulated by the Superintendency of Banks and Insurance Institutions.

Trading methods

The Bogotá Stock Exchange, unlike other exchanges in Colombia, uses two systems for operations: open outcry floor trading, for shares, rights and tax refund certificates licences given by the government to exporters; and the Electronic Transaction System (Sistema Electrónico de Transacciones, SET), for the trading of all other securities.

The Colombian stock exchanges also use an auction system for trading shares. Shares may be either listed or unlisted on the respective stock exchanges, but must be registered in the National Securities Register.

Hours

Bogotá Stock Exchange open outcry trading operates between 10.00 and 12.00 and the SET trades between approximately 08.00 and 16.15.

Settlement time and clearing

There is a clearing and settlement house located in and managed by the Bolsa de Bogotá, whose functions include registering, settling and clearing all credit or cash operations carried out on the Stock Exchange. With the participation of the three stock markets, the Banker's Association and fifty-seven financial institutions, the Central Securities Depository (DECE-VAL) was created to provide custody of securities, collection services, electronic registration of stock transfers, the administration of issues, and the clearing and settlement of transactions. The services of DECEVAL also reinforce and complement the activities of the organization operating on the Stock Exchange. On the Bogota Exchange, settlement takes place within five trading days of the transaction (T+5). On the Medellín Exchange, settlement takes place on the trading day following the transaction.

Types of shares

Equity shares may be either ordinary or preferred.

Stock indices

The IBB includes the twenty shares with the highest trading volume frequency during the last two years.

Taxes

Dividends for non-residents are taxed at 12%, while interest on money market accounts and bonds is subject to a withholding tax of between 6% and 7%. Capital gains are subject to a tax of 31%.

Disclosure of financial statements

All local companies registered with the National Securities Register must disclose quarterly financial statements within thirty calendar days following the end of the March, June and September quarters. Financial statements for the period ending in December must be submitted to the National Securities Register by March 1 of the following year, along with notes and the auditor's review. Foreign companies listed on the Colombian stock exchanges must submit quarterly financial statements within forty-five days of the end of the respective quarters.

Ownership limits for non-residents

Non-residents are allowed to invest in the stock market directly or through a mutual fund. In both cases, a local manager must be appointed the fund's legal representative. There is no restriction on the overall level of foreign investment in a company, but no foreign institutional investment fund may control more than 10% of a company's outstanding voting shares.

There can be no foreign investment in sectors related to national defence and the disposal of toxic waste. Foreigners are also required to obtain prior approval from the National

Planning Department (Department Nacional de Planeación) to invest in telecommunications, postal service, press and public services. For investments in financial institutions, where the sum exceeds 5% of the subscribed voting stock, authorization from the Superintendency is also required.

Take-over bids and large stakes
In order to make a public offering on the primary securities market, the respective security must be listed on the National Securities Register and authorization must be obtained from the Superintendent of Securities. For a public offering on the secondary securities market, the securities need only be listed in the National Securities Register.

Sectors
The banking sector dominates the IBB index with approximately 42% market weight, followed by the cement sector (24%), and the beverage and insurance sectors (14% each).

ADRs
As of April 1996, eight Colombian companies have listed ADRs, of which two (Banco Ganadero and Banco Industrial Colombiano) trade on the NYSE.

■ DEBT

The Superintendencia Nacional de Valores (SNV – Securities Superintendency) regulates the capital markets and authorizes securities offerings.

The most common and heavily traded debt securities in Colombia are short-term money-market instruments. They include treasury bills, commercial paper, CDs and bankers' acceptances. The medium- and long-term bond market is undeveloped.

Public debt
Titulos de Tesoreria (TES)
TES are issued by the Central Bank for maturities of 3, 6, 9, 12 and 15 months and for 3 years. They are discount bills, in bearer form and are offered for sale in daily Dutch auctions.

Titulos de Participacion
These are discounted bills issued by the central bank as an instrument of its open market operations. They have maturities of 7, 15, 30, 90, 180 and 360 days. They are offered for sale through a US treasury-style auction. Other instruments include Certifico de Cambio, which are issued by the central bank to absorb export earnings; and longer dated bonds named after the law or decree which authorized their issue (i.e. Decreto and Law 55).

Private debt
Commercial paper
CP is issued by private companies for maturities ranging from 30 to 270 days. They are sold in US treasury-style auctions and are in bearer form. The market is embryonic, and secondary market trading is thin.

CDT (Certificados de Depositos a Termino)

CDTs with minimum maturities of 30 days are issued by commercial banks and other financial institutions. They amortize on an accrual basis and are discount securities.

Bankers' acceptances (BAs)

BAs are discount instruments with a maximum maturity of 180 days, although 90 days is the most common.

Secondary market trading is either over the counter (OTC) or on the stock exchanges of Bogotá (via the electronic system SET – Superintendencia Nacional de Valores), Cali and Medellin. OTC dealings involve the exchange of physical securities.

Central bank administered or issued securities are deposited at the Deposito Central de Valores (Central Securities Deposit); other securities are deposited at DECEVAL.

Settlement for bearer securities is normally on trade date, but is negotiable. It is performed through physical exchange of cash and securities; foreign investors transfer funds through the SWIFT payments system.

Non-residents can buy treasury bills and private debt instruments through investment funds, subject to 35% withholding tax.

Eurobonds

The Republic issued a small eurodollar bond in 1987, but started to issue more regularly in US dollars and yen from 1993 onwards. It also raises money in the US domestic market (yankees) and in Japan (samurais). Private enterprises and domestic banks also raise bond finance, especially through euro medium-term notes and private placements.

Eurobond issues (US$m)

	1990	1991	1992	1993	1994	1995	1996
Sovereign	—	—	150.0	316.6	575.0	389.2	1,085.3
Private	—	—	—	100.0	125.0	240.0	306.7

Resheduled debt

1988 and 1990 public sector loans were refinanced and consolidated into tradeable loan packages, called Keystone, Concorde, Challenger and Hercules. They are denominated in several major currencies in registered form and are repayable in semi-annual instalments for terms up to thirteen years. Colombia has not had a Brady-style restructuring of its external debt.

■ COLOMBIA: Economic indicators

Population and development	1990	1991	1992	1993	1994	1995	1996e
Population, million	32.3	32.8	33.4	34.0	34.5	35.1	35.7
Population growth, %	1.8	1.7	1.7	1.7	1.7	1.7	1.7
Nominal GDP per capita, US$	1247	1256	1322	1498	1951	2258	2437

National accounts	1990	1991	1992	1993	1994	1995	1996e
Nominal GDP, US$bn	40.3	41.2	44.1	50.9	67.3	79.3	87.0
Change in real GDP, %	4.3	2.0	4.0	5.2	5.7	5.3	3.0
Gross fixed capital formation, % of GDP	16.6	14.6	15.5	18.8	19.6	20.0	20.5

Money supply and inflation	1990	1991	1992	1993	1994	1995	1996e
Narrow money, change %, Dec/Dec	27.9	31.7	41.0	30.0	25.3	19.7	16.6
Broad money, change %, Dec/Dec	39.7	20.8	45.0	37.5	34.6	21.5	—
Consumer price inflation (avg.) %	29.1	30.4	27.0	22.5	22.9	20.9	20.9
Producer prices (avg.) %	26.60	27.60	20.10	14.20	17.10	18.10	—

Interest rates	1990	1991	1992	1993	1994	1995	1996e
Discount rate, end of period	46.5	45.0	34.4	33.5	44.9	40.4	—
Deposit rate, annual average	36.4	37.2	26.7	25.8	29.4	32.3	—
Prime lending rate, annual average	45.2	47.1	37.3	35.8	40.5	42.7	—
Government bond yield, monthly average							

Government finance	1990	1991	1992	1993	1994	1995	1996e
Government expenditure, % of GDP	23.8	24.8	25.0	25.0	28.0	29.0	34.8
Government balance, % of GDP	-0.3	0.1	-0.3	-0.2	2.5	-0.2	-1.0

Exchange rates *lc=local currency*	1990	1991	1992	1993	1994	1995	1996e
Exchange rate, annual average, lc/US$	502.26	633.05	759.28	863.06	844.84	913.46	1036.48
Exchange rate, end of year, lc/US$	568.73	706.86	811.77	917.33	831.27	987.65	1001
Real exchange rate 1990=100	100.0	99.1	99.4	106.5	130.9	130.5	136.9

Balance of payments	1990	1991	1992	1993	1994	1995	1996e
Exports of goods & services, US$m	8679	9101	9241	9174	11949	13812	13900
Change %	18.5	4.9	1.5	-0.7	30.3	15.6	0.6
Imports of goods & services, US$m, fob	6858	6360	8067	10735	13946	16270	16000
Change %	12.0	-7.3	26.8	33.1	29.9	16.7	-1.7
Trade balance, of goods only, US$m, fob-fob	1972	2959	1233	-1659	-2284	-2548	-2000
Current account balance, US$m	542	2349	912	-2102	-3219	-4116	-4000
as a % of GDP	1.3	5.7	2.1	-4.1	-4.8	-5.2	-4.6

Foreign exchange reserves	1990	1991	1992	1993	1994	1995	1996e
Foreign exchange reserves, US$m	4212	6029	7389	7552	7750	8102	7700
Gold at ⅔ of market price, US$m	160.9	208.2	110.7	72.4	75.0	68.3	77.5
Import cover (reserves/imports), months	7.4	11.4	11.0	8.4	6.7	6.0	5.8

Foreign debt and debt service	1990	1991	1992	1993	1994	1995	1996e
Short-term debt, US$m	1856	1530	2096	3129	3562	4639	5000
Total foreign debt, US$m	17555	16975	16833	18271	21669	24197	27000
as a % of GDP	43.6	41.2	38.1	35.9	32.2	30.5	31.0
as a % of foreign exchange receipts	174.3	151.1	145.5	165.0	157.1	154.6	172.0
Interest payments, US$m	1644	1492	1325	1188	1387	1894	2000
Principal repayments, US$m	2158	2275	2523	2702	3353	2734	3000
Total debt service, US$m	3802	3767	3848	3890	4740	4628	5000
as a % of goods exports	53.7	50.2	53.0	52.4	54.1	44.6	47.6
as a % of foreign exchange receipts	37.8	33.5	33.3	35.1	34.4	29.6	31.8

Côte d'Ivoire

Area (thousands of km²):	322
Population (1995, millions):	14.3
Population projection (2025, millions):	34
Population younger than 15 yrs (1991, % of total):	48.2
Urbanization rate (1993, % of population):	42
Life expectancy (1993, years at birth):	51
Gross domestic product (1996, US$bn):	10.1
GDP per capita (1996, US$):	689
Average annual GDP growth rate (1990-96, %):	1.4
Average annual inflation rate (1990-96, %):	7.4
Currency (CFA franc per US$, average 1996):	518.0
Structure of production (1994):	41% agriculture, 32% services, 26% industry
Main exports:	cocoa, coffee, timber, fuel products
Main imports:	manufactures, primary commodities, fuel
Main trading partners:	France, Nigeria, Netherlands, Germany, Italy, US, Ghana
Market capitalization of Stock Exchange (December 1996; US$bn):	0.9
Total foreign debt (% of GDP):	191.1
Next elections due under normal circumstances:	presidential scheduled Oct. 1999; legislative scheduled Nov. 1999
Credit rating: (Jan 1997, Standard & Poor's, Moody's)	not rated

FORECAST: 1997-2000 (average)

	Worst case	Most likely	Best case
Real GDP growth (%)	4.0	5.9	6.3
Inflation (%)	4.0	3.0	2.0

■ POLITICS

Historical overview

Prior to the arrival of the French in the 1840s, Côte d'Ivoire consisted of a number of isolated communities. Small Muslim empires controlled parts of the country, but no national power was ever established because of the thick jungle environment that made transport and communication difficult.

With few natural harbours, the region was not discovered by European traders until the mid-19th century. It became a French colony in 1893, and with the help of French investment grew to be the wealthiest colony in French West Africa.

The move towards independence was led by Felix Houphouët-Boigny, a cocoa farmer who led the farmers' union. During the 1940s and 1950s, there was some debate over whether Côte d'Ivoire should become an independent country or part of a French West African federation. In 1946, Houphouët-Boigny was elected head of the sub-region's main independence party – the Rassemblement Démocratique Africain (RDA) – which had close links with the Parti Démocratique de Côte d'Ivoire that Houphouët-Boigny had formed earlier.

Under Houphouët-Boigny's leadership, talk of a federation diminished, and in 1960 Côte d'Ivoire was declared independent, with Houphouët-Boigny as inaugural president.

Following independence, Houphouët-Boigny dominated Ivoirian politics until his death in 1993. Elections were held, but without any opposition. The country grew wealthy under the one-party system in the 1970s but, as economic instability began to creep in during the 1980s, criticism of the Houphouët-Boigny regime surfaced.

In 1990, a multiparty political system was set up. Laurent Gbagbo was chosen to lead the Front Populaire Ivoirien (FPI), the leading opposition party. In the October 1990 presidential elections, Houphouët-Boigny won 81.7% of the vote, a result Gbagbo disputed.

In the November 1990 legislative elections, Houphouët-Boigny's PDCI-RDA party won 163 seats. In an attempt to steer the economy away from recession, Houphouët-Boigny appointed the World Bank economist Alassane Dramne Ouattara as prime minister.

Political unrest increased following the elections, with opposition leaders organizing large rallies. In 1992, a 20,000-strong demonstration was violently broken up, and opposition leaders, including Gbagbo, were arrested.

Following the death of Houphouët-Boigny, Konan Bédié, the leader of the assembly and fierce critic of Ouattara, took power. Ouattara and nine of his supporters left the RDA to set up the Rassemblement des republicains (RPR), a centrist party.

Recent events

President Bédié consolidated the RDA's grip on power since taking over from Houphouët-Boigny in 1993. In December 1994, he introduced a new electoral code preventing non-Ivoirian-born residents from voting in the elections. This led to unrest among the country's large immigrant population, but had the desired effect of preventing his main rival Ouattara (who has a Burkina-Faso-born mother) from participating in the 1995 elections.

In the run-up to the elections, the two opposition parties joined forces, but were unable to develop a solid power base to challenge the RDA, and subsequently boycotted the elections. With no opponent of note, Bédié won 96% of the vote in the presidential elections held in October 1995. The following month, his Democratic Party won 133 of the 175 seats in the assembly. The RPR won 9 seats, as did Laurent Gbagbo's Front Populaire Ivoirien.

Bédié's government, both before and after the 1995 elections, has been notably less tolerant than the Houphouët-Boigny regime. Political violence has also increased. At least ten people were killed during the run-up to the elections, and there was an aborted coup in May 1996. Nevertheless, Côte d'Ivoire has remained one of the most stable West African countries.

Chronology

1885	Berlin Conference starts European scramble for African colonies
1893	Côte d'Ivoire becomes official French colony
1906	French governor Gabriel Angoulvant launches pacification campaign
1944	African Agricultural Union is set up
1958	Côte d'Ivoire achieves self-government within the French community
1960	Côte d'Ivoire is granted independence
1968	Student unrest forces partial withdrawal of French influence
1975	Constitution is changed to allow president of assembly to succeed president
1980	Constitution is changed to allow president to appoint vice president
1985	Houphouët-Boigny wins uncontested presidential election
1989	Economic austerity programme is introduced
1990	Houphouët-Boigny beats Laurent Gbagbo in first contested presidential election
1993	Houphouët-Boigny dies, and is replaced by Konan Bédié
1995	Bédié wins presidential election

Constitution and government

The constitution was signed in October 1960, but has been changed many times since. Under the present constitution, the country elects a president every five years. There is a unicameral multiparty parliament, the Assemblée Nationale, which is also elected every five years. If the president dies, he is replaced by the head of the assembly.

Despite the introduction of a multiparty political system in 1990, Côte d'Ivoire has effectively been a one-party state since independence. There is a 175-seat national assembly elected every five years, and a 120-member social and economic advisory council, the Counseil Economique et Social, appointed by the president. The country is divided into 49 departments, each of which has its own elected council, and 129 municipalities.

Current government

President	Henri Konan Bedie
Prime Minister	Daniel Kablan Duncan
Economy and Finance Minister	Ngoran Niamien
Governor, central bank	Charles Konan Banny

■ ECONOMICS

Historical overview

The absence of coups during the early years of independence allowed Côte d'Ivoire to prosper for much of the 1960s and 1970s. Between 1960 and 1979, the gross national product grew by almost 8% a year at a time when many of its neighbours were showing minimal or negative growth. The principal sources of growth were coffee and cocoa exports. The government set up agro-industry companies to try to replace the manufactured goods it had formerly imported from Senegal.

But when world commodity prices fell in the early 1980s, Côte d'Ivoire's economic fortunes deteriorated. Between 1980 and 1990 national GDP fell by 20%. Concerned that the recession might undermine political stability, Houphouët-Boigny appointed a World Bank economist, Alassane Ouattara, as prime minister in 1990. The following year, the country agreed to adopt a programme of structural reform under the guidance of the IMF and the World Bank. Stricter fiscal policies were introduced, and markets liberalized.

The economy continued to contract during the early 1990s, however, largely because of the over-valued currency. Following the 50% devaluation of the CFA at the beginning of 1994, the economy slowly began to revive; but, with inflation rising, the government agreed to accelerate the pace of its reform programme.

Share of GDP by sector

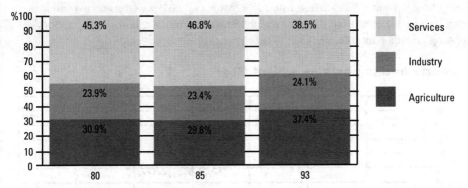

Source: Official data

Recent developments

The recovery continued during 1995, with GDP growing by 7% and inflation falling below 15%. The outlook for investment improved with French investors, in particular, showing great interest in the privatization programme. A further thirty-one companies have been scheduled for sale in 1997. The main areas of interest are utilities, minerals, agro-industry and tourism.

With the government running a budget surplus, and its tight fiscal policies finding favour with the IMF, there appear to be no major obstacles to Côte d'Ivoire receiving additional foreign credits to cover its financing requirements. The country is likely to qualify for an 80% reduction of its Paris Club debt, having already achieved a similar cut in its commercial bank debt through a Brady plan. Before this happens, the US$18.8 billion debt burden, which is equivalent to around 200% of GDP, is likely to remain a considerable hindrance to development.

Population

A census taken in 1990 estimated Côte d'Ivoire's population to be 10.8 million, although official estimates made in 1994 suggest that 13.6 million may be a more accurate estimate. This gives a population density of 42.5 per square kilometre. Only 3.5 million people are officially economically active.

The economy

Agriculture dominates the Ivoirian economy, with over half of all workers employed in this sector. Key crops are cocoa and coffee – Côte d'Ivoire is the world's largest and second largest producer of these two crops respectively. Manufacturing is dominated by the agro-industry.

Despite agriculture's continuing economic importance, the development of oil and gas fields in the late 1980s has begun to reduce the country's vulnerability to shifts in coffee and cocoa prices. Meanwhile, France continues to play an active role in financing and directing economic development.

Savings and investment

Investment levels have increased in recent years, with investment as a proportion of GDP rising from 9.3% in 1993 to an estimated 15% by the end of 1996. Overseas aid and loans are vital to investment in Côte d'Ivoire, with international institutions such as the World Bank playing an important role.

Exports and imports as a % of GDP

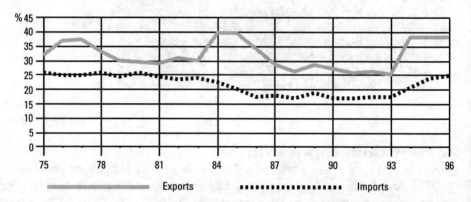

Source: Official data

Balance of payments

The principal exports are commodities such as cocoa beans, timber, coffee and cotton. Main imports are industrial machinery, transport equipment, and food and drink. In 1995, exports were valued at an estimated US$3.7 billion, and imports US$2.2 billion, leaving a healthy trade surplus. However, this was offset by the high cost of servicing the sizeable foreign debt. France is Côte d'Ivoire's main trading partner, although Nigeria makes a significant contribution to imports.

Economic policy

The central bank has followed a tight monetary policy since the introduction of an IMF-sponsored reform programme in 1994. Inflation has been brought down from 30% in 1994 to around 4% in 1996. Before the devaluation, Côte d'Ivoire ran high budget deficits as the authorities tried to off-set the deflationary impacts of an overvalued currency. The

devaluation corrected some of the imbalances in the economy, helping to bring down the
deficit to around 1% of GDP in 1996 from more than 10% in 1994.

Current account as a % of GDP

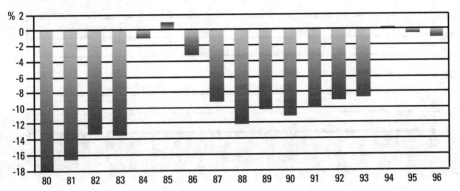

Source: Official data; UBS estimates

Currency

Côte d'Ivoire is one of a number of West African Francophone countries that use the CFA
franc. The CFA franc (XOF) was pegged to the French franc at a rate of XOF 50 = 1 French
franc between 1948 and 1994, when it was devalued to XOF 100 = FRF 1.

CFA franc/US dollar exchange rate

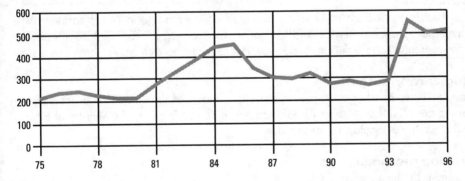

■ EQUITIES

Index performance (in local currency)

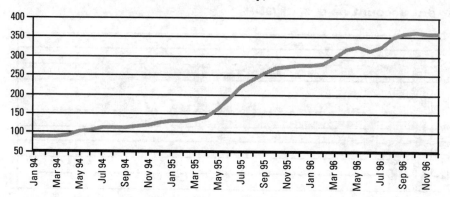

Key indicators

	Index performance %, in US$ terms	Market Cap. US$bn	P/E	Div. Yield
1994	-19.7	0.4	11.6	10.1
1995	140.8	0.9	12	10.1
1996	4.9	0.9	8.4	4.8

Sources: Abidjan Stock Exchange, IFC, Bloomberg, Datastream, UBS

Structure

The Abdijan Stock Exchange (ASE) is the only stock exchange in French-speaking West Africa. It was opened in 1976 and has twenty-six companies listed. Market capitalization stood at around US$520 million at end 1996. Foreign residents own around 70% of the shares.

Regulatory authority

The ASE is regulated by a ten-person committee known as the Conseil de la Bourse, comprising the President of the Stock Exchange, a representative from the Ministry of Finance and a number of employer's organizations.

Trading methods

Trading is by open outcry.

Hours

The ASE is open for trading 9.00 to 10.00, Tuesday to Friday.

Settlement time and clearing

Settlement is on an on-the-spot basis. There is no central clearing system.

Types of shares

Ordinary shares only.

Stock indices
There are two indices, a general index (BVA) and one following the top twelve companies (12VB).

Taxes
There is a 12% withholding tax on dividends, but no capital gains tax.

Disclosure of financial statements
Companies must submit annual reports to the Stock Exchange.

Ownership limits for non-residents
There are no restrictions on foreign ownership.

Capital and foreign exchange controls
There are no restrictions on repatriation of capital.

Brokers
There are six brokers.

Sectors
The principal sectors are banking, finance, oil, transport, food, textiles and construction.

ADRs
There are no Ivoirian ADRS.

Market comment
The ASE is a small market with limited liquidity. However, plans to privatize up to thirty state-owned companies could boost market size considerably.

■ DEBT

Government bonds are listed on the Bourse des Valeurs Mobilières d'Abidjan (BVA), and number about thirty. In addition, two international bonds issued by the Lomé-based BOAD (Regional Development Bank) are also listed on the exchange. In the primary market, in the case of over-subscription, residents are given preference over foreign participants. There are no restrictions on overseas investment in the secondary market, however. A 12% withholding tax is charged on securities with maturities of less than five years, and 6% on securities of more than five years. There are plans to make the BVA the regional exchange for the seven UEMOA countries. If it is formed, then the bonds of those seven West African countries will be traded there. Côte d'Ivoire rescheduled interest and principal due to commercial bank creditors in 1985 and 1986, through a rescheduling of the debt into loan notes – US$589 million in a Refinancing Credit Agreement (including new money) and US$851 million in a Multi-Year Rescheduling Agreement denominated in several currencies. Payments on these notes are in arrears. They are likely to be restructured through a Brady-style plan in 1997.

■ CÔTE D'IVOIRE: Economic indicators

Population and development	1990	1991	1992	1993	1994	1995	1996e
Population, million	11.7	12.2	12.7	13.2	13.7	14.3	14.8
Population growth, %	4.1	4.0	3.9	4.0	3.9	4.5	3.5
Nominal GDP per capita, US$	845	861	866	790	526	657	689

National accounts							
Nominal GDP, US$bn	9.9	10.5	11.0	10.4	7.2	9.4	10.1
Change in real GDP, %	-9.1	8.0	-5.9	-0.7	1.8	6.9	6.2

Money supply and inflation							
Broad money, change %, Dec/Dec	-2.6	0.1	-1.2	-1.4	46.8	17.0	10.0
Consumer price inflation (avg.) %	-0.8	1.7	4.2	2.2	26.1	14.7	3.4

Government finance							
Government expenditure, % of GDP	33.4	32.9	30.0	27.9	29.3	26.2	24.3
Government balance, % of GDP	-11.6	-13.0	-9.6	-11.2	-7.5	-4.4	-3.6

Exchange rates lc=local currency							
Exchange rate, annual average, lc/US$	272.26	282.11	264.69	283.16	555.20	499.15	509.00
Exchange rate, end of year, lc/US$	256.45	259.00	275.33	294.78	533.70	490.70	524.40

Balance of payments							
Exports of goods & services, US$m	3503	3319	3596	3257	3310	3835	4140
Change %	10.1	-5.2	8.3	-9.4	1.6	15.8	8.0
Imports of goods & services, US$m, fob	3445	3175	3429	3104	2533	3790	4220
Change %	14.5	-7.8	8.0	-9.5	-18.4	49.6	11.3
Trade balance, of goods only, US$m, fob-fob	1094	923	995	851	1309	1500	1590
Current account balance, US$m	-1214	-1074	-1013	-916	13	-150	-100
as a % of GDP	-12.3	-10.2	-9.2	-8.8	0.2	-1.6	-1.0

Foreign exchange reserves							
Foreign exchange reserves, US$m	4.0	13.4	6.9	2.3	200.0	400.0	600.0
Gold at ⅔ of market price, US$m	11.4	10.7	10.2	10.7	11.4	11.4	11.5
Import cover (reserves/imports), months	0.0	0.1	0.0	0.0	0.9	1.3	1.7

Foreign debt and debt service							
Short-term debt, US$m	3618	3948	4436	5751	4241	4350	4240
Total foreign debt, US$m	16622	17557	17988	19147	18560	18860	19500
as a % of GDP	167.9	167.3	164.0	184.0	257.8	200.6	191.1
as a % of foreign exchange receipts	422.8	462.8	447.5	545.2	514.2	491.8	471
Interest payments, US$m	641	663	565	501	556	700	600
Principal repayments, US$m	571	569	535	479	718	600	600
Total debt service, US$m	1212	1232	1100	980	1274	1300	1200
as a % of goods exports	41.6	45.5	37.3	36.9	44.3	39.4	34.4
as a % of foreign exchange receipts	30.8	32.5	27.4	27.9	35.3	33.9	29.0

Croatia

Area (thousands of km²):	57
Population (1995, millions):	4.8
Population younger than 15 yrs (1991, % of total):	19.4
Urbanization rate (1993, % of population):	51
Life expectancy (1993, years at birth):	70
Gross domestic product (1996, US$bn):	18.8
GDP per capita (1996, US$):	3944
Average annual GDP growth rate (1990-96, %):	-5.1
Average annual inflation rate (1990-96, %):	431.2
Currency (kuna per US$, average 1996):	5.4
Structure of production (1994):	62% services, 25% industry, 13% agriculture
Main exports:	consumer goods, machines, chemical products
Main imports:	machines, mineral, consumer goods
Main trading partners:	Germany, Italy, Russia
Total foreign debt (% of GDP):	25.8
Next elections due under normal circumstances:	presidential August 1997; legislative October 1999
Credit rating: (Jan 1997, Standard & Poor's, Moody's)	BBB-; Baa3

FORECAST: 1997-2000 (average)

	Worst case	Most likely	Best case
Real GDP growth (%)	2.5	5.0	7.5
Inflation (%)	8.0	4.0	2.0

■ POLITICS

Historical overview

Croatia is not a new nation. It is newly reborn as an independent country, but has an ancient and rich history as an independent state, governing its own affairs with its own assembly or parliament. Even periods of Hungarian or Austrian rule were based on laws and treaties ratified by its own parliament. The exception was the agreement that saw the country unite with Serbia and Montenegro in 1918: Croatia has always viewed its position in a federal state with Serbia as artificial.

The first written records from Croatia date from the 9th century. Duke Tomislav, crowned in 925, is recognized as the first King of Croatia. He succeeded in uniting the various Croatian dukedoms by driving out the invading Hungarians and acknowledged the authority of the Roman bishops over the Croatian bishops. Since that time, Croatia has been firmly under the influence of Roman, Western European cultural traditions. In 1102, Croatia entered into the Personal Union with Hungary, which lasted until the end of the First World War. Throughout this time, the country had its own assembly (the Diet), viceroys (ban), regional administrators (zupan) and tax system.

In October 1918, as the Austro-Hungarian Empire collapsed after its defeat in the first World War, the Croatian parliament broke all links with the empire and, together with Slovenia, Bosnia-Hercegovina and Voivodina, formed the State of Slovenes, Croats and Serbs with a government in Zagreb called the National Council. The Council had a Slovene president and two vice-presidents, one Croat and one Serb. The Serbian vice-president led a delegation to Belgrade, which accepted the declaration of the unified kingdom of Serbs, Croats and Slovenes by Prince Regent Alexander. Meanwhile, the National Council in Zagreb, which was opposed to the declaration, rescinded the delegation's authority to negotiate. The unification of Serbia, Croatia and Slovenia was ratified by the Serbian assembly but no political body of the State of Slovenes, Croats and Serbs ever ratified the establishment of the union.

A new National Assembly of the Kingdom of Serbs, Croats and Slovenes was established, although its deputies were not elected but were chosen by the Belgrade authorities. In November 1920, King Alexander dissolved the Croatian parliament and imposed the Vidovdan constitution. This was the first time Croatia lacked its own assembly in a thousand years. After the assassination of Croatian politicians in the Belgrade National Assembly in June 1928, King Alexander instituted a personal dictatorship, renaming the country the Kingdom of Yugoslavia. Extensive political persecution in the 1930s resulted in the rise of extremist opposition groups. In 1934, King Alexander was assassinated. Political activity revived and in 1939, an autonomous Croatian banovina was established and the Croatian parliament reconstituted.

Germany invaded Yugoslavia in April 1941. The occupying powers installed Nazi sympathizers in Zagreb and Belgrade and set up the so-called "Independent State of Croatia" under the leadership of the fascist Ante Pavelič.

After the Second World War, the Croatian parliament formally continued the work of the banovina parliament of 1939. The Communist Party came to power in Belgrade under the leadership of Marshal Tito and set up the Socialist Federal Republic of Yugoslavia (SFRJ). Initially allied with Stalin's USSR, the Yugoslav leadership refused to yield to Soviet hegemony and split with Stalin in 1948. Croat Communists were solid supporters of Tito's break with Stalin and of the economic liberalization and decollectivization of agriculture which followed. The federal structure of the SFRJ did dissolve real powers to the republics, but Tito tended to take Croatian compliance with his policies for granted.

A gradual polarization of interests emerged in the 1950s and 1960s between the republics (especially Slovenia and Croatia) and the centralized bureaucracy in Belgrade, which was closely linked to powerful and wealthy companies engaged in foreign trade. A privileged position was given to Serbs outside Serbia who tended to be viewed as more loyal to the "Yugoslav" idea.

In 1971, the Croatian Communist leadership called for greater autonomy within a confederal Yugoslavia. After some hesitation, Tito dismissed the entire leadership and a series of purges followed, with thousands of moderates losing their positions and some being imprisoned. In the 1980s, after the death of Tito, the interests of the constituent republics started to diverge more rapidly. In response, the Belgrade government tried to centralize more powers, which helped encourage the rise of Serb nationalism. The fall of Communism throughout Europe in 1989 hastened the demise of the Communist government and set in train a process which led to the rapid disintegration of the country.

Recent events

Following the decision of the Central Committee of the League of Communists of Croatia to give up its monopoly on power, the Croatian parliament (Sabor) legalized the creation of political parties in September 1989. In Croatia's first postwar multiparty elections in April 1990, the Croatian Democratic Union (HDZ) won an overall majority and its leader, Dr Franjo Tudjman, was elected head of state by the Sabor. While democratic changes were occurring in Slovenia and Croatia, the strength of extreme nationalism was growing in Serbia, and President Miloseviç consolidated his power over all former socialist government institutions. In June 1990, Miloseviç called in a speech to the Serbian parliament for Serb areas of other republics to be incorporated into Serbia and the Yugoslav National Army (JNA), foreseeing the collapse of Yugoslavia, made preparations to take over other parts of the country.

In December 1990, a new Croatian constitution was drawn up. This sought a confederal Yugoslavia. Serbian communities in Croatia, strongly encouraged by the nationalist government in Belgrade, opposed this new constitution and Croat government institutions. As the former Yugoslavia slid further into crisis, Croatia and Slovenia initiated negotiations to transform the SFRJ into an alliance of sovereign states. All proposals were repeatedly rejected by Serbia.

In May 1991, a referendum (boycotted by the Serb population in several regions) was held on full independence and produced a 93% vote in favour. The decision by Slovenia to proclaim independence in June prompted Croatia to declare its own independence. In response, the JNA attacked Slovenia's national militia forces, but after a brief conflict withdrew under an EC plan, under which both Croatia and Slovenia agreed to defer their declarations of independence for three months in order to search for a negotiated solution. It was during this three-month period that full hostilities commenced. The JNA intervened in support of the Serbian forces and heavy fighting spread around the country.

After several years of failure of UN peacekeeping, Croatian government forces retook Serb-held Western Slavonia and the Krajina in the summer of 1995. Eastern Slavonia, Baranja and western Srijem are the only areas of Croatia still not under government control.

In November 1995, the Erdut agreement was signed to return the region of Eastern Slavonia to Croatian government rule. The plan contemplates transitional rule over the area for a period of one year (now extended to July 15, 1997) before the region comes under direct rule from Zagreb. The UN mandate is now terminated and new international forces under the command of IFOR in Bosnia-Hercegovina will guarantee the agreement and human rights. The agreement allows for the demilitarization of the area and the return of refugees.

Chronology

7th century	Croats migrate from northern Europe to present-day Croatia and Bosnia-Hercegovina
1102	Personal Union between Croatia and Hungary
1527	Croatian nobility elects Habsburgs to the monarchy
1627	Creation of the Military Frontier (krajina) under direct Austrian rule
1815	Congress of Vienna. Dalmatia transferred to Austrian rule.
1918	October 29: Croatian parliament breaks all links with the Austro-Hungarian Empire and proclaims the State of Slovenes, Croats and Serbs
1920	King Alexander dissolves the Croatian parliament and imposes the Vidovdan Constitution
1929	Country renamed the Kingdom of Yugoslavia
1934	Assassination of King Alexander
1939	Establishment of an autonomous Croatian banovina and revival of Croatian parliament
1941	Germany invades Yugoslavia; establishment of puppet "Independent State of Croatia"
1943	Anti-Fascist Council under Josip Broz Tito lays framework for federal postwar Yugoslavia
1974	New Federal Yugoslav constitution creates quasi-confederal country
1980	Death of Tito
1989	Croatian Communist Party cedes monopoly on power. Creation of new political parties.
1990	April: first multiparty elections. HDZ under Dr Franjo Tudjman wins 205 out of 350 seats.
1990	June: President Milosevic of Serbia calls for Serb-inhabited lands to be incorporated into Greater Serbia
1990	September: first armed clashes between Croat government forces and Serb paramilitaries
1990	November: Yugoslav National Army (JNA) intervenes in support of Serb insurrectionists
1990	December 22: promulgation of current constitution of the Republic of Croatia
1991	May: Referendum produces 93% vote in favour of independence
1991	June: Declaration of independence
1991	October: JNA attacks Croatian coastal resorts and city of Dubrovnik
1991	December 7: EC Badinter Commission declares that Yugoslavia had ceased to exist
1991	Vance Plan; deployment of UN forces in Croatia
1992	January 3: fifteenth cease-fire of the conflict; full-scale military activities draw to a close
1992	Republic of Croatia recognized by all twelve EC member states
1992	Republic of Croatia admitted to the United Nations
1994	Washington Agreement creates alliance between Bosnian Muslims and Croats
1995	May: Croatian army launches Operation Flash to liberate Western Slavonia
1995	August: Croatian army launches Operation Storm to liberate the so-called Krajina
1995	Erdut Agreement on re-integration of Eastern Slavonia, Baranja and Western Srijem
1996	Extension of UNTAES mandate in Eastern Slavonia until July 15, 1997

Constitution and government

The Republic of Croatia (Republika Hrvatska) is a constitutional democracy. It is divided into twenty-one counties (zupanije), and has Zagreb as its capital. According to its constitution, promulgated on December 22, 1990, its head of state, the president, is elected by popular vote for a five-year term. The current president is Dr Franjo Tudjman, elected by parliament in April 1990, and re-elected by popular vote on August 2,1992. The head of government, the prime minister, is nominated by the president and confirmed by parliament.

Current government

Prime Minister   Dr Zlatko Matesa
Finance Minister   Bozo Prka
Foreign Minister   Mate Graniç
Defence Minister   Gojko Susak

Croatia's bicameral parliament, the Sabor, comprises a lower house, the House of Representatives (Zastupniïki Dom), and an upper house, the House of Counties (Zupanijski Dom). The House of Representatives has 127 seats, 80 elected by proportional representation from party lists, 28 elected on a first-past-the-post system in the constituencies, and 12 elected by proportional representation by the Croatian diaspora. Seven seats are reserved for national minorities. Members are elected for a four-year term. There is a 5% threshold for parties and 11% threshold for alliances. The last elections were held on October 29, 1995. The House of Counties has 63 elected members, 3 from each zupanija, and 5 members nominated by the president.

Election results

	Share of total	No. of seats
Croatian Democratic Union (HDZ)	45.23%	75
5-party centre-left coalition	18.26%	18
Croatian Social-Liberal Party (HSLS)	11.55%	12
Social Democratic Party (SDP)	8.93%	10
Others	16.03%	12

Central bank

The National Bank of Croatia (NBH) became Croatia's central bank in December 1991, and is chartered by the NBH Law. Croatia has a two-tier banking system in which the NBH acts as a central bank but does not engage in commercial banking. The NBH operates as an independent institution and is solely responsible to the Sabor. Principal responsibilities of the NBH are monetary and foreign exchange policy, as well as bank regulation and supervision. The NBH is specifically responsible for the money supply; determining the general liquidity of banks; maintaining general liquidity of payments abroad; issuing banknotes and coins; supervising banks; maintaining the country's gold and foreign exchange reserves; and acting as general banker to the government. Guidelines for monetary policy are established by the NBH in co-ordination with the government, although it is the NBH which has the authority (in consultation with the Sabor) to make the final decisions on policy. General exchange rate rules are also independently established by the NBH in co-ordination with the government, although they are not subject to government approval. The implementation of exchange rate and monetary policy is within the sole authority of the National Bank of Croatia. The governor and members of the board are appointed by the Sabor for six-year terms and can only be removed by the Sabor.

■ ECONOMICS

Historical overview

The Croatian economy emerged from four decades of socialist management in a stronger condition than most economies of Central and Eastern Europe. Under the former Yugoslav economic system, enterprises were "socially owned" by their current and former employees rather than directly by the state, and were managed in a decentralized manner. Enterprises were generally free to make their own pricing and investment decisions, without the widespread bureaucratic central planning more prevalent in other socialist economies.

The foreign trade regime was liberal, with few restrictions and tariff barriers. There were few monopolies in the economy and enterprises were encouraged to compete. Extensive trade took place with Western Europe, largely on market terms. Citizens of the former SFRJ were usually free to travel abroad and so the economy was much more open to foreign ideas and developments. Before independence, the Croatian economy was already able to compete internationally in a range of industrial sectors, including electrical engineering, pharmaceuticals and shipbuilding, and had attracted significant subcontracting business from Western European companies.

Post-independence developments

Croatia was expelled from the Yugoslav monetary system two days after the country's declaration of independence in June 1991. The central bank of the former Yugoslavia kept all the country's foreign exchange reserves, leaving Croatia with no hard currency reserves at independence. Simultaneously, the conflict meant that external sources of financing dried up.

The 1991 war left around one third of the country's territory outside of government control and severely disrupted lines of communication, not only across the country but also with many of Croatia's trading partners. Hostilities also caused extensive infrastructure, housing and industrial damage to the country (estimated at a minimum of U$15,000 million, approximately equivalent to Croatia's pre-war gross domestic product). It also displaced hundreds of thousands of people and dramatically reduced tourism, which had been a major foreign exchange earner.

Since 1992, Croatia has given refuge to approximately 300,000 refugees from Bosnia-Hercegovina, imposing a large strain on the resources of the government. Croatia's industrial base was disrupted by the loss of markets in the former Yugoslavia and the cutting of trade routes to the south and east. Between 1989 and 1993, Croatia's real economic output shrank by some 40%, disposable incomes fell sharply and the public deficit rose, pushing the country to the brink of hyperinflation.

Background to the 1993 Stabilization Plan

The decline in Croatia's GDP started well before the outbreak of war in 1991 and was principally a result of the imbalances within the economic structure of the former Yugoslavia. Another factor was the rapid fall in economic activity in the transition economies of Central and Eastern Europe, which were major trade partners, as well as the recession in Western Europe. Although very different from the Soviet economic system, the former Yugoslav system of "social ownership" or "self-management" shared with other socialist systems a lack of microeconomic incentives. However, a two-tier banking system and free prices for most consumer goods gave rise to a healthy degree of competition. Shortages of consumer goods prevalent in Soviet-style economies rarely occurred in the former Yugoslavia.

However, problems such as unclear property rights, the permanent monetization of fiscal deficits and heavily regulated markets for foreign exchange and imports gave rise to persistent economic problems in the former Yugoslavia. The most prominent of these were high levels of inflation and frequent balance of payments problems. In the twenty years before Croatian independence, inflation averaged an annual 69%, and in the 1980s, Yugoslavia's commercial bank debt was rescheduled four times. Multiple foreign exchange rates disguised many subsidies and government control of banks meant that enterprise losses were automatically covered: there were no bankruptcies in this period.

At the start of the 1991 war, Croatia was still using the currency of the former Yugoslavia. The country had no foreign exchange reserves at independence and external borrowing was impossible: the country was not recognized internationally at this stage, and war risks meant that commercial lenders were unwilling to extend credit. The government's deficit, therefore, could only be financed by money creation, further fuelling an already high inflation rate.

Croatia introduced its own currency, the Croatian dinar (HRD), in December 1991 and initially maintained a fixed exchange rate. At first, this helped to reduce inflation, but the lack of public confidence in the new currency led to further currency substitution (the sale of HRD and use of hard currencies, principally the deutschmark) and a return of inflation.

The 1993 Stabilization Programme

In October 1993, the government adopted an economic stabilization programme. It was implemented without the assistance of multilateral financial organizations, and proved successful. The programme is not simply an anti-inflation process, but is aimed at the long-term restructuring of the Croatian economy.

The programme:

1 The first phase was a short-term anti-inflation programme, using various stabilization tools, such as exchange rate, monetary and fiscal policy, to reduce the government's deficit and break the inflationary cycle.

2 The second phase, started in December 1993, is designed to fulfil the conditions for long-term low inflation by eliminating fiscal imbalances. The main aims are:
   ◆ rapid privatization and de-monopolization
   ◆ balancing the central government budget
   ◆ restructuring commercial banks

3 The goals of the third phase are to establish the full external convertibility of the currency, to achieve permanent price stability, and to establish the conditions for sustainable growth.

At the start of the programme, only the exchange rate and wages were frozen; all other prices were liberalized. From November 1993 to July 1994, Croatia experienced disinflation of 3% in consumer prices and 13% in industrial producer prices (see below). The exchange rate was initially fixed at HRD 4,444 = 1 DEM. Shortly after, as the foreign exchange market started to operate, it appreciated by some 20%. This came as a shock to most people and helped to break inflation. Not only did imported goods fall in price, but there was also no indication of future inflation. This was an important element in curbing inflationary expectations and deflating the inflationary bubble. Restrictive income policies also helped. The government set severe limits on the total wage bill of the state-controlled sector through decree laws.

In addition, formal wage and pension indexation was eliminated. Tight income policies will most probably be assured through collective bargaining processes between the trade unions and the government. This is an important area of the stabilization programme, as budget constraints are still soft in some areas, such as in large non-privatized companies, and a rapid increase in real wages above the increase in labour productivity could easily lead to increasing aggregate demand, thus reviving inflation. Now that initial monetary stabilization has been achieved, the government has embarked on the second stage of the plan, with the rehabilitation of the banking system and an acceleration of privatization.

The economy

Croatia has a relatively modern, diversified economy. Services account for around 60% of GDP, agriculture only around 10% and industry the balance. The country is not overdependent on any one economic activity.

Because of the previous system of "social ownership", where companies were "owned" (at least in theory) by their current and former employees, the government had little direct involvement in the economy of the former Yugoslavia and its influence was therefore much less pronounced than in other socialist countries. As a result, market forces had a significant effect on the shaping of the economy and industrial production. Services have made up more than 50% of the economy for more than twenty years, while in other socialist economies, the service sector was very small.

The government did, however, intervene to support export-orientated sectors, which received large subsidies often hidden behind a system of multiple exchange rates. For example, imports of raw materials by favoured companies benefited from an overvalued foreign exchange rate whereas export earnings could be converted at a market rate. Consequently, Croatia became the third largest shipbuilding nation in the world in the 1980s (although this sector has since diminished substantially) as well as being a significant producer of finished foodstuffs, electrical machinery and textiles, all of which became substantial export industries.

Croatia was, until recently, able to meet most of its energy needs through domestic production and transit fees from international pipelines which cross the country. For four years, the major oil fields and pipelines were in Serb-held territory, but now the country should once again become self-sufficient in energy.

Manufacturing and mining generally account for just under one third of GDP and employ around one third of the labour force. The largest sectors in terms of production are electrical engineering, textiles, foodstuffs, chemicals, wood-processing and shipbuilding. Croatia's reputation for high-quality manufacturing and its close proximity to major Western European markets made it an attractive subcontracting destination for Western European – particularly German and Italian – manufacturers in the 1970s and 1980s. Agriculture, forestry and fishing represent around 10% of GDP and employ approximately 5% of the labour force. Croatia is generally self-sufficient in agricultural products, despite the fact that much of the country's most fertile land in eastern Slavonia is outside of the government's control, and had been a net exporter of food products prior to 1991. Croatia's experiment with collectivized farming ended in 1953 after Tito severed relations with Stalin's Soviet Union. As a result, Croatian agriculture has been significantly more productive than other former socialist countries, and the food processing industry has become a major exporting sector of the economy. Following the disruption of war and the loss of almost one-third of Croatia's territory in 1991, both agricultural and cultivable land decreased by approximately 30%, resulting in extremely low crop yields. Agricultural production increased somewhat in 1993 and has been rising ever since, although it is not expected to return to pre-1991 levels for some years.

Before the war, Croatia was a net exporter of construction services, with workers employed on projects around the world, especially in the former Soviet Union, Africa, and the Middle East. The construction industry in Croatia is divided into large state-owned concerns and smaller privately owned construction companies. It is the state-owned companies that have been more affected by recessionary conditions, and the government is now launching restructuring and privatization. Smaller companies have, by and large, begun to increase activity as part of the initial phase of reconstruction. Currently, the construction industry employs around 6% of the labour force, but this is expected to rise significantly as part of postwar reconstruction.

Tourism was Croatia's most important source of foreign currency earnings before the war, even though it represented only around 4% of GDP. Until independence, some of this revenue went to the federal authorities of the former SFRJ. At its peak in 1989, when the country received over ten million tourists, the industry employed approximately 5% of the labour force. The actual percentage, however, was much higher, as much tourism activity is unrecorded.

Share of GDP by sector

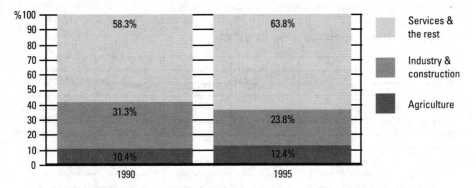

Source: EBRD

Inflation
The start of the stabilization plan in October 1993 saw inflation fall very rapidly, and for seven consecutive months, retail prices actually fell. Strict monetary and fiscal policies have

kept price pressures subdued. The government has put much effort into achieving price stability, prioritizing the control of inflation. Thus, despite the very large budgetary demands of reconstruction, there should be no easing of policy. With the expectation that postwar reconstruction will encourage foreign investment and the repatriation of capital, the government believes that inflationary pressures can be kept subdued for the foreseeable future.

Currency

Croatia used the Yugoslav dinar (YUD) before and immediately after independence. The country introduced its own currency, called the Croatian dinar (HRD), on December 23, 1991. Initially the HRD was introduced at parity to the YUD, but the exchange rates rapidly diverged. The Croatian dinar was replaced by the kuna (HRK) on May 30, 1994 at the rate of HRD1,000=HRK1; the kuna is divided into 100 lipa. The Croatian kuna is officially a free-floating currency as there is no official currency management plan. However, in effect the central bank operates a "dirty float" by intervening in the foreign exchange market to limit daily fluctuations of the currency and to prevent its rapid appreciation. Banks are free to set any foreign exchange rate but are required to report their transactions to the central bank.

Foreign trade

Approximately two thirds of Croatia's trade is now with EC countries and over 80% is with European countries (both Eastern and Western). Croatia's exports are heavily concentrated in just two countries, Germany and Italy, which account for nearly half of the country's exports. This leaves the country vulnerable to external factors such as recession in Germany. The government has recently tried to expand the country's export markets in Latin America and the Far East, sending trade delegations to promote the country and its products. However, it is not likely that the overall structure of trade partners will change significantly in the foreseeable future. Before the war, there were wide and extensive trade links between enterprises in the various Yugoslav republics, and when bilateral relations become normalized, Serbia is likely to become a significant trading partner.

Imports and exports as a % of GDP

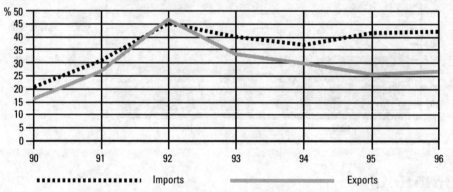

Source: EBRD

Current account as a % of GDP

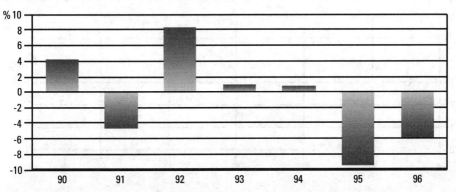

Source: UBS

Privatization

The aim of the privatization programme is to sell approximately 3,000 socially owned enterprises.

At the beginning of 1995, the Ministry for Privatization was established to handle the final stage of the process: privatization of Croatia's utilities and the mass voucher privatization programme, both governed by the Privatization Act of December 1995.

By September 1996, just over 1,000 companies had been wholly privatized, 1,318 companies had a majority of private shareholders and a further 228 companies had some private shareholders but with the majority of their common stock held by the CPF and two state pension funds.

Debt

Croatia has moderate levels of internal and external debt. Foreign debt amounts to about US$5 billion, or 30% of GDP. The government's fiscal restraint means the country has plenty of scope to use debt financing for reconstruction projects. Croatia's public debt is mostly inherited from the former SFRJ. Less than 20% of the country's total external debt has been contracted since independence.

Economic policy
Monetary policy

The National Bank of Croatia is responsible for monetary policy. Since the introduction of the stabilization programme, the main goal of the NBH has been to maintain exchange rate and price stability. It seeks to achieve this through intervening in the foreign exchange market to resist sharp fluctuations in the exchange rate of the kuna and by regulating the money supply. The NBH is also responsible for setting interest rates.

Croatian kuna/US dollar exchange rate

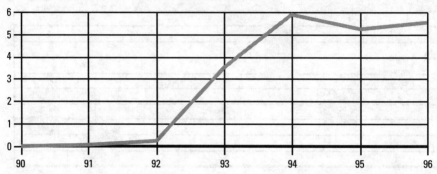

■ EQUITIES

Key indicators

	Market Cap. US$bn	P/E
1994	0.6	15.8
1995	0.6	—
1996	3.0	14.0

Sources: Local stock exchange, IFC, Bloomberg, Datastream, UBS

Background

Stock Exchange activity in Croatia goes back to late 1918, when a small group of entrepreneurs formed the Zagreb Stock & Commodities Exchange. However, in 1931, following the Great Depression, the Exchange ceased trading in stocks. Until the end of the Second World War the Exchange continued to trade commodities, but after the Communists seized power in 1945 it was closed. In July 1991, a group of Croatian banks combined forces to relaunch the Stock Exchange. Consequently, the Zagreb Stock Exchange (ZSE) was formed, with the first trading session taking place on March 31, 1992. In addition, there are OTC exchanges in Varazdin, Osijek and Zagreb.

Structure

The ZSE is dominated by banks and brokerages, as well as a relatively high proportion of private investors (one in eight Croatians own shares). The Exchange is split between fully quoted and TN (OTC) quoted companies. Currently, sixty-three shares are listed on the ZSE, but only two companies (PLIVA and ZB) are fully listed with the remaining sixty-one having a TN quotation. Companies tend to favour the TN quotations as they have less stringent listing requirements.

Regulatory authority

The ZSE is regulated by the Croatian Securities and Exchange Commission (CROSEC).

Trading methods
Trading on the ZSE takes place using two systems. The Telecommunications Supported Trading System (TEST-1) is an off-line electronic trading system. In addition, the ZSE has an agreement with the Croatian Privatization Fund whereby stocks are sold at weekly auctions. TEST-2, an on-line electronic trading system for the ZSE, is currently under development in a joint project between the ZSE and the German government.

Hours
Trading is between 09.00 and 14.00, Tuesday to Friday on TEST-1. Special one-way auctions for Croatian Privatization Fund portfolio stocks are on Monday and Thursday at 10.00.

Settlement time and clearing
Settlement takes place on a trade date plus five business days (T+5) basis. There is no central clearing house – settlements take place directly between buyers and sellers.

Limits on price movement
None

Types of shares
Ordinary shares are traded on the ZSE.

Stock indices
There are no stock indices calculated by the ZSE because there are too few fully listed companies at present.

Taxes
There are no taxes on the ZSE. There are no capital gains or withholding taxes.

Dividends
Interest and dividend income is subject to 25% corporation tax. Realized gains are tax-free.

Disclosure of financial statements
Listed companies are required to produce an annual report, a semi-annual report and an auditor's report at the end of the year.

Ownership limits for non-residents
There are no limits on foreign ownership.

Capital and foreign exchange controls
Portfolio investment and repatriation of capital are freely transferable. Currency is freely convertible.

Brokers
There are forty-five banks or brokerage firms operating on the ZSE. Typically, commission rates are 1%.

Sectors

The pharmaceuticals company PLIVA has a market capitalization and turnover larger than any other sector, with around 47% of total market value. Other sectors that make significant contributions, in terms of capitalization, include banking, food processing and tourism.

ADRs

There are no Croatian ADRs.

Derivatives

There is no derivatives market in Croatia.

■ DEBT

Bonds are defined by the Company Act, and the legal status of short-term securities (one year or less) is defined in the Law on the Money-Market.

The markets are regulated by the Securities and Exchange Act (1995). Bonds are traded on an electronic, decentralized system developed by the Zagreb Stock Exchange in March 1994.

NBC treasury bills

The National Bank of Croatia (NBC) issues discounted treasury bills with maturities of 35, 91 and 182 days. Bills are auctioned every Wednesday. Domestic banks and other financial institutions make competitive bids for themselves and their customers.

Non-residents can only buy bills in the secondary market, and must set up a kuna account at a local bank. The seller (normally a bank) must provide the NBC with full details about the buyer within 2 days of the transaction date. Redemption value is par and payments are made in kuna.

MOF treasury bills

The Ministry of Finance organizes ad hoc auctions of MOF bills to cover public revenue shortfalls. Maturity dates are determined by the timing of government expenditure payments. Orders are filled at the weighted average price of all bids.

Titles to ownership of bills are held in the Registration Ledger, managed by ZAP (Croatian Public Audit Bureau), a centralized payment agency, which also administers transfers.

Ministry of Finance Bonds

During the breakup of Yugoslavia in 1991, Croatian foreign exchange deposits were frozen by the National Bank of Yugoslavia. The Croatian government assumed responsibility for these obligations as "The Public Debt of the Republic of Croatia", to restore confidence in the country's banking system. It converted the debt into DEM5 billion 10-year government bonds, which, after a 4-year grace period, would begin an amortization schedule of 20 semi-annual instalments and pay a 5% coupon.

In December 1995 the Ministry of Finance refinanced the first of the amortizations, which was due in June 1995 and issued DEM153.7 million Croatian MinFin Tranche 1 Bonds. In June 1996, it refinanced the second amortization payment due in December 1995, and issued DEM147 million Croatian MinFin Tranche 2 Bonds.

The bonds can only be traded through authorized brokers, but there are no restrictions on the repatriation of profits abroad. Interest and principal cannot be stripped and traded separately. Further payments of the amortizing "frozen foreign exchange deposit" bonds will be met with cash, rather than refinanced.

Other bonds issued by the Croatian government which represent frozen deposits include DEM1.3 billion of "Big Bonds". Formerly called "Government Bonds for the Restructuring of the Croatian Economy" they pay a 5% coupon and a term of twenty years. They are listed on the Zagreb Stock Exchange, but are not transferable. The government has indicated that it will replace them with transferable bonds, which will form part of its overall plan to open the domestic bond market to overseas investors.

Former Yugoslavia (FRY) debt

On July 31 1996, Croatia came to an agreement with its London Club commercial bank creditors over its share of the Former Yugoslavia's debt, following a rescheduling accord reached in April. It assumed responsibility for US$1.46 billion, which accounts for 29.5% of the total owed by the FRY. Two tranches of US dollar bonds have been issued, which pay 13/16% over libor. The first represents US$833 million of matured principal repayable over 14 years with a grace period of 3½ years. The second tranche represents US$643 million of interest arrears, repayable over 10 years with no grace period. 4% of the debt will be paid annually for the first 7 years, rising to 14% each year nearer the maturity date.

■ CROATIA: Economic indicators

Population and development	1990	1991	1992	1993	1994	1995	1996e
Population, million	4.8	4.8	4.8	4.8	4.8	4.8	4.8
Population growth, %	0.2	0.2	0.3	0.3	0.2	0.2	0.2
Nominal GDP per capita, US$	3690	2971	2232	1916	2906	3836	3944

National accounts							
Nominal GDP, US$bn	17.6	14.2	10.7	9.2	14.0	18.3	18.8
Change in real GDP, %	—	—	—	-3.6	0.8	1.5	5.0

Money supply and inflation							
Consumer price inflation (avg.) %	609.5	123.0	665.5	1517.0	97.5	2.0	3.6

Interest rates							
Discount rate, end of year	—	—	1889.4	34.5	8.5	8.5	6.5
Money market rate, monthly average	—	—	951.2	1370.5	26.9	21.1	19.5
Deposit rate, monthly average	—	—	658.5	379.3	6.5	5.5	5.9
Prime lending rate, monthly average	—	—	1157.8	1443.6	22.9	20.2	23.2

Government finance							
Government balance, % of GDP	—	—	—	—	-0.7	-0.8	-1.5

Exchange rates lc=local currency							
Exchange rate, annual average, lc/US$	11.2	19.6	264	3574	6.0	5.2	5.5
Exchange rate, end of year, lc/US$	—	—	—	—	5.6	5.3	5.4

Balance of payments							
Exports of goods & services, US$m	2913	3280	6097	5710	65931	7169	9500
Change %	3.70	12.60	85.88	-6.35	15.46	8.75	32.51
Imports of goods & services, US$m, fob	4426	3830	4460	6308	7278	9508	7800
Change %	25.28	-13.47	16.45	41.42	15.38	30.63	-17.96
Trade balance, of goods only, US$m, fob-fob	-1513	-550	137	-763	-900	-2200	-3000
Current account balance, US$m	-621	-589	822	278	100	-1700	-800
as a % of GDP	-3.53	-4.15	7.68	3.02	0.71	-9.29	-4.26

Foreign exchange reserves							
Foreign exchange reserves, US$m	—	—	167	612	1400	2000	2400
Import cover (reserves/imports), months	—	—	0.4	1.2	2.3	2.5	3.7

Foreign debt and debt service							
Total foreign debt, US$m	3062	2719	2541	2660	3200	3700	4500
as a % of GDP	17.4	19.1	23.7	28.9	22.9	20.2	23.9
as a % of foreign exchange receipts	—	—	41.7	41.7	43.9	45.4	47.4
Interest payments, US$m	—	—	—	—	400	400	600

Czech Republic

Area (thousands of km²):	79
Population (1995, millions):	10.3
Population projection (2025, millions):	11
Population younger than 15 yrs (1991, % of total):	21.2
Urbanization rate (1993, % of population):	65
Life expectancy (1993, years at birth):	73
Gross domestic product (1996, US$bn):	53.5
GDP per capita (1996, US$):	5189
Average annual GDP growth rate (1990-96, %):	-1.4
Average annual inflation rate (1990-96, %):	17.9
Currency (koruna per US$, average 1996):	27.1
Real exchange rate: (1990=100, average 1996)	142.1
Structure of production (1994):	55% services, 39% industry, 6% agriculture
Main exports:	industrial products
Main imports:	oil, investment goods, raw material & semi-finished products, consumer goods
Main trading partners:	EU
Market capitalization of Stock Exchange (October 1996; US$bn):	17.6
Total foreign debt (% of GDP):	33.6
Next elections due under normal circumstances:	presidential: January 1988; parliamentary: June 2000 at the latest
Credit rating: (Nov 1996, Standard & Poor's, Moody's)	A; Baa1

FORECAST: 1997-2000 (average)

	Worst case	Most likely	Best case
Real GDP growth (%)	2 to 3	4 to 6	7 to 10
Inflation (%)	9 to 12	6 to 8	3 to 5

■ POLITICS

Historical overview

In the 5th and 6th centuries, Slavonic tribes settled in the territory of Bohemia and Moravia. In 1212 Bohemia was declared a kingdom, which reached its height of power during the reign of King Charles IV (1346-78). He established Charles University in Prague in 1348 – the first university north of the Alps – and was crowned Roman Emperor in Rome in 1355. Following the brief reign of the Jagellon dynasty (1471-1526) the Habsburgs succeeded to the throne of Bohemia. Ferdinand II (1619-37) was determined to re-introduce Catholic faith in Bohemia, and to replace Hussite reformation and religious freedom. His attempt led to the outbreak of the Thirty Years' War (1618-48), which brought political disorder and economic devastation to Bohemia. Although Austria suffered severe losses with the Peace of Westphalia (1648), the Catholic faith was re-introduced in Bohemia, the throne was made hereditary in the Habsburg dynasty and most important political offices were transferred to Vienna.

The Czech national movement began in the late 18th century, initially aspiring to revive Czech language and culture, but soon striving for political emancipation. The compromise in 1867 between Austria and Hungary, which eventually established the Austro-Hungarian dual monarchy, crushed Czech hopes for independence. The empire was divided in two halves, one ruled by the Germans the other by the Magyars, and in both the Czechs remained in political inferiority.

The defeat of the Austro-Hungarian monarchy in the First World War cleared the way for an independent Czech state. On October 28, 1918 the Czech National Committee assumed responsibility for Czech lands following the dissolution of Austria-Hungary. Within three days, the Slovak National Council declared its intention of closer political ties with the Czechs and, by mid-November, the Czechoslovak Republic was formed. The government was led by T.G. Masaryk, the inaugural president. The 1919 Treaty of St Germain-en-Loye recognized the Czechoslovak Republic encompassing Bohemia, Moravia, parts of Silesia, and Slovakia plus the formerly autonomous province of Subcarpathian Ruthenia.

During this period the Czechoslovak Republic was an advanced, prosperous, country with individual wealth on a par with Austria, until the Munich Agreement in 1938 dismantled the country. In March the following year, the German-backed Slovak government declared independence. Meanwhile, Germany incorporated the Sudeten regions into the Reich and put the remaining regions into the "Protectorate of Bohemia and Moravia". German rule ended in May 1945 when Czechoslovak sovereignty was restored (with the exception of Subcarpathian Ruthenia, which was integrated into the USSR).

In the election following liberation, the Communist Party received almost two-fifths of the vote. Consequently, a Communist prime minister, Klement Gottwald, led a coalition government, winning an incredible 89% of votes in 1948. After twenty years of Communist rule, increasing pressure for liberalization led to the resignation of hard-line leader Antonin Novotny in 1968. Consequently, the Communist Party introduced a number of reform measures during the Prague Spring which was suddenly ended by Soviet troops in August 1968.

During the late 1980s demonstrations demanding reform re-emerged, leading the "Velvet Revolution" and the downfall of the Communist regime. On November 30, 1989, the Federal Assembly abolished the Communist Party's right to govern, and founded a new government presided over by Vaclav Havel. However, despite the end of Communist rule, Czechoslovakia's future was short-lived. The 1992 elections saw the Movement for a Democratic Slovakia campaign for Slovak independence. By mid-July the Slovak National Council had declared its sovereignty and, by the beginning of September, outlined an independent Slovak Constitution (effective from January 1, 1993). On November 25, the Federal Assembly voted for the dissolution of the federal Czechoslovak Republic.

Recent events

Elections in June 1996 witnessed Vaclav Klaus enter a second term as prime minister. He leads a coalition government consisting of three conservative parties, including Klaus' Civic

Democrats, the Christian Democrats, and the Civic Democratic Alliance, but is in a minority with only 49.5% of parliamentary seats. In elections to the less important Senate in November 1996 the government coalition won a majority of 64.2%. However, the speed of free market reforms, of which Klaus is a strong proponent, may slow because of difficulties in gaining parliamentary approval. The country became a member of OECD in 1996, and is on track towards NATO (1999) and EU membership.

Chronology

600	Slavonic settlements in Bohemia
1212	Kingdom of Bohemia
1348	Charles University in Prague is established
1419	Reformer Jan Hus is executed
1526	Ferdinand of Habsburg succeeds to the throne of Bohemia as Louis, King of Bohemia and Hungary and is killed by the Turks in the Battle of Mohács
1618-1648	Thirty Years' War ends with Peace of Westphalia (1648). Catholic faith re-introduced in the crownlands of Bohemia, which become part of the Habsburg Empire.
1918	Czechoslovak state is formed following the dissolution of Austria-Hungary
1918	State declared a republic by Czechoslovak National Assembly with T.G. Masaryk as president
1919	Czechoslovak Republic recognized by the Treaty of St Germain-en-Loye, understood to comprise Bohemia, Moravia, parts of Silesia, Slovakia, and Subcarpathian Ruthenia
1938	Czechoslovak Republic broken up by the Munich Agreement
1939	Slovak government declares Slovakia independent. The Sudetenland is incorporated into Germany, the rest becomes the German "Protectorate of Bohemia and Moravia".
1945	Liberation by American and Soviet troops. Former Czechoslovak territory resumes sovereign rule minus Subcarpathian Ruthenia, which is incorporated into USSR
1946	Communists receive almost two-fifths of the vote in elections. A Communist prime minister, Klement Gottwald, leads a coalition government.
1948	Twelve non-Communist MPs resign over police interference by Communist Party members. Gottwald goes on to form a predominantly Communist government.
1968	Strong pressure for liberalization leads to resignation of Stalinist Communist Party leader Antonin Novotny. Consequently, the Communists introduce a far-reaching package of reforms.
1968	Soviet forces occupy Czechoslovak Republic and force the government to reverse liberalization process
1989	Mass demonstrations demanding urgent reform begin culminating in the collapse of the Communist government
1989	The Federal Assembly removes the Communist Party's right to govern. A new government is formed, led by Vaclav Havel.
1992	Election campaigning by the Movement for Democratic Slovakia leads to the Slovak National Council declaring independence from the Czechoslovak Republic
1993	The Czechoslovak Republic separates peacefully into the Czech Republic and the Slovak Republic
1996	Prime Minister Vaclav Klaus enters second term leading a minority coalition government. OECD membership.

Constitution and government

The current constitution was approved on December 16, 1992 and effective from January 1, 1993. It provides for a bicameral parliament. The 200-member House of Representatives is elected for four-year terms by a proportional representation system while the eighty-one members of the Senate sit for six-year terms. Elections to both chambers are held during the last thirty days before the end of the electoral term. If the Chamber of Deputies is dissolved then elections take place within sixty days. The president, who acts as Chief of State, is elected for a five-year terms by both chambers of parliament. The prime minister is named by the president at the speaker's suggestion.

Current government
President Vaclav Havel (no party affiliation)
Prime Minister Vaclav Klaus (ODS)

Deputy prime ministers:
Minister of Finance Ivan Kocarnik (ODS)
Minister of Agriculture Josef Lux (KDU-CSL)
Minister of Justice Vlasta Parkanova (ODA)

Local government
The Czech Republic comprises eight regions, or kraj.

Political parties
Coalition parties

Civic Democratic Party (ODS)
Christian Democratic Party – Czechoslovak People's Party (KDU-CSL)
Civic Democratic Alliance (ODA)

Opposition parties

Czech Social Democratic Party (CSSD)
Communist Party of Bohemia and Moravia (KCSM)
Association for the Republic – Republican Party of Czechoslovakia (SPR-RSC)

Result of the January 1993 presidential election:
Vaclav Havel elected president by the National Council on January 16, 1993

Results of the June 1996 parliamentary election:

	% votes	Seats
Civic Democratic Party (ODS)	29.6	68
Czech Social Democratic Party (CSSD)	26.4	61
Communist Party of Bohemia and Moravia (KCSM)	10.3	22
Christian Democratic Party – Czechoslovak People's Party (KDU-CSL)	8.1	18
Association for the Republic – Republican Party of Czechoslovakia (SPR-RSC)	8.0	18
Civic Democratic Alliance (ODA)	6.4	13
(Turnout 76.4%)		

Next elections
Presidential – January 1998; parliamentary – June 2000 at the latest

Central bank

The Czech National Bank (Ceská Národní Banka, CNB) was established on January 1, 1993 following the dissolution of the Czech and Slovak Federal Republic and the State Bank of Czechoslovakia. Most assets and liabilities of the former State Bank were split at a ratio of two to one in favour of the CNB.

The CNB is independent of any government instructions. The Bank Board of seven members, its highest managing body, is appointed by the President of the Republic. Board members are appointed for a term of six years. The Czech National Bank is currently governed by Josef Tosovsky, who was already governor of the former State Bank. The prime objective of the CNB is to maintain the stability of the national currency, the Czech crown (koruna).

■ ECONOMICS

Population

In 1994 the IMF estimated the Czech Republic's population to be 10.33 million. Approximately one-fifth is aged fifteen or under, with a similar number of retirement age (over 60 for men, over 55 for women), thus giving a sizeable dependency ratio. The population has grown by around 30% since 1950 with an annual growth rate of 0.6% between 1950 and 1995. The population is projected to grow by 12% during the next thirty years. In 1995 5.8 million (51%) were active in the labour market.

Performance under central planning

The four decades after the First World War were characterized by the long-term decline of GDP growth. According to the OECD, growth of net material product declined from 8% in the 1950s to 2% in the 1980s, and labour productivity growth dropped to 1.5% compared to 4.3% in the 1970s. Several attempts to reform the economy were undertaken, but all were brought to an end. One of the most far-reaching in the 1960s was stopped abruptly after the "Prague Spring" in 1968. The next reform moves were introduced after 1986, inspired by Perestroika in the Soviet Union and by reforms in Hungary and Poland.

In some respects, however, Czechoslovakia was initially less prepared for economic transition than some of its neighbours. The private sector was almost non-existent at the beginning of the 1990s. Czechoslovakia's economy was tightly closed, given that at the end of 1989 only fifty joint ventures were registered against about five hundred in both Hungary and Poland; Czechoslovakia was more dependent on socialist trade, and thus more vulnerable to a collapse of CMEA trade than Hungary or Poland. Prices were almost completely controlled in 1989 and not even contract pricing had been introduced.

On the other hand, Czechoslovakia missed some economic imbalances which plagued some of its neighbours during transition, and partly still do. Hard currency debt was only 15% in 1989, considerably less than in Hungary and Poland. Monetary overhang was relatively small since the consumer goods market was more or less in balance, and pent-up inflationary pressures also seemed relatively small.

Economic transition

Like all other former socialist countries, Czechoslovakia could not escape the initial cycle of transition-recession-inflation that followed the Soviet collapse. GDP plunged by 21% between 1990 and 1993, and inflation rose from 1.5% in 1989 to more than 56%. Restrictive fiscal, monetary and income policies were introduced to achieve macroeconomic stabilization. Considerable employment and social safety schemes helped to dampen the negative effects of transition but also slowed structural adjustment. Uncertainty was created by the dissolution of the Czech and Slovak Federal Republic in 1993 and the termination of the Czech and Slovak monetary union in February of that year. Nevertheless, the continued commitment to stabilization helped to overcome the renewed shock of political and monetary separation.

Transition-recession-inflation

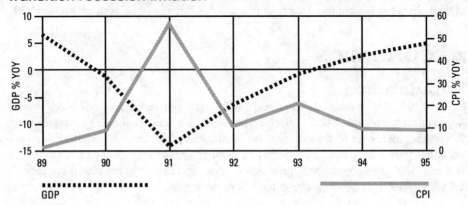

Source: Czech Statistical Office

Recent economic performance

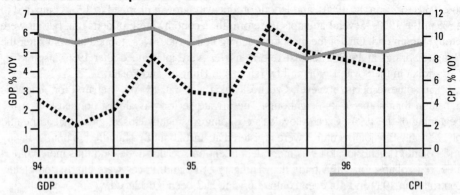

Source: CSU

Turnaround started in 1994 with GDP rising by 2.6% and inflation falling to 10%, and in 1995 GDP grew by 4.8% while inflation decelerated to 9.1%. Throughout the whole transition period, unemployment remained remarkably low, and excepting 1992 the government managed to run budget surpluses. Available statistical data for 1996 confirm solid GDP growth and gradually declining inflation. The combination of strong fixed investment growth, accelerating private consumption growth and cautious fiscal and monetary policies should lead to continued stable economic growth and steadily falling inflation.

The economy
The structure of GDP by origin has changed in a similar way to all former socialist countries. There has been a shift from manufacturing to services as a share of GDP, while agriculture remained broadly stable. The separation from Slovakia removed some of the burden of heavy industries, mainly producing for former COMECON markets. These industries were heavily subsidized and not particularly competitive.

Gross fixed investment accounts for a relatively high share of GDP at 31.5%, reflecting the continued structural change of the domestic economy. Infrastructure improvement and enhancement of capacity is set to continue. However, private consumption, already the biggest GDP component, is beginning to gain even more in importance. Real wages have risen considerably in the last two years and were expected to reach pre-reform levels during 1996. Hence, with real incomes projected to rise, private consumption should further increase its share in GDP.

Foreign direct investment inflows have been smaller than in Hungary and Poland. Total investment at the end of 1995 amounted to US$5.8 billion, while Poland attracted US$6.8 billion and Hungary US$12.7 billion. However, foreign direct investment (FDI) in the Czech Republic in 1995 grew by 8%, considerably faster than in other CEFTA countries.

Share of GDP by sector

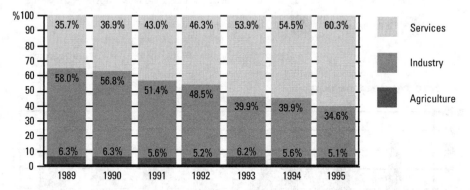

Source: CSU

Balance of payments
The Czech Republic successfully re-orientated its trade from East to West. Initially, the export industry was more dependent on COMECON markets than its neighbouring transition economies. In contrast, the commodity structure of Czech exports – relatively small shares of agricultural products and mineral fuels – enabled a quick shift. With the exception of steel, access to EU markets is less restricted for industrial products than for agricultural products and coal. Company links associated with FDI also eased access to EU markets.

The trade balance has steadily deteriorated since 1993 due to import growth, mainly driven by the need for capital goods. According to the Czech National Bank, investment goods accounted for 39% of all imports in 1995, raw material and semi-finished products for 42% and consumer goods for 19%. The Czech Republic is still largely dependent on gas and oil imports from Russia, which supplies 93% of all natural and heating gas and 67% of all oil imports. However, the opening of the Ingolstadt-Kralupy-Litvinov (IKL) pipeline in March 1996 reduces dependency on Russian oil. Exports mainly comprise materials and semi-finished goods (32.2%), machinery and transport equipment (30.4%), and chemicals (9.3%). Growth dynamics have been dominated by economic performance: while export growth to the EU slowed moderately, reflecting lower growth in Western Europe, export growth accelerated to CEFTA countries.

Trade and current account

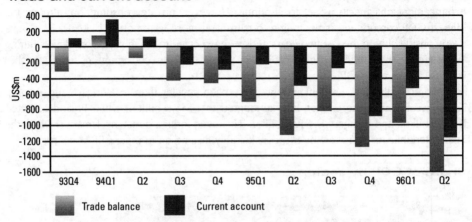

Source: CNB

Exports by destination

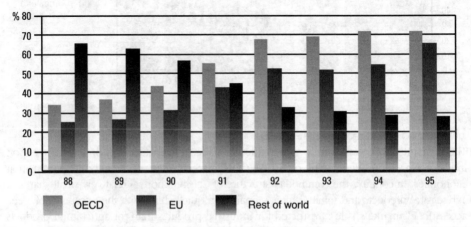

Source: CSU

Since 1994 the current account deficit has been rising steadily and is likely to remain negative. The high level of fixed investment suggests that the buildup of capital stock should generate adequate returns on capital inflows. In addition, completion of economic restructuring should result in a declining trade deficit.

Fiscal policy

Czech fiscal policy has been prudent throughout the whole transition process, while stabilization has been achieved at a relatively early stage. The main aims of fiscal policy are balanced budgets and reduction of central and local government expenditure in GDP. The consolidated general government budget has been in surplus since 1993. The separation of the Czech and Slovak Republics resulted in windfall gains to the Czech budget, since transfers from the Czech part to the Slovak part had grown from CZK9 billion in 1990 to CZK23 billion in 1992 (2% of GDP). After these transfers the Czech budget was left with a notional surplus of about CZK20 billion, considerably higher than the recorded state budget of CZK4.7 billion.

Gross foreign debt in mid-1996 stood at US$16.7 billion or 33.3% of GDP. The Czech debt is among the lowest in the OECD and about one third of it is in foreign currency. This particularly low indebtedness and the continued cautious fiscal policy are major reasons of macroeconomic stability. It is likely that the government will continue to target balanced budgets as well as further reduction of fiscal burdens.

Budget balance and foreign debt

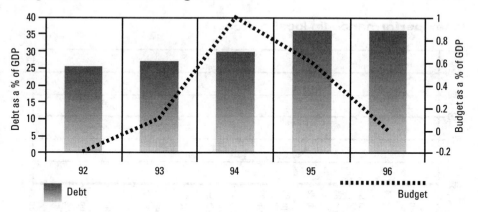

Source: OECD

Currency

The Czech koruna (CZK) was introduced on February 8, 1993 shortly after the separation of the Czech and Slovak republics. A stable nominal exchange rate is one of the cornerstones of Czech stabilization policies. Pegged to a basket of DEM (65%) and US$ (35%), the exchange rate regime remained unchanged from May 1993 until the end of February 1996, when the CNB announced a widening of the fluctuation band to +/- 7.5% from +/- 0.5%. This took some appreciation pressure off the koruna but also led to short-term funds outflow of about US$1 billion. Subsequently, the CNB successfully employed its reserves to calm the markets.

The koruna has remained fairly stable and even appreciated, which reflects the currency's underlying strength as well as market confidence in CNB policies. The koruna has steadily appreciated in real terms since 1989, eroding the devaluation buffer created in 1990.

Koruna/US dollar/German deutschmark exchange rate

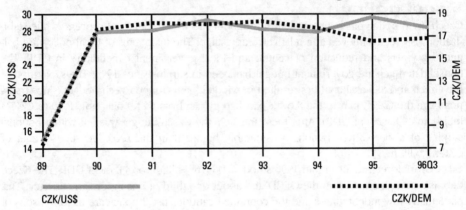

CZK/US$ CZK/DEM

■ EQUITIES

Index performance (in local currency)

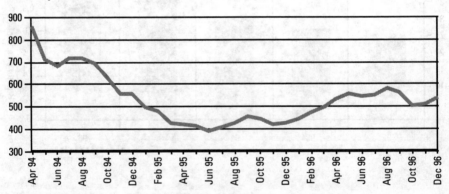

Key indicators

	Index performance %, in US$ terms	Market Cap. US$bn	P/E	Div. Yield	Weight in IFCI	IFCG
1994	—	5.9	16.3	1.1	—	—
1995	-21.5	15.7	11.2	1.4	0.8	—
1996	20.0	18.1	17.6	1.4	0.5	0.9

Sources: Local stock exchange, IFC, Bloomberg, Datastream, UBS

Background

There is a long tradition of Stock Exchange activity in Czech lands. Following the establishment of the Chamber of Commerce and Small Business in 1850, trading in commodities and securities began to develop. The Exchange closed during the First World War, re-opening in 1919. However, the Second World War, together with the subsequent rise of Communism in Eastern Europe, caused the Exchange to close again from 1939.

Following Communism's collapse and the adoption of the Stock Exchange Act, the Prague Stock Exchange (SEP) re-opened for trade in April 1993 for the first time in more than fifty years. The Czech capital market was recreated primarily to aid the mass privatization programme and, as the Czech economy remains buoyant (with debt as a percentage of GDP minimal and a small budget surplus), the government has not had an incentive to use the Stock Exchange to raise finance. Consequently, the market has developed in an ad hoc manner.

Structure

The SEP is split into three segments: the Main Market, the Secondary Market and the Free Market. Listed firms are quoted on the Main and Secondary markets, and unlisted firms on the Free Market. The latter comprises numerous small firms, which in many cases are not actively traded. Entry criteria to listed markets are based on transparency and liquidity, with the Main Market the more strict of the two.

In addition to segmenting the three markets, the Exchange also divides securities between three trading groups. Trading Group 1 is used for securities on the Main Market that are included in daily continuous trading at varying prices. Trading Group 2 is for securities admitted to all three markets that are included in daily trading at a fixed price. Finally, Trading Group 3 is used for securities registered in the Free Market that are included in trading at a fixed price, with trading twice weekly. There are currently 43 shares and unit trusts on the Main Market, 51 on the Secondary Market, and 1,600 on the Free Market.

Regulatory authority

The market is regulated by the Ministry of Finance. A legal framework is in place but is not stringently enforced. The SEP lacks regulation in two main areas: control of investment funds and pricing. Foreign investors tend to avoid these pitfalls by favouring high capitalization blue chip stocks where regulation is stronger. Legislation for the creation of a semi-independent regulatory body, based on the US Securities Exchange Commission (SEC) model has been prepared, but not yet implemented.

Trading methods

Trading takes place using three main methods: the Stock Exchange computer order-driven system (KOBOS), the unregulated OTC market, and the RMS system.

On the Stock Exchange system, orders are inputted in the early morning session, after which a price that maximizes volume transacted is then fixed. This price is used for the rest of the day for all stocks (except the top five in which continuous trading takes place). However, the bulk (around 90%) of total volume is traded off the Exchange over the phone.

Prices on the OTC market can be different from the fixed price of the Exchange. There are no charges on the OTC market. Trades negotiated this way can be settled through the Exchange. The RMS-type system is designed primarily for retail business, as the size of trades are too small for institutional clients.

Hours
Trading takes place between 08.00 and 10.00 for Order Input-type trading, at 11.00 for price fixing-type trading, and between 11.30 and 14.00 for continuous trading.

Settlement time and clearing
Settlement takes place on a trade day plus three business days (T+3) basis on the Exchange, but is negotiable on the OTC market.

Limits on price movement
In the Main Market shares are limited to 8% daily fluctuations. In the Secondary and Free Markets there is a 10% share price fluctuation limit.

Types of shares
Common shares are traded on the SEP. Preference shares are not traded.

Stock indices
The SEP produces twenty-two indices. The most widely quoted is the PX 50 Index, which, based on the IFC's methodology, is a weighting of fifty issues based on market capitalization and liquidity.

There are two other aggregate indices: the PXL Indicator and PX-GLOB, as well as nineteen sectoral indices BI 01 to BI 19. In addition, the Czech National Bank produces the CNB 120 Index.

Taxes
Trading through the Stock Exchange system attracts an Exchange fee of 0.125% (for the Main and Secondary market stocks) and 0.5% (for Free market stocks). This fee is not charged on OTC trading. Capital gains on the sale of securities held for more than one year are liable to an income tax which ranges between 20% and 47%. Dividends and interest income is taxed at 25%.

Disclosure of financial statements
Companies listed on the Main Market are required to produce an annual report by no later than the end of July, and a semi-annual report by no later than the end of the month following the end of the calendar quarter. Those on the Secondary market must provide a statement of their financial position every six months.

Shareholders' rights
Shareholders have the right to vote in the General Meeting of Shareholders in person or by proxy. For every CZK1000 (approximately US$35) of shares they get one vote, but are limited to no more than 20% of the total vote.

Ownership limits for non-residents

Non-resident investors must get central bank permission to own bank stocks (although they can trade freely in banking GDRs in London); otherwise, there are no limits to foreign ownership. A shareholder (or group of shareholders) are obliged to disclose their position upon acquiring 10% of a company's share capital.

Capital and foreign exchange controls

Investment inflows and repatriation of profits are (less tax) freely permitted.

Takeover bids

In June 1996, new laws obliged acquirers to bid to minority shareholders.

Brokers

There are approximately seventy brokerages operating on the SEP. Commissions are negotiable, but typically range between 0.4% and 1.3%.

Sectors

The three largest sectors, in terms of market capitalization, are power generation, transport and communications, and finance and banking, which have a combined value equivalent to more than half of total capitalization. Although smaller, the refining and distribution of steel, engineering and chemicals sectors also make a significant contribution to capitalization.

GDRs

There are a number of Czech GDRs, namely KB, Ceska Sporitelna (both banks) and CEZ (electricity generation).

Derivatives

There is no market for futures or options in the Czech Republic. However, steps are being taken towards the introduction of a derivatives market in 1997.

■ DEBT

The Ministry of Finance regulates the bond market, which was opened by the Debt Securities Act in 1990.

Increases in foreign capital inflows due to the koruna's strength have led to the expansion of the Czech money markets. The independent Czech National Bank (CNB), established in 1993, conducts open market operations to withdraw excess liquidity from the system, but government indebtedness to the banks is low, and this precludes significant buy-sell transactions. Therefore the CNB is forced to issue short-term securities to sterilize these inflationary flows.

Hence, the increasing importance of money-market instruments for monetary policy. CNB pressure on commercial banks to manage their liquidity has meant short-term instruments – inter-bank deposits, bills and repos – have developed quite rapidly.

Public debt
SPP treasury bills (Statni Pokladnicni Poukazky)
Ministry of Finance T-bills have 1-,3-,6- and 12-month maturities, and are sold by the CNB in multiple-price US treasury-style auctions. One-month bills are auctioned every other Thursday and settled the next day, and 3-month bills are sold each month, usually on a Wednesday for 2-day settlement. Bills for 14 days, 4 and 9 months are also sometimes issued. SPPs trade OTC in bearer form for same day (negotiable) settlement. Yields are calculated on an actual/365 day basis.

Overseas investors can buy MOFs if they open an account with the CNB.

PP CNBs (Pokladnicni Poukazky Ceske Narodni Banky)
Czech National Bank liquidity bills are issued to absorb excess liquidity caused by foreign capital inflows. They are issued by Dutch auction and can only be bought by domestic banks.

FNMs
National Property Fund Bills have 6-month maturities, and were originally issued to cover shortfalls in privatization receipts. They trade OTC, but are illiquid. Overseas investors can buy FNMs if they open an account with the NCB.

Bills and other money-market securities with maturities of less than one year settle and clear in book-entry form through Sysdem Evidence a Vyborani (SEV) operated by the CNB.

Bonds
Foreign investors hold approximately 20% of the bond market – predominantly corporate and bank issues. Older government and municipal bonds are illiquid, and because of punitive tax treatment are less attractive to foreign investors than bank and corporate issues.

New state issues are free of tax. Trading takes place on the Prague Stock Exchange and OTC at the Central Securities Registry.

Government bonds
The CNB organizes US treasury-style auctions for short- and medium-term notes in the first week of the second month. Only domestic financial institutions can participate. A MOF-authorized bank administers each issue. Participants must bid for at least Kc50 million, but no more than 35% of the total issue size. Non-competitive bids are limited to Kc50 million. Secondary market trades settle between two and seven days later, and yields are calculated on a 30/360 day basis.

Municipal bonds
Bonds have been issued by Pilzen, Smrzovka and Liberec and other cities.

Private debt
BEs
Bills of Exchange are issued by banks and corporates, placed privately and trade in the OTC market.

Corporate bonds
Most are privately placed, although some are now listed on the Prague Stock Exchange. Issues include CEZ and Chemapol and SPT Telecom.

Bank bonds
Most are syndicated by the issuer among other banks. Issuers include the Komercni Bank and Investicni Postovni Bank.

Eurobonds
Eurobond issues denominated in US dollars, yen and deutschmarks, for the CNB, Komercni Bank, Calex, Radegast, the City of Prague and CEZ (electricity company) have been well received in the market at tight spreads. In addition, Czech borrowers have issued koruna eurobonds, which have been placed with European investors.

Eurobond issues (US$m)
Pre-1993 figures refer to Czechoslovakia

	1990	1991	1992	1993	1994	1995	1996
Sovereign	433.5	275.7	—	694.3	—	—	—
Private	—	—	15.0	—	150.0	—	297.0

■ CZECH REPUBLIC: Economic indicators

Population and development	1990	1991	1992	1993	1994	1995	1996e
Population, million	10.36	10.31	10.32	10.33	10.33	10.34	10.34
Population growth, %	-0.10	-0.48	0.12	0.10	0.02	0.03	0.05
Nominal GDP per capita, US$	1956	2358	2754	3065	3493	4566	5067

National accounts							
Nominal GDP, US$bn	20.3	24.3	28.4	31.7	36.1	47.2	52.4
Change in real GDP, %	-1.2	-14.2	-7.1	-1.0	2.6	4.8	4.3
Gross fixed capital formation, % of GDP	23.0	26.1	30.3	28.3	32.3	32.2	33.0

Money supply and inflation							
Narrow money, change %, Dec/Dec	—	—	19.9	12.5	24.3	10.6	10.0
Broad money, change %, Dec/Dec	—	—	23.0	17.2	22.9	20.2	15.5
Consumer price inflation (avg.) %	8.3	61.1	11.2	20.7	9.7	9.1	8.8

Interest rates							
Discount rate, end of year	—	—	—	8.00	8.50	9.50	10.50
Deposit rate, average	—	—	—	7.03	7.07	6.96	6.82
Prime lending rate, monthly average	—	—	—	14.07	13.12	12.80	12.54

Government finance							
Government expenditure, % of GDP	—	43.7	41.4	36.2	35.0	36.2	36.3
Government balance, % of GDP	—	2.7	2.7	0.0	1.1	0.6	-0.1

Exchange rates lc=local currency							
Exchange rate, annual average, lc/US$	28.00	29.48	28.26	29.15	28.78	26.50	27.13
Exchange rate, end of year, lc/US$	18.27	28.55	28.59	30.00	28.20	26.60	27.23
Real exchange rate 1990=100	—	100.0	106.7	130.5	141.0	147.7	156.9

Balance of payments							
Exports of goods & services, US$m	—	—	8448	12997.20	14016	21463	20000
Change %	—	—	—	53.84	7.84	53.12	-6.81
Imports of goods & services, US$m, fob	—	—	10350	13309	14905	25140	25000
Change %	—	—	—	28.59	11.99	68.67	-0.56
Trade balance, of goods only, US$m, fob-fob	-252	340	-1902	-312	-889	-3678	-5000
Current account balance, US$m	-338	1143	-305	115	-49.7	-1362	-4200
as a % of GDP	-1.67	4.70	-1.07	0.36	-0.14	-2.89	-8.02

Foreign exchange reserves							
Foreign exchange reserves, US$m	732	2127	755	3790	6145	13900	124000
Gold at ⅔ of market price, US$m	426.2	448.4	508.4	467.2	511.8	509.5	512.3
Import cover (reserves/imports), months	—	—	0.7	2.7	3.9	5.6	4.4

Foreign debt and debt service							
Short-term debt, US$m	1155	799	901	1040	1207	1187	1200
Total foreign debt, US$m	5390	6743	7082	8496	11252	15000	18000
as a % of GDP	26.6	27.7	24.9	26.8	31.2	31.8	34.4
as a % of foreign exchange receipts	—	—	57.7	47.7	56.8	50.1	62.1
Interest payments, US$m	506	396	520	646	799	1256	1300
Principal repayments, US$m	550	733	908	841	2234	2014	3631
Total debt service, US$m	1056	1129	1428	1487	3033	3270	4931
as a % of goods exports	22.6	19.4	16.9	11.4	21.6	15.2	24.7
as a % of foreign exchange receipts	—	—	11.6	8.4	15.3	10.9	17.0

Ecuador

Area (thousands of km²):	284
Population (1995, millions):	11.5
Population projection (2025, millions):	18
Population younger than 15 yrs (1991, % of total):	38.9
Urbanization rate (1993, % of population):	57
Life expectancy (1993, years at birth):	69
Gross domestic product (1996, US$bn):	18.5
GDP per capita (1996, US$):	1583
Average annual GDP growth rate (1990-96, %):	3.1
Average annual inflation rate (1990-96, %):	38.8
Currency (sucre per US$, average 1996):	3140.7
Real exchange rate: (1990=100, average 1996)	124.8
Structure of production (1994):	51.9% services, 21.1% industry, 11.9% agriculture, 10.5% petroleum and mining, 4.6% construction
Main exports:	petroleum and derivatives, bananas, shrimp, coffee
Main imports:	inputs for industry, transport equipment, non-durable consumer goods
Main trading partners:	US, Colombia, Japan, Germany, Brazil, Mexico
Total foreign debt (% of GDP):	78.8
Next elections due under normal circumstances:	legislative May 1998; presidential May 2000

FORECAST: 1997-2000 (average)

	Worst case	Most likely	Best case
Real GDP growth (%)	1.5	3	4
Inflation (%)	28	22	18

■ POLITICS

Historical overview

The conquest of the Incas began in 1534 and marked the beginning of centuries of Spanish rule in Ecuador. During this time, the region remained a peaceful colony where agriculture flourished. Towards the end of the 18th century, however, discontent and disillusionment with Spanish domination led to a number of rebellions, which resulted in victory for the indigenous population in 1822. Ecuador was subsequently attached to the Republic of Greater Colombia. The collapse of this republic in the late 1820s paved the way for Ecuadorian independence. Despite several attempts to implement democracy and develop the region, rivalry between the liberals from Guayaquil and Quito's conservatives resulted in political division and turmoil for more than a century. In fact, from independence in 1830 until 1979, only seventeen of some ninety presidents remained in office for their full term. The constitution was changed no fewer than eighteen times and the military took power on several occasions. This political turmoil was accompanied by economic difficulties resulting partly from the collapse of the cocoa market in the 1920s and partly the Great Depression of the 1930s.

In 1972, the military took power for the last time. The discovery and exploitation of petroleum in the Orient jungle provided the revenues needed to implement profound economic reforms and led to a period of unprecedented prosperity. The armed forces returned the country to civilian rule at the end of the 1970s. Further liberalization of the economy came in 1984, when León Febres Cordero from the centre-right Partido Social Cristiano (PSC) became president. His reforms, which broke from the traditional interventionist policies of the previous military regimes, led to constant political turmoil and the victory of the centre-left Izquierda Democrática (ID) in the 1988 congressional and presidential elections. However, the new administration of Rodrigo Borja saw its popularity wane as the economy contracted sharply; the ID lost its congressional majority by 1990.

Recent events

In July 1992, Sixto Durán Ballén, from the centre-right Partido Unión Republicana (PUR), won the presidential election. But his party did not receive a majority in Congress, despite the President's coalition with the Partido Conservador (PC). Due to this weakness, the opposition controlled all legislative committees, government proposals were frequently rejected and several ministers were impeached. This political constellation frequently resulted in deadlock, paralyzing the political system and thereby hindering further economic reforms.

The border dispute that has existed between Ecuador and Peru since the early 1940s led to an armed conflict again in January 1995. The war resulted in dozens of dead and wounded and negatively affected Ecuador's economy. Despite a cease-fire agreed in March, Ecuador still claims sovereignty over the disputed territory.

During the 1996 presidential elections, Abdalá Bucaram Ortiz, from the populist Partido Roldosista Ecuatoriano (PRE) won the second round with 54% of the vote, against his main rival Jaime Nebot of the Partido Social Cristiano (PSC). Since her inauguration on August 10, 1996 Bucaram has faced increasing public discontent and waning congressional support. This dissatisfaction culminated in Bucaram's removal from office by Congress in February 1997. Congressional President Fabián Alarcón will serve as interim president until August 1998.

Chronology

1534	Beginning of the Spanish conquest
1739	Transfer of Ecuador to the Viceroyalty of Colombia (or Nueva Grenada)
1819	Creation of the Republic of Greater Colombia
1822	Defeat of the Spanish
1822	Ecuador is incorporated into the Republic of Greater Colombia
1830	Ecuador gains independence
1895	Revolution

1920s	Collapse of the cocoa market
1930s	Great Depression
1942	Rio Protocol settled the border conflict between Peru and Ecuador
1972	Military government led by General Guillermo Rodríguez Lara
1978	Constitutional referendum
1979	The populist Jaime Roldós Aguilera becomes president
1979	Present constitution comes into force
1981	President Roldós dies and Vice-President Osvaldo Hurtado Larrea is invested as president
1984	Conservative León Febres Cordero wins the presidential elections
1988	Rodrigo Borja Cevallos of the Izquierda Democrática is elected president
1990	The Izquierda Democrática loses its congressional majority
1992	Conservative Sixto Durán Ballén, of the Partido Unión Republicano, wins the presidency
1995	Border conflict with Peru breaks out again
1996	Jaime Nebot Saadi of the Partido Social Cristiano is defeated by the populist Abdalá Bucaram Ortiz of the Partido Roldosista Ecuatoriano during the presidential election
1997	Bucaram ousted by Congress after six months in office. Fabián Alarcón appointed as interim president.

Constitution and government

The constitution of the Republic of Ecuador was adopted in 1979 and established a unicameral system. The Chamber of Representatives (Congress) consists of twelve members nationally elected for a period of four years and seventy members chosen on a provincial basis for a two-year term. The president, who is elected by universal suffrage for a nonrenewable four-year term, holds considerable executive authority since the constitution provides him with veto power. He also appoints and leads the Council of Ministers. The federal judiciary is elected by Congress for four-year terms from lists of candidates submitted by the head of state.

Main political parties

Izquierda Democrática (ID)
> Centre-left
> Founded in 1970
> led by andrés vallejo arcos and rodrigo borja cevallos

Partido Social Cristiano (PSC)
> Centre-right
> Founded in 1951
> Led by Jaime Nebot Saadi

Democracia Popular (DP)
> Centre-left
> Founded in 1978
> Led by Rodrigo Paz

Partido Roldosista Ecuatoriano (PRE)
> Centre-left

Founded in 1984
Led by Abdalá Bucaram Ortiz
Pachakutik-Movimiento Nuevo País (P-MNP)
Left-wing
Founded in 1995
led by luis mADAS

Results of the 1996 elections to Congress
PSC (27 seats), **PRE** (19), **DP** (12), **P-MNP** (8), ID (5), **others** (11)

Next elections
Congress: May 1998; presidential: May 2000

Other political forces
Military
The military traditionally exerts considerable power in Ecuador. The resurgence of the border conflict with Peru in 1995 further reinforced the armed forces' position and prevented cuts in defence spending. The military played an important role in the February 1997 political crisis by insisting on a democratic resolution of the conflict.

Central bank
The Banco Central del Ecuador is not legally independent, but it enjoyed a great degree of autonomy under the direction of Augusto de la Torre during the Durán Ballén presidency. Although de la Torre continues at the helm of the bank, the independence of the institution will be limited under the Bucaram administration.

The central bank's principal objectives are to control inflation and provide incentives to increase national savings, improve financial intermediation and strengthen productive investment. For this purpose, the bank has refined the management of monetary and exchange rate policies through mechanisms such as weekly auctions.

■ ECONOMICS

Historical overview
In the past, Ecuador was highly dependent on its agricultural sector, whose products, mainly bananas, accounted for most of the country's exports. But the discovery of oil in the early 1970s dramatically changed the structure of the economy. In 1973, petroleum exports started to rise, allowing the country to post impressive economic growth. However, the oil boom hid important economic problems, such as the stagnation of the agricultural sector, high tariff barriers and an increasing dependence on petroleum revenues.

Sinking oil prices in the second half of the 1980s, the March 1987 earthquake (which cut Ecuador's oil production and exports for six months) and tight monetary and fiscal policies implemented in 1988–89 to reduce inflation resulted in a dramatic decline in output by the end of the 1980s. Despite the tight monetary policy, inflation reached record levels. Consequently, the government initiated a profound economic transformation by opening its economy and introducing a new tax system, monetary laws and labour reforms. Strong banana, shrimp and mineral exports, combined with the increasing domestic demand induced by substantial public sector wage hikes, led to a modest economic recovery at the beginning of the 1990s. Inflation, however, remained at high levels and the current account deficit increased dramatically.

Ecuador's economic performance

	Average annual real GDP growth, %	Average annual consumer price inflation, %
1961-1965	4.5	4.0
1966-1970	4.4	5.0
1971-1975	11.4	13.5
1976-1980	6.5	11.7
1981-1985	2.1	27.5
1985-1990	2.0	45.7
1991-1995	3.5	39.1

Source: IMF

Recent developments

After 1992, the congressional opposition systematically rejected most of the government's proposals and thus delayed important reforms, such as the privatization of state-controlled companies and a planned restructuring of the judicial system. Nevertheless, the Durán Ballén administration succeeded in implementing tight monetary and fiscal policies. In addition, Ecuador's withdrawal from OPEC in November 1992 allowed the country to increase oil production and exports. Consequently, the economy expanded 4.3% in 1994 while the year-end inflation rate declined from 60.2% in 1992 to 25.4% in 1994.

The political crisis surrounding former Vice-President Alberto Dahik, energy shortages experienced in the latter half of 1995, and poor export performance resulted in a slowdown of economic growth, which reached 2.3% and 1.8% in 1995 and 1996, respectively. In addition, inflation remained at uncomfortably high levels and the budget deficit increased due to the high cost of the border conflict with Peru. In order to address these problems, President Abdalá Bucaram announced an austerity programme and structural reforms that included the implementation of a currency board regime. However, strong opposition to the measures implemented by the president precipitated his fall from power, clouding prospects for economic reform.

The economy

Thanks to its natural beauty (particularly the Galápagos Islands), Ecuador is strongly orientated towards tourism. However, tourism earnings have increased only modestly over the last few years, reducing the industry's share in the services sector. Services in general accounted for nearly 52% of GDP in 1995.

The mining industry (including oil), which is totally controlled by the state, remains an important sector of the Ecuadorian economy. Since the country's withdrawal from OPEC in 1992, oil production has boomed. The mining sector has grown about 30% over the past ten years, and accounted for about one fifth of Ecuador's 1995 GDP.

Share of GDP by sector

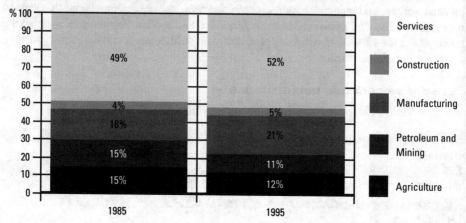

Source: Banco Central del Ecuador

Ecuador's manufacturing base remains small, underdeveloped and overprotected next to that of other Latin American countries. It generated none the less about 21% of GDP in 1995. Manufacturing has grown steadily since the beginning of the decade, due to trade liberalization and the abolition of many business restrictions.

Agriculture, forestry and fishing are also important sectors of the economy, collectively accounting for about 12% of total GDP.

Saving and investment

Domestic investment boomed in the 1970s due to oil revenues. However, the dramatic economic slowdown of the late 1980s resulted in decreasing investment, which has not amounted to more than 22% of GDP since that time.

The gap between domestic saving and domestic investment has been filled by foreign investment. The latter occurred mainly in the oil sector since the 1990s. Liberalization of the economy, combined with new legislation facilitating foreign direct investment and the opening of all sectors (except the media) to foreign capital, attracted foreign investors in the mid-1990s. As a result, foreign investment has more than doubled since the end of the 1980s. However, it remains relatively low, averaging US$490 million a year.

Privatization

In 1993, the government initiated an ambitious privatization programme, which aimed to raise US$10 billion from the sale of 80% of the 167 state-owned companies by mid-1996. However, the plan met severe opposition in Congress and the necessary legal changes were not approved. Thus, privatization proceeds were meagre during the past three years. In 1996, the government managed to sell the airline Ecuatoriana de Aviación and the telecommunication company EMETEL. To avoid more pronounced opposition from Congress, the government omitted oil and gas companies from its privatization programme and promised to use privatization revenues to create a social fund. The opening of these protected sectors to private investment is likely to raise strong opposition.

Trade

Ecuador is highly dependent on foreign trade. Exports account for about 40% of GDP. Fishing and agricultural commodities, such as shrimp, bananas and coffee, provide nearly half of all export proceeds. Petroleum and derivatives follow, representing 32% of exports, while non-traditional exports, such as flowers, chemicals and timber, remain low. In 1995, capital goods and raw materials made up 34.2% and 40.8% of imports, respectively, while 22.5% of Ecuador's total foreign purchases were consumer goods. Fuel and lubricants accounted for the rest of imports.

As a result of the almost complete elimination of trade barriers among the members of the Andean Pact trade group (comprising Bolivia, Colombia, Ecuador, Peru and Venezuela), Ecuador's intra-regional trade has increased significantly during the past four years. The US remains, however, the country's principal trading partner.

Imports and exports US$m

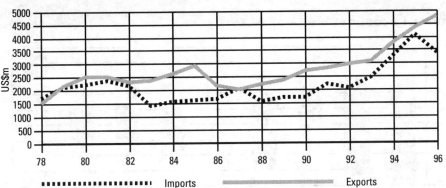

Source: IMF

Breakdown of exports (1995)

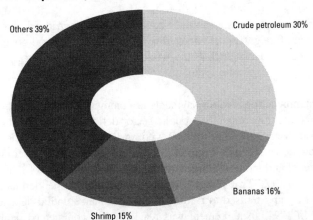

Others 39%
Crude petroleum 30%
Bananas 16%
Shrimp 15%

Source: Banco Central del Ecuador

Balance of payments

Ecuador has traditionally posted trade surpluses, thanks to large petroleum revenues. However, low banana and oil prices, the continued real appreciation of the sucre and the Andean Pact trade association have, in recent years, resulted in a more rapid rise of imports than exports. Thus, Ecuador's trade surpluses shrank from more than US$1 billion in 1990 to US$0.3 billion in 1995. In 1996, the sluggish economy, combined with energy shortages, the war with Peru, and international political strife, led to a sharp fall of imports, while exports stagnated. As a consequence, the trade surplus increased again.

Since 1992, Ecuador's current account shortfall has worsened because of an increase in the services deficit, which has been fuelled by interest payments and the boycott of the Galápagos Islands (Ecuador's leading attraction) by many North American tourist groups to protest against the over-fishing of endangered species. The current account deficit amounted to 4.5% of GDP in 1995. In 1996, however, the improvement in the trade account resulted in a current account surplus.

Current account as a % of GDP

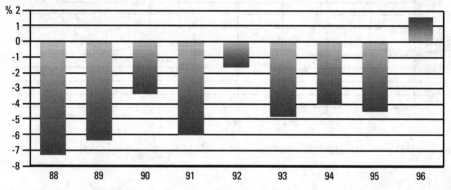

Source: IMF

Ecuador's current account shortfalls have largely been financed by oil-related foreign direct investment, foreign capital attracted by high interest rates on government debt and multilateral official creditors (such as the World Bank and the IDB).

Debt

Ecuador unilaterally suspended all payments to commercial bank creditors in 1987. In the following years, the government cut public sector deficits and restricted credit expansion. Ecuador's efforts were rewarded in 1989 with an IMF stand-by agreement, and debt was rescheduled by the Paris Club's group of official creditors. But the government's inability to comply with fiscal and monetary targets resulted in the suspension of IMF disbursements in 1990 and again in 1992. That year, the country once again suspended its debt servicing to commercial banks and refused to resume interest payments until a debt restructuring deal was secured. In 1994, an agreement was reached with commercial bank creditors for a Brady Plan, Ecuador agreed to a new stand-by facility with the IMF, and the Paris Club rescheduled some of the debt maturing in 1995.

The foreign debt of Ecuador's public and private entities totalled US$14.6 billion, or 78.7% of GDP, in 1996, compared to 112% in 1990. Total debt service amounts to about 10% of the country's GDP and 25% of foreign exchange receipts.

Economic policy
Monetary policy
The fight against inflation is one of the monetary authorities' main goals. For this purpose, the central bank traditionally adopts a tight monetary policy. As a consequence, Ecuador has avoided a period of hyperinflation similar to that in Argentina, Peru or Brazil. Nevertheless, the tight monetary policies and austerity measures regularly launched by various governments (restriction of credit to the public sector and to private business, for example) have been offset by loose fiscal policies and several devaluations. As a result, annual inflation remains well above 20%.

Fiscal policy
Budget surpluses were generated in the second half of the 1980s due to well-conceived fiscal policies, including a reorganization of the tax system, increases in public sector tariffs (such as fuel prices), public investment cuts and a privatization programme. However, fiscal revenues fell sharply in 1991 because of a decline in oil prices and severe losses of several state-owned companies. In addition, a steep rise in external interest payments induced by escalating US interest rates in 1994, the resurgence of the border conflict with Peru in 1995, public-sector wage increases and an easing of policy before the May 1996 elections resulted in a deterioration of the fiscal account, from a surplus of 0.2% of GDP in 1994 to deficits of 1.1% and 3.0 % of GDP in 1995 and 1996 respectively.

Ecuador sucre/US dollar exchange rate

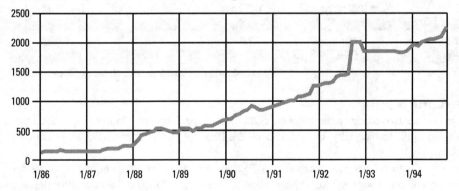

Currency
Ecuador adopted a crawling peg system in December 1994. Since then, the sucre is allowed to float within a band set by the central bank in accordance with an annual inflation target. On August 12, 1996, the central bank adjusted this band by 8% and increased the rate at which the sucre depreciated against the dollar, to 18.5% a year, from 16.5%. As a consequence, Ecuador's currency depreciated both in nominal (-18.9%) and real terms (-1.3%) against the US dollar in 1996.

Banking system

The banking system is regulated by the Superintendency of Banks. Since its deregulation in the first half of the 1990s, the financial sector has grown significantly. Although there are numerous banks and financial institutions, financing costs are excessive and the sector remains underdeveloped.

■ EQUITIES

Index performance (in local currency)

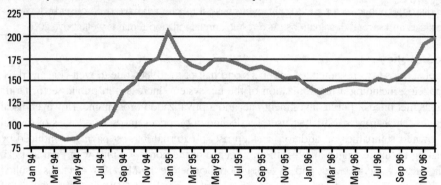

Key indicators

	Index performance %, in US$ terms	Market Cap. US$bn	P/E	Div. Yield
1994	38.8	2.5	11.3	3.6
1995	-31.4	2.6	7.6	5.0
1996	-15.5	1.9	12.2	6.0

Sources: Local stock exchange, IFC, Bloomberg, Datastream, UBS

Structure

Ecuador has two stock markets – one in Quito, the capital, and one in the busy coastal town of Guayaquil. Traditionally, Quito has been the larger of the two but Guayaquil overtook its rival in 1993.

Trading on Guayaquil totalled US$573 million in 1994 (of which equity accounted for US$408 million), taking market capitalization to $2.5 billion. Quito still accounts for the lion's share of government bond and promissory note trading, and had a market capitalization of US$2.01 billion at the end of 1995. Between the two markets, there are 115 companies listed.

Regulatory authority

The Consejo Nacional de Valores (CNV) was set up in 1995 to examine market practices but as of October 1996 it had not gained any concrete powers of regulation.

Trading methods
Trading is by open outcry. However an electronic system has been put in place for transactions between 09.00 and 11.00.

Hours
The market is open from 11.00 to 13.00 on weekdays, although electronic trading is permitted between 09.00 and 11.00.

Settlement time and clearing
Settlement is on a T+2 basis. A centralized clearing system is planned for 1997.

Types of shares
There are two classes of shares, voting and non-voting.

Stock indices
There are three indexes: the Quito Index, based on the eight largest stocks; the Guayaquil Index, following nine stocks; and the Interinvest index, covering the seven largest and most active stocks on the two exchanges.

Taxes
There are no taxes on dividend income or capital gains.

Disclosure of financial statements
Ecuadorian accounts generally conform to accepted principles. However, consolidated statements are rare. The banking companies are required to submit income statements and balance sheets every month, while corporates have to do so every year.

Ownership limits for non-residents
There are no restrictions on foreign investment.

Capital and foreign exchange controls
Investors can convert holdings into hard currencies freely, without taxes, and on the same day.

Brokers
There are eighty registered brokers.

Large companies
The largest companies listed (in descending order) are La Cemento Nacional, Cervecerias Nacionales, Conticorp, La Favorita, Banco del Progreso, Banco Continental, Banco Popular, Banco del Pichincha, Banco del Pacífico, Banco de Guayaquil, Ecuatoriana Aviacíon, Hotel Colón, Cemento Chimborazo, Cemento Selva Alegre, Banco Amazonas, Cerveceria Andina, Banco Previsora, Banco Bolivariano, Aymesa and Banco Tungurahua.

ADRs
A number of Ecuadorian companies have ADR listings, including La Cemento Nacional, Grupo Financiero Conticorp, Banco Previsora and Banco Amazonas.

Market comment
The Interinvest index has been influenced primarily by political events in recent years. The 31% fall in 1995 had less to do with the "Tequila effect" than with fears that the border conflict with Peru might disrupt regional trade.

■ DEBT

In May 1993, the New Capital Markets Law introduced a new regulatory infrastructure for the securities markets. The Consejo Nacional de Valores (CNV) determines the rules that are enforced by the Superintendencia de Companias (SIC) and the Superintendencia de Bancos (SIB) monitors market participants. The Law also provided for the establishment of brokerage firms, created a clearing system and drafted plans for a central depository (DECEVALE – Deposito Centralizado de Valores) and rating agencies.

Public debt
BEMs (Monetary Stabilization Bonds)
BEMs are sucre-denominated discount bills, and are the most heavily traded debt securities in the market. They have maturities of 90, 180 and 360 days, and are sold by the Banco Central del Ecuador (central bank) as agent for the Ministry of Finance on a weekly basis in Dutch auctions. Only financial institutions can participate in the primary market. BEMs are bearer securities.

Bonos de Gobierno (Government Bonds)
Bonos have been issued by the Ministry of Finance since September 1995, primarily to fund infrastructure and social welfare projects. They are sold by the central bank through Dutch auction and are then listed on the exchange. They can be indexed to the CPI, and either US dollar or sucre denominated. They are in bearer form and are tax-free.

In addition, the government issues US dollar denominated bonds, and structures containing imbedded dollar currency options, which are free of tax.

Private debt
Polizas de Acumulacion
These are issued by financial institutions for maturities up to 360 days, in either bearer or registered form.

Aceptaciones ("Avales" – bankers' acceptances) and Pagares a la Orden (promissory notes)
BAs and promissory notes are denominated in sucre (BAs can be in US dollars too), are in registered form and are issued with maturities of up to one year.

Depositos a Plazo

These are denominated in sucre or US dollars, have a flexible interest payment schedule and are issued with maturities of 30, 60, 90, 120, 180 and 360 days. They can be in either bearer or registered form.

Obligaciones (commercial paper)

Commercial paper, issued by private corporations for maturities of 1 to 5 years, are in bearer form and are sold in minimum denominations of 1 million sucres. Bonds trade over the counter (OTC) in the interbank market or on the stock exchanges in Quito, Cuenca and Guayaquil. Arbitrage opportunities sometimes exist because there is no electronic connection between the exchanges. There is no central depository yet, although one is planned. Settlement for trades transacted on the same exchange and OTC is the same day; for bargains that require a transfer of securities between exchanges, settlement is normally 2 days later.

Foreign investment

Non-residents can invest in debt securities without registering with any official body, and can repatriate capital and profits freely.

Eurobonds

Ecuador has not yet issued a plain vanilla sovereign eurobond, although there are plans for a US$200 million 5-year bond in 1997. In September 1996 a special purpose vehicle, guaranteed by the Republic, called The Synthetic Ecuador Bond Company raised DEM150 million for seven years at 637 basis points over German bonds. Two private banks also raised small amounts through dollar euro medium-term notes in 1995.

Eurobond issues (US$m)

	1990	1991	1992	1993	1994	1995	1996
Sovereign	—	—	—	—	—	—	100.0
Private	—	—	—	—	—	26.0	—

Brady bonds

Ecuador issued Brady bonds in February 1995. The bank loans were replaced by discount bonds and par bonds with a 30-year maturity. Ecuador also issued past due interest bonds (PDIs) against interest arrears. Ecuador had made partial and unequal interest payments in the years preceding the Brady agreement and so also had issue interest equalization (IE) bonds, which brought all creditors into line. The par and discount bonds are collateralized with 30-year zero coupons and have a 12-month rolling interest guarantee.

Bond	Coupon	Collateral	Maturity	Currencies
Discount	6mth L+13/16	Principal+Interest	2025	US$
Par	Step up	Principal+Interest	2025	US$
PDI	6 mth L+ 13/16 (early years capitalization option)		2015	US$
IE	6mth L+13/16		2004	US$

■ ECUADOR: Economic indicators

Population and development	1990	1991	1992	1993	1994	1995	1996e
Population, million	10.3	10.5	10.7	11.0	11.2	11.5	11.7
Population growth, %	2.3	2.3	2.3	2.2	2.2	2.1	2.1
Nominal GDP per capita, US$	1041	1119	1178	1303	1480	1595	1583

National accounts							
Nominal GDP, US$bn	10.7	11.8	12.7	14.3	16.6	18.3	18.5
Change in real GDP, %	3.0	5.0	3.6	2.0	4.3	2.3	1.8
Gross fixed capital formation, % of GDP	18.4	19.7	19.5	19.9	18.8	18.6	18.5

Money supply and inflation							
Narrow money, change %, Dec/Dec	52.2	46.5	44.5	49.4	35.7	12.7	15.0
Broad money, change %, Dec/Dec	96.0	58.5	52.2	63.0	51.6	36.8	25.0
Consumer price inflation (avg.) %	48.5	48.7	54.6	45.0	27.3	22.9	24.3

Interest rates *=latest figures							
Deposit rate, annual average	43.55	41.54	46.81	31.97	33.65	43.31	30.00*
Prime lending rate, annual average	37.50	46.67	60.17	47.83	43.99	55.67	46.60*

Government finance							
Government balance, % of GDP	-0.3	-1.0	-1.7	-0.4	0.2	-1.1	-3.0

Exchange rates lc=local currency							
Exchange rate, annual average, lc/US$	768	1046	1534	1919	2197	2517	3141
Exchange rate, end of year, lc/US$	878	1271	1844	2044	2269	2889	3562
Real exchange rate 1990=100	100.0	103.4	105.5	121.4	129.5	126.2	124.8

Balance of payments							
Exports of goods & services, US$m	3253	3408	3631	3716	4589	5216	5700
Change %	13.3	4.8	6.5	2.3	23.5	13.7	9.3
Imports of goods & services, US$m, fob	2373	2925	2831	3273	4204	5078	4400
Change %	1.8	23.3	-3.2	15.6	28.4	20.8	-13.4
Trade balance, of goods only, US$m, fob-fob	1003	644	925	588	562	267	1400
Current account balance, US$m	-366	-707	-215	-682	-680	-823	300
as a % of GDP	-3.4	-6.0	-1.7	-4.8	-4.1	-4.5	1.6

Foreign exchange reserves							
Foreign exchange reserves, US$m	838.5	924.0	868.2	1379.9	1844.2	1627.6	1700.0
Gold at ⅔ of market price, US$m	113.9	106.9	101.3	99.2	105.9	105.9	106.9
Import cover (reserves/imports), months	4.2	3.8	3.7	5.1	5.3	3.8	4.6

Foreign debt and debt service							
Short-term debt, US$m	297	254	301	286	261	428	800
Total foreign debt, US$m	12030	12651	12660	13220	14024	13906	14600
as a % of GDP	112.6	107.6	100.0	92.4	84.5	76.1	78.8
as a % of foreign exchange receipts	354.2	355.3	333.7	340.1	291.9	250.6	242.5
Interest payments, US$m	1108	1017	846	804	872	831	912
Principal repayments, US$m	775	796	893	690	1395	2070	600
Total debt service, US$m	1883	1813	1739	1494	2267	2901	1512
as a % of goods exports	69.4	63.6	57.8	48.8	59.0	66.5	31.5
as a % of foreign exchange receipts	55.4	50.9	45.8	38.4	47.2	52.3	25.1

Egypt

Area (thousands of km²):	1001
Population (1995, millions):	59
Population projection (2025, millions):	86
Population younger than 15 yrs (1991, % of total):	39.1
Urbanization rate (1993, % of population):	44
Life expectancy (1993, years at birth):	64
Gross domestic product (1996, US$bn):	67.5
GDP per capita (1996, US$):	1123
Average annual GDP growth rate (1990-96, %):	3.8
Average annual inflation rate (1990-96, %):	12.2
Currency (pound per US$, average 1996):	3.39
Structure of production (1994):	17% agriculture, 21.9% industry, 61.1% services
Main exports:	cereals, chemicals, machinery, transport equipment, manufactures
Main imports:	machinery & transport equipment, livestock, chemical industries
Main trading partners:	US, Germany, France, Italy
Market capitalization of Stock Exchange (October 1996; US$bn):	10.9
Total foreign debt (% of GDP):	28.6
Next elections due under normal circumstances:	presidential 1999
Credit rating: (Nov 1996, Standard & Poor's, Moody's)	BBB-; Ba2

FORECAST: 1997-2000 (average)

	Worst case	Most likely	Best case
Real GDP growth (%)	3.0	4.5	5.0
Inflation (%)	9.0	5.2	4.0

■ POLITICS

Historical overview

Egypt was a province of Turkey's Ottoman Empire from the 16th century, until it was occupied by British forces in 1882. From 1882 to 1922, British officials controlled Egyptian administration, although the country remained an Ottoman province in name until 1914. Egypt was granted independence on February 28, 1922, although British forces continued their occupation. After the Second World War, British forces withdrew from Egypt, although they maintained a military presence in the Suez Canal zone. The proclamation of the State of

Israel in 1948 met with opposition from the Arab armies, but a cease-fire was agreed in 1949, leaving Egyptian forces occupying the Gaza Strip.

In October 1956 Egypt and the United Kingdom signed an agreement providing for the withdrawal of all British forces from the Suez Canal, but as a result the US and British governments withdrew their offers of financial assistance for Egypt's construction of the Aswan High Dam. The same year the newly elected president, Gamal Abdel Nasser, responded with the announcement of the nationalization of the Suez Canal Company, so that revenue from canal tolls could finance the dam's construction. The takeover of the canal caused concern in Israel, Britain and France. Israel invaded the Sinai Peninsula on October 29, and two days later, Britain and France launched military operations against Egypt. On November 6, the UN and the US arranged a cease-fire, and the withdrawal of the foreign forces from Egypt.

President Nasser died suddenly in September 1970. He had enjoyed enormous prestige throughout the Arab world and was recognized internationally for being the founder of modern Egypt. He was succeeded by Colonel Anwar El Sadat.

President Sadat came to rely increasingly on US aid, and relations with the US became closer. In 1973 Egyptian troops crossed the Suez Canal to recover territory lost in 1967. In 1974 and 1975 Dr Henry Kissinger, the US Secretary of State, negotiated a truce. Israel evacuated territory in Sinai, and Israeli and Egyptian forces were separated by a buffer zone under the control of UN forces.

In September 1978, after talks at Camp David in the US, President Sadat and Menachem Begin, Prime Minister of Israel, signed the Camp David Agreement. Israel made phased withdrawals from the Sinai Peninsula, the last of which took place in April 1982.

Political parties, which had been banned since 1953, were allowed to participate in the 1976 elections of the People's Assembly. In 1978 Sadat formed the National Democratic Party (NDP), with himself as leader.

At a summit of Arab leaders in Jordan in 1987, Syria's Hafiz Assad proposed to re-admit Egypt to the League of Arab States. However, the conference approved a resolution placing the establishment of diplomatic links with Egypt at the discretion of member governments. In May 1989 Egypt was re-admitted to the League, despite Libya's opposition.

Chronology

1922	End of the British protectorate. Egypt is recognized as an independent and sovereign state on February 28.
1948	The State of Israel is declared
1948	Egypt and other Arab League countries declare intentions of military intervention
1956	June 19: the last British soldiers leave Egypt
1956	Nasser is elected president
1956	The Suez Canal Company is nationalized
1957	The Suez Canal is reopened in April
1967	Nasser orders the closing of the straits of Tiran, thus cutting off Israeli shipping to the port of Eilat. The Israelis move into the Sinai, occupy the whole of Sinai and reach the east bank of the Suez Canal.
1970	September 28: Nasser dies

1970	October 15: Anwar El Sadat is elected as new president
1970	The Muslim Brotherhood is tolerated again by the government
1973	October: Egypt unsuccessfully invades Israeli-occupied Sinai
1973	The restrictions on foreign investment and exchange control are lifted and the "open door" policy allows greater involvement in Egyptian business by Western companies.
1978	A peace treaty is signed with Israel (Camp David Agreement). Egypt is isolated from the Arab countries.
1981	October 6: President Anwar El Sadat is assassinated by a group of religious dissidents. Muhammad Hosni Mubarak becomes the new president.
1991	The government sends 35,000 soldiers to the Gulf to fight with the Allies against Iraq. Egypt again becomes a major political power in the region.

Constitution and government

The president, who must be of Egyptian parentage and over forty years old, is nominated by at least one-third of the members of the People's Assembly, approved by at least two thirds, and elected by popular referendum. His term is for six years and he may be re-elected for another subsequent term. (President Mubarak was elected for a third term.) He has the possibility to take emergency measures, but these must be approved by referendum within sixty days.

The president appoints one or more vice-presidents, a prime minister and a council of ministers. He has the right to dissolve the Assembly prematurely, but his action must be approved by a referendum and elections must be held within sixty days. He may also dismiss the vice-presidents and ministers. The president has the right to refer important matters to the people.

The government is described as "the supreme executive and administrative organ of the state". Its members, whether full ministers or deputy ministers, must be over thirty-five years old. Further sections define the roles of local government, specialized national councils, the judiciary, the higher constitutional court, the armed forces, the national defence council and the police.

The unicameral Majlis ash-Sha'ab, or People's Assembly, elected for five years, is the legislative body. It approves general policy, the budget and the development plan, and also nominates the president. It must have 350 or more elected members, at least half of whom must be workers or farmers. The Assembly may pass a vote of no confidence in a deputy prime minister, a minister or a deputy minister, provided three days' notice of the vote is given, and the minister must then resign. In the case of the prime minister, the Assembly may prescribe his responsibility and submit a report. The matter is put to a referendum if the Assembly persists. Public support for the president results in the dissolution of the Assembly, support for the Assembly means that the president must accept the resignation of the government. The People's Assembly currently has 454 members: 10 nominated by the president and 444 directly elected from 222 constituencies.

In 1993 President Mubarak was nominated for a third term of office. His nomination was approved by some 94.9% of the valid votes cast in a national referendum. The government's claim that 84% of the electorate had participated in the referendum was regarded with scepticism by many. Parliamentary elections were held in November 1995; the next presidential election will be in 1999.

Current government
President   Muhammad Hosni Mubarak

Council of Ministers
Prime Minister   Kamal Ahmad AL-Ganzouri
Deputy Prime Minister
(and Minister of Agriculture, Livestock,
Fisheries and Land Reclamation)   Dr Yousuf Amin Wali
Minister of Defence   Field-Marshal Muhammad Hussain Tantawi
Minister of Foreign Affairs   Amr Muhammad Moussa
Minister of Supply and Internal Trade   Ahmed Gueily
Minister of Finance   Mohieddin El-Gharib
Minister of the Interior   Hussain Muhammad Al-Alfi
Minister of Economy and
International Co-operation   Nawal Et-Tatawi
Minister of the Public Sector
(and Minister of State for Administrative
Development and for the Environment)   Dr Atif Muhammad Obeid
Minister of State for Economic Affairs   Dr Youssef Boutros Ghali

Political parties

Article Five of the constitution describes the political system as multiparty. There are four main parties: the ruling National Democratic Party, the Socialist Workers (the official oppos-ition), the Liberal Socialists and the Unionists' Progressive. (The legality of the reformed New Wafd Party was established by the courts in January 1984.) The formation of any political party must be approved by the government. It tolerates limited political activity by the tech-nically illegal Muslim Brotherhood. Trade unions and professional associations are officially sanctioned. The constitution forbids sectarian-based parties, and this has encouraged the Muslim Brotherhood to ally itself with the Socialist Labour Party. In April 1984 President Mubarak promised the first "free, honest and sincere" elections in Egypt in more than thirty years. He allowed the re-emergence of the original Wafd Party, perhaps the only opposition party with the prospect of wide popular support. In April 1990, three new political parties, the Green Party, the Democratic Unionist Party (DUP) and the Young Egypt Party (YEP), were legalized, bringing the total number of officially recognized political parties in Egypt to ten:

Government party:
National Democratic Party (NDP)
> Established in 1978 by President Anwar El Sadat
> Has absorbed the Arab Socialist Party
> Led by President Hosni Mubarak

Opposition:
New Wafd Party (NWP)
> Original Wafd Party founded in 1919
> Disbanded in June 1978, it was reformed in August 1983. In its present form, the New

Wafd Party is more heterogeneous than before, comprising Coptics, Nasserites, Muslim Fundamentalists, former army officers and socialist and liberal businessmen.
Led by Fouad Sreat Ed-din

Socialist Labour Party
Founded in September 1978, it is considered the official opposition party.
Led by Ibrahim Shukri

Ikhwan (Brotherhood)
Officially illegal, the (Muslim) Brotherhood advocates the adoption of the Shari'a or Islamic law, as the sole basis of the Egyptian legal system.
Sec-Gen.: Maamoun Al-Hodaiby

Other opposition parties:
National Progressive Unionist Grouping, or Tagammu (NPUG), Socialist Liberal Party (SLP), Democratic Unionist Party (DUP), Umma (National) Party, Misr Al Fath Party (Young Egypt Party) and the Green Party

Military
The military is the basis of power. It takes advantage of several economic and social privileges, but does not interfere in day-to-day politics.

The armed forces number 440,000 on active duty and 254,000 reserves. There is a selective three-year period of national service. Defence expenditure for 1995-96 was budgeted at US$2.96 billion (about 4.7% of GDP).

The first of three five-year military modernization plans was launched in 1983. The aim has been to replace the Soviet-dominated inventory with Western, primarily US, equipment by 2005. In 1994, 45% of Egypt's tanks, 40% of its combat aircraft and 505 of its ships were still of Eastern-bloc origin.

Central bank
Egypt's central bank controls the banking system and directs monetary, credit and general banking policies through the usual means of discount and interest rates, liquidity and reserve ratios.

Central bank policy is highly restrictive for new Egyptian entrants into banking. The central bank had expected a new banking law adopted in 1995 to streamline the sector and promote mergers because of its higher capital requirements for local banks, EGP50 million (US$14.7 million), but most banks chose to raise the additional capital and the country still remains overbanked.

Due to successful negotiations with the IMF beginning with a stand-by credit line in 1991, Egypt's external position has improved. The last US$4 billion of debt relief expected from the agreement was held up by the IMF's refusal to approve Egypt's reform programme, originally scheduled for June 1994. It was finally approved in October 1996, along with a new stand-by credit line.

Both the World Bank and the IMF believed the currency was overvalued, and that the effectively fixed exchange rate was harmful to exports and encouraged imports. At one point, the IMF made devaluation a core requirement for further borrowings under its

Extended Fund Facility. The central bank argued that the majority of the country's foreign exchange earnings came from tourism, Suez Canal revenues, workers' remittances and oil sales. These were denominated in US dollars and unaffected by local exchange rate movements. Devaluation would therefore have little effect on foreign earnings, but would push up the cost of imports, especially capital goods. It would also raise the cost of food subsidies, impacting directly on the budget. At the end of 1995, the IMF backed down on the point.

■ ECONOMICS

Historical overview

Egypt's public sector was built up by Nasser. He brought banking, insurance, transport, major trading operations, mining, and even agriculture under the overall control of the state. Anwar El Sadat attempted to reduce state control through his "open door" policy, which encouraged foreign and domestic private investment. This was followed by an improvement in economic performance as real GDP rose by an average of over 9% per year from 1974 to 1981. Four main sources financed the government's rapid expansion during this period: oil exports, Suez Canal tolls, tourism receipts and workers' remittances. However all of them are heavily dependent on external factors.

When Hosni Mubarak became president in 1981 he inherited chronic economic problems. The government attempted to cover its commitments to the welfare state, despite insufficient resources, by borrowing. This led to rising inflation, foreign exchange shortages, balance-of-payments deficits, declining growth, and a massive foreign debt. By the end of 1987 Egypt was the most indebted country in the Middle East and foreign debt had grown to over US$51.3 billion.

In May 1991 Egypt and the IMF agreed to a three-year stand-by accord, which was followed by a US$300 million structural adjustment loan (SAL) from the World Bank. A Paris Club agreement covering half its debt, at the time estimated to be US$27–28 billion of official and government-guaranteed civilian and military debt, was also achieved in 1991. The agreement linked debt relief to progress on economic reform.

These measures improved macroeconomic performance. Tight fiscal and monetary policies substantially reduced the budget deficit and lowered inflation. The balance of payments moved into surplus. Prices were freed except on sensitive goods such as edible oil, rationed sugar, and drugs. And the banking sector and capital markets were liberalized and invigorated. A framework was developed for public-sector reform and privatization and for liberalization of trade and investment policies, although actual progress in these areas was slight. Egypt completed its IMF and World Bank programmes in March 1993 and a new three-year IMF Extended Fund Facility (EFF), concentrating on structural reforms, was approved by the IMF in September 1993.

In June 1994 economic reform was hindered by a major disagreement between the government and the IMF. The IMF insisted on a 20-30% devaluation of the Egyptian pound to encourage investment and improve export competitiveness. The government feared that a devaluation would erode confidence in the currency and threaten capital repatriation. It strongly – and correctly – denied that any devaluation would take place. Egypt also moved only gradually towards a market-orientated economy, remaining reluctant to sell off its huge, inefficient and non-competitive public-sector industries until 1996, when a large wave of privatizations began.

Today privatization is seen in Egypt primarily as a means of mobilizing domestic savings for investment rather than altering the nature of the state sector. This approach, which has successfully drawn funds into the stock market, is unlikely to be changed because of fears that the privatization process will lead to large-scale redundancies. The balancing act of cutting subsidies without increasing the speed of privatization has been difficult. By the middle of 1995 four state-owned companies had been sold outright, while shares in 1,749 local government projects had been sold to the private sector. However, assuming the authorities carry out their revised plans for 1995-96, the public sector could be left with about 134 marginally profitable enterprises and 114 loss-making enterprises. They are seeking strategic partners to assist with the restructuring of these enterprises.

The economy

In 1995 agriculture contributed 17% of GDP, industry 21.9% and services 61.1%.

Share of GDP by sector

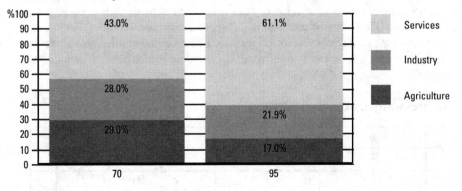

Source: Official data

Egypt's principal exports in 1995 were petroleum and petroleum products, cotton and cotton textiles, and food and live animals. The principal imports were cereals, chemicals, machinery and transport equipment, and basic manufactures.

Egypt has had chronic trade deficits because of its inability to boost productivity and output in its traditional goods export industries, especially cotton, cotton textiles, oil and refined products, and because of a lack of dynamism in non-traditional export sectors. A surge in imports since 1993 has reflected faster economic growth and also growing demand for capital equipment.

Breakdown of exports (1995)

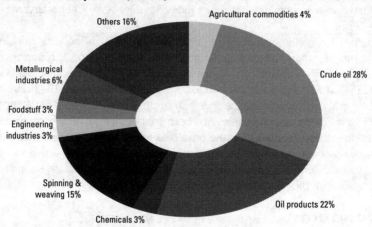

Source: Official data

The current account improved substantially in the early 1990s, with relatively large surpluses arising from stronger exports of both goods and services and, from 1990 to 1993, falling imports. Current account surpluses essentially disappeared after 1993, as growth accelerated. Egypt's main source of current account receipts, besides goods exports, are tourism, Suez Canal fees and transfer receipts, including remittances of Egyptian workers abroad.

The growing trade gap (US$bn)

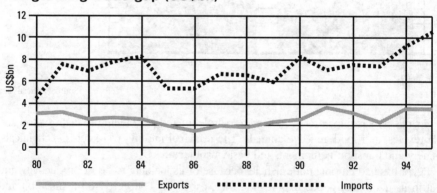

Source: Official data

Current account surpluses

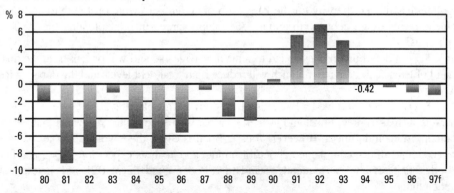

Source: Official data

Debt

In the early 1980s Egypt had a large public sector deficit financed by increasing oil exports. A widening trade deficit was funded by rising tourism revenue and workers' remittances. Foreign borrowing rose to such an extent that external debt reached over US$50 billion in 1987-88, equivalent to about 185% of GDP in 1988. Because of Egypt's membership of the anti-Iraq coalition in the 1990-91 conflict, however, more than US$13 billion in debt was immediately written off. A Paris Club deal, including a phased US$10 billion debt reduction agreement, also was signed in 1991. Egypt's total foreign debt fell to US$28.6 billion (42.7% of GDP) and debt service declined to 11.6% of foreign exchange receipts by the end of 1996.

Egypt reduced its short-term debt from 18% of total external debt in 1989 to 10.3% in 1996. This is a substantial achievement. As a result of the debt cancellation and the economic policies associated with it, Egypt's overall economic performance has improved dramatically.

Decreasing debt and inflation

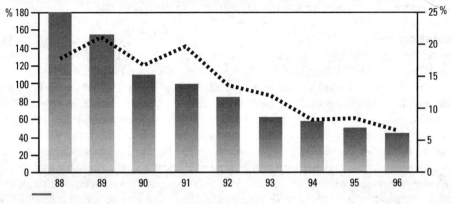

Source: Official data

In October 1996 the government signed a 24-month stand-by credit agreement with the IMF that cleared the way for the Paris Club of creditors to write off the third and final tranche of sovereign debt worth about US$4 billion agreed in principle after the 1990-91 Gulf crisis.

Egypt's debt burden is expected to remain manageable and will benefit from the final round of Paris Club debt relief, which will reduce both total debt levels and the debt-service burden.

Egypt recently received a Ba2 rating by Moody's. This places it above other emerging markets such as Turkey, Brazil and Jordan, on a par with Mexico and Venezuela, but below Bahrain, Israel and Tunisia. However, Youssef Boutros Ghali, the Egyptian minister of state for economic affairs, complained about this rating, and analysts expect it to be raised after Moody's first review. Subsequently, Standard & Poor's rated Egypt BBB-, an investment grade rating.

Economic policy
Government role
With the help of the IMF and the World Bank, the government has begun to reform Egypt's predominantly state-controlled economy. After a slow start the privatization programme began to pick up speed during 1996, with the sale of majority stakes in state companies for the first time.

Monetary policy
After a series of devaluations in 1990-91, the government established a single, unified exchange rate. The Egyptian pound has remained stable since then and the IMF is now no longer arguing for a depreciation.

The government is expected to maintain a tight monetary policy, allowing interest rates to trend down with inflation. This will help stimulate domestic and foreign investment. The government will also be keen, however, to limit the fall in rates to safeguard portfolio capital inflows. Thus it will maintain a positive interest differential between Egyptian pound and US dollar rates, although the size of this differential may be allowed to decline. In addition, the government intends to keep official foreign exchange reserves high, currently at above ten-month import cover, to provide confidence in the pound.

Fiscal policy
The budget deficit, which persistently ran at over 5% of GDP until 1991 and averaged more than 10% in 1982-86, is estimated to have fallen below 1.5% since 1994/95.

The government will continue to pursue a tight fiscal policy and will aim to keep the budget deficit down to about 2% of GDP or less. However, certain difficulties lie ahead. In particular, cuts in tariff rates, agreed with the IMF, will reduce revenues, and due to the continuation of subsidies, higher food import costs will have to be borne by the government. Since no new taxes are planned, revenue increases to offset such costs will have to come from elsewhere. Some gains are expected from more efficient tax collections, but more especially the government will be looking to use the proceeds from privatizations to finance the budget. Although such funds have also been earmarked to clear state companies' liabilities as a precursor to privatization, it is expected that finance for the budget will receive priority.

Consequently, although the budget is expected to come under pressure, the deficit-to-GDP ratio is expected to be contained.

Recent reforms

In 1990 the principle of economic reform was first established and real steps were taken to liberalize prices, abolish subsidies and controls on foreign exchange and capital, and move towards liberalized interest rates. Under the extended arrangement with the IMF, the government arranged to sell 25% of the assets of public sector companies between 1993 and 1996.

The IMF launched the third phase of Egypt's economic liberalization and structural adjustment programme. The programme involved trade liberalization, deregulation, strengthening and deepening of the financial system and the modernization of the fiscal system. In October 1996, to fulfil some terms of the previous agreement, the government removed the final barrier to the IMF's review of the agreement and the passage of a new two-year stand-by agreement by implementing across-the-board tariff cuts of up to 25%. The maximum tariff on goods other than luxuries was reduced from 70% to 55%. It is hoped that this and other earlier agreed actions will increase Egypt's rate of investment to between 23% and 25% of GDP from its current rate of 17%, and raise the growth rate to between 7% and 8%. The second strand of the new IMF agreement tackles Egypt's bloated public sector and attempts to streamline its bureaucracy.

Foreign exchange rate

The liberalization of the foreign exchange system in February 1991, coupled with the establishment of the primary and free foreign exchange markets, was a strong impetus to the external transactions sector. There has been an increasing inflow of foreign exchange as well as a general move to savings in local currency instead of foreign currencies.

Since Cairo convinced the IMF that no devaluation of the exchange rate was needed, the exchange rate is expected to hold at close to EGP3.39:US$1 in 1997-98. Foreign exchange reserves are currently able to provide over ten-month import cover, and the government intends to try and maintain such a level of cover to secure confidence in the exchange rate. Currently there is no market pressure for depreciation.

Banking system

The privatization programme also includes the banking sector. Compared with the privatization of industry, mass dismissals are not expected. However, the four big public-sector banks (65% of the assets of all banks) will not be privatized. These four banks have little chance attracting investors because of their large holdings of low-yielding and non-performing debts of the state and state companies, together with their large bureaucracy.

According to the latest IMF agreement the four public-sector banks are expected to abandon their twenty-four participations in joint ventures held with foreign institutions. This began in 1996 with the sale of shares in several of the joint ventures by the Egyptian banking partners.

■ EQUITIES

Index performance (in local currency)

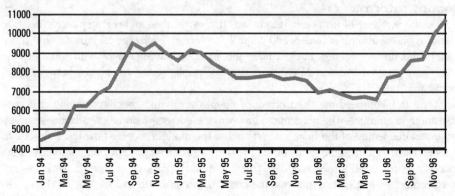

Key indicators

	Index performance %, in US$ terms	Market Cap. US$ bn	P/E	Div. Yield
1994	167.2	4.3	—	—
1996	-10.6	8.1	—	—
1996	38.8	14.2	11.3	4.9

Sources: Local stock exchange, IFC, Bloomberg, Datastream, UBS

Structure

Set up in 1883, the Cairo Stock Exchange was the busiest in Africa until the nationalization programme of the early 1960s. In 1994, it was unified with the Alexandra Exchange into one electronically linked market. At the end of 1995, there were 746 companies listed, bringing the market's capitalization to EGP27.42 billion (US$8.1 billion). Turnover rose sharply during 1995 to 72.2 million shares, worth a total of EGP3.84 billion (US$1.1 billion).

Regulatory authority

The Capital Market Authority (CMA) is responsible for implementing the Capital Markets Law which was introduced in 1994.

Trading methods

Trading is fully automated via a computer-based screen trading system. The two exchanges are linked electronically on a real time basis.

Hours

11.00 to 15.00, Sunday to Thursday.

Settlement time and clearing
Clearance and settlement procedures are all computerized, although settlement is on a cash basis within two days after a deal is struck. A central depository system was introduced in 1996.

Types of shares
Ordinary and preference shares are traded.

Stock indices
There are many indices, including a general index, a public subscription index and a number of sectoral indices covering individual industries such as construction. There are also a number of privately compared indices.

Taxes
There is no withholding tax on dividends, although a 2% capital gains tax is imposed.

Disclosure of financial statements
Companies wishing to list on the exchange must complete a lengthy prospectus. They are also obliged to provide semi-annual reports plus full-year financial statements and the reports of the board and the auditor. Companies must all immediately disclose any material changes in their financial structure.

Ownership limits for non-residents
There are no limits on foreign ownership or on repatriation of capital or income.

Brokers
There are over one hundred local brokers, most of them small.

Sectors
The largest sectors are banking, cement and construction. There are also a number of chemicals, milling, oil and pharmaceutical companies.

ADRs
There is only one Egyptian company with an ADR, the Commercial International Bank of Egypt.

Market comment
Foreign interest in the Egyptian market has risen sharply in 1995 and 1996. The EFG-Hermes Index increased by 34% in the first six months of 1996. The average price to earnings ratio in mid-1996 was 8.5%. The privatization programme which was restarted in May 1996 has been a significant driver of growth. More than ninety-one state-owned companies are scheduled for sale in 1996/1997.

■ DEBT

The Capital Market Authority (CMA) was formed in December 1979 to develop and supervise stock market activity, including bond trading. It reports directly to the Ministry of the Economy. Bonds are listed on the Cairo or Alexandra Stock Exchanges.

Treasury bills

T-bills with maturities of 3, 6, and 12 months are auctioned by the central bank on Wednesday, Monday and Sunday respectively, although not every maturity is always offered each week. Bids can be submitted two days earlier and allocations are announced and settled the following day. Banks and non-bank financial institutions can make multiple-price bids for their own and their customers' accounts.

Treasury bonds

In 1995 parliament authorized the central bank to raise EGP15 billion (US$4 billion) through bond issues, to lengthen the term of the government's domestic debt and to establish a yield curve for corporate issuance. In May of that year the central bank offered EGP3 billion (US$1 billion) of 5-year bonds, and in October 1996 auctioned a second issue for EGP4 billion with a 7-year maturity, callable after five, at a yield of 11%.

Corporate bond issuance has expanded with the development of the equity market during the mid-1990s. Previously the only bonds available were 20-year government housing bonds, which were issued through the central bank with a fixed coupon of 8%. Since 1994, corporations and foreign and domestic banks have issued 5- and 7-year bonds with either fixed rate or floating rate coupons linked to the 3- or 6-month T-Bill rates.

If the issuer is the government or a listed or state-owned enterprise, then withholding tax is generally not payable on bond interest. Interest income on other bond issues is taxed at 32%, although this may be mitigated in the case of foreign investors if a double-taxation treaty exists.

Non-residents can participate in primary auctions for both bills and bonds, by bidding through a domestic bank or broker. There are no restrictions on the remittance of sale proceeds or interest income.

■ EGYPT: Economic indicators

Population and development	1990	1991	1992	1993	1994	1995	1996e
Population, million	52.7	53.9	55.2	56.5	57.9	59.2	60.1
Population growth, %	2.4	2.3	2.3	2.4	2.4	2.4	1.5
Nominal GDP per capita, US$	673	635	757	834	892	1021	1123

National accounts							
Nominal GDP, US$bn	35.5	34.2	41.8	47.1	51.6	60.5	67.5
Change in real GDP, %	5.7	1.1	4.4	2.9	3.9	4.6	4.0
Gross fixed capital formation, % of GDP	27.6	25.0	20.6	16.2	16.6	21.2	22.4

Money supply and inflation							
Narrow money, change %, Dec/Dec	16.6	8.1	8.8	12.1	10.7	8.5	11.0
Broad money, change %, Dec/Dec	28.7	19.3	19.4	13.2	11.2	9.9	10.4
Consumer price inflation (avg.) %	16.8	19.7	13.7	12.0	8.2	8.4	7.4
Producer prices (avg.) %	16.8	17.9	12.1	8.5	11.1	—	—

Interest rates							
Discount rate, end of year	14.0	20.0	18.4	16.5	14.0	13.5	13.0
Money market rate, annual average	14.0	20.0	18.4	16.5	14.0	—	—
Treasury bill rate, annual average	—	—	—	—	—	—	10.06
Deposit rate, annual average	12.0	12.0	12.0	12.0	12.0	11.8	109.0
Prime lending rate, annual average	19.0	—	20.3	18.3	16.5	16.5	15.5

Government finance							
Government expenditure, % of GDP	31.6	35.4	41.6	38.2	36.3	32.6	32.1
Government balance, % of GDP	-5.7	-1.0	-3.5	-3.5	-2.1	-1.2	-1.3

Exchange rates lc=local currency							
Exchange rate, annual average, lc/US$	2.71	3.25	3.33	3.34	3.39	3.39	3.39
Exchange rate, end of year, lc/US$	2.87	3.33	3.34	3.37	3.39	3.39	3.39

Balance of payments							
Exports of goods & services, US$m	9895	10947	11386	11440	12114	12990	14184
Change %	35.1	10.6	4.0	0.5	5.9	7.2	9.2
Imports of goods & services, US$m, fob	14091	13195	13768	15290	15642	16123	18343
Change %	16.2	-6.4	4.3	11.1	2.3	3.1	13.8
Trade balance, of goods only, US$m, fob-fob	-6379	-5667	-5231	-6378	-5953	-6850	-7867
Current account balance, US$m	185	1903	2812	2299	31	493	-79
as a % of GDP	0.5	5.6	6.7	4.9	0.1	0.8	-0.1

Foreign exchange reserves							
Foreign exchange reserves, US$m	2684	5325	10677	12761	13316	15998	17300
Gold at ⅔ of market price, US$m	625.2	586.6	556.2	582.7	622.3	622.2	627.9
Import cover (reserves/imports), months	2.3	4.8	9.3	10.0	10.2	11.9	11.3

Foreign debt and debt service							
Short-term debt, US$m	3832	3832	2516	2003	2252	3300	3400
Total foreign debt, US$m	38454	32873	32230	30699	29888	28690	28592
as a % of GDP	108.4	96.1	77.2	65.2	57.9	47.4	42.3
as a % of foreign exchange receipts	224	191	166	157	165	152	139
Interest payments, US$m	1427	892	1230	1226	1349	1232	1293
Principal repayments, US$m	1879	1724	1487	975	931	1095	1009
Total debt service, US$m	3306	2616	2717	2201	2280	2327	2302
as a % of goods exports	84.3	62.8	74.0	62.1	56.4	52.9	44.6
as a % of foreign exchange receipts	19.2	15.2	14.0	11.3	12.6	12.3	11.2

Estonia

Area (thousands of km²):	45
Population (1995, millions):	1.6
Population projection (2025, millions):	2
Population younger than 15 yrs (1991, % of total):	22.3
Urbanization rate (1993, % of population):	73
Life expectancy (1993, years at birth):	69
Gross domestic product (1996, US$bn):	4.3
GDP per capita (1996, US$):	2945
Average annual GDP growth rate (1990-96, %):	-2.8
Average annual inflation rate (1990-96, %):	212.5
Currency (kroon per US$, average 1996):	12.1
Structure of production (1994):	55% services, 36% industry, 10% agriculture
Main exports:	agricultural products, machines, electrical appliances
Main imports:	mineral products, fuel, raw material
Main trading partners:	Finland, Russia, Sweden, Germany
Total foreign debt (% of GDP):	9.3
Next elections due under normal circumstances:	March 1998

FORECAST: 1997-2000 (average)

	Worst case	Most likely	Best case
Real GDP growth (%)	1 to 3	4 to 7	5 to 8
Inflation (%)	20 to 30	10 to 20	5 to 10

■ POLITICS

Historical overview

The Estonians are a Finno-Ugric people, related to the Finns, the peoples of northern Russia and, more distantly, the Hungarians. The other Baltic peoples, the Latvians and Lithuanians, form a subgroup of the Indo-European language group not related to Estonian. Despite their cultural distinctiveness, however, the Estonians have been influenced by their neighbours for many centuries.

In the early 13th century, the Danes, under King Waldemar II, and an order of German knights, the "Brothers of the Sword", invaded and forcibly christianized Estonia. These knights were to form an aristocracy in the region that prevailed until the 20th century. During this time all or part of the territory was disputed between Denmark, Sweden, Poland and finally Russia, which in 1721 was finally able to assert control over the region.

The collapse of the Russian Empire allowed the Estonians to declare independence in 1918. Independence was short-lived, as in 1940 the USSR invaded Estonia. Following the Soviet annexation, a reign of terror began. After the German attack on the USSR in 1941, the country came under German occupation and further round-ups began, this time of Estonia's small Jewish population. In 1944 the Soviets re-occupied the country, and the terror grew more intense. Thousands were exiled to Siberia and almost 100,000 people fled to the West. It has been estimated that by 1945 nearly 40% of the population had been exiled or killed. An anti-Soviet guerrilla movement continued until 1953. The Soviet period saw a large influx of Russians, and by 1989 the Estonian population had shrunk from 88% to 66%, while the overall population had stayed stable at 1.2 million.

Recent events

By the mid-1980s the Estonians had begun to recreate the national movement of the previous century. In the famous "Singing Revolution" of 1988, there was a mass demonstration of 300,000 singing Estonians in Tallinn, who restated a previous declaration of sovereignty. The August coup of 1991 in Moscow gave the Estonians just the opportunity they needed to restore independence.

The first elections took place in September 1992. The current government coalition between the Coalition Party-Rural Union (KMU) and the Reform Party (R) came to power after parliamentary elections in October 1995. Estonia's major political goals, EU and NATO membership, will remain unchanged and economic policy will move, if anything, with the entrance of the liberal Reform Party to the right.

Chronology

13th century	Estonia is invaded by Danish and Germans, and forcibly christianized
1558-85	Livonian war. Northern part of Estonia under Swedish rule, southern part under Polish-Lithuanian rule.
1710-21	Great Northern War between Sweden and Russia. Russia asserts control over the region.
19th century	Emergence of national movement: start of first Estonian newspaper (1806), abolition of slavery (1816-19), publication of national epic *Kalevipoeg*
1918	February 24: declaration of independence
1918-20	War of Liberation
1920	Tartu peace treaty between Estonia and Soviet Russia. Soviet Russia recognizes unconditionally Estonian independence.
1940	Soviet Union occupies Estonia
1941-44	German occupation. Deportation and execution of the Jewish population.
1944	Soviet re-occupation, followed by a reign of terror
1988	"Singing Revolution"
1991	August 20: Estonia declares independence after attempted coup in Moscow
1992	Republic of Estonia re-established. Election of parliament (Riigikogu) and president.
1993	Estonia becomes a full member of the Council of Europe
1995	Estonia becomes an associated member of the EU

Constitution and government

The Republic of Estonia (Eesti Vabariik) is a constitutional democracy. It is divided into fifteen counties, with Tallinn as its capital. Power is split between parliament (Riigikogu), the president, the government and supreme court. The legal system is based on that of civil law; there is no judicial review of legislative acts.

According to the Estonian constitution, adopted on June 28, 1992, the president is elected by parliament for a five-year term. Since October 21, 1992, Lennart Meri has been president, re-elected for a second term on September 22, 1996. The president nominates the prime minister.

The unicameral Riigikogu is the Estonian parliament. Elections are held every four years on the first Sunday in March. There is a 5% threshold to enter parliament. The 101 members currently in office were elected on March 5, 1995. Since the Reform Party left the coalition the KMU – the Coalition Party (K) and Rural Union and Union of Families and Pensioners (MU) – is running a minority government.

Current government

Prime Minister	Tiit Vähi (KMU, K), elected November 3, 1995
Foreign Minister	Toomas Hendrik Ilves,
Finance Minister	Mart Opmann (KMU, K)

Election results

	% vote	seats
Coalition party and Rural Union KMU	32.2	41
Estonian Reform Party (liberal) R	16.2	19
Estonian Centre Party K	14.2	16
Pro Patria and ENIP Union I&ERSP (moderate) M	7.9	8
Our Home is Estonia MKOE (right-wing) W	5.9	6

Next elections
March 1, 1998

Central bank

The central bank is the Bank of Estonia (Eesti Pank). Originally founded in 1919, the bank was re-established in 1990 after its activities had been interrupted in 1940 by the Soviet occupation. Parliament passed the law on the Bank of Estonia on May 18, 1993 and its statute was adopted on November 23, 1993.

The Bank of Estonia is independent of all government agencies, and reports only to parliament. The government has considerable influence on the bank's monetary policy, however, with the finance minister sitting on the board of the bank. According to the law, the Bank of Estonia determines the monetary and exchange rate policy of Estonia. However, this in turn has been limited by the law governing the security of the Estonian kroon.

A board of one chairman and eight members govern the Bank of Estonia. The chairman is appointed by parliament for a five-year term. Members of the board are nominated by the chairman and are also appointed by parliament for five-year terms. The president of the bank and the finance minister are ex officio members of the board. The other members are not permitted to be government members or bank employees. The president of the bank is nominated by the board and appointed by the head of state for a five-year term.

■ ECONOMICS

Collapse of the former Soviet Union

Estonia's economy was profoundly affected by the final collapse of the former Soviet Union's central planning system in 1990-91. It disrupted trade and financial links. Estonia, like its Baltic neighbours, lost its export markets, suffered shortages of raw materials and goods, and experienced disruption of payments and monetary arrangements. Moreover, in early 1992 Russia moved to world market prices for fuel exports and increased prices for other raw materials. All these external shocks resulted in a rapid fall in output volume and hyperinflation. Real gross domestic product declined by 34% between 1990 and 1994, and inflation rocketed to 1076% in 1992.

Real GDP growth

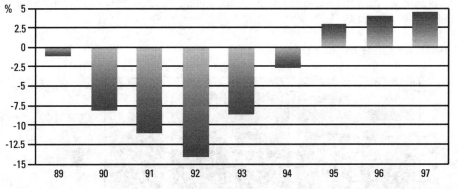

Source: Official data

Stabilization programme

Estonia adopted a stabilization and reform programme to bring down inflation and increase output. To insulate itself from further external shocks, it introduced its own currency and set up a currency board to stabilize monetary policy and to establish credibility. For this, gold reserves deposited by Estonia in 1940 in Western central banks became available in 1992. In addition, the government adopted strict fiscal policies by increasing tax revenues and cutting expenditures.

The programme has been successful in curbing hyperinflation. Inflation continues to decline, although at a lower pace. Mainly regulated price rises keep inflation from falling faster. However, considerable confidence in monetary policy has been established and, in addition, output has begun to recover as well. GDP grew by 2.9% in 1995 and is projected to grow even faster in the next five to ten years.

Control of hyperinflation

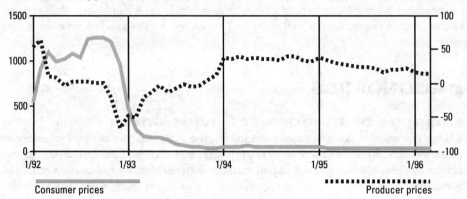

Consumer prices   Producer prices

Source: Official data

Structural changes

Estonia is now in the process of structural reform, increasingly shifting economic orientation away from the agricultural and industrial sectors in favour of the service sector. In addition, the private sector is gaining in importance, accounting for about 65% of GDP at end 1995, up from 40% at end 1993.

Share of GDP by sector

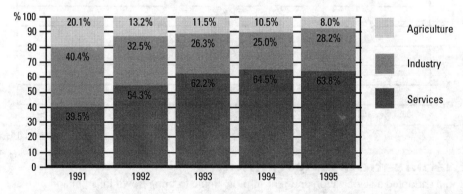

Source: Official data

Trade

Up to the end of 1991, more than 90% of Estonia's foreign trade was with Russia and other countries of the former Soviet Union (FSU). Since then, foreign trade has been successfully diversified from the FSU to industrialized countries. Although Russia has remained Estonia's second biggest trading partner, Finland is now the most important foreign market, followed by Sweden and Germany respectively. Mineral products form by far the largest part of imports from Russia, indicating Estonia's continuing dependence on Russian fuel and raw material exports.

The recent economic boom, mainly fuelled by foreign investment, has resulted in a sizeable current account deficit (1995: 7.9% of GDP). Investment demand will probably continue growing and consumer demand is projected to increase in the medium term. The current account will therefore most likely remain in deficit for the time being.

Economic policy

Monetary policy

Estonia's currency, the kroon, is pegged under a currency board arrangement to the deutschmark at a rate of 8 to 1. Base money supply is fully backed by foreign reserves and the currency board prevents the central bank from extending credits to state enterprises, agriculture and government. This system has been successful in bringing down inflation, but the fixed exchange rate has also resulted in a substantial real appreciation of the kroon.

Estonian kroon/US dollar/German deutschmark exchange rate

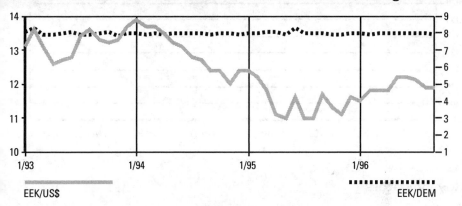

EEK/US$ EEK/DEM

Real exchange rate appreciation

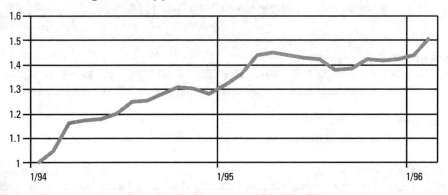

Balanced budget

Estonia's budget has to be balanced by law and, with the exception of 1993, all governments managed to achieve surpluses. The balanced budget law together with the pegged exchange rate disciplines government and is one of the lynchpins of Estonia's reform success. Yet, pressure to abandon strict budgetary discipline is increasing, particularly from agricultural interests, which are pushing for more government subsidies. However, it seems unlikely that any government would change the law for fear of jeopardizing Estonia's budgetary reputation and risking retaliation from international lenders.

■ EQUITIES

Index performance (in local currency)

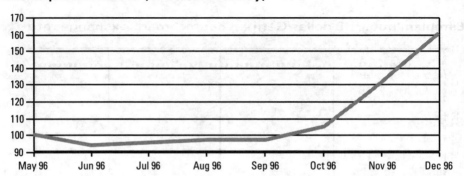

Key indicators

	Index performance %, in US$ terms	Market Cap. US$bn	P/E	Div. Yield
1996	194.0	0.6	13.0	0.6

Sources: Tallinn Stock Exchange, IFC, Bloomberg, Datastream, UBS

Background

The Tallinn Stock Exchange (TSE) was registered in August 1995 and began trading on May 31, 1996. Market capitalization is approximately EEK5200 million (US$ 433 million).

Structure

Trade on the TSE is divided between the Main Market, the Free Market and the OTC market.

Regulatory authority

The TSE is regulated in line with the Rules and Regulations of the Exchange by the TSE Stock Exchange Disciplinary Committee (SEDC). The SEDC comprises five representatives from the Estonian Securities Board, the TSE, the Ministry of Finance, Law Office Raidla & Partners and ICI Trust Ltd.

Trading methods
Trading takes place through two systems. For listed securities traded by two or more recognized dealers, transactions are performed on the Dealer Market system. However, listed securities that do not have two or more officially recognized dealers or are quoted on the Free Market are traded through the Public Order Book system. The main difference between the two is that the Dealer Market is quote-driven whereas the Free Market is order-driven.

Hours
Trading takes place between 10.00 and 14.00, Monday to Friday.

Settlement time and clearing
Settlement takes place on a trade date plus three days (T+3) basis. Settlement and clearing are undertaken by the Estonian Central Depository for Securities.

Limits on price movement
None.

Types of shares
Common shares are traded on the TSE. There are no preference shares.

Stock indices
The TSE produces two main indices. The most widely quoted is the TALSE Index, a capitalization-weighted index comprising the top five shares listed on the Main Market. The EVK Index, uses the same methodology as the TALSE but incorporates fifteen shares.

Taxes
Dividend and interest income is taxed at 15%.

Disclosure of financial statements
Listed companies are required to produce quarterly, semi-annual and annual reports.

Ownership limits for non-residents
Although the Law on Foreign Investment gives the government the legal basis to restrict foreign ownership, there are currently no limits. However, in a number of sectors licences are required prior to investment taking place.

Capital and foreign exchange controls
The Estonian kroon is fully convertible.

Brokers
There are ten brokerage firms on the TSE. Typically, brokers charge commission rates between 0.4% and 1%.

Sectors
The banking sector dominates the TSE – banks contribute around 80% of capitalization. Other significant companies include the Saku Brewery, Tallinn Department Store, and Norma.

ADRs

There are no Estonian ADRs.

Derivatives

There is no derivatives market in Estonia.

■ DEBT

The government issued bonds worth 300 million kroons during the 1992 banking crisis to provide income for banks whose accounts had been frozen at Moscow's Vnesheconombank. They were separated into ten tranches with various maturities. Secondary market trading is negligible. Estonia has run a balanced budget since, so there has been no need for further issuance.

However, the State Compensation Fund, which receives 50% of all privatization revenues for reinvestment, issues bonds for vouchers in the primary market. The first Fund bonds were issued in September 1995. Recent issues pay an annual coupon of 7% with tenures of 5 to 6 years. The non-government sector is more active. There have been several corporate and municipal issues. In addition foreign banks with local branches have issued kroon-denominated eurobonds (the Finnish Postipank OY and Merita Bank Ltd, for example).

Eurobonds

In November 1995, the Estonian Investment bank issued DEM20 million 3- and 4-year bonds at libor plus 150 basis points. In April 1996, the City of Tallin raised DEM60 million through a 3-year bond with a 6% fixed-rate coupon, priced to yield 221 basis points over German government bonds.

■ ESTONIA: Economic indicators

Population and development	1990	1991	1992	1993	1994	1995	1996e
Population, million	1.58	1.58	1.54	1.51	1.51	1.49	1.48
Population growth, %	0.13	0.06	-2.47	-1.95	-0.13	-1.19	-0.67
Nominal GDP per capita, US$	—	6825	732	1144	1544	2445	2945

National accounts							
Nominal GDP, US$bn	—	10.78	1.13	1.73	2.33	3.64	4.36
Change in real GDP, %	10.29	-11.80	-19.29	-2.11	-2.70	2.90	3.50

Money supply and inflation							
Consumer price inflation (avg.) %	17.2	210.6	1069.3	89.4	47.7	29.0	24.5

Interest rates *=latest figures							
Money market rate, monthly average	—	—	—	—	5.70	4.90	3.60
Deposit rate, monthly average	—	—	—	—	11.50	8.70	6.10
Prime lending rate, monthly average	—	—	30.5	27.30	23.10	16.00	14.87

Government finance							
Government expenditure, % of GDP	—	22.1	21.2	26.7	31.7	—	—
Government balance, % of GDP	—	0.4	1.1	-2.0	2.9	0.8	0.0

Exchange rates lc=local currency							
Exchange rate, annual average, lc/US$	0.17	0.17	12.65	13.22	12.98	11.46	12.10
Exchange rate, end of year, lc/US$	1.17	0.17	12.52	13.88	12.39	11.46	12.40

Balance of payments							
Exports of goods & services, US$m	—	—	461	812	1321	1849	2145
Change %	—	—	—	76.2	62.7	40.0	16.0
Imports of goods & services, US$m, fob	—	—	551	957	1684	2569	2880
Change %	—	—	—	73.6	76.0	52.6	12.1
Trade balance, of goods only, US$m, fob-fob	—	—	-90	-145	-363	-720	-735
Current account balance, US$m	—	—	36	21	-164	-185	-300
as a % of GDP	—	—	3.2	1.2	-7.0	-5.1	-6.9

Foreign exchange reserves							
Foreign exchange reserves, US$m	—	10.0	170	386	412	576	650
Import cover (reserves/imports), months	—	—	3.7	4.8	2.9	2.7	2.7

Foreign debt and debt service							
Total foreign debt, US$m	—	—	40	65	175	260	390
as a % of GDP	—	—	3.5	3.8	7.5	7.1	8.9
Interest payments, US$m	—	—	—	4.0	6.5	17.5	20.0
Principal repayments, US$m	—	—	—	8.0	15.0	20.0	30.0
Total debt service, US$m	—	—	—	12.0	21.5	37.5	50.0
as a % of goods exports	—	—	—	1.5	1.6	2.0	2.3

Ghana

Area (thousands of km²):	239
Population (1995, millions):	17.7
Population projection (2025, millions):	36
Population younger than 15 yrs (1991, % of total):	46.8
Urbanization rate (1993, % of population):	35
Life expectancy (1993, years at birth):	56
Gross domestic product (1996, US$bn):	7.4
GDP per capita (1996, US$):	402
Average annual GDP growth rate (1990-96, %):	4.2
Average annual inflation rate (1990-96, %):	31.3
Currency (cedi per US$, average 1996):	1650
Structure of production (1994):	46% agriculture, 39% services, 16% industry
Main exports:	gold, cocoa related, timber
Main imports:	manufactures, fuels, non-fuel primary products
Main trading partners:	UK, Nigeria, Germany, US, Togo
Market capitalization of Stock Exchange (December 1996; US$bn):	1.5
Total foreign debt (% of GDP):	82
Next elections due under normal circumstances:	2000
Credit rating: (Jan 1997, Standard & Poor's, Moody's)	not rated

FORECAST: 1997-2000 (average)

	Worst case	Most likely	Best case
Real GDP growth (%)	3.5	5.0	6.0
Inflation (%)	55	20	10

■ POLITICS

Historical overview

The Akan, who are the largest ethnic group in present-day Ghana, have played a dominant role in the region since the 15th century. During the late 1600s, armed Akan chiefs overcame their rivals and established the Ashanti kingdom. Largely through military superiority, the Akan controlled most trade routes to the Gold Coast and, as a consequence, they prospered in comparison to other tribesfolk. In the early 19th century, however, the Akan's authority was crushed by the slave trade.

The final quarter of the 19th century saw the British invasion of the Ashanti kingdom and subsequent colonization of the Gold Coast. Britain had full control by 1901, and the

Gold Coast developed into a leading African colony in the early 20th century, with cash crops and gold the main products.

Following the Second World War, political independence movements, which were previously dominated by the educated elite, diversified into wider social bands. By 1949, many nationalists supported the Convention People's Party (CPP) led by Kwame Nkrumah. The British authorities drafted a constitution which provided for a government under the British crown. Three general elections were won by the CPP. In 1957, Ghana became an independent state within the Commonwealth.

In 1964, the socialist CPP government created a single-party state. Ghana's first military coup occurred in 1966. Elections followed in 1969, but the new government was overturned by a second military coup in 1972. A National Redemption Council (NRC), consisting of senior military and police officials took charge.

The NRC's initial popularity declined as the economy deteriorated. This culminated in leader Ignatius Acheampong being ousted by defence chiefs during the late 1970s. Before new elections could be held, Jerry Rawlings' Armed Forces Revolutionary Council (AFRC) initiated a further coup proposing to purge corruption and stabilize the situation until new elections could be held. The June 1979 general election was won by a majority of one seat by the People's National Party (PNP)

Following a period of political instability and widespread public strikes, Rawlings seized power for a second time at the end of 1981. This time he resisted a quick return to civilian rule and instead formed the Provisional National Defence Council (PNDC). He initially led the government with a radical, socialist agenda. However, the PNDC's early socialist philosophy was replaced by free-market reform as Ghana complied with the conditions attached to IMF structural adjustment loans.

Recent events

International donor pressure to move towards a multiparty system resulted in presidential and legislative elections in 1992. Following the presidential elections (which Jerry Rawlings won easily), a number of opposition parties claimed that they had been disadvantaged. Consequently, they boycotted the legislature elections and were therefore not represented in that parliament.

In the December 1996 presidential elections, Jerry Rawlings obtained 57.2% of the vote against 39.9% for his main rival, John Kufor. The voter turnout was 76.8%. In the parliamentary elections, held at the same time, Rawlings' National Democratic Congress (NDC) won 130 of the 200 seats. Kufor's New Patriotic Party obtained 59 seats.

Chronology

1874	The British invade the Ashanti kingdom with a view to colonization
1901	After years of resistance, the British gain control of the "Gold Coast"
1947	The United Gold Coast Convention (UGCC) is formed to spearhead protest against British rule. Led by lawyer Dr J. B. Danquah, the group is chiefly composed of the educated elite.
1949	Nationalist radicals strongly support the Convention People's Party (CPP) and its leader Kwame Nkrumah, the former secretary of the UGCC.
1960	July 1: Ghana is officially declared a republic

1964	The socialist CPP government creates a one-party state
1966	February 24: Conservative generals instigate Ghana's first military coup
1969	A civilian government is elected
1972	A second coup follows
1975	The NRC's leader, Ignatius Kutu Acheampong, forms a new Supreme Military Council (SMC) in order to quell increasing rivalry
1978	Defence chiefs led by Lt-Gen. Frederick Akuffo instigate a military coup
1979	Before new elections take place, Flight Lieutenant Jerry Rawlings leads a further coup. The African Forces Revolutionary Council is installed in office. Subsequently, a weak government is elected to power.
1981	After barely two years in power, the civilian government is ousted by another Rawlings-led coup on December 31. The AFRC install themselves in government as the Provisional National Defence Council (PNDC) and, after initial socialist policies, introduce World Bank-inspired economic reforms during the 1980s.
1994	In February disturbances between the Konkomba and Nanumba ethnic groups cause five hundred deaths in the Northern Region. A state of emergency is imposed for three months.
1996	December 7: Jerry Rawlings and his National Democratic Congress are returned to power

Constitution and government

Ghana's current constitution was adopted in 1992, laying the foundations for the Fourth Republic. The constitution is influenced by the US model, giving the president executive power. The president is elected for four-year terms and appoints the cabinet on the approval of the unicameral parliament. Ghana has ten regions, which are divided into one hundred districts.

The Bank of Ghana is the central bank, having responsibility for advising the government on monetary policy as well as regulating the banking system. The bank's board is selected by the government.

■ ECONOMICS

Recent developments

Since the inception of Ghana's structural adjustment programme in 1983, the country's economic policy has been heavily influenced by conditions laid down by the IMF and the World Bank. This has led to a degree of fiscal and monetary prudence which has reversed huge budget deficits and brought inflation down from the triple-digit figures registered in the early 1980s. Liberalization measures, higher investment, and greater macroeconomic and political stability have also seen economic growth rising steadily. Since its inception in 1988 Ghana's privatization programme has overseen the transfer of state-owned companies to the private sector at an increasing rate. Between 1988 and 1994, some 53 state-owned companies were sold outright, with another 39 involved in the selling of shares, joint ventures and leases. In 1995 the government indicated its intention to further speed up the process unveiling a plan to transfer a further 113 companies to the private sector. The excellent progress that Ghana had made up to the early 1990s was, however, tarnished by loose monetary and fiscal policies in the run-up to the 1992 elections, and the inflationary consequences thereafter. Prior to the elections, there was a big increase in fiscal spending, with a deficit of 5% of GDP – at a time when Ghana was targeting a surplus. As a result of the lagged effects of these policies, and rising food prices (which comprise a large component of the consumer price index) inflation peaked at over 70% in 1995. In 1996, inflation had begun a downward trend, but the average rate (estimated at 45%) was still more than double previous targets.

The economy
Agricultural production dominates Ghana's economy, accounting for around 45% of GDP, down from around 60% a decade ago. Key crops include maize, cocoyam, cassava and other root vegetables. Agricultural exports are dominated by cocoa, which in 1996 was estimated to have generated around US$0.5 billion in revenues (second only to gold's estimated US$0.6 billion). Industrial production is underdeveloped, contributing less than 15% to GDP. Inside the industrial sector, manufacturing is the key player (contributing almost 60%), although it has been growing more slowly during the 1990s. Gold output has more than doubled since the early 1990s. As new mining facilities come fully on stream, gold output will rise further. This will also benefit Ghana's manufacturing sector. Services occupy a growing proportion of GDP as a consequence of increased liberalization measures and faltering agricultural value.

Share of GDP by sector

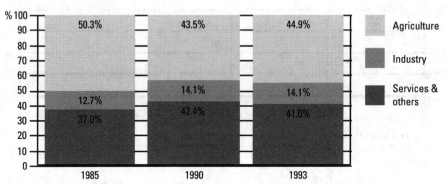

Source: Official data

Population
Ghana's population is estimated to be around 17 million. The annual growth rate (currently around 3% a year) is predicted to fall to 2.3% by 2025 from its 3.9% peak in the mid-1980s. However, even with this falling rate of growth, the population is predicted to number 38 million by 2025. Almost half the population is under 15 years old.

Savings and investment
For the government to achieve its goal of sustainable 8% growth, investment will need to double to over 30%. Given the low per-capita earnings in the Ghanaian economy, such

levels of investment are unlikely to stem from private savings: in 1995 national savings were equivalent to just over 8% of GDP. The government is therefore actively seeking to increase foreign investment in order to boost growth.

Gross fixed investment was 16.4% of GDP in 1995, with the public sector accounting for the bulk. However, this situation is likely to change within the next few years as the economy becomes more open to private activity.

Balance of payments

Since the early 1980s both exports and imports have grown steadily as a proportion of GDP, although import growth has been more marked, leading to an annual trade deficit each year since 1987. In 1996 this deficit was estimated at US$0.3 billion.

Exports consist predominantly of primary goods like cocoa, timber, and gold, whereas imports are largely capital-intensive. Gold is the largest export item, accounting for around 40% of the US$1.5 billion export revenues estimated for 1996.

The level of exports varies in response to factors such as climatic conditions and world commodity prices. In contrast, imports are influenced predominantly by exchange rate policy.

Imports and exports as a % of GDP

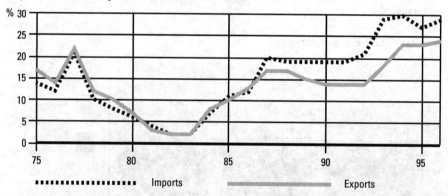

Source: Official data

Ghana's current account largely shadows the performance of visible trade. During the 1980s the current account deficit was low, fluctuating around 1% of GDP. However, the early 1990s witnessed rapid growth, with the deficit approaching 10% of GDP in 1993 before it began to fall.

The services balance has been in deficit throughout the 1980s and early 1990s. This is partly because Ghana's tourism industry is smaller than other African countries, and partly because of its underdeveloped financial sector. However, both have attracted greater investment in recent years, and are likely to show further improvement.

Ghana's total external debt, around US$6.1 billion in 1996, is equivalent to 94% of GDP. Debt servicing is lower than the level of indebtedness might suggest, however, because the bulk of Ghana's debt is official debt, obtained under more favourable terms.

Breakdown of exports (1994)

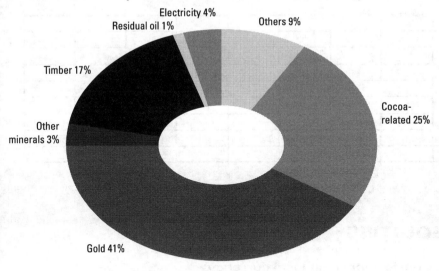

Electricity 4%
Residual oil 1%
Others 9%
Timber 17%
Other minerals 3%
Cocoa-related 25%
Gold 41%

Source: Official data

Current account as a % of GDP

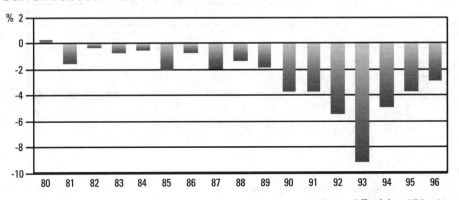

Source: Official data; UBS estimates

Currency

Against the background of high inflation and current account pressures, the cedi has continued to weaken substantially against the US dollar, falling by about 80% in nominal terms in the five years to 1996. Stabilization of the currency only becomes a realistic prospect once the inflation rate gets down to a more manageable level.

Ghanaian cedi per US dollar

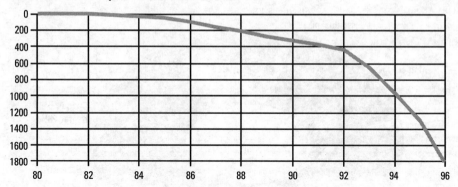

■ EQUITIES

Index performance (in local currency)

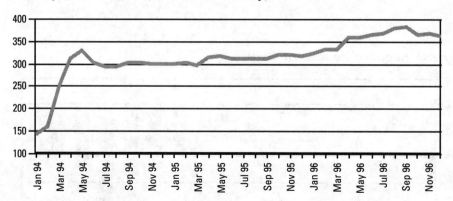

Key indicators

	Index performance %, in US$ terms	Market Cap. US$bn	P/E	Div. Yield
1994	68.8	1.9	2.5	2.5
1995	-22.2	1.7	8.0	3.7
1996	-22	1.5	11.9	3.7

Sources: Ghana Stock Exchange, IFC, Bloomberg, Datastream, UBS

Structure

Set up in 1990, the Ghana Stock Exchange (GSE) has nineteen listed companies. Market capitalization has risen sharply over the past two years, due to an acceleration in the government's privatization programme, and now stands at GHC3,181 billion (US$2.2 billion). Total trading volume during 1995 was GHC27.09 billion (US$18.8 million).

Regulatory authority
The Accra-based GSE is regulated by the Securities Industries Commission. A thirteen-man council representing the licensed dealers, listed companies, banks, insurance companies and private investors also plays a supervisory role.

Trading methods
The GSE uses a call-over system of trading by which all transactions executed by the dealers on the floor are presided over by an exchange official. Trading takes place in lots of 100 shares.

Hours
The GSE is open 10.00 to 12.00 Monday, Wednesday and Friday.

Settlement time and clearing
A new clearing and settlement house was established in November 1996, and the clearing and settlement period is now five working days.

Types of shares
Ordinary shares and government bonds are traded.

Stock indices
There are two indices: the GSE all-share index and the Databank Stock Index, which is a composite index of all equity shares listed on GSE and measures change in aggregate value.

Taxes
There is a 10% withholding tax on dividend income. Capital gains are not taxed.

Disclosure of financial statements
Companies must notify the GSE of any dividend recommendations, any meetings, any capital calls, any changes in directors, any acquisition of shares, and any proposed alterations to the company's regulations. They must also submit half and full-year financial statements.

Ownership limits for non-residents
Foreign investors cannot own more than 10% of a single company, or over 74% on a grouped basis.

Capital and foreign exchange controls
Remittance of capital and dividends is free.

Brokers
There are twelve brokerage houses.

Companies
The market is dominated by Ashanti Goldfields, which accounts for 88% of total market capitalization. The other principal stocks are Standard Chartered Bank, Social Security Bank,

Unilever Ghana, Mobil Oil Ghana, Pioneer Tobacco, Accra Brewery, Fan Milk and Home Finance. Kumasi Brewery, Enterprise Insurance and CFAO Ghana also trade (relatively) actively.

ADRs

Ashanti Goldfields is the only Ghanaian company with an ADR listing.

■ DEBT

On March 1, 1996 the central bank (Bank of Ghana) introduced a wholesale auction system for money-market instruments to improve secondary market efficiency and liquidity. The intention was also to enhance competition among distributors.

Treasury bills of 91 and 180 days, and 1-year and 2-year notes are now distributed through a syndicate of banks and discount houses, rather than sold directly by the Bank of Ghana. They can be bought in round lots of 50,000 cedis. In addition, an underwriting facility for government securities is being developed.

Secondary market trading is largely confined to dealings among banks, and between banks and discount houses to manage liquidity positions. A high rediscount rate deters banks from selling bills back to the central bank. Most bills and notes are held to maturity.

The Ghana Stock Exchange has initiated a Long-Term Debt Development Project for establishing a corporate bond market, and listings for government medium- and long-dated bonds.

■ GHANA: Economic indicators

Population and development	1990	1991	1992	1993	1994	1995	1996e
Population, million	15.0	15.5	16.0	16.5	16.9	17.7	18.3
Population growth, %	3.1	3.1	3.1	3.1	3.0	4.4	3.3
Nominal GDP per capita, US$	415	452	431	368	310	353	402

National accounts							
Nominal GDP, US$bn	6.2	7.0	6.9	6.1	5.3	6.2	7.4
Change in real GDP, %	3.3	5.3	3.9	5.0	3.8	4.5	4.7
Gross fixed capital formation, % of GDP	12.2	12.7	12.8	21.9	15.0	15.0	15.0

Money supply and inflation							
Broad money, change %, Dec/Dec	22.2	68.3	50.6	23.0	35.3	55.0	30.0
Consumer price inflation (avg.) %	37.2	18.0	10.1	24.9	24.9	59.4	45.0

Interest rates							
Discount rate, end of year	33	20	30	35	33	45	—
Treasury bill rate, annual average	21.78	29.23	19.38	30.95	27.72	35.38	—

Government finance							
Government expenditure, % of GDP	12.5	13.2	16.6	20.7	22.5	20.3	19.7
Government balance, % of GDP	0.2	1.5	-4.8	-2.5	2.1	-0.7	-1.4

Exchange rates *lc=local currency*							
Exchange rate, annual average, lc/US$	326	368	437	649	957	1300	1650
Exchange rate, end of year, lc/US$	345	391	521	820	1053	1438	1725

Balance of payments							
Exports of goods & services, US$m	970	1093	1097	1200	1366	1544	1650
Change %	9.9	12.7	0.4	9.4	13.8	13.0	6.9
Imports of goods & services, US$m, fob	1490	1638	1829	2156	1981	2130	2280
Change %	17.0	9.9	11.7	17.9	-8.1	7.5	7.0
Trade balance, of goods only, US$m, fob-fob	-314	-321	-470	-664	-353	-300	-300
Current account balance, US$m	-224	-251	-375	-558	-264	-142	-210
as a % of GDP	-3.6	-3.6	-5.5	-9.2	-5.0	-2.3	-2.9

Foreign exchange reserves							
Foreign exchange reserves, US$m	218.8	550.2	319.9	409.7	583.9	697.5	700.0
Gold at ⅔ of market price, US$m	60.4	64.2	62.9	65.9	70.4	70.4	—
Import cover (reserves/imports), months	1.8	4.0	2.1	2.3	3.5	3.9	3.7

Foreign debt and debt service							
Short-term debt, US$m	312	394	414	476	582	580	590
Total foreign debt, US$m	3810	4351	4477	4835	5389	5700	6000
as a % of GDP	61.2	62.2	65.0	79.8	102.5	91.4	81.6
as a % of foreign exchange receipts	270.2	282.2	279.8	276.0	287.7	271.0	278.4
Interest payments, US$m	58	112	121	120	117	136	150
Principal repayments, US$m	134	191	201	183	228	267	240
Total debt service, US$m	192	303	322	303	345	403	390
as a % of goods exports	21.6	30.4	32.6	28.5	28.1	28.8	26.0
as a % of foreign exchange receipts	13.6	19.6	20.1	17.3	18.4	19.2	18.1

Greece

Area (thousands of km²):	132
Population (1995, millions):	10.4
Population projection (2025, millions):	11
Population younger than 15 yrs (1991, % of total):	18.6
Urbanization rate (1993, % of population):	64
Life expectancy (1993, years at birth):	78
Gross domestic product (1996, US$bn):	120.9
GDP per capita (1996, US$):	11624
Average annual GDP growth rate (1990-96, %):	1.2
Average annual inflation rate (1990-96, %):	14.1
Currency (drachma per US$, average 1996):	240
Real exchange rate: (1990=100, average 1996)	116
Structure of production (1994):	60.7% services, 15.7% agriculture, 15.5% manufacturing, 6.1% construction, 2% mining
Main exports:	manufactures, food & beverages, petroleum products
Main imports:	capital goods, petroleum products, food
Main trading partners:	EU Countries (Germany, Italy, France, UK)
Market capitalization of Stock Exchange (October 1996; US$bn):	24.7
Total foreign debt (% of GDP):	44.7
Next elections due under normal circumstances:	Parliament before September 2000; Presidential scheduled May 2000
Credit rating: (Nov 1996, Standard & Poor's, Moody's)	BBB-; Baa3

FORECAST: 1997-2000 (average)

	Worst case	Most likely	Best case
Real GDP growth (%)	1.5	2.8	3.8
Inflation (%)	9.0	5.3	4.0

■ POLITICS

Historical overview

In 1829, Greece gained independence after nearly four centuries of Ottoman rule. The country was first governed by a Bavarian prince until he was replaced in 1862 by the King of Denmark's son, who remained in power for the next fifty years; a parliament was first established in 1864. The boundaries of today's Greece were largely drawn in 1923 by the Lausanne Treaty.

Twentieth-century Greece saw several major political changes, including the return to monarchy in 1935, German occupation during the Second World War, and military rule from 1967 to 1974. The country finally became a republic in 1975. The conservative New Democracy Party, led by Constantine Karamanlis, remained in power from 1974 to 1981, when he succeeded in bringing Greece into the European Community. The October 1981 elections were won by Andreas Papandreou's Pan-Hellenic Socialist Movement (PASOK) party, which ruled Greece from 1981 to 1989. The 1989-90 period saw political turbulence, with three general elections. The New Democracy Party, under Constantine Mitsotakis, won the April 1990 elections with a small margin and stayed in power until October 1993. This time, Papandreou's PASOK won a decisive victory and obtained 170 seats in the 300-seat parliament. However, Papandreou's continued health problems caused him to step down in November 1995, and PASOK selected Constantinos Simitis as the new prime minister. He is known to be a reformist within PASOK and to be strong in economic issues. After the death of Andreas Papandreou, Simitis began to unify PASOK under his leadership and easily won early general elections in September 1996.

Chronology

1821-29	War of Independence
1833	Monarchy is established
1864	A constitution envisaging a parliamentary government takes effect
1923	Treaty of Lausanne establishes the boundaries of modern Greece
1935	Monarchy is restored
1941	German invasion of Greece during the Second World War
1967-74	Military junta rule
1974	November: Karamanlis' New Democracy (ND) Party wins the elections
1974	December: monarchy is abolished in a national referendum, and the country is declared a republic
1975	June: current constitution is adopted
1981	January: Greece becomes a full member of the EEC
1981	October: Andreas Papandreou's Pan-Hellenic Socialist Movement (PASOK) party wins the general elections
1985	June: PASOK re-elected
1990	April: New Democracy government wins by a slim majority
1993	October: early general elections. Papandreou's PASOK wins a decisive majority
1995	November: Papandreou's health problems cause him to step down as the prime minister. Konstandinos Simitis becomes the new PM.
1996	January: Papandreou dies
1996	July: Simitis is elected as PASOK leader
1996	September: Simitis' PASOK wins the early general elections

Constitution and government

The current Greek constitution, effective from 1975, establishes the country as a parliamentary republic, headed by a non-executive president. The president is elected by the parliament for a five-year term by a two-thirds majority in the first two rounds of voting or a three-fifths majority in the third round. If this fails, the parliament is dissolved, and new general elections are held. President Constantinos Stephanopoulos was elected in March 1995 in the third-round ballot.

The Hellenic Republic has a unicameral parliament ("vouli") of 300 members directly elected for a four-year term through a system of reinforced proportional representation. Of its 300 MPs, 288 are elected from 56 constituencies, and the remaining 12 are deputies of state allocated to the parties according to the percentage of the votes received. A political party needs to exceed the 3% national threshold to enter the parliament.

Current government

President	Constantinos Stephanopoulos
Prime Minister	Constantinos Simitis
President of Parliament	Apostolos Kaklamanis
Central Bank Governor	Lucas Papadademos

Ministers:

Finance, National Economy	Yannos Papandoniou
Foreign Affairs	Theodoros Pangalos

Political parties

In the most recent general election, on September 22, 1996, Costas Simitis' PASOK received 41.5% of the votes and won 162 seats.

Results of the September 1996 general election

		% of vote	seats
PASOK	Social democratic	41.5	162
New Democracy	Conservative	38.1	108
KKE	Communist	5.6	11
Coalition of the Left	Socialist/Communist	5.1	10
Democratic Social Movement	Socialist	4.4	9
Political Spring	Conservative/Nationalist	2.9	0
Others		2.3	0

Central bank

The Bank of Greece is the central bank. It can extend short-term advances to the Treasury as well as borrow from the international markets. The Greek banking system was tightly controlled until 1987, when a reform package was introduced in line with the required adjustments to the single European market. The Bank of Greece eliminated most of the controls by April 1993, and the last controls on short-term capital movements were eliminated in May 1994.

International relations

Greece is part of a historically unstable region, where conflicts have traditionally concerned questions of nationality.

By 1997, Greece had steadily improved its relations with all of its neighbours, with the exception of Turkey. Relations between Greece and Turkey have been strained for several centuries. In the 1960s the status of Cyprus became an issue and relations with Turkey deteriorated further after the Turkish military intervention in Cyprus in 1974. In addition, Greece and Turkey are at odds over jurisdiction in the Aegean Sea. Since both countries are NATO members, the general assumption is that other NATO members would seek to prevent an escalation of tensions that may lead to armed conflict.

■ ECONOMICS

Population
Greece has a population of around 10.5 million. The growth rate has been declining, reaching an average 0.5% per annum between 1985 and 1996. The size of the labour force is about 4.2 million in 1995. Unemployment has been rising in recent years, from 7% in 1990 to 10% in 1996. While per-capita income is more than US$11,000, there are large disparities in income distribution.

The economy
The economy of Greece is divided between agriculture (16%), industry (24%), and services (60%). The agricultural sector is largely self-sufficient. Principal agricultural products are wheat, corn, barley, sugar beets, olives, tomatoes, wine, tobacco and potatoes.

Share of GDP by sector

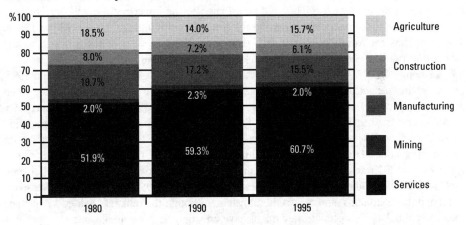

Source: Official data

Greece also has significant reserves of bauxite and lignite and deposits of oil, nickel, chromite, magnesite, asbestos, gypsum and marble. The share of Greece's mining and quarrying sector in GDP is about 2%, but the sector provides about 5% of exports.

The Greek maritime sector and its merchant fleet is the largest in the world. It embraces more than 1,050 ships over 1,000 gross registered tons (GRT), totalling 29 million GRT. There are also ships owned by Greeks under Liberian, Panamanian, Cypriot, Maltese, and Bahamian registry.

Economic policy

Current economic policies focus on bringing economic performance in line with the Maastricht criteria for European monetary union. This involves cutting the budget deficit from around 10% to 3% of GDP, reducing the ratio of domestic debt to GDP from 112% towards 60%, and bringing inflation and long-term interest rates to the level of the three best-performing EU countries. Such a transformation requires substantial economic restructuring and painful reforms. Based on 1996 data and projections, Greece would not qualify for monetary union if the first group of countries form such a union in 1999.

Inflation and economic growth

	Real GDP growth (%)	Inflation (%)
1954-1973	7.1	3.8
1974-1979	3.8	16.2
1980-1984	1.1	21.8
1985-1989	2.4	17.2
1990-1993	0.8	17.6
1994-1995	2.0	9.3
1995-1996	2.2	8.5

Slow growth has characterized the Greek economy after 1980. Real GDP growth averaged just 1.5% between 1980 and 1994, less than half the levels achieved in the 1970s. A structural break appears to have occurred in 1981 after PASOK came to power. The savings rate fell dramatically, which might have contributed to the lower real-growth performance since 1980. The gross national saving rate fell from 29% of nominal GDP in 1980 to 13% in 1985, and has recovered only to the 17-18% level since 1988. The main reason is the increase in public debt and budget deficits. General government liabilities, which stood at 23% of nominal GDP in 1980 climbed to 48% in 1985, 78% in 1990, and to 115% in 1995. Similarly, the budget deficit amounted to 2.6% of GDP in 1980, but averaged 9% between 1981 and 1986, and further increased to an average of 12% of GDP between 1987 and 1995. Reductions in the heavy debt burden will depend on the success of new revenue generation as well as progress in lowering inflation and real interest rates, and more crucially, on expenditure cuts. Financial transfers from the EU mask a larger deterioration in public finances. Net EU transfers amounted to an average of 2.5% of GDP per annum between 1981 and 1989 and about 4.5% of GDP between 1990 and 1995. The EU has progressively tightened the conditions attached to the transfers. Although the transfers helped to alleviate the external balance constraint, they might have encouraged loose fiscal policy.

Greece's efforts to keep fiscal balances under control may be assisted by privatization, but progress has been slow, with difficulties in the sale of the state telecommunications company, OTE, and the Hellenic shipyards (the biggest in the Eastern Mediterranean). Progress in privatization and structural reforms will be a key factor in Greece's overall performance, and will be instrumental in ensuring continued financial support from the EU.

Inflation

Greece has traditionally experienced inflation of between 10% and 25%. Trends in consumer prices also reflect the deterioration in the internal balance since the early 1980s. Against a background of a 14.3% average increase in consumer prices between 1970 and 1980, inflation reached an average of 19% between 1981 and 1990. Inflation then eased gradually to 8% at the end of 1995 – its lowest since 1973. The main factors behind the gradual lowering of inflation were the government's tighter fiscal stance, which produced a primary budget surplus of more than 2% of GDP since 1994, consistently high real interest rates (around 6%), and a strong drachma. Despite the progress in bringing inflation down to single figures, 1996 year-end inflation of 7.5% in Greece is still the highest in the EU.

Monetary policy

The Bank of Greece uses M3 as an intermediate policy target and monitors the growth of M4 in its attempts to control inflation. This is coupled with a fairly strict drachma policy. M3 and M4 grew by 10.4% and 8.3% in 1995, respectively, against the targets of 7-9% and 9-11%. Domestic credit grew by 7.9%, remaining within the projected growth rate of 6-8%. The overshoot in M3 largely reflects a portfolio shift rather than monetary easing given the tightening in the growth of M4. The Bank of Greece set a target of 6-9% growth for M3 in 1996.

Currency

Greece is a member of the European Monetary System (EMS), but it does not participate in the Exchange Rate Mechanism (ERM). The drachma is included in the ECU basket. The Bank of Greece determines the value of the drachma against other currencies in a daily fixing. Commercial banks quote their own rates in the domestic spot market. Credit institutions are allowed to conduct foreign exchange transactions, including foreign currency swaps and options. All transactions of more than ECU 2,000 have to be notified to the Bank of Greece.

Greek drachma/US dollar exchange rate

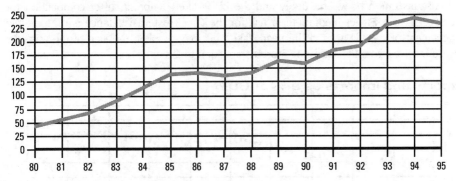

The central bank currently pursues a hard drachma policy aimed at establishing an anchor that weakens inflationary expectations and reduces import price inflation. Since Greece has experienced high inflation, curbing the inflationary expectations is of prime importance. Moreover, imports are high in raw materials and semi-finished products, so a depreciation may feed more price pressures into the economy because of higher input costs. Another reason behind the hard drachma policy is to steadily reduce exchange rate volatility until the drachma participates in the ERM, an objective of Greece's convergence programme to EMU. Nevertheless, Greece's participation in the ERM will require the approval of the other ERM members. In 1996 the inflation differential between Greece and the ERM members was still too high.

The Bank of Greece's main foreign exchange rate target is the drachma/ECU rate. The bank successfully targeted a 3% depreciation of the drachma (GRD) against the ECU in 1995. The bank further announced a 1% depreciation of the drachma against the ECU in 1996.

The bank has had a good record of commitment and ability to contain pressures on the currency, evidenced by its policies to deal with the speculative run in May 1994 (when controls on short-term capital movements were lifted) and during the period of uncertainty in late-1995/early-1996 over the successor to Papandreou.

Trade

Greece has traditionally experienced large foreign trade deficits. The trade balance registered an average of US$5.3 billion between 1980 and 1989. The deficit, however, reached the US$10 billion level between 1990 and 1994, and deteriorated further to US$16.7 billion in 1995. The 1996 deficit estimate is US$18.4 billion. The recent worsening in the trade balance is linked to the hard drachma policy. The current account balance has also come under pressure. However, the deterioration is less visible due to EU transfers, tourism revenue, and workers' remittances. Nevertheless, the Greek tourism sector was also adversely affected by the hard drachma policy, frequent public sector strikes, natural disasters, and poor infrastructure.

European Union countries absorb about 50% of Greek exports. Germany is the leading importer, followed by Italy, France and the UK. Thus, a slowdown in these countries also affects Greek exports. Furthermore, about one quarter of all exports are fresh and processed food, followed by clothing and textiles, while manufactured goods account for about half. The customs union between Turkey and the EU is likely to bring stiffer competition for Greek textiles. A bigger medium-term risk for the Greek external balance is the possible enlargement of the EU around the year 2000. This may threaten the size of the transfers Greece receives from EU and bring more competition to Greek exports.

Exports and imports as a % of GDP

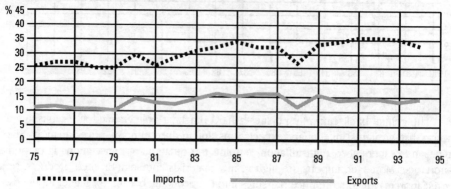

Source: Official data

Breakdown of exports

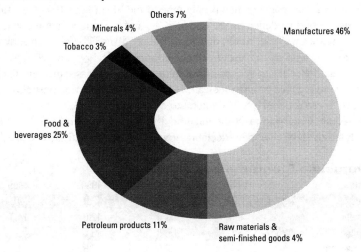

Others 7%

Minerals 4%

Tobacco 3%

Manufactures 46%

Food & beverages 25%

Petroleum products 11%

Raw materials & semi-finished goods 4%

Source: Official data

Current account as a % of GDP

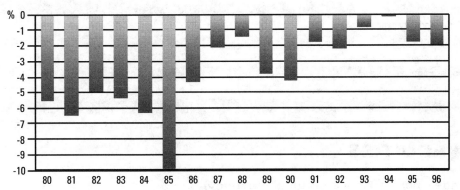

Source: Official data

Debt

In 1996 the level of external debt was estimated at US$55.2 billion, equivalent to almost 46% of GDP. The proportion of Greece's external debt to GDP has increased since 1980, when it was about 21%. Short-term debt as a proportion of total external debt is about 31%, with 80% of this amount owed to commercial banks. Debt servicing costs in 1995 and 1996 amounted to around US$9 billion and US$6.5 billion, respectively, which amounts to 49% of the revenue from the exports of goods and services in 1995 and 35% in 1996. Despite a tight payments schedule and increasing proportion of external debt to GDP, Greece has not experienced external payments difficulties. However, a further worsening in current account balances and the need to defend the drachma may lead to increased pressure on the foreign exchange reserves.

Greece and the European Union

Greece submitted a four-year convergence programme to the EU in June 1994 (see Table), aimed at eliminating the budget deficit by the end of 1999, and bringing inflation down. The decision on which countries will take part in the third stage of EMU will be made in early 1998 using 1997 data. Greece is unlikely to meet any of the EMU criteria in 1997, and will be among the non-core countries (for which a second convergence phase and assistance are likely to be in place) and its convergence programme can, at best, be seen as a demonstration of its willingness to move towards the Maastricht criteria to qualify for further EU assistance. This would, however, require Greece to meet the inflation, the interest rate, and the deficit criteria along with a domestic debt/GDP ratio declining towards 60% "at a satisfactory pace".

Greek Convergence Programme targets

Annual growth rates	1996	1997	1998	1999
GDP at market prices	1.7	2.6	3.0	3.5
Fixed public investment	9.5	11.0	12.0	14.0
Fixed private investment	3.5	6.8	8.4	10.1
Private consumption deflator	6.1	3.9	3.5	3.3
Short-term interest rate	10.6	7.9	6.8	6.2

General government (% of GDP)				
Revenue	38.1	38.3	38.4	38.5
Current primary expenditure	30.5	30.0	29.6	29.1
Interest due	11.9	9.3	7.8	7.0
Net borrowing	7.6	4.2	2.4	0.9
Primary surplus	4.9	5.1	5.4	6.1
Debt	115.3	113.4	109.3	103.4
Transfers from EU	1.0	1.4	1.9	2.6

■ EQUITIES

Index performance (in local currency)

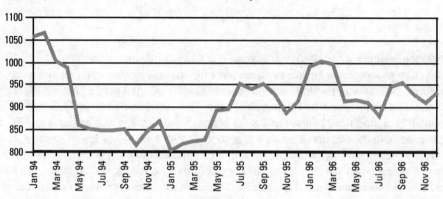

Key indicators

	Index performance %, in US$ terms	Market Cap. US$bn	P/E	Div. Yield	Weight in IFCI	Weight in IFCG
1994	-2.1	14.9	10.4	4.6	1.8	0.9
1995	5.5	17.1	10.5	4.5	1.6	0.9
1996	-1.0	24.2	10.5	3.7	1.5	1.0

Sources: Local stock exchange, IFC, Bloomberg, Datastream, UBS

Structure
There are two exchanges in Greece – the Athens Stock Exchange (ASE) and the new Thessalonika Stock Exchange, which was set up in 1995 and is concentrating on developing an alternative market for companies from Northern Greece and the Balkans. At the end of September 1996, there were 184 companies listed on the ASE, and 34 on the parallel market for medium-sized companies. The market capitalization was over US$24 billion, and daily turnover was US$29 million.

Regulatory authority
The Capital Market Committee was set up in 1991 as an independent public entity operating under the auspices of the Ministery of National Economy.

Trading methods
The ASE uses an automated trading system called ASIS, which covers all listed companies.

Hours
Trading hours have been set out between 10.15 and 10.45 – pre-opening period for the determination of the opening price – and between 10.45 and 13.30 – the main trading session for the execution of orders.

Settlement and clearing
The clearing and settlement process, both for the domestic and for cross-border transactions, is performed by the Central Securities Depository S.A. The CSD follows the delivery versus payment system (DVP) on a T+2 basis.

Types of shares
Ordinary shares account for 96% of all shares issued. Preference shares (which do not carry voting rights) account for the remaining 4% (preferred shares are obliged to pay a minimum dividend amounting to 6% of their par value which is cumulative and therefore is merely postponed, as opposed to being foregone, in event of one or more loss-making fiscal year(s).

Shares of banking, insurance and leasing sector enterprises are registered. A law introduced in September 1994, requires corporations with over 60% of their net worth invested in real estate to have registered shares. Moreover, shares of companies involved in public sector services or supplies should also be registered.

Stock indices
The ASE General Index comprising seventy-five companies accounting for over 60% of market cap. and trading volume is the principal index. There are nine sector indices: Banking, Insurance, Investment, Leasing, Holding, Industrial, Miscellaneous, Construction and Parallel.

Taxes
Distributed dividends carry no tax liability as taxes are applied on profits prior to distribution. The normal corporate tax rate for listed companies is 35%. Capital gains are not taxed.

Disclosure of financial statements
Companies are required to produce half-year reports and full audited full-year results.

Ownership limits for non-residents
Foreign investors can buy shares in any Greek company although re-registration of a change of national status is required for a majority holding in shipping companies. Moreover, the maximum foreign ownership in a media company is 25%.

Capital and foreign exchange controls
Foreign investors can repatriate income from the sale of securities including capital gains and dividends.

Brokers
There are a large number of local brokers including more than fifty major firms.

Sectors
At the end of September 1996, the sectoral breakdown by market capitalization was banking 24%, investment 1.7%, insurance 1.4%, leasing 0.7%, holding companies 1.3%, construction 5.4% and industrial 65.5%.

ADRs
There are a number of Greek companies with ADR listings including John Boutari and Son Wines and Spirits, the Globe Group and the Alpha Credit Bank.

Market comment
The Greek market is relatively small in size compared to other Western European exchanges. There had been hopes that the privatization programme would boost the market in 1994 and 1995. However, progress has been slow. The value of listed shares rose by 11% in 1995 as foreign investors began to take a more active interest in the market.

■ DEBT

All Greek government securities are listed on the Athens Stock Exchange, whose Council supervises secondary market trading. The Capital Markets Committee (CMC) is an autonomous body operating under the auspices of the Ministry of National Economy. One of its functions is to protect investors, ensure market transparency and approve bond issues.

The Bank of Greece uses various methods, including repurchase agreements which charge the interbank overnight intervention rate, 2-week and 4-week auction bid rate, the Lombard rate or the discount rate, for its money-market operations. The introduction of the Athens Interbank Offered Rate (ATHIBOR) in 1992 was an important benchmark and encouraged the development of a derivatives market.

The Ministry of Finance is keen to develop the bond market to reduce the cost of financing the government's budget deficit. It is likely that benchmark issues will be established to facilitate the development of a yield curve, which should help meet the needs of the country's large state-owned banks.

Treasury Bills

Discount T-bills are issued with maturities of 3, 6 and 12 months by the Bank of Greece (BOG) acting as agent for the treasury. Most are sold at fixed prices, but since 1995 bills have been sold through competitive auctions.

Treasury Notes

Floating-rate T-notes are offered through competitive auction, for maturities of 3, 5 and 7 years. The first coupon, set by the Ministry of Finance, pays a spread (as risk premium) over the equivalent bond yield of the 1-year T-bill. Auctions are held monthly.

In November 1996, the finance ministry launched its first issue of fixed rate bonds. It auctioned Dr100mn of 3-year bonds with an 11% coupon, which was 100 basis points lower than the rate on 12-month treasury bills. The finance ministry has plans to issue 5-year fixed rate bonds early in 1997, and will later introduce zero coupon and index-linked instruments.

Treasury bills and notes are tax-free investments.

Foreign currency bonds

These are floating rate bonds targeted at foreign investors, who pay for the bonds in drachmas, but can receive the proceeds at maturity in a prescribed foreign currency. Issues have been denominated in US dollars, yen, deutschmarks, sterling and ecu, with maturities of one to three years. In addition, they offer a two-day currency option after issuance, in case of drachma devaluation, which can raise the coupon's spread over libor. Custody is provided by domestic banks.

Primary market

Competitive auctions were introduced for bill and note issuance in June 1995. They normally take place in the middle of the month. Financial institutions submit bids at two prices for each new issue, which are filled at or above a minimum price determined by the Ministry of Finance. Bills of 3 and 6 months are normally offered at the end of the month, and 12-month bills in the middle of the month.

Secondary market trading was conducted by a double auction, open outcry system, but in 1996 moved to an electronic matching system. Most trades are transacted through banks rather than through the Stock Exchange. Stripped bond coupons are also traded. During the final few months before expiry, foreign currency bonds trade at a similar level to 12-month T-bills: they are bought by domestic investors who transact a forward foreign exchange contract.

The clearing and settlement process is performed by the Central Securities Depository (CSD), which is partly owned by the Athens Stock Exchange. Settlement is delivery versus payment, but securities will be dematerialized soon.

Marathon bonds

These have been issued by international financial institutions since 1994. They are denominated in drachmas, pay fixed coupons and have maturity dates ranging between two and five years. They are tax-free to foreign investors.

Corporate bonds

Greek companies must satisfy certain requirements before they can issue bonds. These include minimum share capital of GRD 1 billion, the issuer must have a five-year history of satisfactory operating profits, and have published five consecutive balance sheets, and the value of the bond issue should not exceed half of the book value of the company's equity, but no less than GRD 20 million. Requirements for listing on the Parallel market are less stringent.

Eurobonds

By November 1996, Greece had issued sixty-four eurobonds denominated in nine different currencies.

Eurobond issues (US$m)

US$ millions	1990	1991	1992	1993	1994	1995	1996
Sovereign	620.2	1543.0	2453.9	3473.2	3652.4	2310.8	3637.5
Private	0.0	0.0	0.0	140.0	0.0	0.0	0.0

■ GREECE: Economic indicators

Population and development	1990	1991	1992	1993	1994	1995	1996e
Population, million	10.0	10.2	10.3	10.4	10.4	10.5	10.5
Population growth, %	0.1	1.5	0.8	0.8	0.5	0.5	0.5
Nominal GDP per capita, US$	8291	8730	9597	8868	9388	10907	11740

National accounts							
Nominal GDP, US$bn	82.9	89.0	99.0	92.0	97.9	114.3	123.6
Change in real GDP, %	0.0	3.1	0.4	-1.0	1.5	2.0	2.2
Gross fixed capital formation, % of GDP	22.6	23.2	22.1	21.0	20.4	21.3	21.9

Money supply and inflation							
Narrow money, change %, Dec/Dec	24.4	13.5	13.3	11.2	11.1	12.4	18.0
Broad money, change %, Dec/Dec	15.3	12.3	14.4	15.0	8.8	10.4	10.9
Consumer price inflation (avg.) %	20.4	19.3	15.9	14.4	11.0	9.3	8.5

Interest rates *=latest figures							
Discount rate, end of year	19.0	19.0	19.0	21.5	20.5	18.0	17.5
Treasury bill rate, annual average	—	22.5	22.5	20.25	17.5	13.8	12.0*
Deposit rate, annual average	19.50	20.67	19.92	19.33	18.92	15.75	12.00*
Prime lending rate, annual average	27.62	29.45	28.71	28.56	27.44	23.05	21.00*

Government finance							
Government expenditure, % of GDP	36.1	33.8	32.7	35.9	38.1	37.2	37.4
Government balance, % of GDP	-14.9	-12.4	-7.3	-11.4	-10.3	-9.9	-8.0

Exchange rates lc=local currency							
Exchange rate, annual average, lc/US$	158.5	182.3	190.6	229.3	242.6	231.7	240.6
Exchange rate, end of year, lc/US$	157.6	175.3	209.2	245.3	242.8	237.9	245.4
Real exchange rate 1990=100	100.0	101.4	104.3	106.3	107.7	111.5	113.8

Balance of payments							
Exports of goods & services, US$m	13018	14126	16231	14614	15829	17060	18300
Change %	117.2	8.5	14.9	-10.0	8.3	7.8	7.3
Imports of goods & services, US$m, fob	19570	20073	22900	20434	21792	26359	29500
Change %	46.3	2.6	14.1	-10.8	6.6	21.0	11.9
Trade balance, of goods only, US$m, fob-fob	-10199	-10136	-11628	-10576	-11442	-14475	-17200
Current account balance, US$m	-3626	-1539	-2105	-721	-133	-2951	-4800
as a % of GDP	-4.4	-1.7	-2.1	-0.8	-0.1	-2.6	-3.9

Foreign exchange reserves							
Foreign exchange reserves, US$m	3412	5189	4794	7790	14488	14780	16600
Gold at ⅔ of market price, US$m	874.1	826.2	785.2	822.5	882.3	885.5	893.6
Import cover (reserves/imports), months	2.1	3.1	2.5	4.6	8.0	6.7	6.8

Foreign debt and debt service							
Short-term debt, US$m	7589	7942	8352	9237	12279	16417	17225
Total foreign debt, US$m	31733	34397	35518	38045	46813	52361	55236
as a % of GDP	38.3	38.6	35.9	41.3	47.8	45.8	44.7
as a % of foreign exchange receipts	175.8	165.9	152.6	172.5	195.2	198.5	200.1
Interest payments, US$m	1824	2014	2262	2086	2102	2682	2550
Principal repayments, US$m	2323	2585	4528	3815	4102	6444	3950
Total debt service, US$m	4147	4599	6790	5901	6204	9126	6500
as a % of goods exports	65.2	67.7	113.0	117.2	118.9	158.1	98.5
as a % of foreign exchange receipts	23.0	22.2	29.2	26.8	25.9	34.6	23.5

Hong Kong

Area (thousands of km²):	1
Population (1995, millions):	6.3
Population projection (2025, millions):	6
Urbanization rate (1993, % of population):	95
Life expectancy (1993, years at birth):	79
Gross domestic product (1996, US$bn):	158.3
GDP per capita (1996, US$):	25101
Average annual GDP growth rate (1990-96, %):	5.1
Average annual inflation rate (1990-96, %):	8.9
Currency (Hong Kong dollar per US$, average 1996):	7.74
Real exchange rate: (1990=100, average 1996)	145.02
Structure of production (1994):	83% services, 27% finance, 9.3% manufacturing sector
Main exports:	miscellaneous manufactured articles, machinery, transport equipment, manufactured goods by materials
Main imports:	intermediate goods, consumer goods, capital goods
Main trading partners:	China, US, Japan, Taiwan, Germany
Market capitalization of Stock Exchange (October 1996; US$bn):	403.5
Total foreign debt (% of GDP):	17.5
Next elections due under normal circumstances:	In 1999 subject to the introduction of acceptable new electoral arrangements
Credit rating: (Nov 1996, Standard & Poor's, Moody's)	A; A3

FORECAST: 1997-2000 (average)

	Worst case	Most likely	Best case
Real GDP growth (%)	2 to 3	4 to 5	6 to 7
Inflation (%)	8 to 10	6 to 7	4 to 5

■ POLITICS

Historical overview

Hong Kong Island was little more than a backwater before China ceded it to Britain in 1841, during the First Opium War. Soon, however, it began to flourish as a burgeoning trade entrepôt between the Chinese Empire and the rest of the world. Britain pushed on to the Mainland in 1860, taking possession of Kowloon Peninsula and Stonecutters Island following the Second Anglo-Chinese War. The demands of other European colonial powers for territorial concessions from China peaked after Japan's military defeat of the Chinese Empire in 1895. The encroachment of the imperialist powers spurred Britain to seek a defensive zone for Victoria harbour. A Sino-British convention signed in 1898 granted Britain a 99-year lease of the New Territories. Except during the period of the Second World War, when Hong Kong was occupied by Japan, Britain has since ruled Hong Kong as a Crown colony through its appointed governor.

The Chinese in Hong Kong thrived under liberal British rule. Racial discrimination was banned in 1865, and with a laissez-faire economic policy and political stability, Chinese immigration to Hong Kong was rapid. Huge numbers of people found asylum in Hong Kong following the Chinese Revolution of 1911 and after the 1948–49 civil war. The Chinese population grew to nearly 1.6 million at the outbreak of the Second World War. The population fell to around 600,000 by the end of the war, but surged to 2.2 million by 1950. In 1997, the People's Republic of China (PRC) will assume sovereignty over a highly affluent city of more than 6 million inhabitants.

Transition to Chinese sovereignty

Ahead of the expiry of the lease on the New Territories, the Sino-British Joint Declaration was signed in December 1984. This bilateral agreement described the terms by which sovereignty over Hong Kong will revert to the PRC on July 1, 1997. The Joint Declaration provides for the future Hong Kong Special Administrative Region of China to enjoy a high degree of autonomy in judicial, legislative, economic and financial affairs. Defence and foreign affairs are reserved to the sovereign government in Beijing.

The PRC has established "one country, two systems" as the guiding principle of its rule over Hong Kong. In April 1990, China's National People's Congress promulgated the Basic Law, Hong Kong's mini-constitution after 1997. The Basic Law guarantees that Hong Kong's capitalist system and way of life shall remain unchanged for fifty years. These documents envisioned a "convergence" of pre- and post-1997 institutions in order to ensure a seamless transition to PRC sovereignty over Hong Kong. However, Sino-British relations began to deteriorate after the traumatic events in Beijing's Tiananmen Square in June 1989. Mutual suspicion prevented the two sides from coming to timely decisions over key issues, such as financial arrangements for the new airport and the establishment of a Court of Final Appeal.

In October, 1992 Chris Patten, Britain's last governor in Hong Kong, outlined his proposals for broadening the franchise of the Hong Kong electorate in the selection of the Legislative Council (Legco). Despite China's objections, the proposals were unilaterally introduced in time for the 1995 elections, the last under British rule. The PRC government subsequently confirmed that the Legco would be replaced by a Provisional Legislature in 1997 until electoral arrangements in accordance with the Basic Law could be introduced. The principle of convergence was damaged.

Nevertheless, with only months remaining before Hong Kong reverts to Chinese sovereignty, confidence appears high. Stock and property prices have rebounded, consumer spending is recovering, and emigration from Hong Kong has stabilized. Nagging questions remain about such issues as limitations on press freedoms, civil service morale, encroaching corruption, the influence of business interests, and the style of governance after 1997, but Beijing seems eager to reassure the Hong Kong public. Although the electorate had no direct influence over the choice for the first chief executive, a leading criterion appeared to be the acceptability of the candidates to the people of Hong Kong.

Chronology

1840–42	First Opium War.
	January: Convention of Chuanbi cedes Hong Kong island to Britain
1856-58	Second Anglo-Chinese War
1860	Convention of Peking cedes Kowloon Peninsula and Stonecutters Island to Britain
1895	Japanese military defeat of China
1898	Convention grants Britain a 99-year lease on the New Territories
1911	Chinese Revolution inaugurates period of rapid immigration into Hong Kong
1942-45	Japanese occupation of Hong Kong
1948-49	Chinese civil war. Nationalist defeat results in renewed immigration
1966-67	Onset of China's Cultural Revolution. Civil disturbances disrupt Hong Kong's economy
1979	Introduction of Deng Xiaoping's "Open Door" policy begins era of Hong Kong direct investment on the Mainland
1984	Sino-British Joint Declaration provides for sovereignty transfer to the PRC on July 1, 1997
1985	Establishment of Joint Liaison Group (JLG) to oversee the transition to PRC sovereignty
1989	Tiananmen Square in Beijing. Demonstrations.
1990	China's National People's Congress (NPC) promulgates the Basic Law
1991	JLG agreement approving new airport construction
1992	Chris Patten arrives as Britain's last Governor. Outlines plans for broadening the electoral franchise.
1993	China establishes "Preliminary Working Committee" in retaliation for the Patten-plan
1994	NPC votes to abolish the elected Legco in 1997
1995	Sino-British agreement that the Court of Final Appeal will be established on July 1, 1997. Final airport financial arrangements are also agreed.
1995	Legco elections result in victory for pro-democracy candidates
1996	Preparatory Committee established in accordance with the Basic Law to supervise final transition process
1996	Selection Committee names post-97 chief executive and members of the Provisional Legislature

Constitution and government

The Letters Patent, the basis of colonial law mandated by the British government, will be replaced by the Basic Law on July 1, 1997. Hong Kong will become a Special Administrative Region (SAR) of China on that date. The Basic Law guarantees autonomy in all areas except defence and foreign affairs. Hong Kong's capitalist way of life is to be preserved for at least fifty years. China's National People's Congress has the power of interpretation and amendment of the Basic Law.

During its colonial past and until 1997, Hong Kong has been ruled by its British-appointed governor in consultation with the Executive Council (Exco) and the 60-member Legislative Council (Legco). Legislation requires passage by Legco before implementation. Before 1990 political parties were illegal and Legco members were appointed by either the governor or functional constituencies. Under the principle of convergence agreed by the

PRC and the UK, the 1995 elected Legco was originally meant to straddle the 1997 transition and remain in office until 1999, but will now be replaced by a Provisional Legislature. Members of the Provisional Legislature will be chosen by the 400-member Selection Committee.

Results of the September 1995 Legco election

The Democratic Party won 11 of the 20 directly elected geographical constituencies seats, with pro-democracy independents and members of smaller parties winning a further five. The main pro-China party, the Democratic Alliance for the Betterment of Hong Kong, won only two of the directly elected seats, but did better in the indirectly elected functional constituencies. Of the total of 60 seats, pro-democracy parties won half outright and pro-Beijing parties took 9. The pro-business Liberal party garnered 10 seats and mostly democracy-leaning independents won 12 seats.

Next elections

These should take place in 1999, subject to the introduction of acceptable new electoral arrangements.

Political forces

Governor

Given the acrimony of recent Sino-British relations and the virulent reaction of the Chinese to Governor Patten's electoral reforms, the governor's ability to shape events in the run-up to the transition is extremely limited. The UK government can still exercise some influence via world opinion and commercial lobbying.

Chief executive

In December 1996, Tung Chee-hwa was elected as Hong Kong's first chief executive, by a Beijing-appointed Selection Committee, for a five-year term. The new SAR chief executive must have the confidence of the PRC government, but is also expected to be acceptable to the Hong Kong public. The chief executive will therefore play the key mediating role, seeking to carry out the wishes of Beijing and its representatives in Hong Kong while striving to fulfil the aspirations of the people of Hong Kong.

Legislature

As under colonial administration, both the Provisional Legislature and any future Legco will be subordinate to a powerful chief executive. The legislature cannot introduce bills without the consent of the chief executive, but it can play a strong advisory role.

Political parties

Parties will continue to exist under SAR administration, but their role is unclear. Democratic Party members have so far refused to consider appointment to the Provisional Legislature.

Business

Hong Kong business interests wield considerable influence in Beijing and, presumably, will have a strong voice in the conduct of the SAR administration after 1997.

Military

The People's Liberation Army (PLA) is a key political actor in Beijing, and could play a similar role in post-97 Hong Kong. Its extensive business interests on the Mainland and coming presence in Hong Kong would appear to lend it considerable influence in the SAR.

Central bank

The only aim of the Hong Kong Monetary Authority is to maintain exchange rate stability within the framework of the link of the Hong Kong dollar to the US dollar. The linked exchange rate is maintained by a currency board system requiring Certificates of Indebtedness, which give note-issuing banks the authority to issue currency notes. Inaugurated in October 1983, the exchange rate peg has provided currency stability during a period of political volatility.

■ ECONOMICS

Historical overview

With only a small territory and limited natural resources, Hong Kong's principal assets are its skilled labour force and strategically located deep-water harbour. As the gateway to southern China, and with its strong links to the Chinese diaspora throughout the Pacific region, Hong Kong's economy is dependent on its role as a merchandise trade entrepôt. Despite its small size, Hong Kong was the eighth largest trading centre in the world in 1995. The container port vies with Singapore's as the busiest in the world.

The government has refrained from promoting specific industries as it has in the other Asian "Tiger" economies, and has followed a liberal, non-interventionist policy of a low tax regime, fiscal prudence, and a transparent rule of law. Following the Second World War, economic development was concentrated in low-cost, labour-intensive manufacturing. Real GDP growth averaged 9% a year during the 1960s and 1970s.

With the introduction of China's Open Door policy in the late 1970s, Hong Kong's economy embarked on a dramatic course of structural change. Its manufacturing capacity was rapidly shifted to lower-cost locations chiefly in neighbouring Guangdong Province of the PRC. Hong Kong itself has thrived as a service centre and regional headquarters for companies doing business in China. Economic integration with the Mainland has proceeded rapidly, with Hong Kong providing some 60% of total realized foreign direct investment in China.

Despite a number of severe shocks to the economy during the 1980s, real GDP growth remained rapid at an average 6.9% a year. The loss of confidence resulting from the conclusion of the Sino-British Joint Declaration in 1984 led to the abandonment of the floating exchange rate regime in favour of a linked exchange rate to the US dollar. A rapid emigration of much of the professional and skilled workforce also ensued. With monetary policy constrained by the exchange rate peg, inflation averaged a high 8.3% a year during the decade.

Domestic and foreign sentiment was again shaken by the violence of Tiananmen Square in 1989. As China imposed a strict economic austerity policy, trade and investment flows to the Mainland dwindled and domestic consumer spending plummeted. Hong Kong's real GDP growth dropped to an average 3% a year during 1989–90.

Recent developments

Economic prospects improved dramatically with Deng Xiaoping's famous tour of Shenzen in January 1992 and his promotion of accelerated economic reform in China. Trade and investment flows through Hong Kong picked up rapidly. A protracted period of US monetary policy easing during the early 1990s resulted in negative real interest rates in Hong Kong, which led to rapid asset price appreciation and a surge in consumer spending. The party ended in early 1994 with US monetary policy tightening, the introduction of administrative measures aimed at curbing the property price bubble, and a renewed period of austerity in China. While private consumption growth slumped in Hong Kong, overall economic expansion remained relatively robust in 1995 due to public sector investment in infrastructure construction. Real GDP growth averaged 5.5% a year during 1991–95.

The economic outlook for the post-1997 period is mixed. Hong Kong's financial and re-export sectors will continue to benefit from enhanced integration with China. But the loss of manufacturing capacity to the Mainland and contraction of domestic merchandise exports will probably lead to continued widening of the trade deficit. The growth of services exports is unlikely to compensate fully, resulting in a growing current account deficit during the coming decade. The trend decline in the real GDP growth rate since the mid-1980s is likely to continue during the next decade.

Population

Hong Kong's population is estimated at 6.3 million. For the past ten years, population growth averaged 1.3%, but the growth rate has fluctuated significantly, falling well below 1.0% during the 1988–90 period because of rapid emigration. Since 1994, population growth accelerated to above 2% p.a. as many previous émigrés returned and the number of expatriates rose. Moreover, a policy promoting family reunification allows 150 mainland Chinese to enter Hong Kong daily.

Post-1997 immigration from mainland China into Hong Kong is likely to continue at a rapid pace, increasing the income gap between new arrivals and highly skilled service sector employees.

The economy

Hong Kong began to relocate its manufacturing capacity to neighbouring Guangdong province on a massive scale in the early 1980s. In the process, it has undergone a rapid structural shift into services and achieved a high level of economic integration with the mainland. The manufacturing sector accounted for 9.3% of GDP in 1994, less than half its tally only five years before. The economy has shed some 50% of its manufacturing workforce during the past ten years. The services sector accounted for 83% of GDP in 1994, up from 70% only ten years earlier. Finance, which includes insurance, real estate and business services, made up nearly 27% of GDP in 1994.

Savings and investment

Like other Asian economies, Hong Kong has a high savings ratio. Gross domestic savings averaged 33.5% of GDP during the 1980s, but declined to 32.6% in 1995 as the economy matured and the propensity to consume began to rise. The rate of investment has been more volatile and somewhat below the norm for Asian "Tiger" economies. Gross domestic investment averaged 27.2% of GDP during the 1980s, but plummeted to just 21.6% in 1985 following announcement of the impending handover to China and the deterioration in investment sentiment. However, gross domestic investment rose to 33.5% of GDP in 1995 as a result of public sector investment in infrastructure. The investment ratio will most likely decline to trend following completion of the new airport in 1998.

Balance of payments

Hong Kong does not publish balance of payments statistics, but current account trends are reflected in the merchandise trade and national accounts statistics. The positive gap between gross domestic savings and investment averaged nearly 8% of GDP during the past ten years, indicating the size of the current account surplus. However, as public sector investment in infrastructure surged in 1995, retained import growth accelerated and Hong Kong recorded its first deficit on goods and services trade since 1982. While construction-related imports have peaked and the goods and services balance is set to improve during 1996–97, the trend towards structural current account deficits is probably irreversible.

Re-export growth averaged a robust 21.6% a year during 1990–95, but the balance of payments has been adversely affected by the transfer to China of domestic manufacturing capacity. The result has been stagnant domestic export growth, averaging only 0.6% a year between 1990 and 1995 against average retained import growth of 10.3%. This has led to a remorseless rise in the merchandise trade deficit, which amounted to US$19.0 billion (13.2% of GDP) in 1995. Services exports increased by a strong 14.7% a year during 1990–95, but was matched by similar growth of services imports. The services trade surplus has remained steady at about 10% of GDP for the last ten years, and is not likely to boost the current account balance significantly in coming years.

Given the openness of Hong Kong's capital account, recording the magnitude of capital flows is difficult. A proxy for the capital account is the change in the foreign currency assets of the Exchange Fund, Hong Kong's official foreign exchange reserves. These doubled in size between 1991 and June 1996 to US$57.3 billion, indicating a healthy overall balance of payments surplus during the period.

Shares of GDP by sector

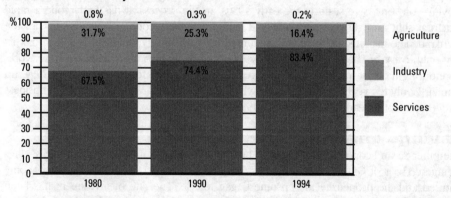

Source: Official data

Exports and imports as a % of GDP

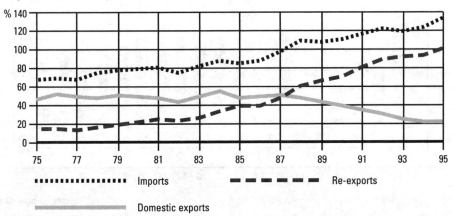

●●●●●●●●●●●●●●●●●●● Imports　　　　■ ■ ■ ■ ■ ■ Re-exports

━━━━━━ Domestic exports

Source: Official data

Breakdown of exports (1995)

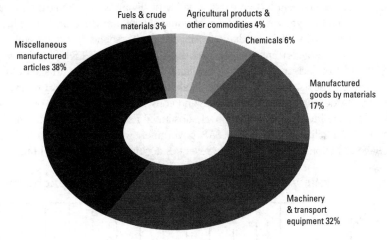

Fuels & crude materials 3%

Agricultural products & other commodities 4%

Chemicals 6%

Miscellaneous manufactured articles 38%

Manufactured goods by materials 17%

Machinery & transport equipment 32%

Source: Official data

Economic policy
Monetary policy

Given the restrictions of the currency board arrangement for the Hong Kong dollar, the monetary environment is determined externally by the US Federal Reserve and cross-border capital flows. Although domestic interest rates closely follow the level of US interest rates, the Hong Kong Monetary Authority (HKMA) can influence short-term rates and adjust liquidity conditions to maintain exchange rate stability. Aside from this kind of fine-tuning, the HKMA has occasionally acted aggressively to defend the exchange rate peg against speculation. The exchange rate peg to the US dollar effectively prevents any counter-cyclical use of monetary policy to smooth business cycle fluctuations, combats a consumer price inflation rate that has admittedly been too high, and contributes to asset price inflation during periods of negative real interest rates.

Goods and services balance as a % of GDP

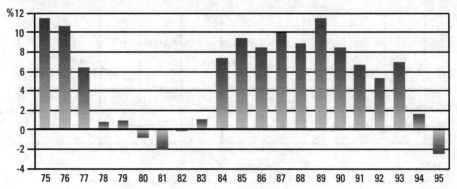

Source: Official data

Fiscal policy

Maintaining confidence in the exchange rate peg also dictates a conservative approach to fiscal policy. The government has an explicit policy of "living within its means", meaning limiting total expenditure growth to the level of nominal GDP growth. Hong Kong has recorded budget surpluses since 1985, but due to increased capital spending on the new airport and related projects, the government incurred a small deficit of HK$2.5 billion in 1995-96. The 1996–97 budget projects a return to surplus, and, given Chinese concerns about overspending on welfare benefits, fiscal prudence is likely to be maintained under Chinese sovereignty after 1997. A decade of budget surpluses and consistent underspending on capital projects in the past has led to the accumulation of substantial fiscal reserves amounting to HK$150 billion (US$19.4 billion). The future SAR government will receive a windfall transfer of around US$22 billion from the land-sale revenues accumulated in the land fund.

Hong Kong dollar/US dollar and nominal effective exchange rate

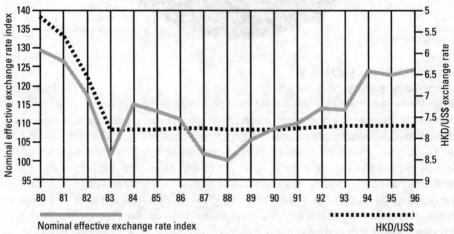

Nominal effective exchange rate index
Nov 83 = 100

HKD/US$

Currency

The revelation of Sino-British negotiations over the future of Hong Kong led to political uncertainty and a run on the Hong Kong dollar in 1983. In order to stem capital flight, the currency was linked to the US dollar at 7.8:1 in October of that year. While debate has raged over the fundamental merits of the peg, it must be seen as a political imperative which has provided the stability under which Hong Kong has since thrived. The Basic Law stipulates that the Hong Kong dollar will continue to circulate as the legal tender in the Hong Kong Special Administrative Region, and that it must be backed by a 100% reserve fund. The Chinese authorities have openly supported the linked exchange rate arrangement and expressed their willingness, in case of speculative attacks, to support the currency with their own reserves.

■ EQUITIES

Index performance (in local currency)

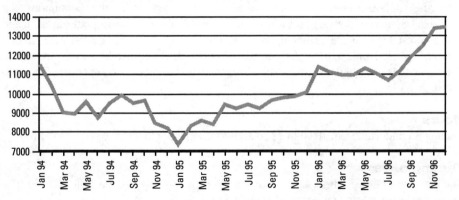

Key indicators

	Index performance %, in US$ terms	Market Cap. US$bn	P/E	Div. Yield
1994	-28.8	269.5	19.4	4.1
1995	37.2	303.7	17.5	3.6
1996	18.4	440.1	14.9	2.9

Sources: Local stock exchange, IFC, Bloomberg, Datastream, UBS

Structure

The Stock Exchange of Hong Kong was capitalized at HK$3.4 trillion (US$437 billion) at the end of November 1996. There were 575 listed companies, of which twenty-two were Chinese and another twenty-two foreign. During 1996, thirty-nine new companies became listed on the exchange, bringing the total number of listed securities to 1,219.

Regulatory authority
The Securities and Futures Commission (SFC) is a statutory regulatory body overseeing the operations of the securities industry in Hong Kong. The Stock Exchange of Hong Kong is a self-regulatory organization operating within a statutory framework. But the SFC has reserved powers to step in if the Exchange fails to discharge its responsibilities. The Companies Ordinance and the Exchange Listing Rules have recently been altered in order to enhance the surveillance of corporate actions.

Trading methods
All stocks are traded through a computerized system called Automatic Order Matching and Execution System (AMS). This system, introduced in 1993, supports both automatic order matching as well as the old semi-automatic quotation system, which comprises an information dissemination system and a trading system. Under this old system, traders enter orders without the order quantity into the system which then displays the broker numbers under each of the two best bid/ask prices. The information is then displayed on the trading floor, where traders would strike deals.

After AMS became operational, listed stocks settled under the Continuous Net Settlement System in the Central Clearing and Settlement System were gradually admitted into automatching. At the beginning of 1996, the exchange introduced the AMS Second Terminal, an electronic trading platform placed in the offices of members of the exchange. This system is designed to enable the Exchange to face future competition from off-exchange trading.

Hours
Trading is conducted from 10.00 to 12.30 and from 14.30 pm to 15.55, Monday to Friday.

Trading rules
The maximum number of outstanding orders per broker number in the system is 200. The number of order in each order queue is limited to 1,000.

Custody
Both global and regional custodians are well represented in Hong Kong. Investors may hold physical stock and there are no restrictions on where the scrip is held. Most institutional investors hold stock in a nominee name using a broker or a bank as settlement agent and custodian. Delivery takes place two days after trading (T+2).

Stock indices
Hong Kong's most popular index is the Hang Seng Index (HSI). First published in 1969, the HSI is a value weighted index of thirty-three of the largest and most liquid stocks. The index's original base date was July 31, 1964, set at 100. When four sub-indices were introduced in 1985, the base date was shifted to January 13, 1984 (the revised base date index was 975.47, the closing for that day). Other indices are the Hang Seng China Enterprises Index and the Hang Seng MidCap 50 Index.

Disclosure of interests

The Securities (Disclosure of Interests) Ordinance requires investors to disclose their interests in the share capital of listed companies, regardless of their place in incorporation. Shareholders that hold more than 10% of a company's issued shares are required to disclose their interests to the Exchange and to the listed company. Directors, chief executives and their families have to disclose their interests, however small, to the Exchange and to the company. When companies themselves do research into their shareholders, they are required to inform the Exchange of the result of their inquiries.

Foreign investment

Hong Kong enjoys one of the world's highest levels of foreign participation in its securities market. There are no restrictions on foreign investment into Hong Kong, except for in the main television broadcasting company Television Broadcasts Ltd. Foreigners cannot hold more than 10% per shareholder and 40% in aggregate of this company.

Taxes

There are no withholding taxes in Hong Kong, and no capital gains tax.

Commission

Minimum commission set by the Exchange is 0.25%, subject to a minimum transaction of HK$50. Both buyer and seller are liable for a transaction levy of 0.013%. Stamp duty amounts to 0.15%. Transfer deed duty, payable by first seller only, is HK$5.

Foreign exchange controls

There are no foreign exchange controls in Hong Kong. Sale proceeds and dividend/interest may be freely repatriated.

Stock Exchange members

There are 563 members of the Stock Exchange of Hong Kong. Of this number, 497 are actively involved in trading while the remainder is non-trading. The members hold 928 shares.

■ DEBT

The bond market has grown rapidly since 1991 due to changes to the structure of the market and the requirements of the banking sector for funds to finance large infrastructure projects. The market is small compared to bank debt and equities. Yet trading of exchange fund bills and notes is now the most liquid public sector market in Asia.

Since 1989, the independent Securities and Future Commission (SFC) has been the main regulator, but listed corporate bonds must meet the requirements of the Stock Exchange of Hong Kong, and deposit-taking institutions are monitored by the Hong Kong Monetary Authority (HKMA).

Hong Kong has no exchange controls so there are no restrictions on foreign participation in the bond markets. The HKMA's Liquidity Adjustment Facility (LAF) offers banks a discount window to manage their liquidity. Eligible securities are exchange fund bills and notes, and private sector debt (minimum Standard and Poor's ratings of A- for banks and A for other issuers), if registered and cleared through the Central Money Market Unit Service (CMU), are marketable and approved by the HKMA.

Public debt

Hong Kong runs a large budget surplus so it has no need to borrow. In 1990, however, it introduced a debt programme that has led to a rapid growth of the government securities market, particularly since 1993.

Exchange fund bills

Ninety-day bills were first offered by the HKMA in March 1990, and 182-day bills the following October. In addition, 364-day bills are now also offered. Tenders are accepted from recognized dealers who submit bids at competitive auctions, and they must hold two accounts with the HKMA: one for their own holdings and the other for their clients.

The HKMA issues bills to manage liquidity, and banks can discount them at the Monetary Authority's LAF.

Exchange fund notes

Two-year notes were introduced in May 1993, and were followed by a 3-year in October, a 5-year in September 1994 and a 7-year in November 1995. Tenders are accepted from recognized dealers who submit bids at competitive auctions.

Notes are issued to give the domestic capital market a benchmark yield curve, and also qualify for borrowing at the LAF.

The CMU was set up in 1990 to provide a computerized clearing and settlement facility for exchange fund bills and notes. It processes immobilized debt (bills and notes held in the CMU) and transfers are made in book entry form. In December 1993 the HKMA extended the facility to non-government securities, and in the following year linked the CMU to euroclear and cedel in an effort to attract foreign investors. From 1996, non-HK dollar bonds were also admitted.

Private debt

The government offers tax incentives to persuade domestic and overseas borrowers to issue bonds in Hong Kong. Nine supranational organizations benefit from profit tax exemption. In contrast to Singapore, Hong Kong has allowed the internationalization of its currency and permits foreign governments and corporates to issue debt denominated in HK$.

The major credit rating agencies, Standard and Poor's, Moody's and Thomson Bank Watch, have offices in Hong Kong.

Commercial paper (CP)

The market is shrinking because of competition from deposit-taking banks and a 17% tax on interest income.

Negotiable certificates of deposit (NCDs)

Issued by banks for terms of up to 3 years to finance high-cost projects.

Corporate bonds

Although the Mass Transit Railway Company (MRTC) issued the first Hong Kong corporate bond in 1976, the market has only developed since the government began issuing exchange fund notes, which offer investors benchmarks for pricing corporate debt.

If the issuer intends to list its bonds on the SEHK, it must comply with the exchange's listing rules and the statutory conditions contained in the Securities Ordinance, Protection of Investors Ordinance and the Companies Ordinance. These include requirements that the company's shares are listed or that shareholder's funds exceed HK$100 million (US$13 million), and that the bond issue size must be a minimum of HK$50 million (US$6 million) and be transferable.

The secondary market is illiquid, but issues registered with and cleared through the CMU qualify as eligible securities for repo transactions at the LAF.

Dragon bonds

The market in international bond issues listed in Hong Kong was launched by an Asian Development Bank offering in 1991. In practice the market is indistinguishable from the conventional eurobond market, and many issues are placed privately and outside the region.

Derivatives

Interest rate swaps can be transacted out to ten years, and a large variety of instruments are available, including forward rate agreements, interest rate caps and floors, swaptions (options into swap agreements) and currency options.

Eurobonds
Eurobond issues (US$m)

	1990	1991	1992	1993	1994	1995	1996
Sovereign	—	—	—	—	—	—	—
Private	50.0	0.0	271.9	6631.4	5389.7	2100.0	1717.5

■ HONG KONG: Economic indicators

Population and development	1990	1991	1992	1993	1994	1995	1996e
Population, million	5.7	5.8	5.8	5.9	6.1	6.2	6.3
Population growth, %	0.3	0.9	1.0	1.8	2.4	2.1	2.0
Nominal GDP per capita, US$	13110	14948	17325	19601	21629	23148	25101

National accounts							
Nominal GDP, US$bn	74.8	86.0	100.7	116.0	131.1	143.3	158.3
Change in real GDP, %	3.4	5.1	6.3	6.1	5.3	4.8	4.3
Gross fixed capital formation, % of GDP	26.4	26.6	27.4	27.3	29.7	30.3	32.4

Money supply and inflation							
Narrow money, change %, Dec/Dec	13.3	19.5	21.1	20.6	-1.2	2.8	—
Broad money, change %, Dec/Dec	22.4	13.3	10.8	15.9	12.9	14.0	—
Consumer price inflation (avg.) %	9.8	11.6	9.3	8.5	8.2	8.6	6.0

Interest rates							
Money market rate, average	—	—	4.06	3.56	5.88	5.88	—
Deposit rate, average	5.50	3.50	1.50	1.50	3.75	—	—
Prime lending rate, average	10.1	9.5	7.4	6.5	7.2	8.9	—
Overnight interbank offer rate (HIBOR)	8.2	5.8	3.6	3.0	3.9	5.6	—

Government finance							
Government expenditure, % of GDP	14.7	13.8	14.5	16.4	16.1	16.5	16.1
Government balance, % of GDP	0.7	3.4	2.8	2.1	1.1	-0.2	0.1

Exchange rates lc=local currency							
Exchange rate, annual average, lc/US$	7.79	7.77	7.74	7.74	7.73	7.74	7.74
Exchange rate, end of year, lc/US$	7.80	7.78	7.74	7.73	7.74	7.73	7.74
Real exchange rate 1990=100	100.0	111.9	118.1	126.1	149.7	143.6	145.0

Balance of payments							
Exports of goods & services, US$m	100414	119283	143956	163119	182880	211195	226400
Change %	12.3	18.8	20.7	13.3	12.1	15.5	7.2
Imports of goods & services, US$m, fob	93742	113212	138172	154557	180214	213941	224300
Change %	15.2	20.8	22.0	11.9	16.6	18.7	4.8
Trade balance, of goods only, US$m, fob-fob	-341	-1685	-3920	-3406	-10388	-19021	-16900
Current account balance, US$m	6672	6071	5783	8562	2666	-2746	2100
as a % of GDP	8.9	7.1	5.7	7.4	2.0	-1.9	1.3

Foreign exchange reserves							
Foreign exchange reserves, US$m	28900	35300	43000	49300	55400	56400	58000
Import cover (reserves/imports), months	3.1	3.1	3.3	3.3	3.1	3.0	3.0

Foreign debt and debt service							
Short-term debt, US$m	—	6274	6897	7210	8073	9452	—
Total foreign debt, US$m	—	13456	14417	15283	17492	18908	—
as a % of GDP	—	15.6	14.3	13.2	13.3	13.2	—
as a % of foreign exchange receipts	—	11.3	10.0	9.4	9.6	9.0	—
Interest payments, US$m	—	822	538	487	750	1051	—
Principal repayments, US$m	—	645	1074	1171	1235	1243	—
Total debt service, US$m	—	1467	1612	1658	1985	2294	—
as a % of goods exports	—	1.5	1.3	1.2	1.3	1.3	—
as a % of foreign exchange receipts	—	1.2	1.1	1.0	1.1	1.1	—

Hungary

Area (thousands of km²):	93
Population (1995, millions):	10.4
Population projection (2025, millions):	9.6
Population younger than 15 yrs (1991, % of total):	20
Urbanization rate (1993, % of population):	65
Life expectancy (1993, years at birth):	69
Gross domestic product (1996, US$bn):	44.3
GDP per capita (1996, US$):	4331
Average annual GDP growth rate (1990-96, %):	-2.0
Average annual inflation rate (1990-96, %):	25.6
Currency (forint per US$, average 1996):	155
Real exchange rate: (1990=100, average 1996)	130
Structure of production (1994):	60% services, 33% industry, 7% agriculture
Main exports:	raw material, food, machines
Main imports:	raw material, machines, consumer goods
Main trading partners:	EU (Germany, Austria, Italy, Russia, France & US)
Market capitalization of Stock Exchange (October 1996; US$bn):	4.7
Total foreign debt (% of GDP):	66.7
Next elections due under normal circumstances:	Legislative scheduled May 1998; presidential scheduled June 2000
Credit rating: (Nov 1996, Standard & Poor's, Moody's)	BBB; Ba1

FORECAST: 1997-2000 (average)

	Worst case	Most likely	Best case
Real GDP growth (%)	3.0	4.5	5.0
Inflation (%)	15.1	13.25	11.5

■ POLITICS

Historical overview

In 896, seven nomadic tribes took over the land that would later become Hungary. It took until 1001 for the country to become a kingdom under Saint Stephen I, who introduced Christianity. In the 16th century, a substantial part of Hungary fell to advancing Ottoman troops, and remained under their control for about 150 years. During the 17th century Hungary was integrated with Austria, although the country was permitted a substantial degree of autonomy. In 1867 it became Austria's partner in the Dual Monarchy of the Austro-Hungarian Empire.

Following the collapse of the Austro-Hungarian Empire in 1918, Hungary became a fully independent state and a democratic republic was proclaimed. In 1920 the monarchy was re-installed with a former Austro-Hungarian admiral, Mikós Horthy, as regent. As a result of the Treaty of Trianon following the First World War, the Hungarian government had to accept the loss of two-thirds of its previous territory and about 3 million native Hungarians living in neighbouring states. In the Second World War, Hungary was allied with and later occupied by Nazi Germany. In October 1944, Soviet armies occupied Hungary.

According to the Potsdam Treaty, Hungary, together with the other Central and Southern Eastern European countries, came into the Soviet sphere of interest. In 1948, Communist rule was installed with Mátyás Rákosi as Secretary-General of the Communist Party. Nationalization and overly aggressive collectivization of agricultural land, based on the Soviet model, together with economic hardship and political terror, led to an uprising in 1956, which was brutally suppressed by Soviet troops. The following "Kádár era" was less repressive, with some political relaxation and economic reforms, most notably in the agricultural sector in 1957 and the overall "New Economic Mechanism" (NEM) in 1968. In foreign policy, however, the regime remained careful not to antagonize the USSR. The NEM loosened centralized planning and control of the economy and introduced a limited number of market economic elements. As a result, Hungarian enterprises were directly confronted with domestic and foreign markets and Hungary became strongly integrated into the world economy. The simultaneous existence of elements of both planned and market economies caused disturbances to the system, however, and led to internal and external imbalances, which helped the hard-liners to hit back between 1974 and 1979. The NEM was partially taken back, direct controls were re-introduced, and special credits and subsidies increased again. The reform policy of stop and go continued until the middle of the 1980s.

Recent events

Already intense under the short era of Andropov, political discussion in Hungary increased after 1985 under Gorbachev. In 1988 János Kádár resigned as secretary-general of the Communist Party after thirty-two years. Under the new Communist secretary-general, Károly Grósz, further steps towards political liberalization became possible.

These steps were symbolized in the official rehabilitation and reburial of Imre Nagy, the executed prime minister of 1956, together with four other victims of the Hungarian uprising. Official terminology described the events of 1956 as a "counter-revolution" to a "popular uprising against the existing state power". In February 1989, the Communist Party gave up its "leading role in society" and agreed to the establishment of a multiparty system. The constitution was revised to provide a democratic system, regular elections were announced for March 1990 and the name of the country was changed from the "People's Republic of Hungary" to the "Republic of Hungary". The country's symbolic removal of the "Iron Curtain" from the border with Austria in May and the official opening of the Hungarian-Austrian border allowed for the exodus of thousands of East Germans seeking to emigrate to West Germany in September 1989. These constituted two important steps for radical change in Eastern Europe.

In 1990 a coalition of centre-right parties won the parliamentary majority in the first free legislative elections since 1949. The newly formed National Assembly elected Árpád Göncz as the President of Hungary. In the second regular elections in 1994, the Hungarian

Socialist Party (HSP), the reform wing of the former Communists, won the majority and formed a coalition government with the Association of Free Democrats (AFD).

Since the first free democratic elections of May 1990, Hungary's political system has remained remarkably stable, in spite of four decades of totalitarian rule. One major reason for Hungary's political stability is its largely homogenous demographic structure, which has prevented clashes between different ethnic minorities. However, the status of Hungarian minorities in the formerly autonomous province of Voivodina – part of Serbia since 1990 – is far from satisfactory. Slovakia is also home to a sizeable Hungarian majority. Although this problem was addressed by a treaty signed with Hungary at the beginning of 1995, laws apparently flouting this agreement have recently been passed by Slovakia which limit the use of Hungarian in schools and on signposts for places inhabited mainly by Hungarian speakers. In September 1996, following long and acrimonious negotiations, a similar treaty was signed with Romania. This treaty, which is a precondition for EU and NATO membership, still has to be ratified and implemented.

The popularity of the current mid-left coalition government revived again after reaching a low in mid-1995 following the unveiling of an unpopular austerity programme. The coalition stands a good chance of winning the next elections, due in 1998 despite the growing unpopularity of Prime Minister Horn. The government's austerity programme has received international acclaim, and this will make it possible to ease the current tough measures without jeopardizing the stability achieved. An expected growth acceleration in 1997 should raise real incomes again after two years of decline and thus improve the government's standing among the population.

Chronology

896	Seven tribes settle the land which constitutes present-day Hungary
1001	Establishment of Hungary as a Western Christian kingdom by Saint Stephen I
1526	Beginning of Ottoman occupation (150 years) and division of Hungary into three parts (Hungarian, Hapsburg and Ottoman spheres)
1686	End of the Ottoman occupation; Hungary is integrated into the Hapsburg Empire
1848	Hungarian civic revolution and uprising against Hapsburg rule
1867	Reorganization of the Hapsburg Empire as the Dual Monarchy of Austria and Hungary
1914	The Austro-Hungarian Empire enters the First World War.
1918	The disintegration of the Austro-Hungarian Empire, followed by Hungary's independence. Hungary is declared a republic.
1920	The restoration of the monarchy
1920	According to the Treaty of Trianon, Hungary loses two-thirds of its previous territories and about 3 million native Hungarians to its neighbouring countries
1941	Hungary enters the Second World War in alliance with Germany and Italy
1945	The Soviet Army liberates Hungary from German occupation. According to the Potsdam Treaty, Hungary enters the "Soviet Interest Sphere".
1948	Communists take over
1949	Amendment of the constitution and establishment of the "Socialist People's Republic"
1956	Uprising under Imre Nagy against Soviet occupation and Communist rule
1956	János Kádár is installed by the USSR as the new orthodox Communist leader
1957	Economic reform in agriculture

1968	Introduction of the "New Economic Mechanism"
1982	Hungary becomes a member of the IMF and the World Bank
1988	János Kádár resigns as secretary-general of the Communist Party and is replaced by Károly Grósz. The National Assembly votes to allow the establishment of independent political organizations as well as the right to demonstrate.
1989	Amendment of the Hungarian constitution. Removal of the "Iron Curtain" from the Austrian border.
1990	The Hungarian Democratic Forum (HDF) and its allies win the first free elections since 1949. Hungary becomes a member of the Council of Europe.
1992	Hungary becomes an associated member of the EU
1994	Hungary applies for full membership in the EU
1996	Hungary becomes a member of the OECD

State organization

Hungary is divided into 19 counties and further into 97 districts. There are 168 town authorities, of which 5 cities claim separate county status. In rural areas villages have their own representative bodies. Elections for local governments are held every four years.

Constitution and government

The first Hungarian constitution in written form was introduced in 1949, followed by the establishment of the Hungarian People's Republic. The constitution was amended several times, with the latest radical amendments in October 1989, abolishing the People's Republic and proclaiming the Republic of Hungary.

National Legislature

Hungary's highest body of state authority is the unicameral National Assembly. According to the referendum of 1990, the National Assembly enacts the constitution and law, elects the president, and determines the state budget. The National Assembly consists of 386 deputies, made up of 176 individual constituency winners, 125 allotted by proportional representation and 85 from a national list, who are elected for a four-year term. The president is the head of the state and also serves as the commander-in-chief of the armed forces. The president is elected by the National Assembly for a period of four years.

The government, currently headed by Prime Minister Gyula Horn, is the supreme executive body of the state. The prime minister and other members of the government are elected by the National Assembly on the recommendation of the president.

Current government
President (re-elected June 19, 1995)   Árpád GÖNCZ

HSP and AFD coalition government (formed June 25, 1994, took office July 25, 1994)

Prime Minister	Gyula Horn (HSP)
Deputy Prime Minister	Gábor Kuncze (AFD)
Defence Minister	György Keleti (HSP)
Finance Minister	Péter Medgyessy (HSP)

Foreign Affairs Minister	László Kovács (HSP)
Interior Minister	Gábor Kuncze (AFD)
Trade and Industry	Szabolcs Fazakas (independent but nominated to the post by the HSP)
Speaker of Parliament	Zoltán Gál (HSP)
President, central bank	György Surányi

Political parties

Between 1949 and 1989, no party except the Hungarian Socialist Worker's Party was allowed. In 1989, it gave up its "leading position in the society" and made way for a democratic multiparty system.

Main parties

Hungarian Socialist Party (HSP) (Magyar Szocialista Párt)
Founded in 1989 from the reform wing of the Hungarian Socialist Worker's Party.
The Party leader is Gyula Horn, former minister for foreign affairs in the last (pre-1989) government and current prime minister. The HSP was the winner of the 1994 elections with 54% of the parliamentary seats. A government coalition with the AFD was formed in 1994.

Alliance of Free Democrats (AFD) (Szabad Demokraták Szövetsége)
Centre-left
Founded in 1988
Led by Iván Petö
The second strongest in the 1994 elections after the HSP, its government coalition partner

Hungarian Democratic Forum (HDF) (Magyar Demokrata Fórum)
Populist wing of the old conservative right-oriented HDF Founded in 1987
Led by Sándor Lezsák
Winner of 1990 elections, it formed the government coalition until 1994 with the ISP and the Christian Democrats

The Hungarian Democratic People's Party (HDDP) (Magyar Demokrata Néppárt)
Centre right
Led by former finance minister Iuàn Szabo
Split in March 1996 from the right-wing (60%) majority of the HDF. After the split there were seventeen HDPP deputies in parliament.

Independent Smallholder's Party (ISP) (Független Kisgazda Párt)
Right wing
Founded in 1988
Led by József Torgyán
The party was split into two groups in early 1993. One remained loyal to the government and the other, led by József Torgyán, left the coalition and went into opposition. After the split of the HDF, the ISP, together with its populist leader, József Torgyán, is the most dynamic force in the opposition.

Christian Democratic People's Party (CDPP) (Kereszténydemokrata Néppárt)
Right wing
Founded in 1989
Led by György Giczy

Federation of Young Democrats (FYD) (Fiatal Demokraták Szövetsége)
Centre right
Founded in 1988
Led by Viktor Orbán

Election results

	1990 seats	1994 seats	constituency seats	regional proportional	national transferable
Hungarian Socialist Party	33	209	149	53	7
Alliance of Free Democrats	92	69	16	28	25
Hungarian Democratic Forum	165	38	5	18	15
Independent Smallholders' Party	43	26	1	14	11
Christian Democratic People's Party	21	22	3	5	14
Federation of Young Democrats	21	20	0	7	13
Others	11	2	2	0	0
TOTAL	386	386	176	125	85

Having won 54% of the seats, the Hungarian Socialist Party emerged as the clear winner of the May 1994 elections. The runners up, with 18% of the seats, were the Alliance of Free Democrats. Although – given their absolute majority – the HSP could have governed on their own, they decided nevertheless to form a coalition with the Free Democrats. This move was probably triggered by fears of in-fighting between left- and right-wingers within the HSP, which could even have jeopardized the party's majority in parliament and, hence, the Socialists' ability to stay in power. Moreover, a two-thirds majority is required for amendments to the constitution, which is only possible with the participation of the liberals in the coalition.

Central bank

In 1987 a two-tier banking system was introduced. The new Law of the National Bank of Hungary (NBH) was approved by the National Assembly at the end of 1991 and came into force in 1992. While the NBH continued to be the central bank of the state and the bank of issuing currency, it was deprived of its commercial-bank functions. The new law gave the NBH freedom in shaping monetary policy and limited financing of the state budget. According to law, the president and vice-president of the NBH are appointed for a six-year term by the president of the Republic following the nominations by the prime minister. The members of the board of the central bank have a three-year term of office.

Membership of international organizations

Since 1955, Hungary has been a member of the United Nations (UN) and many of its agencies (UNESCO, FAO, UNIDO, WHO etc.). It is a signatory to the World Trade Organization (WTO). Hungary joined the International Monetary Fund (IMF) and World Bank in 1982. It has been a member of the International Finance Corporation (IFC) and the International Development Association (IDA) since 1985, and in 1990 it became the first Eastern European country to be admitted to the European Council. Hungary is member of the Bank for

Reconstruction and Development (EBRD) and the Central European Free Trade Agreement (CEFTA). Hungary has been associated with the European Union since the beginning of 1992 and signed a free-trade agreement with EFTA in mid-1992. It applied for EU membership in 1994 and also intends to join NATO.

■ ECONOMICS

Historical overview

The transformation of the Hungarian economy in accord with Communist politics began in the 1950s. Economic development was mainly focused on heavy industry, while little attention was paid to the country's lack of natural resources. Industries were nationalized and agriculture organized on a collective basis. Treaties on economic co-operation with the USSR and other Communist countries were concluded. Hungary joined the Council for Mutual Economic Aid (COMECON) in 1949 and the Warsaw Pact in 1955. The strict central planning in the early 1950s was partly relaxed with the reform of the agricultural sector in 1957 and more pronounced after 1968 with the implementing of reforms, known as the New Economic Mechanism (NEM). The NEM abolished the detailed imperative central planning on the level of the enterprises and transferred certain responsibilities from the ministries to individual plant managers. At the same time, reforms re-orientated the economy away from heavy industry towards consumer goods. A gradual liberalization of (retail) prices, exchange rates and foreign trade also began. The introduction of the reforms led initially to a rapid improvement both in the economy and in living standards. The simultaneous existence of elements of both planned and market economies caused, however, disturbances to the system, leading to a reversal of reforms from 1974 until 1979. During this time, moves were made towards recentralization, restrictions in the decision-making processes of enterprises were reintroduced and price regulations were applied again.

Following the growth of foreign trade deficits and of foreign debt, there was another change in policy in 1979 which sought to improve the foreign trade balance. Domestic consumption and investment were curbed in order to raise exports. Import restrictions followed in 1982. Although this austerity policy resulted in a trade surplus, the price paid was in lower GDP growth and higher inflation. The economic decline intensified the pressure for reform. Small private enterprises (with a maximum of thirty employees) and joint ventures were allowed in 1981. In 1982 the issuing of company bonds was allowed as one of the early financial market instruments. The new two-tier banking system was introduced in 1987, followed by the introduction of VAT and a Western-style personal income tax, and – most remarkably for a socialist country – the introduction of unemployment benefits. The reopening of the Stock Exchange took place in June 1990 after an interruption of more than five decades and opened up the possibility, together with the revised Company Act, to convert state-owned enterprises into joint stock companies.

Recent developments

After the fall of Communism in Eastern Europe in 1989 the reform process in Hungary accelerated. The simultaneous implementation of the new bankruptcy law, the banking act and the law on corporate accounting in 1992 triggered a microeconomic "big bang", forcing companies to operate in a genuine market environment. After the early implementation of market economic reforms a macroeconomic "big bang" was not necessary. While industrial production declined and GDP fell sharply until 1994, the cumulative decline in Hungary between 1990 and 1993 was 18.2%, among the lowest in the region (Slovakia: 24.7%, Czech Republic: 22%, Slovenia 18.6%, Poland 13%). The budget deficit and public debt increased rapidly as a result of bank recapitalization and measures to aid a number of large enterprises by taking over parts of their debt by the budget. Rapidly rising domestic demand was fuelled by a decline in household savings, caused by negative real interest rates and high bank liquidity. This led to a sharp deterioration of the current account in 1993.

Unfortunately, the new HSP-AFD coalition government took more than eight months to introduce an urgently needed macroeconomic stabilization programme. The package, introduced on March 12, 1995, included the devaluation of the forint by 9% coupled with the introduction of a crawling peg devaluation (by 1.9% per month initially and by 1.2% per month since the beginning of 1996) and the introduction of an import surcharge of 8%. A tight wage policy intended to reduce consumption and imports lowered pressures on the budget. Since the introduction of the programme, Hungary has improved its budget and foreign trade balance considerably. In late 1995 the forint was made fully convertible for current account transactions. Both Hungarians and foreigners can freely exchange the forint into foreign currencies for any current account transactions. According to the IMF criteria this classifies the forint as a convertible currency. There remain, however, restrictions in capital account transactions.

The economy

The rapid industrialization programme pushed through by the Communist government in the 1950s and 1960s transformed the country from an agrarian to an industrial society. Even after 1980, however, the agricultural sector accounted for 17.5% of GDP – well above the Western European average. The second big economic restructuring, which took place after 1989, was felt hardest by the agricultural sector: its share of GDP then declined to 6.7% by 1994. This is probably below its potential, given that Hungary's climatic and topographic conditions are ideal for agriculture. The halving of agriculture's contribution to gross domestic product between 1990 and 1994 was accompanied by a sharp downturn in GDP of almost 16%. By 1994, industry's contribution to GDP had declined to 30.5%, with the result that the service sector now accounts for more than 60% of economic activity in Hungary. The size of the shadow economy is estimated to be about 30%.

Since 1990 – and for the first time in the last forty years – Hungary has been confronted with the problem of open unemployment. Compared with the other Central Eastern European countries, Hungary's unemployment rate is in the middle range, between that of the Czech Republic (3%) and the high rates prevailing in Poland and Slovenia (14%).

Unemployed (000s)/unemployment rate (%) at end of period

	1990	1991	1992	1993	1994	1995	1996
Number of unemployed	79.5	406.1	663.0	632.1	519.6	495.9	—
Unemployment rate (%)	1.9	7.5	12.3	12.1	10.4	10.4	10.5

Source: Hungarian National Bank

Share of GDP by sector

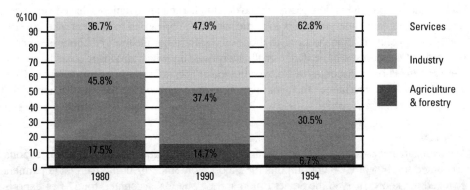

Source: Official data

Savings and investment

Investment in Hungary has undergone a transformation since the collapse of the Communist system, in which most investment was channelled through state-administrated enterprises. While in 1987 83% of total investment came from the public sector, in 1995 it was just 19.8%. Foreign direct investment (FDI) increased markedly between 1989 and 1995, amounting to US$12 billion. A large share of the State Property Agency's (SPA) revenues came from foreign investors, reaching over 90% in 1995. In May 1996 cumulative FDI (since 1990) from Germany made up 37% of the total, followed by US (19%) and French (13%) investment. Investment in enterprises was largely financed by retained earnings or by foreign borrowing. The share of enterprise borrowing on total foreign debt grew between 1990 and 1995 from 5.8% to 17.5%. The share of bank loans on investment financing has been low owing to high cost and difficult access. Over half of equity investments was undertaken by firms with foreign participation, with imported machinery and equipment accounting for about two-thirds.

Gross fixed capital fell in real terms between 1990 and 1992 (-7%; -10%, -2.7%), practically stagnated in 1993, but grew quite strongly in 1994 and 1995 (12.2%, 9%). Gross national savings declined from 21% of GDP in 1990 to the minimum of 13% in 1993 and grew again to 19% in 1995.

Privatization

The base for privatization in Hungary was made in 1988 and 1989 by the Company Act, the Foreign Investment Act and Transformation Act. The real start was in 1990, when the State Property Agency (SPA) was established and began to work. From the planned privatization of first twenty enterprises, six had been fully privatized by 1993 and five others had gone bankrupt. Progress on privatization was initially rapid and then slowed after 1993 before accelerating sharply again in the second half of 1995. A state holding company, AV Rt, was created 1995, and is under the control of the minister without a portfolio for privatization.

There has been no mass privatization in Hungary. Each individual enterprise has been treated separately, under a variety of schemes by a "British-style" case-by-case procedure. The main part of privatized firms were sold off to foreign investors for foreign currency (approximately 93% of privatization-revenues in 1995). The revenues of AV Rt in 1995 were about US$3.5 billion, of which US$3 billion was foreign investment. A variety of concessions, such as subsidized government loans and favourable leasing arrangements, have been introduced to tempt Hungarian investors to participate in the privatization process. The government issued compensation coupons to those who suffered or incurred certain losses under the former Communist regime. Only small enterprises, for which no buyer could be found, were privatized by manager and employee buy-outs. The share of the private sector to GDP is about 70%. Most machine manufacturing is already privatized, and the privatization of the energy sector began recently.

Trade

The Hungarian economy's reliance on foreign trade is relatively high: in 1995, exports accounted for 43% of GDP and imports for almost 49%. Since 1990 the main trade partners changed markedly. In 1986 the Soviet Union and COMECON accounted for 57% of exports and 51.6% of imports. By 1995 the European Union accounted for 64.3% of exports and 61.5% of imports. This share has grown rapidly since Hungary acquired EU associate status in 1992, even though trade barriers and quotas have continued to limit trade in agricultural products, textiles and steel.

Regional structure of foreign trade (%)

Merchandise exports	1980	1989	1990	1995
Germany	9.9	11.9	16.8	28.7
Austria	4.2	6.5	7.5	10.1
Italy	4.6	4.7	5.9	8.5
Russia	31.0	25.3	20.7	6.4
France	1.8	2.4	2.7	4.0
US	1.3	3.3	3.5	3.2
Merchandise imports				
Germany	12.2	16.0	17.3	23.4
Russia	28.8	22.1	19.1	11.8
Austria	5.5	8.6	9.9	10.7
Italy	3.2	3.4	4.1	7.9
France	2.3	2.2	2.0	4.0
US	2.6	2.5	2.6	3.1

Source: OECD; Hungarian National Bank

Hungary's main trading partners – for both exports and imports – are Germany, Austria, Italy, Russia, France and the US. The signatories to the Central European Free Trade Agreement (CEFTA, of which Hungary is also a member) are substantially less important than these countries.

As might be expected, Russia's share of Hungarian exports declined drastically after 1989 and particularly so after COMECON was disbanded in 1990. On the import side, Russia is still the second biggest supplier, accounting for almost 12% of Hungary's imports. This is attributable in large part to Hungary's shortage of raw materials and the infrastructure already in place for oil and gas supplies.

Regional structure of foreign trade by country group

	Exports		Imports	
	1989	1995	1989	1995
Transitional/non-market economies	47.3	24.9	44.3	24.0
of which E. European countries	35.7	20.5	33.1	22.1
Market economies	52.7	75.1	55.7	76.0
of which industrialized countries	44.2	71.1	49.7	70.4
of which EU	24.8	64.3	29.0	61.5
of which developing countries	8.4	4.0	6.0	5.5
TOTAL	100.0	100.0	100.0	100.0

Source: Hungarian National Bank

Structure of exports by product group

	1980	1986	1989	1990	1995
Energy/power	1.8	1.9	2.4	2.5	2.4
Intermediates	29.8	30.2	36.3	37.8	39.5
Machinery	27.7	31.1	24.0	20.1	11.3
Industrial consumer goods	17.2	16.5	15.7	16.5	25.0
Foods	23.5	20.3	21.6	23.1	21.8
TOTAL	100.0	100.0	100.0	100.0	100.0

Source: OECD; Hungarian National Bank

Structure of imports by product group

	1980	1986	1989	1990	1995
Energy/power	13.3	18.4	11.0	13.8	10.8
Raw materials, intermediates	49.2	45.3	50.6	46.3	42.3
Machinery	20.3	17.4	18.1	17.9	20.1
Industrial consumer goods	9.0	11.8	13.1	14.4	20.9
Foods	8.2	7.1	7.2	7.6	5.9
TOTAL	100.0	100.0	100.0	100.0	100.0

Source: OECD; Hungarian National Bank

In 1995, Hungary's principal exports were intermediates (39.5%), food (21.8%), industrially manufactured consumer goods (25%) and machinery (11.3%). With a growth rate close to 10 percentage points, the share of industrially manufactured consumer goods has increased most rapidly. That machinery's share of exports has dropped below half its original level can undoubtedly be put down to the loss of the former COMECON markets and to the problems that Hungarian manufacturers have so far experienced in selling their products on world markets. Where imports are concerned, the leading products are raw materials and intermediates (42.3%), machinery (20.1%), industrially manufactured consumer goods (20.9%) and energy (10.8%). Here again, the share of industrially manufactured consumer goods has shown the sharpest rise since 1989 (up 6%) due mainly to the deregulation of imports into Hungary.

Exports and imports as a % of GDP

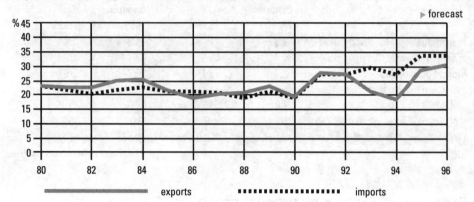

Source: IIF Database

Breakdown of exports (1995)

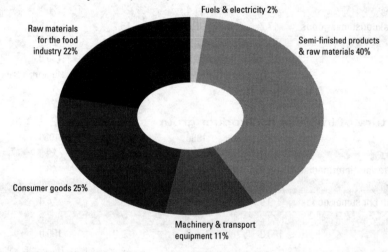

Source: National Bank of Hungary

Balance of payments

Whereas Hungary's trade balance was in surplus in the years immediately following 1989, large deficits were registered in 1993 and 1994 owing to the collapse of the export sector. The microeconomic "big bang", which – through the simultaneous implementation of new laws on bankruptcy, banks and corporate accounting – triggered the closure of a large number of companies, also destroyed a sizeable part of Hungary's export industry. It took two years – until 1995 – for exports to recover. The trade deficit narrowed from US$3.6 billion in 1994 to US$2.4 billion in 1995, though imports increased at the same time by 35%.

The macroeconomic stabilization programme helped to reduce the trade imbalance. The one-time devaluation of the forint by 9% plus the introduction of a crawling peg has improved exporters' competitiveness on the cost side. With private consumption hit by the decline in real incomes, export markets have become increasingly important to the sales and growth potential of Hungarian companies. The introduction of an import surcharge of 8% has certainly helped to fill government coffers and thus also to cut the budget deficit. However, it has had only a limited impact on imports. With demand for imported capital goods remaining high, any attempt to limit these would be a strategic mistake.

Hungary posted a deficit on invisibles every year from 1993 to 1995. This was mainly due to the high rates of interest on its external indebtedness. During this period, Hungary's foreign debt, which was already fairly large, registered an unusually strong nominal increase, rising by 15% in US dollar terms in 1993, by 16% in 1994 and 11% in 1995. Owing to a 10% decline in gross indebtedness during the first half of 1996 and falling interest rates, lower interest payments for the year as a whole are expected. With Hungary's traditional surpluses from tourism and from the net inflow of transfer payments, the invisible balance is likely to be in surplus again this year, which will partly offset the deficit in the trade balance.

Current account as a % of GDP

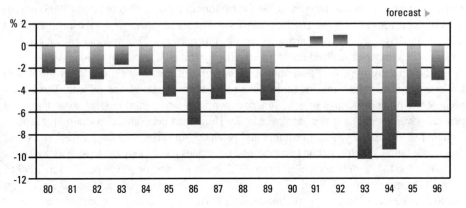

Source: Official data

Currency

The official Hungarian currency is the Hungarian forint (HUF; 1 forint=100 filler). Since March 1995, the forint has been under a crawling peg exchange-rate system against a basket of currencies giving 70% weight to the ECU and 30% to the US$ with a monthly average devaluation ratio of 1.2% throughout 1996. Before the new Foreign Exchange Act was adopted in November 1995, the forint was only "internally convertible". Since November 1995 the Hungarian forint has been convertible on current-account transactions in line with Article 8 of the IMF statute.

Hungarian forint/US dollar exchange rate

Economic policy
Fiscal policy

The 1987 tax reform was pioneering in the region in introducing value-added tax (VAT) and personal income tax (PIT) to replace corporate- and commodity- specific direct taxes as main sources of government revenue. One substantial problem is the arrears on taxes and social insurance payments rising from 136 billion forint in 1993 to 205 billion in 1995 or from 0.9% of tax revenues to 3.7%. The bulk arrears are to social insurance funds and the largest debtors are large state-owned firms, especially the railways. The majority of outstanding arrears are to under-capitalized companies or those with little apparent residual value.

The structure of general government expenditures is heavily weighted in favour of welfare spending and wages, making budget control and fiscal consolidation difficult. These categories account for about half of government expenditure and a third of GDP. In addition, the general government is a major employer in the Hungarian economy, accounting for around a quarter of total employment. Consumer and producer subsidies decreased, except the subsidies to the farming sector, public transport and medicines (both lately decreasing as well).

The total state debt increased from 827.7 billion forint, or 39.6% of GDP, in 1990 to 2068.6 billion forint, or 47.7% of GDP, in 1994. The Hungarian National Bank is limited by law to finance more than 3% of the budget deficit. Treasury bills became the most important source of budget financing, while the NBH financing declined continuously. Since the introduction of the macroeconomic stabilization programme in March 1995 Hungary is expected to reduce the budget deficit from 8.2% of GDP in 1994 to a targeted 4% of GDP in 1996.

Monetary policy

The main objective of monetary policy was to reduce the high current account deficit to an extent that would stop the further growth of external debt, while being in line with sustainable economic growth based on exports. An additional goal is the further curbing of inflation, in order to encourage domestic saving.

Inflation was double-digit since 1988, peaking at 35% in 1991 before the devaluation of the forint in the macroeconomic stabilization programme of March 1995 boosted inflation again to an average rate of 28% in 1995. In the second year of the stabilization programme, inflation was reduced to 23.6%.

Banking system

At the beginning of 1987 a two-tier banking system was created, abolishing the monopoly of the NBH. Its two main credit sections were transformed into two commercial banks, the Hungarian Credit Bank and the Commercial and Credit Bank. A third major bank, the Budapest Bank, was also established. In late 1990 the first foreign banks were allowed to set up retail banking services. The Bank Act distinguishes between commercial banks, specialized financial institutions, investment banks and savings banks. By the end of 1995 there were 34 Hungarian commercial banks, 7 specialized financial institutions, one investment bank and 252 saving banks; 36% of the bank shares were owned by foreigners, 44% by the state, the rest by local owners. The NBH remains the bank of issue and has considerable power to regulate the activities of commercial banks.

From 1990 to 1993, the government purchased outright non-performing loans from banks at either a discount or the net value on the bank's balance sheet against 20-year Treasury bonds. Banks were also given the incentive to try to recover as much as they could from bad performing loans through creating special bad debt workout departments. Recapitalization proceeded in several stages, progressively raising the capital asset ratio. By the end of 1995 loss-making banks accounted for a mere 3% of the total Hungarian banks.

In July 1995, 25% of the Hungarian Foreign Trade Bank was sold to the Bayerische Landesbank of Germany, and another 17% to the European Bank for Reconstruction and Development. Some months later 27.5% of the Budapest Bank was sold to GE Capital and another 32.7% to the European Bank for Reconstruction and Development. A third large bank, OTP (National Savings Bank), was privatized through the London Stock Exchange in May 1995. The Hungarian Credit Bank (MHB) was taken over with an 89% stake by the Dutch Bank ABN AMRO in late 1996, and the Commercial Bank is to be privatized by 1997.

Foreign debt

One of the early consequences of Hungarian economic reform and the country's opening up to foreign trade was the sharp growth in its foreign debt burden, from the second half of the 1960s onwards. Although its debt service payments reached a peak in 1987 at 75.6% of its foreign exchange revenues, which placed a great burden on the country, Hungary has always continued to service its debt and is one of the few countries in Eastern Europe, along with Slovakia and the Czech Republic, which have never applied for debt rescheduling. As a result of the serious macroeconomic imbalances after 1989, near the end of the first Conservative government's term of office, foreign indebtedness took an unusually strong leap, with a nominal increase in US$ terms of 15% in 1993, 16% in 1994 and 11% in 1995, to reach a total of US$31.7 billion.

Following the opening in 1989 and the ensuing heavy inflow of direct foreign investments, Hungary's foreign currency reserves rose sharply, peaking at US$12 billion in 1995. The high level of income from privatizations in 1995 was utilized in the first half of 1996 to trim the country's gross foreign debt to US$28.4 billion by mid-1996, thus reducing indebtedness to its end-of-1994 level. The share of foreign debt in terms of Hungary's GDP has gradually diminished since 1994, reaching a level of 65% in 1996. Gross indebtedness is likely to decline to approx. US$29.5 billion by the end of 1996, which is a fall of 7% year-on-year.

■ EQUITIES

Index performance (in local currency)

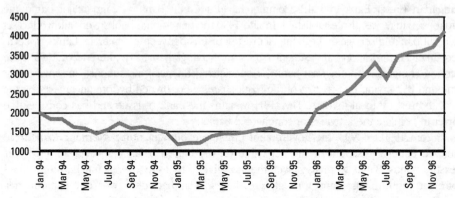

Key indicators

	Index performance %, in US$ terms	Market Cap. US$bn	P/E	Div. Yield	Weight in IFCI	IFCG
1994	-17.5	1.6	-55.2	2.7	0.1	0.1
1995	-29.4	2.4	12.0	3.1	0.1	0.1
1996	94.6	5.3	17.5	1.1	0.5	0.3

Sources: Local stock exchange, IFC, Bloomberg, Datastream, UBS

Background

Exchange activity in Hungary dates back to 1864, to the foundation of the Pest Commodity and Stock Exchange. At the turn of the century, the Exchange was Europe's fourth largest in terms of capitalization.

The rise of Communism brought trading to a halt with the Exchange closing for more than four decades from 1948. However, Hungary was the first Eastern Bloc country to begin preparations for re-opening the Stock Exchange. Initially, the re-establishment of the securities market was limited to bonds, but the foundation of the Budapest Stock Exchange (BSE) in June 1990 changed this. The BSE has a capitalization in the region of HUF420 billion (US$3 billion). The OTC market is roughly three times the size of the Stock Exchange.

Structure

The BSE is the only stock exchange in Hungary. There is one official board and an OTC market. Listed equities account for around one third of total market capitalization, with bonds, investment funds and compensation notes also traded. The market is dominated by foreign investors, with more than half of trading and investment undertaken by non-residents. There are forty shares listed in the official market and fifty shares listed in the OTC market.

Regulatory authority
The BSE is regulated by the State Securities and Exchange Commission (SSEC).

Trading methods
There are two trading systems – the open outcry system and the automatic trading system. More active shares tend to be traded through the automatic system. Open outcry trading occurs within the range of the Price Order Book price spread. The computerized trading system is a continuous electronic market where the larger stocks trade in three groups for thirty minutes each.

Hours
Trading takes place between 11.00 and 14.00 on the BSE and between 09.00 and 17.00 on the OTC market.

Settlement time and clearing
Settlement takes place on a trading date plus three business days (T+3) basis, but can be negotiated to T+5. The Central Clearing House and Depository (KELER) is a separate body from the BSE and oversees clearing. KELER is half-owned by the central bank.

Limits on price movement
If a stock price fluctuates by 10%, trading is temporarily suspended (for about ten minutes) to allow brokers to contact clients. If the fluctuation reaches 20% of the previous day's level, trading is suspended for the day.

Types of shares
Ordinary shares are traded on the BSE.

Stock indices
The main index of the BSE is the Budapest Stock Exchange Index (BUX). Prior to 1995 this was published unofficially, but has since been formally recognized by the BSE.

Taxes
Capital gains are taxed at 18% for non-residents. Interest income is taxed at 18% for companies and 0% for individuals while dividends are tax-free for companies and 10% for private investors. A number of countries operate tax treaties with Hungary giving lower rates of taxation.

Disclosure of financial statements
Issuers are required to submit an annual report by May 31 each year. In addition, semi-annual reports and quarterly reports must be published within forty-five days of the time period ending.

Ownership limits for non-residents
Non-residents can purchase up to 100% of a company's shares. However, for stakes greater than 50% (10% for banking institutions) regulatory approval is required.

Capital and foreign exchange controls

No specific permission is required when making portfolio investment. However, repatriation of profits arising from movable or immovable property must be first approved.

Brokers

There are fifty-six brokerage firms on the BSE. Commission rates typically vary between 0.4% and 1%.

Sectors

In terms of market value, pharmaceuticals and petroleum are the most important sectors, with around 60% of capitalization. Banking and chemicals, although of lesser importance, make a significant contribution.

ADRs

Most Hungarian securities listed on the BSE are also traded on markets outside Hungary. London is the largest foreign market for Hungarian equities.

Derivatives

A futures market was launched in March 1995. There are five contracts traded, namely 3-month treasury bills, BUX Index, and US$, DEM and ECU currencies against HUF.

■ DEBT

The National Bank of Hungary, the Magyar Nemzeti Bank (NBH) is authorized by the annual budget laws to act as fiscal agent for the Ministry of Finance, and organizes auctions for the issuance of treasury bills and government bonds.

Treasury bills

Discounted T-bills are issued by the central bank, for maturities of 1, 3, 6 and 12 months. They are auctioned at the Money and Capital Market Department of the NBH. Bills of 1 and 3 months are auctioned weekly, on Tuesdays and Wednesdays respectively. Bids must be no more than 1% different from the average yield of bills of the same maturity sold at the previous auction. Bills of 6 and 12 months are auctioned twice a week. The size and minimum acceptable price is published in advance by the NBH.

The bank can buy bills from its own account at the average price to help provide liquidity. Settlement is five days later, and bills are listed on the Budapest Stock Exchange.

In addition, small amounts of interest-bearing bills are privately placed or issued by subscription, mostly to individuals.

Government bonds

Notes are issued by the NBH for a maximum maturity of three years. They can have fixed or floating rate coupons – floating rate coupons pay a margin over T-bill yields. Financial institutions bid at auctions held once a month, details of which are announced a month earlier. The value of the domestic bond market is about HUF600 billion (US$4.8 billion).

Stock Exchange and OTC (although these can be settled directly between counterparties) trades are settled in Keler, the central depository and clearing house, although cash in a deal is transferred between respective custodians.

Foreign investors must apply for a Forex Authority Permit from the NBH and can trade with domestic holders, but they cannot buy securities with original tenures of less than one year.

Eurobonds

Hungary, through the National Bank has accessed the international bonds markets since the 1980s. It is a particularly active issuer of bonds denominated in yen both in the eurobond and samurai markets.

Eurobonds issues (US$m)

	1990	1991	1992	1993	1994	1995	1996
Sovereign	949.9	1,234.9	1,485.1	4,800.9	1,724.5	3,108.4	331.3
Private	—	—	—	—	—	—	—

■ HUNGARY: Economic indicators

Population and development	1990	1991	1992	1993	1994	1995	1996e
Population, million	10.4	10.3	10.3	10.3	10.3	10.2	10.2
Population growth, %	-0.2	-0.2	-0.3	-0.3	-0.2	-0.2	-0.2
Nominal GDP per capita, US$	3176	3230	3612	3744	4061	4274	4331

National accounts							
Nominal GDP, US$bn	32.9	33.4	37.2	38.5	41.7	43.8	44.3
Change in real GDP, %	-3.5	-11.9	-3.0	-0.8	2.9	1.5	1.0
Gross fixed capital formation, % of GDP	17.8	19.7	15.4	20.6	23.0	22.8	23.3

Money supply and inflation							
Narrow money, change %, Dec/Dec	35.2	17.1	31.0	10.3	10.3	—	—
Broad money, change %, Dec/Dec	29.2	29.4	27.3	16.8	13.4	18.1	—
Consumer price inflation (avg.) %	28.5	35.0	23.0	22.5	18.8	28.2	23.5
Producer prices (avg.) %	22.0	32.6	12.3	10.8	11.3	28.9	—

Interest rates							
Discount rate, end of year	22.00	22.00	21.00	22.00	25.00	28.00	23.00
Treasury bill rate, annual average	30.10	34.50	22.70	17.20	26.90	32.00	23.73
Deposit rate, annual average	24.70	30.40	24.40	15.70	20.30	26.10	—

Government finance							
Government expenditure, % of GDP	52.4	54.2	56.5	58.3	59.4	51.9	44.9
Government balance, % of GDP	-0.1	-3.3	-6.9	-5.5	-8.2	-6.6	-4.0

Exchange rates lc=local currency	1990	1991	1992	1993	1994	1995	1996e
Exchange rate, annual average, lc/US$	63.21	74.81	79.00	92.20	104.75	125.66	155.00
Exchange rate, end of year, lc/US$	61.45	75.62	83.97	100.75	110.70	139.47	164.00
Real exchange rate 1990=100	100.0	110.5	119.2	130.9	132.7	126.3	131.0

Balance of payments							
Exports of goods & services, US$m	9005	11949	13791	11392	11407	17816	19200
Change %	16.8	32.7	15.4	-17.4	0.1	56.2	7.8
Imports of goods & services, US$m, fob	9793	12543	14326	15579	16226	21426	22090
Change %	5.8	28.1	14.2	8.7	4.2	32.0	3.1
Trade balance, of goods only, US$m, fob-fob	272	189	-49	-3247	-3634	-2442	-2500
Current account balance, US$m	-44	267	324	-3455	-3911	-2480	-1500
as a % of GDP	-0.1	0.8	0.9	-9.0	-9.4	-5.7	-3.4

Foreign exchange reserves							
Foreign exchange reserves, US$m	1070	3936	4428	6771	6811	11968	11000
Gold at ⅔ of market price, US$m	77.1	62.2	23.3	27.3	28.1	25.6	25.8
Import cover (reserves/imports), months	1.3	3.8	3.7	5.2	5.0	6.7	6.0

Foreign debt and debt service							
Short-term debt, US$m	2940	2177	2286	2005	2397	3203	3072
Total foreign debt, US$m	21326	22352	21539	24782	28763	31713	27500
as a % of GDP	64.8	66.9	57.8	64.4	69.0	72.5	62.1
as a % of foreign exchange receipts	219.0	174.5	146.9	204.4	233.5	167.4	134.5
Interest payments, US$m	1657	1628	1635	1586	1947	2357	2140
Principal repayments, US$m	2564	2408	3096	3322	4267	6058	3590
Total debt service, US$m	4221	4036	4731	4908	6214	8415	5730
as a % of goods exports	64.7	43.6	47.2	60.6	81.6	65.7	43.4
as a % of foreign exchange receipts	43.3	31.5	32.3	40.5	50.5	44.4	28.0

India

Area (thousands of km²):	3288
Population (1995, millions):	936
Population projection (2025, millions):	1370
Population younger than 15 yrs (1991, % of total):	35.8
Urbanization rate (1993, % of population):	26
Life expectancy (1993, years at birth):	61
Gross domestic product (1996, US$bn):	359
GDP per capita (1996, US$):	377
Average annual GDP growth rate (1990-96, %):	4.9
Average annual inflation rate (1990-96, %):	10.2
Currency (rupee per US$, average 1996):	35.9
Real exchange rate: (1990=100, average 1996)	70.67
Structure of production (1994):	42% services, 30% agriculture, 28% industry
Main exports:	gems & jewellery, ready-made garments, engineering goods, cotton yarn and fabrics & leather manufactures
Main imports:	petroleum, crude oil, precious stones, machinery, chemicals, iron and steel
Main trading partners:	US, Germany, Japan & UK
Market capitalization of Stock Exchange (December 1996; US$bn):	122.6
Total foreign debt (% of GDP):	26.5
Next elections due under normal circumstances:	presidential scheduled July 1997; legislative required by May 2001
Credit rating: (Jan 1997, Standard & Poor's, Moody's)	BB+; Baa3

FORECAST: 1997-2000 (average)

	Worst case	Most likely	Best case
Real GDP growth (%)	5.0	6.3	8.0
Inflation (%)	12.5	9.0	6.0

■ POLITICS

Historical overview

A diverse country

With a population of more than 900 million people, 3,500 years of history, fourteen major languages and two hundred dialects, India is ethnically, culturally and linguistically among the most diverse countries in the world. In terms of population, it is also the world's largest democracy. Folk, tribal and classical cultures co-exist side by side, as do ultra-modern and traditional lifestyles.

Constitution and government
A quasi-federal system of government
The Republic of India was founded in 1950. It has a quasi-federal political system with powers constitutionally divided between the centre and states. It follows a parliamentary form of democracy. New Delhi is India's political capital. State governments administer each of the twenty-seven states and six union territories. Parliament is comprised of the Lok Sabha (the lower house of parliament) and the Rajya Sabha (the upper house). These serve as the political machinery at the centre while the state legislatures and legislative councils provide the institutional framework at the state level.

Parliament
The Lok Sabha is the most powerful governing body in India. The prime minister is the head of government. He wields executive power, unlike the president, whose powers are largely ceremonial. Furthermore, the prime minister and his council of ministers are responsible to the Lok Sabha and the Rajya Sabha. Once every five years the Lok Sabha members are elected from 543 constituencies across the country. Most candidates tend to be affiliated to political parties, but there is also a sprinkling of independents. The Rajya Sabha contains 250 members who are either nominated by the president or elected by the electoral college made up of members of the state legislative assemblies.

The state legislative assemblies play the role of governing bodies in the states. State elections are also held once every five years. The powers and responsibilities of the union and the state government differ and are delineated in the Indian constitution. This invests the union government with the more crucial powers. The central government manages external affairs, defence, and fiscal policy while the state governments focus more on regional or local issues. The central government does have powers to enforce economic policy across states.

Political parties
The Congress Party has dominated the national political scene since India became independent in 1947. Except for two brief periods 1977-80 and 1989-91 (when the Janata Party and the National Front (NF) government were in power), the Congress had always ruled at the federal level until June 1996. Furthermore, it has benefited greatly from there being no long-standing, united opposition party and efforts made by breakaway groups (from the Congress or other parties) to form a united opposition party, have not been sustainable.

Population and society
The world's second largest population
According to the 1991 national census, India's population was 844 million. Forty percent of the population is below 14 years of age, 83% of the population is Hindu and 11% Muslim. Sikhs and Christians each comprise about 2% of the population. The major Indian language is Hindi, spoken by 40% of the population. Population density rose from 216 per sq. km. in 1981 to 267 in 1991. The most densely populated state is Kerala, with 747 per sq. km. The

largest urban agglomerations are Mumbai (13m), Calcutta (11m), Delhi (9m) and Chennai (6m).

■ ECONOMICS

The world's sixth largest economy

The economy has a large agricultural base alongside a rapidly growing services sector accounting for over 50% of gross domestic product.

While India is the world's sixteenth largest economy by conventional measures, it is the world's sixth biggest in purchasing power parity (PPP) terms after the US, China, Japan, Russia and Germany.

India is also the world's tenth largest industrialized country and is technologically advanced, with established industries in nuclear energy, space and satellite communications, oceanography, deep sea oil drilling and armaments.

A large parallel economy

India also has a fairly substantial unaccounted or parallel economy, estimated by some to be as high as 70% over and above the official economy. With agriculture being untaxed since 1947 and tax evasion being substantial (less than 1% of the country pays income taxes and many firms are either unregistered or tend to understate profit figures to avoid tax), tax revenues are barely 10% of GDP. However, government revenues are expected to rise as tax reforms are implemented. Until the end of the 1970s the maximum income tax rate was as high as 97%.

Only in 1985 was it reduced to 40%. High marginal tax rates resulted in widespread tax evasion and channelling of funds into avenues like gold and cash holdings. There was also a tendency to show income as accruing from agricultural activities rather than keeping money in bank deposits and investing in the capital markets.

Business advantages

India has one of the largest (and cheapest) pools of world-class scientific and engineering talent and an affluent non-resident population (particularly in the US, UK, Canada, Hong Kong, Singapore, and the Middle East).

Multinationals and foreign companies have long benefited from the country's major advantages, such as a strong industrial/agricultural production base, an increasingly consumerist middle class, the widespread use of English as the national business language, and a large skilled workforce.

Natural resources

India produces many minerals, including fuel, metallic and non-metallic minerals. It is the world's largest producer of mica blocks and is also a major producer of chloride, iron ore, manganese, barytes and kyanite. Of the fifty-two minerals produced, India is self-sufficient in about thirty, which constitute primary raw materials for industries such as power generation, iron and steel, cement, aluminium and ferro alloys.

Economic reforms

In June 1991, the Congress party led by Narasimha Rao came to power. Rao led a shift from personality-centred politics to institutionalized politics via the delegation of power to various ministries.

Rao began the process of liberalizing the economy, which had pursued socialist development policies for over forty years since the country gained independence in 1947. He inherited an economy in deep trouble, plagued by fiscal and external deficits, and immediately began liberalization. For the first time, experienced and respected professionals such as Dr Manmohan Singh were invited to join the administration, bringing with them a fresh approach to policy-making akin to the technocrats who have managed policy in the East Asian "tiger" economies.

Will economic reform continue?

Notwithstanding the economic progress which much of India has enjoyed following the reforms introduced in the early 1990s, the collapse of the Congress-dominated government in the 1996 elections and the formation of the United Front (UF) coalition government has raised concerns about the support for continued economic reform. Doubts about the willingness to open the economy to foreign investment and trade have resurfaced following highly publicized disputes in recent years regarding foreign direct investment in the power generation and consumer goods sectors of the economy. Moreover, the disparate nature of the UF government and the diminished prospects for aggressive measures to reform tax and expenditure policies or to cut the government budget deficit have further raised concerns about macroeconomic policy management. Although a sharp reversal of the reforms initiated in the early 1990s is not likely, further substantial liberalization measures are less likely to be implemented for India to join the ranks of the most successful Asian "tiger" economies.

Macroeconomic improvement

The Indian economy has improved considerably. Real GDP, which increased only 1.8% in 1991, rose 7% in 1995. Industrial production has benefited the most in the ensuing five years. The industrial production index, which had declined 1% in 1991, rose 12% in 1995 as industry recovered strongly from recession of the early 1990s and, along with agriculture, benefited from eight successive good monsoons. The rupee has held firm against the dollar despite full current account convertibility in March 1993, and there is now talk of making the rupee fully convertible on the capital account by the year 2000.

Foreign currency assets are now more than US$18 billion, covering around five months of current imports of goods. The 1996 fiscal deficit is targeted at 5% of GDP, but will probably come in at 6%, which is nevertheless down from 8.4% of GDP in 1991. The maximum import duty has been slashed in stages to 50% today from more than 225% in 1991, and is likely to be cut back further to 25-30% by the year 2000. Corporate taxes have been reduced from 57% to 40%, and are likely to be lowered further over the next few years.

The restructuring programme was primarily aimed at building up the foreign exchange reserves, narrowing the fiscal deficit and rationalizing the tax system. The government also decided to embark on a privatization programme to encourage private investment in infrastructure sectors such as telecommunications, refineries and power. With the lowering of the import duties, Indian industry, which had been sheltered, was gradually opened up to foreign competition.

Share of GDP by sector

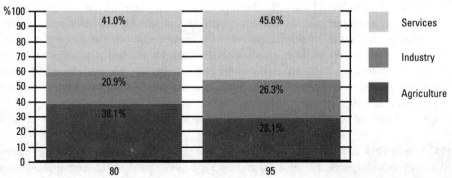

Source: RBI Annual Report 1995/96

Foreign investment inflows

Foreign investment has been wooed since September 1992 when Indian companies were allowed to raise capital abroad. Access to the Euromarkets has enabled corporates to raise funds at internationally competitive levels. In 1995 total foreign investment of over US$4.2 billion flowed into India, and the government has set a target of attracting annual foreign direct investment (FDI) of US$10 billion. In particular, higher FDI in sectors like power and telecommunications are expected as the policy framework for infrastructure is rationalized. Portfolio investment has also risen with already over US$6.5 billion invested in the stock market.

Considerable challenges remain, including reducing still high inflation and fiscal deficits. Reforms have also been slow to alleviate poverty, and the socio-economic position of many people remains precarious. The persistence of poverty and destitution seems to be attributable more to the delayed pace of structural changes designed to expand opportunity rather than to any basic defects in the programme.

Agriculture a dominant force

Three quarters of the population owe their livelihood, directly or indirectly, to agriculture, which with forestry, mining and fisheries accounts for one third of GDP. It has been the main source of raw material supply for industries such as cotton and jute textiles, sugar, oils and plantations. Agricultural products account for almost 20% of India's exports. Many small-scale and cottage industries such as handloom weaving, oil crushing and rice husking also depend on agriculture for their raw materials.

There is no tax on agricultural income and the farm lobbies' support is necessary to win any election, whether state or national. While there is a growing use of new agricultural technology, such as high yielding seeds, fertilizers, and irrigated land, approximately two thirds of cultivated land is still dependent on the annual monsoon.

India is a major producer of rice, wheat, tea, coffee, sugarcane and cotton, and is self-sufficient in food. About 43% of the country's geographical area is used for agriculture, although only about one third of this is irrigated. Policy focuses on infrastructure investment in agriculture in order to generate more value-added exports. The focus is now on improving per capita production and ensuring better distribution.

A rural consumer class

For many years, consumer goods companies concentrated on the urban markets on the mistaken assumption that the purchasing power of the urban consumer was far more than that of the rural consumer. In addition, distribution difficulties hampered rural sales. However, the structure of the rural economy and consumption patterns are changing discernibly. With no taxation, and huge investments being made in agriculture, farmers' disposable incomes have grown and they now have higher marketable surpluses from better crop yields. This has greatly increased rural demand for packaged urban consumer goods.

Industrial production

Industrial production rose 12% in 1995 and over 9% in 1994 as industry began to adjust to the newly liberalized environment. Thus far, in the current fiscal year (1996-97), the index of industrial production has risen some 9%, led by a 23% rise in transport equipment, a 23% rise in electrical machinery and an 18% increase in metal products.

Interest rates

The Reserve Bank of India (RBI) deregulated prime lending rates in October 1994. Interest rate regulation had led to market distortions since industry preferred to tap the capital market for funds and bank margins were under pressure due to rising inflation. In October 1996, the Reserve Bank lowered the maximum rate on short-term deposits (under one year) from 11% to 10%. In view of its concern about continuing high real interest rates, an easier monetary policy is likely in 1997.

Longer-term, the RBI is seriously considering reducing both the cash reserve ratio (CRR) and the Statutory Liquidity Ratio (SLR) to ensure a longer-term easing of liquidity. However, there is unlikely to be substantial relaxation due to the government's annual (budgeted) market borrowing programmes and strong private sector credit demand. No major decline in prime lending rates (PLRs) is expected over the next two to three years.

Inflation and money supply

Inflation should continue at around 10% through 1997 and 1998, with prime lending rates at around 15%. The freeing of bank deposit rates could be the next phase of interest rate liberalization. Further, unless India curtails unproductive expenditure, and keeps money supply growth firmly under control, inflation and the budget deficit will not fall significantly. While increased tax revenue and borrowings are targeted for the coming years, curtailment of capital expenditure, both planned and non-planned, is expected to maintain the fiscal deficit in real terms.

Worrying fiscal deficit

India is seeking to achieve budgetary stability through its economic reforms, but even if government expenditure is lowered, higher tax revenues are crucial if the budget deficit is to be reduced. The deficit still remains at 6% of GDP. The government's long-term fiscal deficit target of 4% of GDP is unlikely to be met unless tax collections rise, the privatization process speeds up and the government curbs its borrowings.

Fiscal deficit

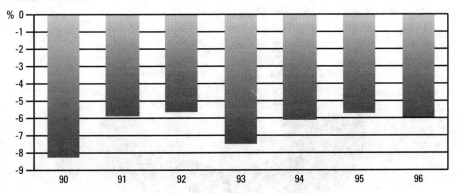

Source: Official data

Trade

India's exports have only represented about 0.5% of world exports for more than forty years and trade as a percentage of GDP is barely 25%. Moreover, the country has always had a trade deficit. Export gains have been matched by a steady rise in imports. The biggest imports are oil and petroleum products, accounting for almost a quarter of total imports. Trade policy reforms began in August 1991 and have been extended, with encouraging results.

Exports and imports as a % of GDP

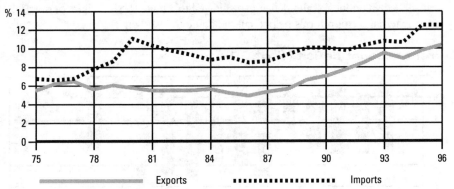

Source: IFS

India's export structure is typical of most developing countries. Its main trading partners are the US, Germany, Japan and the UK. The nation has traditionally exported agricultural raw materials and agri-products. Currently, the major exports are gems and jewellery, ready-made garments, engineering goods, cotton yarn and fabrics and leather goods. Major imports are petroleum and crude oil, precious stones, machinery, chemicals, and iron and steel. Tourism is India's second largest foreign exchange earner, with annual tourist arrivals of around 2 million.

Breakdown of exports (1995)

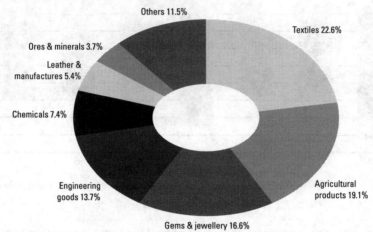

Others 11.5%
Textiles 22.6%
Ores & minerals 3.7%
Leather & manufactures 5.4%
Chemicals 7.4%
Engineering goods 13.7%
Agricultural products 19.1%
Gems & jewellery 16.6%

Source: RBI Annual Report 1995/96

Foreign reserves and capital flows

India's foreign currency reserves are now above US$18 billion and sufficient to cover around five months' imports of goods. Reserves have risen sharply since the exchange rate was unified in March 1993. Foreign exchange reserves covered barely two weeks of imports when the reforms programme began in June 1991. Since then reserves have risen more than nine fold.

In 1991 the current account deficit had spiralled to a huge US$10 billion, or over 3% of the GDP. External sector reforms helped cut the figure to less than 2%.

Current account deficit (% of GDP)

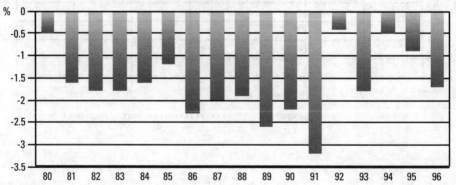

Source: IFS

Investment inflows

Total foreign investment, which was just US$154 million in 1991, rose almost thirty fold to US$4.35 billion in 1995, with the government targeting US$10 billion in 1997. This, coupled with other capital inflows including worker remittances by non-residents' portfolio investment, should boost total foreign investment inflows to new highs. India has a huge and affluent non-resident population in countries ranging across the world, and if the right policies are formulated and investment avenues made available to tap these funds, the inflow of foreign capital could be huge.

Foreign investment inflows

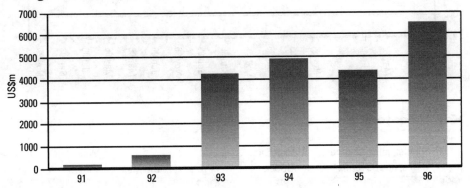

Source: Official data

Currency

India's currency and exchange rate system has been gradually reformed. Until 1992, the rupee exchange rate was fixed by the government on a trade-weighted basis. Following a series of trade-weighted devaluations of the rupee, a floating exchange rate system was adopted in March 1993. Although in August 1994 the rupee became convertible on the current account, full convertibility is likely to still be a few years away.

Indian rupee/US dollar exchange rate

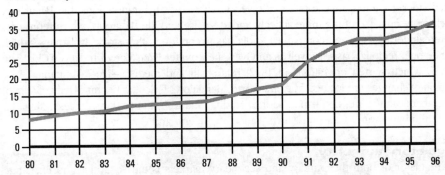

■ EQUITIES

Index performance (in local currency)

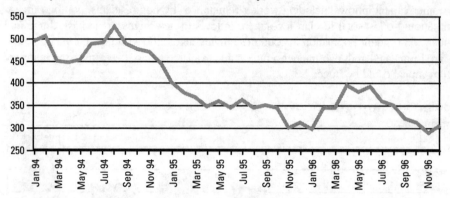

Key indicators

	Index performance %, in US$ terms	Market Cap. US$bn	P/E	Div. Yield	Weight in IFCI	IFCG
1994	6.5	127.5	26.7	1.0	3.4	7.0
1995	-35.2	127.2	14.2	1.8	2.2	5.3
1996	-3.5	122.6	12.3	1.7	1.9	4.8

Sources: Local stock exchanges, IFC, Bloomberg, Datastream, UBS

Structure

The two main stock exchanges in India are the Bombay Stock Exchange (BSE), first set up in 1875, and the National Stock Exchange (NSE). Both are in Mumbai. Prior to its establishment, the BSE was known as the "Native Share Brokers Association". The BSE's market capitalization was US$107 billion at the end November 1996, with six thousand companies listed.

There are three categories of listings: the A group, comprising the sixty most actively traded stocks wherein investors are allowed to carry forward transactions; the B1 group, which represents 420 of the more actively traded stocks; and the B2 group, which represents the remainder of the listed companies. India has twenty-one other stock exchanges, which operate on a regional basis, as well as an Over-The-Counter Exchange of India (OTCEI). The OTCEI, which started operations in 1992, lists small and medium-sized companies. The regional exchanges are located in Ahmedabad, Bangalore, Calcutta, Cochin, Delhi, Gauhati, Hyderabad, Mangalore, Ludhiana, Madras, Madhya Pradesh, Pune, Uttar Pradesh, Magadh, Jaipur, Bhubaneswar, Saurashtra-Kutch, Vadodara, Meerut and Coimbatore.

Regulatory authority

The regulator of both the primary and secondary markets is the Securities and Exchange Board of India (SEBI). Set up in 1988, this independent body functions under the Securities and Exchange Board of India Act, 1992.

Trading methods

Four types of shares are traded on India's exchanges: common equity shares; preference shares; debentures/bonds; and securities, which are issued by central and state governments and by corporates and institutions promoted by the government and units of mutual funds.

At the BSE in two-way auction, sellers compete with each other for the highest possible price and buyers compete for the lowest possible price. On the NSE, trading takes place through a traditional auction system.

Hours

The Bombay Stock Exchange and the National Stock Exchange both trade between 10.00 and 15.30, Monday to Friday.

Settlement time and clearing

Settlement for the most actively traded companies (A and B1 group) is 7 days. For the less actively traded companies (B2 group), settlement is 14 days. A depository sponsored by the NSE is expected to commence operations in end 1997 with an initial list of eleven stocks.

Commission on equity trading

On each transaction, brokers are allowed to charge a maximum commission of 2.5%. The average commission charged is 1-1.5%. The minimum size of a transaction is 25 rupees (around US$40.8).

Foreign investors

Foreign investors have to be approved by the SEBI before they can operate directly on India's Stock Exchanges. This process takes on average three months. Currently, there are around 250 foreign investors listed, of which about 100 are active.

Stock indices

The most widely used index is the Bombay Stock Exchange Sensitive Index. It includes the thirty most actively traded shares.

The value of this index is currently placed at around the 3,000 level. The BSE reconstituted this index in August 1996, in order to give a better reflection of activity in the market.

The revamped index has a larger representation of the market capitalization. The top five stocks represent 38% of the index weight, compared to approximately 55% formerly. Previously unrepresented industries with a large share of the BSE are now included. They are infrastructure industries such as telecommunications, power, oil and refineries, banking and finance.

Taxation

Dividends and capital gains are taxable under India's Income Tax Act. This tax may be reduced for investors residing in countries with a tax treaty with India. The tax on dividends is 10% and on long-term capital gains (more than one year) is 20%.

Investment limits

Investments by international investors are subject to a ceiling of 24% of a company's issued share capital. One investor cannot hold more than 10% of a single company's issued shares. These ceilings include convertible bonds as well.

Depository receipts

In order to facilitate international investors with an exposure to their stock, scores of Indian companies issued Global Depository Receipts (GDRs) in recent years. These are mainly listed in London and Luxembourg. They are actively traded and mostly follow the local markets. Among the market-makers are UBS, HSBC James Capel, ING Baring, Jardine Fleming, Peregrine, Morgan Stanley, Paribas Capital Markets, BZW, CS First Boston and Caspian Securities, all in London. NatWest Markets has also announced it will start market-making in early 1997.

Several of the market-makers are quoting their prices on the Stock Exchange Automated Quotation (SEAQ) system and run indices. There is no tradeable index for the GDRs yet, but CS First Boston is working on one. There are hardly any agency brokers in London. Most of the GDRs are trading at a premium of between 10 and 20% to the underlying stock.

With the development of the Central Depository, this premium might decline over the next few years, as most foreign investors invest in GDRs mainly in order to avoid the settlement and clearing difficulties and risks.

Exchange controls

There are no exchange controls in India for foreign institutional investors (FIIs).

■ DEBT

The bond markets are regulated by the Reserve Bank of India (RBI), the Securities Exchange Board of India (SEBI), the Ministry of Finance, the Department of Company Affairs and the Government of India. The SEBI is emerging as the main regulator, and in 1992 was mandated by the Ministry of Finance to foster the development of India's capital markets to reach international standards. India continues its programme of financial sector reform initiated in 1991.

In 1995, the National Stock Exchange began offering screen-based facilities for trading debt instruments. Issuance of bills and bonds now takes into account internal debt and monetary management – that is, a deliberate policy of controlling the cost and composition of government debt – and short-term liquidity management.

Overseas investors are only allowed to buy listed debt securities; all publicly placed issues are listed. Since 1996, they can invest 100% of their Indian portfolios in corporate debt (previously restricted to 30%). They must register with the SEBI.

The Government regulates the issue of securities to foreign investors, although some corporates have issued Foreign Currency Convertible Bonds through Global Depository Receipts.

Public debt

Banks must satisfy a Statutory Liquidity Reserve (SLR) requirement of 25% of their net demand and time liabilities. Eligible securities include central government securities (GoISecs), treasury bills, state government securities and government-guaranteed bonds. Government debt accounts for 60% of total issuance, and last year the RBI set up a system of primary dealers.

Treasury bills

Ninety-one and 364-day treasury bills are issued by the RBI on behalf of the Government of India. Ad hoc issuance to replenish cash balances with the RBI will be phased out in 1997. Bills are issued on tap to investors (principally commercial banks) every working day, but the most important method for selling bills is by regular auction.

Since 1993, 91-day bills have been auctioned by the RBI for a notified amount each Friday. Bids are accepted at a cut-off price at market determined yields. Non-competitive bids are accepted at the weighted average price of successful bids. Issue sizes range from Rs1 to 5 billion, and the RBI has reduced its role as an end-buyer – bills are not eligible for rediscounting with it. Settlement is next day.

364-day auctions are held every other Wednesday, for an amount unspecified but within the range of Rs3 to 10 billion. Settlement is two days later.

Central government securities (GoISecs)

GoISecs are medium- and long-term securities issued by the RBI for the Government of India. They are normally semi-annual fixed-rate bonds with bullet redemptions. Zero coupons and partly paid bonds have also been introduced. Coupons are paid net of (variable) withholding tax, and bonds are registered in the name of the holder at the Public Debt Office (PDO) of the RBI, which also acts as a depository. Settlement is book-entry.

Since 1992 the RBI has adopted an auction-based issuance method. The RBI announces details of a forthcoming offering of a specific amount through a press release two days before, and acts as the selling agent. There is no fixed calendar. Successful bids are allotted from the lowest yield until the issue is placed. Multiple bids are permitted without provision of collateral. Alternatively, participants can choose to convert treasury bill holdings into the longer dated bond.

The RBI uses GoISecs for its open market operations. Commercial banks are the largest investors, and increasingly trade the bonds. They are required to market 30% of their portfolios. The Securities Trading Corporation of India Ltd (STCI) and the Discount and Finance House of India Ltd (DFHI) are the principal market-makers in government securities. There are proposals for improving the primary dealer system, establishing an automated settlement system at the RBI and introducing bond trading on the National Stock Exchange. Following the April 1992 "Securities Scam" when money was illegally diverted out of the bond market into the Stock Exchange, dealers have been banned from taking short positions and from conducting repo and reverse transactions.

State government securities (SGSs)

Each state is allocated a market borrowing limit by the RBI, which offers SGS bonds in a pool, although large, fiscally sound issues are rated higher by the market. In a particular year, all have the same coupons and bullet redemption dates. Bonds are fixed rate and pay semi-annually. The RBI acts as depository, and settlement is book-entry two to three days after subscriptions close.

The market has increased ten fold during the last twenty years. Issue sizes range between Rs0.1 billion and Rs50 billion. Trading volume is small.

Government-guaranteed bonds

Government-guaranteed bonds are medium- and long-term securities issued by government agencies and public sector bodies. Interest and principal payments are explicitly guaranteed by either central or state governments. They are issued with fixed semi-annual coupons for bullet redemption, and are normally in physical form and registered with the issuer, who is responsible for coupon payments, payable net of withholding tax.

Bonds are tightly held in the banking sector, and secondary market trading is thin.

Examples of issuers are infrastructure enterprises, house finance companies and state-owned utilities.

Government securities settle through an automated SGL transfer system. Over-the-counter trades normally take 2 days, and transactions on the exchanges take 14 days to settle.

PSU bonds

Public sector entities (more than 50% government owned) issue 5- to 10-year bonds to large domestic institutional investors. Most are private placements, and many pay interest free of tax to some categories of investor. Structures include fixed rate, FRNs, deep-discounts and bonds with embedded put or call options. They must be listed on the Stock Exchange and be rated by one of India's three agencies.

Separate coupon restrictions on taxable and non-taxable bonds were lifted in 1992; yields are normally lower than on corporate issues because of their quasi-sovereign status.

PSUs can be bought by foreign investors, who are partly attracted by lower transaction costs (for example no stamp duty) than for comparable securities. The market is more liquid than for SGS and government-guaranteed bonds. PSUs also issue long-term debentures to domestic institutions.

Private debt
Certificates of Deposit (CDs)

CDs are rupee denominated deposits made with commercial banks and Development Finance Institution (DFIs). They are traded as unsecured, negotiable promissory notes and are transferable by endorsement and delivery. Bank CDs are discount instruments, usually with 91-day maturities and DFIs are often coupon bearing with 1- to 3-year terms. They need not be rated, and because they are not Stock Exchange listed, overseas investors can-not buy them. Corporates are the largest purchasers.

CDs attract high stamp duty, so trading in them is negligible.

Commercial paper (CP)

CP was first issued in 1991, mainly by manufacturing companies. They are usually discount instruments with 91-day maturities, but can extend to 1 year. Until 1994, many poorly rated companies issued CPs supported by stand by guarantees from banks. Now issues tend to be higher rated.

Foreign investors can buy CP in the secondary market because issues are stock exchange listed. However trading in them is thin, because most are tightly held by banks and insurance companies.

Corporate debentures

Corporate bonds can be secured or unsecured and have a variety of coupon structures. Public issues with terms of more than 18 months must be rated, and the maturity range for most non-convertible bonds is 3 to 12 years. Issue sizes are Rs50 million to Rs2 billion.

In the primary market, new public bonds are allotted on a pro rata basis to subscribers over a period which might extend to 2 months. Private placements are made after the issuer receives written bids during a 2-week selling period.

Credit rating agencies

In 1988, the RBI required all public corporate bond issues to carry a rating, in order to protect small investors. There are three domestic agencies:

◆ **Credit Rating Information Services of India Ltd (CRISIL)**
◆ **Investment Information and Credit Rating Agency of India Ltd (IICRA)**
◆ **Credit Analysis and Research Ltd (CARE)**

Eurobonds

Indian state-owned enterprises, banks and corporates have tapped the eurobond market since 1985. They have issued a total of thirty-two, denominated in US dollars, yen, deutschmarks and Swiss francs.

Eurobond issues (US$m)

	1990	1991	1992	1993	1994	1995	1996
Sovereign	507.3	226.9	—	—	100.0	100.0	—
Private	—	—	—	—	250.0	270.0	300.0

■ INDIA: Economic indicators

Population and development	1990	1991	1992	1993	1994	1995	1996e
Population, million	834.7	844.0	870.0	901.5	918.6	935.7	953.2
Population growth, %	2.1	1.8	2.4	3.6	1.9	1.9	1.9
Nominal GDP per capita, US$	367	319	313	291	328	368	377

National accounts							
Nominal GDP, US$bn	306.0	271.2	272.1	262.7	301.4	344.0	359.0
Change in real GDP, %	5.7	0.4	5.3	3.9	6.3	7.0	6.0
Gross fixed capital formation, % of GDP	23.2	22.1	22.5	21.5	22.5	24.5	25.6

Money supply and inflation							
Narrow money, change %, Dec/Dec	15.2	23.4	7.6	19.0	27.6	11.2	—
Broad money, change %, Dec/Dec	15.4	18.6	17.0	17.1	20.4	11.1	16.5
Consumer price inflation (avg.) %	8.9	13.9	11.8	6.4	10.2	10.3	9.0

Government finance							
Government expenditure, % of GDP	17.3	17.0	16.9	17.4	16.0	16.6	17.1
Government balance, % of GDP	-8.1	-5.8	-5.6	-7.3	-6.1	-5.8	-6.0

Exchange rates *lc=local currency*							
Exchange rate, annual average, lc/US$	17.50	22.74	25.92	30.49	31.37	32.43	35.90
Exchange rate, end of year, lc/US$	18.07	25.83	26.20	31.38	31.38	35.18	37.00
Real exchange rate 1990=100	100.0	85.1	78.1	72.2	73.6	72.1	70.7

Balance of payments							
Exports of goods & services, US$m	22911	23020	24945	29224	34824	43000	49000
Change %	13.0	0.5	8.4	17.2	19.2	23.5	14.0
Imports of goods & services, US$m, fob	29326	26768	28473	33735	43749	57400	63750
Change %	4.6	-8.7	6.4	18.5	29.7	31.2	11.1
Trade balance, of goods only, US$m, fob-fob	-5151	-2992	-2131	1112	-876	-8900	-7500
Current account balance, US$m	-10042	-4028	-4105	-315	-2315	-5500	-5700
as a % of GDP	-3.1	-1.5	-1.5	-0.1	-0.8	-1.6	-1.6

Foreign exchange reserves							
Foreign exchange reserves, US$m	1521	3627	5757	10199	19698	17922	18200
Gold at ⅔ of market price, US$m	2748.7	2721.4	2595.5	2744.9	3019.5	3269.8	3299.8
Import cover (reserves/imports), months	0.6	1.6	2.4	3.6	5.4	3.7	3.4

Foreign debt and debt service							
Short-term debt, US$m	8522	8613	10883	11743	14532	14655	16029
Total foreign debt, US$m	81177	84234	92243	96305	103678	91200	95000
as a % of GDP	26.5	31.1	33.9	36.7	34.4	26.5	26.5
as a % of foreign exchange receipts	309.8	312.1	321.7	288.2	250.2	176.1	163.8
Interest payments, US$m	4347.7	4666.5	4169.5	4479.1	4824.3	5249.5	5250.3
Principal repayments, US$m	4116.6	4156	4255.1	5250.9	7122.3	7645.8	9200
Total debt service, US$m	8464.3	8822.5	8424.6	9730.0	11946.6	12895.3	14450.3
as a % of goods exports	46.3	48.8	42.1	42.9	44.6	39.7	38.5
as a % of foreign exchange receipts	32.3	32.7	29.4	29.1	28.8	24.9	24.9

Indonesia

Area (thousands of km²):	1905
Population (1995, millions):	193.5
Population projection (2025, millions):	265
Population younger than 15 yrs (1991, % of total):	35.8
Urbanization rate (1993, % of population):	33
Life expectancy (1993, years at birth):	63
Gross domestic product (1996, US$bn):	221
GDP per capita (1996, US$):	1123
Average annual GDP growth rate (1990-96, %):	7.3
Average annual inflation rate (1990-96, %):	8.6
Currency (rupiah per US$, average 1996):	2327
Real exchange rate: (1990=100, average 1996)	101.15
Structure of production (1994):	40% services, 44% industry, 16% agriculture
Main exports:	petrol & natural gas, textiles, leather & footwear, wood and cork
Main imports:	raw material, capital & intermediate goods
Main trading partners:	Japan, US, Singapore, Germany
Market capitalization of Stock Exchange (December 1996; US$bn):	91.0
Total foreign debt (% of GDP):	51.8
Next elections due under normal circumstances:	legislative scheduled June 1997; presidential March 1998
Credit rating: (Jan 1997, Standard & Poor's, Moody's)	BBB; Baa3

FORECAST: 1997-2000 (average)

	Worst case	Most likely	Best case
Real GDP growth (%)	6.0	7.5	9.0
Inflation (%)	10.0	8.5	6.5

■ POLITICS

Historical overview

European traders, led by the Portuguese, established commercial relationships with Indonesia from the early 16th century. Gradually, the Dutch East Indies Company set up a colonial empire, concentrating primarily on trade with the island of Java. By the end of the 18th century, the colonial administration had become too complex, and responsibility was passed to the Dutch government, which continued the conquest of the entire archipelago. Dutch rule ended when Japanese forces occupied Indonesia in early 1942. After the

Japanese surrender, Sukarno and Hatta declared independence on August 17, 1945. The formal transfer of the colony took place in 1949, after a four-year negotiation period.

As the country's first president, Sukarno led the country from a federal to a centralized state. Lack of skills and resources to fight social and economic problems progressively weakened the government. Following the first national election in 1955, which resulted in a political impasse and heightened social pressures, President Sukarno declared martial law in 1957 and gradually started to replace the parliamentary government with an authoritarian system, known as "Guided Democracy". The elected legislature was replaced by an appointed one, political activity was restricted and the army became deeply involved in the administration. The economy deteriorated and social discontent rose. An abortive coup led by a group of army officers, with the alleged involvement of the Communist Party (PKI), ended with the downfall of the government. Although President Sukarno remained head of state, his power was gradually eroded, until he was formally replaced by General Suharto in 1967.

President Suharto's "New Order" regime re-established political stability, and the economy opened up to foreign investment. A set of vague principles concentrating on personal and public responsibility, known as the "Pancasila", was turned into national ideology. Ever since, elections have regularly ensured victory for Golkar, President Suharto's ruling party.

Recent events

Although certain trends point to an easing of political restrictions, Indonesia's stability has recently been tested by several events. These include the ousting of Mrs Megawati, daughter of the late President Sukarno, from her position as leader of the Indonesian Democratic Party (PDI, one of Indonesia's three permitted parties) and the subsequent street rioting in Jakarta in July 1996. Furthermore, as the president, born in 1921 and now in his sixth five-year term, is ageing, uncertainty about his successor is acute.

The issue of succession

The next presidential elections will take place in 1998. It seems likely that Suharto will run for a seventh term. If he decides to stand, he would almost certainly be re-elected by the People's Consultative Assembly. The succession issue is becoming crucial, but no clear candidate has been identified. In the event of Suharto's demise, the armed forces are likely to play a key role in the transition. The military emergence of Suharto's son-in-law, Prabowo, may be pivotal.

Chronology

16th century	European incursion begins, led by the Portuguese
1602	Dutch East India company conquers the East Indies and replaces the Portuguese
1798	Dissolution of the Dutch East India company
1811-1816	British occupation under Sir Stamford Raffles
1816-1945	Administration of the colony under the Dutch government
1941-1945	Japanese occupation
1945	August 17: Declaration of independence by Sukarno and Hatta

1949	Formal transfer of sovereignty from the Dutch
1965	Coup of left-wing junior army officers against Army High Command
1966	March: military commanders under General Suharto take over the executive power; Communist Party is outlawed; National Front is dissolved
1967	Suharto becomes acting president, full president a year later
1967	Indonesia is a founding member of the Association of South-East Asian Nations (ASEAN)
1969	Irian Jaya is incorporated into Indonesia
1976	East Timor is incorporated into Indonesia
1989	Indonesia chairs the Paris Conference on Cambodia
1990	Diplomatic relations with China are restored
1994	Indonesia hosts the Asia-Pacific Economic Co-operation forum (APEC) in Bogor
1994	June: Revocation of publishing licences of three widely read news magazines
1996	July: Megawati Sukarnoputri ousted as leader of the Indonesia Democratic Party
1996	Streets riots in Jakarta
1996	October: Nobel Peace Prize awarded to Jose Ramos Horta and Bishop Carlos Filipe Belo, leading defenders of human rights in East Timor

Constitution and government

Indonesia has had three provisional constitutions, adopted in August 1945, February 1950 and August 1950. The 1945 constitution was re-enacted by presidential decree in 1959, and supplemented by the General Elections Law in 1969. The constitution is based on the "Pancasila" principle, which includes: belief in the One Supreme God; just and civilized humanity; the unity of Indonesia; democracy led by the wisdom of deliberations among representatives; and social justice for all the people of Indonesia.

The People's Consultative Assembly (PCA) is the highest authority of the state, and numbers 1,000. The PCA sits once every five years, and its main job is to elect the president and the vice-president. The House of People's Representatives (500 members), part of the PCA, acts as the legislative body proper. Seventy-five members (100 until 1997) are appointed by the president from the armed forces, and 425 members are elected every five years. The judicial branch of the state acts independently from the executive.

Current government

President	General Suharto
Vice-President	Try Sutrisno

Ministers:

Finance	Muhammed Mar'ie
Foreign Affairs	Ali Alatas
Interior	Yogie Suardi Memet
Industries and Trade	Tungky Ariwibowo
Governor, central bank	Sudradjad Djiwandono

Opposition (in conflict with government)
Fretilin
> Revolutionary Front for an Independent East Timor. Seeks independence for East Timor.

National Council of East Timorese Resistance
> Front organization for the East Timorese resistance
> Led by José Ramos Horta

Free Papua Movement
> Seeks unification with Papua New Guinea

State organization
Indonesia is divided into 27 provinces, each under the control of a governor appointed by the lresident. The provinces are subdivided into 246 districts, 55 municipalities and 3,592 subdistricts.

Political parties
The president can dissolve any party whose membership does not cover one quarter of Indonesia, or whose policies are deemed to be at variance with the aims of the state. There are three officially permitted political parties in Indonesia.

Golongan Karya (Golkar)
> Founded in 1964, reorganized 1971
> President: Gen. Suharto
> Chairman: Harmoko

Indonesian Democratic Party (IDP)
> Founded in 1973
> Merger of five nationalist and Christian parties
> Chairman: Soerjadi (replaced Megawati in July 1996)

United Development Party (UDP)
> Founded 1973
> Merger of four Islamic parties
> President: Hassan Metareum

Results of the June 1992 election of 400 members to the House of Representatives:
Golkar (282 seats, 68% of votes), **UDP** (62 seats, 17%), **IDP** (56 seats, 15%)

Next elections
May 1997 House of Representatives elections
March 1998 presidential elections

Other political forces
Army
The armed forces exercise a dual function, combining conventional defence duties with involvement in most areas of political and social life.

Nahdlatul Ulama
Largest Muslim organization.

Ikatan Cendekiawan Muslim Indonesia
(Association of Indonesian Muslim Intellectuals)
Founded in 1990, with governmental support;
Chairman: Jusuf HABIBIE

Central bank
The Bank of Indonesia (BoI) acts as the central bank and is wholly owned by the state. Its functions and responsibilities are prescribed by the Central Bank Act of 1968. The bank's tasks are currency issuance, supervision and regulation of financial institutions, lender of last resort to the banking system, government banker and holder of official international reserves, as well as the state's treasury accounts.

Monetary policy has traditionally been exercised through the setting of credit growth targets. The bank uses open market operations and discount facilities.

Banking system
Until the late 1980s, Indonesian commercial banking was dominated by five large state-owned banks, which concentrated on specific sectors of the economy and accounted for 80-90% of total credit volume. Strict direct credit controls over commercial banks, including credit volume and interest rate restrictions to promote small-scale national businesses, helped keep inflation down despite a rapid increase of reserve money following the oil price shocks. However, they also led to inefficient capital allocation. Balance of payments pressures, following the oil price collapse and devaluation of the currency in 1986, provoked several bouts of capital flight. The Bank of Indonesia launched drastic reforms of the financial sector, in line with overall economic liberalization efforts. Interest rate and credit ceilings were abolished and the BoI returned to indirect credit controls. A special form of discount instrument, known as Bank of Indonesia Certificates (SBI), was introduced to complement money market securities for the regulation of the liquidity in the financial system. The reforms culminated in the new banking law in 1992, aimed at the liberalization and simplification of the banking structure. The categories of recognized banking institutions were reduced to two: commercial banks and small-scale credit banks. Foreign banks, previously allowed to operate mainly in Jakarta, were given permission to open branches in other regions.

The financial sector reforms of the late 1980s, together with the new banking law, helped to boost the sector. By the end of March 1996, there were 10 foreign banks, 31 joint banks and 172 national (state and private) commercial banks.

■ ECONOMICS

Historical overview

The assumption of power by President Suharto and his "New Order" resulted in economic stability, after a near collapse of the economy in the mid-1960s. Under the new government, there were three broad phases of development. While the period 1967–73 was one of adjustment, stabilization and liberalization, a rapid increase in oil and other commodity earnings allowed the government to focus on development of the economy in the second half of the 1970s. This period, however, was also marked by a reversal of the economic liberalization of the late 1960s. The industrial base was upgraded by strengthening the role of state-owned enterprises (including banks) and intensifying investment controls (in particular of foreign investment) through a comprehensive licensing system. By the early 1980s, a restrictive trade regime had been developed, characterized by a multitude of tariff and non-tariff restrictions. The discrimination against exports resulted in heavy dependence on oil revenues, while eroding competitiveness of the non-oil economy due to an appreciation of the exchange rate. Credit allocations at subsidized interest rates further enhanced the distortions of the trade regime.

A sharp decline in the terms of trade, largely due to lower oil prices, presented major tests for the Indonesian economy during the 1980s. GDP growth plunged, the value of exports dropped and the trade deficit spiralled. Two adjustment periods followed: 1982-85 and 1986-88. The currency was devalued (1983, 1986), import controls reduced and the import-substitution policy abandoned. Robust growth had resumed by the late 1980s. Furthermore, the economy became increasingly reliant on strong private sector investment. Overall development was supported by dramatic reforms of the financial sector and by policies of macroeconomic stability.

To reduce the dependency on oil revenues, the government sought to stimulate non-oil exports. While agricultural development had always been a target of the New Order government, it increasingly strove to encourage industrialization, focusing on basic manufacturing. Today, Indonesia is moving up the value-added ladder, with an 80% share of non-oil exports in total exports in 1995, compared with only 25% in 1975. Since 1988, growth has been driven predominantly by non-oil exports.

Indonesia's economic performance

	Average annual real GDP growth, %	Average annual consumer price inflation, %
1961-1965	1.6	141.4
1966-1970	5.8	279.8
1971-1975	8.1	20.3
1976-1980	7.9	14.7
1981-1985	4.8	9.7
1985-1990	6.3	7.5
1991-1995	7.8	8.9

Recent developments

Liberalization of the financial sector led to a rapid increase in money and credit growth. During 1989-91, the economy was booming, inflationary pressures intensified and the balance of payments position deteriorated. To counteract inflation pressures, the authorities tightened credit policy by raising interest rates in 1990-91. Growth in some sectors declined, until monetary policy was relaxed in mid-1992. By June 1993 interest rates attained their lowest levels for seven years, and the economy started to recover. A doubling of the current account balance in 1995 induced the authorities to apply the brakes again. To avoid repeating the past experiences of shock therapy, the Bank implemented indirect measures, including an increase in reserve requirements, and tightened credit restraint. It also opted for gradually widening the intervention bands of the currency, thus transferring exchange rate risk to the market.

In spite of the restrictive monetary and credit policy, the economy is surging ahead. Growth is expected to continue at 8% rates in 1997, driven by private investment, with foreign capital playing a key role. The country is embarking on a new stage of development, characterized by a rising tide of foreign investment, which could upgrade its productive and export structure. Foreign direct investment (FDI) more than doubled in 1995, and a surge in FDI approvals in 1996 foreshadows continued rapid inflows.

The economy

Over the last thirty years, the economic structure has been transformed profoundly. Until 1990, agriculture was the predominant sector. Indonesia has a rich and diverse base of natural resources, and the soil – particularly in Java – is extremely fertile. Although agriculture has fallen to 16% of GDP in 1995, it remains the most significant sector in employment terms. The most important sub-sector is food crops, in particular rice and other food staples. The importance of rice for the country explains the relatively high weights in various price indices used to measure inflation. Self-sufficiency in rice has generally been a main policy objective and considerable efforts have been put into increasing production. These were particularly successful during the 1980s and early 1990s. Subsequent decline in rice output, however, forced Indonesia to import rice in 1995.

Share of GDP by sector

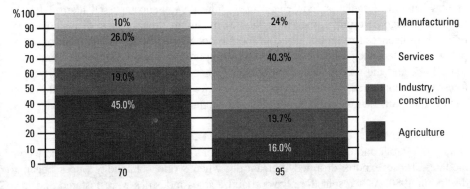

Source: Official data

The contribution of mining (including oil and natural gas) and quarrying to total domestic output has been declining. Although the output of the mining and quarrying sector has not been decreasing in absolute terms, the manufacturing sector has been growing much faster, increasing its share of total production. Industrialization has been given priority since the accession of the New Order government, which has established numerous state-owned enterprises, and encouraged private investors to participate in building a sound industrial base. Indonesia is now replacing traditional non-oil export products, such as textiles and plywood, with commodity-based but higher value-added products such as paper, chemicals, ceramics and glass.

The services sector is dominated by tourism and trade-related services. Banking and financial services are also on the rise.

Savings and investment
Private investment

Indonesia's saving and investment ratios as a percentage of GDP have been rising over the last three decades. Substantial incomes during the oil boom resulted in a rapid increase of domestic saving, and with some lag, in investment. The external shocks Indonesia experienced during the 1980s inevitably led to a decline in both. Sustained rapid growth and positive real interest rates, together with a foreign investment boom, have pushed savings and investment rates up to above 33% and 37% in 1995 respectively.

National saving has on average been slightly lower than domestic investment, mirrored by the chronic current account deficit. Although the government's development programmes have tried to enhance the role of the private sector in establishing and upgrading the economy since the mid-1980s, private investment as a percentage of total investment only rose slowly between 1980 and early 1990s, but has increased markedly since 1994.

Foreign investment

Since the New Order regime, foreign investment policy in Indonesia has undergone swings from liberalization to restriction and back again. Foreign direct investment (FDI) received a boost from a wide-ranging set of deregulatory reforms in the early 1990s. A significant move came in 1992 when 100% foreign ownership was allowed for certain types of investment. The big bang in deregulation, however, came in June 1994. It encompassed alternative structures for foreign investment, the elimination of minimum capital requirements, automatic renewals of licences for foreign investors and the opening up by the government of sectors previously closed, such as telecommunications and ports. As a result, FDI has been booming since 1995, and the recent surge in approvals (exceeding US$81 billion since early 1994) foreshadows continued, rapid inflows. The bulk of foreign investment has gone into manufacturing, in particular the metal processing and chemical industries.

Trade and balance of payments

During the stabilization period of the late-1960s, non-oil exports were mostly primary commodities. These exports dropped dramatically when world commodity prices began to decline in 1980. As a result, the plywood and textiles industries were fostered and have become major (and, since 1994, ailing) export products. While the share of trade in total national output increased markedly, it is the composition of export products that has shifted most notably since. Overall, petrol and natural gas remain Indonesia's main export products, accounting for nearly 15% of the total (down from 75% in 1975). The bulk of the non-oil export goods consists of primary and semi-processed agricultural goods (such as plywood, food and coffee), as well as textiles and footwear. Several of these key traditional non-oil exports have been suffering price and competitiveness problems.

Breakdown of exports (1995)

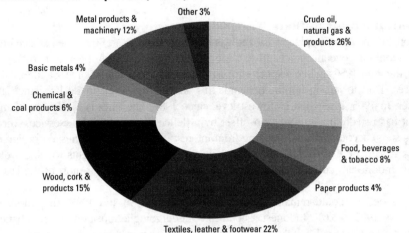

Metal products & machinery 12%

Other 3%

Crude oil, natural gas & products 26%

Basic metals 4%

Chemical & coal products 6%

Food, beverages & tobacco 8%

Wood, cork & products 15%

Paper products 4%

Textiles, leather & footwear 22%

Source: Official data

Imports and exports as a % of GDP

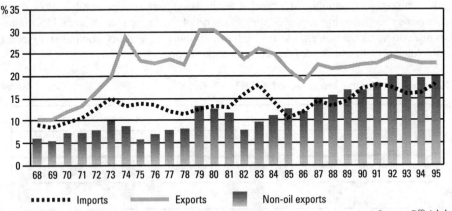

•••••••• Imports ——— Exports ■ Non-oil exports

Source: Official data

After growing 48% a year in 1990-92 in the wake of strong Japanese investment, exports of textiles and related products came under attack from lower-cost producers in the region. These exports expanded by only 3.6% a year in 1993-95. This constituted a major drain on overall trade performance, as they represented 24% of total non-oil exports. Similarly, plywood as a share of total non-oil exports declined by roughly half. A wide range of other manufacturing goods is assuming an increasingly important proportion of the country's exports. In particular, chemical, metal and paper products are emerging as extremely dynamic export products.

Indonesia's imports consist largely of raw materials, capital and intermediate goods. Consumer goods imports, which accounted for 5% of total non-oil imports in 1995, have been growing rapidly, adding to the overall pressure on the country's current account.

Current account deficits

Traditionally, the trade surplus on oil and gas has exceeded the non-oil trade balance deficit. Thus, Indonesia's overall merchandise trade balance has constantly been in surplus, even during the mid-1980s when export earnings suffered from the decline of international oil prices. Due to strong import demand, this surplus has been in decline since 1993, however. In 1995, it reached its lowest level since 1987. The surplus on the merchandise account has usually been more than offset by a deficit of the invisibles (services, income and transfers) account, largely resulting from interest payments on Indonesia's foreign debt and the repatriation of profits by foreign investors, as well as payments for trade-related services. Indonesia's current account has therefore been in deficit for most of the last two decades.

This deficit should remain around 4% of GDP in 1996 and 1997, after more than doubling in 1995 to 3.6%. Indonesia is currently undergoing a transition period, characterized by marked external imbalances. Sustained strong import growth is inevitable, as it is related to significant investment, notably foreign investment, which is needed to upgrade and diversify the economy.

While this investment boom will maintain pressure on the trade balance, it is likely to lead to stronger non-traditional export growth in due course. Indonesia's 1996 export performance illustrates the improved diversification of the exports structure and its minimal exposure to a global semiconductor setback. Indonesian exports continued to record double-digit growth in 1996 despite a region-wide slump.

Current account as a % of GDP

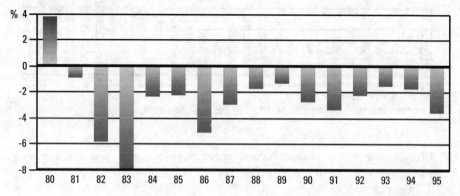

Source: Official data

Trade restrictions
Only Indonesian nationals can be authorized as importers of merchandise, although foreign investors are permitted to import the items required for their own projects. Imports of certain goods are restricted to approved importers, most of which are state enterprises. These include, rice, fertilizer and certain heavy equipment, as well as motor vehicles. Exporters need trade permits, issued by the Ministry of Trade, and exports of certain domestically produced commodities must have prior authorization.

Financing the current account deficit
Since the capital account was fully liberalized in 1971, foreign capital inflows have generally been plentiful, allowing for current account financing and reserve accumulation. In the 1990s, balance of payments surpluses have kept the country's foreign exchange reserves above four months of merchandise imports. Net foreign capital inflows more than doubled in 1995 and continued to surge in 1996, bringing the level of foreign exchange reserves to over US$16 billion. The composition of these capital inflows has shifted towards a higher private capital exposure, reflecting the country's improved access to international capital markets, but also increasing the vulnerability to external liquidity shocks. While foreign direct investment (FDI) has been booming since 1995, the contribution of official aid to the capital account has been declining steadily. In fact, taking into account debt repayment and debt servicing costs, Indonesia currently records a negative net transfer on official aid.

Debt
Indonesia went through several periods of heavy external borrowing. The country borrowed excessively in the early 1960s, in 1975 and again in the early 1980s.

Estimates and forecasts of foreign debt composition

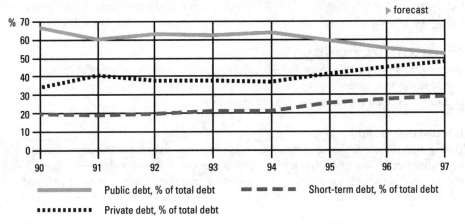

Source: Official data

Although external borrowing has been managed more prudently since 1986, the country's foreign debt has constantly been rising in absolute terms. Total foreign debt as a percentage of GDP, on the other hand, has gradually fallen from 70% in 1991, to some 55% in

1995. At the end of 1994, Indonesia's external debt stood at some US$100 billion, and was estimated at nearly US$110 billion by the end of 1995.

Of this amount, about two-thirds were public medium- and long-term debt (including state-owned enterprises). With the liberalization of regulations governing foreign borrowing by Indonesian banks, private debt as a percentage of total debt has been increasing, in particular through commercial banks. The ratio of short-term debt to official reserves remains close to 200%, reflecting the increasing share of short-term debt in total foreign debt. In 1994, 38% of the long-term debt was denominated in yen, compared to 20% in dollars. Since the early 1980s, the share of yen-denominated debt has been increasing gradually.

Although the growth of export earnings has kept up with the country's rising debt burden, debt amortization and servicing costs continue to absorb about 30% of total export receipts. In line with the relative increase of private debt, debt servicing by private borrowers has been increasing over the last years. The average interest rate of new commitments stood at 4.9% for official credits in 1994 and at 5.0% for private creditors.

Public debt repayments have been intensified in recent years, therefore mitigating the impact on total debt of the constantly growing private debt. In particular, privatization proceeds have been used to repay external debt recently. The government used privatization receipts from the listings of PT Indosat, PT Tambang Timah and PT Telkom to settle US$1.5 billion of high-cost foreign liabilities over the past two years. It has also pledged to use funds from last year's budget surplus to prepay an additional US$580 million in 1996. Further privatization, such as the recently completed initial public offering (IPO) of shares in the state-owned Bank Negara Indonesia (BNI), should provide additional resources for debt reduction.

The World Bank recently went further, recommending the generation of much larger fiscal surpluses that could be used to reduce public foreign debt. Management of the external debt has been improving due also to the creation of a governmental regulatory body, the Commercial Offshore Loan Team (COLT), which sets ceilings on commercial foreign borrowing by the central bank, state banks, state-owned companies and state-related projects.

Economic policy

Since the accession of the "New Order" government, economic policy has maintained a relatively steady course. Main policy goals have included macroeconomic stability, agricultural and rural development and improvement in infrastructure.

Monetary policy

During the last three decades, Indonesia has experienced several bouts of inflationary pressures. Controlling prices has therefore been a major objective of the central bank. Since the financial market liberalization of the late 1980s, monetary policy is generally carried out through interest rates, as well as by the usual indirect measures. Credit growth rates are monitored closely.

Recent overheating has been dampened by indirect measures, mainly higher reserve requirements, as international capital flows can complicate monetary management, given Indonesia's managed currency regime and open capital account. In particular, a hike in interest rates can attract large short-term inflows, which, unless sterilized, feed into base money growth.

In 1990-93 Bank of Indonesia Certificates (SBI) were introduced to sterilize the accumulation of foreign exchange reserves, but they put upward pressure on domestic interest rates. After peaking in early 1994 at Rp24 trillion, SBIs were aggressively unwound. Since 1994, fiscal policy strongly came to the support of monetary policy. By running surpluses and depositing them in Bank of Indonesia's vaults, the government de facto sterilized excess foreign capital inflows, while keeping base money growth under control.

In the first half of 1996, capital inflows intensified and challenged the authorities' pledge to curtail monetary expansion. Broad money accelerated to nearly 30% by mid-year, compared with an official year-end target of 17%. In the second quarter, the authorities responded by renewed fiscal tightening and contractionary open market operations.

Fiscal policy

Soon after its accession to power, the government adopted a balanced budget policy. Concessional inflows of foreign capital in the form of project and programme aid, classified as revenues, are used to fill the gap between domestic revenue and domestic expenditure. Budget surpluses can be deposited with the central bank, which can be withdrawn for extra-budgetary funding of government spending in times of reduced revenues. As the government was not reliant on domestic borrowing and money creation, fiscal excesses were avoided and fiscal dilemmas have been unravelled by fiscal reforms.

Revenues are derived from a wide range of sources, including direct taxes, indirect taxes (a VAT came into effect in April 1985) and non-tax revenues. Taxes on oil company profits have also been an important source of government receipts since the mid-1970s. They represent some 22% of total fiscal receipts today. Reforms of the tax system, including a widening of the tax base in 1994, led to a relative increase of domestic consumption taxes as a share of overall government revenues. Import duties make up for roughly 4.5% of total revenues.

Overall fiscal expenditures have decreased relative to GDP in recent years, reducing fiscal reliance of foreign aid. The foreign aid component was reduced significantly from 7% of GDP in fiscal year 1988-89 to 2.8% in 1994-95, and is budgeted to remain at about this level over the next two years. As budget surpluses would help mitigate the current account deficit, tighter fiscal policy would be desirable. Higher oil prices in 1996 are likely to support public finances.

Currency

The rupiah was devalued in both 1983 and 1986 by more than 40% against the US$. Since February 1988, it has evolved within a managed crawling peg system against a trade-weighted basket of currencies. Although the composition of the basket is undisclosed, it appears very heavily dollar-weighted. Thus, the US$ can de facto be considered as the nominal anchor for Indonesian exchange rate policy.

Every trading day, the central bank announces the level of the IDR/US$ mid-rate. To compensate for inflation differentials with the US and maintain the real competitiveness of the currency, Bank of Indonesia has been depreciating the rupiah's mid-rate against the US$ by an average of 4% a year. The exchange rate is allowed to evolve freely within a trading range, which has been gradually widened in recent years. The last widening, to 8% around the official mid-rate vis-a-vis the US dollar, took place on September 11, 1996.

Indonesian rupiah/US dollar exchange rate

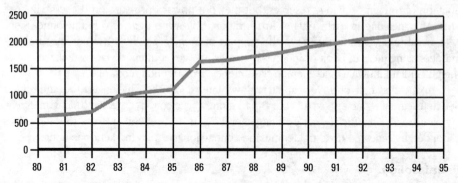

Exchange controls

There are no limitations on the remittances of capital in the form of foreign exchange. Both residents and non-residents are permitted to hold foreign currency deposits with foreign exchange banks. The latter are subject to Bank of Indonesia directives with respect to borrowing abroad and the acceptance of deposits of non-residents. Foreign commercial loan transactions are supervised by the COLT. Indonesian citizens and residents also may freely transfer, negotiate, import and export securities denominated in rupiah or in foreign currency.

Deregulation

In 1985, the government began to reduce and simplify regulations in order to encourage the private sector. Deregulation has gathered momentum since 1994, when regulations banning 100% foreign ownership across a wide range of industries were scrapped and tariffs on a large variety of goods were cut. Import tariffs were cut further in 1995 and 1996. In line with its AFTA and WTO commitments, the government plans to bring tariffs down from their current average of 12% to 7% by 2003. These moves will clearly strengthen the non-oil export industry and improve the investment environment.

Privatization

At the end of 1994, there were 180 state enterprises, most of which were in areas that are now dominated by the private sector, such as industry and finance. Overall, the privatization process in Indonesia has been somewhat slower than elsewhere in the region. An ambitious privatization programme was launched in 1989, but had only limited success. The programme gained new impetus in 1994-96, with the greatest advances being made in telecommunications. The government sped up privatization outside telecommunication. The listing of shares in state-owned Bank Negara Indonesia (BNI) is a prime example.

■ EQUITIES

Index performance (in local currency)

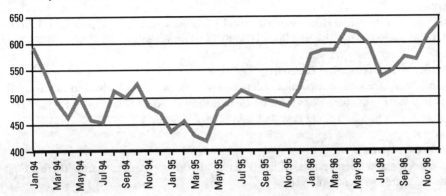

Key indicators

	Index performance %, in US$ terms	Market Cap US$bn	P/E	Div Yield	Weight in IFCI	Weight in IFCG
1994	-20.6	47.2	20.2	1.5	2.7	2.4
1995	9.9	66.6	19.8	1.9	3.2	3.5
1996	18.0	91.0	21.6	1.4	4.5	4.7

Sources: Local stock exchanges, IFC, Bloomberg, Datastream, UBS

Structure

The Indonesian stock market exists largely on one exchange, in Jakarta (JSE). There is a second exchange in Surabaya, East Java, but trading here is minimal. A third exchange is being set up in Medan, North Sumatra.

Trading can be on six separate boards, of which the regular board (blocks of 500 shares), the crossing board (for internal cross trades by one broker) and the foreign board (for trading shares in companies in which the 49% foreign ownership limit has been reached) account for 97% of trading volume and 98% of trading value. As of September 1996, there were 247 equity shares listed in Jakarta.

Regulatory authority

BAPEPAM (the Capital Market Executive Agency to the Ministry of Finance), established in 1977, is Indonesia's equivalent of the US Securities and Exchange Commission or the Securities Investment Board in the UK. BAPEPAM has supervisory powers over all institutions in the Indonesian primary and secondary markets.

Trading methods

The JSE began automated trading in May 1995. The Jakarta Automated Trading System (JATS) can process as many as 50,000 transactions in a single day. JATS is order-driven and not quote-driven as in the UK. The computer matches orders by price, followed by the time they were entered. All entries into the JATS are made from terminals on the exchange floor by members of the stock exchange. By 1998, remote trading from terminals located in member broker offices will be possible.

Hours
Trading starts at 09.30 and closes at 16.00, Monday to Friday. The JSE is closed from 12.00 to 13.30 on Monday to Thursday and from 11.30 to 14.00 on Friday.

Settlement time and clearing
Settlement time for both buying and selling is T+4. Shares are typically held in custodian banks in Jakarta. All transactions must be cleared through KDEI (Kliring and Deposit Efek Indonesia). This makes clearing easy and usually problem-free.

Types of shares
From a stock market perspective, all listed shares are ordinary voting shares. There are no "A" or "B" shares with multiple votes.

Stock indices
There is one main index for the JSE, the JSE Composite Share Price Index. The JSE Index includes all listed stocks, weighed by market capitalization. In 1996, the JSE introduced a number of sector indices covering basic industries, financial institutions, property, consumer and other sectors. These sub indices have made redundant those quoted by JF Nusantara.

Taxes
There is a deduction of 15% at source on dividends and 10% on interest made by resident companies on payments to investors resident in countries in which Indonesia has a double tax treaty. Most companies run on a January to December calendar. Dividends are paid at varying times throughout the year, mostly during the third quarter. Transactions on the JSE are subject to a 10% VAT on commissions paid plus a 0.04% levy on transaction value. Selling transactions are also subject to a 0.1% sales tax on transaction value. There is no capital gains tax for foreign investors.

Disclosure of financial statements
Financial statements must reflect the true and accurate position of the company. In many respects, the Indonesian GAAP is substantially the same as the US GAAP, although there are far fewer rules. Companies must have their accounts audited and approved by external registered companies (often the "big six" accounting firms). Every listed company must disclose their financial statements twice a year. Furthermore, banks must disclose their financial statements on a quarterly basis.

Shareholders' rights
Shareholders can vote by proxy in Indonesia. All shareholders must be informed of any upcoming extraordinary and annual general meetings.

Ownership limits for non-residents
There is a foreign ownership limit of 49% of the listed shares of all companies on the JSE.

There is no distinction made between privatized state enterprises and other companies, nor with banks and other sectors, although changes in the rules regarding the latter have been discussed. There are no foreign exchange controls in Indonesia.

Take-over bids and large stakes
Available to all shareholders for the number of shares they intend to buy. The company may set a minimum acceptance limit for which the offer is valid. If a company tries to buy more than 50% of another company it must make a bid for all of the company's shares and is required to buy all those that the shareholders are willing to sell.

Brokers
There are nearly two hundred brokers in Indonesia. It is only possible to do trades on the exchange through these official brokers. However, the industry is fairly concentrated and the top twenty brokers will typically account for about half of the trading value in any particular month. The largest brokers are associated with foreign banks or securities companies or with local banks.

Sectors
The biggest sectors by market capitalization and volume represented on the JSE are the consumer goods (with about 25% of market capitalization), telecommunications and cement sectors. Also important are the finance, property and forestry sectors as well as the automotive sector.

ADRs
There are five Indonesian ADRs: Telkom, Indosat, APP, APRIL and Tripolyta. GDRs exist for Telkom and Tambang Timah. Warrants exist for six different companies: Bank Bali, Indah Kiat, Apac Centrix, Ometraco Corp., Perdana Cipta Multifinance and Surabaya Agung.

■ DEBT

Informal capital markets have existed in Indonesia since the 17th century, but the modern bond market came with the deregulation of interest rates in 1983, which raised the cost of commercial bank lending. The market is small compared to other ASEAN countries, but grew at an annual rate of 64% between 1988 and 1995, due to the funding needs of property developers and financial institutions.

The Capital Markets Law (1952) empowered the Ministry of Finance (MoF) to organize and regulate a capital market. In 1976, the MoF delegated the regulatory role to an agency, Badan Pelaksana Pasar Modal (BAPEPAM), which has limited powers to make independent decrees. The central bank's jurisdiction extends to the banking system, money market activities and debt issues with maturities up to one year.

Public debt
In 1967, the New Order government adopted a balanced budget policy which, by forbidding deficit spending, prevented government bond issuance. Government debt is thus restricted

to money-market instruments, issued through the central bank, in its exercise of monetary policy.

Bank Indonesia Treasury Notes (Sertifak Bank Indonesia – SBI)

SBIs were first issued by the central bank in 1984 to act as a monetary policy tool. The 1-month bill is the most important and is a key interest rate, although 7-, 14-, 91- and 182-day maturities are also available. Volume is thin beyond 1 month.

Bills of one year were introduced in 1988. They are discounted instruments with rates calculated on a 360-day basis and are usually priced lower than interbank rates to deter foreign speculation.

Auctions are held each day for 7-, 14-, and 28-day bills; regular weekly auctions for 91- and 182-day bills are held on Wednesday, but the central bank has discretion to auction bills on other days. Only banks and qualifying financial institutions can make bids, which are accepted within a band either side of the average yield of the last auction: 25 basis points for daily auctions and 50 basis points for weekly auctions. Allotments are made from the highest price down to a clearing level (Stop-Out-Rate) where small banks are allocated bills. Settlement is book-entry and investors receive a Bilyet Deposit Simpanan (BDS).

In the secondary market, SBIs are traded over the counter (OTC), quoted on a yield basis and settlement is trade date plus two days in book-entry form.

Surat Berharga Pasar Vang (SBPUs)

SBPUs are promissory notes discounted by the central bank with maturities up to 1 year, and were introduced in 1983 to help control liquidity.

Private debt

Until 1988 only state-owned companies were allowed to raise money in the bond market and they remain the principal issuers, although issues from private companies have increased since 1993. But high costs and a lengthy issuance process has led corporates to raise funds in the commercial paper and medium-term note markets. However, investors are not protected by the BAPEPAM regulator and so the market is dominated by the strongest credits.

Commercial Paper (CP)

CP is unsecured debt privately placed by corporates, denominated in rupiah or US dollars, and quoted on a discount basis. Maturities range from 7 days to 1 year. Issues are usually backed by an underlying transaction, a bank-stamped acceptance or a corporate credit. Paper is issued in bearer form and trades settle for physical delivery, T+5. The market is unregulated, and evolved from the restrictions imposed on bank lending in 1991.

Certificates of deposit (CDs)

A syndicate of financial institutions receives the CDs from an underwriter, and sells them to investors. Issues now extend to 3 years, are traded OTC in bearer form and settlement is T+5.

Medium-term notes (MTNs)

Like CP, MTNs are privately placed corporate issues but with maturities of 1 month to 3 years – although longer-dated programmes are sometimes available. They are bearer securities, denominated in either rupiah or dollars and are transferable. The issuer, through the arranger and placement agent, can sell notes of different structures and maturity dates until the programme reaches its specified size (up to Rp100 billion – US$40 million).

Corporate bonds

Most are issued by financial, infrastructure or general purpose state-owned companies, which are required by law to provide collateral or sinking funds to support their issues. They are fully underwritten, listed on the Stock Exchange but increasingly trade OTC. Payment for bonds in the primary market is one to two days before the issue date; buyers receive a certificate. A "when-issued" market operates during the interim. Market quotes are on a clean price basis, and settlement is physical DVP. The first private sector bond was launched in 1988, but a greater number of corporates subsequently have preferred to tap the private placement market. Public issues are normally over-collateralized by the issuer's assets, have a 5-year maturity, and are issued at par in bearer form.

Many issues have initial fixed-rate coupons that change to floating-rate payments, but after the "Gebrakan Sumarlin" shock in 1990, which pushed interest rates up in the early nineties, investors have insisted on straight FRNs. The Indonesian authorities impose no restrictions on foreign purchases of domestic bonds. International investors have been significant buyers of CP and MTNs, which offer higher yields than those available on SBIs.

In 1993, the Indonesian Depository and Clearing Agency (KDEI) was formed, sponsored by seven state banks and the Jakarta and Surabaya stock exchanges, and has devised a system that allows for the immobilization of bonds. Market participants prefer to trade bonds in registered form because it reduces the risks of forgery, and the KDEI system should be able to accommodate their preference.

An electronic monitoring system called Parallel Information Bonds System (PIBS), providing real-time information on bond prices and secondary market transactions was set up by the Surabaya Stock Exchange in 1995. It will be linked to the KDEI depository, and transactions will be settled through book-entry.

Safe custody of bearer bonds remains a problem to foreign investors.

Credit Rating Agency

PT Pemeringkay Efek Indonesia (PEFINDO) was set up in September 1994, and is jointly owned by seventy shareholders. It fulfils a legal requirement for all debt issues by awarding its own short-term and long-term ratings, but caps short-term local debt at PA+ (A+ equivalent) because Standard and Poor's has rated Indonesia BBB for all its foreign currency borrowing.

Derivatives

Rupiah bonds can be hedged into dollars using 3- to 6-month swaps, and major international banks provide dollar/rupiah cross-currency swaps out to 5 years. Interest rate swaps are transacted with reference to the Indonesian Rupiah Swap Offer Rate (IRSOR).

Taxation

In January 1995, a 35% capital gains tax was replaced by 0.1% transaction tax. Withholding tax for domestic investors is 15%, but banks and pension funds are exempt. Non-residents pay 20% unless there is a double taxation agreement.

Eurobonds

After the fall in the stock market and rise in interest rates in 1990, corporates turned to foreign investors by issuing euro-convertibles denominated in dollars and Swiss Francs. Indonesian enterprises have also issued vanilla eurobonds and yankees. There has been a total of forty issues, denominated in US dollars, yen and Swiss francs.

Eurobond issues (US$m)

	1990	1991	1992	1993	1994	1995	1996
Sovereign	—	—	—	—	—	—	400.0
Private	50.0	—	—	485.0	1170.0	1605	2837

■ INDONESIA: Economic indicators

Population and development	1990	1991	1992	1993	1994	1995	1996e
Population, million	179.3	182.0	184.0	187.1	190.3	193.5	196.8
Population growth, %	1.6	1.5	1.1	1.7	1.7	1.7	1.7
Nominal GDP per capita, US$	592	641	756	844	923	1026	1123

National accounts							
Nominal GDP, US$bn	106.1	116.6	139.1	158.0	175.7	198.5	221.0
Change in real GDP, %	7.2	7.0	149.4	7.3	7.5	8.1	8.0
Gross fixed capital formation, % of GDP	28.4	28.1	25.8	26.3	27.8	28.8	30.0

Money supply and inflation							
Narrow money, change %, Dec/Dec	18.4	10.6	9.3	28.7	23.5	15.2	18.0
Broad money, change %, Dec/Dec	44.2	17.0	20.2	22.2	19.9	27.6	27.6
Consumer price inflation (avg.) %	7.8	9.5	6.9	9.7	8.5	9.4	8.0

Government finance							
Government expenditure, % of GDP	25.3	22.9	20.6	19.5	18.9	17.8	17.6
Government balance, % of GDP	0.0	0.0	0.0	-0.5	0.3	0.8	0.5

Exchange rates *lc=local currency*							
Exchange rate, annual average, lc/US$	1842	1950	2029	2087	2158	2244	2327
Exchange rate, end of year, lc/US$	1901	1992	2062	2110	2198	2284	2363
Real exchange rate 1990=100	100.0	98.0	95.4	98.7	99.2	96.0	101.1

Balance of payments							
Exports of goods & services, US$m	29704	33374	38005	41530	45552	51025	55785
Change %	16.9	12.4	13.9	9.3	9.7	12.0	9.3
Imports of goods & services, US$m, fob	33110	37896	41356	44174	48855	58547	64337
Change %	23.3	14.5	9.1	6.8	10.6	19.8	9.9
Trade balance, of goods only, US$m, fob-fob	5352	4801	7022	8231	7901	5710	5748
Current account balance, US$m	-3240	-4392	-3122	-2298	-2960	-7222	-8152
as a % of GDP	-3.1	-3.8	-2.2	-1.5	-1.7	-3.6	-3.7

Foreign exchange reserves							
Foreign exchange reserves, US$m	7459	9258	10449	11263	12133	13674	15290
Gold at ⅔ of market price, US$m	799.8	750.4	709.3	742.9	793.5	793.4	800.7
Import cover (reserves/imports), months	2.7	2.9	3.0	3.1	3.0	2.8	2.9

Foreign debt and debt service							
Short-term debt, US$m	14109	15890	16924	19189	21395	27900	31500
Total foreign debt, US$m	72795	82186	85406	92452	100684	109200	114500
as a % of GDP	68.6	70.5	61.4	58.5	57.3	55.0	51.8
as a % of foreign exchange receipts	241.7	244.3	221.4	219.3	218.0	211.5	203.1
Interest payments, US$m	4589	4888	4705	4825	5000	6200	7000
Principal repayments, US$m	6010	6204	6569	7079	9000	10000	10900
Total debt service, US$m	10599	11092	11274	11904	14000	16200	17900
as a % of goods exports	39.5	37.4	33.4	32.5	34.8	35.6	35.7
as a % of foreign exchange receipts	35.2	33.0	29.2	28.2	30.3	31.4	31.7

Israel

Area (thousands of km²):	21
Population (1995, millions):	5.8
Population projection (2025, millions):	8
Population younger than 15 yrs (1991, % of total):	30.9
Urbanization rate (1993, % of population):	90
Life expectancy (1993, years at birth):	77
Gross domestic product (1996, US$bn):	94
GDP per capita (1996, US$):	15632
Average annual GDP growth rate (1990-96, %):	5.8
Average annual inflation rate (1990-96, %):	13.1
Currency (shekel per US$, average 1996):	3.19
Real exchange rate: (1990=100, average 1996)	107.0
Structure of production (1994):	35.8% services, 32.2% industry, 14.9% transport, 9% construction, 8.1% agriculture
Main exports:	metal, machinery & electronics, diamonds (worked), chemical goods, textiles
Main imports:	investment, goods, diamonds (net), fuel
Main trading partners:	EU & United States
Market capitalization of Stock Exchange (December 1996; US$bn):	35
Total foreign debt (% of GDP):	51.1
Next elections due under normal circumstances:	presidential scheduled March 1998; legislative required by May 2000
Credit rating: (Nov 1996, Standard & Poor's, Moody's)	A-; A3

FORECAST: 1997-2000 (average)

	Worst case	Most likely	Best case
Real GDP growth (%)	3.0	4.5	6.0
Inflation (%)	10.5	9.0	7.5

■ POLITICS

Historical overview

The State of Israel was founded in 1948. The idea of a Jewish homeland in what was then British Palestine was accepted in international agreements by the British authorities in the Balfour Agreement in 1917. In 1920, the League of Nations gave this explicit mandate to the British as part of its agenda in Palestine. Although there had always been a Jewish presence, Jews started emigrating to the area in greater numbers from the late 1800s. In part, this move back to Palestine was driven by Zionist idealism fuelled by discrimination against Jews in Europe and the region in the last years of the 19th century. Faced with rising anti-Semitism in the 1920s and 1930s, Jewish emigration to the area increased in earnest.

At the time, the area was under British control, following the British and French division of the collapsed Ottoman Empire. After the Second World War and the Holocaust, a homeland for the Jews was made a priority of the postwar settlement. A British backed UN initiative resolved to divide Palestine into two states – a Jewish and an Arab state. This arrangement pleased neither side. The Jews saw this as only a partial return of their historical homeland, whereas the Arabs in the region believed that the Jews were being given Arab land. This grievance has led to attacks on Israel in 1948, 1967 and 1973, and goes to the root of present-day problems in the Middle East. The 1978 Camp David Accord, which brought peace with Egypt, marked a fundamental change in relations between the Arabs and Israel. Thereafter, despite setbacks, the change in the geo-political environment with the collapse of the Soviet Union, the fall-out from the Gulf War and increase in the influence of the United States in the region all accelerated this process. Another major attempt in the long and arduous struggle for accommodation in the region was the 1993 Oslo Accord.

Recent events

The Oslo Accord is based on the principle of land for peace. Thus far, the agreement has delivered a Palestinian Authority with limited jurisdiction over some of the West Bank and most of Gaza. Further discussions on more comprehensive powers being bequeathed gradually to the Authority and talks on the status of Jerusalem were also envisaged. Even though the Oslo Accord still remains the basis for negotiation, events in 1996 have shown that this accommodation is still far from painless.

The victory of Binyamin Netanyahu over Shimon Peres in the May 1996 election, marked a change in policy towards the peace process. The new government had been elected following a sharp increase in terrorism in Israel since the Oslo Accord signing. It therefore took a more conservative stance on the pace of implementing the Accord.

Chronology

1947	Proposed creation of the Jewish State
1948	War of Independence; Israel repels attacking armies
1948-52	Accelerated immigration of Jews
1956	Suez Crisis, occupation of Sinai
1967	Six-day War. Israel repels attacking armies and captures the West Bank, Golan and Sinai.
1973	Yom Kippur War. Israel repels attacking armies.
1978	Camp David Accord
1982	Security situation in northern Israel deteriorates. Israel invades Lebanon.
1985	Israel withdraws from Lebanon (except the security zone)
1987	Palestinian intifada begins
1990	Collapse of the Soviet Union
1991	Gulf War
1993	Oslo Accord

1995	Assassination of Yitzhak Rabin
1996	Election of Yasser Arafat as chairman of the Palestinian Authority
1996	Election of Binyamin Netanyahu as prime minister

Constitution and government

Israel has no formal constitution, but has a number of Basic Laws covering key areas of public life, such as human rights, the electoral system, the Knesset and the legal system.

The present government is a coalition, headed by Binyamin Netanyahu. His position is unique in the history of the state as, for the first time, in May 1996, the country voted for both the prime minister and the parliament. Netanyahu's victory gave him the post of prime minister for four years, irrespective of the make-up of the coalition. The separate election of a prime minister is aimed at elevating this post relative to the rest of the political system.

The main parties are the Likud (Conservative), Labour (Left), Shas and Mafdal (both religious parties), and the Israel ba-Aliya (Immigrants' Party). The Likud-led coalition represents a more conservative approach to security issues and questions the wisdom of relinquishing large tracts of land to the Palestinian Authority. Netanyahu's margin of victory – less than 1% of the population (although within the Jewish population the margin was 12%) – underlines the split over the peace process. On the economic front, the coalition has indicated that it will preside over a broad policy of balanced budgets, lower inflation, liberalization and privatization. Labour is the main opposition party and still the biggest party in the Knesset. In terms of ideology Labour is more social-democratic on economics and argues that the only way to proceed politically is to accelerate the Oslo process.

Current government

President   Ezer Weitzmann
Prime Minister   Likud   Binyamin Netanyahu

Results of the May 1996 elections
(of a total 120 Knesset seats) :
Labour Party (33); **Likud Party** (31); **Shas** (11); **Mafdal** (9); **Third Way** (5); **Israel ba-Aliya** (7)
Meretz (6); **Agudat Yisrael** (3);. **Arabs** (7); **Moledet** (2)

Next elections
May 2000 at the latest

Central bank

Israel's central bank is responsible for issuing banknotes, implementing exchange rate and monetary policies and aiming for lower inflation by taking into account the government's development plans and annual programmes, as well as advising the government on financial matters and overseeing aspects of the banking system. In practice, since 1991 the Bank has been increasingly independent in the operation of monetary policy.

Jacob Frenkel, the present governor, was first nominated in 1991 for a five-year term and in 1996 was reconfirmed in the post until 2001.

■ ECONOMICS

Historical overview

Since 1989, the Israeli economy has grown at a pace approaching that of the dynamic economies of South East Asia. What makes this performance all the more spectacular is that Israel is already an industrialized country, more akin in structure to the small open economies of north-west Europe than its immediate neighbours. Analysis of the complexion of the economy bears this out, with 24% of the workforce employed in industry as against 4% in agriculture, enabling Israel's main export categories – machinery and electronics – to outstrip by a factor of five times the corresponding figure for agriculture. Furthermore, despite its size, Israel is an economic giant in the region. Israeli GDP, at around US$93 billion, is only about 12% less than the combined GDP of Egypt, Lebanon, Jordan and Syria, with only about 7% of their population.

Over the past eight years, and particularly recently, domestic demand has been surging. While Israeli exporters have made significant gains in newly opened export markets, they have also consolidated their position in more established markets such as the EU and the USA, where Israel has free-trade arrangements. At the same time, this external dynamism has been mirrored domestically in the labour market, with unemployment falling sharply in the past eighteen months and nearing accepted "full employment" levels.

Economic background

Despite being a small open economy, with goods and services exports and imports totalling just over 75% of GNP, the economy's growth patterns have diverged quite markedly from the global economic cycle. The reasons for this stem from the fact that Israeli economic history has been largely determined by two central factors: successive waves of immigration, and ongoing conflicts with its neighbours. Unique movements in the cycle appear to be driven by these forces and domestic policy reactions to them.

Israeli economic history over the past two decades can be neatly subdivided into three sections. The first period, 1975-85, was characterized by an explosion of government expenditure, surging inflation and a falling exchange rate, driven in the main by a surge in military spending. The economy stagnated, growth slumped, unemployment rose and debt ballooned. The second subperiod, 1985-89, saw the authorities come to grips with the imbalances in the economy, slashing inflation, reining in expenditure and thus, ensuring an improvement in the external imbalance. In addition, the authorities began the process of liberalizing the economy in an effort to place it on a more competitive footing. The final period, 1989-96, has been characterized by a new wave of immigration (mainly from former Communist countries), movements towards a "normalization" in external relations and the opening of foreign markets. These factors have served as catalysts, kick-starting the economy precisely as the supply side reforms of the 1985-89 period were bearing fruit.

The lost years

Israel grew at extremely strong rates throughout the 1960s and early 1970s, but the economy endured a protracted period of stagflation between 1973 and 1985, with output growth moderating and inflation ballooning. Triggered by the Yom Kippur War and the first oil crisis, this period saw the state's role in the economy greatly enhanced. In response to the increased external threat, military expenditures peaked at 35% of government spending in 1976. This pressure drove the budget deficit up to 14% of GDP. Inflation, which averaged around 150% per annum in the early 1980s, reached 445% in 1984, while external debt increased from 25% to 80% of GDP over the period. To finance increased expenditure, a myriad taxes were levied on nearly all aspects of economic activity which, in tandem with near hyperinflation, led to an extremely inefficient allocation of resources.

Adjustment

In 1985, the government, faced with little choice, introduced a stabilization programme with the dual aims of bringing down inflation and reducing the its own role in the economy. In tandem with short-term austerity measures, a programme of deregulation, tax reduction and privatization was introduced. Inflation was brought down in two short years from 445% to 20%, while by the early 1990s, foreign debt and debt servicing as a percentage of exports had fallen to manageable levels. The budget registered a surplus in 1986, and small deficits have been registered since then. Total government debt fell from a staggering 170% of GDP to 90% by 1992. The process of deregulation has been largely completed in the area of trade and the financial markets, while privatizations have continued apace. The total tax burden has been reduced to 40% of GDP, lower than the comparable figure in Germany or France.

Immigration, dynamism and growth

By the early 1990s, the economy appeared, for the first time in almost two decades, to be in a relatively strong position to respond to global economic trends in an efficient manner. Inflation and the budget deficit were under control, debt servicing had ceased to be a drain on the nation's resources and the process of deregulation ensured that the Israeli economy could capitalize on its primary natural resources – a highly educated labour force and extremely high levels of research and development per employee. What was needed was a catalyst to harness this productive potential. The trigger came from the collapse of the Soviet Union.

For Israel, the implosion of the Soviet Union presented three unique opportunities. First, there was the prospect of mass immigration of well-educated labour. Second, it brought the opening up of markets previously sealed by the animosity of Soviet backed regimes in Eastern Europe and elsewhere. Third, although not apparent at the time, the collapse of the Soviet Union made possible a thawing of relations between Israel and its neighbours as the ideological sting was gradually removed from many previously intractable regional disputes.

The arrival of the new immigrants at the beginning of 1989, more than anything else, re-invigorated the Israeli economy. It grew by 6% per year for the next six years. Initially, the explosion in population – an increase of 12% or about 600,000 in all – led to a frenzy of activity, spearheaded by the construction sector. In the drive to house the influx, the government boosted public housing projects, causing the deficit to rise modestly. However, when it became apparent that the private sector was responding with such gusto to the new opportunities, the state reined in their expenditure, enabling the deficit to ease back.

Following the initial burst, the economy returned to a more normal footing, with a sharp fall in construction spending exerting significant downward pressure on aggregate GDP. On the other hand, domestic consumption remained strong, underpinned by rising income expectations, falling taxes and a positive wealth effect associated with the surging stock market and non-residential investment held up well. The fall in residential construction was primarily a correction following the frenzied building activity of 1991-92 and the return of immigration to more manageable levels.

At this stage the second benign factor kicked in – newly opened markets. By 1992, booming exports were beginning to contribute more significantly to growth. With Israel's major trade partner, the US, growing strongly and Israeli exporters making significant gains in the newly opened and growing markets of South East Asia, China and India, exports took off sharply. This external fillip supported industrial production, which had been accelerating apace since 1990.

Over the period the domestic economy displayed considerable dynamism in responding to the population explosion. Nowhere has this flexibility been more evident than in the labour market. Unemployment, which lurched upwards following the initial bloating of the labour force, fell rapidly, surprising even the most optimistic commentators. From its all-time high of 11.2% in 1992, unemployment fell to 6.4% in 1996.

Recent overheating

Despite these impressive structural improvements, the economy has not been able to avoid the business cycle. Thus, following almost seven successive years of growth, the economy in 1996 appeared to be overheating and all indications pointed to a slowdown. The perennial trade and current account deficits were spiced with stubbornly high levels of inflation and an expanding government deficit. This cocktail caused the central bank to raise real interest rates, which also had the effect of driving up the currency. The strong shekel affected exports, choking off a potential source of non-inflationary growth.

Population

Population has been the key influence on both Israeli politics and economics. The population now stands at 6 million, of which about 600,000 arrived in the country since 1989. The influx of immigrants is set to continue at about 60,000 a year until the turn of the century.

Trade

The EU and the US remain Israel's major trading partners. The country has a free trade agreement with both. Israel has consistently recorded deficits on its trade account, and in 1996 the deficit was estimated to have expanded to over 11% of GDP. Up to now financing such a shortfall has not been a problem due, in the main, to unilateral transfers and US loan arrangements. The strikingly large trade deficit is largely a function of the population explosion. As the immigrants become more absorbed, the trade deficit should shrink.

Main trading partners (% of total)

Exports to:	1992	1993	1994
Total EU	34.5	29.6	29.2
UK	7.7	5.4	6.3
Belgium-Luxembourg	5.0	5.4	5.5
Germany	5.8	5.3	5.4
France	4.7	3.9	3.8

Netherlands	4.2	3.7	4.2
US	31.5	30.9	30.6
Japan	5.3	5.1	6.9
Hong Kong	5.1	4.8	5.2
Imports from:	**1992**	**1993**	**1994**
Total EU	50.2	60.9	53.7
UK	8.0	8.6	8.7
Belgium-Luxembourg	13.0	12.2	12.7
Germany	11.9	10.4	10.4
France	4.5	4.2	4.5
Netherlands	3.3	3.4	3.3
Switzerland	7.2	7.5	6.5
Italy	7.0	7.3	7.8
US	17.2	17.7	17.9
Japan	5.3	5.1	4.1

Source: Central Bureau of Statistics

Share of GDP by sector

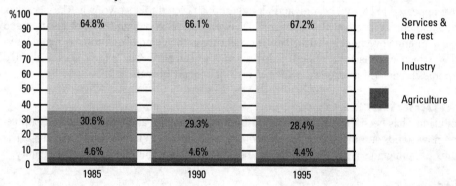

Source: Bank of Israel

Savings and investment

The general macroeconomic background has been characterized by Israelis reducing their saving, causing the ratio of saving to investments to fall and paying the price through higher real interest rates. The current account deficit is simply the external manifestation of this internal process. Up to the end of 1995, a fall in the saving rate relative to investment has been a dominant macro trend in Israel.

Balance of payments

Clearly the external corollary of this fall in saving relative to investment has been a deterioration of the current account. Potentially, the current account deficit could become a problem. The new government has acknowledged this and is committed to reducing the shortfall.

Government spending driving the current account deficit (as % of GDP)

	Current account	Private Saving	Public saving	National savings	Investment
1990	1.1	22.85	-2.5	20.3	20.0
1991-93	-0.9	23.8	-0.1	23.7	24.9
1994	-3.3	20.4	0.4	20.9	24.5
1995	-4.7	20.7	-0.7	20.0	24.9

Source: Bank of Israel

Imports and exports as a % of GDP

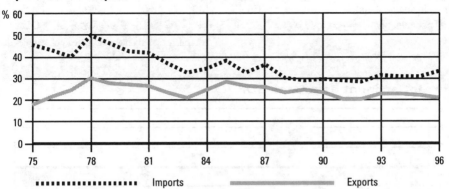

Source: IMF

Breakdown of exports (1995)

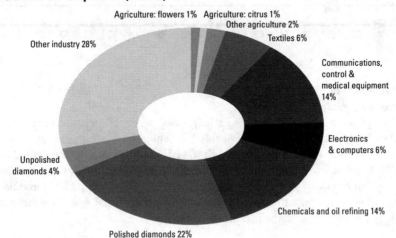

Source: Bank of Israel

Foreign investment, 1991-95

Net foreign investment in Israel grew markedly during the early 1990s, faltered slightly in 1994, but recovered thereafter. Between 1991 and 1995 net non-resident investment increased by over 550% from US$366 million to US$2.03 billion. Direct investment represents the lion's share of net foreign investment (equivalent to US$1.6 billion in 1995 – more than four times the 1991 total). However, net investment in traded securities has also improved of late, increasing from a net loss in 1992 to US$393 million in 1995.

Net investment (US$m, at current prices)

	1991	1992	1993	1994	1995
Net investment by non-residents	366	504	756	604	2030
of which:					
Investment in traded securities, net	15	-35	176	183	393
Direct investment, net	375	519	560	393	1611
Total net investment from abroad	-320	-1414	-695	-442	1433

Source: based on Central Bureau of Statistics data

Current account as a % of GDP

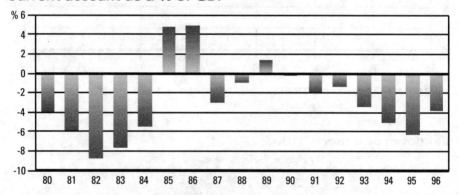

Source: IMF

Economic policy
Monetary policy

The main plank of monetary policy is exchange rate policy. The inflation target has been 8% to 10% a year since 1995. To achieve this the central bank allows the exchange rate to depreciate by 6% a year against a traded basket of currencies. Around this central rate, there is a ±7% comfort band within which the currency can fluctuate. This depreciation, taken together with estimated global inflation of 3% a year, is consistent with a domestic inflation rate of between 8% and 10%. Any change in the inflation target will be facilitated by a change in the rate of exchange rate depreciation.

Fiscal policy

In summer 1996, fiscal policy became a problem, with expenditures running well ahead of revenues. This would not normally give cause for alarm, but because the economy had been growing so strongly and was expected to slow, there has been some cause for concern. The extent of the overshoot in 1996 led the government to put together a fiscal adjustment package of NIS4.9 billion to be effected in 1997. However, the fear has been that this may not be sufficient to bring the deficit back to the government's desired target of between 2% and 2.5% of GDP. The deficit for 1996 as a whole is estimated to be about NIS14.5 billion – NIS5 billion above target. This overshoot, and the fact that the government's growth assumptions for 1997 could turn out to be too optimistic, argue against the government meeting its 1997 target of 2.8% of GDP.

New Israeli shekel/US dollar exchange rate

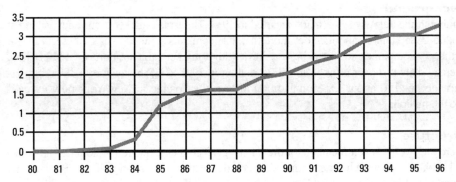

Investment outlook

In general, the investment outlook for Israel is broadly favourable. The economic fundamentals are positive and the expanding educated labour force gives Israel a unique advantage over many of its competitors. The large imponderable remains the future course of the peace process. Politics aside, however, investors will be closely watching the economic liberalization measures being pursued by the new government.

■ EQUITIES

Index performance (in local currency)

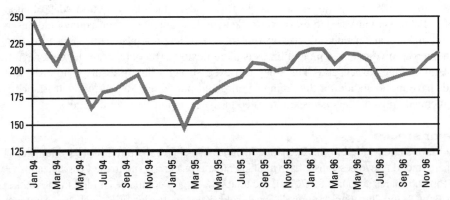

Key indicators

	Index performance %, in US$ terms	Market Cap. US$bn	P/E	Div. Yield
1994	-33.4	32.7	—	—
1995	10.0	36.8	17.1	1.1
1996	-2.7	40.0	14.7	1.4

Sources: Local stock exchange, IFC, Bloomberg, Datastream, UBS

Background

Trading in the Tel Aviv stock market started in 1935. The Israeli market is currently valued at around US$40 billion, and includes more than 625 companies traded over 1,100 securities. A further 75 companies are listed in New York with a market capitalization of US$17 billion. Average daily turnover grew from US$15 million in 1991 to US$65 million in 1994, but has since declined to about US$30 million. However, the volume in New York now exceeds US$100 million.

Structure

There are twenty-seven members of the exchange. The members are the commercial banks and brokerage firms who meet admission criteria relating to reputation, financial standing, integrity and experience. In addition, there is a group of mutual fund managers and portfolio managers who are allowed to take part on the floor, trading as "associate members". The members of the exchange are also its owners.

Free float and major players

The free float is approximately 35% to 40%. The term "interested parties" refers in most cases to the founders of the companies. Most of the pension fund money in Israel is held by the labour organization union (the Histadrut – through its seven funds). Pension funds are not invested heavily in the market due to limitations on their investment portfolio structure by the capital market division in the finance ministry.

The provident funds accumulate monthly provisions made by the employer and the employee (5% each). The money is held by the fund for fifteen years before the saver can draw out the money, and is invested in the market. The provident funds are allowed to invest up to 50% of their assets in shares. The funds, which hold around NIS90 billion (US$30 billion) are invested in the stock market and have increased their equity holdings in the last three years, mainly due to government proscribing non-negotiable bonds carrying high interest. Investment in mutual funds is more flexible. The public can draw money on demand. During stock market falls, they can exert strong selling pressure. The provident funds have more latitude on the timing of sales and purchases. Mutual funds in Israel are open-ended. Most of their assets are invested in shares and in short-term bonds.

Major stocks

The list of shares traded in the Exchange includes 100 shares that are listed as "blue chips" and are traded at two sessions a day (multilateral and bilateral). The market capitalization of the top 100 shares accounts for 70% of the total. The largest companies traded in the market are: Bank Hapoalim, Bank Leumi, Teva, Bezeq, Koor industries, ICL. Each has a market capitalization exceeding US$1 billion. In addition some 75 companies are traded exclusively on NASDAQ or the NYSE, accounting for a further US$17 billion in capitalization. Major companies quoted in the US include ECI, Tadiran Ltd, Tadiran Telecommunications, Teva (joint listing), Chip Express, Blue Square and Scitex.

Trading methods
There are two trading systems on the Tel Aviv Stock Exchange. First, the Computerized Call Market (multilateral trading) under which all shares, convertible stocks and bonds are traded. Dealings are processed through a computer system. A fixed price is set once a day and all transactions are executed at this price during the day. The trading hours of the CCM are 10.00 to 15.30.

Second, there is the Auction System, under which the one hundred most active companies are traded. Trading hours are between 11.30 and 15.30. Trades are handled as follows:

◆ **The auctioneer announces the name of the share next scheduled for trading.**
◆ **The exchange members through public negotiation buy or sell according to clients' orders. A transaction is made when the seller and buyer agree on a price and the auctioneer announces the terms.**
◆ **When trading in the security has ceased, the auctioneer announces the name of the next security.**
◆ **At the end of the day a quick "crossing round" is conducted. In this round, trades are matched and no negotiation on price is allowed.**

Trading is conducted in round lots of US$5000, as opposed to the morning session when any amount is allowed. The closing price is calculated according to the last three transactions executed. The top one hundred companies are traded in the morning CCM short-version session as well.

Hours
Trading days are Sunday to Thursday. Trading times are 10.30 to 16.00 for shares, warrants and convertibles, and 10.30 to 11.30 for bonds. Trading is held in several halls simultaneously.

Settlement time and clearing
The settlement period is T+0 for domestic investors and T+1 for non-residents.

Types of shares
There are a variety of securities traded including ordinary, preference, bearer, preferred common and registered shares.

Stock indices
The main indices are: the General Index, which aggregates all shares traded; the Mishtanim Index, of the leading one hundred companies; the Maof Index, of selected twenty-five blue chips; and the Karam Index, of shares traded under the multilateral trading system.

Taxes
Although the nominal corporate tax rate in Israel is in the 35% to 37% range, the effective tax rate is substantially lower due to liberal investment incentive schemes. Interest tax is 35% and dividend tax is 25% – both are paid by private investors and corporates alike.

Disclosure of financial statements
Listed companies are required to publish an audited annual report within four months of the fiscal year ending and at least ten days before their annual meetings. In addition, quarterly reports, changes in the board of directors, intentions to sell substantial proportions of assets and plans to cease business must also be disclosed.

Brokers
The Tel Aviv Stock Exchange limits commissions to a maximum of 1%.

Sectors
The sectors which have the greatest impact in the market are industry and investment and holdings. There is much double counting in the market, and many of the holding companies publicly traded carry the value of their publicly traded subsidiaries

Derivatives
Although only active for three years, the derivatives market has been growing fast in terms of volume. The daily turnover, in terms of the underlying asset, is about NIS500 million (about US$150 million). The market is trading Call and Put European options for three, six, and nine months on the Maof index, mainly for speculation rather than for hedging. There are no immediate plans for trading options on shares

■ DEBT

The Israeli government and corporate bond markets are regulated by the Securities Authorities and the Tel Aviv Stock Exchange, where bond market trading is transacted. The Bank of Israel also acts as a central depository.

Makam bills
Bank of Israel Makam bills are zero-coupon unlinked certificates with durations of 3 months to 1 year, issued by the central bank to absorb liquidity in the market. Transaction volumes average NIS50 million (US$16 million) a week.

Government bonds
Government bonds make up the largest asset class in the Israeli capital market. Turnover averages NIS60 million (US$18 million) a week. CPI and US$-linked bonds pay floating rate coupons and non-linked bonds pay fixed rate coupons.

Bills and bonds are auctioned by the central bank according to the requirements of the bank; there is no fixed calendar.

There is no repo market.

Recent reforms provide that savings earmarked for pensions would receive tax incentives, be tax-free and be channelled into high yielding government bonds; savings not earmarked for pensions but designated for 10-year bonds would receive tax-free interest but no tax incentives; savings in instruments with less than 10-year maturities would be taxable. Index and currency linked deposits will pay interest, as well as T-bills and bank deposits.

Large investors are provident funds, who own 60% of tradeable bonds, commercial banks, which own 25% to cover savings schemes, mutual funds, and life insurance companies.

In the Futures Exchange there is a stock index contract but no bond contract.

■ ISRAEL: Economic indicators

Population and development	1990	1991	1992	1993	1994	1995	1996e
Population, million	4.7	5.0	5.2	5.4	5.6	5.8	6.0
Population growth, %	3.1	6.2	5.1	3.8	3.7	3.6	3.4
Nominal GDP per capita, US$	11199	12023	12613	12045	13160	14893	15632

National accounts							
Nominal GDP, US$bn	52.2	59.5	65.6	65.0	73.7	86.4	93.8
Change in real GDP, %	5.8	6.2	7.2	3.4	6.5	7.1	4.0
Gross fixed capital formation, % of GDP	20.0	25.4	25.0	25.1	25.0	25.3	25.0

Money supply and inflation							
Narrow money, change %, Dec/Dec	30.6	13.8	32.0	27.9	7.7	15.1	12.3
Broad money, change %, Dec/Dec	19.4	17.7	26.5	22.0	24.6	21.7	19.3
Consumer price inflation (avg.) %	17.2	19.0	11.9	11.0	12.3	9.9	10.5
Producer prices (avg.) %							

Interest rates *=latest figures							
Discount rate, annual average	13.00	14.20	10.40	9.80	17.00	14.20	14.70*
Deposit rate, annual average	13.90	13.90	11.30	10.40	12.20	14.10	14.40*
Prime lending rate, annual average	25.30	26.40	19.90	16.40	17.40	20.20	16.20*

Government finance							
Government expenditure, % of GDP	49.3	38.3	51.8	49.1	45.9	48.8	48.8
Government balance, % of GDP	-5.1	-5.8	-5.4	-3.9	-2.3	-3.4	-4.5

Exchange rates lc=local currency							
Exchange rate, annual average, lc/US$	2.02	2.28	2.46	2.83	3.01	3.01	3.19
Exchange rate, end of year, lc/US$	2.05	2.28	2.76	2.99	3.02	3.14	3.24
Real exchange rate 1990=100	100.0	102.4	100.6	100.6	102.0	103.6	107.0

Balance of payments							
Exports of goods & services, US$m	16726	16834	19216	20928	23288	26710	28007
Change %	50.4	0.6	14.1	8.9	11.3	14.7	4.9
Imports of goods & services, US$m, fob	20118	22333	23942	27233	30526	35991	39195
Change %	54.2	11.0	7.2	13.7	12.1	17.9	8.9
Trade balance, of goods only, US$m, fob-fob	-2981	-4854	-4946	-5607	-5886	-7684	-10588
Current account balance, US$m	557	-416	219	-1373	-2468	-4087	-5838
as a % of GDP	1.1	-0.7	0.3	-2.1	-3.3	-4.7	-6.2

Foreign exchange reserves							
Foreign exchange reserves, US$m	6275	6279	5131	6385	6795	8158	11000
Gold at ⅔ of market price, US$m	215.7	101.6	2.1	2.2	2.3	2.3	2.3
Import cover (reserves/imports), months	3.7	3.4	2.6	2.8	2.7	2.7	3.4

Foreign debt and debt service							
Short-term debt, US$m	11622	12001	12329	12692	14248	16198	17426
Total foreign debt, US$m	33510	34117	34915	36919	41151	44274	47493
as a % of GDP	64.2	57.3	53.2	56.8	55.8	51.3	50.6
as a % of foreign exchange receipts	140.8	136.9	129.4	130.8	135	127.4	128.7
Interest payments, US$m	2577	2418	2314	2203	2395	2759	2410
Principal repayments, US$m	1710	2213	1865	1943	2204	2219	2238
Total debt service, US$m	4287	4631	4179	4146	4599	4978	4648
as a % of goods exports	35.3	38.3	31.4	28.0	27.6	26.3	24.5
as a % of foreign exchange receipts	18.0	18.6	15.5	14.7	15.1	14.3	12.6

Jordan

Area (thousands of km²):	89
Population (1995, millions):	4
Population projection (2025, millions):	9
Population younger than 15 yrs (1991, % of total):	43.6
Urbanization rate (1993, % of population):	70
Life expectancy (1993, years at birth):	70
Gross domestic product (1996, US$bn):	7.2
GDP per capita (1996, US$):	1676
Average annual GDP growth rate (1990-96, %):	6
Average annual inflation rate (1990-96, %):	6.5
Currency (dinar per US$, average 1996):	0.71
Structure of production (1994):	66.7% services, 27.7% industry, 5.6% agriculture
Main exports:	chemicals, machinery & transport equipment, basic manufactured, food
Main imports:	machinery & transport equipment, basic manufactured, food & live animals
Main trading partners:	India, Iraq, US, Saudi Arabia, Germany
Market capitalization of Stock Exchange (October 1996; US$bn):	4.4
Total foreign debt (% of GDP):	91.4
Next elections due under normal circumstances:	1997
Credit rating: (Nov 1996, Standard & Poor's, Moody's)	BB-; Ba3

FORECAST: 1997-2000 (average)

	Worst case	Most likely	Best case
Real GDP growth (%)	4.2	5.2	6.2
Inflation (%)	5.3	3.1	2.3

■ POLITICS

Historical overview

The Romans ruled over the region that is now Jordan for more than four hundred years, and with them they brought Christianity. In the 7th century, however, the Islamic armies ended Roman control, since which time Jordan has been Islamic. The country belonged to the Ottoman Empire until the First World War, when, between 1916 and 1918, the Arabs, with British support, resisted Ottoman rule. In 1920, following a League of Nations mandate, Palestine and Transjordan were placed under British administration. In 1923 Transjordan formally separated from Palestine. It was declared an independent state on March 22, 1946 by a treaty signed with Great Britain, and on May 25 (which has also become Jordanian Independence Day) the Amir Abdullah received the title of King. In 1949, the country was renamed Jordan.

Between 1949 and 1950, the area of Palestine belonging to the Arabs (excluding the Gaza Strip) was placed under Jordanian rule and incorporated into Jordan. In 1967, Jordan lost its authority over the West Bank, when it was occupied by Israel. In 1974, Jordan accepted a resolution passed by an Arab summit conference that designated the Palestine Liberation Organization as the sole legitimate representative of the Palestinian people. To enable the Palestine Liberation Organization to represent the Palestinian people, King Hussein severed ties between Jordan and the West Bank in 1988, announcing the dissolution of legal and administrative ties with the Israeli-ruled territory.

Recent events

Iraq's invasion of Kuwait in 1990 deeply affected Jordan. Iraq remains Jordan's principal trading partner, and Jordan relied on supplies of Iraqi petroleum, so the subsequent imposition of economic sanctions against Iraq damaged Jordan's economy. Although King Hussein was against Iraq's invasion of Kuwait, Jordan refused openly to oppose the invasion, prompting the US to review its military and economic assistance to Jordan, as well as the deterioration of relations with Egypt and Saudi Arabia (which contributed armed forces to the US-led coalition).

Following the Gulf War, Jordan concentrated on improving relations with its Arab neighbours, which by now have essentially returned to normal. On July 25, 1994 a declaration was signed between Jordan and Israel that ended formally the state of war between these two countries. This declaration was followed a few months later by a full peace treaty. As a result, US President Clinton promised to cancel Jordan's official debts to the US. In 1995 the US and Jordan signed an agreement cancelling US$420 million of Jordan's outstanding debt, and in 1996 the US offered US$300 million in military aid. Jordan and Israel have also signed a trade agreement.

Chronology

1923-27	The formation of the Shura Council, the first step towards democracy
1927	Establishment of the first Jordanian political party
1928	Peaceful relations with Saudi Arabia are established
1946	The Amir Abdullah is proclaimed King of the Hashemite Kingdom of Jordan. May 25 becomes the independence day of Jordan.
1948	The British government ends its mandate on Palestine and proclaims the birth of the Jewish State in Palestine
1948	First military conflict between Israel and its Arab neighbours
1952	The constitution of the Hashemite Kingdom of Jordan is promulgated. It separates executive, legislative and judicial powers.
1953	King Hussein bin Talal ascends the throne
1955	Jordan becomes a permanent member of the United Nations
1967	Six-Day War with Israel, in which the West Bank is lost
1973	Ramadan (Yom Kippur) War with Israel

1974	Rabat Conference, after which the Palestine Liberation Organization becomes the sole representative of the Palestinian people
1989	General elections are held and the twelfth representative council is formed
1990-91	Iraq's invasion of Kuwait and the Gulf War
1994	Peace Treaty is signed with Israel

State organization

Jordan is divided into eight governorates: Al Balqa', Al Karak, Al Mafraq, 'Amman, At Tafilah, Az Zarqa', Irbid, Ma'an. Each of these is subdivided into districts and counties. Local affairs are handled by city or village councils. There are 152 municipalities and 340 village councils.

Constitution and government

The constitution, passed on January 8, 1952, established the Hashemite Kingdom of Jordan as an independent sovereign Arab State; its system of government is parliamentary with a hereditary monarchy.

Legislative power is vested in the National Assembly and the king. The National Assembly consists of a Senate, which has forty members appointed by the King for eight years, and a Chamber of Deputies, which has eighty members elected by universal suffrage for four years. A 1993 law restricts each elector to a single vote, replacing a system in which electors had several votes depending on the number of seats in the constituency.

Executive power is vested in the king, who exercises his power through his ministers in accordance with the provisions of the present constitution.

Judicial power is exercised by the courts of law.

Current government
Head of state
King Hussein ibn Talal (proclaimed king on August 11, 1952; crowned on May 2, 1953)

Cabinet (Ministers):

Prime Minister, Defence and Foreign Affairs	Abdul-Karim Kabarati
Finance	Marwan Awad
Justice	Abdul Karim ad-Dughmi
Labour and Social Affairs	Abdul Hafez Shakhanbeh
Public Works and Housing	Abdul Hadi al-Majali
Parliamentary Affairs	Muhammad Thweib
Prime Ministry Affairs	Hisham at-Tall
Foreign Affairs	Khalid Madadha
Trade and Industry	Ali Abu ar-Ragheb

Political parties

Political parties were legalized in 1992 and in 1993 King Hussein dissolved the House of Representatives to allow the country's first multiparty general election on November 8, although the first parliamentary elections in twenty-two years were held in 1989.

Results of the 1989 parliamentary elections

	Seats	
Independent centrists	44	
Islamic Action Front	16	Sec. Gen.: Ishaq al-Fahran
Independent Islamists	06	
Independent leftists	04	
Al-Ahd	02	Sec. Gen.: 'Abd al-Hadi al-Majali
Jordanian Arab Democratic Party	02	Sec. Gen.: Mu'nis al-Razzaz
Others	06	
TOTAL	80	

Central bank

The Central Bank of Jordan (CBJ) began operations on October 1, 1964. It is the monetary authority in the kingdom and has the status of an autonomous corporate body.

The main objectives of the CBJ, which are established by the law, are to maintain monetary stability, to ensure the convertibility of the Jordanian dinar and to promote the sustained growth of the kingdom's economy in accordance with the general economic policy of the government. The CBJ is the fiscal agent for the government. It provides treasury functions, keeping accounts of revenues and expenditures for ministries and government departments, and disbursing, transferring and collecting funds domestically and abroad.

The CBJ is headed by Governor Ziad Fariz, who is the chief executive officer responsible for the implementation of bank policy and the management of its affairs. He also represents the Bank in all its relations with other parties. The governor is appointed by the Council of Ministers, with the approval of the king, for a term of five years. After this period the governor is eligible for re-appointment. Governor Fariz was appointed in 1996.

■ ECONOMICS

Historical overview

Jordan's economy has always relied on foreign aid, primarily from the UK, the US and the Arab oil producers, and increasingly from the EU, in part to help a structural shortfall of national income. Jordan's economy faced many setbacks, especially during the late 1960s and early 1970s. Agriculture and the tourist economy suffered from the loss of the West Bank; before the 1967 war, the West Bank produced 25% of Jordan's grain, 40% of the vegetables and 70% of the fruit production. The agricultural workforce decreased from 37% in 1965 to 7% in 1987. Industrial production declined by about 20% after the war. Now, only 5% of Jordan's land is arable. Internal instability hampered business confidence, commercial activity and economic planning. After 1973, the increase of oil income of the Gulf States improved Jordan's economy, especially with the help of higher levels of Arab aid and remittances sent home by Jordanian workers in neighbouring countries.

Remittances and Arab aid decreased in the late 1980s and Jordan's growth slowed to an average of roughly 2% per year. The state cut capital spending and increased its borrowing to soften the adverse political effects of increasing unemployment. The country's foreign debt rose steadily, while foreign currency reserves decreased. Imports – oil, capital goods, consumer durables and food – surpassed exports, with the difference covered by aid, remittances, and borrowing. In mid-1989, the Jordanian government began debt-rescheduling negotiations and agreed to implement an IMF programme to complete a general rescheduling of the kingdom's external debt. This required Jordan to reduce the fiscal deficit and to contain credit expansion. The 1990-91 Gulf crisis, however, forced the government to postpone the programme The international economic embargo against Iraq meant that Jordan lost a lucrative export and re-export market. The consequences of the Gulf War were a significant drop in external trade, a drop in real income, an increase of unemployment (mainly caused by the return of some 300,000 Jordanians from Kuwait), and a further decline of aid and remittances.

A second programme was agreed to by Jordan and the IMF in 1991. The second accord contains a seven-year time horizon, lasting until 1998. Over this period, the IMF aims for Jordan to reduce its budget deficit, to increase real GDP, to cut consumption, to stabilize inflation around 4.5%, to cut foreign and domestic borrowing, and to reduce the current account deficit.

From 1987 to 1993, Jordan's GDP per capita fell, in real terms, at an average annual rate of 2.7%, due in part to rapid population growth, which averaged 4.7% over the same period. Real gross domestic product (GDP) increased at an average annual rate of 1.9%. Subsequently, growth resumed, with real GDP expanding at a 6% rate and per capita GDP rising at a 2.5% rate from 1993 to 1995. Inflation has also declined to moderate levels since the early 1990s.

The Jordanian economy has been subject to significant performance swings, in part due to variable political conditions.

Jordan's economic performance, 1981-1995

	Average annual real GDP growth, %	Average annual consumer price inflation, %
1981–1984	3.2	5.4
1984–1987	4.8	0.9
1987–1990	-3.5	16.1
1990–1993	2.9	5.6
1993–1995	6.0	3.0

Source: Official data

The economy

Jordan has about 4 million inhabitants and is a lower-middle-income country. Annual per-capita income was US$1,676 in 1996. Service-related activities account for about two thirds of the GDP, and about three quarters of the total labour force. Jordan's economy is highly dependent on imports, which equal nearly 60% of GDP. Compared to domestic economic activity, the size of the public sector is large. It provides basic services, such as health and education, public utilities, water and electricity, and other infrastructural support, transportation, communication and irrigation. Government expenditures are about 35% of GDP.

Poverty and inequality have increased steadily since the late 1980s. In 1991, estimates put 8.7% of the population below the severe poverty line, and 19.8% below the general poverty line (compared with none in 1986). Jordan's official response has been to invest in safety-net programmes, consisting of generalized food subsidies, food coupons, health cards, and transfers through the established National Aid Fund, which provide direct income support to the extremely poor. In 1990, total food subsidies were around 3.5% of GDP, accounting for almost 10% of central government current expenditure.

Share of GDP by sector

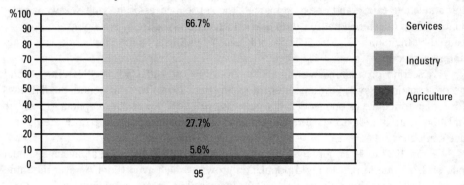

Source: Official data

Breakdown of the services sector

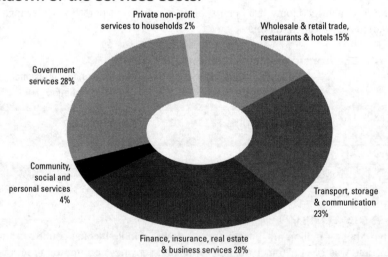

Source: Official data

The Gulf crisis was the main cause of the increase in unemployment in Jordan – some 300,000 Jordanians were forced to return from abroad. Between 1986 and 1991, the unemployment rate exploded, climbing from 8% to 40%. However, in recent years, the economy has been able to re-absorb these people, who also brought with them substantial savings and technical know-how to revitalize the private sector. By 1994 unemployment had fallen back to 16% of the labour force.

Figures for 1995 show that import growth has remained strong, but export growth has been stronger. The dinar value of goods and services exports rose nearly 18% and imports rose 10.3% in 1995. Export growth is expected to increase in the future due to growth of phosphate and potash production. Jordan's principal exports are: natural calcium phosphates, natural potassic salts, chemicals, vegetables, fruits, and nuts, basic manufactures, and machinery and transport equipment. Its main imports (based on 1993 data) are: machinery and transport equipment (26.9%); basic manufactures (20.7%); food and live animals (17.7%); and fuels and lubricants (12.8%).

Breakdown of exports (1993)

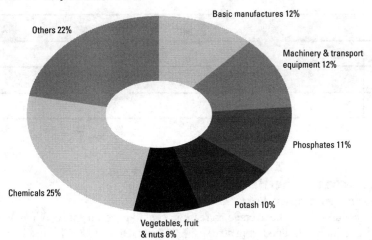

Source: Official data

Exports and imports as a % of GDP

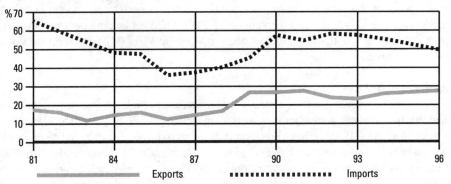

Source: IMF; UBS

Annual inflows of transfer payments, in the form of foreign aid and expatriate worker remittances, permitted Jordan to register only a relatively small current account deficit in

1995. These transfer receipts were in some years more than US$1 billion. Although Jordan has always had a high trade deficit, it has always been able to limit the current account deficit, and in several years it actually registered surpluses. In 1996 Jordan had a current account deficit of US$0.3 billion, while its trade balance deficit was US$1.6 billion.

Current account as a % of GDP

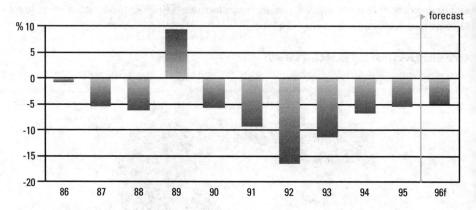

Source: IMF and UBS

Economic policy
Government spending
From 1989 until 1995, the average increase in central government spending was 8.2%, while total expenditures declined from 40.6% to 33.5% of GDP in 1996. This result was achieved in spite of the subsidization of staple food, higher interest payments on foreign debt, supplementary expenditures on housing and education, and emergency stockpiling of food supplies for the large number of Jordanian workers returning from neighbouring countries. To contain spending, the government stopped extra-budgetary expenditures, and cut both current and capital expenditures as a percentage of GDP, while net lending became negative. The share of military outlays in GDP has been reduced by 3% of GDP, and food subsidies have also declined.

Monetary policy
Since 1970, the Jordanian banking system improved steadily. Bank intermediation has been enhanced, the payment system improved, and an active stock exchange established. From the early 1980s until 1988, money and credit policies were conducted to stimulate domestic economic activity by supporting bank liquidity and encouraging domestic lending. In 1989 the authorities began to tighten monetary policy. Inflation subsequently fell to record levels by 1994 as private sector credit expansion declined, along with the persisting excess of credit to the banking sector. In the next few years, tight fiscal and monetary policy will be maintained. The government is expected to promote privatization by offering incentives to banks to finance local business ventures. It will also seek to raise the quality of locally produced goods, help businesses to expand their Arab markets, and introduce new legislation to encourage investment.

Currency

In 1995, the CBJ changed its exchange rate policy. Under this amendment, it was decided to keep the dinar's exchange rate stable against the US dollar and to allow it to fluctuate against other foreign currencies. The aim was to give more transparency to the stability of the Jordanian dinar exchange rate, to help interest rate policy and to increase the attractiveness of keeping assets denominated in Jordanian dinars rather than US dollars. The government will continue to keep the exchange rate fixed (JOD0.709 per US$). The demand for dinars will depend especially on the development of the Middle East peace process.

Jordanian dinar has been pegged to the US dollar

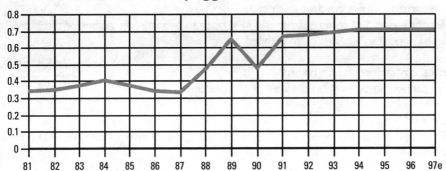

■ EQUITIES

Key indicators

	Index performance %, in US$ terms	Market Cap. US$ bn	P/E	Div. Yield	Weight in IFCI	Weight in IFCG
1994	-11.7	4.6	20.8	2.4	0.2	0.3
1995	10.6	4.7	18.2	1.9	0.2	0.3
1996	-3.6	4.6	16.9	2.3	0.1	0.3

Sources: Local stock exchange, IFC, Bloomberg, Datastream, UBS

Structure

The Amman Financial Market (AFM), established in 1978, is one of the most developed in the Middle East. It is divided into a regular market, a bond market, a legal transfers market (for off-floor trading) and a parallel market for companies preparing for a listing.

Market capitalization at the end of 1995 was JOD3.5 billion (US$4.7 billion). Daily turnover is around US$1 million. The number of ASE listed companies fell from 117 in 1994 to 97 at the end of 1995. Average price to earnings ratio is around 13:1. Arab Bank accounts for around 32% of the market.

Regulatory authority
The AFM is self regulating, although an SEC-style authority is being prepared.

Trading methods
Trading is by continuous auction. Shares are traded on the floor in units and prices are quoted in Jordanian dinars, although automation is imminent.

Hours
The AFM is open between 10.00 and 12.00, Saturday to Wednesday. The parallel market is open between 09.00 and 09.30 on the same days.

Settlement time and clearing
Settlement is on a T+3 manual basis. The AFM plans to become fully computerized in 1997. A central depository system is also planned.

Limits on price movement
Shares cannot moved by more than 5% in a single day.

Types of shares
Ordinary and preferred shares are traded on the AFM as well as corporate bonds and treasury bills.

Stock indices
The AFM has five indices tracking the overall market movement, banking, insurance, services and industrial stocks respectively.

Taxes
There is a 10% tax on dividends but none on capital gains.

Disclosure of financial statements
Companies must present annual financial statements. They must also inform the AFM of any changes in the capital structure or financial structure that may affect its operations.

Ownership limits for foreign investors
The limit is 50%, unless the percentage was higher at the time of the IPO, in which case the latter percentage is the limit.

Capital and foreign exchange controls
There are no restrictions on the repatriation of capital or income.

Brokers
There are eighteen local brokers.

Sectors
Banks 49.6%, Industrials (mainly potash and phosphate companies) 40.6%, service and

insurance companies 9.9%. The largest companies (in descending order) are the Arab Bank, Arab Potash Company, Jordan Cement Factories, Jordan Phosphate Mines, The Housing Bank, Jordan National Bank, Jordan Petroleum Refinery, Arab Banking Corporation, Jordan Islamic Bank, Dar Al Daw Development and Investment, Arab International Hotels, Cairo-Amman Bank, Arab Pharmaceutical Manufacturing, Bank of Jordan, Arab Jordan Investment Bank, Jordan Investment and Finance Bank, Arab Inter. for Investment and Education, Arab Aluminium Industries, Jordan Hotel and Tourism and the Jordan Worsted Mills.

ADRs
There are no Jordanian ADRs.

■ DEBT

The legal bases for bill and bond market primary issuance, secondary market transactions, repayment, tax treatment and insurance are contained in The Public Debt Law of 1971. In 1995, several measures were introduced to encourage domestic and foreign investment, in particular by creating an independent Investment Promotion Corporation (IPC). The IPC's mandate includes simplifying investment procedures and reducing regulatory barriers.

The distinction between Arab and non-Arab investors has now been abolished, and non-residents may repatriate their capital, profits and dividends freely in any foreign convertible currency. Jordanian banks can effect transfers without central bank approval.

In October 1996, the central bank reduced the reserve requirements on foreign currency deposits with domestic banks to 14% from 35%. The released money can be invested in either the domestic or international capital markets. Banks are also allowed to place 20% of the new reserve levels on local inter-bank markets, provided they can still cover the full reserve requirements at the end of each month.

The total nominal value of bonds issued cannot exceed the capital expenditures estimated in the Government Budget Law in a particular year, and cannot exceed 20% of the actual capital spending of the previous year.

Treasury bills
The central bank issues bills on behalf of the government after consultation with the Ministry of Finance. The most common term is 90 days, but bills can be offered with 1-year maturities. Only Jordanian banks are allowed to bid and subscribe at tenders, and trade the bills (minimum denominations of JOD10,000) in the secondary market. Individuals can invest in bills through their banks. The central bank can reduce individual allocations if primary tenders are oversubscribed.

The value of treasury bills cannot exceed 25% of the higher of the average domestic revenues collected in the previous three years or of currency in circulation

Treasury bonds
Bonds normally have maturities of 2 to 5 years, but can be issued for a maximum term of 15 years. They are tendered by the central bank each month. Owners of securities can choose to hold either bearer or registered bonds. Presentation of bonds at the central bank

provides evidence of ownership. In addition, bond holders can choose to receive their value in cash rather than new bonds, if the Government decides to make an exchange. The central bank can set up a Satisfaction Fund to guarantee future payments of maturing bond issues.

Long-term development bonds

There is no regular schedule for the issuance of these bonds, which have maturities of 5 to 10 years. Long-term development bonds trade on the Secondary Amman Financial Market, coupon payments are semi-annual and are free of tax.

Eurobonds

One state utility, Jordan Telecommunications Corporation issued a US$50 million 7-year eurobond in September 1995. It pays a floating rate coupon of libor plus 110 basis points, and carries a sovereign guarantee.

Brady bonds

Jordan issued Par Bonds, Discount Bonds and PDIs in a Brady-style restructuring of debt principal and interest arrears in 1993. The Par and Discount bonds are collateralized by zero coupon US Treasuries and the Discount Bonds also have a 6-month interest rolling guarantee. They are rated Ba3 by Moody's and BB- by Standard and Poor's.

■ JORDAN: Economic indicators

Population and development	1990	1991	1992	1993	1994	1995	1996e
Population, million	3.5	3.7	3.8	4.0	4.1	4.3	4.3
Population growth, %	3.1	4.2	5.2	5.8	5.3	5.7	5.7
Nominal GDP per capita, US$	1159	1134	1336	1379	1446	1538	1676

National accounts							
Nominal GDP, US$bn	4.0	4.2	5.1	5.5	6.0	6.6	7.2
Change in real GDP, %	1.0	1.8	16.1	5.9	5.9	6.4	4.1
Gross fixed capital formation, % of GDP	26.0	23.7	30.0	34.2	33.2	32.8	31.8

Money supply and inflation							
Narrow money, change %, Dec/Dec	9.4	15.5	4.2	0.2	1.3	-0.2	2.4
Broad money, change %, Dec/Dec	8.3	15.8	3.3	4.5	3.3	5.7	7.0
Consumer price inflation (avg.) %	16.1	8.2	4.0	4.7	3.6	2.3	6.4

Interest rates							
Discount rate, end of year	8.50	8.50	8.50	8.50	8.50	8.50	—
Deposit rate, end of year	6.75	3.25	3.25	3.25	3.25	3.25	—
Prime lending rate, end of year	10.00	10.00	9.75	9.00	9.00	9.75	—

Government finance							
Government expenditure, % of GDP	37.6	36.5	32.2	33.7	32.9	34.6	34.8
Government balance, % of GDP	-3.5	0.4	5.2	1.8	2.5	-2.9	4.6

Exchange rates *lc=local currency*

	1990	1991	1992	1993	1994	1995	1996e
Exchange rate, annual average, lc/US$	0.66	0.68	0.68	0.69	0.70	0.70	0.71
Exchange rate, end of year, lc/US$	0.66	0.68	0.69	0.70	0.70	0.71	0.71

Balance of payments							
Exports of goods & services, US$m	2511	2481	2668	2820	2987	3430	3605
Change %	6.9	-1.2	7.6	5.7	5.9	14.8	5.1
Imports of goods & services, US$m, fob	3569	3425	4324	4492	4397	4860	5075
Change %	21.1	-4.0	26.3	3.9	-2.1	10.5	4.4
Trade balance, of goods only, US$m, fob-fob	-1237	-1173	-1780	-1899	-1579	-1620	-1630
Current account balance, US$m	-227	-394	-835	-629	-398	-350	-342
as a % of GDP	-5.6	-9.4	-16.3	-11.4	-6.6	-5.3	-4.7

Foreign exchange reserves							
Foreign exchange reserves, US$m	849	826	767	1637	1693	1973	2050
Gold at ⅔ of market price, US$m	193.6	190.3	180.5	189.5	203.2	202.9	204.0
Import cover (reserves/imports), months	2.9	2.9	2.1	4.4	4.6	4.9	4.8

Foreign debt and debt service							
Short-term debt, US$m	158	240	150	55	60	50	60
Total foreign debt, US$m	7276	7792	7180	6904	7051	7129	7070
as a % of GDP	181.0	185.6	139.8	125.3	117.8	108.0	98.1
as a % of foreign exchange receipts	196.6	219.8	177.5	158.4	156.4	141.4	135.3
Interest payments, US$m	321	294	287	212	203	233	249
Principal repayments, US$m	239	341	388	348	302	278	305
Total debt service, US$m	560	635	675	560	505	511	554
as a % of goods exports	52.6	56.2	55.4	44.9	35.4	29.2	29.2
as a % of foreign exchange receipts	15.1	17.9	16.7	12.8	11.2	10.1	10.6

Kazakstan

KEY FACTS

Area (thousands of km²):	2717
Population (1995, millions):	16.4
Population projection (2025, millions):	22
Population younger than 15 yrs (1991, % of total):	31.6
Urbanization rate (1993, % of population):	57
Life expectancy (1993, years at birth):	70
Gross domestic product (1996, US$bn):	22.8
GDP per capita (1996, US$):	1397
Average annual GDP growth rate (1990-96, %):	-8.4
Average annual inflation rate (1990-96, %):	778.1
Currency (tenge per US$, average 1996):	67.8
Structure of production (1994):	29.5% services, 18.4% agriculture, 52% industry
Main exports:	mineral & metals, oil & oil products, textiles
Main imports:	machines, food, chemical products
Main trading partners:	China, Germany, Switzerland
Total foreign debt (% of GDP):	18.1
Next elections due under normal circumstances:	presidential election 2001
Credit rating: (Jan 1997, Standard & Poor's, Moody's)	BB-; Ba3

FORECAST: 1997-2000 (average)

	Worst case	Most likely	Best case
Real GDP growth (%)	1.5	3.5	5.0
Inflation (%)	35	15	10

■ POLITICS

Historical overview

The Kazaks are an ethnic group in Central Asia who take their origin from both Mongols and Turks. The Kazak language belongs to the Turkic branch of the Ural-Altaic family of languages. Kazakstan as a political entity appeared as a confederation in the late 15th century under the name "Kazak Orda" ("Kazak Horde"). Nevertheless, the confederation lasted until the early 16th century, and about a century later, the Kazak khanates sought protection from Russia against the Chinese-backed Oirat Mongols. The Kazak/Kyrgyz steppes of Central Asia consequently passed into the control of tsarist Russia between 1731 and 1854, and following further Russian expansion into the rest of Central Asia between 1865 and 1881, the region was named Turkestan. The Kazaks made a bid for independence in 1918, creating the Kazak Autonomous Region, with Orenburg as the capital. However, the

Bolsheviks took control of the region, and created the Kyrgyz Autonomous Soviet Socialist Republic (ASSR) in August 1920. This name was changed to the Kazak ASSR in October 1924. (Kazaks were generally referred to as Kazak-Kyrgyz to distinguish them from ethnically unrelated Cossacks.)

The compulsory collectivization of land and cattle caused the Kazaks much hardship, starvation, and migration between 1930 and 1934. The human cost of collectivization is said to be about one million lives, or about 25% of the Kazak population at that time. Meanwhile, the Kazak ASSR was upgraded to full Soviet Socialist Republic (SSR) in 1936. (The Karakalpak region was separated from the Kazak SSR and included in the Uzbek SSR as an ASSR.)

The Kazak SSR became the destination of a large number of forced immigrants during the Second World War. The largest groups were Germans, Koreans, Crimean Tatars, and other Caucasian nationalities including Chechens. After the death of Stalin in 1953, Khrushchev unveiled the Virgin Lands programme to increase output of food, meat, cotton, and tobacco as a means of reducing the USSR's dependence on imported agricultural products. The Virgin Lands campaign brought about 60% of Kazak SSR's arable land under cultivation, predominantly in the northern parts of the Republic. The region turned into a major grain-growing area, with an increase in the cultivated land from 7 million hectares in 1953 to 23 million hectares in a couple of years. With a large number of Russian migrants coming to the Kazak SSR to work in agricultural production, the native Kazak population was reduced to a minority: despite its higher birth rate, the Kazak population made up less than 40% of the population in 1989. During the Brezhnev era (1964–82), the Kazak SSR grew in importance. In addition to traditional agriculture, Kazak territory was given over to nuclear testing (at Semipalatynsk) and also became home to Baikonur space centre.

Administration in the Kazak SSR was headed by Dinmukhamed Kunayev (a native Kazak and a Brezhnev loyal), the First Secretary of the Communist Party of Kazakhstan (CPK) from 1962 to 1986. Nevertheless, Gorbachev appointed Gennady Kolbin (a Russian-Kazak) to replace him. This led to ethnic conflicts, and resulted in the transfer of Kolbin to Moscow. A native Kazak, Nursultan Nazarbayev, was appointed as the first secretary of the CPK in June 1989. Nazarbayev initially opposed the dissolution of the Soviet Union and in March 1991, the Kazak SSR voted in favour of retaining the USSR. As the USSR officially came to an end, however, the Kazak SSR declared its independence on December 16, 1991, making it the last to leave the USSR. The Republic of Kazakstan was chosen as the new name of the country. Nazarbayev remained in power through an unopposed direct presidential election held at the same time (winning 95% of the votes).

Recent events

Kazakstan has remained politically stable since the independence. Nazarbayev extended his presidency until the end of the year 2000 in a national referendum in April 1995. The official successor to the president is the vice-president, currently Eric Asanbaev.

Russia remains a key country for economic and social stability in Kazakstan. Russians make up about 37% of Kazakstan population, inhabiting the more developed north. Furthermore, Kazakstan depends mainly on Russia for accessing external markets. In theory, Russia has the power to disrupt Kazakstan's external trade. In view of the strategic importance of Russia for the economic development of Kazakstan, Nazarbayev's foreign policy aims to maintain close ties with Russia. There are, however, some disputes involving dual citizenship and the demarcation of the Caspian Sea. In an attempt to bring closer ties to Russia and Russians in Kazakstan, Mr. Nazarbayev issued a decree in July 1994 to move the capital from Almaty to Akmola in Central Kazakstan (mainly Russian-populated) by the year 2000. It is not clear whether this plan will be carried out at this stage, but despite the strategic gains it could provide, it is likely to be a costly operation in financial terms.

Chronology

1731-1854	Russia conquers the Kazak/Kyrgyz steppes
1865-1881	Russia completes its takeover of Central Asia, and names the region Turkestan
1916	Muslim insurrection is crushed by Russia
1917	Third All Kazak National Congress forms Provisional People's Council of Alash Orda in Orenburg
1918	June: Kazak Autonomous Region is declared
1920	August: Kyrgyz Autonomous Soviet Socialist Republic (ASSR) is formed
1924	October: the Kyrgyz ASSR was named Kazak ASSR
1929	Latin script for Kazak is adopted
1930	Collectivization causes famine and starvation
1936	Kazak ASSR is upgraded to SSR
1940	Cyrillic script for Kazak is adopted
1954	Communist Party of Kazakstan (CPK) backs Khrushchev's Virgin Land programme
1960	Dinmuhammad Kunayev becomes the First Secretary of the CPK
1971	Kunayev becomes a full member of the Communist Party of the Soviet Union's Politburo
1986	December: Kunayev's replacement by Gennady Kolbin as the First Secretary of the CPK leads to violent protests
1989	June: Nursultan Nazarbayev replaces Kolbin
1990	September: Kazak Supreme Soviet declares the superiority of Kazak laws to Soviet laws
1991	August: coup attempt in Moscow. Nazarbayev opposes the coup after initial hesitation.
1991	August: Nazarbayev resigns from the CPK
1991	December: Kazak Supreme Soviet declared Kazakstan's independence on December 16. Nazarbayev, running unopposed, gains 95% of the vote in presidential elections.
1992	May: Kazakstan agrees to dispatch its tactical nuclear weapons to Russia
1993	January: Kazak Supreme Soviet ratifies a new constitution
1994	July: parliament votes in favour of moving the capital from Almaty to Akmola by 2000
1995	March: parliament is dissolved by President Nazarbayev after the constitutional court rules that the 1994 elections were unlawful
1995	April: the presidential elections in 1996 are postponed until December 2000 in a referendum, effectively extending Nazarbayev's term until then
1995	December: new parliamentary elections are held. Nazarbayev rules by decree between March and December 1995.
1996	June: the government led by Prime Minister Akezhan Kazhegeldin tables and obtains a vote of confidence after the government's pension reform bill was voted down in May. If the parliament had rejected the bill for the second time, President Nazarbayev would have had to either dissolve the parliament or dismiss the government.

Constitution

The current constitution was approved on January 28, 1993. The Kazak constitution affirms the Republic of Kazakstan as a unitary, democratic, secular and law-based social state with a presidential form of rule. Kazak is the state language, while Russian can be used officially in state bodies and local governments on a par with Kazak. The constitution prohibits the establishment of religious parties and funding of political parties and trade unions by foreign states/citizens or international organizations. Double citizenship by Kazak citizens is not allowed.

The president is defined as the head of state and the highest official. Any citizen of the Republic by birth, who is between thirty-five and sixty-five years of age, speaks Kazak fluently and has lived in Kazakstan for not less than fifteen years may be elected the president of the republic on a five-year term. More than 50% of the electorate must take part for the elections to be considered valid. The president is elected with at least 50% of the vote in the first round. Otherwise, the two candidates with the largest number of votes go to a second round of elections.

The constitution gives the power to the president to dissolve parliament on three accounts: if parliament passes a vote of no confidence in the government; if parliament refuses to consent to the appointment of the prime minister; or if there is a political crisis resulting from insurmountable disagreements between the chambers of parliament and other branches of state power. However, the president cannot exercise this power during the last six months of a presidential term, for one year following parliamentary dissolution, or if there is a state of emergency or martial law. The current president's term was extended in April 1995. The next presidential election is expected to take place in the year 2001.

Government

The parliament includes a Majlis (lower house) and a Senate (upper house). The senate is partly elected and partly appointed by the president. The Majlis is elected from single-mandate territorial constituencies. The term of parliament is four years. The last general elections were held in December 1995. Both houses are mainly dominated by President Nazarbayev's supporters. There also exist a number of opposition parties. The main nationalist parties are the National Democratic Party of Kazakstan, the Jeltoqsan and the Republican Party, while the Socialist Party and the Communist Party comprise the left-wing. In addition, there are small ethnic-orientated parties, including most notably the Russian minority movement, the Lad (Harmony), Russian nationalists, and Cossack groups.

In theory, parliament can reject legislation proposed by the government, but as the Kazak constitution allows the president considerable leverage to pass legislation, in such circumstances he is free either to dissolve parliament or to dismiss the government. In 1996, for example, the parliament voted against a bill proposing to increase the retirement age. However, the parliament passed the bill when it was submitted a second time, given the implied threat of dissolution. It should also be noted that Nazarbayev suspended the parliament in early 1995 for several months. During this period, he enacted a large number of presidential decrees, mostly in favour of speeding up economic and structural reforms.

Current government

President	Nursultan A. Nazarbayev

Council of Ministers

Prime Minister	Akezhan Kazhegeldin
Deputy Prime Minister (Finance)	Viktor Sobolev
Chairman, central bank	Uraz Dzhandosov

Central bank

According to the Kazak constitution (Article 53/5), the governor of the central bank is appointed by the president with the consent of parliament. The regulations pertaining to the central bank are mainly prescribed by laws. The central bank is permitted to provide credit to the government, but this function is currently restricted to meet IMF targets on domestic credit growth. Current monetary policy largely aims at controlling the expansion in domestic credit and narrow money supply. Domestic credit fell more than one third in real terms in 1995, while broad money expanded by one third in real terms between end-1994 and May 1996. Narrow money supply, on the other hand, contracted by more than 20% in real terms in 1995.

■ ECONOMICS

Historical overview

Kazakstan served as a major agricultural production centre during the Soviet era, making up 6% of Soviet agricultural net material product (NMP) in 1988. However, Kazakstan has also a developed industrial base, especially because of heavy industries transferred to the republic during the Second World War. Its rich energy resources and mineral base complete the diversity in the economic structure. It is estimated that agriculture, industry, and services sectors made up approximately 22%, 50%, and 28% of the GDP in 1991, respectively.

To date, over the transition years, agriculture's share in GDP appears to have declined to 18%, while the shares of industry and services increased to 52% and 29.5%, respectively.

A distinct feature of Kazakstan among the Central Asian countries is the share of urban population, now reaching 56%. This is consistent with the large share of industry in GDP. However, the structure of agriculture in Kazakstan differs from that in other Central Asian countries: grain production and livestock are main activities, and cotton is of lesser importance. Farming in southern Kazakstan largely depends on irrigation systems and availability of water, while the production in the north is rain fed. Further deterioration in the Aral Sea levels and droughts (as in 1991) render long-term agricultural production estimates difficult.

Kazakstan is also undergoing a notable demographic change, with two main trends: the increase in the share of the Kazak population, and the increasing participation of the Kazak youth in the labour force; in fact it is estimated that half of the population will be made up of Kazaks in the early 2000s. This raises the question of ethnic harmony in the country, as there are already existing tensions between Russian and Kazak communities, but these are unlikely to threaten economic progress. It is also worth noting that the initial outward emigration of Russians has slowed down, and some Russians have indeed returned to Kazakstan.

Population by ethnic group (1992)

	Number ('000)	(%)
Kazak	7,297	43.2
Russian	6,169	36.5
Ukrainian	875	5.2
German	696	4.1
Uzbek	364	2.2
Tatar	335	2.0
Belarusian	184	1.1
Others	972	5.7
TOTAL	16,892	100.0

The economy

Following the break-up of the USSR, the disruption in inter-republican trade and payments, end of central subsidies from Moscow, the collapse of the rouble zone, and economic disintegration in other post-USSR countries also led to a massive collapse in real GDP in Kazakstan.

The measured collapse in output amounts to about 50% between 1991 and 1995. However, economic data are scarce, their reliability are questionable, and there are measurement problems when one switches from NMP to GDP. It is likely that the output collapse is overstated.

Share of GDP by sector

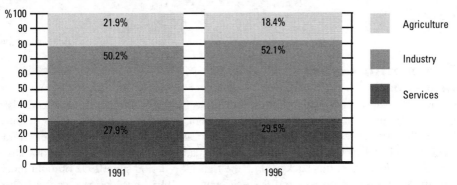

Source: Official data

Exports and imports as a % of GDP

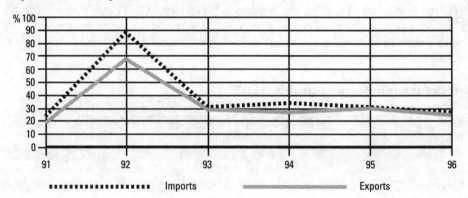

Source: Official data

Breakdown of exports, 1995

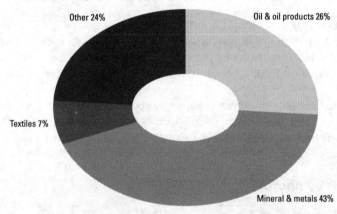

Source: Official data

Economic policy
Background

As with the other post-Soviet countries, Kazakstan is undergoing a transition towards a market economy. The legacy from the Soviet era includes environmental problems, such as the nuclear-test site Semipalatynsk, desiccation of the Aral Sea, obsolete infrastructure and fuel-inefficient machinery, inadequate distribution systems, and a large bureaucracy. In view of this background, the transition period since 1992 brought much hardship to the Kazak people and the economy. In 1995, the economy contracted in real terms to 51% of its level in 1990. Inflation came close to 3000% (year-on-year) in 1992 and it remained above 1000% until 1995. The introduction of the national currency, the tenge, in May 1993 and the IMF-backed economic reform programme in January 1994, however, set the course for macroeconomic stabilization. In addition, the country's rich mineral base attracts foreign investors, who bring in much-needed hard currency. When still part of the USSR, Kazakstan produced all the union's output of beryllium and tantalum, 95% of its chromite, half of its silver, tungsten and lead, one third of its copper, a quarter of the union's coal output, about 10% of its gold and iron ore, and 5% of its oil.

Current account as a % of GDP

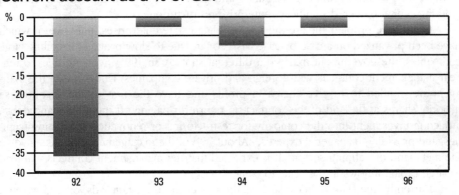

Source: Official data; UBS estimates

Main issues

Economic recovery in Kazakstan is constrained by the same structural factors affecting many other Commonwealth of Independent States (CIS) countries. These include the existence of Soviet-era enterprises which are adjusting with difficulty to the demands of a market economy, the need for large-scale investment to modernize sectors, and the uncertainties of a changing legal and tax environment.

Another factor depressing the economy is the massive inter-enterprise debt, that now extends across international borders (the former Soviet republics). Against this background, Kazakstan's economic and social policies since independence in December 1991 focused on six areas with varying intensity over time: (1) macroeconomic stabilization, (2) price liberalization, (3) trade liberalization and current account convertibility, (4) enterprise reform and privatization, (5) the creation of a social security safety net, and (6) the development of the institutional and legal framework for a market economy, including an efficiently functioning financial system.

Much progress has been registered in all areas to date. The rate of economic decline has slowed, with the economy expected to grow in real terms from 1996. Inflation was reduced to 40% from more than 1100% in 1994. The tenge proved stable over time, and established an anchor to stimulate further stabilization. It is now fully convertible.

Additional structural steps, such as enterprise reform and privatization, take time to implement. The record to date has involved small enterprises in the service sector. Even then, only about half of the target, 16,000 enterprises, was reached in the first half of 1996. In the agricultural sector, more than 90% of state and collective farms were privatized since 1994, and in principle land was fully privatized by a presidential decree in December 1995. Nevertheless, uncertainty over property rights, and lack of know-how and equipment remain as bottlenecks. The privatization of medium and large enterprises are being conducted under a voucher program, which are to be pooled in private investment funds (PIFs). According to Kazak authorities, mass privatization of medium-sized enterprises (200–500 employees) has largely been completed: about 16,000 enterprises have been sold in 22 auctions. However, the experience of the privatized enterprises showed that weak corporate governance and continued shortages of investment and working capital hindered significant enterprise restructuring.

Even more problematic are the 180 very large state enterprises, only five of which have been privatized on a case-by-case basis so far. Due to slow progress in selling large companies, the government initiated a different strategy in 1995 involving five- to ten-year management contracts with foreign and private companies. Under these, the managers are entitled to receive shares in profits and have the first option to purchase majority shares at the end of the contract, in return for paying off the arrears and debts, attracting investment into the company for restructuring or renovation of existing facilities, and providing managerial expertise. About 75% of the management contracts involve the metal and oil-refining sectors. It is expected that the management contracts will lead to large capital inflows in the years to come.

Currently, the state utilities, such as the power industry, railroads, oil and gas and most of the air transportation sector remain in state ownership.

Banking sector

Kazakstan's main problem with its banking sector is the existence of a large number of weak and undercapitalized banks. It was found in a study by international auditors that about 50% of loans, equivalent to 15% of GDP, were non-performing.

The new Bank and Banking Activity Law took effect in September 1995. The new law provided additional rights and responsibilities to the National Bank of Kazakstan. The central bank started to move decisively against problem banks, cancelling the licences of fifty-five banks in 1995 and a further thirteen in 1996. It was also announced by the State Property Committee that Kazakstan privatized forty banks in 1995, yielding US$6 million in revenue. Despite these moves, there still remain 117 banks in the sector. The Banking Law allows foreign banks to open on their own or in joint-ventures with local banks. However, a bank with foreign capital is classified as a "second-tier bank", which involves some operating restrictions.

Fiscal policy in 1996

Kazakstan pursued tight fiscal and monetary policies in 1995 and 1996. Budget deficit was 2.3% of GDP in 1995, below the IMF target of 3.5%, and well below 6.8% in 1994. The main reasons for this achievement are improved revenue collection and the cuts in government expenditure in response to less than expected foreign financing. The 1996 budget deficit target is 2.8% of GDP, with a primary deficit amounting to 1.3% of GDP. The government is also taking steps to increase revenue collection and create new sources. These measures include increasing excise duties, improving natural resource taxation, eliminating some import duty exemptions, and strengthening tax administration. Kazakstan was granted a three-year US$450 million credit facility by the IMF in July 1996 to assist with the country's transformation process. Kazakstan received a BB- rating from Standard & Poor's and a Ba3 rating from Moody's for its long-term foreign currency debt in November 1996. The ratings were given in view of Kazakstan's US$200 million three-year Eurobond issue in December 1996.

Macroeconomic balances in 1996

In response to tight fiscal, monetary and credit policies and a stable exchange rate (see below), inflation performance has improved substantially. Monthly consumer price increases averaged 2.5% - down from 4.5% in the same period of 1995. The prospect of continued tight fiscal and monetary policies for the rest of the year, should help bring year-end inflation close to the 28% target agreed with the IMF. Indeed, targeting even lower inflation (between 9 and 12% by 1998) is one of the aims of the three-year government programme to restructure the economy and improve the macroeconomic performance.

CPI changes (% MOM)

	1996	1995	1994
January	4.1	8.9	42.6
February	2.5	6.7	24.2
March	1.7	5.1	17.4
April	2.9	3.2	31.8
May	2.0	2.7	33.8
June	2.5	2.3	45.9
July	1.8	2.9	25.4
August	0.7	2.1	3.3
September	1.2	2.4	9.7
October	2.9	4.1	21.4
November	2.4	4.4	14.2
December	0.8	3.6	3.6

There remain problems with the current account, which may show larger deficits in the coming years. However, this is likely to be the result of investment recovery and return to macroeconomic growth, which will eventually boost the country's infrastructure and help increase natural resource exports. Furthermore, equity investment and net lending, expected to be about 10% of GDP a year in 1997 and 1998, should be sufficient to finance both the current account deficit and a further increase in reserves, which now covers about three and a half months of imports.

Competitiveness

Despite low local wages, the large real appreciation in the Kazak tenge, brought about by tight fiscal and monetary policies, led to a deterioration in Kazakstan's external competitiveness. The tenge has appreciated in real terms by about 80% against the US$ since January 1995.

Currency

After its independence, Kazakstan tried to stay in the Russian rouble zone. However, Russia's hard-to-meet conditions for continued membership in the rouble zone led Kazakstan to introduce its own currency, the tenge (1 tenge=100 tiyan) in November 1993. The initial rate was set at KZT/US$=4.75. The tenge traded at 50.5 against the US$ one year after its introduction, which still represented a large real appreciation. The tenge stabilized after January 1995, and depreciated by less than 20% in nominal terms since then. Kazakstan joined Article 8 of the IMF Charter on July 19, 1996, which envisages full convertibility of the tenge. This move made Kazakstan the fourth ex-Soviet country (after Kyrgyzstan, Moldova, and Russia) to join the Article.

Kazak tenge/US dollar exchange rate

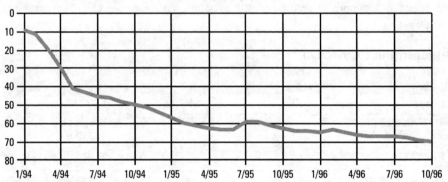

Oil and gas sector

The extent to which Kazakstan was integrated with its neighbours is particularly evident in the energy sector. Kazakstan has vast oil reserves, but the country is land-locked and the existing transport and pipeline structure has proved inadequate to meet high hopes of the newly independent state. Moreover, projects have been held up by the need to negotiate new inter-state treaties. As a consequence of these and other disruptions, oil output fell from 26.6 million tonnes (or some 540,000 barrels per day) in 1991 to 20.9 million tonnes in 1994, before recovering slightly to 20.6 million tonnes in 1995. For 1996, the government is targeting 23.3 million tonnes.

In May 1996, the US oil company, Mobil, signed an agreement with Kazakstan for a 25% share of the Tengiz oil field, which is estimated to hold recoverable reserves of at least 6 billion barrels. Output from Tengiz oil field was 83,000 barrels per day (bpd) in the first quarter of 1996, and the company expects this figure to rise to 130,000 bpd by the end of the year. Output is projected to peak at 700,000 bpd by 2010.

The lack of a viable export route is the main factor which hinders the development of Kazakstan's large oil and gas sector. A positive step in overcoming this difficulty was the tentative agreement in April 1996 by eight oil companies to provide US$1.2 billion towards financing construction of a pipeline from the Tengiz field to the Black Sea. In addition, an oil-swap agreement was concluded with Iran recently, under which Kazak crude oil will be shipped to Iranian refineries and in return Iran will export an equal amount of crude oil. This is expected to boost oil exports by 15–20% a year starting from late-1996. In principle, Kazakstan should find increasing access to international markets for its oil and its dependence on Russia should diminish gradually as alternative transport routes are developed.

■ EQUITIES

Structure
There are two stock exchanges in Kazakstan – the Central-Asian Stock Exchange (CASE) and the Kazakstan Interioantla Stock Exchange. The CASE is the larger of the two with twenty-two companies listed. Total market capitalization was T11.8 billion (US$184 million) at the end of 1995. Turnover between April 1995 and April 1996 was T2.7 million (US$0.04 million).

Regulatory authority
The main regulatory body for the CASE is the National Securities Commission, which oversees trading and sets the rules for ownership limits.

Trading methods
Trading takes place using an open outcry system between 10.00 and 13.00, Monday to Friday. Settlement is on a manual T+5 basis. All share certificates are held by investors. There is no central depository or registry system. There are no indices measuring the exchange performance. There is a 15% withholding tax on dividends, but capital gains are tax free. Non-residents face no limits on the repatriation of capital. There are a small number of local brokers.

Sectors
Banks and trading companies account for almost all companies listed apart from one furniture manufacturer.

ADRs
There are no Kazakstan ADRs.

Market comment
Foreign participation in Kazakstan has been virtually non-existent due to perceived problems with settlement and clearing. Plans are under way to modernize the exchange.

■ DEBT

The Ministry of Finance began to issue treasury bills at the end of 1994, and uses the National Bank of Kazakstan (NBK) as its selling agent.

Three-, 6- and 12-month bills are auctioned by the NBK, and the Ministry of Finance intends to launch 12-month National Savings Obligations, which will be targeted at individual investors.

Overseas participation in auctions is limited to 10-20%, but there are no restrictions on secondary market purchases. Non-residents obtain foreign exchange licences and can then buy bills from domestic banks.

Kazakstan issued its first eurobond in December 1996 ($200 million, 3-year maturity at a spread of 350 basis points over Treasuries).

■ KAZAKSTAN: Economic indicators

Population and development	1990	1991	1992	1993	1994	1995	1996e
Population, million	16.8	17.0	16.9	16.7	16.5	16.4	16.3
Population growth, %	—	1.2	-0.6	-1.2	-1.2	-0.6	-0.6
Nominal GDP per capita, US$	5060	3253	323	995	753	1078	1397

National accounts							
Nominal GDP, US$bn	85.0	55.3	5.5	16.6	12.4	17.7	22.8
Change in real GDP, %	-0.4	-11.5	-12.3	-10.7	-20.0	-8.2	1.0

Money supply and inflation							
Consumer price inflation (avg.) %	—	78.8	1381.0	1662.3	1877.0	176.3	40.6
Consumer price inflation, change %, Dec/Dec	104.6	136.8	2984.1	2162.5	1160.5	60.4	28.0

Government finance							
Government expenditure, % of GDP	31.4	32.9	31.7	23.4	24.6	18.9	18.3
Government balance, % of GDP	1.0	-7.9	-7.0	-1.3	-6.7	-2.3	-3.0

Exchange rates *lc=local currency*							
Exchange rate, annual average, lc/US$	—	—	—	—	36.20	61.40	67.84
Exchange rate, end of year, lc/US$	—	—	—	6.30	54.30	63.76	74.00
Real exchange rate 1990=100	100.0	77.3	29.2	56.9	55.7	75.7	79.8

Balance of payments							
Exports of goods & services, US$m	14270	10210	4062	5219	3712	5733	6360
Change %	739.4	-28.5	-60.2	28.5	-28.9	54.4	10.9
Imports of goods & services, US$m, fob	24550	13370	5828	5748	5667	6163	6810
Change %	862.7	-45.5	-56.4	-1.4	-1.4	8.8	10.5
Trade balance, of goods only, US$m, fob-fob	-10280	-3160	-1121	-414	-920	-222	-200
Current account balance, US$m	—	25	-1889	-439	-905	-518	-1040
as a % of GDP	—	0.0	-34.6	-2.6	-7.3	-2.9	-4.6

Foreign exchange reserves							
Foreign exchange reserves, US$m	—	—	83	359	806	1100	1600
Gold at ⅔ of market price, US$m	—	—	45.7	71.9	89.6	89.5	90.4
Import cover (reserves/imports), months	—	—	0.2	0.7	1.7	2.1	2.8

Foreign debt and debt service							
Short-term debt, US$m	—	—	1246	22	150	224	272
Total foreign debt, US$m	—	—	1478	2245	3327	4125	4594
as a % of GDP	—	—	27.1	13.5	26.8	23.3	20.2
as a % of foreign exchange receipts	—	—	35.9	42.1	87.3	70.8	71.0
Interest payments, US$m	—	—	175	20	48	102	210
Principal repayments, US$m	—	—	0	104	182	112	230
Total debt service, US$m	—	—	175	124	230	214	440
as a % of goods exports	—	—	4.9	2.6	7.0	4.1	7.6
as a % of foreign exchange receipts	—	—	4.3	2.3	6.0	3.7	6.8

Kenya

Area (thousands of km²):	580
Population (1995, millions):	30.5
Population projection (2025, millions):	47
Population younger than 15 yrs (1991, % of total):	51.1
Urbanization rate (1993, % of population):	26
Life expectancy (1993, years at birth):	58
Gross domestic product (1996, US$bn):	9.1
GDP per capita (1996, US$):	290
Average annual GDP growth rate (1990-96, %):	2.6
Average annual inflation rate (1990-96, %):	21.6
Currency (shilling per US$, average 1996):	57
Structure of production (1994):	29.7% agriculture/forestry/fishing, 21.1% government services, 15.5% trade,restaurants & hotels, 11% manufacturing
Main exports:	tea, coffee & horticultural products
Main imports:	industrial machinery & motor parts
Main trading partners:	Europe, Kenya, Tanzania, Uganda
Market capitalization of Stock Exchange (December 1996; US$bn):	1.8
Total foreign debt (% of GDP):	81.3
Next elections due under normal circumstances:	presidential and legislative December 1997
Credit rating: (Jan 1997, Standard & Poor's, Moody's)	not rated

FORECAST: 1997-2000 (average)

	Worst case	Most likely	Best case
Real GDP growth (%)	3.5	4.5	5.0
Inflation (%)	11.0	9.5	7.5

■ POLITICS

Historical overview

After nearly seventy years as part of the British Empire, during which time local tribes fought hard to remove their colonial masters, Kenya finally became independent in 1963. Its political history has since been dominated by the Kenyan African Union (KANU) Party founded by Jomo Kenyatta in 1947, which has remained in power for the past fifty years. For much of this period, Kenya has been a one-party state. Attempts, during the 1960s, to set up rival opposition parties were strongly resisted by the authorities.

Following the death of Kenyatta in 1978, Daniel arap Moi took over as president, but did not immediately deviate from the one-party system. International pressure by donor countries began to grow, however, and multiparty politics were introduced in 1991. Rivalry between leading opposition politicians prevented the launch of an effective challenge to KANU. In the December 1992 elections, Moi was re-elected and, in the legislative elections that followed, KANU won 100 of the 188 elected seats in the National Assembly. Since the election, there have been further outbreaks of tribal violence, particularly in the Rift Valley.

Relations with the international community cooled in the early 1990s when several countries including the US, withdrew aid after concerns over human rights abuses.

Recent events

Following various political and economic reforms, overseas donors now appear to be taking a more flexible line towards the Moi administration. Early in 1996, the IMF agreed to release a long-blocked structural adjustment credit. Other bilateral donors have also resumed aid.

Presidential and legislative elections are scheduled for December 1997. Divisions between opposition parties have been a feature of Kenyan politics, but if KANU are to face a sterner test next time, a unified front would be required.

Chronology

1895	Kenya becomes part of the British Empire
1944	Kenya African Union (KANU) is set up
1947	Jomo Kenyatta becomes president of KANU
1952	Mau Mau campaign begins
1961	KANU candidates win majority in general election
1963	Kenyatta becomes prime minister
1963	Kenya becomes independent
1966	Oginga Odinga forms rival Kenya People's Union (KPU)
1966	Senate and House of Representatives merge into unicameral assembly
1969	KPU is banned and Odinga jailed
1969	KANU wins unopposed general election
1974	Kenyatta wins third term in office in unopposed election
1978	Daniel arap Moi takes over as leader of KANU after Kenyatta dies
1982	Airforce disbanded after attempted coup
1983	Moi calls and wins early election
1986	Amnesty International accuse government of human rights abuses
1988	Moi is returned to office in unopposed election
1991	Odinga forms Forum for the Restoration of Democracy (FORD)
1991	Multiparty political system introduced
1992	Political rallies banned after two thousand are killed in tribal clashes
1992	FORD splits into Ford-Kenya and Ford-Asili
1992	Moi and KANU win first multiparty elections
1993	Three thousand are killed in tribal clashes in the Rift Valley
1994	Kijana Wamalwa takes over as leader of FORD-Kenya after Odinga dies
1995	Dr Richard Leakey launches Safina Party

| 1995 | Aid suspended after allegations of human rights abuses and lack of transparency in certain government accounts |
| 1996 | Electoral Commission set up to create new constituencies |

Constitution and government

The one-party state constitution drawn up by KANU in the early years of independence was changed in 1991 to allow rival parties to participate in the 1992 elections. Executive power is held by the president, who is directly elected for five-year terms. The president is currently limited to serving only two terms. There is a unicameral National Assembly of 188 elected members, plus 12 presidential appointees, the attorney general and speaker.

Current government

President	Daniel arap Moi
Finance Minister	Musalia Mudavadi
Foreign Affairs Minister	Kalonzo Musyoka

Results of the December 1992 presidential election

Daniel arap Moi (KANU) (36.4%), Kenneth Matiba (FORD-Asili) (26.2%), Mwai Kibaki (DP) (19.1%), Oginga Odinga (FORD-Kenya) (17.6%).

Results of the December 1992 general election

Kenyan African National Union (KANU) (100 seats), Forum for the Restoration of Democracy-Asili (FORD-Asili) (31 seats), Forum for the Restoration of Democracy-Kenya (FORD-Kenya) (31 seats), Democratic Party (DP) (23 seats), Kenyan Social Congress (KSC) (1 seat), Kenyan National Congress (KNC) (1 seat), Independent (1 seat).

■ ECONOMICS

Historical overview

Kenya's economy is dominated by agriculture. Large numbers of people live at subsistence level. However, the service and manufacturing sectors are growing, particularly food processing, textiles and tobacco. Tourism is also a significant hard currency earner, and despite a decline in 1995, continues to be the country's main source of foreign currency earnings.

In the years after independence, the government concentrated on redistributing land held by white farmers to the indigenous population. Agricultural production in Kenya flourished as coffee and tea led exports. Between 1963 and 1980, the economy prospered on the back of increased demand for these products.

The onset of the 1980s signalled a change in fortune for the Kenyan economy, as a combination of deteriorating terms of trade, escalating government expenditure and high levels of borrowing de-stabilized the economy, culminating in poor growth rates during the early 1980s.

A stabilization programme was introduced by the IMF in 1983, but a severe drought in 1984 held back the recovery. From the mid-1980s the economy prospered on the back of rising commodity prices for its key agricultural exports. Growth between 1984 and 1993 averaged 3.5% a year, making Kenya one of the best-performing economies in sub-Saharan Africa.

In 1991, aid payments were suspended by Kenya's creditors, who announced that they would withhold payment until certain reforms were implemented. Partly because of this, the economy stagnated in the early 1990s.

In December 1993, the government introduced a development plan that aimed to reduce the number of public sector employees, decrease government subsidies, eliminate currency controls and accelerate privatization. The agricultural sector was liberalized and de-regulated. The implementation of these reforms has not been entirely smooth. As of October 1996, the only major privatization to have been completed was that of Kenya Airways.

Historically, Kenya's main trading partners have been in Europe. However, closer inter-regional co-operation has led to a surge in local trade. Attempts to diversify the export base away from tea and coffee into new industries such as cut flowers have been relatively successful.

Population

In 1989, a census put the population at 21 million. It is now estimated at around 27.5 million. The heaviest concentration is in the western highlands, the coastal strip and the lake area. In 1985, the country's average birth rate was 5.4%, the highest in the world. By 1993, this had fallen to 3.6%.

The economy

Agriculture – chiefly maize, tea, wheat and coffee – has traditionally dominated the Kenyan economy. Agriculture employs around three-quarters of the working population and accounts for around 30% of GDP. However, this proportion is lower than in many countries in the region, largely because of a history of commercial activity amongst European settlers.

Share of GDP by sector

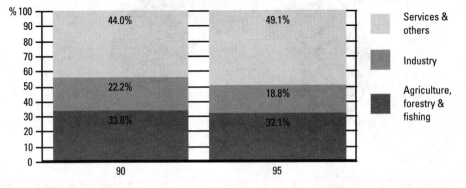

Source: Official data

Kenya has the most developed industrial base in East Africa, backed by a relatively good infrastructure and considerable private-sector activity. Despite this, the manufacturing sector (traditionally dominated by food processing, petroleum refining, metal transportation and beverage industries) only contributes around 18% to GDP. Throughout the post-independence period and up until the 1980s, manufacturing grew rapidly at around 10% per annum, in line with the economy as whole. Manufacturing growth fluctuated, however, during the 1980s and early 1990s, whilst never approaching the buoyant growth witnessed following independence.

Exports and imports as a % of GDP

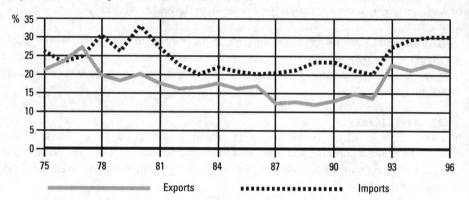

Source: Official data

Breakdown of exports (1995)

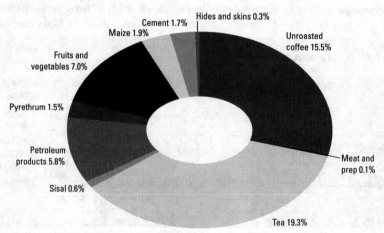

Source: Central Bank of Kenya

Relative to other East African countries, Kenya has a large export sector equivalent to around a quarter of GDP. Tea, coffee, horticulture and petroleum products are the leading export sectors, accounting for around half of total exports. Uganda, the UK and Tanzania are the biggest importers from Kenya, purchasing in the region of KES15 billion (US$270 million) worth of goods. Imports into Kenya are predominantly from developed nations. The UK, the UAE and Japan are the three leading exporters to Kenya, earning combined receipts equivalent to over a tenth of Kenyan GDP. Imports consist largely of capital goods, fuel and industrial materials, with industrial and electrical machinery, crude petroleum, motor vehicles and chassis, and iron and steel accounting for 40% of total imports.

Recent developments

Kenya's GDP expanded by over 4.5% in 1995 and 1996, largely on the back of higher coffee and tea prices. With the population growing at about 4% a year, however, Kenya is under pressure to make the recent economic recovery last.

A key event was the IMF's decision to approve a US$216 million facility in April 1996 which strengthened Kenya's image among international lenders. The agreement should allow Kenya to regain access to around US$800 million of suspended overseas aid. Under the terms of the facility, the government has promised to make further progress on economic reform, to try to limit inflation to 5% and extend the independence of the central bank.

In his 1996-97 budget, Finance Minister Mudavadi announced that the budget deficit had been reduced to 0.7% of GDP in the year ending June 1996, from 2.8% in the previous fiscal year. He stated that the aim was to balance the budget. Much of this success can be attributed to the implementation of measures suggested by the IMF, such as improved tax collection, accelerating the privatization process, reforming the civil service and cutting spending on lower priority projects.

Current account as a % of GDP

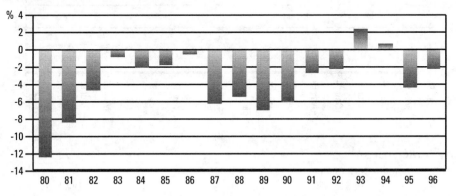

Source: Official statistics, UBS estimates

Currency

The official currency is the Kenyan shilling (100 cents). The Kenyan shilling (KES) floats freely on world exchanges, with the central bank increasingly allowing open market operations to govern the supply of money and credit in the economy. Notably, in 1994, the government signed Article VIII with the IMF, committing them to a current account convertibility. Since reverting to a floating currency system in October 1993, the shilling stabilized against the US$ after eighteen months of initial volatility. This trend continued in 1996.

Kenyan shilling/US dollar exchange rate

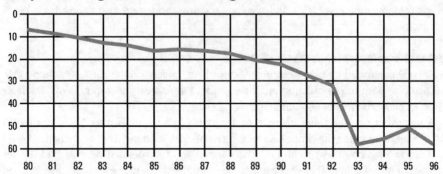

■ EQUITIES

Index performance (in local currency)

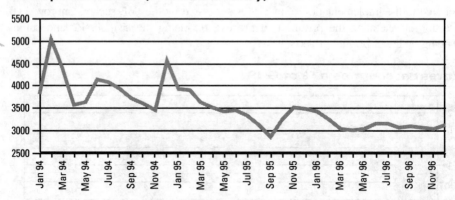

Key indicators

	Index performance %, in US$ terms	Market Cap. US$bn	P/E	Div. Yield
1994	179.0	3.1	9.8	5.0
1995	-38.9	1.9	12.4	4.3
1996	-9.0	1.8	6.6	10.3

Sources: Local stock exchange, IFC, Bloomberg, Datastream, UBS

Structure
The Nairobi Stock Exchange (NSE), one of the oldest in Africa, was set up in 1954. There are fifty-six companies. Total market capitalization increased during the early 1990s to stand at US$1.7 billion by late 1996.

Regulatory authority
The Capital Markets Authority (CMA) is the main regulator.

Trading methods
The NSE uses an open outcry floor-based continuous auction method of trading.

Hours
The market is open 10.00 to 12.00 Monday to Friday.

Settlement time and clearing
The NSE acts as a central clearing house. Delivery occurs on T+7 basis with settlement occurring on D+7. There are penalties for late delivery.

Types of shares
Ordinary and preference shares are traded as well as corporate bonds and debenture stocks.

Stock indices
The NSE 20 share index tracks the twenty largest shares by market capitalization.

Taxes
There is no capital gains tax. Dividends are taxed at source at a rate of 10% for foreign investors.

Disclosure of financial statements
Companies must inform the NSE of any significant changes within twenty-four hours of a decision being taken. They must also produce half yearly and annual results not later than three months after the end of the financial year.

Ownership limits for non-residents
The market was opened to foreign investors in 1995. Institutional investors cannot own more than 40% of a single company, while individuals cannot own more than 5%.

Capital and foreign exchange controls
There are no restrictions on the repatriation of capital or income.

Brokers
There are twenty brokers operating on the NSE.

Sectors
Agriculture KES4.2 billion (US$75.1 million), commerce and services KES7.1 billion

(US$127.0 million), finance and investment KES50.6 billion (US$905.2 million) and industrials KES38.9 billion (US$695.9 million).

ADRs
There are no Kenyan ADRs.

■ DEBT

Money and capital markets began to evolve in Kenya in the mid-1980s, and have now grown to about US$1 billion. Interest rate liberalization and the abolition of exchange controls in 1995 have provided an impetus for further development and expansion.

The Central Bank of Kenya manages the auctions of treasury bills, which are issued with maturities of 28, 91, 182 and 270 days. Auctions are held every Thursday, for settlement on Monday. Bills of other terms are also issued, but 91-day bills account for more than the combined total of all other maturities. More than half the bills are held by domestic banks.

Treasury bonds paying fixed coupon rates are also issued with maturities of 1 to 5 years and are in registered form. Longer-term bonds have been issued in the past. A secondary market is expected to develop over the next year.

Several Kenyan companies have issued commercial paper, and a corporate bond sector is likely to grow following an inaugural issue from the East African Development Bank. There are proposals to trade bonds on the Nairobi Stock Exchange – up to now trading has been conducted over the counter.

■ KENYA: Economic indicators

Population and development	1990	1991	1992	1993	1994	1995	1996e
Population, million	24.0	25.9	25.7	28.1	29.3	30.5	31.5
Population growth, %	-3.4	7.8	-0.8	9.4	4.2	4.2	3.2
Nominal GDP per capita, US$	355	310	309	196	240	294	290

National accounts							
Nominal GDP, US$bn	8.5	8.0	8.0	5.5	7.0	9.0	9.1
Change in real GDP, %	4.2	1.4	-0.8	0.4	2.7	4.4	4.8
Gross fixed capital formation, % of GDP	20.7	19.3	17.1	17.6	19.2	21.6	19.9

Money supply and inflation							
Broad money, change %, Dec/Dec	14.3	23.7	32.3	28.7	48.8	25.0	23.0
Consumer price inflation (avg.) %	15.6	19.8	29.5	45.8	29.0	0.8	8.0

Interest rates							
Discount rate, end of year	16.50	19.43	20.27	20.46	45.50	21.50	24.50
Treasury bill rate, annual average	13.86	14.78	16.59	16.53	49.80	23.32	18.29
Prime lending rate, annual average	17.25	18.75	19.00	21.07	29.99	36.24	28.80

Government finance							
Government expenditure, % of GDP	27.5	28.9	24.9	27.1	28.9	28.3	28.7
Government balance, % of GDP	-3.8	-2.6	-0.4	-3.6	-3.3	-2.8	-0.7

Exchange rates *lc=local currency*

	1990	1991	1992	1993	1994	1995	1996e
Exchange rate, annual average, lc/US$	22.92	27.51	32.22	58.00	56.05	51.43	57.00
Exchange rate, end of year, lc/US$	24.08	28.07	36.22	68.16	44.84	55.94	55.00

Balance of payments							
Exports of goods & services, US$m	2229	2200	2151	2326	1654	2949	2931
Change %	15.9	-1.3	-2.2	8.2	-28.9	78.3	-0.6
Imports of goods & services, US$m, fob	2705	2330	2172	2079	2462	3524	3189
Change %	5.4	-13.9	-6.8	-4.3	18.4	43.1	-9.5
Trade balance, of goods only, US$m, fob-fob	-915	-512	-500	-247	-238	-738	-377
Current account balance, US$m	-527	-213	-180	71	98	-400	-178
as a % of GDP	-6.2	-2.7	-2.3	1.3	1.4	-4.5	-2.0

Foreign exchange reserves							
Foreign exchange reserves, US$m	205.4	116.9	53.0	405.6	557.6	353.4	690.0
Gold at ⅔ of market price, US$m	20.6	19.3	18.3	19.2	20.5	20.5	20.7
Import cover (reserves/imports), months	0.9	0.6	0.3	2.3	2.7	1.2	2.6

Foreign debt and debt service							
Short-term debt, US$m	840	708	777	903	688	610	590
Total foreign debt, US$m	6947	7455	6906	7120	7274	7290	7415
as a % of GDP	81.4	92.7	86.9	129.0	103.6	81.4	81.3
as a % of foreign exchange receipts	261.5	286.5	271.3	273.3	361.5	207.1	214.0
Interest payments, US$m	287	319	259	264	342	259	256
Principal repayments, US$m	280	396	407	363	547	494.0	444
Total debt service, US$m	567	715	666	627	889	753	700
as a % of goods exports	52	60.3	60.1	49.7	57.8	39.3	34.8
as a % of foreign exchange receipts	21.3	27.5	26.2	24.1	44.2	21.4	20.2

Latvia

KEY FACTS

Area (thousands of km²):	64
Population (1995, millions):	2.5
Population projection (2025, millions):	3
Population younger than 15 yrs (1991, % of total):	21.7
Urbanization rate (1993, % of population):	70
Life expectancy (1993, years at birth):	69
Gross domestic product (1996, US$bn):	5.4
GDP per capita (1996, US$:	2152
Average annual GDP growth rate (1990-96, %):	-8
Average annual inflation rate (1990-96, %):	182
Currency (lats per US$, average 1996):	0.5
Structure of production (1994):	56% services, 21.1% manufacturing, 10.1% agriculture, 6.3% construction, 6.1% electricity & gas, 0.3% fishing & mining
Main exports:	wood, wood products, textiles, foodstuffs, mechanical & electrical products
Main imports:	energy, agricultural products, chemical products
Main trading partners:	Russia, Germany, Sweden, Commonwealth of Independent States
Total foreign debt (% of GDP):	11.1
Next elections due under normal circumstances:	October 1998

FORECAST: 1997-2000 (average)

	Worst case	Most likely	Best case
Real GDP growth (%)	1 to 3	4 to 7	5 to 8
Inflation (%)	15 to 30	8 to 14	5 to 7

■ POLITICS

Historical overview

The culture of the Baltic (Selonians, Semgallians, Couronians, Latgallians) and Finno-Ugric tribes was formed during the second millennium BC in the territory of today's Latvia. By the 1270s German crusaders had conquered Latvia and established the state of Livonia, a political union of the Livonian Order of Knights and the Catholic Church. In 1282 Riga, founded in 1201, was admitted to the Hanseatic League of northern Germany, thereby gaining a mediating role in East–West trade. After the Livonian Wars (1558–83), fought over demands by the state of Moscow for access to the Baltic Sea, Livonia was divided between Sweden and Poland-Lithuania. The division resulted in the formation of the Duchy of Kurzeme, a semi-independent state paying tribute to Poland.

In the 17th century, the Duchy became so successful that for a short while it held colonies in Gambia and on the Caribbean island of Tobago. After the Great Northern War (1700-21) Latvia was included in the Russian Empire.

The 19th century witnessed the evolution of the Latvian nationalist movement, countered by deliberate russification. The revolution of 1905 was an outright struggle against German landowners and Russian oppression.

After the First World War, independence of the Republic of Latvia was declared. Latvia's constitution in 1922 established a democratic political system. But independence was short-lived, ending in 1939 with the signing of the Molotov-Ribbentrop Pact. Soviet troops invaded the country in 1940, followed by German invasion in 1941 and re-invasion by Soviets in 1944. By the end of the war, Latvia had lost about one third of its population.

The annexation of Latvia was followed by years of deportations, mass imprisonment and forced mass immigration of Russians. Before Soviet occupation, Latvians made up approximately 75% of the population. By 1989 this figure had dropped to below 51%.

The pro-independence movement began to recover under Mikhail Gorbachev's policy of glasnost and perestroika. In March 1990 the Latvian Popular Front (LTF) gained a majority of seats in the Supreme Council (former Supreme Soviet), and on May 4, 1990, the Council voted to reinstate both the 1922 constitution and the country's official name, the Republic of Latvia. Moscow declared these moves illegal. After assaults by Soviet special forces in January 1991 and a general referendum in March, the parliament restored Latvia's pre-war independence on August 21, 1991.

Recent events

The latest parliamentary elections in October 1995 led to a fragmented parliament with nine parties holding seats. Parliament split into two coalition blocs: the right-of-centre National Conservative-Latvian Way bloc, comprising the Latvian Way, Fatherland and Freedom, LNNK-Greens and the Farmers' Union alliance; and the National Reconciliation bloc, which included the leftist Saimnieks, Harmony and Latvian Unity, and also the extreme right People's Movement for Latvia.

With neither coalition bloc able to form a government that would be ratified, President Ulmanis selected neutral candidate Andrijs Shkele to form a new government. Shkele eventually succeeded in forming a six-party coalition. Nevertheless, Shkele's government has made some progress in tackling economic and political reforms and despite the difficulties attached to a six-party coalition, the government seems stable.

Chronology

1270	Conquest of Latvia by German Knights
1629	Latvia is captured by Sweden
1721	Treaty of Nystad passes part of Latvia to the Russian Empire
1918	Republic of Latvia announces declaration of independence for the first time

1922	Democratic political system is established under the first Latvian constitution
1934	Dictatorship established by Karlis Ulmanis
1939	Molotov-Ribbentrop Pact brings Latvia into the Soviet Union
1940	Soviet troops invade Latvia
1941	German invasion of Latvia
1944	Soviet forces return Latvia to the Soviet Union
1988	Pro-independence movement gathers momentum, with the inaugural congress of the Latvian Popular Front (LTF)
1989	Latvia declares sovereignty and economic independence
1991	Formal independence is achieved and recognized by the United Nations
1993	Latvia's Way-Farmers' Union coalition government is established following the parliamentary elections. Guntis Ulmanis (great-nephew of Karlis Ulmanis) is elected president by parliament.
1995	Elections result in a coalition government involving a broad range of political parties, with Andrijs Shkele as prime minister
1996	Guntis Ulmanis re-elected president

State organization

Latvia is divided into 26 counties and 7 municipalities. The capital is Riga

Constitution and government

The Republic of Latvia (Latvijas Republika) is a constitutional democracy. Power is divided between parliament (*saeima*), the president, the government and the Supreme Court. In 1993, the newly elected parliament restored the constitution of 1922, which had been amended in 1933.

Legal system

Based on civil law system: no judicial review of legislative acts.

Head of state

President of the Republic, elected by parliament for a three-year term (term in office will be extended in two stages to four years).

Guntis ULMANIS has been in office since July 7, 1993, having been re-elected for a second term on June 18, 1996.

Head of government

Prime minister, nominated by the president.

Parliament (*saeima*):

The unicameral parliament has one hundred members, elected every three years on the first Sunday in March (term in office will be extended in two stages to four years). There is a 5% threshold to enter parliament. The last elections were held on September 30/October 1, 1995. The next elections are scheduled for October 1998.

Current government

Prime Minister   Andrijs Shkele, approved December 14, 1995
Foreign Minister   Valdis Birkavs
Finance Minister   Aivar Kreituss

Political parties

There is currently a coalition government, made up of the Democratic Party "Saimnieks", Latvian Unity Party, Alliance "Latvia's Way", Union "For Fatherland and Freedom", Latvian National Conservative Party, Christian Democrats and Farmers' Union

Election results

	% vote	seats
Democratic Party "Saimnieks"	15.2	18
People's Movement for Latvia (Siegerist Party)	14.9	16
Alliance "Latvia's Way"	14.6	17
Union "For Fatherland and Freedom"	11.9	14
Latvian Unity Party	7.1	8
United List of Latvia's Farmers' Union	6.3	8
Latvian Christian Democratic Union		
Latgale Democratic Party		
Latvian National Conservative Party and Latvian Green Party	6.3	8
National Harmony Party	5.6	6
Latvian Socialist Party	5.6	5

Population

Latvia has a small and decreasing population. It was 2.5 million in 1995, having fallen by 36,000 since the beginning of 1994. In 1994 the population comprised 54% ethnic Latvian, 33% ethnic Russian, 4% Belarusian and 2% Polish. (The current proportion of Russians in the population is in contrast to the situation in 1939, prior to the Soviet annexation, when 77% of the population was ethnic Latvian.) Since 1950 the population has become increasingly older, perhaps because of rising levels of healthcare provision and higher standards of living. Estimates of life expectancy in 1995 were 60 years for males and 73 years for females, with birth and death rates standing at 13.7 and 12.5 per 1,000, respectively.

Central bank

The history of the central bank of Latvia begins with the declaration of independence in 1918. The right to issue the national currency was charged to the central bank, the Bank of Latvia, which was founded in September 1922 by the Constitutional Assembly. However, from 1940 to 1990, except for the brief period of German occupation during the Second World War, Latvia was incorporated into the Soviet financial system, during which time the State Bank of the USSR controlled the monetary system in Latvia, and Latvia merely had its own branch of the Soviet State Bank. In 1990 the Bank of Latvia was recreated, although it was not until the collapse of the Soviet Union in 1991 that the bank regained its status as a central bank with the exclusive right to issue the national currency.

The bank is administered by a board of governors, consisting of the governor, the deputy governor and six other members. The governor is appointed by parliament upon the recommendation of the chairman of the parliament, and the other members are appointed by the parliament on the governor's recommendation. Members of the board are appointed for a six-year term.

The objective of the bank is to control the amount of money in circulation to maintain price stability. Legislation grants the central bank independence from government policy. The Minister of Finance is entitled to sit in on meetings of the board of governors of the bank but does not have voting rights on these occasions. The minister can postpone for ten days the execution of a policy chosen by the board, but cannot prevent its execution if the board wishes to uphold its decision. Policy decisions are made by the board of governors, whereas the day-to-day execution of the adopted policies is performed by the executive board, which consists of six members.

Legislation also stipulates that the bank does not have the right to conduct commercial operations. As a consequence the decision was taken to restructure and privatize the bank's forty-nine commercial branches, established during Latvia's years in the Soviet Union.

■ ECONOMICS

Historical overview

During the interwar years Latvia's market-based economy performed reasonably well, trading predominantly with Scandinavia and Western Europe. After annexation by the Soviet Union in 1944, agricultural collectivization and rapid industrialization policies were introduced, with particular attention on heavy industries, such as chemicals and engineering. During this period Latvia grew dependent upon imports of raw materials from the other Soviet states, particularly Russia, and also became a near-monopoly producer of certain manufactured products exported to the other states; Latvia, for example, was the key producer of Soviet railway passenger cars, buses, diesel engines, and radio sets.

Recent developments

After regaining independence in 1991, Latvia adopted a reform package, involving price and trade liberalization, small-scale privatization and macroeconomic stabilization. The process of transition has not been easy, and the first few years of reform were characterized by structural change, industrial stagnation and economic hardship.

However, the macroeconomic stabilization programme has been favourably regarded by international economic institutions. Between 1991 and 1993 GDP fell by more than 50%. Industrial production collapsed in the initial period of reform, falling by 32% in 1992 and 38% in 1993 according to the IMF. Alongside the decline in the industrial sector has been a significant rise in unemployment, which has stabilized at above 6% having risen from 0.2% in 1991. Inflation rose in 1991 to 124% and peaked in November 1992 with 1444.7%.

Economic recovery began in late 1993, although statistical problems, particularly with respect to the shadow economy, make it difficult to gauge its true extent. Latvia adopted tight fiscal and monetary policies to achieve stabilization. In May 1992, the introduction of a new central bank law signalled the shift to a strong anti-inflationary monetary policy. On the fiscal side, Latvia managed to run budget surpluses or small deficits throughout 1991 to 1993. However, recovery was temporarily halted in 1995 by a banking crisis, which had repercussions throughout the rest of the economy. As a consequence of the ensuing payments difficulties, the government was less able to finance its deficit through the Treasury-bill market and had to respond with massive cuts in budget expenditure.

The economy

The main trend in the composition of GDP since independence has been a shift away from agriculture and industry towards services. The agricultural sector has witnessed massive structural change since independence, having been transformed from a centrally planned collectivized agricultural system to a private ownership system.

Share of GDP by sector (1995)

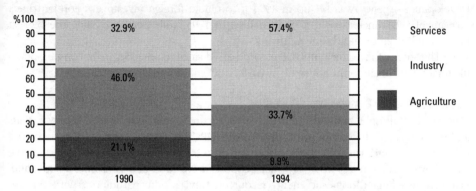

Source: Official data

Productivity decline in agriculture and industrial sector

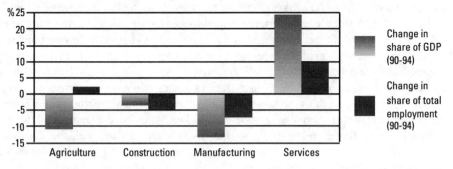

Source: Official data

Privatization created more than 58,000 private farms, some of which, however, may prove to be too small to be financially viable. The combined shock of transition from a centrally planned to a market economy, price liberalization and the breakdown of the Soviet

Union led to a sharp decline the industrial sector's relative importance. However, the drop in share of GDP was not accompanied by a similar drop in employment. Employment in the industrial sector declined less sharply and employment in agriculture even increased. Despite recent signs of industrial recovery, the sector will face more restructuring in order to improve productivity.

One key reason of this development is that the privatization process has failed to change the industrial property structure with any rapidity, resulting in continued dominance of the public sector (see Economic Policy).

Savings and investment

In November 1991 Latvia passed the Foreign Investments in Latvia law, which established two acceptable forms of foreign ventures, namely the joint-stock company and the company with limited liability. The latter is the most commonly used for joint ventures, which have increased in number from only two in 1989 to more than 1,200 in 1995. The Latvian Development Agency was set up in 1994 to promote foreign investment. Foreign direct investment (FDI) increased to US$378 million in 1995, with Denmark being the biggest investor, followed by the US and Germany.

The share of investment in GDP has decreased since reforms began; in constant prices the total fixed capital formation share in GDP fell from 32% in 1990 to only 14% in 1994.

Balance of payments

Latvia is a small open economy, and is highly dependent on international trade; imports and exports account for approximately 70% of GDP. The vast majority of all trade during the Communist era was with the Soviet Union, and 96% of exports were destined for the other Soviet states in 1991. Latvia's main exports were food and consumer goods, and, given its very limited domestic energy resources, Latvia's principal imports were energy-related.

In 1990 more than 90% of total domestic demand for primary energy was satisfied by imports, predominantly from Russia. In early 1992 Latvia suffered a shock in terms of trade when Russia moved to world market prices for fuel exports to the Baltic countries. This 30-40% deterioration in Latvia's terms of trade helped trigger higher inflation in the early years of reform. As prices are further liberalized in Russia, the prices charged to Latvian importers of Russian raw materials may be expected to rise, which could create both inflationary pressures and trade deficits in Latvia in the future.

Since the collapse of the Soviet Union, Latvia's trading partners have changed dramatically. Although Russia remains the largest single market for Latvian exports and the largest supplier of imports, more than 50% of trade is now done with countries outside of the former Soviet Union. The main trend is a sharply rising share of trade with the European Union, especially Germany and Sweden, and a declining share with the members of the Commonwealth of Independent States (CIS). The appreciation of the new national currency, the lats, in 1994 is partly responsible for the shift from a small trade surplus in 1993 to a large trade deficit of LVL300 million in 1994.

Latvia has adopted import tariffs to shelter domestic industry until it is capable of successfully competing in world markets. This policy aims to balance the general process of liberalization of trade with the maximum increase of exports of Latvian commodities and services. Tariff rates fluctuate considerably, depending upon the policy selected by the Tariff Council, although there is a standard tariff of 20% on most imports. For goods that directly compete with those produced by Latvian producers, the imports are often considerably higher. Companies within Latvia can apply for exemptions on imported raw materials and components.

During the first half of 1996 Latvia's most profitable exports were wood and wood products, an industry which has grown substantially in Latvia in recent years in response to rising world timber prices. Other significant exports are textiles, foodstuffs, vehicles, electrical equipment and metals. On the import side fuels, machinery, chemicals and vehicles are most important. Exports to the European Union tend to concentrate in wood products, textiles, base metals and animal products, whereas exports to the CIS are predominantly foodstuffs, vehicles, and mechanical and electrical equipment.

Structure of exports in the first half of 1996

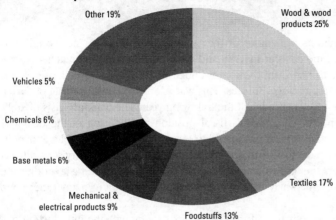

Source: Ministry of the Economy

Foreign trade by country

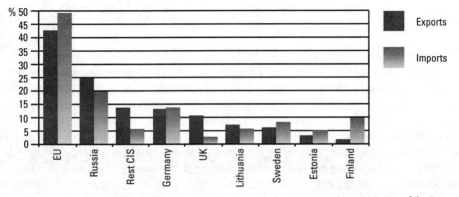

Source: Ministry of the Economy

Economic policy

The privatization programme has been slower in Latvia than in many other former Soviet states. While 83% of small companies had been moved into the private sector by the end of 1994, the figure for larger companies, at only 14%, was less impressive. As a consequence the share of state property in the structure of industry remains dominant, followed by a large and rising share of intermediary property forms, involving public-private and foreign-domestic mixes.

Part of the reason for the slower progress in the privatization programme was due to the lack of a centralized privatization agency. This was rectified in March 1994 by the establishment of the Latvian Privatization Agency, which is largely based on the Estonian equivalent. In addition, a State Property Fund was set up to oversee the operation of those companies still in the public sector. At the beginning of 1995 voucher privatizations commenced, and in July 1995 a stock exchange began trading shares in privatized companies.

Fiscal policy

During Latvia's years as a member of the Soviet Union, it was a net contributor to the Soviet budget, with the transfer in 1988 and 1989 believed to have reached 14% of GDP. When the transfers to and from the centre ended in 1991 with the collapse of the Union, Latvia managed to run a budget surplus. This was short-lived. Rising social outlays plunged the government's finances into deficit the following year. The banking crisis of 1995 placed an added strain on the government's fiscal position as financing of the deficits became more difficult. The government was forced to respond with cuts in public expenditure and delays in wage payments to civil servants, jeopardizing the country's fragile economic recovery. However, the government has succeeded in maintaining a budget deficit of around 3% of GDP, which may be considered small in relation to many other countries in transition.

In 1994, there were major reforms of the tax system, with the introduction of 25% flat rate corporate and income taxes, replacing the previous progressive tax rate system. However, the financial crisis of 1994-95 led to the introduction of an additional 10% tax rate on top of the flat rate for higher income earners. As a consequence, the relative contribution of personal income tax to government revenue rose significantly in 1995, although the social tax and value-added tax remain the most important sources of revenue at about 36% and 29%, respectively.

Currency

At an early stage of the adjustment programme Latvia introduced its own currency, enabling the Bank of Latvia to pursue an independent monetary policy. The transition from Soviet roubles to a Latvian national currency was performed in two stages. In May 1992, Latvia introduced a parallel currency, the Latvian rouble, which circulated in addition to the Soviet rouble. Later that year, Latvia left the Soviet rouble bloc and the Latvian rouble became effectively the sole legal tender. In March 1993, once the Latvian rouble was sufficiently strong the new national monetary unit of Latvia, the lats, was introduced. On October 18, 1993 the freely floating Latvian rouble ceased to be legal tender and the lats became the sole currency. Since February 1994 the Bank of Latvia has operated a currency-board-type exchange rate system, with the monetary base almost fully backed by gold and foreign exchange reserves. The exchange rate was fixed to the Special Drawing Rights basket of currencies at a rate of LVL0.799:SDR1. (The currencies within the SDR currency basket are the US dollar, the British pound, the German deutschmark, the Japanese yen and the French franc). Latvia has adopted a fixed exchange rate with the aim of reducing uncertainty and eliminating exchange rate risk. The Bank has achieved full convertibility of the lats, for both current account and capital account purposes; there are absolutely no restrictions on capital account transactions and capital movements, therefore allowing foreigners to repatriate profits in any currency. Both Latvian residents and foreigners are allowed to open accounts in lats and foreign currencies without any restrictions.

■ EQUITIES

Index performance (in local currency)
There is no index in Latvia.

Background
The Riga Stock Exchange (RSE) was established in December 1993. It is a non-profitmaking joint stock company. Trading began in the summer of 1995. The market was launched with the help of the SBF-Paris Bourse and the Central Depository of France. The RSE is the only licensed securities exchange in Latvia.

Structure
The market is divided between the Central Market (CM) and the Block Market (BM). The CM comprises the Official List, which has strict listing requirements, and a less stringent Second List. On the BM large blocks of securities are traded, with the RSE ensuring clearing and settlement procedures. Currently, there are only two equities listed on the Official List (Unibanka and Rigas Transporta Hote) and twenty-five equities listed on the Second List.

Regulatory authority
The RSE is supervised by the Securities Market Commission (SMC). However, until the SMC is formally established, the Ministry of Finance acts as regulator.

Trading methods
Trading on the RSE occurs in an order-driven, centralized manner. Brokers submit orders to the Exchange for price matching. In each trading session a security's price is fixed for all participants. Prices are set in order to maximize turnover.

Hours
Trading days are Tuesday, Wednesday and Thursday. Buy and sell orders are submitted from 10.00 and the Stock Exchange opens at 11.00.

Settlement time and clearing

Settlement takes place on a trade plus three business days (T+3 basis). The clearing process is undertaken by the Latvian Central Depository (LCD). All public issues must be registered at the LCD.

Limits on price movement

Prices are not permitted to fluctuate by more than 15% during a trading session.

Types of shares

Ordinary shares are traded on the RSE.

Stock indices

There are no stock indices published by the RSE.

Taxes

A tax of 0.1% is charged for transactions on the CM and a set fee of LTL10 for direct transactions. Dividends are subject to a withholding tax of 10%. Interest income is charged at 10% for related parties (including all offshore companies) and 0% for non-related parties.

Disclosure of financial statements

Listed companies are required to submit quarterly financial reports and an audited annual report.

Shareholders' rights

Shareholders must own a minimum 5% of equity to attend an emergency general meeting. Shareholders with 10% or more of equity have the right to inspect companies' financial reports, require the supervisory board to inspect the commercial operations of management, propose issues for discussion at the general meeting and propose the liquidation of a joint stock company.

Shareholders with more than 25% of equity can require the Company Register to approve the foundation process of a company and postpone the approval of the annual report until an extraordinary general meeting.

Ownership limits for non-residents

There are no limits on foreign ownership, but they must report to the SMC within three days and the issuer within ten days after acquiring 10%, 25% and 33.3% of shares in a company.

Capital and foreign exchange controls

Profits are freely repatriated, currency is freely convertible.

Brokers
Brokers and brokerage departments of banks are the sole entities allowed to trade on the RSE. There are thirteen brokerages on the RSE, which charge varying rates of commission between 0.5% and 1.3%. However, typically, a charge of 1% can be expected.

Sectors
The two companies on the Official List, Unibanka (a bank) and Rigas Transporta Hote (in the transport sector), dominate the RSE with a combined market capitalization of around LVL55 million (US$100 million) or 88% of total capitalization. Because of the limited number of listings on the RSE, there is no official market analysis by sector.

ADRs
There are no Latvian ADRs.

Derivatives
There is no derivatives market in Latvia.

■ DEBT

The Bank of Latvia regulates the domestic bond market, and organizes primary auctions as the agent of the Ministry of Finance. The central bank also awards licences to commercial banks permitting them to trade bills in the secondary market. Dealers must be members of the Riga Stock Exchange and the Central Depository of Latvia, which is owned by the central bank.

Treasury Bills
Bills are issued at a discount in registered form by the Ministry of Finance for 1, 3, 6 and 12 months. Yields are calculated on an actual/360-day basis.

Only Latvian commercial banks can directly participate in auctions. Foreigners, like domestic investors, must open a securities account with a local bank, which enables them to participate indirectly in the primary market and trade in the secondary markets. Hence, there are no restrictions for overseas investment.

One-month bills are auctioned every Wednesday and 3-month bills each month. Successful competitive bids are filled at the bid price submitted, for settlement 2 days later. There are no non-competitive bids. Bills trade on the Riga Stock Exchange and are settled on the same day.

Mortgage bonds
One Latvian bank, Latvijas Hipoteku un Zemes banka, has issued mortgage bonds, which are listed on the stock market. Trading in the bonds is thin.

Eurobonds

In August 1995, Latvia raised 4,000 million yen with a 2-year eurobond, paying a coupon of 5.4% and priced to yield a spread of 378 basis points over Japanese Government Bonds. In addition, the municipality of Riga plans to issue bonds in the eurobond market.

Eurobond issues (US$m)

	1990	1991	1992	1993	1994	1995	1996
Sovereign	—	—	—	—	—	45.0	—
Private	—	—	—	—	—	—	—

■ LATVIA: Economic indicators

Population and development	1990	1991	1992	1993	1994	1995	1996e
Population, million	2.67	2.66	2.61	2.58	2.57	2.53	2.51
Population growth, %	-0.22	-0.41	-1.92	-1.15	-0.23	-1.56	-0.80
Nominal GDP per capita, US$	7751	280	511	918	1362	1779	2152

National accounts							
Nominal GDP, US$bn	20.68	0.74	1.33	2.36	3.50	4.50	5.40
Change in real GDP, %	-3.50	-8.30	-33.80	-11.70	0.60	-1.60	2.50
Gross fixed capital formation, % of GDP	—	—	—	—	15.80	14.50	15.50

Money supply and inflation							
Narrow money, change %, Dec/Dec	—	—	—	—	31.1	0.8	9.0
Broad money, change %, Dec/Dec	—	—	—	—	50.3	-21.4	11.8
Consumer price inflation (avg.) %	10.5	124.5	951.2	109.1	36.6	25.2	18.0

Interest rates							
Discount rate, end of year	—	—	—	27.00	25.00	24.00	10.00
Money market rate, monthly average	—	—	—	—	37.18	22.39	14.00
Treasury bill rate, monthly average	—	—	—	—	—	28.24	17.40
Deposit rate, monthly average	—	—	—	34.78	31.68	14.79	12.10
Prime lending rate, monthly average	—	—	—	86.36	55.86	34.56	26.50

Government finance							
Government expenditure, % of GDP	—	11.1	31.9	29.5	27.6	18.9	18.0
Government balance, % of GDP	—	8.1	-1.4	25.1	-2.0	-3.7	-1.3

Exchange rates lc=local currency							
Exchange rate, annual average, lc/US$	0.59	30.00	136.60	0.67	0.56	0.53	0.51
Exchange rate, end of year, lc/US$	0.60	90.00	168.50	0.67	0.56	0.52	0.51

Balance of payments							
Exports of goods & services, US$m	—	4403	1091	1587	1657	2066	2500
Change %	—	—	—	45.5	4.4	24.7	21.0
Imports of goods & services, US$m, fob	—	5272	996	1256	1597	1974	2450
Change %	—	—	—	26.1	27.1	23.6	24.1
Trade balance, of goods only, US$m, fob-fob	—	-869	-40	3	-300	-600	-700
Current account balance, US$m	—	-120	193	416	202	0	-0.1
as a % of GDP	—	-0.6	14.5	17.6	5.8	-0.6	-3.9

Foreign exchange reserves							
Foreign exchange reserves, US$m	—	24.4	71.2	230.0	460.0	420.0	600.0
Import cover (reserves/imports), months	—	—	0.9	2.2	3.5	2.6	2.9

Foreign debt and debt service							
Total foreign debt, US$m	—	60	65	73	400	400	600
as a % of GDP	—	8.1	4.9	3.1	11.4	8.9	11.1
as a % of foreign exchange receipts	—	—	5.5	4.3	21.7	19.4	36.3
Interest payments, US$m	—	—	6	7	7	30	40
Principal repayments, US$m	—	—	13	15	20	40	50
Total debt service, US$m	—	—	19	22	27	70	90
as a % of goods exports	—	—	2.4	2.1	2.7	5.4	5.6
as a % of foreign exchange receipts	—	—	1.6	1.3	1.5	3.4	6.5

Lithuania

Area (thousands of km^2):	65
Population (1995, millions):	3.7
Population projection (2025, millions):	4
Population younger than 15 yrs (1991, % of total):	22.5
Urbanization rate (1993, % of population):	71
Life expectancy (1993, years at birth):	70
Gross domestic product (1996, US$bn):	7.6
GDP per capita (1996, US$):	2051
Average annual GDP growth rate (1990-96, %):	-9.1
Average annual inflation rate (1990-96, %):	256.8
Currency (litas per US$, average 1996):	4
Structure of production (1994):	57% services, 34% industry, 9% agriculture
Main exports:	mineral, textiles, chemical products
Main imports:	machines, textiles, chemical products
Main trading partners:	Russia, Germany, Latvia, Ukraine
Total foreign debt (% of GDP):	17.1
Next elections due under normal circumstances:	2000
Credit rating: (Nov 1996, Standard & Poor's, Moody's)	Ba2

FORECAST: 1997-2000 (average)

	Worst case	Most likely	Best case
Real GDP growth (%)	1 to 3	4 to 7	5 to 8
Inflation (%)	20 to 30	10 to 20	5 to 10

■ POLITICS

Historical overview

The formation of Lithuania dates back to 1230, with the establishment of the Grand Duchy of Lithuania by the country's first grand duke, Mindaugas, crowned king in 1251. In 1385 Grand Duke Jogaila married Queen Jadvyga of Poland and established the union of crowns between Lithuania and Poland.

With the union of Lublin in 1569, the Lithuanian-Polish kingdom was merged in a commonwealth, ruled by a monarch. In 1795, Russia annexed Lithuania and started a period of russification. By the end of the 19th century, however, anti-Russian sentiment was growing, and led Lithuania to use the opportunity presented by the aftermath of the First World War to declare its independence from Russia. A constitution creating a parliamentary democracy was adopted in 1922, but a successful military coup in 1926 by the nationalist Tartinkai Party led to the establishment of a dictatorship. In 1939 Lithuania lost its independence when the Nazi-Soviet pact was signed. Attempts to secure independence from the Soviet Union and the invading German army during the Second World War proved ineffective, and Lithuania returned to Soviet rule when Soviet forces recaptured the country in 1944.

Under the Soviet Union's policy of glasnost in the 1980s, the Lithuanian press became more open and the independence movement gained increasing recognition. In October 1988, the Lithuanian Movement for Restructuring (Sajudis), founded only four months earlier, persuaded the Lithuanian Communist Party (LCP), part of the Lithuanian branch of the Communist Party of the Soviet Union (CPSU), to support the campaign for independence. Later that year Algirdas Brazauskas, the reformist leader of the LCP, broke the party's links with the CPSU. In February 1990 the Sajudis won the first free elections to the Supreme Council, and on March 11, 1990 the Supreme Council declared the restoration of Lithuanian independence. Moscow responded with economic sanctions and embargoes on fuel and sent Soviet troops to seize government buildings in Vilnius, the Lithuanian capital, leaving thirteen dead.

Recent events

Mounting pressure from the Kremlin forced the declaration of independence to be suspended in June 1990, only to be re-instated in January 1991 by Vytautas Landsbergis, chairman of the Lithuanian Supreme Council. In the aftermath of the failed coup in Moscow in August 1991 independence was finally achieved, and the collapse of the Soviet Union followed. By the end of the 1992 Lithuania had become a member of the United Nations and had been admitted to the IMF and World Bank. But all three Baltic states refused to participate in the Commonwealth of Independent States (CIS).

In October 1992 the renamed Communist Party, the Lithuanian Democratic Labour Party (LDDP), won a convincing victory over the Sajudis in the parliamentary elections and established a government that restored relations with Russia, and in February 1993 Mr Brazauskas, then leader of the LDDP, won the presidential elections.

The LDDP's grip on power suffered setbacks in 1995, notably when a government scandal, involving the collapse of the two largest banks in the country, engulfed the prime minister, Adolfas Slezevicius. Slezevicius survived two no-confidence motions in 1995, but was eventually forced to resign by President Brazauskas in February 1996. His replacement, Mindaugas Stankevicius, formed a new LDDP government. After parliamentary elections in October 1996, the Conservative Homeland Union and the Christian Democrats formed a new coalition government.

Chronology

1230	Creation of Grand Duchy of Lithuania, under Grand Duke Mindaugas
1385-1795	Various forms of unification with Poland
1410	Battle of Grunwald (Zalgiris, or Tannenwald), defeat of Teutonic order
1569	Union of Lublin, Lithuania and Poland form a Commonwealth
1795	Lithuania comes under Russian rule
1918	Lithuania declares independence from Russia
1926	Successful military coup by the nationalist Tartinkai Party results in a dictatorship under Andenaes Smetona

1939	Nazi-Soviet pact places Lithuania under Soviet rule; invasion by USSR
1941-1944	German invasion of Lithuania
1944	Lithuania re-occupied by USSR
1988	Sajudis (Lithuanian Movement for Restructuring) set up
1988	Lithuanian Communist Party (LCP) expresses support for independence
1989	LCP breaks off links with the Communist Party of the Soviet Union
1990	Lithuanian independence reinstated but invasion by Soviet troops and economic embargoes force reversal
1991	Independence finally achieved on September 6, after failed coup in Moscow
1992	Lithuania admitted to IMF and the World Bank
1992	Lithuanian Democratic Labour Party (LDDP) wins resounding victory in general election
1993	Algirdas Brazauskas, Chairman of the LDDP, wins the presidential election
1995	Municipal elections won by the Fatherland Union
1995	Political tension concerning government ministers' response to collapse of the two largest banks in Lithuania
1996	Homeland Union and Christian Democrats form new government after winning parliamentary elections

Constitution and government

The constitution initially adopted in 1992 by the newly independent Republic of Lithuania was a modified version of the Soviet-style constitution. Adjustments to the constitution were made following a referendum in October 1992 when the people voted for a more parliamentary approach, in contrast to the attempts of the Sajudis government to establish a stronger presidency.

The current constitution of Lithuania was adopted by referendum on October 25, 1992. The powers of the state are exercised by the Seimas (parliament), the president, the government, and the judiciary. Law is adopted by parliament if the majority of the members participating in the sitting vote in favour.

The Seimas is a inicameral parliament with 141 members, who are elected for a four-year term on the basis of universal, equal and direct suffrage. The parliament is deemed elected when at least three-fifths of its members have been elected.

President

The president is the head of state and has the power to appoint and dismiss the prime minister with the approval of the legislature (the Seimas). The president is elected by the citizens of Lithuania and cannot serve more than two consecutive terms. The president may be removed from office only for gross violation of the constitution, breach of the oath of office, or conviction of an offence.

Prime minister

The prime minister is the head of government and nominates the members of the cabinet, known as the Council of Ministers. Once nominated by the prime minister, the president must approve the composition of the government and then appoint the ministers. The government must resign if the majority of all the parliament deputies express a lack of confidence in the government or in the prime minister.

Current government

President	Algirdas Brazauskas
Prime Minister	Gediminas Vagnorius
Chairman, central bank	Reinoldijus Sharkinas

Political parties

There are twelve political parties in Lithuania's parliament. The ruling government is a coalition between the Conservative Party, led by Vytautas Landsbergis, and the Christian Democratic Party, led by Algirdas Saudargas. The new government is expected to speed up reforms. The former ruling party, the Democratic Labour Party, lost 61 seats and has been relegated to the opposition benches. Other parties include the Centre Union and the Social Democratic Party.

Results of the October/November 1996 parliamentary elections

	seats
Conservative Party CP (Homeland Union)	70
Lithuanian Christian Democratic Party LDCP	16
Centre Union of Lithuania CU	13
Lithuanian Social Democratic Party LSDP	12
Lithuanian Democratic Labour Party LDDP	12
Others	14

Next election
October 2000

Local government

There are fifty-six communes, which are self-governed through local government councils. Members of these councils are elected for two-year terms on the basis of universal, equal and direct suffrage by all Lithuanian citizens resident in their administrative unit. In 1995 there was political reform of local government. Elections to self-governing councils were held under a new proportional elective system, and the Lithuanian Association of Self-Governments was founded to protect the interests of self-governments and represent them at state authority institutions. Also in 1995 ten higher administrative units, called counties, were established. These are governed by district governors, who are appointed by the national government.

Central bank

One of the first fundamental reforms adopted by newly independent Lithuania was the establishment of a central bank, the Bank of Lithuania. It is owned by the state and has the exclusive right to issue bank notes, the litas. The bank is directed by a bank board, consisting of the chairman, the deputies to the chairman, and the board members. The chairman is appointed for a five-year term by parliament on the nomination of the president.

Compared to the central banks of other Baltic states, the Bank of Lithuania has a relative lack of independence.

■ ECONOMICS

Recent developments

In the post-Second World War period when Lithuania was under Soviet rule, the Lithuanian economy was restructured along Soviet lines, with collectivization of agriculture, Soviet-style industrialization, and central planning from Moscow.

Since independence in September 1991, Lithuania has advanced rapidly towards a market economy through the adoption of comprehensive stabilization and reform programmes. An extensive privatization programme has transferred nearly 50% of state property (mainly small and medium enterprises) into the private sector, and trade has gradually shifted away from former Soviet markets to Western markets.

Lithuania has experienced economic hardship during the transition from state planning to a market economy, however. In response to Lithuania's declaration of independence in 1990, Moscow initiated a fuel embargo, crippling the economy, which is dependent on external energy, particularly Russian natural gas and petroleum, for almost two-thirds of its fuel requirements.

Even when relations with Russia had improved, Russia penalized Lithuania for not joining the Commonwealth of Independent States (CIS) by charging world prices for fuel, rather than the lower price charged to CIS members. Both GDP and industrial output in Lithuania suffered from this shock, which created severe energy shortages in 1992. In 1993 industrial output was less than half the 1991 level, and in 1992 alone GDP fell by 35%.

Real growth and consumer prices

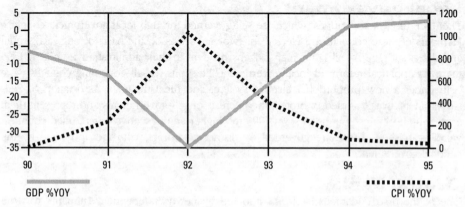

Source: Official data

The terms of trade shock and high inflation during early 1992 required rapid action to prevent a prolonged decline in output. By 1994 Lithuania appeared to have pulled out of recession, although estimates of the extent of the recovery vary. Recovery was hindered by the 1995 banking crisis, which had both economic and political ramifications. In 1994 the IMF granted an extended funding facility to Lithuania as an official endorsement of its economic policies, the latest tranche of which was approved in June 1996.

Population

Lithuania's population is 3.7 million, growing at 0.2% a year, with the male to female ratio at 47.5 to 52.5. Since 1950 the population has grown by nearly 50% and the structure has become increasingly elderly. The strongest proportionate growth over the 1950-95 period was in the economically active 25-59 age group, which stood at about 46% of the population in 1995. Life expectancy in Lithuania stands at 67 years for males and 76 years for females. The birth rate in 1993 was 13 per 1,000 and the death rate was 11 per 1,000.

The composition of the population is as follows: 80.1% Lithuanians, 8.6% Russians, 7.7% Poles, and 3.6% people of other nationalities. Approximately 68% of the population live in urban areas, compared to 32% in rural areas.

The economy

The composition of Lithuanian GDP has changed markedly since independence. In 1989 industry and agriculture were the two largest sectors, totalling more than 60% of GDP. The collapse of industry following the disintegration of the Soviet Union significantly reduced the share of industry, and unsuccessful privatization of agriculture combined with a severe drought in 1992 served to decrease its relative contribution. The agricultural sector has been further hindered by the poor payment record of food-processing companies, which are the main purchasers of their produce. Attempts to encourage more entrepreneurial farmers to expand their holdings were introduced at the beginning of 1994, when Lithuania passed a law permitting the transfer of land between citizens.

Most industrial companies are engaged in producing machinery and machine parts, food processing and light industrial products. Within agriculture, animal husbandry is dominant and the main crops are grain, maize, potatoes, fodder crops, sugarbeet and flax.

Share of GDP by sector

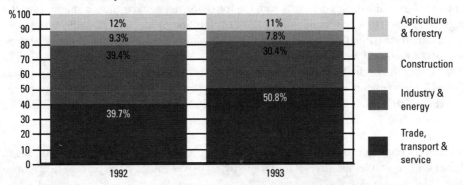

Source: Lithuanian Investment Agency

According to the Lithuanian Ministry of Statistics data, trade and services are the most important sectors of the economy, accounting for nearly half of GDP between them. These two sectors are also the most highly privatized, and were the only two sectors to record an increase in employment between 1984 and 1992.

Savings and investment

Lithuania has been cautious about the extent of foreign investment it permits. In 1992 it amended its foreign investment law so that foreign investors are allowed to acquire shares in newly privatized enterprises as well as to establish companies, and a 1996 amendment allowed foreign investors to own non-agricultural land. However, this amendment does not come into force until all fifteen European Union members have ratified the EU Association agreement signed in 1995.

Joint ventures are the most popular form of foreign investment. Foreigners are still not allowed to invest in certain strategic industries, such as defence, public utilities and energy exploration, and face restrictions in transport and communications. Foreign investment is being encouraged, however, in some projects that have been given special priority, such as the completion of a hydrostation, construction of an oil terminal in Butinge, and the reconstruction of Zokniai airport.

There are a number of international financial institutions providing loans and/or guarantees to investments in the Baltic states, including the World Bank, International Finance Corporation, European Bank for Reconstruction and Development, and the European Investment Bank. By the end of 1995 Lithuania had received loans in excess of US$730 million.

Balance of payments

The former Soviet Union remains Lithuania's main trading partner, although the main trend in its foreign trade is the increasing share with non-Commonwealth of Independent States (non-CIS) countries. This is reflected in the rising proportion of Lithuanian exports to European Union and Nordic countries. The neighbouring Nordic countries in particular have strong purchasing power and high labour costs, so provide an obvious market for low cost exporters. Although Lithuania's trade mix has altered significantly since independence, it has none the less maintained good links with the former Soviet markets. Russia still remains the biggest trading partner, accounting for 20% of exports and 31% of imports in 1994. Lithuania lacks important natural resources other than agricultural land and remains dependent on imports of fuels and raw materials.

Under the centrally planned Soviet regime, trade outside of the Communist bloc was minimal and exporters were restricted through a system of licences. Import and export control is now carried out through customs tariffs. In 1992-93, liberalization of exports replaced licences with tariffs and abolished most export quotas.

Import tariffs vary from 5% to 25%, with the higher rates used on products such as tobacco, alcohol and some manufactured goods. Agricultural tariffs, except those on sugar, butter and vegetable oils, are set to decline by 60% over the next six years in accordance with Lithuania's Free Trade Agreement with the European Union, which came into effect on January 1, 1995. Lithuania is also a member of the Baltic Free Trade Association and has Most Favoured Nation status with all members of the OECD except Japan.

Breakdown of exports (1995)

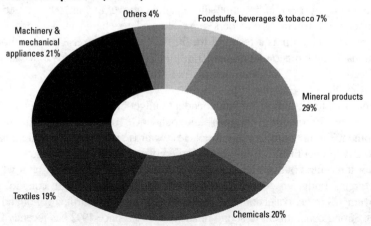

Others 4%

Foodstuffs, beverages & tobacco 7%

Machinery & mechanical appliances 21%

Mineral products 29%

Textiles 19%

Chemicals 20%

Source: Department of Statistics to the Government of the Republic of Lithuania

Economic policy

Privatization in Lithuania began in 1991, largely based on a voucher system. This was used principally to transfer farms and housing into the private sector and, at its close in 1996, was estimated to have privatized 45% of all state assets. The government has made plans for a second wave of privatizations, based on cash sales of large state enterprises. This is due to commence in January 1997, when as many as 1,700 companies will be sold. Some fear that such a system may jeopardize Lithuania's strategic interests, particularly if large stakes in its energy sector are bought up by Russian corporations. In response to these criticisms, the government has set up an independent privatization agency to co-ordinate strategy and investment interests. The head of the privatization commission has announced that even companies within the energy, transport and communication sectors may soon be privatized.

Monetary policy

Under Russian rule, Lithuania had very low inflation, because the centrally planned system involved the control of virtually all prices. But once the Soviet Union collapsed, the price of energy charged by Russia rose. The authorities were forced to pass these cost increases on to consumers. The higher price of resources, combined with the removal of food subsidies, led to an explosion of prices, with inflation reaching 1,021% in 1992.

Initial undervaluation of the currency may explain a large part of the inflation experience, with price increases, rather than changes in the exchange rate, being the chief channel for real appreciation until mid-1993.

Under its reform programme Lithuania strove to re-align domestic prices with world prices by rapidly completing price and trade liberalization. The Baltic countries were quick to introduce their own currencies to insulate themselves from inflationary pressure in the former Soviet Union. Following the introduction of the new currency, the litas, in June 1993, and a change in the management of the Bank of Lithuania in October 1993, monetary policy was tightened by an increase in the reserve requirement ratio and by making foreign currency deposits subject to reserve requirements.

The programme of economic stabilization successfully brought inflation down to double figures by 1994, although it still remained above 30% in 1995. In 1995 prices were fully liberalized when shopkeepers were allowed to charge market prices. Inflationary pressures may pick up as a result of the 1996 increases in excise taxes, although calls for reductions in the tariffs on food imports may help in the fight against price increases.

Fiscal policy

Lithuania adopted its first wholly independent budget in 1991, after budgetary links with the former Soviet Union were ended by independence. Under its stabilization policies, the government attempted to gear fiscal policies towards achieving balanced budgets, to avoid inflationary budget financing. The IMF set the government stringent targets of 5% and 1% of GDP for the central budget deficit in 1993 and 1994 respectively. After narrowly missing the 1994 target, budgetary discipline has been tightened, through cuts in expenditure, improvements in tax collection, and higher excise taxes on petrol, alcohol and high-tar cigarettes. Strong commitment to sound financial policies since 1992 has recently helped establish the credibility of strong monetary policies. In July 1994, the Bank of Lithuania started Treasury Bill auctions to partially finance the deficit.

Currency

To insulate the domestic economy from economic shocks in Russia, Lithuania introduced an interim coupon currency, the talonas, in May 1992. However, the talonas circulated in parallel and at par with the rouble until October 1992, and stability was not achieved. Only in June 1993 was a permanent currency, the litas, introduced.

Tighter monetary policy during the first year of its introduction caused the litas to appreciate against the US dollar, damaging the industrial and export base. In response to this appreciation and the resultant interest group pressure exerted on the monetary authorities Lithuania adopted a currency board system in April 1994 whereby the litas was pegged to the US dollar at a rate of 4 to 1, although initially the currency was not fully backed by net reserves.

Expectations of a devaluation in early 1995 were not fulfilled, although technically the collapse of the dollar at the beginning of 1995 dragged the value of the litas down. While in 1996 there have been calls for a looser system of exchange rates, the currency board system is likely to prevail until late 1997.

The Law on Foreign Exchange limits the use of foreign currencies in the country. In order to undertake transactions in foreign currencies, institutions must obtain general licences from the Bank of Lithuania.

■ EQUITIES

Index performance (in local currency)

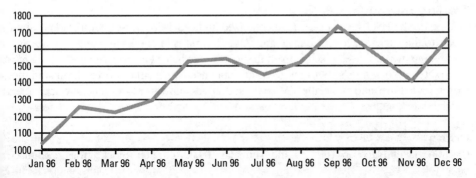

Key indicators

	Index performance %, in US$ terms	Market Cap. US$bn	P/E	Div. Yield
1994	—	0.04	31.6	17.7
1995	—	0.2	9.8	—
1996	8.1	0.9	-23.9	1.2

Source: National Stock Exchange of Lithuania, IFC, Bloomberg, Datastream, UBS

Background

Although the Vllinius Stock Exchange traded between 1926 and 1936, Lithuania does not have a grand history of stock market activity. However, following independence in 1990, the Stock Exchange of Lithuania was established to serve the mass privatization programme. During early September 1992, the government of Lithuania, with the help of SBF-Bourse de Paris, established the National Stock Exchange of Lithuania (NSEL). The first trading session was on September 13, 1993, and capitalization reached LTL3080 million (US$770 million) by November 1996. However, equities only play a small part, with government securities accounting for over two-thirds of total value.

Structure

The NSEL is split between the Central Market (CM) and the Block Market (BM). The vast majority (95%) of turnover occurs on the BM. On the CM, companies are listed on the Current Trading List, which is divided between Groups A and B. For a Group A listing, companies must adhere to certain criteria including a statement of profit and at least three months' trading history.

Companies not meeting Group A's criteria are listed on Group B. In addition to the Current List, there are plans to introduce an Official Trading List in the near future. At present 454 securities are traded on the Stock Exchange Current Trading List, 209 of which are quoted.

Regulatory authority

The NSEL is regulated by the Securities Commission.

Trading methods

Trading on the NSEL takes place in a centralized and order-driven manner. Brokers submit orders to the Exchange for price matching. All transactions in one-issue shares are executed at the same market price, which is fixed in order to maximize turnover. In addition, there is a market for block trades, but they have no influence over market price. The majority of shares traded are traded on the CM. Banking shares, however, are generally transacted through block trades.

Hours

CM trade takes place on Tuesday and Thursday, 09.00 to 12.00. Block trades take place daily.

Settlement time and clearing

Settlement takes place on a trade day plus three business days (T+3) basis. Settlement is performed by the Settlement Centre of the Bank of Lithuania, the clearing bank, and is supervised by the Settlement and Clearing Department of the Exchange.

Limits on price movement

Limits vary from 0% to 100%, but 20% is the most common.

Types of shares

Shares are traded in public companies, investment companies and banks.

Stock indices

On October 24, 1996 the NSEL unveiled the National Stock Exchange Index (LITIN), which it had been recording from January. LITIN is a capitalization-weighted, price-based index based on IFC methodology. The LITIN takes two forms: the LITIN-A, which incorporates the twenty-three shares of the twenty-two companies in Group A of the Current Trading List; and LITIN-G, which includes all securities listed on the Current List.

Taxes

Transaction fees range from 2.5% on for deals up to US$20,000 to 0.5% for deals in excess of US$2.5 million. Dividends to foreign investors are tax-free.

Disclosure of financial statements

Companies must disclose annual and biannual reports.

Ownership limits for non-residents

There are some limits on foreign ownership for banks (where 10% is the maximum stake permitted) and other sectors deemed to be of strategic importance, where a 30% limit is imposed.

Capital and foreign exchange controls
Profits can be freely repatriated.

Brokers
There are three classifications of brokerages on the NSEL: Brokerage Companies of Banks (of which there are twelve), A-category Brokerage Companies, and B-category Brokerage Companies (twenty-seven). B-category Brokerage Companies are not officially approved by the Securities Commission.

Sectors
The largest single listing on the Exchange is Mazeikiu nafta, an oil processing company, which has a market capitalization of LTL838 million (US$209 million). This is more than double the capitalization of the next largest company, Lietuvos dujos (a gas supplier). Clearly, energy-related industries dominate the NSEL.

ADRs
There are no Lithuanian ADRs, but there is a GDR (Vilniaus Bankas).

Derivatives
There is no derivatives market in Lithuania.

■ DEBT

In 1995, trading of government securities constituted 70% of total turnover on the National Stock Exchange of Lithuania (NSEL). They are the most liquid of all securities, including equities, that are currently traded. There is no corporate bond issuance in the domestic market.

The market is regulated by the Central Securities Depository of Lithuania and the Bank of Lithuania, which are authorized by the Securities Law 1994.

Lithuanian government securities
Issue sizes average 50 to 55 million LTL, and are auctioned by the Bank of Lithuania for 1-, 3- and 6-month maturities. Bids can be competitive or non-competitive. Multiple bids are accepted on a yield basis, with priority given to the lowest yields tendered.

By far the largest investors are commercial banks. There are no restrictions on non-resident purchases; repatriated profits are not taxed. At times, participation by foreigners has exceeded 40% of the total bids submitted at treasury bill auctions.

In the past, bills were traded every Tuesday at the NSEL. Increased turnover in 1995 prompted the NSEL to allow block trading and to conduct trading sessions in two cycles, five days a week. Transactions are executed at the highest offer price, if matched by a buy order. Each cycle ends in the registration of all trades; orders that were not, or only partly, executed are carried over to the second cycle. Other innovations were also introduced, including computer-based trading – brokers submit orders through e-mail facilities.

Trades are settled for delivery versus payment the day after the transaction, through the Settlement Centre of the Bank of Lithuania. Securities are registered in book-entry form at the Central Securities Depository. Broking firms contribute to a Guarantee Fund to indemnify victims of default or fraud.

The market received a setback at the end of 1995 following the Lithuanian banking crisis. Two of the country's largest banks, Litimpeks and Joint-Stock Innovation, who were also important participants in the government securities market, became bankrupt.

Eurobonds

Lithuania has issued eurobonds denominated in US dollars (and also Japanese samurai bonds). Its maiden issue was in December 1995, when the Republic launched a US$60 million 2-year bond, paying a 10% coupon which was priced to yield a spread of 445 basis points over US Treasuries. Eight months later, Lithuania was able to issue a second 2-year eurodollar bond at a tighter spread of 375 basis points.

Eurobond issues (US$m)

	1990	1991	1992	1993	1994	1995	1996
Sovereign	—	—	—	—	—	60.0	100.0
Private	—	—	—	—	—	—	—

■ LITHUANIA: Economic indicators

Population and development	1990	1991	1992	1993	1994	1995	1996e
Population, million	—	—	3.7	3.7	3.7	3.7	3.8
Population growth, %	—	—	—	-0.3	-0.3	-0.3	1.3
Nominal GDP per capita, US$	—	—	511	686	1148	1606	1916

National accounts							
Nominal GDP, US$bn	—	—	1.9	2.6	4.3	6.0	7.2
Change in real GDP, %	—	—	—	-30.3	1.0	3.0	3.5

Money supply and inflation							
Narrow money, change %, Dec/Dec	—	—	—	—	—	41.7	—
Broad money, change %, Dec/Dec	—	—	—	—	105.0	14.3	—
Consumer price inflation (avg.) %	—	—	—	409.6	72.1	39.1	25.0
Producer prices (avg.) %	—	—	—	397.10	30.90	28.30	15.80

Interest rates							
Money market rate, monthly average	—	—	—	—	69.50	26.80	21.00
Treasury bill rate, monthly average	—	—	—	—	—	26.90	22.58
Deposit rate, monthly average	—	—	—	48.70	27.40	8.40	6.00
Prime lending rate, monthly average	—	—	—	91.90	62.30	27.10	22.60

Government finance							
Government expenditure, % of GDP	—	—	—	22.3	25.3	25.5	25.0
Government balance, % of GDP	—	—	—	—	-1.8	-1.7	-1.7

Exchange rates lc=local currency							
Exchange rate, annual average, lc/US$	—	—	1.77	4.34	3.98	4.00	4.00
Exchange rate, end of year, lc/US$	—	—	3.79	3.90	4.00	4.00	4.00

Balance of payments							
Exports of goods & services, US$m	—	—	—	2224	2351	3191	3990
Change %	—	—	—	—	5.7	35.7	25.0
Imports of goods & services, US$m, fob	—	—	—	2433	2611	3902	5540
Change %	—	—	—	—	7.3	49.5	42.0
Trade balance, of goods only, US$m, fob-fob	—	—	—	-155	-205	-300	-600
Current account balance, US$m	—	—	—	-86	-94	-614	-500
as a % of GDP	—	—	—	-3.4	-2.2	-10.3	-6.6

Foreign exchange reserves							
Foreign exchange reserves, US$m	—	—	45.3	350.4	525.5	757.1	800.0
Gold at ⅔ of market price, US$m	—	—	42.5	44.5	47.6	47.6	47.6
Import cover (reserves/imports), months	—	—	—	1.7	2.4	2.3	2.4

Foreign debt and debt service							
Total foreign debt, US$m	—	—	—	—	—	800	1300
as a % of GDP	—	—	—	—	—	13.3	17.1

Malaysia

Area (thousands of km²):	330
Population (1995, millions):	20.1
Population projection (2025, millions):	30
Population younger than 15 yrs (1991, % of total):	38.6
Urbanization rate (1993, % of population):	52
Life expectancy (1993, years at birth):	71
Gross domestic product (1996, US$bn):	95.4
GDP per capita (1996, US$):	4638
Average annual GDP growth rate (1990-96, %):	8.7
Average annual inflation rate (1990-96, %):	3.7
Currency (ringgit per US$, average 1996):	2.51
Real exchange rate: (1990=100, average 1996)	106.15
Structure of production (1994):	43% industry, 42% services, 14% agriculture
Main exports:	semi-conductors, consumer electronics, computers & peripherals, crude petroleum, palm oil, logs & timber, rubber & rubber products
Main imports:	machinery & transport, basic manufactures, energy
Main trading partners:	Japan, US, Singapore, Germany, UK
Market capitalization of Stock Exchange (October 1996; US$bn):	294.1
Total foreign debt (% of GDP):	50
Next elections due under normal circumstances:	legislative scheduled April 2000
Credit rating: (Nov 1996, Standard & Poor's, Moody's)	A+; A1

FORECAST: 1997-2000 (average)

	Worst case	Most likely	Best case
Real GDP growth (%)	7.3	8.4	8.8
Inflation (%)	4.1	3.8	3.8

■ POLITICS

Historical overview

Malaysia's modern history begins with the foundation of the Malacca sultanate in 1400. This evolved into the dominant trading centre in the Asian region. Malacca was captured by the Portuguese in 1511, and remained under nominal Portuguese control until 1641 when Dutch traders began to extend their commercial links. By the mid-18th century, a rough federation of Malay states had emerged, but local sultans maintained their rule over individual regional states. British traders began to move into the Malay peninsula in the late 18th century. They bought Penang in 1786 and Malacca in 1795 as part of a long-term strategy of securing a trade route from their Indian operations to the Chinese market. A trading settlement was set up on the island of Singapore in 1819. In 1826 the three colonies were merged into a single administrative unit, the Straits Settlements, which remained under the control of British India until responsibility was transferred to the colonial office in London in 1867.

Outlying states such as Perak were added in 1874 to form the Federated Malay States with a federal capital at Kuala Lumpur. The four northern states were finally brought under British control in 1909. Executive power during this period lay nominally in the hands of the sultans, although the British governor-general, or "resident", had considerable influence.

The demographic balance in the Malay states began to change in the early 20th century with the arrival of thousands of Chinese labourers shipped in to work on the tin mines and rubber plantations. By 1931, the Chinese represented 39% of the population. More entrepreneurial than the local Malays (most of whom were subsistence rice farmers), the Chinese quickly began to extend their control over the lucrative rubber and tin industries.

The political structure of the islands changed dramatically following the Japanese invasion and occupation of Malaysia in 1941-42. Keen to undermine support for the local sultans, who had stayed on after the British left, the Japanese began to encourage the development of a pan-nationalist movement. The occupation was resisted by the Malayan People's Anti-Japanese army composed mainly of ethnic Chinese and Communists.

On returning to Malaysia after the defeat of the Japanese in 1945, the British set up a centralized political structure called the Malayan Union in which all races (Indians, Chinese and native Malayans) would be given equal rights of citizenship. This was opposed by the United Malays National Organization (UMNO), the main Malay party, who forced the British to extend the political rule of the individual sultans.

In 1948, the Federation of Malay was inaugurated. The Chinese-dominated Communist Party violently opposed the new constitution. However, resistance soon died out, and a pan-racial ruling party centred around the UMNO began to emerge in the early 1950s. In 1952, the UMNO and Malayan Chinese Association (MCA) stood together as one party in the Kuala Lumpur municipal elections. Two years later, in 1954, the Malayan Indian Congress (MIC) joined the alliance.

With independence drawing near, the UMNO agreed to water down the restrictions on Chinese and Indian citizens' rights, but insisted that the Yang di-Pertuan Agong (paramount ruler) be given special rights to safeguard the position of the native Malay population. Independence was finally granted in August 1957. Tunku Abdul Rahman, president of UMNO, became the federation's first prime minister.

The early years of independence were dominated by attempts to reduce the commercial power of the Chinese by increasing the political power of the Malays. The largely Chinese island of Singapore was barred from joining the federation until 1963 when Borneo and Sarawak (both dominated by Malays) also gained entry. Two years later, Singapore was formally expelled from Malaysia after trying to interfere in local elections.

Ethnic tension increased in 1969 after two opposition parties, the Parti Gerakan Rakyat Malaysia (GERAKAN) and the Democratic Action Party (DAP) based their electoral campaign on reducing Malay political power. The government reacted by banning public discussion of sensitive political issues such as the power of the sultans. Unable to put up effective opposition to UMNO, the two opposition parties decided to join the ruling coalition which then became known as the Barisan Nasional (BN).

Throughout the 1970s, the Malay-dominated BN followed a programme of positive discrimination aimed at increasing the economic power of ethnic Malays. Malays were appointed to key political posts, and subsidies granted to Malay-owned businesses.

In 1981, Dr Mahathir Mohamad replaced Hussein bin Onn as prime minister. The following year, in 1982, the BN performed strongly in the federal elections, giving Mahathir a strong power base within the House of Representatives.

The early years of Mahathir's rule were characterized by attempts to reduce the power of the sultans. There were numerous reports of financial scandals and alleged government corruption. Meanwhile, the central alliance's control over the outlying states began to weaken. In 1986, a local party, the Parti Bersatu Sabah (PBS) won 34 of the 54 seats in the State Assembly elections in Sabah (formerly North Borneo).

However, the BN maintained its strong position in the general elections of 1986 (thanks in part to Mahathir's success in persuading the two Sabah parties to join the coalition). The BN retained control of all 11 state assemblies, and won 148 of the 177 seats in the House of Representatives.

During the late 1980s, Mahathir consolidated his powerbase within the BN by introducing tight controls on press freedom, and by dismissing a legal challenge to the validity of the 1987 leadership elections. In March 1988, he announced that the UMNO party was to be reformed, and that all new members would have to be registered. Over 100 deputies including his main rival Tan Sri Razaleigh, the former trade and industry minister, refused to do so, and were expelled from the party.

But opposition to the UMNO grip on power began to grow. In September 1988, Razaleigh set up an opposition party with fourteen former UMNO deputies. The following year, his Semangat '46 party formed an alliance with the Islamic-based PAS party, called the Angkatan Perpaduan Ummah (APU-Muslim Unity Movement).

Four years later, in 1992, a number of ethnic-based parties joined Razaleigh's opposition coalition, including DAP, the main Chinese party, the Indian Progressive Front and the Kongres Indian Muslim Malaysia. However, the alliance proved unable to dislodge the BN from power in subsequent elections.

During the early 1990s, the principal political issues facing Mahathir's BN government were the role of the sultans and the growing support for regional parties. In 1993, the government removed the legal immunity enjoyed by the sultans. The following year, the power of the monarch was reduced. Meanwhile, unrest in Sabah was quelled by Mahathir's promise to rotate the post of chief minister between the three ethnic groups.

Recent events

In the general elections of April 1995, the ruling BN coalition scored a notable victory, winning 162 of the 192 seats in the House of Representatives (with around 64% of the votes cast).The pro-Chinese DAP party won only 9 seats (down from 10 in 1990). The Islamic party, the PAS, won 7 seats (the same as in 1990) and Semangat '46 secured just 6 seats. Significantly, the BN retained control in 10 out of the 11 state assemblies.

Despite his overwhelming victory, Mahathir's position within his own UMNO party seemed uncertain during the months that followed. Several of his supporters were forced out of office, and there was speculation that Deputy Prime Minister Anwar might launch a challenge. However, following Anwar's declaration in October that he did not intend to run for prime minister, Mahathir announced he would retire in the near future, and named Anwar as his successor.

Meanwhile, the power-sharing agreements set up in outlying states such as Sabah and Kedah began to run into trouble. UMNO deputies attempted to prevent the removal of UMNO chief ministers in these two states in early 1996, but Mahathir was able to persuade both to step down.

Attempts to revive the activities of the banned Islamic fundamentalist sect known as Al-Arqam were quickly quashed in June 1996, when a number of activists, including the sect leader's wife, were arrested.

In June 1996, the ruling BN coalition received a boost when Razaleigh led his Semangat '46 party back into the fold, after support for the party had been dwindling and a number of deputies had deserted. This may increase the BN's chances of recapturing control of the state of Kelantan, presently under PAS rule.

In foreign affairs, Malaysia continues to play a leading role in the development of a South-East Asian power bloc through the Association of South-East Asian Nations (ASEAN).

The main political issue of 1997 and 1998 is likely to be the election of a successor to Mahathir who is expected to retire in 1999. The principal candidate is Deputy Prime Minister Anwar Ibrahim, who has established himself as a leading light within the UMNO. This could change, however, if Razaleigh (once one of the most powerful figures in the BN) decides to back another candidate. The campaign to elect the three UMNO vice-presidents in 1996 was fiercely contested, suggesting that political in-fighting within the UMNO could increase during the coming years.

Chronology

1400	Malacca sultanate is established
1511	Malacca is captured by Portuguese
1786	British acquire Penang
1795	British buy Malacca
1819	British trading settlement is set up in Singapore
1824	Anglo-Dutch treaty secures UK control
1840	Fighting breaks out in Perak
1873	British take control in Perak
1896	Federated Malay states set up with capital at Kuala Lumpur
1909	Four northern states come under British rule
1930	Communist party of Malaya (CPM) set up
1941-2	Japan invades and occupies Malaya
1945	Japanese are defeated, and withdraw from Malaya
1946	British unite north and south states into Malayan Union
1946	United Malays National Organization (UMNO) is established
1948	Federation of Malaya is established
1951	British high commissioner is assassinated by Communist rebels

1957	Independence is granted. UMNO leader Tunku Abdul Rahman becomes prime minister.
1959	Singapore secures internal self-government
1963	North Borneo and Sarawak join Malaysian federation
1965	Singapore expelled from Malaysia
1967	Association of South-East Asian Nations (ASEAN) set up
1969	Ethnic riots leave hundreds dead in Kuala Lumpur
1970	Tun Abdul Razak takes over as prime minister
1970	Alliance changes its name to Barisan Nasional (BN)
1970	Bahasa Malaysian introduced as national language
1976	Hussein bin Onn becomes prime minister
1981	Dr Mahathir Mohamad becomes prime minister
1986	Muta Hitam challenges Mahathir's leadership
1986	BN wins 148 of 176 seats in elections
1987	Mahathir defeats Razaleigh in leadership vote
1988	One hundred deputies expelled from UMNO
1989	Razaleigh forms Semangat '46 opposition party
1990	UMNO wins smaller majority in federal elections
1992	ASEAN announces plans to set up free trade area within the next fifteen years
1992	Opposition coalition led by Razaleigh registered
1993	Sultan rulers lose legal immunity
1993	Mahathir retains leadership of UMNO unopposed
1993	Anwar Ibrahim replaces Ghafar as deputy president
1993	Mahathir extends federal control over states
1994	New constitution reduces power of monarchy and judiciary
1995	BN wins 162 of 192 seats in federal elections
1996	Semangat '46 rejoins BN
1996	Mahathir and Anwar retain posts in leadership elections

Constitution and government

The constitution of the Federation of Malaysia was signed and became effective in August 1957. It provides for a supreme head of state, elected by a conference of rulers, a federal bicameral parliament, a cabinet formed by the prime minister and appointed by the king. It also includes rights for each of the country's thirteen states, each of which also have their own constitution.

Malaysia is a federation of thirteen states. The capital, Kuala Lumpur, is a separate federal territory, as is the island of Labuan. Each of the states has its own written constitution and state assembly, which (in some areas) has legislative power over and above that of the federal government.

Malaysia has a bicameral federal parliament – the Dewan Negara (Senate) with 68 members elected every six years, and the Dewan Rakyat (House of Representatives) with 180 members elected every five years.

The current national government is a coalition called the Barisan Nasional (BN), which is dominated by Mahathir's United Malays National Organization (UMNO), a Malay-based party. The other minority partners are the Malaysian Chinese Association (MCA), the Malaysian Indian Congress (MIC), Gerakan, Parti Pesaka Bumiputera Bersatu (PPBB) and the

Sarawak National Party (SNP). The major opposition parties are the Parti Islam Sa-Malaysia (an Islamic-based party), the Democratic Action Party (Chinese-based) and the Parti Bersatu Sabah (PBS), a regional party from the Sabah state.

Current government

Supreme Head of State	Tuanku Abdul Rahman
Deputy Head of State	Salahuddin Abdul Aziz
Prime Minister	Dr Mahathir Mohamad
Deputy Prime Minister	Anwar Ibrahim
Minister of Foreign Affairs	Abdulah Ahmad Badawi
Minister of Trade and Industry	Rafidah Aziz

Results of the April 1995 House of Representatives election

United Malay National Organization	88 seats
Malaysian Chinese Association	30 seats
Sarawak National Front parties	26 seats
Malaysian Indian Congress	7 seats
Gerakan Rakyat Malaysia	7 seats
Sabah National Front parties	14 seats
Barisan Nasional	162 seats
Democratic Action Party	9 seats
Parti Bersatu Sabah	8 seats
Parti Islam Sa-Malaysia	7 seats
Semangat '46	6 seats

Next elections
April 2000

Other political forces
Monarch
The country is nominally ruled by the head of state, the Yang di-Pertuan Agong, who is elected for a five-year term by the Conference of Rulers. The monarch is always drawn from one of the federation's nine hereditary rulers. He has almost no executive power, and is compelled to approve legislation passed by the House of Representatives within thirty days.

Sultans
Nine of the federation's thirteen states retain a sultan as head of state. In practice, they have little legislative power, and have lost most of their commercial and legal privileges. All are known as sultans except for the ruler of Perlis, who has the title of Raja, and the ruler of Negri Sembilan, who is known as Yang di-Pertuan Besar.

Central bank
The central bank of Malaysia is the Bank Negara, which plays a key role in the development and maintenance of stable economic conditions. In practice, it is controlled by the Ministry of Finance.

■ ECONOMICS

Historical overview

Blessed with extensive natural resources such as tin, copper, gas, rubber, timber, gas and oil, Malaysia is one of the fastest-growing economies in South-East Asia. In the last ten years, it has also developed a strong manufacturing sector exporting consumer goods and textiles.

On gaining independence, the government inherited a predominantly agricultural economy sustained by extensive tin mining and rubber plantations. It quickly began to develop the country's industrial base by an import-substitution policy. Processing plants were set up to turn the country's natural resources into usable products.

In 1969, the government launched a twenty-year economic development programme, the New Economic Policy, which aimed to raise living standards (particularly among poor native Malays) via the creation of state-sponsored industries. Tax incentives were offered to companies setting up manufacturing factories to reduce the country's dependence on agriculture.

During the 1970s, the government began to switch from import-substitution to an export-orientated economic policy, utilizing the country's large pool of low-cost labour. Textiles and electronics factories were set up, financed by foreign investment. In the late 1970s, the discovery of petroleum and gas reserves led to the development of an energy industry.

The palm oil industry also expanded rapidly during this period. Total palm oil production increased by nearly 20% a year between 1970 and 1980. In 1975, the government set up a large number of palm oil mills, aiming to broaden the industry to include producing, refining, manufacturing and selling oil-based products.

The timber industry was booming as well. Production of saw logs and wood-processing soared during the 1960s and 1970s, with the increase in world demand for hardwoods. But it soon became clear that the forests were being destroyed with little thought for the future, and in 1978, the government set up a National Forestry Policy aimed at encouraging sustainable development.

The 1980s saw a rapid expansion of heavy industries such as steel and car production. New factories were set up manufacturing a wide range of consumer products ranging from televisions, toys and videos to computers, typewriters and refrigerators. Most of the investments were organized by the government through centralized industrial development agencies. In 1985, the government began to encourage foreign companies to set up in Malaysia, helping local firms to gain access to new industrial technology. Restrictions on foreign equity ownership were relaxed, and tax breaks were offered to overseas investors.

To ensure the rapidly expanding industrial sector had sufficient power, the government allowed several privately owned energy companies to be set up. By 1994, they were producing so much power there was an energy surplus.

Rubber production, once Malaysia's largest export, declined during the 1980s and early 1990s, however, because of rapid fluctuations in world rubber prices, and the scarcity of labour due to urban migration. The government continued to support the rubber industry via the Federal Land Development Authority, which offered grants to small-scale farmers.

The rapid industrialization of the economy led to a sharp increase in the country's gross domestic product. Between 1970 and 1990, GDP grew on average by 6.7% a year.

There were periods of lower growth (notably during the world recession of 1981-1983), but expansion continued at a rapid rate.

In the first half of the 1990s, following the introduction of Malaysia's sixth five-year economic plan, the government concentrated on upgrading the country's infrastructure. A large number of construction projects were launched. This led to a rapid acceleration in economic growth with GDP expanding by an average of 8.4% between 1991 and 1994. Manufacturing and electronics production grew by over 15% a year during this period.

Nevertheless, agriculture (which still employed 21% of the labour force) saw production figures drop during this period as world food prices fell. The palm oil industry was hit particularly hard by the collapse of the Soviet Union (one of the biggest importers of palm oil), as was the tin industry.

Recent developments

The first official sign that the Malaysian government recognized the dangers of pursuing persistently high growth targets came in May 1996, when it introduced the Seventh Malaysia Plan (1996 to 2000). This aims to slow GDP growth to a more sustainable 8% a year.

The government hopes that, by slowing growth and thus demand for imports, it will be able to reduce the current account deficit. Economists feared the deficit could undermine the confidence of overseas investors and lead to a capital flight, as it did in Mexico in 1994.

Worries over the current account deficit eased during 1996 after the trade balance improved. However, it remains to be seen whether the government's aim of eliminating the deficit by the year 2000 can be achieved. Demand for credit remains high, and the bulk of the deficit is likely to be financed by foreign rather than domestic capital.

Over the past two years, the government has repeatedly tried to reduce Malaysia's dependence on foreign capital by tightening up on foreign direct investment, and encouraging Malaysian companies to borrow funds domestically rather than overseas. Foreign direct investment fell during 1995 and 1996 as a result. But the Seventh Malaysia Plan offers few concrete strategies for increasing local savings to a level where they can provide sufficient finance to cover investment needs.

Meanwhile, government spending seems set to continue at a high level. Late in 1995, the government promised to review spending on large infrastructure projects. However, the Seventh Malaysia Plan has allocated M$200 billion to infrastructure spending on roads, ports, railways, power and telecommunications, considerably higher than the M$112 billion spent between 1991 to 1995. This will ease the infrastructure bottlenecks that have disrupted production during 1995 and 1996. It will do little to ease growth or external borrowing, however.

The government is likely to continue to direct investment away from labour-intensive fields such as basic manufacturing and component assembly to technology-led industries such as electronics, aerospace and skilled service sectors. Applications for new manufacturing projects must now pass a capital-labour ratio threshold before being approved by the government.

This, and the decline in world commodity prices, is likely to lead to a further decline in the agricultural sector, which is expected to grow by 2.4 % a year compared to 10.7% a year for manufacturing. Palm-oil production is likely to remain the dominant agricultural industry as rubber, logging and mining production decline.

GDP is expected to continue to expand by 8% a year in 1997 and 1998, providing the current account deficit does not rise out of control. Much of the growth will be investment-led and export-driven, with demand from the fast-moving Asian economies compensating for weak growth in Europe and North America. The outlook, therefore, is positive, with long-term economic growth likely to remain at or above 7.5% a year.

Population

Malaysia's population is estimated to be over 21 million. Of these, at least 15 million live in or around Kuala Lumpur on the main Malay peninsula. Sabah and Sarawak both have around 2 million each. The ethnic mix in Malaysia is very varied. On the mainland, about 60% are native Malays; Chinese immigrants (who arrived in the 1930s) represent around 31% and the Indian immigrants 9%. Most native Malays are Muslims. In the outside states such as Sabah, the immigrant population is smaller, and there are fewer Muslims.

The economy

Over the past five years, manufacturing has become the dominant economic activity in Malaysia. In 1995, the manufacturing sector – comprising such industries as electronic component and consumer goods production – accounted for just over 33% of GDP. The sector's share of GDP is expected to rise to over 37% by the year 2000 as production of cars and other high-value manufactured products increases.

Financial services are an important part of the economy, representing 10.7% of GDP. This sector is expected to expand significantly over the next five years as local capital markets develop in line with the government's policy of reducing Malaysia's reliance on overseas capital.

The government's plan to increase infrastructure spending between 1996 and 2001 is likely to boost production in retailing, hotels, and transport and communications sectors. Retailing and hotels account for 12% of GDP – a proportion certain to rise to nearer 15% within the next five years as new hotels are built, and the number of overseas visitors increases. Transport and communications which accounted for 7.3% in 1995 should also rise to around 8.2% by the year 2000.

Share of GDP by sector

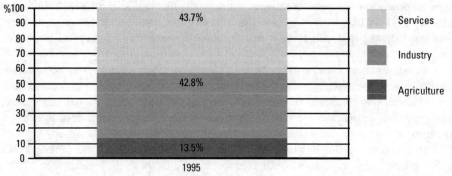

1995

Source: Official data

Production in the electricity, water and construction sectors is expected to rise slowly in the coming years. Economists expect the two sectors to account for 2.6% and 4.8% of national GDP respectively by the year 2000.

Two sectors likely to see a decline are agriculture (which, despite the rise in urban migration still accounts for 13.6% of GDP) and government services. With increasing amounts of land being transferred from rubber and food crop production to more cash-productive uses, agriculture's share of GDP is expected to fall to around 10% within the next five years. Government services should also fall to around 8% of GDP by the year 2000 as state-sponsored industry gives way to private sector enterprise.

Savings and investment

Malaysia has a relatively high savings rate. At the end of 1995, gross national savings stood at M$69 billion, or almost one third of GDP. Nevertheless, because the amount of capital required to finance the construction of new factories and infrastructure has been so large, local savings have not been able to cover investment needs. A saving-to-investment deficit has been run since 1990 and is expected to reach nearly M$20 billion by the end of 1996.

In the 1960s and 1970s, the bulk of Malaysia's investment was financed by state investment funds which borrowed money from overseas lenders. However, private sector borrowing and foreign direct investment have played an increasingly significant role since the mid-1980s.

As the government has sought to reduce Malaysia's dependence on overseas capital by encouraging local companies to borrow more funds from domestic lenders, FDI approvals fell by 19% in 1995, reflecting tighter scrutiny of applications.

The maintenance of high local interest rates has helped to slow the pace of net corporate investment, expected to fall to M$7.8 billion in 1996. Nevertheless, given the large amount of new investment, savings rates will need to rise significantly in the next five years if Malaysia is to reduce its reliance on foreign direct investment (FDI) and overseas borrowing. External debt is forecast to rise from 47% of GDP in 1996 to around 53% in 1997.

Balance of payments

Malaysia's balance of payments situation is dominated by one inescapable fact – almost all of its exported goods are made with imported parts. Thus, to make televisions or computers for sale abroad, it needs to import semi-conductors and factory machinery. By granting subsidies to exports and imposing tariffs on imports, the government has been able to keep its trade deficit at a manageable level.

But the task has become harder. Exports have been undermined by the establishment of new factories in China and Vietnam where production costs are lower, while import demand has risen steadily. In 1995, the trade balance was US$0.3 billion.

This is likely to increase during 1997 thanks to the ringgit's rise against the yen (which will reduce the cost of imported goods from Japan), the recent decline in semi-conductor prices, and a surge in global electronics sales. As Malaysian industry becomes more self-sufficient, trade problems should ease. But there may be some anxious moments on the way.

Because domestic savings are insufficient to cover local financing needs, Malaysia has been forced to source a significant proportion of its capital from overseas. In combination with the trade deficit, this has resulted in a current account deficit totalling US$7.4 billion in 1995. The government has taken steps to reduce this (such as reducing external borrowing and foreign capital inflows) but a deficit (albeit declining) is likely to exist for the next four years.

Imports and exports as a % of GDP

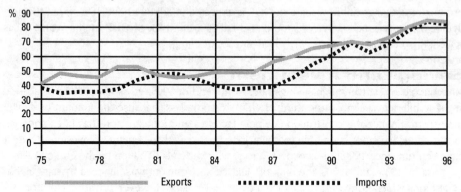

Source: Official data

Breakdown of exports (1995)

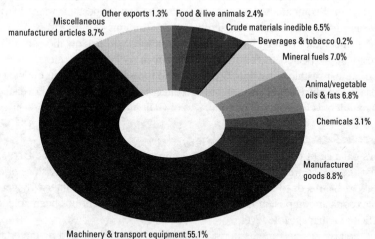

Machinery & transport equipment 55.1%

Source: Official data

Economic policy
Monetary policy

With the economy growing at such a spectacular rate, the Bank Negara has had to maintain tight control over monetary policy to curb rises in inflation. Since 1990, when inflation began to rise, basic interest rates have been kept at over 7% in a bid to dampen domestic consumption and investment. Price controls have been introduced on basic goods ranging from cement to chickens.

According to the local consumer price index, the government's anti-inflationary strategy has been reasonably successful. Consumer price inflation has been kept below 4% a year since 1994. However, sharp rises in broad money supply in the first half of 1996 indicate that inflationary pressures are rising.

Attempts by the central bank to combat this rise (by increasing the statutory reserve requirement ratio of lending banks to 13.5%, and raising interest rates) have enjoyed mixed results. Domestic consumption has fallen, but investment demand has not. Nevertheless, inflation is not expected to rise above 5% in 1997 or 1998.

The future monetary policy of the central bank is likely to be dictated by two main concerns. It does not want to raise interest rates too high for fear of attracting hot money from international investors, thereby triggering a rise in the ringgit and a fall in export competitiveness.

On the other hand, it cannot reduce interest rates without encouraging a rise in domestic consumption and lending, thereby stoking inflation. For these reasons, the basic interest rate is expected to remain within a fairly narrow 8% to 9% band over the next two years, barring a sharp fall in GDP growth.

Fiscal policy

Outwardly at least, the government appears committed to reducing public spending and eliminating the small budget deficit it has run for some years.

The 1996 budget showed a fall in the deficit. However, the planned increase in infrastructure spending announced in May 1996 indicates that the commitment may not be as strong as is thought.

Current account as a % of GDP

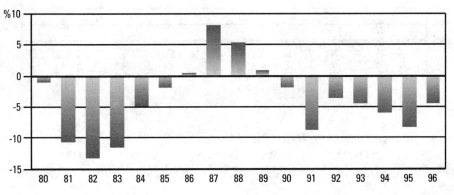

Source: Official data

Currency

The Malaysian currency is the ringgit. During the 1960s and 1970s, it remained relatively strong against the major world currencies. However, in the 1980s it began to depreciate significantly in real terms as a result of falling prices for key exports. Currency movements are strictly controlled by the Bank Negara, which introduced temporary restrictions on inflows of overseas capital in 1994.

Malaysian ringgit/US dollar exchange rate

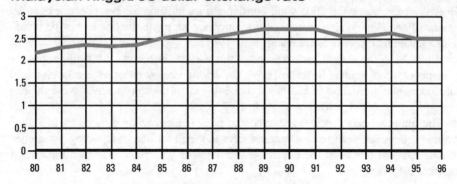

■ EQUITIES

Index performance (in local currency)

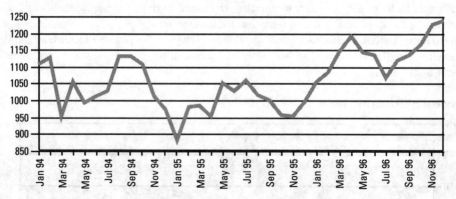

Key indicators

	Index performance %, in US$ terms	Market Cap. US$bn	P/E	Div. Yield	Weight in IFCI	Weight in IFCG
1994	-22.8	199.3	29.0	1.8	24.8	13.4
1995	1.8	222.7	25.1	1.7	19.7	13.1
1996	22.9	307.2	27.1	1.2	22.9	16.1

Sources: Local stock exchange, IFC, Bloomberg, Datastream, UBS

Structure

The Kuala Lumpur Stock Exchange comprises a Main and Second Board. Larger companies are listed on the Main Board and smaller companies on the Second Board. There are 588 equity shares listed on the two markets, 394 on the Main Board and 194 on the Second. The Main Board accounts for more than 92% of total stock market capitalization. There is an average free float of 30%.

Regulatory authority

The Securities Commission is responsible for both the equities and futures market. The Registrar of Companies is responsible for the incorporation of companies. The Licensing Officer (Securities/Futures Trading) is responsible for the issuance of licences. The KLSE is responsible for the conduct of members, market surveillance and enforcement of listing requirements. The Foreign Investment Committee regulates the acquisitions, mergers or take-overs and major issues of foreign investments.

Trading methods

All shares listed on the official market are traded on the SCORE system.

Hours

Trading takes place from 09.30 to 12.30 and 14.30 to 17.00, Monday to Friday.

Settlement time and clearing

Physical settlement is on a T+4 basis, and financial settlement on T+7. Most shares in the official market are deposited in the Central Depository System (CDS). Delivery of shares is through book-entry, and there is no physical movement of script, making clearing more efficient and convenient.

Limits on price movement

The upper and lower limit of price is fixed at 30% of the closing price of the previous trading session.

Types of shares

Most are ordinary voting shares with just two preferred shares. The preference share is non-voting and bears a fixed preferred dividend in addition to the ordinary dividend earned by the other shares.

Other types of securities include bonds, loan stocks, loan notes, property trust units, warrants, TSRs and call warrants.

Stock indices

The KLSE computes an index for each of the main sectors traded on the bourse, but the most widely followed is the KLSE Composite Index. This is made up of one hundred companies and is generally accepted as the local stockmarket barometer.

Taxes

There is a deduction of 30% corporate tax at source for all dividends other than tax exempt dividends. A non-resident shareholder may receive the full amount of the dividend less corporate tax. There is no capital gains tax derived from transaction of securities in Malaysia.

Dividends

Dividends are paid once a year or bi-annually with an occasional special dividend. Management proposes the dividend, which is then approved by shareholders at an annual assembly before disbursement.

Disclosure of financial statements

A public company should comply with approved accounting standards and generally accepted accounting principles of financial records and preparation of financial statements and reports.

All reports must be prepared by professional accountants. The information disclosed must be in accordance with best practice and must meet minimum standards under the Companies Act 1965 and international accounting standards approved by the relevant Malaysian accounting standard-setting bodies.

All listed companies must disclose financial statements twice a year. Some companies report quarterly.

Shareholders' rights

Shareholders can vote by proxy in Malaysia. All shareholders must be informed of any forthcoming extraordinary and annual general meetings.

Ownership limits for non-residents

Foreign ownership of companies is generally restricted to 30%. If foreigners own shares in a company that has reached the 30% limit, they must queue for registration under foreign ownership, and in the process lose their dividend and voting rights.

Take-over bids and large stakes

When a company has acquired more than 50% stake of a company it must make a general offer to acquire the remaining shares.

Brokers

There are sixty stockbroking companies in Malaysia. It is only possible to trade on the exchange through a licensed dealer or agent engaged by these companies.

Commissions

Stocks, ordinary shares and preference shares

less than 50 sen	1/2 sen per share
between 50 sen and RM1.00	1 sen per share
on the first RM500,000 (US$200,000)	1.0%
on the next RM500,000 to RM2,000,000 (US$200,000 to US$ 500,000)	0.75%
on amounts exceeding RM2,000,000 (US$500,000)	0.5%

Other debentures (non-convertible)

less than RM50,000 (US$20,000)	1%
RM50,000 to RM100,000 (US$20,000 to US$40,000)	0.5%
more than RM100,000 (US$40,000)	0.25%

Minimum brokerage

The minimum brokerage (payable by both buyer and seller) on loan transactions is RM2.00 and on any other transactions is RM5.00.

Sectors

The biggest sectors by market capitalization represented on the KLSE are trading/services (29%), finance (15%) and industrial products (14%). Other sectors include consumer products, properties, construction, plantations, mining, hotels and the infrastructure project companies.

■ DEBT

The Minister of Finance sets the broad policies for creating the bond market's framework, and Bank Negara Malaysia (BNM – the central bank) is the main promoter of its activities and development. Both BNM and a second regulator, the Securities Commission (SC) report to the Minister.

Public debt

Malaysian Treasury Bills (MTBs)

Bank Negara sells 91-, 182- and 364-day bills for the Federal Treasury through weekly tenders made by principal dealers, who are obliged to bid for them and who underwrite all MTB issues. Auctions for 91-day bills occur weekly: dealers submit bids every Wednesday for issue and settlement on Friday; 182-day bills are auctioned fortnightly and 364-day bills monthly. MTBs are issued on a simple discounted interest basis, and the standard transaction size is RM1,000,000 (US$400,000).

Bank Negara Bills (BNBs)

BNBs were first issued in February 1993 for use by the central bank in its open market operations and, in particular, to absorb foreign speculative flows. They have the same primary and secondary market features as MTBs. Banks can use them as repo collateral to cover overnight deficits, and offer them to satisfy statutory reserve requirements.

Malaysian Government Securities (MGS)

In previous years, Bank Negara offered at least three MGS issues each year, but more recently issuance has been determined by the budget deficit forecast for the year.

Bonds of more than 1-year to 10-years maturity are offered at a "best price" tender basis to primary dealers, and yields are determined by the weighted average rates of successful bids. Longer-dated issues are placed with major institutional investors at par with an administratively chosen coupon. Domestic financial institutions hold MGSs for compliance reasons and pension funds have a statutory requirement to invest in them – the Employees Provident Fund (EPF) is the largest holder of MGSs.

Government Investment Certificates (GICs)

The Government Investment Act 1983 authorized issuance of government debt based on Islamic principles, which Islamic banks can hold to satisfy liquidity requirements.

Principal dealers in government securities act as intermediaries between the government and investors, and also act as authorized depository institutions with responsibility for paying interest and principal.

Private debt

Corporate bonds

The impetus for the corporate bond market was the creation of the Cagamas Berhad (National Mortgage Corporation) in October 1987. Cagamas repackages housing mortgages into debt instruments, which are traded in the interbank market and qualify as liquid assets for banks. It was specifically devised to help develop Malaysia's financial markets. Since 1988, corporate bond issuance has increased while government issuance has declined, largely because the government's Privatization Master Plan transferred more responsibility for financing and maintaining infrastructure projects to the private sector.

Bank Negara ensures that funds raised through private bond issues are used for their stated purpose, and since the publication of the PDS (Private Debt Securities) Guidelines in January 1989, all corporate debt issues (except Cagamas bonds) need its approval. Mandatory rating by Rating Agency Malaysia Berhad (RAM) was introduced in 1992. The minimum rating required for long-dated issues is BBB, and for short-dated paper is P3; an issuer must have shareholders' funds of at least RM25 million (US$10 million). In addition, all bond issues must be underwritten by a bank (unless an irrevocable undertaking for subscriptions has been secured), have a maturity date of not less than 3 years, and a minimum issue size of RM25 million.

The Securities Commission also regulates securities issuance and dealings and acts as a one-stop agency to coordinate approvals from Bank Negara and other regulatory bodies. The multiple approval process causes delays and raises borrowers' costs.

The majority of corporate bonds have initial 5-year tenures and often have equity warrants attached. New issues are bought by primary subscribers, who sell them to regional financial intermediaries or end-investors. Most are quoted on a yield basis. Bonds guaranteed by banks are similarly priced because financial institutions are perceived to have equal risk, but prices of non-guaranteed issues vary greatly. Trading takes place on the Stock Exchange (KLSE), through money brokers or over the counter. But the secondary market is illiquid because bonds are tightly held by domestic institutions for compliance reasons.

Trades are settled through the electronic SPEEDS system, which is made up of the Interbank Funds Transfer System (IFTS) and Scripless Securities Trading System (SSTS), via computer terminals. Approved dealers hold separate accounts with BNM for themselves and their clients, and an additional cash settlement account for repo trades.

Islamic PDSs (Private Debt Securities)

The concept of Islamic PDSs emerged at the same time as GICs in 1983, but the first issue, a RM125 million (US$50 million) deferred payment sale facility for Shell MDS Malaysia Bhd, was not launched until 1990. Subsequent issues have been structured in one of three ways according to three principles to avoid usury prohibitions: Al-Bai-Bithaman (deferred payment sale), Al-Musharakah (joint participation), Al-Qardul Hassan (interest-free loan).

RUFs and NIFs

RUFs are issued with 1-, 2-, 3- and 6-month maturities to fund a company's working capital requirements. They are 5-year renewable facilities which pay discounted interest on roll-over dates rather than principal at redemption. Rates are pegged to KLIBOR (lower than Base Lending Rate), and because issues are fully underwritten by a Tender Panel of eligible investors (usually the discount houses) the cost is capped. NIFs are similar to RUFs, but are not underwritten.

Eurobonds

London or Luxembourg listed eurobonds and euro-convertibles have been issued by Malaysian corporates since 1990. But Exchange Control Notice ECM10 and 15 restricts off-shore borrowing to specific purposes: to increase productive capacity to generate foreign exchange earnings for Malaysia, or to produce import substitution goods and hence save on the future outflow of foreign exchange. The exception to the rule is financing for infrastructure projects.

Eurobond issues (US$m)

	1990	1991	1992	1993	1994	1995	1996
Sovereign	200.0	190.2	—	—	—	—	—
Private	—	—	—	—	1785.0	815.0	150.0

■ MALAYSIA: Economic indicators

Population and development	1990	1991	1992	1993	1994	1995	1996e
Population, million	17.8	18.2	18.6	19.1	19.7	20.1	20.6
Population growth, %	2.4	2.4	2.4	2.4	3.1	2.3	2.3
Nominal GDP per capita, US$	2411	2591	3117	3323	3594	4243	4638

National accounts							
Nominal GDP, US$bn	42.8	47.1	58.0	63.3	70.6	85.3	95.4
Change in real GDP, %	9.7	8.4	7.8	8.3	9.2	9.5	8.3
Gross fixed capital formation, % of GDP	32.4	35.6	34.3	35.2	38.2	37.2	38.4

Money supply and inflation							
Narrow money, change %, Dec/Dec	14.5	11.0	27.3	35.3	16.8	13.2	—
Broad money, change %, Dec/Dec	10.6	16.9	29.2	26.6	12.7	20.0	—
Consumer price inflation (avg.) %	2.7	4.4	4.7	3.6	3.7	5.3	3.5
Producer prices (avg.) %							

Government finance							
Government expenditure, % of GDP	31.3	30.7	30.9	25.3	24.3	23.0	21.5
Government balance, % of GDP	-0.2	-0.4	1.3	-0.4	-0.8	1.2	-0.6

Exchange rates lc=local currency							
Exchange rate, annual average, lc/US$	2.70	2.75	2.55	2.57	2.62	2.50	2.51
Exchange rate, end of year, lc/US$	2.70	2.72	2.61	2.70	2.55	2.54	2.52
Real exchange rate 1990=100	100.0	97.0	103.5	103.3	102.1	102.7	106.2

Balance of payments							
Exports of goods & services, US$m	32665	38086	44812	51444	63452	79028	88260
Change %	18.2	16.6	17.7	14.8	23.3	24.5	11.7
Imports of goods & services, US$m, fob	31765	39885	44009	51255	64208	80400	86450
Change %	25.6	25.6	10.3	16.5	25.3	25.2	7.5
Trade balance, of goods only, US$m, fob-fob	2526	391	3150	3025	1581	300	2600
Current account balance, US$m	-870	-4183	-2167	-2809	-4147	-7400	-4300
as a % of GDP	-2.0	-8.9	-3.7	-4.4	-5.9	-8.7	-4.5

Foreign exchange reserves							
Foreign exchange reserves, US$m	9754	10886	17228	27249	25423	23774	29400
Gold at ⅔ of market price, US$m	604.1	566.8	546.6	572.6	611.6	611.5	617.1
Import cover (reserves/imports), months	3.7	3.3	4.7	6.4	4.8	3.5	4.1

Foreign debt and debt service							
Short-term debt, US$m	3934	5363	7630	12853	7600	7468	8502
Total foreign debt, US$m	20458	22758	26306	28600	34400	40200	47700
as a % of GDP	47.8	48.3	45.3	45.2	48.7	47.1	50.0
as a % of foreign exchange receipts	58.8	57.3	56.3	53.2	52.1	48.3	51.5
Interest payments, US$m	1613	1468	1201	1285	1598	2075	2190
Principal repayments, US$m	1775	1606	3255	3854	3631	3269	3820
Total debt service, US$m	3388	3074	4456	5139	5229	5344	6010
as a % of goods exports	11.8	9.1	11.2	11.1	9.2	7.4	7.6
as a % of foreign exchange receipts	9.7	7.7	9.5	9.6	7.9	6.4	6.5

Mexico

Area (thousands of km²):	1958
Population (1995, millions):	94.8
Population projection (2025, millions):	136
Population younger than 15 yrs (1991, % of total):	37.6
Urbanization rate (1993, % of population):	74
Life expectancy (1993, years at birth):	71
Gross domestic product (1996, US$bn):	299.6
GDP per capita (1996, US$):	3102
Average annual GDP growth rate (1990-96, %):	1.9
Average annual inflation rate (1990-96, %):	21.7
Currency (peso per US$, average 1996):	7.6
Real exchange rate: (1990=100, average 1996)	91.13
Structure of production (1994):	60.9% services, 32% industry, 7.1% agriculture
Main exports:	cars, machinery and equipment, chemicals, tobacco
Main imports:	transport equipment, data processing machinery, electrical goods
Main trading partners:	US, Japan, EU
Market capitalization of Stock Exchange (December 1996; US$bn):	106.5
Total foreign debt (% of GDP):	58.4
Next elections due under normal circumstances:	Chamber of Deputies: July 1997; presidential and Senate: August 2000 Presidential & Senate: August
Credit rating: (Jan 1997, Standard & Poor's, Moody's)	BB; Ba2

FORECAST: 1997-2000 (average)

	Worst case	Most likely	Best case
Real GDP growth (%)	3.2	4.2	4.8
Inflation (%)	18	12	10

■ POLITICS

Historical overview

In 1521, the Spanish conquest of Mexico marked the beginning of three hundred years of Spanish rule. During this period, the country saw the dawn of economic development. But, social inequality between the Indian and mestizo populations on the one hand, and the conquistadors on the other triggered Mexico's fight for independence. Rebellion against the Spanish began in 1810 and independence was eventually achieved with the creation of the Republic of Mexico in 1821. Subsequently, war with the US, conflicts between governments and the Catholic church, economic problems and social disorder caused by the concentration of land ownership contributed to a period of political and economic instability, spanning some one hundred years. Dictatorships and civilian governments alternated until the mid-1920s. The election of Plutarco Elías Calles as president in 1924 did much to influence the country's future political development. He created the National Revolutionary Party (the Partido Nacional Revolucionario, predecessor of the Institutional Revolutionary Party, PRI) in 1929 and declared that all government members – army officers, civil servants and judges – had to be members of the party. Since then, Mexican politics have been PRI-dominated, although other parties have nominally been free to contest elections. While the PRI remains the leading political force, its predominance is diminishing and several states are ruled by opposition parties.

Recent events

In 1994, Mexico experienced the most traumatic political events of many years. On January 1, the uprising of the Zapatista National Liberation Army (EZLN) in the state of Chiapas broke out just as the North American Free Trade Agreement (NAFTA) came into force. Although the uprising did not pose a serious threat to Mexico's stability, the subsequent peace talks prompted reform of the electoral system. In March, Luis Donaldo Colosio, the PRI's candidate for the 1994 presidential election, was assassinated. In September, José Francisco Ruiz Massieu, the secretary-general of the PRI's national executive council, was murdered.

Political uncertainty receded somewhat with the triumph of Ernesto Zedillo in the presidential election of August 1994. At the same time, the PRI won 59% of the 500 seats in the Chamber of Deputies and 75% of the 64 seats in the Senate. But, since a two-thirds majority is required for constitutional amendments, the PRI's representation in the lower house is not sufficient to change the constitution without support from at least one of the opposition parties.

Chronology

1521	Aztec empire is brought to an end by the Spanish conquest
1810	Rebellion against the Spaniards
1821	Mexican independence
1845	War between Mexico and the US. Texas, California, Arizona and New Mexico are annexed to the US.
1863	French forces occupy Mexico City
1867	Withdrawal of the French troops
1876-1910	Authoritarian government under General Porfirio Días
1910-29	Alternating dictatorships and civilian government
1917	New constitution
1929	Creation of a governmental party, the National Revolutionary Party (Partído Nacional Revolucionario, or PNR) by President Plutarco Elías Calles. The PNR is renamed the Institutional Revolutionary Party (Partido Revolucionario Institutional , or PRI) in 1945.
1934-40	Presidency of Lázaro Cárdenas

late 1960s	Cuban revolution and left-wing movements in Latin America produces social tensions in Mexico
late 1970s	Discovery of the Chiapas oil field
1976-82	Presidency of José López Portillo
1982	Debt crisis and decline of public support for the PRI
1988	Carlos Salinas becomes president
1988	First non-PRI members in the Senate
1994	The North American Free Trade Agreement (NAFTA) enters into force
1994	Social unrest in Chiapas
1994	Assassination of the PRI's presidential candidate, Luis Donaldo Colosio and of the secretary-general of the PRI's national executive council, José Francisco Ruiz Massieu.
1994	Ernesto Zedillo wins the presidential election.
1994-95	Currency crisis and further decline of public support for the PRI
1996	Electoral and political reform

Constitution and government

Mexico is a democratic, federal republic. The 1917 constitution separated the executive, legislative and judicial powers. The president is directly elected for a single six-year term and represents the supreme executive authority. He appoints the members of the Council of Ministers, the senior military and civilian officers as well as the mayor of Mexico City. Legislative power is vested in the Congress, which is divided into a 500-member Chamber of Deputies and a 64-member Senate – representing the individual states and the federal district. Senators are elected every six years, whereas deputies are elected every three years, 300 of them from single-member constituencies and 200 chosen under a system of proportional representation. Judicial power is mainly vested in the Supreme Court, whose 21 magistrates are appointed for 6 years by the president and approved by the Senate.

Major electoral and political reforms were passed in 1996 for implementation in 1997. Included are 18 constitutional changes, such as the right to vote for Mexicans living abroad, the direct election of the Mexico City mayor, limits to campaign spending and greater independence for the Federal Electoral Institute. Overall, the legislation aims to free the electoral system from the grip of the PRI and the government.

State organization

The country consists of thirty-one states and the federal district of Mexico City. Each state is free and sovereign in all internal affairs and has its own constitution, whereby it can legislate and set taxes. Each state is administered by a governor directly elected for six years and a unicameral legislature whose members are chosen for a three-year term. Judicial officers are appointed by the state governments.

Political parties

Winning most of the presidential, gubernatorial and senatorial elections since its creation in 1929, the Institutional Revolutionary Party (PRI) has been virtually identical to the government. Despite a setback in 1988, when the left-wing alliance Frente Democrático Nacional (FDN) won seats in the Senate for the first time, the PRI still dominates Mexican politics. Nevertheless, the power of opposition parties has been growing since the beginning of the 1990s.

President Zedillo has promised to reform the PRI, but the party old guard is blocking any efforts to democratize the party and separate it from the government.

Institutional Revolutionary Party (PRI)
>Party of the revolution
>Founded 1929
>Led by Humberto Roque Villanueva

National Action Party (PAN)
>Conservative, largest opposition party
>Founded 1939
>Led by Felipe Calderon

Democratic Revolution Party (PRD)
>Left-wing
>Founded 1989
>Led by Andrés Manuel Lopez Obrador

Labour Party (PT)
>Left-wing
>Founded 1990
>Led by Alberto Anaya Gutierrez

Result of 1993 elections to the Senate and Chamber of Deputies
Senate: PRI (61 seats), PRD (2), PAN (1)
Chamber of Deputies: PRI (300 seats), PAN (119), PRD (71), PT (10)

Next elections
Chamber of Deputies: presidential July 1997 and Senate August 2000

Other political forces
Zapatista National Liberation Army (EZLN)
The main goals of the Zapatistas are to mobilize public opinion against the government's economic programme and a political system they deem authoritarian. They have succeeded by forcing the government to reform the educational system and to improve indigenous rights. They enjoy substantial support mainly within the peasant population in the south-eastern state of Chiapas.

At the beginning of 1996, the EZLN initiated peace negotiations with the Zedillo government. But as these talks have made little progress, a resurgence of political violence cannot be ruled out.

Central bank
The Bank of Mexico has acted as the country's central bank since 1925. However, it gained autonomy over monetary policy only in 1993, while exchange rate policy is still determined jointly with the Finance Ministry.

According to the Mexican constitution and the regulatory law of the Bank of Mexico, the central bank's primary objective is to maintain the stability of the domestic currency's purchasing power by controlling the expansion of the monetary base.

Target for 1996

Inflation	20.5%
Growth of M0	27.0%
Domestic credit growth	24%

■ ECONOMICS

Historical overview

Mexico's economic development took off after the Second World War as a result of restored political stability and a sharp increase in world demand for natural resources in which the country was rich. Until 1970, Mexico enjoyed high economic growth, low inflation and negligible public deficits. Encouragement of import substitution provided grounds for rapid industrialization, though finished goods were often expensive and of poor quality. Political turmoil at the end of the 1960s and the 1971 recession ended this success story. To regain public support, the Mexican government opted for populist policies, producing the desired economic growth, but also large budget deficits, soaring inflation and rising current account deficits. By late 1976, the peso had to be devalued for the first time in more than thirty years.

After a period of IMF-imposed austerity, the government had returned to aggressive spending and monetary expansion by the end of the 1970s. Accelerating inflation along with the fixed exchange rate provoked a rapid real appreciation of the peso. Both the budget deficit and the defence of the exchange rate were financed by foreign banks, leading to a sharp increase in external debt. But, as oil prices fell, speculation intensified on an eventual devaluation of the Mexican currency. This, coupled with an increase in US interest rates and the reluctance of foreign banks to lend more to Mexico, forced the government to announce, in August 1982, its inability to meet the amortization payments due on its foreign debt. This triggered the global debt crisis and ended four decades of economic growth. Inflation climbed, the budget deficit reached 17% of GDP and economic output fell 4.2% the following year. The economic reforms and the Programme of Immediate Economic Re-ordering, launched after the 1982 crisis, opened up the Mexican economy, resulting in increasing competition from abroad and tight government macroeconomic policies. As a consequence, Mexico experienced a long period of stagnation. Its real output and the inflation rate returned to the level attained in 1981 only in the late 1980s.

Mexico's economic performance, 1961-95

	Average annual real GDP growth, %	Average annual consumer price inflation, %
1961-1965	7.2	1.9
1966-1970	6.9	3.6
1971-1975	6.5	12.0
1976-1980	6.7	21.3
1981-1985	1.7	66.6
1985-1990	1.4	69.7
1991-1995	0.7	17.6

Source: IMF

Recent developments

The main reason for the modest growth of the early 1990s was the government's austerity programme. This aimed to reduce inflation and improve the country's competitive position within a future North American Free Trade Area (NAFTA). This austerity reduced the pace of nominal demand and output growth, resulting in rising unemployment. But inflation fell from 29.9% in 1990 to 7% in 1994.

The 1994 currency crisis

In 1994, investment opportunities in industrialized countries and monetary tightening in the US slowed inflows to Latin America. At the same time, Mexico's rising demand for imports resulted in a huge current account deficit. Because the growing external imbalance could no longer be financed by capital inflows, foreign exchange reserves had to be drawn upon. When capital started to leave Mexico in early 1994, the central bank provided liquidity by expanding domestic credit, but initially allowed interest rates to rise along with US interest rates.

In November, however, reserves dropped sharply after renewed unrest in the State of Chiapas and Mario Ruiz Massieu's accusation that high-profile PRI members had impeded the investigation into his brother's assassination. Owing to the negative effect of sharply increased Mexican interest rates, particularly on financial institutions, the central bank was reluctant to tighten monetary policy further in response to the changes in international capital flows. The authorities also feared that a sharp monetary tightening would spark investor suspicion, triggering further outflows. They also decided not to use the credit swap lines of US$6.5 billion that were available from Mexico's NAFTA partners. Since Mexican interest rates were not high enough to contain capital outflows, the authorities were eventually forced to widen the peso's floating band.

But the lifting of the peso/dollar ceiling on December 20, 1994, did not alleviate pressure on the country's foreign exchange reserves. On the contrary, reserves dropped sharply and two days later the government had to abolish the peso band completely.

The 1994 collapse of the peso brought strong capital outflows, high exchange rate volatility, sharply higher interest rates, a scarcity of liquidity and depressed domestic demand. As a result, 1995 output shrank by 6.9% and inflation rose to an annual average of 34.8%. The US dollar value of exports surged during 1995 and the beginning of 1996 as a result of Mexico's improved competitiveness after the peso devaluation. At the same time, year-over-year inflation fell to about 28% by the end of 1996 and, thanks to renewed access to international capital markets, Mexico's emergency borrowings from the US were repaid ahead of schedule.

The economy

Mexico's economy is characterized by low productivity in the agricultural sector and by relatively well-developed manufacturing and service sectors.

Agriculture and mining account for 7.4% and 3.4% of GDP, respectively. Silver is the most important mining product, followed by copper, lead and zinc. Manufacturing (mainly vehicles, machinery, chemicals and textiles) and the construction sectors generate 22.5% and 5.5% of total output, respectively.

Oil extraction and processing are also important contributors. Services account for about 60% of GDP. Commerce, restaurants and hotels represent one fourth of GDP, followed by financial services, insurance and real estate, at 11.5%.

Share of GDP by sector

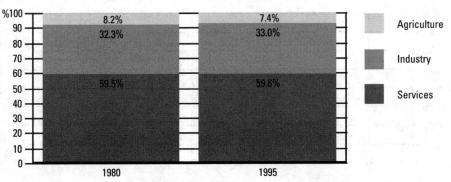

Source: Banco de Mexico

Saving and investment

Saving and investment ratios of Mexico have been low by international standards. After picking up in 1983, gross national saving declined to 15.9% of GDP in 1994 and rebounded to 16.7% in 1995. Investment remained around 22% of GDP for more than a decade until the end of 1994 but shrank to 17% in 1995 because of the economic crisis.

The gap between saving and investment has been financed mainly by foreign direct investment (FDI). In 1995, despite the high degree of uncertainty resulting from the peso crisis of December 1994, FDI flows amounted to US$5.5 billion. The maquiladora sector (see section on trade) was the largest recipient of FDI.

Trade

Mexico's dependence on foreign trade was modest until the 1994/95 crisis. But the country's improved international competitiveness after the peso devaluation resulted in a 40% rise of the dollar value of exports in 1995. This raised the share of exports as a percentage of GDP from 16% in 1994 to 32% in 1996.

The maquiladora sector includes companies whose production is orientated exclusively to foreign demand. These companies are located primarily along the US border and import semi-finished goods that are assembled and re-exported. They enjoy favourable tax treatment. Maquiladora exports account for 40% of total Mexican exports.

Mexico's export structure has diversified considerably in recent years. In 1983, oil accounted for two-thirds of total exports. But this portion declined to less than 11% in 1995 because of weaker oil prices, growing domestic demand for oil and the expansion of non-oil export products. Manufactured goods, such as cars, machinery and equipment, chemicals and tobacco, represented more than 83% of exports, up from about one quarter in 1983, while agricultural goods remained at 4%.

The composition of imports has also changed substantially during the last ten years. The share of intermediate goods in total imports increased from 7% in 1983 to 80% in 1995, reflecting the expansion of Mexico's processing industry, above all the maquiladora industry. Capital goods accounted for 18% of imports in 1995, while in the wake of the peso devaluation, imports of consumer goods collapsed from 12% of imports in 1994 to only 2% in 1995.

Balance of trade in US$m (excluding maquiladore)

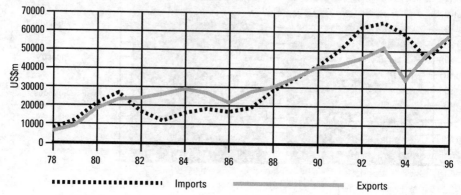

Source: IMF

Mexico's main trading partner is the United States, which purchased 85% of 1995 exports, while 69% of Mexican imports came from its northern neighbour. Japan and the European Union are also important partners, whereas trade with other Latin American countries is marginal, although closer links are desired.

Trade restrictions

Except for temporary imports of raw materials and intermediate goods for export industries, no import licence is required, but all imports must be accompanied by an exporter's declaration of shipment. The import tariff structure is based on the item's description and coding system of the General Agreement on Tariff and Trade. Export is free except for a few specific products.

Breakdown of exports (1995)

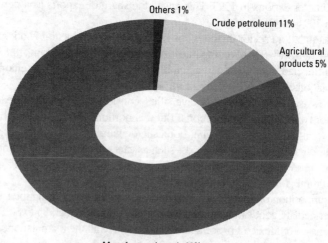

Source: IMF

Balance of payments

Strong import growth in the early 1990s created huge foreign trade deficits, amounting to US$18.5 billion in 1994, up from a roughly balanced account in the late 1980s. In 1995, due to Mexico's improved international competitiveness after the peso devaluation, the US dollar value of exports rose 30%. At the same time, the economic crisis led to a sharp drop in imports, resulting in a trade surplus of US$7.1 billion. Since the invisibles and transfer balances are traditionally slightly negative and interest payments increased sharply because of the higher risk premium, the current account remained slightly in deficit. However, compared to a current account deficit of US$29.4 billion or 7.8% of GDP in 1994, the 1995 deficit of US$720 million was very modest. The trade surplus decreased somewhat in 1996, due to a slowdown in US import growth and the acceleration of Mexican imports of consumer and capital goods in line with the general economic recovery.

In the beginning of the 1990s, Mexico's large current account deficits could be financed by capital inflows. Net capital inflows averaged US$28.1 billion per year between 1991 and 1993, including an annual US$24.4 billion of foreign direct and portfolio investment. However, higher US interest rates and increased political uncertainty after the Chiapas uprising and the Colosio assassination sharply reduced net inflows in 1994. Foreign direct investment resumed somewhat in 1995, reaching US$5.49 billion by the end of the year, and boomed again in 1996.

Current account as a % of GDP

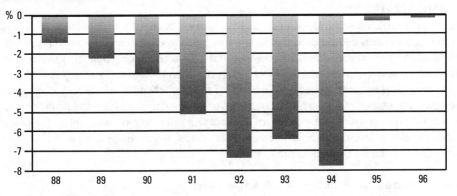

Source: IMF

Debt

In 1982, the government of Mexico said that it could no longer service its debt, an announcement that heralded the start of the international debt crisis. In the following years, several debt reschedulings were agreed, including a Brady Plan which reduced Mexico's foreign debt servicing to commercial creditors by about 35%. Although privatization proceeds allowed for the redemption of outstanding debt, Mexico's nominal foreign debt continued to increase in the 1990s and stood at US$175 billion in 1996. Mexico's debt service as a percentage of foreign exchange receipts declined from about 70% in 1982 to less than 30% in 1996. The proportion of total external debt to GDP was reduced significantly from 65% in 1987 to 43% in 1994, but increased again to about 60% in 1996, as a result of the currency crisis.

Economic policy

Monetary policy

The national bank of Mexico and the government have followed a monetary policy focused on price stability since the beginning of the 1990s. Money supply was controlled, trade restrictions and tariffs were cut and interest rates were kept attractive for foreign investors to ensure the continuation of capital flows. In the aftermath of the 1994-95 currency crisis, inflation soared and the Mexican government agreed with labour and business on an emergency economic plan, which resulted in a further tightening of monetary policy (including wage constraints and limits on growth of the monetary base and domestic credit). This allowed inflation to come down from 52% at end-1995 to 28% at end-1996.

Fiscal policy

Fiscal policy has been a key factor in Mexico's strategy to fight inflation, given that much of the inflation-fuelling money growth of the 1980s was due to central bank financing of the government budget deficit. The authorities were able to steadily reduce the public sector deficit from more than 14% of GDP in 1987 to a surplus of 0.2% in 1995. These improvements resulted mainly from a reduced interest burden (thanks to lower rates and to privatization, the revenues from which were partly used to redeem outstanding debt), and more efficient collection of direct taxes. In 1995 and 1996, despite the recession, fiscal policy remained tight and the budget was balanced.

Privatization

Many of the most attractive Mexican assets have already been sold. Legislation was passed during 1995 to open telecommunications services, satellite communication, natural gas distribution and the railroad system to foreign and private investors. But the privatization programme experienced a setback in October 1996, when the government announced that it was scrapping its earlier scheme for privatizing the petrochemical industry. According to the new plan, instead of selling off 100% of sixty-one secondary petrochemical plants owned by the state oil company Pemex, the government will offer no more than 49% of existing plants to private investors. The government also plans to privatize electricity generation plants and warehouse facilities in the near future.

Mexican peso/US dollar exchange rate

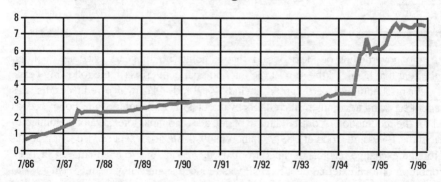

Currency

In December 1994, the Mexican peso was allowed to float freely, and the exchange regime based on the crawling peg was abandoned. This caused a dramatic currency drop, with the annual average of the exchange rate rising from 3.4 pesos/US$ in 1994 to 6.4 pesos/US$ in 1995. Since the crisis, the authorities have continued to pursue a floating exchange rate policy. Given low foreign exchange reserves, direct intervention of the Central Bank has been rare; the monetary authorities have pledged to use only interest rate changes to curb peso fluctuations. Nevertheless, the nominal value of the peso remained relatively stable from the end of 1995 to December 1996, while inflation continued well above that of the US, making the real effective exchange rate appreciate considerably in 1996.

Exchange controls

A free exchange rate applies to all export and import transactions without limits or special requirements.

Banking system

Although the Mexican banking system was privatized in the early 1990s, it remained characterized by poor asset quality and insufficient reserve coverage. As a consequence, the currency crisis of 1995 nearly led to a collapse of the banking system and the government had to implement debt relief programmes for mortgage holders and rescue plans for commercial banks whose solvency was jeopardized by the dramatic increase in loan defaults resulting from the sharp rise in interest rates. Having intervened in the affairs of seven commercial banks and purchased the bad debts of several others, the public sector now controls about one quarter of the banking sector's assets. Yet recapitalization (including the injection of fresh capital from foreign institutions), the improvement of asset quality and the reprivatization of institutions in public hands are essential to the sector's recovery, since one half of total loans in the system (about US$100 billion) are estimated to be non-performing.

■ EQUITIES

Index performance (in local currency)

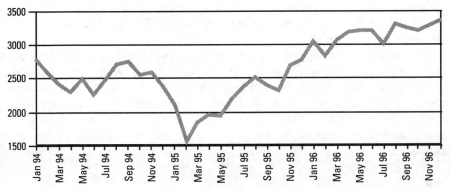

Key indicators

	Index performance %, in US$ terms	Market Cap. US$m	P/E	Div. Yield	Weight in IFCI	IFCG
1994	-41.6	130.2	17.1	1.8	23.9	12.9
1995	-27.0	90.7	28.4	1.1	9.2	5.6
1996	16.2	106.5	16.8	1.5	9.8	6.8

Sources: Local stock exchange, IFC, Bloomberg, Datastream, UBS

Structure

The Mexican Stock Exchange (BMV) is located in Mexico City. The exchange is split into two: the main market, and the intermediary (or second-tier) market.

Larger companies are listed in the main market, and medium-sized companies in the intermediary market. As at December 1994, there were 428 equity shares from 206 companies listed in the two markets. One hundred and seventy-six companies are listed in the main market, with only thirty in the second-tier market. The main market accounts for more than 99% of the market capitalization of the total stock market. As at November 1996, 189 domestic companies were listed on the BMV, with a total market capitalization of US$103.1 billion.

Regulatory authority

The National Banking and Securities Commission (CNBV) is Mexico's equivalent of the NYSE's Securities and Exchange Commission or the Securities and Investment Board in the UK. The CNBV is an independent public entity with administrative and financial autonomy. It has supervisory powers over all institutions in the Mexican primary and secondary markets. The CNBV's purpose is to supervise and regulate financial entities, in order to ensure their stability and adequate operation, as well as to maintain and promote the healthy and balanced development of the financial system as a whole, while seeking to protect the public.

Trading methods

In 1989, the indice de bursatilidad (marketability index), a system for ranking an equity issuer's marketability, was introduced, which categorizes stocks as having either high, medium, low or minimal marketability. Medium and high marketability issues continue to be traded using the open outcry system. Open outcry transactions on the trading floor are initiated by a quote made by a floor broker, who indicates whether the quote is a bid or an ask, the type of security, the ticker symbol, the series, the amount or nominal value of the securities involved and the price of the transaction.

Once executed, the trade is registered on the Stock Exchange. Low and minimal marketability shares (about half of the shares listed on the main and second-tier markets) are traded on the Automated Securities Trading System (SATO). This provides an electronic framework for the buying and selling of securities. Users of the system and regulatory authorities are provided with real-time trading information, and supervision and surveillance are carried out to ensure transactions are made in accordance with the relevant laws and regulations.

Hours

Trading starts at 08.30 and closes at 15.00, Monday to Friday.

Settlement time and clearing

Physical settlement is on a T+2 basis. S.D. Indeval is the Central Securities Depository of Mexico, regulated by the National Banking and Securities Commission (CNBV) and the Ministry of Finance. According to the Securities Market Act, its functions are the custody administration, transferring, clearing and settlement of the securities, and all securities listed on the Mexican Stock Exchange (with the exception of Federal Government issues) are deposited here. The custody agent is responsible for the settlement of cash and securities. Transfer is completed through book-entry procedures. S.D. Indeval also performs the administration of securities, which consists of collecting interest, dividend and redemption payments and distribution among holders. S.D. Indeval provides its depositors access to on-line information on their positions, as well the amounts to be paid for their securities.

Limits on price movement

The price of a share without a listed ADRs can only move 5% before trading is halted for thirty minutes. This can only happen three times in one day before trading of the stock is halted for the session. If a share has a listed ADR, there is no limit on the movement of a share price.

Stock indices

The IPC is the main index for the Mexican Stock Exchange. It is calculated from a sample ranging from thirty-two to forty of the most actively traded listed stocks (market capitalization-weighted). The IPC is updated every two months. There are also other indices such as the INMEX and the Mexican Intermediate Market Index, but these are used less often.

Taxes

Capital gains earned on shares sold through the bolsa are exempt from taxation. Non-residents investing in the Mexican stocks are not required to file any kind of Mexican tax return.

Dividends

There is no withholding tax on dividends. All companies run on a January to December fiscal calendar. Dividends are paid throughout the year (there are no limits on the frequency at which dividends can be paid).

Disclosure of financial statements

The National Securities and Banking Commission (CNBV) requires listed companies to file audited annual financial statements, unaudited quarterly (for some issuers, monthly) financial statements, and other financial information.

Shareholders' rights

Shareholders can vote by proxy in Mexico. All shareholders must be informed of extraordinary and annual general meetings.

Under the Securities Market Act, the National Securities and Banking Commission (CNBV) regulates the activities of brokerage firms which are required to:

1 Assume responsibility for the authenticity and integrity of the securities traded and guarantee the buyer that all securities were acquired legitimately.

2 Issue numbered, non-negotiable receipts made out to the investor backing the deposit.

3 Establish the commissions to be paid by investors, which may not exceed the maximum levels established by the National Securities and Banking Commission.

4 Assume responsibility for holding securities that have been deposited.

5 Deposit securities with S.D. Indeval.

6 In the event of disputes between a brokerage firm and its customers in connection with the contracting of services or transactions, the investor will have the option of filing a complaint with the National Securities and Banking Commission before entering into arbitration.

7 For further investor protection against the bankruptcy of a brokerage firm, the Stock Exchange and intermediaries have set up a Contingency Fund.

Ownership limits for non-residents

There are no restrictions on foreigners acquiring Free Subscription Series ("B" shares), since they are not reserved exclusively for Mexican nationals. In the past, investment in "B" shares was the most commonly used mechanism through which foreign investors acquired shares in Mexican companies.

Since 1989 foreign investment regulations have allowed foreigners to acquire series "A" shares through a trust fund (Neutral Fund), presently managed by Nacional Financiera (NAFINSA), a Mexican development bank. NAFINSA then issues Certificates of Ordinary Participation (CPOs) to the foreign investor. These certificates grant the foreign shareholder all pecuniary rights except voting rights. Foreign investors may acquire series "C" or "L" stocks, which are shares with limited voting rights.

Capital and foreign exchange controls

Aside from the above restrictions on foreign ownership of "A" shares, foreign investors may invest without restriction in all other equity instruments. Since December 1994, the peso has been allowed to float freely.

Brokers

There are currently thirty-three brokers in Mexico. It is only possible to do trades on the exchange through these official brokers.

Sectors

The largest (market capitalization-weighted) sectors represented on the Mexican exchange are telecommunications (23% of market capitalization), diversified industrials (13%), cement (10.2%) and financials (9.0%). Also important are the commerce/retail, beverage, entertainment, mining and paper sectors.

ADRs

As at April 1996, there are eighty-eight Mexican ADRs listed for sixty-five Mexican companies on US stock exchanges.

■ DEBT

The domestic bond markets are regulated by the Comision Nacional de Valores (CNV – Mexican Banking and Securities Commission), which is overseen by the Ministry of Finance.

Public debt

Bills and bonds are issued by the government through the Banco de Mexico, and registered at the Registro Nacional de Valores y Intermediaries (RNVI – National Securities and Intermediaries Register).

Cetes (treasury certificates)

Cetes are discount bills with maturities of 1, 3, 6, 12 and 24 months. Most repo agreements are transacted using Cetes, and the 1-month (28-day) Cetes rate is the benchmark interest rate for the market.In November 1995, Mexico issued a US$1.5 billion LIBOR/Cetes linked note with a 1-year maturity. At redemption, the note paid the higher of 12-month libor (fixed on the issue date) and the 28-day Cetes rate minus 6%, compounded each month over the life of the note. The libor option effectively provides a floor for the investment. Redemption proceeds were paid in US dollars at the exchange rate prevailing at maturity.

Bondes (federal government development bonds)

Development bonds are discount instruments with maturities of 12 and 24 months. They have floating rate coupons and pay interest every 28 days, based on the highest yielding 28-day security, plus or minus a spread.

Ajustabonos (inflation-indexed bonds)

Ajustabonos are issued with maturities of 3 to 5 years. Interest is paid quarterly, and is based on the principal amount of the bond adjusted by the CPI.

Tesobonos (treasury bonds)

Tesobonos were discount securities issued with maturities of 1, 3, 6 and 12 months. They were US dollar-indexed and payable in pesos converted at the free market exchange rate. Mexico assumed the currency risk. They were all redeemed in 1995 using some of the cash injected by the US as part of its rescue package. There have been no further issues since.

Primary market

Government securities are auctioned by the central bank on Tuesdays and settle two days later. Details of the week's auctions – size and whether single or multi price bidding – are announced by the Banco de Mexico on the preceding Friday. Cetes are auctioned every week and Adjustabonos every fortnight. Only eligible financial institutions can participate.

They must register each transaction with the central bank, and distinguish between proprietary and customer purchases.

Most secondary market trading is OTC, but deals can be transacted on the exchange. Trades settle in book entry form on the same day or up to two days later at Indeval, which also acts as custodian.

Repo agreements are allowed up to 360 days, and are transacted using all types of bill and bond instruments.

There is a new derivatives market for warrants (linked to the CPI and the Stock Exchange index), swaps, currency and interest rate futures.

Overseas investors receive interest from government securities tax-free, and some qualify for exemption from CGT. Foreign investors can operate their own peso accounts as long as they only receive proceeds from foreign exchange transactions.

Private debt

Banks issue promissory notes and bankers' acceptances with maturities of up to one year. They are discount securities. In addition, corporates issue debentures, subordinated debt and convertibles, and banks raise money for urban renovation, infrastructure construction and development by issuing bonds.

Commercial paper is issued by Mexican companies through domestic brokers with tenures of up to 360 days. A longer-dated domestic corporate bond market has not yet developed. Top-quality enterprises raise money through issuing international bonds.

Eurobonds

Although government-owned agencies and enterprises as well as private companies had some limited access to the international bond markets throughout the 1980s, Mexico did not issue using its sovereign name – the United Mexican States (UMS) – until eight years after the start of the debt crisis. In December 1990, it took a first tentative step by launching a US$ 40 million Yankee bond with a 10-year maturity, and over the next year issued bonds in the domestic markets of Germany, Spain and again the US. Its first eurobond arrived in November. Denominated in sterling with a 7-year maturity, it was priced at 227 basis points over UK government bonds and raised £100 million.

Over the next four years the UMS continued to issue in several domestic markets, launch euro medium term notes and make small eurobond offerings. In January 1994, it raised US$1 billion through Banamext SNC, and in July 1995 issued US$1 billion in floating rate notes using its sovereign name.

During the next year, UMS made several "jumbo" bond offerings, and then in July 1996 issued a US$6 billion floating rate 5-year note at 200 basis points over libor with a 2-year grace period. At the time, this was the largest ever eurobond issue to be launched. Standard & Poor's awarded the issue a BBB- rating, which was the first time Mexico had ever been given an investment grade rating. It was achieved because the bond was collateralized by a portion of the dollar earnings from state oil company Pemex, which are kept in an account at in the Federal Reserve Bank of New York.

In April 1996, Mexico exchanged US$1.75 billion of collateralized Brady bonds for a 30-year US dollar denominated global eurobond, which yielded 552 basis points over US treasuries. The swap meant that Mexico could sell back an equivalent proportion of the zero coupon US Treasury bonds which provided the collateral. The 30-year term of the eurobond signals Mexico's continued purpose of developing a yield curve for its international debt and, in particular, lengthening the maturity profile of its liabilities.

Eurobond issues (US$m)

	1990	1991	1992	1993	1994	1995	1996
Sovereign	288.8	1,323.2	886.1	2,788.9	2,617.1	5,477.0	10,679.2
Private	480.0	920.0	1991.8	5661.1	1796.5	—	2,575.0

Brady Bonds

Mexico was the first country to restructure its commercial bank under the Brady initiative. The agreement between creditor banks and the government was reached in 1989 and the new bonds issued in March 1990. The bank loans were replaced by discount bonds and par bonds with a 30-year maturity. The bonds are collateralized with 30-year zero coupons and have an 18-month rolling interest guarantee. They were issued with 'value recovery rights', which are indexed to the price of oil, paying an extra dividend when oil prices rise above a certain level.

Bond	Coupon	Collateral	Maturity	Currencies
Discount	6mth L=13/16	Principal+Interest	2019	Multiple
Par	6.25%	Principal+Interest	2019	
Aztec	6mth L +1 5/8	Principal and interest	2008	

Aztec bonds trade alongside the Bradys. They were issued in 1988 as part of an earlier restructuring and received collateral at the time of the Brady issue to ensure they enjoyed equal standing with the newer bonds. As the price approaches par the Aztecs are expected to be called by the debtor.

■ MEXICO: Economic indicators

Population and development	1990	1991	1992	1993	1994	1995	1996e
Population, million	86.2	87.8	89.5	91.2	93.0	94.8	96.6
Population growth, %	2.2	2.0	1.9	1.9	2.0	1.9	1.9
Nominal GDP per capita, US$	2868	3308	3734	4030	4054	2640	3102

National accounts							
Nominal GDP, US$bn	247.1	290.5	334.3	367.6	377.1	250.2	299.6
Change in real GDP, %	4.4	3.5	2.7	0.4	3.5	-6.2	4.9
Gross fixed capital formation, % of GDP	18.4	19.2	20.5	20.0	20.3	16.3	16.8

Money supply and inflation							
Narrow money, change %, Dec/Dec	63.1	123.9	15.1	17.7	5.2	10.0	41.5
Broad money, change %, Dec/Dec	75.8	49.3	22.8	14.4	22.7	42.0	30.0
Consumer price inflation (avg.) %	26.7	22.7	15.5	9.8	7.0	34.8	35.3
Producer prices (avg.) %							

Interest rates *=latest figures							
Money market rate, annual average	34.70	19.30	15.60	14.90	14.10	48.60	28.00
Treasury bill rate, annual average	34.76	19.28	15.62	15.03	14.10	48.44	29.57*
Deposit rate, annual average	31.24	17.10	15.68	15.46	13.26	39.18	23.61*

Government finance							
Government balance, % of GDP	-2.2	-0.3	1.6	0.7	-0.3	0.2	0.0

Exchange rates lc=local currency							
Exchange rate, annual average, lc/US$	2.81	3.02	3.09	3.12	3.38	6.41	7.60
Exchange rate, end of year, lc/US$	2.95	3.07	3.12	3.11	5.33	7.66	7.88
Real exchange rate 1990=100	100.0	110.0	119.3	128.8	120.9	82.5	91.1

Balance of payments							
Exports of goods & services, US$m	48843	51557	55471	61403	71205	89831	105330
Change %	15.3	5.6	7.6	10.7	16.0	26.2	17.3
Imports of goods & services, US$m, fob	51915	60955	74089	77413	92271	81861	97380
Change %	21.7	17.4	21.5	4.5	19.2	-11.3	19.0
Trade balance, of goods only, US$m, fob-fob	-844	-7308	-15934	-13481	-18464	7096	6950
Current account balance, US$m	-7451	-14888	-24442	-23400	-29418	-720	-500
as a % of GDP	-3.0	-5.1	-7.3	-6.4	-7.8	-0.3	-0.2

Foreign exchange reserves							
Foreign exchange reserves, US$m	9446	17140	18394	24886	6101	15250	17000
Gold at ⅔ of market price, US$m	236.3	222.6	157.4	116.0	109.0	131.5	128.0
Import cover (reserves/imports), months	2.2	3.4	3.0	3.9	0.8	2.2	2.1

Foreign debt and debt service							
Short-term debt, US$m	15368	28220	41374	57779	59676	43118	45000
Total foreign debt, US$m	105333	121597	132713	153573	162392	174081	175000
as a % of GDP	42.6	41.9	39.7	41.8	43.1	69.6	58.4
as a % of foreign exchange receipts	187.7	210.2	215.2	226.7	206.6	178.5	154.8
Interest payments, US$m	9222	9215	9611	10934	11807	13333	14400
Principal repayments, US$m	5451	5604	6749	6803	8625	7245	12550
Total debt service, US$m	14673	14819	16360	17737	20432	20578	26950
as a % of goods exports	36.0	34.7	35.4	34.2	33.6	25.9	28.6
as a % of foreign exchange receipts	26.2	25.6	26.5	26.2	26.0	21.1	23.8

Morocco

Area (thousands of km²):	447
Population (1995, millions):	27.1
Population projection (2025, millions):	43
Population younger than 15 yrs (1991, % of total):	40.7
Urbanization rate (1993, % of population):	47
Life expectancy (1993, years at birth):	64
Gross domestic product (1996, US$bn):	38.9
GDP per capita (1996, US$):	1407
Average annual GDP growth rate (1990-96, %):	3
Average annual inflation rate (1990-96, %):	5.6
Currency (dirham per US$, average 1996):	8.7
Structure of production (1994):	50.1% services, 34.2% industry, 15.7% agriculture
Main exports:	textiles, phosphoric acid, phosphate rock, citrus fruits
Main imports:	capital goods, energy products, consumer goods
Main trading partners:	EU (France, Spain, Germany, Italy), US
Market capitalization of Stock Exchange (October 1996; US$bn):	7.6
Total foreign debt (% of GDP):	60.3
Next elections due under normal circumstances:	June 1999

FORECAST: 1997-2000 (average)

	Worst case	Most likely	Best case
Real GDP growth (%)	0.7	4.7	5.8
Inflation (%)	4.7	2.9	2.4

■ POLITICS

Historical overview

Morocco's strategic location has traditionally attracted foreigners who traded in, settled or invaded the land. Romans, Vandals, Visigoths and Byzantine Greeks successively ruled the area until Arab forces began occupying Morocco in the late 600s, bringing with them Arab civilization and Islam. Berbers ruled the country from about 1050 until 1268, extending into Spain. Competition among the European powers for control over Morocco began as early as the 15th century.

The presently reigning Alaouite dynasty gained power towards the middle of the 17th century. The first Alaouite, Moulay Rachid, took hold of the north of Morocco. His successor, Moulay Ismail, a contemporary of Louis XVI, extended his authority to the Berbers and successfully fought the Turks in Algeria. Several Alaouite sovereigns succeeded.

In 1912, a protectorate treaty was signed first with France, then with Spain, who assumed protection of the northern and southern (Saharan) zones. A manifesto of the Istiqlal Party in 1944 was one of the earliest public demands for independence – "Istiqlal" means "independence, and the party subsequently provided most of the leadership for the nationalist movement. France's exile of the highly respected sultan Mohammed V in 1953 and his replacement by the unpopular Muhammad Ben Aarafa, whose reign was perceived as illegitimate, sparked active opposition to the French protectorate. France allowed Mohammed V to return in 1955 and negotiations leading to independence began the following year. In 1956 Mohammed V gained Morocco its independence. Moroccan control over certain Spanish-ruled areas was restored through agreements with Spain in 1956 and 1958. On October 29, 1956, the signing of the Tangier Protocol politically reintegrated the former international zone.

After the death of his father, Mohammed V, King Hassan II succeeded to the throne on March 3, 1961. He recognized the Royal Charter proclaimed by his father on May 8, 1958, which outlined steps towards establishing a constitutional monarchy. A constitution providing for representative government under a strong monarchy was approved by referendum on December 7, 1962. Elections were held in 1963. In June 1965, following student riots and civil unrest, the king invoked Article 35 of the constitution and suspended parliament. He assumed all legislative and executive powers and named a new government not based on political parties.

In July 1970, King Hassan submitted to referendum a new constitution providing for an even stronger monarchy. An unsuccessful coup on July 10, 1971, organized by senior military officers at Skhirat, was followed by Morocco's third constitution, in 1972. The new constitution kept King Hassan's powers intact but enlarged from one third to two thirds the number of directly elected parliamentary representatives. In August 1972, after a second coup attempted by Moroccan Air Force dissidents and the king's powerful interior minister General Oufkir, relations between the opposition and the Crown deteriorated further, due to disagreement on opposition participation in elections.

Chronology

788	First Muslim dynasty
1649	Beginning of Alaouite rule
1912	Protectorate treaty signed with France, then with Spain
1953	France exiles Sultan Mohammed V, sparking active opposition to the French protectorate
1956	After being allowed to return, Mohammed V gives Morocco its independence from France
1961	The Crown Prince is enthroned under the name of Hassan II
1962	Constitution providing for representative government under a strong monarchy is approved by referendum and leads to the first elections
1970	July: new constitution providing for an even stronger monarchy
1971	July: unsuccessful coup by senior military officers
1972	Third constitution, approved by popular referendum

1972	August: second coup attempt by Moroccan Air Force dissidents and interior minister General Oufkir
1974	Rapprochement between the king and the opposition begins
1992	September: king appoints the prime minister to head government; parliamentary powers are expanded
1996	September: referendum to create two houses of parliament, with the direct election of new lower house

Constitution and government

The king is head of state, and his son, the Crown Prince, is heir apparent. He also controls the military and ensures loyalty by catering to its welfare. But the king is also the spiritual leader, and as son of Mohammed V, national hero, with Alaouite ancestry, King Hassan has unquestioned authority. Most major political decisions are made by King Hassan himself, although he relies on a few key advisers.

Under the constitutional monarchy, the king rules with a parliament, the Chamber of Representatives. All cabinet members are appointed by the king and are directly responsible to him. Parliament can be dissolved in case of national emergency and the king governs by decree, as was the case from the mid-1960s to the mid-1970s. Subsequently, King Hassan allowed for a limited democracy, but using competition between the major parties to extract promises in exchange for participation in the cabinet. Under the 1972 constitution, two-thirds of parliamentary representatives are directly elected, while the remainder are chosen by local councils, chambers of commerce and salaried worker unions. The limited degree of democratic expression has produced a diversified political life by Arab or African standards. Nevertheless, the role of the monarchy and Morocco's Islamic status is unquestionable. The parliament is not the legislative body, and has no power over the budget, cabinet or j-udiciary. Instead it acts to build national consensus. And, while it can pass laws, they are subject to ratification by the king.

New constitution

Under the 1992 constitution, which preserved the constitutional monarchy and authority of the king, a prime minister appointed by the king is head of government, which is now responsible to the legislature rather than directly to the king, as before. The constitution strictly forbids a single-party structure. Of the 333-seat unicameral parliament, two thirds of the members are chosen directly by universal adult suffrage; the remaining third is indirectly elected by community councils and business, labour, artisan, and farmer groups.

The parliament's powers, though limited, were expanded by the 1992 constitution and include budgetary matters, approving bills presented by the king and establishing ad hoc commissions of inquiry to investigate actions by the executive branch. Yet in 1993, following opposition parties' refusal to join a minority cabinet, King Hassan appointed a non-political cabinet responsible only to him.

Nevertheless, the political system is opening up progressively and opposition parties are being allowed greater party involvement. A referendum in September 1996 approved a change in constitution to set up a second house of parliament. The new lower house will be directly elected, and its creation paves the way for decentralized power. However, the role of the monarchy is not questioned. The king will preserve wide-reaching powers and maintain control in key areas.

The highest court in the independent judicial structure is the Supreme Court, the judges of which are appointed by the king (who also appoints the provincial governors). The legal system is based on Islamic law and French and Spanish civil law system. There is judicial review of legislative acts in the Constitutional Chamber of the Supreme Court. Members of the National Assembly serve six-year terms. The last elections were held on June 25, 1993, and the next are scheduled for June 1999.

Current government
Executive branch:

Chief of State	King Hassan II
Prime Minister	Abdellatif Filali

Officials:

Agriculture	Hassan Abouyoub
Energy and Mines	Abdellatif Gueraoui
Finance and Foreign Investments	Mohamed Kabbaj
Foreign Affairs and Co-operation	Abdellatif Filali
Foreign Trade	Mohamed Alami
Industry, Commerce and Privatization	Driss Jettou
Information	Driss Alaoui M'daghri
Interior	Driss Basri
Justice	Abderrahmane Amalou
Labour & Social Affairs	Amine Damnati
Post & Telecommunication	Hamza Kettani
Public Works	Abdelaziz Meziane Belfkih
Tourism	Mohamed Alaoui Mohamadi
Transport	Said Ameskane

State organization

Morocco is divided into sixty provinces and five urban prefectures, all of which are governed by non-elected officials from the Ministry of Interior. Cities and rural communes elect communal councils headed by presidents chosen by the council members. Several of Morocco's larger municipal councils elect a president of the Urban Commune and have recently been granted greater budgetary authority by the Moroccan parliament. Most local authority, however, remains in the hands of the non-elected officials of the Ministry of the Interior.

Political parties

The pro-government RNI and UC parties won the largest number of seats in local elections in 1992. In 1993, parliamentary elections gave 50% of the vote to the six parties of the previous governing coalition, but the two largest opposition parties, the Istiqlal and USFP, which ran common candidates, received the highest individual party vote totals. Together they took 41% of the seats contested (four smaller parties and independents won the remainder). These elections demonstrated a significant increase in the opposition's representation. The expansion of parliament's authority under the September 1992 constitution was another indicator of Morocco's political liberalization.

Pro-government parties
Berber-based Popular
Promotes and protects Berber culture Movement (MP) and interests
Led by Mohamed Laenser
Total seats: 51
National Popular Movement (MNP)
Promotes and protects Berbers
Led by Mahjoubi Ahardane
Total Seats: 25
The Constitutional Union Party (UC)
Centre-right
Founded 1983
Led by former prime minister Maati Bouabid.
Total seats: 54
The National Democratic
Break-away from RNI (see below); Party (PND) mainly rural-based
Founded 1981
Led by Arsalane El Jadidi
Total seats: 24

Opposition parties
Istiqlal (IP)
Morocco's oldest political party; strongly nationalistic; active on pan-Arab issues
Founded 1944
Led by M'hamed Boucetta
Total seats: 50
Party of Progress
Communist; illegal from 1969 until and Socialism (PPS) 1974; urban and young supporters
Founded 1943
Led by Secretary General Ali Yata
Total seats: 10
Organization for Democratic and Popular Action (OADP)
Strongly leftist on domestic issues
Led by Mohammed Ben Said
Total seats: 2
Union of Socialist Popular
Social democrat; urban and organized Forces (USFP) labour supporters
Founded 1974
Led by Mohammad al Yazghi
Total seats: 52

Independent parties
The National Rally of Independents (RNI)
> Founded 1977
> Led by Ahmed Osman
> Total seats: 41

Three other independent parties account for nine parliamentary seats. Labour unions and community organizations, which are indirectly elected only, share a total of fifteen seats in parliament.

Other political forces
Military
While there were earlier coup attempts in 1971 and 1972, the king now has a loyal army. The army fully supports Hassan II and he, in turn, provides the army with substantial benefits. About a third of government spending goes to the military. The war in the Sahara served to enhance the army's prestige and to increase its capabilities. Moreover, the war helped keep the military out of daily politics and away from the king.

Western Sahara
In 1969, the Polisario Front (Popular Front for the Liberation of the Saguia el Hamra and Rio de Oro) was formed to combat Spanish colonization. The Polisario claims to represent the aspirations of the Western Saharan inhabitants for independence. Morocco's claim to sovereignty over the Western Sahara is based largely on the historical argument of traditional loyalty of the Saharan tribal leaders to the Moroccan sultan as spiritual leader and ruler. The International Court of Justice, to which the issue was referred, has judged the claims as insufficient to establish Moroccan sovereignty. In 1975 Spain, Morocco, and Mauritania announced a tripartite agreement for an interim administration under which Spain agreed to share administrative authority with Morocco and Mauritania, leaving aside the question of sovereignty. Spain's role in the administration of the Western Sahara gradually ceased altogether. Mauritania withdrew from the territory in 1978. Later, local elections and the election of representatives to the National Assembly took place and Morocco proclaimed the area reintegrated into Morocco. It has since built fortifications that control about three-quarters of the Western Sahara and protect the economic and population centres. War between Morocco and the Polisario took place in the 1980s following Morocco's installation.

In 1988, Moroccan and Polisario representatives, meeting separately with United Nations officials, agreed on a peace plan proposed by the UN Secretary General. A cease-fire and project for a referendum went into effect in September 1991 between Morocco and the Polisario. The referendum, which aims at determining whether the region will choose integration with Morocco or independence, was originally scheduled for 1992 but has yet to be held because of differences between the two parties regarding the details of implementation.

Central bank
The central bank operates as an independent entity. It is headed by the governor (currently Mohamed Seqat), who is appointed by the king. Following economic reform measures, the central bank has been markedly successful in restoring domestic and international

confidence in the value of the local currency. The dirham has been made convertible for an increasing number of transactions over the last few years. The central bank sets the exchange rate for the dirham against a basket of currencies of its principal trading partners. The rate against the basket has been steady since a 9% devaluation in May 1990, with changes against the dollar generally caused by movement of the dollar against major European currencies.

Bank Al-Maghrib lifted all ceilings on interest rates in February 1996. Interest rates are now determined freely, allowing for competition between banks. An interbank money market was developed, so that banks now trade with each other on a daily basis. The central bank adopted new instruments to manage liquidity – commercial banks can bid for liquidity via the central bank's 7-day repurchase agreements; 5-day and 24-hour agreements are also available at penalty rates. A secondary market of government paper has not yet developed and the central bank is hence, not in a position to regulate liquidity through open-market operations. In June 1996, the interbank foreign exchange market began operating, which allows Moroccan banks to trade any foreign currency on the spot market and take forward positions for trade operations. Banks that exceed the authorized limits are required to buy or sell currency to the Bank Al-Maghrib at the end of the day. Although banks may now trade foreign exchange, the central bank still controls the nominal exchange rate and it sets a buy-sell rate against the dirham for each of the currencies at the beginning of each trading session. The central bank can provide the government with substantial credit to finance the budgetary gap. The government is somewhat constrained in financing via issues of public debt instruments, partly because the central bank lowered the requirement to hold government paper as a proportion of bank deposits from 25% to 20% and then to 15% early this year. This in turn has reduced bank purchases of government paper.

■ ECONOMICS

Historical overview

Morocco faces the typical challenges of other countries, especially those with a history of central authority – restraining government spending, reducing constraints on private activity and foreign trade, and keeping inflation within bounds. Severe economic problems beginning in the 1980s resulted in social unrest and violent clashes with police. The onset of payment imbalances and high foreign debt led Morocco to request IMF assistance in 1983. The IMF granted a stand-by agreement on condition that Morocco cut the budget deficit and liberalize foreign trade. However, not all targets were implemented for fear of popular protest, resulting in the suspension of IMF credit on several occasions. In 1988, credits were granted again, conditional on the adoption of tighter monetary and fiscal policy and on clearance of debt arrears. Social unrest led King Hassan to introduce mitigating measures in 1991, including a higher minimum wage, new jobs for unemployed university students and institutionalized annual negotiations with unions on wage increases and benefits. The last IMF credit extension, from January 1992 to March 1993, targeted the budget and current account deficits. However, by 1993, continued droughts had aggravated economic difficulties, once again leading to discontent and a wave of strikes. Emergency programmes were implemented to alleviate the hardship and reduce the increasing rural-urban shift.

The Moroccan economy has been subject to significant performance swings during the 1990s as a result of variable agricultural conditions.

	Average annual real GDP growth, %	Average annual consumer price inflation, %
1971-1975	6.0	7.5
1976-1980	5.0	9.7
1981-1985	3.4	9.9
1986-1990	4.4	4.7
1991-1995	1.2	6.0

The economy

Since the IMF programme expired, the government has attempted a continuation of tight monetary and fiscal policies, further liberalization of the economy and debt servicing. Yet the need to overcome social problems, especially related to droughts, often resulted in expansionary policy instead.

Food represents 45% of the consumer price index, and rises in inflation can largely be attributed to higher agricultural prices. Currently, Morocco is implementing a comprehensive economic and social programme in a five-year plan, calling for austerity measures that would reduce the budget deficit to 1% of GDP by the year 2000, while maintaining a 5-6% maximum rate of inflation. Reduced revenues and higher capital expenditure have widened the deficit since 1992. To offset the fall in revenue, the government plans to expand the tax base and improve tax collection. Privatization has become one of the most important means of raising revenue. Despite several setbacks, the kingdom continues to strive to loosen capital controls, strengthen the banking sector, and privatize state enterprises. High unemployment, vulnerability to external economic forces and servicing the large debt remain long-term problems for Morocco. Over the last decade, government reforms have contributed to rising per capita incomes, lower inflation, and narrower fiscal and current account deficits.

The Moroccan economy has difficulty employing the existing labour force. Each year sees about 350,000 new job-seekers entering the market, 100,000 of which at least secondary-school graduates. There is thus a growing number of disappointed youths who have begun joining popular revolts and radical Islamic groups, or have even disassociated themselves from the official system to create their own forms of employment, manufacturing, trading and selling goods outside the economy. Population growth, rural-urban migration, and higher labour force participation rates (particularly among women) are contributing to rising urban unemployment, in spite of generally strong economic growth and job creation. The rapid increase in secondary and university (but not primary) enrolments in the 1980s exceeded the economy's capacity to create jobs, resulting in rising unemployment rates for graduates, which are about 33% for high school graduates and 11% for university graduates.

Importance of agriculture

The Moroccan economy has substantial assets, including the world's largest phosphate reserves, diverse agricultural and fishing resources, a sizeable tourist industry, a growing manufacturing sector, and remittances from Moroccans working abroad. Morocco is poor in natural resources, but it is one of the world's major suppliers of phosphate rock. In addition, there is some production of iron ore, lead, manganese, copper, fluorite and zinc. About one third of the Moroccan manufacturing sector is related to phosphates and one third to agriculture with most of the remaining third divided between textiles, clothing, and metal-working. The clothing sector has shown consistently strong growth over the last few years as foreign companies established large-scale operations geared towards exporting garments to Europe. Fishing is also important to Morocco, employing more than 100,000 people (including canning and packing workers). But agriculture remains singularly important. Severe droughts in 1992-93 and in 1995 depressed economic activity and held down exports.

The agricultural sector accounts for almost half of the country's workforce, yet provides less than a fifth of its income. Given the importance of agriculture in the kingdom's social setting, the success or failure of harvests has a significant impact on the well-being of the population. Not only is agricultural production at the mercy of rainfall, it suffers from other constraints as well. Just one third of agricultural land is actually considered favourable with sufficient precipitation, but farmers still attempt to cultivate unsuitable land, resulting in poor harvests. In addition, 85% of farmland is privately owned, while the rest is owned by indigenous or religious groups and therefore often inefficiently cultivated. Better irrigation techniques are needed but financing is constrained by relatively high interest rates and by efforts to reduce the budget deficit restricting government expenditure. Moreover, the government has made no attempt at land reform.

Share of GDP by sector

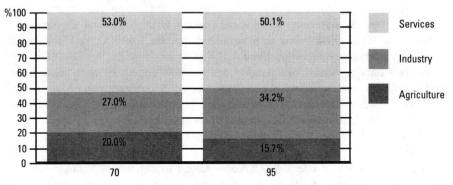

Source: Official data

Economic growth has fluctuated significantly as a result of substantial variations in agricultural output that are transmitted to the rest of the economy because of important linkages with secondary and tertiary activities. Agriculture experienced major disasters in 1992 and 1993, followed by a recovery in 1994, before being hit by the worst drought in Moroccan history in 1995. Real GDP contracted by 4.4% in 1992, 1.1% in 1993 and a staggering 7.5% in 1995. Favourable rainfall in 1994 boosted agricultural production by 40%, resulting in economic growth of 11% for the year. The trade deficit also rose sharply in 1995, as the drought forced the import of 2.4 million tonnes of cereals. Yet Morocco's industrial sector is remarkably diversified, including food processing, textiles, car assembly, cement, ceramics and paper industries. Although manufacturing contributes 18% of GDP and agriculture 19%, the much larger share of employment in the agricultural sector guarantees that any changes in agricultural output will have a magnified effect on the overall economy. The importance of weather conditions, specifically rainfall, therefore explains the sharp fluctuations seen in overall output and points to a major source of instability in the Moroccan economy.

Savings and investment

Morocco's saving and investment levels have been slowly decreasing this decade, although they are on a comparable level with other emerging economies. National saving has fallen from 25% of GDP in 1990 to about 15% in 1995, while investment has fallen from 26% to 22% in the same period. However, the privatization programme has the potential to bring in significant portfolio investment, as in 1994 when it reached US$238 million.

Direct investment has also become significant for the economy, reaching close to US$600 million in 1994. The poor economic prospects and slowdown in privatization, however, restricted investment inflows in 1995. Nevertheless, inflows should rise again as privatization picks up pace and as investors take advantage of the new investment laws.

Chronic trade deficits

The kingdom's principal exports are textiles, phosphoric acid, phosphate rock, and citrus fruits, while its main import is cereals. The export of phosphates and its derivatives alone account for more than a quarter of Moroccan exports and together with food and other mineral products, they account for about 40% of total exports. The combination of falling demand, lower prices and rising foreign competition is taking its toll on exports of phosphate rock. Textiles and fishing each account for roughly 10% of exports. Textiles also face trade barriers from the European Union.

Morocco runs a chronic merchandise trade deficit, largely because of its import dependence for most of its energy needs as well as for a significant portion of its cereal requirements, which is generally offset by earnings from tourism, workers remittances and foreign investment. Approximately 1.7 million Moroccans work abroad, mainly in France, the Netherlands, Belgium, Italy and other EU countries, as well as in Libya, Algeria and the Gulf States.

Overall, the current account deficit has remained moderate and Morocco does not have great difficulty in covering the balance of external financing requirements through conventional sources. Official loans have gradually lessened in significance. Morocco's foreign exchange reserves grew steadily in recent years, reaching seven months' worth of merchandise imports by the end of 1994. A major boost in reserves came from Gulf States' payments in connection with the Gulf War, in appreciation of Morocco's alliance. A recent widening of the merchandise trade deficit and falling receipts from tourism, workers remittances and foreign investment have begun to put pressure on Morocco's foreign exchange reserves, which started to fall in 1995 and will continue to do so in 1996 and 1997.

The trade deficit widened in 1994 as imports grew slightly more than exports. The growth in exports was led by an increase in phosphates and phosphate derivatives. Agricultural exports also rose thanks to good harvests. The deficit widened further in

1995 due to increased cereals imports and lower growth in exports of phosphates and agricultural products. Exports are projected to grow faster than imports in 1996 and 1997, generating a slight reduction in the trade deficit. Tourism receipts fell considerably in 1994, when the Moroccan government closed its border with Algeria, and in 1995. Remittances also fell in both 1994 and 1995, reflecting in part the tighter immigration policies in Europe and diminishing ties between Moroccans already in Europe and their homeland.

Tourism receipts and remittances are expected to recover in 1996 and 1997. Overall, the current account deficit will remain largely unchanged in 1997 following a significant drop from US$1.5 billion in 1995 to US$0.8 billion in 1996; it is expected to rise to US$1 billion in 1997. Economic prospects for 1996 were promising in view of heavy rainfalls expected to boost GDP growth, reducing upward pressure on prices. To sustain growth over the medium term, however, the authorities must increase efforts to remove structural imbalances and to generate foreign capital and investment.

Exports and imports as a % of GDP

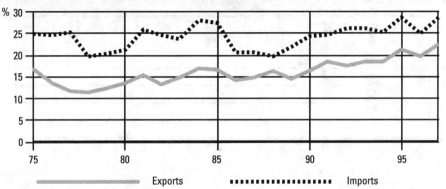

Source: Official data

Breakdown of exports (1994)

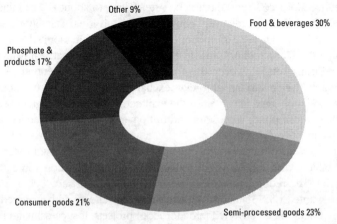

Source: Official data

The EU is Morocco's principal trading partner, accounting for almost two thirds of exports and imports. Trade and co-operation agreements have been the norm with the EU, although these have proved disappointing for the kingdom in light of an increased EU protectionist stance. Consequently, Morocco requested a partnership agreement, with the ultimate goal of full membership in the EU. In February 1996, an accord was signed giving Morocco association status, creating a free-trade zone for European industrial goods and services within twelve years. The EU will also be given preferential treatment relative to other trading partners. In return, the kingdom will receive EU funds to help its own industries adapt to the increased competition. The agreement also resolves a dispute over fisheries, reducing EU access to Moroccan territorial waters.

Current account as a % of GDP

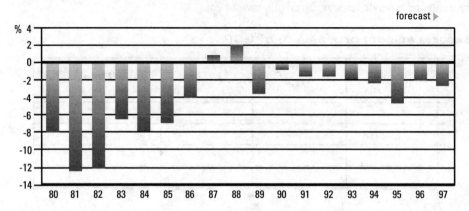

Source: Official data

Debt

In the early 1980s, Morocco's external debt rose to a critical point, leading to several reschedulings with official and commercial creditors. Debt reschedulings and write-offs have managed to reduce Morocco's substantial debt. After falling to about US$22 billion in 1990, the level of debt has remained relatively constant, although it has steadily decreased as a share of GDP, from 122% in 1985 to about 74% in 1995. The kingdom's last rescheduling agreement with Paris Club creditors was in 1992 and the government can now borrow on international credit markets. However, the end of reschedule agreements has raised debt-service considerably. Given substantial foreign exchange reserves, Morocco should not face future problems with debt repayment. Since the expiration of the IMF programmes, the kingdom has followed a firm policy of prompt and full payment of its debt-service and intends to increase its payments on past debt.

Financial support from donors, following the 1995 drought, raised external debt to almost US$24 billion with only a slight reduction to US$23.4 billion forecast for 1996. Government efforts to reduce its debt and debt-service burden are beginning to come through. France granted US$75 million worth of debt forgiveness and has agreed to auction US$120 million of debt to be converted into Moroccan projects. If successful, additional conversions will be used in the future.

Economic policy

Government role

The government's pursuit of the IMF economic reform programme has led it to restrain government spending, revise the tax system, reform the banking system, follow appropriate monetary policies, ease import restrictions, lower tariffs and liberalize the foreign exchange regime. Further reforms are still needed in some areas, notably trade and agriculture. Yet the Moroccan government has reduced considerably its role in the economy over the last decade, eliminating direct credit and foreign exchange allocation, reducing trade barriers, cutting government spending and taxes, and implementing a privatization programme. Overall, reforms have contributed to lower inflation, narrower fiscal and current account deficits, and modest growth in per-capita income during the last decade. Despite an overall positive trend, there have been wide year-to-year fluctuations due to exogenous factors such as rainfall and conditions in Morocco's export markets.

Monetary policy

In the early 1990s, monetary authorities were focusing on monetary restraint via increases in the reserve requirements. The Bank Al-Maghrib is currently attempting to move away from instruments of direct monetary control. Consequently, interest rates have been liberalized and the reserve requirement for banks has been lowered from 25% to 15%. The system of linking bank lending rates to banks' cost of funds was changed in 1994 in order to lower lending rates, although they remain relatively high.

The Bank Al-Maghrib has recently adopted new instruments to manage liquidity. Commercial banks are now able to bid for liquidity through 5-day, 7-day and 24-hour repurchase agreements. These reforms should allow the private sector easier and cheaper access to credit, which in turn, will boost investment. In addition, a legal framework was established to introduce new financial instruments, including mutual funds, commercial paper, and certificates of deposit.

The central bank has also granted exceptional financing for the government's fiscal deficit. Such financing, however, is unsustainable in the long run, and could lead to higher inflation or pressure on reserves.

Fiscal policy

While the Moroccan government has reduced its budget deficit over the last decade, in recent years it has experienced increasing difficulty meeting budget targets, as projected increases in the tax base and revenues have not materialized (largely because of the droughts), and current expenditure has not been stemmed. Meanwhile, budget financing requirements are putting pressure on the domestic capital market.

After declining to about 2% of GDP, the budget deficit widened substantially between 1993 and 1995, to reach almost 6% of GDP. Much of the deterioration resulted from a combination of reduced tax revenues and higher capital expenditure. Agriculture does not contribute to revenue enhancement as it is outside the direct tax base. The tax has further narrowed as a result of growing evasion and smuggling. On the other hand, adjustments in spending are limited by the large share of personnel, interest and subsidy expenditure. Another factor complicating fiscal management is the downward pressure on import duties stemming from trade liberalization within GATT and the recently completed association agreement with the European Union. The government is attempting to offset the resulting revenue loss by broadening the tax base and improving tax collection. Budget deficits are largely financed through the domestic sale of government paper. The government also relies increasingly on the sale of assets under its privatization programme to offset higher spending.

Fiscal performance in 1996 improved. Measures to reduce the deficit included a 1% increase in value-added tax, the targeting of tax evaders and smugglers, improved tax administration, and limiting new personnel hiring. The government plans to eliminate the deficit altogether by the year 2000, based partly on expectations of a revitalized privatization programme to accelerate receipts.

Recent reforms

The Moroccan government is embarking on a programme to encourage foreign investment. It has opened virtually all sectors (other than those reserved for the state such as air transport and public utilities) to foreign investment. The government has also made a number of regulatory changes designed to improve the investment climate in recent years, including tax breaks, streamlined approval procedures, and access to foreign exchange for the repatriation of dividends and invested capital.

Morocco's commitment to open its economy has resulted in full convertibility of the dirham, rewriting of the banking law, revitalization of the stock exchange, and the extension of privatization to include strategic industries. Liberalization of foreign investment in 1982 abolished the requirement for majority Moroccan shareholding in all foreign capitalized companies and offered better terms for repatriation of profits. Foreign trade is being progressively liberalized through the removal of state controls on exports as well as the reduction of tariffs and duties on imports. Import licences were eliminated for all products except sugar, cooking oils and cereals, and the state monopoly on the trade of tea and sugar was abolished in 1994. Import duties on many commodities have also been lowered and a high-level committee is in charge of compressing and simplifying the tariff structure. Having satisfied GATT pressures to reduce tariffs on industrial goods, Morocco has now begun to lower tariffs on agricultural products.

The privatization programme was launched in 1989, limited to 112 companies in the agricultural sector, food, textiles, industrial production, banking and financial, tourism, and services. The programme only gained momentum, however, in 1993, fuelling activity on the Casablanca stock exchange (BVC), where market capitalization tripled from 1993 to early 1995. Despite a significant rise in trading and volume, 1995 was still a disappointment as inadequate transparency and information prevented the market from responding to investor requirements. Moreover, the effects of the drought that severely constricted growth last year depressed the stock market, creating by mid-1995 a poor environment for privatization. In 1996 the government intensified its efforts to renew interest in privatization, sparking considerable progress. To revive privatization, the authorities began to issue privatization bonds. Holders of the bonds can convert them into shares in privatized companies, and will be given priority access, or they can sell them back for a minimum 8% return per year. Bonds not exchanged by the end of the three-year period will be reimbursed based on their nominal value plus a bonus of 8.5% per year. To encourage conversion, bond holders are given priority over other investors.

An additional 114 enterprises are due to be sold by the end of 1998, including the telecommunications utility as well as all mining companies. In 1996 the biggest refinery, SAMIS, and the biggest oil distribution company, SOMAS, were both privatized.

By mid-1996, 23 companies and 17 hotels have been sold, raising about US$1 billion altogether. Foreign industrial operators and financial investors account for over one third of the privatization revenues. In the second half of 1996, two more industrial companies and three financial institutions were privatized. Morocco is the sole Middle-Eastern country in which such high levels of foreign investment have been drawn from state sell-offs.

To encourage foreign investment, the authorities have changed the legal structure regarding new investment, the capital market, and corporate business organizations. The aim is to modernize business, encourage financial innovation and promote investment. Consequently, an investment law was ratified in October 1995 to liberalize the tax code, guarantee the right to repatriate earnings and capital from investments, provide tax breaks for export industries, create an investment promotion office and attempt to cut the paperwork required for investment. Full foreign ownership is now allowed in several sectors, including manufacturing, mining, tourism, and exports. Moreover, fewer restrictions are applied to sectors where 100% foreign ownership is allowed, and foreign investors no longer have to wait for permission from the Office des Changes before starting investment in a project or company. Thus, foreign investors are given the freedom to take shares in new firms, raise the capital of the firm or trade with other foreign firms, and any investment application with no grounds for rejection after two months is automatically accepted.

Foreign exchange

The Moroccan dirham is convertible for all current transactions, as well as for some capital transactions, namely capital repatriation by foreign investors. Foreign exchange is available through the commercial banks. Moroccan companies may borrow abroad without prior government permission. The nominal exchange rate is set by the central bank against a basket of currencies of its principal trading partners.

Moroccan dirham/US dollar exchange rate

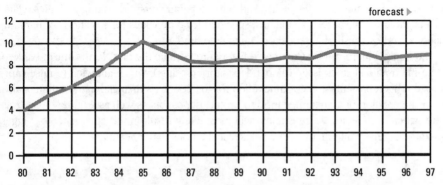

The rate against the basket has been steady since a 9% devaluation in May 1990, with changes in the rates of individual currencies reflecting changes in cross rates. The dirham has therefore appreciated against the dollar during the first half of 1995 as the dollar has depreciated against many of the other currencies in the basket. The real effective rate has appreciated somewhat and may now be slightly overvalued.

The most radical financial market reform freed exchange rates and set up a domestic foreign exchange market on June 2, 1996. Banks are now allowed to manage exchange rates and to hedge their positions through swaps, while authorized dealers can buy and sell freely within a margin set by the central bank.

Banking system

Morocco has a well-developed banking system, modelled after the French system, but currently in the process of modernization. There are 12 major banks in the country plus 5 government-owned specialized financial institutions, about 15 credit agencies and about 10 leasing companies. Until 1991, credit and money supply were controlled directly by the old French-style encadrement system allocating sectoral lending among banks based on historical patterns. Financial liberalization now allows for the free allocation of credit, with the central bank using indirect methods to control the interest rate and volume of credit. The banking system is still used by the government as a way to channel domestic savings to finance government debt, and the banks are required to hold a part of their assets in bonds paying below market interest rates. Following liberalization, the pace of credit expansion appeared to threaten price stability as interest rates rose to record levels. Consequently, the central bank moved partially back to administrative controls by raising the discount rate and setting an administrative ceiling on interest rates, calculated as a markup over the banks' average cost of funds.

In an effort to strengthen the banking system and broaden financial markets, the government has relaxed the requirement for banks. Interest-rate ceilings were lifted to encourage competition between banks and to improve companies' access to loans. Banks are now allowed to offer loans at preferential rates according to their assessment of individual customer risk ratings. In addition, the reserve requirement was reduced to 15% of deposits and the ceiling on equity lending was raised from 7% to 10% of the bank's equity. A new bank reform law promulgated in 1993 clearly laid out the parameters of banking activities, clarified oversight and control responsibilities, specified legal penalties for violations of banking regulations, and established a depositors' guarantee fund.

The Banque Marocain du Commerce Exterieure became the first North African bank to make an international stock issue (global depository receipts), which allows it to raise capital abroad. This represents a major innovation for the country's financial market. Banks also hope for the creation of a guarantee fund to protect depositors as well as a lifting of controls on external credit. Freeing of constraints will most likely result in the emergence of bigger banks and mergers, while many of the weaker institutions may not survive.

■ EQUITIES

Index performance (in local currency)

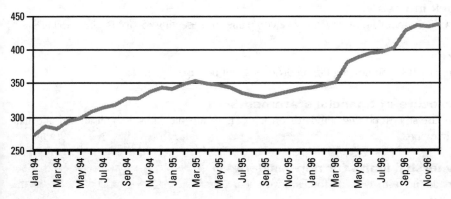

Key indicators

	Index performance %, in US$ terms	Market Cap. US$bn	P/E	Div. Yield
1994	40.3	4.4	14.0	2.5
1995	5.8	6.0	21.5	2.5
1996	38.4	8.7	13.8	2.1

Sources: Local stock exchange, IFC, Bloomberg, Datastream, UBS

Structure
The Casablanca Stock Exchange (CSE) is the largest in Africa apart from South Africa. Market capitalization stood at around US$8 billion in June 1996. Daily trading volume is US$0.7 million. It has over fifty listed companies. The average price to earnings ratio in mid-1996 was 15:1.

Regulatory authority
The Conseil Deontologique en Valeurs Mobiliere (CDVM) was set up in 1993.

Trading methods
There are two trading systems – an open outcry system and an OTC market.

Hours
The official market is open from 11.00 to 12.15, Monday to Friday. The OTC market is open until 16.00.

Settlement time and clearing
Settlement is on a T+2 basis for the official market, and a T+5 basis for the OTC market.

Types of shares
Ordinary and preference shares are traded.

Stock indices
The CFG 25 Index follows twenty-five companies representing 85% of market capitalization.

Taxes
There is a 10% withholding tax on dividends, but no capital gains tax.

Disclosure of financial statements
There are strict reporting standards on the CSE. Companies must submit annual and half-yearly reports.

Ownership limits for non-residents
There are no restrictions on foreign investment.

Capital and foreign exchange controls
There are no restrictions on the repatriation of capital or income.

Sectors
Investment holding companies, banking, finance, construction and cement represent the majority of listings.

ADRs
BMCE is the only Moroccan firm to have an ADR listing.

Market comment
The government's privatization programme has been the biggest driver of growth for the CSE. However, there is a lack of new private companies seeking listings. The market rose by 180% between 1991 and 1995, and by 24% in the first ten months of 1996. From 1997 onwards Morocco will be included in the IFC Global Composite Index with an expected 0.4% weighting. Seventeen local mutual funds with total funds under management of Dh1 billion (about US$100 million) were set up in 1996.

■ DEBT

The Moroccan central bank provides the regulatory framework of the market, incorporating the monitoring of primary auctions and secondary market activities, the execution of orders and settlement procedures.

Treasury bills are auctioned by the central bank for 13, 26 and 52 weeks. Treasury bonds are auctioned for 5, 10 and 15 years. The corporate bond market was launched this year.

Laws and regulations for the creation of a Moroccan secondary bond market were made at the start of 1996. Trades are settled through the central bank, which also acts as central depository for the bonds. Custody agreements can be arranged with local Moroccan banks.

Foreign investors pay no income or capital gains tax, and there are no restrictions on repatriation of profits or capital.

A total of US$2.4 billion Moroccan medium-term loans were restructured and refinanced under 1983-4 and 1985-8 Refinancing Agreements in the Restructuring and Consolidation Agreement Tranche A, and US$450 million US$ bankers' acceptances were refinanced in the Restructuring and Consolidation Agreement Tranche B in September 1990. In the same year Restructuring and Consolidation Agreements – fixed and floating rate tranches, were issued.

Eurobonds

In July 1996, Morocco issued its first and only eurobond, partially guaranteed by France (FRF1,500 million with a 6-year maturity and a 6.5% coupon at 48 basis points over government bonds).

■ MOROCCO: Economic indicators

Population and development	1990	1991	1992	1993	1994	1995	1996e
Population, million	24.5	25.0	25.6	26.1	26.6	27.1	27.6
Population growth, %	2.0	2.2	2.1	2.0	2.0	2.0	1.8
Nominal GDP per capita, US$	1060	1105	1125	1062	1241	1261	1407

National accounts							
Nominal GDP, US$bn	26.0	27.6	28.8	27.7	33.0	34.2	38.9
Change in real GDP, %	3.5	6.8	-4.0	-1.0	11.6	-7.6	12.0
Gross fixed capital formation, % of GDP	23.8	22.3	23.4	22.9	22.0	21.8	21.5

Money supply and inflation							
Narrow money, change %, Dec/Dec	19.4	14.4	6.1	6.4	9.6	6.4	6.0
Broad money, change %, Dec/Dec	18.5	16.8	9.3	9.1	9.1	7.1	4.1
Consumer price inflation (avg.) %	7.0	8.0	5.7	5.2	5.2	6.1	4.0
Producer prices (avg.) %	4.6	6.4	2.8	4.5	2.4	6.5	7.0

Interest rates							
Deposit rate, annual average	8.50	10.87	11.72	11.50	8.50	10.90	11.70

Government finance							
Government expenditure, % of GDP	28.7	28.0	29.7	30.0	28.1	29.6	27.3
Government balance, % of GDP	-2.2	-2.1	-1.4	-2.3	-3.9	-5.7	-3.8

Exchange rates lc=local currency							
Exchange rate, annual average, lc/US$	8.24	8.71	8.54	9.30	9.20	8.54	8.75
Exchange rate, end of year, lc/US$	8.04	8.15	9.05	9.65	8.96	8.47	8.65

Balance of payments							
Exports of goods & services, US$m	6238	6712	7135	6986	7555	8867	10040
Change %	25.2	7.6	6.3	-2.1	8.1	17.4	13.2
Imports of goods & services, US$m, fob	7783	8285	9044	8594	9378	11328	11870
Change %	24.9	6.4	9.2	-5.0	9.1	20.8	4.8
Trade balance, of goods only, US$m, fob-fob	-2109	-1764	-2463	-2065	-2107	-2397	-2050
Current account balance, US$m	-196	-413	-433	-521	-720	-1520	-800
as a % of GDP	-0.8	-1.5	-1.5	-1.9	-2.2	-4.4	-2.1

Foreign exchange reserves							
Foreign exchange reserves, US$m	2066	3100	3584	3655	4352	3600	3534
Gold at ⅔ of market price, US$m	181.0	169.8	161.0	168.7	180.1	180.1	181.8
Import cover (Reserves/imports), months	3.2	4.5	4.8	5.1	5.6	3.8	3.6

Foreign debt and debt service							
Short-term debt, US$m	1567	1650	1633	1543	1925	1780	1880
Total foreign debt, US$m	21905	22838	22693	22119	23210	23873	23445
as a % of GDP	84.3	82.6	78.9	79.9	70.3	69.8	60.3
as a % of foreign exchange receipts	226.0	220.0	204.5	205.2	229.0	209.1	186.7
Interest payments, US$m	1002	1220	1178	1370	1300	1470	1330
Principal repayments, US$m	1115	1140	1530	1786	1865	2035	1840
Total debt service, US$m	2117	2360	2708	3156	3165	3505	3170
as a % of goods exports	50.1	46.3	54.1	63.9	57.1	51.0	41.2
as a % of foreign exchange receipts	21.8	22.7	24.4	29.3	31.2	30.7	25.2

Nigeria

Area (thousands of km²):	924
Population (1996, millions):	108.9
Population projection (2025, millions):	217
Population younger than 15 yrs (1991, % of total):	46.5
Urbanization rate (1993, % of population):	38
Life expectancy (1993, years at birth):	51
Gross domestic product (1996, US$bn):	29.5
GDP per capita (1996, US$):	271
Average annual GDP growth rate (1990-96, %):	4.0
Average annual inflation rate (1990-96, %):	42.9
Currency (naira per US$, average 1996):	82.0
Structure of production (1994):	42% services, 42% agriculture, 15% industry
Main exports:	crude petroleum, cocoa
Main imports:	machinery & transport equipment, manufactured goods, chemicals
Main trading partners:	US, UK, Germany, France
Market capitalization of Stock Exchange (December 1996; US$bn):	3.6
Total foreign debt (% of GDP):	126.1
Next elections due:	under military rule
Credit rating: (Jan 1997, Standard & Poor's, Moody's)	not rated

FORECAST: 1997-2000 (average)

	Worst case	Most likely	Best case
Real GDP growth (%)	2.5	3.5	4.0
Inflation (%)	40.0	25.0	19.0

POLITICS

Historical overview

Nigeria's history has been bloody and violent. Since gaining independence from Britain in 1960, it has suffered a civil war resulting in the death of more than a million people, countless political assassinations and no fewer than five military coups. For much of this period, it has been governed by military juntas.

One of the largest and most resource-rich countries in Africa, Nigeria has been an active trader for centuries. In the 17th and 18th centuries, Nigeria was the hub of the slave trade but, following its abolition in the early 19th century, new markets, such as the trading of palm-oils, grew.

Moves towards Nigerian independence grew steadily from the 1920s onwards, gathering pace following the establishment of a new constitution in 1947. This legislated for a federal system of government in an attempt to avoid tribal tensions. By 1954, the federation had achieved self-governance, with Tafawa Balewa becoming the first prime minister in 1957. Full independence was not gained until October 1963, however, when Nigeria was declared a federal republic. Dr Nnamdi Azikiwe of the National Council for Nigeria and the Cameroons (NCNC) became the inaugural president.

Attempts to govern Nigeria centrally have been hampered by the country's ethnic diversity. The first government was formed by an uneasy coalition between the NCNC and the Northern People's Congress (NPC). Tension between the two parties increased following independence, culminating in the NCNC declining to participate in the 1964 elections, whilst a third party, the Action Group (AG) was pressing for full independence for the Western region. With the country close to anarchy, the military seized power in January 1966.

The following year civil war erupted after leaders of the Eastern region declared an independent republic. The Biafran war was to cost the lives of more than a million people before the army triumphed in 1970. The army's commander, Colonel Yakuba Gowon, promised to return the country to civilian rule but was overthrown in a coup in 1975. The new leader, General Murtala Muhammad, lasted only seven months before his assassination in February 1976.

Under the leadership of General Olusegun Obasanjo, the country moved quickly towards civilian rule. A constituent assembly and new constitution were drawn up, and in 1979 a general election was held. The new political landscape was similar to that of 1960 – ethnically based and very unstable. The election was won by the narrowest of margins by the National Party of Nigeria, the successor to the NPC.

Split by factional differences, the NPN proved unable to govern effectively. Following allegations of vote-rigging in the elections of 1983, the military junta took over again. In August 1985, General Ibrahim Babangida took power and launched a phased programme of return to civilian rule in which the number of political parties would be limited to two: the National Republican Convention (NR) and the Social Democratic Party (SDP), each containing components of the former ethnically based parties.

In June 1993, a third civilian general election was held. This was won by Chief Abiola of the SDP, but Babangida declared it illegal before resigning three months later. Chief Shonekan headed an interim government with a mandate to supervise a re-run of the election in 1994. Shonekan also resigned, however, and the interim government was replaced by the Provisional Ruling Council, led by General Abacha.

Recent events

Following a lengthy national constitutional conference, the PRC drew up a new constitution in June 1995 that proposed establishing a system of rotational power-sharing between the six newly created zones. A three-year transition programme was launched, whereby state elections were scheduled for 1997, and legislative and presidential elections in 1998.

In November 1995, the PRC aroused strong international criticism after executing Ken Saro-Wiwa and eight other Ogoni activists. Saro-Wiwa had led demonstrations in the Ogoni delta region pressing for more regional autonomy. Nigeria was subsequently suspended from the Commonwealth.

However, the Organization of African Unity has refused to condemn General Abacha, while few Western countries have appeared willing to support an embargo on imports of Nigerian oil.

Chronology

1200	Hausa city states are set up
1400	Islam arrives
1890	George Goldie forms United African Company
1899	Southern Nigeria is brought under control of the UK Colonial Office
1914	Northern and Southern Nigeria are merged
1920	National Congress of British West Africa is set up
1960	Nigeria becomes independent
1966	Military coup
1967-70	Biafran war
1975	General Murtala Muhammed overthrows General Gowon
1976	Muhammed is murdered, General Obasanjo takes over
1979	Civilian elections are won by Shehu Shagari's NPN
1983	General Buhari overthrows NPN government
1985	General Babangida overthrows Buhari
1993	Babangida suspends civilian elections after Abiola looks set to win
1993	General Abacha takes charge of PRC
1995	Obasanjo is imprisoned. Ogoni activists are executed.
1995	Nigeria is suspended from Commonwealth. Government announces a three-year transition to civilian rule.

Government

Nigeria is a federation of thirty different states. Government is carried out at local, state and federal level. The national government is the Provisional Ruling Council (PRC) made up of senior army officers. A Federal Executive Council was set up in November 1993, but its power is limited. The PRC has agreed to hand over to a civilian government in 1998.

Head of State	General Sani Abacha
(also Chairman of the cabinet	
and Defence Minister)	
Minister of Finance	Anthony Ani
Governor, central bank	Paul Ogwuma

■ ECONOMICS

The economy

One of the most resource-rich countries in Africa, Nigeria has the potential to be a major economic power. But over-dependence on the oil industry (which generates more than 95% of export revenues), widespread corruption and poor management have hampered the development of its economy.

Agriculture is a leading economic activity. However, the bulk of production is consumed locally, and cash crops make little contribution to the overall economy. The manufacturing sector remains relatively small. There are a number of light consumer industries, but these are heavily dependent on imports.

The development of the oil industry began shortly after independence in 1960, when the government started full-scale exploitation of its extensive reserves. When oil prices rose in the early 1970s, Nigeria attempted to develop its industrial base by investing in state-run industrial and manufacturing projects such as steel plants. The programme was implemented poorly, however, with few feasibility studies carried out.

With rising oil revenues driving up wages, and the currency beginning to appreciate, the agricultural economy (which employs the majority of people) collapsed. Exports of commodities like groundnuts and cotton all but disappeared. Between 1970 and 1982, agriculture's share of exports fell from 70% to just 2%.

Population

Nigeria is the most populous nation in Africa, with an estimated 110 million people. According to a UN report, Lagos could become the world's third largest city by 2015. It is ethnically diverse, with over 250 different languages spoken.

Exports and imports as a % of GDP

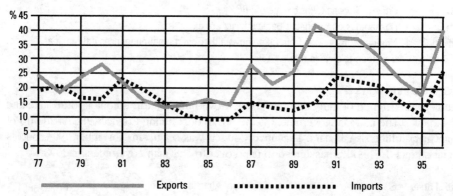

Source: Official data

Economic policy

In 1986, General Babangida launched a structural adjustment programme (SAP) to get the economy and public finances back on track. The currency was devalued (to promote exports), and subsidies and tariffs were cut. This had a positive effect on agricultural production, which was a major factor in the subsequent rise in economic growth. Between 1984 and 1993, growth averaged 4.2% a year.

The government launched a "guided de-regulation" programme in 1995 in a bid to promote economic activity and foreign investment. The 1989 Enterprises Promotion Act, which limited or forbade foreign equity participation in certain areas, was repealed along with the Exchange Control Act of 1962, creating a more liberal investment environment.

Current account as a % of GDP

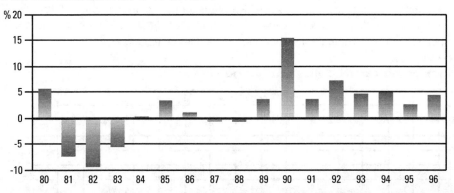

Source: Official data, UBS estimates

Although there has been some improvement in the economic situation following the introduction of the de-regulation programme, deep-rooted problems remain. High inflation has increased production costs for farmers and manufacturers. Unemployment remains high and living standards are pitifully low, particularly in rural areas. GDP per capita is estimated at just US$230 a year.

The government appears committed to further economic de-regulation as part of its 1996-98 national rolling plan. Interest rates (which were previously capped at 21%) were freed in 1996. Measures have also been introduced to improve revenue collection and fiscal management. Tax incentives have been extended to encourage greater private sector involvement in the economy. The energy sector looks set to remain the lynchpin of the Nigerian economy. Several overseas oil companies launched new exploration and development programmes in 1995 and 1996, with a view to doing more deep-water exploration. Reserves are expected to rise from 20 billion barrels to 25 billion barrels by the year 2000.

The natural gas sector is also expected to expand significantly in the next ten years. Several projects have been signed and are expected to begin production by 1998. There are also plans to develop iron ore and coal production.

The biggest economic problem is the country's external debt. Nigeria owes around US$35 billion to foreign creditors. It currently meets about half its annual debt servicing obligations of US$4 billion a year, leaving the rest to accumulate as payments arrears. Moves within the Paris Club of creditors (representing government-to-government loans) to try to restructure the debt ground to a halt in early 1996. The IMF, meanwhile, has been reluctant to provide financial support to Nigeria until further reforms are implemented.

The government has adopted a more cautious approach to monetary and fiscal policy in a bid to improve Nigeria's image among international lenders. Once a debt refinancing package is secured, economic development could accelerate, although the oil industry is likely to remain the driving force of export earnings.

Monetary policy

Monetary policy has been characterized by excessive control, and extensive periods of negative real interest rates. However, the 21% cap on interest rates was removed in October

1996. There are two exchange rates (an official one which values the naira at around 22 to the US dollar, and a black market rate which offers around 80 to the dollar). Inflation has been a major problem in recent years, rising to over 70% in 1995. Tighter controls and a temporary improvement in the fiscal position saw inflation trend lower in 1996.

Nigerian naira/US dollar exchange rate

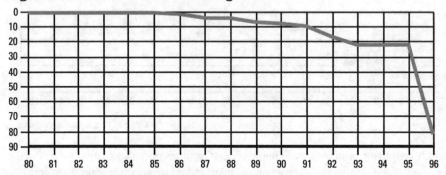

Fiscal policy

Nigeria has run annual deficits on its federal budgets for a number of years. The main problems have been the volatility of the price of oil (which accounts for the lion's share of government revenues), and the revenue allocation policy whereby federal money is allocated to state and local governments. In the past, the government used to exclude certain expenditures from its budget, and ran an off-budget account for special investments. This tactic was reportedly stopped in 1995.

Following a reduction in public spending in the 1994 budget, and some improvement in tax collection methods, the government showed a small surplus in 1995.

■ EQUITIES

Key indicators

	Index performance %, in US$ terms	Market Cap. US$bn	P/E	Div. Yield	Weight in IFCI	IFCG
1994	168.8	2.7	6.0	8.4	—	0.2
1995	-26.9	2.0	12.5	5.7	—	0.1
1996	55.6	3.6	10.1	4.1	—	0.2

Sources: Local stock exchange, IFC, Bloomberg, Datastream, UBS

Structure

The Nigerian Stock Exchange (NSE) is among the largest in Africa. Capitalized at US$2.1 billion, the exchange has 182 listings. Nigeria's largest companies, such as Nigerian National Petroleum Corporation and Nigeria Telecommunications, are not listed on the exchange, but if they were, they would triple the NSE's market capitalization.

The market was opened to foreigners in July 1995, when the Nigerian Investment Promotion Commission was set up. Foreign investors need to obtain a certificate of capital importation from a Nigerian bank in order to buy stock from brokers. The secondary market is virtually non existent.

Turnover

The NSE's turnover ratio was 0.1 for most of 1996, apart from in May, when it reached 0.3 and June, when it was 0.2 times capitalization.

Hours

Trading takes place from 11.00 to 13.00, Monday to Friday.

Taxes

A 5% tax on dividends is levied. Capital gains tax is 20%, levied each time a security changes hands, as well as a 10% withholding tax.

Foreign market participation

The Nigerian government changed its regulations concerning international market participation in July 1995. International brokers are allowed to enlist as dealers on the NSE. The new regulations also allow NSE listed companies to have cross-border and multiple listings abroad.

Stock indices

The country's main index is the Nigerian Stock Exchange All Shares Index, which includes all NSE listings. The International Finance Corporation IFCG Nigeria Index tracks thirty-five stocks, representing around 80% of the market's capitalization. However, neither index includes Nigeria's ten largest companies, as these are not listed.

■ DEBT

Capital markets developed in Nigeria in the 1970s. Domestic and foreign capital inflows were required to help the country's recovery from civil war. The market structure is based on UK and US models. The Ministry of Finance formulates regulations enforced by the Central Bank of Nigeria (CBN), and the market is directly supervized by a Securities and Exchange Commission (SEC).

The Ministry of Finance, using the central bank as agent, issues treasury bills for maturities of 90, 120 and 365 days at fixed rates. The CBN also conducts repurchase agreements as part of its open market operations.

Blue chip Nigerian enterprises issue debentures and secured bonds at fixed rates for maturities of more than one year. Secondary market dealing takes place on the Nigerian Stock Exchange in Lagos, and trades are settled by payment before delivery of securities. Payment can be either in naira or foreign currency. Local banks and brokerage houses offer custodial services and can act as agents for investments by overseas investors.

Interest income and capital gains are taxed at 10%. There are no restrictions on non-residents repatriating profits or capital.

Brady bonds

As part of a Brady-style debt restructuring, Nigeria issued US$2,050,961,000 Par bonds on January 21, 1992. The issue is collateralized by 30-year zero coupon US Treasury bonds and a 12-month interest payment guarantee. It has detachable value recovery rights indexed to the price of oil, and bonds are eligible for tendering in the country's debt-equity swap programme.

In 1988, Nigeria issued US$4,800,000,000 of Promissory Notes, which mature in 2010 and are eligible for tendering in the country's debt conversion programme. Nigeria has not issued a eurobond.

■ NIGERIA: Economic indicators

Population and development	1990	1991	1992	1993	1994	1995	1996e
Population, million	96.2	98.2	100.2	102.3	104.5	106.7	108.9
Population growth, %	-8.4	2.1	2.1	2.1	2.1	2.1	2.1
Nominal GDP per capita, US$	337	333	317	309	391	414	271

National accounts							
Nominal GDP, US$bn	32.4	32.7	31.8	31.6	40.8	44.2	29.5
Change in real GDP, %	8.2	5.1	5.8	2.3	1.3	2.8	3.5
Gross fixed capital formation, % of GDP	11.9	11.7	11.0	11.8	14.5	14.2	14.1

Money supply and inflation							
Broad money, change %, Dec/Dec	37.8	31.9	61.8	40.0	35.0	30.0	20.0
Consumer price inflation (avg.) %	7.4	13.0	44.6	61.3	76.8	72.8	44.2

Government finance							
Government expenditure, % of GDP	23.5	20.8	19.6	25.0	20.0	23.0	24.0
Government balance, % of GDP	-8.5	11.0	-10.2	-14.5	-7.9	-3.1	-1.0

Exchange rates lc=local currency							
Exchange rate, annual average, lc/US$	8.04	9.91	17.30	22.07	22.00	36.50	81.00
Exchange rate, end of year, lc/US$	9.00	9.86	19.65	21.88	22.00	80.00	82.00

Balance of payments							
Exports of goods & services, US$m	14550	13140	12844	12063	10971	11500	12500
Change %	84.9	-9.7	-2.3	-6.1	-9.1	4.8	8.7
Imports of goods & services, US$m, fob	5379	10261	8991	9826	8507	7200	8000
Change %	45.7	90.8	-12.4	9.3	-13.4	-15.4	11.1
Trade balance, of goods only, US$m, fob-fob	10182	4441	4610	3800	5100	4300	4500
Current account balance, US$m	6518	1203	2268	1500	2000	1100	1300
as a % of GDP	20.1	3.7	7.1	4.7	4.9	2.5	4.4

Foreign exchange reserves							
Foreign exchange reserves, US$m	3864	4435	967	1600	1600	1200	1300
Gold at ⅔ of market price, US$m	176.6	165.7	157.1	164.6	175.8	175.8	177.4
Import cover (reserves/imports), months	8.6	5.2	1.3	2.0	2.3	2.0	2.0

Foreign debt and debt service							
Short-term debt, US$m	1561	377	1013	1519	1890	2990	3410
Total foreign debt, US$m	34539	34436	30999	32500	34100	35600	37200
as a % of GDP	106.5	105.3	97.5	102.9	83.6	80.5	126.1
as a % of foreign exchange receipts	237.4	262.1	241.4	269.4	310.8	309.6	297.6
Interest payments, US$m	1880	2259	1696	1321	1396	1498	1437
Principal repayments, US$m	1495	1117	2081	509	480	482	533
Total debt service, US$m	3375	3376	3777	1830	1876	1980	1970
as a % of goods exports	24.8	27.6	32.0	16.8	17.7	17.2	15.8
as a % of foreign exchange receipts	23.2	25.7	29.4	15.2	17.1	17.2	15.8

Pakistan

Area (thousands of km²):	796
Population (1995, millions):	130
Population projection (2025, millions):	243
Population younger than 15 yrs (1991, % of total):	44
Urbanization rate (1993, % of population):	34
Life expectancy (1993, years at birth):	67
Gross domestic product (1996, US$bn):	65.1
GDP per capita (1996, US$):	485
Average annual GDP growth rate (1990-96, %):	5
Average annual inflation rate (1990-96, %):	11
Currency (rupee per US$, average 1996):	37
Real exchange rate: (1990=100, average 1996)	85.6
Structure of production (1994):	50% services, 25% industry, 25% agriculture
Main exports:	cotton fabrics, cotton yarn & thread, rice, raw cotton
Main imports:	machinery & transport equipment, minerals, fuels, chemicals
Main trading partners:	US, Japan, UK, Germany, Kuwait, Saudi Arabia
Market capitalization of Stock Exchange (December 1996; US$bn):	10.6
Total foreign debt (% of GDP):	43.9
Next elections due under normal circumstances:	legislative scheduled February 1997; presidential scheduled December 1998
Credit rating: (Jan 1997, Standard & Poor's, Moody's)	B+; B2

FORECAST: 1997-2000 (average)

	Worst case	Most likely	Best case
Real GDP growth (%)	3.2	5.5	6.8
Inflation (%)	15	11	7

■ POLITICS

Historical overview

In 1997 Pakistan celebrates fifty years as an independent state. Despite several elections, the democratic process in the country remains fragile, after twenty-four years of intermittent military rule.

Having been designated as a homeland for the Muslims of India, Pakistan gained independence from Britain on August 14, 1947. At the outset, the new state found itself facing serious political problems as a result of border disputes and inter-ethnic strife. East Pakistan and West Pakistan were divided by more than 1,600 km of Indian territory as well as by cultural differences.

At the time of independence, millions of Hindus and Muslims suddenly found themselves living in the 'wrong' country. Around 600,000 people were killed in the ensuing riots while millions had to be resettled in new areas. Kashmir, on the border between Pakistan and India, was another flashpoint. The state had a predominantly Muslim population, but a Hindu ruler chose to join India.

Late in 1947 fighting broke out between the armies of India and Pakistan. The UN oversaw a cease-fire in 1949, but the dispute over the area continued.

The country found itself in a crisis following the death of the first governor-general, Mohammed Ali Jinnah, in 1948, and the assassination of his successor, Liaquat Ali Khan, in 1951. Attempts to appease East Pakistan resulted in constitutional changes being made in 1956, but the internal political situation did not improve. Following the declaration of martial law in 1958, the army took power.

War broke out between India and Pakistan in 1965 over Kashmir. A peace agreement was signed the following year, although the dispute was not settled.

Bangladesh declares independence

Elections were held in 1970. The proponents of independence in East Pakistan gained an overwhelming majority. Following military intervention by West Pakistan, the East proclaimed itself the independent republic of Bangladesh. Troops from West Pakistan were unable to prevent this move. With millions of refugees fleeing to India, the Indian army intervened. The Pakistani army was eventually forced to surrender in the East. When Britain recognized the new state, Pakistan withdrew from the Commonwealth.

The new leader of the smaller Pakistan, Zulfikar Ali Bhutto had to address the difficult legacy of the country having to do without the revenues from the east. He subsequently pursued a nationalization programme. The first elections in seven years were held in 1977, which saw an overwhelming victory by Bhutto's Pakistan People's Party (PPP). However, the opposition claimed that the elections had been rigged, and widespread unrest followed.

The army takes power

Bhutto called in the army, under General Zia ul-Haq, to take charge of the worsening situation. Soon after, however, Zia ul-Haq imposed martial law and arrested Bhutto on charges of conspiracy to murder a political opponent. The military then took power again, with General Muhammad Zia al-Huq heading the regime. Bhutto was subsequently executed in 1979.

Upon assuming power, Zia ul-Haq imposed strict censorship. Martial law, though it had existed before, distanced Pakistan further from the Western World, as did efforts to reform the judicial system along Islamic lines.

Nevertheless, after the Soviet invasion of Afghanistan in 1979 and the emergence of a fundamentalist Iran in the Middle East, the West increasingly viewed Pakistan as a strategic ally in the region. Pakistan's commitment to the Afghan cause brought it closer to the West. The US provided considerable aid lasting until the withdrawal of Soviet troops from Afghanistan in 1989.

After eight years of military rule, President Zia al-Huq organized elections. But the elections were boycotted by major parties. Mohammed Khan Junejo was hand-picked as prime minister, but was sacked by the president in 1988 on charges of incompetence. Zia al-Huq subsequently died in an air crash.

Civilian rule restored

In 1988 Benazir Bhutto, daughter of Zulfikar Ali Bhutto, was elected prime minister in the first party-based elections since 1977. However, Bhutto found herself facing a hostile establishment, and after only twenty months in power, her PPP government was dismissed by President Ghulam Ishaq Khan on charges of corruption and incompetence.

New elections were held in October 1990, with Nawaz Sharif's nine-party Democratic Alliance winning a two-thirds majority in the federal parliament. Bhutto complained that these elections were rigged. This government, too, was unable to serve its full term in office because in April 1993 the President dismissed Sharif's government on charges of corruption. Subsequently, the Supreme Court reinstated the Sharif government, ruling that the president had exceeded his constitutional powers. The head of the army then oversaw a deal whereby both Sharif and President Ishaq Khan would step down and new elections would be held.

Recent events

The October 1993 elections produced mixed results with no single party gaining a clear majority. But after various by-elections, the senate elections of March 1994 and coalitions, the PPP was able to form a government under the leadership of Benazir Bhutto.

In November 1996, however, Bhutto's nominee for president, Farooq Leghari, dissolved the National Assembly and dismissed Bhutto's three-year-old PPP government, citing corruption, obstruction of justice and lowering the esteem of the judiciary as reasons for his actions. The president appointed an interim government, headed by the former speaker of the National Assembly, Malik Meraj Khalid. This time, the Supreme Court upheld Ms Bhutto's dismissal and new elections were held in February 1997. Sharif's Pakistan Muslim League won the election, controlling almost two thirds of the seats in the National Assembly.

1988-90	Benazir Bhutto, Pakistan Peoples Party (PPP)
1990-93	Nawaz Sharif, Pakistan Muslim League (PML)
1993-1997	Benazir Bhutto (PPP)
1997	Nawaz Sharif (PML)

Government structure

The executive

At the federal level, the executive arm of the government consists of an indirectly elected president and a cabinet, led by the prime minister, which reports to the parliament. At the provincial level, the federation appoints the governor as its representative. The chief minister is the leader of the house in the provincial assembly. The federal parliament is the chief legislative body, comprising the National Assembly with 207 Muslim and 10 minority seats. There are 87 senators in the Senate, with 19 belonging to each of the 4 provinces, 3 from the federal capital and 8 from FATA. The federal supreme court and provincial high courts constitute the superior judiciary. The judiciary is constitutionally independent of the executive body.

Provincial assemblies

	Muslim seats	Minority seats	Total seats
Punjab	240	8	248
Sindh	100	8	108
NWFP	80	4	84
Baluchistan	40	2	42

The conflict with MQM

One of the most important issues that needs to be resolved is a political settlement with the leadership of the Mohajir Qaumi Movement (MQM), which essentially demands provincial autonomy for urban Sindh. Although the PPP has had a majority in rural Sindh, the MQM still dominates the two largest cities of Karachi and Hyderabad. With the army withdrawn from Sindh, it is increasingly difficult to ignore the demands of MQM. No resolution is expected in the near term and sporadic violence may continue.

■ ECONOMICS

Population and society

Pakistan has the world's ninth largest population (estimated at 140 million in 1996), and a population growth rate of around 3%. A recent UN study projects that by the year 2050, Pakistan will be the world's third most populous state after India and China, with around 360 million inhabitants. Integrating the large teenage population into the workforce will pose a great social and economic challenge to Pakistan in the future. Though Urdu is the national language, English is widely spoken among the business community. The four major cities of Pakistan, Islamabad, Peshawar, Lahore and Karachi, reflect the many historical influences that have gone into creating modern Pakistan. Its four provinces, Sindh, Punjab, Baluchistan and the North West Frontier Province (NWFP) all have a distinct character and culture.

Natural resources

Pakistan is rich in natural resources, including coal and natural gas. Most of the mineral wealth is concentrated in the mountainous regions. Its main minerals are coal, natural gas, crude oil, marble, china clay, limestone and magnesite. A mineral development policy has been framed to enlarge the mining sector's role and exploit deposits. Pakistan's most important energy resource is natural gas, found at Sui and other locations in the Indus plains and piped thence to Lahore, Karachi and other towns. Exploration has also revealed a number of oil fields, and the country could achieve a high degree of self-sufficiency in petroleum in the next century.

Agriculture

Agriculture contributes about a quarter of the country's GDP. It provides employment to half the total labour force and is the single largest source of foreign exchange earnings. Agricultural growth has averaged 4% per annum over the past decade. Direct agricultural products supplied almost a quarter of total exports while processed products such as cotton yarn, textiles, leather and carpets constitute nearly half of all exports. Major cash and food crops include cotton, wheat, rice, and sugar cane, accounting for around 10% of GDP.

Pakistan is the world's fourth largest cotton producer and until three years ago was the world's third largest cotton exporter. The country's climate and soil are well suited to the cotton crop. However, the crop has become increasingly vulnerable to pests. In the longer term, agricultural productivity will depend on a more effective use of fertilizers, pesticides and irrigation facilities. But with favourable weather conditions, sector growth of 5-6% per annum over the next five years appears achievable.

Industrial growth

Pakistan has averaged industrial growth of 6.8% per year over the past decade, with industry now contributing one quarter of GDP. The cotton textile industry, which is central to the country's industrial and agricultural sector, has already benefited greatly from investments to enhance productivity. It accounts for about 60-65% of total export earnings and one third of the industrial workforce. Access to cotton below world prices has allowed the sector to grow rapidly since 1980. However in 1997, for the third year in a row, Pakistan, once the world's second largest cotton exporter, will have to import cotton to make up for harvests hit by bad weather, the curl leaf virus and pests.

Rapid growth

Pakistan has traditionally had a steadily growing economy. Real GDP growth averaged over 6% per annum during the 1980s with agricultural growth averaging 4% and industrial growth 7%.

The country's political stability, together with fiscal and monetary policy discipline, will be of key importance if rapid growth is to continue. Pakistan had three governments in the four years to October 1993, an uncertain situation which resulted in short-term political considerations taking precedence over long-term economic goals. GDP growth enjoyed a moderate recovery in 1995-96 due to a good cotton crop, although the 6.1% rate of expansion was still below the government's growth target.

Share of GDP by sector

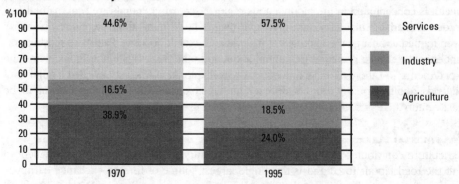

Source: State Bank of Pakistan

Reducing deficits

The overriding objective of economic policy in Pakistan is to reduce the fiscal and external account deficits to sustainable levels. These imbalances have persisted and worsened in the 1990s. Large fiscal deficits of the recent past have been financed increasingly by borrowings. This has directly increased the volume of outstanding public debt and debt servicing costs. Expansionary deficits have also boosted inflation to double digit levels, in part because monetary financing has boosted liquidity. The deficit problem has been exacerbated by low tax revenues and high spending on defence and mandatory interest costs. The tax/GDP ratio has stagnated around 14% since the 1980s and defence expenditure and debt servicing alone almost equal total revenues.

Monetary sector

The World Bank has highlighted fiscal policy measures as the weakest area of implementation in its Pakistan structural adjustment programme. In view of growing financial imbalances and underlying structural weaknesses, there is a need to increase both tax and non-tax revenues. A weak tax administration process and numerous tax concessions have depressed government revenues. Moreover, key sectors such as agriculture enjoy low taxes for political reasons. Defence, interest payments and administrative expenses, which are largely unproductive, account for the majority of expenditure. The result is that there are inadequate resources available for development projects that can directly and indirectly generate future revenues for the government. To improve its fiscal position, the government aims to broaden direct taxation and improve tax administration and compliance, while relying less on import and excise duties which have strong distortionary effects.

Inflation

Poor harvests, floods, increases in farm support prices and the impact of earlier structural reforms have combined to keep inflation high. A sustained reduction in inflation, however, will only be possible if the monetary authorities are able to keep monetary and credit expansion under control. Over time this will require lower fiscal deficits to reduce the need for monetary financing of public debt.

External imbalances

Pakistan's large trade and current account deficits pose immediate risks of a possible balance of payments crisis. The deficits have not fallen significantly despite the sharp decline in the rupee's value in the 1990s. Following the conclusion of an agreement with the IMF in October 1996, Pakistan will receive the remaining tranches of its US$600 million stand-by loan with the IMF. The funds will enable the country to tide over a looming balance of payments crisis.

At the time the agreement was signed, foreign exchange reserves had fallen to US$600 million, equal to just two weeks' import cover. The agreement with the IMF was held up until the government announced a US$1 billion supplementary budget which imposed new taxes on agriculture and delivered expenditure cuts. In the long run, Pakistan will have to focus on increasing national savings (including cutting the public sector deficit) in order to bring down the current account deficit to sustainable levels. In addition, the country will have to diversify its export base, which presently relies heavily on cotton-based products.

Breakdown of exports (1995)

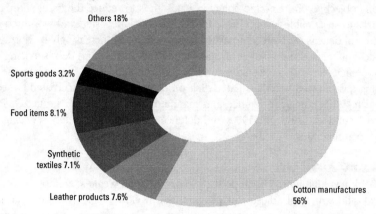

Others 18%

Sports goods 3.2%

Food items 8.1%

Synthetic textiles 7.1%

Leather products 7.6%

Cotton manufactures 56%

Source: Official data

Imports and exports as a % of GDP

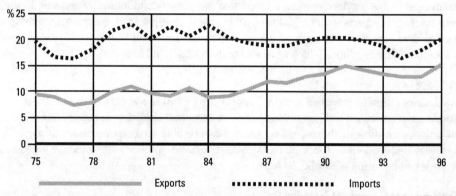

Exports ▬▬▬▬▬ Imports ▪▪▪▪▪▪▪▪▪▪▪▪▪▪▪▪▪

Source: Official data

Capital flows

The chronic current account deficit has meant that Pakistan has had to borrow extensively overseas. Total foreign debt now stands at about US$29 billion, or 44% of GDP. Nevertheless, the country will require continuous private foreign investment as well as multi-lateral assistance (from agencies such as the World Bank and the IMF) to meet its development needs.

In 1997, further stringent aid conditions will probably be set in an effort to ensure the medium-term sustainability of Pakistan's external accounts and foreign capital needs. Although the relatively high level of foreign debt does not pose a critical short-term debt servicing problem (since most of the long-term debt is on a soft loan basis), over a longer period the country needs to better manage its external financing needs in order to avoid more serious balance of payments problems.

Current account as a % of GDP

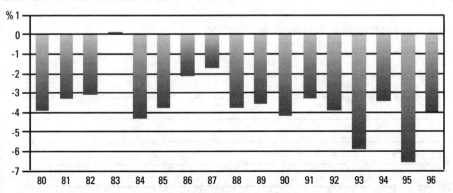

Source: Official data

Currency

The caretaker government of Moin Qureshi devalued the rupee by 10% in July 1993, following a 4.6% depreciation in the proceeding twelve months. Until recently this was the largest currency realignment since the country moved to a managed floating system against a basket of currencies in 1982. In 1996 there have been two additional sharp devaluations of the rupee designed to boost Pakistan's competitiveness. Although the currency is convertible for current account transactions, capital account convertibility will not be introduced until the fiscal and external deficits are firmly under control.

Pakistani rupee/US dollar exchange rate

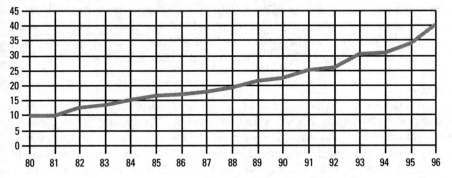

■ EQUITIES

Index performance (in local currency)

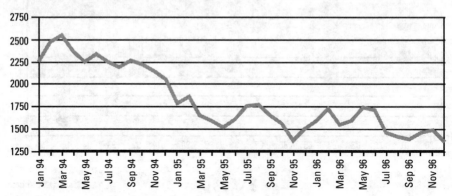

Key indicators

	Index performance %, in US$ terms	Market Cap. US$bn	P/E	Div. Yield	Weight in IFCI	IFCG
1994	-9.8	12.3	23.3	1.6	1.0	0.8
1995	-32.6	9.3	15	2.4	0.8	0.6
1996	-21.8	10.6	11.7	3.2	0.5	0.4

Sources: Local stock exchange, IFC, Bloomberg, Datastream, UBS

Background
The Pakistan stock market gained prominence in 1991 when the government initiated its privatization programme, allowed foreign investment and began deregulation of the economy. Foreign portfolio investment was fully deregulated and 100% ownership was permitted in all but a few sensitive industries. Capital gains and dividends became freely repatriable.

Structure
Pakistan has three stock exchanges, in Karachi, Lahore and Islamabad. The Karachi Stock Exchange (KSE) is the largest, accounting for 82% of turnover. Established in 1948, it has 200 members, of which 140 are active. Corporate memberships were allowed in 1991 and there are now sixteen. Management comprises an elected president and sixteen directors, including one each from state-owned National Investment Trust (NIT) and Investment Corporation of Pakistan (ICP). Management elections are held annually.

Regulatory authority
The main regulatory body governing the capital markets is the Corporate Law Authority (CLA), a part of the Ministry of Finance. The CLA is responsible for ensuring that all companies conform to the guidelines regarding listing and post-listing requirements, as stipulated by the Companies Ordinance 1984 and the Securities and Exchange Ordinance 1969. The CLA works closely with the KSE to monitor companies and safeguard investor interests. Until

recently, all companies wishing to raise capital were required to seek prior permission from the Controller of Capital Issues. However, the Controller of Capital Issues Act was repealed in the 1995–96 budget to reduce bureaucratic controls.

Laws governing the corporate sector
Companies Ordinance 1984
Securities & Exchange Ordinance of Pakistan 1969

Trading methods
Each counter is traded in sequence through an open outcry system.

Hours
Trading takes place 10.15 to 14.00, Monday to Thursday, and 10.15 to 12.15 on Friday.

Settlement time and clearing
All trades made between Tuesday (T+13) and Monday (T+7) are settled on the Monday of the following week through a centralized clearing house. Physical settlement of shares is the norm. Due to increasing share volumes, timely settlement has become a key problem. The IFC has sponsored the establishment of a Central Depository System.

Stock indices
The KSE 100 is the prime indicator of stock market performance and is quoted daily. It was introduced in November 1991, based on market capitalization, with a base level of 1,000 points. Since 1991, however, a number of new issues such as Fauji Fertilizer, Hubco and PTC came on to the market. The index was revised in December 1994 and again in August 1996, to incorporate the new large issues.

Taxes
Capital gains have been made exempt from tax until 1998. There is 7.5% withholding tax on dividend along with Rs0.25 per share Zakat (tax on surplus assets). Bonus issues, until recently exempt from tax, are now taxed at 10% for private companies and 15% for public companies.

Badla
Although futures trading is not allowed, investors can carry forward positions through settlement periods by paying badla (interest), usually 2–3% per month, to brokers. However, during periods of strong speculation, badla rates can reach as high as 7-8% per month.

■ DEBT

Significant changes have been made to the domestic money and bond markets since March 1991. In particular, new instruments were introduced and auctions replaced taps for the issuance of new government debt.

Public debt

Domestic banks are large buyers of government bonds to meet their 25% statutory reserve requirements.

6-month short-term federal bonds

Federal bonds replaced 6-month discount treasury bills in July 1996. The new bonds are issued at par and pay a coupon after auction.

Federal Investment Bonds (FIBs)

Three-, 5- and 10-year maturity FIBs are issued at par with coupons of 13%, 14% and 15% respectively.

Repurchase agreements

More than 90% of daily interbank lending is transacted on a repo basis, with government securities used as collateral for cash transferred simultaneously at the central bank. Repos can be made for up to six months, but most are overnight.

Private debt
Term Finance Certificates (TFCs)

In 1996 public companies were authorized to issue corporate bonds called TFCs, with coupons ranging between 15% and 18%, payable semi-annually. By September 1996, four enterprises had issued bonds.

The bond market is open to overseas investors. Individuals pay 10% and institutions 30% withholding tax, unless a dual taxation treaty exists.

Eurobonds

Pakistan tapped the eurobond market for the first time in December 1994, with a US$150 million 5-year issue at 540 basis points over US treasuries. By September 1996 the spread had tightened to 240 basis points. The Republic issued a second bond – a four-year floating rate note – at libor plus 200 basis points in June 1996.

Eurobond issues (US$m)

	1990	1991	1992	1993	1994	1995	1996
Sovereign	—	—	—	—	150.0	—	150.0
Private	—	—	—	—	—	—	—

■ PAKISTAN: Economic indicators

Population and development	1990	1991	1992	1993	1994	1995	1996e
Population, million	112.0	115.5	119.1	122.8	126.5	130.3	134.1
Population growth, %	3.1	3.1	3.1	3.1	3.0	3.0	3.0
Nominal GDP per capita, US$	352	371	405	389	406	453	485

National accounts							
Nominal GDP, US$bn	39.4	42.9	48.3	47.7	51.4	59.0	65.1
Change in real GDP, %	4.5	5.5	7.8	1.9	3.8	4.5	6.1
Gross fixed capital formation, % of GDP	17.3	17.4	18.6	19.1	17.9	17.2	17.9

Money supply and inflation							
Narrow money, change %, Dec/Dec	17.3	20.2	21.5	1.7	15.1	12.8	14.5
Broad money, change %, Dec/Dec	11.6	18.9	29.3	18.1	17.4	13.8	14.9
Consumer price inflation (avg.) %	9.1	11.8	9.5	9.9	12.4	12.4	10.8

Government finance							
Government expenditure, % of GDP	22.4	23.3	24.3	24.6	24.3	23.2	23.0
Government balance, % of GDP	-5.4	-7.6	-7.9	-8.9	-6.9	-4.8	-5.8

Exchange rates *lc=local currency*							
Exchange rate, annual average, lc/US$	21.71	23.80	25.08	28.11	30.57	31.64	33.70
Exchange rate, end of year, lc/US$	21.90	24.72	25.70	30.12	30.80	34.25	35.00
Real exchange rate 1990=100	100.0	97.0	92.7	94.4	92.2	85.3	85.6

Balance of payments							
Exports of goods & services, US$m	6803	7905	8433	8327	8827	9880	10200
Change %	13.8	16.2	6.7	-1.3	6.0	11.9	3.2
Imports of goods & services, US$m, fob	10157	10945	12342	11962	11829	13140	14850
Change %	12.0	7.8	12.8	-3.1	-1.1	11.1	13.0
Trade balance, of goods only, US$m, fob-fob	-2714	-2261	-2790	-2575	-2228	-2300	-3400
Current account balance, US$m	-1654	-1396	-1868	-2887	-1804	-2100	-4300
as a % of GDP	-4.2	-3.3	-3.9	-6.0	-3.5	-3.6	-6.6

Foreign exchange reserves							
Foreign exchange reserves, US$m	296.0	527.0	850.0	1197.0	2929.0	1733.0	1900.0
Gold at ⅔ of market price, US$m	501.1	473.0	462.2	489.7	523.0	525.8	530.6
Import cover (reserves/imports), months	0.3	0.6	0.8	1.2	3.0	1.6	1.5

Foreign debt and debt service							
Short-term debt, US$m	4790	4961	5773	7006	7533	7558	6112
Total foreign debt, US$m	20661	23046	24194	26173	29579	29000	28600
as a % of GDP	52.4	53.7	50.1	54.8	57.5	49.2	43.9
as a % of foreign exchange receipts	212.6	212.3	201.8	244.3	249.0	221.2	223.1
Interest payments, US$m	829	944	1005	1114	1302	1500	1800
Principal repayments, US$m	1088	1066	1366	1399	2121	2028	2500
Total debt service, US$m	1917	2010	2371	2513	3423	3528	4300
as a % of goods exports	35.6	31.5	34.5	37.2	48.3	43.6	51.2
as a % of foreign exchange receipts	19.7	18.5	19.8	23.5	28.8	26.9	33.5

Data on fiscal year basis (ending June 30).

Panama

KEY FACTS

Area (thousands of km²):	76
Population (1995, millions):	2.6
Population projection (2025, millions):	4
Population younger than 15 yrs (1991, % of total):	34.6
Urbanization rate (1993, % of population):	53
Life expectancy (1993, years at birth):	73
Gross domestic product (1996, US$bn):	7.7
GDP per capita (1996, US$):	2898
Average annual GDP growth rate (1990-96, %):	5
Average annual inflation rate (1990-96, %):	1.2
Currency (balboa per US$, average 1996):	1
Real exchange rate: (1990=100, average 1996)	84.06
Structure of production (1994):	73% services, 16% industry, 11% agriculture
Main exports:	sugar, bananas, shrimp
Main imports:	machinery, chemicals, petroleum, road vehicles
Main trading partners:	US, Costa Rica, other Central American countries
Total foreign debt (% of GDP):	69.2
Next elections due under normal circumstances:	presidential & legislative scheduled May 1999
Credit rating: (Jan 1997, Standard & Poor's, Moody's)	BB+; Ba1

FORECAST: 1997-2000 (average)

	Worst case	Most likely	Best case
Real GDP growth (%)	3.0	3.8	4.0
Inflation (%)	2.0	1.9	1.7

■ POLITICS

Historical overview

In 1502 the Spanish arrived in Panama, from which point they were to launch their conquest of Peru. The country was ruled by governors appointed by the Spanish king until 1821. Panama then became a province of Colombia, which signed a treaty allowing the United States to construct a railway across the isthmus, stretching 80 kilometres from the Atlantic to the Pacific coast. An attempt by the French-Panama Canal Company to build a canal failed in 1888, and the Colombians opposed French intentions to sell the project to the US. Enraged by this opposition, Panama declared its independence in 1903, supported by the

US. The sovereign rights over the Canal Zone as well as the right of intervention to protect the Canal, completed in 1914, were ceded to the US. The US intervened militarily in Panama's affairs several times until 1936 when it abandoned its right to use troops outside the Canal Zone.

Relative governmental stability prevailed until 1941, when President Arnulfo Arias Madrid was brought down. Several presidents followed in quick succession. In 1968, a period of internal stability began under Omar Torrijos. He headed a populist government and adopted left-wing sympathies in foreign policy, blaming US intervention for the country's plight. His biggest achievement was the conclusion of the Canal Treaty in 1977, signed with US President Jimmy Carter, which returned the Canal and the adjacent Zone to Panama, and set a deadline of 1999 for US military withdrawal.

Recent events

General Manuel Noriega, former president of Panama's secret police and a CIA operative, took control in 1983. Because of his association with drug trafficking and criminal activity, the US imposed sanctions and froze Panamanian assets. Noriega appointed himself president in 1989 and declared war on the US. The US overthrew Noriega and installed Guillermo Endara as president. It then lifted sanctions and restored diplomatic relations.

The new government abolished the Panamanian military, restructured and privatized state companies and attempted, but failed, to reform the constitution, eventually losing public confidence. Ernesto Pérez Balladares, a member of Noriega's party, was elected president in 1994. He privatized various state-run companies, implemented educational reforms and sought, with mixed success, to attract foreign investment.

Chronology

1510	First Spanish settlement on the Caribbean coast
1538-1821	Panama is ruled by governors appointed by the Spanish king
1821	Panama becomes a province of Colombia
1846	Colombia signs a treaty permitting the US to construct a railway across the isthmus and to defend it with military force
1880-1900	French attempt to build a canal fails
1900-03	Civil war
1903	Independence
1903	Treaty cedes sovereign rights over the canal to the US
1914	The US finishes building the canal
1941	Coup against President Arias Madrid
1941-68	Period of instability and political unrest
1968	General Omar Torrijos Herrera takes control
1977	Treaty with the US establishes 1999 as the deadline for US military withdrawal from the Canal area
1983	General Manuel Noriega takes control
1989	Noriega appoints himself president and declares war on the US
1989	The US invades Panama and replaces Noriega with Guillermo Endara
1994	Abolition of the army
1994	Ernesto Pérez Balladares is elected president

Constitution and government

The present constitution was adopted in 1972 and amended in 1978 and 1983. The seventy-two members of the unicameral legislative assembly are elected for five-year terms. Executive power is held by the president and the ministers of state. The president is elected by popular vote for five years and is assisted by two vice-presidents. The judiciary consists of the Panama Supreme Court, five high courts, forty-four circuit judges, and eighty-four municipal judges.

State organization

Panama consists of nine provinces, one autonomous Indian reservation and the Colón Free Trade Zone. Each province consists of electoral districts which have their own mayors, and are represented in the legislative assembly by one representative for every 30,000 inhabitants of the district, plus one representative for every additional 10,000 inhabitants.

Government

Head of State and Head of Government	Ernesto Pérez Balladares
First Vice President	Tomas Altamirano Duque
Second Vice President	Felipe Alejandro Virzi
Planning & Economics	Guillermo Chapman
Treasury & Finance	Miguel Heras Castro
Foreign Relations	Ricardo Alberto Arias
Director, National Bank	José Antonio de la Ossa
National Banking Commission President	Nestor Moreno

Main political parties

Partido Revolucionario Democrático (PRD)
> Founded 1978
> Supports policies of former president Torrijos
> Combination of Marxist, Christian Democrat and business interests
> Led by Ernesto Pérez Balladares

Partido Arnulfista (PA)
> Nationalists
> Founded early 1940s
> Led by Mireya Moscoso De Gruber

Movimiento Pápá Egoró (MPE)
> Populist, rejecting traditional political leadership
> Founded 1992
> Leaders: Ruben Blades

Legislature:
PRD (30 seats), **PA** (13 seats), **MPE** (6), **others** (23 seats)

Next elections
Unicameral legislature in 1999; presidency in 1999

Other political forces
Labour
The small labour movement has only limited influence in the government. During the election campaign, important labour groups supported Ernesto Pérez Balladares, but have since criticized his economic policies.

Military
President Pérez Balladares abolished the military and established the Public Force (PF) as a police rather than a military force. However, most of its members belonged to the military under Noriega. All police, naval, presidential guard and intelligence units are included in the Public Force. However, the PF exercises no direct political influence, and mechanisms are in place to keep it in check. It is not likely to have an influential role in the foreseeable future.

Central Bank
No central bank exists in Panama. However, the National Banking Commission and the Banco Nacional de Panama, a state-owned commercial bank, carry out central bank functions. The National Banking Commission supervises the banking system, sets up reserve requirements and regulates interest rates. The Banco Nacional de Panama serves as the government's principal depository, manages the country's international reserves and is the clearing house for the banking system.

■ ECONOMICS

Historical overview
Panama had one of the highest growth rates (8%) in Latin America during the 1960s due to booming business in the Canal Zone. However, the Vietnam War and the 1973-74 oil crisis caused growth to fall below 2% in the first half of the 1970s. The 1977 Canal Treaty ended the economic slowdown and political uncertainty. Banking and other service sectors expanded, but Panama was severely hit by the Latin American debt crisis at the beginning of the 1980s. In 1985 the International Monetary Fund and the World Bank demanded readjustment programmes, which brought structural reforms and economic expansion until the US imposed sanctions against the Noriega regime. The lifting of sanctions, together with economic reforms and debt rescheduling by the Endara government, boosted output, which has grown almost 5% a year in the 1990s.

Panama's economic performance

	Average annual real GDP growth, %	Average annual consumer price inflation, %
1981-1985	3.7	3.2
1986-1990	0.2	0.4
1991-1995	5.0	1.2

Recent developments

The Pérez Balladares government has set out several reforms to modernize and open one of the most protected economies of the world to international competition. Reforms include the deregulation of the economy, privatization, overhauling the tax code, lowering import barriers, and restructuring foreign debt. Nevertheless, growth fell to 3.7% in 1994 and below 2% in 1995, compared with an average of 5.7% between 1991 and 1994. The construction sector which was mainly responsible for the increase in activity in earlier years, slumped significantly, due to excess capacity in commercial property. Activity in the Colón Free Trade Zone, which accounts for more than 60% of imports and 90% of exports, also shrank, due to the economic slowdown in other Latin American countries.

The modernization programme caused uncertainty in the domestic market, leading to declines in private consumption and industrial output. High foreign debt, amounting to 73.4% of GDP, posed another challenge. However, in April 1996, Panama signed a US$ 3.5 billion Brady bond restructuring deal that will allow it to return to international capital markets. The economic reform programme will eventually bear fruit in 1997, when ecomomic activity should accelerate.

The economy

Unlike other Latin American countries, where agriculture accounts for a large share of output, Panama is a service-based economy generating its revenues mainly from the Canal and offshore banking activities. The largest sectors are transport, storage, communications and finance, and there are plans to develop the tourist sector. Manufacturing and construction generate 9.3% and 6.5% of total output, respectively. Processing of agricultural goods is the main manufacturing activity. Panama is self-sufficient in energy, due to abundant hydroelectric power.

Share of GDP by sector

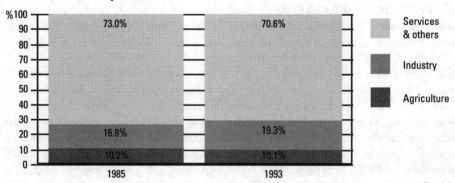

Source: Official data

Trade

As a small country, Panama, excluding the Colón Free Trade Zone, traditionally had a deficit on visible trade and used its earnings from services to obtain foreign exchange. Sugar, bananas and shrimps are the principal export products. But exports of bananas fell almost 12% in 1995 due to the quota system imposed by the EU. Similarly, exports of sugar have declined due to US quotas. Shrimp exports rose 17% to US$81.5 million in 1995, however, and coffee exports, which profited from high international prices, climbed from almost US$14 million in 1994 to US$32 million in 1995. The industrialized countries, especially the US, are the most important consumers of Panamanian exports, accounting for 70% of the total. Some 25% go to other Central American countries, especially Costa Rica.

Machinery represents the biggest category of imports, with 18%, followed by chemicals (13%), petroleum (12%) and cars (12%). About 70% of crude oil consumption is imported from Mexico and Venezuela. About two thirds of intermediate and capital goods are imported from the US, the balance coming from other industrialized countries.

The Colón Free Trade Zone specializes in the re-export of clothing, radios, television sets, watches and pharmaceuticals. Most of the re-exports go to developing countries, mainly Latin America.

Trade restrictions

There are no import quotas on industrial products, but they exist for some agricultural goods such as timber, fishmeal, milk, salt and sugar. The tariffs for most agricultural products range from 30% to 100%. However, the agricultural market will be opened and tariffs lowered over the next ten years through the entry of Panama into the World Trade Organization.

Panama also agreed to a 40% ceiling on tariffs in the industrial sector, formerly protected by high tariffs to promote local industries. Tariffs will drop to 30% over the next five years.

Breakdown of exports (1994)

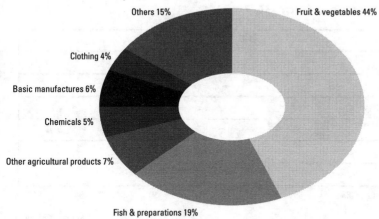

Source: Official data

Export taxes are levied on gold, silver, platinum, manganese and other minerals, unrefined sugar, bananas and assorted agricultural products. For some non-traditional goods, tax credit certificates, equal to 20% of value added, are required. There are no duties on imports to and exports from the Colón Free Trade Zone and the newly established export-processing zones.

Balance of trade in US$m

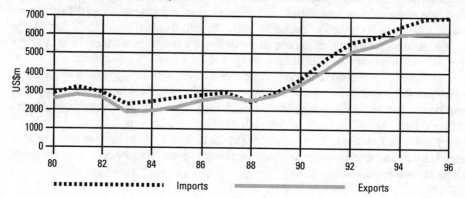

Source: Official data

Balance of payments

Panama has traditionally posted trade and current account deficits. When US sanctions were imposed, imports fell by 18.6% and exports by 6.3%, leading to a trade surplus. However, a deficit appeared again when sanctions were lifted and imports resumed. In 1995 the deficit almost doubled due to an economic slowdown in the Colón Free Trade Zone. The deficit is likely to have widened further in 1996, since world prices of manufactured goods rose that year and imports were boosted by a recovery in domestic demand.

Current account as a % of GDP

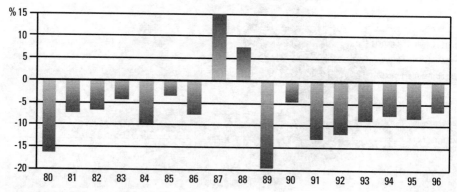

Source: Official data

Economic policy

Monetary policy

Panama's use of the US dollar constrains its monetary policy and curbs consumer price inflation. Thus, the inflation rate is similar to that of the US. It is Panama's balance of payments that influences most of its monetary developments. Since 1990, net foreign assets have increased, causing monetary conditions to be very liquid. However, this trend has slowed since 1994.

Fiscal policy
The budget deficit, which stood at 9.6% of GDP in 1982, fell to 0.4% in 1986. But it rose again in 1988 and 1989 to 11% of GDP, due to the conflict between General Noriega and the US. Economic sanctions and the withholding of canal tolls by the US caused significant revenue losses and cuts in government spending. Since 1993, the government's fiscal accounts have again been in deficit. To meet the fiscal deficit target of US$22 million the government froze expenditures in the spring of 1996 for a few months. Large payments to foreign creditors under the Brady plan impede further progress in reducing the deficit.

Currency
The balboa is at parity with the US$ (one balboa is equal to one dollar). The balboa is limited to coins, and the US dollar circulates freely in Panama.

Exchange controls
There are no exchange controls and no central monetary authority. No official guarantees exist against non-convertibility. Foreign-exchange transactions are not subject to any controls or taxes.

Banking system
The Banco Nacional de Panamá is in charge of the fiscal matters of the government and the Comisión Bancaria Nacional is responsible for supervising the banking system, granting banking licences and supporting the development of Panama as an international banking centre. Other state-owned financial institutions are the Banco Hipotecario Nacional, the Caja de Ahorros, and the Banco de Desarrollo Agropecuario.

The commercial banking sector comprises 109 banks: 62 operate under a general licence, which enables them to do domestic and international business, 30 under an international licence, limited to off-shore business, and 17 are representative offices. Panama is an important international banking centre in the region, and some 75% of deposits are from abroad.

To combat money laundering, the government has signed an accord requiring anti-laundering safeguards. And under a new law in 1996, banks and other financial institutions must identify customers carrying out large transactions. Further changes are under review to broaden the power of the Comisión Bancaria Nacional, to close troubled banks, and to increase minimum capital requirements for establishing banks from US$2 million up to US$40 million.

■ EQUITIES

Index performance (in local currency)

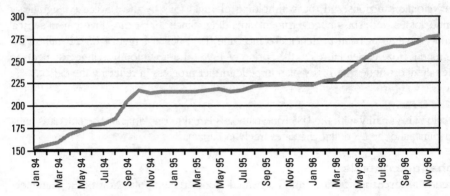

Key indicators

	Index performance %, in US$ terms	Market Cap. US$bn	P/E	Div. Yield
1994	44.1	0.7	11.0	2.8
1995	3.1	0.8	9.4	4.0
1996	24.9	1.3	17.8	3.6

Sources: Local stock exchange, IFC, Bloomberg, Datastream, UBS

Structure
The official Panamanian exchange, Bolsa de Valores de Panama, is made up mainly of bonds, with 70% of the market capitalization in corporate bonds, 22% commercial paper, 6% equities and 2% government paper. The secondary market is much smaller, amounting to about one sixth of the official market. Equity market capitalization stood at US$1.33 billion at end 1996.

Regulatory authority
The National Securities Commission regulates all fixed income and equity trades and has the power to licence brokers and regulate the Stock Exchange.

Trading methods
The exchange runs a traditional in-the-pit system but an electronic trading system is planned and will be introduced some time in 1998.

Hours
The market is open from 08.00 to 17.00 although trading only takes place between 11.00 and 12.00 Monday to Friday.

Settlement time and clearing
Financial settlement is currently T+5 but is expected to become T+3 with the introduction of the electronic trading system.

Types of shares
Almost all shares are ordinary voting shares.

Stock index
The PSI (Panama Stock Index) has one hundred listings, of which only twenty-five are equities. Only eleven stocks are regularly traded.

Taxes
There is a withholding tax of 10% on dividends.

Ownership limits for non-residents
No ownership limits exist on non-residents.

Capital and foreign exchange controls
There are no capital or foreign exchange controls and the US dollar is the official currency.

Brokers
There are seventeen brokers in Panama. The brokers act on behalf of their clients and execute the trades directly through the clearing system.

Sectors
The biggest sector in terms of market capitalization is breweries and soft drink companies, making up about 40% of equities, followed by 35% in banks and the remaining 25% in insurance companies and other industries.

■ DEBT

The Ministry of Planning and Finance regulates the country's bond markets through the National Security Commission. Issues by banks and private companies, often family owned, make up about 90% of volume on the Bolsa de Valores de Panama.

Government domestic debt instruments are limited to 180-day Certificado Tesoros (Treasury Certificates), issued by the Ministry of Planning and Finance through the Banking Commission. Bills are offered once a year at a fixed yield (7% for December 1996's issue) and are fully underwritten by the Banco Nacional de Panama.

Private Debt
Bonds with maturities ranging from one to ten years are offered by Panamanian companies at fixed rates of between 8% and 10%. Approximately PAB100 million are offered each month. Domestic banks also issue bonds at similar rates and tenures.

In addition, private enterprises raise short-term finance by placing Valores Comerciales Negiciables (VCNs) – equivalent to commercial paper, with local banks and finance companies. About PAB20 million is issued each month.

Most trades are transacted on the Bolsa, which is a private organization owned by market participants. Settlement is normally three days through the Bolsa's Panaclear system.

Income and capital gains from transactions outside the exchange are subject to tax. There are no restrictions for foreign investors, but their involvement is small. There are currently plans to create a local credit rating agency.

Brady bonds

Panama has recently completed a Brady-style restructuring of its external commercial bank debt. The menu included collateralized Discount and Par bonds, Past Due Interest and Interest Reduction Bonds.

Eurobonds

Panama is now beginning to access the eurobond market. In July 1996 a private bank, Banco Ganadero issued a US$75 million three-year eurobond paying a 10% coupon and a US$75 million euro medium-term note with the same terms.

Eurobond issues (US$m)

	1990	1991	1992	1993	1994	1995	1996
Sovereign	—	—	—	—	—	—	—
Private	—	—	—	—	—	150.0	—

PANAMA: Economic indicators

Population and development	1990	1991	1992	1993	1994	1995	1996e
Population, million	2.4	2.4	2.5	2.5	2.6	2.6	2.7
Population growth, %	2.1	1.7	2.0	1.6	2.0	1.9	1.5
Nominal GDP per capita, US$	2247	2426	2683	2808	2876	2888	2898
National accounts							
Nominal GDP, US$bn	5.4	5.9	6.7	7.1	7.4	7.6	7.7
Change in real GDP, %	7.4	7.9	7.2	4.1	3.7	1.9	1.5
Gross fixed capital formation, % of GDP	8.4	14.8	18.4	23.7	24.5	25.3	26.6
Money supply and inflation							
Narrow money, change %, Dec/Dec	41.0	28.7	14.8	10.8	13.5	1.4	4.5
Broad money, change %, Dec/Dec	36.6	31.0	25.0	17.1	15.5	7.9	7.3
Consumer price inflation (avg.) %	0.8	1.3	1.8	0.5	1.3	1.0	1.5
Interest rates							
Prime lending rate, annual average	11.98	11.79	10.61	10.06	10.15	11.10	—
Government finance							
Government expenditure, % of GDP	22.7	22.4	21.7	21.1	21.6	21.9	22.5
Government balance, % of GDP	-2.4	-1.4	1.6	-1.4	-0.3	-0.1	-0.5
Exchange rates lc=local currency							
Exchange rate, annual average, lc/US$	1.00	1.00	1.00	1.00	1.00	1.00	1.00
Exchange rate, end of year, lc/US$	1.00	1.00	1.00	1.00	1.00	1.00	1.00
Real exchange rate 1990=100	100.0	96.7	93.2	91.9	88.4	84.7	84.1
Balance of payments							
Exports of goods & services, US$m	4489	6676	7846	8291	8788	9541	9423
Change %	18.4	48.7	17.5	5.7	6.0	8.6	-1.2
Imports of goods & services, US$m, fob	4429	7686	8965	9137	9536	10355	10141
Change %	18.2	73.5	16.6	1.9	4.4	8.6	-2.1
Trade balance, of goods only, US$m, fob-fob	-236	-509	-506	-462	-444	-831	-800
Current account balance, US$m	-238	-723	-724	-576	-526	-587	-400
as a % of GDP	-4.4	-12.2	-10.8	-8.1	-7.1	-7.7	-5.2
Foreign exchange reserves							
Foreign exchange reserves, US$m	343.5	499.1	504.4	597.4	704.3	781.6	887.0
Gold at ⅔ of market price, US$m	0.0	0.0	0.0	0.0	0.0	0.0	0.0
Import cover (reserves/imports), months	0.9	0.8	0.7	0.8	0.9	0.9	1.0
Foreign debt and debt service							
Short-term debt, US$m	215	215	176	175	224	249	334
Total foreign debt, US$m	5319	5482	4989	5231	5328	5571	5356
as a % of GDP	98.6	92.6	74.7	73.6	71.8	73.4	69.2
as a % of foreign exchange receipts	85.5	78.4	60.3	60.9	58.9	56.8	55.2
Interest payments, US$m	395	393	290	291	354	422	250
Principal repayments, US$m	149	114	583	154	201	178	169
Total debt service, US$m	544	507	873	445	555	600	419
as a % of goods exports	16.2	12.1	17.1	8.2	9.2	9.9	7.1
as a % of foreign exchange receipts	8.7	7.3	10.6	5.2	6.1	6.1	4.3

Peru

KEY FACTS

Area (thousands of km²):	1285
Population (1995, millions):	23.5
Population projection (2025, millions):	36
Population younger than 15 yrs (1991, % of total):	37.1
Urbanization rate (1993, % of population):	71
Life expectancy (1993, years at birth):	66
Gross domestic product (1996, US$bn):	61.9
GDP per capita (1996, US$):	2577
Average annual GDP growth rate (1990-96, %):	3.7
Average annual inflation rate (1990-96, %):	1151.2
Currency (sol per US$, average 1996):	2.45
Real exchange rate: (1990=100, average 1996)	122.11
Structure of production (1994):	56% services, 37% industry, 7% agriculture
Main exports:	copper, gold, fishmeal
Main imports:	intermediate goods, capital goods, consumer goods
Main trading partners:	US, Japan, UK, Germany, Brazil
Market capitalization of Stock Exchange (December 1996; US$bn):	13.8
Total foreign debt (% of GDP):	48.5
Next elections due under normal circumstances:	presidential & legislative April 2000
Credit rating: (Jan 1997, Moody's)	B2

FORECAST: 1997-2000 (average)

	Worst case	Most likely	Best case
Real GDP growth (%)	4.0	5.2	6.0
Inflation (%)	11.0	8.5	7.0

■ POLITICS

Historical overview

The Inca empire was engaged in civil war when Francisco Pizarro began his conquest of Peru on behalf of the Spanish, in 1532. Pizarro captured, ransomed and executed the Inca emperor, Atahualpa, and some seven thousand of his men. Pizarro then founded the city of Lima, and in 1544, the Viceroyalty of Peru was established.

Over the next two hundred years, Peru enjoyed a peaceful period, with Lima as the major political, social and commercial centre of the Andean nations. Peru remained loyal to Spain until 1821, when it declared its independence, helped by the forces of the Argentinean general José de San Martín and the Venezuelan Simón Bolívar. In the War of the Pacific with

Chile (1879-83), Peru lost the province of Tarapacá, and with it the lucrative nitrate fields in the northern Atacama Desert.

Peru had another border dispute with Ecuador in 1941, and as a result the area north of the Río Marañón was ceded to Peru under the treaty of Rio de Janeiro in 1942. However, this decision is still contested by Ecuador today. In 1968, a left-wing military regime was installed by General Juan Velasco who nationalized banks, telecommunications, railways and heavy industries as well as large haciendas, which were converted into agricultural co-operatives. In 1980, military rule was ended, and a new constitution came into effect, but a series of nationwide strikes and violent insurgency by the Maoist Shining Path (Sendero Luminoso) guerrillas resulted in political instability throughout the decade. At the same time, the Túpac Amaru Revolutionary Movement (MRTA), another guerrilla group, gained in influence. The populist regime of President Alan García (1985-90) was one of fiscal excess that destabilized the nation economically as well.

Recent events

In 1990, Alberto Fujimori, a political outsider of Japanese descent, was elected president. His surprising victory and the rise of his newly created party, Cambio 90, underscored the failure of the traditional parties to address the economic and political concerns of the population. In 1992, Fujimori, alleging corruption and an obstructive attitude on the part of Congress toward his policies, suspended the constitution, dissolved the bicameral legislature, and reorganized the judiciary. However, international pressure to restore a democracy resulted in the election of a Democratic Constituent Congress (CCD), whose primary task was to draft a new constitution by November 1992 and organize municipal elections in early 1993. The pro-government majority in the newly formed Congress supported the president's far-reaching reform programme and approved the extension of the special powers sought by Fujimori. In 1993, 53% of Peru's voting population approved the new constitution.

Abimael Guzmán and other members of the Sendero Luminoso were arrested in 1992. Since then, violence has decreased. In early 1995, the old border dispute with Ecuador began anew, with an eighteen-day military conflict. Although peace talks have made some progress, the border dispute will not be settled permanently in the foreseeable future.

In 1995, Fujimori was re-elected with 64.4% of the vote, while his major rival, former United Nations Secretary-general Javier Pérez de Cuellar, garnered only 21.8%. Fujimori suffered a political defeat in November 1995, when his political protégé Jaime Yoshiyama was defeated by independent candidate Alberto Andrade in the mayoral elections of Lima. Although in recent years Fujimori has enjoyed one of the highest approval ratings of any Latin American leader, his popularity has begun to wane, due to the economic slowdown and his bid for a third consecutive presidential term. On December 17, 1996, MTRA rebels took over the Japanese ambasssador's Lima residence, initially retaining over 500 hostages. The traumatic event diverted the president's attention from his political and economic agenda.

Chronology

1532	Beginning of the conquest of Peru by Francisco Pizarro
1544	Creation of the Viceroyalty of Peru
1572	Rebellion of the last Inca leader, Manco Inca, is suppressed

1821	Independence
1824	Battle of Ayacucho; the Spanish are defeated by the Republicans
1879-83	War of the Pacific; Peru loses the province of Tarapacá
1928	Foundation of the left-wing and populist Alianza Popular Revolucionaria Americana (APRA)
1930-60	Political instability
1968-80	Military government
1980	The new constitution takes effect
1980	"People's War" initiated by the Maoist group Sendero Luminoso
1985	The ARPA candidate Alan García wins the presidential election
1990	Independent candidate Alberto Fujimori wins the presidential election
1992	Self-coup by Fujimori and suspension of the constitution and the legislature
1992	Capture of Sendero Luminoso leader Abimael Guzmán and decrease of violence
1992	Election of the Democratic Constituent Congress
1993	Adoption of the new constitution
1995	Eighteen-day military conflict with Ecuador
1995	Re-election of Alberto Fujimori
1996	MTRA hostage-taking at the Japanese ambassador's residence

Constitution and government

In 1993, a new constitution replaced the 1979 charter. It enlarged the already considerable power of the president as the executive authority. It also allows the president, who is elected by universal suffrage, to run for a second term.

The president appoints the Council of Ministers as well as senior military officials, and has the right to dissolve Congress under certain circumstances. Since 1993 the legislature has consisted of a single chamber of 120 members, who are elected for five-year terms by universal suffrage. Judicial power is vested in the Supreme Court of Justice and other tribunals.

State organization

Politically the country is divided into twenty-four departments and a constitutional province (Callao).

Main political parties

Cambio 90
> Independent
> Founded 1990
> Led by Alberto Fujimori

Unión Por el Perú
> Independent
> Founded 1995
> Led by Javier Pérez de Cuellar

Partido Aprista del Perú
  Democratic, left-wing
  Founded 1994
  Leaders: Luis Alva Castro

Legislature
Cambio 90–Nueva Majoría (67 seats), **Unión Por el Perú** (17 seats), **Partido Aprista del Perú** (8 seats), **Frente Independiente Moralizador** (6 seats), others (22 seats).

Next elections
Presidential and legislative elections in April 2000

Other political forces
Labour
Labour unions were once powerful, but have recently declined in influence. The number of strikes has also fallen significantly. The General Confederation of Labour of Peru, controlled by the political left, is the strongest labour group.

Military
Since Fujimori's rise to power in 1990, the military has grown in influence. It has special powers to root out subversives during emergencies. President Fujimori is trying also to reform the army into a body to carry out social tasks.

Central bank
The Central Reserve Bank of Peru was founded in 1922 and received its present name in 1931. Its function is to preserve monetary stability, and it is responsible for regulating money in circulation, credit to the financial system and international reserves, for the issuance of notes and coins, and for providing information on national finances. It is autonomous.

■ ECONOMICS

Historical overview
There was little direct government involvement in the economy until the 1950s, when the government began to protect domestic manufacturing with high import tariffs. Until the 1970s, Peru experienced positive growth. This ended when an expensive nationalization programme, a fall in exports and a rise in imports caused a recession in 1977-78.

In subsequent years the economy continued to contract, and Peru suffered annual inflation rates of more than 100%. In August 1985, President Alan García launched a stabiliz-ation programme based on price and wage controls and a fixed exchange rate. However, expansionary policies accompanied the stabilization programme. After a short recovery, progress ground to a halt due to the conflict between continuing high inflation rates and a fixed exchange rate.

Between 1988 and 1990, the economy fell by a cumulative 24.5% in real terms. Consumer prices, which rose a record 397% year-over-year in August 1990, rocketed to

3,337% a year between 1988 and 1990. As a result, relative prices were severely distorted and the economy was dollarized.

Peru's economic performance

	Average annual real GDP growth, %	Average annual consumer price inflation, %
1961-1965	6.2	9.0
1966-1970	4.4	9.8
1971-1975	5.2	11.5
1976-1980	2.7	51.0
1981-1985	0.1	104.9
1986-1990	-1.2	2342.2
1991-1995	5.5	112.7

Recent developments

Soon after taking office in 1990, President Fujimori launched a stabilization programme aimed at balancing the central government budget and restraining monetary growth. The exchange rate was allowed to float freely. Moreover, to achieve long-term stabilization, the government embarked on an ambitious programme of labour market and tax reform, trade liberalization, and privatization of public-sector enterprises.

Since 1993, the economy has staged an impressive recovery. The continuation of restrictive monetary and fiscal policies resulted in a fall in inflation to 10.2% in the twelve months ending December 1995. This new stability resulted in a rise in disposable income for a large part of the population, triggering a rebound in domestic demand. The economy grew 6.4% in real terms in 1993, 13.1% in 1994, and 7% in 1995. However, it slowed considerably in 1996, registering real GDP growth of about 2.5% for the full year. Despite the success of the economic programme, the social costs were substantial. Almost all sectors of the economy initially experienced a considerable contraction of output in 1992. Unemployment rose to 9.9% in 1993, and underemployment to 77.4%. However, the expansion has recently alleviated those pressures. Furthermore, at his re-election, President Fujimori pledged that since hyperinflation has been tamed, his second term would focus more on job creation and export promotion, with additional resources dedicated to education and health. Despite this promise, fiscal policy remained tight in the first year of his second term, in an effort to achieve the macroeconomic targets agreed with the International Monetary Fund.

The economy

The services sector is the most important contributor to Peruvian output, accounting for 45% of GDP and employing more than 50% of the economically active population. Fujimori's adjustment programme significantly reduced the size of the state bureaucracy, however, causing a loss of more than 20,000 jobs. Industry and mining are also important sectors, with the former generating 33% of GDP and the latter providing half of Peru's export earnings. Agriculture accounted for more than 20% of GDP in the 1950s, but fell below 15% by 1970 and contributed only 11-13% in the 1990s. President Fujimori has attempted to revive the agricultural sector, but his success has been limited because of the lack of credit to farmers and the over-valuation of the currency.

Saving and investment

At the same time the privatization programme was launched, the government founded a private pension system (managed through administradoras de fondos de pensiones, AFP), modelled on the Chilean system, to replace the chaotic state-run social security system. The goal was to increase domestic savings and to develop local capital markets. The number of affiliates increased considerably during the first eighteen months, although the total funds under the AFP's management are still equivalent to only 1% of GDP. Consequently, the government has liberalized the investment climate to encourage private inflows. Foreigners are as free as Peruvian nationals to invest. Since 1990, gross domestic investment has increased by 7.8%. Spain is the dominant foreign investor in Peru, followed by the US, the UK, Holland and Chile.

Trade

Imports were very low in the 1980s due to the heavily protected economy and the recession. Through liberalization of the economy in 1990, imports increased considerably. Intermediate goods represented the most important components in 1995, amounting to 41.9% of total foreign purchases. Capital goods accounted for 30.7%, while 22.8% of total imports were consumer goods.

As for exports, traditional products (mining, fishmeal oil and agricultural products) accounted for 80% of the total in 1995. Mining was the most important export industry, representing 47% of total foreign sales, and new investment projects in the copper and gold industries will boost the share of mining exports in the second half of the 1990s. Exports of fishmeal, which increased considerably in 1993-94 due to large investments and abundant harvests, represented 14% of total exports in 1995. Non-traditional products (textiles, agricultural goods, steel, chemical and metal products, etc.) accounted for 20% of total exports.

In 1995, 17.2% of exports went to the US, by far the most important trading partner. Japan followed with 8.4%. The UK, China and Germany were Peru's other principal export partners. The largest share of imports (25%) come from the US, whereas Colombia's share is 8.1%, followed by Japan (7.0%) and Brazil (5.6%).

Balance of trade in US$m

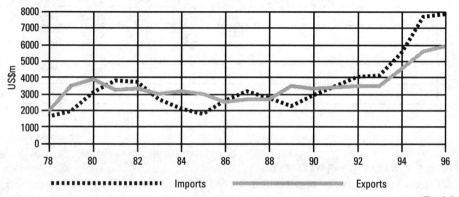

Source: Official data

Breakdown of exports (1995)

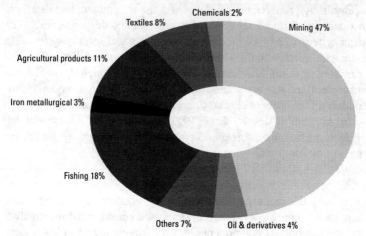

Source: Official data

Trade restrictions

There are generally no restrictions on imports, with the exception of a few products (for social, health or security reasons). There is a uniform value-added tax of 18 per cent of the CIF value of imports in addition to the import duty. Agricultural products are subject to a variable import surcharge. The only items that are prohibited for export are wildlife, plants, cottonseed cakes, natural rubber, and mineral ores. The state monopoly over the export of mining and petroleum products was abolished in 1991. Proceeds from exports are not subject to a repatriation requirement.

Current account as a % of GDP

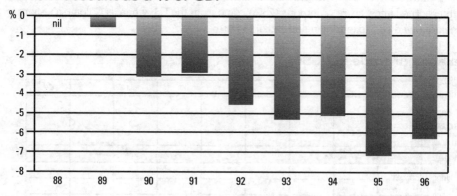

Source: Official data

Balance of payments

Peru's trade balance has deteriorated from a US$1.24 billion surplus in 1989 to a US$1.95 billion deficit in 1996, largely because of trade liberalization, a sharp increase in domestic demand for imported goods, and the sol's real appreciation against other currencies. The current account has traditionally posted deficits, owing to large shortfalls in the invisibles balance. The deterioration in the trade balance has recently swelled the current account deficit dramatically, from US$2.54 billion in 1994 (5.1% of GDP) to US$3.9 billion in 1996 (6.3%). Thus far, the capital account surplus has been sufficient to offset the current account shortfall and boost foreign exchange reserves, which rose from US$1.0 billion in 1990 to US$10.5 billion at the end of 1996. Moreover, capital inflows have largely consisted of direct investment that is not easily reversed, while short-term foreign financing has been mainly trade-related.

Debt

When Fujimori took office in 1990, he inherited a country ineligible to borrow in international financial markets. To comply with IMF requirements for financial assistance, the authorities ended the debt moratorium, launched an austerity programme, and embarked on structural reforms to deregulate the economy and open it to foreign competition. In March 1993, the IMF granted the country a US$1.4 billion Extended Fund Facility loan, US$860 million of which was used to settle arrears to the Fund.

In October 1995, Peru reached a preliminary Brady-style debt restructuring accord with its foreign commercial bank creditors. Although the Brady plan will reduce Peru's external obligations, the resumption of all debt-service payments will exert pressure on the fiscal and current accounts. The country's interest payments due amounted to an estimated 33.8% of its foreign exchange receipts in 1996, a considerable debt-service burden.

Economic policy

Monetary policy

President Fujimori curtailed net credit to the public sector, expanded loans to the private sector and encouraged capital repatriation with high real interest rates. In addition, since 1993, central bank currency and reserves have been fully covered by foreign exchange reserves. However, despite the central bank's efforts to sterilize strong capital inflows, monetary aggregates have expanded rapidly.

To slow this expansion and to prevent an overheating of the economy, the central bank tightened its monetary stance in mid-1995. The central bank's control over monetary policy is limited, however, since about 70% of all deposits in Peru are denominated in dollars.

Fiscal policy

Fujimori has also dramatically reduced the central government deficit since 1990. To raise revenues, fuel prices were increased and the tax system reformed. Tax privileges for firms were eliminated, many VAT exemptions reduced, and penalties were imposed for tax evasion. At the same time, public expenditures were curtailed, transfers to public enterprises cut, and real wages of public employees lowered.

In addition, the government embarked on an ambitious privatization programme. These policies, along with strong economic expansion and extraordinary privatization revenues, have reduced the total public sector fiscal deficit from 7.3% of GDP in 1989 to 1.3% in 1996.

Currency

Due to high inflation, two new currencies were introduced between 1985 and 1991. In 1985, the inti replaced the sol at a rate of one inti per 1,000 sols, and in 1991 this currency was replaced by the new sol at a rate of one new sol per one million intis. The central bank allows the currency to float freely and intervenes only to avoid dramatic fluctuations in the market. Peru's economic success has strengthened capital inflows and put upward pressure on the currency.

Although the strength of the sol has helped to control inflation, it has eroded export competitiveness and caused the trade deficit to increase. In November 1995, nervousness over the rising current account deficit and the likelihood of lower inflows in 1996 caused the sol to depreciate by about 3.5% in nominal terms within ten days. The government responded by selling dollars through the Banco de la Nación, and succeeded in stabilizing the sol. In the third quarter of 1996, however, the central bank began buying dollars in the foreign exchange market, causing the sol to depreciate to 2.58 per US dollar at year-end.

Peruvian sol per US dollar exchange rate

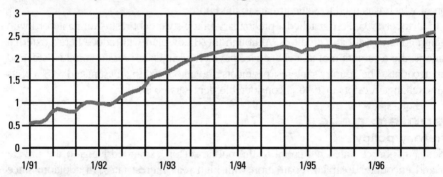

Exchange controls

Since 1991, the sol has been allowed to float freely. Companies and individuals are allowed to hold foreign exchange balances abroad and in domestic banks. Forward cover against exchange rate risk is available only from commercial banks. Foreign currency-denominated accounts may be opened in domestic banks.

Banking system

A 1993 law regulates the banking system. The Superintendencia de Bancos y Seguros (SBS) supervises the banking sector, and state interference is minimal. Banks are subject to the norms of the Bank of International Settlements, which limits total assets plus risk-weighted contingent credits to 12.5 times net worth.

About three quarters of all deposits are in the hands of four banks. Nevertheless, new financial institutions are beginning to operate in Peru. The relative stability of the currency has meant that Peruvians have begun saving in sols. Still, almost 70% of bank deposits in 1995 were denominated in dollars. Despite an increase in deposits (which have doubled to over US$800 million since 1992), Peru remains underbanked. Since 1993, an increasing number of foreign banks, which are attracted by the growth potential and high spreads, are investing in Peru. A 45% reserve requirement is imposed by the central bank on foreign currency deposits.

■ EQUITIES

Index performance (in local currency)

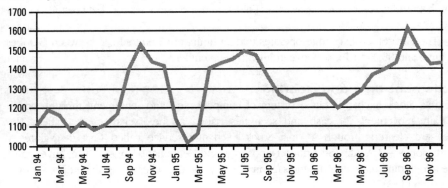

Key indicators

	Index performance %, in US$ terms	Market Cap. US$bn	P/E	Div. Yield	Weight in IFCI	IFCG
1994	52.1	8.2	44.0	0.7	1.0	0.6
1995	9.3	11.8	14.5	1.3	1.1	0.7
1996	0.7	13.8	14.2	2.4	1.0	0.7

Sources: Local stock exchange, IFC, Bloomberg, Datastream, UBS

Structure

The market is composed of Exchange Floor shares (registered on the exchange) and Over the Counter shares (not registered on the exchange floor). As at November 1996, there are 241 registered securities listed on the Bolsa de Valores de Lima, with a total market capitalization of almost US$14 billion.

Regulatory authority

The National Securities Commission (CONASEV) was established in 1970 to contribute to the efficiency of the capital market. The stock market was converted into a non-profit civil association and renamed the Lima Stock Exchange. CONASEV is a public institution affiliated with the Economy Ministry. It is responsible for promoting the securities market, ensuring that companies are correctly managed and that their accounting is up to standard.

Trading methods

Trading is undertaken on an integrated electronic order and floor-based system. Member brokers may post bids and offers on an electronic system with price and time priority. On the floor there is a stock exchange official (or "director") who can improve on the price displayed on screen if a better price is available from the floor, when a bid or offer is accepted. A significant amount of business is generated by floor-based brokers.

Hours

Exchange Floor and Over the Counter continuous trading is between 09.00 and 12.45. In addition, there is a pre-opening session between 08.00 and 09.00 for entry of firm offers through the Electronic Trading System (ELEX), and a closing session between 12.45 and 13.30.

The Lima Stock Exchange operates trading hours of 09.00 to 13.30 between October and June, and 08.00 to 16.00 between July and September.

Settlement time and clearing

The Lima Stock Exchange has a system of compensation and settlement, through which the daily movements of cash and securities traded at the Exchange are settled. The trades are cleared through a Lima Stock Exchange service called Caja de Valores y Liquidaciones – CAVALI (Securities Depository and Settlement House). The buyer must settle two trading days after the transaction (T+2), while the seller settles three days after the transaction (T+3).

Types of shares

Common or capital stock: this type of share is issued by public companies and represents a cash contribution to capital, with a view to earning a profit. Common or capital shares incorporate the rights and duties of the shareholders. Employee stock: this type of share was created in 1977 and issued by industrial, fishing and mining companies to grant workers direct participation in the company's equity. These stocks grant their holders the right to receive dividend payments, in cash or stock, but they have no voting rights or representation at the General Shareholders' Meetings. However, in the case of a company's liquidation, holders of employee stock have preference over common stockholders.

Stock indices

The General Index of the Lima Stock Exchange (IGBVL) was created on December 30, 1981. Since 1995, the IGBVL portfolio has been revised, and its index constituents are subject to review every six months, on January 2 and July 1. Factors considered in selecting the constituents include frequency and volume traded. At present the index is composed of forty-six companies.

The Selective Index of the Lima Stock Exchange has been calculated since July 1993. The Selective Index consists of the fifteen most frequently traded "representative" shares.

Taxes

Dividends are subject to a 10% withholding tax. Capital gains on the sale of shares are exempt from tax. The Stock Exchange Fee is 0.10%; and the Peruvian SEC charge is 0.05%. Every purchase and sale on the Lima Stock Exchange, whether by a local or foreign party, is subject to 18% VAT.

Disclosure of financial statements

Equity issuers must present to CONASEV and those markets on which their securities are registered, non-audited financial information as of March 31, June 30, September 30 and December 30 of each year, within thirty calendar days following the closing dates.

Ownership limits for non-residents

Only approved institutional investors/broker-dealers can invest directly in Peru and an Investor ID (CAVAL code) must be disclosed prior to trading. Tax implications for non-Peruvian investors are the same as those for local investors (see above).

Brokers

According to Peruvian market legislation, stock market intermediaries are brokerage houses (Sociedades Agentes de Bolsa), acting with the authorization of CONASEV. Brokerage houses are the only parties entitled to membership in the Lima Stock Exchange. The authorization has no fixed duration and may be suspended or revoked as a penalty for grave misconduct or inactivity over a six-month period.

The General Law of Banking, Financial and Insurance Institutions authorizes banks to set up subsidiaries to operate in the stock market. Financial companies are also allowed to create special departments or offices for the same purpose.

Commissions

Commissions collected by brokers as the result of the sale of shares are negotiated between broker and client. Commissions usually range from 0.55% to 1.45% of the transaction.

Sectors

The telecommunications sector is the largest in Peru's IGBVL index with a 33% market weight in the Bolsa, followed by the mining and cement sectors, each with 19%, and banks (14.2%). The Bolsa's sectoral indices are classified into both common stock and employee stock sub-sectors.

Common stock sectoral indices include banks and financial institutions, industrials, mining, utilities, insurance and diverse industrials. Employee stock sub-sectors include only industrial companies and mining.

ADRs

There are nine publicly listed Peruvian ADRs, with two (Banco Wiese and Telefónica del Peru) listed on the NYSE.

■ DEBT

The National Supervisory Commission of Companies and Securities (CONASEV) regulates the Bolsa de Valores de Lima (Lima Stock Exchange). The National Commission for Foreign Investment and Technologies (CONITE) has broad responsibility for overseas investment. The framework and practice of the capital markets are governed by Legislative Decree 755. The bond markets are still undeveloped. Government securities are tightly held, primarily by pension funds to satisfy reserve requirements. The largest sector is the CD market, mainly denominated in sols (some in dollars). Secondary market activity is low.

Primary market
There is no regular auction system, but auctions are usually held on Mondays or Fridays. Bids are submitted during the morning up to a cut-off time and allocations announced later in the day.

CDs (Certificado de Deposito del BCRP)
CDs are issued by the central bank at a discount, with maturities of 30, 60 and 90 days. Primary placement is by weekly Dutch auction and settlement is in physical form 1 or 2 days later.

Repurchase agreements
Repos are transacted by financial institutions, for 30, 60, 90 and 180 days at discount. Settlement is T+1, book entry form.

Corporate bonds (Bonos Corporativos)
Bonos are issued by enterprises for maturities ranging from 2 to 5 years. The coupon can be either fixed or floating, and payments are made quarterly or semi-annually. New offerings are underwritten by financial institutions.

Leasing and subordinated bonds
(Bonos de Arrendiamiento y los Subordinados)
The structure and mechanism is similar to corporate bonds. They are issued by financial institutions with maturities of 2 to 4 years. Coupons can be fixed or floating, and payments are made quarterly or semi-annually. Bonds are sold on an underwritten basis.

CAVAL (Caja de Valores) is the central depository for securities which settle in book-entry form. The Caja de Liquidaciones is the clearing house for all trades. Both institutions are part of the Lima Stock Exchange.

Foreign investors
Non-residents are treated the same as domestic investors. Legislative Decree 662 stipulates that they can repatriate profits and avoid CGT payment if they transact their bargains in the exchange.

Eurobonds
Peru has not issued a eurobond, but in 1994 a private company raised US$40 million through three-year euro medium term notes, and a smaller securitized deal was privately placed in the US for Pesquera Austral SA.

Eurobond issues (US$m)

	1990	1991	1992	1993	1994	1995	1996
Sovereign	—	—	—	—	—	—	—
Private	—	—	—	—	40.0	—	—

Brady bonds

Peru is expected to issue Brady bonds in the first quarter of 1997, the last of the Latin countries to complete a Brady restructuring. The bank loans, supplier credits and working capital lines will be replaced by discount bonds and par bonds with a 30-year maturity and front-loaded interest reduction bonds (FLIRB). Peru will also issue past due interest bonds (PDIs) against interest arrears. The par and discount bonds are collateralized with 30-year zero coupons and have a 6-month rolling interest guarantee. Peru also bought back over US$1 billion of principal with a similar amount of interest arrears attached as part of the restructuring agreement.

Bond	Coupon	Collateral	Maturity	Currencies
Discount	6mth L+13/16	Principal+Interest	2027	US$
Par	Step up	Principal+Interest	2027	US$
PDI	Step up		2022	US$
FLIRB	Step up		2016	US$

■ PERU: Economic indicators

Population and development	1990	1991	1992	1993	1994	1995	1996e
Population, million	21.6	22.0	22.5	22.6	23.1	23.5	24.0
Population growth, %	2.1	2.1	2.1	0.8	2.0	1.9	2.0
Nominal GDP per capita, US$	1572	2151	1877	1824	2171	2501	2577

National accounts							
Nominal GDP, US$bn	33.9	47.3	42.1	41.3	50.1	58.9	61.9
Change in real GDP, %	-3.8	2.9	-1.8	6.4	13.1	7.0	2.4
Gross fixed capital formation, % of GDP	14.8	12.9	15.2	16.8	21.0	23.4	24.1

Money supply and inflation							
Narrow money, change %, Dec/Dec	5529.0	95.2	76.0	55.1	68.3	24.4	12.5
Broad money, change %, Dec/Dec	6384.2	230.7	88.2	71.8	39.5	26.8	40.7
Consumer price inflation (avg.) %	7482.0	409.2	73.5	48.5	21.0	11.5	11.6
Producer prices (avg.) %							

Government finance							
Government expenditure, % of GDP	14.2	11.0	13.7	13.6	13.0	14.5	15.1
Government balance, % of GDP	-4.6	-3.3	-3.0	-2.5	-2.2	-2.7	-1.3

Exchange rates lc=local currency							
Exchange rate, annual average, lc/US$	0.19	0.77	1.25	1.99	2.20	2.25	2.45
Exchange rate, end of year, lc/US$	0.52	0.96	1.63	2.16	2.18	2.33	2.58
Real exchange rate 1990=100	100.0	120.8	123.2	110.9	118.9	120.7	122.1

Balance of payments							
Exports of goods & services, US$m	4162	4275	4530	4425	5718	6810	7200
Change %	-4.7	2.7	6.0	-2.3	29.2	19.1	5.7
Imports of goods & services, US$m, fob	4095	4846	5426	5559	7170	9703	9850
Change %	19.4	18.3	12.0	2.4	29.0	35.3	1.5
Trade balance, of goods only, US$m, fob-fob	399	-189	-340	-600	-972	-2112	-1950
Current account balance, US$m	-1066	-1369	-1921	-2170	-2545	-4224	-3900
as a % of GDP	-3.1	-2.9	-4.6	-5.3	-5.1	-7.2	-6.3

Foreign exchange reserves							
Foreign exchange reserves, US$m	1040	2443	2849	3408	6992	8222	10500
Gold at ⅔ of market price, US$m	568.1	441.7	449.9	529.5	468.5	466.2	335.0
Import cover (reserves/imports), months	3.0	6.0	6.3	7.4	11.7	10.2	12.8

Foreign debt and debt service							
Short-term debt, US$m	2397	2784	3396	3210	3867	4535	4900
Total foreign debt, US$m	22534	26364	27855	27977	30159	32108	30000
as a % of GDP	66.5	55.7	66.1	67.8	60.2	54.5	48.5
as a % of foreign exchange receipts	482.2	536.9	538.4	547.5	453.0	407.5	375.0
Interest payments, US$m	1768	1758	1394	1423	1623	1936	1500
Principal repayments, US$m	299	1021	483	1688	615.	607	1200
Total debt service, US$m	2067	2779	1877	3111	2238	2543	2700
as a % of goods exports	62.2	81.6	51.3	88.3	48.9	45.6	45.8
as a % of foreign exchange receipts	44.2	56.6	36.3	60.9	33.6	32.3	33.8

Philippines

Area (thousands of km²):	300
Population (1995, millions):	68.6
Population projection (2025, millions):	115
Population younger than 15 yrs (1991, % of total):	39.2
Urbanization rate (1993, % of population):	52
Life expectancy (1993, years at birth):	67
Gross domestic product (1996, US$bn):	83
GDP per capita (1996, US$):	1184
Average annual GDP growth rate (1990-96, %):	2.8
Average annual inflation rate (1990-96, %):	10.7
Currency (peso per US$, average 1996):	26.23
Real exchange rate: (1990=100, average 1996)	128.25
Structure of production (1994):	42% services, 36% industry, 22% agriculture
Main exports:	semi-conductors, garments, coconut products, copper rods
Main imports:	machines & transport equipment, basic manufactures, mineral fuels
Main trading partners:	US, Japan, Hong Kong, Saudi Arabia, Germany
Market capitalization of Stock Exchange (December 1996; US$bn):	80.6
Total foreign debt (% of GDP):	54.2
Next elections due under normal circumstances:	presidential scheduled May 1998; legislative scheduled May 1998
Credit rating: (Jan 1997, Standard & Poor's, Moody's)	BB; Ba2

FORECAST: 1997-2000 (average)

	Worst case	Most likely	Best case
Real GDP growth (%)	3.0	5.8	6.2
Inflation (%)	12.5	8.0	6.7

■ POLITICS

Historical overview

Unlike other countries in South-East Asia, the Philippines has never had a traditional monarchy. In pre-colonial times, the state consisted of little more than scattered communities (baranguay), each housing between thirty and one hundred families. This political fragmentation was mainly responsible for the weak resistance to European settlements, which began in the 16th century.

In March 1521 a Spanish expedition landed in the Philippine archipelago, but it took more than fifty years for the Spanish to extend their control over most of the country. Under Spanish rule, the archipelago remained isolated and little effort was made to exploit the country's economic resources. Only in the early 19th century was the port of Manila opened to other European nations for trade mainly in agricultural products. Slowly, economic activity gained importance and a new entrepreneurial class based on land ownership emerged. By the end of the century, discontent with the colonial power culminated in a popular rebellion against Spanish rule, led by members of the newly emerging business class. The uprising ended in June 1898 when the Philippines achieved independence from Spain only to fall under the rule of the United States. With the defeat of Japan the Philippines gained full independence and proclaimed the Republic of the Philippines on July 4, 1946.

Between the late 1940s and early 1950s a Communist-inspired rebellion broke out, but was put down with the help of the US. In November 1965, Ferdinand Marcos was elected president. Near the end of his second term, in September 1972, he declared martial law and began a long period of autocratic rule. The fall of Marcos was initiated by the assassination of his main political rival, Benigno Aquino, in August 1983, which led to massive anti-Marcos rallies. Attempts by Marcos to legitimize himself through an early presidential election in February 1987 backfired when he was narrowly defeated by Corazon Aquino, widow of Benigno. After a vain bid to cling to power, Marcos was finally forced to leave the country by a popularly supported military revolt.

The new government led by Corazon Aquino took office in March 1986. Although Aquino was backed by popular support, her administration encountered various difficulties in implementing reforms, including tensions within the coalition of forces that had brought her to power, as well as attempts by the former dictator to destabilize the new regime. Military unrest persisted throughout the presidential term, and Aquino survived no fewer than seven military coup attempts. Nevertheless, with the ratification of a new constitution in February 1987, the new government achieved a major success. Furthermore, the transition of the presidential post to Fidel Ramos in 1992 was realized by democratic means under relatively peaceful circumstances.

Recent events

The term of President Fidel Ramos has been marked by continuity in economic and political policies. The economy has recovered, although deep-rooted economic and social problems still remain to be solved. In domestic politics, President Ramos has mastered the conflicting interest groups in Congress and managed to secure a "cessation of hostilities" from dissident military groups. He also set up a process of peace negotiations with both Communist and Muslim secessionist rebels.

In September 1996, after three years of discussion, the Moro National Liberation Front (MNLF) signed a peace settlement. The MNLF, operational since 1972, is a moderate Muslim rebel movement fighting for an autonomous Mindanao. The constitution does provide for the establishment of autonomous regions, but a national referendum needs to be called. The government and the MNLF agreed to set up a Southern Philippines Council for Peace and Development (SPCPD) in Mindanao, which will serve as a temporary administrative body for the region until the issue is put to popular vote in three years' time.

With only one year until the end of the presidential term, the unofficial race for the presidential election has already begun. Some would like to see Ramos in the presidential seat again, but the constitution prohibits a second term. This could be suitably amended, but only if three million citizens sign a "peoples' initiative". Efforts in this direction have already started. But Ramos has so far not made it known that he is willing to run for a second term. Apart from Ramos, Vice-President Joseph Estrada has the best prospects as a potential candidate for the presidency.

Chronology

1521	Spanish expedition reaches the Philippines
1565	First Spanish settlements
1834	Port of Manila is opened to foreign trade
1896	Uprising against Spanish colonial rule
1898	Independence from Spain, US rule
1941-44	Japanese occupation
1946	Full independence; proclamation of the Republic of the Philippines
1965	Ferdinand Marcos elected president
1972-86	Marcos rules with martial law
1986	Overthrow of Ferdinand Marcos. President Corazon Aquino takes office.
1987	New constitution adopted
1992	Fidel Ramos elected president
1992	August: unconditional amnesty offered to Communist and Muslim rebels
1996	September: peace treaty with MNLF

State organization

The Philippines is divided into 15 regions, 76 provinces, 60 cities, more than 1,000 municipalities and 40,000 baranguays, the latter representing units of no fewer than 1,000 inhabitants. Each province is headed by an elected governor, while cities and municipalities have elected mayors.

Traditionally government in the Philippines was tightly centralized, but since the adoption of a new constitution in 1987, a region may become autonomous by majority decision. Two regions have since reached autonomy: the Cordillera region of Northern Luzon and most of Mindanao. The autonomous authorities are responsible for personal and property relations, education, economic and social development. Furthermore, a reform passed in October 1991 allows all local governments to use 40% of local tax revenues.

Constitution and government

The current constitution was ratified by national referendum in February 1986. The president is chief executive, head of state and commander-in-chief, and is limited to one single six-year presidential term. The legislature is vested in the bicameral Congress, consisting of a 24-member Senate elected for a six-year term, and a 250-member House of Representatives elected for a three-year term. Only 204 are elected by district, while the rest include appointees from either sectors of society or party lists. The president is elected by popular vote. Members of the cabinet are selected by the president from outside of

Congress but are subject to congressional approval, after which they may only be removed by the president.

Current government
Given the number of cabinet portfolios, policy is often formulated by cabinet committees. The National Economic and Development Authority (NEDA) is responsible for co-ordinating all departments in areas important to economic development during the presidential term.

President	Fidel Ramos
Vice-President	Joseph Estrada
Ministers:	
Finance	Roberto de Ocampo
Foreign Affairs	Domingo Siazon
Economic Planning	
(also Director-General of NEDA)	Cielito Habito
Trade and Industry	Rizalino Navarro
Defence	Renato de Villa
Agrarian Reform	Ernesto Garilao
Budget and Management	Salvador Enriquez
Governor, central bank	Gabriel Singson

Political parties
There are few ideological differences between the parties represented in Congress – party members tend to support personalities rather than adhering to a party line. Alliances are therefore constantly shifting, and support in Congress for the president may be stronger at times than the election results would indicate. However, as the end of Ramos' presidential term comes near, more splinter groups tend to appear as presidential hopefuls emerge.

Lakas ng Edsa-National Union of Christian Democrats (Lakas-NUCD)
Formed in 1992 to support the election of President Ramos. Government party.

Laban ng Demokratikong Pilipino (LDP)
Formed in 1988, out of two pro-Aquino parties. Lost a substantial amount of its members to the Lakas-NUCD in the House of Representatives. Although the party initially kept its majority in the Senate, it split in two groups in late 1995.

Nationalist People's Coalition (NPC)
Formed in late 1991 to support the presidential candidate Eduardo Cojuangco. At the moment the NPC is the only formal opposition in the House of Representatives.

Results of the May 1995 elections to the House of Representatives
Lakas-NUCD (141 seats), **NPC** (23), **LDP** (21), **Others** (16)

Next elections
May 1998 (general elections)

Other political forces

The Philippines has a long history of rural rebellion. Hostility is strongest in the former Muslim-dominated region of Mindanao, where attempts to break away from Manila's control date as far back as the Spanish conquest in the 16th century. Various rebel movements have emerged over the years and have contributed to a permanent instability in this area. But the rebel groups themselves find it difficult to maintain internal discipline, and have a tendency to fragment.

Although the Ramos government has recorded some major successes on the road towards political stability, there is still a long way to go.

Moro Islamic Liberation Front (MILF)

The Moro Islamic Liberation Front (MILF) is the strongest militant Islamic movement. In contrast to the Moro National Liberation Front (MNLF), which signed a peace pact in September, it continues its military struggle for an independent Islamic state in Mindanao.

The movement was formed from a faction that broke away from the MNLF in 1978. Its armed forces are thought to number 40,000. However, the MILF does not have the backing of the Organization of Islamic Conference (OIC), suggesting that the Islamic countries in the region are committed to furthering the peace process.

National People's Army (NPA)

An umbrella organization for the Maoist Communist Party and its military wing, the National People's Army (NPA) was founded in 1969. The movement had its heyday in the mid-1980s but since then has gradually eroded.

The Ramos government has successfully pursued a policy of offering unconditional amnesty for rebels while simultaneously prosecuting an active military campaign. As a result, the strength of the NPA has declined from over 20,000 in mid-1985 to 6,000 in late 1995. The government has started informal peace talks with the NPA, and a settlement of the dispute is likely in the near future.

Religious groups

Religious groups are significant political factors in the Philippines, most notably the Catholic Church, to which 82% of the population belong.

In 1986, the Catholic Church played an active part in bringing down the Marcos regime when its head in the Philippines, Cardinal Jaime Sin, called the people onto the streets in support of the military revolt.

Central bank

Banko Sentral ng Pilipinas acts as the central bank. Its principal aim is price stability, while maintaining sound economic development and employment. The bank was reformed in 1992 making it one of the most independent central banks in Asia.

In the 1993 restructuring, the government assumed the massive debts accumulated by the central bank during the 1980s.

■ ECONOMICS

Historical overview

The Philippine economy has long been hamstrung by a relatively low growth rate punctuated by cycles of boom and bust. Underlying this laggardly performance were an overly protected economy, heavy state intervention and excessive concentrations of economic power. Other characteristics of the Philippine economy have been its dependence on foreign capital flows and exposure to fluctuations of international commodity prices.

To reduce the country's high dependence on imports, the Philippine government adopted an import-substitution policy in the early 1950s. This resulted in remarkable economic and especially industrial growth rates, but it also caused serious distortions in the allocation of resources. In particular, it fostered capital-intensive production in a country where labour was cheap and abundant. Structural deficiencies became apparent when strong population growth started to dampen the expansion of agricultural production and led to declining export incomes, while imports continued to rise, culminating in a rapid deterioration of the current account in the 1960s.

The economic situation improved only after 1972, when a policy of encouraging manufactured exports and foreign investment was adopted. Booming commodity prices, together with buoyant world demand, boosted exports by 20% on average annually between 1970 and 1979, thereby reviving the economy.

The availability of petrodollar-derived capital on international markets induced the government to adopt a programme designed to widen the industrial base, with special emphasis on heavy industry. As a result, foreign debt rose from about US$3 billion in 1970 to more than US$17 billion in 1980, while debt-servicing costs surged, thus increasing pressure on the balance of payments.

Adverse developments in the international markets, such as a decline in commodity prices, the worldwide recession and rising international interest rates, led to an economic downturn in the late 1970s and early 1980s. Fundamental policy problems were unveiled: heavy state intervention, protectionism and a backward financial and fiscal system. The structure of power in the state further added to economic mismanagement. Under President Marcos, economic power was concentrated among his family and a group of close associates, who dominated the economy by means of cartels and monopolies.

In 1983, the economy slipped into a profound recession, precipitated by the assassination of President Marcos' leading opponent, Benigno Aquino. Real GDP growth contracted by 7.3% in 1984 and 1985. The country's current account balance turned deeply negative and international confidence collapsed, leading to massive withdrawals of capital by foreign investors. A moratorium was declared on the repayment of external debts, rigorous exchange rate controls were imposed, the peso was devalued and a severe austerity programme under IMF supervision was adopted.

Economic stabilization made rapid progress. The current account deficit was on its way down by 1984 and was eliminated by 1985. Inflation, which had risen to over 50% by 1984, was down to about 1% in 1986. The IMF programme failed to reduce state interventionism, but succeeded in promoting labour-intensive and agricultural production.

The Philippines' economic performance

	Average annual real GDP growth, %	Average annual consumer price inflation, %
1961-1965	5.2	5.5
1966-1970	5.1	5.8
1971-1975	6.1	17.4
1976-1980	6.2	12.4
1981-1985	-1.3	21.4
1985-1990	4.7	7.9
1991-1995	2.2	10.5

Recent developments

When the Aquino government took power in 1986, the economy had just emerged from one of its worst recessions since the war. Formulated in response to this crisis, the Medium-Term Philippine Development Plan for 1987–92 had economic recovery as its immediate aim and sustainable development as its ultimate objective. But growth could not, in the event, be sustained, although it accelerated rapidly by the end of the 1980s. Inflation also accelerated and growth started to lapse again in the early 1990s, undermined by energy bottlenecks, a decline in global demand following the Gulf crisis, and persistent structural weaknesses in the economy itself.

The Ramos administration has started to pursue economic reforms with more vigour, aiming to shift economic policies towards an outward-orientated and free-market approach. Nearly all foreign-exchange controls have been removed, telecommunications, transport, insurance and other major sectors have been liberalized, while the pace of privatization has been stepped up and more sectors opened to foreign investors.

To prevent future boom-and-bust cycles caused by infrastructure bottlenecks, a national programme to upgrade infrastructure was implemented via a build-operate-transfer (BOT) scheme, by which the private sector finances and, for a contracted period, operates new facilities. At the end of the contracted period, these facilities are transferred to the government. BOT schemes originally concentrated on the energy sector, but have since been extended to other sectors, such as roads, railways and the development of special economic zones.

Supported by vigorously implemented reforms and by a sharp rise in capital inflows from overseas workers as well as foreign investors, the economy has been gaining momentum since 1994. Driven by buoyant investment, real GDP growth accelerated from 0.3% in 1992 to 4.8% in 1995. This trend is likely to persist through the rest of President Ramos' term until 1998. Ambitious targets include GNP growth between 5.7% and 7.4% on average, an upper limit on inflation of 6.1%, and investments rising to nearly 30% of GDP by 1998.

The economy
Agriculture
The Philippines has a rich and diverse base of natural resources, and the soil is extremely fertile. Agricultural production, however, is constantly challenged by droughts and other adverse weather conditions. In 1995, the agriculture, fishing and forestry sector contributed 21.7% of GDP, 13% of exports and employed nearly half the working population.

Farming is very diverse and includes a large number of rice, maize and coconut holdings that are worked by agricultural tenants or labourers. Rice and maize are the principal food crops, but considerable quantities must be imported periodically, in order to satisfy growing domestic demand. Sugar haciendas, coconut plantations and large agri-business plantations also are part of the landscape. The Philippines today is the world's leading exporter of coconut products. The sugar industry used to generate about 15% of export earnings, helped for many years by a guaranteed share of the US market. The sector went into crisis when world sugar prices plummeted in the mid-1980s, which led to a rapid decline in cultivated area. Today, sugar no longer dominates agricultural exports. The Philippine forests, one of the country's major resources, have suffered severe depletion as the result of population pressure, shifting cultivation and illegal logging. Substantial areas of virgin forest, mainly on the island of Mindanao, succumbed to the chainsaw during the 1970s. The 45 million hectares of virgin forest in 1945, had fallen to 1.2 million hectares in 1991.

Peaking in the 1970s, the agricultural sector has since rarely grown at more than 1.5% in real terms annually. Agricultural production received a slight boost after 1988, when the Aquino Government launched the Comprehensive Agrarian Reform Programme. The land reform encompassed all agricultural land, with a total of more than 5 million hectares allocated between 2 million landless farmers. Some large estates are to be preserved, but will be placed under co-operative ownership. Implementation in three phases is due to be completed in 1998, but some delay is likely.

Composition of GDP by sector, 1995

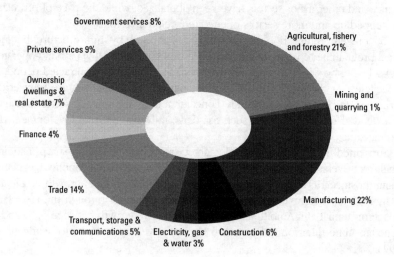

Source: Official data

Manufacturing

Manufacturing was developed relatively early in the Philippines, accounting for 20-25% of GDP since the early 1960s. Supported by import quotas and tariffs, the manufacturing sector was long orientated towards the domestic market, but extensive tariff cuts and the establishment of export-processing zones have expanded the market and by 1995 manufacturing exports had increased to 81% of total exports. Manufacturing consists predominantly of labour-intensive production, mainly textiles and electronic components.

Trade and balance of payments

The structure of Philippine exports has changed substantially during the last three decades. While essentially four commodities (coconut, sugar, timber and copper) accounted for more than half of total exports in 1970, the share of manufacturing in total exports has reached 80% today. Driving export sectors are electronics, electrical equipment and to a lesser extent clothing, all with a high import component. The trend of imports in volume terms therefore closely tracks that of exports. Apart from its manufacturing inputs, the Philippines imports energy, although it has limited oil and coal reserves, as well as hydro-electric power. Fuels, minerals and related products account for about 13% of total imports.

Breakdown of exports, 1995

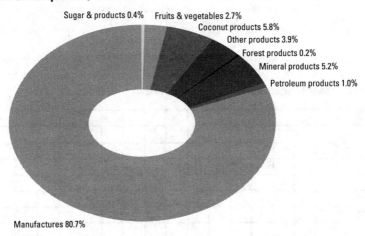

Sugar & products 0.4% Fruits & vegetables 2.7%
Coconut products 5.8%
Other products 3.9%
Forest products 0.2%
Mineral products 5.2%
Petroleum products 1.0%

Manufactures 80.7%

Source: Official data

Japan and the US are the main trading partners of the Philippines, accounting for more than half of the exports and nearly 43% of imports. In recent times, their share has been declining, however, as exports expand to other Asian countries, in particular to the ASEAN nations.

Fluctuations in international prices for commodities resulted in a sluggish export performance during the 1970s and early 1980s. In 1982, following the oil price shock, the Philippines entered the worst of its many balance of payments crises. The government then placed severe restrictions on imports, and the trade deficit improved rapidly. But since

1986, imports have been growing faster than exports when measured as a percentage of GDP, thereby contributing to a gradual but constant widening of the trade deficit.

In mid-1995, exports received a boost as the peso plunged against the Japanese yen. Exports soared to Japan and the US, and registered a record annual growth of 28.8%. Although export growth has since slowed, the Philippines is one of the few countries in East Asia to have escaped an exports slump in 1996, reflecting the resilience of its low value-added export sector.

Trade balance

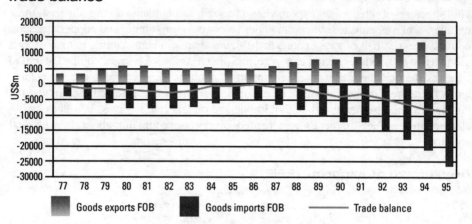

Source: Official data

Exports and imports as a % of GDP

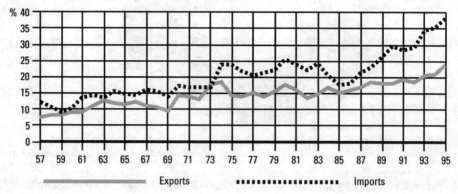

Source: Official data

While the trade balance has traditionally been in deficit, the Philippines has recorded a surplus on the balance of services for most of the last two decades, supported by income from tourism. More importantly, since 1992, remittances from Filipinos working abroad have pushed the balance on income into surplus. The turnaround in the income balance has been supported further by lower debt service payments, achieved through the stabilization of external debt and the reduction of interest rates in the 1990s. Thus, the rapid increase in the trade deficit since 1991 has not been matched by a correspondingly sharp rise in the current account deficit. Although the trade gap widened to US$9.2 billion in 1995, the current account deficit accounted for only US$1.9 billion or 2.6% of GDP, down from 4.6% in 1994.

Current account as a % of GDP

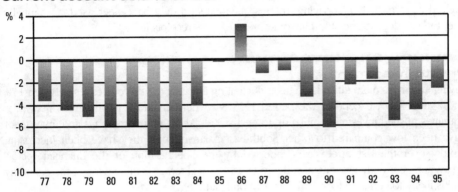

Source: Official data

Trade restrictions
There are three categories of import goods: freely importable, regulated (for reasons of public health and safety, national security, international commitments and protection of local industries), and prohibited. Applications to import freely importable products may be processed by authorized agent bans without prior approval of any government agency. A clearance of permit is needed from the appropriate government agency to import regulated imports.

Financing the current account deficit
For most years (the major exception being the period 1981–84), the capital account has more than offset the current account deficit, therefore allowing for reserve accumulation. Balance of payments surpluses have kept the country's foreign exchange reserves above two-and-a-half months of merchandise imports over most of the 1990s, and have raised them from US$6.4 billion at the end of 1995 to US$9.7 billion in September 1996. Current account financing has traditionally been met by private and public sector borrowing; long-term official capital is providing the principal support for external payments.

Foreign debt
The Philippines has been through several periods of heavy external borrowing. Regular rounds of debt relief have been necessary to deal with the Marcos regime's legacy of foreign debt, which amounted to fully 99% of GDP in 1986.

Debt negotiations have been backed by the IMF, which has exacted as its price structural changes and programmes of fiscal austerity. Given the improving economic fundamentals and a desire to exclude outside influence on domestic policy-making, the current 3-year Extended Fund Facility (EFF), approved in June 1994, is likely to be the last such arrangement.

External debt stood at some US$45 billion by the end of 1995 (55% of GDP), about three-quarters public medium- and long-term debt. The ratio of short-term debt of total debt is likely to increase over the next years, while net inflows from official creditors are likely to be limited by large repayments. In 1994, 38% of the long-term debt was denominated in yen, compared to 30% in dollars. The average interest rate on external debt has gradually fallen over the last five years (4.2% in 1994). Fluctuations in debt repayment have produced a cyclical pattern of debt servicing. Interest payments on debt have decreased substantially over the last decade and stood at some 7% of exports receipts in 1995.

Savings and investment
Private investment
Saving and investment ratios have been fluctuating over the last three decades between 15% and 23% of GDP, except for the period 1975–84, when ambitious public investment programmes pushed investment ratios up to nearly 30%. Although both savings and investment have been low compared to other South-east Asian nations, they have been increasing rapidly over the last three years, boosted by the liberalization of the financial sector. Investment, currently growing at roughly 13-15% in real terms, is the engine of the economy and is likely to continue to sustain the economic take-off.

On average, national saving has been slightly lower than domestic investment, mirrored by the chronic current account gap. Although the government's economic development programmes have generally fuelled national investment, private investment as a percentage of total investment has remained relatively high, at rates between 70 and 90% over the last three decades.

Foreign investment
Together with structural reforms implemented by the government since the early 1990s, a more liberal policy towards foreign investment was adopted. In particular, special conditions are offered to export-orientated industries in export-processing zones (also known as Ecozones), including 100% foreign ownership and temporary tax and import-duty exemptions. As a result, foreign direct investment (FDI) inflows increased from US$228 million in 1992 to US$799 million in 1995 and are likely to exceed US$1,000 million over the next two years. The introduction of alternative financing schemes for foreign investment in 1995 resulted in a drop of FDI inflows registered at the Board of Investment, the government agency responsible for overseeing investments, while registration with special projects, including the Clark Special Economic Zone and the Subic Bay Freeport Zone in the central part of Luzon, are capturing a growing proportion of FDI. Although the majority of investment traditionally comes from Europe, Asian investment, in particular from Japan and Hong Kong, accounted for the largest share, at 75% of total approved investment in 1995.

Economic policy
Monetary policy
Each year, in conjunction with the IMF, the central bank sets targets for money supply growth that strike a balance between accommodating rapid economic growth and controlling inflation. The M3-target under the IMF-programme for 1996 is 25.8%.

The opening of the capital account in 1993 had an impact on both interest rates and the exchange rate, reflecting the inverse character of the relationship between the nominal peso/US$ exchange rate and interest rates. Coping with the expansionary effects of a rapid rise in capital inflows, both from overseas workers and portfolio investors, is a major problem for the monetary authorities. The government sterilizes these inflows by selling peso debt (T-bills) and depositing the proceeds with the central bank. Rising central bank liabilities to the government therefore offset the rise in foreign assets, dampening base money growth. Cuts in reserve requirements combined with an acceleration in foreign fund inflows following the liberalization of the banking system led to an increase in the money multiplier in the first half of 1995. This, together with the eagerness to boost economic growth, led to an easy money policy, with broad money supply (M3) growth averaging 36.8% yoy during the first six months of 1995, well above the IMF target of 31% for 1995. Exacerbated by a food price hike, the inflation rate soared in September 1995. The central bank reacted with a hike in overnight borrowing rates in November. Monetary policy has remained rather restrictive since, with a tight watch on money supply levels.

Fiscal policy

The Philippine public sector has been in deficit for most of the last three decades, and fiscal consolidation on the basis of an improved tax system has long been one of the targets set by the IMF. In particular, the tax base is regarded as too low, with government revenues between 18–19% of GDP. Fiscal deficits were usually contained below 5%, but deteriorated sharply during the early 1980s-recession. Since the early 1990s, the public sector deficit has narrowed significantly, as expenditures increased in line with revenues. In 1994 and 1995, the exceptional proceeds from privatization allowed the government to post a surplus for the first time in twenty years.

In order to reduce reliance on privatization proceeds, the government has intensified its efforts to broaden the tax base. A first step forward in fiscal consolidation was taken by implementing an extension of value-added tax (EVAT) in early 1996. A more substantial improvement should be achieved if the Comprehensive Tax Reform Package (CTRP), held up in the Congress for some time, is finally accepted. The package is aimed at reforms of individual and corporate income taxes and tax administration, as well as excise taxation. A surprise compromise excise tax bill passed Congress on the eve the 1996-APEC summit, hosted by the Philippines. After numerous delays, the passage of this key component of the Comprehensive Tax Reform Package will increase the likelihood of effective fiscal reform becoming a reality in 1997. The excise tax will raise about 6 billion pesos in 1997, about half of the targeted increase for the year. Completion of the tax reform package would represent a major step forward in the Ramos administration's programme of economic overhaul and help ensure a continued balanced budget as privatization proceeds wane.

Privatization

Privatization was launched under the Aquino administration in 1989. Under Ramos' government, privatization was pursued with even greater vigour. Philippine privatization has been carried out in two phases. The first included the state airline, the Philippine National Bank, the national steel company and the state petrol corporation. In the second wave, privatization was extended to public-sector infrastructure, in particular transport and power generation infrastructure. A new round of privatization was announced at the end of 1996, and plans to sell off state-controlled social security and pension funds.

Banking system

In August 1992, following the election of President Ramos, all controls on foreign exchange transactions were lifted, setting the stage for a more aggressive push towards foreign investment in the Philippines and towards an export-orientated economy. Moreover, restrictions on new branches and on deposit rates were liberalized, giving banks a freer hand to determine to compete. With the restructuring of the domestic banking system complete by February 1995, the government re-opened the banking system by granting commercial banking licences to ten new foreign banks, and by allowing numerous additional joint ventures. To minimize risks in the financial system, minimum capital at universal banks was raised to P2.5 billion (US$100 million) and at commercial banks to P1.25 billion (US$50 million) in December 1995.

Exchange rate

The peso has been floating freely since February 1970. The central bank intervenes when necessary to dampen volatility. Although the currency started out with a gradual depreciation against the US$, it made big jumps between 1982 and 1984 and again in 1990. The exchange rate remained highly volatile until early 1995, when the Mexican crisis also put pressure on the peso. Since then, however, strong capital inflows have buoyed the currency. Heavy central bank buying of dollars has recently kept the peso exchange rate among the most stable in Asia, at around 26.2 versus the US$.

Philippine peso/US dollar exchange rate

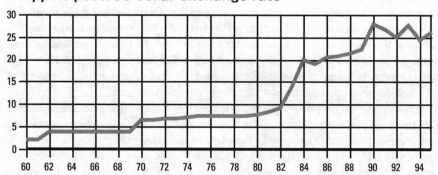

Exchange rate controls

Foreign currency can be sold for pesos without restrictions. The purchase of foreign currency from the banking system is, however, subject to certain restrictions and procedures, depending on the purpose of the purchase. Additionally, non-residents may purchase foreign exchange from authorized agent banks only up to the amount they have previously sold to a bank. For trade purposes, commercial banks may sell foreign exchange to importers for letters of credit, open account arrangements, and other guarantees. Foreign currency lending, on the other hand, is strictly regulated.

■ EQUITIES

Index performance (in local currency)

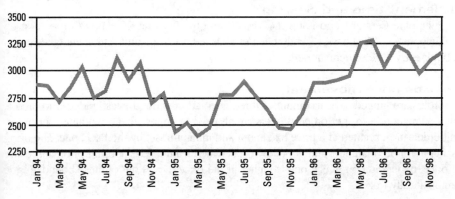

Key indicators

	Index performance % in US$ terms	Market Cap. US$bn	P/E	Div. Yield	Weight in IFCI	IFCG
1994	-1.1	55.5	30.8	0.4	3.9	3.2
1995	-14.6	58.9	19.0	0.6	2.8	2.9
1996	19.1	80.6	20.0	0.8	3.3	4.6

Sources: Local stock exchange, IFC, Bloomberg, Datastream, UBS

Structure

There are 212 companies listed on the Philippine Stock Exchange, and its total capitalization at end 1996 was US$74.3 billion. Stocks listed on the PSE can be classified in four categories: commercial and industrial, property, mining, and oil. These companies pay regular dividends, have regular business operations and a history of earnings.

Stocks of companies not listed on the PSE are traded over-the-counter (OTC) by brokers outside PSE trading hours.

Regulatory authority

The securities industry is regulated by the Securities and Exchange Commission in Manila. This is a quasi-judicial government agency.

Trading methods

Stock trading is fully automated in the Unified Trading System (UTS). The UTS uses the Single-Order-Book system, where all orders are posted and matched in one computer.

OTC transactions are carried out by direct inquiries and negotiations among the dealers by mail, telephone or other forms of communications. The dealers in the OTC market often act as principals, that is, they buy and sell for their own accounts in transactions with customers and other dealers.

Hours
The market is open from 09.30 to 12.00, Monday to Friday.

Settlement time and clearing
The Philippine Central Depository, Inc. (PCDI) and the Securities Clearing Corporation of the Philippines (SCCP) have recently been established. Clearing and settlement takes place via book entry. The settlement period is T+3.

Limits on price movement
Buy orders are limited to a maximum of three fluctuations from the last traded price and a cap of 30 million Pesos per order. Brokers are allowed to impose their own limits per order. Limit orders are executed at a price maximum and minimum set by the Exchange. The band is set at not more than 50% and 40% down, calculated from the last closing price or the last bid price, depending on which one is higher. If the price moves out of these boundaries, it is automatically frozen.

Stock indices
The main index is the Philippine Stock Exchange Composite Index. It is composed of thirty stocks, representative of the four major sectors on the Exchange.

Taxes
Foreign corporations investing in the Philippines are subject to a 35% dividend tax. Non-residents must pay a 30% tax on dividends received in the Philippines.

Types of shares
Most of the stocks traded on the PSE are common stocks with voting rights attached to them. Common shares can be divided into Class A and Class B shares. Local investors can own both types, but international investors can only possess Class B shares. There is no difference between the two sets of shares. They have the same privilege and the same dividends. The separate classification of shares is done to monitor the equity ownership of local and international investors. Preferred stocks are also traded on the PSE. Holders of this type of stock are entitled to receive dividends before these are paid to holders of common stock.

Ownership limits for foreigners
Under the Philippine constitution, no more than 40% of a company can be owned by foreign investors. Some industries, such as mass media, rural banks and retail trade are reserved solely for local investors.

Non-resident transactions are registered with the Bangko Sentral ng Pilipinas, the Philippines central bank. All registered foreign investments in Philippine securities, including profits and dividends, net of taxes and charges may be repatriated.

Brokers
The PSE had 185 members by the end of 1995. Of these, thirty-six are international, 169 are operating actively and seventeen are non-operating. In the course of 1995, eight new members were admitted, of which six were international.

■ DEBT

The market is dominated by national government (NG) bills and bonds, issues from local governments, state corporations and monetary institutions, and central bank bills. Until 1986, external debt made up the largest proportion of the country's total indebtedness. After a Brady restructuring, domestic debt increased substantially, fuelled by recurrent budget deficits, central bank losses, and treasury bill issuance to absorb excess liquidity caused by large foreign exchange reserves in the early 1990s.

Most debt maturities are less than one year, so the market has the characteristics of a money rather than a bond market. Major investors in government securities include the Social Security Service (SSS) and Government Service Insurance System (GSIS), which represent a large contractual savings sector. The Securities and Exchange Commission (SEC), a government agency, enforces capital markets regulations. In 1989, the Financial Executives Institute of the Philippines (FINEX) initiated a Capital Markets Development Project with USAID funding, which is still in progress.

Public debt

Reforms to the structure of the government debt market are currently under way. Among changes at various stages of development are moves to liberalize accreditation guidelines for dealers in T-bills and to extend the treasury note yield curve. In addition, to improve secondary market liquidity, more timely price information is required, as is a central depository and an automated settlement and clearing system. The Bangko Sentral ng Pilipinas (BSP) imposes constraints on dealers financing their T-bill inventories by treating their holdings as deposits subject to reserve requirements.

NG treasury bills

The most important issues are the 91-, 182-, and 364-day bills; 35-, 49-, and 63-day bills are also issued to absorb liquidity. The current primary market system was created in 1986. The Government Securities Department of the BSP manages weekly auctions, and jointly with representatives from the National Treasury and the Department of Finance determine issue sizes, which are contingent on government financing needs and BSP open-market requirements. Thirty accredited dealers bid for bills on a yield basis, and the auction committee determines a clearing level. The system is not automated. Since 1991, the BSP has experimented with several tap issues. The yield rate is based on the lowest accepted bid rate of the immediately preceding auction for the same maturity. Since July 1994, the Philippine Postal Savings Bank has offered T-bills in small denominations to the general public.

NG treasury notes

Recognizing the need to create a market for medium- and long-term bonds, the government issued a 3-year floating rate note (FRTN) in 1991. It was priced at par with a coupon paying a margin over 91-day T-bills. Other notes followed in 1994. Also in 1994, a 2-year fixed rate note (FXTN) was issued. It paid a semi-annual coupon based on the lowest accepted yield in an auction, was transferable in bearer form (but with a registered option) in denominations ranging from P10,000 to P10 million (US$400 to US$400,000), and was eligible for liquidity and reserve requirements. Subsequently, 3-, 5- and 7-year FXTNs have been launched.

Municipal bonds

The first municipal bond was issued in 1991, when Cebu Equity Bond Units (CEBU) launched a 3-year bond, convertible into shares of Cebu Property Ventures Development Corporation. Other issues followed in 1994 after the BSP published new guidelines for bond flotations by local government units (LGUs). However, LGUs cannot secure long-term credits from private financial institutions.

Private debt

Commercial paper (CP)

Commercial paper is issued for maturities up to one year especially by non-financial corporations. CP pays a credit-determined margin over treasury bills, and since 1976 have to be registered with the SEC. Rates are low compared to bank loans, and there is no reserve requirement for short-term paper. Long-term commercial paper functions as de facto corporate bonds, and has been issued for terms up to seven years.

Corporate bonds

Corporate issues are restricted to a few blue-chip companies. Philippine Corporation law requires that bond issues gain the approval of two thirds of a company's shareholders, whereas commercial paper programmes can be launched after a board decision.

Brady bonds

In September 1996, the Philippine government proposed a Brady bond exchange offer. Holders of the Par bonds were offered a choice of 20-year fixed rate bonds at 225 basis points over US treasuries or 15-year floating rate notes at 175 basis points over 6-month libor. The new bonds are unsecured by US treasuries, so represent pure Philippine sovereign risk. They are rated BB by Standard and Poor's. The bonds exchanged (most were held by Philippine commercial banks), amounting to about US$700 million are:

Collateralized Fixed Rate Par Bonds (PCIRBs) Series A	US$153.490 million
Collateralized Fixed Rate Par Bonds (PCIRBs) Series B	US$1740.60 million

Other Brady bonds issued in 1990 or 1992, which are not affected by the exchange offer are: Front-Loaded Interest Reduction Bond (two series), Debt Conversion Bonds (two series) and New Money Bonds.

Eurobonds

The Philippines returned to the eurobond market in February 1993, after a ten-year absence. Other borrowers from the public and private sector followed. In 1996, the BSP gave its approval for corporates to issue euro medium-term note programmes.

Eurobond issues (US$m)

	1990	1991	1992	1993	1994	1995	1996
Sovereign	—	—	—	350.0	100.0	150.0	368.2
Private	—	—	—	205.0	415.0	470.0	875.0

▇ PHILIPPINES: Economic indicators

Population and development	1990	1991	1992	1993	1994	1995	1996e
Population, million	61.5	62.9	64.3	65.7	67.1	68.6	70.1
Population growth, %	2.3	2.3	2.2	2.2	2.2	2.2	2.2
Nominal GDP per capita, US$	721	722	824	828	956	1081	1184

National accounts							
Nominal GDP, US$bn	44.3	45.4	53.0	54.4	64.1	74.1	83.0
Change in real GDP, %	3.0	-0.5	0.3	2.1	4.4	4.8	5.3
Gross fixed capital formation, % of GDP	23.1	20.0	20.9	23.8	23.6	22.3	25.2

Money supply and inflation							
Narrow money, change %, Dec/Dec	14.3	15.9	9.1	22.3	11.3	21.7	—
Broad money, change %, Dec/Dec	22.5	17.3	13.6	27.1	24.4	9.9	—
Consumer price inflation (avg.) %	14.2	18.7	8.9	7.6	9.1	8.1	8.4

Government finance							
Government expenditure, % of GDP	19.6	19.2	19.7	18.5	18.3	17.9	18.8
Government balance, % of GDP	-3.5	-2.1	-1.2	-1.5	1.1	0.5	0.4

Exchange rates lc=local currency							
Exchange rate, annual average, lc/US$	24.30	27.50	25.51	27.12	26.42	25.71	26.23
Exchange rate, end of year, lc/US$	28.00	26.65	25.10	27.70	24.42	26.21	26.40
Real exchange rate 1990=100	100.0	99.4	110.8	108.1	116.7	120.6	128.3

Balance of payments							
Exports of goods & services, US$m	11430	12494	14566	16048	20251	26795	31350
Change %	3.5	9.3	16.6	10.2	26.2	32.3	17.0
Imports of goods & services, US$m, fob	13967	13855	16827	20687	25987	33317	39150
Change %	16.6	-0.8	21.5	22.9	25.6	28.2	17.5
Trade balance, of goods only, US$m, fob-fob	-4020	-3211	-4695	-6222	-7850	-8944	-12200
Current account balance, US$m	-2695	-1034	-1000	-3016	-2950	-1980	-2600
as a % of GDP	-6.1	-2.3	-1.9	-5.5	-4.6	-2.7	-3.1

Foreign exchange reserves							
Foreign exchange reserves, US$m	924	3246	4403	4676	6017	6372	11800
Gold at ⅔ of market price, US$m	742.4	811.9	640.0	771.7	740.0	915.9	—
Import cover (reserves/imports), months	0.8	2.8	3.1	2.7	2.8	2.3	3.6

Foreign debt and debt service							
Short-term debt, US$m	5912	6398	6474	7318	9689	10987	12012
Total foreign debt, US$m	31145	32671	32874	35931	42511	43300	45000
as a % of GDP	70.3	72.0	62.1	66.1	66.3	58.4	54.2
as a % of foreign exchange receipts	226.6	213.7	181.2	183.2	169.5	127.3	114.8
Interest payments, US$m	2154	2157	1898	1822	1900	2350	2300
Principal repayments, US$m	1095	1360	1136	3177	2272	2854	3300
Total debt service, US$m	3249	3517	3034	4999	4172	5204	5600
as a % of goods exports	39.7	39.8	30.9	43.9	30.9	29.8	27.9
as a % of foreign exchange receipts	23.6	23.0	16.7	25.5	16.6	15.3	14.3

Poland

Area (thousands of km²):	313
Population (1995, millions):	38.6
Population projection (2025, millions):	41
Urbanization rate (1993, % of population):	64
Life expectancy (1993, years at birth):	71
Gross domestic product (1996, US$bn):	129.9
GDP per capita (1996, US$):	3353
Average annual GDP growth rate (1990-96, %):	0.6
Average annual inflation rate (1990-96, %):	116.9
Currency (zloty per US$, average 1996):	2.72
Real exchange rate: (1990=100, average 1996)	208
Structure of production (1994):	43% services, 47% industry, 10% agriculture
Main exports:	vehicles, machinery, chemical products, paper, textiles, plastics
Main imports:	machinery, transport equipment, chemical products, crude oil
Main trading partners:	EU (especially Germany, Italy), US, Russia
Market capitalization of Stock Exchange (October 1996; US$bn):	8.0
Total foreign debt (% of GDP):	34.6
Next elections due under normal circumstances:	legislative Sept. 1997, presidential Nov. 2000
Credit rating: (Nov 1996, Standard & Poor's, Moody's)	BBB; Baa3

FORECAST: 1997-2000 (average)

	Worst case	Most likely	Best case
Real GDP growth (%)	4.0	5.0	6.0
Inflation (%)	14.5	12.5	11.5

■ POLITICS

Historical overview

The Polish kingdom was once powerful and prosperous, but declined in the 17th and 18th centuries. Between 1795 and 1918 it was partitioned by Russia, Prussia and Austria. Poland re-emerged as an independent state on November 11, 1918, at the end of the First World War. After a turbulent period of parliamentary democracy from 1919 to 1926, Poland was governed by an authoritarian military regime. This prevailed until the Second World War broke out in September 1939. Poland was invaded by both Germany and the USSR and partitioned between the two powers. After Germany declared war on the USSR, in June 1941, its forces occupied the whole of Poland until they were expelled by Soviet troops in March 1945. The Yalta and Potsdam Agreements assigned Poland to the Soviet sphere of interest.

At the end of the war, a pro-Communist "Polish Committee of National Liberation", was established under Soviet auspices in July 1944, and formed the basis of a provisional government. A People's Republic was established in February 1947, with the Polish Worker's Party (PWP), led by Wladislaw Gomulka, as the dominant group. Gomulka's reluctance to implement certain aspects of Soviet economic policies, notably the collectivization of agriculture, led to his dismissal as First Secretary of the PWP in 1948. In December 1948 the PWP merged with the Polish Socialist Party to form the Polish United Worker's Party (PUWP). Two other parties were also allowed, but were closely controlled by the PUWP, and Poland effectively became a one-party state.

After the death of Stalin in 1953 and the end of the Stalinism period in Poland, Gomulka was rehabilitated and returned to power. After the strike at Gdansk in 1970, when workers were killed as police repressed the strikes and protests, he was shunted aside by Edward Gierek. In 1980 higher prices for meat prompted strikes in factories near the capital, Warsaw, and soon labour unrest spread throughout the country. In addition to economic claims, shipyard employees in the Baltic ports, notably at Gdansk, demanded the right to form free trade unions. The most important trade union was "Solidarity" (10 million members in 1981) with Lech Walesa as leader.

Gierek was replaced in 1980-81 for "health reasons" by an unknown Communist leader, Stanislaw Kania. Poland was in effect ungoverned until December 13, 1981, when the defence minister, General Wojciech Jaruzelski, spurred by the fear of Soviet intervention (as in Hungary in 1956 and in Czechoslovakia in 1968) declared martial law. Solidarity leaders and activists were interned and Solidarity was suspended. Protests and strikes against martial law came immediately and were forcibly dealt with. After eighteen months, in June 1983, martial law was withdrawn and an amnesty was given to most political prisoners.

Recent events

Facing a wave of strikes in 1988, the Communists agreed to partially free elections. In the June 1989 elections, Solidarity candidates won most of the available seats in the parliament, as an early signal of the end of the political monopoly of the Communist Party. After the fall of Communism in the Central Eastern European countries, and the victory of Solidarity in the local elections in May 1990, Lech Walesa persuaded Jaruzelski to resign as president. In the presidential elections of December 1990 Walesa won 74% of the votes in the second round and became the first freely elected president of Poland since the Second World War.

The first free elections for the entire parliament, held in October 1991, resulted in a fragmented legislature that included twenty-nine parties. The largest controlled 12% of the seats. Four successive weak coalition cabinets were forced to leave office after brief periods following the loss of their parliamentary majorities. After the right-wing coalition of Hanna Suchocka fell in March 1993, new elections were held. The Democratic Left Alliance (SLD), formed by the moderate wing of the old Polish Communist Party, won with 171 seats – the largest number of seats in a legislature dominated by the centre-left. To minimize popular opposition to a government that includes former Communist Party members, SLD leader Aleksander Kwasniewski picked Waldemar Pawlak, leader of the Polish Peasant Party (PSL; 132 seats), to head the new SLD-PSL coalition government. The two coalition parties hold 66% of the seats in the lower house, the Sejm, and 73% of the seats in the upper house, the Senate. The Pawlak government resigned in March 1995, in part because of Walesa's refusal to co-operate with it, and SLD member Jozef Oleksy became Prime Minister, leading a restricted SLD-PSL coalition. In the November 1995 election, Kwasniewski defeated Walesa and became president. Prime Minister Oleksy resigned in January 1996 following accusations that he had been recruited by the Soviet intelligence Service. Deputy speaker of Parliament and member of the SLD, Wlodimierz Cimoszewicz became prime minister in February 1996.

Chronology

976	The first historical ruler of Poland, Prince Mieszko I, converted to Christianity
1493	A bicameral parliament (Sejm) was established
1772	The first partition of Poland, between Russia, Prussia and Austria, takes place
1793	The second partition of Poland
1795	The third partition extinguished the Polish state
1918	November: Joszef Pilsudski assumes power in Warsaw. Poland was declared an independent republic.
1919	June 28: the Treaty of Versailles recognizes Polish independence
1932	A non-aggression pact is signed with the USSR
1934	A non-aggression pact is signed with Germany
1939	August 23: the German-Soviet Pact is signed, including a secret agreement between the USSR and Germany to partition Poland
1939	September 1: Germany invades western Poland and the Second World War begins
1939	September 17: the USSR invades eastern Poland
1941	June 22: Germany invades the USSR; Poland is now entirely occupied by German forces
1945	In the Treaty of Yalta the eastern border of Poland is agreed by Churchill, Roosevelt and Stalin. Stalin promises "free and unfettered elections" in Poland after the war. In the Potsdam Conference former German territories east of the Oder-Neisse line are given to Poland.
1947	Elections to the Sejm were won by the Democratic Bloc, a grouping dominated by the Polish Workers Party (PWP). The UK and the US complain that the elections did not meet the requirements agreed at Yalta. The People's Republic of Poland is established
1956	June: riots in Poznan by industrial workers because of food shortages and price rises
1956	October: Gomulka is appointed First Secretary of the Polish United Workers Party (PUWP) and introduces some political liberalization
1970	Gomulka, First Secretary of the PUWP and Spychalski, Head of State, resign after workers are killed when police suppress strikes and protests. Edward Gierek is appointed First Secretary of the PUWP
1980	August: strikes at the Lenin Shipyards in Gdansk and Szczecin lead to agreements that include the right to form free trade unions and the right to strike
1981	December: General Wojciech Jaruzelski declares martial law
1983	June: withdrawal of martial law
1989	June 4: Solidarity candidates win most of the freely elected seats at the elections to the National Assembly.

1989	August 20: first non-Communist government in Eastern Europe, with Tadeusz Mazowiecki as prime minister
1989	December: amendment to the constitution, including an end of the PUWP's monopoly of power and restoration of the official name and flag of prewar Poland
1990	Lech Walesa (Solidarity) is elected president
1990	Start of reforms towards free market economy
1993	The Democratic Left Alliance (SLD) wins the largest number of seats in parliament
1995	Aleksander Kwasniewski (SLD) defeats Lech Walesa (Solidarity) in the presidential election

State organization

Poland is divided into 49 provinces ("voivodships"), each administrated by an appointed governor. The voivodships are further divided into 822 towns and 2,121 wards ("gmina"). Under reforms introduced in 1990, complete autonomy was granted to the directly elected local councils, which are the basic form of the organization of public life in the rural community.

Constitution and government

The Soviet-style constitution adopted on July 22, 1952 was amended in 1989 to incorporate reforms, such as the establishment of an upper legislative chamber, and again in 1990, to permit the holding of direct presidential elections. In December 1992 an interim "Small Constitution" came into force, designed principally to regulate relations between the legislative and executive authorities, pending a full revision of the constitution, initiated in November 1992. The constitution establishes Poland as a democratic republic with a bicameral parliament, a president as head of state, a Council of Ministers and an independent judicial system.

President

The president of the Republic is directly elected for a five-year term and may be re-elected only once. Any Pole over thirty-five years of age with full electoral rights may stand as a presidential candidate; a minimum of 100,000 signatures are required to secure nomination. The president is the highest representative of the Polish State. Presidential powers include the right to initiate legislation, to call for elections to the Sejm, Senate and local councils. The president commands the armed forces, retains overall responsibility in setting guidelines for foreign policy and internal security, appoints the members of the Supreme Court and nominates the prime minister and the president of the national bank, although his nomination can be overruled by the parliament. He can (when necessary) impose martial law and introduce a state of emergency for a maximum of three months on the entire country or a segment of it, with the approval of the Senate and Sejm for another three months. The president has the right to dissolve the parliament, and must do so after three vetoes on the same law, passed by the parliament and cancelled by the president.

National Assembly

The supreme organ of power is the parliament. The constitution provides for two houses of parliament, a Senate of one hundred members and a Sejm of 460 deputies, elected for four years. All one hundred senators are elected by a majority vote on a provincial base. Each province is represented by two senators, with the exception of Warsaw and Katowice, which elect three delegates. Sejm deputies are elected under a complex system of proportional representation: 391 members are chosen from lists for multiseat electoral districts, the remaining 69 deputies being elected from national lists. Since 1993 there is a 5% hurdle limiting the number of parties represented in parliament.

The prerogatives of the Sejm include the adoption of laws and state financial plans; the appointment and recall of the chairman of the Council of Ministers (at the motion of the president), the appointment and recall of the members of the Council of Ministers (at the motion of the chairman presented in conjunction with the president or on the chairman's own initiative); the appointment of the civil rights ombudsman (with approval of the Senate); the adoption of a resolution concerning a state of war; and the expression of consent for prolongation (at most for three months) of a state of emergency imposed by the president. The Sejm can overturn any presidential veto by means of a two-thirds majority.

The Senate reviews the laws adopted by the Sejm; it may suggest comments and proposals on these laws or even propose their rejection in full. The Senate can be overruled by the Sejm by a qualified majority of two-thirds.

Council of Ministers

The Council of Ministers is the supreme executive and managing agency of state authority, serving functions typical for the executive branch and carrying out the decisions adopted by the Sejm. The Cabinet is responsible to the Sejm for its activities, and to the president between the sessions of the Sejm. The president chooses the prime minister, with the consent of the parliament. The prime minister selects a cabinet, but ministers must be approved by the parliament. The Council of Ministers co-ordinates actions of the entire state administration.

Current government

President: Aleksander Kwasniewski (sworn in December 23, 1995)

The current government is a coalition of the Democratic Left Alliance (SLD), the Polish Peasant Party (PSL) and independents.

Prime Minister:	Wlodzimierz Cimoszewicz (appointed February 1, 1996)
Minister of Finance:	Marek Belka
Industry and Trade:	Klemens Scierski (PSL)
Foreign Affairs:	Dariusz Rosati (independent)
Interior:	Leszek Miller (SLD)
Justice:	Leszek Kubicki (independent)
Privatization:	Miroslaw Pietrewicz (PSL)
President, National Bank:	Hanna Gronkiewicz-Waltz

Political parties

The Communist Party, the PUWP, played the leading role in Polish political life for about forty years, until 1989. In January 1990, it held its final congress and disbanded. Under the 1990 law, political parties are not obliged to file for registration, but by May 1, 1992, a total of 135 parties had been registered.

Main parties

Democratic Left Alliance
Sojusz Lewicy Demokratycznej (SLD)
Founded: 1991

Leader: Jozef Oleksy

Electoral coalition of Social Democracy of the Republic of Poland (founded 1990; over 60,000 members in 1995; Former Polish United Worker's Party) and the All Poland Trade Union. Dominant position in urban areas. Government coalition with PSL.

Polish Peasant Party
Polskie Stronnictwo Ludowe (PSL)
Founded: 1989

More centre-right and Catholic-Church-orientated

Leader: Waldemar Pawlak

Government coalition with SLD. Stresses development in agriculture and food-processing.

Members: 200,000 in 1993

Freedom Union
Unia Wolnosci (UW)
Centrist. Leading anti-Communist party in the Sejm. Strongly pro-reform.

Founded: 1994 by merger of Democratic Union (Unia Demokratyczna/UD) and the Liberal Democratic Union (Kongres Liberalno Demokratyczny/KLD)

Leader: Leszek Balcerowicz.

Solidarity Trade Union
Founded: 1981 in Gdansk

Members: 10 million in 1981, 1.8 million in 1993

Solidarity Electoral Action (AWS)
Political voice of the Solidarity trade union

Movement for the Reconstruction of Poland (ROP)
Populist and nationalist group of former anti-communists

Leader: former Prime Minister Andrzej Olszewski

Results of the September 1993 elections

Sejm (total 460)**:** Democratic Left Alliance (SLD), 171; Polish Peasant Party (PSL), 132; Democratic Union (UD), 74; Labour Union, 41; Confederation for an Independent Poland, 22; non-party Block (BBWR), 16; German Minority, 4

Senate (total 100)**:** Democratic Left Alliance (SLD), 37; Polish Peasant Party (PSL), 36; Solidarity, 10; Democratic Union (UD), 2; non-party Block (BBWR), 2; Labour Union, 2; others, 9.

Next elections Sejm
September 1997, at latest

Central bank

In 1989 the "monobank" structure of the National Bank of Poland – the "Narodowy Bank Polski" (NBP), established in 1945 – was broken down and nine commercial banks were removed from the NBP. Most of the commercial tasks of the NBP were given to these banks (in 1988 NBP granted 90% of available credits), while the NBP transformed itself into a typical central bank.

The NBP is now responsible for monetary, credit and exchange rate policy, together with bank regulation and supervision. It is especially responsible for issuing banknotes and coins. It acts as banker to the central government, as banker to other banks in the domestic banking system, as custodian of the country's gold and foreign exchange reserves, as a bank of rediscount and lender of last resort. In fulfilling its central bank functions, the NBP has been granted considerable autonomy, although it is required each year to submit to parliament a draft of the guidelines for monetary policy that is voted on by parliament along with the budget act. The implementation of the monetary and exchange rate policy is within the sole authority of the NBP.

A new Act on the National Bank of Poland and a Banking Law came into force in February 1989. The President of the National Bank is nominated by the President of Poland for a six-year term. During this term, the NBP President may be replaced only in the event of resignation, the loss of capability to discharge responsibilities through prolonged illness, the sentencing for a criminal offence by a court, or on the basis of a ruling of the Tribunal of State. The term of the current president of the NBP, Mrs Hanna Gronkieicz-Waltz expires in March 1997. She would like the NBP to be independent. The goal of the NBP leadership is to introduce a Monetary Council system, as in France, while keeping a similar level of autonomy (as Germany's Bundesbank).

International relations

Poland is a founding member of the United Nations and belongs to most relevant international organizations. In 1967 Poland joined the General Agreement of Tariffs and Trade (GATT) and in 1986 Poland re-joined the International Monetary Fund (IMF) and the World Bank (IBRD), having withdrawn in 1950. Poland is also a member of the International Finance Corporation (IFC) and was a founding member of the European Bank for Reconstruction and Development (EBRD).

Since the fall of Communism, foreign policy has stressed the integration of Poland with Western Europe. In 1991, Poland signed an association agreement with the European Union that provides a Free Trade Agreement for industrial products and quotas for agricultural products, textile, coal and steel. Application for full membership in the EU was made in 1994.

Although not formally required to do so, Poland will attempt to achieve as many of the Maastricht criteria as possible. As of 1996, two of the five Maastricht criteria have been fulfilled: a budget deficit of 3% of GDP or less (in 1995: 2.6%) and a public debt of 60% of GDP or less (in 1995: 57.6%). But both inflation (with an average rate of 19.9% in 1996 and interest rates are far above the Maastricht criteria and are not expected to fall to Maastricht levels before possible entry into the EU. Entry into the EU is likely to occur between 2001 and 2005 (the timetable is expected to be clear in late 1998/early 1999). In 1992 Poland signed an agreement on free trade with the member countries of EFTA, which seeks to abolish tariff barriers for almost all trade between EFTA and Poland by January 2001.

In 1993 the agreement on free trade within the Central European Free Trade Area (CEFTA), which includes Poland, Hungary the Czech Republic and Slovakia, came into force.

The date of entry to NATO is likely to be announced in July 1997 and could be as early as 1999. A defence co-operation agreement was duly signed by Poland and NATO in March 1994.

Good relations with the US are important, since Poland enjoys economic and political support and private foreign investment from the US in general, as well as from its large Polish minority. In 1991–92 Poland established diplomatic relations with the former republics of the USSR, developing particularly strong links with Ukraine. Relations with neighbouring Lithuania were initially strained by concerns over the status of the Polish minority. Relations improved in 1993-94, and in April 1994 Poland and Lithuania signed a treaty of friendship and co-operation.

■ ECONOMICS

Historical overview

In the years following the Second World War, Poland became an industrial economy. As in the other Eastern European countries, central planning had been installed by the late 1940s. With the westward shift in Poland's borders after the war, the country lost the underdeveloped eastern regions and gained more industrialized and developed German territories. The fast industrialization in the 1950s, with central planning as the instrument to allocate resources, resulted in high industrial output growth. But consumption and living standards increased only slowly. Although the agricultural sector was left mainly in private hands, discrimination in favour of state-owned institutions and the lack of bank credits did not allow any improvement of productivity, which remained at very low levels.

The 1970s again brought an official promise of reform, but there was little change. Nevertheless, the Polish economy became more open towards Western countries. By the mid-1970s the government substantially overestimated the capability of the economy. Trade and current account balances showed increasing deficits which were financed through growing external debt. As the burden of debt service rose dramatically, the country declared its insolvency at the end of the decade and remained, as a consequence, isolated from international financial markets for more than a decade.

After the introduction of martial law in 1981, economic reforms were at least partially taken back again, and central planing and state control intensified. The economy remained fragile, with double-digit inflation and slowing growth.

Recent developments

New market-orientated reforms were introduced in 1990, also known as the "Balcerowicz plan" after the new finance minister. The reform was accompanied by a macroeconomic stabilization programme that included a commitment to reduce the fiscal deficit sharply, the introduction of a temporarily fixed exchange rate to break emerging hyperinflationary tendencies, and a tax-based income policy to restrain wage increases. The liberalization of most prices and international transactions cleared the way for emerging market reform. A two-tier banking system with an independent central bank and new commercial banks was also established by the Act of NBP (1989). The tax system was unified in 1989 and now applies to both the state-owned and private enterprises.

In the first two years of reform and macroeconomic stabilization, GDP fell rapidly, by 11.6% in 1990 and 7.1% in 1991. The turnaround in GDP came in 1992, the earliest among the Eastern European countries, with a real growth rate of 2.6%. Subsequently GDP growth accelerated resulting in a sustainable rate of 5-6% by 1996. The main reasons for the sharp GDP fall were the introduction of the macroeconomic stabilization programme and the start of structural adjustment on top of the collapse in trade among the previous Council of Mutual Economic Assistance (COMECON) partners and the attendant worsening in the terms of trade. As one of the first results of structural adjustment, the share of the services and the private sector on GDP rose substantially.

There are several reasons why Poland in 1992, two years ahead of the other Central Eastern European countries, posted real economic growth. The most important is that the reform programme, introduced in 1990, was the first and was completed under extraordinarily favourable psychological conditions.

At the beginning of 1990, the mood among the Polish people was for two reasons particularly conducive to the introduction of radical reforms likely to cause considerable social pain. To start with, Poland was the first to introduce a non-Communist government in mid-1989, and was once again at the forefront of change. The wave of political renewal throughout Eastern Europe in the second half of 1989 added to this euphoria.

Secondly, the reform programme of the new Polish government in 1990 was able to build on more than ten years of reform drafting by the Balcerowicz Group, an expert commission of the University of Planning and Statistics in Warsaw formed in 1978. Although the imposition of martial law in 1981 prevented the reform programme from being launched, it continued to be the subject of academic discussion and was constantly reworked in the following years.

Finance minister Balcerowicz was given the task of introducing economic reform. He believed in the programme and his competence was largely recognized by the public. Since the old system had prevented reform measures ten years earlier, their ultimate implementation took on an added symbolic character that considerably increased the Polish people's willingness to accept social hardship.

Although Balcerowicz finally had to resign, later governments never fundamentally questioned his reform programme despite statements to the contrary. Concessions were primarily made in the area of privatization and not on essential reform measures.

The economy

After the beginning of reforms towards a market economy in 1990, the Polish economy made a structural transition from an industry-dominated and state-owned economy towards private sector and growing services.

The share of GDP accounted for by the state-owned sector fell from 81.7 % in 1989 to only 55 % in 1993. The share was already relatively low compared with the 95-97% average in other Eastern European countries, largely due to the size of private agriculture, which was also private in Communist times. Nevertheless, large-scale privatization was delayed until 1994 as the legislation was long disputed in parliament.

Share of GDP by sector

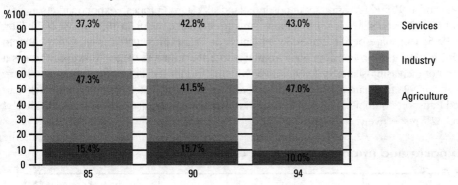

Source: Official data

Investment

Gross fixed capital formation as a percentage of GDP fell from 22.5 % in 1988 to 15.9 % in 1994, but increased again to 19% in 1995 and was expected to reach 20.5 % in 1996. Two-thirds of investment in the enterprise sector was financed in 1995 by enterprise profits, while only 10% was due to loans from the banking sector. While GDP growth in 1993 was mainly reflected in a rise in private consumption, since 1994 real GDP gains mainly reflect increased investment.

Foreign direct investment (FDI) inflows have accelerated from US$10 million in 1990 to US$1.3 billion in 1995, but the cumulative level equalled only US$75 per capita at the end of 1995, still well below potential. By comparison, the Hungarian per-capita level at the same time was US$1,153, and the Czech level was US$705. The main part of foreign currency inflows recently has been portfolio investment, concentrated on highly profitable treasury bills and equities. The Stock Exchange was reopened in Warsaw in 1991.

Trade

Since the beginning of economic reforms and liberalization of foreign trade in 1990, the main trading partners and the commodity structure of external trade changed considerably. While before 1990 Polish foreign trade was primarily COMECON-orientated (41% of trade in 1988), after the disintegration of the Eastern trading block, the European Union, especially Germany, became the most important trading partner. In 1994 63% of Polish exports were to the EU and 58% of Polish imports originated in the EU. Thus, access to the EU market is extremely important for the economy. Regarded from the EU-side, Poland's share of all EU exports was a mere 0.9% and Poland delivered only 0.8% of all EU imports. Main export products to the EU were agricultural products, metals and metal goods and light industry products, together accounting for 52%. Since 1995 all Polish exports into the EU, with the exception of textiles, coal and steel, are free of customs duties. All imports from the EU will be duty-free beginning in 1999. A free trade agreement between Poland and EFTA came into effect on November 15, 1993.

According to official balance of payment statistics, Poland's merchandise exports in nominal US dollar terms grew from US$10.9 billion in 1990 to US$22.9 billion in 1995. This growth occurred despite a 33% contraction in officially recorded industrial output between 1990 and 1991 and recessionary trends in Poland's Western European export markets in 1992 and 1993. Poland's merchandise imports grew from US$8.6 billion in 1990 to US$24.7 billion in 1995. The share of the former Soviet Union on Polish imports fell from 33% in 1988 to 6.8% in 1994 and on Polish exports from 28% to 5.4%. In the last years, however, there is a trend of increasing shares of foreign trade with the former socialist countries.

In 1994 the main export products were non-food raw materials (39%) and machinery and transport equipment (22%). The main imports were the same product groups with 41% and 32% respectively.

Exports and imports as a % of GDP

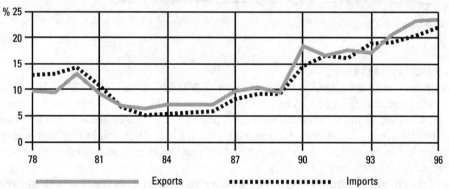

Source: Official data

Breakdown of exports (1994)

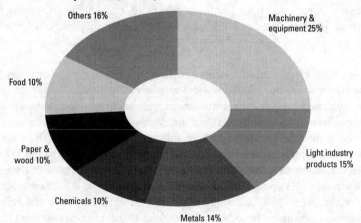

Source: Official data

Balance of payments

The structure of the balance of payments has been significantly influenced by debt-related flows. The two recent agreements with the Paris Club (1991) and the London Club (1994) reduced the burden of the foreign debt-service to under 10% of export earnings.

A structural speciality of Polish foreign trade is the large weight of so-called cross-border trade (informal trade by individuals). On the German border it consists of Poles carrying cheaper merchandise to Germany, and Germans buying food, clothing, simple consumer durables and petrol in Poland. There is also some cross-border trade on the eastern frontier of a less sophisticated kind.

Since there is little doubt that a part of sales and purchases of foreign exchange to the Polish banking system, which used to appear in the capital account, is in fact used for current account purposes, the Polish Statistical Office integrated these estimated inflows into the trade statistics in early 1996 while revising the trade figures back to 1994. According to the revised figures both the trade and current account balances were positive since 1994. The asset repatriation of residents rose in the last years reaching US$3.5 billion in 1995. This all allowed the NBP to increase the official reserves from US$5.8 billion in late 1994 to some US$17.3 billion in late September 1996.

Current account as a % of GDP

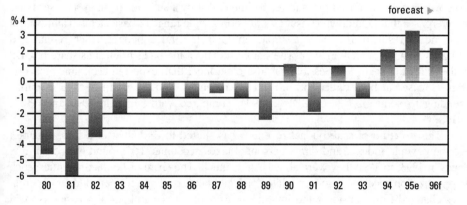

Source: Official data

Employment

Poland is the largest country in Central Eastern Europe with an estimated 38.6 million people. Employment in the economy, excluding private agriculture, fell from 13.5 million in 1989 to 11.4 million in 1993. In 1993, 6 million people were employed in the state sector, 5.3 million in the private sector and around 4 million on private farms. The share of industry in total employment declined from 28.4% in 1985 to 25.4% in 1993 and the share of agriculture (including fishing and forestry) declined from 29.9% in 1985 to 25.8% in 1993. Only the share of employment in trade rose from 8.5% in 1985 to 13.9% in 1993, underlining the structural adjustment in the transformation process towards a market economy.

Unemployment rocketed in 1990 as the economic reform and macroeconomic stabilization programmes began. At the end of 1990 6.3% of the economically active population were registered as unemployed, but at the end of 1995 some 15.0% were without work. In 1996 unemployment fell substantially and reached 13.2% in October. Unemployment especially affected young people: the 18-24 age group accounts for 36.9% of the total at the end of 1995, with a further 25.9% aged 25-34 and 24.1% aged 35-44. Geographically, unemployment is mainly concentrated in the northern provinces (over 25%), while in Warsaw and Upper Silesia, unemployment is lower than the Polish average.

Economic policy

The main aims of economic policy are economic growth and meeting the requirements of the Maastricht criteria. As two of the five Maastricht criteria (budget deficit and public debt) were fulfilled in 1996, Polish economic policy is currently focused on the inflation target. The Polish government's extraordinarily ambitious middle-term economic policy, "Package 2000", was accepted in mid-April 1996. The intention is to maintain real GDP growth at an average of 5% per year; to bring inflation down to 5% by the end of the decade; to cut taxes while reducing the budget deficit to 1.7 % of GDP; and to reduce unemployment to 10%.

Fiscal policy

The state budget was in deficit throughout most of the 1980s. In October 1989 the Solidarity-led government announced plans to reduce the deficit by a substantial cut in state subsidies to enterprises that held down consumer prices on a wide range of basic items. Tight control of spending resulted in a budget surplus in 1990. In 1991 a budget deficit re-emerged and grew to 4.9% of GDP in 1992. The significant cut of the budget deficit as share of GDP in the following years was possible because of stronger than expected economic recovery, with increases in both direct and indirect tax revenues, and the sharp decline in public spending to some 32.7 % of GDP in 1994, compared with 34.5% in 1990 and 53.1% in 1981.

The structure of state budget revenues has shifted towards that of a typical market economy: while indirect and direct personnel taxes accounted for around 65% of all revenues in 1993, in 1990 they were about half as much. The share of non-tax revenues, such as privatization receipts, rose too, while corporate taxes declined further. Budget expenditures changed from subsidies and investment to debt service and social security as main items. Subsidies were cut sharply from 42% of all state spending in 1988 to only 4% in 1993. Debt service expenditure increased from 4% in 1991 to 12% in 1993, declined in the following years because of agreements with the Paris and London Clubs, but are expected to grow again in the future. Social security expenditures grew rapidly and reached about 20% of budget spending in 1994. Such expenditures could cause deficit blowouts after the turn of the century if social security reform is not approved and implemented soon. As in all former Eastern Bloc countries, social security reform is urgently needed, but not yet started.

The main part of the deficit in 1991–93 (about 90%) was financed by domestic banks, particularly the NBP. Since 1993 the share of the NBP and other banks declined, and the share of foreign financing grew. Main debt financing instruments were short-term treasury bills and long-term bonds (with a share of about 75%). Poland's public debt in relation to GDP is expected to shrink from 59.5% in 1995 to about 55% in 1996 because of the higher growth rate of GDP than that of public debt.

Monetary policy

The main aim of the Polish government and policy-makers of the NBP are to reduce inflation and maintain convertibility of the zloty. Because of relatively high budget deficits in 1991–93 and the legal requirement for the NBP to buy government's bills, a tight monetary policy was not easy to effect. This was complicated by high foreign currency inflows which to hold down the exchange rate had to be acquired by the NBP but then offset by other asset sales to avoid a higher than desired growth of domestic money supply.

Real domestic credit declined sharply in 1990–93, but grew by 30% in 1994 and a further 17% in 1995. Net credit to the government grew slower than to the non-government sector, as the latter climbed to 30% of domestic credit in 1995 from 25% in 1994. Although interest rates were lowered by the NBP, they are seen by the government to be too high to stimulate growth and investment and minimize the cost of budget financing.

Inflation has been reduced from 586% in 1990 to 35.3 % in 1993, to 19.9% in 1996. The official government target is single-digit inflation in 1999. Inflation has been reduced despite significant deficit financing by banks because the amount of private saving intermediated through the banking system has increased.

A very important policy instrument to reduce inflation is the exchange rate. Since late-1991 the NBP has used a crawling peg system, depreciating the zloty on a monthly basis against a basket of five currencies. In 1996 the average monthly devaluation rate was 1% with a +/- 7% band around the mid-rate. Since 1995 the zloty appreciated steadily in real effective terms as the depreciation remained substantially lower than the inflation differential to the currencies in the basket. Since the beginning of 1996, the NBP tried to control the money supply by undertaking open market transactions to sterilize the liquidity overhang of the banking system.

Banking system

As a first step after the new Act of National Bank of Poland and a Banking Law 1989, the "monobank" structure was broken and nine state-owned banks were spun off from the central bank. These players were each centred in a different major city and its surrounding region. The goal now is to privatize these banks, and two of them were already privatized in 1996. One difficulty has been to attract Western strategic investors.

One of the most important barriers is the large size of bad debt portfolios on the books of state banks. In late 1995, there were more than 80 commercial banks and 1,660 co-operative banks in the country. Most banks are undercapitalized and have poor loan portfolios.

Foreign banks are entering the Polish market in growing numbers and, as from 1997 are free from any special restrictions in Poland. There were 83 private banks in 1994, most of them undercapitalized and about 15 threatened by liquidation or collapse. These private banks hold about 10% of banking sector assets. The co-operative banks, which were initially under the umbrella of BGZ, are small, with an average total asset of PLZ2 billion zloty, and service the agriculture sector. Since September 1992 the NBP ordered the co-operative banks to affiliate with one of four "associate" banks, so currently the co-operative banks are no longer fully autonomous; credit decisions are to be taken by a credit committee that includes representation from the associate bank. They also have been prohibited from issuing guarantees. Deposits in co-operative banks are fully guaranteed by the Treasury.

Privatization

The large-scale privatization of state-owned enterprises was started in late 1994 with 444 middle and big enterprises. During 1995, fifteen national investment funds (NFI) were established to oversee the privatization and restructuring of enterprises. Each NFI was given a lead shareholding in some enterprises and a minority stake in the others. Of the capital of each privatized firm, 33% went a to lead NFI, 27% was spread among the other fourteen NFIs, the employees were given 15% and 25% was retained by the state. On November 22, 1995 Polish mass privatization began. Citizens were able to purchase, for a nominal PLZ20 (US$8), share certificates giving them a stake in each of the fifteen NFIs. The certificates were on sale for one year, until the end of November 1996. The book value of the capital represented by each certificate will be "at least PLZ134". Within two years the certificates will be exchangeable for fifteen individual shares in each NFI and these in turn will be freely tradeable.

About 12 million Poles had bought certificates by August 1996. At the end of 1994, 1308 of the 8441 registered enterprises had been privatized. The share of the private sector on GDP rose from 55% in 1993 to more than 60% in 1995. The Stock Exchange was reopened in Warsaw in 1991 with sixty-one companies listed on the first tier and a further thirteen on the second tier at the end of May 1996. The stock market capitalization was about US$8billion in 1996.

Foreign debt

Total foreign debt (public and private) rose from US$26.5 billion in 1981 to US$49 billion in 1990 and declined to US$44 billion in 1995. As a percentage of GDP, foreign debt rose from an average of 35% in 1978–84 to 51% in 1985–89, soared to 83% in 1990 because of the sharp fall in GDP and since then declined to 64% in 1991 and an estimated 37% in 1995. The main creditors are official bilateral creditors (Paris Club) and commercial banks (London Club), which hold, together, about 80% of Polish debt.

In April 1991, the Paris Club agreed to an unprecedented debt-forgiveness package which pledged to cancel the equivalent of 50% in net present value of the US$30.5 billion owed to Western governments in two tranches of 30% and 20%. The deal was conditional on Poland agreeing to a three-year adjustment programme with the IMF, and this was duly signed. In September 1994 one more agreement was signed with the London Club, yielding 46% relief on private debt. Interest payments declined in the past years from US$3.9 billion to an estimated US$1.5 billion in 1995, what accounts for only 4.3% of foreign exchange receipts for goods, services and factor income. Poland's membership in the OECD and an investment grade rating from both Moody's and Standard & Poor's now allow the country to borrow on quite favourable terms.

Currency

The currency of Poland is the zloty (1 zloty=100 groszy). After the nominal exchange rate of the Polish zloty (PLZ) reached very high levels due to rocketing inflation in the beginning of the 1990s, the authorities cut the face value of the currency by a factor of 10,000 on January 1, 1995 resulting in single-digit exchange rates to the US dollar. The Ministry of Finance and the National Bank of Poland (NBP) are responsible for foreign exchange policy and control the restrictions and limitations imposed by the Foreign Exchange Law. The zloty is fully convertible for current account transactions. Restrictions exist only for capital account transactions and borrowing from abroad, which require a permit of the NBP. There are no restrictions on remittances of interest, principal, royalties and fees.

Polish zloty/US dollar exchange rate

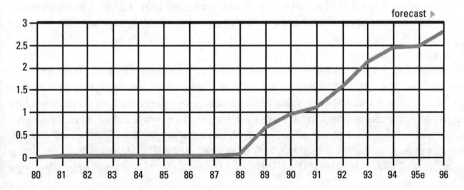

In 1995 monetary reform eliminated four zeros from the exchange rate. Dates shown before 1995 are on a comparable basis.

■ EQUITIES

Index performance (in local currency)

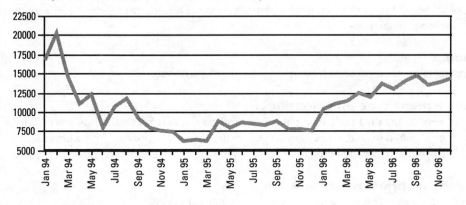

Key indicators

	Index performance %, in US$ terms	Market Cap. US$bn	P/E	Div. Yield	Weight in IFCI	Weight in IFCG
1994	-42.6	3.1	12.9	0.4	0.4	0.2
1995	-9.2	4.6	7	2.6	0.3	0.2
1996	71.2	8.4	14.3	1.2	0.8	0.6

Sources: Local stock exchange, IFC, Bloomberg, Datastream, UBS

Background

Stock exchange activity in Warsaw goes back to 1817. Prior to its closure in 1939, more than 130 securities were traded on the Warsaw Stock Exchange (WSE) – equivalent to 90% of the trading that occurred in Poland at the time. However, first Nazism and then Communism in Eastern Europe led to the WSE's prolonged closure until April 1991. The WSE was reopened with the assistance of Societé des Bourses Françaises and the French Depository SICOVAM.

Structure

The Polish equity market comprises three segments, each with different listing requirements. These are the Main Market, which is the official market with the most stringent listing requirements, the Parallel Market, favoured by smaller companies because of its less stringent listing requirements, and the Free Market for companies that fail to meet the listing requirements of the other two markets, but wish to be traded publicly. There are sixty-one listed companies on the Main Market and fourteen on the Parallel Market. Total capitalization is around PLN27.5 billion (about US$10 billion).

Regulatory authority

The WSE is regulated by the Polish Securities Commission.

Trading methods

Trading takes place using a computerized single price auction order matching system with price set to maximize trading volume. In extra-time trading, bids or offers can be made to balance excess buy or sell orders at the fixed price. Each stock has a specialist who supervises the stock and will scale back orders if an imbalance persists. In 1996 a new "crossing session" was introduced where new orders can trade at a fixing price. There is strictly no off-exchange trading.

Hours

Trading takes place between 09.00 and 12.30, Monday to Friday.

Settlement time and clearing

Settlement occurs on a trade date plus three business days (T+5) basis. All members of the WSE are required to hold a securities account in the National Depository for Securities and a cash account in a clearing bank.

Limits on price movement

During a trading session, shares are permitted to fluctuate by 5%.

Types of shares

Ordinary shares are traded on the WSE.

Stock indices

The WSE produces three main stock indices. The most widely quoted is the Main Market Index (WIG), which is calculated in line with IFC methodology and includes all companies listed on the Main Market. In addition, there is the Parallel Market Index (WIRR), which is similar to the WIG Index but comprises all the shares listed on the Parallel Market. Finally, there is the WIG20 Index, which is a price index comprising the twenty highest ranking companies on the Main Market.

Taxes

There is a Stock Exchange fee of 0.16% plus the 0.06% fee charged by the depository, payable on all trades. Capital gains tax is 40% but may be reduced by a relevant tax treaty. Capital gains tax is usually not paid in Poland. Dividend and interest income is taxed at 20%, although some countries operate tax treaties with Poland, reducing the rate to 5–15%.

Disclosure of financial statements

All companies involved in public trading must produce quarterly, semi-annual, and (audited) annual reports.

Ownership limits for non-residents

There are no limitations specific to non-residents, but investors wishing to hold a majority stake must seek the advice of the Ministry of Finance.

Capital and foreign exchange controls

There are no restrictions on capital and foreign exchange with reference to portfolio investment. Foreigners are free to repatriate profits from their investments.

Brokers

There are twenty-seven member and eight non-member brokers on the WSE. Commissions are typically between 0.3% and 1.2% depending on the size of the transaction.

Sectors

Banking, trading and chemicals are the three leading sectors on the WSE with over 70% of market capitalization between them. Food is the only other sector with capitalization in excess of 10%.

ADRs

There are no Polish ADRs, but Bank Gdanski is a GDR.

Derivatives

There is no derivatives market in Poland.

■ DEBT

The government securities market re-opened in 1991, and many restrictions on foreign investment were lifted two years later. The National Bank of Poland (NBP) acts as fiscal agent for the Ministry of Finance (MOF), and arranges auctions for treasury bills and bonds. Since 1992, it has conducted open-market operations through the use of repo/reverse transactions with licensed banks and money-market dealers.

According to the 1991 Act on Public Trading of Securities and Trust Funds, securities trading must be conducted exclusively through brokerage houses, licensed by the Warsaw Securities Commission.

Treasury bills

The NCB organizes auctions of 8-, 13-, 26-, 39- and 52-week bills on the first business day of each week. Bills are sold according to a bid-price system, where bids are only accepted at or above a minimum price. Orders must be for at least PLZ100,000. Settlement is two days later. Primary market participants must satisfy turnover thresholds to qualify – 0.2% of the nominal value of quarterly secondary market turnover. They hold their securities in the Central Register of T-bills at the NPB.

T-bills have been dematerialized since June 1, 1995, and trade on the Warsaw Stock Exchange through continuous quotation on a book-entry basis.

Treasury bonds

Treasury bonds were first issued in 1989. There are five main types:

One-year indexed bonds (IR & RP)

Coupon interest is paid at redemption, and is currently set at 3% over base rate. The base rate is determined by the CPI indicies for one year, starting two months before the issue date of a particular series.

RP bonds with a face value of PLZ1,000 are sold at auctions, and IR bonds are issued in smaller denominations (PLZ100 face value) and sold to the general public at service outlets. RP bonds are usually issued every two months. Investors in IR bonds can roll over the proceeds from one issue on maturity into a new issue.

Three-year floating rate bonds (TZ)

The interest rate is fixed quarterly at 110% of the weighted average rate of return of the first four 13-week T-bill auctions in the preceding month. Bonds are issued each quarter through auctions and customer service outlets fourteen days before the official launch of a series.

Two-year fixed rate bonds (OS)

These were introduced in February 1994. Fixed rate bonds have a nominal value of PLZ1,000, and have annual paying coupons of 16%, 17% and, most recently, 18%. Auctions take place every third Thursday of the month.

Five-year fixed rate bonds (OS)

Details are the same as for two-year bonds, but coupons are 12%, 13%, 14% and, most recently, 15%.

Ten-year floating rate bonds (DZ)

DZ bonds were first issued in December 1995. Quarterly auctions are held on the second Tuesday of the month, but the NBP can hold additional auctions in the fallow months. Unsold bonds are re-offered a month later. Members of the National Depository bid at auctions both for their own accounts and on behalf of their clients (including foreigners). The minimum bid is PLZ 1 million; competitive bids are filled at the price offered above a clearing level set by the MOF.

Annual coupons are 100 basis points over the weighted average return for 52-week T-bills during the two months prior to the first month of an interest period. Rates are posted in the Official Gazette (Dziennik Urzedowy) of the Ministry of Finance. The MOF has the right to call the bonds after five years.

Passive bonds

In addition, "passive bonds" were issued for special reasons: to re-capitalize commercial banks, for instance and to finance the implementation of the London Club agreement. Some bonds convert into shares of privatized companies on redemption. They are in registered form, and were placed with the NBP and commercial banks.

Secondary markets

Bonds trade on the Warsaw Stock Exchange for 3-day settlements (large lots settle two days after trade date). Volumes traded OTC between the dealing departments of domestic banks are larger. Bills and bonds are bearer instruments.

Municipal bonds

Several large cities have issued municipal bonds. Issue sizes are small, but meet strong investor demand.

Corporate bonds and commercial paper (CP)

A dozen companies have launched small commercial paper programmes. CP pays a margin over treasury bills and are normally held to maturity. A few illiquid longer-dated bonds are also tightly held, yielding less than treasury bonds.

Zloty-linked bonds

The Polish zloty is not fully convertible, and so all zloty-linked bonds are settled in hard currencies. These bond issues – for the General Electric Capital Corporation and the International Finance Corporation – allow foreign investors to gain exposure to the currency.

Eurobonds

The Ministry of Finance launched the Republic's first eurobond in July 1995, denominated in US dollars. A second issue for DM250 million followed in July 1996.

US$250 million Republic of Poland 7.75%, 13 July 2000
DM250 million Republic of Poland 6.125%, 31 July 2001

In addition, the MOF has given tax breaks to Polish banks to encourage issuance. Consequently, Bank Handlowy and Bank Rozwoju Exportu have issued dollar eurobonds.

Eurobond issues (US$m)

	1990	1991	1992	1993	1994	1995	1996
Sovereign	—	—	—	—	—	250.0	164.1
Private	—	—	—	—	—	—	—

Brady bonds

In October 1994, Poland normalized relations with its external creditors through a Brady Plan debt and debt-service agreement. There are six structures:

(US$)	Name	Coupon	Maturity
138m	New Money Bonds	6mth libor + 13/16	27 Oct 2009
2.7bn	Past Due Interest Bonds (PDIs)	3.25-7%	27 Oct 2014
393m	Debt Conversion Bonds (DCBs)	4.5-7.5%	27 Oct 2019
3bn	Collateralized Discount Bonds	6mth libor + 13/16	27 Oct 2024
930m	Collateralized Par Bonds	2.75-5%	27 Oct 2024
900m	Collateralized RSTA Bonds	2.75-5%	27 Oct 2024

■ POLAND: Economic indicators

Population and development	1990	1991	1992	1993	1994	1995	1996e
Population, million	38.1	38.2	38.4	38.4	38.5	38.6	38.7
Population growth, %	0.4	0.3	0.3	0.2	0.2	0.3	0.3
Nominal GDP per capita, US$	1633	2038	2200	2240	2359	3093	3353

National accounts

	1990	1991	1992	1993	1994	1995	1996e
Nominal GDP, US$bn	62.3	77.9	84.4	86.1	90.9	119.5	129.9
Change in real GDP, %	-11.6	-7.6	2.6	3.8	5.2	7.0	5.0
Gross fixed capital formation, % of GDP	28.6	20.3	14.5	14.8	14.9	14.9	16.9

Money supply and inflation

	1990	1991	1992	1993	1994	1995	1996e
Narrow money, change %, Dec/Dec	401.1	14.4	37.0	36.0	29.0	22.0	—
Broad money, change %, Dec/Dec	160.1	37.0	57.5	36.0	35.2	25.2	—
Consumer price inflation (avg.) %	585.8	70.3	45.3	36.7	32.2	27.8	19.9

Interest rates

	1990	1991	1992	1993	1994	1995	1996e
Discount rate, end of year	48.00	36.00	32.00	29.00	28.00	25.00	—
Money market rate, annual average	—	49.90	29.50	24.50	23.30	25.80	—
Treasury bill rate, annual average	—	—	44.00	33.20	28.80	25.60	—
Deposit rate, annual average	41.70	53.50	37.80	34.00	33.40	26.80	—
Prime lending rate, annual average	54.20	54.60	39.00	35.30	32.80	33.50	—

Government finance

	1990	1991	1992	1993	1994	1995	1996e
Government expenditure, % of GDP	43.7	49.5	56.9	32.1	44.1	31.6	31.2
Government balance, % of GDP	3.1	-6.0	-5.2	-3.4	-3.1	-2.7	-2.6

Exchange rates *lc=local currency*

	1990	1991	1992	1993	1994	1995	1996e
Exchange rate, annual average, lc/US$	9500	10576	13626	18115	23115	2.41	2.72
Exchange rate, end of year, lc/US$	9500	1095	15767	21217	24370	2.47	2.89
Real exchange rate 1990=100	n/a	100.0	102.5	109.6	113.2	121.6	131.8

Balance of payments

	1990	1991	1992	1993	1994	1995	1996e
Exports of goods & services, US$m	14666	18653	20690	20115	25401	37744	41080
Change %	93.6	27.2	10.9	-2.8	26.3	48.6	8.8
Imports of goods & services, US$m, fob	15486	21567	23000	24911	25899	34006	42850
Change %	111.1	39.3	6.6	8.3	4.0	31.3	26.0
Trade balance, of goods only, US$m, fob-fob	2214	-711	824	-2189	599	1948	-3700
Current account balance, US$m	3066	-2164	-1844	-4036	666	3723	-2000
as a % of GDP	4.9	-2.8	-2.2	-4.7	0.7	3.1	-1.5

Foreign exchange reserves

	1990	1991	1992	1993	1994	1995	1996e
Foreign exchange reserves, US$m	4492.1	3632.6	4099.1	4091.9	5840.0	14774.0	18000.0
Gold at ⅔ of market price, US$m	121.3	114.1	108.2	113.3	121.0	121.0	122.1
Import cover (reserves/imports), months	3.5	2.0	2.1	2.0	2.7	5.2	5.0

Foreign debt and debt service

	1990	1991	1992	1993	1994	1995	1996e
Short-term debt, US$m	1541	1583	1327	1163	182	1085	1200
Total foreign debt, US$m	49040	49288	48045	47907	43506	44409	45000
as a % of GDP	78.8	63.2	56.9	55.6	47.9	37.2	34.6
as a % of foreign exchange receipts	285.5	253.8	227.1	229.5	163.8	117.7	110.2
Interest payments, US$m	3910	2495	2265	1834	1764	1511	1450
Principal repayments, US$m	310	455	543	520	1219	1883	1175
Total debt service, US$m	4220	2950	2808	2354	2983	3394	2625
as a % of goods exports	38.8	20.5	18.9	15.8	15.3	11.8	8.5
as a % of foreign exchange receipts	24.6	15.2	13.3	11.3	11.2	9.0	6.4

Portugal

KEY FACTS

Area (thousands of km²):	92
Population (1995, millions):	10.5
Population projection (2025, millions):	10
Population younger than 15 yrs (1991, % of total):	20.2
Urbanization rate (1993, % of population):	35
Life expectancy (1993, years at birth):	75
Gross domestic product (1996, US$bn):	103
GDP per capita (1996, US$):	9500
Average annual GDP growth rate (1990-96, %):	1.8
Average annual inflation rate (1990-96, %)	7.5
Currency (escudo per US$, average 1996):	154.8
Real exchange rate: (1990=100, average 1996)	117.48
Main exports:	textiles, transport, machinery, chemicals & minerals
Main imports:	machinery & transport equipment, animal, vegetable & food products, chemicals
Main trading partners:	Germany, Spain, France, UK, Italy
Market capitalization of Stock Exchange (December 1996; US$bn):	24.6
Total foreign debt (% of GDP):	12.6
Next elections due under normal circumstances:	legislative required by Oct. 1999; presidential scheduled Jan. 2001
Credit rating: (Jan 1997, Standard & Poor's, Moody's)	AA-; A1

FORECAST: 1997-2000 (average)

	Worst case	Most likely	Best case
Real GDP growth (%)	1.0	2.5	3.9
Inflation (%)	4.5	2.5	1.5

■ POLITICS

Historical overview

Portugal, a neutral country during the Second World War, was a founding member of NATO in 1949, and also joined the United Nations. However, during the decades that followed, Portugal was an introspective country under the leadership of Antonio Salazar. Industrialization was slow and the government happy to have a high proportion of the labour force in agriculture. A large amount of wealth and industry was controlled by the "20 Families", while widespread rural poverty led to emigration as workers sought higher wages in the United States, France and Germany.

In 1961, Portugal fought a war in Africa as its colonies rebelled. The military effort was not helped by Portugal's small size and the fact that none of its many colonies was adjacent to each other. The war was long and expensive, both in financial and human terms. It also added to Portugal's political isolation. Growing dissatisfaction within the military resulted in a revolt by some army commanders in 1974 which toppled the government.

The rebel commanders were embraced by the population and the 1974 bloodless revolution occurred under three guiding lines called "the three Ds" (democracy, decolonization and development). The first two were achieved quickly: decolonization occurred in 1975 with the independence of the African colonies while in 1976 Portugal had democratic elections. The last, development, is a much longer and more complex process.

As part of the development programme, Portugal underwent a period of rapid nationalization. In other areas, however, economic policy was lacking in clarity. Successive governments – 13 in total between 1976 and 1986 – sought to follow conflicting objectives of social justice and fiscal stability. Some reform was carried out and the welfare state expanded, but pressing problems stemming from the country's economic structure and lack of competitiveness were largely untouched. Economic growth averaged just 2% a year over the period.

Chronology

1487	Portugal commences two centuries of empire-building
1822	Brazil is granted independence from Portugal
1908	Assassination of the monarch, King Carlos and Luis Filipe, his son
1910	Abolition of the monarchy
1926	Military revolt ends parliamentary rule
1932	Oliveira Salazar becomes prime minister and establishes the autocratic Estado Novo regime
1949	Founding member of NATO
1968	Salazar suffers a stroke and is succeeded by Marcelo Caetano
1974	Military coup and bloodless revolution bring democracy and an end to the Portuguese colonial empire in Africa
1976	Parliamentary and presidential elections are held. Ten years of mostly short-lived governments follow.
1985	The PSD (Social Democrats), under Cavaco Silva, is voted into power
1995	The Socialist Party (PS) under António Guteres wins legislative elections, ending ten years of PSD rule
1996	Former Lisbon mayor Jorge Sampalo wins presidential elections

Constitution and government

Portugal is a parliamentary democracy. The constitution was drawn up in 1975–76 and amended in 1982, 1989–90 and 1992 (the latter following the Maastricht Treaty of the European Union). Portugal has been a member of the European Union since 1986. Executive power is vested in the parliament (Assembly of the Republic), consisting of 230 members elected under a system of proportional representation for a maximum term of four years. In addition, Portugal has a president, elected every five years.

Portugal is a highly centralized country. There is no federal system in place. Regional development is both determined and financed by the central government. However, in its 1995 election campaign, the Socialist Party (PS) vowed to establish a regional political system while at the same time seeking to avoid increased bureaucracy or spending. The objective is to even out the growing disparities of wealth between the booming coastal areas and the poorer inland regions.

Results of the October 1995 parliamentary election
The PS won 112 of the 230 seats in the October 1995 elections, leaving it 4 seats short of an absolute majority. Despite this, PS leader António Guteres was able to form a government, thus ending a decade of Social Democrat (PSD) rule.

Socialist Party, PS: 112, **Social Democrats, PSD:** 88, **Communists, CDU:** 15,
Popular Party, PP: 15

Main political parties
Socialist Party (PS)
The PS, headed by prime minister António Guteres, has evolved into a moderate centre-left party. It espouses policies of fiscal austerity, privatization, economic modernization and, above all, Portugal's participation in a single currency.

Social Democrats (PSD)
Since Cavaco Silva's resignation in early 1995, the PSD has been in disarray. The interim leader, Fernando Nogueira, was forced to step down after the party's defeat in the October 1995 elections and has been replaced by Marcelo Rebelo de Sousa. The PSD is a centre-right moderate party, professing much the same ideas as the PS.

Communist Party (CDU)
The party is left wing, advocating heavy state participation in the economy. Its leader is Carlos Carvalhas.

Popular Party (PP)
Previously known as the Centre Democrats (CDS), the PP is a new right-wing party, opposed to Maastricht and Portugal's participation in a European single currency. Its leader is Manuel Monteiro.

Results of the January 1996 presidential election
Jorge Sampaio, former Lisbon mayor and Socialist candidate, won the presidential election in January 1996, succeeding fellow Socialist, Mario Soares.

Central bank
In 1994, the Bank of Portugal gained full independent status. Technically, it has exclusive power in the formulating and carrying out of monetary policy, although it tends to work in close co-operation with the government. According to its constitution, its sole objective is monetary stability.

The board consists of between five and eight members. It has one president, one or two vice-presidents and three to five senior officials. All members are nominated for a five-year term and can stand for a maximum of two terms. The board is appointed by the incumbent finance minister. The current central bank president is Antonio de Sousa, appointed in August 1994 under the previous PSD administration.

Central bank board meetings are held weekly, usually on Thursdays, when monetary policy decisions are taken. In exceptional circumstances, interim meetings can be summoned. The bank has at its disposal three main instruments for the management of money markets: an overnight credit facility (emergency lending rate), mechanisms to absorb liquidity (absorption rate) and repurchase agreements (or repos, sometimes referred to as the injection rate). Under normal market conditions, the former two act as the ceiling and the floor for short term interest rates. Within this band, the central bank steers money market rates through variable rate repos.

■ ECONOMICS

Historical overview

Nineteen eighty-six marked the beginning of a new era. First, after a decade of political turbulence, the centre-right PSD under Cavaco Silva won a landslide victory, allowing single-party majority rule for the first time. The new government brought wide-ranging, market-orientated reforms to almost all sectors of the economy. Second, Cavaco Silva took Portugal into the European Community. These complementary forces, and an influx of foreign investment and European aid, allowed the economy to prosper.

Recent developments

Since joining the EC in 1986, Portugal has gone through two distinct periods of economic development. From 1986 to 1990, growth averaged 5.3% a year, supported by easy fiscal and monetary policy, access to European markets, and an inflow of European aid.

Since 1991, a new era of economic conservatism has emerged. Growth priorities have been replaced by a commitment to rapid economic restructuring and long-term competitiveness. The signing of the Maastricht Treaty in 1991, outlining proposals to move to a European single currency by the end of the decade, was the catalyst for this policy reassessment. Portugal would have to undergo a period of rapid adjustment if it wished to participate in the single European currency.

The intermediate focus of the new economic policy has been currency stability. As a highly open economy (exports plus imports of goods and services represent 88% of GDP), a stable currency is seen as vital in forcing rapid disinflation and restructuring. In 1992, the Portuguese escudo became a member of the European Exchange Rate Mechanism (ERM). Maintenance of the escudo's central parity within the EMS has become the prime target of interest-rate policy. Over the period, complementary policies of fiscal consolidation, privatisation and economic liberalization have also been put into place.

The new regime has been highly successful. Since 1991, inflation has fallen from 14% to 3%, the fiscal deficit has narrowed from 7% to 4% of GDP and the exchange rate has depreciated by only 6% on a trade-weighted basis – but the cost has been economic slowdown. Between 1991 and 1995 growth averaged just 1.1% a year, 1% below the EU average. A lacklustre European environment, combined with tight monetary and fiscal conditions have taken their toll on Portuguese activity. Unemployment has risen from 4% in 1991 to more than 7%.

Population

The population (including the islands of the Azores and Madeira) has been static throughout the 1990s at around 9.8 million. The low and declining birth rate (1.4 children per family) could pose demographic problems over the next century as the population ages and the dependency ratio rises. The low birth rate is largely due to the rapid modernization of the economy and increased female participation in the workforce.

Large migration during the 1960s and 1970s has created a sizeable emigrant population. Latest estimates put the number of Portuguese living abroad at 4.5 million, equivalent to almost half of the resident population. The main countries of residence are South America, France, South Africa and the United States. However, improving economic conditions at home have stemmed the flow of migrants and encouraged many to return.

Employment

Portugal has the benefit of a cheap labour market. Permanent contracts, which grant full employment rights and generous severance payments, account for 89% of all employment contracts. Nevertheless, conciliatory union attitudes and the fact that unemployment benefits are low and short-lived allow real wages to respond rapidly to changes in the level of unemployment.

Recession, economic restructuring and increased female participation in the workforce have caused unemployment to accelerate. Economic recovery is unlikely to lead to a return to previous low levels. A jobs and skills mismatch, particularly in the older, less-educated generations, is likely to persist.

The economy

Since joining the EU, the structure of the Portuguese economy has moved towards services at the expense of industry and agriculture. The agricultural sector has almost halved in size and now constitutes only 5.1% of total GDP, leaving Portugal dependent on imports for its food supply. Services have grown rapidly, and now make up 60% of output.

As important has been the change in the structure of firms. Portugal's traditional family-run firms are gradually being replaced by high-tech international businesses. A loss of comparative advantage in cheap, labour-intensive products to the Far East has forced Portugal to re-focus its business and upgrade its products.

Savings and investment

Portugal has the highest investment ratio of all its EU partners, at around 28%. The ratio has risen from 22% in 1986, due to EU aid and foreign direct investment (FDI). As one of the four poorest members of the EU, Portugal receives substantial Structural Fund money, which is channelled into infrastructure, education and industrial restructuring. The current 1994–1999 Delors Two programme grants Portugal funds equivalent to nearly 4% of GDP a year. Currently, EU aid all but makes up the shortfall between Portugal's 23% savings ratio and the investment ratio. Net foreign direct and portfolio investment into Portugal has fallen back sharply over the last few years and turned negative in 1995.

Share of GDP by sector

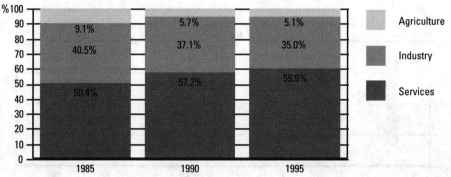

Source: Official data

Breakdown of exports (1996)

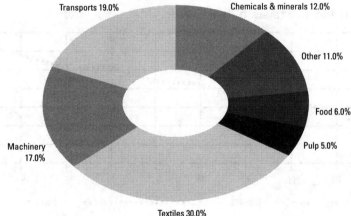

Source: Official data

Balance of payments

Since 1986, Portugal's current account balance has fluctuated between a modest surplus and a modest deficit (+1 to -1% of GDP). This stability has been maintained despite a sizeable and increasing trade deficit (which reached a peak of 11% of GDP in 1992). A commitment to a stable exchange rate, despite a substantial cost and inflation disadvantage versus its main trading partners, has led to a gradual erosion of competitiveness. This loss is being clawed back through company restructuring, internal modernization and a re-focusing of trade, but the process is slow. The trade deficit was still nearly 10% of GDP in 1995.

Three factors explain the sizeable ex-trade surplus: tourism receipts, EU transfers and emigrants' remittances. The latter two will diminish over time, particularly after 1999 when the current Delors Two aid programme ends. By then, Portugal will need to have taken action on its structural trade imbalance.

Current account as a % of GDP

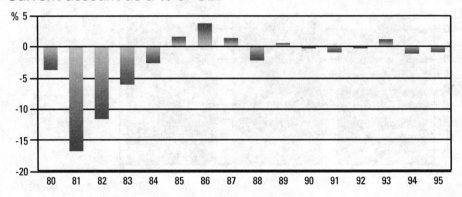

Source: Official data

Exports and imports as a % of GDP

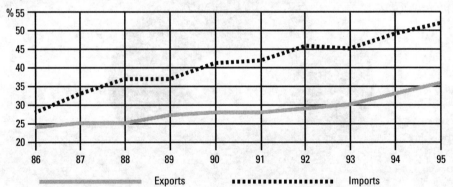

Source: Official data

Economic policy
Monetary policy

The central bank does not set any intermediate or final monetary targets, at least not overtly. However, it is insistent that while other variables are monitored, currency stability, specifically within the EMS, is the only intermediate target of monetary policy.

Given Portugal's tenuous trade position, the central bank has maintained high real interest rates to contain domestic demand and attract capital inflows. During periods of exchange rate tensions, the bank has been quick to raise rates and draw on its foreign exchange reserves (US$21 billion, equivalent to 20% of GDP) to stem speculative attack. Only during periods of wider devaluations have the Portuguese authorities sanctioned a currency realignment.

The success in beating inflation has allowed nominal short-term interest rates to fall sharply. The official injection/repo rate has declined from 16% to 6.5% over the last four years. Long-term rates have also fallen considerably, as improving prospects attract investors into the Portuguese market.

Fiscal policy

After an extended period of lax fiscal policy, the government has taken aggressive steps to rein in its mounting fiscal problems. Between 1986 and 1993, the ratio of gross government debt to GDP rose from 56% to 67%, driven up by high and mounting debt servicing costs, inefficient tax collection and economic recession.

The urgency with which the government has tackled its fiscal problems stems from the demands of the Maastricht Treaty, which requires budget deficits to be no more than 3% of GDP and outstanding debt below 60% of GDP before its currency will be admitted into the European single currency bloc. Assessment for first-round 1999 monetary union will take place in 1997.

Over the last three years, a restructuring of the tax system, a clampdown on tax evasion and modest indirect tax hikes have helped boost tax receipts. Falling interest rates have helped ease the debt-servicing burden. Public sector wage control, departmental spending efficiencies and restructuring of loss-making public companies have all eased spending pressures. In 1996, the fiscal deficit is expected to be 4% of GDP, down sharply from the 7.1% of GDP recorded in 1993.

Currency

The Portuguese escudo joined the European Exchange Rate Mechanism (ERM) in April 1992 at a central parity of 174.788 against the European Currency Unit (ECU), within 6% fluctuation bands. This central rate has since been realigned three times and now fluctuates within 15% bands at a central parity of 195.792 against the ECU. On a trade-weighted basis, the escudo has depreciated by just 9% since joining the ERM and has been stable for the last three years.

Portuguese escudo/US dollar exchange rate

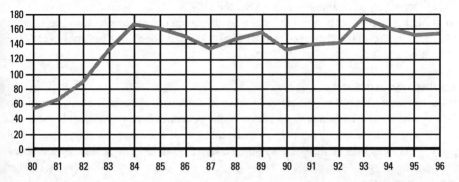

■ EQUITIES

Index performance (in local currency)

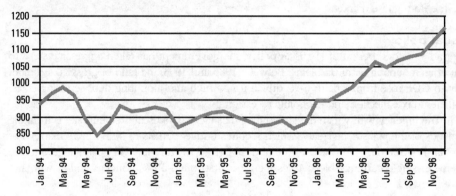

Key indicators

	Index performance %, in US$ terms	Market Cap. US$bn	P/E	Div. Yield	Weight in IFCI	IFCG
1994	16.5	16.2	20.3	3.2	1.7	1.2
1995	-4.1	18.4	14.8	3.3	1.4	1.0
1996	25.3	24.7	18.1	2.3	1.9	1.6

Sources: Local stock exchange, IFC, Bloomberg, Datastream, UBS

Structure
The Lisbon Stock Exchange comprises three parts: the Official Market, the Second Market and the Market Without Quotes. Larger companies are in the Official Market, smaller ones are in the Second and companies with financial problems and/or a low free float are relegated to the Market Without Quotes.

As at June 1996 there were 173 shares listed in the three markets. Eighty-three shares from seventy-seven companies were listed in the Official Market, with only sixteen in the Second Market and seventy-one companies in the Market Without Quotes. The Official Market accounts for more than 90% of total market capitalization, and has an average free float of 30%.

Regulatory authority
The Commisão de Mercados de Valores Mobiliares (CMVM) is Portugal's equivalent of the NYSE's Securities and Exchange Commission or the Securities Investment Board in the UK. The CMVM is financially independent, with administrative and financial autonomy. It has supervisory powers over all institutions in the Portuguese primary and secondary markets.

Trading methods
Most of the shares listed on the official market are traded on an automated order-driven continuous system. Eventually all the stocks on the official market will be traded in this way.

The computer matches orders by price, followed by the time they were entered. The computer system is called TRADIS and only registered brokers may use this.

Hours
Trading starts at 10.00 and closes at 16.30, Monday to Friday. There is a pre-opening period from 9.30 to 10.00.

Settlement time and clearing
Physical settlement is on a T+3 basis, and Financial settlement is T+4. Hence there is free delivery and the seller has to deliver the shares one day before he receives the cash. Most shares in the official market have their shares deposited in the CVM (Central de Valores Mobiliares or just the "central"). This makes clearing easy and usually problem-free.

Limits on price movement
The price of a share may not change by more than 15% in a single session.

Types of shares
Most shares are ordinary voting shares. There are no "A" or "B" shares with multiple votes. There are few preferred shares. A typical Portuguese preferred share is non-voting and bears a fixed preferred dividend in addition to the ordinary dividend earned by the other shares.

Stock indices
The two most used stock indices are the BVL-30 (Bolsa de Valores de Lisboa) index and the PSI-20 index. The BVL-30 index is the official index of the thirty largest stocks and takes into account the re-investment of dividends. It includes all listed stocks, weighed by market capitalization. The PSI-20 is an index of the top twenty stocks on which there is a future contract traded on the derivatives market in Oporto.

Taxes
There is a withholding tax on dividends of 20% (previously 25%).

Dividends
All companies run on a January to December calendar and usually pay dividends once a year around April. Management proposes the dividend payment, and then shareholders approve it at the annual assembly before March 31. It is then paid in April. Stocks are suspended from trading for four days while dividends are paid.

Disclosure of financial statements
Financial statements must reflect the true and accurate position of the company. Companies must have their accounts audited and approved by external registered accounting firms (often one of the "big six" accounting firms). Several EU directives are incorporated in the generally accepted accounting principals. Every listed company must disclose their financial statements twice a year, and banks must disclose their financial statements on a quarterly basis. Companies may not publish forecasts for annual profits until disclosure of half-year results.

Shareholders' rights
Shareholders can vote by proxy in Portugal. All shareholders must be informed of any forthcoming extraordinary and annual general meetings.

Ownership limits for non-residents
Some of the privatized companies listed in the market have ownership limits for non-residents. This has been a matter of fierce debate since these have been circumvented in a number of cases. Non-residents buying shares in BTA, for example, will not be able to register and will lose voting rights. However, they will still be able to receive dividends.

Capital and foreign exchange controls
With the liberalization of capital movement at the end of 1992, there are currently no major restrictions. Foreign exchange deposits may be held in banks in Portugal, currency exchanges made, and exported from Portugal.

Take-over bids and large stakes
Available to all shareholders for the number of shares it intends to buy. The company may set a minimum acceptance limit for which the offer is valid. If a company tries to buy more than 50% of another company it must make a bid for all of the company's shares.

Brokers
There are nineteen brokers. It is only possible to do trades on the exchange through them. Most of the brokers were either created or acquired by commercial banks (which cannot themselves directly do brokerage). Brokers which can only act as agents are designated as "sociedades corretoras" (of which there are eleven) while "sociedades financeira de corretagem" (eight) may deal as principals.

Sectors
The biggest sectors by market capitalization and volume of trading are banking, retailing and construction, building materials and utilities. Also important are the beverage, glass and ceramics sectors as well as insurance.

ADRs
Several stocks are listed in New York, including PT, Cimpor, Portucel and BCP. However, liquidity in these stocks is usually much higher in Portugal.

Derivatives
Futures are traded between 09.45 and 16.45 at the Bolsa de Derivados do Porto (BDP). The contract, the PSI-20 Index Future, is traded in sizes of PSI-20 x PTE 100.

■ DEBT

The bond markets are regulated by the Security Exchange Commission, the Comissao Marcados Voloras Modiliareos (CMVM). Reforms were introduced in the two years following the liberalization of capital movements in December 1992.

Treasury bills
Discounted bills of 91,182 and 364 days are issued by the treasury and are sold through competitive auction. Auctions are normally held each week, on Thursday, Monday and Wednesday respectively. Details of auctions are announced a few days earlier, and bids are submitted to the treasury the day before.

Government bonds
OTs (Obrigações Tesouros)
Introduced in 1991, OTs are fixed rate bonds with 3-, 5-, 7- and 10-year maturities. Since 1994 they have been issued with annual coupons.

The Public Debt Office, the Junta de Credito Publico (JCP), administers auctions, which are held each Tuesday according to a monthly calendar, and which usually amount to about 25 billion escudos (US$170 million). The JCP auctions existing issues to help establish benchmarks.

Market makers (OEVTs) can make up to five bids at different yields. They can also buy additional bonds from the JCP at the cut-off price in the auction. The size of the OT market is about US$15,063 million.

FIPs and OTRVs
These are floating-rate notes which, although less liquid than OTs, make up more than half the volume of government bond issues.

Secondary market trading normally begins on the Lisbon Stock Exchange a week after auction, through an electronic-based system called Continuo. Larger orders above 175 million escudos (US$1.2 million) are transacted via Special Market for Bulk Transactions (MEOG). However, intra-day trading is not possible on MEOG – a dealer cannot sell bonds bought earlier the same day.

Most trades are settled domestically, through the National Clearing House, the Central de Valores Mobiliarios (CVM), four days after trade date. They can be settled through euroclear and cedel, but because the clearing houses do not have a direct link with the CVM, there is a two-day delay.

Withholding tax is 20%, but non-residents and some domestic institutions are exempt.

Corporate bonds
The introduction of Lisbon Interbank Offered Rate (LISBOR) in 1992 provides corporate borrowers with a reference rate, but the market is still in its infancy.

Caravelas bonds (navigator)
From the late 1980s, supranationals issued escudos denominated bonds, which, because they were tax free to non-residents, traded with lower yields than OTs. In 1992, foreign

holders of government bonds were also exempted from withholding tax, thereby reducing the appeal of navigator bonds.

Eurobonds

Portugal began to raise money in the international capital markets again in 1993 after a four-year absence. Since then it has been a regular borrower, issuing seventeen eurobonds in seven currencies.

Eurobond issues (US$m)

	1990	1991	1992	1993	1994	1995	1996
Sovereign	0.0	0.0	0.0	2544.9	2468.2	1908.4	2322.0
Private	0.0	373.4	173.8	150.0	1350.9	1208.8	45.4

Derivatives

The BDP (Bolsa de Derivados do Porto) futures market opened in June 1996. Its screen-based system is similar to the Spanish Meff-RF. Trading hours are 09.00 to 16.45pm.

The 10-year bond futures contract has a notional size of 10 billion escudos (US$70 million) and 8% coupon. The initial margin is 400 million escudos (US$2.7 million) per contract. Deliverable bonds have a minimum maturity of 6.5 years, and delivery dates are the third Wednesday in March, June, September and December.

The prospect of a more active repo market should help improve liquidity.

■ PORTUGAL: Economic indicators

Population and development	1990	1991	1992	1993	1994	1995	1996e
Population, million	9.9	9.9	9.9	9.9	9.9	9.9	9.9
Population growth, %	-0.4	-0.3	-0.1	0.1	0.5	-0.2	0.3
Nominal GDP per capita, US$	6792	7786	9856	8758	9056	10789	11110

National accounts							
Nominal GDP, US$bn	67.2	76.4	92.1	81.9	84.7	100.9	104.1
Change in real GDP, %	4.1	2.3	1.9	-1.1	0.7	1.9	2.5

Money supply and inflation							
Narrow money, change %, Dec/Dec	4.7	15.6	18.1	10.2	7.0	11.0	7.3
Broad money, change %, Dec/Dec	12.5	29.9	22.8	11.4	11.0	9.2	8.9
Consumer price inflation (avg.) %	13.4	11.4	8.9	6.8	4.9	4.0	3.0

Interest rates							
Money market rate, monthly average	13.12	15.5	17.48	13.25	10.62	8.91	7.20
Treasury bill rate, monthly average	13.51	14.2	14.59	11.06	8.37	8.38	7.00
Deposit rate, monthly average	13.99	14.8	14.59	11.06	8.37	8.38	7.00
Government bond yield, monthly average	18.55	18.27	15.38	12.45	10.83	11.23	8.28

Government finance							
Government expenditure, % of GDP	38.0	40.3	39.9	40.3	40.1	40.5	40.7
Government balance, % of GDP	-5.6	-6.7	-3.3	-6.9	-5.7	-5.2	-4.3
Government debt, % of GDP	65.5	70.2	62.4	67.3	69.6	71.7	71.0

Exchange rates *lc=local currency*							
Exchange rate, annual average, lc/US$	142.6	144.5	135.0	160.8	166.0	151.1	156.1
Exchange rate, end of year, lc/US$	133.6	134.2	146.8	176.8	159.1	149.4	155.0
Real exchange rate 1990=100	100.0	107.8	117.2	114.5	114.4	118.4	117.5

Balance of payments							
Exports of goods & services, US$m	21554	21622	23845	22777	25396	32101	33578
Change %	29.6	0.3	10.3	-4.5	11.5	26.4	4.6
Imports of goods & services, US$m, fob	27146	28499	32467	29462	32185	38949	40896
Change %	33.0	5.0	13.9	-9.3	9.2	21.0	5.0
Trade balance, of goods only, US$m, fob-fob	-6683	-7688	-9387	-8050	-8078	-8485	-9005
Current account balance, US$m	-181	-716	-184	233	-1505	-299	-490
as a % of GDP	-0.3	-0.9	-0.2	0.3	-1.8	-0.3	-4.9

Foreign exchange reserves							
Foreign exchange reserves, US$m	14485	20629	19129	15840	15513	15850	17851
Gold at ⅔ of market price, US$m	4070	3828	3673	3848	4112	4112	4149
Import cover (reserves/imports), months	6.4	8.7	7.1	6.5	5.8	4.9	9.0

Foreign debt and debt service							
Short-term debt, US$m	6466	8429	9948	12306	14337	14988	16057
Total foreign debt, US$m	23994	28710	27859	31450	33845	34661	36625
as a % of GDP	35.7	37.6	30.2	38.4	40.0	34.3	35.2
as a % of foreign exchange receipts	81.8	97.8	91.6	89.2	100.6	98.9	81.9
Interest payments, US$m	1378	1268	1299	2308	1940	1720	1910
Principal repayments, US$m	2469	4766	5087	4947	5060	4710	4160
Total debt service, US$m	3847	6034	6386	7255	7000	6430	6070
as a % of goods exports	23.4	36.8	34.8	45.5	37.6	26.9	24.3
as a % of foreign exchange receipts	13.1	15.3	12.0	25.7	24.8	16.2	21.3

Romania

Area (thousands of km²):	238
Population (1995, millions):	22.6
Population projection (2025, millions):	23
Population younger than 15 yrs (1991, % of total):	23.1
Urbanization rate (1993, % of population):	55
Life expectancy (1993, years at birth):	70
Gross domestic product (1996, US$bn):	32.5
GDP per capita (1996, US$):	1435
Average annual GDP growth rate (1990-96, %):	-1.5
Average annual inflation rate (1990-96, %):	120.3
Currency (leu per US$, average 1996):	3550
Structure of production (1994):	46% services, 33% industry, 21% agriculture
Main exports:	manufactures, fuels, non-fuel primary products
Main imports:	manufactures, fuels, non-fuel primary products
Main trading partners:	Former Soviet Union, Germany, Italy, France, Austria
Total foreign debt (% of GDP):	23.8
Credit rating: (Nov 1996, Standard & Poor's, Moody's)	BB-; Ba3

FORECAST: 1997-2000 (average)

	Worst case	Most likely	Best case
Real GDP growth (%)	below 0	2 to 4	5 to 7
Inflation (%)	above 55	20 to 55	below 20

■ POLITICS

Historical overview

Modern Romania was formed under the Treaty of Berlin in 1878 and recognized as a kingdom in 1881. The new kingdom did not unite all ethnic Romanians, as Transylvania remained in Hungary, and Bessarabia (today's Republic of Moldova) remained under Russian control.

In 1916 Romania entered the First World War on the side of Britain, France and Russia. With the defeat of Austria-Hungary in 1918, Banat, Transylvania and Bucovina were unified. These territorial acquisitions doubled the country's size, but between the two world wars it failed to integrate and develop them.

In June 1941 Romania joined Germany's invasion of the Soviet Union but later switched sides. At the end of the war, Romania ceded Bessarabia and northern Bucovina to the USSR, southern Dobrogea to Bulgaria, and northern Transylvania to Hungary. The country fell under Communist rule until 1989, after the forced abdication of King Michael in 1947.

From 1964 the country's undisputed leader, Nicolae Ceausescu, and members of his family developed a concentration of power and a personality cult unparalleled in Eastern Europe since Stalin. This era ended with the fall of Communism in December 1989, and the trial and execution of Ceausescu and his wife.

After the fall of Ceausescu, the National Salvation Front (NSF), an umbrella organization of groups from all points of the political spectrum took power. Ion Iliescu, a former official and then opponent of the Romanian Communist Party, became president. In the subsequent first free election in May 1990, Iliescu was elected president, with 85% of the popular vote, and the NSF won 67% of the seats in the bicameral parliament. Petre Roman was appointed prime minister.

In March 1992 the NSF split and Roman, who had resigned in September 1991, remained NSF leader. The breakaway NSF members formed the Democratic National Salvation Front (DNSF) and supported Iliescu. The DNSF, which is now known as the Party of Social Democracy of Romania (PSDR), emerged as the largest party in the September 1992 general elections, with 34% of the seats in parliament. Iliescu was re-elected as president in October 1992 and Nicolae Vacaroiu appointed prime minister of a minority government. Other important parties are the National Liberal Party, the former NSF (DP-NSF) and the Hungarian Democratic Union of Romania (HDUR).

The prime minister's programme, which he describes as "social democratic" and "a combination of liberalism and elements of marked social protection", seeks to ease social decline and open the economy, with less government control. The government tried several times to pass reform programmes through legislation, but was hindered by opposition groups. Despite a strong opposition and regular no-confidence attempts in parliament, Vacaroiu's minority government survived until 1996.

Recent events

In the November 1996 parliamentary elections, the ruling PSDR was soundly defeated by the Democratic Convention (CDR). Two weeks later CDR leader Emil Constantinescu won the presidential elections over Iliescu, and the CDR formed a coalition government with Petre Roman's Social Democratic Union (USD). The result reflected voter dissatisfaction with the economy. Despite the economic reforms started under Iliescu, the average worker has seen little gain. The results are also expected to lead to improved relations with Romania's neighbouring Hungary.

Chronology

1878	Treaty of Berlin: Romania is recognized as an independent state
1919-20	Romania absorbs Bessarabia, Bucovina, Transylvania, Banat and Crisana-Maramures
1940	Bessarabia and northern Bucovina are ceded to the USSR, southern Dobrogea to Bulgaria and northern Transylvania to Hungary

1941	Romania joins German invasion of the USSR
1944	Romania joins the Allies after pro-German Prime Minister Antonescu is arrested
1944	Soviet troops in Romania
1945	Soviet-controlled government
1967	Nicolae Ceausescu elected First Secretary of the Romanian Workers' Party (later Romanian Communist Party)
1968	Romania refuses to join Warsaw Pact's suppression in Czechoslovakia
1971	Admitted to GATT
1972	Admitted to IMF and World Bank
1989	December 22-25: after civil unrest, Ceausescu and his wife try to flee, but are captured and executed
1989	December 26: Ion Iliescu declared president and Petre Roman prime minister
1990	First free elections

Constitution and government

The Romanian National Assembly adopted a new constitution in November 1991, subsequently approved in a national referendum. The constitution guarantees private property rights and a market economy. Legislative power is based on a bicameral parliament consisting of the 341-seat Chamber of Deputies and the 143-seat Senate. Members of parliament are elected for four years. Members are elected on the basis of proportional representation. There is a constitutional court.

The president is elected by direct vote for four years, can only be elected for two terms and may not belong to a political party after taking office. The prime minister is appointed by the president and on a vote of confidence by the parliament. The president may dissolve parliament and can call a referendum on matters of national interest.

Current government

Head of State	Emil Constantinescu
Prime Minister	Victor Ciorbea
Finance Minister	Mircea Ciumara
Foreign Affairs Minister	Adrian Severin
Defence Minister	Victor Babiuc
Governor, central bank	Mugur Isarescu

Political parties

Democratic Convention (CDR)

Winner of the November 1996 election. Formed the current coalition government with its major partner, the Social Democratic Union. Market-orientated, strongly pro-reform and centre-right.

Emil Constantinescu succeeded Iliescu as president.

Party of Social Democracy in Romania (PSDR)

Emerged from the former Democratic National Salvation Front; formed by Iliescu after the fall of the old regime. United many of the former state party members.

Social Democratic Union (USD)
> Pro-reform; centre-left.
> Led by Petre Roman, the first post-Communist prime minister.

Hungarian Democratic Union (UDMR)
> Formed by minority Hungarians to represent their interests. Based in Transylvania.

Results of the November 1996 election

	Senate	Deputies
Democratic Convention (CDR)	30.7 %	30.1 %
Party of Social Democracy (PSDR)	23.0 %	21.5 %
Social Democratic Union (USD)	13.1 %	12.9 %
Hungarian Democratic Union (UDMR)	6.8 %	6.6 %
Greater Romania Party (PRM)	4.5 %	4.4 %
National Unity Party (PRM)	4.2 %	4.3 %

■ ECONOMICS

Historical overview

State planning and nationalization followed the Communist take-over in 1947. Romania's economy was traditionally agricultural, with 75% of the population engaged in farming in 1950. By 1990 this had fallen to 28%.

Under Ceausescu, industrial growth was a priority. The economy became strongly linked to those of the COMECON bloc. In the 1970s, import-orientated growth resulted in a buildup of foreign debt, eliminated in a harsh and costly pay-back scheme in the 1980s. Most foreign exchange receipts were used for debt reduction at the cost of further industrial investment and modernization. As a result, most industrial installations were outdated by the time the Ceausescu regime collapsed.

The transformation from a centrally planned to a market-orientated economy has been difficult. Under Iliescu, moves towards privatization and market reform were often hindered by concerns over the high social costs of re-structuring. Half-hearted reform led to a longer economic decline than in other Eastern European transition economies.

Romania's economic performance

	Average annual real GDP growth, %	Average annual consumer price inflation, %
1991-1995	-1.9	160.3

The economy

Industry accounts for roughly one third of GDP and agriculture one fifth. The service sector is growing, and natural resources such as coal, oil and gas are also important. Trade accounts for 11% of GDP and transport/communications for 6.5%. Real GDP growth fell from -5.6% in 1990 to -8.8% in 1992, but has showed positive growth since then, peaking in 1995 at 6.9%. The pace slowed to around 4.8% in 1996, and is expected to slow further, to 3%, in 1997.

Unemployment rose from virtually nil in 1991 to almost 10% in 1996, and there have been regular strikes. Although economic indicators have shown impressive growth, the average worker has seen little gain. Inflation remains on a high level, but has been significantly reduced. Inflation reached a record level of over 250% in 1993, but has now slowed to 35%.

Share of GDP by sector

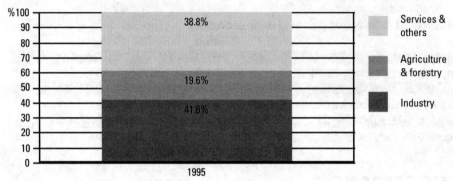

Source: Official data

Trade

With the changes in the Romanian economy, trade patterns, too, have altered. Exports more than doubled between 1991 and 1996, from US$3.2 billion to US$6.9 billion. Germany is now Romania's largest trading partner, accounting for 17.8% of exports in 1995, followed by Italy (15.6%). Russia, once its main trading partner, now accounts for only 1.9% of exports compared with exports to the EU of 53.5%. However, Russia still accounts for 12.6% of imports, reflecting the supply of gas, crude oil and raw materials. There is a persistent trade deficit and the current account has also shown a deficit since 1990. This currently stands at some US$1 billion, and is unlikely to change in the foreseeable future.

Imports and exports as a % of GDP

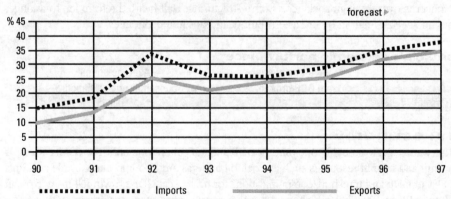

Source: Official data

Breakdown of exports (1995)

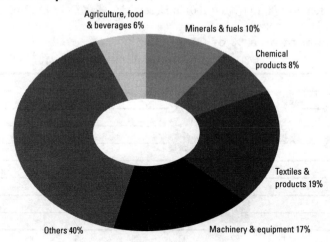

Agriculture, food
& beverages 6%

Minerals & fuels 10%

Chemical
products 8%

Textiles &
products 19%

Machinery & equipment 17%

Others 40%

Source: Official data

Privatization

A focal point of economic restructuring has been privatization. Although the government announced large-scale privatization plans, progress has been slow. The old guard, strongly represented in the Iliescu era, were reluctant to push quick reforms, while pro-reform groups, supported by international organizations, have advocated speedy action.

Privatization started in 1993 with small companies. As a result, 80% of industrial output was still being produced by large state-controlled companies in 1995. A voucher-based privatization scheme started in September 1995, covering about 4,000 companies. At the start of 1996, some 1,500 companies had been privatized while 5,500 remain in state ownership. Most privatized companies have been sold to the old management, adding almost no new capital or technology.

So far large public monopolies such as power, telecommunications, oil and gas have not been part of privatization. Foreign direct investment has been minimal. Foreign companies have bought only three major manufacturing concerns. Foreign investment is deterred by slow bureaucracy, an unfriendly business environment and uncertainty over laws and government policies. The new government has announced a more investor-friendly environment.

Fiscal and monetary policy

Economic decline has produced higher budget deficits, rising from 2.8% of GDP in 1993 to 3.5% in 1996. In recent years the government financed these deficits mainly through external loans and treasury bill issues bought by domestic banks. On the revenue side, tax evasion and tax arrears caused by illiquidity are a major concern. On the expenditure side, increases in pensions and wages have put a heavy burden on the budget.

The national currency, the leu, has been under constant pressure in the last two years. After a period of stabilization in 1994, the lack of foreign exchange reserves and growing current account deficit pushed down the value of the leu substantially. The election period in 1996 added to uncertainty, further lowering the value of the leu. The real effective exchange rate fell from 90.1 (1,990 = 100) in December 1994 to 78.8 in 1996.

Current account as a % of GDP

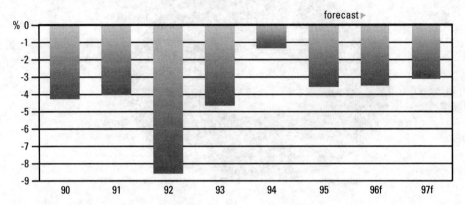

Source: Official data; UBS estimates

Romanian leu/US dollar exchange rate

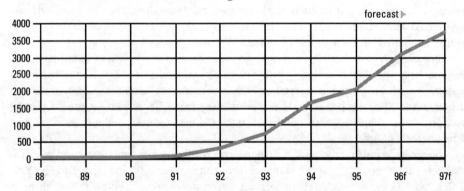

Debt

Romania's net foreign debt has increased substantially since 1990. After the old regime's painful pay-back period, Romania raised its total foreign debt from US$1.2 billion (3.1% of GDP) in 1990 to US$7.7 billion (23.8%) in 1996.

About one third of debt was borrowed from international financial institutions (the IMF, IBRD and others), another third from official bilateral creditors and the rest from commercial banks and private creditors. Further debt growth will be inevitable, given the substantial current account deficits.

While the relative debt burden is still considerable, but manageable, Romania has access to the international markets and in 1996 acquired credit ratings just below investment grade from major agencies (Moody's: Ba3 / Standard & Poor's: BB-).

■ EQUITIES

Index performance
There is no index in Romania.

Background
The original Bucharest Stock Exchange (BSE) was established in 1882, but its current version, prohibited under Communism, re-opened in 1995. The OTC market was officially opened in September 1996 and is still in its early stages. The mass privatization programme will involve the sale of almost four thousand companies. These will be initially traded on the OTC market, but there are no restrictions preventing them from eventually being listed on the BSE. In late 1996, the BSE had a market capitalization of around ROL147 billion (US$45 million).

Structure
There are two markets in Romania: the BSE (which is further divided between the higher "first tier" and the "base tier") and the non-regulated OTC market. There are fourteen securities listed on the BSE with a total market capitalization of around US$55 billion. All companies are currently listed in the "base" category with none yet meeting the more stringent requirements of the "first tier".

Regulatory authority
The BSE is regulated by the National Securities Commission (CNVM).

Trading methods
The BSE uses a computerized order-driven system, and trading is continuous. Each session comprises two stages: pre-opening and actual trading. Pre-opening clears the market at the opening price, seeking to maximize volume. Investment by non-residents must be made on the basis of an application to the Romanian Development Agency. On registration the foreign investor receives a Certificate of Investor, enabling them to invest in the Exchange via brokers.

Hours
Trading takes place between 09.30 to 10.00 (opening) and 10.00 and 10.30 (continuous trading), twice weekly on Tuesdays and Thursdays.

Settlement time and clearing
Settlement takes place on a trade date plus three business days (T+3) basis. No margin or short selling is permitted.

Limits on price movement
Shares are not permitted to fluctuate by more than 10% from the daily opening trading price.

Types of shares
Ordinary shares are traded on the BSE.

Stock indices

The BSE currently produces no indices, but there are plans to introduce one.

Taxes

Capital gains are tax-free and there are no stamp duties. However, profits are taxed at 38% and dividends at 10%.

Disclosure of financial statements

Companies listed on the Exchange are obliged to publish annual and semi-annual statements.

Ownership limits for non-residents

There are no ownership limits for foreigners in Romania, but investors are obliged to take certain steps when they own a "significant" shareholding position (5% of capital/voting rights), a "control" position (30%) or a "majority" position (more than 50%).

On achieving the "significant" position, the investor must inform the BSE and CNVM, and make subsequent trading public.

Upon reaching the "control" position, the investor must make a public offer. Finally, upon reaching a "majority" position, the investor must make a public offer for all the shares of the issuer in circulation.

Capital and foreign exchange controls

Repatriation of profits requires clearing authority from the National Bank of Romania.

Brokers

The BSE has sixty members of which thirty-nine are authorized to trade. In accordance with CNVM rules, brokers can charge up to a maximum commission rate of 8%.

Sectors

Turnover on the Exchange is dominated by Azomures, a chemicals company. Other companies occupying a significant portion of turnover are Sanevit (a precision engineering company) and Foraj Sondes (involved in oil and gas drilling).

ADRs

There are no Romanian ADRs.

Derivatives

There is no derivatives market in Romania.

■ DEBT

The National Bank of Romania (BNR) regulates the country's developing treasury bill market. The first auction for fifty years was held in April 1994, and raised more than 327 billion lei (US$185 million) to part-finance 1993's budget deficit, through the issue of 91-day bills. Subsequent issues have also been for 3 months.

In August 1995, the BNR set rules for the start-up of open market operations, which will allow banks to use bills and other future government securities as collateral for credits from the central bank. This move has encouraged the growth of secondary market trading in these instruments.

Domestic banks and their clients, insurance companies and unit trusts can bid in auctions, which are held twice a month. Foreigners cannot participate. T-bill yields are lower than the average weighted interest rate of interbank operations. Significant end-buyers of bills include state funds, for example the social insurance fund, which run large surpluses.

In August 1996, Romania issued a US$104 million hard currency bond which was placed with local banks. It had a 366-day maturity and paid interest of 7.1% to produce a yield spread of 250 basis points over libor.

Eurobonds

In 1996 Romania launched its first international bond issues for half a century. In May it issued a 52-billion yen samurai, and in the following month it raised US$225 million with a 3-year eurodollar priced to yield 305 basis points over US treasuries. The bond was rated BB- by Standard and Poor's and Ba3 by Moody's.

Eurobond issues (US$m)

	1990	1991	1992	1993	1994	1995	1996
Sovereign	—	—	—	—	—	—	769.1
Private	—	—	—	—	—	—	—

ROMANIA: Economic indicators

Population and development	1990	1991	1992	1993	1994	1995	1996e
Population, million	23.2	23.2	22.8	22.7	22.6	22.6	22.6
Population growth, %	0.3	-0.1	-1.9	-0.3	-0.2	0.0	0.0
Nominal GDP per capita, US$	1648	1247	860	1163	1329	1570	1435

National accounts	1990	1991	1992	1993	1994	1995	1996e
Nominal GDP, US$bn	38.3	28.9	19.6	26.4	30.1	35.5	32.5
Change in real GDP, %	-5.6	-12.9	-8.8	1.5	3.9	6.9	4.8
Gross fixed capital formation, % of GDP	30.2	28.0	31.4	29.0	26.9	25.7	21.0

Money supply and inflation	1990	1991	1992	1993	1994	1995	1996e
Narrow money, change %, Dec/Dec	13.7	221.2	41.6	95.0	107.8	64.7	40.0
Broad money, change %, Dec/Dec	25.1	101.0	73.6	152.2	135.9	71.0	50.0
Consumer price inflation (avg.) %	7.4	166.6	210.0	256.1	136.8	32.2	36.4

Interest rates	1990	1991	1992	1993	1994	1995	1996e
Discount rate, end of period	—	—	—	—	—	66.90	41.30
Deposit rate, annual average	—	—	—	151.50	44.90	57.00	36.50

Government finance	1990	1991	1992	1993	1994	1995	1996e
Government expenditure, % of GDP	31.4	24.2	26.9	20.6	21.9	21.9	24.0
Government balance, % of GDP	-2.8	-1.9	-4.4	-2.8	-3.5	-4.1	-3.5

Exchange rates lc=local currency	1990	1991	1992	1993	1994	1995	1996e
Exchange rate, annual average, lc/US$	22.4	76.2	308	760	1655	2033	3100
Exchange rate, end of year, lc/US$	34.8	186	460	1276	1767	2578	3550
Real exchange rate 1990=100	100	72.8	57.8	81.0	71.5	78.7	—

Balance of payments	1990	1991	1992	1993	1994	1995	1996e
Exports of goods & services, US$m	3908	3969	4997	5676	7291	9094	8640
Change %	-34.5	1.6	25.9	13.6	28.5	24.7	-5.0
Imports of goods & services, US$m, fob	5671	5340	6746	7130	8002	10799	10100
Change %	66.5	-5.8	26.3	5.7	12.2	35.0	-6.5
Trade balance, of goods only, US$m, fob-fob	-1743	-1254	-1373	-1130	-411	-1231	-1040
Current account balance, US$m	-1657	-1182	-1685	-1240	-428	-1336	-1050
as a % of GDP	-4.3	-4.1	-8.6	-4.7	-1.4	-3.8	-3.2

Foreign exchange reserves	1990	1991	1992	1993	1994	1995	1996e
Foreign exchange reserves, US$m	524	209	96	42	592	334	926
Gold at ⅔ of market price, US$m	567.6	542.0	527.7	567.8	671.7	691.6	697.9
Import cover (reserves/imports), months	1.1	0.5	0.2	0.1	0.9	0.4	1.1

Foreign debt and debt service	1990	1991	1992	1993	1994	1995	1996e
Short-term debt, US$m	973	1279	693	892	966	1266	1334
Total foreign debt, US$m	1203	2528	3143	4249	5490	6550	7744
as a % of GDP	3.1	8.7	16.1	16.1	18.2	18.4	23.8
as a % of foreign exchange receipts	30.0	60.8	62.1	72.1	72.5	69.2	85.6
Interest payments, US$m	5	77	144	204	233	293	405
Principal repayments, US$m	4	13	300	148	404	796	990
Total debt service, US$m	9	90	444	352	637	1089	1395
as a % of goods exports	0.3	2.8	10.4	7.2	10.4	14.5	20.0
as a % of foreign exchange receipts	0.2	2.2	8.8	6.0	8.4	11.5	15.4

Russia

Area (thousands of km²):	17075
Population (1995, millions):	147.9
Population projection (2025, millions):	153
Population younger than 15 yrs (1991, % of total):	22.6
Urbanization rate (1993, % of population):	75
Life expectancy (1993, years at birth):	65
Gross domestic product (1996, US$bn):	475.7
GDP per capita (1996, US$):	3305
Average annual GDP growth rate (1990-96, %):	-9.2
Average annual inflation rate (1990-96, %):	439.1
Currency (rouble per US$, average 1996):	5123
Structure of production (1994):	55% services, 38% industry, 7% agriculture
Main exports:	fuels, metals & raw material
Main imports:	machinery & equipment, foodstuff, chemicals
Main trading partners:	EU, Eastern European countries
Market capitalization of Stock Exchange (December 1996; US$bn):	37.2
Total foreign debt (% of GDP):	23.9
Next elections due under normal circumstances:	legislative required by December 1999
Credit rating: (Jan 1997, Standard & Poor's, Moody's)	BB-; Ba2

FORECAST: 1997-2000 (average)

	Worst case	Most likely	Best case
Real GDP growth (%)	3.5	4.0	4.5
Inflation (%)	20	13	10

■ POLITICS

Historical overview

Kievan Rus, founded in 862 in present-day Ukraine, was the first independent Slavonic state in the region. The first centralized and fully independent Russian state, Moscovy principality, emerged at the end of 15th century, after almost three centuries of domination by the Tatars. Over the following two centuries the Russian state gradually strengthened and expanded its territory.

In the 18th century, the development of Russia accelerated rapidly under Peter the Great, and there was a drive to "Westernize" the country. Civil and military institutions were modernized and there was a notable increase in trade. The gains of the Russian empire, formally established in 1721, were consolidated in the latter part of the century during the reign of Catherine the Great. By the early 19th century Russia had come to be seen as a great European power. Economically and institutionally, however, it still lagged behind the West.

In 1905, following Russia's defeat in the war against Japan, widespread strikes and demonstrations forced Tsar Nicolas II to introduce limited political reforms setting up a parliament ("duma"). Subsequent reforms between 1906 and 1911 resulted in high economic growth. However, the reforms were derailed by the outbreak of the First World War, and Russia's only period of democratic rule prior to 1991 came to an end.

Tsarist rule collapsed in March 1917 and after a short-lived government of social democrats, power was usurped by the Communists in November 1917. The Russian Federation was proclaimed as the successor to the Russian empire, and in 1922 the Union of Soviet Socialist Republics was formed, in which the Russian Federation became the dominant force.

For the next seventy years the Soviet Union pursued hardline Communist policies, during which the private ownership of the means of production was outlawed and any public dissent to government policies suppressed. High economic growth in the first few decades of Communist rule was achieved by diverting massive resources to strategic projects, especially the military-industrial complex. Great strides were made in education and health. Consumer goods, however, were neglected and of poor quality. On the whole, the Soviet system proved to be inherently inefficient as well as repressive, reflected in chronic shortages of the most basic goods.

By the time Mikhail Gorbachev came to power in the 1980s, the USSR's economy was already stagnating. After several years of attempted reform, the Soviet Union disintegrated in 1991.

Recent events

Russia emerged as one of fifteen newly independent republics, inheriting the international assets and liabilities of the former Soviet Union. In June 1991, Boris Yeltsin became the first Russian head of state to be democratically elected.

In the presidential elections of June 1996, Yeltsin gained 35% of the vote against the 32% of his Communist rival, Gennady Zyuganov. General Alexander Lebed received 15% and liberal reformer Grigory Yavlinksy 7%, while nationalist Vladimir Zhirinovsky's share fell under 6%.

In the run-off, Yeltsin triumphed with 54% of the vote, albeit with Lebed on his team as national security adviser. Russia's democratic process was strengthened by virtue of the elections being held as scheduled, and perceived as free and fair.

They alleviated fears that Russia would abandon its reform policies and withdraw into a narrow nationalism. However, given concerns about President Yeltsin's health, speculation as to his succession came to the fore soon after his re-election for a four-year term. A few months after Yeltsin's election victory, Lebed was dismissed from the administration. At the end of 1996 opinion polls placed Lebed well ahead of other Russian politicians.

Chronology

15th century Consolidation of Russian domains into centralized state
1686-1725   Reign of Peter the Great who significantly modernized the country and established the
                 Russian Empire

1762-1796	Under the rule of Catherine II, the Russian Empire expands, becoming a powerful state in Europe
1855-1881	First significant legal, administrative and economic reforms are introduced by Alexander II. However, the reforms still lag behind those in the West at the time.
1905	Uprisings and strikes, followed by the Russia's defeat in war with Japan. Tsar is forced to introduce a parliament (Duma).
1917	Revolution sweeps away the old order. Communism rules for the next seven decades.
1922	The Soviet Union is established. Russia becomes one of fifteen Soviet republics.
1985	Mikhail Gorbachev becomes head of the USSR. Political and economic reforms are introduced.
1991	USSR disintegrates. Russian Federation inherits international assets and liabilities of the USSR. Boris Yeltsin is elected president.
1992	Authorities start radical economic reforms.
1993	New constitution replaces Communist-era government structures
1995	Dissatisfaction over inconsistent implementation of economic reforms, in particular high inflation and declining living standards, produces strong showing for the Communists in parliamentary elections
1996	Boris Yeltsin re-elected as president

State organization

For a time during 1992 and 1993 it appeared as though the Russian Federation itself might break up into various regions, with some of the richer areas evaluating the benefits of leaving the federation.

In addition, Tatarstan and Chechnya refused to sign the federation treaty on the supremacy of the Russian federal government. The 1993 constitution states that the Russian Federation consists of twenty-one republics, sixty-six provinces of varying status and two cities with an autonomous provincial status (Moscow and St Petersburg). Eight of Russia's twenty-one autonomous republics have signed special treaties with Moscow. The treaty with Tatarstan declares that Tatarstan is a sovereign state, associated with Russia on the basis of the constitutions of the two states. A peace agreement was negotiated with Chechnya in August 1996. According to the agreement, the region's future political status will be decided in five years' time.

Constitution and government

In December 1993, about 60% of the country's voters approved a newly drafted constitution to replace the 1978 Soviet constitution. The new constitution created a presidential republic, with powers separated along executive, legislative and judicial branches. The president and the members of parliament are directly elected by the people in separate elections. Unlike most of his Western counterparts, however, the Russian president retains enormous powers.

The president:
◆ proposes candidates for top government posts;
◆ has control over foreign policy, defence and state security;
◆ can issue decrees and call referendums;
◆ can declare war on other countries and states of emergency in Russia;

◆ can reject a vote of no confidence in the government by the legislature;
◆ has the power to dismiss the government without the approval of the legislature;
◆ can dissolve the legislature and call new elections;
◆ acts as final arbiter in conflicts between the republics which comprise the Russian Federation, as well as between these republics and the federation. (The president, therefore, also has some judicial powers.)

Legislature

This consists of the State Duma (lower house) with 450 elected members and a Federation Council (upper house) of 178 members, which represent Russia's 89 regions. The legislature has the power to impeach the president, although the procedure is cumbersome. It can oppose the nomination for prime minister (but then faces being dissolved by the president). The Duma can initiate legislation and vote on the government's fiscal and monetary policies, but in case of a deadlock, the president has the upper hand.

Members of the legislature are elected according to separate "party" and "individual" lists. Half the seats in the Duma are reserved for parties obtaining 5% or more of the vote.

The prime minister is appointed by the president and approved by the State Duma. Viktor Chernomyrdin was re-appointed prime minister in 1996. In the case of the president becoming incapacitated, the prime minister temporarily assumes the presidential functions. New elections have to be held within three months of this transfer of power.

Current government

President	Boris Yeltsin
Prime Minister	Victor Chernomyrdin
Finance Minister	Alexander Livshits
Presidential Chief of Staff	Anatoly Chubais
Governor, central bank	Sergei Dubinin

Political parties

Communist Party of the Russian Federation

Re-launched in 1993, following the banning of the Communist Party of the Soviet Union. Became the single largest party in the Duma in 1995 with 149 seats (22% of the total vote).
"Reformed" Communists.
Led by Gennady Zyuganov.

Liberal Democratic Party of Russia

Founded in 1990. Won 11% of the vote in 1995 (down from 23% in 1993); i.e. 51 seats in the Duma.
Far-right, nationalists.
Led by Vladimir Zhirinovsky.

Our Home is Russia

Founded in 1995. Gained 10% of the vote (55 seats).
Centrist.
Led by Victor Chernomyrdin (current prime minister).

Yabloko
> Founded in 1993.
> Gained 7% of the vote in 1995 (46 seats).
> Centrist, pro-reform.
> Led by Grigory Yavlinsky.

Other parties include **Russian Regions** (42 seats), the **Agrarian Party** (35), and the **Popular Party** (37). Another 35 deputies are not registered in a faction. The Russian party system is still in flux and is likely to look distinctly different at the time of the next elections.

The judiciary

The Constitutional Court is the main arbiter between the executive and the legislature. The rest of the judiciary consists of a Supreme Court and lower courts. The Constitutional Court has a complicated task because of a lack of clarity on the conflicting status of presidential decrees and laws. This leaves open the possibility of ongoing legislative battles between the executive and the legislature.

Central bank

Russia's central bank was established in 1989, but its role in providing inflationary credits to finance the government's budget led to an amendment of the law in 1995. The new law proclaims the bank's independence and places restrictions on issuing credits to the government. The governor of the bank is nominated by the president and confirmed by the State Duma. The appointment lasts four years and the governor cannot be removed for reasons other than violating federal laws or the bank's charter.

■ ECONOMICS

Russia's changing economy

Since the demise of the Soviet Union, the composition of the Russian economy has undergone drastic changes. Agriculture officially now accounts for only about 8% of GDP, nearly half its share five years earlier, industry is down to 31% of GDP, from nearly 40%, while services have expanded to nearly 50%, up from 37% of GDP in the same period. Most services now originate in the private sector.

Russia is rich in natural resources. The country is estimated to have over one third of world gas reserves, nearly 12% of coal reserves and 5% of the world's oil reserves. It is a significant producer of nickel, platinum and palladium.

Population

With a population of 147.9 million (1995), the Russian Federation accounts for about 50% of the total population of the former USSR. The annual growth rate of the population averaged 0.7% in the 1970s and 1980s, but turned negative in the early 1990s.

Although about 82% of population is ethnically Russian, the Russian Federation includes dozens of other nationalities including Tatars (3.8%), Ukrainians (3%) and Belorussians (0.8%).

Share of GDP by sector

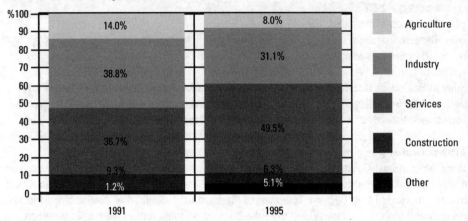

Source: Official data

The end of GDP contraction

Since 1989 Russia's GDP has contracted each year, so that in 1996 it was less than half of its size in 1989, according to official statistics. A number of overlapping causes generated the disintegration of the economy of the former Soviet Union, notably the progressive weakening of the centrally planned linkages and growing chaos as enterprises had to seek new suppliers and customers. The GDP contraction accelerated with the 1992 stabilization programme, which curtailed subsidies and liberalized prices. In the initial phases of the post-Soviet depression, energy, steel, heavy engineering and defence sectors contracted most, but light industry followed suit as consumers preferred imported goods. In 1996 official GDP figures showed the economy declining by 6%, compared with 4% in 1995 and nearly 13% in 1994.

Then again, Russia's economy may have been growing for the last two years, as official data on economic trends are incomplete. The expanding private sector is captured in the statistics only to a minor degree, in part for technical reasons (Goskomstat, the organization responsible for providing Russia's official statistics, is ill-equipped to follow the rapidly expanding private sector), in part because of tax evasion. The size of Russia's informal or uncounted economy is estimated by the authorities at up to 40% of GDP, compared to 5% or 10% for the Western industrial economies. There are indications that, with few exceptions, private-sector companies have been growing since 1994, some very rapidly. Yet a sizeable proportion (perhaps well over 50%) of private sector production, sales and profits are not reported to Goskomstat and, therefore, are not reflected in the official statistics.

Monetary and fiscal policies

Price stabilization is a key issue in Russia's economic recovery. After the collapse of the Soviet Union in 1989, Russia continued to supply cheap credits to other former Soviet republics and to the state enterprises which kept on producing unsaleable products even while inventories were accumulating. The budget deficit of 11% in 1992, mainly caused by the price liberalization in the beginning of the year, together with an increase in the broad money supply of around 550% produced a huge inflation of over 1,500% in 1992. In the course of 1993 the rouble zone disintegrated after Russia imposed a measure of fiscal discipline and reduced the fiscal deficit to 7% of GDP, but the money supply still increased by over 400%. When in 1994 the budget deficit again reached over 10% of GDP, the run on the rouble by Russia's emerging financial markets late that year convinced the government to return to a restrictive fiscal policy, and 1995 ended with a federal deficit of 4% of GDP. Similarly, the central bank followed a more restrictive monetary policy after the rouble crisis, and the expansion of the money supply was reduced from over 200% in 1994 to 130% in 1995.

In 1996, the fiscal deficit crept up again to an estimated 5% of GDP (using the government definition which excludes interest on certain government debt instruments), due to the declining tax base in the "official" economy. Thus, the most urgent structural problem in 1996 was insufficient tax collection. At the same time pressures for higher expenditures increased, in part related to the elections. Substantial arrears to miners, pensioners and others aggravated social problems.

The effect on consumer prices of tighter fiscal and monetary policies was a drastic reduction from the over 300% increase in 1994 to 200% in 1995. In 1996 inflation averaged around 50%, ending the year at close to 20%.

Inflation

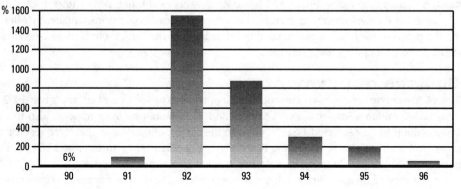

Source: Official data

Privatization

The privatization of state enterprises on a large scale was launched in the autumn of 1992 through vouchers distributed to all citizens. These vouchers could be exchanged for shares in enterprises, transferred to an investment fund, or sold for cash.

Bidding for shares in these enterprises began in December 1992 and ended in June 1994. By mid-1995, 116,400 firms of all sizes, about 70% of the total, had been formally transferred to "private" ownership, employing 90% of the labour force. However, in many instances, this simply meant the designation of managers and employees as partial owners with the state continuing to hold large or controlling interests in these companies. In the aggregate, the state still owned about one third of the industrial sector, as measured by the official statistics.

Privatization targets in 1996 included the sale of residual state-owned shares in at least a thousand of the partially privatized enterprises and the outright sale of at least five major companies. Restructuring of many formally privatized companies has been lagging, as the managers have done little to improve efficiency, relying instead on privileged relations with the government. Urban real estate, now under the control of local governments, is to be privatized to make it more accessible to private businesses.

The banking sector and stock market

The banking sector has undergone fundamental changes as the monolithic Soviet-style state banks broke up, many of their branches made into independent banks or closed and a large number of private banks created. At the end of 1995, 2,250 commercial banks were registered in Russia, but well over 150 lost their licences in 1996 as they failed to meet capitalization requirements. The banking system remains undercapitalized, oversized and illiquid. The number of banks is expected to shrink substantially in the next few years as banks consolidate or fold. The central bank is improving bank regulation and supervision.

The privatization programme by voucher distribution created some 40 million shareholders, thereby providing propitious conditions for the emergence of stock markets. The first stock market opened in 1991 in Moscow and by 1995 some one hundred trading places were in operation. The range and volume of securities traded has been rapidly expanding, although inadequate regulation and custody registration systems have hampered development. A Commission for Securities and Stock Market was established late in 1994.

Russian equities remain undervalued relative to international norms, apparently offering the potential for large capital gains if the risk discount declines, there is greater political stability and economic growth resumes.

Balance of payments

Russia's exports to convertible currency markets have expanded substantially since 1992, from US$26 billion to an estimated US$69 billion in 1996, but so have imports, also from US$26 billion to an estimated US$51 billion in the same period. Russia therefore recorded substantial trade surpluses, increasing from near balance in 1992 to an estimated US$18 billion in 1996. With rapidly rising imports, this surplus is expected to decline.

The general trends indicate that a rapid expansion of trade with partners in convertible currency areas is taking place, with the trade surplus being counterbalanced by an increasing deficit on services, so that the current account is heading for balance or even deficit again in the short term. On the capital account, lending by the IMF, the World Bank and official bilateral sources is counterbalanced to a major extent by private capital outflows. Foreign direct and portfolio investments are minimal at perhaps US$2 billion a year. With the current account surpluses of recent years, foreign exchange reserves have recovered from zero at the end of 1991 to US$14 billion at the end of 1995, providing four months of import cover. In addition, Russia holds some US$4 billion in gold reserves.

Exports are dominated by fuels, metals and raw materials, which account for about 60% of the total. Machinery and equipment constitute the main imports. About 70% of exports go to convertible currency markets, while 45% of imports come from non-convertible currency areas. As with the figures on national income, Russian trade statistics are incomplete; the capital account data in particular are fragmentary.

Currency

A floating rouble rate was introduced in January 1992. The exchange rate of the rouble fell dramatically from 1992 to 1995 as a result of high inflation and capital flight. Following the introduction of a more restrictive monetary policy, a band of 4,300 to 4,800 roubles per US dollar was introduced in July 1995. From January to July 1996 the band was set at 4,550 to 5,150 roubles per dollar.

In June 1996 Russia's central bank signed a series of IMF regulations, including Article 8, which made the rouble convertible for current-account operations.

In July 1996 the government abandoned the rouble band in favour of a "crawling peg". The currency was thus set to depreciate from an initial range of 5,000–5,600 roubles per dollar to 5,500–6,100 by the end of 1996, with daily fluctuations consistent with a 1.5% depreciation per month. However, to prevent a renewed creeping inflation-adjusted appreciation of the rouble, as happened in 1995, a higher rate of depreciation may be required to offset inflation fully.

Debt

Russia's convertible currency external debt was estimated at US$120 billion at the end of 1995, equivalent to about one third of nominal GDP. Of this amount, over 80% was medium and long-term debt, and the balance consisted of interest in arrears and short-term debt. Official bilateral lenders held around 55% of this debt, commercial banks and other private creditors around 30%, and the IMF and World Bank about 15%. The external debt has been rising steadily, partly because of new borrowings (mostly from the IMF, the World Bank and official bilateral lenders), and partly because of debt reschedulings. In April 1996, the Paris Club rescheduled US$40 billion of official debt mostly over twenty-five years, with six years of grace. The London Club of creditors provided a similar arrangement for the stock of outstanding principal.

The debt reschedulings have eased Russia's debt servicing burden by some US$6 billion a year in principal repayments, from nearly US$10 billion in 1991 to about US$4 billion in 1996. Russia also was to pay about US$5 billion a year in interest, but has made only partial payments, accumulating arrears that have grown to over US$8 billion by 1995. On the basis of interest payments due and principal repaid, the overall debt service burden dropped from US$14 billion in 1991 to US$6.4 billion in 1992, increasing to US$7.3 billion in 1994 and an estimated US$9 billion in 1995, equivalent to 12% of foreign exchange receipts. In October 1996, the rating agencies Standard & Poor's and Moody's assigned Russia's long-term foreign debt a BB- and Ba2 rating respectively. At the time this meant that the former agency placed Russia's creditworthiness below Mexico's, whereas the latter agency had both countries in the same category.

Structural problems

Without doubt, Russia has made progress on its road to a viable democracy and to a private-enterprise economy responsive to market forces. Nevertheless, formidable obstacles inhibit the unfolding of its potential. The structure of the Russian economy reflects the requirements of its centrally planned past. Heavy industry and defence still predominate, aside from the extractive industries. Huge, largely self-sufficient monopoly enterprises from the Soviet era find it difficult to produce quality goods for the domestic market and for export. Managers struggle in an increasingly competitive environment. The workforce acquires new skills and work habits only slowly.

Labour mobility is inhibited by Russia's chronic housing shortage. The breakup of the highly integrated former Soviet Union created new obstacles, as roads, railroads and pipelines now cross new borders, with new customs, currency and other complications. Investment aimed at maintaining and expanding the transportation, power and telecommunications infrastructure remains far short of requirements, as many projects have been postponed in a climate of fiscal austerity and tight money.

Payment arrears, primarily within the enterprise sector, but also between the companies and the government, especially including the latter's wage arrears, have risen in the last two years, substantially reducing liquidity in the whole economy. The consequences – besides social hardship – are to restrain investment and overall growth possibilities.

One of the most serious problems undermining the market in Russia is the legal foundation for a market economy, as yet incomplete. The independent judiciary is still feeling its way in the new environment. Grey areas in Russian law relate to private property, corporate organization and financial liability. Judiciary and law enforcement agencies are understaffed and poorly paid. The Russian "mafia" targets them just as it does businesses.

Under the mass privatizations, much of the nation's wealth has been transferred to vaguely identified private individuals under nebulous terms and conditions. "Self-privatization" by the "managers" probably was common especially for smaller enterprises in the provinces.

A small but quickly rich class of new entrepreneurs and "businessmen" is largely responsible for capital flight, estimated at about US$60 billion between 1991 and 1995. Privatization has been slow in agriculture as land was excluded from the 1992 privatization programme. Only 2% has been fully privatized. In many regions, only limited privatization, mostly in the form of leases of collective farmland, has been permitted. The cultural, social and political support necessary for a market economy to flourish is only slowly and painfully taking root.

The IMF monitors reforms

In March 1996 the Russian government entered into an agreement with the IMF under which it will receive US$10.2 billion over three years in monthly disbursements under an Extended Fund Facility (EFF). It commits the authorities to reduce the fiscal deficit to 2% of GDP by 1998 from 4.7% in 1995 and to begin implementing a comprehensive package of structural reforms designed to encourage a strong and sustainable expansion of market-orientated output. To assure progress on structural reforms, disbursements under the EFF are linked to quarterly benchmarks on structural measures and monthly financial targets. Benchmarks for 1996 related to: improving fiscal performance, especially tax collection and expenditure controls; strengthening the banking system through improvements to the payments, supervision and regulatory system; liberalizing external trade by eliminating export tariffs and most remaining restrictions on foreign trade; selling shares the government holds of privatized state enterprises; improving the financial performance of state enterprises; and reinforcing the regulation of capital markets. For 1997 and 1998 planned measures should intensify progress in these areas and extend reforms to agriculture, the social safety net, health and education.

The first quarterly review under the EFF noted mixed progress, with reform most advanced in banking and slowest in agriculture and privatization. In the second quarterly review, the burgeoning fiscal deficit, due principally to severe deficiencies in tax collections and the extraordinary expenditures arising from the elections, threatened to undo the progress achieved in reducing inflation. This prompted the IMF to delay some disbursements.

Russia's longer-term prospects

Modern capitalism was built up in the West over centuries. Russia, with only a distant cultural memory of its brief fling with a market economy in the early part of this century, is at a distinct disadvantage. While the country can leapfrog in certain areas by making use of technology, its economic structure and legal environment remain serious handicaps. Without a legacy of market experience, prospective Russian entrepreneurs face higher hurdles than those experienced by entrepreneurs elsewhere. These impediments to wealth creation mean that the Russian economy will continue to perform below its capability for many years to come. While Russia's economic growth over the next decade or so should exceed growth rates in more mature economies, and perhaps rates in some emerging market countries, this will be more a reflection of a recovery from a low, and slowly restructuring economic base, than of any revolutionary high growth recipe.

The present structure of the Russian economy still reflects the requirements of the country's centrally planned, command-driven past, when heavy industry and defence constituted the hub of the system. Around 8 million workers, or about one fifth of the industrial labour force, worked primarily to fill defence orders. The highly specialized requirements placed on the defence industry make conversion to products saleable in a free market a cumbersome task. In Russia, the transformation process is further hampered by the retention of incumbent state managers, with the result that not much has changed inside the typical defence enterprise. The quality of non-defence manufacturing is poor, the result of decades of guaranteed orders, and lack of competition. The Russian economy is still burdened by gigantic, unprofitable industries employing a workforce with skills for which there is no ready market, but which are striving to adapt to the freeing up of markets.

Savings and investment

While the rates of savings and investment in Russia appear satisfactory, between 25% and 30% of national income, the quality of investment remains very low. With very little financial intermediation of any sort, investment typically goes where surplus funds are generated; existing enterprises with a positive cash flow. This leaves little room for investment by new competitors or innovative projects. There is also a massive backlog in infrastructure investment, and it seems unlikely that the money will be available for upgrading and rebuilding in the near future.

Picking winners

Against this background, it is difficult to envisage from where the stimulus will come in the next few years to enable Russia to change from an exporter of fuels, minerals, raw materials, and armaments into a dynamic participant in world markets for manufactured goods and increasingly complex services. Without an internationally competitive economy, Russia will not generate the consistently high growth and development needed to sustain an economic miracle.

So far the behaviour of foreign investors matches this view of Russia's future. Foreign direct investment in the Russian Federation is around 1% of gross domestic product, low by the standards of other states in the region. Moreover, the bulk of the investment in Russia is in oil and gas where high risks are offset by hopes for quick returns in many other parts of the world as well. Russia is not yet seeing significant foreign investment in industry, services or even local distribution networks, that suggests a country poised to export a widening range of manufactured goods in the near future.

Relatively low foreign investment in Russia

(1995 stocks of foreign direct investment)

	US$ millions	% of GDP
Hungary	11770	26.9
Poland	6490	5.4
Czech Republic	7260	15.4
Russia	3808	0.9
Romania	1406	4.1
Slovakia	1010	5.8
Ukraine	566	1.7
Estonia	524	15.0
Bulgaria	514	4.0
Slovenia	500	2.9
Latvia	380	7.2
Lithuania	253	4.4

Source: UN Economic Commission for Europe and UBS estimates

In Russia's favour

Despite this unfavourable legacy, it would be wrong to assume that Russia's cannot in time become the large, rapidly developing economy that might be expected of a country with abundant natural resources, a labour force well trained in the sciences and high levels of specialized technology. With the appropriate policies it would become a question of when, rather than if, the necessary quality and quantity of investment will be forthcoming to stimulate the economy, and significantly improve the quality of life for all its citizens.

Various studies conclude that Russia has the potential to achieve high, sustainable, growth rates if it pursues non-inflationary budgets and measures that emphasize competition in markets including the development of a sound legal framework for business. Such "with-reform" scenarios show Russia achieving sustainable annual average growth rates of 7-8% for some time if it has political stability and opens up the economy.

In contrast, a more realistic muddle-through scenario, with Russia continuing to move towards becoming a market economy, but with important gaps left unfilled, suggests a more modest 4-6% annual average growth. Still worse scenarios might also be considered, with Russia's government pursuing populist free spending, producing one or more boom-bust cycles with even lower average growth.

Yet, as the chart shows, even the most optimistic scenario is still no panacea. It would take Russia nearly fifteen years to regain average Eastern European income levels. The bottom line is that a decade from now Russia will most likely have a market economy characterized by protected monopolies, a high degree of regulation and inefficiencies that are glaring by the standards of more successful emerging market economies. Russia, it appears, will enter the next century as it began this one: with living standards well behind its European contemporaries.

Russia will lag without reform

(Real income per capita in constant 1995 US dollars)

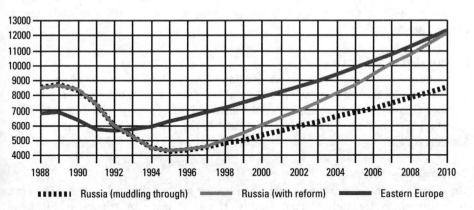

ıııııı Russia (muddling through) ——— Russia (with reform) ▬▬▬ Eastern Europe

Source: UBS projection

■ EQUITIES

Index performance (in local currency)

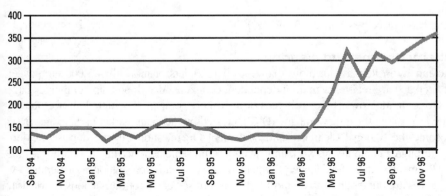

Key indicators

	Index performance % in US$ terms	Market Cap. US$bn	P/E	Div. Yield
1994	—	30.0	—	—
1995	-30.6	15.9	—	—
1996	155.9	37.2	6.3	0.9

Sources: Local stock exchange, IFC, Bloomberg, Datastream, UBS

Structure
The Russian equity market historically developed as an over-the-counter market (OTC). Some 90% of all equity trades are made on the OTC market, which is mainly (80%) traded outside Russia. The OTC market lists seventy-seven companies with a capitalization of US$19.2 billion.

Regulatory authority
The Russian Federation Commission on Securities and Capital Markets supervises the market. The Russian Brokers Association (PAUFOR) is a self-regulatory organization. It has 162 members, mostly brokerages, and set up the Russian Trading System (RTS), a screen-based quotation system. RTS is modelled after PORTAL, the market-making system for major Russian brokers.

Trading methods
The RTS system transacts a significant part of trading on the OTC market. Portal is on-line and share-prices are updated continuously. Deals are made by telephone. Blocks of shares representing between 15 and 25% of the equity capital of a company are sold through auctions and tenders. On the primary market, approximately twenty companies are classified as blue chips with a high liquidity and trading volume. Continuous trading is based on a bid/offer system. Daily turnover has been between US$6 million and US$40 million.

Hours
Trading takes place between 10.00 and 18.00.

Settlement time and clearing
Any company in Russia with more than 500 shareholders or more than 5,000 employees must keep a share register with an independent company. Most blue chip companies have depositories in Moscow. There are scores of depository companies scattered all over Russia, but the Depository Clearing Company (DCC), created by the main market participants, is set to become the National Clearance and Settlement Organization. All the depositories are linked through a computer network and clearance and settlement occurs on a trade-by-trade basis. Payment is due after delivery, which in Russia means registration at a depository. Stock-prices are quoted in roubles and US dollars, but settlement of transactions is primarily in roubles. Settlement in hard currencies is only permitted for non-residents and Russian banks with a licence from the Central Bank of Russia. Investments in Russian equity remitted in US dollars are entered in a so-called I (investment) account and converted at the exchange rate of the Moscow Interbank Currency Exchange (MICEX) on the date of transaction. Conversion and account maintenance fees depend on size of the operation and the status of the customer.

Taxes
Foreign legal entities with no operation in Russia are subject to a withholding tax on returns made in Russia. However, bilateral treaties that prevent double taxation will allow the investor to eliminate or reduce this tax.

Ownership limits for foreigners

Foreigners can hold up to 20% of a company. To buy more, permission must be obtained from the Ministry of Finance and the State Antimonopoly Committee.

However, de facto, 25% of shares is usually the maximum ownership allowed without prior permission. There is no limit to LUKoil, the oil company, but the limit for Gazprom is 10%.

■ DEBT

Rapidly developing domestic market

Government securities are issued by the Ministry of Finance. The Central Bank of Russia (RCB) is the MOF's agent for the issuance of treasury bills, and VneshEconombank (Bank of Foreign Economic Affairs) for the country's foreign currency bonds. The largest part of the market consists of state bonds and bills with maturities of 6 months.

Government debt
GKOs

Guaranteed by the central bank, GKOs were first issued by the Ministry of Finance in May 1993. They are discounted bills with 3-, 6- and 12-month maturities, denominated in rouble lots of RUR1,000,000 (about US$200) and issued as global certificates. They make up the largest proportion of tradeable Russian debt, are the principal instrument of government funding and provide an important source of income for the country's banking system.

GKOs trade at the Moscow Interbank Currency Exchange (MICEX), which also acts as the Central Depository.

Foreign investors

Prior to August 1996, foreigners could only buy GKOs at primary auctions through external agents of the RCB. They had to transact a 3-month forward foreign exchange contract, which capped yields at 19%, through special schemes offered by two off-shore Russian banks, despite considerably higher yields available to domestic investors (220% during the final stages of the July 1996 presidential campaign, for example).

To circumvent restrictions, international investment banks devised various schemes, usually involving special off-shore vehicles and informal arrangements with local banks, to access the higher returns availabe to domestic investors.

However, since August 15, 1996 foreigners can buy GKOs in the secondary market if they open new S-accounts with one of twenty-one authorized Russian banks. In September 1996, the RCB proposed changes that will open the market further and which aim to make rouble-denominated bonds internationally traded.

The forward rate for the foreign exchange transaction was scheduled to be reduced to two months in January 1997, and then to one month in May.

In each quarter of 1997, the RCB would reportedly cut by 25% the requirement that Russian commercial banks must sell foreign currency earned from overseas GKO purchases to the RCB. In addition, from 1997, foreign banks may be allowed to become brokers for the sale of GKOs to non-residents.

OFZs (Federal Loan Bonds)

OFZs are medium-term bonds with variable-rate coupons, issued by the Ministry of Finance. The RCB acts as market-maker and paying agent. They were first issued in June 1995 with maturities up to 2 years. The rate is set as the weighted average of the yields of GKOs that mature 30 days or more before (but no longer than 30 days after) its next quarterly payment.

Primary market

GKO and OFZ primary placements are conducted each Wednesday on MICEX, which also acts as a clearing and depository centre. The amount and maturity date are announced a week earlier by MICEX, and RCB-nominated dealers make competitive and non-competitive bids (the Ministry of Finance sets a maximum for each individual auction). Since July 1996, primary dealers must bid for at least 1% of an issue, and in return receive priority Lombard credits from the RCB and can conduct repo operations.

Secondary market

GKOs and OFZs are registered securities and trade at MICEX, Monday to Friday. Dealers trade through an electronic book-entry system for one-day settlements. GKO principal repayments are covered by new issues. Short-positions are prohibited.

Other domestic debt

Municipal bonds

Municipal and other federal issuers register bond issues with the Ministry of Finance. The market is growing, with St Petersburg the major issuer. They are issued in physical form and retained by domestic holders or custodians.

Bank promissory notes ("Veksels")

Veksels are issued by major banks, sold at the sight of the issuer and trade on the exchanges in roubles and dollars. Maturities range from 3 days to 18 months, and represent a credit chain linking corporate suppliers and customers in the Russian economy. Yields range from 25% to 70%, and are largely bought by banks who hold a diverse portfolio of notes, recognizing that a proportion will default. Veksels are subject to reserve requirements, and can be used as collateral for repo transactions.

Derivatives

Rouble-denominated bonds can be hedged with rouble/US dollar futures contracts traded at the Moscow Exchange, and also at the Moscow Central Stock Exchange (MCSE), Russian Exchange and Moscow Financial and Futures Exchange. Most forward contracts are for 1, 2 and 3 months. Small volumes of GKO futures are traded on the MCSE, and repos are transacted on MICEX.

External tradeable debt

MinFins (Taiga bonds)

MinFins are hard currency bonds which were issued in five tranches in May 1993, as compensation for holders of foreign currency accounts held at VneshEconombank, which were frozen two years earlier. The first tranche, out of a total US$7.7 billion, matured in May 1994.

Ministry of Finance compensation bonds – MinFins (Taiga bonds)

Tranche III	May 14, 1999	US$ 1,307,000,000
Tranche IV	May 14, 2003	US$ 2,627,000,000
Tranche V	May 14, 2008	US$ 2,167,000,000
Tranche VI	May 14, 2006	US$ 1,302,000,000
Tranche VII	May 14, 2011	US$ 1,298,000,000

They are dollar-denominated obligations of the Ministry of Finance of the Russian Federation, which pay fixed 3% annual coupons. All bonds are in physical form, and most are held in safe custody accounts at Vneshtorgbank or with local sub-custodians. All trades are settled in Russia with Vneshtorgbank acting as central clearer. A dozen banks are selected as paying agents, who intermediate the transfer of coupon and principal payments to the bond owner. Annual coupons are paid in arrears, and should be presented seven days before payment. Bonds are in bearer form, and their theft has been a continuing problem. Settlement is made in dollars or roubles, delivery versus payment

Vneshekonombank Loans (Vnesh)

Vnesh loans represent defaulted syndicated loans payable to international creditors. They are denominated in US dollars, deutschmarks and Swiss francs. Vnesh are actively traded, but there are plans to restructure them into Interest Arrears Notes (IANs) and Principal Notes (PRNs). IANs and PRNs currently trade on a "when and if issued" basis.

Eurobonds

On November 21, 1996, Russia issued its first eurobond. It raised US$1 billion for a 5-year maturity, with a coupon of 9.25% and was priced to yield a spread of 345 basis points over US Treasuries.

Municipalities, for example Moscow, St Petersburg and Nizhny Novgorod, and corporates such as Gazprom and Lukoil have indicated that they will tap the international bond markets soon.

Eurobond issues

US$ millions	1990	1991	1992	1993	1994	1995	1996
Sovereign	294.9	—	—	—	—	—	1000
Private	—	—	—	—	—	—	—

■ RUSSIA: Economic indicators

Population and development	1990	1991	1992	1993	1994	1995	1996e
Population, million	148.0	148.5	148.3	148.2	148.0	147.9	146.3
Population growth, %	0.0	0.3	-0.1	-0.1	-0.1	-0.1	-1.1
Nominal GDP per capita, US$	7252	5146	576	1167	1870	2476	3250

National accounts							
Nominal GDP, US$bn	1,073.3	764.1	85.5	172.9	276.6	366.2	475.7
Change in real GDP, %	-3.6	-5.0	-14.5	-8.7	-12.6	-4.0	-6.0
Gross fixed capital formation, % of GDP	30.1	39.3	23.9	22.5	25.2	21.9	21.5

Money supply and inflation							
Broad money, change %, Dec/Dec	—	140.0	783.3	286.6	216.5	114.0	—
Consumer price inflation (avg.) %	5.6	92.5	1542.1	842.7	433.4	205.2	52.9

Government finance							
Government expenditure, % of GDP	—	41.6	26.3	19.4	22.7	16.7	17.2
Government balance, % of GDP	—	-15.7	-10.5	-6.5	-10.4	-4.2	-5.3

Exchange rates lc=local currency							
Exchange rate, annual average, lc/US$	0.60	1.70	222	992	2205	4575	5123
Exchange rate, end of year, lc/US$	0.60	1.70	414	1247	3388	4631	5554

Balance of payments							
Exports of goods & services, US$m	36100	39900	32300	45600	76667	94060	96732
Change %	-42.7	10.5	-19.0	41.2	68.1	22.7	2.8
Imports of goods & services, US$m, fob	36600	35300	40900	44000	63446	79440	88200
Change %	-26.5	-3.6	15.9	7.6	44.2	25.2	11.0
Trade balance, of goods only, US$m, fob-fob	5000	10800	-100	9500	19713	22754	21957
Current account balance, US$m	-500	6200	-5600	4400	11369	12261	7300
as a % of GDP	0.0	0.8	-6.6	2.5	4.1	3.4	1.5

Foreign exchange reserves							
Foreign exchange reserves, US$m	6700	15.0	1955	5835	3981	14382	19000
Gold at ⅔ of market price, US$m	3986.5	2251.5	2020.7	2442.5	2153.8	2408.6	2323.8
Import cover (reserves/imports), months	2.2	0.0	0.6	1.6	0.8	2.2	2.6

Foreign debt and debt service							
Short-term debt, US$m	12785	8500	8076	7776	8395	9203	10662
Total foreign debt, US$m	57100	61400	76471	83845	95545	106894	115409
as a % of GDP	5.3	8.0	89.5	48.5	34.5	29.5	23.9
as a % of foreign exchange receipts	158.2	148.0	216.6	173.2	118.6	107.6	114.7
Interest payments, US$m	4700	4400	5400	5400	5000	5800	5500
Principal repayments, US$m	9802	9559	955	1425	2273	3170	3800
Total debt service, US$m	14502	13959	6355	6825	7273	8970	9300
as a % of goods exports	48.2	40.9	24.3	17.7	10.7	11.0	11.1
as a % of foreign exchange receipts	40.2	33.6	18.0	14.1	9.0	9.0	9.2

Saudi Arabia

KEY FACTS

Area (thousands of km²):	2150
Population (1995, millions):	18.6
Population projection (2025, millions):	69
Population younger than 15 yrs (1991, % of total):	43
Urbanization rate (1993, % of population):	79
Life expectancy (1993, years at birth):	70
Gross domestic product (1996, US$bn):	134.9
GDP per capita (1996, US$):	7106
Average annual GDP growth rate (1990-96, %):	3.5
Average annual inflation rate (1990-96, %):	2.1
Currency (riyal per US$, average 1996):	3.75
Structure of production (1994):	50.3% industry, 42.7% services, 7% agriculture
Main exports:	crude oil & refined petroleum, petrochemicals & plastics
Main imports:	transport equipment, machinery & mechanical appliances, base metals & textiles
Main trading partners:	US, Japan, UK, Singapore
Market capitalization of Stock Exchange (October 1996; US$bn):	39.6
Total foreign debt (% of GDP):	18.7
Next elections due under normal circumstances:	king appoints Council; next term 1997

FORECAST: 1997-2000 (average)

	Worst case	Most likely	Best case
Real GDP growth (%)	0.3	2.0	2.5
Inflation (%)	4.2	1.8	0.5

■ POLITICS

Historical overview

The history of modern Saudi Arabia began in 1902, when Abd al-Aziz ibn Abd ar-Rahman regained his family's former domain by capturing the city of Riyadh. Subsequent conquests allowed Abdul Aziz to be proclaimed King of the Hejaz and Sultan of Najd. In 1933, he merged the lands under his control into the Unified Kingdom of Saudi Arabia. Since Saudi Arabia's legendary founder, four kings have led the country: King Saud Bin Abdul Aziz (1953-64), King Faisal Bin Abdul Aziz (1964-75), King Khalid Bin Abdul Aziz (1975-82), and

King Fahd Bin Abdul Aziz, the current leader. King Saud began modernizing the country by establishing roads and basic communications, introducing modern technology and improving education, healthcare, and agriculture. King Faisal took more direct control of fiscal policy and began the five-year development plans in 1970, which boosted progress. He was also noted for promoting Islamic unity and co-operation. King Khalid implemented the second and third development plans in 1975 and 1980. During those years, the Kingdom achieved political and economical respect regionally as well as internationally, and standards of living increased significantly. King Fahd began efforts to diversify the country's economic base, which has depended too much on oil, and to support the growth of the private sector.

Islam has deeply affected the history and development of Saudi Arabia. The Qur'an has become the constitution of Saudi Arabia its legal system is based on Shari'ah (Islamic law). The Shari'ah governs all aspects of the public and private, social and economic, religious and political life of every Muslim. By tradition, the king's legitimacy has been tied to his role as religious protector and custodian of the two holy mosques in Mecca and Medina, which are among the most important sites in Islam.

Recent events

Afraid of Iraqi expansionism, King Fahd allowed US troops into the Kingdom following the invasion of Kuwait, to block a possible attack on the country. In response to criticism that he did not consult enough before allowing the entrance of foreign troops, King Fahd announced the imminent creation of a Consultative Council in 1992. The council can question government decisions and discuss disagreements on policy with the king, but has no legislative powers. The new system gives a more formalized structure to better meet the requirements of the modern state. In 1995 King Fahd suffered a minor stroke, and was hospitalized. The king temporarily handed over management of government affairs to his half-brother, Crown Prince Abdullah bin Abdel-Aziz al-Saud, during 1996.

Chronology

1902	Abd al-Aziz captures Riyadh and proclaims himself ruler of Najd
1932	Hejaz and Najd are merged to form the Unified Kingdom of Saudi Arabia
1953	Saud bin Abdul Aziz becomes king
1964	King Saud is forced by the royal family to abdicate in favour of Faisal bin Abdul Aziz
1973	Saudi Arabia leads a movement by Arab petroleum producers to exert pressure on Western countries by reducing supplies of crude oil
1975	King Faisal is assassinated and succeeded by Kahlid bin Abdul Aziz
1981	Saudi Arabia forms, with five other Gulf countries, the Gulf Co-operation Council (GCC)
1982	King Khalid dies and is succeeded by Fahd bin Abdel Aziz al-Saud
1989	King Fahd signs a pact of non-aggression with Iraq
1990	The Gulf War
1993	Consultative Council is inaugurated by the king
1995	International criticism over the increasing number of executions during 1995 (191 people received the death penalty in 1995 compared with 53 in 1994 and 85 in 1993)
1995	King Fahd is hospitalized
1996	King Fahd temporarily transfers power to his half-brother, Crown Prince Abdullah bin Abdel-Aziz, then resumes control of the affairs of state

Constitution and government

The Kingdom of Saudi Arabia is a monarchy, with no legislature or political parties. Its constitution is the Qur'an and the Sunnah, which call for peace, equality, tolerance, justice, consultation, and respect for the rights of the individual.

One of the king's duties is to ensure the application of the Shari'ah and supervise the protection and defence of the nation. In 1953 the Council of Ministers was established in order to assist the king. It consists of the prime minister, who is the king, the first deputy prime minister, the second deputy prime minister, twenty-one ministers with portfolio and six ministers of state. The Council was restructured in 1993 and now consists of a chairman and sixty members appointed by the king for a four-year renewable term. The country's judicial system is based on the Shari'ah.

The Executive power is vested in the king, and in the cabinet, which is the council of ministers. Ministers are appointed by the king and the majority are royal family members. Legislative power is vested in the Consultative Council. Judicial power is exercised by the Supreme Council of Justice.

Saudi Arabia is divided into thirteen provinces. Their governors and appointed councils of prominent citizens have the rights and responsibilities to monitor development for each region and advise the government.

Current government

Head of State	King Fahd bin Abdel Aziz al-Saud (acceded June 1982)
Prime Minister	King Fahd bin Abdel Aziz al-Saud
Deputy Prime Minister	Abdullah bin Abdel-Aziz al-Saud
Second Deputy Prime Minister,	
Minister of Defence & Aviation	Sultan bin Abdel-Aziz al-Saud
Agriculture & Water	Abdullah bin Abdel-Aziz bin Muammar
Commerce	Osama bin Jaafar bin Ibrahim Faqih
Finance & National Economy	Ibrahim Abdel-Aziz al-Asaf
Foreign Affairs	Saud al-Faisal al-Saud
Industry & Electricity	Hashem bin Abdullah bin Hashem Yamani
President of the Consultative Council	Mohammed bin Ibrahim al-Jubair
President of the Board of Grievances	Nasser bin Hamad al-Rashid
President of the Supreme Judicial Council	Salih bin Mohammed al-Lihaydan
Governor, central bank	Hamad Saud al-Sayari

Infrastructure

Saudi Arabia has a population of some 19 million, and is one of the richest countries in the Middle East. Its urban infrastructure is highly developed and technologically sophisticated. There are excellent hospitals, clinics, schools, colleges, and universities, together with free medical care and education. .

Central bank

The central bank of Saudi Arabia, called the Saudi Arabian Monetary Agency (SAMA), was formed in 1952 with United States technical assistance. SAMA is responsible for overall monetary policy and currency stability, the regulation of commercial banks, exchange dealers and money changers, and serves as the depository for all government funds. The bank is regulated by Islamic law. SAMA is allowed to extend credit to the government.

■ ECONOMICS

Historical overview

Pilgrimage to Mecca and Medina and the export of dates were the two major sources of revenue before 1930, when oil was discovered. Large-scale oil production began after the Second World War. Since then Saudi Arabia has made rapid economic progress, addressing education, health, transport, agriculture, and industry. The country now has a large industrial base and supplies a substantial portion of its domestic market needs. Government funding in agricultural development reduced Saudi Arabia's dependence upon imported food and raises the standard of living in rural areas, despite the short supply of natural water and the small proportion of arable land (only 1%). Saudi Arabia is one of the fastest developing countries in the world.

The main objective of the authorities has been to diversify the economy. To accomplish this, Saudi economic development since 1970 has been guided by a series of five-year plans. Between 1970 and 1992, GDP increased three-fold to US$113 billion and the non-oil sector's share of GDP increased from 46% to 67%.

From 1987 to 1993, Saudi Arabia's real GDP per capita increased at an annual rate of only 0.8%, partly because of a rapid growth in population (which averaged 3.9% over the period). Real GDP increased at an average annual rate of 4.7%. Subsequently real GDP growth slowed to a 1.0% rate and per capita GDP fell at a 1.9% rate from 1993 to 1995.

Saudi Arabia's economic performance

	Average annual real GDP growth, %	Average annual consumer price inflation, %
1982-1984	-4.2	-0.8
1985-1987	-1.8	-2.7
1988-1990	5.2	1.3
1991-1993	3.3	1.9
1994-1995	1.0	2.3

Source: Official data

The Sixth Five-Year Development Plan

The sixth plan began in 1995, and will last until the year 2000. It concentrates on the development of technical skills of the workforce, places more emphasis on the private sector, particularly industry and agriculture to further reduce dependence on oil, and aims to lower the cost of government services without cutting them. To achieve these goals, the plan calls for limiting government spending, the encouragement of private capital in government projects, the improvement of financial conditions for small-scale enterprises and the expansion of the Saudi Credit Bank's activities, the privatization of electric utilities and the establishment of new industrial cities in locations with favourable growth potential. The plan aims to reach an average growth rate of 3.8-3.9% growth in non-oil GDP, and a 4.9% and 19% increase in private sector and government investment, respectively.

The oil industry

Saudi Arabia's oil reserves are the largest in the world, and the kingdom is the greatest producer and exporter of oil. Oil accounts for more than 90% of the country's exports and nearly 75% of government revenues. Saudi ARAMCO produces more than 95% of all Saudi oil on behalf of the Saudi government and is the world's largest fully integrated oil company. To maximize production, the kingdom has continuously expanded and upgraded existing refineries and built new ones. Saudi Arabia has a refined product capacity of more than 1.8 million barrels per day. Given the large dependence of the economy on oil, price movements and the volume of oil exports have a major impact on economic performance.

Recent developments

After enjoying high petroleum revenues from the end of the 1973 Arab-Israeli war until the early 1980s, the country has faced previously unknown problems such as budget deficits and rising unemployment. The first budget deficit was recorded in 1983, due to weak oil prices and a high level of government spending. To finance its budget deficit, the government drew down its foreign assets: deposits around the world fell from US$85.8 billion in 1990 to US$54.2 billion in 1994, and its net assets went down from US$73 billion to US$39.5 billion. The government also cut subsidies (particularly for growing foodstuffs), delayed the start of some investment projects and encouraged private-sector investment and privatization. The private sector has been encouraged with cheap credit, land, infrastructure and utilities. The non-oil private sector now accounts for 48% of GDP, compared with 35% in the oil sector and 17% for the government sector. In 1994, King Fahd announced plans for the privatization of the telephone company, the national airline and the eight electricity companies.

The economy
Share of GDP by sector

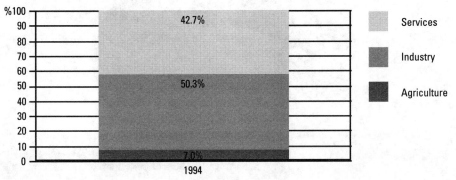

Source: Official data

Breakdown of the service sector

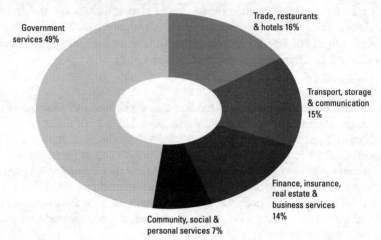

Government services 49%

Trade, restaurants & hotels 16%

Transport, storage & communication 15%

Finance, insurance, real estate & business services 14%

Community, social & personal services 7%

Source: Official data

The trade account has been in surplus for many years, due to oil exports, and in 1995 totalled US$23.4 billion. The current account, however, has been in deficit since 1982 for a variety of reasons: lower oil prices, war-related payments in the early 1990s and large private transfer payments abroad by foreign workers in Saudi Arabia. This deficit has been declining since 1991 and a surplus of US$0.5 billion was expected in 1996 due to higher oil prices. Main imports are transport equipment (24% of the total), machinery and mechanical appliances (21%), base metals and base-metal products (9%), and textiles and textile products (8%).

Breakdown of exports (1994)

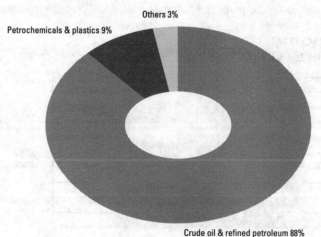

Others 3%

Petrochemicals & plastics 9%

Crude oil & refined petroleum 88%

Source: Official data

Imports and exports as a % of GDP

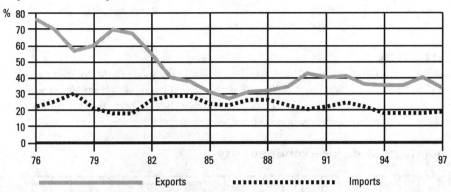

Source: Official data

Current account as a % of GDP

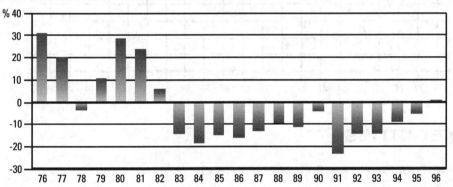

Source: Official data

Economic policy
Monetary policy
A statutory reserve requirement obliges each commercial bank to maintain minimum non-interest-bearing deposits with the central bank. Banks also must hold additional liquid assets equal to part of their deposit liabilities. Bank activities consist of providing credit, deposit facilities, securities trading, investment banking, foreign exchange services, government finance, and development of a secondary government bond-treasury bill market.

Fiscal policy
The budget forecast for 1996 showed expenditure of SR150,000 million (the same as in 1995), while revenue was expected to decline 2.6% to SR131,500 million, leaving a budget deficit of SR18,500 million (US$4.9 million).

The budget problem became serious in 1991 when Saudi Arabia experienced a big rise in government payments for foreign services. Since then the current account deficit on government services and official transfers, a measure of the budget components, has declined from US$30.1 billion to US$6.9 billion. Government services alone declined from US$24.4 billion to US$6.3 billion over the same period.

Currency

In 1986, the Saudi Arabia central bank fixed the official selling rate of the Saudi riyal (SR) at SR3.745 to US$1. The official riyal/dollar rate is revalued at intervals to keep within a narrow band, although no such change has occurred since 1986. There is no restriction on converting or transferring the SR outside the country.

Saudi riyal/US dollar exchange rate

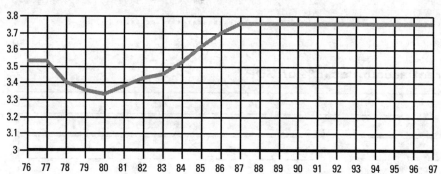

■ EQUITIES

Index performance (in local currency)

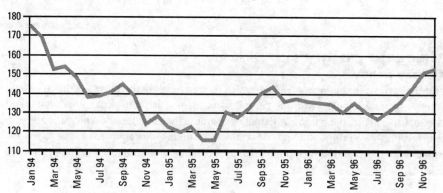

Key indicators

	Index performance %, in US$ terms	Market Cap. US$bn	P/E	Div. Yield
1994	-28.7	38.7	13.6	3.4
1995	6.6	41.0	11.8	5.0
1996	12	45.9	—	—

Sources: Local stock exchange, IFC, Bloomberg, Datastream, UBS

Structure
The Saudi stock market exists mainly for the initial public offering of previously state-owned companies in the process of being privatized. The official market is thin, with only about ten shares traded regularly. There are seventy-two companies listed and the market capitalization of the exchange is US$43 billion.

Regulatory authorities
Two bodies regulate all shares traded: the Saudi Shares Registration Company, which acts as an integrated central registry for all shares traded in the market; and the central clearing unit at SAMA (The Saudi Arabian Monetary Agency), equivalent to the Saudi central bank.

Trading methods
All trades are executed through the Kingdom's banks who act as brokers. In 1990, a computerized dealing system, Electronic Securities Information System (ESIS), was introduced but is now rarely used.

Hours
Shares are traded during bank hours, which are 08.30 to 12.00 and 17.00 to 19.00 from Saturday to Wednesday and mornings only on Thursdays in the western and central regions of the country, and from 08.00 to 11.30 and 16.00 to 18.00 Saturday to Wednesday and mornings only on Thursdays in the eastern regions.

Stock index
The NCFEI All Share Index lists all of the country's shares.

Taxes
Dividends are calculated on a six-monthly basis and there is no withholding tax on dividends.

Capital and foreign exchange controls
There are no foreign exchange controls and capital can move freely both into and out of the Kingdom.

Disclosure of financial statements
Companies are required to publish quarterly financial statements, but these tend to be sketchy and uninformative.

Ownership limits for non-residents

The Saudi equity market is not open to non-Saudi nationals although nationals of GCC (Gulf Cooperation Council) countries are allowed to buy shares in the market, except those in banks. Tentative plans are being made to open the market to other foreign nationals but this is likely to be through mutual funds, and officials at the Ministry of Finance say foreign share-holding in any company will be limited to less than 20% of its market capitalization.

Sectors

The largest sector is made up of industrial companies, such as the Saudi Arabian Basic Industries Company (SABIC) and the Saudi Arabian Fertilizer Company (SAFCO), which are heavily involved in export. The electricity sector is also large and in 1991 accounted for 44.1% of the total paid-up capital of the stock market.

■ DEBT

The Saudi Arabian Monetary Agency (SAMA) regulates the domestic bond market by providing guidelines that specify the status of bonds.

Saudi government treasury bills

T-bills are issued through the central bank with maturities of 28, 91, 182 and 364 days. The rate is linked to money market rates. The 364-day bills are offered on the last Tuesday of every month and the others sold each Monday. Settlement is two days later.

SGDBs (Saudi Government Development Bonds)

The government issues SGDBs with maturities of 2, 3 and 4 years for budget deficit financing. Contractor bonds are issued by the Ministry of Finance in lieu of receivables. They are auctioned every Saturday by the central bank to commercial banks and "autonomous government institutions", who bid a yield spread over benchmark US treasuries. SGDBs pay semi-annual coupons and interest is calculated on a 30/360 day basis. Investors can buy bonds from domestic banks in the secondary market, and the bonds can be used for transacting repo agreements with the central bank.

SSGBs (Special Saudi Government Bonds)

The central bank has issued about US$3 billion dollars worth of SSGBs over the past two years to repay contractors owed money by the government. Bonds have been issued with maturities up to five years. Most contractors have discounted them at banks, who now hold most of the securities.

Eurobond issues (US$m)

	1990	1991	1992	1993	1994	1995	1996
Sovereign	0.0	0.0	0.0	0.0	280.0	0.0	0.0
Private	—	—	—	—	—	—	—

■ SAUDI ARABIA: Economic indicators

Population and development	1990	1991	1992	1993	1994	1995	1996e
Population, million	15.9	16.5	17.0	17.6	18.1	18.6	19.0
Population growth, %	3.8	3.5	3.3	3.1	2.9	2.7	2.2
Nominal GDP per capita, US$	6566	7154	7227	6743	6644	6838	7106

National accounts							
Nominal GDP, US$bn	104.7	118.0	123.2	118.5	120.2	127.0	134.9
Change in real GDP, %	10.7	8.4	2.8	-0.6	0.5	0.8	1.8
Gross fixed capital formation, % of GDP	18.8	21.5	22.4	25.3	21.1	24.0	23.5

Money supply and inflation							
Narrow money, change %, Dec/Dec	11.6	17.7	2.9	-1.6	0.4	1.6	1.7
Broad money, change %, Dec/Dec	4.6	14.6	2.1	3.4	0.2	1.2	1.7
Consumer price inflation (avg.) %	2.0	4.9	-0.1	1.0	0.5	4.9	1.5
Producer prices (avg.) %	1.7	3.0	1.3	0.7	1.8	7.2	-0.2

Government finance							
Government expenditure, % of GDP	58.3	51.7	45.8	42.3	38.0	31.5	30.1
Government balance, % of GDP	-18.0	-15.9	-9.0	-10.5	-9.3	-3.2	2.6

Exchange rates *lc=local currency*							
Exchange rate, annual average, lc/US$	3.75	3.75	3.75	3.75	3.75	3.75	3.75
Exchange rate, end of year, lc/US$	3.75	3.75	3.75	3.75	3.75	3.75	3.75

Balance of payments							
Exports of goods & services, US$m	47333	50700	53750	45679	45854	48656	57677
Change %	67.3	7.1	6.0	-15.0	0.4	6.1	18.5
Imports of goods & services, US$m, fob	43900	64768	62028	50193	40108	43270	44519
Change %	128.3	47.5	-4.2	-19.1	-20.1	7.9	2.9
Trade balance, of goods only, US$m, fob-fob	22793	21832	20032	16522	21296	21886	29548
Current account balance, US$m	-4152	-27546	-17760	-17268	-10256	-7014	458
as a % of GDP	-4.0	-23.3	-14.4	-14.6	-8.5	-5.5	0.3

Foreign exchange reserves							
Foreign exchange reserves, US$m	11668	11673	5935	7428	7378	8622	15961
Gold at ⅔ of market price, US$m	1181.5	1108.6	1051.2	1101.1	1176.1	1175.9	1186.7
Import cover (reserves/imports), months	3.2	2.2	1.1	1.8	2.2	2.4	4.3

Foreign debt and debt service							
Short-term debt, US$m	13400	10500	10780	11900	14900	17730	17960
Total foreign debt, US$m	15600	17450	17520	19650	21660	23100	25240
as a % of GDP	14.9	14.8	14.2	16.6	18.0	18.2	18.7
as a % of foreign exchange receipts	27.6	29.4	28.7	37.9	43.3	43.2	40.3
Interest payments, US$m	1220	1930	1945	2300	2400	2300	2600
Principal repayments, US$m	575	600	725	690	3490	2630	810
Total debt service, US$m	1795	2530	2670	2990	5890	4930	3410
as a % of goods exports	4.1	5.3	5.3	7.1	13.8	10.9	6.3
as a % of foreign exchange receipts	3.2	4.3	4.4	5.8	11.8	9.2	5.4

Singapore

KEY FACTS

Area (thousands of km²):	1
Population (1995, millions):	3
Population projection (2025, millions):	4
Population younger than 15 yrs (1991, % of total):	23.1
Urbanization rate (1993, % of population):	100
Life expectancy (1993, years at birth):	75
Gross domestic product (1996, US$bn):	92.0
GDP per capita (1996, US$):	30281
Average annual GDP growth rate (1990-96, %):	8.1
Average annual inflation rate (1990-96, %):	2.6
Currency (SG$ per US$, average 1996):	1.41
Real exchange rate: (1990=100, average 1996)	116.09
Structure of production (1994):	64% services, 36% industry
Main exports:	office machines, semi-conductors, telecomm unications equipment, petroleum products
Main imports:	office machines, telecommunications equipment, crude petroleum
Main trading partners:	US, Japan, Malaysia, Hong Kong, Thailand
Market capitalization of Stock Exchange (December 1996; US$bn):	186.5
Total foreign debt (% of GDP):	50.7
Next elections due under normal circumstances:	general election is postponed until January 1997
Credit rating: (Jan 1997, Standard & Poor's, Moody's)	AAA; Aa1

FORECAST: 1997-2000 (average)

	Worst case	Most likely	Best case
Real GDP growth (%)	5	7.2	8.4
Inflation (%)	2.3	2	21.8

■ POLITICS

Historical overview

Between the 11th and the 14th centuries, when Singapore was part of the great Sri Vijaya Empire that encompassed much of modern Indonesia and Malaysia, the island became an international melting pot of cultures and commodities. It then passed under the control of the kingdom of Majapahit, later falling to the Malacca sultanate as part of Johore. The modern city was founded in 1819 by Sir Thomas Stamford Raffles and deeded in perpetuity to the British East India Co. in 1824 by the sultan of Johore. Two years later, it was incorporated into a colony of the Straits Settlements. Singapore soon became an important naval base for the British Empire, and its role as an entrepôt was enhanced by its strategic location on the narrow Malacca Straits connecting the Indian Ocean to the South China Sea.

Singapore became a separate crown colony in 1946, and became subject to the ideological (and ethnic) conflicts that engulfed British Malaya over the next decade and a half. The Communist Party of Malaya (CPM) – ostensibly representing the interests of the rural Chinese peasantry, and heavily influenced by the PRC – began a guerrilla war in Malaya. This delayed Malaya's independence until 1957. Singapore's ethnic-Chinese majority provided fertile recruiting ground for the CPM, while the British attempted to nurture conservative political forces in both Malaya and Singapore. They succeeded in the former, but had much less success in the latter, where the 1955 legislative election was won by the left-wing Labour Front, headed by David Marshall, at the expense of the two conservative parties. Led by a young Lee Kuan Yew, the socialist People's Action Party (PAP) emerged as the largest opposition party (although it had only contested a third of the seats).

The PAP was, until 1962, split almost equally between a moderate nationalist wing (with socialist aspirations, but overt opposition to Communism) and a leftist wing. Broadly, the latter represented politicians who had been educated in Chinese-language (or other local language) schools, while the former were largely English-educated. The PAP advanced a nationalist agenda that included the provision of social services, economic development and merger with Malaysia by 1963. A bid by the left to capture the PAP was thwarted via a public campaign by Lee. Advocating independence, the PAP won 53.4% of the vote (and 43 of 51 legislative seats) in the 1959 election, and Singapore became a self-governing state on June 3 of that year. Lee Kuan Yew became prime minister, and an ethnic-Malay, Inche Yusof bin Ishak, became head of state.

The internal conflict within the PAP came to a head in July 1961 over the issue of merger with Malaya, with the leftists quitting the PAP to form the Barisan Socialist. The PAP survived a vote of confidence by a single vote. A referendum secured the Singaporeans' overwhelming assent to a merger of the Malayan peninsular states with Singapore, Sabah and Sarawak in 1963. Differences soon arose, however, between the socialist/egalitarian orientation of the PAP and the conservatism of Malaysia's ruling UMNO – particularly over the latter's emphasis on the economic rights of the Malays. The PAP advocated a national identity shorn of ethnic differentiation, while the UMNO's *raison d'être* played on the Malay people's historic grievance at the loss of their assets during the colonial period (and their consequent need for compensation). Political differences spiralled out of control, and Singapore became independent from Malaysia on August 9, 1965.

Chronology

1959	Lee Kuan Yew becomes prime minister of Singapore
1961	PAP split gives rise to the Barisan Socialis
1963	Merger with Malaysia, and the beginnings of an attempt at import-substitution – PAP wins overwhelming victory in a general election
1965	August 9: independence from Malaysia
1966	The Housing Development Board, Public Utilities Board, the Economic Development Board (EDB) and the Central Providence Fund (CPF) formed in order to lead the way in the

provision of public services, particularly a massive programme of subsidized public housing

1967   Finance Minister Lim Kim San outlines a strategy of export-orientated development based principally on attracting foreign capital, technology and marketing skills to Singapore (as recommended in the Winsemius Report)

1968   The British depart from their naval base in Singapore. The Winsemius report is officially adopted as the government's economic strategy, following a massive victory in the general election (PAP wins all 58 seats, 51 of them without a contest). EDB's Industrial Promotion division begins to play a key role in attracting foreign investment.

1970   Labour shortages begin to emerge, and are relieved via the import of foreign workers

1971   Five-Power Defence Pact with Australia, NZ, UK and Malaysia. Tripartite National Wages Council (NWC) formed to steer future increases in wages.

1975-78   Wage restraint in the face of the global recession ensures real GDP growth averaging 8%

1979   June: the Second Industrial Revolution (SIR) aims to squeeze investment away from labour-intensive manufacturing, and the NWC raises wages by 20%

1982   J.B. Jeyaratnam wins Anson by-election, the first parliamentary seat lost by the PAP in seventeen years

1984   December: PAP wins 79 of 81 seats in the general election; Jeyaratnam (WP) and Chiam See Tong (SDP) represent the opposition. Despite the high-wage policy, real GDP grows at a 9-10% pace through 1980-84, but a slowdown begins in 4Q/84.

1985   Recession. Blue-ribbon committee headed by B.G. Lee Hsien Loong asserts that the high-wage policy was the ultimate cause of the recession; wages are frozen for two years, and the employer contribution to CPF is reduced from 25% to 15%.

1988   PAP wins 63.2% of the vote at the general election and 80 of 81 seats in parliament, with the SDP's Chiam the lone opposition member

1990   Goh Chok Tong succeeds Lee Kuan Yew as prime minister, while the latter becomes senior minister

1991   August 31: PAP wins 59% of the vote in the general election and the opposition manages to win 4 seats

1992   Economic slowdown (to 4.6% GDP growth in 2Q/92) is successfully tempered with the help of fiscal and monetary expansion

1993   Ong Teng Cheong is elected, with 57% of the vote, in the first election to the newly enhanced position of President of Singapore

1994   Real GDP grows more than 10% for the second consecutive year, and Singapore's per-capita GDP passes that of the UK, its erstwhile imperial power

1996   Evidence of a sharp economic slowdown emerges in the third quarter

1997   General election due

Constitution and government

The 1959 constitution was amended to make Singapore a republic in December 1965, and Inche Yusof was re-elected president. While the president's role was largely ceremonial, a further amendment in 1992 provided for direct elections for the presidency, and gave the president overall control of the country's foreign exchange reserves and some power to veto legislation.

Most legislative power rests in the 81-member unicameral parliament, whose members are elected in a mix of single-member constituencies and multi-member seats (called GRCs, for Group Representation Constituencies) with all seats filled on a "winner-take-all" (the party that wins the most votes in a GRC wins all the seats). A recent amendment introduced by the ruling PAP will extend the number of GRCs, possibly reducing single-member seats to as few as eight. The leader of the ruling party becomes prime minister, the office in which most executive authority actually rests. Lee Kuan Yew was prime minister from 1959 until 1990, and Goh Chok Tong has held the post since. The prime minister chooses a cabinet to help in his executive and legislative functions, and he usually chooses to have one or two deputy prime ministers. The Finance Minister also functions as ex-officio chairman of the Monetary Authority of Singapore. The state plays a key role in the economy, through its control over the Central Provident Fund (CPF), the savings fund towards which employers and employees are obliged to contribute, and through the government's stake in most of the largest Singaporean companies. Government ministers are among the most highly paid in the world. This guards against corruption and ensures that some of the leading lights of the private sector are attracted to political careers (DPM Tony Tan, for instance, was formerly the CEO of local banking major, OCBC).

The opposition is weak and, despite a sharp economic slowdown and disenchantment over spiralling prices of homes and cars, most Singaporeans recognize the crucial contribution to Singapore of the PAP's political leadership. A high proportion (at least 85%) of Singaporeans live in Housing Development Board apartments that they own. Nevertheless, many in the younger generation aspire to own private homes, the prices of which have soared more than 300% in the past five years. In the face of this rise, the government announced several measures in May 1996 to rein in speculative property transactions (via a stamp duty) and foreigners' purchases of residential property in Singapore (including a tax on capital gains for property sold within three years of purchase, and strict limits on loans to foreigners). These strictures have helped cap property prices and reduce transactions in the residential property market. Prices are expected to decline 10-15% before mid-1997, which will enhance the PAP's popularity.

Political parties

People's Action Party (PAP)
Ruling party since 1959
Key members: PM Goh Chok Tong, DPMs Tony Tan Keng Yam and Lee Hsien Loong, finance minister Richard Hu Tsu Tau, foreign minister S. Jayakumar
77 seats in parliament

Singapore Democratic Party (SDP)
One member (Chiam See Tong) often votes against the rest of the party.
Key personality: Chee Soon Juan, secretary-general, but not yet a member of parliament.
3 seats

Worker's Party
Non-MP J.B. Jeyaratnam is its most prominent member
1 seat

■ ECONOMICS

Historical overview

Singapore's role as an entrepôt grew during the first half of this century, but manufacturing did not begin to play a significant role until after the imperial preferences of the Great Depression (aimed against Japan) began to nurture a small textile industry, plus some tin and rubber processing. The mercantile interests of Singapore businessmen, however, led to a predilection towards free trade and a hostility towards the system of preferences (the latter finding greater support in peninsular Malaysia). In 1960, manufacturing still accounted for only 11.9% of GDP and re-exports accounted for 94% of total exports.

Import substitution was the economic basis of the merger with Malaysia. But its demise meant a new strategy, dependent on attracting multinational capital into export-orientated sectors, had to be adopted. Singapore returned to its status as a free port, but with a slew of fiscal incentives encouraging foreign direct investment (FDI) into the country's manufacturing sector. This strategy – led not by local entrepreneurs (as in Japan, Taiwan and Korea), but explicitly by multinational companies (MNCs) – was pioneered by Singapore (and has since been emulated by other ASEAN countries, and partially by China and recently India). The contrast with Latin America is also worth noting. During the 1960s and 1970s, Brazil, Argentina and Mexico also depended on MNC investment, but the rationale for FDI there was the protectionist barriers accorded to MNCs. In Singapore, MNCs were invited to invest in areas where Singapore had a comparative advantage – and MNC profit margins depended on the strength of global demand rather than the artificial profit margins flowing in Latin America from protectionist barriers.

The Economic Development Board (EDB) served as the agency charged with the responsibility of attracting foreign investors into the country. It scoured the globe looking for potential investments, consulting key MNCs to gauge the nature of their needs and aiming to find a match with Singapore's economic endowments. It shepherded Singapore up the value-added ladder successfully, focusing on honing Singapore's advantages: a highly skilled labour force, aided by subsidized skills-training, and top-quality physical infrastructure.

In vivid contrast to Hong Kong, Singapore retained a large and rapidly growing manufacturing sector marked by sharp increases in labour productivity (mainly a consequence of high levels of investment, and the high capital-to-labour ratio for the overall economy, particularly for the manufacturing sector). Manufacturing still accounts for 28% of GDP, and domestic exports remain the key driver of economic activity.

The services sector has also grown over the years, however. Singapore is the fourth largest foreign exchange trading centre in the world, is the centre of the Asian dollar market, and is now engaged in greatly expanding its role as a fund management centre (in which it is still a distant second to Hong Kong in ex-Japan Asia).

In recent years, new FDI has become concentrated in two sectors – semi-conductors and petrochemicals – that are highly susceptible to global cycles. The coincidence of a downturn in both cycles (a consequence of over-capacity in the Asian region following massive investments in the past two years) is the proximate cause of the current Singapore slowdown. However, Singapore has always succeeded in insulating its tradeable goods sector from inflationary impulses – which have instead concentrated on non-tradeable goods, services and assets. The real effective exchange rate of the Singapore dollar has not appreciated significantly in the past decade despite a large and growing current account surplus. When the upturn in global electronics demand comes, Singapore will be a prime beneficiary – and real GDP is expected to recover to 7.1% growth in 1997 after dipping to a decade-low of 5.5% (estimated) in 1996.

Balance of payments, savings and investment

Singapore suffers from a problem of plenty arising from its twin surpluses – fiscal and BoP basic balance. Its gross domestic savings rate reached 51% in 1995, while investment accounted for 34% of GDP, and the country posted a current account surplus equivalent to over 17% of GDP. While the CPF system ensures a structurally high private savings rate, public savings (or the budget surplus, without accounting for capital receipts from parastatal agencies) amounted to 7.8% of GDP in 1995.

The principal contributor to the current account surplus was a large surplus in services trade. Singapore also receives considerable net inflows of long-term capital that contribute to its large basic balance surplus – which primarily accumulates as foreign exchange reserves.

Singapore's economic slowdown
Sharpest slowdown since 1985

In 1996 Singapore found itself in the midst of its sharpest economic slowdown in a decade. The downturn was particularly severe for the trade-related sectors – manufacturing, transport and commerce. With economic policy emphasizing the need to rein in asset inflation, sentiment in asset markets worsened, causing activity in the financial and business services sector to decelerate. Pockets of residual strength, primarily in construction, were scant. Export weakness, especially in electronics which accounts for more than half of non-oil domestic exports and over 45 per cent of manufacturing value-added, was a key factor behind the 1996 slowdown.

Weaker productivity performance

Estimates indicate that the second half of 1996 marked the first half-year of actual declines in labour-productivity in Singapore for fifteen years. The prevailing view is that this is a cyclical phenomenon that has also afflicted competitor countries. Thus *relative* unit labour costs have not risen significantly, although the absolute gains in unit labour costs appear excessive. In a chronically labour-scarce economy like Singapore's, employers have a natural aversion towards cutting employment in the midst of a temporary slowdown. This form of "labour hoarding" does not become a serious problem unless the cyclical downturn is prolonged.

Rising relative prices of non-traded goods a reflection of rapid productivity growth in the traded-goods sector

There is no doubt that Singapore's currency management has successfully forced manufacturers to move up the value-added ladder. Rising productivity (ultimately underpinned by strong investment spending), coupled with fiscal and other incentives, has helped ensure the enduring competitiveness of Singapore's exporters.

Singapore's export prices have declined steadily in the past five years at a slightly faster pace than that at which the trade-weighted exchange rate has appreciated. However, the CPI inflation differential between Singapore and its trading partners has been lower (about 1.5-2%) than the pace of the Singapore dollar's annual appreciation (3.5-4%), implying real Singapore dollar appreciation, based on a CPI comparison, of 2-2.5% annually. Because of declining import and export prices, there has been little change in the real exchange rate, at least based on goods and services that are traded. Within the context of the domestic economy, this merely implies that the relative prices of traded goods have declined because of higher productivity in that sector of the economy.

Exports and imports as % of GDP

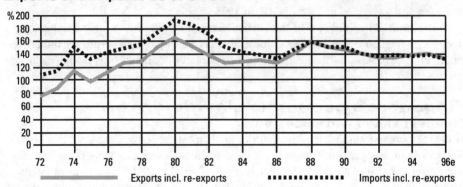

Source: Official data

Current account balance as a % of GDP

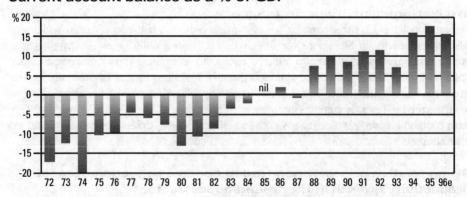

Source: Official data

Breakdown of exports (1995)

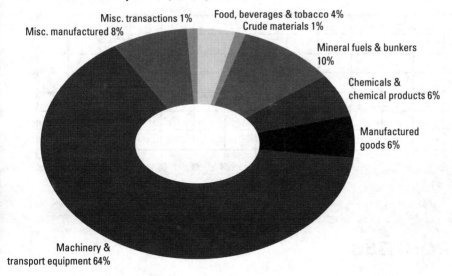

Misc. transactions 1%
Misc. manufactured 8%
Food, beverages & tobacco 4%
Crude materials 1%
Mineral fuels & bunkers 10%
Chemicals & chemical products 6%
Manufactured goods 6%
Machinery & transport equipment 64%

Source: Official data

Monetary policy

The trade-weighted exchange rate of the Singapore dollar is the key instrument of monetary policy. Singapore aims to keep CPI inflation below 2.5%, and rarely fails. The MAS has allowed the NEER to appreciate 3.5-4% annually over the past decade – more during periods of over-heating, less during slowdowns such as those of 1985 and 1992. Despite the primacy of the current fight against asset inflation, the pace of the currency's appreciation is expected to moderate during the current economic slowdown – effectively implying a marginal easing of monetary policy.

Currency

The Monetary Authority of Singapore manages the Singapore dollar against a trade-weighted basket of currencies. The weights are also adjusted to take account of third-country competitors in key export markets and the key country-sources for imported inputs used in exports. In other words, competitor currencies (such as the currencies of Malaysia, South Korea and Taiwan) likely have a higher weight than suggested by their trade-shares, as does the Japanese yen (because it is the largest source of imported intermediate inputs). Countries with a rigid dollar peg (such as Hong Kong and Thailand) have felt the recent impact of US dollar strength much more than Singapore, where the impact has been tempered by the much higher weights accorded to currencies other than the greenback. The direct impact of yen weakness has been further dampened by the fact that a relatively small proportion of Singapore's exports compete with Japanese production.

Singapore dollar/US dollar exchange rate

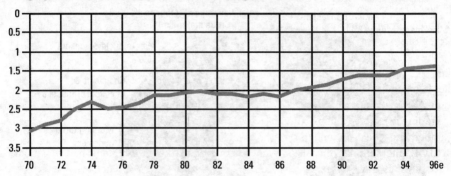

■ EQUITIES

Index performance (in local currency)

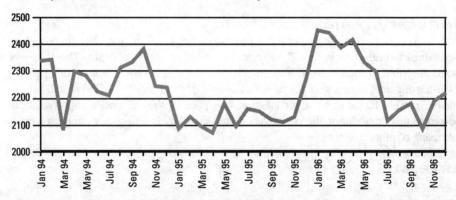

Key indicators

	Index Performance %, in US$ terms	Market Cap.	P/E	Div. Yield
1994	-2.8	169.8	24.7	—
1995	11.9	202.3	23.6	1.3
1996	-7.3	186.5	21.7	1.3

Sources: Local stock exchange, IFC, Bloomberg, Datastream, UBS

Structure

The Stock Exchange of Singapore (SES) was established in June 1973. It operates four markets for the trading of securities and derivatives: the Main Board, SESDAQ, Stock Options and CLOB International.

A total of 215 Singapore and 39 foreign companies were listed on the Main Board as of August 1996, with a market capitalization of US$200.6 billion. The SES is keen to encourage eligible foreign companies to list on the SES in line with its efforts to develop Singapore into a regional securities market.

The Stock Exchange of Singapore Dealing and Automated Quotation (SESDAQ) market, the second oldest board, was launched in February 1987. It is aimed at enabling smaller companies with a shorter track record to tap the stockmarket for long term funds. As at August 1996, 48 companies were listed with a total market capitalization of US$2.6 billion.

Trading of equity options commenced on March 1993. Currently, call and put options on 7 underlying stocks are traded on the Options market.

CLOB International, the SES's over-the-counter market, was established in January 1990 to allow investors to trade in a number of international securities listed on foreign stock exchanges. As of August 1996, 10 Hong Kong stocks, 112 Malaysian stocks and 7 other international stocks were quoted on CLOB, with a total market capitalization of US$161 billion. Companies quoted on CLOB do not have to adhere to the disclosure policy that applies to companies listed on the Main Board or SESDAQ. However, corporate announcements of companies quoted on CLOB are disseminated as timely as possible to investors.

The SES has recently established a Foreign Board to accommodate foreign companies and infrastructure projects that do not meet the stringent mainboard listing criteria. All listings will be in US dollars. To date, three companies have applied for listing.

Regulatory authority

The SES is regulated by the Securities Industry Act of 1986 and supervised through a set of rules and regulations enforced by the nine-member Stock Exchange of Singapore Committee.

Brokers and commissions

There are thirty-three member companies, of whom seven are international members, that is they can be wholly owned by foreigners. These can deal freely in SES-quoted securities with non-residents and companies controlled by or beneficially owned by non-residents.

Commission rates are set by the SES and are payable as follows:

On the first S$250,000 (US$180,000)	1%
On the next S$250,000	0.9%
On the next S$250,000	0.8%
On the next S$250,000	0.7%
On the next S$500,000	0.5%
On amounts exceeding S$1.5 million (US$1 million)	Negotiable, subject to a minimum of 0.3%

Trading methods

Shares are traded mainly in board lots of 1,000 shares. All securities are traded through the computerized Central Limit Order Book (CLOB) trading system. The CLOB system maintains an order book for every traded security and matches buy and sell orders that are electronically transmitted to the SES's computer system.

Hours

Trading takes place from 09.00 to 12.30 and from 14.00 to 17.00, Monday to Friday.

Settlement time and clearing

Trading on the SES markets is scripless. All transactions are reflected in securities accounts that shareholders maintain with the Central Depository (CDP), a subsidiary of the SES which acts as a central nominee.

Trades are dealt on a ready basis for seven-day settlement. New issues are traded on "when issued" basis, that is trading commences on the next market day after the shares are balloted.

In addition to brokerage fees, the following charges are payable:

◆ a clearing fee of 0.05% on the value of the contract, subject to a maximum of S$100
◆ a contract stamp duty of 0.2% on the value of the contract
◆ a goods & services tax of 3% on brokerage and clearing fees.

Dividends and taxes

Singapore does not levy dividend tax nor withhold tax on dividends paid to non-residents. However tax at the corporate tax rate of 26% is deducted from the gross dividends payable, representing the corporate tax on the listed company's profits out of which dividends are franked.

Limits on foreigners

There are no foreign exchange controls or capital gains tax on the trading of securities by non-residents. Purchases and sales of securities are not subject to any restrictions with the exception of banking stocks and certain strategic companies. When foreign limits are reached, a separate foreign board is established. There are also no limitations on the repatriation of income, capital gains and capital.

Types of shares

Most shares are ordinary voting shares. There are few preferred shares.

Stock indices

The most commonly used indices locally are the Straits Times Index, a thirty-stock unweighted index comprising industrial stocks, and the DBS 50 Index, a broad based fifty-stock index weighted by market capitalization. The SES also computes a Mainboard Index (all listings), an All-share index (S$ listings) and sub-indices for the property, industrial, hotel, finance and electronics sectors and for foreign companies.

Sectors

The main sectors in the market are banks (which take up 19.8% of market capitalization), telecommunications (29%,) property (14.7%) and airlines (10.6%).

Disclosures

Listed companies are encouraged to provide as full a disclosure as possible. Minimum disclosure standards are provided by the SES. Listed companies must disclose their financial results twice a year.

Shareholders' rights

Shareholders can vote by proxy. The Companies Act sets out minimum periods for sending out notices of upcoming shareholder meetings.

Take-over bids

The take-over trigger level in Singapore is 25%. Any shareholder holding more than 25% but less than 50% of the shares also needs to make a general offer if he buys more than 3% within twelve months.

ADRs

There are seventeen ADRs.

Market performance and outlook

The market had a good rally towards the turn of 1996, driven by improved sentiment toward the property sector. However valuations became stretched, and the onset of disappointing corporate results brought about a correction.

The imposition of anti-speculation measures in the property sector in May, the sharp downturn in exports in June, as well as more earnings disappointment in August to September, further eroded the market's performance.

Looking ahead, there may be more downside risk as the economy continues to languish amid continued weakness in most sectors in the market. This will affect confidence towards the property sector, and in turn affect stock market performance. No pick-up is expected until the spring of 1997.

■ DEBT

The Government of Singapore (GOS) intends to make the country the major regional bond market centre. It is already larger than the equity market, but 99% is made up of Asian Dollar issues – a counterpart of the London eurodollar market. Singapore limits foreign participation in its bond markets and has not internationalized its currency.

The Monetary Authority of Singapore (MAS) is fully responsible for developing and regulating the bond markets. Prior to the 1986 Securities Act, the market was self-regulated by practitioners under the guidance of the Singapore Stock Exchange (SES).

Public debt

Singapore has huge cash reserves and usually runs a fiscal surplus. Government debt is issued to help develop the domestic, corporate bond market by providing a benchmark yield curve and, more importantly, to absorb the country's substantial contractual savings held in the Central Provident Fund (CPF). Government bonds secure a guaranteed return for CPF contributors. Higher returns are earned by the Government of Singapore Investment

Corporation (GSIC), which converts the proceeds from the CPF's bond holdings into hard currencies for overseas investment.

Money market intervention by MAS is conducted through buying and selling treasury bills, foreign exchange swaps, interbank lending and repurchase agreements in government bonds.

Treasury bills

The MAS affects domestic liquidity and interest rates through issuing 91-, 182- and 364-day treasury bills. Volumes auctioned vary each week.

Treasury bonds

The bond market was restructured in 1987 and is based on the US model. Two-, 5- and 7-year bonds are auctioned on a yield basis and allotted at par. Subscribers bid through one of seven primary dealers and pay the full price on application. Non-competitive bids are restricted to S$500,000 million (about US$360,000) and are allocated at the weighted average yield of successful bids. Settlement is book-entry. In addition, issues with longer maturities are placed with the CPF, usually at administratively determined yields.

Private debt

Asian Currency Units (ACU) are traded on the interbank market and are a conduit for transferring capital to Asia. Asian Dollar credits are most commonly issued on a 3- and 6-month roll-over basis, and carry a variable interest rate pegged to SIBOR or LIBOR.

Asian Dollar Market

The sector was set up in 1968, and now dominates Singapore's domestic bond market. Asian Dollar bonds are issued in bearer form and are free of withholding tax. They are listed on the Singapore Stock Exchange, regulated by the MAS and placed through management, underwriting and selling groups with Asian investors. Issues fall outside the jurisdiction of the government in whose currency the bond is denominated – usually US dollars. Structures include fixed coupons, FRNs and convertibles. Secondary market activity is over the counter but illiquid because issues are tightly held, mostly by banks, to meet reserve requirements. Settlement is through euroclear or cedel. Non-residents can purchase a limited number of approved Asian Dollar bonds.

Derivatives

The Singapore International Monetary Exchange (SIMEX) was established in 1984 to provide risk management services to international investors, and is now the most active futures exchange in the region. The following contracts are traded:

◆ 3-month eurodollar, 3-month euroyen, 3-month euromark, 3-month eurosterling
◆ Nikkei-225 Stock Index, Nikkei-300 Index, MSCI Hong Kong Stock Index
◆ Japanese Government Bond 10-year futures, US$/yen and US$/deutschmark deferred spot currency contracts
◆ Gold, Sulphur fuel, Oil

In 1984 SIMEX, jointly with the Chicago Mercantile Exchange (CME), formed the SIMEX-CME Mutual Offset System, to trade eurodollars in two time zones.

Eurobond issues (US$m)

	1990	1991	1992	1993	1994	1995	1996
Sovereign	—	—	—	—	—	—	—
Private	75.0	0.0	62.5	0.0	330.0	379.4	405.0

■ SINGAPORE: Economic indicators

Population and development	1990	1991	1992	1993	1994	1995	1996e
Population, million	2.7	2.8	2.8	2.9	2.9	3.0	3.0
Population growth, %	2.2	2.1	2.0	2.0	2.0	1.9	1.8
Nominal GDP per capita, US$	13844	15781	17643	20299	24181	28652	30281

National accounts							
Nominal GDP, US$bn	37.4	43.6	49.7	58.3	70.9	85.6	92.0
Change in real GDP, %	8.1	7.0	6.4	10.1	10.1	8.8	6.1
Gross fixed capital formation, % of GDP	31.8	33.3	35.6	35.0	33.7	33.0	34.1

Money supply and inflation							
Narrow money, change %, Dec/Dec	11.0	7.7	12.7	23.6	2.3	8.3	11.0
Broad money, change %, Dec/Dec	20.0	12.4	8.9	8.5	14.4	8.5	11.3
Consumer price inflation (avg.) %	3.4	3.4	2.3	2.3	3.0	1.8	1.4

Government finance							
Government expenditure, % of GDP	21.0	21.2	19.6	17.4	13.0	12.9	14.9
Government balance, % of GDP	10.6	8.6	12.6	15.5	8.5	7.6	4.8

Exchange rates lc=local currency							
Exchange rate, annual average, lc/US$	1.81	1.73	1.63	1.62	1.53	1.41	1.41
Exchange rate, end of year, lc/US$	1.74	1.63	1.64	1.60	1.46	1.41	1.41
Real exchange rate 1990=100	100.0	104.3	106.1	107.5	113.2	115.1	116.1

Balance of payments							
Exports of goods & services, US$m	67489	75154	82503	96372	121284	148394	156520
Change %	21.9	11.4	9.8	16.8	25.8	22.4	5.5
Imports of goods & services, US$m, fob	64956	70528	77885	91778	110123	134028	141416
Change %	22.9	8.6	10.4	17.8	20.0	21.7	5.5
Trade balance, of goods only, US$m, fob-fob	-1633	-110	-1823	-2724	1351	1625	-100
Current account balance, US$m	3097	4884	5615	4205	11284	15093	14400
as a % of GDP	8.3	11.2	11.3	7.2	15.9	17.6	15.6

Foreign exchange reserves							
Foreign exchange reserves, US$m	27958	34436	40115	48591	58413	68800	78100
Import cover (reserves/imports), months	5.2	5.9	6.2	6.4	6.4	6.2	6.6

Foreign debt and debt service							
Short-term debt, US$m	25223	24931	29786	32441	35461	38481	—
Total foreign debt, US$m	28697	28844	33464	37113	40363	43335	—
as a % of GDP	76.6	66.2	67.3	63.6	57.0	50.7	—
as a % of foreign exchange receipts	38.7	34.8	36.8	35.5	31.0	27.1	—
Interest payments, US$m	2474	1856	1362	1377	1577	1982	—
Principal repayments, US$m	1150	652	724	671	845	870	—
Total debt service, US$m	3624	2508	2086	2048	2422	2852	—
as a % of goods exports	6.6	4.1	3.1	2.6	2.5	2.4	—
as a % of foreign exchange receipts	4.9	3.0	2.3	2.0	1.9	1.8	—

Slovakia

KEY FACTS

Area (thousands of km²):	49
Population (1995, millions):	5.4
Population projection (2025, millions):	5.7
Population younger than 15 yrs (1991, % of total):	23.0
Urbanization rate (1993, % of population):	58
Life expectancy (1993, years at birth):	71
Gross domestic product (1996, US$bn):	19.1
GDP per capita (1996, US$):	3505
Average annual GDP growth rate (1990-96, %):	-1.3
Average annual inflation rate (1990-96, %):	19
Currency (koruna per US$, average 1996):	30.7
Structure of production (1994):	33.2% industry & construction, 51% services, 5.6% agriculture, 9.5% other
Main exports:	machinery & transport equipment, misc. manufactured goods, chemicals
Main imports:	machinery & transport equipment, fuel, intermediate manufactured products
Main trading partners:	EU, Czech Republic, Former Soviet Union, Germany
Total foreign debt (% of GDP):	34
Next elections due under normal circumstances:	September 1998
Credit rating: (Nov 1996, Standard & Poor's, Moody's)	BBB-; Baa3

FORECAST: 1997-2000 (average)

	Worst case	Most likely	Best case
Real GDP growth (%)	2 to 5	5.to 7	8 to 10
Inflation (%)	7 to 12	4 to 7	2 to 4

■ POLITICS

Historical overview

Between AD 500 and 700, Slavonic tribes settled in the area of Slovakia, and in early 800, the empire of Great Moravia was established. After the Battle of Bratislava in 907, Great Moravia became part of the kingdom of Hungary. Following the Turkish invasion of Hungary, Bratislava (Pressburg, Pozsony) became the capital of the remaining Hungarian kingdom, which was now under Habsburg rule.

Slovak nationalism started to emerge in the 19th century, but was stifled by Hungary. After the accord between Hungary and Austria in 1867, the Hungarian government adopted a policy of magyarization, which sought to create a homogenous Magyar state.

After the defeat of the Austro-Hungarian Empire in the First World War, the Prague National Committee declared an independent Czecho-Slovak state in October 1918. The Slovak National Council adopted a resolution declaring the right of self-determination for Slovaks and endorsed the principle of Czecho-Slovak unity. By the beginning of the Paris peace conference in January 1919, Czecho-Slovak troops had already occupied essentially all territory to which they aspired, creating a fait accompli for the conference. Czecho-Slovakia's population of 13.6 million was formed by Czechs (6.7m), Slovaks (2.05m), Ruthenians (0.46m), Germans (3.2m), Magyars (0.69m), Jews (0.18m) and Poles (0.08m).

The Munich Agreement in 1938 ended the independence of Czechoslovakia. The Sudeten district was assigned to Germany, President Benes resigned and the new president granted Slovakia autonomy. Backed by the Nazi regime in Germany, the Slovak Diet declared independence in March 1939, while Hungary annexed Ruthenia and parts of eastern and southern Slovakia. On March 15, German troops occupied the remaining parts of Czechoslovakia. But after the end of the Second World War, Slovakia joined forces with the Czech Republic once more. This time (unlike 1918) concessions were made to Slovak demands for autonomy, including the establishment of a regional legislature (the Slovak National Council) and an executive based in Bratislava, Slovakia's capital. However, the seizure of power by the Communists led by Gustav Husak in 1948 halted the movement towards a federal system.

Under Communist rule, expressions of nationalism were suppressed, and in 1954 Husak and others regarded as nationalists were imprisoned. In 1960, the Slovak National Council (SNC) was abolished. The country enjoyed a short period of liberalization in 1968, the so-called Prague Spring, under the leadership of Alexander Dubcek. But in August 1968, some 600,000 Soviet troops invaded (supported by Husak), and the government was purged of liberals.

Husak, despite his early nationalist credentials, did little to advance Slovak autonomy during the 1970s. The dissident movement began to grow in the early 1980s, culminating in the anti-government demonstrations of 1988, and the "Velvet Revolution" of 1989 when Husak ceded control to Vaclav Havel without a fight.

A coalition government was set up in 1990 following the first civilian elections since 1946. But the principal coalition partners – the Civil Forum (Czech), Public Against Violence (Slovak) and Christian Democratic Movement (Slovak) – soon began to fall out. The Christian Democratic Movement joined the pro-federal wing of Public Against Violence and, together with two Hungarian parties, established a majority in the Slovak National Council. Vladimir Meciar, founding member of Public Against Violence, was ousted from the Praesidium of the National Council and replaced by Jan Carnogursky.

In the 1992 elections, Meciar and his new party, the Movement for a Democratic Slovakia (HZDS), won 74 of the 150 seats of the Slovak National Council, while Vaclav Klaus and his Civic Democratic Party (ODS) emerged as winners in the Czech Republic. Both parties agreed to form a federal government on the basis of symmetric power-sharing. However, fundamental differences between the two leaders eventually lead to the separation of the Slovak and Czech republics, which took place on January 1, 1993.

Recent events

Within months of becoming independent, Slovakia's coalition government began to fragment. In 1993, Meciar sacked the deputy prime minister, Milan Knazko, who went on to set up a new party, the Alliance of Democrats of the Slovak Republic (ADSR). In February 1994, two other parties were set up: the National Democratic Party-New Alternative (NDP-NA), and the Democratic Union of Slovakia (DUS) led by the foreign minister, Jozef Moravcik.

In March 1994, Meciar lost a no-confidence motion, and the government was replaced by a new coalition based around the Christian Democratic Movement (CDM). Under the new leadership of Moravcik, Slovakia began to assume a more Western stance than Meciar.

Meciar bounced back in the 1994 elections after a highly populist campaign. Despite the achievements of the Moravcik regime which had successfully reduced inflation and tackled the Hungarian minority question, Meciar's HZDS party won 35% of the vote giving it 61 seats in the council.

Desperate attempts were made to patch together a coalition government, but without success. So Moravcik continued to rule until mid-December when the HZDS finally persuaded the right-wing Slovak National Party and the left-wing Association of Workers of Slovakia Party (ZRS) to form a new government.

But the coalition between Meciar's HZDS, the far-left ZRS and the far-right Slovak National Party (SNS) looks highly unstable. It barely survived in June 1996 and it is doubtful whether it will stay together in its present form until the next general elections, scheduled for June 1998. Meciar, however, who continues to enjoy strong public support, will try to prevent early elections.

Another serious political concern is the continued conflict between President Kovac and Prime Minister Meciar, which dominates domestic politics and is felt also at international levels. In March 1994, President Kovac asked the parliament to vote against Meciar's minority government.

Since regaining power after elections in October 1994, Meciar has been trying to oust the president. This struggle has not only dominated domestic politics but also alienated the European Union and the US. Slovakia's ambition to join the EU at the same time as the other Visegrad-countries (Poland, Czech Republic and Hungary) may have suffered as a result.

Chronology

500-700	Settlement of Slavonic tribes
833	Great Moravia is set up
907	Battle of Bratislava, destruction of Great Moravia
1000	Slovakia becomes part of Hungary
1848–49	Slovakian uprising
1863	Origin of Matica Slovenska
1867	Compromise between Austria and Hungary, Austro-Hungarian dual monarchy takes power
1915	Pittsburgh Agreement is signed by Czech and Slovak emigration leaders
1918	First Czecho-Slovak Republic
1938	Munich agreement, Sudeten district annexed to Germany

1939	March 14: Slovak National Council declares independent Slovakia with backing from Germany
1939	March 15: German troops occupy remaining Czech provinces, Bohemia and Moravia
1946	May 26: elections to the Constituent National Assembly of Czechoslovakia, Communists strongest party with 38%
1948	Communist coup in Prague, Czechoslovakia becomes part of the Soviet bloc
1968	January: Alexander Dubcek elected First Secretary of Communist Party
1968	April: Prague Spring, Communist Party announces new action programme which comprises gradual political and economic liberalization
1968	August 21: Warsaw Pact troops invade Czechoslovakia; Dubcek and other reformers are kidnapped. Gustav Husak takes over the top job at the Communist Party.
1989	Communist Party drops claims to "leading role"; President Husak is replaced by playwright and dissident Vaclav Havel
1990	June: first free elections since 1946. Civic Forum, Public Against Violence and Christian Democratic Movement emerge as the strongest parties
1992	June: Vladimir Meciar's HZDS wins Slovak federal elections
1993	January 1: Separation of Slovak and Czech republics
1994	Meciar's HZDS wins Slovak general elections

Constitution and government

The Slovak constitution was passed by the Slovak National Council on September 1992. It became fully effective on January 1, 1993 when the Slovak Republic formally split from the Czech Republic.

Supreme power is invested in the National Council of the Slovak Republic, whose 150 members are elected every four years. The president (head of state) is elected every five years.

Current government

Head of State	President Michal Kovac
Prime Minister	Vladimir Meciar
Deputy Prime Minister	Sergei Kozlik

Central bank

The National Bank of Slovakia was set up in January 1993 as a successor to the Czechoslovak State Bank. It is the central bank and bank of issue. Governor Vladimir Masar has often stated his commitment to bringing down inflation. In 1996, its lon-term debt was upgraded from BB+ to BBB- by the rating agency Standard & Poor's.

Political parties

The current government, led by Vladimir Meciar, is made up of an uneasy coalition between Meciar's Movement for a Democratic Slovakia, the right-wing Slovak National Party and the left-wing Association of Slovak Workers. Together it has 83 seats in the 150-seat parliament.

The principal opposition parties are: the right-of-centre Christian Democratic Movement led by Jan Carnogursky; the Democratic Union Party, led by Jozef Moravcik; and the Party of the Democratic Left which with the Social Democratic Party of Slovakia, the Farmers' Movement of Slovak Republic and the Green Party of Slovakia form the Common Choice coalition, led by Jozef Migas. There is also a Hungarian coalition, led by Vojtech Bugar.

Results of the September 1994 elections

Movement for a Democratic Slovakia (HZDS)	61 seats	35.0%
Common Choice (SV)	18 seats	10.4%
Christian Democratic Movement (KDH)	17 seats	10.1%
Hungarian Coalition (HK)	17 seats	10.2%
Slovak Democratic Union (DU)	15 seats	8.6%
Association of Slovak Workers (ZRS)	13 seats	7.3%
Slovak National Party (SNS)	9 seats	5.4%

Next election
The next legislative election will be held in September 1998.

■ ECONOMICS

Historical overview

The Communist coup in 1948 was soon followed by the transformation of the economy into a centrally planned system. The first five-year plan was introduced that October, revised in 1950 and again in 1951. This and all subsequent plans emphasized the buildup of heavy industries, predominantly military production, power generation and chemical industries. These newly created industries depended mainly on the Soviet Union for their export market as well as for raw materials and energy.

The agricultural sector was divided into co-operatives and state farms, although members of collective farms were allowed to cultivate their own small allotments. The industrial economy, meanwhile, suffered when the energy supply from Russia began to dry up in 1984. To compensate, the government began to commission a number of nuclear power plants. During the 1980s, the economy grew slowly but steadily.

After the collapse of the Soviet Union, the Czechoslovak government started a series of radical market-orientated reforms. Subsidies were phased out, and government support for state-owned companies reduced. Prices on imported goods were liberalized. Nearly eight thousand small enterprises were privatized by public auction in 1990 and 1991.

Slovakia's heavy industries were hit hard by these reforms – many could not survive without cheap energy, and suffered from the decline in demand from their key markets in the East. Manufacturing could not compete with imported goods. Starved of the support which had fostered it for decades, industrial output fell in 1990 and 1991. Unemployment rose, leading to a sharp fall in living standards. With domestic demand dampened by the anti-inflationary policies of the new government, the economy plunged into recession. Meciar struggled to reduce the impact of the changes by slowing the pace of reform. GDP, however, continued to fall, by 2.5% in 1990, 14.5% in 1991, 7% in 1992 and 4.1% in 1993.

Transition-recession-recovery

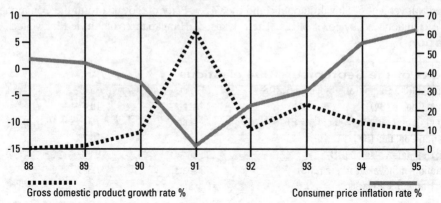

▪▪▪▪▪▪▪▪▪
Gross domestic product growth rate %   Consumer price inflation rate %

Source: IFS

After the removal of Meciar as prime minister in 1994, the coalition pressed ahead with further structural reforms. A second wave of coupon privatization was introduced to include the sale of some two hundred state-owned companies with a nominal value of SK80 billion (US$2.6 million).

As a result of these changes, Slovakia's macroeconomic performance began to improve steadily in 1994. Exports of chemicals, oil products and steel increased as producers switched to new markets in Western Europe. The construction industry took advantage of its lower production costs to win new orders abroad. GDP grew for the first time in four years, by 4.3%. Annual inflation fell from 23% in 1993 to 12%. Unemployment was well below forecast, at 14.6%.

Most of its IMF-approved targets were met, and in June 1994 Slovakia qualified for a US$254 million IMF standby loan and a second US$90 million tranche of its Systematic Transformation Facility. By the end of September 1994, its foreign currency reserves had tripled from their end-of-1993 total. Exports of basic industrial goods such as chemicals, oil products and steel soared in 1993 and 1994.

Recent developments

Economic recovery continued in 1995 with GDP growth up to 7.3%. Inflation fell further to just 9.9% for the year as a whole. However, much of the recent growth has been driven by domestic demand, which could fall away when increased structural reforms create higher unemployment. Fixed capital formation is likely to remain strong, mainly due to large investments in the energy and oil sector.

The National Bank of Slovakia has expressed its concern about the rising trade and current account deficits incurred by rising domestic demand. Export growth is expected to continue to slow in 1996 in the wake of the koruna's recent real appreciation.

A recent IMF survey published in the summer of 1996 warned that Slovakia, like other Central European economies, needed to prevent its main competitive advantage – low-cost labour – from being eroded by wage increases. Many of the country's largest companies are facing demands for higher wages, despite remaining less productive than their overseas competitors.

Inflation

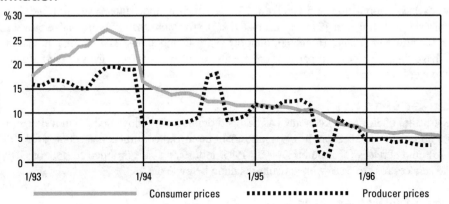

Source: IFS

The reliance of the Slovakian economy on heavy industries is likely to hamper development. Unlike the Czech Republic, it has few consumer-orientated manufacturing industries that could take advantage of its low wage costs. Efficiency remains low in many companies.

Export and import growth (% YOY)

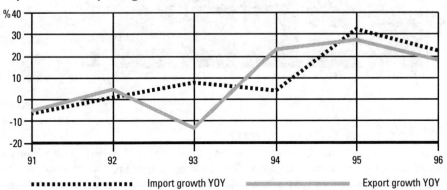

Source: UBS

The future of the agricultural and forestry sectors also remain uncertain. The return of land to pre-1945 owners has yet to be completed, deterring farmers from developing small-scale farms. The forestry industry, meanwhile, remains bedevilled by pollution caused by the country's power industry. Official figures show that 14% of the country's forests have been destroyed or damaged by acid rain, with 80% affected.

At the same time, Meciar's administration has been reluctant to press ahead with controversial privatizations that will probably lead to a further rise in unemployment.

Nevertheless, the second wave of privatization has been completed, and Slovakia hopes to join the OECD in 1997.

Population

Slovakia has a population of 5.4 million, 23% of which is under fifteen years of age. The population growth rate in 1995 was estimated at 0.54%. More than 85% are native Slovaks. There is, however, a large Hungarian minority representing almost 11% of the population, who have their own political party. There are also as many as 500,000 gypsies who are not on the electoral register.

The economy

The structure of Slovakia's economy has changed dramatically following the removal of subsidies and price liberalization. In 1991, industrial output and construction accounted for 60% of GDP and services for around 35%. By 1995, industry's share dropped to 33% of GDP, while services rose to 52%, with agriculture falling below 6%.

Share of GDP by sector

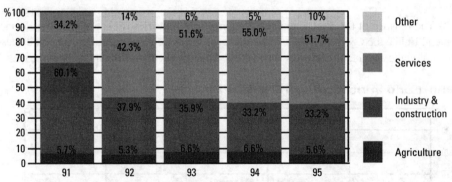

Source: IFS

Savings and investment

Slovakia's economy is in need of investment, but capital inflows have been relatively small compared to other transition economies. The stock of foreign investment amounted to US$732 million by the end of 1995, a rather modest level given the investment needs of the country. However, the growing number of companies with foreign capital participation is positive. These increased from 5,143 in 1993 to 8,740 by the end of 1995. Gross fixed investment accounted for 29% of GDP in 1995.

Balance of payments

Despite a massive fall in exports in the early 1990s when demand in its key Eastern markets disappeared, Slovakia's balance of payments has never been unduly troubled. Exports fell, but so, too, did imports, and in 1994, Slovakia registered a trade surplus of US$109 million. But both the current account and trade balances deteriorated in 1996 on the back of falling exports, and the country remains vulnerable to shifts in demand for its manufactured exports. The country's principal trading partners are the EU, which accounted for an estimated 37.4% of exports and 34.7% of imports, and the Czech Republic. The former Soviet Union, the country's dominant partner for most of its postwar history, now only accounts for 7% of exports. The main export products are machinery and transport equipment, chemicals, and black-market manufactured goods.

Current account as a % of GDP

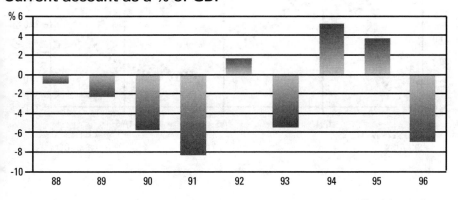

Source: Official data; UBS estimates

Economic policy
Monetary policy
The National Bank of Slovakia (NBS) has played a major role in macroeconomic stabilization. The most tangible proof is the steadily falling inflation rate, which provided scope for lower official and market interest rates. In addition, the NBS gained credibility in domestic and foreign financial markets. The primary objective of the NBS is to maintain currency stability. The NBS monitors the development of the monetary aggregate M2. Growth rates are set in advance, based on macroeconomic expectations and these rates can be adjusted according to economic performance. The target for 1996 is 11.6% (+/-0.6%).

Fiscal policy
Slovakia has run a small budget deficit for the past year. In April 1996, the state budget deficit was US$147 million. Planned revenue for the year is US$5.2 billion against expenditure of US$6.1 billion. However, it should reach its target of restricting the annual deficit to US$880 million or 4.1% of GDP. Slovakia's gross foreign debt has risen in recent years from US$2.7 billion in 1991 to an estimated US$5.8 billion in 1995. However, it is still not large enough to cause concern.

Currency
The Slovak koruna (crown, SKK) replaced the Czecho-Slovak crown on February 8, 1993 as the legal currency of Slovakia. The SKK is fixed against a dollar/deutschmark basket. The fluctuation band was widened from +/-3% to +/-5% on July 17, 1996. The Lombard rate was raised to 15% from 13% and minimum reserve requirements were increased from 3% to 9%, effective from August 1. The SKK has gradually devalued since the beginning of 1995. The

sharp appreciation at the beginning of 1995 and the gradual depreciation since late 1995 result from changing US dollar exchange rates.

Slovakian koruna/US dollar/DEM exchange rate

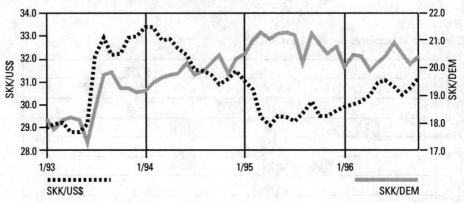

SKK/US$ SKK/DEM

■ EQUITIES

Index performance (in local currency)

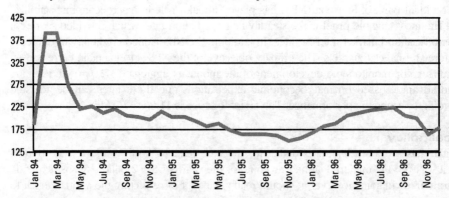

Key indicators

	Index performance %	Market Cap. US$bn	Market P/E	Div. Yield
1994	—	1.1	27.6	3.3
1995	-24.2	1.2	17.5	3.9
1996	15	2.2	8.5	3.3

Sources: Local stock exchange, IFC, Bloomberg, Datastream, UBS

Background
The Bratislava Stock Exchange (BSSE) was formed in 1992 following independence from Czechoslovakia. Total market capitalization in June 1996 was SKK190 billion (US$6.3 billion), of which SKK52.6 billion (US$1.75 billion) comprised listed shares.

Structure
The BSSE divides securities between three boards: the Senior Market of Listed Securities, the Junior Market of Listed Securities, and the unlisted Market of Registered Securities.

The unlisted market is by far the largest, with trading in 907 shares compared to just eight on the Junior Market and eleven on the Senior Market. Block trades have been permitted on the BSSE since December 1995 with the aim of increasing liquidity.

Regulatory authority
The BSSE is a self-regulatory body with the Stock Exchange Chamber its executive body. It is owned by banks, brokerages and other financial institutions.

Trading methods
Trading on the BSSE takes place using the Electronic Stock Exchange Trading System (EBOS). It is an on-line computerized system and operates on all three boards. In addition, there is also an RM-S market trading system.

Hours
Trading takes place between 10.30 and 14.00, Monday to Friday.

Settlement time and clearing
Settlement takes place on a trade date plus three business days (T+3) basis.

Limits on price movement
For direct trades, share prices can only fall by a maximum of 10%; there is no upper limit. However, for anonymous trades there is an upper and lower limit of 10%.

Types of shares
Ordinary shares are traded on the BSSE.

Stock indices
The main index of the BSSE is the Slovak Share Index (SAX). The SAX index is a capitalization-weighted average of the twelve leading shares listed on the BSSE accounts for 70% of market capitalization.

Taxes
Interest, dividend and capital gains income is taxed at 15%.

Disclosure of financial statements
All listed companies are required to publish an audited annual financial statement within three months of the financial year end and an annual report without delay following the

General Assembly. In addition, companies with issues on the Senior Market are required to produce quarterly financial statements, while those on Junior Market are obliged to publish semi-annual financial statements.

Ownership limits for non-residents
None.

Capital and foreign exchange controls
Capital and foreign exchange used for the portfolio investment are not subject to any particular controls. Currency is freely convertible.

Takeover bids and large stakes
If an investor attempts to purchase more than 30% of share capital in a company they are obliged by law to make a takeover bid for all remaining shares. A single investor is prohibited from owning more than 80% of a single issue.

Brokers
There are forty-four members licensed to trade on the BSSE floor. Commission rates vary between 0.2% and 3% depending on the brokerage company and volume of trade. Rates are usually negotiable.

Sectors
The small number of listings on the BSSE means that sectoral analysis is largely absent. However, in terms of capitalization four companies dominate listed securities, with Slovnaft (involved in oil refinery), VSZ (steel production), Nafta (oil and gas) and VUB (banking) accounting for around 70% of the market total.

ADRs
Shares in the oil refinery company Slovnaft are traded in the US.

Derivatives
There is currently no market for derivatives in Slovakia but the BSSE has plans to introduce one in the second half of 1997. Attempts to open the Bratislava Options Exchange collapsed after it failed to acquire a licence.

■ DEBT

The Bond Act (1990) set the regulatory framework for the creation of Slovakia's bond market. The National Bank of Slovakia has concentrated on developing the short-end of the market, so investors had to look to the bank and corporate sector to lengthen maturity. But the government is by far the largest issuer of debt securities, accounting for more than 80% of issuance in 1995. Trading takes place on the Bratislava Stock Exchange (BCPB), established in 1991, but most business is transacted OTC through the computer-based RMS (Register Manual System). However, most investors follow a buy and hold strategy.

There are few restrictions for overseas investors, who can buy debt securities through brokers on the Stock Exchange or directly through the RMS. Income from investments maturing in more than one year can be repatriated if an agreement has been reached with the host country. Custody arrangements are provided by the Security Centre Bratislava Central Depository. The value of the bond market is about SKK75 billion (US$2.5 billion).

Treasury bills

NBS T-Bills are issued by the National Bank to sterilize excess liquidity in the money markets. Their maturities range from one week to one month, and investors are subject to 15% withholding tax. MOF T-Bills are issued by the NBS on behalf of the Ministry of Finance to fund the budget deficit. Their maturities range from 1 to 9 months, and are free of tax. Bills are issued weekly by the NBS through multiple price auctions. Only domestic investors can participate in auctions.

T-bills are bought by banks, who also use them in repo transactions – although, because of punitive tax and accounting treatment, bills are presented for physical delivery at both trade dates. Bills and bonds are settled at the NBS registration centre, which allocates the securities when payment is confirmed.

Treasury bonds and state guaranteed issues

Government bonds are most commonly issued with maturities of 2 to 5 years. Some 5-year issues have 3-year call options. They are sold at multiple price auctions, which occur on an irregular basis.The government has also guaranteed corporate issues if their proceeds are used for developing the country's infrastructure, such as the two Doprastav issues that will help finance the construction of the Slovak highway network.

National Privatization Fund (NPF) bonds are expected to begin trading as soon as the MOF completes the necessary regulatory guidelines.

Corporate bonds

Commercial paper is rarely issued because domestic investors are taxed at 40% on interest payments, compared to just 15% on alternative interest income.

Slovak companies are keen to issue bonds rather than dilute ownership through equity offerings. Several have tapped the markets, and the sector is likely to increase further.

Eurobonds

Slovakia has issued three yen bonds – two private placements and a samurai in 1993/4. The City of Bratislava (without a sovereign guarantee) also issued in yen at 227 basis points over the 5-year JGB in 1995, and Calex (guaranteed by the Republic) raised US$21 million with a private placement in 1994, for three years at 325 basis points over treasuries.

Two multilateral organizations, the EBRD and the IFC, have issued eurobonds denominated in Slovakian koruna.

Eurobond issues (US$m)

	1990	1991	1992	1993	1994	1995	1996
Sovereign	—	—	—	239.0	275.2	—	—
Private	—	—	—	—	—	—	—

■ SLOVAKIA: Economic indicators

Population and development	1990	1991	1992	1993	1994	1995	1996e
Population, million	5.3	5.3	5.3	5.3	5.3	5.4	5.4
Population growth, %	0.4	-0.4	0.4	0.4	0.4	0.4	0.4
Nominal GDP per capita, US$	2515	1799	2015	2081	2400	3246	3505

National accounts							
Nominal GDP, US$bn	13.3	9.5	10.7	11.1	12.8	17.4	19.1
Change in real GDP, %	-2.5	-14.5	-7.0	-4.1	4.8	7.4	7.0
Gross fixed capital formation, % of GDP	26.0	26.7	29.5	32.6	29.5	29.0	29.1

Money supply and inflation							
Narrow money, change %, Dec/Dec	-8.3	27.6	-3.7	8.9	8.0	17.6	6.0
Broad money, change %, Dec/Dec	-0.7	26.7	4.4	18.0	18.8	17.5	7.6
Consumer price inflation (avg.) %	8.4	62.0	10.1	23.2	13.4	9.9	5.8

Interest rates							
Discount rate, end of year	—	—	—	12.00	12.00	9.75	8.80
Deposit rate, monthly average	—	—	—	8.02	9.32	9.01	6.77
Prime lending rate, monthly average	—	—	—	14.41	14.56	15.64	13.87

Government finance							
Government expenditure, % of GDP	—	56.3	56.1	51.0	40.7	32.9	27.3
Government balance, % of GDP	—	—	-10.6	-7.6	-2.8	-1.6	-4.1

Exchange rates lc=local currency							
Exchange rate, annual average, lc/US$	18.27	29.48	28.26	30.70	31.90	29.74	31.31
Exchange rate, end of year, lc/US$	28.00	28.55	28.59	32.84	31.40	29.60	31.17

Balance of payments							
Exports of goods, US$m	1326	2525	3430	5447	6732	8543	10000
Change %	6.0	90.4	35.8	58.8	23.6	26.9	17.1
Imports of goods, US$m, fob	1859	3312	3633	6379	6647	8483	10400
Change %	44.6	78.2	9.7	75.6	4.2	27.6	22.6
Trade balance, of goods only, US$m, fob-fob	-533	-787	-203	-932	85	60	-400
Current account balance, US$m	-767	-786	173	-601	712	800	300
as a % of GDP	-5.8	-8.3	1.6	-5.4	5.6	5.0	1.7

Foreign exchange reserves							
Foreign exchange reserves, US$m	367	1063	356	415	1605	3423	3600
Gold at ⅔ of market price, US$m	213.1	224.1	244.7	309.1	330.1	330.0	333.1
Import cover (reserves/imports), months	2.4	3.9	1.2	0.8	2.9	4.8	4.2

Foreign debt and debt service							
Short-term debt, US$m	968	878	567	715	864	925	960
Total foreign debt, US$m	2695	3083	2829	3341	4144	5800	6500
as a % of GDP	20.2	32.4	26.5	30.2	32.3	33.3	34.0
as a % of foreign exchange receipts	—	—	—	—	45.0	41.8	41.4
Interest payments, US$m	253	198	260	184	236	350	400
Principal repayments, US$m	171	247	368	424	576	661	597
Total debt service, US$m	424	445	628	608	812	1011	997
as a % of goods exports	32.0	17.6	18.3	11.2	12.1	11.8	10.0
as a % of foreign exchange receipts	—	—	—	—	8.8	8.6	7.5

Slovenia

KEY FACTS

Area (thousands of km²):	20
Population (1995, millions):	2
Population projection (2025, millions):	1.9
Population younger than 15 yrs (1991, % of total):	20.3
Urbanization rate (1993, % of population):	62
Life expectancy (1993, years at birth):	73
Gross domestic product (1996, US$bn):	17
GDP per capita (1996, US$):	8572
Average annual GDP growth rate (1990-96, %):	-1.1
Average annual inflation rate (1990-96, %):	134.8
Currency (tolar per US$, average 1996):	135
Structure of production (1994):	56% services, 38% industry, 5% agriculture
Main exports:	intermediate goods, consumption goods, capital goods
Main imports:	intermediate goods, consumption goods, capital goods
Main trading partners:	Germany, Italy, Croatia, Austria, France
Total foreign debt (% of GDP):	25.6
Next elections due under normal circumstances:	2000
Credit rating: (Nov 1996, Standard & Poor's, Moody's)	A; A3

FORECAST: 1997-2000 (average)

	Worst case	Most likely	Best case
Real GDP growth (%)	3.5	4.5	5.8
Inflation (%)	7.8	6.8	6.0

■ POLITICS

Historical overview

Like many of its former partners in the Yugoslav Republic, Slovenia has waited a long time for its political freedom. Until the 16th century, it was part of the Habsburg Empire, which encompassed vast swathes of Europe. It was then taken over by the Turks, who merged it into the Ottoman Empire.

Following the disintegration of the Ottoman Empire at the end of the First World War, Slovenia became part of a unified state, drawing together the three main powers of the region – the Serbs, Croats and the Slovenes. Despite plans to introduce a degree of regional autonomy, the Kingdom of the Serbs, Croats and Slovenes was a highly centralized state dominated by the Serbs.

Both the Croats and the Slovenes quickly became disaffected with the lack of political power, and it came as little surprise when, during the Second World War, the three countries split up into different militias. After the war, however, the country continued to be ruled centrally by the new leader, Marshal Tito, who became prime minister of a government of national unity in March 1945. Seven months later, the monarchy was established and the Federal People's Republic of Yugoslavia was set up.

Tito, although a Communist by ideology, refused to submit to the directives sent to Belgrade by the Soviet leaders in Moscow. In 1948, Yugoslavia was expelled from the Communist bloc. Assisted by Western arms and aid, Yugoslavia maintained its autonomy, and by the late 1950s had achieved a partial reconciliation with the Warsaw Pact states. However, it continued to insist on full independence and the right to find its own "road to socialism". During this time, Yugoslavia remained a Communist country, albeit with its own peculiar characteristics. The country was governed by a single party – the League of Communists of Yugoslavia (SKJ) – but a federal constitution promulgated in 1963 allowed individuals much greater power than was possible under the Soviet system. The economic system was known as "self-management". In addition, each region had its own constituent republics that could legislate for, but not over-rule, the SKJ.

In 1980, Tito died at the age of eighty-seven. Surprisingly, the federal system he set up continued to survive, due to the then unique system of power-rotation, in which the president of the SKJ rotated on an annual basis between the different republics. In 1989, Janez Drnovsek (Slovene) and Borisav Jovic (Serb) introduced a system of direct election whereby each regional president would be elected for five years by popular vote rather than by the earlier procedure of republican or parliamentary selection.

But tension was not far below the surface. The prosperous Slovenes had long resented the power wielded over them by the more numerous Serbs, and in September 1989, the Slovene Assembly voted to change the country's constitution to one that confirmed Slovenia's sovereignty and its right to secede from Yugoslavia. A number of opposition parties such the Slovenian Christian Democrats (SCD), and the Democratic Opposition of Slovenia coalition (DEMOS) were set up in preparation for the planned multiparty elections.

In January 1990, the Slovenian delegation withdrew from the annual meeting of the SKJ. Not long after, it suspended all links with the SKJ and renamed itself the Party of Democratic Reform (PDR).

In multiparty elections in April 1990, DEMOS won the majority of the votes and formed a coalition government under Lojze Peterle, leader of the SCD. In July, Slovenia declared itself a sovereign republic, and resolved that its republican laws should take precedence over federal laws. The government took control of the local defence force, bringing the country into direct confrontation with the Serbian-led Yugoslavian army. In January, Slovenia and Croatia signed a mutual defence pact, and the following month the Slovene assembly voted for phased secession from Yugoslavia.

During the first half of 1991, several moves were made to create a federation of sovereign states. But Slovenia indicated it would be unwilling to support the poorer republics, while Croatia was worried that the Serbs of Krajina would split from Croatia if a federation was set up. Both Croatia and Slovenia declared their independence in June 1991.

Their declaration of independence led to full-scale confrontation. However, unlike Croatia, which was drawn into intense fighting, Slovenia escaped much of the conflict. By October all Yugoslav army units had withdrawn from Slovene territory.

With no independence battle to fight, Peterle's coalition government began to crumble. In October 1991, one of the main coalition partners, the Slovenian Democratic Union, split into the Liberal Democratic Party (DP) and the more right-wing National Democratic Party (NDS). DEMOS was dissolved, and in April 1992 Peterle resigned.

In the elections of December 1992, the Liberal Democratic Party (LDP) under Janez Drnovsek won the largest number of seats in the ninety-member assembly. The following month, a coalition government was set up with a new party at its head, the Liberal Democracy of Slovenia (LDS), comprising the LDP, the Greens and the DS. Soon after, tension between the coalition's members began to surface. In January 1996, the ULSD withdrew from the coalition, leaving the government with only 45 out of the 90 seats.

Recent events

Without a majority, the government has been left in a precarious position. In January 1996 it was forced to back down on its economic austerity programme after a series of public sector strikes were supported by opposition parties, and to agree to wage increases.

Three months later, in May 1996, a more serious problem occurred when a junior partner, the SKD, joined the opposition in a vote of no confidence in the foreign minister, Zoran Thaler, over the delay in the signing of the Association Agreement with the EU. With a new foreign minister, Davorin Kracun, the agreement was signed in June 1996. The agreement has been seen as a sign that Slovenia is likely to become one of the first former Communist countries to join the EU.

In the November general elections Janez Drnovsek's LDP won 25 seats, the largest number in the 90-seat parliament.

Chronology

1918	Kingdom of Serbs, Croats and Slovenes is formed
1929	Kingdom is renamed Yugoslavia
1941	German invasion is resisted by Tito's Partisans
1945	Marshal Tito becomes prime minister
1945	Federal People's Republic of Yugoslavia is set up
1948	Yugoslavia is expelled from Communist bloc
1953	Tito is elected life-time president
1963	Self-management system is extended
1980	Tito dies
1989	Slovene Republic votes for right to secede
1990	DEMOS coalition wins multiparty regional election
1991	Slovenia declares its independence
1991	Ljubljana is bombed by Serbs
1992	Liberal Democratic Party wins election
1996	Slovenia signs EU Association Agreement

Constitution and government

Under the terms of the constitution adopted in December 1991, legislative power is vested in the Drzavni Zbor (National Assembly) which has 90 deputies elected for a term of four years by popular vote. Of this 90, 38 are directly elected and 50 are selected on a proportional basis by an electoral commission from those parties that have secured at least 3% of the vote. Two seats are reserved for the Italian and Hungarian minorities. There is also an advisory council, the Drzavni Svet (National Council) which can veto decisions made by the National Assembly. There are 40 members elected for five-year terms.

The Republic of Slovenia is a democratic republic. The constitution provides for a National Assembly and a second 40-member chamber, the Council of State, which has the power to delay legislation but not make it. This is made up of 22 local interest members, 12 members representing employers and employees and 6 representing non-economic activities. There are 60 administrative divisions and 148 municipalities, although power is firmly centred with the government in Ljubljana.

Current government

Head of State	President Milan Kucan
Prime Minister	Janez Drnovsek
Minister for Finance	Mitja Gaspari
Minister for Economic Activities	Metod Dragonja

The former government coalition was made up of the **Liberal Democracy of Slovenia (LDS)** and the **Slovene Christian Democrats (SKD)**. By February 1997, parliament had still not approved a new cabinet and acting prime minister Drnovsek was trying to form a coalition with the Slovene's People's Party.

Results of the November 1996 elections

Liberal Democracy of Slovenia (LDS)	25 seats
Slovene People's Party (SLS)	19 seats
Social Democratic Party of Slovenia (SDSS)	16 seats
Slovene Christian Democrats (SKD)	10 seats
United List (former Communists)	9 seats
Democratic Party (DP)	5 seats
Slovene National Party (SNP)	4 seats
Hungarian minority	1 seat
Italian minority	1 seat

Next elections
November 2000

Central bank

The Bank of Slovenia was established in 1991. It is formally autonomous, although the Ministry of Finance exerts some influence, and responsible for monetary policy, exchange rate management and the commercial banking network. Since 1991, it has maintained high interest rates in an effort to keep down inflation.

■ ECONOMICS

Historical overview

With only 2 million people, Slovenia lacks the potential to develop into a major economic power. But its long tradition of inventing and manufacturing, which made it the richest country within the Yugoslav Republic, with a per-capita income more than double the national average, suggests that once the political situation becomes more stable, its economy could become one of the most productive in the region.

Under Tito, the Slovenian economy, as in other Yugoslav countries, was run on a system of "self-management" which divided the country into companies and enterprises that were run by local councils of employees and managers. This allowed Slovenia to develop faster than many other former Communist countries that had to endure collectivization and state planning programmes. At the same time, it was not a capitalist system, so the economy lacked the dynamism that drove growth in Western Europe.

During the 1970s and 1980s, Slovenian companies obtained Western technology through licensing agreements, and by the end of the 1980s, the European Union was already the Slovenian republic's main export market. Its principal industries are chemicals, heavy industry such as the manufacture of machinery, automotive components and transport equipment, and the production of white goods such as refrigerators.

Having escaped the fighting that engulfed Croatia and Bosnia, of the former-Yugoslav countries Slovenia was in the best economic position. But the disintegration of the Yugoslav Republic left Slovenia without a large domestic market, and growth during the early years of independence was slow. Real GDP fell by 15% during 1991 and 1992.

Many of Slovenia's heavy industry producers lost market share to their rivals in Hungary and the Czech Republic, where wages were lower and companies were not run on the self-management principle. A number were forced to lay off workers, and unemployment rose to 8%, three times its 1989 level.

In an effort to reduce inflation, which had risen to 247% in 1991, the government launched an economic austerity programme. State spending was cut drastically. Meanwhile, disagreement over the privatization process held up company reform while uncertainty caused by the war discouraged corporate investment. Economic output continued to decline as a result.

The austerity programme finally began to bear fruit in 1993, when inflation slowed to 23%. Companies started to increase production, and introduce new products suited to their new markets in Western Europe. GDP growth began to pick up as a result, expanding by 10.3 % between 1993 and 1995.

Recent developments

Despite signs of growth in 1993 and 1994, Slovenia's economic revival has been fitful. Many firms continue to be less competitive than their main rivals in Eastern Europe because of rises in local wages and the continued appreciation of the tolar. Export demand, meanwhile, remains subdued because of the slow pace of growth in its main export markets in Western Europe. The evolution of the Slovenian economy has been further hindered in recent years by an increase in public sector strikes, which has disrupted production and put added pressure on companies to raise wages.

The privatization programme has been held up by disagreement between the incumbent company councils and a number of influential politicians who wanted to raise money via open sale. This has delayed the reform of local companies, much needed to make them more competitive and market-orientated. A compromise solution was introduced in 1995. This gave all Slovenians a chance to buy shares by offering vouchers to workers. However, as of September 1996, few companies had completed privatization.

The slow pace of growth apart, Slovenia's macroeconomic position is one of the best in Eastern Europe. Thanks to the government's maintenance of high interest rates, inflation stood at around 10% in 1996, making it one of the lowest in the region. Public spending remains low, and small budget deficits are a regular feature.

Efforts have also been made to encourage more foreign investment. But the small size of the country, and continued uncertainty over political stability in the region once UN troops withdraw, have deterred foreign companies. Foreign direct investment in Slovenia remains far lower than in countries such as Hungary and the Czech Republic. It could increase, however, once the EU Association Agreement is ratified.

Economic growth remained subdued during 1996. However, GDP growth is expected to pick up in 1997 as the tolar falls to a more competitive level, and the export markets in Western Europe pick up. Nevertheless, until the privatization process accelerates, structural problems such as over-manning will continue to thwart economic development.

Population

The population of Slovenia was estimated at just over 2 million in July 1995. Almost 70% of people were estimated to be between 15 and 64 years old. Population growth stands at around 0.24%. The vast majority are Slovenes (91%) although there are small numbers of Italians, Hungarians, Croats, Serbs and Muslims.

The Slovene economy

Slovenia is a very service-orientated economy. In 1995, services such as tourism and banking accounted for 61.5% of GDP. Manufacturing, including the production of electrical equipment, food processing, textiles, paper products and chemicals, accounted for 33.7%. Unlike many of its neighbours, the agricultural sector is very small, accounting for only 4.8% of GDP in 1995.

Savings and investment

Slovenia has a relatively healthy savings base. Gross national savings are estimated at around 22.5% of GDP. Investment levels are rising due to the introduction of a new law in July 1996 which allows companies to set 40% of investment against profits tax. Gross fixed investment was expected to reach an estimated 20% in 1996. Nevertheless, savings will probably cover financing needs.

Share of GDP by sector

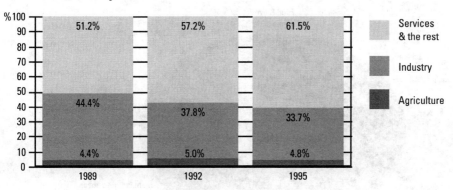

Source: EBRD

Balance of payments

After splitting from Yugoslavia in 1991, the Slovenian government was able to run budget surpluses because of low public spending and the slow pace of public consumption until 1993. Since 1994 small deficits were registered which remained under 0.2% of GDP. A fall in exports during the second half of 1995 led to a US$15 million deficit in the first quarter of 1996. The deficit is not large enough to cause problems, however, given the anticipated rise in foreign investment levels.

Exports and imports as a % of GDP

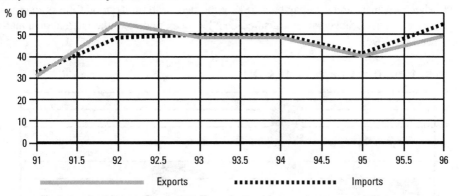

Source: Central Bank

Economic policy
Monetary policy

The Bank of Slovenia has pursued tight monetary policies since independence in 1991. Interest rates have been maintained at high levels to keep inflation down. With inflation standing at only 10% in 1996, a cut in interest rates is technically possible but the Bank of Slovenia is expected to maintain a firm stance on inflation.

Breakdown of exports (1995)

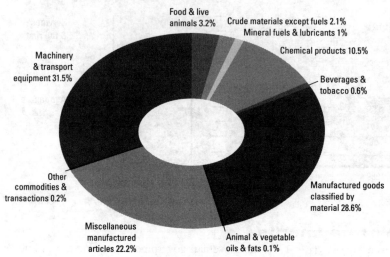

Food & live animals 3.2%
Crude materials except fuels 2.1%
Mineral fuels & lubricants 1%
Chemical products 10.5%
Machinery & transport equipment 31.5%
Beverages & tobacco 0.6%
Other commodities & transactions 0.2%
Manufactured goods classified by material 28.6%
Miscellaneous manufactured articles 22.2%
Animal & vegetable oils & fats 0.1%

Source: IFS

Fiscal policy

Slovenia's public finances are in a strong state. Budget surpluses were run every year until 1994 when a deficit equivalent to 0.23% of GDP was incurred. External debt has stayed steady at US$1.4 billion, easily covered by reserves of US$1.8 billion.

The potential problem of the Yugoslavian external debt was worked out in January 1996 when Slovenia agreed to pay back 18% of the debt with the London Club of international bank creditors. Slovenia's restructured debt has been trading in the international market since June 1996.

Current account as a % of GDP

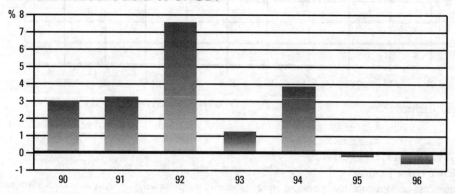

Source: Central Bank

Currency

The tolar is available for purchase and sale with the exchange rate allowed to float freely. Since independence it has depreciated from 28 tolar per US dollar in January 1992 to 135 tolar per US dollar at the end of 1996. The future direction of the tolar is a matter of some debate. Increased capital inflows from foreign investors could boost the tolar's value. However, the Bank of Slovenia is expected to intervene in the market in order to keep the tolar low enough to sustain export competitiveness.

Slovene tolar/US dollar exchange rate

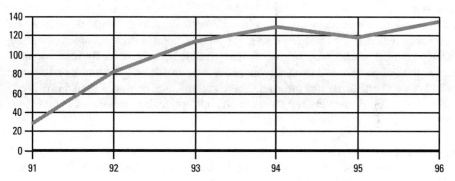

■ EQUITIES

Index performance (in local currency)

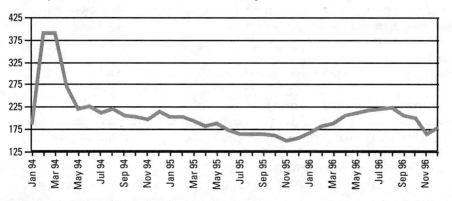

Key indicators

	Index performance %, in US$ terms	Market Cap. US$bn	P/E	Div. Yield
1994	—	0.6	—	—
1995	1.0	0.3	—	—
1996	4.0	0.7	12.7	3.2

Sources: Local stock exchange, IFC, Bloomberg, Datastream, UBS

Background
Stock exchange activity in Slovenia goes back to 1924 when the Ljubljana Stock, Commodities, and Foreign Exchange was established. However, the Second World War led to the Exchange's closure in 1941, and in 1953, with Communism dominating Eastern Europe, the Exchange was abolished. New laws governing capital markets were passed in 1989, enabling the Ljubljana Stock Exchange (LSE) to re-open in 1990. Equity market capitalization has grown from SIT422.9 million (US$5.2 million) at the end of 1991 to SIT87 billion (US$636 million) in late 1996.

Structure
The LSE is split into three segments: A, B and C. Securities in markets A and B are traded on the exchange, whereas the C market is used for over-the-counter trade. Companies seeking admission to the A market have to meet tougher criteria than those on B-market. Equities dominate the LSE with share trading accounting for around 80% on the A and B markets and almost 90% on the C market of turnover. There are 18 common and 8 preference shares listed on the A and B- markets and 23 common and 3 preference shares quoted on the C market.

Regulatory authority
The Slovenian Securities Act of 1994 lays the foundations on which the LSE is regulated, including the role of the Agency for Securities which oversees LSE activity. New laws governing securities are imminent.

Trading methods
Trading on the LSE takes place using the electronic trading system BIS. Trading is continuous and trades occur automatically if an offer and a bid match. Trades must be carried out by authorized banks and brokerages.

Hours
Trading on the LSE takes place between 09:30 and 13:00, Monday to Friday.

Settlement time and clearing
Settlement takes place on a trade date plus two business days (T+2) basis. Clearing and settlement is overseen by the Central Securities Clearing Corporation of Slovenia (KDD).

Limits on price movement
Shares on Tiers A and B are not permitted to fluctuate by more than 10% during a session. Furthermore, should a cumulative fluctuation reach 30% the companies are obliged to submit a press release.

Types of shares
Ordinary and preference shares are traded on the LSE.

Stock indices
The main Stock Exchange index is the SBI index. This is calculated by taking the arithmetic

mean of changes in ten companies' share prices. From early 1997, the LSE will introduce a new index which reflects the increased depth of the market as a consequence of the privatization programme.

Taxes

There is a transaction fee of 0.085%. Dividends are taxed at 15%. Interest income and capital gains are taxed indirectly through corporation tax (from 30%) but are tax-free for individuals.

Disclosure of financial statement

Listed companies are required to submit balance sheets, revenue accounts, and cash flow statements.

Ownership limits for non-residents

Legislation governing portfolio investment in Slovenia is not yet in place, but new laws are expected during the first half of 1997.

Capital and foreign exchange controls

New laws on capital movements are under review.

Brokers

The LSE has forty-six members. Brokerage rates vary but are typically between 1% and 2%.

Sectors

Pharmaceuticals, banking and food processing are the three largest sectors on the LSE, with a combined market capitalization equivalent to 80% of the total. The pharmaceuticals sector on its own has a market value of SIT36.7 billion (US$268 million) or 42% of the total.

ADRs

There are no Slovenian ADRs.

Derivatives

Futures and options are traded at the Derivatives Exchange. Live trading began during March 1996 after a month-long simulation. As well as a number of currency contracts, there are futures and options contracts on the SBI (the stock index) and the BIO (the bond index).

DEBT

The Securities Market Act, passed in March 1994, regulates all aspects of the securities market. Government and corporate debt securities trade on the Ljubljana Stock Exchange and over the counter (OTC).

In addition to acting as agent for the treasury by issuing short-term bills, the Bank of Slovenia issues 6-month CDs, denominated in tolars and deutschmarks. Some are inflation linked, where the discount is based on the difference between real and forecast inflation.

Other tolar CDs have warrants attached, providing investors an opportunity to buy 1-year deutschmark or US dollar notes.

Government bonds with initial maturities of 7 and 10 years have been issued in deutschmarks and ECU, with a nominal value of about DEM550 million in October 1996. A small municipal bond, for the Community of Zagorje, has been issued with an 11% coupon and 7-year maturity.

Bargains settle through a new clearing system in dematerialized form. KDD (Central Securities Clearing Corp) was set up in November 1995. One innovation from the previous system is the existence of a guarantee fund, supported by payments from KDD members.

In October 1995, the Ljubljana Stock Exchange started to publish the BIO Bond Index, composed of five domestic corporate issues which must meet certain turnover criteria. The composition of the index is reviewed every six months.

The majority of corporate issues are denominated in deutschmarks and pay fixed-rate coupons. Almost all are issued by domestic banks. Maturities range from 4 to 10 years.

Exchange controls operate in Slovenia so there is no foreign participation in the domestic bond market.

Futures contracts and options on the BIO Index are traded on the Ljubljana Derivatives Exchange, which opened for business on March 28, 1996.

Eurobonds

On July 22, 1996 the Republic of Slovenia issued a US$325 million 7% 5-year bond at 58 basis points over US treasuries. In June 1996, government bonds with a value of US$812 million were listed on the Luxembourg Stock Exchange. The bonds represented Slovenia's share of the former Yugoslavia's debt, and were issued in two series denominated in US dollars and two in deutschmarks with a maturity of 2006. They were simultaneously offered for trading OTC in London. Subsequently, the Republic has called bonds with a nominal value of US$125 million.

Eurobond issues (US$m)

	1990	1991	1992	1993	1994	1995	1996
Sovereign	—	—	—	—	—	—	325.0
Private	—	—	—	—	—	—	—

■ SLOVENIA: Economic indicators

Population and development	1990	1991	1992	1993	1994	1995	1996e
Population, million	2.0	2.0	2.0	2.0	2.0	2.0	2.0
Population growth, %	-0.2	-0.1	-0.1	-0.1	-0.1	-0.3	-0.2
Nominal GDP per capita, US$	8679	6353	6206	6365	7056	8637	8572

National accounts							
Nominal GDP, US$bn	17.3	12.7	12.4	12.7	14.0	17.1	17.0
Change in real GDP, %	-4.8	-9.4	-5.4	1.3	4.9	3.5	2.5
Gross fixed capital formation, % of GDP	17.0	15.8	17.9	20.1	20.2	22.3	23.3

Money supply and inflation							
Narrow money, change %, Dec/Dec	—	—	92.8	41.2	49.1	—	—
Broad money, change %, Dec/Dec	—	—	45.1	63.3	62.2	—	—
Consumer price inflation (avg.) %	549.7	117.7	201.3	32.8	19.8	12.6	9.8
Producer prices (avg.) %	390.4	124.1	215.7	21.6	17.7	12.8	—

Interest rates							
Discount rate, end of year	—	—	25.00	18.00	16.00	10.00	10.00
Money market rate, annual average	—	—	60.40	39.15	29.08	12.18	—
Deposit rate, annual average	—	673.60	151.53	32.65	27.89	15.32	—
Prime lending rate, annual average	—	853.50	203.84	49.61	39.42	24.84	—

Government finance							
Government expenditure, % of GDP	49.2	41.2	46.4	47.1	47.1	46.2	—
Government balance, % of GDP	-0.2	-0.7	0.3	0.3	-0.2	0.0	-0.6

Exchange rates *lc=local currency*							
Exchange rate, annual average, lc/US$	11.32	27.57	81.29	113.24	128.80	118.50	134.90
Exchange rate, end of year, lc/US$	10.52	57.73	96.19	129.37	128.10	125.60	135.00

Balance of payments							
Exports of goods & services, US$m	4252	3974	7902	7411	8682	10706	10950
Change %	24.8	-6.5	98.9	-6.2	17.1	23.3	2.3
Imports of goods & services, US$m, fob	4199	3682	6931	7254	8296	10788	11100
Change %	30.6	-12.3	88.2	4.7	14.4	30.0	2.9
Trade balance, of goods only, US$m, fob-fob	53	292	791	-154	-338	-957	-1150
Current account balance, US$m	794	400	926	192	540	-36	-100
as a % of GDP	4.6	3.2	7.5	1.5	3.8	-0.2	-0.6

Foreign exchange reserves							
Foreign exchange reserves, US$m	—	112	716	788	1499	1821	1850
Import cover (reserves/imports), months	—	0.4	1.2	1.3	2.2	2.0	2.0

Foreign debt and debt service							
Short-term debt, US$m	278	223	123	162	124	152	166
Total foreign debt, US$m	2089	1987	2627	2751	3136	3905	4350
as a % of GDP	12.1	15.7	21.2	21.7	22.3	22.8	25.6
as a % of foreign exchange receipts	—	—	32.8	36.5	35.5	35.7	38.8
Interest payments, US$m	176	145	158	147	143	190	200
Principal repayments, US$m	188	196	255	272	320	545	590
Total debt service, US$m	364	341	413	419	463	735	790
as a % of goods exports	8.6	8.6	6.2	6.9	6.8	8.8	9.5
as a % of foreign exchange receipts	—	—	5.2	5.6	5.2	6.7	7.0

South Africa

Area (thousands of km²):	1221
Population (1995, millions):	41.2
Population projection (2025, millions):	69
Population younger than 15 yrs (1991, % of total):	38.6
Urbanization rate (1993, % of population):	50
Life expectancy (1993, years at birth):	63
Gross domestic product (1996, US$bn):	124.8
GDP per capita (1996, US$):	2968
Average annual GDP growth rate (1990-96, %):	1
Average annual inflation rate (1990-96, %):	11.2
Currency (rand per US$, average 1996):	4.3
Structure of production (1994):	65% services, 31% industry, 5% agriculture
Main exports:	gold; semi-precious stones; iron and steel; mineral fuels; ores; machinery
Main imports:	machinery, vehicles, crude oil
Main trading partners:	Germany, UK, US, Italy, Japan
Market capitalization of Stock Exchange (December 1996; US$bn):	241.6
Total foreign debt (% of GDP):	25.2
Next elections due under normal circumstances:	early 1999
Credit rating: (Jan 1997, Standard & Poor's, Moody's)	BB+; Baa3

FORECAST: 1997-2000 (average)

	Worst case	Most likely	Best case
Real GDP growth (%)	3.0	3.9	4.4
Inflation (%)	9.0	7.9	7.5

■ POLITICS

Historical overview

Around AD 300, Bantu speakers began migrating from North Africa to the south-eastern part of the continent, where the San and Khoikhoi peoples were already long established. European settlement began during the mid-17th century with the arrival of the Dutch East India Company in the Cape region.

The company's need for labour resulted in the importation of slaves from the Far East and from other parts of Africa. Hence, from the earliest days, society at the Cape was composed of groups of people who were culturally different and unequal in the eyes of the law.

The expanding European settlements came into conflict with the indigenous population and there were several frontier wars.

In the early 19th century, Britain annexed the Cape and there followed an influx of British settlers. Subsequently, the descendants of the Dutch settlers, whose cultural ties to the Netherlands had by then been largely severed, migrated north on the so-called Great Trek. This led to the formation of the Boer republics: Transvaal and the Orange Free State. Following British victory in the Anglo-Boer War (1899–1902), both Afrikaner states became British colonies. This, and the fierce Boer-Zulu fighting that had occurred on the Great Trek, helped galvanize the Afrikaners' sense of national identity.

In 1910 the Union of South Africa was created, bringing together the British colonies. The Union embraced territories that differed in their interpretation of civil liberties, so that blacks retained certain voting rights in the Cape, but had negligible or no parliamentary representation elsewhere. In time, convergence resulted in the Union becoming less liberal, as the remaining freedoms accorded to blacks were removed from the statute book. Further racially biased legislation quickly followed, with better-paid mining jobs legally reserved for whites from 1911 and land acts restricting black ownership from 1913. In response to these developments, and in order to campaign for the franchise of blacks, 1912 witnessed the establishment of the South African Native National Congress – later called the African National Congress. However, a year later, the formation of the National Party (NP) represented the start of a drive to unite Afrikaners politically and push for greater white power.

In the years immediately following the Second World War, there was a renewed focus on human rights throughout the world. South Africa was already out of step, and on India's request the United Nations condemned racial discrimination against Indians in South Africa. This was followed by India imposing trade sanctions against the country. In 1948 the National Party – which was even more isolated from mainstream views – won power (a minority of votes but a majority of seats) on its policy of separate but equal racial development: "apartheid". This marked the start of over forty years of apartheid rule and the introduction of scores of repressive laws. One of the NP's first acts was to ban the Communist Party of South Africa under the Suppression of Communism Act. Later, the Soviet diplomatic mission was closed down, reinforcing South Africa's position in the East-West conflict and helping to postpone serious Western sanctions.

During 1952, the increasingly powerless ANC embarked on a non-violent defiance campaign, but with little real success. The last remaining "non-whites" in the Cape were stripped of their right to vote in 1956, and ten black homelands were formed in 1959, giving the white minority 87% of the land. During the 1960s, the granting of independence to their colonies by the main European countries sharpened the contrast between political liberation elsewhere and the position of blacks in South Africa. Human rights violations in the country began to make international headlines. The 1960 Sharpville massacre witnessed a demonstration in which sixty-nine blacks were shot dead by police and hundreds more injured. After this event, the government outlawed the ANC, signifying the end of a long chapter of non-violent opposition to white rule. The ANC subsequently established an underground military wing, which began to attack infrastructure targets. In 1964, Nelson Mandela was jailed for life on charges of sabotage and plotting terrorism.

The 1970s marked the beginning of the end for the apartheid system, with the 1976 Soweto uprising seen by many as the turning point. Following student protests against inferior educational opportunities for blacks, over six hundred people were killed in nation-wide demonstrations. Thousands of youths left the country to join the ANC armed wing. More and more members of the government began to realize the necessity for fundamental change. Economic factors were at work as well as the fact that South Africa's relations with the West were deteriorating.

Gradually, reformers began to gain the upper hand. By 1979 the black trade union movement was legalized and, in 1983, Asians and coloureds regained the vote, albeit within racially segregated parliamentary chambers. This new constitution had the opposite effect of what the government had intended, galvanizing black resistance to the reforms. The increased political tensions coincided with a sharp deterioration in the country's economic fortunes as commodity prices collapsed and sanction pressures were stepped up. Widespread rioting followed and in 1985 a state of emergency was declared.

Despite the outward deterioration, behind-the-scenes informal meetings between the government and the ANC became more frequent. As the decade closed, F.W. de Klerk replaced P.W. Botha as head of the National Party. Sweeping policy changes followed. In 1990, the prohibition on the ANC and other illegal parties was lifted and formal talks between the government and ANC began in earnest, although the Zulu Inkatha Freedom Party was increasingly concerned about exclusion and insisted on a strong federal constitution. Following the launch of democracy negotiations between nineteen parties in 1991, whites voted overwhelmingly in a referendum in favour of De Klerk's reforms and, during 1993, the government and ANC agreed to share power for five years after all-race elections. In response, the international community began to lift sanctions. In April 1994, the ANC won 63% of votes in the country's first universal franchise election and formed the Government for National Unity (GNU). This comprised a partnership between the ANC, the National Party, and the Inkatha Freedom Party with Nelson Mandela, freed from prison only four years earlier, becoming president.

Recent events

In April 1996 the National Party decided to withdraw from the coalition in order to establish itself as the main opposition party. While this initially unsettled the markets, it means that by the time the next election is held in early 1999 the ANC would have had a track record of several years in government. This will provide the markets with a clearer view of the type of policies pursued by the ANC governing on its own.

Chronology

c. 300	Bantu-speaking peoples begin settling in southern Africa
1652	First white settlement follows the arrival of the Dutch East India Company
1688	French Huguenots arrive. Together with Dutch and, later, German settlers, they form the Afrikaner segment of the population.
1795	Britain occupies the Cape, before later returning it to the Dutch
1806	Britain re-occupies the Cape
1820	Influx of British settlers
1836-40	Afrikaner farmers, already living in isolated communities, flee British rule, trekking to the north. They create the Boer republics (Transvaal and Orange Free State) in the 1850s.
1867	Diamonds discovered, some gold

1886	Huge gold discovery on the Witwatersrand
1899-1902	War between British and Boers kills tens of thousands, ending with defeat of the Boer republics
1910	Union of South Africa created, joining four provinces. Blacks excluded from the vote, except in the Cape.
1912	South African Native National Congress – later renamed African National Congress (ANC) – is formed
1913	Land acts passed, restricting blacks to owning land in specified areas
1948	The National Party wins power on the platform of apartheid and Afrikaner nationalism. This marks the start of over forty years of apartheid rule and the introduction of scores of repressive laws.
1952	ANC starts a non-violent defiance campaign
1959	Ten black homelands created, giving whites 87% of the land and leaving 13% to the black majority
1960	Sharpville massacre. ANC and Pan-Africanist Congress banned.
1964	Mandela and other ANC leaders sentenced to life for sabotage and plotting terrorism
1976	Soweto uprising
1979	Black trade union movement is legalized
1984	New racially based constitution (which extends voting rights to Asian and coloured people, but excludes Africans) is introduced against massive opposition. The start of widespread rioting. Desmond Tutu wins Nobel Peace Prize.
1985	Government declares state of emergency. International sanctions stepped up. Increased informal contacts between South African business, opposition groups and government leaders with the ANC.
1989	F.W. de Klerk takes over National Party from P.W. Botha
1990	De Klerk lifts ban on ANC, PAC and Communist Party, and frees Mandela. First formal talks between government and ANC. ANC suspends armed struggle.
1993	Government and ANC agree to share power for five years after first all-race elections. United Nations lifts most sanctions. Mandela and De Klerk jointly win Nobel Peace Prize
1994	First all-race general elections. ANC wins 63% of the vote, winning seven of the nine provinces. The National Party and the Inkatha Freedom Party participate in the Government of National Unity.
1994-96	Negotiations for a final constitution. The Inkatha Freedom Party does not participate.
1995/96	ANC does very well in local elections, largely confirming the 1994 elections
1996	National Party withdraws from the Government of National Unity
1997	New constitution becomes law

Constitution and government

South Africa's new constitutional order is a radical break with the country's past. As a reaction to centuries of injustice, the constitution is characterized by its strong emphasis on equality, human rights and the protection of civil liberties. The new constitution is also a break with the parliamentary system that South Africa originally copied from Britain, borrowing more from the American and German models. A powerful Constitutional Court upholds an extensive Bill of Rights and has the power to strike down any Act of Parliament which is found to be unconstitutional.

The new rights and freedoms listed in the constitution are comparable with the most liberal Western constitutions and stand in stark contrast to most of the constitutions prevailing in the rest of Africa. A US-style freedom of information clause gives everyone "the right of access to any information held by the state", whereas unfair discrimination on the following grounds is outlawed: "race, gender, sex, pregnancy, marital status, ethnic or social origin, colour, sexual orientation, age, disability, religion, conscience, belief, culture, language and birth". The new constitution also broke the unitary mould of the previous system, introducing principles of regionalism and federalism.

Parliament consists of a lower house of up to four hundred delegates, known as the National Assembly, and an upper house, the National Council of Provinces. Members of the Assembly are elected by voters for a five-year term on the basis of proportional representation. In turn, they elect the president of the country, who has to be a member of the Assembly. The president, who may not serve more than two terms, is assisted by a Deputy-President. The National Council represents the nine provinces to ensure that provincial interests are taken into account. Each province delegates ten representatives to the National Council. The provinces have their own legislatures and executives that have jurisdiction over certain provincial matters. The devolution of power to the provinces does not go as far as some would like, and this is likely to remain a contentious issue.

Results of the April 1994 elections
African National Congress (62.7%, 252 seats), **National Party** (20.4%, 82 seats), **Inkatha Freedom Party** (10.5%, 43 seats), **Freedom Front** (2.2%, 9 seats), **Democratic Party** (1.7%, 7 seats), **Pan-African Congress** (1.3%, 5 seats), **African Christian Democratic Party** (0.5%, 2 seats), **12 other parties** (0.9%, no seats).

Next general elections
Under normal circumstances, in early 1999

Political forces
The interim constitution provides for a ruling coalition with any party achieving more than 5% of the vote. In April 1996 the National Party withdrew from the Government of National Unity, leaving the ANC and the Inkatha Freedom Party in the coalition.

Government of National Unity
African National Congress (ANC)
> Formed in 1912.
> Led by Nelson Mandela.

Inkatha Freedom Party (IFP)
> Relaunched in 1975.
> Led by Mangosuthu Buthelezi.

Other parties
National Party (NP)
> Formed in 1912. In power from 1948 to 1994; in coalition from 1994 to 1996.
> Led by F.W. de Klerk

Freedom Front (FF)
>Right-wing. Formed in 1994.
>Led by Constand Viljoen

Democratic Party (DP)
>Formed in 1989, following the merger of the Independent Party, the National Democratic Movement, and the Progressive Federal Party

Pan-Africanist Congress (PAC)
>Formed in 1959; broke away from the ANC because it opposed "multiracial" policies

Central bank

The South African Reserve Bank is the central bank and its powers and functions are regulated in terms of an Act of Parliament. According to the 1997 constitution, the Bank's primary objective is "to protect the value of the currency in the interest of balanced and sustainable economic growth". In pursuit of this objective, the bank "must perform its functions independently and without fear, favour or prejudice, but there must be regular consultation between the Bank and the Cabinet member responsible for national financial matters".

While the constitution stresses the independence of the Reserve Bank, the Bank's terms of reference are broad enough to make the choice of governor a crucial issue. The present governor of the Reserve Bank, Dr Chris Stals, appointed in 1989, has earned a reputation as an inflation fighter, and has managed to break the long-held perception that South African inflation could not fall to single digits.

South African financial markets react nervously whenever there are rumours that the governor may leave. They have reason to do so for, despite the constitutional framework, markets know that disagreements between governments and central banks occur the world over. Governments want high growth; good central bankers want low inflation. There is usually a shorter-term trade-off between the two. In South Africa's case, the pressures for growth are particularly high. In the years ahead, the chemistry between the head of state, the finance minister and the governor will be a significant issue determining how the central bank interprets its constitutional mandate. Meanwhile, there has been growing criticism of the authorities in the business community for not lifting exchange controls.

■ ECONOMICS

Historical overview

Following the discovery of diamonds and gold in the 19th century, the South African economy developed apace as an abundance of minerals facilitated the development of heavy and light industry. This is partly responsible for agriculture's relatively small contribution to national wealth, accounting for less than 5% of GDP in the early 1990s. South Africa's topographical structure, which limits irrigation, serves as a barrier to a substantial expansion of agriculture. Also, the lack of irrigated land means that in many areas agriculture is rain-reliant and thus severely disrupted during dry years.

The industrial sector dominates the South African economy, with mineral extraction the basis for a strong manufacturing sector (contributing over a fifth of GDP). Although mining now accounts for less than 10% of GDP, it remains important in export terms, accounting for around 60% of the total, as well as forming the backbone to much of the country's manufacturing output.

South African industry is principally located in four areas: Gauteng (meaning "place of gold"; this new province includes Johannesburg and Pretoria), western Cape, Durban-Pinetown, and Port Elizabeth. Gauteng is the engine-room of the industrial economy with the majority of industry located there. Through the use of regional policy, attempts have been made to promote the location of industry away from the established areas.

The service sector makes the main contribution to the economy. Financial services, in particular, are highly developed. Following years of political turmoil, tourism is underdeveloped, with the proportion of South Africa's GDP from tourism only a third of the world average. Since the political transition, the situation has improved, although the high crime rate may undermine rapid development in this area.

Share of GDP by sector

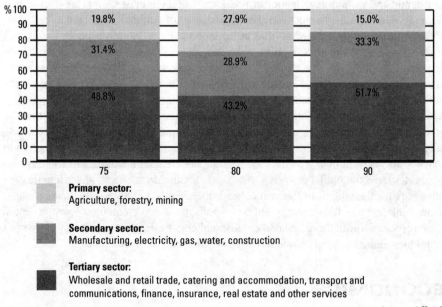

Primary sector:
Agriculture, forestry, mining

Secondary sector:
Manufacturing, electricity, gas, water, construction

Tertiary sector:
Wholesale and retail trade, catering and accommodation, transport and communications, finance, insurance, real estate and other services

Source: Official data

Recent developments

Unlike developments on the political scene, recent economic reforms in South Africa have not been particularly noteworthy in an international context. The country still trails well behind the liberalization curve when compared to the measures undertaken by various emerging market countries. Tough foreign exchange restrictions on residents remain in force; there has been no major privatization drive; and the rigidities of the labour market are reminiscent of Britain in the 1970s.

However, an assessment of the extent of South African reforms should take account of where the debate started and what its driving force is. Within this context, there would be progress to report. The ANC-led government has reduced import tariffs faster than required by its commitments to GATT. Privatization and equity partnerships are now stated government policy. The government has committed itself to a Maastricht-level budget deficit of 3% of GDP by 1999, while the policies of the Reserve Bank, coupled with a more open economy, meant that 1996 registered the fifth consecutive decline in the average annual rate of inflation.

These are not the economic policies that one would have expected from an ANC government when the organization was legalized in February 1990 or, for that matter, when looking at the party's April 1994 election manifesto.

In terms of the ability of residents to make economic choices freely, the business environment within South Africa is unquestionably more liberal today than it was five years ago. This is the result of a combination of the deregulation measures started by the previous government, the new freedoms enshrined in the new constitution, and the lifting of foreign restrictions on business ties with the country.

While these political and economic developments have helped to raise the country's longer-term growth potential from around 1.5% in recent years to perhaps close to 3%, this level of growth is insufficient to reduce the unemployment rate anytime soon or to bring about tangible increases in living standards for the majority of the population. Both are required if the government is to satisfy its key constituency.

Population

In late 1996 the authorities conducted the country's first post-apartheid census to try and obtain a more accurate picture of the size of the population. Until the new figures are published, the working assumption is that in 1996 South Africa had a population of around 42 million. Nearly 77% of the population is African (growing at around 2.5% per year), whites comprise around 12.5% (growing at around 0.7% per year), "coloureds" (or people of mixed origin) account for 8.5%, while the Asian population represents about 2.5% of the total. The rate of population increase for the latter two categories is around 1.5% annually. As a whole, the country's population is now growing at just over 2% (or nearly 900,000 people) annually, down from 2.7% in the 1970s.

The latest census might throw some light on the question of how many illegal persons presently reside in the country. Estimates speak of several million. It is also unclear whether that figure is in addition to the current estimate for the population. Given that South Africa is significantly wealthier than its neighbours, many of which are also struggling with very high unemployment rates, it is logical that the country is seen as offering new opportunities to the residents of neighbouring states.

AIDS (Acquired Immune Deficiency Syndrome) has gradually spread south from central Africa. It is unclear what effect the illness will have on the population growth rate in the next decade or on the national health bill. A study in 1994 found that nearly 5% of the sexually active population were HIV positive.

South African society is one of the most unequal in terms of a broad range of socioeconomic indicators. The country's longer-term stability will depend on the extent to which these inequalities can be reduced.

Medium-term growth prospects

Achieving sustained growth above 3% will require nothing less than sweeping structural changes, supported by an unambiguous, investment-friendly policy environment. In June 1996 the authorities unveiled a macroeconomic plan to push growth up to 6% annually by the year 2000 which, on the government's calculations, should produce around 400,000 new jobs a year. The jobs issue is particularly important because the level of unemployment is estimated at around 33% (or nearly 5 million people). The labour force is growing by around 350,000 job-seekers annually. In 1996, at best, perhaps 100,000 found employment. If this trend were to continue, the ranks of the unemployed would swell by another 1.5 million over the next five years. This is clearly untenable. While the country's ability to achieve growth of 6% by the year 2000 is debatable, it is reasonable to expect higher growth rates in the years ahead as a result of an improving policy environment, a more open economy and greater political stability. However, the obstacles on the road to higher growth include the legacy of the past (which have saddled the country with enormous backlogs and inequalities) and the costs of the transition process which include the uncertainties generated by major structural changes, high crime rates and an increase in the emigration of highly skilled labour.

Savings and investment

South Africa's savings rate of around 17% is a record low. In the early 1980s the savings rate was boosted by the windfall profits of the gold mines and was nearly double present levels. Since the mid-1980s, however, savings have been on a downward trend as the macro-economic picture deteriorated. Rising taxes, inflation and political concerns distorted investment decisions. In addition, deteriorating government finances meant that by the early 1990s the authorities were dissaving (borrowing money to finance government consumption expenditure) by more than 4% of GDP. The pool of domestic savings available for investment was consequently reduced by that amount. Thus, just reversing government dissavings would already make a substantial contribution to the country's savings rate. The government's macroeconomic strategy aims to cut government dissavings from around 3% of GDP in 1996 to a projected 0.6% by the year 2000, and at the same time measures are being taken to boost the level of private savings, which should gradually push the overall savings rate closer to the longer-term average of around 22%.

Balance of payments

Even at that rate, South Africa would still require capital inflows equivalent to around 2–3% of GDP to finance the shortfall in its projected investment requirements. This has been the country's Achilles heel for much of the last decade. Foreigners were unwilling to finance a South African current account deficit from the mid-1980s until 1994, when strong capital inflows finally resumed following a successful transfer of power. A large portion of this was volatile, short-term capital.

In early 1996, however, portfolio investors were reassessing their South African exposure in the light of an overvalued currency, ambiguous macroeconomic policy statements by the authorities, and the prospect that a sudden lifting of exchange controls would see a flood of capital leaving the country, pulling down the currency and thereby reducing the international value of South African-held assets.

The opening up of new markets to South African goods since the lifting of economic sanctions, and the increased competitiveness of those goods following the sharp devaluation in 1996, are boosting exports. In US dollar terms, exports in 1996 were estimated to be 20% higher than in 1990, the year the main reforms got under way.

Despite efforts to diversify its export base, South Africa still remains reliant on the export of primary and intermediate exports to industrialized countries. Gold accounts for around 20% of exports, down from a peak of about 50% in 1980. Manufactured exports (including vehicles, machinery, chemical products, paper, textiles and plastics) are rising too, especially in the African market, and manufactured goods now account for around 70% of exports to the rest of the continent.

In 1995 South Africa's imports were about 20% of GDP, up from around 15% in the early 1990s. The main imports are machinery, transport equipment, chemical products, and crude oil.

At around 24% of GDP in 1995, South Africa's level of foreign indebtedness compares very favourably with many other emerging market countries (Indonesia, Israel and Malaysia, for example, had debt to GDP ratios of around 50%). This suggests that, given the right macroeconomic framework, South Africa would have the option to substantially increase its foreign borrowing.

Current account as a % of GDP

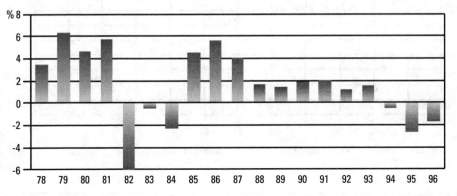

Source: Official data

Currency

For the three decades up to early 1996, the rand/US dollar exchange rate had closely tracked its underlying purchasing power parity, or more accurately, the inflation differential between the two countries. In March 1995 the rand underwent a dramatic change when the financial rand (used for capital transfers) was abolished. This caused the rand to weaken initially, because the unitary currency also reflected capital movements. Yet, as the abolition occurred against the background of a sharp fall in the value of the dollar and strong capital inflows, the rand quickly recovered. What followed was nearly a year of remarkable stability in the rand/dollar exchange rate. However, given that South Africa's inflation rate was 4–5% higher than US inflation, the real value of the rand continued to appreciate, making imports more attractive, while weakening the country's export sector. By February 1996 the imbalances of a rapid increase in the money supply and a deteriorating current account deficit had increased South Africa's risk profile for short-term investors. The result was a substantial outflow of short-term capital, pulling the currency down with it. By the end of 1996, the rand had fallen by 22% against the US dollar compared to the end of 1995. This represented a 15% decline on an average annual basis.

South Africa maintains stringent foreign exchange controls on residents. The authorities have stated that they will gradually phase out these controls, and the process has already begun. The markets, however, have been clamouring for a "big bang" abolition of controls. The most likely outcome will probably be the continuation of the gradualist course, meaning that more and more avenues are created for residents to invest abroad in the years ahead.

The best-case scenario would be an improving investment environment allowing capital inflows to offset the pent-up demand for foreign assets by South African residents. Under this scenario, the lifting of controls (or what remains of them) would probably occur when the government feels it has made considerable progress on deficit reduction, privatization proceeds are on track, and foreign capital inflows have picked up.

South African rand/US dollar exchange rate

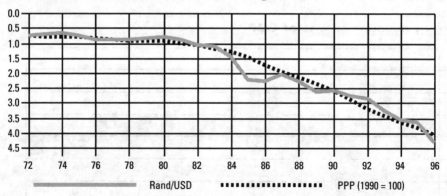

South Africa's macro plan

In June 1996 the South African government announced its medium-term macroeconomic strategy, entitled "Growth, Employment and Redistribution". The aim of the strategy is to achieve 6% economic growth and create 400,000 new jobs annually by the year 2000.

The baseline scenario is an average 2.8% GDP growth over the next five years and represents the economy muddling through with no substantial restructuring. "High growth" is an average 4.2% (starting at 2.9% in 1997 and rising to 6% in 2000), simulating the potential effects of the government's macroeconomic strategy.

In order to achieve its higher growth and employment targets, and making full use of the depreciation of the rand, the government's strategy concluded that the following policy elements are required:

◆ A tighter fiscal policy stance, reducing the deficit from 5.1% budgeted for the 1995/96 fiscal year to 3% by 1999. This would have the effect of increasing the level of savings in the economy, which would lower interest rates and stimulate growth.

◆ Speeding up tariff reductions to improve competitiveness and keep downward pressure on inflation. The average tariff (as a percentage of imports) would have to come down from 10% in 1996 to 6% by 2000.

◆ Greater labour market flexibility; moderating the rate of wage rises; and sectoral shifts towards more labour-intensive industry.

◆ Boosting investment by public authorities and public corporations; increasing non-gold exports, especially manufacturing; and attracting additional foreign direct investment.

Adherence to the government's new macroeconomic strategy has the potential to lay the basis for sustainable higher growth and to create more jobs, although this might not be at the high levels the authorities are hoping for. The additional obstacles to higher investment levels over the medium term include exchange controls, an inflexible labour market, crime and political uncertainties.

Potential effect of the macroeconomic strategy on the unemployment rate (%)

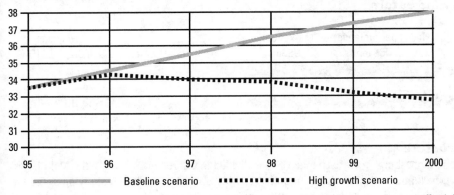

Source: Official data

■ EQUITIES

Index performance (in local currency)

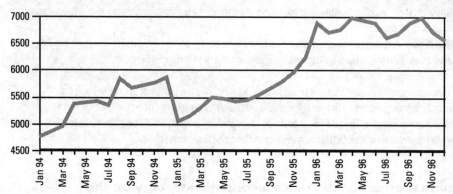

Key indicators

	Index performance %, in US$ terms	Market Cap. US$bn	P/E	Div. Yield	Weight in IFCI	IFCG
1994	28.5	225.7	21.3	2.2	—	—
1995	14.8	280.5	18.8	2.3	26.7	15
1996	-19.2	241.6	16.3	2.7	12.6	8.2

Sources: Local stock exchange, IFC, Bloomberg, Datastream, UBS

Structure

The Johannesburg Stock Exchange (JSE) is divided into three main boards: the Main Board, the Development Capital Market and the Venture Capital Market. When applying to the JSE, a company should qualify for one of these three possible listings.

The main requirements for the Main Board are:

◆ a subscribed capital, excluding revaluations of assets, of at least R2 million in the form of not less than one million shares in issue;
◆ a satisfactory profit history for the preceding three years, the last of which reported an audited profit before taxation of at least R1 million;
◆ a minimum of 10% of each class of equity shares to be held by the public;
◆ a minimum of three hundred public shareholders for equity shares
◆ the minimum initial issue price of shares to be not less than 100 cents per share.

To promote the socio-economic development of South Africa, the JSE has recently introduced the Financial Redevelopment sector to the Main Board, and, to promote industrial development in South Africa, it has also introduced the Industrial Development sectors to the Main Board. Listings in these sectors are subject to certain modified criteria.

As at June 1996, there were 635 companies listed on the JSE. The number of listed securities stood at 828, and liquidity in the market was 9.8% on an annualized basis. The top ten companies, ranked by market capitalization, accounted for 30.2% of the total market capitalization.

Regulatory authority
The JSE is governed by statutory law in terms of the Stock Exchanges Control Act of 1985 (SECA) but, in common with the international trends, this Act requires self-regulatory rules and directives which are drawn up by the JSE Committee. Insider trading is monitored by the Securities Regulation Panel; the responsibilities and powers of the Panel follow closely those of the Take-over Panel of the UK and include the powers of investigation and prosecution. Additionally, the Panel has responsibility for regulating take-overs and mergers through its own Code.

Trading methods
All the shares listed on the Johannesburg Stock Exchange are traded on the Johannesburg Equity Trading (JET) System, which came into effect in March 1996. With the introduction of the JET System, the structure then changed to continuous order-driven on a time-priority basis with central market principles. A dual trading capacity was also introduced, complemented by member firms voluntarily acting as market makers. Fixed brokerage fell away, enabling brokers to negotiate commissions with their clients for the first time. It is charged at an agreed rate in an agency transaction, but may not be charged when the firm is acting as a principal.

Hours
Jet trading takes place 09.30 and 16.00, Monday to Friday, excluding public holidays. There is a pre-opening period from 08.45 to 09.30. A facility allows for after-hours trade.

Settlement time and clearing
All trading settlements at the JSE between members are operated through the JSE clearing house in terms of a fixed settlement period (generally on the following Tuesday or thereafter). Rolling settlement, ultimately three days after trade (T+3) is expected to be introduced during 1997. Settlement of private trades must be done within seven trading days from the date of the deal.

Types of shares
Most shares are ordinary voting shares. There are also A and B shares, and "N" shares, which have limited voting rights. There are also a limited number of preference shares and debentures.

Stock indices
The main indices are the JSE Actuaries All Share Index (ALSI), the JSE Actuaries All Gold Index (GLDI), and the JSE Actuaries Industrial Index (INDI). However, the most used stock indices are the All Share 40 (ALSI 40), the All Gold 10 (GLDI 10), and the Industrial 25 (INDI 25). The numbering relates to the most significant stocks included in each index.

These indices are important as they are the basis of the equity-futures market in South Africa.

Sectors

There are forty-two sectors represented on the Johannesburg Stock Exchange. The biggest sectors by market capitalization are industrial holdings (with about 17% of market capitalization), mining houses (14%) and banks and other (8%). Other sectors include insurance (8.2%), beverages and hotels (5.6%) and diamonds (5.5%).

Dividends and taxes

A marketable securities tax (MST) of 0.5% is payable in respect of every purchase of marketable securities through the agency of or from a member of the JSE. The tax is not payable by a person who is not ordinarily resident in South Africa, Namibia, Lesotho or Swaziland, but if registration of transfer is sought, stamp duty would become payable unless a specific exemption applies. VAT is payable on brokerage charged in agency transactions. Dividends on listed shares, and interest on debentures, bonds and bank account credit balances owned by foreign investors, are freely transferable to countries outside the Common Monetary Area of Southern Africa. Dividend and interest payments are exempt from normal and withholding taxes.

Disclosure

Announcements of dividends and/or interest payments on listed securities should be notified to the holders of the relevant securities immediately upon declaration either by means of a circular or by a press announcement.

Interim reports will be published in the press and be distributed to all shareholders as early as possible after the expiration of the first six-month period of a financial year, but no later that three months after that date. While interim and preliminary reports are not required to be audited, the reports must be reviewed by the listed company's auditors who should confirm that they have been prepared in accordance with the principles applied in the preparation of the most recently published annual financial statements and in accordance with GAAP. Non-compliance with any of these requirements can lead to the suspension and possible de-listing of a company. Listed companies are obliged to notify shareholders of any negotiations or transactions which may influence their share price.

Limits on non-residents

Exchange control restrictions require that foreign-owned securities carry on the share certificate the restrictive endorsement non-resident against transferability in the ownership of the stock. The purpose is to restrict South African residents from selling their shares overseas.

Take-over bids and large stakes

A controlling interest exists when a shareholder can exercise, or cause to be exercised, 50% or more of the voting rights at meetings of the relevant company, or can appoint or remove, or cause to be appointed or removed, directors exercising more than 50% of the voting rights at directors' meetings of the relevant company.

Brokers and commissions

There are currently forty-six member firms of the Johannesburg Stock Exchange. The JSE operates an equities market, but many member firms also trade bonds and financial futures. Traditional options are traded by member firms on an OTC basis. Corporate limited liability membership with ownership by non-stockbrokers was introduced on November 8, 1995 supplementing the present membership of sole traders, partnerships or unlimited liability corporate members. However the member firm will be the trading entity and not the individual. Foreigners may also operate as member firms. Brokerage is fully negotiable between the investor and the member firm. It is charged at an agreed rate in the agency instance but may not be charged when acting as principal.

■ DEBT

Bond market activity is regulated through the Stock Exchange Act and Financial Markets Control Act. The Bond Market Association (BMA) was set up in 1989 as a self-regulatory and supervisory body, after a decade of market evolution, triggered by the liberalization of inter-est rate controls in 1977. Domestic banks and brokerage houses began to trade bonds both for their own and their customers' accounts, and a few years later parastatals made markets in their own bonds.

Treasury bills

The Reserve Bank offers bills of 3 and 6 months every Friday in competitive US treasury-style auctions. Bids are submitted by 11.00, and allocations are made at noon. The auction size and maturity are announced earlier. Foreign participation is permitted, but most bills are bought and held to maturity by domestic banks to satisfy compulsory reserve requirements.

Government bonds

Republic of South Africa (RSA) bonds pay fixed rate coupons semi-annually and are issued for tenures up to twenty years. Auctions for longer-dated bonds are held irregularly but turnover in the secondary market is high, accounting for more than 95% of total turnover on the Exchange and over the counter (OTC) markets. Domestic institutions are captive investors because they are prevented from making overseas investments, and the market's volatility encourages strong foreign participation. Transaction volume in 1995 was about 2.5 trillion rand (US$700 billion), and was marginally higher in 1996.

Corporate and parastatal bonds

The largest issuers are the state utility companies – Eskom (electricity), Telkom (telecommu-nications) and Transnet (transport). Frequency of interest payments vary and bonds have been issued for maturities up to twenty years.

Trading of RSA and non-government bonds occurs on the Johannesburg Stock Exchange and OTC. Volumes are about even. Settlement is for physical delivery against pay-ment until a central depository is created. Trades used to settle on the second Thursday after dealing, but now settle T+2 days. The South African Reserve Bank also functions as a clear-ing house for all debt securities.

Foreign investors

International investors are required to use a local custodian for settlement of bill and bond transactions. Otherwise they face no restrictions. They can repatriate capital and profits, and since the unifying of the commercial and financial rands into a single free floating currency in March 1995, they face no foreign exchange controls. Foreigners do not pay taxes on their investments or trading activities.

Derivatives

Bond futures trade on the South African Futures Exchange (SAFEX), and options trade OTC. Transaction volumes in interest rate contracts are huge, reflecting the high turnover in the cash bond market. A forward foreign exchange market is normally active out to one year.

Eurobonds

The Republic of South Africa tapped the international capital markets with a few small ECU-denominated issues in 1984/5, but had to wait until 1991 before it could access the markets in larger size. It launched a DEM400 million 5-year bond, paying a 10.5% coupon at a yield spread of 170 basis points over German government bonds. The RSA's next significant issue came three years later, after the official ending of apartheid, with a US$700 million 5-year bond at 193 basis points over US treasuries. In the meantime, South African utilities also raised funds in the eurobond market.

Eurobonds issues (US$m)

	1990	1991	1992	1993	1994	1995	1996
Sovereign	58.7	418.7	724.0	—	750.0	545.1	289.5
Private	—	22.1	262.8	—	—	—	—

■ SOUTH AFRICA: Economic indicators

Population and development	1990	1991	1992	1993	1994	1995	1996e
Population, million	37.1	38.0	38.8	39.6	40.4	41.2	42.0
Population growth, %	2.4	2.4	2.1	2.1	2.0	2.0	2.0
Nominal GDP per capita, US$	2874	2955	3081	2966	3010	3231	2968

National accounts							
Nominal GDP, US$bn	106.7	112.3	119.6	117.5	121.6	133.5	124.8
Change in real GDP, %	-0.3	-1.0	-2.2	1.1	2.7	3.4	3.0
Gross fixed capital formation, % of GDP	19.6	17.8	16.6	15.5	16.0	16.9	17.4

Money supply and inflation							
Narrow money, change %, Dec/Dec	14.3	17.7	16.2	16.6	24.8	16.8	21.0
Broad money, change %, Dec/Dec	13.1	16.1	10.8	3.9	16.0	15.3	13.7
Consumer price inflation (avg.) %	14.3	15.3	13.9	9.7	9.0	8.7	7.4

Interest rates							
Discount rate, end of year	18.00	17.00	14.00	12.00	13.00	15.00	17.00
Money market rate, annual average	19.46	17.02	14.11	10.83	10.24	13.07	15.50
Deposit rate, annual average	18.86	17.30	13.78	11.50	11.11	13.54	15.13
Prime lending rate, annual average	21.00	20.31	18.91	16.16	15.58	17.90	19.50
Government bond yield, end of year	16.00	16.70	14.90	12.30	16.80	14.60	16.10

Government finance (year ending 31 March)							
Government expenditure, % of GDP	28.2	28.2	28.8	32.0	31.5	31.1	31.4
Government balance, % of GDP	-1.5	-2.7	-4.1	-7.9	-6.4	-5.6	-5.3
Government debt, % of GDP	38.6	37.2	39.5	44.5	48.6	54.8	56.2

Exchange rates lc=local currency							
Exchange rate, annual average, lc/US$	2.59	2.76	2.85	3.27	3.55	3.64	4.30
Exchange rate, end of year, lc/US$	2.56	2.77	3.01	3.38	3.54	3.64	4.68

Balance of payments							
Exports of goods & services, US$m	27952	27775	28314	28540	29737	34051	34039
Change %	—	-0.6	1.9	0.8	4.2	14.5	0.0
Imports of goods & services, US$m, fob	25946	25589	27032	26872	30411	36874	36219
Change %	—	-1.4	5.6	-0.6	13.2	21.3	-1.8
Trade balance, US$m, fob-fob	6782	6133	5429	5775	3197	1611	1978
Trade balance, of goods only, US$m, fob-fob	2077	2259	1387	1800	-629	-2790	-2128
as a % of GDP	1.9	2.0	1.2	1.5	-0.5	-2.6	-1.7

Foreign exchange reserves							
Foreign exchange reserves, US$m	1008	899	992	1020	1700	2824	941
Gold at ⅔ of market price, US$m	1051.4	1560.6	1521.0	1140.4	1074.7	1100.2	930.0
Import cover (reserves/imports), months	0.7	0.6	0.7	0.7	0.9	1.3	1.6

Foreign debt and debt service							
Short-term debt, US$m	11098	10766	10204	8624	11246	13264	13250
Total foreign debt, US$m	26200	25600	27200	25500	27883	31800	32000
as a % of GDP	24.6	22.8	22.8	21.7	22.9	23.7	25.6
Interest payments, US$m	2464	2078	1890	1905	1876	1980	1950
Principal repayments, US$m	2251	1757	1565	1923	2092	2256	2430
Total debt service, US$m	4715	3835	3455	3828	3968	4236	4380
as a % of goods exports	20.0	16.5	14.6	15.9	16.1	14.9	15.1
as a % of foreign exchange receipts	16.9	13.8	12.2	13.4	13.3	12.4	12.9

South Korea

Area (thousands of km²):	99
Population (1995, millions):	44.8
Population projection (2025, millions):	53
Population younger than 15 yrs (1991, % of total):	24.8
Urbanization rate (1993, % of population):	78
Life expectancy (1993, years at birth):	71
Gross domestic product (1996, US$bn):	489.2
GDP per capita (1996, US$):	10814
Average annual GDP growth rate (1990-96, %):	7.7
Average annual inflation rate (1990-96, %):	6.3
Currency (won per US$, average 1996):	804.5
Real exchange rate: (1990=100, average 1996)	101.29
Structure of production (1994):	50% services, 43% industry, 7% agriculture
Main exports:	semiconductors, passenger cars, woven fabrics, ships
Main imports:	machinery & transport equipment, mineral fuels, crude materials
Main trading partners:	US, Japan, Hong Kong, Singapore, Germany, Saudi Arabia
Market capitalization of Stock Exchange (December 1996; US$bn):	138.8
Total foreign debt (% of GDP):	25.6
Next elections due under normal circumstances:	presidential scheduled December 1997; legislative scheduled April 2000
Credit rating: (Jan 1997, Standard & Poor's, Moody's)	AA-; A1

FORECAST: 1997-2000 (average)

	Worst case	Most likely	Best case
Real GDP growth (%)	4 to 5	6.5 to 7.5	8 to 9
Inflation (%)	6 to 7	4 to 5	3 to 4

■ POLITICS

Historical overview

Until the beginning of the 20th century, Korea remained a feudal society governed by powerful families such as the Yi dynasty, which ruled from 1392 until 1910. Political life revolved around a small court, which controlled the country through patronage. In the 1860s, Korea became known as the Hermit Kingdom when the Yi rulers closed Korea's borders to foreign visitors. In 1882, however, Chinese forces seized power after an aborted military coup. Twelve years later, Japan invaded. Under Japanese rule, Korean culture was repressed and locals denied political power. This led to the killing of hundreds when Japanese police broke up an independence rally in Seoul in 1919.

The defeat of Japan in the Second World War gave Korea its first chance of full independence. But with the United States and Russia both determined that the country should not fall into the other's sphere of influence, Korea was split along the 38th Parallel, with the Soviets in charge of the North and the Americans in charge of the South. In 1948, the US withdrew from South Korea, and the Republic of Korea was formally proclaimed, with Syngman Rhee as its first president.

Fighting soon broke out between the North and the South. In June 1950, the North Korean military (backed by Soviet and Chinese forces) invaded South Korea and occupied Seoul. Four months later, a counter-offensive was launched and the South Korean forces reclaimed their territory south of the 38th Parallel. The fighting continued until July 1953, by which time thousands of civilians and soldiers had died and most of South Korea was reduced to rubble.

In 1961, General Park Chung-hee seized power in a military coup. He quickly introduced a new constitution known as the Yusin, giving him extensive powers of appointment. He set up a national assembly, which he packed with his supporters. After eighteen years in power, Park was assassinated in 1979 and replaced by General Chun Doo-wan, who introduced martial law and jailed opposition politicians such as Kim Young-sam. Popular opposition to his rule increased following the Kwangju incident of 1980, when more than two hundred people died as soldiers suppressed a student rally.

Real political reform began in the mid-1980s, and by 1987, Kim Dae-jung's Party for Peace and Democracy (PPD) and Kim Young-sam's Reunification Democratic Party (RDP) were both allowed to take part in the first democratic elections ever to be held in Korea. The political structure underwent considerable change in the early 1990s, when Kim Young-sam's party joined forces with the ruling Democratic Justice Party (DJP), led by President Roh Tae Woo, to form the Democratic Liberal Party (DLP). In the 1992 elections, the DLP held on to power, albeit with a much smaller majority, and Kim Young-sam took over from Roh as president. In 1993, Kim began economic and political reform. He launched an anti-corruption drive, banning false-name bank accounts. He also ratified the GATT trade treaty.

Recent events

The government's popularity declined in 1994 and 1995 after revelations that two of the DLP's former presidents, Chun Doo-hwan and Roh Tae-woo, had amassed huge slush funds during their political careers. Kim Dae-jung's Democratic Party (DP) scored well in the 1995 local elections but was undermined when Kim announced he was leaving to set up the National Congress for Politics. In April 1996, the ruling DLP (now called the New Korea Party) failed to win an outright majority in the legislative elections, but nevertheless emerged as the clear winner, with 133 of the 299 national assembly seats.

After the election, Kim Young-sam consolidated his grip on power by reshuffling his cabinet, and launching a crackdown on Communist sympathizers. Increased co-operation between the two major opposition leaders, Kim Dae-jung and Kim Jong-pil, has made life difficult for the new government, however. In June 1996, the opening of the assembly was delayed for a month. South Korea's relations with North Korea also came under severe strain. Already hit by disagreements over the funding of a nuclear reactor in North Korea, relations took a turn for the worse when a North Korean submarine ran aground off the coast. This led to recriminations over the military's handling of the affair. Now, the big political question is who will take over from Kim Young-sam as president in February 1998. Given the absence of any credible opposition leaders, the NKP candidate seems likely to win.

Chronology

668	Silla Dynasty begins
918	Koryo Dynasty takes power
1392	Yi Dynasty emerges
1592	Japan invades Korea
1882	Chinese seize power after aborted military coup
1910	Korea formally annexed by Japan
1943	Japan defeated by the US
1943	Korea split into two on the 38th Parallel
1948	Elections held in South Korea
1950	Korean War begins
1953	Cease-fire negotiated
1960	President Rhee resigns under pressure from the US
1961	Military junta replaces Democratic Party government
1962	New Yusin constitution gives more power to the president
1972	Park declares martial law after third election win
1979	Park is assassinated, and replaced by General Chun Doo-wan
1980	Martial law is extended after student riots
1981	Chun's Democratic Justice Party (DJP) wins elections
1987	First multiparty elections are held
1988	New constitution is approved
1988	Seoul Olympics
1990	DJP merges with RDP to form Democratic Liberal Party (DLP)
1992	Kim Young-sam replaces Rhee as president and leader of DLP
1993	South Korea ratifies GATT agreement
1995	Roh is arrested over slush fund scandal
1996	DLP wins legislative elections

Constitution and government

The new constitution was approved by national referendum on October 29, 1987. Executive power lies with the president who is elected by popular vote every five years and can only serve one term. The president appoints the State Council (cabinet) composed of the president, the prime minister and between fifteen and thirty ministers.

The legislature is a unicameral national assembly (Kuk Hoe), which has a minimum of two hundred members (currently 299) elected for four-year terms. Of these, 253 have been elected by popular vote, with the remaining 46 distributed between parties in proportion to their share of the national vote.

Current government

President   Kim Young-sam
Prime Minister   Lee Soo-sung
Deputy Prime Minister   Han Seung-soo

Results of the April 1996 legislative elections

New Korea Party	139 seats	34.5% of vote
National Congress for New Politics	79 seats	25.3% of vote
United Liberal Democrats	50 seats	16.2% of vote
Democratic Party	15 seats	11.2% of vote
Independents	16 seats	11.9% of vote

Next elections
April 2000. A presidential election is due in December 1997.

Political forces

The national government is dominated by the Democratic Liberal Party which changed its name to the New Korea Party in December 1995. It won 139 seats in the April 1996 elections, leaving it eleven short of an overall majority, but was able to take power with the assistance of eleven independent deputies. There are three main opposition parties – the National Congress for New Politics (NCNP), the United Liberal Democrats (ULD) and the Democratic Party (DP).

Central bank

South Korea's central bank, the Bank of Korea (BOK), implements monetary policy in conjunction with the Ministry of Finance. The primary monetary policy tool is the targeting of broad money supply (M2) growth to control inflation. The BOK intervenes in the money market via open market operations, and regulates the bank foreign exchange positions to adjust liquidity conditions.

■ ECONOMICS

Historical overview

Prior to the arrival of the Japanese in 1910, Korea had an agriculture-based economy with little exposure to international trade. The Japanese occupiers set up a basic transport infrastructure, but almost all of this was destroyed during the civil war (1950-53). Since the civil war, the South Korean economy has expanded at a rapid rate. Average income has grown from less than US$50 a year in the mid-1950s to more than US$8,500 in 1996. It is now one of the world's largest producers of ships, semi-conductors and electronic consumer products.

The roots of this rapid expansion lie in the five-year economic reconstruction plans launched by General Park in 1962. Under the first of these plans (which drew closely on the Japanese example), the banking system was nationalized and large amounts of capital channelled into export-orientated industries such as textiles and light industry. The government also launched a major construction programme to revitalize South Korea's power, transportation and communications infrastructure. In the late 1960s and early 1970s, the government began investing heavily in electronic and petrochemicals industries. Foreign technology was imported from the US, Europe and Japan. Favoured conglomerates (known as chaebol), such as Daewoo, Samsung and Hyundai, were granted subsidised loans to finance investment in new industries such as chemicals and steel.

Industrial production increased rapidly in the 1960s and 1970s. Thanks to the country's low labour costs, South Korea was able to undercut rival producers in Japan and the US, and began to establish itself as a major manufacturer of consumer and industrial goods. Throughout this period, the local market was protected from overseas producers by high import taxes and tariffs. In the mid-1970s, the government began to shift investment into high-technology industries such as shipbuilding and electronics.

Following Park's death in 1979, the government implemented an IMF-backed austerity programme to reduce external debt and eliminate the current account deficit. The won was devalued, and subsidies to heavy industry cut. The breakneck pace of investment continued in the 1980s, however, as the chaebol expanded into new industries such as car manufacturing and semi-conductors. Thanks to an appreciation in the Japanese yen, exports rose sharply during the second half of the decade. Real GDP increased by more than 10% a year between 1986 and 1991.

Recent developments

In recent years, the civilian government has tried to reduce the role of the state in the economy, to improve the efficiency of the private sector and reduce government spending. Subsidized loans have been reduced, and in 1994, the Economic Planning Board (which had channelled capital and labour into favoured industries and companies) was abolished. The domestic market has also been gradually opened to foreign competition as part of Kim's globalization programme. A trade liberalization agreement was signed in 1993, and tariffs on imported goods gradually reduced.

A commitment to financial sector liberalization was taken in 1993 with the introduction of the five-year Blue Print for Financial Reform. Much of the programme has already been implemented, and the remainder has been accelerated in conjunction with membership in the OECD. The role of the government in the allocation of credit has been greatly reduced, and interest rates have been almost completely deregulated. However, the inability of the authorities to ease policy substantially in the face of the current economic downturn underscores the need to deepen reforms.

The legacy of General Park's interventionist economic policies lives on. The economy continues to be dominated by a small group of large diversified companies which operate in many different industries. Many of the chaebol are heavily in debt and are increasingly vulnerable to downturns in world demand for key exports such as semi-conductors. The banking sector and local capital markets remain underdeveloped due to the restrictions placed on the entry of foreign competitors. The government has announced plans to remove many of the restrictions governing capital flows and foreign investment in 1997, also required by the OECD membership.

Population

In mid-1996, the population was estimated at 45.2 million, with an annual growth rate of just under 1%. About 24% is under the age of fourteen. Almost all are Koreans, although there are an estimated 20,000 ethnic Chinese.

The economy

In 1995, manufacturing accounted for 29.9% of GDP, financial and business services 17.2%, trade, restaurants and hotels 12.5%, construction 11.4%, transport, storage and communications 7.9%, agriculture, forestry and fishing 6.5%, government services 5.8%, electricity, gas and water 2.4% and mining 0.3%.

Share of GDP by sector

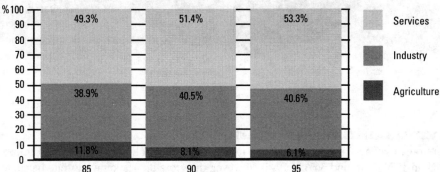

Source: Official data

Exports and imports as a % of GDP

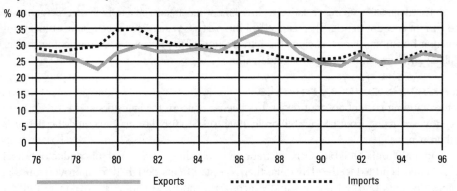

Source: Official data

Breakdown of exports (1995)

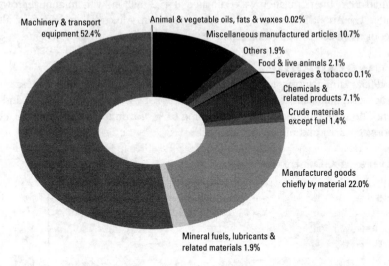

Machinery & transport equipment 52.4%

Animal & vegetable oils, fats & waxes 0.02%

Miscellaneous manufactured articles 10.7%

Others 1.9%

Food & live animals 2.1%

Beverages & tobacco 0.1%

Chemicals & related products 7.1%

Crude materials except fuel 1.4%

Manufactured goods chiefly by material 22.0%

Mineral fuels, lubricants & related materials 1.9%

Source: Official data

Savings and investment

South Korean savings rates have increased rapidly over the past thirty years from about 15% of GDP in 1970 to around 36% in 1995. However, the gross domestic savings rate began to fall in the 1990s. Gross domestic investment as a proportion of GDP has also increased over the past three decades, although not as rapidly as savings, from levels of 24% of GDP in 1970 to around 37% in 1995. However, the 1990s also marked a period of weakening investment rates.

The decline in savings relative to investment has been reflected in the emergence of the current account deficits characteristic of the past six years. Recent government measures aimed at boosting savings, such as the introduction of tax incentives, are welcome but are unlikely to do much to narrow the trade gap.

Balance of payments

The expanding current account deficit has been a concern for investors and economists in recent years, rising from US$4.5 billion in 1994 to US$8.9 billion in 1995, and the deficit is still growing.

In 1996, unfavourable terms of trade due to falling prices of semi-conductors, steel and chemicals added to the deficit. Furthermore, tariff cuts designed to improve industrial competitiveness boosted imports and exacerbated the trade gap. Yen weakness and the semi-conductor overhang persisted and restrained any export recovery. Import expansion waned, however, in response to slowing investment growth. The deficit is estimated at US$23 billion for 1996. An export rebound in 1997 will improve the current account balance only slightly, given a structural services trade deficit. Still, at around US$23 billion, the deficit is a manageable 4.5% of GDP.

Economic policy
Monetary policy
Interest rates have begun to fall in the past three years as regulations governing bank deposit rates have been lifted. Some controls still exist, but interest rates are now mostly market-determined. Nevertheless, they remain substantially higher than in most other OECD countries. The government aims to lower rates to "global" levels in order to minimize the potential impact of hot money inflows resulting from capital account liberalization, but it has made little progress. In 1996, the plunge in export revenues, mounting inventories, and currency depreciation raising debt servicing costs on substantial US dollar liabilities have raised working capital requirements. The increased corporate demand for funds has put a floor under rates. The removal of capital controls will expose South Korea's relatively under-developed capital markets to competition. The OECD has accepted a plan for the gradual removal of remaining restrictions on capital inflows, which would allow a lowering of interest rates. Phased liberalization of capital flows should minimize disruption to monetary and exchange rate policy. Nevertheless, financial opening runs the risk of exchange rate appreciation. Current central bank targeting of broad monetary aggregates has long been considered inadequate, and explicit inflation-targeting may become a policy option.

Fiscal policy
The South Korean government has achieved effective control of its budget, maintaining an average surplus of 0.1% of GDP between 1990 and 1995. Revenue from taxation increased at an average rate of 17% in the first five months of 1995, while value-added tax, which accounted for 28.5% of total tax receipts in 1994, is the biggest source of revenue. The government has pledged to reduce spending in coming years, but small budget deficits are still expected in the 1996-98 period.

Currency
South Korea introduced a market average rate (MAR) system for exchange rate determination in 1990. Under the MAR system, the South Korean won is effectively free-floating and its exchange rate per US dollar largely determined by demand in the interbank market. The won is allowed to fluctuate within a band, currently set at +/-2.25%, around the previous day's weighted average rate in the interbank spot market.

South Korean won/US dollar exchange rate

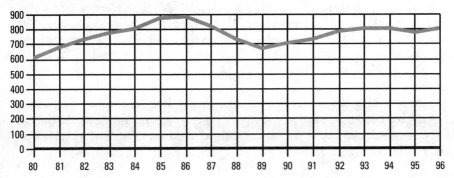

■ EQUITIES

Index performance (in local currency)

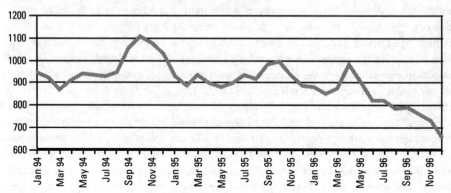

Key indicators

	Index performance %, in US$ terms	Market Cap. US$bn	Market P/E	Div. Yield	Weight in IFCI	IFCG
1994	16.3	191.8	34.5	1.3	3.3	13.3
1995	-7.0	182.0	19.8	1.4	2.8	11.4
1996	-39.2	138.8	11.7	2.3	2.4	6.9

Sources: Korea Stock Exchange, IFC, Bloomberg, Datastream, UBS

Background

The securities market in Korea really began with independence following the end of the Second World War. There is evidence of share trading in Korea prior to 1945, but only on a very small scale. In 1956, the formation of the Daehan Stock Exchange enabled bond trading, but failed to create a market place for equities.

However, during May 1963, the Exchange was reorganized as a non-profit-making, government-owned, corporation and renamed the Korea Stock Exchange (KSE), thus laying the foundations for future equity market development in Korea. During the 1960s and 1970s the market grew apace, but it was not until 1981 that the government announced plans to relax rules on foreign investment. The 1990s have witnessed continuing internationalization of the KSE, with direct investment by non-residents permitted since January 1992.

Structure

The KSE is divided into three main areas: the stock market, the bond market and the beneficial certificates market. In addition, the stock market is split into two sections. There are 738 companies listed and 1,050 issues on the KSE with a market value of KRW133314 billion (around US$160 billion).

Regulatory authority

The Securities and Exchange Commission (SEC) and its executive arm, the Security Supervisory Board (SSB), act as regulators of the KSE. The Comprehensive Surveillance and Information System (COSIS) electronically monitors the market for malpractice.

Trading methods

Trading takes place using the computerized Stock Market Automated Trading System (SMATS). Orders are entered directly into SMATS by brokerage house dealers and sent to the electronic "post" where they can be matched automatically or semi-automatically by an Exchange employee. Continuous trading occurs throughout the session.

The system for foreigners is separated into two parts. For stocks where the foreign ownership limit has not been reached, brokers put in orders in the normal way – a broker can "lock-up" the whole system from 08.00. However, if (as is historically the case) the full quota for foreign ownership has been reached, trading is done over the counter (OTC) by negotiation. All crossing must be done through the market.

Foreign investors must obtain a foreign investor number from the Korean Securities Board when they set up custody and standing proxy. This number must be displayed whenever the trades are and settled via the central depository, the Korean Securities Settlement Corp.

Hours

Trading takes place between 09.30 and 11.30, Monday to Saturday and between 13.00 and 15.00, Monday to Friday.

Settlement time and clearing

Settlement occurs on a trade plus two business days (T+2) basis.

Limits on price movement

Minimum limits on price movement depend on the price of the share:-

Share price (KRW)	Variation unit (KRW)
Less than 10,000	10
Between 10,000 and 100,000	100
Between 100,000 and 500,000	500
More than 500,000	1,000

Furthermore, to prevent excessive price fluctuation there is a 6% ceiling on price movement from the previous day's closing prices. This limit is expected to rise to 10% in early 1997 in line with the continuing liberalization.

Types of shares

Common shares and preferred shares are traded, as well as debt securities.

Stock indices

The main index exchange of the KSE is the Koreas Composite Stock Price Index (KOSPI). This is a weighted value average of all common and preferred stocks listed on the Exchange, with the exception of bond-type preferred stocks and newly listed stocks. In addition, the KOSPI 200 is a weighted value average of two hundred stocks and is used as the underlying index for futures trading. Other sector, section, and stock size based indices are also published.

Taxes

Floor-based Transaction Tax (on sales)	0.30%
Special Tax (on sales)	0.15%
OTC-based Transaction Tax (on sales)	0.5%
Dividend and interest income withholding tax	15%*
Capital gains tax	10%/25%*

*Some countries have treaties with South Korea which give more favourable tax rates.

Disclosure of financial statements

Listed companies are required to produce an annual report within ninety days of the closing of the business year, and a semi-annual report within forty-five days of closing of the first half of the year.

Ownership limits for non-residents

Foreigners are limited to owning 20% of a company's capita (limits for KEPCO and POSCO are set separately). During 1997 foreigners are expected to be given access to the OTC market. The limit on ownership will be 10% in aggregate or 3% for a single investor.

Capital and foreign exchange controls

There are no restrictions on foreign exchange, but foreign investors are required to register with the appropriate body.

Brokers

Securities trading on the KLSE is restricted to member firms. Non-member firms are required to transact customers' orders to member firms, giving the member 50% of the commission or 30% if the non-member is a member of the Korea Securities Dealers Association (KSDA). Brokers are free to determine their own commission rates between 0.3% and 0.6%. However, in general, a sale of shares up to the value of KRW500,000 (about US$600) results in a 0.6% charge and 0.4% charge thereafter.

Sectors

In terms of market value, fabricated metals, machinery and equipment, finance, and electricity and gas are the leading sectors with a combined value equivalent to 57% of total capitalization. Chemicals and chemical products, basic metal industries, and construction are smaller, but still make an important contribution.

ADRs

There are three Korean companies listed on the NYSE: POSCO, Korea Electric Power, and Korea Mobile Telecom.

Derivatives

On May 3, 1996 the KOSPI 200 futures market opened. Trade occurs between 09.30 and 11.30 and 13.00 and 15.15 with contract sizes of KOSPI 200 x KRW 500,000. An options market is scheduled for early 1997.

■ DEBT

The bond market is one of the largest in East Asia, and comprises issues by the government, municipalities, state enterprises and corporates. A financial sector reform programme should be completed in 1997. Already the liberalization schedule has been accelerated to comply with forthcoming membership of the OECD. For instance, interest rates on new government bill and bond issues are now market determined (except for the shortest maturities), rather than administratively decided.

The Korean Securities and Exchange Commission (KSEC) and its executive body, the Securities Supervisory Board (SSB) were established under the Securities and Exchange Law of 1977. The KSEC and SSB are mandated to develop and regulate the markets and are accountable to the Ministry of Finance and Economy (MFE). The KSEC and MFE also have control over foreign participation in the domestic market and authorize Korean issuers access to international markets. In addition to the KSEC, a self-regulatory body, the Korean Securities Dealers Association (KSDA) helps operate the exchange and the OTC markets.

Treasury bills have not been issued since 1994, but the Bank of Korea (BOK) issues Monetary Stabilization Bonds for its money market operations. Other government securities are national investment bonds, grain securities, national housing bonds and Seoul metropolitan subway bonds. The medium- and long-dated sector includes industrial finance debentures and long-term credit debentures, but the largest component is corporate bonds.

Public debt
Monetary stabilization bonds (MSBs)

The Bank of Korea (BOK) issues MSBs to absorb liquidity for its open market operations and uses them for repo agreements. The BOK operating desk determines the size and timing of MSB auctions, maturities range up to 2 years and interest rates, which are administratively determined, are based on time deposits. Bonds are issued to a captive group of bank and non-bank financial institutions, who can be included the Government Bond Underwriting Syndicate. Since 1994 there has been limited over the counter (OTC) secondary market trading.

In the fourth quarter of 1996, the total outstanding was 29,107.4 billion won (about US$40 billion).

Private debt
Corporate bonds

New issuance volume is controlled by the Corporate Bond Coordinating Committee of the KSDA. Stock Exchange listed and registered companies can issue bonds, with or without a bank guarantee – non-guaranteed issues, which have increased in popularity since 1993, require a rating from one of Korea's three agencies. According to the Companies Act, an issuer must submit a securities report and a preliminary prospectus to the Korea Securities Supervisory Board. According to the statutory Commercial Code, bonds can be issued for amounts up to twice the paid-in capital plus reserves of the company. They must be issued through a public offering and underwritten by a syndicate of financial institutions. To gain a listing on the KSE, the company's capital must be at least 500 million won (US$650,000) and the issue size at least 300 million won (US$400,000).

Until 1981, coupons were subject to a maximum rate. They are still restricted to within a 2% band around base rate. Most issues have fixed-rate coupons, but convertibles are becoming more common. Mortgage bonds, secured by property collateral provide investors with an alternative to bank-guaranteed issues.

Although more than 75% of issues are listed on the KSE, almost all secondary market trading is conducted OTC. Bonds are quoted on a yield basis, the usual trading unit is 100,000 won (US$130) and settlement is normally for cash.

In the fourth quarter of 1996, the total outstanding was 67,897.6 billion won (about US$90 billion).

Foreign investors

Overseas investors have been permitted to buy non-guaranteed convertible bonds, listed on the KSE, since 1992. They can also bank guaranteed bonds as long as the yield is comparable to international interest rates – which is rarely the case. A foreign investor's holding of Korean securities cannot exceed 30% of its total portfolio; holdings of an individual company's issue is restricted to 5%. The restrictions imposed on foreign participation in the markets is a major problem.

Eurobonds

South Korean state agencies, private enterprises and banks are regular borrowers in the eurobond market, particularly through floating rate notes placed in the region. By November 1996, issuance amounted to 285 offerings, denominated in eight currencies, which is by far the greatest volume to date from an Asian country.

Eurobond issues (US$m)

	1990	1991	1992	1993	1994	1995	1996
Sovereign	—	—	—	—	—	—	—
Private	450.0	1258.8	1507.7	2018.0	3485.9	6480.8	5528.4

■ SOUTH KOREA: Economic indicators

Population and development	1990	1991	1992	1993	1994	1995	1996e
Population, million	42.9	43.3	43.7	44.1	44.5	44.8	45.2
Population growth, %	1.0	0.9	0.9	0.9	0.9	0.9	0.9
Nominal GDP per capita, US$	5917	6799	7053	7554	8565	10149	10814

National accounts							
Nominal GDP, US$bn	253.7	294.2	307.9	332.8	380.7	455.1	489.2
Change in real GDP, %	9.5	9.1	5.1	5.8	8.6	9.0	6.6
Gross fixed capital formation, % of GDP	37.1	38.4	36.6	36.0	35.7	36.6	34.2

Money supply and inflation							
Narrow money, change %, Dec/Dec	11.0	36.8	13.0	18.1	11.9	18.9	—
Broad money, change %, Dec/Dec	17.2	21.9	14.9	16.6	18.7	15.6	17.9
Consumer price inflation (avg.) %	8.6	9.3	6.2	4.8	6.2	4.5	5.1

Government finance							
Government expenditure, % of GDP	16.2	16.5	17.0	16.8	17.6	17.7	21.4
Government balance, % of GDP	-0.7	-1.6	-0.5	0.6	0.3	-0.2	-0.3

Exchange rates lc=local currency							
Exchange rate, annual average, lc/US$	707.76	733.35	780.65	802.68	803.70	771.90	804.50
Exchange rate, end of year, lc/US$	716.40	760.80	788.40	808.10	788.70	774.70	822.00
Real exchange rate 1990=100	100.0	100.5	94.9	94.1	96.6	98.3	101.3

Balance of payments							
Exports of goods & services, US$m	74331	81802	87919	96495	113490	149446	158950
Change %	3.6	10.1	7.5	9.8	17.6	31.7	6.4
Imports of goods & services, US$m, fob	76395	89983	92138	95804	117351	155834	180150
Change %	15.3	17.8	2.4	4.0	22.5	32.8	15.6
Trade balance, of goods only, US$m, fob-fob	-2004	-6980	-2146	1860	-3146	-4746	-20000
Current account balance, US$m	-1745	-8291	-3939	1016	-3855	-8251	-23262
as a % of GDP	-0.7	-2.8	-1.3	0.3	-1.0	-1.8	-4.8

Foreign exchange reserves							
Foreign exchange reserves, US$m	14793	13701	17121	20229	25639	32677	33100
Gold at ⅔ of market price, US$m	82.3	77.4	73.9	77.6	83.2	83.7	84.4
Import cover (reserves/imports), months	2.3	1.8	2.2	2.5	2.6	2.5	2.2

Foreign debt and debt service							
Short-term debt, US$m	14342	17237	18511	19165	28143	45376	62000
Total foreign debt, US$m	38531	46246	50746	54168	71043	94530	125000
as a % of GDP	15.2	15.7	16.5	16.3	18.7	20.8	25.6
as a % of foreign exchange receipts	48.9	53.4	54.5	53.3	59.7	60.5	75.1
Interest payments, US$m	3133	3292	3451	2957	3900	5700	6980
Principal repayments, US$m	5678	3369	3739	5284	6710	6100	7360
Total debt service, US$m	8811	6661	7190	8241	10610	11800	14340
as a % of goods exports	14.0	9.6	9.6	10.2	11.3	9.6	11.0
as a % of foreign exchange receipts	11.2	7.7	7.7	8.1	8.9	7.5	8.6

Taiwan

KEY FACTS

Area (thouands of km²):	36
Population (1995, millions):	21.3
Population younger than 15 yrs (1991, % of total):	26.3
Urbanization rate (1993, % of population):	75
Life expectancy (1993, years at birth):	75
Gross domestic product (1996, US$bn):	273.3
GDP per capita (1996, US$):	12,704
Average annual GDP growth rate (1990-96, %):	6.3
Average annual inflation rate (1990-96, %):	3.8
Currency (New Taiwan dollar per US$, average 1996):	27.46
Structure of production (1994):	59.1% services, 37.9% industry, 3% agriculture
Main exports:	machinery, electrical & electronic equipment, textiles
Main imports:	intermediate goods, capital goods, consumer goods
Main trading partners:	US, Japan, Hong Kong
Market capitalization of Stock Exchange (October 1996; US$bn):	239.7
Total foreign debt (% of GDP):	17.9
Next elections due under normal circumstances:	legislative required by December 1998; presidential scheduled for March 2000
Credit rating: (Nov 1996, Standard & Poor's, Moody's)	AA+; Aa3

FORECAST: 1997-2000 (average)

	Worst case	Most likely	Best case
Real GDP growth (%)	5.8	6.3	6.8
Inflation (%)	6.0	5.2	4.7

■ POLITICS

Historical overview

Situated between China and Japan, the island of Taiwan has had an eventful past. Portuguese, Spanish and Dutch traders arrived in the early 17th century, but were expelled by a Chinese renegade, Zheng Zheng Gong, in 1661. In 1663, the Qing emperor Kang Xi invaded, and the island became part of the Chinese empire. During the 18th and 19th centuries, thousands of Chinese from the mainland moved to Taiwan. The island was ceded to Japan at the end of the Sino-Japanese War of 1895, but was regained after Japan was defeated in the Second World War.

Taiwan's roots as an independent country separate from mainland China go back to the years following the Chinese revolution, when the country split into two separate political forces – the Communists led by Mao and the right-wing Chinese National People's Party, the Kuomintang (KMT), led by Chiang Kai-shek. Following a long and bloody civil war, Kai-shek was forced out of office in 1949, and fled to Taiwan along with 2 million of his supporters. Once in Taiwan, the KMT took over the local National Assembly and filled it with politicians formerly in power on the mainland. Ignoring demands for democracy from the native Taiwanese, the KMT extended their terms of office indefinitely, and set about building a powerbase that could eventually lead to re-unification with mainland China.

For a while, the KMT became the official international face of China, occupying the country's UN seat until 1971. Its position was severely weakened in the 1970s when foreign countries began to recognize Communist rule in China. However, the KMT continued to dominate Taiwanese politics. Surviving members of Kai-shek's KMT force were not obliged to stand for office in the National Assembly, while opposition parties lacked sufficient power to provide a meaningful challenge.

Relations with mainland China remained frosty for much of the 1970s and 1980s. The KMT stuck to its official "three nos" line: no compromise, no contact and no negotiation. However, under its new leader, President Lee Teng-hui, the KMT began to adopt a more conciliatory line, and in 1990 Lee announced that Taiwan would formally end the state of war with mainland China. Political reform had begun in 1987, when martial law was abolished and opposition parties were allowed to form. In December 1991, the first open elections to the National Assembly were held in which the Democratic Progressive Party (DPP) won 75 seats. The KMT remained the dominant political force, winning 319 seats. The following year, in December 1992, the first open elections to the legislative council (Yuan) took place. This time the DPP did rather better, winning 31% of the votes cast. However, the KMT retained 102 of the 161 legislature votes, and a KMT candidate, Lien Chan, became premier.

The pace of political change accelerated in July 1994 when the constitution was changed to allow open presidential elections, in which the public rather than just the assembly would vote. In March 1995, President Lee agreed to opposition demands to set up a committee to investigate corruption within the KMT. A key issue within Taiwanese politics has been whether or not to make Taiwan fully independent and separate from China. Opposition deputies made regular attempts to force a referendum on the subject during the early 1990s. In 1990, DPP members were barred from the National Assembly for refusing to swear allegiance to the Republic of China (Taiwan's official name). The same year, a DPP leader was jailed for ten years for "preparing to commit sedition". The rift between conservative elements in the KMT (which remained committed to re-unification) and the younger reformers who supported independence widened in 1993, when thirty liberal KMT deputies resigned to form the New Alliance Nationalist Party (or New Party).

Recent events

Since 1995, the KMT has seen its grip on power eroded by growing support for opposition parties. In December, it won only 85 seats in the elections for the Legislative Yuan. The DPP secured 54 seats, while the hard-line re-unification New Party won 21 seats. Four months later, in March 1996, President Lee held on to power in the presidential elections, but the result was narrower than many expected – he won 54% of the vote, against Peng Ming-min (DPP) 21%, Ling Yang-kang (NP) 15% and Chen Li-an, an independent candidate, who secured 10%. Meanwhile, relations with mainland China have deteriorated. In March 1996, the Chinese carried out a series of missile tests off the Taiwan coast in an attempt to destabilize the KMT regime in the run-up to the elections. With Hong Kong set to return to Chinese rule in 1997, the Chinese have adopted a less confrontational stance towards Taiwan. However, Chinese pressure on Taiwan to consider re-unification is likely to increase once the Hong Kong changeover has been absorbed.

The key domestic political issue of 1997 is the division of power between the legislative assembly and the presidential office. At present, power resides with the presidential office. However, opposition parties (who have presented a more united front in 1996 despite disagreements over the independence issue) are pressing for more power for the legislative assembly. The first signs of this conflict came in May 1996, when the opposition parties successfully blocked the government's plan to build a US$4.1 billion nuclear power plant north of Taipei. Prime Minister Lien Chan then sent back the bill for reconsideration. Further disagreement between the two sides is expected to continue in 1997.

Chronology

1663	Taiwan becomes part of the Chinese empire
1894	Taiwan is ceded to Japan after the Sino-Japanese War
1945	Taiwan returns to Chinese rule
1949	Chiang Kai-shek flees to Taiwan
1949	The KMT takes control of the National Assembly
1954	US signs mutual defence pact with Taiwan
1971	European countries recognize the People's Republic of China
1986	Democratic Progressive Party is set up
1989	Opposition parties legalized
1990	State of war with China dropped by President Lee
1991	First open elections for National Assembly
1993	Thirty KMT politicians split to form New Party
1995	The KMT wins by a narrow margin in legislative elections
1996	President Lee wins 54% in presidential election
1996	China steps up missile tests in the Taiwan Strait

Constitution and government

Taiwan's original constitution was signed in 1949 when the KMT took power. Following a long process of reform, the constitution was amended in 1991 to provide for democratic legislative elections. Further amendments in 1994 provided for direct election of the president beginning in 1996.

Taiwan is a representative democracy born out of a one-party state. The head of state is the president (elected for six years) who appoints a prime minister to head the Executive Yuan (cabinet). The Executive Yuan is composed of the ministries and the Executive Yuan Council nominally the supreme policy-making body. In practice, all decisions are taken by the leaders of the ruling party. There is also a legislative Yuan which approves policies set by the Executive Yuan. The National Assembly, which before constitutional reform elected the president and vice-president, now has a reduced role in government.

Current government

President	Lee TENG-HUI
Vice President	Lien CHAN
Vice President	Hsu LI-TEH
Secretary General	Chao SHOU-PO

Results of the December 1995 legislative elections

Kuomintang (KMT)	85 seats
Democratic Progressive Party (DPP)	54 seats
New Party (NP)	21 seats

Results of the March 1996 presidential elections

Lee Teng-hui (KMT)	54.0%
Peng Ming-min (DPP)	21.1%
Lin Yang-kang (NP)	14.9%
Chen Li-an (Independent)	10.0%

Political forces

The Kuomintang remains the dominant political party in Taiwan, and maintains eventual reunification with the mainland as its ultimate political goal. The main opposition party, the Democratic Progressive Party (DPP), promotes independence for Taiwan as one of its key policies. In 1993 several KMT members seeking to safeguard party ideals broke away to form the New Party.

Central bank

The Central Bank of China (CBC) serves as Taiwan's central bank. The CBC has traditionally maintained tight control over money supply growth to limit inflation. Since the liberalization of foreign exchange controls in 1987, the CBC has used its considerable foreign exchange holdings to dampen exchange rate fluctuations.

■ ECONOMICS

Historical overview

Taiwan's rapid economic development began soon after the KMT came to power in 1949, and has led to a transformation of an agrarian economy to a manufacturing and services one. Between 1952 and 1993 the average real GDP growth rate was an impressive 8.6%. The first stage of growth was financed by the US, which provided US$1.4 billion of aid between 1951 and 1965. In 1953 a four-year programme of economic reform was introduced, including land reform, the rapid development of industry and the establishment of a nine-year free public education system. The government concentrated specifically on agricultural growth and the development of import-substitute industries, in an effort to secure some level of self-sufficiency in the economy.

In the 1960s, particular attention was given to developing export-orientated industries such as fertilizers, electrical items and chemicals. Tax incentives for exporters were introduced, and imported goods were restricted to encourage development of the domestic manufacturing sector. Agriculture (principally rice and sugar), which had formed the backbone of the Taiwanese economy in the 1940s, was gradually replaced by consumer goods as the country's main source of exports. Furthermore, in 1974, the government launched ten major construction projects in an effort to develop the country's infrastructure. Two new ports, an airport, a nuclear plant, an integrated steel plant, a petrochemical complex and shipbuilding facilities were set up.

During the 1980s, amid rising real wages and shortages of skilled labour, Taiwan gradually shifted away from labour-intensive industries into more capital and technology-intensive industries such as semi-conductors and electronics. In 1980, a Science Industry Park was set up. Imports were still closely regulated in the 1980s until 1987 when US pressures forced the government to cut tariffs across the board. This was the start of the most recent trend of liberalization and internationalization of the economy. Foreign investment increased dramatically in the late 1980s, with Taiwanese companies investing heavily in China and Hong Kong. Since the 1980s, Taiwan has also adopted a more prominent role in the formation of regional policies.

Taiwan's economy has matured in ways similar to industrial countries and, since registering double-digit growth rates in the mid-1980s, is now characterized by more moderate growth and a loss in external competitiveness in some sectors. These problems are associated in part with Taiwan's remarkable economic success of the late 1980s – huge balance of payments surpluses led to a 40% appreciation of the currency against the US dollar, while rising real wages and land prices also slowed productivity gains. Simultaneously, private investment moved offshore as labour-intensive industries shifted to low-wage countries in South-East Asia and China. In parallel, there has been an increased emphasis on social development, with rising spending on health, the environment, education and ambitious public infrastructure investment.

Recent developments

Taiwan's economic record began to show the first signs of faltering in 1995 when GDP growth slowed to 6%. The downturn continued into 1996 with growth expected to average 5.4%. Foreign investment and domestic spending have been weak following political tensions in early 1996; industrial production has been sluggish and the unemployment rate has also increased to a ten-year high of 3.1% in October 1996. Nevertheless, the long-term outlook is positive. Intra-regional trade with Southeast Asian countries is expected to improve, and a growth rate of 6% is forecast for 1997.

A key issue in the run-up to 1997 will be the development of closer links with the Chinese mainland where Taiwanese companies have already invested between US$20-25 billion. Owing to a ban on direct investment in the mainland, almost all has been routed via affiliates in Hong Kong. Taiwanese business leaders have started exerting pressure on the government to ease investment restrictions, and policy changes are currently under consideration. In 1996, the two state-owned oil companies of Taiwan and China signed an agreement on joint oil exploration. The pace of reform is also being pushed by China which published regulations governing shipping links with Taiwan (currently banned by Taiwan) in August 1996. Meanwhile, the Taiwan government has suggested a phased plan for establishing direct shipping links with China. The first stage, trans-shipment of sea cargo, which could take two years to complete, would be followed by a gradual intro-duction of direct sea links, cargo air links, passenger transit links and finally passenger flights.

Population

The population was estimated at 21.4 million in mid-1996, with some 24% believed to be under the age of fourteen. The growth rate was around 0.93%. Around 84% of the population are descendants of mainland Chinese who emigrated to the island between the 17th and early 20th centuries. About 2 million mainland Chinese fled to Taiwan as a result of the civil war. Peoples originally indigenous to Taiwan comprise another 2% of the population.

The economy

In 1995, manufacturing accounted for the lion's share of GDP (28.2%). Finance/real estate and commerce were also significant, accounting for 21.2% and 16.1% respectively. Transport and communications represented 6.6%, construction 5.2%, agriculture 3.5%, utilities 2.6% and mining 0.3%.

Breakdown of exports 1995

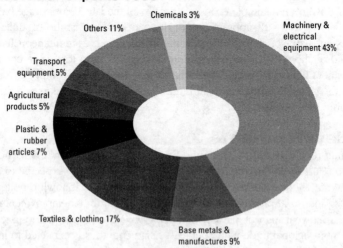

Source: Official data

Share of GDP by sector

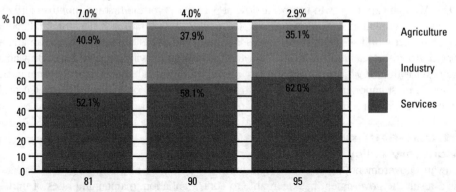

Source: Official data

Exports and imports as a % of GDP

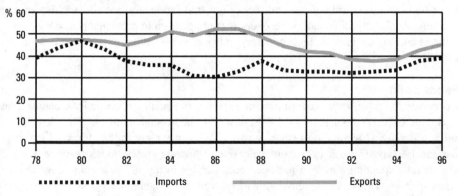

Source: Official data

Savings and investment

Traditionally Taiwan, like other Asian economies, has had a high gross domestic savings rate. An average rate of 33.4% of GDP was registered in the 1980s. However, savings rates have fallen consistently in the 1990s, hitting a twenty-year low of 25.6% of GDP in 1995. This trend reflects a maturing economy, rising wages and an increasing propensity to consume. Gross domestic investment, on the other hand, has remained fairly constant over the past decade. Averaging 22.6% between 1985 and 1995, domestic investment rates in Taiwan have fallen below the average prevailing in other Asian economies. A significant amount of investment has been diverted to mainland China and Hong Kong.

Balance of payments

Historically, Taiwan has maintained a healthy current account surplus and has essentially had an export-led economy. However, as specific export industries have faced losses in competitiveness and the economy has become more services-led, the current account surplus has fallen from around 20% of GDP in the mid-1980s to a low of 1.9% of GDP in 1995. Average export growth has been slow at 3.2% (yoy) for the first ten months of 1996, against 20% growth in 1995. However, this is largely a cyclical rather than a structural problem. Stronger world semi-conductor prices, a more competitive exchange rate and an anticipated growth acceleration in major industrialized countries will probably boost Taiwan's export growth in 1997. Hong Kong (and, by extension, mainland China) is fast becoming the country's most important trading partner. In 1995, it accounted for 23.4% of exports (second only to the US with 23.6%).

Economic policy
Monetary policy
Taiwan's government has pursued a tight monetary policy for much of the past five years. As a result the government has been able to control inflation, maintaining rates of under 5% since 1990. Given the recent slowdown in the economy, however, the government has made concerted efforts to ease liquidity and bolster investment and consumption in the real economy. Rediscount rate cuts of 25bp in both May and August 1996 encouraged commercial banks to cut interest rates. But demand for credit is weak. Depressed consumer sentiment, political tension and weak industrial production are all weighing on the economy. A meaningful economic recovery is contingent on improvements in cross-Straits relations and export growth, and monetary policy alone is unlikely to stimulate domestic demand.

Fiscal policy
Between 1970 and 1988 the government managed to run small budget deficits, maintaining an average of -0.7% of GDP. In the 1990s, however, the average annual deficit grew to 6%, and is widening. Government revenue growth has been stalling in the 1990s, falling from 18.8% in 1992 to -0.56% in 1995, principally due to slowing growth in tax revenue. On the other hand, expenditure growth has been considerable in the 1990s, averaging 8% due to higher spending on health, the environment, education and ambitious public infrastructure. The mismatch in expenditures and revenues does not pose any immediate threat given Taiwan's immense foreign reserves, low external debt and trade surpluses. The government aims to balance the budget by 2000-01.

Currency
Between 1961 to 1973, the New Taiwan dollar (TWD) was fixed at 40 to the US dollar. It was then devalued to 38:1. The currency appreciated gradually during the 1970s and early 1980s, but the appreciation accelerated dramatically in the late 1980s due to massive current account surpluses. The currency was made convertible for current account transactions in 1987, but some capital account restrictions remain in place. The exchange rate is largely market-determined, but the central bank frequently intervenes in the market to smooth fluctuations. Chinese missile testing in the Taiwan Strait in March 1996 led to a flight from the TWD, but the central bank spent considerable resources to stabilize the exchange rate at 27.5 per US dollar. Following the relaxation in political tension, the market was allowed to push the exchange rate beyond the previously defended level.

New Taiwan dollar/US dollar exchange rate

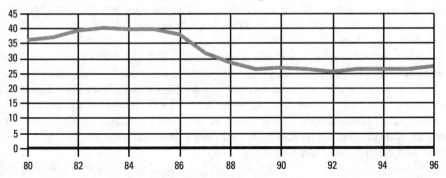

■ EQUITIES

Index performance (in local currency)

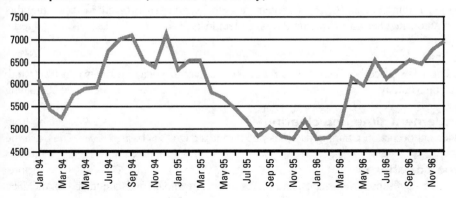

Key indicators

	Index performance %, in US$ terms	Market Cap. US$bn	P/E	Div. Yield	Weight in IFCI	IFCG
1994	21.5	247.3	36.8	0.7	3.2	17.1
1995	-31.4	187.2	21.4	1.2	2.8	10.4
1996	36.1	273.6	28.2	0.9	7.3	14.4

Sources: Local stock exchange, IFC, Bloomberg, Datastream, UBS

Background

The Taiwan Stock Exchange (TSE) was established in 1962 following the inauguration of the Securities and Exchange Commission in September 1960. Share trading in Taiwan had been growing since the 1952 land reform campaign, which compensated landlords in the form of bonds and shares, thus developing an OTC market. Up until the late 1980s the TSE grew steadily, but began to soar in 1988 as a consequence of a new computerized trading system and the licensing of new brokerage firms. However, in recent years, trading has been less spectacular.

Structure

The TSE stock market is split into three sections: Category A, Category B, and Category C. In terms of listed stocks and trading value, Category A is by far the largest (equivalent to over 80% of total value) while Category C is relatively insignificant. Companies are categorized in accordance with various criteria based on, inter alia, capital amount, profitability, capital structure, and shareholder distribution.

Regulatory authority

The Securities and Exchange Commission (SEC) regulates the TSE in line with Securities and Exchange Law (SEL).

Trading methods

Trading is fully computerized, with all trades passing through the Exchange's Computer Assisted Trading System (CATS). In recent years this system has evolved, incorporating the Fully Automated Securities Trading (FAST) system in 1993.

Hours

Trading takes place between 09.00 and 12.00, Monday to Friday and between 09.00 and 11.00 on Saturday.

Settlement time and clearing

Settlement occurs on a trading day plus one business day (T+1) basis.

Types of shares

Common shares, preferred shares, and shares from convertible bonds are traded on the TSE. Around 90% of issues are common shares, equivalent to 99% of total value.

Stock indices

The TSE produces fourteen indices. The most widely quoted is the TSE Capital Weighted Stock Index (TAIEX). Its calculation includes all listed stocks with the exception of preferred stocks, full-delivery stocks, and stocks that have been listed less than one month. Other measures include both market value and price average indices differentiated by sector or category.

Taxes

The Securities Transaction Tax is levied at 0.3%. Cash dividends are subject to a 15% with-holding tax for residents, rising to 35% for non-residents. However, this figure may be reduced to 20% if investments had the approval of the Statute for Investment by Foreign Nationals. There is a 10% withholding tax on interest income for residents which rises to 20% for non-residents. There is no tax on capital gains.

Disclosure of financial statements

Listed companies are required to produce annual and semi-annual reports for auditing and public display. In addition, a monthly sales report and quarterly financial statement must also be submitted for public consumption. Any event that significantly affects shareholder's interests or security prices must be immediately reported to the Exchange and made public forthwith.

Shareholders' rights

The Security Investors Protection Fund (SIPF) was devised to protect investors in cases of brokers' default. For investors to make claims, they must have completed their settlement obligations in accordance with Exchange rules.

Ownership limits for non-residents

Non-residents are limited to owning 20% of stock.

Brokers

There are 233 brokers and forty-four dealers on the TSE with a fixed local brokerage rate of 0.1425%, with a TWD20 minimum charge. However, foreign ownership is only permitted through special Broker Facilities authorized by the Ministry of Finance. These facilities can be taken out by a broker or institutional investor and are for a fixed dollar amount. The approval process has become increasingly liberal. Facility-holders may trade as a local within the market subject to the 20% non-resident ceiling per stock.

Sectors

Banking and insurance and textiles are the most important sectors of the TSE, accounting for around 30% of total value. The electronic, steel, and construction and building materials sectors, although less significant, all occupy close to a tenth of total value.

■ DEBT

In 1991, the Ministry of Finance (MOF) and the Central Bank of China (CBC) introduced reforms to the bond market following the presentation of Taiwan's National Six-Year Infrastructure Plan, which launched major public works programmes. The government has run a budget deficit since 1992, which has provided an additional catalyst market for growth.

The issuance procedure for government bonds was changed from a fixed-price allocation to an auction system. In addition, bullet repayment of principal was made standard – in which principal is repaid at the bond's maturity and interest was repaid in equal instalments – which was intended to facilitate secondary market trading. The government sector is significantly larger than the corporate debt market, whose expansion is limited by the absence of a local credit rating agency. Additional changes were made to the treasury bond market in 1995 to improve trading.

Public debt
The treasury bill market is small. Medium-dated bonds are issued by the central, provincial and municipal governments, and by government enterprises.

Treasury bonds
The Ministry of Finance manages state funding and issues bonds through the central bank, acting as its agent, in an auction system that began in 1991. Until July 1995, new issuance was on an ad hoc basis, depending on the immediate needs of the MOF. Now a fixed schedule of one issue each month is auctioned to licensed primary dealers whose bids are accepted in descending order from the highest price. Non-competitive bids are filled at the weighted average price of successful competitive bids, and usually make up 30% of the total. Individual investors can either bid through primary dealers or buy bonds at the post office. A "when-issued" market has existed since 1993, but is small and volatile.

Treasury bonds are issued for 2 to 15 years, 7-year maturities are the most common, and in 1995, the MOF issued a 3-year zero coupon bond. Yields are calculated on an actual/365-day basis. Domestic banks are large buyers of treasury bonds and hold them as secondary reserves. They value their holdings at cost and are reluctant to realize a capital loss, which creates an illiquid secondary market. Liquidity is enhanced by a repo market for traders to fund positions, who also exploit an arbitrage created by the different tax treatment of individual and institutional investors. The normal trading unit is NT$50 million and transactions settle three days after bargain date for physical delivery through the Taiwan Securities Central Depository Company. Bonds are usually issued in bearer form.

Provincial and municipal government bonds
Coupon rates are determined after the launch date by the issuer consulting agency banks, who are then allocated bonds.

Private debt
Commercial paper (CP)
CP is the most important source of finance for small- and medium-sized companies. Criminal penalties against bank officers who make bad loans mean that CP is now more important than bank lending. The benchmark rate is 3-month CP.

Corporate bonds
Most issues have tenures under five years, and in recent years new structures, for example deferred coupons and Bull-Bear floaters, have entered the market. Large issues are offered for auction, while small deals are privately placed. There is no credit rating agency in Taiwan so many issues are bank-guaranteed.

Bank debentures and NCDs
Savings banks issue floating-rate debentures, which are placed with domestic financial institutions.

Taxation
A transaction tax of 0.1% is payable by the seller of bank debentures and corporates.

Domestic institutions pay income tax on an accrual basis and individuals pay on receipt of cash. Foreigners pay 20% withholding tax.

Foreign institutional investors

Qualified overseas investors can buy government and corporate bonds, bank debentures and money market instruments through a programme for QFIIs, set up by the Securities and Exchange Commission. Holdings of government bonds are limited to 30% of their Taiwanese portfolios to encourage equity investment and cap repo dealings.

Value of outstanding domestic debt, May 1996 (millions NT dollars)

Treasury bonds	786,675
Provincial govt. bonds	45,407
Municipal govt. bonds	20,429
State enterprise bonds	22,910
Commercial paper	828,927
Corporate bonds	102,672

Eurobond issues (US$m)

	1990	1991	1992	1993	1994	1995	1996
Sovereign	—	—	—	—	—	—	—
Private	0.0	229.0	60.0	78.3	1804.4	698.6	858.1

■ TAIWAN: Economic indicators

Population and development	1990	1991	1992	1993	1994	1995	1996e
Population, million	20.4	20.6	20.8	20.9	21.1	21.3	21.5
Population growth, %	1.3	1.2	1.0	0.5	1.0	1.0	1.0
Nominal GDP per capita, US$	7866	8709	10198	10652	11453	12243	12704

National accounts							
Nominal GDP, US$bn	160.2	179.4	212.1	222.6	241.7	260.8	273.3
Change in real GDP, %	5.6	7.6	6.8	6.3	6.5	6.1	5.4
Gross fixed capital formation, % of GDP	22.4	22.2	23.2	23.7	22.9	23.0	23.0

Money supply and inflation							
Narrow money, change %, Dec/Dec	-6.6	12.1	12.4	15.3	12.2	0.8	—
Broad money, change %, Dec/Dec	10.5	19.7	19.6	15.5	15.2	9.6	12.5
Consumer price inflation (avg.) %	4.1	3.6	4.5	2.9	4.1	3.7	3.1

Government finance							
Government expenditure, % of GDP	26.2	29.9	27.2	27.3	30.2	13.7	15.7
Government balance, % of GDP	1.6	-0.9	-2.4	-1.3	-1.2	-0.3	-2.1

Exchange rates lc=local currency							
Exchange rate, annual average, lc/US$	26.89	26.82	25.16	26.39	26.39	26.49	27.46
Exchange rate, end of year, lc/US$	27.11	25.75	25.40	26.63	26.24	27.27	27.50

Balance of payments							
Exports of goods & services, US$m	74037	84137	91006	97734	105702	125968	135699
Change %	1.1	13.6	8.2	7.4	8.2	19.2	7.7
Imports of goods & services, US$m, fob	66440	76255	86761	93687	101191	121108	126465
Change %	5.2	14.8	13.8	8.0	8.0	19.7	4.4
Trade balance, of goods only, US$m, fob-fob	14928	15754	12767	11587	11942	13540	16684
Current account balance, US$m	10769	12015	8154	6714	6154	4824	8900
as a % of GDP	6.7	6.7	3.8	3.0	2.5	1.8	3.3

Foreign exchange reserves							
Foreign exchange reserves, US$m	72441	82405	82306	83573	92454	90310	94500
Gold at ⅔ of market price, US$m	3480.0	3265.3	3097.8	3248.2	3471.2	3470.6	3499.4
Import cover (reserves/imports), months	13.1	13.0	11.4	10.7	11.0	8.9	9.0

Foreign debt and debt service							
Short-term debt, US$m	18932	21275	21386	24747	26599	27164	27820
Total foreign debt, US$m	21755	24412	25572	30297	36730	43700	48900
as a % of GDP	13.6	13.6	12.1	13.6	15.2	16.8	17.9
as a % of foreign exchange receipts	26.3	26.1	25.3	28.4	31.9	32.0	34.8
Interest payments, US$m	1647	1491	1602	1409	1773	2587	2380
Principal repayments, US$m	572	597	675	782	834	1188	1429
Total debt service, US$m	2219	2088	2277	2191	2607	3775	3809
as a % of goods exports	3.3	2.8	2.8	2.6	2.8	3.4	3.2
as a % of foreign exchange receipts	2.7	2.2	2.3	2.1	2.3	2.8	2.7

Thailand

Area (thousands of km²):	513
Population (1995, millions):	60.1
Population projection (2025, millions):	81
Population younger than 15 yrs (1991, % of total):	32.4
Urbanization rate (1993, % of population):	19
Life expectancy (1993, years at birth):	69
Gross domestic product (1996, US$bn):	183.8
GDP per capita (1996, US$):	3017
Average annual GDP growth rate (1990-96, %):	8.6
Average annual inflation rate (1990-96, %):	5.2
Currency (baht per US$, average 1996):	25.35
Real exchange rate: (1990=100, average 1996)	105.33
Structure of production (1994):	49% services, 40% industry, 11% agriculture
Main exports:	textiles, rubber, rice, tapioca
Main imports:	non-electronic machinery, chemicals, crude petroleum
Main trading partners:	Japan, US, Singapore, Germany
Market capitalization of Stock Exchange (December 1996; US$bn):	99.8
Total foreign debt (% of GDP):	51.4
Next elections due under normal circumstances:	parliamentary required by November 2000
Credit rating: (Jan 1997, Standard & Poor's, Moody's)	A; A2

FORECAST: 1997-2000 (average)

	Worst case	Most likely	Best case
Real GDP growth (%)	4.0	7.0	8.5
Inflation (%)	6.5	5.2	4.0

■ POLITICS

Historical overview

The first unified Thai kingdom was established in Sukothai in the 13th century, and populated by people originally from the Yunnan Province in China. A new centre of power was set up further south, at Ayudhya. The kingdom gained importance in the development of rice production and trade. In the 16th century, trade relations with European trading nations started to flourish.

Internal reforms and concessions enabled Siam, as the kingdom was called from then on, to remain independent of colonial rule. Under Rama IV (1851-68) and Rama V (1868-1910), Western advisors were accepted to modernize the administration. A modern state emerged. Bangkok, the new capital, developed into a trading centre dominated by European firms. The established monarchical order and democratic forces increasingly conflicted. In a bloodless coup in 1932, the absolute monarchy was turned into a constitutional monarchy with a bicameral parliament.

Until 1992, Thailand was ruled chiefly by a succession of military regimes. These were usually characterized by strong leaders, who, by restoring stability, were generally respected by the public. Over the decades, as the economy boomed, Thailand's democratic forces grew stronger, and the military governments became more moderate and progressively sought civilian support. Brief periods of civilian governments interrupted the sequence of military regimes. These civilian coalitions have, however, often been characterized by factionalism and infighting among competing interest groups, precipitating further military take-overs.

Recent events

Following pro-democracy demonstrations in Bangkok, which led to a military crackdown in May 1992 and provoked an unprecedented intervention by the King, new elections were held in September 1992. These were won by a pro-democracy coalition, headed by Prime Minister Chuan Leekpai, leader of the Democrat Party. Despite little public confidence, the coalition survived its first two years without major crisis, but failed in a no-confidence vote in 1995 following a series of troubles beginning in late 1994.

A new coalition under the former opposition party, Chart Thai, took over the leadership of the country after the July 1995 elections. Struggles within the coalition parties rapidly weakened the government under Prime Minister Banharn Silpa-archa. The coalition was further shaken by a no-confidence vote in May 1996, which was followed by a major cabinet reshuffle, including the appointment of a new finance minister. Pressure on the Banharn government revived, however, with the rapid deterioration of the country's economic performance, which was partly blamed on mismanagement by the government.

When his own coalition allies forced the Prime Minister to resign, Banharn decided to call fresh elections instead. New elections were held on November 17, 1996. They were won by a six-party coalition led by the New Aspiration Party leader General Chavalit, whose major challenge will be to restore confidence in the economy by tackling structural deficiencies.

Chronology

1826	Treaty of Amity and Commerce with Great Britain
1833	Diplomatic exchanges with the US
1932	Absolute monarchy is changed into constitutional monarchy
1938-45	Rule by Marshal Phibun Songkhram
1939	Siam is renamed Thailand
1946	King Bhumibol Adulyadej crowned ninth monarch of Chakri dynasty
1948-57	Second rule by Phibun Songkhram
1958-72	Authoritarian government under General Sarit Thanarat and successors
1972-73	Student-led demonstrations lead to the collapse of military rule
1973-76	Several civilian governments
1976	Violent crackdown of a student sit-in at Thammasat University. Military-dominated

	National Administrative Council takes over, dissolving the National Assembly.
1977-80	Moderate military government under General Kriansak Chomanan
1980-88	Coalition government between military forces and centre-right parties under Prem Tinsulanonda
1983	Constitutional amendments
1988-91	Coalition government between military forces and centre-right parties under Prime Minister Chatichai Choonhavan
1991	Bloodless military coup. National Peacekeeping Council takes command of the country. Anand Panyarachun is appointed prime minister
1991	New constitution
1992	Elections result in a weak coalition; non-elected General Suchinda Kraprayoon takes over premiership
1992	Military crackdown of demonstration in Bangkok
1992	King appoints Anand Panyarachun as interim prime minister. Constitutional amendments: prime minister must be an elected member of the National Assembly.
1992	New elections result in a coalition government under Chuan Leekpai
1995	Coalition falls after a no-confidence vote. Election results in a seven-party coalition under Prime Minister Banharn Silpa-archa.
1996	May: unsuccessful no-confidence motion
1996	September: Banharn Silpa-archa resigns and calls new elections
1996	November: elections are won by a six-party coalition under NAP leader Gen. Chavalit

Constitution and government

Thailand is a constitutional monarchy. The constitution provides for two houses of parliament, a Senate, appointed by the National Peacekeeping Council, with 270 members, and a 360-member House of Representatives, elected for four-year terms. The government can usually rely on the appointed Senate, which reflects the importance of the armed forces. The current constitution was drawn up by the military government in 1991, with the amendment in 1992 that prime ministers should be elected members of the legislative. Further amendments, aimed at strengthening democracy, were passed in January 1995.

Current government

Head of State	King Bhumibol Adulyadej
Prime Minister	Chavalit Yongchaiyudh (NAP)
Deputy Prime Ministers	Sukavit Rangsitphol (NAP)
	Amnuay Viravan (NAP)
	Korn Dabbaransi (CPP)
	Montree Pongpanich (SAP)
	Samak Sundaravej (PTP)
Finance Minister	Amnuay Viravan (NAP)
Foreign Affairs Minister	Prachuab Chaiyasarn (CPP)
Interior Minister	Snoh Thienthong (CPP)
Governor, central bank	Rerngchai Marakanond

State organization

Thailand is divided into 76 provinces, each under the control of a governor. The provinces are subdivided into 655 districts, 88 subdistricts and many more communes and villages that together form the local government. Administrative power lies firmly with the central government. Apart from the Bangkok Metropolitan Administration, local government does not have tax authority and therefore depends on central government transfers.

Political parties

Political parties in Thailand do not differ much ideologically. A few leading individuals, often representing commercial interests, are at the core of each party. Most parties are relatively young, often formed by group divisions or mergers of established parties. Conflicting interests between and within parties often lead to coalition changes.

Main parties
New Aspiration
> Split from Chart Thai
> Founded 1990
> Led by Gen. Chavalit Yongchaiyudh, former army and armed forces commander

Democrat Party
> Liberal, reformist, centre, powerbase in the south
> Founded 1946
> Led by Chuan Leekpai

Chart Thai
> Right-wing, represents Thai business interests
> Founded 1981
> Led by Silpa-Archa Banharn

Social Action
> Conservative
> Founded 1981
> Led by Montree Pongpanit

Chart Pattana
> Split from Chart Thai
> Founded 1992
> Led by Gen. Chatichai Choonhavan

Results of November 1996 elections to the House of Representatives:

New Aspiration (125 seats), **Democrat Party** (123), **Chart Pattana** (52), **Chart Thai** (39), **Social Action** (20), **Prachakon Thai** (18), **Solidarity** (8), **Seritham** (4), **Prachakorn Muanchon** (2), **Thai** (1), **Palang Dharma** (1)

Coalition parties
New Aspiration (NAP), **Chart Pattana** (CPP), **Social Action** (SAP), **Prachakorn Thai** (PTP), **Seritham** (SRP), **Muanchon** (MC)
Total seats: 221

Next elections
November 2000 at the latest

Other political forces
Monarch
The monarch is head of state and of the armed forces. Although the king has little direct influence in government, the royal family has proven to be a stabilizing factor during times of political volatility. The present monarch, King Bhumibol Adulyadej, who has been on the throne since 1946, is highly respected.

Military
Historically, the army largely controlled politics. It sees itself as the guardian of the wider national interest. Most military coups reflected a conflict of interests between the military and civilian political parties. While earlier civilian government policy aimed at co-operation with the army, after the May 1992 crackdown the coalition government under Chuan Leekpai pursued a cautious policy of slimming down the armed forces. It appears that under the current government the influence of the military has again increased.

Central bank
The Bank of Thailand acts as the central bank. Its principal aim is price stability. A decade of remarkable monetary management has rendered the central bank highly credible. Although its position vis-à-vis the Ministry of Finance is uncertain, the Bank of Thailand has generally been relatively independent.

Credit growth is increasingly gaining importance as a main monetary target. However, the bank has been unable to rely on discount rate or bond prices, as the domestic bond market is not large or liquid enough. Hence, in pursuing its monetary objectives, the central bank relies heavily on a policy of "moral suasion" by trying to get the commercial banks to co-operate.

Financial system
During the early 1990s, the Thai government intensified its efforts to become a regional financial centre. All controls of interest rates have been lifted since 1992, while the regulatory and supervisory framework of the financial sector was strengthened. In 1992, in an effort to increase saving, the Bank of Thailand spearheaded the establishment of a Securities and Exchange Commission, as an independent agency to supervise the operations of the capital markets. The central bank's efforts culminated in the introduction of the Bangkok International Banking Facility in March 1993.

Bangkok International Banking Facility

As an offshore market, the BIBF is internationally orientated, and offers investors and financial institutions special advantages owing to its liberal fiscal legislation. BIBF is under the jurisdiction of the central bank. For most of the twenty-four foreign banks operating on the BIBF, the principal attraction is tax privileges. These include lower corporate taxes than for domestic commercial banks, as well as tax-exempt operations. Another incentive is the access BIBFs have to bank licences to operate in the Thai money market, subject to a relatively large capital requirement of Bt1 billion. Currently, only a few foreign banks have a licence that enables them to engage in business in Thailand.

Originally, the BIBF was created with the aim of promoting the use of the baht within South-East Asia, thus supporting Thailand's aim to become a financial centre and a hub for trade in the Mekong region. Money from the BIBF has, however, increasingly been used to fund credits in Thailand (so-called "out-in investment"). Of the total outstanding loans of the BIBF, some 80-90% are loans to Thai banks (or foreign banks operating in Thailand).

The loans are primarily short-term and the interest rate is determined in the interbank market. As the loans are denominated in baht, the BIBF-interest rate is linked to the risk premium associated with the exchange rate.

Banking system

There are currently fifteen commercial banks in Thailand, besides a number of specialist banking institutions in the public and semi-public sector, which serve to provide capital to various sectors.

The banks' profitability was supported by the authorities' policy to grant commercial banks access to cheap foreign financing while maintaining uncompetitive domestic price setting. Thus, Thai banks have long benefited from a large spread between the interest rates offered on deposits and those charged for loans. Although the spread has narrowed in the last few years, it still stood at around 380 basis points by the end of 1996. By 1996, bank earnings accounted for nearly half of the SET's earnings.

Concerns about the health of the banking system have been on the rise since mid-1996, when massive amounts of bad loans were revealed at the Bangkok Bank of Commerce (BBC). Efforts to strengthen the central bank's control over the banking system are likely to be increased. Currently, banks must carry a capital reserve of at least 8% of risk assets. Moreover, the central bank requires each commercial bank to submit its lending plan annually, showing how much was loaned to particular sectors or groups. There is scope for further improvement in financial control and disclosure.

■ ECONOMICS

Historical overview

Thailand began a process of rapid industrialization in the 1960s. Public policy was directed towards the development of an import-substituting industrial sector. External openness and intensive accumulation of capital, together with the adoption of policies designed to maximize private sector investment, further helped rapid development of the industrial base. A strong agricultural sector remained, however, the driving force of the economy. Overall economic expansion was also supported by the US involvement in the Vietnam War, as Thailand became the major provider of US military bases and supplies. US-funded road-building for security purposes rapidly increased communications and transport facilities.

Economic development stagnated during the 1970s and remained centred on primary production and import-substituting industrialization. Although volatile at times, real GDP growth continued at an annual average of 7.4% throughout the decade. By the mid-1970s, the country began to experience problems associated with rapid growth. Consumer prices jumped drastically, fuelled by rising public expenditures reflecting an upturn in defence spending. Moreover, a sharp deterioration of the terms of trade led to a rise in the current account deficit.

The oil shock in 1979-80 and the subsequent fall in non-oil commodities prices precipitated a major economic setback for Thailand. For more than five years, economic growth remained below 6%. The Fifth National Plan (1982-86) was designed to revive economic activity. The plan included tax and financial system reforms and tariff reductions, and focused on the development of an export-orientated, instead of an import-substituting, industrial base. However, progress in implementation was limited and led an interruption of World Bank funding. Yet, tight fiscal and monetary policy, together with the reforms, helped stabilize the economy in the second half of the 1980s and led to an economic boom without precedent in the country's postwar history. Real GDP growth averaged 11.2% annually between 1987 and 1990, and exports nearly doubled in value. This expansion was concentrated in the manufacturing sector, helped by a substantial devaluation of the baht. A surge in foreign direct investment, reflecting plant relocation from East Asian economies, further boosted industrial production.

Thailand's economic performance

	Average annual real GDP growth, %	Average annual consumer price inflation, %
1961-1965	7.3	2.1
1966-1970	9.4	2.5
1971-1975	5.6	10.1
1976-1980	8.0	9.9
1981-1985	5.4	5.0
1985-1990	10.4	3.9
1991-1995	8.4	4.8

Recent developments

By 1990, signs of overheating showed. Infrastructure bottlenecks and labour shortages became serious constraints to continued growth. Inflation edged up to 6% from less than 3% in 1987, and the current account deficit rose from 3.5% of GDP in 1989 to 8.5% in 1990. The authorities responded by tightening economic policy, which, combined with the shock of the 1991 military coup and the political upheaval of May 1992, dampened growth. However, strong investment continued to boost economic output, which has grown by over 8% annually since 1991.

A resurgent trade deficit and rampant consumer price inflation again threatened to overheat the economy in 1995. Much of Thailand's strong growth has been financed through offshore markets, in particular the Bangkok International Banking Facility (BIBF), with loans growing by 76.4% in 1995. To counter overheating pressure through curbs on lending, the Bank of Thailand imposed restrictions on commercial banks and finance houses, thereby stepping back from its policy of financial liberalization. However, the persistent upward trends of the current account deficit, short-term debt and inflation have led to concerns about the ability of the authorities to maintain Thailand's macroeconomic stability. Such concerns have intensified as structural changes in the economy (such as financial liberalization) change the nature of macroeconomic management, and render less effective the usual monetary policy instruments.

Domestic demand started to weaken at the beginning of 1996, given tight credit conditions. A drastic region-wide export slump, due to a cyclical weakness of external demand as well as plunging prices in the semi-conductor and electronics sector, accelerated the economic contraction. Exacerbated by an overall unstable political climate, the economy seems to be heading for more than a cyclical economic downturn. In the face of persistent balance of payments deficits, the Thai economy is likely to converge towards a lower, yet more stable long-term GDP growth path.

The economy

Rapid economic growth has markedly transformed the Thai economy over the last two decades. While Thailand could still be viewed as an agrarian economy in the early 1980s, with crops playing a major role in exports, it now belongs to the club of newly industrializing economies (NIEs), with export-orientated manufacturing covering a broad product range. Agricultural production nevertheless remains important for the economy: Thailand has been the world's largest rice exporter since 1981 and one of the few net food exporters of Asia. Moreover, the agricultural sector remains the basis of the rapidly expanding agrobusiness.

Share of GDP by sector

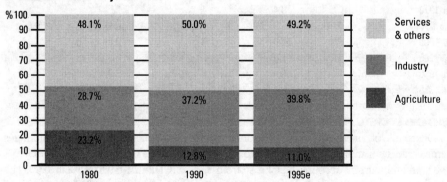

Source: Official data

While the industrial sector contributed 25% to domestic output in 1970, its share has increased to some 40% today. Manufacturing still consists to a large extent of labour-intensive assembly activities, although, since the late 1980s, growth in classic labour-intensive industries was outstripped by growth in medium- and high-tech products, such as computer components, electronics, automobile parts and electrical goods. Foreign direct investment played a major role in both the labour-intensive and medium-tech phases. The classic labour-intensive industries, such as textiles, garments, and wood products have been facing difficulties since the early 1990s, as wage rates rise, and lower-cost countries emerge as competitors.

The growth of manufactured exports has led to a boom in domestic services, as Thai firms take a leading role in trade, communications and development. Thailand's aim to become a regional hub for trade and a financial centre has further boosted the expansion of the tertiary sector.

Savings and investment

Thailand has traditionally had high savings and investment ratios. Although household savings have declined, gross national savings has remained above 30% of GDP for over ten years and stood at 34.4% in 1995. With an investment to GDP ratio above 40%, Thailand has suffered from a structural savings-investment gap for some time. It is ultimately this gap that is hindering a continued rapid economic expansion with GDP growth above 9%.

Thailand's fiscal policy is strongly directed towards higher resources mobilization, with measures that include the creation of provident funds in the public sector and the provision of tax incentives for private savings. The establishment of mandatory provident funds in the private sector, however, remains highly unlikely in the near future.

To fill the gap between savings and investment, substantial foreign direct investment (FDI) has entered the country. Since 1975, over US$15 billion was invested (FDI) in Thailand. During 1988-95, 33.5% of net foreign direct investment was from Japan, 33.4% from Hong Kong, Singapore, Taiwan and South Korea, and 16.6% from the US. The sectorial distribution has shifted from oil and gas to manufacturing since the early 1980s.

The relaxation of controls over capital movements and relatively high Thai interest rates have also attracted large portfolio investment since 1992, which has also helped to finance strong capital formation.

Trade and balance of payments

The share of agricultural exports in total merchandise exports declined from 84.4% in 1960 to 12% in 1995. Manufactured goods exports, however, surged from 2.4% in 1960 to 32.3% in 1980, and 81% in 1995. This spectacular expansion was associated with an increase in the share of import expenditure on machinery and transport equipment, as well as fuel and lubricants.

Today, the main exports commodities are textiles, machines and mechanical as well as electrical appliances. The driving areas, both in terms of share in total exports and growth rates, are computers and parts, electrical apparatus, electric appliances and chemical products. A wide range of commodities, primarily raw materials, intermediate products and capital goods are imported. On the services side, tourism is the most important sector.

The principal trading partners of Thailand are Japan, the US and Singapore (substantially negative trade balance with Japan, positive with the US and Singapore). Over the last years, inter-Asian trade, and particularly within the Association of South-East Asian Nations (ASEAN) has grown rapidly.

Breakdown of exports (1995)

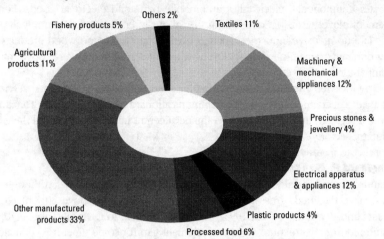

Source: Official data

Thailand has had a negative trade balance for most of the last two decades. The rapid expansion of the economy since 1987 has been accompanied by a sharp increase in imports. In particular, imports have stubbornly outpaced export performance since late 1994. The trade gap thus widened from US$0.42 billion in 1987 to approximately US$17 billion in 1996. In 1996, exports collapsed under the weight of both global-cyclical and domestic-structural factors, resulting in an export growth rate of some 3% in 1996, down from an 18.6% annual average between 1990 and 1995. As import growth continues to exceed export growth, the trade gap is likely to keep on rising in the near future.

Imports and exports as a % of GDP

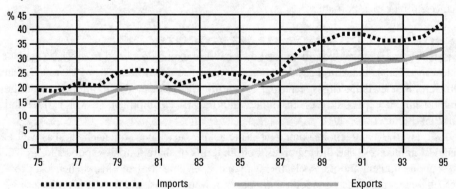

Source: Official data

Trade restrictions

Most commodities may be imported freely, but import licences are required for certain goods. Imports of some goods are prohibited for protective or social reasons. A few agricultural goods are subject to temporary import surcharges. Certain categories of exports are subject to licensing and quantitative restrictions and, in a few cases, to prior approval. All other products may be exported freely.

Current account deficits

Current account deficits, except in 1986, have been a consistent feature of Thailand's economy for over thirty years, given that the import bill for capital goods and raw materials has constantly risen, while export earnings have failed to keep pace. Moreover, the surplus of the invisibles balance has shrunk dramatically in the last few years. Rising private debt servicing costs, rapidly expanding costs for Thais travelling abroad, and a growing freight deficit due to insufficient national freight capacities, largely account for this decline. In 1995, for the third time since the early 1980s, the current account balance deteriorated sharply. Pressures intensified in 1996, given the drastic export growth deceleration. Although the current account position is likely to remain sustainable, ultimately, only higher private savings and/or lower domestic demand can reduce external imbalances.

Current account as a % of GDP

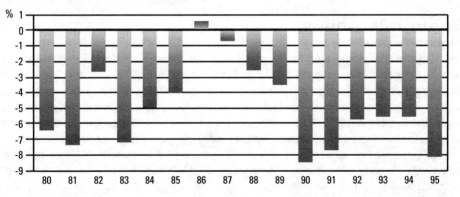

Source: Official data

Since the baht was devalued and pegged to a basket of currencies in 1984, net capital inflows exceeded the current account deficit, therefore feeding into reserves. In relative terms, foreign exchange reserves have represented over six months of imports since 1992. Traditionally, loans and credits represented the bulk of capital inflows. However, since the early 1990s, the composition of fund inflows has undergone a substantial shift towards more short-term and leveraged instruments. In particular, the importance of FDI has declined markedly. Since 1994, the BIBF has become the major provider of funds.

While the surplus of the overall balance is likely to have peaked in 1995 (more than US$7 billion), current account financing should be secured over the next few years. Yet, foreign investor confidence is more vital than ever, and a policy shift away from rapid economic growth towards balance of payments sustainability appears inevitable.

Debt

The persistently high current account deficits of the 1990s have led to a substantial increase in Thailand's external debt. As a percentage of GDP, the gross external debt amounted to approximately 52% in 1995, up from 39% in 1992. Short-term debt accounted for 47.5% of total debt and approximately 114% of foreign exchange reserves in 1995. While public debt increased by 25%, private debt more than doubled between 1992 and 1995.

While debt servicing costs (13.9% of foreign exchange receipts in 1995) are putting additional pressure on the current account balance, it is mainly the structure of the debt that has caused concern recently. Facing higher domestic funding costs in the wake of a tight monetary policy, banks and finance companies have increasingly funded themselves on the BIBF market. These short-term liabilities, denominated in baht, are serviced at the interest rate determined in offshore money markets. Hence, the financing costs of such liabilities are directly linked to the risk premium prevailing on the currency swap markets. The latter, in turn, is highly susceptible to changes in risk perceptions: while the Mexican crisis pushed the country risk premium higher in early 1995, a higher risk profile related to structural economic weaknesses and political instability has again resulted in a higher premium in the second half of 1996.

Economic policy

Monetary policy

The Bank of Thailand, acting as central bank, has generally followed a conservative monetary policy, focusing on price stability. However, the strong inflows of foreign capital that were boosted by the greater integration of national financial markets into international markets, and attracted by relatively high Thai interest rates, have made the task of controlling inflation more difficult. With an exchange rate pegged to a basket of currencies and allowing for free capital movement, Thailand's monetary policy freedom is constrained. To prevent exchange rate appreciation in times of strong capital inflows, the Bank of Thailand intervenes to buy foreign exchange. The latter feeds into foreign reserves and, if unsterilized, creates liquidity in the domestic financial system, fuelling inflation. As the domestic government bond market is not large or liquid enough, sterilization is very limited. Hence, the central bank increasingly resorts to "fiscal sterilization", a process through which the government increases its deposits at the Bank of Thailand. This process, however, compels the government to run fiscal surpluses and postpone necessary public investment.

Fiscal policy

Until 1987, Thailand recorded budget deficits. These were particularly high in the early 1980s. Increased tax revenues, following the introduction of a value-added tax while reducing income and corporate taxes, together with the economic upsurge, have since resulted in substantial budget surpluses. Since 1990, "fiscal sterilization" has also contributed to an increase in budget surpluses.

Currency

The Thai baht is pegged to a basket of currencies of Thailand's major trading partners and has been heavily weighted to the US$ since 1984. The central bank's Exchange Equalization Fund (EEF) announces every morning the daily buying and selling rates for the US$, the intervention currency. Until noon, the EEF purchases and sells US$ at 2 satang (1 satang = 0.01 baht) above or below the fixing rate. In the afternoon, the baht tends to trade on the market's expectations of the following day's fixing rate, plus influences from supply and demand. The baht has remained within the US$/THB 24.4-25.8 range since 1990.

Speculation around an eventual exchange rate devaluation has arisen with regard to Thailand's balance of payments deficits. Thailand's balance of payments problems clearly are not due to an overvalued baht. A devaluation would only trigger massive capital outflows, and is therefore ruled out as an option in tackling the trade deficit. However, should major insolvencies in the banking system develop in a systemic financial crisis, compelling the central bank to act as lender of last resort, monetary policy is likely to be no longer directed towards maintaining the exchange-rate peg, but towards saving the banks.

Thai baht/US dollar exchange rate

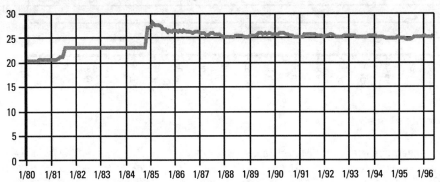

Exchange controls

There are no taxes or subsidies on purchases or sales of foreign exchange. Apart from authorized banks, authorized companies and authorized persons are also allowed to deal in foreign exchange operations. All commercial banks can carry out foreign exchange transactions.

Importers may freely purchase foreign currency or draw foreign exchange from their own foreign currency accounts for payments. Payments for imports may be made through any authorized bank. Foreign exchange transaction forms for transactions whose values exceed THB500,000 have to be completed by importers. Remittances abroad of service fees, royalties, insurance premiums and others are permitted without restriction. Remittances of dividends and profits on all bona fide investments may be made freely.

Exporters are required to surrender foreign exchange proceeds to authorized banks or deposit them in foreign currency accounts with authorized banks in Thailand. Foreign exchange earnings from invisibles must be surrendered to authorized banks or retained in foreign currency accounts with authorized banks in Thailand.

Capital investments in Thailand through equity participation or portfolio investments are permitted freely. Foreign capital may be brought into the country and loans contracted without restriction, but proceeds must be surrendered to authorized banks or deposited in foreign currency accounts. Repatriation of investment funds, loan repayments and interest payments may be made without restriction. External borrowing by the public sector must be approved by the local Foreign Debt Committee.

■ EQUITIES

Index performance (in local currency)

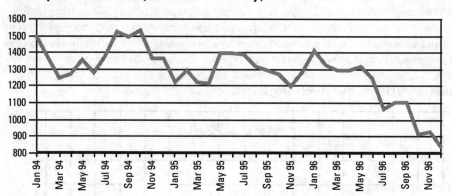

Key indicators

	Index performance %, in US$ terms	Market Cap. US$bn	P/E	Div. Yield	Weight in IFCI	IFCG
1994	-13.1	131.5	21.2	2.0	5.3	8.5
1995	-3.6	141.5	21.7	2.2	4.7	8.8
1996	-38.1	99.8	13.1	3.3	2.9	5.5

Sources: Local stock exchange, IFC, Bloomberg, Datastream, UBS

Background

The Thai capital market goes back to 1953, when Bird Co. Ltd. became the first company to offer brokerage services. Later, in 1963, a group of mostly foreign businessmen established the Bangkok Stock Exchange. However, this venture failed, hindered by a lack of local understanding and government support. In time, the government encouraged a capital market and, following the May 1974 Securities Exchange Act, the Securities Exchange of Thailand opened in 1975. On January 1, 1991 the exchange was renamed the Stock Exchange of Thailand (SET).

Structure

The Stock Exchange of Thailand has four boards: the Main Board for regular trading in round lots, normal size and domestic listings; the Special Board for Odd Lots and reporting Block Trades (currently above THB10 million (US$ 0.4 million) as put-throughs; the Big Lot Board for high-value orders (currently above THB10 million or 10% of total par value); and the Foreign Board for non-residents when a stock has reached its foreign ownership limit on the Main Board. By the end of 1995, there were 536 securities listed on the exchange.

Regulatory authority

The SET is regulated by the Securities Exchange Commission (SEC). In line with the Securities and Exchange Act 1992 (SEA), the SEC regulates all elements of the market including disclosure, investor protection, fund management, take-over procedures and the establishment of securities firms.

Trading methods

The Automated System for the Stock Exchange of Thailand (ASSET) is a screen-based auction system where orders are entered by brokerage house dealers, operating on a price and time priority basis. There are fixed spreads per stock depending on price and an order book is made at each spread level.

Hours

Trading takes place from 10.30 to 12.30 and 14.30 to 16.30, Monday to Friday.

Settlement time and clearing

Settlement takes place on a trade plus three business days (T+3) basis.

Limits on price movement

Stock price movement is limited to 10% above or below the opening price. The smallest price change increment is THB0.1 and the largest THB6.0.

Types of shares

Ordinary shares, preference shares, unit trusts, and warrants are traded on the SET.

Stock indices

The main index is the SET Index, which comprises all the common stocks featured on the Exchange. In addition, there are various sector-based indices and the relatively new SET 50 Index.

Taxes

There are no transaction taxes. Dividends are subject to a 10% withholding tax, although some investors, from countries with tax treaties with Thailand, may pay less.

Dividends

Generally, dividends are paid once or twice yearly.

Disclosure of financial statements

A company listed on the SET is required to produce a quarterly financial statement within forty-five days of the end of each quarter, a fully audited biannual/annual financial statement within two to three months of the end of the accounting period, an annual report within four months of the end of the accounting period, as well as other reports specified by the SET.

Ownership limits for non-residents

Non-resident ownership is restricted by law to a maximum of 25% for financial institutions and 49% for other companies. Companies need not apply for the maximum.

Foreign registered shares can be sold on the Regular or Foreign Board. However, if the quota is not full, there will be no liquidity or premium on the Foreign Board, so shares are sold on the Regular Board.

Capital and foreign exchange controls

Incoming flows of foreign exchange must be made through a correspondent bank, but it is not necessary to report to the central bank.

For repatriation of funds, commercial banks are authorized to approve limitless foreign exchange purchases. Again, central bank approval is not necessary. All trading on the SET must be performed in Thai bahts.

Take-over bids and large stakes

Take-over bids can be made either through the stock market or through public tender.

Brokers

In Thailand, only securities companies are allowed to perform brokerage functions. The brokerage rate for ordinary shares, preference shares and warrants is 0.5% of value traded with a minimum trade of THB50.

Sectors

The banking and finance sectors dominate the SET with a combined value of 36% or THB1015.31 billion (about US$40 billion), as at October 1996. Communications, building, energy, and property are the only other sectors with market value in excess of THB100 billion (about US$4 billion).

Derivatives

Although there is no market for futures or options at present, the SET is undertaking accommodatory steps for future developments.

The SET 50 Index was started on August 16, 1996, comprising the fifty largest stocks, with the derivatives market in mind.

■ DEBT

The Royal Thai Government (RTG), through the Ministry of Finance (MOF) and the Bank of Thailand (BOT), is keen to develop the country's bond market, which has a history extending back to 1933.

Recent deregulatory measures include abolition of interest rate ceilings and reduction of bond-holding reserve requirements, relaxation of foreign exchange control and tax reductions.

Foreign investors have been major investors since the relaxation of exchange controls, but are subject to withholding tax unless a double taxation treaty exists.

Public debt

Treasury bills

The Bank of Thailand began issuing treasury bills on behalf of the Ministry of Finance for open market operations to absorb a large inflow of foreign money in mid-1995, after a six-year lull. The RTG has run budget surpluses since 1987. No regular auction schedules are planned.

Only the BOT underwrites bonds issued by the government, but securities companies are permitted to underwrite government agency and enterprise issues. Since 1995 banks have also been allowed to underwrite debt issues.

Treasury bonds

Budget surpluses since 1987 have meant that the government has had no need to issue treasury bonds. The last (small) series was issued in 1990. However, it is considering issuing debt to provide the market with benchmarks and a risk-free yield curve to price corporate issues.

Prior to 1988, treasury bonds made up 95% of the domestic debt market, comprising various instruments – accumulated loan bonds, coupon loan bonds and others aimed at different categories of investor, but most are due to mature within the next few years.

BOT reserve requirements mean that more than half of government bond holdings are tightly held by commercial banks.

State Enterprise bonds

State Enterprise bonds have been issued since 1990, and the market considers them to be quasi-government debt. The Royal Thai Government intends to increase the role of the private sector in financing infrastructure projects, and there are plans for large public utilities and other state enterprises to be corporatized. They will be encouraged to access the domestic financial markets.

Maturities range from 3 to 10 years, and large issues act as benchmarks for pricing corporate debt. The highest rated bonds are issued by the Industrial Finance Corporation of Thailand.

Private debt

Negotiable Certificates of Deposit (NCDs)

Issuance of NCDs has increased significantly since 1991. Maturities range from 3 months to 3 years, but most are for less than 1 year.

Commercial paper (CP)

Top quality CP, promissory notes, bills of exchange and bankers' acceptances function as surrogate treasury bills for bank investors. Most have 3-month terms, but can be issued for up to 1 year.

Corporate bonds

The Securities and Exchange Act,1992 authorizes any limited company capitalized at Bt500 million (US$20 million) or more to issue unsecured debentures. Previously only SET listed or public companies could do so. Most bonds pay fixed-rate coupons and have a minimum

3-year maturity; although there are FRNs, the market is limited by the lack of a standard reference interest rate. Many are equity-linked – either convertibles or have warrants attached. Corporate bonds now make up nearly half the Thai debt markets.

Primary market

According to SEC regulations, companies that issue bonds must specify how they will use the proceeds, must have a good repayment record and be engaged in a business that benefits the Thai economy. In addition, public issues must be rated by an SEC approved agency.

Secondary market

In November 1994, the Bond Dealers Club was created to standardize secondary market practice, help devise regulations and increase dealer efficiency. It is a professional wholesale market for bonds within the Association of Securities Companies (ASCO); trades are transacted in a computerized trading system called BONDNET via standalone personal computers in each member-dealer's office. Dealers pay a Bt1 million (US$40,000) membership fee.

Settlement

Bonds settle through the Thailand Securities Depository Co. Ltd for DVP via the BAHTNET payment system. Euroclear also accept Thai securities, with Bangkok Bank acting as a depository and cash correspondent.

Credit rating agency

The Thai Rating and Information Services (TRIS) was set up by the BOT in July 1993. It assesses companies' general credit-worthiness, and also a bond issuer's ability to service interest and principal payments on a particular issue. Many ratings are not published.

Eurobonds

Thai borrowers have issued about ninety eurobonds denominated in six hard currencies, and corporate issuers have now gained access to the US Yankee market.

Eurobond issues (US$m)

	1990	1991	1992	1993	1994	1995	1996
Sovereign	0.0	0.0	300.0	168.7	491.4	174.5	283.5
Private	0.0	17.3	259.4	1722.8	3110.6	1920.3	3085.0

■ THAILAND: Economic indicators

Population and development	1990	1991	1992	1993	1994	1995	1996e
Population, million	56.1	56.9	57.8	58.6	59.4	60.1	60.9
Population growth, %	1.6	1.5	1.5	1.4	1.3	1.3	1.3
Nominal GDP per capita, US$	1527	1735	1927	2134	2409	2776	3017

National accounts							
Nominal GDP, US$bn	85.6	98.7	111.3	125.0	143.0	166.9	183.8
Change in real GDP, %	11.2	8.5	8.1	8.3	8.8	8.6	6.7
Gross fixed capital formation, % of GDP	40.2	41.4	39.4	40.2	41.0	42.8	44.1

Money supply and inflation							
Narrow money, change %, Dec/Dec	11.9	13.8	12.3	18.6	17.0	12.1	6.0
Broad money, change %, Dec/Dec	26.7	19.8	15.6	18.4	12.9	17.0	11.8
Consumer price inflation (avg.) %	6.0	5.7	4.1	3.3	5.1	5.8	5.9

Government finance							
Government expenditure, % of GDP	13.9	14.4	15.7	16.5	16.1	15.4	16.7
Government balance, % of GDP	4.9	4.3	2.6	1.9	2.7	3.0	1.6

Exchange rates lc=local currency							
Exchange rate, annual average, lc/US$	25.59	25.52	25.40	25.32	25.16	24.92	25.35
Exchange rate, end of year, lc/US$	25.29	25.28	25.52	25.50	25.10	25.18	25.54
Real exchange rate 1990=100	100.0	100.6	98.8	100.4	102.1	100.6	105.3

Balance of payments							
Exports of goods & services, US$m	29207	35469	41382	47453	56071	70300	72073
Change %	15.8	21.4	16.7	14.7	18.2	25.4	2.5
Imports of goods & services, US$m, fob	36050	42497	46622	53161	63600	82226	86178
Change %	33.1	17.9	9.7	14.0	19.6	29.3	4.8
Trade balance, of goods only, US$m, fob-fob	-9972	-9690	-8086	-8755	-9013	-15002	-17419
Current account balance, US$m	-7277	-7574	-6302	-6364	-8074	-13551	-16117
as a % of GDP	-8.5	-7.7	-5.7	-5.1	-5.6	-8.1	-8.8

Foreign exchange reserves							
Foreign exchange reserves, US$m	13305	17517	20359	24473	29331	36000	38500
Gold at ⅔ of market price, US$m	636.5	597.2	566.3	593.2	633.6	633.5	639.3
Import cover (reserves/imports), months	4.4	4.9	5.2	5.5	5.5	5.3	5.4

Foreign debt and debt service							
Short-term debt, US$m	11014	16209	19826	22600	29200	41100	44000
Total foreign debt, US$m	29342	36783	43378	53751	66904	86470	94500
as a % of GDP	34.3	37.3	39.0	43.0	46.8	51.8	51.4
as a % of foreign exchange receipts	102.0	105.3	107.6	114.9	120.5	125.9	134.9
Interest payments, US$m	2051	2289	2058	1997	2700	4174	5000
Principal repayments, US$m	2320	1829	2031	2670	3422	5389	6000
Total debt service, US$m	4371	4118	4089	4667	6122	9563	11000
as a % of goods exports	19.2	14.6	12.7	12.8	13.8	17.2	19.6
as a % of foreign exchange receipts	15.2	11.8	10.1	10.0	11.0	13.9	15.7

Turkey

Area (thousands of km²):	779
Population (1995, millions):	62.5
Population projection (2025, millions):	92
Population younger than 15 yrs (1991, % of total):	35.2
Urbanization rate (1993, % of population):	66
Life expectancy (1993, years at birth):	67
Gross domestic product (1996, US$bn):	174.0
GDP per capita (1996, US$):	2724
Average annual GDP growth rate (1990-96, %):	4.7
Average annual inflation rate (1990-96, %):	77
Currency (lira per US$, average 1996):	81995
Real exchange rate: (1990=100, average 1996)	90.9
Structure of production (1994):	15% agriculture, 28% industry, 57% services
Main exports:	textiles, processed food, iron & steel, agriculture
Main imports:	electrical machinery, transport vehicles, iron & steel, oil
Main trading partners:	EU, Germany, Italy, France, UK
Market capitalization of Stock Exchange (December 1996; US$bn):	30.0
Total foreign debt (% of GDP):	41.8
Next elections due under normal circumstances:	December 2000 at latest
Credit rating: (Jan 1997, Standard & Poor's, Moody's)	B; Ba3

FORECAST: 1997-2000 (average)

	Worst case	Most likely	Best case
Real GDP growth (%)	2 to 3	4 to 5	6 to 7
Inflation (%)	80	70	60

■ POLITICS

Historical overview

The Republic of Turkey (Türkiye Cumhuriyeti) was founded on October 29, 1923, on the ruins of the Ottoman Empire. Mustafa Kemal Atatürk, who led the War of Sovereignty between 1919 and 1923, was elected as the first president of the republic. A new constitution was drawn in 1924 and, following amendments in 1928, the caliphate, too, was abolished and religion separated from state. The 1920s and 1930s saw a series of reforms designed to turn Turkey into a fully European state. The Latin alphabet was introduced, women were granted suffrage, Islamic laws expunged from the statute books, the Capitulations ended, relations with European powers normalized, and significant progress made towards developing a manufacturing base. The reforms were remarkably successful, and their influence continues to be the major shaping factor in Turkey today.

After the death of Atatürk in 1938, Ismet İnönü became the second president of Turkey. The single-party system (Republican People's Party) continued until 1946. An opposition party, the Democrat Party (DP), won the 1950 general elections. The DP ruled until 1960, when a military coup overthrew the government. The prime minister of the time, Adnan Menderes, along with two other ministers, were charged with corruption and executed. The military stayed in power for only a short period, but put a new constitution in effect.

The 1960s marked the start of planned development in Turkey. A large rural-urban migration that still continues today also started in the 1960s. The 1970s saw the army's warning memorandum to the government (1972), Turkish military intervention in Cyprus (1974), a period of unstable coalitions, escalating street fighting between ultra-nationalists and leftist factions, and external payments difficulties. Against this background, the military intervened again (September 1980), and remained in power until 1983.

The 1980-83 period witnessed a new constitution (1982) and an economic transformation towards a more liberal and open economy. The Motherland Party (ANAP), led by Turgut Özal, who was the architect of the liberalization policies under the military government, won the 1983 general elections. ANAP also won the 1987 general elections and remained in power until 1991. Turkish political life in the 1990s saw a return to coalition governments, Turkey's first woman prime minister (Tansu Çiller, leader of the True Path Party), the rise of the pro-Islamic Welfare Party, and Turkey's first pro-Islamic prime minister (Necmettin Erbakan).

In the 1990s, Turkey has furthered economic liberalization, amended the 1982 constitution to provide more civil rights, and entered into a customs union with the EU (1996). Economic performance, however, followed a less stable path with large variability in real GDP growth rates and no solution to chronic high inflation of around 80% a year.

Recent events

There were two governments in 1996. The first was set up at the beginning of the year between the two main centre-right parties, the ANAP and the True Path Party (DYP), led by Mesut Yilmaz and Tansu Çiller respectively. However, the coalition was riven by personality clashes and proved ineffectual. It finally broke down because of internal strife over an ANAP-supported investigation into Ms Çiller's conduct during her tenure as prime minister (1992-95).

The DYP then went into coalition with the RP, which provided Turkey with its first pro-Islamic prime minister, Necmettin Erbakan. It has eschewed a religious agenda, however, the RP-led government has instead proven seriously populist, adopting and indeed exacerbating many of the social and economic policies of the previous few administrations.

Chronology
Ottoman era

1280	Establishment of Ottoman principality in western Anatolia by Osman I
1453	Conquest of Constantinople. Ottoman capital is moved to Istanbul (formerly Constantinople).
16th-17th centuries	Apogee of Ottoman power. Ottoman conquest of the Middle East and most of North Africa. Borders are extended to Vienna and Tabriz.
1876	First Ottoman constitution is promulgated
1909	Young Turk revolution. Second constitutional period. Power passes to Committee of Progress, led by Enver Pasha.
1914	Ottoman Empire enters war on side of Austria-Hungary and Germany
1918	Ottoman Empire sues for peace
1919	Occupation of Istanbul. Empire is dismembered. Occupation of remaining Turkish-majority territories in Europe and most of Anatolia.
1919-1922	War of Sovereignty. Mustafa Kemal Pasha sets up government in Ankara and persuades occupying powers to leave.

Modern Turkey

1923	October 29: Declaration of Republic. Mustafa Kemal (later Atatürk) first president.
1924-38	Period of reform
1938	Atatürk dies
1939	Republic of Hatay joins Turkey
1945	Turkey enters war on Allied side
1940-70	Turkey drops neutrality, joins OEEC (later OECD), NATO, CENTO and becomes an Associate Member of the EEC
1946	First multiparty elections
1959-1960	Civil disturbances
1960	Military coup d'état. Promulgation of new, liberal constitution. Creation of the Constitutional Court.
1961	Return to civilian rule
1970	Ankara Protocol with EEC previsages customs union and full membership
1977-79	Civil disturbances and economic upheaval
1980	Military coup d'état
1980-81	Serious economic liberalization
1982	New constitution
1983	Return to civilian rule
1986	Trading starts on Istanbul Stock Exchange
1989	Foreign exchange and investment laws fully liberalized
1992	Tansu Çiller becomes Turkey's first woman prime minister
1996	Customs Union with EU
1996	Necmettin Erbakan becomes Turkey's first pro-Islamic prime minister

Constitution and government

Turkey is a parliamentary democracy consisting of seventy-three provinces. Its constitution was adopted on November 7, 1982 and provides for a Grand National Assembly (Buyuk Millet Meclisi), a president, and a prime minister. The Constitutional Court acts as the top level of the judiciary and has wide-ranging powers. In July 1995 a number of amendments to the constitution induced reform in several areas. These included reducing the minimum voting age to eighteen, and removing some of the more onerous provisions of the 1982 constitution.

Turkey has a unicameral legislature. Legislation is passed by the Turkish Grand National Assembly, which has 550 seats. Members are elected for five years through a system of modified proportional representation. Any party which fails to gain 10% of the general election vote is ineligible for any seats in the Grand National Assembly.

The president is elected for a single seven-year term by the Grand National Assembly, and in turn appoints the prime minister. The prime minister nominates the Council of Ministers, who are then approved by the National Assembly and the president.

Current government

President	Süleyman DEMIREL
Speaker of Parliament	Mustafa KALEMLI (ANAP)
Prime Minister	Necmettin ERBAKAN (RP)
Deputy Prime Minister	Tansu ÇILLER (DYP)
Leader of the Opposition	Mesut YILMAZ (ANAP)
Head of the Constitutional Court	Yekta Güngör ÖZDEN

Results of the December 1995 elections
Welfare Party (RP) (21.4%); **True Path Party** (DYP) (19.2%); **Motherland Party** (ANAP) (19.7%); **Democratic Left Party** (DSP) (14.6%); **Republican Populist Party** (CHP) (10.7%); **Other** (14.4%)

Next elections
December 2000 at the latest

Local government
Greater freedom to collect revenues was granted to local governments in reforms during the 1980s. The most important reforms changed municipal structures. The creation of metropolitan authorities (most notably in Istanbul, Ankara, Izmir, Adana and Bursa) provided for the first time a directly elected tier of local government with national presence and authority.

Political forces
Coalition government
DYP and RP formed a coalition in July 1996 after the DYP/ANAP coalition collapsed in acrimony. The RP has sought to bolster its popularity through the adoption of populist spending programmes. The DYP remains committed to centre-right social policies and liberal economics.

Opposition

In terms of ideology there is little to differentiate the ANAP from the DYP. The two other main parties in the National Assembly, DSP and CHP, are both social democratic in terms of social and economic objectives, the former with a slightly nationalistic tinge.

Central bank

Turkey's central bank (Türkiye Cumhuriyeti Merkez Bankasi, TCMB), established on October 3, 1931, is responsible for issuing banknotes, implementing government exchange rate and monetary policies and maintaining price stability. It advises the government on financial matters and oversees numerous aspects of the banking system. The central bank's objectives are determined through consultation with the Undersecretariat of Treasury. Of the share capital, 51% is owned by the state. Consequently, its board is government-appointed, and its operations are strongly linked with government policies.

■ ECONOMICS

Historical overview

Until the 1960s, the main engines of growth in the economy were in agriculture and services, each accounting for around 40-45% of GDP. From the 1960s onwards, the share of the agricultural sector declined steadily, being replaced by strong expansion in the industrial sector. By 1995, agriculture's share of GDP had fallen to 15%, services accounted for 58%, and the remaining 27% was industry. This performance allowed Turkey's economic growth rate, albeit erratic, to be the highest in the OECD.

In the early 1980s a programme of structural change and liberalization was launched to improve competitiveness, lower inflation and boost GDP growth. The reforms involved the removal of price controls, a reduction in subsidies and the role of the public sector in the economy, moves towards the full convertibility of the Turkish lira, encouraging investment and savings, reducing tariffs, easing exchange controls and reforming the tax base. The economy became more diversified, the industrial base broadened out and exports of goods and services rose. GDP growth significantly exceeded 5% during the latter part of the 1980s, after negative growth during 1979-80. In addition, inflation fell sharply from 107% in 1980 to an average of 45% over the remaining part of the 1980s.

Recent developments

In the 1990s, the picture changed. Uncertainties and unfavourable external conditions related to the Gulf War led to a contraction in economic activity, reducing the GDP growth rate to below 1% in 1991. The post-Gulf War recovery was led by real wage increases and fiscal expansion. GDP growth averaged 6.8% during 1992 and 1993.

However, mainly due to the financial crisis and the austerity measures instituted on April 5, GDP declined by 6.1% in 1994. It was a turbulent year for Turkey, with economic management made difficult by the effect of growing public sector budget deficits and rising inflation. The government was unable to raise the funds required without penal rates of interest in the domestic market. Downgradings by both Standard & Poor's and Moody's rating groups at the start of 1994 added to pressure on the exchange rate, resulting from the substantial depreciation in Turkey's external balances. Eventually the crisis of confidence put strong pressure on the currency. To stabilize the situation, the central bank raised interest rates and intervened in the foreign exchange markets. But these moves failed and the lira fell by around 55-60% against the US dollar during the first quarter of 1994. The stabilization package aimed to reduce the rate of inflation, improve the external balances and restore stability in the financial markets. To reduce the fiscal deficit, state sector prices of between 70% and 100% were announced and the government proposed to freeze public sector wages and reduce public investment. Measures to speed structural reform, including privatization, were promised.

By early 1995, it became clear that the emergency package had restored some economic balance. The current account deficit had by then turned into surplus and the economy was once again expanding, with real GDP growth of 7.2% in 1995.

Inflation trended down from 126% in January 1995 to 76% at the end of the year, whilst the fiscal deficit was contained close to 4.0% of GDP. However, with increased political instability during the autumn and the scheduling of general elections on December 24, the economic situation deteriorated as the government began to pursue expansionary fiscal policies. Public sector wage increases of 54% were granted and interest rates started increasing.

During 1996, the Turkish economy continued to recover. GNP growth was close to 7.3% in the first three-quarters of the year. Economic growth continued to be driven by domestic demand and largely consumer-related, given real wage increases to public sector workers. On the negative side, high real interest rates and increased government spending pushed up the fiscal deficit dramatically. The official estimate for the 1996 deficit was around 9.0% of GDP. In tandem with the fiscal expansion, Turkish inflation remained very high, around 80%.

Population

Turkey's population is approximately 63 million. It is comparatively young and grows at an annual rate of around 2%. However, with the transition from an agriculturally based economy to an industrial and service-based one, there has been an accelerating rate of urbanization. About 60% of Turkey's population now live in urban areas. Turkey's high population growth rate is expected to continue. The western and coastal parts of the country are most heavily populated. The capital, Ankara, has approximately 3.4 million inhabitants, and the commercial centre, Istanbul, about 7.4 million.

Labour and employment

Turkey has a large supply of unskilled and semi-skilled workers, with only limited union activity permitted. The growth rate of the working-age population remains high. During the period 1991-95, the total labour force increased by 7%. As of June 1996, unemployment stood at 6.3% of the total workforce. As a share of total employment, 47% of jobs are in agriculture, 37% in services and the remaining 16% in industry.

The economy

In 1995, the industrial sector, which includes metals, iron and steel, chemicals, petroleum refining, electronics and electrical equipment, glass products, vehicles, as well as food, tobacco and textiles, accounted for 27% of GDP compared with 19% in 1980. The share of the agricultural sector to GDP during the same period was 13% in 1995, compared with 26% in 1980. The share of services has trended upwards gradually to stand at 60% of GDP last year. Turkey has a well-developed and increasingly diversified industrial sector. Manufacturing constitutes some 86% of industrial output, with areas of specialization, such as textiles, glass, iron, steel, chemicals and light consumer goods.

As for agriculture, Turkey is less efficient than other European countries, but the country is more or less self-sufficient in foodstuffs. In the services, the largest areas of growth have been in tourism, transport and, until 1993, construction.

Share of GDP by sector

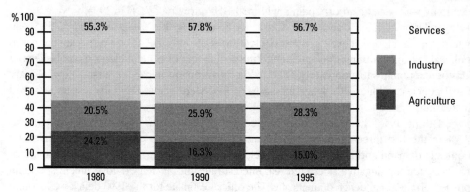

Source: Official data

Savings and investment

Net foreign direct investment has been stimulated in recent years by the move closer to a Customs Union agreement with the European Union. Net foreign direct investment inflows increased from US$18 million in 1980 to US$772 million in 1995.

Furthermore, various reforms, including the relaxation of rules concerning offshore borrowing by Turkish companies, more generous tax allowances for companies resident in Turkey and the reduction of state involvement in a number of areas have encouraged both private domestic and overseas investment. Investments in manufacturing account for two thirds of total direct investment.

Balance of payments

Turkey has a structural trade deficit. This relates to the fact that the Turkish economy is mainly driven by domestic demand, with exports of goods and services accounting for less than 25% of GDP. In recent years the strength of the domestic economy and the real appreciation of the exchange rate have encouraged high import growth, while export volume growth has remained subdued. The trade deficit rose to 8.0% of GDP in 1995.

Imports and exports as a % of GDP

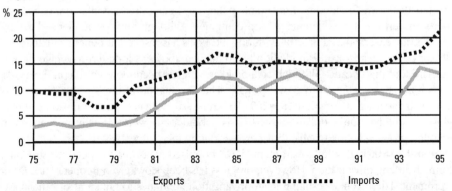

Source: Official data

Breakdown of exports (1995)

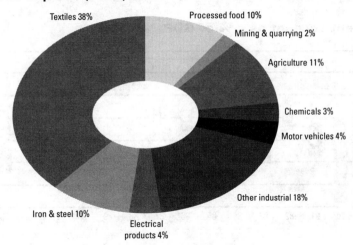

Source: Official data

Turkey continues to have many internationally competitive industries, however. These are primarily companies engaged in the export of textiles, iron and steel, chemicals, consumer durables and automotive parts. The largest export market for Turkish products is Germany. Although trade with Iraq has been suspended (it accounted for 10-15% of total exports), Turkish exports to other Middle Eastern countries have increased overall since 1990. The composition of Turkish exports, in line with the trend in total production, has shifted towards manufactured goods.

Current account deficits continue to be a feature of the Turkish economy. However, the deficit tends to be contained at 3% of GDP, as significant invisible surpluses relating to tourism revenues and workers' remittances partly offset the visible deficits. The current deficit is generally financed by foreign borrowing.

Economic policy

Since the 1980s, the broad aim of economic policy has been to reduce inflation, encourage exports and ensure that economic growth continues. Although inflation moderated during the 1980s, increased political instability during the 1990s has resulted in periods of expansive policies. Consequently, Turkish inflation has remained above its long-term average of 60% during most of this decade. Although economic growth has been more volatile in the 1990s, the economy has continued to grow strongly. The devaluation of the Turkish lira in 1994 and negative real wage growth during 1994-95 have ensured that Turkish companies remain highly competitive. On a dollar-adjusted basis, labour costs were virtually unchanged in 1995, after growing by an average 25% per year during the period 1989-91.

On the structural side, governments have promised measures to speed up structural reform, including privatization. However, progress has been slow, given frequent changes of government. The revenue resulting from privatization continues to fall short of official targets. In 1995, a total of US$576 million was raised against an initial target of US$5 billion. The issues of pensions, taxation and social security reform have been targeted by governments, but so far these structural reforms have also been very slow.

Current account as a % of GDP

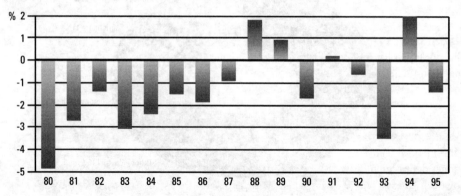

Source: Official data

Monetary policy

The financial difficulties encountered in early 1994, as a result of public sector deficits, together with the widening of the current account deficit, led the central bank to reconsider its monetary policy. Up until that point, the key objective was to limit the growth rate over the medium term of certain components of its balance sheet. The fall in foreign exchange reserves, together with a sharp rise in interest rates, forced the central bank to focus on rebuilding foreign exchange reserves and restoring stability to the financial markets. The fiscal measures in the austerity plan and the improvement in the treasury's domestic borrowing ability helped the central bank to control its balance sheet. Also, the central bank successfully controlled its net domestic assets during 1994. This involved the restriction of credits to the public and banking sector. Furthermore, the reserve requirement system for banks, which previously worked in favour of foreign currency holdings, was switched more in favour of Turkish lira deposits.

1995 was a more stable year for the economy and the financial markets. From the end of 1994, the central bank began pursuing an exchange rate policy to limit the monthly depreciation of a Turkish lira basket (US$1 and DM1.5) to the monthly change in the wholesale price index. Also, monetary policy was conducted under the eyes of an IMF stand-by agreement, with the republic adopting quarterly targets for net foreign exchange reserves, net domestic assets and exchange rates. One outcome of this policy was a rapid increase in foreign exchange reserves, followed by a surge in the money supply during the first three-quarters of 1995. With inflation substantially higher than targeted, the Turkish lira appreciated in real terms. Until end September, the IMF performance criteria were more or less achieved.

In October 1995, however, the economic picture began to change following the collapse of the government. Ahead of the December 24 general elections, fiscal policy was expanded and speculation over a currency devaluation forced the lira to weaken. After the elections, positive trends developed as interest rates fell and the speculation on the lira diminished. The central bank's monetary policy in 1996 focused on limiting the growth of reserve money. In addition, central bank advances to the treasury are being reduced steadily, from an original 15% of total budget appropriations to 3% in 1998. Exchange rate policy continues to focus on keeping the depreciation rate close to wholesale price inflation. In 1996, the wholesale price index (WPI) increased by 84.9%, the exchange rate basket by 72.1%, M1 by 99.3% and M2 by 117%.

Fiscal policy

The public sector in Turkey includes the central government, local government, financial and non-financial economic enterprises (SEEs), social security institutions and extra-budgetary funds. In the run-up to the 1994 financial crisis the budget rose progressively from 2.4% of GDP in 1986 to over 12% in 1993, despite several deficit reduction packages and robust economic growth. Over this period, the consolidated deficit (central government) rose from 2.7% to 6.7%.

In 1994, with various measures taken to improve revenues and reduce expenditure, the budget deficit fell to 8.1% at year-end, and the consolidated deficit dropped to 3.9%. In 1995, however, due to public sector salary increases and pre-election spending, as well as the growing burden of interest payments, the consolidated deficit rose to 4.1%. An improvement in the deficit relating to SEEs allowed the deficit to fall to 6.5%. The 1996 official budget target has been revised several times. The current target is for a consolidated deficit of TL1,300tr, close to 9.5% of GNP. The rise in the fiscal deficit has resulted from expansionary fiscal polices implemented since last October, in particular the government's granting civil servants real wage increases in July, while failing to implement permanent budget savings.

Currency

Turkey has an independent floating exchange rate. Daily rates for foreign exchange are announced at 15.00 on each business day by the central bank. Commercial banks are free to set their exchange rates according to market conditions. Turkey's exchange and trade systems have been liberalized extensively since the 1980s as a part of the economic reform process. Current exchange rate policy targets a monthly lira depreciation rate against the change in wholesale price index. However, during 1995 and 1996, the exchange rate has continued to appreciate in real terms after a fall of 45% during the first four months of 1994.

■ EQUITIES

Index performance (in local currency)

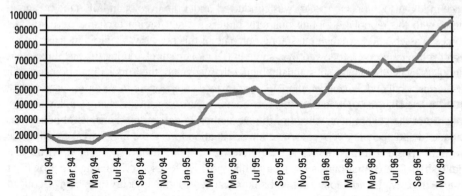

Key indicators

	Index performance %, in US$ terms	Market Cap. US$bn	P/E	Div. Yield	Weight in IFCI	Weight in IFCG
1994	-49.6	21.8	24.8	2.8	3.6	1.6
1995	-4.3	20.8	9.2	3.6	2.3	1.3
1996	29.5	30.0	12.2	2.9	2.4	1.5

Sources: Istanbul Stock Exchange, IFC, Bloomberg, Datastream, UBS

Background

Turkey's stock market is in Istanbul. There are 228 shares (222 companies) listed on the Stock Exchange (up from 176 in 1994) and market capitalization is approximately US$30 billion. Daily trading volume is around US$200 million.

Structure

The Istanbul Stock Exchange has an average free float of 20%, or approximately US$8 billion. Total foreign investment is reckoned to account for 40% of the free float. However, domestic trading accounts for about 90% of daily turnover, and foreign for less than 10%.

Regulatory authority

The Capital Markets Board (Sermaye Piyasasi Kurulu), an autonomous public body located in Ankara has broad control over most aspects of the Turkish capital markets. However, it is not wholly independent of government control, and nominally reports to a designated Minister of State.

The CMB is responsible for almost all capital market regulations and the statutes are purposely vague in order to allow this body to act quickly. Nevertheless, the Turkish legal system, long used to operating under the commercial code, is slow to adapt to the requirements of the relatively recent capital markets regulations.

Trading methods

All shares are traded via a screen-based system called ELIT. There is a continuous auction system. There are exceptions in the case of block trades or orders that involve more than a certain percentage of a company's capital. Only the 161 Turkey-based licensed intermediaries are allowed to use this system.

Hours

Trading hours are 10.00 to 12.00 and 14.00 to 16.00, Monday to Friday.

Limits on price movements

Share price movements are limited to 10% from the weighted average price of the previous session, though exemptions are granted, almost always only on the first day of trading.

Settlement time and clearing

Settlement is generally DVP, and occurs at T+2. There are severe penalties for defaults. The central custodian (Takasbank) has automated the settlement of trades, though these mimic physical movements.

Types of shares

All shares are common shares. While provisions exist for preference shares, there is currently none listed on the ISE. However, there are a few companies with multiple classes of common stock, sometimes with different dividend and voting entitlements. The most obvious example is T. Is Bankasi, with Founders, A, B and C shares.

While all Turkish investors are allowed to vote their shares, it is generally assumed that foreign investors may not unless they register their shareholdings with the Foreign Investment Directorate. This, however, brings upon an obligation to pay capital gains tax.

Stock indices

While foreign institutions have created their own indices, by far the most widely watched is the IMKB-100, which includes the hundred most liquid shares and, by extension, almost all the large companies.

It is a linear index weighted according to free float. However, inclusion is based on the share's liquidity. The index is rebased twice a year. There are two sub-indices: the IMKB Finansal and the IMKB Sinaí, which cover the financial and industrial components of the IMKB-100.

Taxes

Except when foreign investors wish to exercise voting rights, there are no capital gains taxes on investments by institutions, providing that at least 25% of the funds allocated to Turkey is invested in equities and the institution is a proper financial institution. Individuals do not normally pay capital gains tax. There are no withholding taxes.

Dividends

These are paid once a year, generally some time between March and September.

Disclosure of financial statements

Standards are improving. Companies are required to provide fully audited annual, semi-audited semi-annual and unaudited first and third quarter figures with accompanying notes. The information value of the notes may vary widely. There are moves to incorporate EU directives into Turkish regulations.

Ownership limits for non-residents

Non-residents may buy any or all of the free float available on the Istanbul Stock Exchange.

Capital and exchange controls

These were abolished in 1989.

Takeovers

There are no CMB decrees covering these. However, the low free float has meant that there have only been two cases of an unfriendly takeover.

Brokers

There are 161 licensed intermediaries (including most of the banks in Turkey). These range from full-service houses, with the relevant permits to engage in asset management/ research/underwriting, etc. to very small family boutiques.

Sectors

The main sector in the stock exchange is the financials. This covers the banks and holding companies and accounts for 35% of market capitalization. Other large sectors are the cement, consumer durables, oil and steel sectors.

■ DEBT

The impetus for the development of the bond market was the liberalization of the financial sector in the 1980s. In 1982, the Capital Market Board (Sermaye Piyasasi Kurulu) replaced the central bank and the treasury as the regulator of the government securities market.

The central bank and the undersecretariat of treasury supervise the operations of banks and the trading of securities. The capital markets law in the same year initiated a process of deregulation, and, since the early 1990s especially, capital markets have superseded the banking system as the main mechanism for fund allocation.

The bond market is dominated by government issues to finance its budget deficit, which effectively crowds out corporate borrowing. Domestic banks are captive buyers of treasury bills, having to hold bills valued at a fixed proportion of their deposit base.

Bonds are listed on the Bonds Exchange, which is part of the Istanbul Stock Exchange (IKMB).

Treasury Bills

Discounted bills with 1-, 3-, 6-, 9- and 12-month maturities are auctioned every Tuesday by the central bank – normally multiple price auctions. Banks that submit bids must pay a deposit of 1% of the amount bid. Direct sales not exceeding 25% of the total auctioned can be made by the central bank to participants in proportion to their bids, at the average auction price. The central bank requires a range of collateral from bidding institutions. Settlement is seven days later, T+1 for secondary trades.

Issuance expanded after 1984, and the regular weekly system of auctions began in the following year. T-bills are the only Turkish lire denominated debt security available to overseas investors.

Government bonds

Fixed, floating-rate and index-linked bonds are issued with maturities of 1 to 5 years. They are normally auctioned by the central bank as agent of the Treasury, although they can be sold direct to the public through commercial banks.

Secondary market activity in bills and bonds increased in the mid-1980s and was given a further boost when trading was integrated into the IKMB in 1991. A repo market has operated on the IKMB since 1993.

From November 1, 1996, 10% withholding tax was imposed on income from all new bills and bonds issued with a 1997 maturity date.

Eurobonds

The Republic of Turkey has raised money in the eurobond market in US dollars, yen, deutschmarks, ecu and GBP for several years. Other Turkish issuers include the Industrial Development Bank, Export Credit Bank and the City of Ankara.

Private debt

The corporate sector makes up less than 10% of Turkey's bond markets due to the overwhelming supply of government bills and bonds to finance its deficit. At the short-end, bank loans are usually a cheaper source of funding than commercial paper, but there is a small market in bank bills. Other instruments include Revenue Sharing Certificates and Privatization bonds. Asset-Based Securities have gained in popularity during the last four years.

■ TURKEY: Economic indicators

Population and development	1990	1991	1992	1993	1994	1995	1996e
Population, million	56.1	57.3	58.6	59.9	61.2	62.5	63.9
Population growth, %	2.2	2.1	2.3	2.2	2.2	2.1	2.2
Nominal GDP per capita, US$	2686	2636	2715	3012	2133	2644	2724

National accounts							
Nominal GDP, US$bn	150.7	151.0	159.1	180.4	130.5	165.2	174.0
Change in real GDP, %	9.3	0.9	6.0	8.0	-5.5	7.3	6.9
Gross fixed capital formation, % of GDP	24.3	23.5	22.7	24.3	24.2	25.4	25.3

Money supply and inflation							
Narrow money, change %, Dec/Dec	49.9	48.2	66.8	71.9	84.1	75.7	109.9
Broad money, change %, Dec/Dec	48.2	61.4	61.4	49.6	125.4	101.3	120.5
Consumer price inflation (avg.) %	59.3	66.0	70.1	66.1	106.2	89.0	80.4
Producer prices (avg.) %							

Interest rates *=latest figures							
Discount rate, end of year	45.00	45.00	45.00	50.00	50.00	55.00	50.00
Money market rate, annual average	38.70	58.00	57.60	52.90	61.80	83.70	78.00*
Treasury bill rate, annual average	50.90	69.40	72.80	66.50	101.40	133.60	118.00*
Deposit rate, annual average	47.60	62.90	67.80	64.60	87.80	76.10	92.90*

Government finance							
Government expenditure, % of GDP	17.1	20.7	20.3	24.5	24.3	22.5	29.4
Government balance, % of GDP	-7.5	-10.2	-10.7	-12.1	-7.9	-5.5	-9.5

Exchange rates lc=local currency							
Exchange rate, annual average, lc/US$	2609	4172	6872	10985	29609	45722	81995
Exchange rate, end of year, lc/US$	2930	5080	8564	14473	38726	59660	108450
Real exchange rate 1990=100	100.0	102.6	98.8	107.1	80.4	88.9	90.9

Balance of payments							
Exports of goods & services, US$m	21042	22039	24298	26263	29191	36581	41500
Change %	15.7	4.7	10.3	8.1	11.1	25.3	13.4
Imports of goods & services, US$m, fob	25652	24225	26706	33719	26388	40601	48900
Change %	38.9	-5.6	10.2	26.3	-21.7	53.9	20.4
Trade balance, of goods only, US$m, fob-fob	-9555	-7340	-8190	-14160	-4216	-13212	-19700
Current account balance, US$m	-2625	258	-943	-6380	2631	-2339	-7000
as a % of GDP	-1.7	0.2	-0.6	-3.5	2.0	-1.4	-4.0

Foreign exchange reserves							
Foreign exchange reserves, US$m	6050	5144	6159	6213	7112	12353	17874
Gold at ⅔ of market price, US$m	1052.7	1004.2	925.6	965.7	977.5	977.3	967.5
Import cover (reserves/imports), months	2.8	2.5	2.8	2.2	3.2	3.7	4.3

Foreign debt and debt service							
Short-term debt, US$m	9500	9117	12660	18533	11310	15701	20314
Total foreign debt, US$m	49035	50489	55592	67356	65601	73278	78500
as a % of GDP	32.5	33.4	34.9	37.3	50.3	44.3	45.1
as a % of foreign exchange receipts	185.1	179.6	189.2	215.9	197.6	172.6	161.3
Interest payments, US$m	3264	3430	3217	3461	3923	4303	4000
Principal repayments, US$m	3938	4592	4871	4412	6070	7594	7090
Total debt service, US$m	7202	8022	8088	7873	9993	11897	11090
as a % of goods exports	55.3	58.7	54.3	50.4	54.3	54.1	43.5
as a % of foreign exchange receipts	27.2	28.5	27.5	25.2	30.1	28.0	23.4

Ukraine

Area (thousands of km²):	6.4
Population (1995, millions):	51.6
Population projection (2025, millions):	53
Population younger than 15 yrs (1991, % of total):	21.2
Urbanization rate (1993, % of population):	69
Life expectancy (1993, years at birth):	69
Gross domestic product (1996, US$bn):	49.4
GDP per capita (1996, US$):	960
Average annual GDP growth rate (1990-96, %):	-15.2
Average annual inflation rate (1990-96, %):	1.8
Currency (hryvnia per US$, average 1996):	1.83
Real exchange rate: (1990=100, average 1996)	16
Structure of production (1995):	52% industry, 34% services, 13% agriculture
Main exports:	energy equipment, iron metal
Main imports:	oil, natural gas, metal, wood, metal goods
Main trading partners:	CIS, Germany, China, Czech Republic
Total foreign debt (% of GDP):	23.5
Next elections due under normal circumstances:	legislative required by March 1998 presidential scheduled June 1999
Credit rating: (Jan 1997, Standard & Poor's, Moody's)	not rated

FORECAST: 1997-2000 (average)

	Worst case	Most likely	Best case
Real GDP growth (%)	0	2.5	5
Inflation (%)	50	25	10

■ POLITICS

Historical overview

Ukraine has seen many changes and shifting borders since medieval times. Lands east of the Dnepr River were ceded to Russia in 1667 and the remainder were incorporated into the Russian Empire after the second partition of Poland in 1793.

Following the October Revolution in 1917, the Ukrainians established an independent republic. This independence was shortlived. In 1922 Communist Ukrainian delegates joined in the formation of the USSR. Between 1922 and 1939 Ukrainian nationalism was brutally suppressed by Moscow. Collectivization of agriculture and the expropriation of foodstuffs from the countryside resulted in a famine in 1932-33, killing millions of people. Following the Soviet seizure of eastern Poland in 1939, Polish Galicia became part of the Ukrainian SSR. After the German invasion in 1941, Ukrainian territory was under German control and retaken by Soviet forces in 1944. After the war, Ukrainian territory was increased by Transcarpathia, formerly under Czechoslovakian rule, and in 1954 Nikita Khrushchev gave the Crimean peninsula to Ukraine.

Ukraine declared independence on August 24, 1991 after the failed coup in Moscow and the subsequent split-up of the former Soviet Union. The Communist Party was banned and the inaugural presidential elections took place in December 1991. Former Communist official Leonid Kravchuk fought a nationalist campaign to take the presidency. Following elections, nationalist and Communist parliamentarians blocked most of the government's reform plans. With no clear political leadership Ukraine has lagged behind other Eastern European economies in the drive towards significant economic reform.

Recent events

In the 1994 presidential election, Leonid Kravchuk was replaced by former prime minister Leonid Kuchma, who took 52% of the votes. Kuchma's programme was vaguely pro-reform and opposed centralized control of the economy. Kuchma had little support from the opposition Left in parliament, which consolidated its position in the May 1994 elections (see table). Further elections in December 1995 called to fill seats left empty in the general elections did not change the political balance in the 450-seat assembly.

President Kuchma is supported by centrist and right-wing deputies who back his reforms. Left-wing opposition has hindered urgently needed legislative and economic reforms, including privatization. Many other important economic issues are unresolved. In the last three years, Ukraine has seen rocketing inflation, half-hearted reforms, painful economic decline and rising unemployment. A turning point could be in view, as signs of a reversal of the recent continuing decline emerge, and slow progress in reforms and privatization are made.

Chronology

1654	Treaty of Pereyaslav, a military and political alliance signed between Ukraine and Russia, concerning the status of Ukraine under the protection of the Russian state
1905-06	First revolution in Russia. Ukrainians are permitted to form organizations, and the ban on the Ukrainian language is abolished.
1917	The fall of the Russian monarchy and the creation of the Central Rada
1918	Declaration of independence of the Ukrainian National Republic
1919	Soviet Ukrainian government formed by the Bolsheviks
1921	Soviet rule consolidating in Ukraine
1922	The formation of the USSR, including the Ukrainian SSR
1941-44	German occupation
1945	Ukraine becomes a founding nation of the UN
1954	Crimean peninsula is added to Ukraine from Russia
1990	Declaration of the Supreme Rada of Ukraine proclaims the state sovereignty of Ukraine
1991	The Supreme Rada adopts the Act proclaiming the state independence of Ukraine
1996	New constitution

Constitution and government

The Ukrainian parliament adopted its first post-Soviet constitution in June 1996 only after the president challenged the parliament and called for a national referendum. The new constitution provides broader powers for the president and a unicameral parliament. It has not finally settled the question of land ownership (state, private or collective). The constitution states that the Crimea is an integral part of Ukraine but has the status of an autonomous republic. The Autonomous Republic of Crimea has its own government, appointed and dismissed by the Crimean Parliament, but with the Ukrainian president's consent.

The constitution states that the president is elected by direct voting for five years and for not more than two terms. The president has the right to veto laws adopted by the parliament and appoints the prime minister with the parliament's consent. The president is also the supreme commander-in-chief of all military forces. The parliament (Supreme Rada) has one chamber consisting of 450 deputies selected by direct voting for four years.

The parliament is the legislative body that adopts laws, approves and controls the budget and ratifies international agreements. The cabinet of ministers has to be approved by parliament and is subordinate to the president. It resigns if a new president is empowered.

Current government

Head of state	President (sworn in 19 July, 1994) Leonid Kuchma
Head of government	Prime Minister (re-appointed 10 July, 1996) Pavlo Lazaren

Ministers:

Defence	Lt-Gen. Olexander Kuzmuk
Economics	Vasyl Hureyev
Finance	Valentyn Koronevsky
Foreign Affairs	Hennady Udovenko
Foreign Trade	Serhy Osyka
Industry	Valery Mazur
Interior	Yuri Kravchenko

Governor, central bank	Viktor Yushchenko

Political parties

A variety of parties has appeared on the political scene since independence. Over thirty can be counted easily, but only about half of them are present in the parliament. In addition, many members call themselves "independent" and vary in their political orientation. The major political parties are:

Communist Party
    Banned in 1991, but revived in 1993
Socialist Party
    The official successor to the former Communist Party

Agrarian Party

Also known as Peasant Party. The party is the rural counterpart of the Socialist Party.

Rukh

Also called People's Movement of Ukraine. The Rukh was originally (since 1988) the main democratic opposition movement.

Composition of parliament (May 94 election and later additions)

	Political orientation	No. of seats	% of seats
Communist Party		91	
Socialist Party	Left	30	43%
Agrarian Party		52	
Reform Bloc		31	
Inter-regional Bloc for Reforms	Support reform	34	34%
Centre Bloc		37	
Yednist		34	
Derzhavnist Party	Nationalists	30	14%
Rukh		27	
Independents		34	9%

Central bank

The central bank, the National Bank of the Ukraine (NBU), is a government body. It controls the money supply, the depository of government securities, the registering of banks, and, among other major functions of a central bank, fixing the exchange rate and transferring funds from and into foreign currencies. The constitution states that keeping the stability of the currency is the main function of the central bank. The chairman is appointed by parliament upon the proposal of the president of the Ukraine. The Council of the bank is appointed half by parliament and half by the president. The NBU has repeatedly stated it plans to liberalize hryvnia convertibility rules but has not fixed any schedule for action.

■ ECONOMICS

Historical overview

Prior to the 1917 October Revolution, Ukraine was known as Europe's granary. Its rich farm land accounted for around one quarter of Soviet grain production and provided the Union republics with meat and dairy products, as well as sugarbeets. After the Second World War, the sovietized economy invested in heavy industries and agriculture. The newly independent republic inherited these large metallurgical, machine-building, mining and steelmaking industries in 1991. Built up without competitive forces, with cheap energy costs and full employment, heavy industry has since been a key focus of reforms and restructuring. Change will necessitate painful cuts and the closing of obsolete plants.

Recent developments

Following independence, the Ukrainian economy fell into deep recession. Efforts over the first five years to create a market-orientated economy were painful. Strong political opposition to necessary reforms has created a climate resistant to change. Programmes with substantial social costs have faced opposition from parliament. In 1994 real GDP growth fell by a record pace of 23% and by a further 11.8% in 1995. Most economic fundamentals have showed signs of improvement or a slower rate of deterioration – since 1994. GDP was estimated to have declined by 5% in 1996. Industrial output fell faster than overall GDP in 1994 and 1995, reflecting the slow and inflexible process of transformation compared with the rest of the economy. The first three quarters of 1995 showed an improvement compared to 1994. While the annual rate of decline in each quarter of 1994 ranged from 20% to 36%, the range in 1995 was 10% to 17%. The slower low end rates of decline in 1995 are a positive sign when the average declines of earlier years are considered.

Inflation in Ukraine slowed from staggering levels in 1993-94 to a still astronomical 377% in 1995. Inflation remains high and was well above the 1-2% monthly inflation rate the IMF stand-by agreement called for by the end of 1995. Estimates put average inflation for 1996 at 90%, suggesting this target is still unrealistic.

Unemployment is higher than suggested by the official data. Usually, when an employer wants to shed staff, employees are placed on unpaid leave or part-time status. These arrangements allow workers to continue to receive social benefits and businesses to retain flexibility. Privatization and restructuring will certainly generate jobs in the long term while closing unprofitable heavy industry plants will add to short-term unemployment. Lack of cash flow forced many state enterprises to withhold salary payments. Often workers have had to wait months to receive their pay and benefits. The resulting strikes reflect these local difficulties rather than widespread social unrest.

The economy

There is a lack of accurate economic statistics. Estimates show that industry accounts for 34%, agriculture and forestry for 13% and services (including others) for 52%. Due to the transition to a market-orientated economy, further changes in the economic structure can be expected. The service and industrial sector will grow significantly in the near future. Agricultural output will certainly increase productivity, but will be of less importance for the overall economy.

Share of GDP by sector

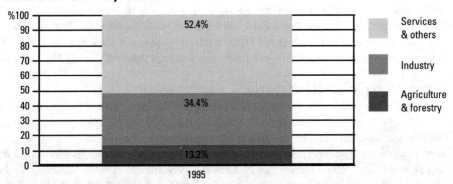

Source: Official data

Trade

Ukraine's main trading partners are still the republics of the former Soviet Union. The republics belonging to the Commonwealth of Independent States (CIS) account for 57% of Ukrainian exports and supply 65% of imports. The Ukraine is heavily dependent on Russia's oil and gas deliveries, leading to regular payment disputes, while the CIS imports Ukrainian agricultural and industrial products. The CIS trade balance has been negative over the last couple of years, while trade with other countries, mainly Germany, has a positive balance. This will continue while Ukraine remains dependent on Russian energy. The trade surplus with the West is effectively used to finance part of the trade deficit with the CIS. Nearly half of CIS trade is based on barter, but Ukraine still does not have enough cash to pay for net imports. Huge arrears on energy payments have accumulated in the last two years.

Breakdown of exports (1995)

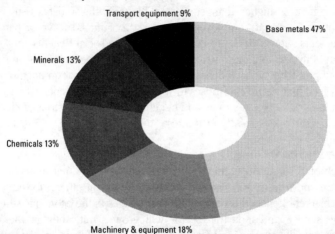

Source: Official data

At the end of 1994 arrears of US$1.4 billion were converted into long-term debt. Partial settlement of principal and interest arrears is planned through the IMF Systematic Transformation Facility and World Bank rehabilitation loans. Because Ukraine is unlikely to meet all the stringent IMF budget and fiscal targets, it is likely that some funds available from the assistance programmes will be not paid out, or at least delayed.

Economic policy

Economic decline and slow progress in structural reform have made it difficult to estimate the state's budget. On the income side, Ukraine's budgeted figures are not very accurate. A lax payment discipline by households and enterprises, missing international loans and the slow pace of privatization generating receipts far below expectations, have led to shortfalls in necessary and planned revenues in the past. Government deficits have usually been almost twice the planned level. Nevertheless, the 1995 deficit (5.2% of GDP) is well down from 1992 (13.8%) and 1994 (9.4%). For 1996 we estimate a budget deficit of 6.1% of GDP.

Despite the improvement, the current deficit remains larger than the 5% target level normally stipulated by the IMF.

Monetary policy was tightened in October 1994, to achieve only minimal credit growth in that year. The central bank increased refinance rates, ceased giving direct credits to enterprises, and removed ceilings on bank interest rates, all of which helped to stabilize 1995 monetary growth (which was much lower than 1994). Further stabilization depends very much on budget discipline.

Current account as a % of GDP

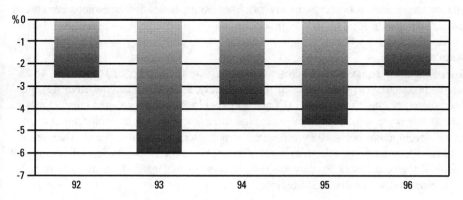

Source: Official data; UBS estimates

Ukraine's administered exchange rate system was eliminated in October 1994. Most trade-related transactions have been convertible since then, and the currency is traded on an interbank exchange market. The new currency, the hryvna, was introduced in September 1996; replacing the karbovanet by knocking off five zeroes. The currency exchange rate is controlled by the central bank and, so far, the new currency cannot be freely transferred into foreign currency.

Debt

Discrepancies between various official documents, mainly in the recording of old obligations to former Soviet republics, make the real amount of debt accumulated in Ukraine difficult to estimate. We estimate total foreign debt was US$8.9 billion at the end of 1995 and will increase to US$11.3 billion in 1996, two-thirds of which will be denominated in US$. Of this US$4.4 billion will be owed to international financial institutions, and US$6.8 billion to official bilateral creditors. Absence of required economic reforms, led the IMF to withhold the third and fourth tranche of a US$867 million stand-by facility for almost one year until it was finally released in May 1996.

Privatization

Hindered by parliament and local administrative officials, the mid-1996 scheduled sale of over 20,000 enterprises (from a total of over 115,000) was not fulfilled. A new plan aims to sell at least 70% of the shares in a total of 5,000 medium and large enterprises, as well as most of the small companies. To improve the process of privatization, preparation procedures are to be streamlined, new privatization certificates circulated to boost demand at auctions, and official intervention to set auction prices abandoned.

■ EQUITIES

Background

Ukraine, one of the younger emerging markets, introduced a new currency in September 1996, switching from coupons to the hryvnia. The country is developing rapidly, introducing new legislation almost on a monthly basis.

Structure

Most of Ukraine's equity trading takes place on the over-the-counter (OTC) market. An estimated 1,000 shares circulate on this market. Recently, a fully automated system was introduced, based on the Russian PORTAL trading system in Russia. There are 46 market-makers and 100 shares are registered. Ukraine also has three stock exchanges, which are in need of further development before they can attract major international investment. They are the Ukrainian Stock Exchange, the Kiev Stock Exchange and the Donetsky Stock Exchange, of which the Ukrainian Stock Exchange is estimated to be the largest. Total market capitalization is estimated at less than US$1 billion.

Regulatory authority

The Ukrainian Stock Exchange Commission was set up in 1995 by presidential decree, but the commission has hardly any power, which is seen as one of this market's main problems in attracting foreign investment. The USEC regulates the market under the guidance of two laws which frequently contradict each other: 'On Business Partnerships' and 'On Securities and the Stock Exchange'.

Trading methods

Apart from the prices on the new OTC trading system, buyers have to hunt around for stock prices. Settlement takes between fifteen and thirty days. Ukraine does not have a central depository. If a company has more than five hundred shareholders, it is obliged to set up an independent registry company. Western custodians do not operate in Ukraine, because title and ownership of stocks is not guaranteed. Foreign investors mainly buy privatization vouchers, or directly into companies.

Privatization

The choice of shares is improving as a mass privatization programme is currently taking off, having fallen short of its targets for the last few years. According to government figures, eight thousand companies of small and medium sizes have been privatized.

Shareholders' rights

Minority shareholders' rights are poorly protected in Ukraine. Unless a shareholder owns more than 25% of all of a company's shares, they cannot veto changes to a company charter or prevent dilution of their investment. The timing of transfer of ownership rights is not clearly spelt out and there are no strict disclosure rules.

■ DEBT

The National Bank of Ukraine is the main source of finance for the government budget deficit, but the development of a domestic bond market is a key element of the government's strategy to create an independent, non-inflationary source of funding. Ukraine's debt programme began in March 1995. It was based on three cabinet resolutions providing for KBV1 trillion (US$5.6 million) of 12-month notes paying 140% and two tranches paying 90%, in addition to 3-, 6- and 9-month bills, for a total of KBV30 trillion (US$170 million) (the hryvnia replaced an interim currency, the karbovanets, in 1996). The first auction was held in June 1995. These first instruments were interest-bearing; since May 1996 they have been replaced by discount bills.

Licensed banks traded and held bills on behalf of clients until the changes introduced in 1996. Individuals can bid at auctions, and as of January 1997, foreigners are permitted to open accounts in local currency at licensed banks for direct trading in government securities. However, there are no specific restrictions against foreign investment anyway, which makes up about 10% of the market.

Treasury bills and bonds

Discount treasury bills, with maturities of 91, 182, 273 and 364 days, are auctioned every Tuesday – the terms are generally announced 2 days earlier. Bids are made through a domestic bank before 10.00; settlement takes place the next day. Bids can be competitive (US treasury-style) or non-competitive; the NBU is considering putting limits on the size of institutional bids at a single price.

Most bills are bought by domestic banks and held to maturity, partly because of unclear tax legislation. Capital gains tax of 30% may be imposed, whether a price rise is due to a fall in yields or a natural accretion to par.

In 1995, all trading was conducted over-the-counter, but there was no standard method of registration within the NBU central depository to confirm transfer of ownership rights. Trades were therefore conducted on a sale-repo basis.

From the beginning of 1996, electronic screen-based trading at the Ukrainian Interbank Currency Exchange (UICE) started, with sessions held each Thursday. Orders submitted via the NBU's electronic mail system are matched by the UICE, and are settled the following day. OTC trading was banned to improve market transparency. The ban has subsequently been lifted to increase trading volumes. All trades are settled through the Exchange, either on the same or the next day.

Securities are in dematerialized form and registered at NBU and commercial bank depositories.

Municipal bills

The City of Kharkiv issued 12-month bills in 1995, and others – Kiev and Dnipropetrovsk, for example – plan to issue municipal bills. Investors are provided with the security of a charge against the city's assets.

■ UKRAINE: Economic indicators

Population and development	1990	1991	1992	1993	1994	1995	1996e
Population, million	51.8	51.9	52.1	51.6	51.3	51.4	51.6
Population growth, %	—	0.2	0.2	-0.9	-0.5	0.2	0.3
Nominal GDP per capita, US$	1819	3264	354	605	699	646	934

National accounts							
Nominal GDP, US$bn	94.3	169.5	18.5	31.2	35.9	33.2	48.1
Change in real GDP, %	—	-12.1	-16.6	-17.4	-23.0	-11.8	-5.0

Money supply and inflation							
Narrow money, change %, Dec/Dec	—	—	—	1551.7	444.0	151.7	—
Broad money, change %, Dec/Dec	—	—	—	1810.3	568.0	115.0	—
Consumer price inflation (avg.) %	23.0	91.2	1210.0	4735.0	1805.3	377.0	90.0

Government finance							
Government expenditure, % of GDP	—	50.8	59.2	56.9	54.3	45.9	50.0
Government balance, % of GDP	—	-8.2	-13.8	-5.1	-9.4	-5.2	-6.1

Exchange rates *lc=local currency*							
Exchange rate, annual average, lc/US$	1.75	1.74	275	4533	31727	153445	1.80
Exchange rate, end of year, lc/US$	1.67	1.67	749	30947	111500	178653	1.95

Balance of payments							
Exports of goods & services, US$m	—	—	11350	15861	14448	15170	17490
Change %	—	—	—	39.7	-8.9	5.0	15.3
Imports of goods & services, US$m, fob	—	—	11961	16755	15750	16030	20690
Change %	—	—	—	40.1	-6.0	1.8	29.1
Trade balance, of goods only, US$m, fob-fob	—	—	-630	-2519	-2367	-1990	-4400
Current account balance, US$m	—	—	-557	-842	-1163	-1152	-1400
as a % of GDP	—	—	-3.0	-2.7	-3.2	-3.5	-2.9

Foreign exchange reserves							
Foreign exchange reserves, US$m	—	482	578	675	1000	1500	2500
Gold at ⅔ of market price, US$m	—	—	0.1	2.8	9.2	12.0	12.1
Import cover (reserves/imports), months	—	—	0.6	0.5	0.8	1.1	1.4

Foreign debt and debt service							
Short- term debt, US$m	—	—	2911	1342	2211	729	728
Total foreign debt, US$m	—	—	3377	5023	7574	8980	11310
as a % of GDP	—	—	18.3	16.1	21.1	27.0	23.5
as a % of foreign exchange receipts	—	—	29.8	31.5	51.7	58.4	63.9
Interest payments, US$m	—	—	—	54	270	630	780
Principal repayments, US$m	—	—	—	148	215	520	705
Total debt service, US$m	—	—	—	202	485	1150	1485
as a % of goods exports	—	—	—	1.6	4.1	9.3	10.2
as a % of foreign exchange receipts	—	—	—	1.3	3.3	7.5	8.4

Uzbekistan

Area (thousands of km²):	447
Population (1995, millions):	22.6
Population projection (2025, millions):	39
Population younger than 15 yrs (1991, % of total):	41.6
Urbanization rate (1993, % of population):	41
Life expectancy (1993, years at birth):	69
Gross domestic product (1996, US$bn):	20.9
GDP per capita (1996, US$):	914
Average annual GDP growth rate (1990-96, %):	-2.5
Average annual inflation rate (1990-96, %):	490.4
Currency (sum per US$, average 1996):	54
Structure of production (1994):	38.1% services, 32% agriculture, 29.9% industry & construction
Main exports:	cotton, natural gas
Main imports:	oil, metals, natural gas
Main trading partners:	Russia, Kazakstan, Switzerland
Total foreign debt (% of GDP):	10
Next elections due under normal circumstances:	2000
Credit rating: (Jan 1997, Standard & Poor's, Moody's)	not rated

FORECAST: 1997-2000 (average)

	Worst case	Most likely	Best case
Real GDP growth (%)	1.5	3.5	6
Inflation (%)	50	20	10

■ POLITICS

Historical overview

Uzbeks are descendants of the Central Asian Turks and Persians, and their language belongs to the Eastern Turkic family of languages. The area that is today's Uzbekistan was the cradle of Central Asian civilization from the 9th to the 10th century – Bukhara was a main scholastic centre, where Ibn-Sina (Avicenna) once lived. There then followed the Mongol-Tatars invasion, which lasted until the 14th century; Timurlane's vast Central Asian empire, stretched from Northern India to Syria. After the collapse of the empire, Uzbek groups established three khanates, in Bukhara, Khiva, and Kokand, but these fell to Tsarist Russia in 1868 and 1873.

Soviet power was established in Tashkent in 1918. The khanates of Khiva and Bukhara retained nominal independence until 1924, when they were incorporated into Turkestan. After the delimitation of the region in 1924–25, the Uzbek Soviet Socialist Republic (SSR) included the Tajik Autonomous SSR (ASSR). The Tajik ASSR was separated in 1929, and the

Karakalpak ASSR was added to the Uzbek SSR in 1936. The Central Asian borders were determined in 1936 under largely political considerations rather than on ethnic or geographic lines. They have changed little since then, and became international borders in 1991, after the collapse of the Soviet Union.

Uzbek leader Rashidov remained in power as the First Secretary of the Communist Party of Uzbekistan from 1961 to 1983. During this time, Uzbekistan served as the main cotton supplier to the Soviet Union. When Mikhail Gorbachev started his anti-corruption drive, he challenged Rashidov and many other Uzbek government officials on the grounds that the cotton production and delivery figures claimed by the Uzbek authorities were falsified. This led to increased ethnic tensions and nationalistic feeling among Uzbeks. Islam Karimov emerged as the next powerful statesman in Uzbekistan, first as the secretary of the CPU, and currently as the president of the Republic.

Uzbekistan declared independence on August 31, 1991, joined the CIS in December 1991, and promoted closer regional economic ties between the Central Asian republics, while taking a stance against Islamic fundamentalist formations in the region. Uzbekistan has the largest population in the region (nearly 23 million), is ethnically the most homogenous of the Central Asian republics, and has minorities living in neighbouring countries; it is likely to become a main regional power, economically and politically. So far, the country is politically stable, with President Karimov in power, constitutionally, at least until the year 2000.

Chronology

1865-1881	Russia completes its takeover of Central Asia and names the region Turkestan
1917	November: Bolsheviks take over in Tashkent
1918	April: Turkestan Autonomous Soviet Socialist Republic (ASSR) is formed in Tashkent
1924	October: Uzbek SSR (including Tajik ASSR) is formed as a result of national delimitation of Turkestan
1956	October: Nuritdin Mukhitdinov, First Secretary of the Communist Party of Uzbekistan (CPU), urges party delegates to develop national culture
1959	Sharaf Rashidov becomes the First Secretary of the CPU
1969	May: Anti-Russian demonstrations in Tashkent
1983	October: Inamjan becomes the First Secretary of the CPU, following Rashidov's death
1988	January: Rafiq Nishanov replaces Usmankhojayev as the First Secretary of the CPU
1989	May: the Birlik (Unity) popular front is formed in Tashkent
1989	June/July: clashes between Uzbeks and Meskhetian Turks in Fergana valley. Islam Karimov replaces Nishanov as the First Secretary of the CPU.
1990	March: elections for the 500-seat Supreme Soviet in Uzbekistan. Communists win 90% of the seats.
1990	April: Democratic Party of Erk is formed
1990	June: Kyrgyz-Uzbek clashes in Osh: 300 dead. Islamic Republican Party is established. Uzbek Supreme Soviet declares Uzbek as the official language to be adopted in 7 years.
1990	October: Uzbek Supreme Soviet declares the superiority of Uzbek laws over Soviet laws
1990	After an amendment in the Uzbek constitution, Islam Karimov is elected as the executive president
1991	August: Uzbek Supreme Soviet declares independence. Republic of Uzbekistan is founded.

1991	September: following its dissolution, the CPU re-emerges as the People's Democratic Party, led by Karimov
1991	December: Uzbekistan joins the CIS
1991	December 29: presidential polls in Uzbekistan. Islam Karimov wins 86% of the vote. His rival Muhammed Saloh gets 13%.
1992	June: Uzbekistan and Russia sign a treaty of political, economic, and cultural co-operation
1994	December 25: parliamentary elections. The Supreme Soviet was replaced with the Oliy Majlis.
1995	March 26: Karimov extends his presidency until the year 2000 in a national referendum
1996	June: Partnership and Co-operation Agreement between Uzbekistan and the European Union is signed

Constitution and government

Under the current Uzbek constitution adopted in December 1992, Uzbekistan is a pluralist democracy. The political system consists of the president, the parliament, and the local authorities. The first presidential elections were held on December 29, 1991, when Islam Karimov received 80% of the vote. In a nationwide referendum on March 26, 1995, Karimov obtained 99% of the vote and extended his presidency until the year 2000. He stresses that political stability during a period of transition and economic reforms is more important than establishing a true pluralist democracy.

The current parliament, Oliy Majlis (Supreme Assembly), comprises 250 seats, and replaces the earlier parliament, the 500-seat Supreme Soviet, which continued until December 1994. The local administrations are headed by governors appointed by the president. The governors are directly responsible to the president.

Current government

President	Islam Karimov
Prime Minister	Utkur Sultanov
Deputy Prime Minister	Viktor Chzhen (also Chairman of State Property Committee)
Foreign Minister	Abdulaziz Komilov
Foreign Trade	Tahir Ghafuriovich Rakhimov
Chairman, Uzbek State Bank	Faizullah Mullazhanov

Political parties
People's Democracy Party
   Led by President Islam Karimov

Pro-government parties
Social Democratic Party, Adolat (Justice) Party, and Vatan Taraqqieti (Fatherland Progressive)

Opposition parties
Erk (Freedom), **Birlik** (Unity), **People's Movement** (BPM), and the **Islamic Renaissance Party** (IRP).

ECONOMICS

Historical overview

Uzbekistan is the most populous of the Central Asian states, with nearly 23 million inhabitants. The country has an educated labour force, and transport facilities and infrastructure are relatively good. Uzbekistan's population is 61% rural, and agriculture, with its related industries, makes up nearly half of the GDP. The private sector's share is estimated to be 25-30%. Uzbekistan is the world's fifth largest cotton producer and second largest exporter. Cotton production accounts for nearly 40% of agricultural production and 75% of exports. Dependence on a single main export is a weakness of the economy. In 1996, for example, it is reported that late planting and harvesting, disruptive weather conditions, and pest infestations will have led to a smaller cotton output than was expected.

Share of GDP by sector

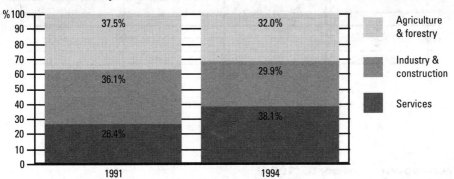

Source: Official data

Uzbekistan also has significant natural resources. Natural gas reserves amount to 1,883 billion cubic metres and oil reserves are estimated to be about 244 million tonnes. In addition, Uzbekistan has the world's fourth largest gold deposits. Its earth also contains rich copper, uranium, wolframite, tungsten, zinc, lead, and silver deposits.

A number of additional factors add to the attractiveness of Uzbekistan for foreign investors. There is a liberal approach to foreign businesses, with foreign joint-ventures in non-mining sectors such as electrical and electronic equipment, manufacture of trucks, agricultural machinery, textiles, consumer goods, and food processing. Uzbekistan's importance in maintaining stability is crucial.

Foreign trade

Cotton exports provide about 75% of Uzbekistan's hard currency earnings. Due to the high price of cotton in world markets, this ratio exceeded 80% in 1995. However, high world prices for cotton, which Uzbekistan enjoyed in 1995, are likely to ease, putting pressure on export earnings. The current account is likely to deteriorate in the medium term with foreign trade liberalization and infrastructure improvement sucking in more capital goods imports.

The most recent detailed breakdown of Uzbekistan's foreign trade shows that in 1994 about two thirds of Uzbekistan exports are to CIS countries, with the latter accounting for about 55% for imports. Among non-CIS countries for exports, Switzerland accounts for 22.3%, the UK 17.4%, the Netherlands 15.2% and China 7.7%. Switzerland (28.5%), Germany (14.6%), US (8.4%), and China (7.8%) are the leading exporters to Uzbekistan. Among CIS countries, the main trading partner is Russia, absorbing about 43% of Uzbekistan's exports and 55% of imports.

Imports and exports as a % of GDP

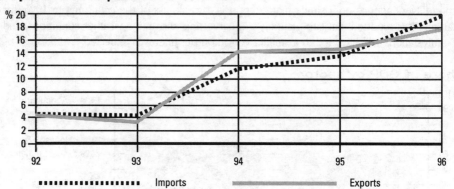

Source: Official data

Breakdown of exports (1994)

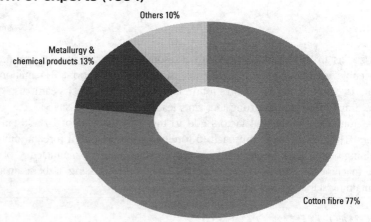

Source: Official data

Current account as a % of GDP, 1992–96

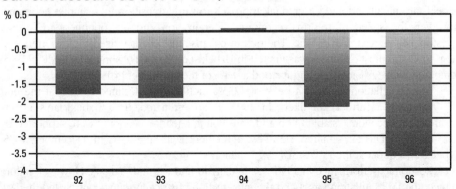

Source: Official data; UBS estimates

Labour market and employment

Uzbekistan has a young population, with an average age of 24. Thus, out of more than 22 million inhabitants in 1994, those of working age (15–65) represent less than half of the population. The table below provides employment market statistics (1994) in Uzbekistan by type and sector of employment.

Employment statistics, in thousands (1994)

Total employment	**8,235**
By type of employment	State sector employees: 4,168
	Collective farm workers: 1,623
	Private subsidy agricultural workers: 1,451
	Leased enterprise employees: 156
	Joint-stock company employees: 105
	Self-employed: 125
	Other: 607
By sector – material sphere	**6,332**
	Agriculture and forestry: 3,754
	Industry and construction: 1,775
	Other: 803
	Retail trade and catering: 501
By sector – non-material sphere	**1,903**
	Culture and art: 990
	Health care, social security, etc.: 480
	Public utilities and personal services: 164
	General administration and defence: 90
	Science and Scientific research: 29

Source: The World Bank, Statistical Handbook 1995:

States of the Former USSR

Economic reform

Uzbekistan initially adopted a gradual approach towards transition to a market economy. However, the speed of reforms, economic liberalization and the openness to foreign investors has increased over time. The output collapse that characterized the experience of the post-Communist countries was limited in Uzbekistan. Real GDP shrank by 1.5% in 1995, compared with 3.5% in 1994, and it stood at 84% of the 1991 level in 1995.

Annual inflation reached a peak of 1233% in 1994, but declined to 78% at the end of 1995, with a further fall likely in 1996 to an estimated 30%. Uzbekistan's efforts towards macroeconomic stabilization and transition to a market economy were supported by a 15-month, SDR124.7 million stand-by agreement with the IMF in December 1995. Uzbekistan's quota at the IMF is SDR199.5 million.

Economic performance in 1996 was initially in line with IMF targets. However, failure to meet the IMF's inflation target and the introduction of strict currency controls led the IMF to suspend the stand-by agreement.

Recent developments

Official figures show that real GDP grew by 1.4% year-on-year in the first half of 1996. Real economic growth is expected to resume in 1997, after stabilization in 1996. The fiscal outlook should also improve, with an estimated budget deficit of 3.5% of GDP for 1996.

The achievements in the fiscal area are remarkable, considering that about 43% of Uzbekistan's 1991 budget revenues came from central transfers and subsidies from Moscow.

While the internal balance will improve, the external balance is likely to deteriorate. This is normal in a transition economy, investing in infrastructure and building up capacity while registering its first year of real economic growth.

In the short term, dependence on a few export items, such as cotton and natural gas, will remain as a weakness, but this dependence is likely to be reduced with the changing structure of production.

Currency

The Uzbek currency, the sum, was introduced in June 1994 at the initial rate of UZS11/US$. The currency was required to be the medium of exchange for all domestic payments in October 1994. Its value is determined in a twice-weekly auction. On other days, the weighted average of the exchange rates at the daily interbank foreign currency market is used. The international cross-rates determine the value of the sum against the currencies not traded in the interbank market.

The Uzbek central bank, the Ministry of Finance and the State Tax Committee have the authority to control foreign exchange transactions. As of April 1996, Uzbekistan maintained bilateral payments agreements with Armenia, Belorus, China, Estonia, India, Indonesia, Islamic Republic of Iran, Kazakstan, Kyrgyz Republic, Latvia, Lithuania, Malaysia, Moldova, Russia, Tajikistan, Turkmenistan, and Ukraine.

The performance of the sum mainly reflected an overvaluation since its introduction. It declined to 25 against the US$ at the end of 1994, reflecting this overvaluation. The sum further depreciated by 43% in 1995, but the year-end inflation figure was 78%. The currency was informally pegged to the US dollar in 1996, to achieve price stability. However, the sum continues to appreciate in real terms, which leads to distortions in the economy.

The difference between the central bank rate and the informal market rate exceeded 40% in 1996. Lengthy delays were also reported by companies applying for foreign exchange, signalling a coming currency crash, especially after the black market premium exceeded 70% in September/October 1996. Furthermore, the Uzbek government introduced strict currency controls in late October (with further tightening in November) in response to a rising trade deficit, triggering the crash. The sum fell from 43.5 per US$ at the end of October to 53 in late November on the Uzbek interbank currency exchange, while the bazaar (black market) rate dived to 130. In early 1997, however, the sum appeared to stabilize around 61 per US$ and the black market premium declined to around 60%.

Uzbek sum/US dollar exchange rate

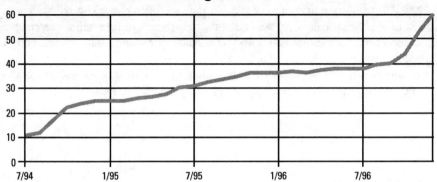

■ EQUITIES

Structure
The Republican Stock Exchange (RSE) and the National Share Depository were established in 1994 on the back of the privatization programme, which is currently taking place under the State Privatization Committee. Five thousand enterprises, of which one thousand are medium and large scale companies, are scheduled to be privatized. Activity in the equity market, however, is extremely illiquid. Given the embryonic phase of the market, new offerings are likely to be the only opportunities to invest in equity as investors are holding on to stocks bought into the existing 570 stocks listed on the RSE. A draft law under way in the last quarter of 1996 aims to encourage increased foreign investment in the secondary market over 1997.

Regulatory authority
Commission on Securities and Stock Exchanges regulates initial offerings and trading.

Ownership limits for non-residents
There are no limits on foreign ownership and investors can own up to 100% stakes in any company, as has often been the case in the newly privatized enterprises.

Capital and foreign exchange controls

Foreign investors are allowed to repatriate 100% of all earnings. However, convertibility of the sum, the official currency introduced in mid-1994, remains a major problem for foreign investors.

Brokers

There is a limited number of Uzbek brokers, and new legislation in October 1996 has given the central government stringent control over licensing dealers.

■ DEBT

The central bank as fiscal agent for the Ministry of Finance began issuing treasury bills in March 1996. Bills with initial maturities of 89 to 91 days are offered in competitive auctions every week to registered dealers. By the end of the year there had been ten issues created through consolidation of existing issues and refinancing of maturing bills. By the end of 1996 Uzbekistan had not yet issued a Eurobond.

Plans are in progress to introduce daily trading of bills, to increase the range and tenure of debt instruments and to permit foreign participation in auctions.

■ UZBEKISTAN: Economic indicators

Population and development	1990	1991	1992	1993	1994	1995	1996e
Population, million	20.2	20.6	21.1	21.6	22.1	22.6	23.1
Population growth, %	1.9	1.9	2.4	2.3	2.3	2.3	2.2
Nominal GDP per capita, US$	—	—	967	990	974	952	914

National accounts							
Nominal GDP, US$bn	—	—	20.6	21.8	21.5	21.4	20.9
Change in real GDP, %	1.6	-0.5	-11.1	-2.4	-3.5	-1.2	0.0

Money supply and inflation							
Broad money, change %, Dec/Dec	—	133.0	470.0	785.0	482.0	—	—
Consumer price inflation (Dec/Dec.) %	3.9	111.1	818.7	1014.5	746.0	78.0	60.0

Government finance							
Government expenditure, % of GDP	—	52.7	43.0	61.0	45.0	51.0	50.0
Government balance, % of GDP	—	-4.1	-12.0	-20.0	-7.1	-3.0	-3.5

Exchange rates *lc=local currency*							
Exchange rate, annual average, lc/US$	—	—	—	—	18.50	30.25	40.94
Exchange rate, end of year, lc/US$	—	—	—	—	25.00	35.80	54.70

Balance of payments							
Exports of goods, US$m	—	—	869	2877	2840	3100	3700
Change %	—	—	—	231.1	-1.3	9.2	19.4
Imports of goods, US$m, fob	—	—	930	3255	2661	2900	4100
Change %	—	—	—	250.0	-18.2	9.0	41.4
Trade balance, of goods only, US$m, fob-fob	—	—	-61	-378	179	200	-400
Current account balance, US$m	—	—	-57	-429	29	-470	-752
as a % of GDP	—	—	-0.3	-2.0	0.0	-2.2	-3.6

Foreign exchange reserves							
Foreign exchange reserves, US$m	—	—	530	1020	1330	1500	2000
Import cover (reserves/imports), months	—	—	6.8	3.8	6.0	6.2	5.9

Foreign debt and debt service							
Short-term debt, US$m	—	—	0	92	291	400	650
Total foreign debt, US$m	—	—	8	981	1156	1500	2100
as a % of GDP	—	—	0.0	0.5	0.5	0.7	1.0
as a % of foreign exchange receipts	—	—	0.1	34.1	40.7	48.4	56.8
Interest payments, US$m	—	—	0.0	8.0	27.0	38.0	55.0
Principal repayments, US$m	—	—	0.0	20.0	85.0	145.0	170.0
Total debt service, US$m	—	—	0.0	28.0	112.0	183.0	225.0
as a % of goods exports	—	—	0.0	1.0	3.9	5.9	6.1

Venezuela

Area (thousands of km²):	912
Population (1995, millions):	21.6
Population projection (2025, millions):	34
Population younger than 15 yrs (1991, % of total):	38.3
Urbanization rate (1993, % of population):	92
Life expectancy (1993, years at birth):	72
Gross domestic product (1996, US$bn):	67.3
GDP per capita (1996, US$):	3040
Average annual GDP growth rate (1990-96, %):	3.1
Average annual inflation rate (1990-96, %):	51.9
Currency (bolivar per US$, average 1996):	414.8
Real exchange rate: (1990=100, average 1996)	108.3
Structure of production (1994):	46.3% services, 24.8% petroleum, 23.1% industry, 5.8% agriculture
Main exports:	oil & derivatives, aluminium, iron, steel, coffee, cacao
Main imports:	machinery, transport equipment, chemicals, foodstuffs
Main trading partners:	US, Colombia, Germany, Brazil, Canada
Market capitalization of Stock Exchange (December 1996; US$bn):	10.0
Total foreign debt (% of GDP):	53.5
Next elections due under normal circumstances:	Congress & presidency December 1998
Credit rating: (Jan 1997, Standard & Poor's, Moody's)	B; Ba2

FORECAST: 1997-2000 (average)

	Worst case	Most likely	Best case
Real GDP growth (%)	2.8	4	6
Inflation (%)	50	35	20

■ POLITICS

Historical overview

A Spanish expedition reached Lake Maracaibo in 1499 and named the region Venezuela ("little Venice") in reference to Amerindian villages built on stilts above the water. Venezuela was ruled by the Audiencia de Santo Domingo until 1717, when it came under the administration of the newly created Viceroyalty of New Granada. During that time, the country's economy was dependent on agriculture, mostly cocoa and coffee. Since the region was considered unimportant by the Spanish, it enjoyed a large degree of autonomy.

In the beginning of the 19th century, Simón Bolívar led a rebellion to obtain independence from Spain. It ended with the foundation of Gran Colombia in 1819. This new state, which consisted of Colombia, Venezuela and Ecuador, was dissolved in 1830, giving birth to Venezuela as an independent country.

The following century was characterized by a series of civil wars and political unrest. Long periods of authoritarian rule alternated with periods of fragile democracy. On the international front, a border conflict with the former British Guyana (today Guyana) and failure to meet debt payment obligations led to serious tensions with some European countries and a blockade of Venezuela's ports by Great Britain, Italy and Germany in 1902.

Although political turmoil continued into the first half of the 1900s, the discovery of oil helped to stabilize the economy, finance development programmes and pay off the country's entire foreign debt. Military rule was abolished in 1958, when Rómulo Betancourt was democratically elected president.

Subsequently, Venezuela enjoyed more than thirty years of democracy, serving as a model of political stability in Latin America during the 1970s and 1980s. However, two successive coup attempts in 1992 and the May 1993 impeachment of President Carlos Andrés Pérez (who was charged with misusing US$17 million in government funds) ended this period of political calm.

Recent events

Venezuela's eighth consecutive presidential and congressional elections in December 1993 resulted in a victory for independent candidate and former president, Rafael Caldera. It also ended thirty-five years of dominance by the traditional political parties Acción Democrática (AD) and the Comité de Organizacíon Política Electoral Independiente (COPEI). However, President Caldera's support in the legislature remains weak, since his two coalition partners, the seventeen-party Convergencia and the left-wing Movimiento al Socialismo (MAS), control only 26% of the seats in the lower house. President Caldera therefore relies on the tacit backing of the AD party to garner congressional support for his policies.

The abstention of an estimated 60% of Venezuela's voting population during the December 1995 regional elections underscored the declining popularity of President Caldera's government.

Chronology

1498	Columbus discovers the Peninsula de Paria
1499	The explorer Alonso de Ojeda names the region Venezuela
1717	Creation of the Viceroyalty of New Granada
1806	Beginning of the war for independence
1819	Proclamation of independence and creation of the Republic of Greater Colombia
1830	Independence from the Republic of Greater Colombia
1840	Border conflict with British Guyana
1902	Blockade of Venezuela's ports by Great Britain, Italy and Germany
1920s	Discovery of oil
1945	Rómulo Betancourt overthrows the government with the support of the majority of the people and some junior army officers

1947	New constitution
1947	Rómulo Gallegos wins the first democratic presidential election
1948	Military coup headed by General Marcos Pérez Jiménez
1958	Return to democratic rule with Betancourt as president
1958-96	Succession of democratically elected presidents
1961	New constitution
1992	Two successive coup attempts led by mid-rank military officers
1993	Impeachment of President Carlos Andrés Pérez
1994	Rafael Caldera, the new elected president, takes office
1995	Regional elections

Constitution and government

Venezuela is a presidential republic. Political power is shared by the president and the Congress, both of which are elected every five years by universal suffrage. The president represents the supreme executive power, heads the armed forces and appoints the Council of Ministers as well as the governors of the federal district of Caracas and the two federal territories. He cannot serve two consecutive terms. The bicameral Congress consists of a 204-member Chamber of Deputies and a 53-member Senate. In addition to the elected members, the 1961 constitution grants seats in the Senate to former presidents and representatives of some minority groups.

State organization

The country is made up of 20 states divided into 156 districts, 2 federal territories, one federal district and 72 federal dependencies (islands). Although states are autonomous and have both legislative chambers and a governor, they must adhere to the laws and constitution of the Republic. The president is the administrator of the federal territories.

Political parties

Causa Radical (Causa R)
> Left-wing
> Founded in 1974
> Led by Andrés Velásquez

Acción Democrática (AD)
> Centre-right
> Founded in 1936
> Led by Pedro Paris Montesinos

Movimiento al Socialismo (MAS)
> Left-wing
> Founded in 1971
> Led by Teodoro Petkoff and Pompeio Márquez

Comité de Organización Política Electoral Independiente (COPEI)
> Centre-left
> Founded in 1946
> Led by Luis Herrara Campins

Convergencia Nacional
    Centre-left coalition of 17 parties
    Founded in 1992
    Led by: Rafael Caldera

Results of 1993 elections to Senate and Chamber of Deputies:
Senate:
AD (16 seats), **COPEI** (14), **Causa R** (9), **Convergencia Nacional** (6), **MAS** (4), **other**: four former presidents, who are life members of the Senate
Chamber of Deputies:
AD (58 seats), **COPEI** (53), **Causa R** (41), **Convergencia Nacional** (26), MAS (26)

Central bank

Legally, the Central Bank of Venezuela (BCV) is independent. However, its autonomy has been severely compromised since President Caldera came to power. The BCV is in charge of monetary policy. In order to meet its inflation and exchange rate targets, the central bank can sell, but not buy, government securities and purchase and sell foreign currencies on the open market. It also fixes the discount rate charged to commercial banks and determines the amount of depository reserves commercial banks must keep at the BCV.

■ ECONOMICS

Historical overview

Venezuela's dependency on the oil sector has expanded dramatically since oil was discovered in the beginning of the 1920s. Despite attempts to diversify production, the country's economy is still dominated by the petroleum industry.

The money that flowed into the country was enough to quell social unrest and to keep the economy growing at a steady pace until the mid-1970s. However, an international recession and the consequent fall in oil demand and world commodity prices, as well as the outbreak of the international debt crisis and subsequent capital outflows, brought economic stagnation from 1978 to 1985. Meanwhile, attempts to liberalize prices along with contin-ually expansionary fiscal policies increased inflation and external indebtedness.

Notwithstanding the decline in world oil prices, fiscal and monetary policies remained expansionary in the second half of the 1980s, stimulating the economy while accelerating inflation. Increased price pressures and shrinking foreign exchange reserves forced the government to institute austerity measures in 1989, leading to a sharp decrease in economic activity. The austerity programme of President Carlos Andrés Pérez also resulted in broad social unrest, which characterized Pérez's tumultuous presidency and contributed to his downfall.

Because of the increase in oil prices stimulated by the Gulf War, Venezuela's economy recovered in the early 1990s, posting one of Latin America's highest growth rates. More restrictive economic policies also allowed the inflation rate and the budget deficit to decline significantly in 1990 and 1991.

Venezuela's economic performance, 1961-95

	Average annual real GDP growth,%	Average annual consumer price inflation, %
1961-1965	7.3	0.4
1966-1970	4.9	1.5
1971-1975	4.8	5.8
1976-1980	3.3	11.2
1981-1985	-1.0	10.9
1985-1990	3.1	36.9
1991-1995	3.0	44.3

Source: IMF

Recent developments

Owing to political turmoil and tight monetary policy, Venezuela's output decreased sharply in 1993 and continued to deteriorate in 1994. Given a pronounced drop in investment, the construction sector shrank dramatically.

Foreign exchange restrictions introduced in June 1994 complicated foreign transactions, significantly reducing imports and boosting both the trade and current account surpluses. Sectors that largely depend on imports, such as the automobile industry, suffered supply shortages and were forced to reduce production. Finally, the banking sector underwent one of its worst crises in history, and state intervention in many financial institutions resulted in a large budget deficit and a rapidly expanding money supply.

In 1995, due to the substantial expansion of the petroleum sector, the current account posted another large surplus and real GDP growth was 2.2%. But the economy as a whole did not improve significantly and output shrank once again in 1996. Meanwhile, inflation was exacerbated by the devaluation of the bolivar and by government spending, which remained high in spite of the 1996 austerity programme.

The economy

Venezuela's economy is poorly diversified, depending largely on its oil industry, which accounts for about 25% of GDP and 73% of total exports. The oil sector includes the production and refining of mainly low-grade crude oil, and is almost entirely owned by the government. The country is one of the largest oil producers outside the Middle East. It has estimated oil reserves of 65 billion barrels (more than seventy years of current production), or 6% of total world reserves.

Non-oil manufacturing and construction generate about 18% and 5% of GDP, respectively. Venezuela produces cement, tyres, automobiles, steel and aluminium products and has an extensive petrochemical industry.

Services account for 46% of GDP. Commerce is the largest segment, accounting for more than one third of the services' share of GDP. The financial sector, including real estate, contracted dramatically during the 1994 banking crisis (see below) and now accounts for 21% of services.

Share of GDP by sector

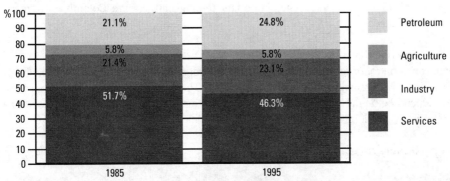

Source: VenEconomy

Although the country is rich in natural resources such as iron ore, coal, bauxite, gold and diamonds, the mining industry remains insignificant. It therefore has large growth potential, particularly iron ore and coal mining. Agriculture accounts for about 6% of GDP. Major crops include sugar, coffee, cocoa, cotton, bananas and rice.

Trade

Venezuela's economy is highly dependent on external transactions, with exports contributing 25% to 1995 GDP – one of the largest shares in Latin America. Oil and derivatives accounted for 73% of Venezuela's total exports in 1995. Other commodities sold abroad include aluminium, iron, steel, coffee and cocoa.

Raw materials and intermediate products represent more than 50% of Venezuela's imports, while capital and consumer goods account for approximately 24% and 26%, respectively. Major import items include machinery and transport equipment, semi-manufactures, chemicals and foodstuffs.

Exports and imports in US$m

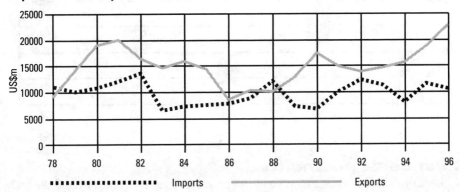

Source: IMF, VenEconomy

Venezuela's main trading partner is the United States, which accounts for 50% of exports and 43% of imports. Other important trading partners are Colombia, Germany, Brazil, and Canada.

Trade restrictions

There is no control or restriction on exports. Some imports require approval from the import office for environmental, health or security reasons. The import tax rate can vary from 5% to 20%, depending on the product. Motor vehicles and agricultural goods are subject to special tariff regimes. Traditionally, exports have exceeded imports, due to the petroleum sector.

Breakdown of exports (1995)

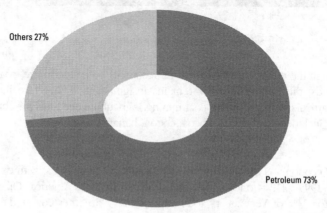

Source: VenEconomy

Current account balance as a % of GDP

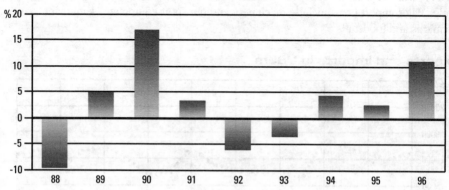

Source: VenEconomy

Balance of payments

Traditionally, Venezuela has enjoyed trade surpluses. Only in 1978 and 1988 did the trade balance post a deficit. Owing to the petroleum sector's large share of overall exports, even a modest change in oil prices generally has a material impact on the trade account. Despite lower oil prices, however, Venezuela's trade surplus widened significantly in 1994, thanks to the strong performance of non-oil exports. Although the volume growth of oil exports is restrained by the country's OPEC quota (Venezuela does not always comply with this production limit, however), the value of US dollar exports expanded 42% from 1994 to 1996. At the same time, a drop in domestic demand and a major devaluation of the bolivar in 1995 resulted in a quasi-stagnation of imports.

The invisibles account is usually in deficit, mainly as a result of large interest payments on external debt. However, since the service and transfer deficit has remained fairly constant, changes in the current account balance have largely reflected changes in the trade balance. Because the latter has improved considerably in the past three years, the current account has registered a surplus since 1994, amounting to 10.9% of GDP in 1996.

Debt

Like many other Latin American countries, Venezuela rapidly accumulated foreign debt in the 1970s, and was consequently forced to reduce its external borrowing after the international debt crisis. Although the second half of the 1980s brought several debt rescheduling agreements, culminating in the Brady debt reduction plan with commercial banks in December 1990, Venezuela remains one of the most highly indebted countries in the region.

Nominal foreign debt increased from US$32.8 billion in 1990 to US$38.2 billion in 1994. However, since portions of the expiring debt could not be refinanced, total nominal indebtedness dropped slightly in 1995 and 1996. Moreover, foreign debt fell from 80% of the country's GDP in 1989 to 53.5% in 1996. Debt service payments, which peaked at over 50% of foreign exchange receipts in 1986, have declined significantly, standing at 19% in 1996. Due to its oil revenues and improved non-oil exports, Venezuela obtained sufficient foreign exchange to avert default on its external liabilities during the 1994 banking crisis.

Economic policy
Monetary policy

Expansionary fiscal policy has made effective monetary discipline very difficult. The central bank followed a relatively tight monetary policy in the early 1990s, with high real interest rates and monetary growth well below that of inflation. However, after Ruth de Krivoy's resignation as president of the central bank in April 1994, monetary policy was abandoned as a disinflationary tool. The narrow monetary aggregate (M1) leapt by 170% between 1994 and 1995, with year-end inflation rates of 70.8% and 56.6%, respectively. In 1996, the central bank again tightened monetary policy, but inflation rose to 103.3%, as a result of the bolivar devaluation in April.

Fiscal policy

As with output growth, the public budget largely depends on oil sales. In the 1970s, the fiscal account was mainly in surplus, but it fell into deficit in the 1980s when oil prices declined. Since then, public expenditures have generally exceeded revenues. In 1994, the public sector's fiscal deficit peaked at 15% of GDP, owing to the extraordinary spending required to avoid a collapse of the banking system. In 1996, however, surging oil revenues significantly improved the fiscal accounts, which posted a surplus equal to 3% of GDP.

Privatization

Since the rash of nationalizations in the mid-1970s, many large companies have remained in public hands, mainly in the mining, transportation and petroleum sectors.

The banking crisis of 1994 also brought numerous financial institutions under state control. The privatization programme is moving very slowly. In 1996, several planned privatizations were delayed or even suspended, and opposition to most privatization plans remains high. Nevertheless, the Caldera administration has stated that government asset sales will continue in 1997. Given strong oil revenues and widespread opposition to privatization, the process is likely to proceed slowly.

Currency

Venezuela has a long history of foreign exchange controls. The exchange rate fell sharply in mid-1994 as a result of the banking crisis. In an attempt to stem the currency weakness, the central bank pegged the exchange rate at 170 bolivars per US dollar in July 1994 and restricted foreign transactions.

Any transactions outside the official system were declared illegal and all exporters were required to sell their foreign currency to the central bank. Moreover, controls were imposed on imports, external debt servicing, spending by travellers and transfers to relatives and students abroad.

The official exchange rate was devalued to 290 bolivar per US dollar in December 1995, and restrictions on foreign transactions were abolished in April 1996. In July 1996, a crawling peg system was implemented.

Since then, the bolivar has been free to fluctuate within a 15% band around a central parity that is adjusted according to inflation expectations. However, the central bank intervened to maintain the currency within a narrower informal band. Since the introduction of the crawling peg system, the bolivar has appreciated in real terms, and now trades at the strong end of the band.

Venezuelan bolivar/US dollar exchange rate

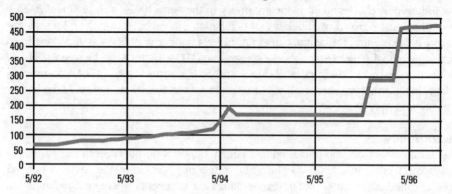

Exchange controls

Restrictions on foreign transactions were abolished in April 1996, and there are currently no capital controls in Venezuela.

Banking system

The banking system is regulated and supervised by the Office of the Superintendency of Banks and the Deposit Guarantee and Banking Protection Fund (Fogade). By the end of 1995, the sector included 39 commercial banks (private and foreign institutions), 21 savings and loan institutions and 9 mortgage banks. Currently, about 25 of these banks are in public hands. Despite the restructuring effort made during the past two years, the sector remains quite inefficient and uncompetitive.

The 1994 banking crisis

In January 1994, the government was forced to take over Banco Latino, the country's second-largest bank. Consequently, financial institutions across the country began to experience large withdrawals of depositors' money. This resulted in a shortage of liquidity among a significant percentage of Venezuelan banks. The state had to intervene in many of these institutions and by the end of 1994 controlled about 40% of the total assets of the commercial banking sector.

■ EQUITIES

Index performance (in local currency)

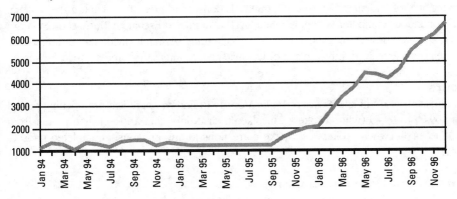

Key indicators

| | Index performance | Market Cap. | | | Weight in | |
	%, in US$ terms	US$bn	P/E	Div. Yield	IFCI	IFCG
1994	-27.2	4.1	18.1	2.5	0.6	0.4
1995	-31.7	3.7	12.0	2.6	0.4	0.2
1996	131.9	10.1	32.5	1.3	0.9	0.7

Sources: Local stock exchange, IFC, Bloomberg, Datastream, UBS

Structure

There are three stock markets operating in Venezuela: the Caracas Stock Exchange, the Maracaibo Stock Exchange and the Electronic Stock Exchange. In 1995, the Caracas Stock Exchange accounted for 85% of the total trading volume of all three Bolsas. In November

1996, there were about 88 companies listed on the Caracas Stock Market, with a total market capitalization of US$9.1 billion.

There are three groups of participants in the market: the regulating authorities, the operating institutions and the supporting agencies. The regulating authorities consist of the Finance Ministry and the National Securities Commission (CNV).

Operating institutions include the three Stock Exchanges, brokerage houses, listed companies, stockbrokers, mutual funds, transfer agents and others. The supporting agencies include the Instituto Venezolano de Mercado de Capitales (the Venezuela Institute of Capital Market) and the Asociación Venezolana de Casas de Bolsas (Venezuelan Association of Brokerage Houses). The Bolsa de Valores de Caracas has sixty-one broker members.

Regulatory authority
The Comisión National de Valores (CNV) is Venezuela's equivalent of the US Securities and Exchange Commission or the Securities Investment Board in the UK. The CNV reports to the Ministry of Finance and is in charge of the regulation of the country's capital markets. The Finance Ministry also acts as a regulating authority for the Caracas Bolsa.

Trading methods
The majority of trading in Venezuelan equities is done on a screen-based automated system. This continuous computer system is called SATB (Automated Exchange Transaction System). Only registered brokers may use this system. The trading session is divided according to buy and sell orders received, buy and sell orders matched, reports issued and post-closing mode.

Hours
Trading starts at 09.45 and closes at 14.00, Monday to Friday. There is a pre-opening period from 09.00 to 09.45 (when brokers can place their orders) and a pre-closing period from 14.00 to 14.30 (when brokers can make corrections to any previously completed transactions).

Settlement time and clearing
Cash: T; T+1; T+2; T+3. Regular: T+5. Forward: from 6 to 60 business days. In May 1994, the Caracas Stock Exchange introduced a multilateral netting system for shares, which handles financial settlement of transactions carried out by the brokers.

Transfer agents, including banks, insurance companies and other institutions authorized by the CVN, are responsible for dealing with the physical transfer of securities, as well as the registration of shareholders' names within two working days of having received any relevant and necessary documents for any purchase/sale of any one security. The Caja Venezolana de Valores (CVV) is Venezuela's Depository Trust company and was established in 1995 to serve as depository of securities and allow for transfer of securities via the electronic system.

Limits on stock price movements
If the price of a share changes by more than 20% throughout any one day, trading of the share is frozen for ten minutes.

Types of shares
Common and preferred shares, fixed- and variable-rate bonds, mutual funds, warrants, ADRs and GDRs are traded on the exchanges.

Stock indices
The most popular stock index is the IBC (Caracas Market Capitalization Index). The index is comprised of the nineteen most liquid shares (there are two classes of shares for four of the index constituents) and is calculated by dividing the daily capitalization by the base year capitalization (as of December 30, 1993) and multiplying by one thousand. Financial and industrial sectors are represented by two sub-indices.

Commissions
Commissions paid by investors for trading in securities are freely fixed by the brokers themselves.

Taxes
The capital gains tax has been replaced with a 1% tax levied on sale of stock. Dividends are tax exempt, however there is a 5% tax on interest income from commercial paper, corporate bonds and certificates of deposits.

Disclosure of financial statements
Listed companies must disclose their financial statements four times a year, within thirty days of the quarter's end. They must also submit audited financial statements within the thirty days following a shareholders' annual meeting. The National Securities Commission also requires a list of salaries and stock holdings of directors, dividend notices, and information that could affect the operation of the company (such as rights issues and changes in accounting practices).

Ownership limits for non-residents
There are no investment restrictions on foreigners other than those applicable to domestic investors and a law which prohibits the foreign ownership of TV and radio broadcasting, Spanish language newspapers, and law firms.

Capital and foreign exchange controls
Restrictions on foreign transactions were abolished in April 1996. Currently there are no capital controls in Venezuela.

Sectors
The largest sectors (by market capitalization) represented by the Caracas stock exchange's IBC index are the electric power sector (29% market weight), financial companies (28%), cement and construction (16%), steel (12%), and food (8%).

ADRs
There are thirteen publicly traded Venezuelan ADRs (some duplicate companies), but only one (Corimon C.A.) is actually listed on the NYSE. However, Corimon has not

actively traded on the NYSE since early February 1996 due to a major restructuring of the company.

■ DEBT

The Capital Markets Law of 1973 (and amended 1974) provides the regulatory framework for the securities markets in Venezuela. The Comision Nacional de Valores (National Securities Commission) enforces those regulations and supervises market practice.

The domestic bond market is predominantly made up of government securities. Top quality corporate borrowers can now raise money by issuing eurobonds.

TEMs (Monetary Stabilization Bonds)

TEMs are issued for maturities ranging up to 180 days, and can be discount or interest bearing securities.

Treasury notes

Treasury notes are discount securities issued for a range of maturities between 50 and 150 days.

Treasury bonds

Treasury bonds are discount securities issued for maturities of 18, 24, 30 and 36 months. All treasury securities are sold by the central bank every Wednesday in Dutch-style auctions. Government debt instruments are in bearer form and trade over the counter in the secondary market for 3-day settlement. A central depository (Caja de Valores) was established in 1996.

Non-residents must obtain a tax ID number before they can open a custody account for trading government securities, and then must appoint a lawyer to submit annual reports of their holdings. Tax laws are complex. Foreign exchange transactions require central bank approval.

Eurobonds

The Republic of Venezuela tapped the eurobond markets in 1988, but was only allowed regular access after the Brady-style restructuring of its external debt was completed in 1990. Venezuela again had difficulty tapping the markets in 1994 due to international concern over its economic reforms. A 3-year deutschmark issue in November 1995 launched at a wide 559 basis points over German government bonds, compared to a 1993 offering at 240 basis points, reflected deteriorating credit perceptions. But in September 1996, the republic issued DM650 million 10.25% seven-year bonds at 440 basis points over the curve, suggesting that perceptions are now more sanguine.

State agencies, for example Bariven SA, and private companies have also issued bonds in several currencies. The country's best credit Petroleos de Venezuela (PDVSA), the state-owned national oil company, was able to issue bonds at a tighter spread even than the sovereign borrower in 1993.

Volume of issuance is small compared to Argentina, Brazil and Mexico.

Eurobond issues (US$bn)

	1990	1991	1992	1993	1994	1995	1996
Sovereign	—	401.8	45.0	1,043.4	—	353.5	429.6
Private	227.0	75.0	145.0	345.7	80.0	—	199.3

Brady bonds

Venezuela issued Brady bonds in December 1990. The bank loans were replaced by discount bonds and par bonds with a 30-year maturity, front-loaded interest reduction bonds (FLIRB) and in addition, Venezuela allowed creditors an option of putting in new money and receiving a more attractive debt conversion bond (DCB) for their original principal. The par and discount bonds are collateralized with 30-year zero coupons and have a 14-month rolling interest guarantee. The bonds also have oil obligation certificates, which require an extra payment once the oil price exceeds an agreed level.

Bond	Coupon	Collateral	Maturity	Currencies
Discount	6mth L+13/16	Principal+Interest	2020	Multiple
Par	6.75%	Principal+Interest	2020	
FLIRB	6mth L+7/8		2007	
DCB	6mth L+7/8		2005	
New Money	6mth L+1		2005	

■ VENEZUELA: Economic indicators

Population and development	1990	1991	1992	1993	1994	1995	1996e
Population, million	19.3	19.8	20.2	20.7	21.4	21.6	22.1
Population growth, %	2.4	2.4	2.3	2.3	3.2	1.2	2.2
Nominal GDP per capita, US$	2514	2701	2984	2900	2725	3782	3040
National accounts							
Nominal GDP, US$bn	48.6	53.5	60.4	60.0	58.3	81.8	67.3
Change in real GDP, %	6.5	9.7	6.1	0.3	-2.8	3.4	-1.6
Gross fixed capital formation, % of GDP	14.1	18.2	21.1	19.3	15.9	15.1	14.8
Money supply and inflation							
Narrow money, change %, Dec/Dec	41.2	51.3	8.3	10.6	130.0	34.2	60.0
Broad money, change %, Dec/Dec	69.0	47.6	14.5	17.6	70.7	36.7	—
Consumer price inflation (avg.) %	40.7	34.2	31.4	38.1	60.8	59.9	98.2
Government finance							
Government balance, % of GDP	0.2	0.7	-5.8	-2.4	-15.0	-5.6	3.0
Exchange rates *lc=local currency*							
Exchange rate, annual average, lc/US$	46.90	56.82	68.38	90.83	148.50	174.78	414.80
Exchange rate, end of year, lc/US$	50.38	61.55	79.45	105.64	170.00	252.10	474.70
Real exchange rate 1990=100	100.0	102.9	107.4	110.9	105.9	134.6	108.3
Balance of payments							
Exports of goods & services, US$m	18806	16388	15514	16119	17679	20130	24500
Change %	34.4	-12.9	-5.3	3.9	9.7	13.9	21.7
Imports of goods & services, US$m, fob	9451	13690	17143	16029	13159	16250	15390
Change %	1.9	44.9	25.2	-6.5	-17.9	23.5	-5.3
Trade balance, of goods only, US$m, fob-fob	10706	4900	1322	3275	7606	7180	12210
Current account balance, US$m	8279	1736	-3749	-1993	2541	2260	7360
as a % of GDP	17.0	3.2	-6.2	-3.3	4.4	2.8	10.9
Foreign exchange reserves							
Foreign exchange reserves, US$m	8321	10666	9562	9216	8067	6283	11170
Gold at ⅔ of market price, US$m	2946.1	2764.3	2621.1	2745.6	2932.5	2932	2942
Import cover (reserves/imports), months	10.6	9.3	6.7	6.9	7.4	4.6	8.7
Foreign debt and debt service							
Short-term debt, US$m	2480	2503	2156	2590	2130	2837	3150
Total foreign debt, US$m	32808	34438	36841	38817	38180	36810	36000
as a % of GDP	67.5	64.4	61.0	64.6	65.5	45.0	53.5
as a % of foreign exchange receipts	149.8	182.0	208.7	213.6	191.7	162.8	133.3
Interest payments, US$m	3198	2529	2682	2208	2382	2235	2400
Principal repayments, US$m	1451	1668	1579	2192	1884	3342	2720
Total debt service, US$m	4649	4197	4261	4400	4266	5577	5120
as a % of goods exports	26.4	27.7	30.0	29.8	26.5	29.9	22.5
as a % of foreign exchange receipts	21.2	22.2	24.1	24.2	21.4	24.7	19.0

Vietnam

Area (thousands of km²):	332
Population (1995, millions):	73.7
Population younger than 15 yrs (1991, % of total):	39
Urbanization rate (1993, % of population):	20
Life expectancy (1993, years at birth):	66
Gross domestic product (1996, US$bn):	22.7
GDP per capita (1996, US$):	303
Average annual GDP growth rate (1990-96, %):	7.9
Average annual inflation rate (1990-96, %):	27.7
Currency (dong per US$, average 1996):	11080
Structure of production (1994):	43% services, 30% industry, 28% agriculture
Main exports:	petroleum, rice, handicrafts & light industrial goods
Main imports:	capital goods, petroleum products, fertilizers
Main trading partners:	Japan, Singapore
Total foreign debt (% of GDP):	28.2
Next elections due under normal circumstances:	legislative required by July 1997

FORECAST: 1997-2000 (average)

	Worst case	Most likely	Best case
Real GDP growth (%)	6.5	8.2	8.9
Inflation (%)	15	7.5	5.0

■ POLITICS

Historical overview

The Vietnamese people established an independent country in the vicinity of Canton during the 4th century BC. In 111 BC, they were conquered by the Han dynasty of China. After more than a thousand years of Chinese rule, they drove out the Chinese and migrated further south to establish a state free of Chinese control in what is now Vietnam. For most of the ensuing period, the empire was ruled from Hanoi by rival dynasties.

European traders established commercial relationships with Vietnam from the early 17th century. Vietnam was occupied by the French in the late 19th century, who merged it with Cambodia and Laos to form the colony of Indochina. Administration was centralized and French governors were appointed to extend control, even down to local levels. After the fall of France in 1940, Japanese troops invaded Indochina. Under Japanese rule, the Communist-inspired independence movement led by Ho Chi Minh gained sufficient momentum for its leader to declare the country independent on September 2, 1945. But the determination of the French authorities to re-assert their control led ultimately to civil war. In 1949-50, France integrated northern Vietnam into the French Union as a sovereign state, but the capital was relocated to Saigon in the south of the country. The ensuing Communist-led Viet Minh offensive culminated in an overwhelming defeat for the French at Dien Bien Phu in 1954. The withdrawal of the colonial power from Vietnam was then formalized by the Geneva Indochina conference, which also provided for the temporary division of the country into northern and southern zones pending a national referendum.

With Hanoi as its capital, the Viet Minh regime then established itself in the northern half of the country as the Democratic Republic of Vietnam (DRV) under the presidency of Ho Chi Minh. A rigorous programme of land reform and industrialization was forced through with the support of China. The USSR also provided military support. In turn, the Hanoi authorities orchestrated a steady escalation of guerrilla activity by the Vietcong movement against the government of South Vietnam, which had meanwhile decided to block the proposed national referendum. The conflict between the Communist north and the US-backed south intensified in the early 1960s, and resulted in direct involvement by the US in 1965. The US troops remained in Vietnam until the 1973 Paris Peace Agreement. Fighting continued until 1975, when Communist troops took Saigon and re-unified the country. The USSR became the principal patron and source of military and economic assistance. Relations with China were broken off in 1978, following the Vietnamese invasion of Cambodia and the installation of a pro-Vietnamese regime in Phnom Penh in place of the Chinese-backed one.

Recent events

Facing a deteriorating economic situation and international isolation, Vietnam's Communist Party introduced free-market reforms (doi moi) at its Sixth Congress in 1986 and intensified its efforts to improve external relations. It was not until 1989, however, that the first serious reforms were implemented. The final withdrawal of the Vietnamese troops from Cambodia in 1989 led to the normalization of political ties with most Western European and Asian countries. In 1992, the National Assembly unanimously approved a new constitution, which confirmed the Communist Party as the leader of the state and society, but which also allowed the public to engage in free enterprise. The reform process gained further support at the Communist Party's Eighth Congress in June 1996. Difficulties in balancing the market economy and Communist ideology are becoming increasingly apparent, however.

A major result of Vietnam's active foreign policy was Washington's lifting of the nineteen-year economic embargo in February 1994. While diplomatic relations between the former enemies have been normalized, Vietnam still lacks Most Favoured Nation status from the US. Relations with neighbouring nations have improved rapidly. In July 1995, Vietnam became the seventh member of ASEAN (Association of South-East Asian Nations) and in January 1996, joined the ASEAN Free Trade Area (AFTA). While the ASEAN and AFTA memberships are of significant political relevance, these moves also force Vietnam to speed up the restructuring of its economy. AFTA is heading for free trade by 2003, thereby reducing tariffs on intra-ASEAN trade and services to 5% or less.

Chronology

14th century- **1887**	Competing dynasties rule over the country
17th century	Start of European incursions
1861-87	In stages, the country falls under French rule (colony of Indochina)
1908, 1930	Unsuccessful rebellions against French administration
1930	Foundation of Ho Chi Minh's independence movement
1940	Japan replaces France as colonial power
1941	Foundation of Communist Viet Minh movement, under Ho Chi Minh
1945	Japanese leave the country
1945	September 2: Ho Chi Minh declares independence
1945	French return to Vietnam
1946-54	Independence war (Indochina war)
1954	Partition of Vietnam along the 17th Parallel, following the Geneva Indochina Conference Agreement
1965	Direct involvement of the US in the Vietnam War
1973	Paris Peace Agreement puts to an end the Vietnam War
1975	Communist troops invade the south and reunify the country
1978-89	Invasion of Cambodia
1986	Economic reform programme (doi moi) launched under Nguyen Van Linh, at the Sixth Party Congress of the Communist Party of Vietnam (CPV)
1991	Seventh Party Congress of CPV; Linh replaced as secretary-general by Do Muoi
1992	New constitution
1994	Lifting of the US trade embargo against Vietnam
1995	Vietnam accepted as a full member of ASEAN
1995	Diplomatic relations re-established between the US and Vietnam
1996	Eighth Party Congress of CPV

Constitution and government

A new constitution was approved by the National Assembly on April 15, 1992. The constitution assigns the Communist Party monopoly of power and the responsibility for guiding the state according to the tenets of Marxism-Leninism and Ho Chi Minh. The 395-member unicameral legislature, the National Assembly, is elected for five-year terms. Candidates may be suggested by the Communist Party (CPV) or the Fatherland Front, or they may propose themselves as individual independents. Over 90% of the assembly members are also CPV members. The assembly sits three times a year, and a permanent standing committee is authorized to act on behalf of the assembly when it is not in session. The assembly elects the prime minister and the president. Recently, it has enhanced its legislative power.

Current government

Secretary-General of the CPV	Do Muoi
Head of the State (President)	Le Duc Anh
Vice-President	Nguyen Thi Binh
Prime Minister	Vo Van Kiet
Finance Minister	Nguyen Sinh Hung

Foreign Affairs Minister	Nguyen Manh Cam
Interior Minister	Le Minh Huong
Governor, central bank	Cao Si Kiem

State organization

The country is divided into provinces and municipalities, which are subordinate to the central government. Municipalities are divided into districts, precincts and cities. Districts are classified into villages and townships.

Local governments are administrated by people's councils, elected by the local people. A revenue-sharing arrangement exists between the central government and the provincial and district levels. Expenditures on local levels have to be authorized by the Ministry of Finance, reflecting the still quite centralized structure of the public sector.

Political organizations

Communist Party of Vietnam (CPV)

Ruling party, founded 1976

Secretary-general of central committee: Do Muoi

Politburo

19 members (expanded from 16 in 1996)

Central Committee

170 members

Vietnam Fatherland Front

A federation of various social organizations

Next elections
1997

Banking system

Until 1988, the financial system consisted of only one bank, the State Bank of Vietnam. After several reforms, a two-tier banking system has been established, with a more clearly defined central banking role for the State Bank of Vietnam, which provides the banking system with its regulatory and supervisory framework. The commercial functions of the State Bank were transferred to four specialized state-owned banks (Vietcombank, Incombank, Vietnam Bank for Agriculture and Bank for Investment and Development of Vietnam). Furthermore, non-state banks have been encouraged, and foreign banks have been admitted since 1992. While the four state-owned banks still represented a dominant share of banking operations, with some 75% of the lending market, there are also fifty-four private joint stock banks, four joint venture banks, as well as some thirty foreign banks.

The authorities have intensified their efforts to increase the competitiveness of the commercial banks and to transform the specialized banks into multipurpose institutions. Nevertheless, the banking system remains underdeveloped and further reforms are vital for the economy.

Performance of the banks is depressed by non-performing loan portfolios, inadequate legal and accounting frameworks, an inefficient payment system and generally underdeveloped money and capital markets. Moreover, the banking sector has continued to be heavily directed towards financing the needs of state enterprises. There also seems to be a widespread suspicion among the Vietnamese against banks, which could in part explain the country's low domestic savings.

■ ECONOMICS

Historical overview

After the reunification of the country in 1976, the north quickly imposed a Soviet-style central planning model on the south, a model that had been in place in the north since 1954. However, collectivization in the agricultural area proceeded very slowly, as food shortages forced the government to change its priority to stimulating food production by lending land to individual families or small production teams, in the "product-contract system". Transformation of industry in the south advanced even more slowly than in the agricultural sector. Most small-scale enterprises remained in private hands, while larger firms, although nationalized, often continued to be managed by the former executives.

Spurred by the success of economic reform in China, the CPV sanctioned the principle of doi moi (economic renovation) at its Sixth Party Congress in December 1986, to fight spiralling inflation, stagnating production and widespread hunger. A major feature of the programme has been to increase support for private enterprise. The Congress elevated the country's leading proponent of economic reform, Nguyen Van Linh, to the senior party post of secretary-general. The reform process yielded impressive early results in agriculture, but did little to prevent the deterioration of Vietnam's fiscal and external position.

Rampant inflation and a balance of payments crisis prompted the acceleration of reform and the introduction of a financial stabilization programme in early 1989. Although this programme met with some early success, it came under threat with the collapse of the Soviet Union. The subsequent withdrawal of Soviet aid and the breakdown of Vietnam's preferential trading arrangements within the Council of Mutual Economic Assistance (CMEA) exposed the vulnerability of Vietnam's economy. Inflation soared again in 1990-91, the value of the currency plunged, and growth in output declined. Deprived of Soviet support, the Vietnamese authorities intensified the adjustment process and opened the economy further to foreign trade and investment.

Recent developments

In 1992, Vietnam's economy emerged from an initial transition period to enter a phase of strong growth and relatively moderate inflation. Within only five years (1991-95), the country managed to nearly double its GDP per capita. Strong foreign direct investment has contributed to a rapid acceleration of investment growth, bringing average annual growth close to 9% since 1992. The private sector, and in particular foreign-invested companies, has become a major source of growth.

Signs of economic overheating raised concern in 1995, as inflation spiked to nearly 17%. Thanks to a bumper rice harvest (rice prices account for some 40% of the CPI basket) and to a tighter credit policy, inflation was tamed at 5.7% in 1996. Buoyant demand for capital goods associated with foreign investment has also resulted in a rapidly widening trade gap.

Continued inflows of foreign capital are likely to sustain strong growth and support a deteriorating balance of payments. However, over the medium term, greater mobilization of domestic resources is vital to sustain strong growth.

Major reforms since 1986
◆ Foreign Investment Law (1987)
◆ Liberalization of most prices (1989)
◆ Decollectivization of agriculture (end of 1980s)
◆ Unification of the two official exchange rates at a rate close to the parallel market rate (1989)
◆ Introduction of the foreign exchange trading floor (1991)
◆ Land Law (1993)
◆ Introduction of interbank foreign exchange market (1994)
◆ Tax reforms
◆ State monopoly on trade abolished

Vietnam's economic performance

	Average annual real GDP growth, %	Average annual consumer price inflation, %
1981-1985	1.3	121.5
1985-1990	5.1	245.8
1991-1995	8.2	31.9

The economy
Although its share of national production decreased from 45% in 1988 to 29% in 1994, agriculture is still the source of livelihood for over 70% of the population.

Share of GDP by sector

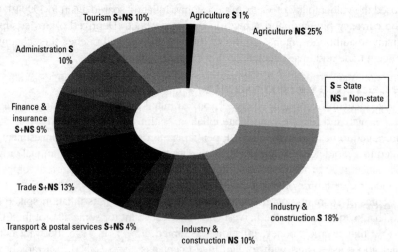

Source: Official data; UBS estimates

Beginning in 1988, a household-based system replaced the collectives and farmers were granted long-term rights to freely transferable land, thereby creating the incentive for investment in land improvement. In 1989, quantitative targets were abolished and prices fully liberalized. These reforms allowed rice production to jump by 12% in 1989. With rice exports of over 2 million tons in 1995 and 1996, Vietnam is the world's third largest rice exporter. The Red River Delta in the north and the Mekong Delta in the south produce 70% of the rice. Total agricultural output grew nearly 4% annually between 1990 and 1995 in real terms.

The industrial sector accounted for some 30% of GDP in 1994, up from 24% in 1988. After a temporary slump in 1989 and 1990, industrial production is now growing at a rate of around 13.5% annually. Manufacturing is dominated by light industry, where food processing is the major component. Other fast growing sectors are textiles and leather production.

The acceleration of the reform process has also led to a rapid expansion of the service sector. In particular, commercial and financial activities have been growing rapidly, reflecting the opening of the country to foreign trade. Booming tourism, partly due to strong foreign participation in hotel development, has also contributed significantly to the expansion of that sector.

Savings and investment

Since the end of the Vietnam War, confidence in the domestic currency has been low. This has contributed to a widespread dollarization of the economy, reinforcing its negative impact on domestically available savings. Lack of appropriate financial instruments, uncertainty about the viability of banks and financial institutions and inappropriate interest rate policy have further dampened savings. Some of these issues have been addressed in the process of restoring macroeconomic stability, and this has since helped increase domestic resource mobilization. However, at an average of 16% of GDP over the past four years, the domestic savings rate remains low compared to other South-East Asian economies.

Propped up by heavy financial support from the Soviet Union, Vietnam's investment rate reached on average 28% of GDP between 1980 and 1985. Investment expenditures dropped drastically in the late 1980s and early 1990s. The US trade embargo blocking access to international development assistance, the ban on multilateral agency financing (imposed in 1985 when Hanoi fell into arrears on its obligations to the IMF) and the financial problems of the CMEA countries forced Vietnam to rely on its own meagre resources. With the restoration of macroeconomic stability and the opening up to foreign investors, investment has been increasing rapidly and currently represents the driving force of the economy. In real terms, investment expenditures are growing at above 30% annually, representing some 28% of GDP in 1995, up from only 15% in 1991. The FDI share of total investment has been rising gradually since 1992, and this is mirrored in a widening domestic investment-savings gap.

Foreign investment

From the start of the transition process, FDI was expected to play a major role in upgrading the country's infrastructure and productive capacity. Thus a liberal investment law was approved in 1987 and enacted somewhat later. The law offers generous tax concessions and duty exemptions, permits 100% foreign ownership and guarantees the unrestricted repatriation of capital and profits. To further promote foreign investment, Hanoi also introduced special industrial and export-processing zones, granting exceptional terms for foreign companies.

While the Foreign Investment Law (1987) and the Joint Venture Law (1995) constitute the legal background for capital investment in Vietnam, legal obstacles and excessive bureaucracy are dampening growth in new investment commitments. Total approved FDI between 1987 and August 1996 reached US$21.9 billion. Inflows have also been increasing over the same period, reaching more than US$5 billion by mid-1996. The sectoral distribution shifted from an initial predominance of investment in the development of offshore oil and gas deposits, to manufacturing (47% between 1988 and 1996), tourism and real estate (37.8% in the same period). Asian countries, including Japan, have provided about 70% of total approved FDI since 1993; Taiwan is the largest single investor.

Trade and balance of payments

The loss of the preferential trading arrangements with the former CMEA countries, together with swiftly growing oil production, resulted in a rapid change in Vietnam's trade structure. While trade with the non-convertible currency area accounted for 80% of the total in 1988, this share fell to less than 10% by 1991. Commercial expansion was helped by improving political and economic relations with Western nations, as well as by trade and exchange rate reforms.

Imports and exports as a % of GDP

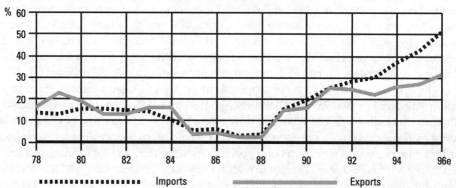

Source: Official data

In line with the rapid expansion of trade with the convertible currency area, total trade has nearly exploded since the late 1980s, helped by a competitive labour force, substantial devaluation of the dong as a result of the 1991 currency reform, and the lifting of the US trade embargo in 1994. Total exports increased by nearly 200% since 1992, while imports grew by almost 300% during the same period. Faster import growth than export growth has widened the trade deficit from US$0.4 billion in 1992 to some US$4 billion in 1996. While capital goods make up for the bulk of imported goods, there is evidence that consumer goods also have also contributed to the upsurge in imports. Since initiating the export boom in the beginning of the 1990s, when mostly FDI-financed oil exploration started coming on stream, oil remains the main export commodity, but it has been gradually declining in importance. Progress in agricultural production, and rice in particular, as well as the development of light industrial products such as leather and textiles, have helped diversify exports.

Capital goods, petroleum products and fertilizer make up for most of Vietnam's imports. To reduce its import dependence and to dampen import growth, efforts have been undertaken to add more value to exports, in particular to petroleum. There are plans to build a refinery which would produce five thousand barrels a day, but talks on the location of the plant have led to substantial delays.

Breakdown of exports (1994)

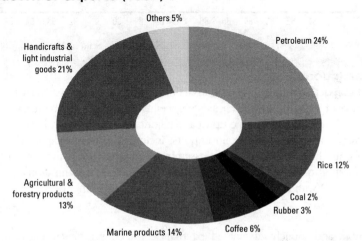

Others 5%

Handicrafts & light industrial goods 21%

Petroleum 24%

Rice 12%

Agricultural & forestry products 13%

Coal 2%

Rubber 3%

Marine products 14%

Coffee 6%

Source: Official data

Rapidly widening current account deficits

Due to a rise in service income (largely from the booming tourism sector), as well as substantial transfers and larger remittances from Vietnamese living abroad, the invisibles balance (recording trade in services, unrequited transfers and income flows generated by factors of production) turned positive in 1994. But steadily rising large dividend payments and transfers abroad, reflecting strong FDI, increasingly present a drain on the services and income balance. The recent emergence of surpluses on the invisibles balance did not suffice to offset the growing trade deficit or avoid the expansion of the current account deficit. Given the drastic rise in the trade deficit, the current account deficit has jumped from a low 0.8% of GDP in 1992 to over 15% in 1996.

Since the early 1990s, the bulk of the current account deficit has been financed indirectly by foreign direct investment. Vietnam's adherence to stabilization and reform policies has helped a gradual expansion of concessional lending by official creditors, while commercial bank lending is also gaining importance. With the capital account slightly in excess of the current account deficit, official reserves have increased from some US$0.5 billion in 1992 to US$1.4 billion in 1996. Overall, foreign exchange reserves remain at a relatively low level, however, with an import coverage of about 1.5 months.

Current account as a % of GDP

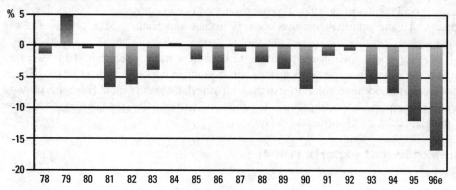

Source: Official data; UBS estimates

Trade restrictions

Some export transactions and all import transactions require a licence issued by the Ministry of Trade. Trade of certain goods such as steel, cement, fertilizer and motorcycles is regulated by quotas. Import tariffs range up to a maximum of 60%. Foreign investment enterprises are exempt from duty on certain imports, including those for capital construction, working tools, machine components and assembling devices. Rice is the only commodity subject to an export quota. Trade is conducted by foreign trade organizations, firms (local and foreign-owned) with direct foreign trading rights and local authorities.

Debt

Vietnam's public and publicly guaranteed external debt in convertible currencies at the end of 1995 amounted to US$5.5 billion (nearly 30% of GDP), including US$0.5 billion in short-term credits and US$0.5 billion in interest arrears. About 14% of the debt was owed to multinational organizations (half of this to the IMF) and 42% to official bilateral creditors. The remaining 44% was owed to private creditors, including commercial banks. Furthermore, Vietnam still has an outstanding debt vis-à-vis Russia and several other former socialist countries, worth 9.6 billion roubles. No agreement about the appropriate dollar-rouble exchange rate has been reached so far.

The debt-service ratio has declined over the last several years, given the sharp rise in export earnings. As a percentage of export receipts, the debt-service ratio fell almost 15% in 1990 to some 7% in 1996. Debt amortization and total interest payments are likely to rise gradually in nominal terms, while maintaining total debt service as a percentage of goods and services exports between 5-7% (assuming continued growth of exports).

Debt restructuring

There have been various agreements between Hanoi and international creditors since 1993. Under increasing international pressure, President Clinton lifted US objections to the clearing of Vietnam's IMF arrears in July 1993. The arrears were repaid in September the same year, with a combination of a US$85 million bridge loan from the commercial banks and US$55 million provided by a Support Group of official donors, led by France and Japan. This gave way to a formal agreement enabling Vietnam to seek fresh funds by the IMF, as well as to a rescheduling arrangement of external arrears outstanding on medium- and long-term loans contracted before January 1990, made with Paris Club creditors at the end of 1993.

In the same year, the World Bank resumed lending to Vietnam. Its pledges reached US$1 billion in mid-1996, all related to highly concessional International Development Fund facilities. In 1994, the IMF granted an enhanced structural adjustment facility (ESAF), a three-year concessional facility, which is to be serviced at 0.5% interest and repaid over ten years. After several rounds of negotiations, Hanoi also accomplished an accord with the Bank Advisory Committee of London Club creditors. This will allow the clearing of nearly US$0.5 billion in interest arrears and the restructuring of US$0.4 billion in principal arrears.

Economic policy
Monetary policy
With the development of a money market and market-based instruments still at a basic level (T-bills have been tradeable since 1994), the authorities have continued to rely on more direct instruments of monetary management. The central bank currently sets targets for over-all banking system domestic credit expansion by varying the volume of credit extended to commercial banks through refinancing arrangements. These arrangements have mainly been used to promote the development of targeted sectors, and have been less successful in curb-ing monetary credit. The central bank also uses reserve requirements as an instrument of monetary management. These requirements, however, have not always been strictly enforced.

Vietnam has experienced several bouts of inflation since unification. From 1978 to 1992, annual inflation never fell below 30% and reached its highest levels in 1986 with an almost 500% rise in prices. High inflation also pushed real interest rates into negative terr-itory, thereby depressing domestic savings. The inflation record has rapidly improved since 1993, however, because the domestic bank financing of the government deficit has nearly been eliminated (now bonds are sold to the non-bank public) and because of prudent mon-etary management. Interest rates have also become increasingly positive in real terms.

Fiscal policy
Vietnam has had a budget deficit in the operations of the general government (including four administrative levels, but excluding activities of the state-owned enterprises) for many years. In a first phase, between 1989 and 1992, the deficit was reduced considerably, mainly by means of higher revenues realized through tax reform that also subjected state-owned enterprises to taxes. In addition, the government began to cut military expenditures. Since 1993, however, higher expenditures for social security, health and education resulted in larger deficits again, amounting to some 1.7% of GDP in 1995 and 1996. While monetization of the government deficit had been a common method until 1992, the gap is now filled with domestic and foreign loans.

Public investment, which is critically required for the economic development of the country, is largely responsible for the recent increase in government spending. On the other hand, a sub-optimal tax system and smuggling (the Asian Development Bank estimates that illegal cross-border trade represents 20% of total recorded trade) are depriving the government of revenue. Together with a reduction of tax revenues from lower import taxes (if the ASEAN Free Trade Area plan is to be met by 2006), revenue shortages will increase pressures on Vietnam to restructure its tax system.

State-owned enterprise reforms

Early reforms of state-owned enterprises (SOEs) consisted mainly of granting greater autonomy, such as free disposal of profits or permitting joint ventures. In 1991, in response to the poor profit performance of many SOEs, the government required all state enterprises to re-register. Only those proving financially viable or having good prospects were granted state enterprise status. Under this re-registration exercise, the number of SOEs and collectives fell from 12,084 in mid-1990 to about 6,600 by mid-1996. To complete the re-registration programme, the government introduced a plan for the equitization of state enterprises in 1992. Shares were to be sold through concessional loans and discounted prices to employees and other parties with a strong interest in the companies. But progress has been very limited and only three SOEs have been "equitized" .

Price liberalization, exposing the SOEs to higher competition, as well as cutting most subsidies, resulted in the improved performance of re-registered enterprises. It is estimated that by mid-1995 only some 10% of state enterprises were still operating with losses. In 1994, net transfers (taxes minus subsidies) to the budget from state enterprises amounted to VND19.7 billion compared to only VND2.5 billion in 1990.

State enterprises continue to receive the bulk of the working capital from the banking system and investment is often supported through the budget or through government-guaranteed borrowing.

Currency

At the heart of Vietnam's export-led growth strategy has been the reform of the exchange rate system. In early 1989, the system of multiple exchange rates, with different rates for trade transactions within the central plan, for invisible transactions, and for trade transactions outside the plan, was abolished. This system had caused large distortions in the structure of relative prices and hidden transfers among the different economic sectors. The new official exchange rate was brought close to the parallel market rate.

At the same time, many administrative controls on the holding and use of foreign exchange were liberalized to increase the amount of foreign exchange in the official market. Foreign exchange trading floors were introduced at the State Bank in 1991, and forty market participants (banks and foreign trade organizations) were allowed to deal in foreign exchange three times a week. In an attempt to bring exchange rate determination closer to the market regime with broader coverage, an interbank foreign exchange market replaced the trading floors in October 1994, and was opened to all big commercial banks. The buying and selling rates are allowed to move within 0.5% on either side of the daily adjusted official reference rate. At the same time, a new foreign exchange regulation package was approved to promote the use of the dong in a still largely dollarized economy and to increase the supply of foreign exchange in the interbank market.

The Vietnamese currency is the dong. The dong has depreciated rapidly since its adjustment to the parallel market rate, rising from some VND/US$4250 in January 1990 to VND/US$10892 in December 1992. Since then, the authorities have kept the rate at roughly VND/US$11000. As the currency has not moved in line with the inflation differentials with its main trading partners, relatively higher inflation has started to erode external competitiveness.

Vietnamese dong/US dollar exchange rate

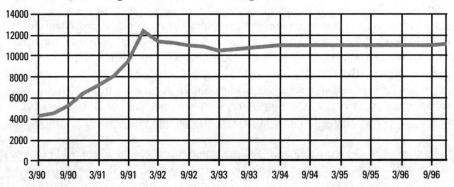

Source: Official data

Exchange controls

Earnings from trade in goods and services are subject to various surrender requirements. Organizations and enterprises must deposit all foreign exchange proceeds in foreign exchange accounts at domestic commercial banks licensed to conduct foreign exchange business in Vietnam. Vietnamese organizations and citizens who need foreign currency for production and business purposes are permitted to borrow foreign currency or obtain a bank guarantee for loans in foreign currency.

■ EQUITIES

At present there is no formal stock market in Vietnam. However, in recent years the government has initiated a process of 'equitization', in an effort to create conditions for a stock market. The process involves the creation of a share structure for State Owned Enterprises (SOEs), with a portion of the shares being sold to employees and the public, and the state maintaining majority control.

Equitization has existed as state policy since 1987, but has only been recognized as a serious policy since May 1993. Progress none the less, has been slow, due to a lack of back-up policies and legal instruments. In May 1996, however, a government decree was issued, stating a decision to change a large number of SOEs into joint-stock companies. This was seen as a milestone in the country's drive for equitization of its enterprises. Similarly, in June 1996, Ho Chi Minh City's Refrigeration Engineering Enterprises (REE), one of the first SOEs to establish a share structure, became the first Vietnamese company to issue convertible bonds in hard currency to foreigners. This was regarded by the international community as a boost to the equitization process.

So far, Ho Chi Minh city plans to list fifty of its enterprises for equitization, while there are plans for seventy others from other regions. The government estimates that by the end of 1997 it will have a total of two hundred joint stock companies equitized from SOEs. Despite government efforts to encourage the issuance of shares, so far only five SOEs have complied. In May 1996, tax breaks were promised to all companies that sold shares to employees and the public. However, SOEs have been reluctant to accept change.

Alongside the process of equitization, plans for the development of a Stock Exchange continue. At present, the deputy governor of the central bank supervises preparations for the bourse. However, the government has already announced its decision to establish a new national securities commission to formally adopt this role. Meanwhile, the International Finance Cooperation (IFC) continues to advise the government on the legal and institutional requirements for establishing a securities market. Similarly, pressure from other Southeast Asian countries for Vietnam, the only ASEAN country not part of APEC (Asia-Pacific Economic Cooperation), to join the APEC accord may prompt progress in its financial market.

In March 1996, Vietnam's Finance Minister stated that a stock market could not begin operating until at least 1999. If and when a stock market is established, possible listings are likely to be food processing companies, banks, property and insurance companies, as Vietnam has no industrial tradition.

■ DEBT

The treasury-bill market opened in mid-1995. The Ministry of Finance, with the State Bank of Vietnam (SBV) acting as its agent, issues 1-, 3-, 6-, 9-, and 12-month bills, denominated in dong, through auctions held every two weeks. The first auction was held in April 1996.

Bills are discount instruments which are transferable, traded OTC and can be used as collateral for loans. They are issued in either registered or bearer form, and proceeds are tax-free.

Investors include domestic banks and insurance companies, and licensed foreign bank branches in Vietnam.

On May 20, 1996, the Bank Advisory Committee (BAC) announced proposals for a Brady-style restructuring of the country's commercial bank (London Club) debt. In addition to a cash buyback of principal and interest, the BAC propose the following bond exchange options: a 30-year discount bond, which incorporates a 50% debt write-off; a 30-year par bond, which amortizes after a 15-year grace period; and an 18-year past due interest (PDI) bond with a variable rate coupon and which amortizes after a 7-year grace period. Of the discount bond principal, 100% will be collateralized, but only half of the Par Bond principal will be backed by zero coupon US treasuries (or equivalent foreign currency securities). All three bonds will be eligible for debt-equity swaps.

Outstanding commercial debt worth about US$400 million will qualify for the exchange. It includes arrears on Vietcombank loans raised before December 31, 1989, and incorporates the 1985 Restructuring Agreement and 1985 Interest Payment Agreement.

It is still uncertain whether either the Vietnamese government or a sufficient majority of commercial bank creditors will accept the BAC's recommendations.

■ VIETNAM: Economic indicators

Population and development	1990	1991	1992	1993	1994	1995	1996e
Population, million	66.2	67.8	69.4	70.8	72.2	73.7	75.1
Population growth, %	2.3	2.3	2.4	2.0	2.0	2.0	2.0
Nominal GDP per capita, US$	124	121	142	181	215	268	303

National accounts							
Nominal GDP, US$bn	8.2	8.2	9.9	12.8	15.5	19.8	22.7
Change in real GDP, %	5.1	5.9	8.6	8.1	8.8	9.5	9.3
Gross fixed capital formation, % of GDP	15.1	15.0	17.6	20.5	24.2	25.0	23.7

Money supply and inflation							
Narrow money, change %, Dec/Dec	58.8	71.9	64.8	34.4	31.2	2.8	—
Broad money, change %, Dec/Dec	53.1	78.8	33.7	19.0	27.8	27.7	26.0
Consumer price inflation (avg.) %	36.4	86.3	37.5	8.4	10.2	16.9	5.7

Government finance							
Government expenditure, % of GDP	22.7	17.2	22.7	28.5	27.1	26.0	26.5
Government balance, % of GDP	-8.0	-3.7	-3.7	-6.2	-2.7	-1.6	-1.7

Exchange rates lc=local currency							
Exchange rate, annual average, lc/US$	5098	9389	11181	10647	10960	11035	11080
Exchange rate, end of year, lc/US$	6500	12990	10565	10786	10995	11011	11150

Balance of payments							
Exports of goods & services, US$m	1698	2560	3161	3622	5057	6670	8360
Change %	37.3	50.8	23.5	14.6	39.6	31.9	25.3
Imports of goods & services, US$m, fob	1834	2329	2978	4184	6281	8890	12490
Change %	62.3	27.0	27.9	40.5	50.1	41.5	40.5
Trade balance, of goods only, US$m, fob-fob	-312	6	-100	-655	-1190	-2200	-4100
Current account balance, US$m	-572	-134	-76	-778	-1166	-1750	-3500
as a % of GDP	-6.9	-1.6	-0.8	-6.1	-7.5	-8.9	-15.4

Foreign exchange reserves							
Foreign exchange reserves, US$m	24.0	27.0	465	404	876	1380	1400
Gold at ⅔ of market price, US$m	264.7	141.0	168.3	191.7	204.7	204.7	206.6
Import cover (reserves/imports), months	0.2	0.1	1.9	1.2	1.7	1.9	1.3

Foreign debt and debt service							
Short-term debt, US$m	150	150	200	110	195	423	597
Total foreign debt, US$m	3341	3522	3969	3889	4722	5480	6415
as a % of GDP	40.6	43.1	40.1	30.3	30.4	27.7	28.2
as a % of foreign exchange receipts	187.4	129.7	119.3	99.0	83.3	70.7	65.8
Interest payments, US$m	300	320	320	253.6	200	210	260
Principal repayments, US$m	29	22	12	80	85	214	302
Total debt service, US$m	329	342	331	334	285	424	562
as a % of goods exports	25.5	16.6	13.6	11.7	7.0	8.0	8.5
as a % of foreign exchange receipts	18.5	12.6	10.0	8.5	5.0	5.5	5.8

Zimbabwe

Area (thousands of km²):	391
Population (1995, millions):	11.5
Population projection (2025, millions):	18
Population younger than 15 yrs (1991, % of total):	44.5
Urbanization rate (1993, % of population):	31
Life expectancy (1993, years at birth):	53
Gross domestic product (1996, US$bn):	7.4
GDP per capita (1996, US$):	617
Average annual GDP growth rate (1990-96, %):	1.6
Average annual inflation rate (1990-96, %):	25.2
Currency (Zimbabwean dollar per US$, average 1996):	9.95
Structure of production (1994):	53.4% services, 32.1% industry, 14.5% agriculture
Main exports:	tobacco, cotton, sugar, maize, meat, gold, ferro-alloy, nickel
Main imports:	machinery & transport equipment, chemicals, manufactures
Main trading partners:	South Africa, UK
Market capitalization of Stock Exchange (December 1996; US$bn):	3.6
Total foreign debt (% of GDP):	60.5
Next elections due under normal circumstances:	legislative required by April 2000; presidential scheduled March 2002
Credit rating: (Jan 1997,Standard & Poor's, Moody's)	not rated

FORECAST: 1997-2000 (average)

	Worst case	Most likely	Best case
Real GDP growth (%)	2.8	4.4	5.0
Inflation (%)	25	20.0	17.0

■ POLITICS

Historical overview

The two main ethnic groups in the area now known as Zimbabwe are the Shona people, who settled over one thousand years ago, and the Ndebele, who arrived from what is now South Africa in the mid-19th century.

The arrival of Europeans in 1890 met with resistance, and administration by Cecil Rhodes' British South Africa Company was not achieved until 1902. Southern Rhodesia was governed by the British South Africa Company until 1923, when the white electorate voted for the status of "self-governing rule". Through a series of acts, a racially stratified and segregated society was established, similar to that of South Africa at the time.

In 1953 the UK joined Southern Rhodesia with Northern Rhodesia (now Zambia) and Nyasaland (now Malawi) to form the Central African Federation, with Salisbury (now Harare) as the capital city. However, increasing opposition from the black population in Northern Rhodesia and Nyasaland led to the collapse of the federation in 1963 when Britain conceded their independence. Meanwhile, white voters in Southern Rhodesia elected the Rhodesian Front (RF) to power in 1962. In 1965, under the premiership of Ian Smith, there was a unilateral declaration of independence (UDI).

The UK responded with economic sanctions, although some countries ignored them and others failed to prosecute companies that broke them. The main challenge to Smith's new white government came from the increasingly militant black nationalist organizations, namely the Zimbabwe African National Union (ZANU) and the Zimbabwe African People's Union (ZAPU), which represented the disenfranchised black majority.

Limited guerrilla activity began in 1966, and a state of emergency was introduced. However, a December 1972 campaign by the ZANU in the north-east marked the beginning of a serious military challenge. In 1976 the two main African parties linked up, creating the Patriotic Front (PF) alliance. This presented a common front in the negotiations for independence.

After a constitutional conference in London, UK-supervised elections took place in February 1980. Robert Mugabe's ZANU and Joshua Nkomo's ZAPU wings of the PF split and contested the elections separately. These were won by Mugabe's ZANU-PF alliance, which has remained in office since, winning elections in 1985, 1990 and 1995. After initially forming a broad-based reconciliatory cabinet, including members of both the RF and the ZAPU, relations deteriorated and Mugabe dismissed the ZAPU members in the mid-1980s.

Following negotiations, a 1987 merger led in December 1989 to the creation of a single party under the ZANU-PF label, with Mugabe as leader and Nkomo as one of two vice-presidents. Mugabe comfortably won the 1990 election against four smaller opposition parties. The victory by the unified ZANU-PF marked the end of the twenty-five-year-old state of emergency and heralded the start of economic reform.

Recent events

In the early 1990s the government's popularity declined as a result of a recession, high unemployment, and austerity measures. Despite student protests and strikes by civil servants, the divided state of the opposition meant there was little serious challenge to the government. The opposition has been torn by leadership quarrels and has failed to present a coherent economic and political programme.

Attempts to defeat the government in the 1995 elections by forming an opposition alliance, the United Front, proved unsuccessful, with the ZANU-PF winning 117 of 120 seats. In 1996 Mugabe won the presidential elections, defeating his opponents Bishop Abel Muzorewa and Ndabaningi Sithole, who both withdrew shortly before the election. Mugabe received 92.7% of the vote, although only 31.8% of the registered voters turned out for the election.

Chronology

1890	Occupation by British South Africa Company (BSA) begins
1902	Conquest by BSA is completed
1923	BSA rule is ended by royal charter and Southern Rhodesia becomes a self-governing colony
1953	Southern Rhodesia, Northern Rhodesia and Nyasaland join to become the Central African Federation
1963	Britain concedes independence to Northern Rhodesia (now Zambia) and Nyasaland (now Malawi)
1965	Southern Rhodesia defies Britain and the United Nations by announcing the unilateral declaration of independence (UDI)
1966-79	War between Smith's ruling Patriotic Front and black nationalist opposition
1980	Mugabe's Zimbabwe African National Union (ZANU) party wins democratic elections under the supervision of the British government
1989	Zimbabwe African National Union (ZANU) and Zimbabwe African People's Union (ZAPU) unite after two years of negotiations
1990	Victory for ZANU-PF in the third general election
1992	Four main opposition parties form a United Front with the aim of defeating the government in the 1995 elections
1992	Police clash with students and trade unionists
1994	Widespread industrial unrest in response to austerity measures
1995	ZANU-PF party wins 117 of 120 seats in the general election
1996	Mugabe wins the presidential elections

Constitution and government

The constitution agreed on 21 December, 1979 at the conference held in London provided for a Westminster-style parliament, with a prime minister heading the executive. Zimbabwe became a republic within the British Commonwealth at independence, with a non-executive president as the head of state. In 1987 the constitution was revised, replacing the office of prime minister with an executive presidency and two vice-presidents.

In 1989 the Senate was abolished by the House of Assembly, and the single remaining house was enlarged to 150 seats. Of these seats, 120 are elected, 8 are provincial governors, 10 are traditional chiefs and 12 are appointed by the president.

Central bank

The central bank is the Reserve Bank of Zimbabwe (RBZ), and operates under the 1964 Reserve Bank Act. The governor and two deputy governors are appointed by the state president for renewable five-year terms. The Bank's primary goal is the maintenance of the internal and external value of the currency, the Zimbabwean dollar. Inflation, however, has been high, averaging 25% a year from 1990 to 1996. This has been the result of high money supply growth, large fiscal imbalances, the phasing out of price controls and the effects of recent severe droughts (1992 and 1995) on food prices.

■ ECONOMICS

The economy

Zimbabwe ranks among Africa's more diversified economies. The service sector represents more than half of GDP. It includes a large public service, financial and business services, and a growing tourist industry. The agricultural sector accounts for around 14% of GDP and provides one quarter of the country's jobs. During years of average or good rainfall, Zimbabwe exports tobacco, cotton, sugar, maize and meat. It is one of the world's largest tobacco exporters and this crop is the main agricultural export and single most important foreign-exchange earner. Land distribution is still biased in favour of the white farmers, which remains a contentious political issue. The industrial sector accounts for about 30% of GDP. The most important activities are heavy engineering and the manufacture of steel, tyres, plastics, paper and consumer goods. Mining accounts for some 7% of GDP and is an important source of foreign exchange: gold, ferro-alloy and nickel exports represent around a quarter of Zimbabwe's exports.

In recent years the mining sector has suffered a large decline in employment, falling by nearly one quarter between 1983 and 1994. However, new investment is likely to help propel growth in this sector over the next few years. Zimbabwe's total mineral output was estimated to have grown by around 20% in 1996 as a result of new exploration and higher production at existing sites. Various projects are attracting interest, including diamond and platinum prospecting. In 1996, the Hartley mine, the largest investment project since independence, started operations and is forecast to produce 150,000 ounces of platinum, 23,000 ounces of gold and other minerals, including rhodium, palladium, copper and nickel. The mine will help make Zimbabwe the world's largest platinum producer after South Africa and reinforce Zimbabwe as Africa's third-largest gold producer. Export earnings from the country's minerals are expected to be in the region of US$0.5 billion in 1997.

Share of GDP by sector

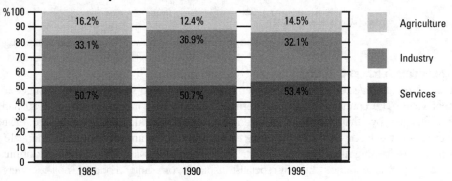

Source: Official data

South Africa is Zimbabwe's main trading partner, taking about 15% of Zimbabwe's exports and supplying about one quarter of its imports in recent years. Since the lifting of international sanctions against South Africa, trade between these two countries has picked up significantly. However, the balance of trade is still heavily skewed in South Africa's favour.

Exports and imports as a % of GDP

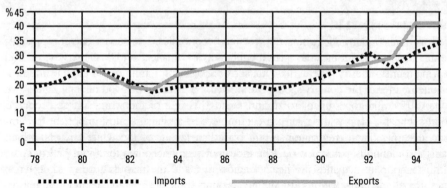

Source: Official data

Breakdown of exports (1995)

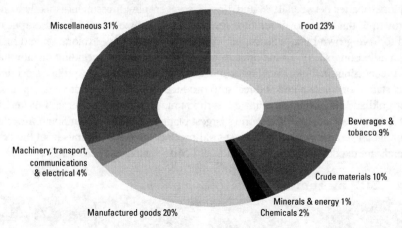

Source: Official data

Economic policy

The new foreign investor interest in Zimbabwe has much to do with the policy changes of recent years. The country Mugabe's government inherited at independence in 1980 had been ravaged by civil war and its economy severely weakened by sanctions. The government was faced with the challenge of restoring peace and stability, rebuilding the economy, redressing the historical inequalities, and addressing the high expectations aroused on independence. Initially socialist-inspired command economy policies were implemented, resulting in an expansion of the state sector. In President Mugabe's first term (1980-85), state expenditure rocketed from one third to nearly half of GDP. Although it has declined from those high levels, the average level of state expenditure since 1980 has been over 40%, much higher than neighbouring South Africa or Kenya (around 30% of GDP).

Government revenue could not match the pace of the rapid rise in expenditure. The result was a series of budget deficits averaging around 10% of GDP since 1991. Subsidies to loss-making parastatals and the maintenance of a bloated civil service, as well as hefty debt payments, became an ever bigger burden to the state.

By the end of the 1980s, it had become clear that the excessive role of the state in the economy was undermining the country's growth. In 1989 the first steps were taken to dismantle the socialist model by partially liberalizing foreign investment. The system for approving investments was streamlined and foreigners were allowed to hold up to 25% of domestic companies.

In 1990 the government co-authored an Enhanced Structural Adjustment Programme (ESAP) with the IMF. The policy paper envisaged a radical liberalization of the economic structures, including deregulation and reducing state intervention; the privatization of parastatals and cutting bureaucracy by 25%, gradually bringing down the fiscal deficit. A strict anti-inflationary stance and currency and trade liberalization have been adopted.

These sweeping reforms, announced in April 1990, and originally scheduled for completion in 1995, were aimed at making Zimbabwe internationally competitive and boosting the country's growth rate.

Following good progress with the first reforms, in 1992 Zimbabwe's agriculture-based economy was severely affected by the worst drought in decades, disrupting the structural adjustment programme. GDP for the year fell by more than 6%, while the current account deficit deteriorated to nearly 12% of GDP – following a sharp drop in exports and the import of large amounts of food. Drought-related shortages, combined with a currency devaluation, also saw a rapid rise in inflation.

After this turbulent hiatus, the government restarted and accelerated the implementation of reforms during 1993, centred mainly on the financial and industrial sectors. Much progress has been made in the abolishing of the extensive system of government controls affecting prices, access to foreign exchange, the labour market, and domestic marketing of agricultural produce. The stock market was also opened to foreign investors.

Following these developments, there was a marked rise in foreign capital flows to Zimbabwe. As a result, Zimbabwe's currency reserves rose to more than four months of import cover in 1996, from a low of only several weeks in 1991.

Fiscal adjustment

In contrast to the significant progress made in the reform of the trade and financial sectors, public sector reform has been particularly slow, with continuing negative consequences for the economy.

Viewed over the longer term, there have been several negative consequences of this situation. First, the obvious crowding out of private sector borrowing and productive investment was evident as the government sought to finance a big part of the deficit on the domestic money market. Second, higher foreign debt (the public sector accounts for the bulk of foreign debt). Third, bouts of high inflation as the government turned to the central bank for additional credits – the creation of new money.

It is one of the aims of the structural adjustment programme not only to lower the public sector borrowing requirement but also to reduce the overall level of government expenditure. This is closely related to the former, and it is clear that privatization or commercialization of the parastatals and the reduction of the large civil service is crucial to the reform process in Zimbabwe.

Progress in terms of privatization and reducing the deficit has been slow. Given that unemployment is over 30%, the government remains acutely aware of the social consequences that could result from the rationalization of government services and the privatization of parastatals in the transition towards a more open economy.

Insufficient progress on getting the deficit under control resulted in the IMF suspending some of its financial support to Zimbabwe in 1995. The budget targets had been missed by wide margins, undermining policy credibility: an original target for a budget deficit of 5% of GDP for the financial year ending June 1995 turned out to be 13.4%, while the 1996 target of 6.7% produced a 10.1% result. The 1997 deficit forecast of 8.5% of GDP will be put to the test by unbudgeted pay increases awarded to civil servants following a strike.

Current account as a % of GDP

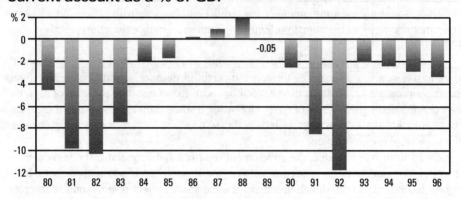

Source: Official data; UBS estimates

Zimbabwe as part of a larger market

Zimbabwe is a member state of the Southern African Development Community. This grouping, which now includes South Africa, aims at greater regional integration. Given the vast size of this region – more than twice the area of the EU 15 – and the conflict that has characterized relations in the area in the past, there is still a very long way to go before any meaningful integration takes place. This is shown by the fact that intra-SADC trade represents less than 5% of total SADC trade, compared with around 60% for the EU. Moreover, the level of development between SADC members is very unequal. Whereas the difference between the average real per-capita income of the richest and poorest EU members is around 3:1, in SADC it is 9:1.

Yet, given that the whole region will benefit from the end of the main conflicts in the area (Angola, Mozambique, South Africa) as well as the growing commitment to democracy and free markets, SADC can play a new role as a forum for enhancing security and democracy in the region and by further opening up markets.

Foreign investors are increasingly being asked to consider the opportunities in the region as a whole. Moreover, as South African foreign exchange controls are phased out, so the likelihood increases that South African companies will diversify production towards neighbouring countries, where labour costs are more competitive. Zimbabwe should benefit accordingly.

Currency

Up until 1994 the value of the Zimbabwean dollar was determined by the Reserve Bank of Zimbabwe (RBZ) on the basis of a trade-weighted basket of foreign currencies. Although regular adjustments were made because of Zimbabwe's higher inflation, there were also a few big devaluations. In 1994 the currency became market-determined, following reforms affecting export earnings and foreign access to the Zimbabwe Stock Exchange. Although the RBZ still reserves the right to intervene in the foreign exchange market to prevent volatility, the currency is largely freely floating. Full convertibility of the current account was achieved in 1995.

Zimbabwean dollars per US dollar (annual average)

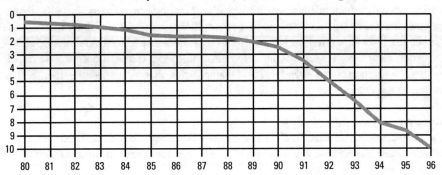

■ EQUITIES

Index performance (in local currency)

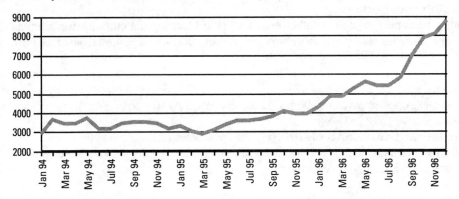

Key indicators

	Index performance %, in US$ terms	Market Cap. US$bn	P/E	Div. Yield	Weight in IFCI	IFCG
1994	22.5	1.8	10.1	4.6	0	0.1
1995	10.6	2.0	7.3	5.2	0	0.1
1996	59.7	3.6	12.9	2.8	0.1	0.2

Sources: Local stock exchange, IFC, Bloomberg, Datastream, UBS

Background

The first stock exchange in Zimbabwe opened in 1896 following the arrival of the pioneer column in Bulawayo. Further exchanges opened in Gwelo and Umtali, but, by 1924, they were all closed after mineral deposits proved disappointing. On January 2, 1946, a new exchange in Bulawayo began trading, with a second floor opening in Salisbury in late 1951. In 1974 the stock exchange moved to its current site in Harare (previously Salisbury) following the Stock Exchange Act. Today, although small in global terms, the Zimbabwe Stock Exchange (ZSE) is the second largest in sub-Saharan Africa after Johannesburg. The ZSE has been open to foreign investment since June 1, 1993.

Structure

The Zimbabwe Stock Exchange (ZSE) is a proprietary body with sixty-three listed companies on a single board. Foreign activity is increasing, with over two thirds of turnover since mid-1993 being from non-residents.

Regulatory authority

The Exchange is regulated in accordance with the Stock Exchange Act by the Committee of the Exchange. The Committee has six members consisting of three nominees from stock-broking firms, two nominees from government and the Secretary of the Exchange.

Trading methods

Trading takes place using the Call-Over system. Board Lots are not officially fixed, but the majority of trades take place in units of 100 shares. Odd Lots are not favoured as price adjustments prove disadvantageous to clients.

Hours

Trading takes place between 09.00 and 12.00, Monday to Friday.

Settlement time and clearing

Settlement occurs on trade date plus five business days (T+5) basis. Brokers settle between themselves on a trade for trade basis.

Limits on price movement

None.

Types of shares

Ordinary shares, preference shares and warrants are traded on the ZSE.

Stock indices

There are two indices in Zimbabwe. The most widely quoted is the ZSE Industrial Index, which is the weighted average of fifty-six of the sixty-three companies listed on the Exchange. The other seven companies' performances are measured by the ZSE Mining Index. Generally, the mining index follows a similar path to the Industrial Index, but tends to be more volatile.

Taxes

Dividends are subject to a 15% Non-Resident Shareholders' Tax (NRST) while interest income faces a 10% tax. Capital gains greater than ZWD5000 (about US$500) are taxed at 10%, but a 15% inflation allowance is given.

Disclosure of financial statements

Listed companies are required to publish interim results and an annual report.

Ownership limits for non-residents

Foreign investors are restricted to 10% per investor or 40% collectively of a company's share value.

Capital and foreign exchange controls

After tax deductions, profits are fully remittable, but approval is required by the Company Transfers Secretary which can be time consuming. Authorized dealers convert foreign currency into ZWD at the Official Exchange Rate.

Brokers

There are ten registered brokerages on the ZSE. There is a Minimum Charge of ZWD15 as well as a Basic Charge of ZWD20 per transaction. In addition, commission rates are as follows:-

Value of transaction	Commission rate
On the first ZWD 50000	2.0%
On the next ZWD 50000	1.5%
Over ZWD 100000	1.0%

Sectors

On the ZSE, companies are divided broadly between industrials and mining. Despite only seven listings, the mining sector accounts for around 40% of market capitalization. This is largely a consequence of Ashanti Goldfields, which individually is equivalent to a third of total market value. The next largest listings on the ZSE are the conglomerate Delta Corporation (which contributes around 17% of total capitalization) and Barclays Bank (6%).

ADRs

There are no Zimbabwean ADRs, but Ashanti Goldfields is a GDR – traded in Ghana and London.

Derivatives
There is no derivatives market in Zimbabwe.

■ DEBT

The Reserve Bank of Zimbabwe acts as fiscal agent for the Ministry of Finance and issues government securities, which are listed and traded on the Zimbabwe Stock Exchange.

The main participants in the market, besides the Reserve Bank, are commercial banks, discount houses, parastatals and corporates, and the Post Office Savings Bank. In addition, pension funds and insurance companies are required to hold more than 50% of their assets in approved investments, which include government securities.

Non-residents can purchase medium- and long-dated bonds after initially exchanging hard currency through Foreign Currency Denominated Accounts (FCDAs). They can later sell the bonds on the secondary market, and repatriate the funds after paying 10% withholding tax, unless a double-taxation treaty exists.

Public debt
Treasury bills
The Reserve Bank issues and redeems treasury bills as part of its monetary policy operations. Bills with maturities of 1, 2, and 3 months are offered either for auction or tender each week. In auctions, the Reserve Bank announces the coupon and issue size, and bids are made on a price basis. In tenders, the Reserve Bank publishes a minimum acceptable price, and orders are allotted at or above that price. Non-residents cannot buy treasury bills.

Government stock (gilts)
Gilts are issued by the Reserve Bank with maturities ranging from 3 to 20 years. They are registered securities, and are designated as either tradeable or non-tradeable. They are issued on a tender basis with a fixed coupon. In the secondary market tradeable stock is priced against a floating rate yield curve interpolated by dealers.

Trades are settled on the same day in negotiable form. Government stocks pay semi-annual coupons, and interest is calculated on an actual/365-day basis.

In November 1996, the RBZ stated that it intended to open more investment opportunities to foreign investors by establishing a formal secondary bond market. In addition, it plans to create an association of market makers in government securities.

Private debt
Bankers' Acceptances and negotiable certificates of deposit (NCDs) are issued with 90-day maturities. Parastatals and corporates issue secured bonds and debentures depending on funding needs and contingent on market conditions, for maturities ranging from 3 to 10 years.

■ ZIMBABWE: Economic indicators

Population and development	1990	1991	1992	1993	1994	1995	1996e
Population, million	9.4	10.2	10.5	10.8	11.2	11.5	12.0
Population growth, %	2.7	8.8	2.7	3.0	3.4	3.4	4.2
Nominal GDP per capita, US$	723	583	482	524	529	575	617

National accounts							
Nominal GDP, US$bn	6.8	5.9	5.0	5.7	5.9	6.6	7.4
Change in real GDP, %	2.2	2.4	-41.3	4.6	7.4	-3.2	6.5
Gross fixed capital formation, % of GDP	19.6	26.7	24.3	22.5	22.1	22.9	21.8

Inflation							
Consumer price inflation (avg.) %	17.3	23.3	42.1	27.6	22.2	22.6	22.0

Government finance							
Government expenditure, % of GDP	35.4	34.5	42.1	44.8	43.9	43.7	40.0
Government balance, % of GDP	-6.9	-6.6	-7.1	-8.8	-7.9	-13.4	-10.1

Exchange rates lc=local currency							
Exchange rate, annual average, lc/US$	2.45	3.62	5.10	6.48	8.15	8.67	9.95
Exchange rate, end of year, lc/US$	2.64	5.05	5.48	6.94	8.39	9.31	10.80

Balance of payments							
Exports of goods & services, US$m	2012	1968	1833	1981	2344	2700	2815
Change %	4.0	-2.2	-6.8	8.1	18.3	15.2	4.3
Imports of goods & services, US$m, fob	2001	2273	2443	2051	2515	2730	2720
Change %	12.7	13.6	7.5	-16.1	22.6	8.5	-0.4
Trade balance, US$m, fob-fob	243	48	-254	122	158	250	400
Current account balance, US$m	-140	-457	-604	-116	-425	-190	-250
as a % of GDP	-2.1	-7.7	-12.0	-2.0	-7.2	-2.9	-3.4

Foreign exchange reserves							
Foreign exchange reserves, US$m	149.2	149.7	222.2	432.0	405.3	595.6	830.0
Gold at ⅔ of market price, US$m	97.4	99.1	125.1	119.8	120.3	194.4	—
Import cover (reserves/imports), months	0.9	0.8	1.1	2.5	1.9	2.6	3.7

Foreign debt and debt service							
Short-term debt, US$m	567	560	706	600	496	520	540
Total foreign debt, US$m	2912	3436	4005	4199	4368	4441	4488
as a % of GDP	43.0	57.8	79.4	74.3	74.0	67.0	60.5
as a % of foreign exchange receipts	130.1	157.2	181.5	183.6	178.9	149.0	152.1
Interest payments, US$m	187	195	207	211	228	258	266
Principal repayments, US$m	371	266	392	409	380	435	425
Total debt service, US$m	558	461	599	620	608	693	691
as a % of goods exports	31.9	27.2	39.2	38.5	31.0	30.8	29.4
as a % of foreign exchange receipts	24.9	21.1	27.1	27.1	24.9	23.3	23.4

Glossary

American depository receipt ADRs are negotiable certificates that are claims on shares in (ADR) non-US companies. They are traded in domestic securities markets and are issued by banks.

Amortization The gradual reduction of debt by means of regular periodic (usually equal) payments that cover the required interest and liquidate debt at maturity, or, more generally, the systematic writing off of an asset, or paying down a liability, over its estimated life.

Asia Pacific Economic Forum (APEC) Forum comprised of Pacific rim countries, including the US, Canada, Mexico, Japan and various East Asian countries to discuss issues of economic cooperation in the Pacific basin.

Appreciation A rise in an asset's value, typically used here to refer to a rise in a nation's currency value, measured in terms of one or more foreign currencies.

Arbitrage The practice of switching funds from one investment or one market to another in order to exploit price or yield differentials. An arbitrage flow of funds will take place between two national financial markets, for example, if the difference in their rates of interest is greater than the cost of covering the currency exchange risk.

Association of Southeast Asian Nations (ASEAN) Regional economic and political forum comprised of Asian Singapore, Malaysia, Thailand, Brunei, the Philippines, Indonesia and Vietnam. Cambodia, Laos and Myanmar have observer status.

Asian Tigers The most advanced East Asian economies: South Korea, Hong Kong, Taiwan and Singapore. Also referred to as NICs and NIEs (see below).

Balance of payments System of recording all economic transactions of a country with the rest of the world during a specific time period using double-entry bookkeeping. The balance of payments is divided into the current account, based on external trade in merchandise and services (including income on investments and transfer payments or grants between countries), capital account (direct and portfolio investments into and out of a country), and capital flows between the central bank and foreign central banks.

Base year The year chosen as the base of comparison for an index number; the weights chosen to construct an index are fixed in that year or measured relative to those in the selected year.

Bearer securities Bearer shares are owned by the bearer, the person who holds or physically possesses the instrument.

Bank for International Settlements (BIS) An international financial institution in Basle, founded in 1930, originally to coordinate war reparations payments between central banks. It continues to serve as a trustee and agent for international transfers and as a forum for discussion of international monetary and banking policy.

Blue chips The shares with the highest status as investments because they are expected to carry a lower risk of earnings failure, dividend omissions or bankruptcy than other shares. Blue chip status is normally assigned to shares of large and well-established companies. The word originally meant diamond chip.

Bond A fixed interest security denominated in a round amount as part of a bond issue. The individual bonds (securities) carry equal rights, with the issue conditions (interest rate, denomination, redemption terms, paying agents, guarantees etc.) uniformly specified. In contrast, medium-term notes are issued continuously, not during a specified period. Also, medium-term notes are not negotiable, while bonds are, and are even listed on the stock exchanges in many countries.

Bond issue A way to borrow funds by issuing securities – mostly fixed-interest – by offering them for public subscription during a specified period (subscription period), usually for a medium- to long-term period.

Book value The value at which assets or liabilities are carried on the books of account based on cost. For example, fixed assets are usually shown at cost less normal depreciation. Many accounts today use market value or a mixture of book and market value measures. The book value of a share is the company's book value divided by the number of shares outstanding.

Boom An unsustainably high level of business activity, usually at the end of a business cycle expansion (see below), frequently accompanied by price pressures and increased speculation in securities, commodities etc.

Brady bonds Bonds introduced in the late 1980s that were issued by developing countries to pay off their defaulted loans from commercial banks. Brady bonds are often collateralized by claims on the US government.

Bretton Woods system The fixed exchange rate system, designed in Bretton Woods New Hampshire at the end of the Second World War, that lasted until 1971.

Broker An independent agent who buys and sells stocks, bonds or other assets for the account of a customer.

Budget surplus or deficit A government's balance on a fiscal account of its receipts and outlays or expenditures for a period of time; the balance is found by subtracting outlays from receipts. A positive balance is called a surplus and a negative balance is called a deficit.

Business cycle An irregular pattern of movements in business activity relative to a long-term sustainable trend in which output and

employment can expand above their trends, reach their peak, then decline in recession, reach their lowest point or trough, then rise, beginning a recovery and eventually a new cycle.

Call option The buyer of a call option acquires the right – but is not obliged – to purchase a certain amount of securities, foreign exchange or precious metals at a predetermined price within a period of time.

Capital account The portion of a nation's balance of payments that includes a country's net foreign investment abroad and net investment flows coming from abroad over a period of time; investment includes direct investment, portfolio transactions in stocks, bonds, other secuities and loans, as well as changes in bank deposits.

Capital exports Flows of capital from one country to another. In the case of remunerative capital exports, the exporting company acquires legal claims, whereas unrequited capital exports can take the form of grants or other types of non-returnable conveyance. In a broader sense, capital exports also include direct investments effected abroad by multinational companies.

Capital gain The difference between the price of an asset and its cost; a negative difference is a capital loss.

Capital gains tax A tax on capital gains, usually levied only on gains that are realized by the sale of an asset. Gains are measured on a net basis and using the original cost of the asset (less any allowed depreciation). Sometimes cost is indexed, or adjusted for inflation to allow for the depreciation in the value of money originally invested.

Capital goods The long-lasting durable goods such as equipment and plant or other buildings that are used as factor inputs in the production of other goods or services.

Capitalization The present value of a flow of income or other recurring cash flow, or the act of computing such a capital value. For a corporation, the market capitalization can be found by multiplying the market price of the corporation's shares by the total number of outstanding shares.

Capital market Where trading, and price discovery for publicly tradeable long-term claims (stocks and bonds) on business enterprises take place; governments and individuals also create claims that compete with capital market assets, such as mortgages and bonds.

cif Abbreviation for cost, insurance and freight. Contract clause common in foreign trade when the seller pays for delivery of the goods to the port of shipment, loading the goods onto the ship, freight from the port of shipment to port of destination and insurance of the goods up to the port of destination. These costs are usually included in the price of the merchandise.

Clearing The settlement of liabilities, often of mutually offsetting claims, between two parties.

Club of Paris International forum of creditor countries that convenes to negotiate rescheduling the debt of heavily indebted countries.

Common stocks See ORDINARY SHARES

Consumer expenditure The rate at which consumers purchase newly produced goods and services over a period of time.

Convertible Bond issued by a corporation that may be converted by the holder into stock of the corporation within a specified time period and at a specified price.

Countercyclical A property of an economic measure indicating that the measure moves inversely to the business cycle – rising in recessions and falling in expansions.

Country risk The risk of default on sovereign liabilities, or the risk of being unable to transfer capital out of a country, arising from political, economic, legal or social factors in a particular country.

Coupon A certificate attached to a bond or share which, when detached and presented to the issuer of the security, entitles the bond or shareholder to receive the interest payment or dividend or to exercise rights.

Crowding out effect The effect of an increase in government spending on private expenditures on GDP, especially business investment, due to government competition for goods and services or the funds necessary to pay for increased spending.

Current account The balance of payments account that records exports and imports of goods and services, as well as transfers and gifts.

Custodian An agent that holds securities or other valuables for its clients and collects dividends and interest on their behalf.

Customs union A group of countries that agrees to eliminate all tariff barriers between themselves and to maintain a uniform common set of external tariffs on goods or services from the rest of the world.

Cyclical unemployment A component of unemployment or employment that occurs because of the cyclical components of national output movements over the business cycle.

Debenture General expression for different types of bonds.

Debt rescheduling Adjustment of the terms of an existing liabilities of a borrower: for example, a reduction of interest rates or an extension of the time required for payment.

Deflation A decline in the general level of prices, or an increase in the purchasing power of money typically brought about by a decrease in the amount of money in circulation relative to the flow of goods and services available.

Depreciation A fall in an asset's value, especially the value of one nation's currency relative to others.

Devaluation Reduction in the external value of a currency. In a system of fixed (or managed) exchange rates, a devaluation is effected by the legal or official lowering of the exchange rate, or parity, of the respective currency in terms of other currencies (formerly against gold). With flexible or floating exchange rates, the term depreciation is typically used to reflect a decline in the exchange rate arising from a rise in supply and/or a decline in demand for the currency.

Dividend A payment to shareholders of a limited company (corporation) or cooperative. The dividend is determined at the General Meeting upon the proposal of the Board of Directors.

Dividends can take the form of a cash dividend (payments in cash), stock dividends (allocation of new shares of the company) and dividends in kind (distribution of material things).

Dividend yield Cash dividends per share paid over a period as a percent of the share price at the beginning of a period.

Downturn General and severe decline in prices or rates (especially on the stock market or foreign exchange market), or in any other measure.

Economic growth A sustainable pace of expansion of a nation's output per capita, based on the growth of supplies of resources and improvements in technology and economic organization.

Equilibrium The absence of pressure for change; in a market, the absence of pressure for price or quantity traded to change unless fundamental factors affecting either supply or demand decisions change.

Emerging markets Usually developing countries that have had, and are expected to continue to have, relatively rapid growth compared with more mature industrial countries, and that usually also have, or are expected to develop, open capital markets, allowing foreigners to invest directly in domestic assets, especially in securities. Some rapidly growing countries with an income per capita among those of the most advanced countries are also commonly called emerging.

Equity The residual or net value of a company's assets after all liabilities (other than those to the holders of ordinary shares) have been deducted, which , when measured accurately, equals the market value of outstanding shares. The equity of a company is the property of the ordinary shareholders, hence shares are called equity.

Eurobonds Bonds issued on the Euromarket (Eurobond market) and denominated in various currencies payable outside the country of origin of the country, generally in Europe.

Eurodollars Eurodollars are dollar balances and dollar liabilities held and traded outside the United States, especially in Europe.

Euromarket International financial market consisting of several specialized markets on which bank loans and bond issues are transacted in Eurocurrencies such as Eurodollars, Euro-DM and Eurofrancs. Although its name refers to Europe, the Euromarket is by no means confined to Europe geographically but is today organized worldwide. In Asia it underwent strong growth under the name of Asian Dollar Market. There have been suggestions that a new expression is necessary to avoid confusion with the proposed new European currency, the euro.

Expansion The period in the business cycle between the end of a recovery, when real GNP reaches the level achieved at the previous cyclical peak, and the peak of the current cycle.

Expansionary fiscal policy A fiscal plan that includes government expenditure increases and/or reductions in taxes aimed at boosting a nation's demand, output and employment.

Expansionary monetary policy A monetary authority's plans for the use of policy instruments to boost demand, output and employment.

Exports Goods and services that are produced in a country and sold to purchasers in other countries.

Factor inputs The labour, capital goods or materials used to produce goods and services, and, therefore, real GDP or GNP.

FDI See FOREIGN DIRECT INVESTMENT

Fiscal policy Government plans to use tax and spending decisions to influence macroeconomic performance.

Fixed exchange rate system An agreement by a group of countries to maintain officially fixed exchange rates of their currencies, with the rate kept within a permitted margin of fluctuations or bands in foreign exchange markets, if necessary, by central bank intervention.

Fixed interest securities Securities on which the borrower must pay interest at a set rate on the original amount loaned for the entire maturity (such as bonds, notes, medium-term notes, debentures, etc.).

Fixed investment Capital goods purchases (plant and equipment and new housing).

Flight capital Common term for capital transferred by the owner to another country to avoid government-policy induced losses in asset value at home, especially when such transactions violate capital export or exchange control laws.

Floating exchange rate system An agreement, even if only tacit, between countries to allow markets to determine the value of the exchange rates between currencies. Clean floating occurs when there is little or no central bank intervention (currency support, buying or selling). In most countries with floating exchange rates, rates are allowed to develop freely, in principle, but central banks intervene on specific occasions for limited times and with limited funds (dirty floating). Also, some countries have managed exchange rates, where bands are set for the permitted movements of the currency's value and the bands are defended by official intervention.

Floating rate note (FRN) A note whose interest rate can change under certain circumstances. On the Euromarket FRNs are generally issued with a stated fixed coupon and variable coupon determined by a stated interest margin over LIBOR.

fob Abbreviation for free on board. Contract clause common in international trade that indicates that the contract price includes transport, insurance and loading costs incurred before merchandise is loaded on board the ship.

Foreign direct investment Investment in business assets (plant and equipment), or the acquisition of established business by foreign companies when they acquire or hold 10 percent or more ownership.

Foreign exchange controls Government regulations on the extent to which the nation's currency can be exchanged domestically for that of another country or moved abroad. Usually regulations are imposed to restrict the outflow of both foreign and domestic currency.

Forwards A contract between a buyer and a seller that provides for the seller to provide the buyer with a fixed amount of the currency or commodity on a fixed future date at a fixed rate of exchange, or price.

Free capital The proportion of equity of a company available for trading by the public on the stock market. Excludes equities held by controlling shareholders.

Free-trade area A group of countries that agree to eliminate tariffs on transactions between themselves while maintaining their own tariff barriers against the rest of the world.

FRN See FLOATING RATE NOTE

Futures Vehicle for the purchase and sale of commodities or financial instruments at a date in the future. Useful for fixing a future price and therefore for hedging current positions, but futures are traded on exchanges and are impersonal in that parties to a future transaction are unknown to each other and, unlike a forward, have no commitment to exercise delivery with each other, but only with the exchange.

Futures transactions The buying and selling of commodities, foreign exchange, or securities under contracts providing for the delivery of specific amounts, at a particular price and at some specified future date, instead of today, as in in a spot transaction.

Global depository receipt (GDR) GDRs are negotiable certificates that are claims on shares in companies traded in their on domestic market. They are traded in global markets and are issued simultaneously in multiple foreign markets.

Gross domestic product (GDP) The monetary value of all final goods and services produced in an economy in a period, measured at an annual rate.

Gross national product (GNP) The monetary value of all final goods and services produced by domestically owned resources,whether used at home or abroad, in a period, measured at an annual rate.

Growth stock Shares of a corporation that have scored faster-than-average earnings gains and are expected to show a high rate of profit growth. As a consequence, they justify a higher p/e ratio, but also have higher risk than average equities.

Hard currency Currency whose exchange rate is stable or tends to go up because the country has little or no domestic inflation, or at least lower inflation than others.

Hedging Forward or futures transaction undertaken by a buyer or a seller to protect assets or receipts or expenditures of goods, services, or money against a change in prices. Used in merchandise, commodities, foreign exchange and securities transactions. Example: an exporter delivers merchandise to Mexico payable after three months in Mexican pesos. To protect himself against the exchange rate risk on the due or payment date, he sells the related peso amount to his bank for delivery three months forward.

High-powered money The central bank's supply of assets that can be used directly as money (currency held by the non-bank public) or as bank reserves necessary for bank depositsa that are used as money. Sometimes called the monetary base, because this total constrains the size of the stock of domestic money

Hot money Another expression for flight capital.

Hyperinflation Unusually high inflation; by one commonly accepted standard, an inflation rate consistently exceeding 25 percent per month.

IBRD The International Bank for Reconstruction and Development. See WORLD BANK

IDA The International Development Association, one of two organizations (along with the IFC) created to further the aims of the World Bank by providing loans to underdeveloped countries at less rigorous terms than the Bank would normally require.

IFC The International Finance Corporation, an organization of the World Bank Group. It was created to further economic development in developing countries by dealing with private investors who do not have government guarantees.

Iliquidity The lack of liquid or easily marketable assets with the result that payment liabilities and obligations cannot be met on time.

Imports The goods and services purchased by individuals, groups, businesses or government in one country from other countries.

Indexed bond A bond that has an interest rate that is adjusted according to an the inflation rate.

Inflation A sustained pace of decline in the purchasing power of money, reflecting a sustained pace of increase in the general level of prices.

Institutional investors Organizations with substantial, mostly continuous investment needs that trade large volumes of securities, e.g. insurance companies, pension funds, investment funds, etc.

Interbank funds Funds borrowed by banks from other banks, usually overnight or for short periods.

Interbank rate Interest rate applied to credit operations between banking institutions. On the Euromoney market the so-called "London Interbank Offering Rate" (LIBOR) is calculated daily and serves as a guide for interest rates used for many international loans in Eurocurrencies. Another example of an interbank rate is the federal funds rate (funds US banks lend one another for short periods).

Interest rate The amount paid for the use of borrowed funds expressed as a percent of the amount borrowed and usually expressed at an annual rate.

Intermediate good Any good that is resold by its purchaser either in its present form or after further processing.

International Monetary Fund (IMF) The most important international organization for monetary policy cooperation and for short to medium term credit to assist macroeconomic adjustment to external payments problems. The IMF was established in 1946 at Bretton Woods New Hampshire in 1946 and based in Washington D.C.

International reserves Assets that are accepted by central banks for settlement of payments between themselves. The principal types of reserves are gold, special drawings rights, foreign currencies or short-term government securities denominated in these currencies, especially the US dollar, yen and German mark,

Inventory investment Changes in the stock of intermediate goods held by business, especially raw materials, parts, and finished goods.

Inverted yield curve Unusual situation where short-term interest rates are higher than long-term rates.

Labour force The number of people willing and able to work, whether currently employed or not.

LIBOR See LONDON INTERBANK OFFERED RATE

Liquidity The property of an asset that indicates its marketability or ability to trade in relatively large amounts over very short periods of time without requiring price sensitivity simply to attract traders. Also a property of a market that indicates the degree to which there is a sufficiently large actual or potential flow of funds to avoid large price adjustments in any of the assets traded in the particular market simply to attract traders whenever there are relatively large variations in supply or demand.

Liquidity trap A situation in which all investors expect asset prices to fall and have an absolute preference for liquidity, especially money, to avoid capital losses due to such price losses. Purely a conceptual construct of some historical interest, however, since such a case would force prices to fall as investors attempted to avoid expected losses by selling assets. Thus, if such a trap could exist, it is not likely that it could ever be observed in practice.

Listed issues or companies Stock issues or companies whose shares are listed on the stock exchange.

London Interbank Offered Rate The rate of interest offered on loans to first-class banks for a (LIBOR) specified period in the the London interbank market.

Long position Owning or holding more of a given financial asset or commodity than one has contracted to deliver in future. One goes long in the expectation that prices will rise and one can realize a profit.

M1 The "narrow" definition of the money supply.

M1 includes money in circulation and current accounts or balances at banks that can be used to make third-party payments by the depositor.

M2 A broader definition of the money supply than M1; comprises M1 (i.e. money in circulation plus current account deposits) plus various measures of time or savings deposits and in some countries money market account balances.

Managed floating An exchange rate policy that allows exchange rates to float subject to some desired band or upward or downward limits on the exchange rate; the central bank defends these limits through market interventions.

Market capitalization The market value of company's entire outstanding share capital (capital stock) or, for an exchange or market, the value of all listed shares on exchange or market.

Maturity The date of payment or settlement of a financial claim; e.g. the date on which a bond becomes due for repayment.

Merchant bank A banking institution whose financial business gradually evolved from its merchant business. The merchant bankers' local knowledge of the countries with which they traded made them specialists in estimating the creditworthiness of their customers, which in turn enabled them to accept bills of exchange and arrange loans at the request of foreign traders. Their business has now extended beyond normal banking transactions to include dealings in foreign exchange, the issue of long-term loans for governments and companies abroad, acting as company advisors, underwriting new issues, managing takeover bids, and engaging in insurance business and investment trust management, etc.

Monetarism A school of thought that generally accepts the views that: inflation is a monetary phenomenon; fiscal policy is ineffective or counterproductive in affecting output and employment; and free markets are efficient in achieving macroeconomic goals, markets are inherently stable and, in the absence of economic policy or other shocks, tend to result in high employment conditions.

Monetary base See HIGH POWERED MONEY; also called central bank money. The monetary base also often includes an adjustment for reserve requirement changes.

Monetary policy Plans by the central bank or other monetary authority to use control of the monetary base, money stock, interbank rate, or a credit measure to achieve its macroeconomic objectives.

Money market The open market for lending or borrowing short-term funds and for dealing in short-term negotiable instruments. In addition to the national money markets, the Euromoney market has developed in recent years into an efficient international market place for dealing in short-dated assets.

Money supply The stock of money that exists in an economy at a given time. There are a number of definitions of what exactly constitutes the money supply. See M1 and M2.

National income Income arising from the production of GNP: net national product less indirect business taxes, plus government subsidies to business and losses on government enterprises.

Net exports Exports minus imports.

New issue market The part of the capital market that provides new long-term capital.

Newly industrializing countries (NICs or NIEs) Usually refers to the most advanced "tiger" countries or economies in East Asia: South Korea, Hong Kong, Taiwan and Singapore. Sometimes used for all of South and East Asia or emerging markets in general.

Nominal GNP or GDP The value of GNP or GDP; see GDP and GNP.

Nominal interest rate An interest rate actually observed on financial assets with given and fixed nominal (local currency) interest and principal.

Note Term used internationally in the lending business meaning essentially a credit instrument consisting of a written unconditional promise to pay a sum of money at some specifies date to a named person or bearer.

Offshore funds Term for investment funds whose domicile is located in one of the offshore financial centres which offer tax advantages to foreign investors. Preferred countries of domicile include the Netherlands Antilles, the Bahamas and Panama.

OPEC Organization of Petroleum Exporting Countries. Member countries include Algeria, Ecuador, Gabon, Indonesia, Iran, Iraq, Kuwait, Libya, Nigeria, Qatar, Saudi Arabia, United Arab Emirates and Venezuela.

Open economy An economy in which there are flows of labour, goods, bonds, and/or money to and from other nations.

Open-market operations Central bank purchases or sales of government bonds for monetary policy or simply asset management.

Option Contract granting the right, but not entailing the obligation, to buy or sell property or assets during a specified period at an agreed price. Also, in the foreign exchange market, a binding contract to buy or sell currency at specific price, the date of the transaction however being left to the choice of the holder of the contract.

Order driven A stock exchange system in which prices react to orders.

Ordinary shares A regular share, without any special voting, income or other ownership limitations.

Over-the-counter market The auxiliary stock market (OTC market) in which securities not listed on regular stock exchanges are traded.

p/bv ratio SEE PRICE/BOOK VALUE RATIO

p/e ratio SEE PRICE/EARNINGS RATIO

Papers Vernacular term for any security, most generally applied to those in the money market.

Par value The value of the security as printed on its face, therefore also called the face value or nominal value. Ordinarily not identical with the market value.

Petrodollars Surplus cash gained by oil exporters (especially OPEC) which they have not spent on imports, but have invested with interest in other countries in varying proportions, mostly on short call. As oil was at one time mainly invoiced and quoted in dollars, the term "petrodollars" was created.

Placing or placement The sale of new shares to institutions or private individuals, as distinct from an introduction or offer for sale.

Portfolio investment An investment in securities for a portfolio holding rather than, in the case of shares at least, an investment enabling or maintaining management control.

Preference shares A share with preference rights that allow holders superior stock rights over ordinary shareholders in a company, especially preferred stocks that pay a fixed dividend that must be paid before any dividend can be paid on other shares.

Price index A measure of prices of a collection of goods or services, such as consumer or purchaser purchases, domestic output, or wages, constructed as a weighted average of the individual prices and stated relative to a base year when the weighted are set at 100, or 100 percent of the base period price measure. There are a variety of techniques for determining the weights and how they might change over time.

Price/book value ratio Total market capitalization divided by the total book value of a company(s). Book value is also called net worth, the difference between total assets and total liabilities, when book value accounting methods are used.

Price/earnings ratio The ratio of total market capitalization to the total earnings of a company(s); earnings are measured over the previous 12 months.

Primary market The market for newly issued securities during the issuing period.

Privatization The sale or transfer to private ownership of a previously nationalized enterprise.

Procyclical An adjective applied to any economic measure that fluctuates in the same direction as cyclical movements of output and employment.

Productivity A measure of output per unit of resource input, typically measured as firm, industry, or national output per unit of labour

input used to produce the output (number of workers or hours worked, or paid for) to obtain labour productivity, or per unit of resources used (where resources are a weighted average of labour and capital employed) to obtain total factor productivity.

Promissory notes A written unconditional promise to pay, issued and signed by the debtor himself, who undertakes to pay on demand or at a fixed or determinable future a certain sum of money to the order of the specified person, or to the bearer.

Protectionist A governmental action (tariff, quota, subsidy or regulatory barrier) to benefit and insulate domestic producers from foreign competition, or simply to reduce imports or raise exports.

Purchasing power parity (PPP) A measure of the foreign exchange value of a currency that provides equivalent purchasing power for the currency in a foreign market or in the domestic economy; computed on the basis of inflation differentials and/or a comparison of foreign and domestic prices of a comparable basket of goods and services.

Put option Gives the buyer the right, but not the obligation, to sell a specified number of securities, a specified amount of foreign currency or a specified quantity of precious metal for a stipulated period at a stipulated price.

Rate of return The earnings from an investment expressed at an annual rate as a percent of the value invested.

Real exchange rate A measure of the exchange value of a currency against one or more currencies adjusted for the purchasing power of the respective currencies; equal to the foreign currency price of a currency times the ratio of what the latter currency will buy per unit of what the equivalent foreign currency could buy. Specifically the price of the domestic currency is multiplied by the ratio of a price index for the domestic economy to the equivalent foreign price index. A real exchange rate rise or fall indicates that a currency's value is rising or falling for reasons unrelated to having a lower or higher inflation rate than its competitors.

Real GDP (or GNP) The value of gross domestic product (or gross national product) measured at constant prices, specifically those in a base period.

Real interest rate Interest rate calculated by subtracting the (annual) inflation rate from the stated (or nominal) interest rate; to measure returns adjusted for the loss of purchasing power on the nominal sums originally loaned or invested.

Real output The concept that is intended to be measured by real GDP or real GNP.

Real wage The nominal wage measured in terms of its purchasing power in goods and services; measured by dividing the nominal wage by the ratio of a price index relative to its base period value.

Recession The stage in the economic cycle in which activity is declining; a growth recession occurs when activity is rising but more slowly than an economy's economic capacity.

Recovery Business cycle period between the trough and the time when real GNP reaches its level at the preceding peak.

Rediscount rate The interest rate applied to bank borrowings from their central bank.

Repurchase agreement (Repo) An agreement to a transaction that allows funds to, in effect, be borrowed; short-term securities are sold with the condition that the securities will be repurchased at a given date and given price.

Revaluation An increase in the external value of a currency in terms of other currencies, that is the opposite to a devaluation (see above.

Rights issue A company's issue to shareholders of transferable rights to purchase additional shares at a fixed price; usually rights are issued in a fixed ratio to the number of shares currently held.

Secondary market Market for trading in securities (such as Eurobonds) subsequent to the initial placement during the issuing period (primary market). The secondary stock market is the market for securities outside the organized exchanges.

Security Share or debt certificates or registered claims that signify the ownership position or rights to ownership which cannot be enforced or transferred without the owners legal direction to that effect.

SDR See SPECIAL DRAWING RIGHT

Settlement Payment of an obligation, e.g. payment in cash for securities.

Sell short Market term for selling an asset that one does not own with the intention of buying the asset later at a lower price to cover the sale. Until the purchase to close the transaction has been made, the trader is said to be short of the asset. Traders taking advantage of expected falling prices by going short are known as bears.

Short position A negative balance of an individual's net holdings of an asset, holdings less short sales, or aggregate short sales of all short sellers.

Sinking fund Provision for the repayment of a loan or security by the issuer, by accumulating a fund through regular payments which, with interest, will amortize the debt.

Soft currency Weak currency that is a less desirable means of payment than other currencies. Soft currency countries tend to have depreciating currencies or frequent currency devaluations, and balance of payments difficulties. Contrast with hard or strong currency.

Special Drawing Right Payment medium and reserve asset used internationally for transactions between central banks; issued by the International Monetary Fund (IMF) to its member nations.

Spot rate In foreign exchange, commodities and security trading, the rate quoted for immediate payment and delivery.

Spot transactions Transaction where delivery and cash payment for the instruments or goods (e.g., securities, foreign currencies or commodities traded on exchanges) are immediate. In the securities business, for example, a spot transaction on the Basle and

Zurich exchanges is usually settled on the working day following the transaction and in the foreign exchange business at the latest two working days later. Opposite: forward or futures transaction.

Spread margin In the commodity and financial markets, the difference between the offered, or bid, and asked prices at any moment. Also name for the difference in the market price between a bearer and a registered share of the same company, the difference in yields on an issuer's liabilities due to differences in maturity or yield differences that come about for some other reason such as various risks, and so on.

Stabilization policy Government plans to use monetary and fiscal policies or actions to achieve macroeconomic goals.

Stagflation Term coined in the seventies to describe the simultaneous occurrence of recession or stagnation and relatively large one-time increases in the general level of prices, or even inflation.

Sterilization Central bank actions to offset the effect on their total assets of foreign exchange purchase or sales by offsetting sales or purchases of other assets, especially securities.

Structural unemployment Unemployment that is independent of cyclical movements in output and arises from structural characteristics of the economy, such as government incentives to conduct excessive search for jobs or to not search at all, disincentives for firms to hire workers, or other costs of finding job matches, hiring or accepting work.

Supply disturbance See SUPPLY SHOCK

Supply shock, or disturbance A disruption in the amount of output that firms are willing and able to produce and sell at the given price level.

Supply-side economics Economic analysis that focuses on factors affecting producer's supply decisions, especially aggregate domestic output supply, including the influence of government stabilization and other economic policies, and changes in tastes or technology. Because it focuses on supply factors, it is concerned at a fundamental level with economic growth.

SWIFT Abbreviation for the Society for World Interbank Financial Telecommunications. Founded by western European and American banks in 1973 with registered offices in Brussels, the company operates a computer-guided communications system to rationalize international payment transfers.

Trade balance The difference between the value of the exports and the imports of a country, but typically exports and imports of goods only, and excluding services. The balance of trade is positive (in surplus or sometimes called favourable) if exports exceed imports and negative (in deficit, or unfavourable) if the opposite is true.

Treasury bills (T-bills) Short-term negotiable state bonds.

Treasury bonds In the USA, any of the series of medium- to long-term bonds issued by the US Treasury. Maturity is usually longer than five years.

Turnover ratio Total value of shares traded during a period (usually a year) divided by market capitalization for the period in currency terms.

Unemployment rate Unemployment (the size of the labour force less the number of persons employed) as a percent of the labour force.

Unit trust An investment organization that offers shares or units in a portfolio it creates and invests the funds subscribed by the public in securities, and that will repurchase the units at any time at their market value.

Unlisted security Securities which are not listed for trading on one of the regular stock exchanges, and are therefore traded in direct negotiations or over-the-counter.

Value added The value that is added to purchased intermediate goods at a given stage of production which equals revenues from sales of goods and the change in the value of inventory value less the cost of intermediate goods purchased during a period of time. It also equals the value of labour and capital employed in a particular stage of the production process during the same period.

Value traded The total value of shares traded during a period of time.

Volume traded The total number of shares traded during a period of time.

Warrant issue An instrument that offers the right to purchase shares or participation certificates in the issuing company at a stipulated price within a certain period.

World Bank Commonly used name for the International Bank for Reconstruction and Development (IBRD) which was established along with the IMF in 1944 at Bretton Woods (USA) and also based in Washington DC. It has some 150 member countries. It grants long-term investment loans to developing countries. The International Development Association (IDA) and the International Finance Corporation (IFC) are affiliated with the World Bank and the three organizations together are the so-called World Bank Group.

Yield The rate of return that equates the present cost of an asset with the present value of its future cash flow. Sometimes measured over one period only and equal to the change in an asset's price over the period plus any distribution of income or principal divided by the value of the asset at the beginning of the period.

Index

Agriculture: Bulgaria 92
  India 285-6
  Morocco 442-4
  Pakistan 467-8
  Philippines 509-10
AMS trading system 256
Andean Community/Pact:
  Colombia 133
  Ecuador 189
Argentina 49-66
  Austral Plan 53
  Convertibility Law 52, 54, 57
  debt 57, 62-5
  economic indicators 66
  equities 59-62
  history: economic 53-4
    political 49-51
  IMF 57
  politics 49-52
  other political forces 52
  political parties 51-2
Army: Indonesia 301
  Pakistan 465-6
  see also Military
Asian competitiveness 20
Asian Dollar Market 610
ASIS trading system 241
ASSET trading system 701

Balance of payments: Argentina
  56
  Brazil 74
  Bulgaria 93
  Chile 106
  China 119-20
  Colombia 134
  Czech Republic 173-4
  Ecuador 190
  Ghana 226-7
  Hong Kong 252-3
  Hungary 272-3
  Indonesia 304-6
  Israel 324-5
  Latvia 376
  Lithuania 390-1
  Malaysia 407-8
  Mexico 425
  Panama 482
  Peru 494-5
  Philippines 511-12
  Poland 533
  Portugal 549-50
  Russia 576
  Saudi Arabia 603-4
  Slovakia 620-1
  Slovenia 633
  South Africa 648-9
  South Korea 664-5
  Taiwan 679-80
  Thailand 695-6
  Turkey 712-13
  Venezuela 748-9
  Vietnam 764-5

Baltic Free Trade Association:
  Lithuania 390
Bangladesh 465
Bank bonds: Czech Republic 181
Bank debentures: Taiwan 684
Bank of Reconstruction and
  Development: Hungary 266-7
Bank promissory notes:
  Indonesia 314-15
  Russia 584
Banking sector: Kazakstan 354
  Russia 576
Banking systems: Argentina 58
  Brazil 76
  Chile 108
  Colombia 136
  Ecuador 192
  Egypt 207
  Hungary 275
  Indonesia 301
  Mexico 427
  Morocco 450
  Panama 483
  Peru 496-7
  Philippines 515-16
  Poland 535
  Thailand 692
  Vietnam 760-1
  Venezuela 751
  see also Central banks
Bills see specific types
Bills of exchange: Czech
  Republic 180
BIS trading system 636
Bond market 10
Bonds: China 125
  Czech Republic 180
  Greece 243
  Mexico 431
  Peru 500
  Poland 540-1
  see also specific types of bond
Brady bonds 38, 39, 41,42
  Argentina 64
  Brazil 82
  Bulgaria 97
  Ecuador 195
  Jordan 344
  Mexico 433
  Nigeria 462
  Panama 486
  Peru 501
  Philippines 520
  Poland 542
  Venezuela 755
Brady Plan: Brazil 75, 81
  Côte d'Ivoire 145
  Ecuador 190
  Mexico 425
Brazil 67-83
  debt: private 80-90
    public 79-80
  economic indicators 83

equities 77-9
history: economic 70-2
  political 67-9
politics 67-70
  other political forces 70
  political parties 69-70
Social Emergency Fund 75
World Bank 75
Bulgaria 84-98
  debt 96-7
  economic indicators 98
  equities 94-6
  history: economic 89-90
    political 84-6
  IMF 89, 90, 94
  international relations 89
  OECD 93
  politics 84-9
    political parties 88
  World Bank 90

Call-Over trading system 229,
  780
Capital see Exchange controls
Capital flows 9, 17
  (by region) 18
Caravelas bonds: Portugal 555
CATS (trading method) 77-8
CCM trading system 329
Central European Free Trade
  Agreement: Hungary 267
Central banks: Argentina 52
  Brazil 70
  Bulgaria 89
  Chile 102
  China 117
  Colombia 130
  Croatia 155
  Czech Republic 171
  Ecuador 186
  Egypt 201-2
  Estonia 214-15
  Greece 234
  Hong Kong 250
  Hungary 266
  Indonesia 301
  Israel 320
  Jordan 336
  Kazakstan 350
  Latvia 373
  Lithuania 387-8
  Malaysia 403
  Mexico 420-1
  Morocco 440-1
  Peru 491
  Philippines 507
  Poland 528
  Portugal 546-7
  Russia 573
  Saudi Arabia 590-1
  Slovakia 616
  South Africa 645
  South Korea 661

Taiwan 676
Thailand 691
Turkey 710, 724
Venezuela 745
Zimbabwe 774
see also National banks
Certificates of deposit: Hong
  Kong 258
  India 294
  Indonesia 314
  Thailand 703
Chile 99-114
  debt 107, 111-12
  Decree Law 600 104, 105
  economic indicators 114
  equities 109-11
  history: economic 102-3
    political 99-101
  indebtedness 107
  politics 99-102
    other political forces 102
    political parties 101-2
China 115-26
  debt, public 124-5
  economic indicators 126
  equities 122-4
    background 122
  Five-Year Plan 119-20
  history: economic 118
    political 115-17
  Hong Kong 247-8
  politics 115-17
    political forces 117
Colombia 127-41
  debt 134-5
    private 139-40
    public 139
  drug dealers 130
  economic indicators 141
  equities 137-9
  guerrilla groups 130
  history: economic 130-1
    political 127
  politics 127-30
    other political forces 130
    political parties 129-30
  World Bank 134
Colón Free Trade Zone 480-1,
  482
  trade restrictions 481
COMECON: Bulgaria 92
  Czech Republic 173
  Hungary 270-1
  Poland 531
  Romania 561
Commercial paper: Colombia 139
  Ecuador 195
  Hong Kong 258
  India 294-5
  Poland 541
  Indonesia 314
  Philippines 520
  Taiwan 684

Thailand 703
Commonwealth of Independent
  States (CIS): Kazakstan 353
  Turkey 726
Competitiveness 19, 20
Convertible bond 43
Corporate bonds: Greece 244
  Hong Kong 259
  Indonesia 315
  Malaysia 414
  Peru 500
  Philippines 520
  Poland 541
  Portugal 555
  Slovakia 625
  South Africa 655
  Taiwan 684
  Thailand 703
Corporate debentures: India 295
Côte d'Ivoire 142-50
  debt 149
  economic indicators 150
  equities 148-9
  history: economic 144-5
    political 142-4
  IMF 145, 146
  politics 142-4
Credit rating agencies: India 295
  Indonesia 315
  Thailand 704
Croatia 151-66
  debt 161, 164-5
  economic indicators 166
  equities 162-4
  history: economic 156-8
    political 151-4
  stabilization plan 157-8
    background 156-7
Current account 16
Current account deficits:
  Indonesia 306-7
  Thailand 697
  Vietnam 765-6
Customs Union: Turkey/EU 712
Czech Republic 167-82
  debt 179-81
    private debt 180-1
    public debt 180
  economic indicators 182
  economic transition 172-3
  equities 176-9 history:
    economic 171-3
    political 167-71
  OECD 171
  performance under central
    planning 171
  politics 167-71
    political parties 170

Debt: Argentina 57, 62-3
  Brazil 79-90
  Bulgaria 96-7
  Chile 107, 111-12
  China 124-5
  Colombia 134-5
  Côte d'Ivoire 149
  Croatia 161, 164-5
  Czech Republic 179-81
  Ecuador 190-1, 194-5
  Egypt 205, 210
  Estonia 220
  foreign 13, 16
  former Yugoslavia 165

Ghana 230
Greece 239, 242-3
Hong Kong 257-8
Hungary 275, 278-9
India 292-5
Indonesia 307-8, 313-15
Israel 330-1
Jordan 343-4
Kazakstan 358
Kenya 368
Latvia 381-2
Lithuania 395-6
local currency 38
Malaysia 413-15
Mexico 431-2
Morocco 446
Nigeria 462
Pakistan 473-4
Panama 485-6
Peru 495, 499-500
Philippines 513-14, 519-20
Poland 539-40
  foreign debt 536
Portugal 554-5
Romania 564, 567
Russia 577, 583-5
  foreign debt 577
Saudi Arabia 596
Singapore 609-10
Slovakia 624-5
Slovenia 637-8
South Africa 655-6
South Korea 669-70
Taiwan 683-5
Thailand 698, 702-4
Turkey 718-19, 728, 729-30
Uzbekistan 740
Venezuela 749, 754
Vietnam 766-7, 770
Zimbabwe 782
see also Indebtedness;
  Rescheduled debt;
  Restructured debt
Derivatives: Argentina 62
  Brazil 79
  Chile 111
  Croatia 164
  Czech Republic 179
  Estonia 220
  Hungary 278
  Israel 330
  Lithuania 395
  Poland 539
  Portugal 554, 556
  Romania 566
  Russia 584
  Singapore 610-11
  Slovenia 637
  South Africa 656
  South Korea 669
  Thailand 702
  Zimbabwe 782
Development bonds: Jordan 344
  Mexico 431
Dragon bonds: Hong Kong 259

EBOS trading system 623
Ecuador 183-96
  debt 190-1
    private 194-5
    public 194
  economic indicators 196
  equities 192-4

market comment 194
history: economic 186-7
  political 183-5
IMF 190
politics 183-6
  other political forces 186
  political parties 185-6
EFTA, Poland 529
Egypt 197-212
  debt 205, 209
  economic indicators 211
  equities 208-9
    market comment 209
  history: economic 202-3
    political 197-9
  IMF 201-2, 206, 207
  politics 197-201
    political parties 200-1
  World Bank 201-2, 206
ELIT trading system 717
Emerging markets: definition of
  787
  share of global output 12, 15
Emerging market debt 35
Employment: Poland 533-4
  Portugal 548
  Turkey 711
  Uzbekistan 737-8
Equity markets (overview) 25-31
  Argentina 59-62
  Brazil 77-9
  Bulgaria 94-6
  Chile 109-11
  China 122-4
  Colombia 137-9
  Côte d'Ivoire 148-9
  Croatia 162-4
  Czech Republic 176-9
  Ecuador 192-4
  Egypt 208-9
  Estonia 218-20
  Ghana 228-30
  Greece 240-2
  Hong Kong 255-7
  Hungary 276-8
  India 290-2
  Indonesia 311-13
  Israel 327-30
    free float 328
  Jordan 341-3
  Kazakstan 357
  Kenya 366-8
  Latvia 379-81
  Lithuania 393-5
  Malaysia 410-13
  Mexico 427-31
  Morocco 451-2
  Nigeria 461-2
  Pakistan 472-3
  Panama 484-5
  Peru 497-9
  Philippines 517-18
  Poland 537-9
  Portugal 552-4
  Romania 565-6
  Russia 581-3
  Saudi Arabia 594-6
  Singapore 606-9
  Slovakia 622-4
  Slovenia 635-7
  South Africa 652-5
  South Korea 666-9
  Taiwan 681-3

Thailand 700-2
Turkey 716-18
Ukraine 728-9
Uzbekistan 740
Venezuela 751-4
Vietnam 769-70
Zimbabwe 779-82
ESIS trading system 595
Estonia 212-21
  debt 220
  economic indicators 221
  equities 218-20
  history: collapse of Soviet
    Union 215
    political 212-13
  politics 212-14
  stabilization programme 215-
    16
Eurobonds 40
  Argentina 64-5
  Brazil 81
  Bulgaria 97
  Chile 112-13
  China 125
  Colombia 140
  Czech Republic 181
  Ecuador 195
  Estonia 220
  Greece 244
  Hong Kong 259
  Hungary 279
  India 295
  Indonesia 316
  Jordan 344
  Latvia 382
  Lithuania 396
  Malaysia 415
  Mexico 432-3
  Morocco 453
  Pakistan 474
  Panama 486
  Peru 500
  Philippines 520
  Poland 541-2
  Portugal 556
  Romania 567
  Russia 585
  Saudi Arabia 596
  Singapore 611
  Slovakia 625
  Slovenia 638
  South Africa 656
  South Korea 670-1
  Taiwan 685
  Thailand 704
  Turkey 719
  Venezuela 754-5
European Bank for
  Reconstruction and
  Development: Poland 528
European Monetary System
  (EMS): Greece 237
European Union (EU): Greece
  238, 240
  Hungary 267
  Lithuania 390
  Poland: membership 529
    trade 531-2
  Portugal 548
  Turkey 712
Exchange controls: Argentina 58
  Chile 108
  Colombia 136

Greece 242
Hong Kong 257
Hungary 278
India 292
Indonesia 310
Jordan 342
Kenya 367
Latvia 380
Lithuania 375
Mexico 427, 430
Morocco 452
Panama 483, 485
Peru 496
Philippines 516
Poland 539
Portugal 554
Romania 566
Saudi Arabia 595
Slovakia 624
Slovenia 637
South Korea 668
Thailand 699-700, 702
Turkey 718
Uzbekistan 740
Venezuela 750, 753
Vietnam 769
Zimbabwe 781
see also Foreign exchange
  rates
Exchange fund bills/notes: Hong
  Kong 258
Exchange Rate Mechanism
  (ERM): Portugal 551

Federal bonds: Pakistan 474
  Russia 584
Fixed-income markets 32-44
Foreign debt 13, 16
Foreign direct investment (FDI) 9,
  17, 18
Foreign exchange rates: Egypt
  207
  Morocco 449-50
  Philippines 516
Foreign investment: Argentina
  55
  Brazil 81
  Bulgaria 95
  Chile 104, 112
  China 119, 125
    limits 124
  Colombia 132
  Hong Kong 257
  India 285, 291
    limits 292
  Indonesia 304
  Israel 325-6
  Kazakstan 357
  Latvia 376
  Peru 500
  Poland 531
  Russia (table) 580
    government debt 583
  Singapore 608
  South Africa 654, 656
  South Korea 670
  Taiwan 685
  Vietnam 763-4
Free Market (trading system) 219

GATT: Morocco 448
  Poland 528
Ghana 222-31

debt 230
economic indicators 231
equity market 228-30
history: economic 224-5
  political 222-4
politics 222-4
Government bonds: Czech
  Republic 180
  Ecuador 194
  Hungary 278-9
  India 294
  Israel 330-1
  Portugal 555
  Saudi Arabia 596
  South Africa 655
  Taiwan 684
  Turkey 719
  see also Development bonds
Government investment
  certificates: Malaysia 413
Government securities: India
  293-4
  Lithuanian 395-6
  Malaysia 413
Government stock (gilts):
  Zimbabwe 782
Greece 232-45
  debt 239, 242-3
  economic indicators 245
  equities 240-2
    market comment 242
  history: political 232-4
  international relations 234-5
  NATO 235
  politics 232-4
    political parties 234

Hong Kong 246-60
  debt 257-8
    private debt 258-9
    public debt 258
  economic indicators 260
  equities 255-7
  history: economic 250-1
    political 246-8
  politics 246-50
    political forces 249-50
Hungary 261-80
  debt: foreign 275
  economic indicators 280
  equities 276-8
  history: economic 267-8
    political 261-4
  membership of international
    organizations 266-7
  politics 261-6
    political parties 265-6

IBRD: Romania 564
IMF see International Monetary
  Fund
Indebtedness: Chile 107
  Mexico 425
India 281-96
  business advantages 283
  debt 292
    private 294-5
    public 293-4
  economic indicators 296
  economic reforms 284
  equities 290-2
    depository receipts 292
  fiscal deficit 286-7

history: political 281-2
interest rates 286
macro-economic improvement
  284-5
natural resources 283
parallel economy 283
politics 281-3
  political parties 282
Indonesia 297-317
  Commercial Offshore Loan
    Team 308
  debt 307-8, 313
    private debt 314-15
    public debt 313-14
  Deregulation 310
  economic indicators 317
  equities 311-13
  history: economic 302-3
    political 297-9
  politics 297-301
    other political forces 301
    political parties 300
  World Bank 308
Inflation: global 15
  Greece 236-7
  India 286
  Pakistan 469
International Development
  Association (IDA): Hungary
  266
International Finance
  Corporation (IFC): Hungary 266
  Poland 528
International Monetary Fund
  (IMF) 10
  Argentina 57
  Bulgaria 89, 90, 94
  Côte d'Ivoire 145, 146
  Ecuador 190
  Egypt 201-2, 206, 207
  Hungary 266
  Kazakstan 354
  Kenya 366
  Lithuania 392
  Peru 495
  Philippines 514-15
  Poland 528
  Romania 564
  Russia 577
    monitoring reforms 578-9
  Turkey 727
  Vietnam 766-7
  see also London Club; Paris
  Club
Israel 318-32 debt 330-1
  economic indicators 332
  equity market 327-30
  history: economic 321-3
    political 318-20
  "Interested parties" 328
  politics 318-20

JATS trading system 311-12
JET trading system 653
Jordan 333-45
  debt 343-4
  economic indicators 345
  equities 341-3
  history: economic 336-7
    political 333-5
  politics 333-6
    poitical parties 335-6
  Public Debt Law (1971) 343

Kazakstan 346-59
  competitiveness 355
  debt 358
  economic indicators 359
  equities 357
    market comment 357
  history: economic 350-1
    political 346-8
  macroeconomic balances
    (1996) 355
  oil and gas sector 356
  politics 346-50
Kenya 360-9
  debt 368
  economic indicators 369
  equities 366-8
  history: economic 362-3
    political 360-2
  politics 360-2
KOBOS trading system 177

Labour: Panama 479
  Peru 491
  Turkey 711
  Uzbekistan 737-8
Latvia 370-83
  economic indicators 383
  equities 379-81
  history: economic 374-5
    political 370-2
  politics: political parties 373
Lithuania 384-97
  debt 395-6
  economic indicators 397
  equities 393-5
  history: economic 388
    political 384-6
  politics 384-7
    political parties 387
London Club: FRY debt 165
  Russia 577
  Vietnam 767

Makam bills: Israel 330
Malaysia 398-416
  debt: private 414-15
    public debt 413
  economic indicators 416
  equities 410-13
  history: economic 404-6
    political 398-402
  monarchs 403
  politics 398-403
    other political forces 403
  Seventh Malaysia Plan 405
  Sultans 403
Manufacturing: Philippines 510-
  11
Marathon bonds: Greece 244
MERCOSUR: Brazil 73
  Chile 105
Mexico 417-34
  1982 debt crisis 32
  currency crisis (1994) 422
  debt: private debt 432
    public debt 431-2
  economic indicators 434
  equities 427-31
  history: economic 421-2
    political 417-19
  politics 417-20
    other political forces 420
    political parties 419-20

Zapatista National Liberation
Party (EZLN) 420
Military: Argentina 52
Chile 102
Ecuador 186
Egypt 201
Hong Kong 250
Morocco 440
Panama 479
Peru 491
Thailand 691
Ministry of Finance bonds:
Croatia 164
Russia 584-5
Monetary Stabilization Bonds:
Ecuador 194
Venezuela 754
Morocco 435-54
debt 447
economic indicators 454
equities 451-2
market comment 452
history: economic 441-2
political 435-6
politics 435-40
other political forces 440
political parties 438-9
recent reforms 448-9
Western Sahara 440
Mortgage bonds: Latvia 381
Municipal bills: Ukraine 730
Municipal bonds: Czech Republic
180
Philippines 520
Poland 541
Russia 584

National banks: Panama 479
NATO: Greece 235
Nigeria 455-63
debt 462
economic indicators 463
equities 461-2
foreign market participation
462
history: political 455-7
politics 455-7

Organization for Economic
Cooperation and Development
(OECD)
reports: Czech Republic 171
South Korea 669
trade deficits: Bulgaria 93-4
OTC trading method 60, 78, 124,
177-8, 729
Ownership limits: Argentina 61
Brazil 78
Chile 111
Colombia 138-9
Croatia 163
Czech Republic 179
Ecuador 193
Egypt 209
Estonia 220
Ghana 229
Greece 242
Hungary 277
Indonesia 312-13
Jordan 342
Kenya 367
Latvia 380
Lithuania 394

Malaysia 412
Mexico 430
Morocco 452
Panama 485
Peru 499
Philippines 518
Poland 539
Portugal 554
Romania 566
Russia 583
Saudi Arabia 596
Slovakia 624
Slovenia 637
South Korea 668
Taiwan 683
Thailand 702
Turkey 718
Uzbekistan 740
Venezuela 753
Zimbabwe 781

Pakistan 464-76
Badla 473
capital flows 470-1
currency weakness 471
debt 473
private debt 474
public debt 474
deficit 469
reducing 469
economic indicators 475
equities 472-3
external imbalances 469-70
history: political 464-6
Mohajir Qaumi Movement 467
monetary sector 469
natural resources 467
politics 464-7
Panama 476-87
debt 485
private debt 485-6
economic indicators 487
equities 484-5
history: economics 479-80
political 476-7
politics 476-9
other political forces 479
political parties 478
Parastatal bonds: South Africa
655
Paris Club debt revisions: Brazil
75
Côte d'Ivoire 145
Ecuador 190
Egypt 205
Poland 533
Russia 577
Peru 488-502
debt 495, 499-500
economic indicators 502
equities 497-9
history: economic 491-2
political 488-90
IMF 495
politics 488-91
other political forces 491
political parties 490-1
Philippines 503-21
Clark Special Economic Zone
514
debt 519
private debt 520
public debt 519-20

economic indicators 521
equities 517-18
history: economic 508-9
political 503-5
IMF 514-15
Moro Islamic Liberation Front
507
National People's Army 507
politics 503-7
other political forces 507
political parties 506
religious groups 507
state organization 505
Subic Bay Freeport Zone 514
Poland 522-43
debt: foreign 536
economic indicators 543
equities 537-9
history: economic 529-31
political 522-5
international relations 528-9
politics 522-8
political parties 527
state organization 525
Political stability 19
Population: China 118
Côte d'Ivoire 145
Czech Republic 171
Ghana 225
Greece 235
Hong Kong 251
India 282-3
Israel 323
Kazakstan (table) 351
Kenya 363
Latvia 373
Lithuania 389
Malaysia 406
Nigeria 458
Pakistan 467
Portugal 548
Russia 573
Slovakia 620
Slovenia 632
South Africa 647
South Korea 663
Taiwan 678
Turkey 711
Portugal 544-57
debt 554-5
economic indicators 557
equities 552-4
history: economic 547-8
political 544-5
politics 544-6
political parties 546
Private debt securities: Malaysia
414
Privatization: Argentina 58
Brazil 75
Bulgaria 90-1
Chile 107
Colombia 135
Croatia 161
Ecuador 188
Hungary 269-70
Indonesia 310
Latvia 378
Mexico 426
Morocco 448-9
Philippines 515
Poland 536
Romania 563

Russia 575-6
Turkey 728, 729
Venezuela 750
Privatization currency bonds:
Brazil 80
PSU bonds: India 294
Public Order Book (trading
system) 219

Rescheduled debt: Colombia 140
Restructured debt: Chile 113
Côte d'Ivoire 149
RMS trading system 177-8, 623
Romania 558-68
debt 564, 567
economic indicators 568
equities 565-6
history: economic 561
political 558-60
IBRD 564
IMF 564
politics 558-61
political parties 560-1
RTS trading system 582
Russia 569-86
debt: external tradable debt
584-5
government debt 583-4
other domestic debt 584
economic indicators 586
economic structural problems
577-8
end of GDP contraction 574
equities 581-3
history: political 569-71
IMF 577, 578-9
long-term prospects 579
politics 569-73
political parties 572
stock market 576
structural problems 577-8
World Bank 577

SATO trading system 428
Saudi Arabia 587-97
debt 596
economic indicators 597
equities 594-6
five-year plan 590-1
history: political 587-8
oil industry 591
politics 587-8
Savings 21
SCORE trading system 411
Secondary market trading:
Argentina 64
Chile 112
Poland 541
SENN trading method 78
SET trading system 137
Shareholders' rights: Argentina
61
Bulgaria 96
Czech Republic 178
Indonesia 312
Latvia 380
Malaysia 412
Mexico 429-30
Portugal 554
Singapore 609
Taiwan 683
Ukraine 729
Singapore 598-612

debt 609
 private debt 610
 public debt 609
economic indicators 612
economic slowdown 603-4
equities 606-9
 market performance and
 outlook 609
history: economic 602-3
 political 598-600
politics 598-600
 political parties 601
Slovakia 613-26
 debt 624-5
 economic indicators 626
 equities 622-4
 history: economic 617-20
 political 613-16
 politics 613-17
 political parties 616-17
Slovenia 627-39
 debt 637-8
 economic indicators 639
 equities 635-7
 history: economic 631-2
 political 627-9
 politics 627-30
 political parties 630
SMATS trading system 667
South Africa 640-57
 debt 655-6
 economic indicators 657
 equities 652-5
 history: economic 645-7
 political 640-3
 macro plan 650-1
 medium-term growth
 prospects 648
 politics 640-5
 political parties 644-5
South Korea 658-72
 debt 669
 private debt 670
 public debt 670
 economic indicators 672
 equities 666-9
 limits on price movement
 668
 history: economic 661-2
 political 658-60
 OECD membership 669
 politics 658-61
 political forces 661
Sovereign risk 13, 18, 37
Soviet Union, collapse of:
 Estonia 215
 Latvia 376
State Enterprise bonds: Thailand
 703
Stock market capitalization 13

Taiwan 673-86
 debt 683
 private debt 684
 public debt 684
 economic indicators 686
 equities 681-3
 history: economic 676-8
 political 673-5
 politics 673-6
 political forces 676
Takeover bids: Colombia 139
 Czech Republic 179

Indonesia 313
Malaysia 412
Singapore 609
South Africa 654
Turkey 718
Telepregon trading method 109
TEST-1/TEST-2 trading systems
 163
Thailand 687-705
 debt 702
 private debt 703-4
 public debt 703
 economic indicators 705
 equities 700-2
 history: economic 692-4
 political 687-9
 monarchs 691
 politics 687-91
 other political forces 691
 political parties 689-90
Trade deficits: Morocco 444-6
 Pakistan 469
 Philippines (table) 512
Trade restrictions: Argentina 56
 Brazil 73-4
 Chile 105
 Colombia 133-4 Indonesia 307
 Panama 481
 Peru 494
 Philippines 513
 Thailand 696-7
 Venezuela 748
 Vietnam 766
Trading methods: Argentina 60
 Brazil 77-8
 Bulgaria 95
 Chile 109
 Colombia 137
 Croatia 163
 Czech Republic 177
 Ecuador 193
 Egypt 208
 Estonia 219
 Ghana 229
 Greece 241
 Hong Kong 256
 Hungary 277
 India 291
 Indonesia 311-12
 Israel 329
 Jordan 342
 Kazakstan 357
 Kenya 367
 Latvia 379
 Lithuania 394
 Malaysia 411
 Mexico 428
 Pakistan 473
 Panama 484
 Peru 497-8
 Philippines 517
 Poland 738
 Portugal 552-3
 Romania 565
 Russia 582
 Saudi Arabia 595
 Slovakia 623
 Slovenia 636
 South Africa 653
 South Korea 667
 Taiwan 682
 Thailand 701
 Turkey 717

Turkey 729
Venezuela 752
Zimbabwe 780
Trading systems: Argentina 60
 Brazil 77-8
 Chile 109
 China 124
 Colombia 137
 Croatia 163
 Czech Republic 177-8
 Estonia 219
 Ghana 229
 Greece 241
 Hong Kong 256
 Indonesia 311-12
 Israel 329
 Malaysia 411
 Mexico 428
 Philippines 517
 Portugal 553
 Russia 582
 Saudi Arabia 595
 Slovakia 623
 Slovenia 636
 South Africa 653
 South Korea 667
 Thailand 701
 Turkey 717
 Ukraine 729
 Zimbabwe 780
TRADIS trading system 553
Treasury bills: Bulgaria 96-7
 China 125
 Croatia 164
 Czech Republic 180
 Egypt 210
 Greece 243
 Hungary 278
 India 293
 Jordan 343
 Latvia 381
 Malaysia 413
 Philippines 519-20
 Poland 540
 Portugal 555
 Saudi Arabia 596
 Singapore 610
 Slovakia 625
 Thailand 703
 Turkey 719
 Ukraine 730
 Zimbabwe 782
Treasury bonds: Brazil 80
 Bulgaria 97
 Egypt 210
 Jordan 343-4
 Mexico 431
 Poland 540
 Singapore 610
 Slovakia 625
 Taiwan 684
 Thailand 703
 Turkey 730
 Venezuela 754
Treasury certificates: Mexico 431
Treasury notes: Greece 243
 Indonesia 314
 Philippines 519-20
 Venezuela 754
Turkey 706-20
 debt 718-719, 728, 729-30
 private debt 719
 economic indicators 720

equities 716-18, 728-9
 market comment 718
European Union 712
history: economic 710-11,
 724-5
 political 706-8
IMF 727
politics 706-10
 political forces 709-10
 political parties 723-4

Ukraine 721-31
 economic indicators 731
 history: political 721-3
 politics 721-4
United Nations (UN): Hungary
 266
United Nations (UN): Poland 528
UTS trading system 517
Uzbekistan 732-41
 debt 740
 economic indicators 741
 economic reform 738
 equities 740
 history: economic 735-6
 political 732-4
 politics 732-5
 political parties 735

Venezuela 742-56
 banking crisis (1994) 751
 debt 749, 754
 economic indicators 756
 equities 751-4
 history: economic 745-6
 political 742-4
 politics 742-5
 political parties 744-5
Vietnam 757-71
 debt 766-7, 770
 debt restructuring 766-7
 economic indicators 771
 equities 769-70
 history: economic 761-2
 political 757-9
 IMF 766-7
 politics 757-60
 major reforms 762
 political organizations 760
 State-owned enterprise
 reforms 768
 World Bank 767

World Bank: Brazil 75
 Bulgaria 90
 Colombia 134
 Egypt 201, 206
 Indonesia 308
 Polish membership 528
 Russia 577
 Vietnam 767
World Trade Organization (WTO):
 Hungary 266

Zimbabwe 772-83
 as part of larger market 778
 debt (public and private) 782
 economic indicators 783
 equities 779-82
 history: political 772-4
 politics 772-4